Industrial Law

Industrial Law

Seventh edition

I T Smith MA, LLB (CANTAB)

of Gray's Inn and Devereux Chambers, Barrister
Clifford Chance Professor of Employment Law
at the University of East Anglia
Member of the ACAS Panel of Industrial Arbitrators

Gareth Thomas LLB, BCL

Senior Lecturer in Law at the University of East Anglia

Butterworths
London Edinburgh & Dublin
2000

United Kingdom	Butterworths, a Division of Reed Elsevier (UK) Ltd, Halsbury House, 35 Chancery Lane, LONDON WC2A 1EL and 4 Hill Street, EDINBURGH EH2 3JZ
Australia	Butterworths, a Division of Reed International Books Australia Pty Ltd, CHATSWOOD, New South Wales
Canada	Butterworths Canada Ltd, MARKHAM, Ontario
Hong Kong	Butterworths Asia (Hong Kong), HONG KONG
India	Butterworths India, NEW DELHI
Ireland	Butterworth (Ireland) Ltd, DUBLIN
Malaysia	Malayan Law Journal Sdn Bhd, KUALA LUMPUR
New Zealand	Butterworths of New Zealand Ltd, WELLINGTON
Singapore	Butterworths Asia, SINGAPORE
South Africa	Butterworths Publishers (Pty) Ltd, DURBAN
USA	Lexis Law Publishing, CHARLOTTESVILLE, Virginia

A CIP Catalogue record for this book is available from the British Library.

1st edn	1980
2nd edn	1983
3rd edn	1986
4th edn	1989
5th edn	1993
6th edn	1996

ISBN 0 406 90411 1

Printed by Redwood Books, Trowbridge, Wiltshire

Visit Butterworths LEXIS *direct* **at: http://www.butterworths.com**

Preface

For the second time in the 20-year history of this book, we have been blown off our intended course of an edition every third year. The time before, we were wrong-footed by an election. This time the culprit was the Employment Relations Act 1999, which from small beginnings in a relatively low-key White Paper, turned out to be a monster of delegated powers, of a distinctly Henry VIII nature. The lot of the employment lawyer is frequently not a happy one, but for the last two years it has been a positively frenetic one. The pace of change, both domestic and EU inspired, has been unremitting, as any subscriber to *Harvey* will know to their cost (intellectual and financial). In a sense, this justifies (if justification is needed) a textbook such as this, because it is in just such times as these that the student or lawyer needs to bear in mind that the subject does actually have underlying principles and (almost) immutable truths, that can sometimes be submerged in the quest for everlasting topicality. This latter quest can be exaggerated by ever more efficient means, especially electronic, to retrieve information on anything that moves. Even before the current information revolution, it was said, for example, that employment law was the most over-reported area of English law. Given the remarkable developments of the last five years or so, the need for the student of this subject to be able to distinguish between the vital development and the merely interesting example has been elevated from the desirable to the essential.

It is in that spirit that we offer this seventh edition. Contrary to pessimistic expectation, we seem to have hit something of a publishing 'window', with most of the 1999 Act either in force or reasonably anticipated. The vital, and most welcome, changes to maternity and parental laws are reasonably well bedded in, and the part-time workers regulations and new ACAS codes of practice have been incorporated. TUPE remains the exception, but then again it always is. We have had to cover the potential large changes at proposal level only. We hope that this edition will help students and practitioners in equal measure in a subject of (if anything) increasing importance, involving fascination and frustration, again in equal measure.

ITS   Norwich
GHT   June 2000

Contents

Chapter 3

Contracts of employment (1): formation and content   77

Chapter 6

Maternity and parental rights 321

Chapter 7

Contracts of employment (2): discharge at common law 355

Chapter 8

The law and procedure of unfair dismissal   401

Chapter 11

Industrial action   628

Chapter 12

Industrial safety (1): compensation for industrial injury   705

Chapter 13

Industrial safety (2): health and safety at work   741

Table of statutes

References in this Table to *Statutes,* are to Halsbury's Statutes of England, Fourth Edition, showing the page at which the annotated text may be found. References printed in **bold** type indicate where the Act is set out in part or in full.

Table of statutory instruments

Decisions of the National Insurance and Social Security Commissioners

Table of cases

C

K

PAGE

L

N

Chapter 1

Introduction

1 GENERAL

Industrial law has been the subject of as rapid a transformation as can have happened to any legal subject in recent times, and is certainly one of the most difficult areas of law in which to keep up to date. In some ways it is a curious mixture of ancient and modern, for much old law lies behind or at the basis of new statutory law and in some cases the old law continues to exist alongside the new (e.g. the continued existence of the separate actions for wrongful dismissal and unfair dismissal, the former being a common law action and the latter entirely a creation of statute). To take one small example, as late as 1969 it could still be seriously debated before the Court of Appeal[1] whether a general hiring of an employee (i.e. one not subject to any express time limitation) was a hiring only for a year, under the old 'presumption of a yearly hiring' which used to apply in the last century and before, principally in order to guarantee year-round employment for agricultural labourers, but which is now totally irrelevant to modern employment law. Ghosts can still clank their chains, particularly in the law relating to contracts of employment where a strictly contractual approach may not always lead to a realistic result. However, the subject is unrecognisable from what it was forty years ago with the enormous increase in statute law and the ever increasing volume of case law on the modern statutes. Thus, the intending student must be able to exercise the lawyer's skill in dealing both with extensive case law and with major statutes, sometimes of astounding complexity. Moreover, he or she must be able to deal with this mass of law with a certain amount of intelligence and discernment, for example being able to tell when a line of old cases, authoritative in themselves, may be so out of line with the modern approach to employment or industrial relations that they are unlikely to be applied in practice, or to tell when a case on a modern statutory provision is merely *illustrative* (however interesting) rather than setting a definite precedent on a point of interpretation, for if this distinction is not borne in mind the student will soon find himself or herself buried alive under the case law, particularly in an area

---

1   *Richardson v Koefod* [1969] 3 All ER 1264, [1969] 1 WLR 1812, CA.

such as unfair dismissal where so much is vested in the discretion of the tribunal and, furthermore, where any actual point of law which does arise should normally be approached primarily by reference to the wording of the statute; the student will soon realise when reading this book (particularly chapter 8) that now, more than ever, this desire to escape from over-legalism in decision making on industrial matters is one of the dominant themes of modern industrial law. Case law of course remains important, but equally clearly some cases are more equal than others. While the approach of this book is avowedly legal, treating the subject as it now has to be treated as an important area of substantive law which leads in practice to a very considerable amount of litigation, at the same time it must be realised that in certain ways this is law with a difference; this must be reflected in the approach of the student, and it is hoped that it is reflected in this book, which in turn reflects the love-hate relationship to the law adopted by so many industrial relations practitioners.

As well as a whole new body of law, industrial law is also subject to a separate jurisdiction exercised by employment tribunals (with appeal to the Employment Appeal Tribunal, and only then into the ordinary court structure, with appeal to the Court of Appeal and then to the House of Lords). Even though tribunals gained some common law jurisdiction (on termination of employment) in 1994, not all matters may go to a tribunal, for many common law actions must still go to the ordinary courts (e.g. an action for breach of the contract of employment during employment, or the sort of action by a union member against his union for unconstitutional action that was so prevalent and so important during the course of the miners' strike of 1984/5). At the level of the High Court it is at first surprising to find that quite a number of employment cases find themselves in the Chancery Division (particularly where the principal aim of the action is an injunction). However, the large majority of cases which are brought do in fact go before the tribunals, and in the last few years the numbers of such cases have increased alarmingly.

This has led to a mushrooming in new specialised sources and materials in industrial law, many ephemeral, but some of major practical use to the industrial lawyer. The two main series of law reports are the Industrial Cases Reports (ICR)[2] and the Industrial Relations Law Reports (IRLR)[3]; preference will be given to citation of these reports throughout this book. The Industrial Tribunal Reports (ITR) commenced publication in 1966 and have now ceased, to avoid further duplication. The leading academic journal is the Industrial Law Journal[4], and the principal up-dating periodicals, so vital in this rapidly developing subject, are:

i)   the IDS Brief[5] – published twice per month; IDS also publish occasional supplements with the brief, covering recent developments in one particular topic, and the more substantial IDS Handbooks which aim to up-date the reader on the major areas of the subject.

ii) The Industrial Relations Review and Report (IR-RR)[6] – also published twice a month; it covers industrial relations matters generally, but also includes a Legal Bulletin (IR-LB – separately numbered from the IR-RR itself) covering

2   These are the official reports, published by the Incorporated Council of Law Reporting for England and Wales; until 1974 they were called the Industrial Court Reports.
3   Published by Industrial Relations Services, 18–20 Highbury Place, London, N5 1QP.
4   Published for the Industrial Law Society by OUP.
5   Published by Incomes Data Services, 140 Great Portland Street, London W1.
6   Also published by Industrial Relations Services, n. 3 above.

recent case law and 'guidance notes' on particular topics, and a Health and Safety Information Bulletin (HSIB – also separately numbered).

iii) The Employment Gazette[7] – this was published monthly, and contained employment statistics and short articles on employment topics; in 1995 it was incorporated into Labour Market Trends, which seems to have had the unfortunate effect of making it concentrate more on purely statistical material, and so become less useful than it was before to the industrial lawyer.

The leading practitioner work is *Harvey on Industrial Relations and Employment Law*[8], a five-volume looseleaf work (updated six times per year, with a monthly Bulletin) which is used extensively by practitioners, advisers and tribunals, and is frequently cited in court judgments (especially in the EAT).

Codes of Practice are of ever increasing importance in industrial law, allowing the statute to lay down merely the general principle on a topic and then amplifying that principle in a way that is likely to be of more use to the people concerned; so far, they have been used in the fields of unfair dismissal, employment protection, union rights, picketing, the closed shop, health and safety at work and disability discrimination, and they should be consulted whenever appropriate. Also, much useful information can be obtained from the Annual Reports of ACAS. In the collective sphere the Donovan Report[9] should still be consulted, for it formed the analytical background to many of the reforms (successful or unsuccessful) in this area. Finally, many of the bodies connected with industrial relations in the widest sense publish from time to time reports or studies with important impacts upon the legal framework[10].

2   THE SCOPE OF THE SUBJECT AND THE LEGISLATIVE FRAMEWORK

The subject of industrial law may be split, for convenience if not for accuracy, into three principal areas – industrial safety law, employment law and the law relating to industrial relations. Each has a different legal and social background, and until recently the level (and type) of legal involvement was markedly different in each. Industrial safety law has a history of statutory intervention dating back to the beginning of the last century, with a formidable volume of case law on the statutes and on the actions which could be brought by an injured employee. Employment law, however, was based almost entirely upon the common law concept of the contract of employment; it attracted little statutory intervention and even much of the common law, though extensive in theory, was a dead letter in practice, principally due to the inadequacies of the remedies for breach of the employment contract by the employer. Industrial relations law was characterised by the voluntary principle and the abstention of the law (once legislation had been used in the latter part of the last century and the first part of this to legalise the operations and purposes of trade unions and to protect them and their members from tortious liability for industrial action); it is true that wage negotiation in certain industries was encouraged by Wages Councils which were the creation of statute,

---

7   Published by the Central Statistical Office.
8   Published by Butterworths. Cross-references are made to *Harvey* in certain parts of this book, especially in the chapter on tribunals and unfair dismissal.
9   Report of the Royal Commission on Trade Unions and Employers' Associations (1968) Cmnd. 3623.
10   The annual reports of, the CAC, the Certification Officer, the EOC, the CRE and the Health and Safety Commission are particularly useful sources of information.

but even here the law merely provided a minimum framework and did not attempt to impose legal rights and duties on the substance of the negotiation itself.

Major developments have occurred in the last two decades which have changed this previous picture, in some areas out of all recognition. In the industrial safety sphere, the major development has been the Health and Safety at Work etc. Act 1974 which creates administrative machinery, provides for more effective enforcement procedures and widens the general duties owed by employers (and others). One possible major development (in the area of compensation for industrial injuries) did not come about in the end, for the Pearson Commission on Civil Liability did *not* recommend the institution of a no-fault system of liability in place of our present tort system which depends essentially upon the ability to prove fault or breach of statutory duty. However, the substance of our safety laws has now been subject to major reform from a different source, namely the EC, with increased emphasis on attempting to harmonise laws on major safety matters throughout the Community[11].

Employment law has been the subject of major revision by the provision of new statutory rights for those in employment (and, in the area of sex, race and disability discrimination, for those seeking employment); moreover, these rights (which usually have little or no dependence upon the theoretical contractual basis of employment) are now the subject of *realistic* enforcement procedures through the tribunal system and so are doubly preferable to most common law rights. These rights are many and various, from what is now a relatively minor matter such as minimum periods of notice according to length of service, to the more important employment protection rights; clearly the most important is the right not to be unfairly dismissed, and these cases constitute a major part of the tribunals' case load.

Industrial relations law suffered a great upheaval with the Industrial Relations Act 1971, which unsuccessfully attempted to impose an overall legislative framework on industrial relations, giving rights and imposing duties by law as is done in some other jurisdictions. The Act was repealed in toto in 1974 (except for the unfair dismissal provisions, which were re-enacted), but ironically we then saw under the same Labour government the enactment of significant new legal rights for trade unions which were capable of having an effect on some of the most fundamental aspects of collective labour relations, such as recognition, bargaining information, standardisation of terms and conditions throughout an industry, prior consultation on impending redundancies and direct union involvement in safety procedures. Certainly, where industrial relations remain on a collective level (and there has been a significant decline in collective bargaining over the past two decades), such relations are still on a voluntary basis and voluntary procedures remain paramount; however, this field is no longer devoid of legal intervention, and the modern legislation has also played an important part in setting up machinery for the settlement of certain industrial disputes (in particular, the Advisory, Conciliation and Arbitration Service and the Central Arbitration Committee) and more recently in placing stringent limitations on what the previous Conservative government saw as unacceptable forms of industrial action or unacceptable purposes behind such industrial action, while at the same time they sought ever greater deregulation of the labour market itself.

---

11   See, in particular the six new sets of regulations which came into force on 1 January 1993 and revolutionised our workplace legislation, ch. 13, below.

The whole subject is thus heavily overlaid with modern statutes[12]. In the employment law area, this process started with the Contracts of Employment Act 1963 (consolidated in 1972) which introduced new rules on notice periods, required an employer to give his employee a written statement of terms of employment, and laid down for the first time the statutory rules on 'continuity of employment' which were to take on much greater significance when more extensive employee rights were later enacted which depended on the concept of continuity (either for qualification for rights or computation of benefits, or both). The first of these rights was the right to a redundancy payment under the Redundancy Payments Act 1965. As well as attempting to introduce a new, but politically unacceptable, framework for industrial relations, the Industrial Relations Act 1971 was notable for introducing the new law on unfair dismissal, and this was re-enacted by the Trade Union and Labour Relations Act 1974 which repealed the 1971 Act and (a) restored the essentially voluntary nature of industrial relations (abolishing, in the process, the National Industrial Relations Court which had adjudicated cases arising under the 1971 Act) and (b) consolidated the law relating to trade union immunities and internal affairs; the 1974 Act was itself amended by the Trade Union and Labour Relations (Amendment) Act 1976 which made the immunities more watertight, abolished the statutory action against a union for unfair expulsion or exclusion, and tightened up the law on the closed shop.

The Employment Protection Act 1975 made significant steps forward in many directions. On the collective side, it gave statutory backing to ACAS, set up the CAC and introduced the important new trade union rights mentioned above; it also set up the Employment Appeal Tribunal (to take the place of the NIRC) and modernised the provisions relating to wages councils. On the individual employment side, it introduced new employment protection rights (e.g. guarantee payments, time off work for union purposes, a right not to be discriminated against on trade union grounds, and the rights relating to maternity pay and leave) and it made significant alterations to the law on unfair dismissal (particularly as regards the available remedies). By this time, the statute law was something of a jungle and indeed was on one occasion castigated in the House of Lords as a bad example of legislation by reference, in that it was frequently the case that a point of law could only be discovered by referring to separate but complementary provisions in two or more Acts. The *individual* aspects were therefore consolidated into the Employment Protection (Consolidation) Act 1978 which covered particulars of terms of employment, employment protection rights, termination of employment, unfair dismissal, redundancy payments, and industrial tribunals and the EAT, and was for years the principal statute.

The Employment Act 1980 marked a major change of direction after the election in 1979 of a Conservative government. Although it adopted, at the very beginning of that government, a 'softly, softly' approach, avoiding a rerun of the Industrial Relations Act 1971, it started the remarkable transformation of industrial law that marked the 1980s. On the collective side, it affected statutory trade union rights by repealing the provisions of the Employment Protection Act 1975 relating to the statutory recognition procedure and the extension of terms and conditions of employment by the CAC ('Schedule 11 claims'). It also affected the internal government of trade unions by allowing financial support for union elections and by reinstating a statutory right of complaint to a tribunal for people unreasonably expelled or excluded from a union where there is a closed shop in

---

12   The statutes currently in force are set out, with annotations, in *Harvey*, Division Q.

operation. The law relating to picketing was altered, and new curbs introduced on secondary industrial action. On the individual side, the Act altered certain aspects of unfair dismissal law (principally those relating to the burden of proof, the closed shop and compensation) and made changes in the rules governing maternity rights and guarantee pay.

The Employment Act 1982, an altogether 'drier' statute by a more established government, contained some new provisions (e.g. altering the law of unfair dismissal in cases where the persons dismissed were on strike) and a host of minor amendments. However, it was principally designed to tighten up the 1980 Act in two areas – the closed shop and the law on industrial disputes. With regard to the former, it imposed more stringent procedural requirements of balloting, radically increased the compensation payable to an employee unfairly dismissed because of a closed shop, and made it more likely that in such a case compensation will in fact be paid by the union rather than the employer. Also, new provisions were introduced to discourage the inclusion of union-labour-only requirements in contracts and tenders. In the area of industrial disputes, the Act basically left alone the restrictions introduced by the 1980 Act (though with a tightening-up of the definition of 'trade dispute' on which the statutory immunities are based); however, the radical change in the 1982 Act was the removal of the union's complete immunity from suit in tort (which the unions had had, with the exception of the years of the Industrial Relations Act 1971, since the Trade Disputes Act 1906), so that now the union itself may be sued (subject to statutory maxima on the damages recoverable) if it contravenes the strengthened laws on industrial disputes.

The Trade Union Act 1984 (following the 1983 election when 'giving unions back to their members' was a prominent Conservative theme) was the third major statute passed by the previous government, but in large part marked a significant departure. While Part II can be seen as following on from the Employment Acts 1980 and 1982 by allowing an employer to sue a union (for damages or an injunction) if the union takes strike or other industrial action without the now obligatory strike ballot, Parts I and III were different in that the causes of action contained within them are vested in the union *members*. Part I obliged a union to hold secret ballots for high union offices and Part III introduced compulsory periodic reballoting on whether a union should continue to operate a political fund. This Act was therefore aimed at the *internal* affairs of a trade union particularly as the events surrounding the miners' strike and certain other major industrial disputes tended to show a greater degree of readiness on the part of union members (or of whole sections of a union) to resort to legal action in order to secure compliance with the union's rules. This process was taken a stage further by the Employment Act 1988 (following the 1987 election and the experiences of the miners' strike), which tightened up some of the provisions of the 1984 Act (in relation to balloting) and introduced certain new statutory rights for union members (e.g. rights to ballots before industrial action, to inspect union accounts, to restrain unlawful expenditure by the union and not to be unjustifiably disciplined); to assist in the enforcement of rights against a union, the Act also established the office of Commissioner for the Rights of Trade Union Members. In one respect, the Act harked back to the early legislation of that government, for it took the changes to the law on the closed shop to their logical conclusion by removing *all* legal protection from it as an institution, so that it is now no longer possible for a union to establish or maintain a legally effective, post-entry closed shop.

While the Employment Act 1989 was largely a tinkering measure, the Employment Act 1990 in several ways set the seal on a decade of change[13], taking several themes first developed in 1980 to their logical conclusions. In particular, it rendered illegal the *pre*-entry closed shop, made illegal *all* secondary action and attacked *un*official industrial action. Thus, by 1990 laws were in place which many Conservatives would have liked to have seen in 1980, had they been able to wave a magic wand. Crucially, of course, by that time there had also been a significant decrease in union membership, a radical decrease in union influence and a very noticeable move away, in many areas, from collectively negotiated terms and conditions of employment, towards more individual contracting, flexibility in employment and more use of what used to be called atypical employments. Indeed, by the early 1990s the encouragement of such moves had been adopted as government policy[14], along with continuing deregulation.

After the fourth Conservative election victory in 1992, another Bill was expected, though possibly of a tinkering nature again, meant politically to show that the government had not run out of steam in the hitherto politically profitable area of industrial relations. However, the Trade Union Reform and Employment Rights Act 1993 turned out to be far more than that. It again addressed union elections and ballots, and the financial affairs of unions; it recast members' rights on disciplining and expulsion; further restrictions were introduced on industrial action (including strike notice and a Citizen's Charter right for individuals to challenge industrial action in the public sector). In the individual field, it altered the laws on maternity, employment particulars, redundancy consultation and transfers of undertakings in response to changes in EC law, and introduced two new heads of unfair dismissal. As a logical, but much criticised, further measure to deregulate the labour market, it finally abolished wages councils.

Outside the above mainstream legislation, the 1980s also saw very significant changes in social security laws relevant to industrial law (especially payment through the employer, through statutory sick pay and statutory maternity pay), and the Wages Act 1986 introduced new laws on deductions from wages that saw quite remarkable development in the early 1990s. In the field of discrimination law there were, again, consistent developments, but this time largely through the intervention of EC law rather than changes in domestic legislation. If all of this does not provide the reader with enough excitement in life, there are always the Transfer of Undertakings Regulations ...

Given this quite remarkable series of statutes (and, often, their supporting regulations and orders) we have at least been fortunate in having five major consolidations in the period 1992–1996, bringing some order to the chaos. The Trade Union and Labour Relations (Consolidation) Act 1992 consolidated the morass of laws (ancient and modern) on collective labour law, replacing in particular the Trade Union and Labour Relations Act 1974 and most of the Conservative Employment Acts 1980–1993. Social security law was consolidated into the Social Security Contributions and Benefits Act 1992 and the Social Security

13   Highly recommended reading to set this series of statutes into their political context is Auerbach *Legislating for Conflict* (1990), commented on in Foch et al, 'Politics, pragmatism and ideology: the wellsprings of Conservative union legislation' (1993) 22 ILJ 14, and Davies and Freedland *Labour Legislation and Public Policy* (1993). The political progress of the three governments of Mrs Thatcher is set out in excellent and highly readable form in Hugo Young *One of Us*.

14   Employment for the 1990s (Cm. 540, 1988); People, Jobs and Opportunity (Cm. 1810, 1992).

Administration Act 1992; it took a particularly strong river to clean out those Augean stables, and shortly after it was done major changes were then made by the Social Security (Incapacity for Work) Act 1994 and the Jobseekers Act 1995 (though largely by amending the two Consolidation Acts, which therefore remain the primary source). The law relating to individual employment matters was finally consolidated in the Employment Rights Act 1996 which replaced the Employment Protection (Consolidation) Act 1978 (as, by then, heavily amended) and the Wages Act 1986, with the law relating to tribunals and the EAT being consolidated at the same time in the Industrial Tribunals Act 1996 (since renamed the Employment Tribunals Act 1996). Outside that framework lie the Equal Pay Act 1970, the Sex Discrimination Act 1975, the Race Relations Act 1976, the Disability Discrimination Act 1995 and the Pensions Act 1995.

The 1997 General Election saw the end of a period of eighteen years of Conservative administrations and a landslide victory for New Labour. Dramatic though this political reversal of fortunes was, it was far removed from the previous return of a Labour government in 1974, when the Trade Union and Labour Relations Act 1974 (sweeping away the previous Conservative government's employment laws) was the first statute passed by that incoming government. Instead, New Labour seemed to put a relatively low priority on employment law changes (reflecting the equally low priority of the subject at the election), and it had been made clear for some time by the 'modernisers' within the party that there were to be no wholesale repeals of the reforms of the Thatcher administration.[15] Indeed, the first statute passed was the Employment Rights (Dispute Resolution) Act 1998 (reforming tribunal procedures and establishing the ACAS arbitration alternative to tribunals for unfair dismissal cases) which was inherited at Green Paper stage from the previous government. The National Minimum Wage Act 1998 enacted one of New Labour's relatively few election commitments on employment law, and the Working Time Regulations 1998 were an obligation under EC law (the previous government's challenge to the legality of the backing Directive having failed in the ECJ); the Public Interest Disclosure (or 'Whistleblowers') Act 1998 was also in many ways relatively uncontroversial and commanded widespread support. It was only with the publication of the White Paper 'Fairness at Work'[16] that a clear idea could be obtained of the likely direction of the new government in this area. Again, however, in spite of some reforms important in themselves, this was hardly a major sea-change, and even then the government were accused of some back-sliding by the unions on the eventual form of the resulting statute, the Employment Relations Act 1999, especially in relation to the union recognition procedure and the mere lifting of the limit on the unfair dismissal compensatory award (from £12,000 to £15,000), rather than its abolition as had been mooted in the White Paper. Moreover, this Act is not to be seen as merely a first step in reforms, because (as the Prime Minister said in the introduction to the White Paper) it 'seeks to draw a line

---

15   'The abolition of the closed shop was one of the many employment law reforms of the 1980s that were justified and will remain ... . Other measures which will remain include those on picketing, secondary action, ballots and notice before strikes, unofficial action, elections for certain trade union offices and rights to join the trade union of one's choice and not to be unjustifiably disciplined': Fairness at Work (Cm. 3968, May 1998), p. 22. For the background political changes, especially in relations with the trade unions, see McIlroy 'The enduring alliance? Trade unions and the making of the New Labour 1994–1997' (1998) 36 BJIR 537.

16   See n. 15, above. See generally Taylor 'Annual review article 1997' (1998) 36 BJIR 293.

under the issue of industrial relations law'. Whether this laudable aim (from the point of view of the harassed employment lawyer) will prove to be realisable remains to be seen.

From this review it will be clear that statute law now dominates much of this subject, but at the same time it must be recognised that there are certain areas where the common law is still very much alive. Further, much of the statute law in both the individual and collective spheres rests on two non-statutory foundations – first the status of a person in question as an *employee* and secondly the voluntary principle which still governs the substance of most industrial relations. It is to these two, fundamental, non-statutory foundations that we must now turn, following that by introductory consideration of two other major influences on the subject, namely the existing and longer-term influence of Europe and the potential influence of the Human Rights Act 1998.

3   THE RELATIONSHIP OF EMPLOYER AND EMPLOYEE

The fact that someone is an employee of someone else is a major jurisdictional factor in several areas of law, for example in tort law on the question of vicarious liability, and in the fields of taxation and social security on the questions of assessment, payment and contributions. In industrial law, both ancient and modern, it is often of fundamental importance; most of the common law on employment only applies to employees, and it is the same with the important statutory rights which usually require the applicant to be an employee and to have served a certain qualifying period as such.[17] As the only definition of 'employee' in the Employment Rights Act 1996 and the Trade Union and Labour Relations (Consolidation) Act 1992[18] is 'an individual who has entered into or works under (or, where the employment has ceased, worked under) a contract of employment', the question of what constitutes a contract of employment is left to the courts and tribunals. The major divide here is between employment and self-employment, between a contract of employment and a contract for services (although other relationships such as agency or partnership could perhaps be used to avoid the relationship of employer and employee). A person with a contract for services is usually referred to as an 'independent contractor' and there may be several reasons why an individual may wish to be classed as such; the prime one is usually taxation, for there may well be tax advantages in being self-employed, of a legal nature (i.e. tax avoidance through being assessed under Schedule D with its payment at least partly in arrears and more generous allowances) or an illegal nature (i.e. tax evasion through part- or non-disclosure of income, not being under the PAYE system for Schedule E taxation of employees). From the employer's point of view it may be desirable to hire independent contractors, for this relieves him of the administrative tasks involved in deducting PAYE deductions and national insurance contributions from wages, and may relieve him of payment of certain levies based upon the number of persons employed (e.g. levies for industrial training); further, it may have certain VAT advantages and help to avoid the need to negotiate with unions (indeed in

17   For the arguments in favour of freeing statutory employment rights from their present basis on the contract of employment, see Hepple 'Restructuring Employment Rights' (1986) 15 ILJ 69.
18   Sections 230(1) and 295 respectively.

an area of large-scale self-employment such as the building industry it may be a long-standing cause of weak unionism generally).[19]

Advantages to the individual, however, tend to be of a short-term nature, and categorisation as 'independent' may have certain serious longer-term disadvantages, for most of the industrial safety legislation, some of the most important social security rights (particularly disablement benefit and jobseeker's allowance) and the modern employment protection legislation only apply to employed persons – to put it shortly, the independent contractor may be in a better monetary position while working, but at a grave disadvantage if he falls off a ladder or is sacked. Moreover, categorisation as independent may indirectly affect the rights of third parties too, for example a passer-by injured by the acts of that person, for the action then lies only against that independent contractor and *not* against the employer who may in the realities of the case be the only person worth suing[20].

i) Definition of the relationship

In spite of the obvious importance of the distinction between an employee and an independent contractor, the tests to be applied are vague and may, in a borderline case, be difficult to apply.[1] Historically, the solution lay in applying the 'control' test, i.e. could the employer control not just what the person was to do, but also the manner of his doing it – if so, that person was his employee[2]. In the context in which it mainly arose in the nineteenth century, of domestic, agricultural and manual workers, this test had much to commend it, but with the increased sophistication of industrial processes and the greater numbers of professional and skilled people being in salaried employment, it soon became obvious that the test was insufficient[3] (for example in the case of a doctor, architect, skilled engineer, pilot, etc.) and so, despite certain attempts to modernise it[4], it is now accepted that in itself control is no longer the sole test, though it does remain a factor and perhaps, in some cases, a decisive one[5]. In the search for a substitute test, ideas have been put forward of an 'integration' test, i.e. whether the person was fully integrated into the employer's concern, or remained apart

---

19   Bird, 'The self-employed: small entrepreneurs or disguised wage labourers?' in Pollert (ed) *Farewell to Flexibility* (1991). In the winter 1997/98 3.3m people were self-employed in their main job, which was 13% of all those in work; of these, 74% were men and 26% women: Moralee 'Self-employment in the 1990s' [1998] Labour Market Trends 121.

20   There are certain exemptions to this general rule, where an employer can be liable for the acts of his independent contractor, but they are narrow and, in some cases, uncertain: see *Clerk and Lindsell on Torts*, paras. 3–36 *et seq.*

1   The tests to be applied are a matter of law, but the *application* of those tests is a question of fact; where it arises in a statutory action, this means that the decision on categorisation lies almost entirely with the employment tribunal with little chance of a successful appeal from their decision: *O'Kelly v Trusthouse Forte plc* [1983] ICR 728, [1983] IRLR 369, CA; *Lee v Chung* [1990] ICR 409, [1990] IRLR 236, PC; see p 408, below, and Leighton (1984) 13 ILJ 62.

2   See, e.g., *Performing Right Society Ltd v Mitchell and Booker (Palais de Danse) Ltd* [1924] 1 KB 762; *Mersey Docks and Harbour Board v Coggins and Griffiths (Liverpool) Ltd* [1947] AC 1, [1946] 2 All ER 345, HL.

3   *Cassidy v Ministry of Health* [1951] 2 KB 343, [1951] 1 All ER 574, CA (a surgeon).

4   See, e.g. *Zuijs v Wirth Bros Ltd* (1955) 93 CLR 561 (concerning the control which could be exercised over a circus acrobat).

5   Particularly where the control demonstrates the reality of the relationship (e.g. in a case where there is more than one possible employer): *Clifford v Union of Democratic Mineworkers* [1991] IRLR 518, CA.

from and independent of it[6]. Once again, this is not now viewed as a sufficient test in itself, but rather as a potential factor (which may be useful in allowing a court to take a wider and more realistic view). The modern approach has been to abandon the search for a single test, and instead to take a multiple or 'pragmatic' approach, weighing up all the factors for and against a contract of employment and determining on which side the scales eventually settle[7]. As Cook J put it, in his much-cited judgment in *Market Investigations Ltd v Minister of Social Security*[8] the question ultimately is whether the person in question is performing the services as 'a person in business on his own account'; factors which are usually of importance are as follows – the power to select and dismiss, the direct payment of some form of remuneration, deduction of PAYE and national insurance contributions[9], the organisation of the workplace, the supply of tools and materials (though there can still be a labour-only sub-contract) and the economic realities (in particular who bears the risk of loss and has the chance of profit); however, even this is not an exhaustive check list, and a court or tribunal must still look at the overall picture in the particular case[10]. A further development in the modern case law (particularly concerning atypical employments) has been the idea of 'mutuality of obligations' as a possible factor, i.e. whether the course of dealings between the parties demonstrates sufficient such mutuality for there to be an overall employment relationship. It is true that such an approach can be disadvantageous to certain particularly irregular workers, making it more difficult to establish that they are employees[11], but on the other hand it has the positive aspect that it is capable of extending employed status to groups of atypical workers (especially of an external or part-time nature) if the relationship with the employer is sufficiently longstanding and stable; thus in *Nethermere (St Neots) Ltd v Gardiner*[12] outworkers making garments at home on a piecework basis were held to be employees of the garment manufacturer, largely because of the regular, longstanding arrangement which showed the necessary mutuality of obligations (to do and to be provided with the work) in practice, even though the outworkers

6   *Stevenson Jordan and Harrison Ltd v McDonald and Evans* [1952] 1 TLR 101, CA per Denning LJ.
7   *Ready Mixed Concrete (South East) Ltd v Minister of Pensions and National Insurance* [1968] 2 QB 497, [1968] 1 All ER 433; *Construction Industry Training Board v Labour Force Ltd* [1970] 3 All ER 220; *Global Plant Ltd v Secretary of State for Health and Social Security* [1972] 1 QB 139, [1971] 3 All ER 385; *Hitchcock v Post Office* [1980] ICR 100; *Andrews v King* [1991] ICR 846, [1991] STC 481 (a fascinating tax case on the legal position of the archaic system of agricultural gang labour). Agency workers may or may not be employees of the agency, depending on the facts (i.e. there is no rule of law either way): *McMeechan v Secretary of State for Employment* [1997] ICR 549, [1997] IRLR 353, CA; they used to be subject to a licensing system under the Employment Agencies Act 1973, but this was repealed and replaced by a much looser protective regime by the Deregulation and Contracting Out Act 1994; this itself is now under review by the present government: Fairness at Work (Cm. 3968, 1998), para. 3.18.
8   [1969] 2 QB 173, [1968] 3 All ER 732, approved and applied by the Privy Council in *Lee v Chung* [1990] ICR 409, [1990] IRLR 236.
9   Though perhaps a potent factor, this is not decisive (being primarily a matter between the person and the tax and insurance authorities) and so the non-deduction of these sums does *not* inevitably point to an independent contract if the other factors are against it; *Davis v New England College of Arundel* [1977] ICR 6; *Airfix Footwear Ltd v Cope* [1978] ICR 1210, [1978] IRLR 396; *Thames Television Ltd v Wallis* [1979] IRLR 136; conversely, deduction of these amounts does not per se mean that the relationship is one of employment: *Hall (Inspector of Taxes) v Lorimer*, n. 1 above.
10 *Hall (Inspector of Taxes) v Lorimer* [1994] ICR 218, [1994] IRLR 171, CA.
11 *O'Kelley v Trusthouse Forte plc* [1983] ICR 728, [1983] IRLR 369, CA; *Wickens v Champion Employment* [1984] ICR 365.
12 [1984] ICR 612, [1984] IRLR 240, CA.

were not covered by a formal contractual obligation to undertake a particular quantity of work; this is an important development, capable of extending employee status (and thereby employment rights) to workers employed otherwise than on a nine-to-five basis on the employer's premises. On the other hand, 'mutuality' was used as an argument *against* employee status for 'casual, as required' power station guides in the rather regressive decision of the House of Lords in *Carmichael v National Power plc*[13], where it was seen as an irreducible minimum for the existence of a contract of employment. Likewise, in *Express Echo Publications Ltd v Tanton*[14] the Court of Appeal viewed personal service by the employee as another irreducible minimum (rather than as just one factor), so that a power to organise delegation of work by the individual was fatal to employment status. Thus, we are seeing certain qualifications on the pure 'balancing of factors' approach. Finally, given the vagueness of the tests, there is considerable scope for an 'instinctive' approach in this area, i.e. that the judge knows a contract of employment when he sees one. In *Cassidy v Ministry of Health*[15], Somervell LJ said:

> 'One perhaps cannot get too much beyond this, "Was the contract a contract of [employment] within the meaning which an ordinary person would give under the words?" '

This may be unsatisfactory from an analytical point of view, but it probably reflects the practical position and indeed may not be as unsatisfactory as it first seems when considered in the context of the modern statutory rights where it falls to be applied by employment tribunals where the lay members may be expected to apply their industrial experience in its resolution[16]. The real problem with a vague test or tests is, however, that it can make advising in advance very difficult; not only is this a problem for the lawyer, but also it concerns an area of fundamental importance for both employer and employee who need to be certain as to the legal basis of their relationship. The parties' primary contact on this matter is likely to be, not with lawyers or tribunals, but with government departments and agencies, in particular the Inland Revenue[17] and the DSS; given the practical importance of such contacts, there has unfortunately been evidence in the past of different departments and agencies giving different advice and using different criteria on a person's employment status[18]. The previous government acknowledged that this can cause problems for employers and undertook to make internal changes to lessen the possibility of it happening[19]. In the context of taxation, the Inland Revenue has published a leaflet 'Tax: Employed or Self-Employed'[20] which attempts to clarify the distinction between employment and

---

13   [1999] ICR 1226, [2000] IRLR 43, HL.
14   [1999] ICR 693, [1999] IRLR 367, CA.
15   [1951] 2 KB 343, [1951] 1 All ER 574, CA at 352 and 579 respectively; see also McKenna J's third condition for a contract of employment in the *Ready Mixed Concrete* case, n 7 above. *Withers v Flackwell Heath Football Supporters' Club* [1981] IRLR 307.
16   *Challinor v Taylor* [1972] ICR 129; *Thames Television Ltd v Wallis* [1979] IRLR 136.
17   In many cases, the parties will in practice consider that they have successfully created the relationship of self-employment if the Inland Revenue have accepted it and not required the employer to operate the PAYE system. As stated above, however, this is not legally conclusive and the Inland Revenue can later decide to reconsider, the second principle of tax law being that the Revenue cannot be estopped (the first principle being that they always win eventually).
18   See Leighton 'Observing Employment Contracts' (1984) 13 ILJ 86.
19   'Lifting the Burden' (Cmnd. 9571, 1985) paras. 4.13, 4.14.
20   IR56. See also IR53 'Thinking of taking someone on?'.

self-employment, using the criteria set out above. While stressing that no one factor is a conclusive test, it suggests that you are an employee if you can answer 'yes' to the following questions[1] : Do you have to do the work that you have agreed to undertake yourself? Can someone tell you what to do, and when and how to do it? Are you paid so much an hour, a week or a month? Can you get overtime pay? Are you expected to work set hours, or a given number of hours a week or month? Are you expected to work at the premises of the person you are working for, or at a place or places they decide? It is then suggested that you are self-employed if you can answer 'yes' to the following questions: Are you ultimately responsible for how the business is run? Do you risk your own capital? Are you responsible for bearing losses as well as taking profits? Do you provide the major items of equipment you need to do your job? Are you free to hire other people, on terms of your own choice, to do the work that you have agreed to undertake? Do you have to correct unsatisfactory work in your own time and at your own expense? While these are not authoritative statements of law, and ultimately the decision on a person's status may have to be taken by a court or tribunal, it is to be welcomed that at least an attempt is being made to standardise the rules of the game (in the most important context in which in practice the issue initially arises, i.e. tax and N.I. contributions), though one might be cynical and say that in marginal cases a game is precisely what it remains[2] .

In addition to the general uncertainties here, one particular problem has caused some disagreement in the cases; it concerns the emphasis (or lack of it) which can be placed upon the statements and intentions of the parties themselves. They may stipulate (orally or in writing) that their contract shall be viewed one way (usually as an independent contract) – how is the court or tribunal to treat that?[3] In the past the usual approach has been to ignore the statements of the parties and apply an objective test[4] , and this can be seen in the decision of the Court of Appeal in *Ferguson v John Dawson & Partners (Contractors) Ltd*[5] where a man taken on at a building site with no written contract but on an oral understanding that he was on the 'lump', i.e. a labour-only sub-contractor, who was later injured, was held to have been in fact an employee (and so able to rely on certain industrial safety provisions in order to bring his action). The majority, Megaw and Brown LJJ, took a clearly objective approach and said that a declaration by the parties, even if incorporated into the contract, should be *disregarded entirely* if the remainder of the contractual terms pointed to the opposite conclusion (though for the purpose of their decision, they were prepared to adopt the less stringent approach

1   The leaflet does not, however, explain what is the position if you answer 'yes' to half of these questions and to half of the next set of questions!
2   With the Inland Revenue permanently having the service, through their ability to raise an assessment on the basis that they have decided upon (usually employment and Schedule E), leaving it up to the employer and/or 'employee' to appeal and challenge the correctness of that basis. In the light of this, the National Federation of the Self-Employed argued for a registration system for self-employment, with registration under it being conclusive of a person's status, and the Institute of Directors put forward the most radical proposal, that people should simply be able to *elect* to be self-employed. Neither of these suggestions has been taken up officially.
3   There may be the added complication that the employee is now trying to *change* the basis of the contract, e.g. where he initially agreed to be self-employed, but has now been injured or dismissed and so needs to show that he was in fact an employee in order to claim the appropriate remedy.
4   For examples, see *Davis v New England College of Arundel* [1977] ICR 6; *Tyne and Clyde Warehouses Ltd v Hamerton* [1978] ICR 661; *Thames Television Ltd v Wallis* [1979] IRLR 136.
5   [1976] 3 All ER 817, [1976] IRLR 346, CA.

that such a declaration or statement can be a relevant, but certainly not conclusive, factor). Lawton LJ dissented strongly, stating[6],

> '... I can see no reason why in law a man cannot sell his labour without becoming another man's servant even though he is willing to accept control as to how, when and where he shall work. If he makes his intention not to be a servant sufficiently clear, the implications which would normally arise from implied terms do not override the prime object of the bargain. In my judgment, this is just such a case.'

In a subsequent Court of Appeal case, *Massey v Crown Life Insurance Co*[7] however, a different approach was taken. In that case a branch manager who was an ordinary employee asked to change the basis of his contract to self-employment (for tax purposes); the employer consented to this and negotiated a new agreement. When the agreement was subsequently terminated, the manager tried to claim unfair dismissal on the basis that he was in fact an employee all along, but the Court of Appeal held unanimously that he could not do so, since the new agreement had effectively altered the basis of his engagement so that he was no longer an employee. It must be said at the outset that the desire to avoid a position whereby a person could claim various tax advantages, and then argue exactly to the contrary to obtain unfair dismissal benefits at a later stage, obviously played a part in this decision[8] but, in spite of that, the approach to the problem was different from that of the previous Court of Appeal. Lord Denning MR said[9],

> 'It seems to me on the authorities that, when it is a situation which is in doubt or which is ambiguous, so that it can be brought under one relationship or the other, it is open to the parties by agreement to stipulate what the legal situation between them shall be. ... So the way in which the parties draw up their agreement and express it can be a very important factor in defining what the true relation was between them. If they declare that one party is self-employed, that may be decisive.'

His Lordship distinguished the *Ferguson* case quite simply 'on its facts' and Lawton LJ did likewise (pointing primarily to the lack of a written agreement or, indeed of any particularly reliable evidence as to the relationship in that case), adding[10],

> '*Ferguson* clearly established that the parties cannot change a status merely by putting a new label on it. But if in all the circumstances of the case, including the terms of the agreement, it is manifest that there was an intention to change status, then, in my judgment, there is no reason why the parties should not be allowed to make the change.'

6   Ibid., at 828 and 351 respectively.
7   [1978] ICR 590, [1978] IRLR 31, CA, applied in *BSM (1257) Ltd v Secretary of State for Social Services* [1978] ICR 894 and *Calder v H Kitson Vickers & Sons (Engineers) Ltd* [1988] ICR 232, CA.
8   See also the dissenting judgment of Lawton LJ in *Ferguson v John Dawson & Partners (Contractors) Ltd*, n. 5 above.
9   *Massey v Crown Life Insurance Co*, n. 2 above, 595 and 33 respectively.
10 Ibid., 597 and 34 respectively.

However, this wider approach in *Massey* was called into question in the further Court of Appeal case of *Young & Woods Ltd v West*[11] where a sheet metal worker who had been engaged on a self-employed basis (and had been treated as such by the Inland Revenue) was held to have in fact been an employee so that after his dismissal he could claim unfair dismissal. The court did not indicate that *Massey's* case was wrong, and did not take as purely an objective approach as the majority in *Ferguson's* case would have liked to do. They did, however, seek to narrow the effect of *Massey's* case; in particular they did not accept that if the parties deliberately set out to create a relationship of self-employment, that intention should normally be put into effect by a court or tribunal. A further contribution of this question was made by Lord Hoffman in *Carmichael v National Power plc*[12], where 'casual, as required' power station guides were held not to be employees; pointing out that in reality many employment relationships will not be contained purely in written form, but will also need to be discerned from correspondence and conduct, he envisaged a significant role for the parties' intentions, at least as a factor:

> 'The evidence of a party as to what terms he understood to have been agreed is some evidence tending to show that those terms, in an objective sense, were agreed. Of course, the tribunal may reject such evidence and conclude the party misunderstood the effect of what was being said and done. But when both parties are agreed about what they understood their mutual obligations (or lack of them) to be, it is a strong thing to exclude their evidence from consideration.'[13]

Thus, the position now seems to be that, as a matter of practice, the declared intention of the parties may be more important if (a) there has been a deliberate *change* in the basis of employment, (b) the work in question was of an unusual nature so that an ambiguity as to its true nature might be found more easily[14], or (c) the arrangement has been entered into in a relatively informal manner and has to be construed in the light of several factors and circumstances, as in *Carmichael*. On the question of the policy behind the earlier decisions, the court in *Young & Woods Ltd v West* thought that the danger of allowing employers to avoid the employment protection legislation simply by labelling people as self-employed was an important consideration. They recognised the fears expressed (particularly in *Massey's* case) of injustice being caused by allowing a person to claim to be self-employed for tax purposes during employment, but then to claim on dismissal to have been an employee all along in order to claim unfair dismissal, but suggested that this could be overcome by a court or tribunal finding that the person was employed (thereby permitting the unfair dismissal action) but then informing the Inland Revenue of that fact, thereby inviting a reassessment of his tax liability for the past years of his employment under

11   [1980] IRLR 201, CA.
12   [1999] ICR 1226, [2000] IRLR 43, HL.
13   At 1235 and 47, respectively. Lord Hoffman disapproved the view of the majority of the Court of Appeal that the relationship had to be considered purely objectively, disregarding the parties' understandings.
14   Both (a) and (b) were considered by Stephenson LJ in *Young & Woods Ltd v West* to have been important aspects of *Massey's* case; on the latter factor, Mr Massey's position as a manager with a separate agency agreement was more unusual employment than Mr West's job of sheet metal worker (working alongside other people doing exactly the same work, but as employees). The Court of Appeal found that Mr West's circumstances did not raise the sort of ambiguity necessary if the label of self-employment was to be decisive.

Schedule E[15]; knowledge that this is a possibility could be a considerable disincentive to the person who is thinking of trying to alter his status at this late stage.

ii)   Three particular applications

In addition to these general principles relating to the existence of a contract of employment, three specific points are worthy of mention. The first is that, although some of the cases cited on this problem are tort cases concerning vicarious liability, some care may be needed, for the test for vicarious liability is not necessarily identical to that for the existence of an employment relationship in industrial law. It is true that it *looks* the same – was there a contract of employment? – but the factors behind it may be different, for in tort (for example in a 'borrowed servant' case[16], where employer A lends B a crane plus driver and, while acting under B's orders the driver injures C – should A or B be liable to C?) the court is essentially looking at the liability question at one moment in time, whereas in an industrial case (e.g. on redundancy rights or unfair dismissal) the tribunal may have to assess the legal consequences of a potentially long-term relationship; it may be, therefore, that 'static' ideas of control may be more important in a tort case than in an industrial case where more factors may need to be taken into account to achieve a realistic result. Thus, in the borrowed servant example, it may be that, on the facts, B is liable to C[17], whereas it is clear that for unfair dismissal or employment protection purposes, A remains his employer. Thus, tort precedents may have to be used with care in other contexts[18].

The second point is that various practical problems may arise over the use of independent contracting, particularly in a system of labour-only sub-contracting as on the 'lump' in the building industry[19]. The Court of Appeal showed some hostility to this in *Ferguson's* case, particularly as there was clear suspicion in that case of unlawful tax evasion; as it stood, that case could perhaps have been developed by subsequent courts as a way of curbing the over-use of sub-contracting by placing stringent limits upon its legal recognition, but even the majority did not feel that they could go as far as to strike down such an agreement as an illegal

15   Thus it could be that the ex-employee would end up owing more to the Inland Revenue than he gained in compensation for unfair dismissal. In *Young's* case, Ackner LJ said that Mr West had probably won a 'hollow, indeed an expensive, victory'. The problem from the employer's point of view is that if this happens he will end up liable to pay the employer's N.I. contributions that should have been paid over the course of the employment; moreover, if the employee is unable to pay the back tax, the Inland Revenue could seek to recover it from the employer on the basis that he should have been operating the PAYE system all along.

16   *Mersey Docks and Harbour Board v Coggins and Griffiths (Liverpool) Ltd* [1947] AC 1, [1946] 2 All ER 345, HL.

17   *Donovan v Laing, Wharton and Down Construction Syndicate Ltd* [1893] 1 QB 629, CA; *Sime v Sutcliffe Catering Scotland Ltd* [1990] IRLR 228, Ct of Sess. For a variation on this, see *McDermid v Nash Dredging and Reclamation Co Ltd* [1987] ICR 917, [1987] IRLR 334, HL.

18   For a clear indication of this, see Denning LJ's judgment in *Denham v Midland Employers' Mutual Assurance Ltd* [1955] 2 QB 437, [1955] 2 All ER 561, CA and more recently, the decision of the Court of Appeal in *Morris v Breaveglen Ltd* [1993] ICR 766, [1993] IRLR 350, CA.

19   Clark 'Industrial law and the labour-only sub-contract' (1967) 30 MLR 6; Drake 'Wage slave or entrepreneur?' (1968) 31 MLR 408; Mordesley 'Some problems of the "lump" ' (1975) 38 MLR 504.

contract and, in the light of the subsequent case law discussed above, a major judicial assault on the lump and other such practices is unlikely. Legislative reforms have been suggested in order to rule out all but bona fide contractors[20] but, except in the area of income tax where provisions have been introduced to extend the PAYE system and counter unlawful tax evasion[1], little has been done.

The third point concerns the position of company directors. An ordinary director will not normally be under a contract of employment, even when in receipt of directors' fees. However, there is nothing to prevent a director from being 'employed' (even by his own one-man company[2]) if the relationship is in fact over and above that of ordinary director, as in the case of an executive or managing director. However, the mere fact that a director performs some duties for the company may not be enough[3] and if he wishes to establish a contract of employment (for example to be able to claim unfair dismissal when his services are dispensed with) he must show further factors. Thus in *Parsons v Albert J Parsons & Sons Ltd*[4] the Court of Appeal held that a director was not 'employed', in spite of working full time for the company, since the company records did not contain a written contract of employment for him or memorandum setting out the terms of an oral contract[5], his sole remuneration was that categorised in the accounts as 'directors' fees' and he had been treated as self-employed for tax and national insurance purposes. Moreover, it may be possible to argue that a director should not be classed as an 'employee' because to do so would be inconsistent with the employment right that that person is trying to claim; the area in which this has arisen to date is the state guarantee for moneys outstanding to employees on a company's insolvency[6], where it had been held by the EAT that it would be improper to allow the de facto owner of a one-man company to claim from the state on his company's insolvency[7]. However, the Court of Appeal later reaffirmed strongly that there was no such rule of law, and that in each case it remains a question of fact – the person's status as a controlling director may well be a *factor* against employment status, but must be balanced against other factors such as the bona fides of the contract, the degree of control exercised by the company, the position of any other directors and the conduct of the parties[8].

20 See the Report of the Committee of Inquiry under Professor Phelps Brown into labour matters in the building industry, (1968) Cmnd. 3714, noted (1969) 32 MLR 75.

1 Finance Act 1971, ss 29–31; Finance (No. 2) Act 1975, ss. 68–71; Finance (No. 2) Act 1979, s. 15.

2 *Lee v Lee's Air Farming Ltd* [1961] AC 12, [1960] 3 All ER 420, PC. On employment by a workers' co-operative, see *Drym Fabricators Ltd v Johnson* [1981] ICR 274.

3 *Stanbury v Overmass and Chapple Ltd* (1976) 11 ITR 7, IT. However, there may be a presumption of employed status if the director is required to work full time for the company in return for a salary: *Folami v Nigerline (UK) Ltd* [1978] ICR 277.

4 [1979] ICR 271, [1979] IRLR 117, CA; *Morley v C T Morley Ltd* [1985] ICR 499; *Eaton v Robert Eaton Ltd* [1988] ICR 302, [1988] IRLR 83.

5 As required by the Companies Act 1985, s. 318.

6 See p. 218, below.

7 *Buchan v Secretary of State for Employment* [1997] IRLR 80.

8 *Secretary of State for Trade and Industry v Botterill* [1999] ICR 592, [1999] IRLR 326, CA (director held to be an employee for insolvency guarantee purposes); reasoning in *Buchan* disapproved.

iii) Atypical, part time, temporary and casual work

It has become increasingly clear that atypical workers such as 'outworkers' (i.e. people who perform work for another at home rather than in a factory) may have their employment protection, etc., rights jeopardised by a finding that they are independent contractors[9]. Part-time workers in factories may have had problems in the past with the old '16 hours per week' rule for computing continuity of employment until its repeal in 1995[10], but at least there was usually no question that they were in fact 'employed', whereas in the case of an outworker even that might be in doubt, for if on the facts it appears that the work is brought to them, and accepted, purely on an ad hoc basis, the tribunal might take the view that the outworker was not in fact 'employed'[11]. Where, however, the outworker works on a regular basis the EAT held in *Airfix Footwear Ltd v Cope*[12] that there is no reason why there should not be a finding of a contract of employment, even though the work is done elsewhere than on the employer's premises, if there is sufficient mutuality of obligations; as seen above, this approach was approved by the Court of Appeal in *Nethermere (St Neots) Ltd v Gardiner*[13]. While an arrangement such as homeworking is still generally considered 'atypical', it is increasingly recognised that nine-to-five employment throughout the year in a manufacturing factory is becoming *less* typical, and so increasingly the law will have to consider the position of those working under more diverse and less full-time conditions. In particular, much of the recent job creation in the economy has been in forms hitherto thought to be atypical, but fast becoming the norm in many sectors of the labour market[14]. At the same time, with the decline of traditional manufacturing industries and the expansion of the service and I.T. sectors, the nature of the employing concern has been changing, with larger numbers of people now being employed by what hitherto would have been considered 'small firms'[15].

---

9   Collins 'Independent contractors and the challenge of vertical disintegration to employment protection laws' (1990) 10 OJLS 353. To take another example, youth trainees are not employees (being in fact in limbo, since they are not self-employed either); for this reason, training agreements have to contain contractual rights akin to those they would have had if they had been employees, and regulations and orders have had to be made in order to extend health and safety legislation and the laws on sex and race discrimination to them specifically.

10 See p. 148, below.

11 *Mailway (Southern) Ltd v Willsher* [1978] ICR 511, [1978] IRLR 322; there is also a possible argument, adverted to in the *Airfix* case (n. 12 below) that there could be a *separate* contract of employment for each job where it is only on a sporadic basis, but no overall contract.

12 [1978] ICR 1210, [1978] IRLR 396. See generally Ewing 'Homeworking, a framework for reform' (1982) 11 ILJ 94, and Hakim 'Homeworking in Britain' [1987] Employment Gazette 92.

13 [1984] ICR 612, [1984] IRLR 240, CA.

14 See, e.g., Fredman 'Labour law in flux: the changing composition of the workforce' (1997) 26 ILJ 337.

15 This was strikingly demonstrated by research undertaken when considering whether to decrease the exemption for small firms from the Disability Discrimination Act 1995. This showed that 1 million employers in the private sector (95% of the total number of employers in the UK) employing 4.5 million workers were firms employing fewer than twenty people: Disability Discrimination Act 1995: the Employment Provisions and Small Employers (DFEE, 1998).

Part-time and temporary work is now more prevalent[16] and in some areas experiments such as job sharing are in evidence[17]. Generally, the workforce has become more flexible[18] and indeed encouraging such flexibility is government policy[19], since it is seen as a way of encouraging more use of individual contracting, flexible pay and payment by results, the antithesis of the collective approach to wage determination. However, this development may cause strains in applying laws evolved basically against the background of full-time, 'normal' employment. While it is important to remember that, for better or for worse, the juristic basis here remains the traditional contract of employment, it is also important to ensure that there is not too much scope for employers to use devices such as temporary or part-time work in order to evade statutory obligations[20]. It is already argued that in Britain we are evolving a two-tier labour force – those in traditional full-time employment with a fair degree of job security and statutory protection, and those (increasingly) in part-time, temporary or otherwise atypical employment with little security, and generally excluded from statutory protection[1]. In fact, the principal moves towards protection of part-time employees have come through EC law. Initially, this was under EC sex equality laws which apply because of the disparate effect on women of rules prejudicing part-timers; the most notable success lay in the enforced removal (first by court action and then by amending

16   In 1998, there were 6.6m part-time workers, comprising 1.3m men and 5.3m women, or 8% of the male workforce and 44% of the female workforce; of those between 25 and 49, 47% of men said they worked part time because they could not find full time work and 34% did not want full time work, whereas 8% of women said they worked part time because they could not find full time work and 90% did not want full time work: [1998] Labour Market Trends 600. According to the same survey, in 1998 there were 1.8m in temporary jobs (8% of the workforce), comprising 880,000 men and 967,000 women: ibid., at 598. The literature on this is voluminous. See e.g. Millward et al. *Workplace Industrial Relations in Transition* (1992), pp. 337 ff; Dickens 'Working time and employment equality' (1992) 21 ILJ 146; views can vary, however, as to how to define 'part-time work' and therefore how prevalent it is: see Hakim 'Employment rights: a comparison of part-time and full-time employees' (1989) 18 ILJ 69 and the reply by Disney and Szyszczak (1989) 18 ILJ 223.

17   Leighton 'Job sharing – some issues for labour law' (1986) 15 ILJ 173.

18   ACAS Annual Report 1987, pp. 14, 18; Hakim 'Trends in the flexible workforce' [1987] Employment Gazette 549; Labour Flexibility in Britain, the 1987 ACAS Survey (ACAS Occasional Paper No. 41, 1988); Wareing 'Working arrangements and patterns of working hours in Britain' [1992] Employment Gazette 88; McGregor and Sproull 'Employers and the flexible workforce' [1992] Employment Gazette 225; Dickens *Whose Flexibility?* (1992); Beatson 'Progress towards a flexible labour market' (1995) Employment Gazette 55; Nolan and Walsh 'The structure of the economy and labour market' in Edwards (ed) *Industrial Relations, Theory and Practice in Britain* (1995).

19   See Employment for the 1990s (Cm 540, 1988); People, Jobs and Opportunity (Cm 1810, 1992) for the previous government's policy; Fairness at Work (CM. 3968, 1998) for the present government's policy.

20   *Lewis v Surrey County Council* [1987] ICR 982, [1987] IRLR 509, HL, at 998 and 516 respectively, per Lord Ackner. One employer's ace wheeze, to avoid employment responsibilities (such as SSP), of putting an employee or to 'daily contracts' (sic) for a total period of nine months was kicked into touch by the Court of Appeal who applied the Employment Rights Act 1996, s. 86(4) which states that any contract for less than a month which in fact lasts for more than three months is deemed to be for an indefinite period (thus requiring notice to end it): *Brown v Chief Adjudication Officer* [1997] ICR 266, [1997] IRLR 110, CA.

1   Dickens 'Falling through the net: employment change and worker protection' (1988) 19 IRJ 139. A current view is that this movement has been a pragmatic reaction to market conditions and business uncertainties rather than deliberate and widespread managerial policy: Sisson and Marquison 'Management: systems, structures and strategy' in Edwards (ed) *Industrial Relations, Theory and Practice in Britain* (1995) 89, at p 113.

regulations) of the requirement of working 16 hours per week in order to gain continuity of employment (for the purposes of qualifying for the major statutory rights)[2]. This approach is now formalised by the Directive on Part-Time Work[3], effective from April 2000. To the extent that the first half of it requires a basic principle of non-discrimination against part-timers, subject to a defence of objective justification, this is enacted in Britain by the Part-time Workers (Prevention of Less Favourable Treatment) Regulations 2000[4]. It may be debatable how much this will add to the position already reached by sex discrimination law (apart from giving a *direct* action to challenge any worse treatment, rather then having to go through the hoops of a discrimination action), since most employers who are well advised already know that it is legally dangerous to treat a part-timer on anything less than a pro rata basis. However, this point is subject to two qualifications. The first is that the second half of the Directive contains some broader aims, requiring employers to give proper consideration to matters such as requests to change from full-time to part-time and vice versa (often a point of some importance for an employee returning from maternity leave), letting existing part-timers know in advance of full-time opportunities, and encouraging part-time work at all levels of the organisation. In the Employment Relations Act 1999, s. 20 the government took a power to enact such provisions by a Code of Practice (awaited at the time of writing). While this would be a 'soft law' option, it could have an important effect on employment practices, especially as the stated aim of the Directive is not just to eliminate discrimination, but more positively to enhance the *status* of part-time work generally. The second qualification is that there may be a greater direct effect on British employment patterns from the *next* Directive in this area (to follow that relating to part-timers), namely the Directive on Fixed-Term Work[5]. When eventually enacted, this will implement again a basic principle of non-discrimination against fixed-term workers, subject to a defence of objective justification. In addition however, it requires further protection in that a member state must choose one of three options to control the *use* of such contracts, namely (1) a need for objective justification whenever such a contract is renewed, (2) a maximum total duration of successive fixed-term contracts, or (3) a limit on the permissible number of such renewals. Given the relatively high incidence of fixed-term employment in Britain and the fact that hitherto it has not been seriously challenged by sex discrimination law, this Directive could have a greater substantive effect here than the Part-time Work Directive.

One legal device that has shown some signs of evolving as a possible remedy in cases where part-time or sporadic work (e.g. on a series of short-term contracts) appears to be being misused is that of the 'umbrella or global contract', i.e. a finding that although the employee was only actually working for certain periods

2   See p 148, below. See also the enforced extension to part-timers of rights under occupational pension schemes, p. 303, below.
3   Directive 98/23; this was the fourth attempt to pass such a directive. The previous government vetoed the previous attempt in 1994: Jeffrey (1995) 24 ILJ 296. This successful directive was the result of a Framework Agreement between the Social Partners, adopted by the Social Affair's Council in December 1997 as Directive 97/81, and then reissued to include the UK as Directive 98/23; for a strong critique of its minimalist approach, see Jeffrey 'Not really going to work?' (1998) 27 ILJ 193.
4   SI 2000/1551.
5   Directive 99/70. As with the Part-time Work Directive, this comes from a framework agreement between the social partners (ETUC, UNICE and CEEP). Interestingly, the Directive defines a fixed-term contract more widely than domestic law, applying not just to a time-limited contract, but also to a contract for a specific task or until the occurrence of a specific event. 'Successive' contracts may be difficult to define.

(possibly on an irregular basis), there was sufficient mutuality between the parties to justify a finding that in law there was one overall contract governing the whole period in question. However, this argument failed in one of the leading cases, *Hellyer Bros Ltd v McLeod*[6], where trawlermen who had sailed exclusively for one company for many years were held unable to claim redundancy payments when dispensed with, since the facts only established a series (albeit a long series) of separate contracts for each voyage. In an appropriate case, however, this could be a useful device, though it is clear that it is no panacea, and that if it does not apply an applicant may be in severe difficulties, for example in establishing the necessary continuity of employment for claiming the statutory right in question.[7]

Casual work has always caused problems legally, especially as there is a persistent folk myth among many employers that *because* a person is termed 'casual', *therefore* they cannot have any employment rights. It is important to realise, however, that 'casual' is not a legal term of art, that the word appears nowhere in the Employment Rights Act 1996, that the only legal distinction is between those who do and those who do not qualify for employment rights, and that a casual worker may or may not so qualify, depending on the facts. On the other hand, it has to be accepted that casual workers can have more problems than most in meeting qualification conditions, obviously in relation to continuity of employment, and more fundamentally in relation to employee status. Although the general trend in the past in the case law has been towards extension of legal rights to casuals, the signs are now that this may no longer be the case. In *Clarke v Oxfordshire Health Authority*[8] a 'bank' nurse (being offered and accepting work or as when it was available at any of the authority's hospitals) who was paid at standard rates and charged to PAYE and NI contributions, but who was not guaranteed any regular work, was held by the Court of Appeal *not* to be an employee (after three years working in the authority's hospitals, with only four breaks totalling fourteen weeks) and so unable to claim unfair dismissal[9]. In *Carmichael v National Power plc*[10] a question was raised as to the employment status of two power station guides employed on a 'casual, as required' basis to show parties around when the need arose, given uniforms and charged to PAYE and NI contributions. The Court of Appeal split, with the majority finding that they were employees, in a thoughtful decision in favour of extending employment status, perfecting the potentially informal relationship by finding implied terms that (a) the employer would offer each guide a reasonable amount of the work available and (b) each guide

6   [1987] ICR 526, [1987] IRLR 232, CA. The possibility of such a finding was, however, considered to be an important possibility (for countering the abuse of short-term contracts by an employer) by Lord Ackner in *Lewis v Surrey County Council*, n. 20, above. Continuity of employment was preserved by the Court of Appeal in *Flack v Kodak Ltd* [1986] ICR 775, [1986] IRLR 255 in a case of irregular, sporadic contracts by the alternative device of resorting to the ERA 1996, s. 212(3)(b) ('temporary cessation of work'), see p. 153, below.

7   For a good example, see *Letheby & Christopher Ltd v Bond* [1988] ICR 480.

8   [1998] IRLR 125, CA.

9   There was, however, a major qualification in the judgment. In the tribunal this issue had arguably been confused by considering not just whether there was an employment contract, but whether there was an umbrella contract covering the whole period (above). What had not been considered was whether there was a series of *individual* contracts (for each stint at one of the hospitals), possibly *linked* by the rules on continuity of employment; the result of the decision was a remission to the tribunal to consider this possibility.

10   [1999] ICR 1226, [2000] IRLR 43, HL. The principal speech is by Lord Irvine LC; the other speech by Lord Hoffman is of interest on the fact/law distinction as applied to the existence of a contract of employment, holding that the Court of Appeal had been wrong to interfere with the tribunal's decision for the employer *at all*.

would accept a reasonable amount of the work offered. However, on further appeal the House of Lords disapproved this completely and held that the guides were not employees, largely due to lack of a level of mutuality of obligations which Lord Irvine LC said was an irreducible minimum for any contract of employment. This is a serious blow to any prospect of further extension of employment status by judicial action, and indeed might even be used to attack existing case law granting such status to certain atypical workers (e.g. homeworkers). In the light of this it is likely that any further moves towards extending employment status and ensuring that employment protection laws continue to apply widely to an ever more diverse workforce will have to come from legislation, which is considered below.

iv) Associated employers

When considering the relationship of employer and employee, 'the employer' will normally be readily identifiable. If an employee decides voluntarily to change employer (e.g. to further his career), it is accepted that he will in doing so lose the rights he has accrued already and have to start again with the new employer. However, in the realities of modern business, the employer is likely to be a body corporate and here it may be more difficult to identify 'the employer' in that the particular company for which the employee works may itself be merely one part of a larger organisation. Such an organisation may be split down into smaller units for reasons (usually financial) which have little to do with employment law. It is, therefore, important that there should be provisions ensuring that employees do not lose their rights as a result of the composition of the employing concern and that an excessively technical view should not be taken of who or what constitutes the employer. Such provisions also serve as an anti-avoidance device, ensuring that employers cannot gain by dividing undertakings artificially into small units.

The provisions in question are those relating to 'associated employers', whereby two or more units (such as companies within one group) can be treated as one employer. The most important application of the concept of associated employers is in the context of continuity of employment (a vital factor in modern employment rights, both as to qualification to claim the right in question, such as unfair dismissal or a redundancy payment, and quantification of the employee's entitlement under that right). Thus, if an employee transfers (or is transferred) from the employment of one employer to the employment of an associated employer, his continuity of employment is *preserved,* and time spent with the first employer can count as time with the second employer[11]. The concept goes further, however, and can be found throughout the employment legislation. Thus for example, when deciding whether an employer can claim to be a 'small employer' (and so entitled to certain exceptions), any employees employed by an associated employer are usually counted in when computing the total number of employees[12]. Also, offers of 'suitable alternative employment' (important in redundancy law and in relation to maternity leave) may be made by the employer or an associated employer[13].

---

11 See p. 159, below. To be an 'associated employer', it is not essential that the company in question was already employing labour when the employee in question transferred to it: *Lucas v Henry Johnson (Packers and Shippers) Ltd* [1986] ICR 384.
12 See for example the maternity leave exemption for small firms.
13 See pp. 335 and 536, below.

From these examples, it is easy to see the importance of the concept of associated employers. The definition is contained in the Employment Rights Act 1996, s. 231:

'… any two employers are to be treated as associated if one is a company of which the other (directly or indirectly) has control, or if both are companies of which a third person (directly or indirectly) has control …'[14].

'Control' is thus crucial, and there must be voting control in some form, not just de facto influence, however strong.[15] An extension to this narrow approach was suggested by the EAT in *Zarb and Samuels v British and Brazilian Produce Co (Sales) Ltd*[16] where it was held that control by a third person could include control by third *persons*, so that if two or more persons between them own more than 50% of the voting shares of the two companies *and* in practice act together, that may satisfy the definition. However, this approach has caused considerable difficulties, since the Court of Appeal in *South West Launderettes Ltd v Laidler*[17] questioned the correctness of *Zarb* and declined to apply it where on the facts it may have been possible to do so. The position is not absolutely clear because it was not necessary for the court to decide the matter and in the subsequent case of *Harford v Swiftrim Ltd*[18] the EAT applied *Zarb* (on the basis that it has been consistently followed) and expressly refused to apply the criticisms of it in *Laidler*. A different division of the EAT under Wood P then declined to follow *Harford* in *Strudwick v Iszatt Bros Ltd*[19], stating obiter that if necessary they would have followed the criticisms in *Laidler* and held against any concept of plural control (largely because of the major problems of discovery, evidence and proof that are capable of arising under such a concept). On the other hand, *Zarb* was applied again by a later EAT in *Tice v Cartwright*[20], which perhaps showed that the present position (until we have a definitive ruling of the Court of Appeal) is that *Zarb* remains there to be used where common sense and justice demand that two organisations be deemed to be one, especially where (or in this case) the facts concern a very restricted shareholding in a family concern, where the necessary de facto control and common action can be shown.

One significant problem which arose under this definition was that it only refers to *companies* as being associated employers. What was to be the position

---

14 This definition, introduced by the Employment Protection Act 1975, is wider than that originally in the Contracts of Employment Acts, which required all parties to be companies, so did not apply to two companies under the control of one person: *Price v Syd Long (Stockton) Ltd* [1976] IRLR 41, IT.

15 *Secretary of State for Employment v Newbold* [1981] IRLR 305; *Umar v Pliastar Ltd* [1981] ICR 727. This even applies when the person in question owns 50 per cent of the shares in one of the companies, for that is *not* a voting majority and so the companies are not associated: *Hair Colour Consultants Ltd v Mena* [1984] ICR 671, [1984] IRLR 386; *South West Launderettes Ltd v Laidler* [1986] ICR 455, [1986] IRLR 305, CA; cf. however *Payne v Secretary of State for Employment* [1989] IRLR 352, CA, where one person held 50% as a nominee of the other person.

16 [1978] IRLR 78. For this principle to apply, it must be the same group of persons exercising control in the case of each company claimed to be associated: *Poparm Ltd v Weekes* [1984] IRLR 388, approved by the Court of Appeal in *South West Launderettes Ltd v Laidler*, n. 19, below.

17 [1986] ICR 455, [1986] IRLR 305, CA.

18 [1987] ICR 439, [1987] IRLR 360.

19 [1988] ICR 796, [1988] IRLR 457; *Russell v Elmdon Freight Terminal Ltd* [1989] ICR 629, EAT.

20 [1999] ICR 769.

where the two employers in question were *not* companies (e.g. in the public sector, bodies such as health trusts, local authorities or universities) or if *one* of the employers was not a company (e.g. where one farmer runs two farms, one constituted as a company and the other as a partnership)? There were conflicting EAT decisions on this point. One view was that the definition was not exhaustive (only governing the position where the two employers in fact are companies) so that other bodies can be 'associated' if that is the practical position[1]. The other view was that the definition *was* exhaustive, so that only companies can be associated[2]. This conflict was resolved in *Merton London Borough Council v Gardiner*[3] where the Court of Appeal held that the definition is exhaustive, so that an employee who was unfairly dismissed by a local authority could only claim to have his compensation calculated by reference to the two years he had worked with that authority, not by reference to the ten years he had previously served with three other local authorities. Thus, except under the first part of the definition ('vertical' associated employers) where one of the employers can be any sort of person provided that he, she or it has control of the company which is the other employer, the bodies claimed to be associated must be companies, which is a significant limitation on the definition (in the absence of any special statutory exception; the most important such exception now is that employees in local government service are covered by regulations which deem their employment to be continuous, for redundancy rights purposes, when they move from one local government body to another[4]).

v) 'Worker' and the wider definition of employment

It can be argued that the traditional legal dichotomy between 'employee' and 'independent contractor' is now too simplistic to fit our diverse workforce, and leaves too many people potentially in a hole in the middle. One way to avoid (or at least mitigate) this, would be to move the goal posts and extend the definition of 'employee'.

This is not a new idea, and it has in the past been done in one of two ways, namely to use the term 'worker' instead (with a correspondingly wider definition) or to retain the term 'employee' but add to the normal definition (i.e. as a person under a contract of employment). Trade union legislation has always used the term 'worker', defining it as 'an individual who works ... (a) under a contract of employment or (b) under any other contract whereby he undertakes to do or perform personally any work or services for another party to the contract who is not a professional client of his'[5]. The extension in (b) is highly significant.

1   *Hillingdon Area Health Authority v Kauders* [1979] ICR 472, [1979] IRLR 197.
2   *Southwood Hostel Management Committee v Taylor* [1979] ICR 813, [1979] IRLR 397.
3   [1981] ICR 186, [1980] IRLR 472, CA.
4   Redundancy Payments (Continuity of Employment in Local Government) (Modification) Order 1999 SI 1999/2277, Harvey R [1186]. See also the Redundancy Payments (National Health Service) (Modification) Order 1993. S.I. 1993 No. 3167, *Harvey* R[755] which performs a similar function in the now-fragmented structure of the NHS, and the ERA 1996, s. 218(7) which preserves continuity through the movement by teachers between schools maintained by a local education authority and that authority.
5   Trade Union and Labour Relations (Consolidation) Act 1992, s. 296; the 'Wages Act' provisions or deductions from wages use a similar term and definition, see now the Employment Rights Act 1996, s. 230(3) and the recovery of commission by a self-employed investment consultant in *Robertson v Blackstone Franks Investment Management Ltd* [1998] IRLR 376, CA.

Discrimination legislation uses the term 'employment' but applies it to employment under a contract of service or apprenticeship or a contract personally to execute any work or labour[6]. The Transfer of Undertakings (Protection of Employment) Regulations 1981 use the term 'employee' but define it as working 'for another person whether under a contract of service or apprenticeship or otherwise but does not include anyone who provides services under a contract for services'[7]. While these definitions contain subtle differences (with the TUPE definition being arguably narrowest, with its exclusion of *anyone* under a contract for services), they do show a deliberate extension of statutory coverage. Perhaps surprisingly, the case law on them has been relatively scarce, though the leading authority of *Mirror Group Newspapers Ltd v Gunning*[8] emphasises the element of 'personal service', and states that that must be the dominant purpose of the contract in question.

This whole matter has, however, become topical again for two reasons. The first is that similar expanded definitions have been used by the present government in the Public Interest Disclosure Act 1998[9], the National Minimum Wage Act 1998[10] and the regulations on working time and part-time workers[11]. The second is that the government have expressed interest in making a similar extension to move mainstream employment legislation, in particular the Employment Rights Act 1996. This was raised in the White Paper Fairness at Work[12] as a possible solution to the problem of the increased use by some employers of unfair forms of contracting such as 'nil hours contracts', which would be difficult to control or ban specifically, but might effectively be negated by wider coverage for employment protection laws. To that end, there is now a power in the Employment Relations Act 1999, s. 23 for the Secretary of State by order to extend any right under the 1996 Act, the trade union legislation or any instrument made under the European Communities Act 1972 to individuals of a specified description. What use is to be made of this? Unfortunately, few clues were given in the Parliamentary debates (which got enmeshed on the question of the employment status of vicars!), and so it all remains to be determined. On the one hand, the power could be used sparingly to extend coverage to district groups of employees currently excluded. On the other hand, there could be a major extension of rights such as unfair dismissal and maternity/parental leave to cover those currently in the hole between employment and self employment. Arguably, legislative action is now necessary here, since the regressive decision of the House of Lords on casual workers in *Carmichael v National Power plc*[13]. A major, across-the-board extension would have the effect of replacing the present,

---

6   Equal Pay Act 1970, s. 1(6)(a); Sex Discrimination Act 1975, s. 82(1); Race Relations Act 1976, s. 78(1); Disability Discrimination Act 1995, s. 68(1). These definitions do not contain the express exclusion of a professional client.

7   S.I. 1981 N. 1794, reg. 2(1).

8   [1986] ICR 145, [1986] IRLR 27, CA, applied by the EAT in *Sheehan v Post Office Counters* [1999] ICR 734 in holding that a sub-postmaster was not covered by the disability legislation. The provision of legal services was held by the House of Lords to be capable of coming within the similar definition in the Northern Ireland fair employment legislation in *Kelly and Laughran v Northern Ireland Housing Executive* [1998] ICR 828, [1998] IRLR 593.

9   This is because the Act puts new sections into the Employment Relations Act 1996 and adopts the latter's definition of 'worker'.

10   S. 54.

11   SI 1998/1833, reg. 2(1); SI 2000/1551, reg 1(2).

12   Cm. 3968, para. 3.18.

13   [1999] 4 All ER 897, [2000] IRLR 43, HL; see p. 21 above, and also *Clark v Oxfordshire Health Authority* [1998] IRLR 125, CA where a PAYE and NI paying bank nurse working for only one authority was held not to be an employee.

essentially exclusive definition of 'employee' with a wider, essentially *inclusive* definition capable of covering much of the present middle ground that causes so much difficulty[14]. The way that this is put in the DTI Guides on the national minimum wage and working time may be significant – they both state that it is only the '*genuinely* self employed' who will not be covered by these laws. Clearly, there will be as many problems defining this as there are currently in defining a person under a contract of employment; however, it does give a flavour of the intent of the legislation, and if the section 23 power is eventually used widely, that could well turn out to be the most radical provision in the 1999 Act.

4   GENERAL PRINCIPLES OF INDUSTRIAL RELATIONS

Of all the 'legal' subjects it is truest of labour law that it does not belong fully to lawyers[15]. A great deal of the background takes its principles from other disciplines – from politics, from economics and from social psychology. Each has its own literature and it is inevitable, though unfortunate, that there is still little synthesis. Tensions inevitably arise. Indeed it is not unknown for the slogan 'keep the law out of industrial relations' to be raised. The reader of this book, aware of the number of pages that follow, must know that those words have a special meaning.

They reflect the belief that British industrial relations are informal rather than formal; collective rather than individual. The best starting point for an understanding of this view is still the Donovan Report[16], already mentioned. That report was a comprehensive overview of our system of industrial relations. In the various notes of dissent and in the vigorous Note of Reservation by Andrew Schonfield the areas where views can sharply diverge are indicated.

Before looking at this central theme it is necessary to point to two trends which may be pulling in the opposite direction. Since 1963[17] great emphasis has been put upon the legal regulation binding employer and employee. Although prior to the Contracts of Employment Act it was clear that the law of contract governed what was archaically referred to by lawyers as the relationship between master and servant, recourse to the law was relatively rare. Indeed the subsidiary terms of the average contract of employment, that is to say features other than wages, hours and holidays, were rarely specified and at best could be determined from recourse to the vague concept of 'custom and practice'. Few knew, or had ready access to, the full terms of their employment contract.

Two factors have changed this. Since 1963 a series of statutes[18] have laid down a considerable number of basic individual rights. There are, as a result, an increasing number of standard terms that apply except where something better is expressly provided. These will be discussed in due course[19]. In addition the provision that each employee should be given a note of the principal terms of his contract has revived the centrality of the legal aspect of the relationship. The

14   It was held under equivalent provisions of the Industrial Relations Act 1971 that the extended definition can cover some self-employed workers, provided giving personal service: *Writers' Guild of Great Britain v BBC* [1974] 1 All ER 574, [1974] ICR 234, NIRC; *Broadbent v Crisp* [1974] 1 All ER 1052, [1974] ICR 248 NIRC.
15   This is also true of family law which, with labour law, is tending to shed legalism.
16   Royal Commission on Trade Unions and Employers' Associations (1968) Cmnd. 3623.
17   Contracts of Employment Act 1963.
18   See pp. 5-9, above.
19   See particularly chs. 3 and 4.

change is remarkable – before 1960, for example, it was exceptionally difficult to answer simple questions such as what the law allowed an employer to do when his employee was regularly absent as a result of ill health.

That difficulty was compounded by the paucity of reported cases. Few cases were litigated, very few indeed found a place in the reports[20]. Those that did tended naturally to concern highly paid employees[1]. This meant that the rules that evolved were by no means of general application. The sparsity of rules also meant that old cases, long since made questionable by a change in social circumstances and attitudes, retained at least the appearance of being good law[2]. It will not be necessary to read far into this book to realise how greatly this has changed. The danger now is that the law is groaning under a surfeit of reported cases.

The reason for the change is not just the swing of attention back to the legal aspect of the employment contract, just described. It arises too because an accessible, cheap forum for disputes has been provided by the establishment and use of the system of employment tribunals. They began in 1964 and the growth in their workload is amazing[3]. This jurisdiction has syphoned off a great deal of decision making that would have traditionally been the business of the employer and his recognised trade unions. It is somewhat surprising that almost no use has been made of the provision that in some areas there can be approved private arrangements[4].

The second development is the closer regulation of collective relationships by statute. Again these will form important topics elsewhere in this book[5]. It is only necessary to pause here to stress that they flow from a different general approach than that traditionally held by industrial relations specialists, by trade unions almost as a whole, and by a considerable number of employers. A continuing spate of statutes since the Employment Act 1980 have attempted to bring the regulation of collective disputes firmly within a legal framework. Of course the law has always been, and must always be, there to define the limits of permitted behaviour. It is the underlying assumption of those statutes that there can be advantage gained by framing the law so that it gives the courts a significant regulating role that is so important, and different.

It has also been the aim of this legislation, taken as a whole, to reduce considerably the disruptive power of trade unions. An earlier debate[6], addressing the question whether trade unions should be protected by positive rights rather than by the current system of immunities has faded, leaving the traditional

---

20   The Law Reports Index 1951–1960 did not have a heading 'Employment'. There are not more than 30 cases reported during that period – and this Index includes the Weekly Law Reports from 1953.

1   *Laws v London Chronicle (Indicator Newspapers) Ltd* [1959] 2 All ER 285, [1959] 1 WLR 698, CA.

2   The law on obedience of orders is a marked example. Text books after World War II were including cases such as *Spain v Arnott* (1817) 2 Stark 256 and *Hallward v Snell* (1886) 2 TLR 836.

3   ACAS has applications referred to it for conciliation. Its statistics show that from 1972 (before ACAS was instituted) there were 200 per week. By 1975 this had risen to 400 per week – see Annual Report 1975. By 1980 the figure was 800 per week – see Annual Report 1980. Having remained stable throughout the 80s, the figures doubled again in the mid-90s, promoting proposals for reform of the system: see p. 403, below.

4   See ERA 1996, s. 110. Only the electrical contracting industry has taken advantage of this provision.

5   See particularly chs. 10 and 11.

6   Cmnd. 8128, January, 1981.

immunities system with its considerable complexity and continuing uncertainty, tending to inhibit trade union actions. It cannot be doubted that a change to a rights system would give the trade unions sounder foundations, with less chance of surprise attacks by the courts and what they see as creeping limitation on their powers.

Despite the legislative changes the basic thinking that underpins the approach of many industrial relations practitioners, though difficult to summarise, is still based upon some form of collective bargaining. Indeed this was the first principle set out in the Industrial Relations Act 1971, despite its different philosophy, and section 1(1)(a) formulated 'the principle of collective bargaining freely conducted on behalf of workers and employers and with due regard to the general interests of the community'. That idea reappeared in the Employment Protection Act 1975, where ACAS was charged in section 1(2) with 'the general duty of promoting the improvement of industrial relations, and in particular of encouraging the extension of collective bargaining and the development and, where necessary, reform of collective bargaining machinery'. We shall see, however, that this formulation was significantly changed in 1993, to drop from 'in particular' onwards, significant in showing at least the desired direction of the previous government. The formulation was changed again in 1999 by the present government, but without reinstating the reference to collective bargaining.

Collective bargaining by its very nature requires the organisation of workers into trade unions. This had increased steadily over the years. It has been estimated that in 1901 12.6% of the workforce were unionised, a figure that had risen to 52.6% in 1976. Those crude figures hide big variations and changing patterns. That process was largely without legislative assistance, although in the Industrial Relations Act[7] and again in the Employment Protection Act[8] statutory recognition procedures were set out. These suffered mixed fortunes and indicate the industrial relations difficulties that prevented the smooth use of a statutory procedure. Indeed ACAS took the view that because of the attitude taken by the courts[9] it found it impossible to work the procedure as it considered it should be worked and the whole procedure was repealed by the Employment Act 1980. There were serious underlying difficulties, e.g. the bad feelings that existed between those trade unions affiliated to the TUC and those that were not, and dilemmas, e.g. where the workers wanted to be represented by a trade union that did not fit into the accepted industrial relations pattern. In the light of all of this, it is perhaps initially surprising that the present government have reintroduced a statutory recognition procedure (under a revamped Central Arbitration Committee). This was, however, an important undertaking to the trade unions, and it was enacted by the Employment Relations Act 1999. However, lessons have certainly been learned and, showing an almost paranoid desire to avoid judicial review (on grounds of perversity) the drafting seeks to define and delineate as much as possible, leaving very little indeed to discretion. The legislation is remarkably long and detailed; its effectiveness remains to be gauged at the time of writing, in the sense of the extent to which it may reverse the hitherto consistent

---

7   Ss. 44–60.
8   Ss. 11–16, repealed by the Employment Act 1980.
9   Especially in *Grunwick Processing Laboratories Ltd v ACAS* [1978] 1 All ER 338, [1978] ICR 231, HL; *UKAPE v ACAS* [1979] ICR 303, [1979] IRLR 68, CA; *National Employers Life Assurance Co v ACAS* [1979] ICR 620, [1979] IRLR 282 and *EMA v ACAS (No 2)* [1979] ICR 637, [1979] IRLR 246, CA. The decisions of the Court of Appeal in *UKAPE v ACAS* and *EMA v ACAS* were eventually reversed by the House of Lords.

decline in recognition, in economic conditions very different from those in the 1970s.

Along with levels of union recognition, the coverage of collective bargaining declined steeply through the 80s and 90s, partly due to deep structural changes in the economy and partly to government policies (privatisation and contracting out having played significant roles). It now appears that for the first time this century only a minority of employees are covered by it.[10] However, again the picture is patchy; reports of its death may be greatly exaggerated, and in the significant areas where it still exists it remains well established (though, like everything else, subject to change and modification). It too has a distinctive flavour. Although some agreements (e.g. those in the engineering industry) look like a properly drawn contract, a great many such agreements are extremely sketchy and it is difficult to separate rules from expressions of intent or to determine exactly what the agreement covers. This is made more confusing to a lawyer by the extensive reliance upon custom and practice. In these circumstances it was no surprise that the attempt in the Industrial Relations Act to make these agreements legally binding failed, neither trade unions nor employers being willing to adopt a more rigorous legal approach[11].

We shall see that the substantive aspects of a collective bargain (i.e. the wage rates and other terms of employment) do gain legal effect by incorporation into the individual contract of the employee covered, but those aspects that bind employer and trade union (e.g. procedures or length of time to elapse before re-negotiation) do so only informally, for the collective bargain itself is *not* legally binding[12].

The same approach colours the areas of dispute regulation. ACAS is an independent, tripartite body[13]. It seeks to persuade the parties to a dispute to settle it by means of conciliation or, less frequently, mediation. In addition it provides facilities for arbitration. All three processes are subject to voluntary co-operation – they are offered, not enforced upon either party. The Grunwick dispute will remain for a long time an example of the clash of two principles. The employer's view was that he need only do what he was required to do by law. That of the trade union (and ACAS when it was called in) followed the traditional course and sought voluntary agreement by compromise. The Scarman Report[14] is an excellent study of these two approaches and its conclusion lends support to the industrial relations rather than the legalistic view.

The law has made little systematic attempt to encourage the use of collective bargaining or influence the form of collective agreements. The initiative has

---

10 Millward et al. *Workplace Industrial Relations in Transition* (1992); Millward *The New Industrial Relations?* (1994); Brown et al. 'Management: pay determination and collective bargaining' in Edwards (ed) *Industrial Relations, Theory and Practice in Britain* (1995). In 1997 8.1m (36% of all employees) were covered by collective bargains over pay and conditions: Culley and Woodland 'Trade union membership and recognition in 1997' [1998] Labour Market Trends 353. In 1998 unions were recognised in 45% of workplaces (down from 66% in 1984 and 53% in 1990); 47% of workplaces had no trade union members at all (up from 36% in 1990): The 1998 Workplace Employee Relations Survey – the First Findings (DTI/ACAS/ESRC/PSI; URN/98/934).

11 See the Industrial Relations Act 1971, ss. 34–36 which give birth to the 'TINA LEA' clause – 'This is not a legally enforceable agreement'.

12 Trade Union and Labour Relations (Consolidation) Act 1992, s. 179. *Monterosso Shipping Co v ITWF* [1982] ICR 675, [1982] IRLR 468, CA. For the (similar) position at common law, see *Ford Motor Co Ltd v AUEW* [1969] 2 QB 303, [1969] 2 All ER 481; Lewis 'Collective agreements: the Kahn-Freund legacy' (1979) 42 MLR 613.

13 TUC and CBI representatives and independent members: three of each plus the Chairman.

14 Cmnd. 6922 (1977).

been generally left to the parties. This is somewhat surprising in view of the emphasis laid upon this aspect of industrial relations by the Donovan Commission.[15] Paragraph 182 summarises the Commission's thinking by indicating that 'orderly and effective' industrial relations would be promoted by the development of 'comprehensive and authoritative' bargaining machinery set up with the trade unions; by the development of grievance and dismissal procedures; by the development of redundancy procedures and by measures to promote health and safety[16].

Several of these aims have been underlined by statutes and will be discussed elsewhere. There are provisions leading to the setting up of grievance and dismissal procedures[17]; the Health and Safety at Work Act etc 1974 has dealt with several aspects of employer-employee relationships in that sphere[18]. But little has been done to further the general objective of developing collective bargaining or other forms of determination of terms and conditions; government policy has for years now indicated a deregulated labour market and the previous government opposed legally-enforceable works councils (though they state that in principle, they were in favour of better communication and participation, but as a matter for the *parties*, not the state). The present government have so far not shown a markedly different approach, in particular where it could lead to compulsion on employers, or lead to them being accused of placing more bureaucratic burdens on businesses[19].

Indeed, one of the uncertainties in the current practical background to much of the law here is the *form* that future industrial relations should take. The old system of collective negotiation through recognised trade unions has declined or changed and in many areas newly-pervasive ideas of 'human resource management' techniques may be seen cynically as a way of avoiding collective negotiation and replacing it, not with new forms of communication, but in fact with very little.[20] This all gives particular significance to two legal developments to be seen in this book. The first is the movement (through the pressure of EC law) towards requirements of forms of consultation with employees through the direct election of employee representatives, even where there are no recognised unions.[1] This now affects collective redundancies, transfers of undertaking and

---

15   Royal Commission on Trade Unions and Employers' Associations, 1965–1968 Cmnd. 3623.
16   Ibid, p. 45.
17   See p. 435, below.
18   See p. 758, below.
19   Fairness at Work (CM. 3968, 1998), para. 1.13.
20   See the conclusion in Millward *The New Industrial Relations?* (1994) at p. 133: 'British industry and commerce appear to be moving towards a situation in which non-managerial employees are treated as a "factor of production". Britain is approaching the position where few employees have any mechanism through which they can contribute to the operation of their workplace in a broader context than that of their own job. There is no sign that the shrinkage in the extent of trade union representation is being offset by a growth in other methods of representing non-managerial employees' interests or views ... Nor is there much of the legal regulation that is so extensive in other developed countries to provide a basic floor of employment rights and minimum labour standards'. In 1998 (taking workplaces with twenty five or more employees) of workplaces with no union presence, only 11% had some form of non-union workforce representation, and 89% had no workforce representation at all: the 1998 Workplace Employee Relations Survey – the First Findings (DTI/ACAS/ESRC/PSI, URN/98/934), p. 17.
1   Collective Redundancies and Transfer of Undertakings (Protection of Employment) (Amendment) Regulations 1995, see pp. 64 and 70; Health and Safety (Consultation with Employees) Regulations 1996, see p. 761 See also the novel concept of the workforce agreement in the Working Time Regulations 1998 (see p. 201) and the Maternity and Parental Leave etc Regulations 1999 (see p. 345).

health and safety; it could provide a model for future developments on a more general basis, even without any formal moves towards works councils. However, if it does it would be a challenge to the unions, not just to management, because it would be significantly different from the old model of the unions being the sole or principal channels of communications. The second development, if increased individualism is to remain dominant in the political and economic fields, is the renewed interest in protection for employees through the medium of the contract of employment and court decisions thereon.

Given this diversity of legal involvement, it is essential to appreciate the tension that can arise between the different approaches of the industrial relations specialist (the company personnel officer or trade union official) on the one hand and the lawyer on the other. The lawyer's virtues – the search for clarity, the anticipation of future difficulty, the demand for good records and the concept of relevance which narrows the area of dispute – all present difficulty when applied to the fluid, amorphous, interlinked problems of industrial relations.

5   EUROPE

The expectation on the part of the trade unions that they would continue to play a part as one of the partners with the employers and government began to wane in the 1980s. The growth of individual rights for workers had progressed well – the Industrial Relations Act 1971 had introduced the concept of unfair dismissal, equality legislation was making progress, albeit rather slowly, on the basis of the Equal Pay Act 1970 and the Sex Discrimination Act 1975. But the central concept of joint regulation, envisaging the trade unions as playing a major part in the regulation of industry and work did not develop well. The final years of the Labour government of 1974–9 were stormy and the advent of Conservative power, in the event to last until 1997, meant the inevitable reconstruction along lines less favourable to the trade unions. What in the early statutes, such as the Employment Act 1980, the Employment Act 1982 and the Trade Union Act 1984 – which showed greater hostility to the enlarged trade union role – might have been regarded as a realignment later showed itself to be a 'step by step' reduction of trade union power and rejection of their aspirations as far as joint regulation was concerned.

Faced with this hostility, one of the consequences was that the trade unions looked to the increasing impact that membership of the European Community (EC) was having. The UK had, by a Treaty of Accession, along with the Republic of Ireland and Denmark joined the community[2].

This had effects on several areas of the law of employment. For example, Article 48 governed the free movement of workers within the community. But the most immediately fruitful area was that of sex equality. Article 119 provided for equal pay for equal work and a number of later Directives expand this – notably Directive 75/117 which introduced the concept of work of equal value, Directive 76/207 which provides more generally for equal treatment and Directive 79/7 which extended the concept of equality to social security.

A difference in statutory interpretation between the English and the European Court soon became obvious. This was clearly demonstrated in cases such as *Garland*

---

2   The treaties were incorporated into the law by the European Communities Act 1972.

v British Rail Engineering Ltd[3] and *Worringham v Lloyds Bank Ltd*[4] in the ECJ in the initial phase of the application of EC equality laws, and the need for the domestic courts to state a novel approach to the interpretation of domestic legislation in order to comply with a backing directive was made equally clear by the House of Lords in *Litster v Forth Dry Dock & Engineering Co Ltd*[5]. Even more revolutionary was the decision of that court in *R v Secretary of State for Employment, ex p Equal Opportunities Commission*[6] that the statutory requirement of 16 hours pw minimum employment in order to qualify for the major statutory rights was indirectly discriminatory (and *not* justified by the British government's political/economic arguments in its favour) and contrary to EC law, with the result that (pending legislative amendment several months later) it had to be 'disapplied' by tribunals, even though it continued to be present in the UK Act of Parliament. When these matters are discussed below at greater length the impact of the European approach will be clear.

Even so, progress from this source has been both patchy and slow. Perhaps the most important impact is in the sphere of health and safety, where underlying political attitudes to trade unions are of minimal importance[7]. Even there it is only since 1990 that rapid strides are being made.

The central feature of the EU, as far as employment relations are concerned, has been the so-called Social Charter – The Community Charter of Fundamental Social Rights. This was adopted in December 1990 at the Strasbourg Summit. Its aim was stated as being 'the completion of the internal market, with the free movement of goods, people, capital and services by 1992'. Its effect was undoubtedly to increase the pace of action.

The Charter has 12 chapters dealing with matters such as uniformity of employment conditions, remuneration, training, living and working conditions, information, consultation, participation and industrial democracy, and protection for children, the elderly and the disabled.

It was at Maastricht in 1992 that a Treaty of European Union was signed. This represented 'a new stage in the process of creating an even closer union among the people of Europe'. The Treaty was adopted by all the countries, but the UK did not sign the Protocol on Social Policy (the 'Social Chapter'). This was the part of the Treaty dealing with the matters which are very much the concern of this textbook, as the list of topics set out in the last paragraph above clearly indicates.

This much-vaunted 'opt out' from the Social Chapter by the previous government was starting to look of dubious longevity even before the 1997 election[8], but it did provoke one of the relatively few disagreements between the parties over employment policy by that time, since the Labour party were in favour of a social dimension to Europe and shortly after their election victory they indicated their intention to sign up to the Social Chapter and end the UK's opt out. This is to be done through the mechanism of the redrafting of the EC Treaty

---

3   [1982] ICR 420, [1982] IRLR 111, ECJ.
4   [1981] ICR 558, [1981] IRLR 178, ECJ.
5   [1989] ICR 341, [1989] IRLR 161, HL.
6   [1994] ICR 317, [1994] IRLR 176, HL.
7   See ch. 13 below.
8   This was particularly so in the case of the Working Time Directive which was passed against the will of the previous government, by the device of classifying it as a health and safety measure (majority voting), not as an employment law measure (unanimity required); the government's challenge to the legality of this was rejected by the ECJ: *United Kingdom v EU Council* C-84/94 [1997] ICR 443, [1997] IRLR 30, ECJ.

as a result of the 1997 Amsterdam Treaty[9]; although the effect immediately is in fact very limited because so little has been done by the signatories to the 1992 Protocol[10], the importance of course lies in the *future* participation by the UK in the negotiation and implementation of social policy initiatives. This is simply one further reason why the interplay between domestic employment law and the EU remains a major player at the centre of the stage.

6 THE HUMAN RIGHTS ACT 1998

At the time of writing, there is much speculation about the impending commencement of the Human Rights Act 1998 in October 2000, enacting into domestic law the European Convention on Human Rights. The overarching effects of this Act, in particular the obligation on public bodies (including courts and tribunals) to act in accordance with the Convention, have aroused much interest, but the likely effects on employment law are very uncertain. On an 'institutional' level, there has been the opinion given by Morison P in *Smith v Secretary of State for Trade and Industry*[11] that an employment tribunal may not be truly independent (as required by Art. 6) when adjudicating on a claim against the Secretary of State, who appoints members and funds the system. Similarly, there may be those wishing to get their proverbial teeth into the Art. 4 prohibition on slavery and forced labour[12]. On a rather saner level, there could be mileage in Arts. 8–11 (right to respect for private and family life, freedom of thought, freedom of expression and freedom of assembly). Certain well-worn employment law chestnuts such as dress codes will doubtless be revisited yet again, and there could be important developments on more significant topics such as an element at least of privacy for an employee while at work, with certain forms of employer surveillance becoming of dubious legality. Overall, however, views vary considerably, from those who view the Act as the New Jerusalem to those who take a much more measured and cautious approach[13]. As with the continuing involvement of EC law, developments in this field will be of particular interest during the currency of this edition.

9   Barnard 'The UK, the "social chapter" and the Amsterdam Treaty' (1997) 26 ILJ 275. The treaty renumbers the relevant Articles, a source of some confusion.

10   The immediate effect was to commit the UK only to the European Works Council Directive 94/95 and the Parental Leave Directive 96/34. To these have now been added directives on the burden of proof in discrimination cases, part-time workers and posted workers.

11   [2000] ICR 69, [2000] IRLR 6.

12   The only definite candidate for protection under this article would be, at the present time, an author of an employment law text, perhaps best defined along with Dr Johnson's 'lexicographer' as 'a harmless drudge'.

13   See particularly Ewing 'The Human Rights Act and Labour Law' (1998) 27 ILJ 275.

Chapter 2

The law relating to industrial relations

I MACHINERY

As seen in chapter 1 above, the voluntary and non-legal nature of British industrial relations has been its dominant characteristic, and there is not an overall statutory framework for compulsory conciliation and arbitration leading to enforceable awards and agreements as may be found in certain other countries. Moreover, we do not formally distinguish between what are conceptually two different types of industrial dispute – those about the negotiation of new and improved terms of employment (disputes of interest) and those about the interpretation, application and enforcement of existing terms (disputes of right)[1]; arguably there should be separate procedures for dealing with them, particularly as the second type is inherently more amenable to legal adjudication, but in this country any such differentiation will be the exception rather than the rule, and so both kinds of dispute tend (in areas where collective bargaining is still the norm) to be subject to voluntarily negotiated procedures of varying quality (or ad hoc arrangements), leading as has been seen to non-enforceable collective agreements. However, although the law has been non-interventionist (except for the period covered by the Industrial Relations Act 1971) it has not abstained totally, and has attempted in various ways at various times to provide certain residual machinery to facilitate industrial relations and minimise industrial conflict. Wages Councils were historically used (prior to their abolition in 1993) to aid collective bargaining in under-unionised trades, and since the Conciliation Act 1896 there has existed machinery (in various forms, but before 1975 principally under the

---

1   Report of the Royal Commission on Trade Unions and Employers' Associations (1968) Cmnd. 3623, para. 60. In recent years there has been interest in 'pendulum' or 'flip-flop' arbitration, where the arbitrator has to make a straight choice between the cases put by the parties, having no discretion to reach an intermediate decision; however, many arbitrations are like that anyway since they concern disputes of right which tend to necessitate an answer one way or the other ('Is this amount payable to these people under this agreement?' or some such question); arbitrations in disputes of interest raise many more issues. For a discussion of the system see Wood 'Last offer arbitration' (1985) 23 Brit J Industrial Rel 415 and Kessler 'Swings and roundabouts of pendulum arbitration' (1987) 19 Personnel Management 38.

Department of Employment and its predecessors) for industrial conciliation. Since the Industrial Courts Act 1919[2] there has also existed machinery for industrial arbitration, previously under the Industrial Court (a tri-partite arbitral body, not to be confused with the NIRC, set up by the Industrial Relations Act 1971) which was renamed the Industrial Arbitration Board between 1971 and 1974, under the 1971 Act; once again, however, the arbitration has always[3] been basically voluntary, i.e. by the consent of the parties. Since 1975, these conciliation and arbitration services have been largely provided by ACAS, and are considered below. In addition to such general provisions, it used to be common to find in statutes establishing or governing major employers in the public sector a standard clause placing them under a duty to seek consultations with appropriate trade unions with a view to concluding agreements for establishing joint industrial negotiating machinery[4]; this applied to the Electricity Council, the British Gas Corporation, Transport Boards, the Independent Broadcasting Authority, the National Coal Board, the UK Atomic Energy Authority, the Post Office, British Shipbuilders, the British Steel Corporation and the Crown Agents[5]. However, such provisions do not apply in the private sector where the establishment of negotiating machinery normally remains a voluntary matter; this has, of course, increasingly been the case because of the previous government's widespread policy of privatisation of bodies or industries previously in the public sector (and, indeed, the mandatory contracting-out of services by bodies still in the public sector). In far more areas, it is now the case therefore that legal intervention is restricted to the provision of outside agencies which the parties may, or may not, decide to call upon in the event of a dispute.

In the resolution of industrial disputes by the intervention of an outside agency there is an important conceptual distinction. On the one hand there is conciliation which is where the conciliator attempts to bring the parties together in the hope that a common discussion will reveal a means of settlement acceptable to both parties; one variation of this is 'mediation' where the mediator takes a more active role in putting forward detailed solutions, though still with a view to

---

2   Now the Trade Union and Labour Relations (Consolidation) Act 1992, ss. 215–216, in relation to courts of inquiry.

3   Except for the period 1940–1959 when, initially as a result of wartime measures aimed at avoiding industrial disruptions, some arbitration was compulsory. In 1951 Order 1376 replaced Order 1305 of 1940; some 1270 cases were heard before its revocation in 1959: see Cooper's *Outlines of Industrial Law* (6th edn, 1972), pp. 446–451; Kahn-Freund *Labour and the Law*, pp. 151–153.

4   The usual wording was that the employer must seek consultation with 'any organisation appearing to it to be appropriate', which meant that such a provision could not be used by a union to *claim* to be consulted (and, in effect, thereby recognised); this can be seen clearly from *R v Post Office, ex p ASTMS* [1981] 1 All ER 139, [1981] ICR 76, CA, where the decision of the Post Office not to consult with and recognise ASTMS (which had recently acquired members within the Post Office and was not within the established federation of post office unions) was upheld by the Court of Appeal as a proper decision that it would not be 'appropriate' so to fragment existing negotiating procedures; cf however *R v British Coal Corpn, ex p UDM* [1988] ICR 36 where the UDM successfully challenged the employers' decision to consult them only in respect of certain categories of workers.

5   Intervention of a very different kind came, in an ad hoc case, following the teachers' strikes in the Teachers' Pay and Conditions Act 1987, see Fredman and Morris 'The teachers' lesson: collective bargaining and the courts' (1987) 16 ILJ 215.

settlement by agreement[6]. These functions are now within the jurisdiction of the Advisory, Conciliation and Arbitration Service (ACAS) which was originally established by the Employment Protection Act 1975 and is the successor to the conciliatory functions of the Department of Employment (and the Commission on Industrial Relations which functioned under the 1971 Act). On the other hand there is arbitration, which is where the arbitrator fulfils a quasi-judicial role in that the parties have agreed to submit their dispute to that person for his *decision* on what should be the result; he therefore has to look into the relevant facts and law, and it is clearly understood that the parties will abide by his decision. This function is now within the jurisdiction of both ACAS and the Central Arbitration Committee (CAC), which also was established by the Employment Protection Act 1975 and is the successor to the Industrial Court and the Industrial Arbitration Board; as we shall see, it may conduct voluntary arbitrations, but also has certain powers of unilateral arbitration under statute and has now been given important new jurisdictions in relation to the statutory recognition procedure and European Works Councils.

i) The Advisory Conciliation and Arbitration Service

The composition of ACAS is governed primarily by Part VI of the Trade Union and Labour Relations (Consolidation) Act 1992. It is directed by a Council consisting of a chairman and between nine and fifteen members (three or four representing employers, three or four representing unions and the rest 'independents'). ACAS itself is set up as a body independent of the government, in particular independent of the Department of Trade and Industry, and appoints its own staff[7]. It maintains a central office in London and regional offices in Scotland, Wales and in five regions in England, and must produce an annual report for the Secretary of State for Trade and Industry to lay before Parliament.

Amongst its staff, it maintains 'conciliation officers'[8] who have particular responsibility for conciliating in statutory actions brought by individual employees.

The functions of ACAS are set out in Part IV of the 1992 Act; in addition to the detailed functions considered below, there is a statement of its general duty in s. 209, as follows:

> 'It is the general duty of ACAS to promote the improvement of industrial relations'.

This apparently simple formulation has in fact gone through three phases, with considerable symbolic significance (if little practical effect). From 1975 to 1993 the section continued '... and in particular to encourage the extension of

---

6   Mediation may be used particularly (a) where issues cannot be presented in a sufficiently clear cut manner for arbitration (e.g. major changes of work, linked to a pay settlement) or (b) where one or both of the parties is or are unwilling to submit the matter formally to arbitration (on the principle that a party who agrees to arbitration must ultimately be able to afford to lose). Either way, mediation must be properly understood by the parties – it does not result in an 'award' by the mediator, though there may be considerable moral pressure to comply with the mediator's suggestions.

7   In 1998 there were 674 staff in ACAS, the majority being located in the regional offices: ACAS Annual Report 1998.

8   Trade Union and Labour Relations (Consolidation) Act 1992, s. 211; they are known as Conciliation Officers Tribunals (COTS) to distinguish them from those specialising in collective conciliation.

collective bargaining and the development and, where necessary, reform of collective bargaining machinery'. That may well have been the ethos of the 1970s, but after a decade in the 1980s of overt government hostility to any such aims it was hardly surprising that the previous government took the opportunity in the Trade Union Reform and Employment Rights Act 1993 to repeal that wording. They substituted '… in particular by exercising its functions in relation to the settlement of trade disputes under sections 210 and 212 [i.e. by conciliation and arbitration.]'. ACAS had certainly proved useful to the previous government in certain disputes (a measure of that use being that they were never seriously threatened with abolition, unlike most tri-partite bodies of the 1970s), and this formulation reflected that. However, it arguably placed too much emphasis on reactive, problem-solving work ('fire fighting' in IR jargon), and too little on long-term advice work ('fire prevention') which ACAS wanted to enhance. With the change of government in 1997, an increased emphasis on fire prevention could be seen to be consistent with the present government's 'partnership' ideas in the White Paper 'Fairness at Work'. As a result, the Employment Relations Act 1999 removed the 1993 wording and left ACAS with the widest possible general duty as set out above. Of course, the cynic could argue that the extent to which ACAS can increase their pro-active work will depend not on a change to their statutory remit but on the resources they are to be given over the next few years.

The specific statutory functions[9] of ACAS are as follows:

a)   Collective conciliation

Where a trade dispute[10] exists or seems imminent ACAS may, at the request of one or more of the parties or on its own initiative, offer its assistance for the purposes of conciliation or mediation. In doing so, it may also refer the parties to a third person for conciliation, and it must where possible encourage the parties to use any existing negotiation or disputes procedures[11]. The traditional form of conciliation is carried out by an individual ACAS officer working directly with the parties, but in recent years there has been an increase in the use of a hybrid form, referred to as 'advisory mediation', aimed at encouraging a co-operative and problem-solving approach by the parties themselves, possibly on a longer-term basis; this tends to be done by the setting up of a joint workshop or joint working party, chaired by the ACAS officer, and may be particularly appropriate for resolving disputes over matters such as handling organisational change[12]. In

9   These services have in the past been free to the parties, but s. 251A of the 1992 Act (inserted by the Trade Union Reform and Employment Rights Act 1993) gives a power to charge fees *and* a power for the Secretary of State to require the charging of fees for some or all services. This change was not wanted by ACAS itself.

10   The wide definition as originally contained in the Trade Union and Labour Relations Act 1974, s. 29 (and now in the Trade Union and Labour Relations (Consolidation) Act 1992, s. 218) continues to apply for this purpose; the narrowed definition for the purpose of immunity from tort action in industrial disputes enacted by the Employment Act 1982 and now in the 1992 Act, s. 244 does not apply here. Perhaps an example of governmental propensity to have cake and consume same.

11   Trade Union and Labour Relations (Consolidation) Act 1992, s. 210. In 1998, 1,214 collective conciliation cases were completed, 91% ending in settlement or progress towards it. Of these cases, 32% were requests from unions, 10% from employers, 41% were joint requests and 17% were initiated by ACAS itself: ACAS Annual Report 1998. Independent research carried out in 1985 and published in 1988 showed a high level of satisfaction with the service provided, by both unions and employers: ACAS Annual Report 1987, p. 26.

12   See 'Joint problem solving' (ACAS Occasional Paper No. 55; Kessler and Purcell).

addition to these forms of voluntary conciliation, ACAS also has statutory conciliation functions at certain stages in union claims for disclosure of bargaining information or under the statutory recognition procedure, which are considered below.

One area of potential difficulty for ACAS in the context of collective conciliation may arise if it transpires in a particular dispute that the employer is seeking to bring a legal action against the union, initially for an injunction to restrain the industrial action or threat of it and then possibly in a suit for damages (both more feasible since the reforms in the Employment Acts 1980 and 1982 and the balloting provisions in the Trade Union Act 1984; see ch. 10 below). In such a case, any ACAS intervention would have to be more circumspect. However, there is another side to it, since such ACAS intervention might in practice be more likely to resolve an impasse than legal proceedings, and the suggestion has been made tentatively that the law should be amended to include provision for a judge to stay proceedings in any action arising from an industrial dispute in order for ACAS to attempt conciliation[13] which, if successful, might well make considerable savings in cost, time, acrimony and accusations against the courts of partiality in industrial disputes; so far, this interesting suggestion has not been taken up. It can be further noted that where the parties engage lawyers the lines of communication may be lengthened and the process of conciliation made more difficult.

b) Individual conciliation

ACAS, through its conciliation officers, has a statutory duty to attempt to conciliate in cases brought before tribunals by individuals claiming unfair dismissal or denial of employment protection rights; this also applies to cases of sex, race and disability discrimination and to the various rights enacted by the legislation for the protection of trade union members, including the statutory redundancy handling procedures[14]. The ACAS regional offices receive copies of originating applications to the tribunals and a conciliation officer must attempt to settle a case without reference to a tribunal if requested to do so by the parties or if, in the absence of a request, he thinks there may be a reasonable prospect of success[15]. In all cases, the conciliation officer must consider encouraging the use of established grievance procedures within the firm. In unfair dismissal cases, the officer must in theory seek to promote a settlement primarily by way of reinstatement or re-engagement, and only attempt a monetary settlement if that

13 ACAS Annual Report 1983, para. 1.16.
14 Employment Tribunals Act 1996, s. 18. See Individual Employment Rights – ACAS Conciliation between Individuals and Employers (ACAS).
15 For many years the total number of such cases was stable at about 35,000 p.a. However they started to climb alarmingly in the 1990s, reaching 79,332 cases received in 1994. This was at a time of some decrease in numbers of staff and placed a severe strain on other ACAS functions. The figures took another lurch upwards in 1995 to 91,568, topped 100,000 in 1996 and stood at 113,636 in 1998. This was the background to the Employment Rights (Dispute Resolution) Act 1998 with its reforms to the tribunal system and inception of the ACAS arbitration scheme for unfair dismissal cases (see below) as an alternative to tribunal proceedings.

Of the cases received and dealt with in 1998, 35% were unfair dismissal claims, 22% concerned unlawful deductions for wages and 21% were breach of contract claims. Of the total, 73% were settled or withdrawn without a tribunal hearing: ACAS Annual Report 1998.

is impracticable, or not wanted by the ex-employee[16]. The conciliation process is confidential, in that anything said to the officer during it is not admissible evidence in subsequent tribunal proceedings without the consent of the person who said it. It must be emphasised that if the conciliation is successful in leading to an agreed settlement as a consequence of action taken by a conciliation officer under his statutory duties, that will bar any future tribunal proceedings in the matter[17], so that the claimant should be certain that he or she is happy with the terms of the proposed settlement before irrevocably agreeing with it. For this reason alone, it is vital that ACAS should behave, and be seen to behave, entirely impartially as between the claimant and the employer when conducting negotiations.

In this respect, a serious problem arose for ACAS through the rise throughout the 1980s of the number of cases submitted to them *without* any formal application having been made to a tribunal. In these cases (referred to as 'non-IT 1' cases in the jargon) the employer would often be wanting ACAS to record an agreement already reached, in order to achieve legal finality, but doubts could arise as to whether the employee had really understood the terms of the agreement. A conflict arose between law and practice. Legally, it was clear from the cases that there was no statutory obligation on an ACAS officer to ensure that it was a *fair* settlement and so an employee could not later challenge the binding nature of the settlement on the grounds that ACAS had not explained his rights to him properly or given him independent advice[18]. On the other hand, it was the established ACAS view that their officers should not simply act as rubber stamps for possibly inequitable settlements and should at least enquire whether the employee understood his position and his rights[19]. Eventually, however, the considerable rise in non-IT 1 cases placed such a strain on resources that ACAS had to reconsider its policy. This was done with effect from July 1990 and the current position is that (a) officers will only act in non-IT 1 cases where the employee claims infringement of specified employment rights; (b) they will decline to conciliate where any qualifying period is clearly not satisfied; (c) they will not become involved where employment ended voluntarily or where a redundancy occurred under fairly applied customary arrangements or agreed procedures; and (d) (most importantly) they will not have any role to play in *any* case (whether or not a non-IT 1 case) where a firm agreement has already been reached independently, *unless* the terms of the agreement are capable of being changed as a result of conciliation[20].

16 Employment Tribunals Act 1996, s. 18(4). This is wholly ineffective in practice, as can be seen from the consistently low rate of re-employment (whether by order or by agreement); see p. 504, below; Williams and Lewis *The aftermath of tribunal reinstatement and re-engagement* (D.E. Research Paper No. 23) pp. 31 and 39.
17 ERA 1996, s. 203(2); Sex Discrimination Act 1975, s. 77(4)(a); Race Relations Act 1976, s. 72(4)(a); Trade Union and Labour Relations (Consolidation) Act 1992, s. 288(2); Disability Discrimination Act 1995, s. 9(2).
18 In *Moore v Duport Furniture Products Ltd* [1982] ICR 84, [1982] IRLR 31, HL, it was held (1) that the action of the conciliation officer in recording an agreement to accept compensation of £300 on the standard form COT3 was sufficient to bar further proceedings, and (2) that where an officer is presented with such an agreement already worked out by the parties, his duty is only to verify the fact of agreement and record it – he is not under a further duty to enquire into the 'fairness' of the agreement or to give the applicant any further advice. Likewise, an ACAS official is under no legal duty to explain the law to the applicant and is not bound to adopt any particular formula or approach: *Slack v Greenham (Plant Hire) Ltd* [1983] ICR 617, [1983] IRLR 271. See further p. 424 below.
19 ACAS Annual Report 1984, p. 63.
20 ACAS Annual Report 1991, p. 45. As a result of this change, the non-IT 1 caseload declined from 17,724 in 1989 to only 2,431 in 1992.

c) Arranging arbitration

Under section 212 of the Trade Union and Labour Relations (Consolidation) Act 1992, ACAS may arrange arbitration for an actual or anticipated trade dispute if one or more of the parties request it *and* all parties consent to it[1]. This is clearly voluntary arbitration, and the resulting decision will not be legally enforceable per se[2], though in practice the arbitrator's decision is invariably complied with. ACAS does not automatically have to arrange arbitration; as well as being satisfied that all parties consent, it must also consider whether conciliation might be successful instead, and should not arrange arbitration unless satisfied that existing negotiation and disputes procedures have been exhausted (unless there are special reasons why arbitration should be used *instead* of such procedures). The conciliation stage is important – if successful it removes the need for an arbitration; if unsuccessful, the ACAS conciliation officer then has the task of determining with the parties the precise terms of reference for the arbitrator, for it is important in an arbitration that the terms are not themselves a subject for dispute; in fact, the terms of reference are usually kept as simple as possible and, further, nothing of what has happened or been said at the conciliation stage is made known to the arbitrator, who approaches the issue afresh. The usual practice is for ACAS to appoint one person to conduct the arbitration (from the panel of approximately eighty appropriate people whom they use), though occasionally a board of arbitration may be convened; officials and employees of ACAS are *not* used, though ACAS do of course provide the necessary secretarial and administrative services[3]. It is also possible for a voluntary arbitration to be referred to the CAC, though there are only a few such cases each year. Legal representation at an arbitration is unusual (and indeed usually discouraged if suggested) and although the proceedings may be conducted in a relatively structured manner (aimed at giving both sides a full opportunity to expand upon their written submissions and to query the other side's case), matters of procedure are largely for the arbitrator to determine and will not normally include legalistic forms, such as prolonged cross-examination.

Certain interesting trends in arbitration might be noted here briefly. First, references may come from *standing* arbitration agreements, usually taking the form of a clause in the disputes procedure section of a collective bargain stating that in the absence of agreement on a disputed point through internal procedures, the matter shall be referred to ACAS for conciliation and/or arbitration. This may be a general reference, or the clause itself may cover the procedure that is to be adopted. Second, it is possible for parties to a dispute to approach ACAS to ask them simply to *nominate* an arbitrator to conduct an arbitration which has already been agreed upon, without going through the

---

1   Mumford 'Arbitration and ACAS in Britain: a historical perspective' (1996) 34 BJIR 287.
2   Part I of the Arbitration Act 1996 does not apply to this form of arbitration: s. 212(5). One rare example of binding arbitration on terms and conditions of employment was contained in the Pilotage Act 1987, s. 5 and the Terms of Employment of Pilots (Arbitration) Regulations 1988, S.I. 1988 No. 1089, but it was meant to be a temporary expedient; see Smith 'The pilots' compensation scheme: a study in arbitration, interpretation and causation' (1994) 32 BJIR 379.
3   In 1998 the number of references to arbitration fell to only 51 (from 117 in 1996, and an average in the previous five years of 106); of these, 22% concerned annual pay, 43% other pay and conditions, 25% discipline and dismissal and 2% (the largest fall) grading issues: ACAS Annual Report 1998. Requests to ACAS simply to nominate an arbitrator for a purely internal arbitration are not included in these figures; on the use of third-party intervention, see Millward et al. *Workplace Industrial Relations in Transition* (1992), pp. 194–196 and 208–211.

normal conciliation procedures; such arbitrations do not figure in the annual ACAS statistics[4]. Third, there has been considerable interest in and publicity about the form of arbitration variously known as 'pendulum', 'flip-flop', 'straight choice' or 'final offer', where the arbitrator is constrained to choose between acceptance in full of one side's case or that of the other[5]. The aim of this is said to be to narrow the field of dispute and ensure that each side puts forward a realistic (rather than a bargaining) case, capable of being accepted in full. While this may be a natural form of adjudication in disputes of right, ACAS are by no means convinced that it is a panacea in disputes of interest such as pay determinations where flexibility in the arbitration may be just as important. Although ACAS will arrange such an arbitration if the parties desire it, they do *not* adopt it as their policy, preferring to encourage responsible bargaining in other ways and pointing out consistently that the fact that an arbitrator is normally given full discretion in coming to his award does *not* mean in practice that all he does is to split the disputed area down the middle, with half a baby to each.

d)   Arbitration in unfair dismissal cases

Although voluntary arbitration has always been available to the parties to a dismissal dispute, it has in the past worked on an informal basis (with a disappointed complainant employee still able to go to a tribunal for a further hearing), and in recent years has declined in numbers along with arbitration generally. Faced with the steep rise in tribunal applications, the previous government explored the possibility of a re-vamped ACAS-run arbitration scheme to act as an *alternative* to tribunal proceedings[6]. This idea was taken up by the present government, and made possible by the Employment Rights (Dispute Resolution) Act 1998 section 7 (inserting the Trade Union and Labour Relations (Consolidation) Act 1992, s. 212A) which gives ACAS the power to produce a scheme for promulgation by the Secretary of State by order. Although this power has existed since August 1998, progress has been slow because of delays in approval at the DTI level. The outlines of the scheme are set out in Chapter 8 on unfair dismissal (see p. 434, below). The major problem for ACAS has been in anticipating the likely level of usage and therefore how many arbitrators to recruit and train. At the time of writing this is entirely uncertain.

4   This however can lead to a problem: the resulting arbitration is *not* an ACAS arbitration within the Act and so the exclusion of the Arbitration Act 1996 by s. 212(5) (n. 2 above) does not apply. Thus the 1996 Act could be applicable (if the agreement to arbitrate is in writing) and so the resulting decision could be legally binding (and any recourse to the courts excluded) under that Act, possibly without the parties realising it at the time.

5   See the CAC Annual Report 1984, ch. 3 for a discussion of this development. This form of arbitration was particularly controversial within the union movement in the mid-1980s, especially where it was combined with a 'no-strike' clause, as in certain innovatory collective agreements negotiated by the EETPU with foreign companies in 'high-tech' industries. For the incorporation of 'no strike' agreements into individual contracts of employment, see p. 115 below. The aim is to avoid the damage arbitration is said to do to conciliation. Parties in negotiation anticipating arbitration tend to 'stand off' leaving a wide band of discretion for the arbitrator. Final offer arbitration encourages them to a adopt a more realistic position, even perhaps to reach agreement. While this is a natural process in disputes of right, where the arbitrator has usually two positions to choose from, it is less certain in its application to disputes of interest. There is considerable North American experience in public sector arbitration. This shows that difficulties arise where there are several issues in the same arbitration: it is difficult to be absolutely clear on the exact form of last positions and it prevents flexibility at the hearing of the dispute. Several devices have been adopted, e.g. issue splitting, to meet these difficulties.

6   Resolving employment rights disputes: options for reform (Cm. 2707).

e) Advice

The statutory power to give advice, contained in the Trade Union and Labour Relations (Consolidation) Act 1992, s. 213, was altered by the Trade Union Reform and Employment Rights Act 1993. It used to contain 11 particular categories of relevant areas, including matters affecting collective bargaining, worker organisation and recognition of unions. It now reads more simply:

> 'ACAS may, on request or otherwise, give employers, employers' associations, workers and trade unions such advice as it thinks appropriate on matters concerned with or affecting or likely to affect industrial relations.'

As with the change at that time (considered above) to the general duty of ACAS, this alteration was likely to have little practical effect, but could be seen (in its removal of express references to collective means of resolving industrial problems) to be symbolic. Again, references to such matters have not been reinstated by the present government.

The power to advise remains wide and will doubtless continue to be heavily used[7]. It covers general advice, specific replies to queries (e.g. on the meaning of modern employment laws), in-depth surveys and projects, giving conferences or seminars and the publishing of advisory booklets[8]. Diagnostic work within a company on a longer term basis may in fact be the result of one particular problem which arose and was settled through ACAS conciliation – the approach may have been made for the ACAS officer to attempt to find a settlement for the immediate problem on the understanding that the whole area in dispute would be looked at, either by the officer himself or, increasingly, by the setting up of a joint working party or workshop under the aegis of ACAS. This latter approach (more recently known as 'advisory mediation', see above) has expanded and largely replaced the older ideas of externally-conducted 'IR audits' for two reasons – (1) it fits the current industrial relations realities better, reflecting their more diverse nature with less chance of one desirable model being appropriate, but (2) at the same time it enables ACAS still to make a distinctive contribution towards ideas of *joint* resolution of problems and employee involvement, even in areas where formal bargaining with unions is no longer the norm[9].

f) Powers of inquiry

ACAS may on its own initiative hold an inquiry into aspects of industrial relations generally or in any particular industry or firm[10]. It may add its advice to its eventual

---

7   In the first ten years of its existence, ACAS had over 3,000,000 general enquiries (often by telephone). This advice function is of great importance in practice: Armstrong 'Evaluating the work of ACAS' [1985] Employment Gazette 143 and 'Asking ACAS' (ACAS Occasional Paper No. 56; Dix, Hawes & Pinkstone).

8   See ACAS Advisory Booklets – No. 1, Job Evaluation; No. 2, Introduction to payment systems; No. 3, Personnel records; No. 4, Labour turnover; No. 5, Absence; No. 6, Recruitment and selection; No. 7, Induction of new employees; No. 8, Workplace communications; No. 9, The company handbook; No. 10, Employment policies; No. 11, Employee appraisal; No. 12, Redundancy handling; No. 13, Hours of Work; No. 14, Appraisal-related Pay; No. 15, Health and Employment; No. 16, Effective Organisations; No. 17, Supervision; No. 18, Teamwork. Advisory Handbooks have also been published on employing people in small firms, and discipline at work, along with the general Employment Handbook.

9   Kessler and Purcell, 'Joint problem solving – does it work? An evaluation of ACAS in-depth advisory mediation' (ACAS Occasional Paper No. 55).

10 Trade Union and Labour Relations (Consolidation) Act 1992, s. 214.

findings, and is empowered to publish both if it thinks publication desirable (after hearing any representations on the question by those involved). In cases of greater public interest, however, the Secretary of State may decide to appoint a Court of Inquiry under the Trade Union and Labour Relations (Consolidation) Act 1992, s. 215 (originally the Industrial Courts Act 1919). This is a more formal procedure than that adopted by ACAS and results in the laying before Parliament and publication of a formal report[11]. In appointing such a court, the Secretary of State lays down rules regulating its procedure, which may include powers to compel witnesses to provide information or give evidence on oath.

g)   Codes of practice

Pursuant to its powers of inquiry and advice, ACAS is empowered by the Trade Union and Labour Relations (Consolidation) Act 1992, s. 199 to issue Codes of Practice. The procedure is that a draft code will be drawn up with a view to comment by interested parties. The final draft is then submitted to the Secretary of State, who, if he approves, may lay it before Parliament. If no objection is taken to it, the Secretary of State may then bring it into force by order. Codes of Practice are of increasing importance in modern industrial law, to attempt to fill out the bare bones of the legislation and give practical advice on how to put that legislation (often of considerable legal complexity) into effect. A Code of Practice is not law in itself, so a person will not be liable for its breach; like the Highway Code in motoring cases, however, breach of its terms may be used as evidence against an employer in any proceedings before a tribunal or the CAC[12]. The first three Codes of Practice issued by ACAS covered disciplinary practices and procedures in employment, disclosure of bargaining information and time off work for trade union duties and activities. In 1987 ACAS submitted the draft of a revised and greatly expanded Code of Practice on discipline and dismissals, but unfortunately the then Secretary of State for Employment refused to approve it (see p. 414, below); it was subsequently published (in part) as the ACAS Handbook 'Discipline at Work', which did not need ministerial approval and has been in wide demand. The three original Codes of Practice were reissued in 1998, but only in order to bring them up to date with current legislation, and not to make any substantive changes. The Code of Practice No. 1 on discipline and dismissal was then reissued in 2000, in an expanded form also covering grievance procedures and the statutory right to be accompanied at a disciplinary or grievance hearing.

ii)   The Central Arbitration Committee

The CAC, successor to the Industrial Court and the Industrial Arbitration Board, was established by the Employment Protection Act 1975 and its procedure is now governed by Part VI of the Trade Union and Labour Relations (Consolidation)

---

11   Use of this device is relatively rare; a notable example was the Report of the Court of Inquiry under Scarman LJ into the dispute between Grunwick Processing Laboratories Ltd and APEX, (1977) Cmnd. 6922.

12   Trade Union and Labour Relations (Consolidation) Act 1992, s. 207(2). Under s. 203 the Secretary of State for Employment may himself issue codes of practice (after consultation with ACAS) and any such COP may replace part or all of one already issued by ACAS. This power has been used to issue the COP's in the politically contentious areas of picketing and the closed shop; it was extended to cover Codes of Practice on union ballots and elections.

Act 1992. It is a permanent arbitration body, independent of both ACAS and the sponsoring department and sitting centrally in London and increasingly elsewhere as the need arises. It consists of a chairman and deputy chairmen and a panel of persons appointed from both sides of industry. It will normally sit with a chairman or deputy chairman and two 'wingmen', though if it cannot reach a unanimous decision, the power of decision lies with the chairman or deputy chairman, acting as an umpire. It may sit in public or in private, and its decisions made in the exercise of its statutory functions (but not its consensual arbitrations) must be published; these decisions are given in the form of arbitral awards, with the emphasis upon a statement of 'general consideration' and then the terms of the award, rather than in the form of a closely reasoned legal judgment. If a question arises as to the interpretation of one of its awards, any party to it may refer the matter back to the CAC for decision. The functions of the CAC were progressively lessened by the previous government (which had a general distaste for third party intervention in industrial disputes) and were restricted to the following:

a) to arbitrate on matters voluntarily submitted to it by the parties through ACAS[13]; the CAC may thus be an alternative to the (more usual) single arbitrator and such a reference may be ad hoc or may be because reference to the CAC is formally built into the relevant procedure agreement between employer and union;

b) to enforce the disclosure of certain bargaining information – see below.

The workload of the CAC was therefore drastically reduced[14]. Under the Labour governments of the 1970s not only was the CAC involved in enforcing the then statutory recognition procedure, but also it had as its major function the determination of claims for the extension of terms and conditions of employment under Schedule 11 to the Employment Protection Act 1975. This form of statutory adjudication over wages was viewed with disfavour by the previous government (having been used extensively in the late 1970s during periods of wage restraint, to which awards under Schedule 11 were not subject) and so Schedule 11 was repealed completely by the Employment Act 1980 (along with the statutory recognition procedure). This decreased the CAC's workload, and this process was taken further when the government revoked the Fair Wages Resolution in September 1983[15]. Moreover, there was no compensating increase in voluntary arbitrations, which remained at a low level[16].

The CAC has, however, seen a revival in its use under the present government, being involved in two major developments. The first, and most high profile, is the new statutory recognition procedure under the Employment Relations Act 1999 (see p. 54, below); jurisdiction to adjudicate on disputes arising from this

13 Trade Union and Labour Relations (Consolidation) Act 1992, s. 212(1)(b).

14 In 1997 the CAC received 22 new references and issued no awards. Disclosure of information cases are usually disposed of by Recommendations and ACAS assistance. The comparable figures at its busiest period in the 1970s were: 1977 – 1,030 references and 308 awards; 1978 – 1,065 references and 836 awards; 1979 – 617 references and 594 awards.

15 In addition to the Fair Wages Resolution, the CAC also had jurisdiction under several particular statutes which imposed requirements analogous to those in the Resolution. However, some of these were repealed (particularly the Road Haulage Wages Act 1938, the Civil Aviation Act 1949, s. 15 and the Broadcasting Act 1981, s. 25) and the remainder (in the Housing Act 1957, s. 92, the Films Act 1960, s. 42 and the Public Passenger Vehicles Act 1981, s. 28) no longer had effect since they were so framed that they only applied while the Resolution itself was in force.

16 In 1997 there were no new references for arbitration received; the 22 references received all related to disclosure of bargaining information: CAC Annual Report 1997.

procedure is given to the CAC[17], and at the time of writing the likely level of usage remains a matter of speculation. The second development is the enactment of the European Worker Councils Directive 94/45/EC (see p. 74, below); here, the CAC is given jurisdiction to adjudicate on certain specified issues concerning employee members, applicability of the new Regulations to a particular company, constituencies and confidentiality of information (with other matters going to a tribunal or the EAT). These important new functions are likely to be sensitive and contentious, as can be seen from three further developments. The first is that when the CAC is operating the recognition procedure, it now has separate procedural requirements as to appointment, composition and decision taking[18], aimed at increasing openness and minimising challenges to its decisions. The second is that its decisions in relation to disputes over European worker councils are subject to appeal on a point of law to the EAT[19]. The third is that, in expanding its membership to cope with the likely increase in its case law, the government were keen to stress (again) openness and adhesion to the 'Nolan principles' on open competition for public appointments. Moreover, the possible legal complexity of these new jurisdictions was reflected in the choice as the new Chairman (to replace the long-serving previous Chairman, Professor Sir John Wood, on his retirement) of not just another employment lawyer, but a High Court judge, Burton J.

iii) The Certification Officer and the Trade Union Commissioners

In addition to ACAS and the CAC the other principal institution which the reader is likely to encounter in the areas of industrial relations and trade union law is the Certification Officer (CO). The office was established by the Employment Protection Act 1975 and is now governed by Part VI of the Trade Union and Labour Relations (Consolidation) Act 1992, though with major changes made by the Employment Relations Act 1999. It takes its name from the major function at that time of certifying trade unions as 'independent', such certification being the key to enjoyment of the new statutory rights given to unions and their members by that Act; the procedure of certification is considered in head 2 below. However, it becomes immediately obvious that in fact this official is, if not misnamed, at least inadequately named, since his functions now extend far beyond certification (which is now of course quantitatively far less important). In fact, he resembles more the old institution of the Registrar of Trade Unions, with a wide supervisory jurisdiction which may be generally split into two functions – administrative and judicial. The administrative functions include the listing of trade unions, dealing with the mechanics of union amalgamations, and receiving the audited annual returns and actuarial reports on members' superannuation schemes that are required of trade unions under the Trade Union and Labour Relations (Consolidation) Act 1992[20]. In addition, however, the CO has judicial

17 In exercising these functions, the CAC 'must have regard to the object of encouraging and promoting fair and efficient practices and arrangements in the workplace': Trade Union and Labour Relations (Consolidation) Act 1992, Sch. A1, para. 171.
18 Ibid. s. 263A. In particular, there *must* be a side member for each side of industry; where there is a split of opinion, but a majority have the same opinion, that is to be the decision (and so the chairman only has the power of umpire to decide the case if there is no majority opinion).
19 Transnational Information and Consultation of Employees Regulations 1999, S.I. 1999 No. 3323, reg. 38(8).
20 These matters are dealt with in ch. 10, below.

functions, in that he has the power to adjudicate on complaints brought by individuals of infringements of the laws relating to (a) political expenditure by a union, the running of a political fund and the necessary balloting thereon; (b) the balloting required for a union amalgamation; and (c) the balloting required for the appointment of union officers. Although the CO is funded and provided with staff through ACAS, he operates independently of it (and of the Department of Trade and Industry). He is expressly empowered to regulate his own procedure on any application or complaint to him, and he produces an Annual Report on his activities, which is an important source of up-to-date information and statistics on trade unions and their operations.

The powers of the CO were markedly increased by the Employment Relations Act 1999. The previous Conservative government had created two politically contentious posts of Commissioners for the Rights of Trade Union Members and Commissioners for Protection Against Unlawful Industrial Action, charged with the duties of assisting union members to assert their rights and members of the public to challenge unlawful strike action. When the present government decided to abolish them they offered the quid pro quo of increasing the CO's powers in most areas previously covered by the Commissioners[1], the idea being to provide an easier and more accessible forum than the ordinary courts. The CO's jurisdiction was extended by the 1999 Act to cover breach of a member's rights to see union accounts and breach of the statutory rules on the use of funds for political objects. In addition, the CO's existing powers in relation to registers of members, disqualification for union office, union office ballots and political resolution ballots were strengthened, largely by allowing him to issue enforcement orders akin to those available in court proceedings[2]. However the most fundamental change was to give him powers to hear complaints by a member of breach of a trade union's own rules (relating to union office, disciplinary proceedings, balloting of members on any issue other than industrial action, the constitution or proceedings of the executive committee or similar body and such other matters as may be prescribed by order, which has not yet been done). Here, as in the other areas affected by the changes, the CO is in effect made into a full alternative to the courts; because of this, the Act also laid down new procedural requirements on the CO when operating in these areas, with an appeal to the EAT on a point of law.

2   THE INDEPENDENCE OF TRADE UNIONS

i)   The importance of independence

For the purposes of the present legislation, the concept of the 'independence' of trade unions was first to be found in the Trade Union and Labour Relations Act 1974, where it was important in the definition of a union membership agreement (closed shop). However, with the advent of the new statutory trade union rights in the Employment Protection Act 1975 (and in other related legislation), the concept took on far greater significance, for the general scheme

1   Areas previously covered by the Commissioners which are *not* covered by the CO's increased powers are the statutory power of an individual to sue on behalf of the union, the right to restrain trustees from unlawful use of union property, the right of a member to restrain union industrial action without a ballot and the member's common law right to challenge breach of the union's rules relating to industrial action.
2   Employment Relations Act 1999, Sch. 6.

is that these new rights may only be exercised by *independent* trade unions, not by any bodies which are liable in any way to be under the influence or control of the employer. Thus, only an independent trade union may receive certain bargaining information as of right, demand to be consulted on pending redundancies or a planned transfer of the employer's undertaking, and appoint safety representatives under the Health and Safety at Work etc. Act 1974[3]; likewise, only a member of an independent trade union has a right to certain time off work, a right not to have detrimental action taken against him or be dismissed because of his union activities, and, in the case of dismissal, a right to apply for interim relief pending the hearing of an unfair dismissal action. The availability of these rights to such a union and its members may be a significant help in recruiting members and, perhaps more to the point, lack of them could be very damaging to any nascent organisation wishing to establish itself as a viable union. In the past this has been particularly important in an area of disputed or growing unionisation, for example in the white collar area, where there is competition for members between a larger, established union and a smaller body such as a staff association, for if that smaller body fails to obtain a certificate of independence it may stand little chance of competing effectively. Staff associations (or 'house' unions) have been particularly at risk in this certification procedure, since they may have evolved from little more than social clubs, and as they only operate with one employer they may be inherently more susceptible to interference (although this is by no means conclusive – the NUM and RMT could be said to be one-employer unions). Also at risk would be non-TUC affiliated bodies and breakaway groups from larger unions[4], where again they may face opposition from established affiliated unions.

ii)   The machinery of certification

A listed[5] trade union may apply to the Certification Officer[6] for a certificate of independence, under the Trade Union and Labour Relations (Consolidation) Act 1992, s. 6. He must decide whether the union is in fact 'independent' within the statutory definition; if his decision is favourable he must grant the certificate, and if unfavourable he must give his reasons for refusal. In coming to his decision he is at liberty to make such inquiries as he thinks fit and 'shall take into account any relevant information submitted to him by any person', which will of course include any other union which has an interest in the area in question and may wish to oppose the application for a certificate. If an applicant union is refused a certificate, it may appeal against that decision to the EAT. Unlike most other appeals to that body, this is an appeal of law *and fact*, so that the EAT may reconsider

---

3   This refers to the position where a trade union of some sort is involved; as will be seen below, the consultation requirements or redundancies and business transfers were extended in 1995 to elected worker representatives, in cases where no trade union is being involved, and similar reforms were made in the case of health and safety representatives in 1996.

4   Non-affiliated bodies would not be able to use, or be bound by, the TUC's internal disputes procedure for the settlement of inter-union rivalries – see p. 604. A particularly newsworthy example of a breakaway group was the Union of Democratic Mineworkers which split from the NUM after the miners' strike, and was granted a certificate of independence.

5   I.e. listed under the Trade Union and Labour Relations (Consolidation) Act 1992, s. 2 – see p. 560, below.

6   See p. 46, above.

the decision completely[7]. It should be noted, however, that the right to appeal is so worded that only a refused applicant union may appeal; if a certificate is in fact granted, there is no appeal against that decision by another union which may have opposed the application[8]. Finally, an application can be made more than once so that if a union is at first refused a certificate (whether after an appeal or not) it may reconsider its organisation etc. (possibly in the light of the reasons given for refusal), make any necessary changes and then apply again[9]. In practice, however, where there is rivalry with an established union this delay might give the latter a considerable tactical advantage.

iii) The tests to be applied

An independent trade union is defined in the Trade Union and Labour Relations (Consolidation) Act 1992, s. 5 as one which (a) is not under the domination or control of an employer or a group of employers or of one or more employers' associations, and (b) is not liable to interference by an employer or any such group or association (arising out of the provision of financial or material support or by any other means whatsoever) tending towards such control. The Certification Officer has evolved certain criteria, particularly on limb (a), and these were approved by the EAT in the first case to come before it on certification, *Blue Circle Staff Association v Certification Officer*[10]. These criteria are the financing of the union (any direct subsidy from the employer being potentially fatal); any other material support from the employer, such as free premises, time off work for officials or office facilities[11]; any interference in the running of the union by the employer; the history of the union, particularly if it started off as the creation of the employer; the union's rules, particularly if they allow intervention by the employer or give much control to senior members of the management; whether the union only operates within a single company (not a fixed criterion, but of course a more broadly based union would be more difficult to influence); the organisation of the union (its structure, financial position, recruiting ability) and its general attitude towards the employer in negotiating, for while it would be going too far to expect industrial chaos as a necessary sign of independence, the nascent union may be expected to have evolved far enough to show some 'robustness' in its negotiations. In the *Blue Circle* case the EAT approved the Certification Officer's refusal of a certificate on the basis that the staff association in question had originated as 'little more than a sophisticated instrument of personnel control' and had not evolved far enough to qualify as independent, in spite of certain changes to its rules and procedures which had, however, not gone far enough:

> '... we are not satisfied that the Association has yet attained that freedom from domination which it has been pursuing since it first decided to reorganise its constitution last year. When the matrix of the new constitution

---

7   Trade Union and Labour Relations (Consolidation) Act 1992, s. 9.
8   *GMWU v Certification Officer* [1977] 1 All ER 771, [1977] ICR 183.
9   *Blue Circle Staff Association v Certification Officer* [1977] ICR 224, [1977] IRLR 20; *HSD (Hatfield) Employees Association v Certification Officer* [1978] ICR 21, [1977] IRLR 261.
10 See n. 9, above.
11 After certification, of course, the union might well bargain for such facilities, and indeed in the case of time off demand it as of right, but before certification it would be wiser not to accept them.

is regarded, it is found to be an organisation whereby the association of the salaried staff members was penetrated at every point by the interference and control of the management. There must be a heavy onus on such a body to show that it has shaken off the paternal control which brought it into existence and fostered its growth, and which finally joined in drafting the very rules by which the control appears to be relaxed[12].'

In order to qualify as independent, the union must satisfy limb (b) of the definition too, for it could be the case that limb (a) is satisfied as things stand, but the union might still in some way be liable to interference, perhaps indirectly[13]. This second stage of the test requires a certain amount of speculation and foresight, and raised a question of interpretation – what was meant by 'liable' to interference? The wider view (i.e. more indulgent to the applicant union) was that 'liable' meant 'likely to suffer in practice', so that even if there were some provisions in the union's rules which might in theory permit interference by the management they should be ignored if in practice that was unlikely to happen. The narrower view was that 'liable' meant 'vulnerable to' or 'exposed to the risk of' interference, so that any factors raising a possibility of interference should disentitle the union to a certificate of independence even if, as things stood at the time of the application, there was little likelihood in practice of it happening. In *Squibb UK Staff Association v Certification Officer*, the applicant association had a proportionally large membership of the employees involved and was recognised by the employer for bargaining purposes; however, it was dependent upon the employer for material support such as accommodation and communications and was in a weak financial position, though there was found to be little likelihood of withdrawal of the employer's support. The EAT gave 'liable' the wider meaning and held that the union was independent[14] but, on the Certification Officer's appeal, the Court of Appeal reversed that decision, holding that the correct interpretation was the narrower view so that on the facts the Certification Officer's decision to refuse the certificate was correct[15]. Thus, the overall test for independence is more stringent than it might have been, in the light of the practical significance of the certificate of independence, and an applicant union or staff association should be quite sure before applying that none of its rules or procedures leave open a way for interference by an employer, so that it can claim to pass limb (b) as well as limb (a) – it is not enough to say that, although interference may be a theoretical possibility it is not likely to happen because of the present attitude of the employer:

'One has to envisage the possibility that there may be a difference of opinion in the future between the employers and the staff association. It does not matter whether it is likely or not. … It may be a mere possibility. But when it arises the questions have to be asked. What is the strength of the employers?

---

12   At 233 and 24 respectively, per Cumming-Bruce J.
13   *HSD (Hatfield) Employees Association v Certification Officer* [1978] ICR 21, [1977] IRLR 261.
14   [1978] ICR 115, [1977] IRLR 355; see also the *HSD (Hatfield)* case, n. 13, above.
15   [1979] ICR 235, [1979] IRLR 75, CA. For an application of these principles, see *A Monk & Co Staff Association v Certification Officer* [1980] IRLR 431, EAT. More recently, the staff association formed at GCHQ, Cheltenham (after the government's decision in 1984 to ban unions there on the grounds of national security) was refused a certificate of independence on this second limb of the test and that refusal was upheld by the EAT: *Government Communications Staff Federation v Certification Officer* [1993] ICR 163, [1993] IRLR 260.

What pressures could they bring to bear against the staff association? What facilities could they withdraw?'[16]

Beneath the legal challenges lies an important principle. The TUC and its affiliated trade unions resist the establishment and growth of non-affiliated unions – often within the one company (the house union). It is difficult for such trade unions to satisfy the criteria of independence and they will rarely, in the early stages of development, be 'effective'[17].

3 RECOGNITION FOR COLLECTIVE BARGAINING PURPOSES

The question of recognition of unions for collective bargaining purposes is not normally a matter for statute; usually it is a question of practical industrial relations and most practical consequences of recognition are extra-legal, particularly in the light of the non-enforceability of collective bargains. The same applies to the withdrawal of recognition, which saw a considerable increase in the 1980s and 1990s. Recognition is expressly covered as a proper subject for a 'trade dispute'[18], and in an appropriate case the parties to such a dispute over recognition may decide to seek the conciliatory help of ACAS in the ordinary way[19]. Other than that, the law has tended to keep out of questions of recognition. However, under the modern legislation, recognition has arisen as a matter of law in two ways. The first, and most obvious, concerns the question whether there should be a residual statutory procedure for a union to claim recognition by an employer (once it has a certain level of membership). Under the Industrial Relations Act 1971 and, more important, during the period from 1976 to 1980 under the Employment Protection Act 1975 there was an attempt to use legal machinery for resolving disputes about union recognition; this was ultimately unsuccessful and the machinery was abolished in the Employment Act 1980, but not before being the source of notable case law going to the root of the problem of how far the courts should control the exercise of its functions by a body such as ACAS when those functions relate to difficult questions of industrial relations[20]. The incoming New Labour government in 1997 were committed to reintroducing a statutory scheme for obtaining recognition, and this featured largely in the 'Fairness at Work' White Paper[1] and the resulting legislation in the Employment Relations Act 1999, which obviously tries to avoid the fatal shortcomings of the pre-1980 legislation.

16 Ibid., at 245 and 78 respectively, per Lord Denning MR. The staff association was eventually granted a certificate by the Certification Officer (Employment News No. 62 (May/June 1979)).
17 The Certification Officer's Annual Report for 1987 showed a cumulative total of 52 refusals of applications in the first 10 years of operation – a large proportion of these were staff associations; 231 certificates had been issued and were still in force at the end of 1987; 140 had been issued and subsequently cancelled (largely due to union amalgamation). Needless to say, the rate of application slowed dramatically; in 1992 six certificates were granted, and by 1995 none: Annual Reports 1992, 1995.
18 Trade Union and Labour Relations (Consolidation) Act 1992, ss. 218(1)(g), 244(1)(g).
19 Ibid, s. 210; see p. 38, above; in 1998 it accounted for 11% of collective conciliation cases.
20 *Grunwick Processing Laboratories Ltd v ACAS* [1978] 1 All ER 338, [1978] ICR 231, HL; *UKAPE v ACAS* [1980] ICR 201, [1980] IRLR 124, HL; *EMA v ACAS (No 2)* [1980] ICR 215, [1980] IRLR 164, HL. For details of the repealed procedure, see the previous editions of this book; particularly interesting is ch. 8 of the ACAS Annual Report 1980, giving their own assessment of the operation of the procedure from 1976 until its demise in 1980.
1 Cm 3968, 1998, paras. 4.11–4.20 and Annex 1.

The second form of legal involvement (always existing independently of the statutory recognition procedures and therefore unaffected by their presence or absence) is that under many provisions of the modern statutes it is necessary to be able to *define* recognition. This is because the key to some of the basic rights is not just that a union is 'independent'[2], but also that it is 'recognised' by the employer in question. Thus, a recognised independent trade union has rights to receive bargaining information[3], to be consulted on impending redundancies[4], to appoint safety representatives[5], to receive information and be consulted about an impending transfer of the employer's undertaking[6], and to be notified about certain matters relating to company pension schemes[7]. Further, the status of a union as recognised also figures in the rights of officers and members to time off work[8]. The definition of recognition must therefore be considered first, then the new statutory recognition procedure and, after that, some incidental aspects of the involvement of the law.

i)   The definition of recognition

As seen above, the question of whether a union can claim to be 'recognised' in law is an important point of jurisdiction for claiming significant legal rights. The clearest case is where there is an express recognition agreement between employer and union. However, the lack of a written recognition agreement (or disputes procedure involving the union) will not be conclusive, for recognition may also be implied if it exists in practice, no matter what the employer might call it[9].

The starting point is the statutory definition, which states that a recognised trade union is one which is recognised by an employer, or two or more associated employers[10], to any extent for the purposes of collective bargaining[11]. The phrase 'to any extent' could have been ambiguous, meaning either (a) that there must be full agreement to recognise the union, though possibly only with regard to certain matters, or (b) that the agreement to recognise might itself only be equivocal or sporadic. However, it has been held that it means the former[12] and

---

2   See pp. 47-51, above.
3   See pp. 59-63, below. The right to receive the information is drafted in such a way that, if recognition is less than total, the *extent* of the recognition can determine not only whether a particular union may make a claim but also what information must actually be disclosed: *R v CAC, ex p BTP Tioxide Ltd* [1981] ICR 843, [1982] IRLR 60. The question is therefore doubly important.
4   See pp. 64-70, below. Most of the case law on the definition of recognition has arisen under this head. As will be seen below, in this area and in that of transfers of undertakings, equivalent rights have now been extended to directly elected worker representatives.
5   Health and Safety at Work etc. Act 1974, s. 2, as amended by the Employment Protection Act 1975, s. 116. Again, there has been an extension to directly elected worker representatives.
6   Transfer of Undertakings (Protection of Employment) Regulations 1981, S.I. 1981. No. 1794, reg. 10; see pp. 70-73, below.
7   Pension Schemes Act 1993, s. 113; Occupational Pension Schemes (Disclosure of Information) Regulations 1996, SI 1996/1655.
8   See p. 581, below.
9   *Joshua Wilson & Bros Ltd v USDAW* [1978] ICR 614, [1978] IRLR 120.
10   For associated employers, see pp. 22-24, above.
11   Trade Union and Labour Relations (Consolidation) Act 1992, s 178(3); collective bargaining is itself defined in s. 178(1), (2).
12   *TGWU v Dyer* [1977] IRLR 93; *NUGSAT v Albury Bros Ltd* [1978] ICR 62, [1977] IRLR 173 (upheld on appeal by the Court of Appeal – n. 13, below).

so, although the recognition may only be partial in coverage, there must still be clear evidence of agreement to recognise.

Further than this, the statutes give little guidance in the sort of case where a problem of definition might arise, for example where a union with no express recognition agreement claims for the first time to be recognised in order to insist on one of the statutory rights (usually in the past, in a case such as this, the right to be consulted about threatened collective redundancies). The task of definition has therefore fallen principally on the courts, and the decisions of the Court of Appeal in *NUGSAT v Albury Bros Ltd*[13] and the EAT in *USDAW v Sketchley Ltd*[14] are particularly instructive. In the former, the Court of Appeal held that the concept of recognition is so important and so fundamental to the statutory union rights that, in the absence of an express agreement, it should not be held to be established unless there was clear and unequivocal evidence of conduct (probably over a period of time) from which recognition could be inferred; on the facts of the case, evidence of recruitment of a few employees by the union followed shortly after by a letter to the employer raising the question of rates of pay, leading to one inconclusive meeting, was held to be too insubstantial to establish the recognition that would have obliged the employer to consult the union over subsequent redundancies. In addition to this general point, the case established a further point of considerable importance in any case where the employer observes terms and conditions negotiated at a higher level – the employer in the case was in fact a member of an employers' association which *did* conduct collective bargaining with the union in question but it was held that that could not of itself be construed as recognition by that employer; this reinforces the point that recognition is ultimately a matter of agreement between a union and an individual employer, which could cause problems for unions in industries which are composed of many small firms, even if there is established bargaining at a higher level, e.g. nationally[15].

So far, discussion has been as to whether a union is recognised or not, and in many industries it is obvious which unions are recognised and that that recognition will cover all foreseeable industrial relations contexts. However, it must be remembered that the statutory definition talks of recognition 'to any extent' and this means that the definition may be satisfied even if the employer has agreed to bargain and negotiate with the union only on certain topics. As long as the necessary level of agreement can be shown, this form of partial recognition will be sufficient in law[16]. However, an important distinction must be drawn here, for

13 [1979] ICR 84, [1978] IRLR 504, CA; *NUTGW v Charles Ingram & Co Ltd* [1977] ICR 530, [1977] IRLR 147. The *NUGSAT* case was applied in *Cleveland County Council v Springett* [1985] IRLR 131, EAT (concerning health and safety representatives) where it was held that the addition of the union to the Burnham Committee by the Secretary of State did *not* per se mean that the union became recognised by one of the employers represented on that committee.

14 [1981] ICR 644, [1981] IRLR 291.

15 A prime example of this is the agriculture industry, where terms and conditions are worked out centrally each year before the Agricultural Wages Board in negotiations between the agricultural section of the TGWU and the NFU, but where any question of union recognition would have to be determined on a farm-by-farm basis. This diversity had long been a cause of weakness of the NUAAW and was one of the reasons for its amalgamation in 1982 with the TGWU.

16 It will be sufficient to claim to be consulted about impending redundancies or transfer and to claim to appoint safety representatives; however, to claim bargaining information the union must be able to go further and show that the information requested is relevant to one of the purposes for which the union is recognised: (*R v CAC, ex p BTP Tioxide Ltd* [1981] ICR 843, [1982] IRLR 60) and this now also applies to the right to time off for union duties (Trade Union and Labour Relations (Consolidation) Act 1992, s. 168(1)(a)).

there also exists in practice a form of 'recognition' involving only the right of a union to represent its members in individual matters, e.g. under a grievance or discipline procedure[17]. This may perhaps be granted while a union recruits a sufficient number of members to warrant full recognition, or may be all that is left after an employer has derecognised the union for most purposes; however it arises, it falls short of an agreement to negotiate and bargain and so does *not* qualify as recognition in law. This can clearly be seen in *USDAW v Sketchley Ltd*[18], where an agreement between the employer and the union in 1978 granting recognition for representation purposes was held by the EAT to be insufficient in itself to entitle the union to be consulted in 1980 about impending redundancies, particularly as the 1978 agreement expressly stated that it did not confer recognition on USDAW for negotiation of terms and conditions. However, the case also shows that recognition is not a static concept, because the evidence showed that in February 1980, when the employer began to select candidates for redundancy, the union threatened strike action if they were not given information about this, as a consequence of which a meeting took place at which it was agreed that, in return for the union calling off the strike threat, the employer would give the union certain advanced information on redundancies, adopt a procedure involving the union and in certain cases make redundancy payments above the legal minimum. While the 1978 agreement could not constitute recognition, the EAT thought it possible that the subsequent events in February 1980 were capable of showing that the union had indeed become accepted as having sufficient negotiating rights (at least in the area of redundancy) to satisfy the definition of recognition, and so they remitted the case to the tribunal for determination of that question.

ii) The statutory recognition procedure

In its manifesto for the 1997 election, the Labour Party stated its intention to reintroduce a statutory recognition procedure. On coming into power, the new government in typical fashion sought to achieve agreement among the 'social partners' (TUC and CBI) on such a procedure, but consultations merely reinforced existing deep divisions. Thus, the government themselves had to take the initiative in the White Paper Fairness at Work and propose a scheme. The failure to discern an agreed version had two principal effects: (i) in an attempt to steer a middle path, the government introduced certain limitations or qualifications to which strong objection was taken by the unions (leading to arguments that there had been resiling from the manifesto pledge of recognition where a simple majority of the workforce voted for it); (ii) the prospect of legal enforcement (raising spectres of the failed 1970s version) meant that there had to be a satisfactory forum, eventually meaning a revamped Central Arbitration Committee[19]. In relation to (i), the White Paper introduced the qualifications that the procedure should not apply to employers of fewer then 20 and that in a ballot those voting in favour of recognition should comprise not just over 50% of those taking part, but also at least 40% of those *eligible* to vote. There was added later the further qualification that, even where there is already a majority union

17 This is now backed by the employee's statutory right to be accompanied by a trade union official (or fellow worker) before a disciplinary or grievance procedure: Employment Relations Act 1999, ss. 10–15; see p. 442, below.
18 N. 14, above; this distinction can also be seen in the *BTP Tioxide* case.
19 See p. 44, above.

membership the CAC may still insist on a ballot if it considers it necessary to gauge 'real' support.

The new statutory recognition procedure was introduced by the Employment Relations Act 1999, which adds a new Schedule A1 to the Trade Union and Labour Relations (Consolidation) Act 1992[20]. The level of detail is stunning; the Schedule entered Parliament 88 paragraphs long and left 172. The intention to avoid the fatal pitfall of its 1970s predecessor (based on broad discretions) is obvious, and was made express by the government minister steering the Bill. He described the main features of the Bill as follows: (a) the legislation would provide the greatest scope for voluntary arrangements to be reached, with compulsion only as a last resort; (b) the threshold for frivolous complaints would be set at 10% of the relevant workforce; (c) the crucial test when determining the appropriate bargaining unit would be effective management, with fragmentation to be avoided; (d) if more than 50% of the workforce were already members of the relevant union, there would be a simplified procedure; (e) if no voluntary arrangement was reached, the dispute would be determined by the CAC; (f) the CAC's determination would be binding *but* would only relate to procedural matters[1]; (g) existing arrangements should, where possible, be left untouched[2]. For most purposes, these statements of principle were adhered to (though with many technical amendments), as was the point that statutory recognition per se would only cover pay, hours and holidays, unless widened by agreement[3].

Part 1 of the Schedule contains the principal provision on statutory recognition, which may be requested by one or more independent trade unions. In keeping with the voluntarist approach, the request is made in the first instance to the employer[4]. If there is agreement (possibly involving ACAS help), that is the end of the procedure[5]. If, however, the employer rejects the request or negotiations fail, the union(s) may apply to the CAC to decide (a) what is to be the appropriate bargaining unit for these purposes and (b) whether the union has the support of the majority of workers in the appropriate bargaining unit[6]. In order to proceed, the CAC must be satisfied that at least 10% of the workers in the bargaining unit are union members[7].

Determination of the bargaining unit may clearly be a crucial factor. Once again, the initial emphasis is on encouraging the parties to agree it, but in default of that the CAC must determine it, taking into consideration the need for effective management, the views of the parties, existing national and local arrangements, the need to avoid fragmentation, the characteristics of the relevant workers and

---

20 For a critical and comparative analysis of these provisions, see Wood and Goddard 'The statutory union recognition procedure in the Employment Relations Bill: a comparative analysis' (1999) 37 BJIR 203; see also Simpson (1998) 27 ILJ 253 and Wedderburn 'Collective bargaining or legal enactment' (2000) 29 ILJ 1, at 33 ff.

1   The government strongly resisted amendments aimed at going further and providing for either a legal duty to bargain in good faith or some form of binding arbitration on substantive claims: HL Committee, 7 June 1999, cols. 1276–1280.

2   See the ministerial statements at HC SC E, 16 March 1999, cols. 344–410.

3   Sch. A1, para. 3(4). Questions of industrial training were originally mooted too, but are now dealt with separately by the Employment Relations Act 1999, s. 5.

4   Para. 4. The exclusion of employers with 20 or less employees is contained in para. 7, which contains a calculation method; employees of any associated employer are included.

5   Para. 10. The CAC may, however be subsequently involved in any dispute over operating the agreement; also, such an agreement may not be unilaterally terminated by the employer for three years: paras. 52–63.

6   Paras. 11, 12.

7   Para. 14.

their location[8]. Once this is determined, the CAC is to proceed to the main question, namely whether there is the necessary support for collective bargaining to make an order for recognition. This can be determined in two ways. The short method is that if the CAC is satisfied that a majority of workers in the unit are union members, it may make the order, *unless* it considers that (a) it would still be in the interests of good industrial relations to hold a ballot, (b) a significant number of members in the unit inform the CAC that they do not want collective bargaining, or (c) there are doubts about the membership evidence[9]. The longer method (where membership numbers are insufficient to trigger the first method) is for the CAC to go straight to a ballot[10]. If the ballot shows that a majority of those voting support the union *and* that those voting in favour constitute at least 40% of the workers in the bargaining unit, the CAC must issue a declaration that the union is entitled to recognition; if not, the application is dismissed[11].

On the making of a declaration, the parties are given a period of 30 working days (or longer by agreement) to negotiate a method by which they will conduct collective bargaining. If no agreement is reached, either side may apply to the CAC for assistance[12]. A further period is determined for CAC-assisted negotiations, but then the CAC is to specify a method[13], which has effect as if in a legally enforceable agreement between the parties, subject to specific performance.

Two further significant matters are covered by the Schedule (in addition to a plethora of highly detailed subsidiary and explanatory provisions). The first concerns subsequent changes in the bargaining unit. Part III (paras. 64–95) sets out complex procedures for dealing with circumstances which necessitate changes to the established collective bargaining structure. The second matter is, of course, derecognition. Normally, this is simply a question of industrial realities, but where recognition has been obtained under the statutory scheme there are special procedures for its removed. These fall into six main categories: (i) where voluntary agreement has been reached under the procedure (where derecognition is not permitted in the first three years); (ii) where the relevant employees fall below the threshold of 21; (iii) where the employer applies for derecognition even though the threshold requirement is still met[14]; (iv) where the request comes from employees; (v) where recognition was originally granted under the short method (i.e. more than 50% membership)[15]; (vi) where the union is not independent[16].

---

8   Paras. 18, 19.
9   Para. 22
10   Para. 23. Procedure for the ballot is set out in paras. 24–28; it must be conducted by an appointed independent person, and may be either workplace or postal. The employer must co-operate, in particular by allowing access to the workforce; this is backed by a DTI Code of Practice.
11   Para. 29.
12   Para. 30.
13   Para. 30. Obviously the hope must be that this power would rarely have to be operated, because compulsion at this stage is an odd concept (analogous to the ancient family law order for restitution of conjugal rights!). To ease the situation if it ever came to such a thing, the Secretary of State has exercised his power under para. 168 to issue a model form of collective bargaining, to be taken into account by the CAC.
14   This is the most significant category; the procedure to be adopted is set out in paras. 104–111, and requires a secret ballot.
15   Part V (paras. 122–133); this again requires a secret ballot. As with voluntary recognition, a request by an employer may not be made until the expiry of three years.
16   Part VI (paras. 134–148). Part VII (paras. 149–155) applies where a union loses its certificate of independence.

As stated above, the complexity of these provisions is remarkable. The overall effect will be watched with great interest during the currency of this edition. At the time of writing, views vary as to the significance of this new procedure. A restrictive view is that this innovation is more important politically than industrially, and is principally aimed at a restricted number of firms which do not recognise unions (or, indeed, may have positively derecognised them in the last decade or more) but where union membership remains quite high. A more expansive view is that the very existence of the procedure may have a normative effect on the renewed acceptability of union involvement more generally. As evidence for this, the TUC stated that in the last three quarters of 1999 (with the statutory procedure imminent) their members negotiated voluntarily over 70 recognition agreements. While this may be significant (though subject to the cynical view that such agreements may have been in order to stave off the inevitable, in a way not involving the complexities of Schedule A1, and thus basically defensive), the question still arises whether this return to formal union recognition is really the government's preferred route towards 'partnership' (a key feature of the White Paper Fairness at Work), rather than the more modern and 'Third Way' concept of EU-inspired consultation with and involvement of the workforce as such, if necessary by direct election of representatives. Further tensions between these two models may be expected.

iii) Further legal provisions

In addition to the legal definition of recognition and the new statutory recognition procedure, three other areas of legal involvement should be noticed at this point – one of general importance and two specific points, one supporting the concept of recognition and the other possibly restricting it.

The general point is that the abolition of the previous statutory recognition procedure in 1980 did not mean the end of all ACAS involvement in such matters. This is because a recognition dispute can of course still be a valid subject for voluntary conciliation by ACAS. This should not be underestimated, and it is interesting to note that according to ACAS during the period 1976–1980 (when the previous statutory procedure was in force) collective bargaining was extended to more workers through voluntary conciliation than by the use of that statutory procedure[17].

The second point is that by virtue of the Transfer of Undertakings (Protection of Employment) Regulations 1981, where an undertaking or part of one is transferred by the original employer to a new employer and it retains an identity distinct from the rest of the transferee employer's business, then if the original employer recognised a particular union, that recognition continues through the transfer and the new employer is deemed to recognise the union to the same

---

17 During that period, 2,292 recognition cases were completed through voluntary conciliation leading to full recognition in 726 cases (concerning 55,500 employees) and partial recognition in 255 cases (concerning 22,000 employees); this total figure of 77,000 employees exceeds the figure of 64,000 employees to whom collective bargaining was extended by virtue of the statutory procedure: ACAS Annual Report, 1980. In 1998, 131 recognition disputes were dealt with by ACAS on a voluntary basis (comprising 11% of collective conciliation cases in that year): ACAS Annual Report 1998.

extent[18]. This was not the case before, for a recognition agreement was viewed as personal to the employer and was not protected on a transfer[19].

The third, restrictive, point is that by virtue of the Trade Union and Labour Relations (Consolidation) Act 1992, ss. 186 and 187 it is unlawful to insert into a contract for the supply of goods or services a condition that a party to that contract must recognise a particular union or unions in relation to persons employed by him; any such clause is declared to be void. Likewise it is unlawful to refuse to contract with or accept tenders from an employer on the ground that he does not recognise a particular trade union. This is to be read along with the wider provisions in sections 144 and 145 aimed at outlawing union-labour-only contracts and tenders[20] and is presumably included to prevent much the same result being reached, not by a direct requirement that contractors or tenderers must employ members of a particular union, but instead by making recognition of the union in question a condition of obtaining the contract. These provisions do not create criminal offences, but the imposition of such a condition or the refusal to contract or accept tenders on the ground of non-recognition is made tortious as a breach of statutory duty (actionable at the suit of the contracting party against whom it is aimed, or 'any other person who may be adversely affected' by it) and section 225 removes the statutory immunities from actions aimed at inducing the incorporation of such a condition or such refusal and from industrial action aimed at disrupting the supply of goods and services because of non-recognition of a particular trade union by the supplier. Thus, not only did the previous government remove the possibility of obtaining recognition through a legal procedure, they also attempted to place legal limits on the ways in which a union may try to obtain it as a matter of practical industrial relations. In practice, these provisions have not had much direct effect – as in the case of industrial dispute cases generally, all that the new legislation does is to remove bars to legal action, but that legal action must be taken, if at all, by individual plaintiffs and therefore must be seen by them to be worthwhile; perhaps it was thought that this may be the case more often with disappointed commercial tenderers (particularly for local government contracts) than in the more usual case of an employer simply being affected generally by industrial action which under the legislation is now illegal (e.g. as being unlawful secondary action or without the necessary ballot – see chapter 11, below), where actual litigation still remains relatively uncommon or, at most, confined to notable exceptions.

One final point to notice is that, in the changed economic and political climate of the eighties and nineties, the question of recognition caused major problems for unions (and indeed for the union movement as a whole), for two reasons. The first is that increasingly any new recognition agreement entered into by an employer may be a part of an overall *single union* agreement (possibly incorporating a no strike and/or compulsory arbitration provision)[1], and the growth of such agreements has caused major splits within the TUC in the past. The second is that in other areas the main problem for unions may not be recognition by new employers, but rather *derecognition* by existing employers. A leading survey published in 1992 and relating to the position in 1990 found that:

---

18   S.I. 1981, No. 1794, reg. 9. For the Regulations to apply at all, the transfer must be a 'relevant transfer'; see p. 160, below. Of course, there is nothing to stop the transferee employer later rescinding the deemed recognition agreement.
19   *UCATT v Burrage* [1978] ICR 314.
20   See p. 669, below.
1   See the ACAS Annual Report 1987, p. 16.

'The clear picture is one of substantial decline in the extent of recognition since 1984. The figure for all workplaces and all employees fell from 66 per cent in 1984 to 53 per cent in 1990. Thus by 1990 only just over half of workplaces were ones where the employer recognised one or more unions for collective bargaining over basic pay for some of the employees present. This is a striking change compared with the 1980 to 1984 period, when there was stability in the overall figures'[2].

This was consistent with the experience of ACAS who suggested that positive derecognition remained relatively unusual, but (1) it remained a possibility if managers continued to question the continuing benefit of the involvement of unions, and (2) even where recognition continued, there were many examples of the *extent* of the union's involvement being amended or restricted[3].

While much of this was a result of major structural changes resulting in a disproportionate rate of closure of large (and heavily unionised) manufacturing plants and their replacement by new enterprises inherently less likely to want union involvement[4], the decline in union membership and the coverage of collective bargaining generally and increased interest in individual contracting[5], rather than of deliberate repudiation of recognition agreements, it remains the case that there have been notable cases of such repudiation (e.g. in the Wapping printing and Dover seamen disputes) and in law there has hitherto been little that a union could do to prevent it, since the collective agreement containing the recognition agreement (where it is so expressed) is itself not legally binding[6]. Whether, and to what extent, this situation will be affected in practice by the new statutory recognition procedure remains to be seen.

4 DISCLOSURE OF BARGAINING INFORMATION

One vestige of earlier times when the law actively encouraged rational collective bargaining is the imposition upon an employer of a duty to disclose certain

2   Millward et al. *Workplace Industrial Relations in Transition* (the ED/ESRC/PSI/ACAS Survey) (1992) at p. 70. The survey goes on to show the variations in the decline across different sectors of industry. The preliminary findings of the equivalent 1998 survey showed a further decline in recognition to 45% of workplaces: the 1998 Workplace Employee Relations Survey – the First Findings (DTI/ACAS/ESRC/PSI; URN/98/934). See also Edwards (ed) *Industrial Relations Theory and Practice in Britain* (1995) at p 139; Gall & McKay 'Trade union derecognition in Britain 1988–1994' (1994) 32 BJIR 433; Milner 'The coverage of collective pay-setting institutions in Britain 1895–1990' (1995) 33 BJIR 69.

3   ACAS Annual Report 1991, p. 21. One form of simplification is the establishment of 'single table' bargaining in place of more traditional multi-unionism: ACAS Annual Report 1989, p. 9.

4   'Workplaces that were less than 10 years old recognised unions in 23% of cases compared with 52% of those that were more than 20 years old': Millward et al., above, p. 73.

5   'The most common reasons for moving towards derecognition were either dwindling trade union membership or the introduction of individual contracts to replace collective bargaining': ACAS Annual Report 1991, p. 37. The Millward et al. survey found that the proportion of employees covered by collective bargaining in all the workplaces surveyed (i.e. of over 25 employees) dropped from 71% in 1984 to 54% in 1990: p. 93.

6   See *National Coal Board v National Union of Mineworkers* [1986] ICR 736, [1986] IRLR 439, where the NUM tried to prevent partial derecognition (and partial recognition of the UDM) by arguing: (i) that the existing arrangements in the collective agreement were legally binding; or (ii) if not, they were incorporated into individual members' terms and conditions and so were contractually binding. They lost on both arguments.

information to an independent trade union which is recognised by him, for the purpose of facilitating the conduct of collective bargaining by that union. This duty was first enacted in the Industrial Relations Act 1971, and is now contained in the Trade Union and Labour Relations (Consolidation) Act 1992, ss. 181–185 and the Code of Practice No. 2 'Disclosure of information to trade unions for collective bargaining purposes', produced by ACAS pursuant to section 181(4)[7].

i)   The duty to disclose

Section 181 lays upon an employer the general duty to disclose information which is in his possession and relates to his undertaking or that of an associated employer, if it is (a) information without which the union would be impeded to a material extent in carrying out collective bargaining with him, *and* (b) information which he ought to disclose in the interests of good industrial relations. This formulation by itself is so vague as to be meaningless, indeed head (a) tends to ignore the fact that effective bargaining is possible (some would say easier) with virtually no information. The scheme is to explain it further in the Code of Practice, which states that the detail, form and depth of information in any given case will vary with the level of bargaining to which it may be relevant, and goes on in paragraph 11 to give particular examples of information which may be amenable to compulsory disclosure. These are under the headings of 'pay and benefits' (including pay systems, job evaluation and grading schemes, total pay bill, fringe benefits and the way that the overall pay bill is analysed), 'conditions of service' (recruitment, training, promotion and redundancy policies; appraisal systems; health and safety matters), 'man-power' (analysis of workforce, manpower and investment plans, any planned changes), 'performance' (productivity, efficiency and their savings; return on capital; state of order book) and 'financial' (cost structures; gross and net profits; sources of earnings; assets; liabilities; allocation of profits; government aid; transfer prices; loans within the group and interest charged). The aim of the Code is to show the *sort* of information within the ambit of section 181; it is at pains to point out that these examples are not an exhaustive check list.[8] Further, the Code stresses the desirability of reaching joint agreement on what should be disclosed, possibly including an agreement to disclose certain information on a regular basis. Where a union wishes to resort to the statutory duty, it must make its request in writing if the employer so wishes, and any information disclosed must also be in writing if the union so wishes.

There is one possible limitation on the right to bargaining information which is inherent in the wording of section 181. As seen above, the union must be 'recognised' in order to make a claim, but that recognition might only be partial (e.g. restricted to negotiating rights only in respect of certain matters). If that is

---

7   See Kahn-Freund *Labour and the Law* (3rd edn, 1983), pp. 106–118; Gospel 'Disclosure of information to trade unions' (1976) 5 ILJ 223; Gospel and Williams 'Disclosure of information: the CAC approach' (1981) 10 ILJ 10; Gospel and Lockwood 'Disclosure of Information for Collective Bargaining: the CAC Approach revisited' (1999) 28 ILJ 233.

8   One marginal area of recent interest is redundancy selection; in *Rolls Royce plc and AEEU* (CAC Award 94/1) the CAC upheld a union request for further information on how a points-based selection system had been applied, accepting that this process fell within the sphere of collective bargaining. In the individual context, this question has caused severe difficulties to the tribunals and courts (see p. 489, below); see the CAC Annual Report 1994 for a contrasting of the CAC and the tribunal approach.

the case, section 181(1) applies to restrict the disclosure of information to matters 'in respect of which the trade union is recognised by him' and so, although the partial recognition is sufficient to qualify the union as 'recognised', the union will not be able to claim information relating to matters outside the scope of that partial recognition. Thus, in *R v CAC, ex p BTP Tioxide Ltd*[9] the union, ASTMS, had bargaining rights in respect of certain terms and conditions of employment, but in respect of a particular job evaluation scheme it only had the right to make representations on behalf of its members seeking re-evaluation of their job[10], not the right to negotiate over the scheme itself. Because of this, the Divisional Court held that the CAC had exceeded its jurisdiction in ordering disclosure by the employer of information relating to the scheme.

ii) Exceptions to the duty to disclose

The duty is not an absolute one, for it is subject to certain exceptions which are contained in section 182, and which should be known to the prudent employer. Three obvious exceptions are where disclosure would be against the interests of national security or in contravention of other legislation, and where the information was obtained by the employer for the purpose of bringing or defending legal proceedings (e.g. resisting an unfair dismissal action). The most important exceptions are likely to be:
a) information which has been communicated to the employer in confidence, or in some way in consequence of a confidence; this is not further defined, either in the Act or the Code, and could lead to litigation[11].
b) information relating specifically to an individual (unless he has consented to its disclosure); thus, while the union may be able to require disclosure of the wages bill for a whole department, the employer may resist a request for details of each individual's salary. This exception has caused some difficulties in areas where the recent trend has been towards individual contracting and performance-related pay[12].
c) information the disclosure of which could cause 'substantial injury' to the employers' undertaking for reasons other than its effect on collective bargaining.
This last category is perhaps the most contentious – what is likely to be substantial injury? Clearly an employer cannot rely on this on the ground simply that he has hitherto as a matter of policy kept the information secret, but on the other hand there will be cases where the employer's genuine interest in preserving secrecy will outweigh the benefits to the union of disclosure. The Code gives some

9   [1981] ICR 843, [1982] IRLR 60. In his judgment, Forbes J said that there were three categories of case where a union would not be entitled to information, on the wording of s. 181 – (i) where the bargaining between employer and union does not meet the statutory definition of 'collective bargaining' because it does not relate to matters referred to in the Trade Union and Labour Relations (Consolidation) Act 1992, s. 178(2); (ii) where dealings between employer and union do not amount to 'collective bargaining' because they cannot properly be described as 'negotiations' (ibid.); (iii) where there is 'collective bargaining' but it does not relate to matters in respect of which the union is recognised. For a good example, see *Babtie Shaw & Morton and UKAPE* (CAC Award 82/4).
10 This form of recognition for representation is not sufficient to qualify as 'recognition' for the purpose of claiming statutory union rights; see p. 54, above.
11 This exception was held to apply to information included in a commercial tender submitted to the employer in confidence: *Civil Service Union v CAC* [1980] IRLR 274.
12 CAC Annual Report 1991, p. 3.

further guidance in paragraphs 14 and 15. It gives as examples of information possibly under this exception – cost information on individual products, detailed analysis of proposed investment, marketing or pricing policies and price quotas or tender prices. It further states:

> 'Substantial injury may occur if, for example, certain customers would be lost to competitors, or suppliers would refuse to supply necessary materials, or the ability to raise funds to finance the company would be seriously impaired as a result of disclosing certain information. The burden of establishing that disclosure of certain information would cause substantial injury lies with the employer.'

Section 182(2) gives some practical protection to an employer by providing that he need not produce original documentation (so that an abstract or precis will suffice) and that he need not compile or assemble information where to do so would involve work or expenditure 'out of reasonable proportion to the value of the information in the conduct of collective bargaining' (a positive invitation to litigation).

One final point concerns the use made of the information by the union. Even if an employer has to divulge information which he would rather have kept secret, the statute only obliges disclosure to the union officials concerned, and then only for the purposes of conducting collective bargaining with that employer; it is thus an open question whether an employer could restrain further use (or, from his point of view, misuse) of that information by the union by the threat of an action for breach of confidence.

iii) Enforcement provisions

If a union considers that an employer is refusing to disclose information which he ought by law to disclose, it may complain to the CAC under section 183. If the CAC thinks that a solution may be reached by conciliation, it must, and most often does, refer the matter to ACAS for that purpose. This is the opposite of the normal ACAS system of conciliation *first*, with arbitration only if that fails; it has been argued that this approach is more effective, with the initial approach to the CAC concentrating the parties' minds on possibilities for conciliation, and this view certainly appears to be supported by the figures, though the statistical basis is small since use of the procedure remains generally low[13]. If the matter is not referred to conciliation (or if it is but no settlement is reached), the CAC must hear and determine the complaint, giving the reasons for its decision. If it upholds the complaint, its declaration to that effect must specify the material which ought to be divulged, the date on which the employer failed to do so, and a period during which the employer should comply by disclosure. If at the expiry of this period the employer has still failed to disclose the specified information, the union may make a further complaint to the CAC under section 184, and this time may attach a substantive claim on behalf of some or all of the employees in question (for higher pay, better benefits, etc.). It is this substantive claim which gives the teeth to this enforcement procedure, for if the CAC finds the union's further complaint well founded (in whole or in part) it may make a declaration to that

---

13   In 1997 there were 22 references to the CAC under ss. 183 and 184, but no awards had to be made to resolve them: CAC Annual Report 1997.

effect *and* award all or part of the attached claim. Any terms and conditions granted in the CAC's award are automatically incorporated into the contracts of employment of the employees concerned, and are then enforceable in the ordinary courts.

One unfortunate limitation upon the power of the CAC under this procedure is that, as it is drafted, the committee is limited to deciding upon information which has in fact already been refused by the employer; this means that it cannot go on to give guidance on information which should be divulged in the future, even if to do so might avoid future litigation on linked matters where it is foreseeable that disputes may well arise[14].

iv) Other obligatory disclosure

The employer must also disclose information to a recognised trade union concerning pending redundancies, under the statutory provisions covering the procedure for handling redundancies[15]. This covers the reasons for the proposed redundancies, the numbers and descriptions of employees involved, the total number affected at each establishment, the proposed method of selection, timing, and the proposed method of calculating any redundancy payments. Further, the employer must publish to his employees a statement of his health and safety policies[16] and divulge certain information relating to such matters to the Health and Safety Commission upon request[17] and to safety representatives appointed under regulations[18]. Also, in a more specialised but linked context, an employer who intends to establish a contracted-out occupational pensions scheme must issue notices to that effect to earners who are to be covered by the scheme, giving certain basic information, and must also convey this information to 'all independent trade unions recognised to any extent for the purpose of collective bargaining in relation to the earners concerned', with whom the employer is then under a statutory obligation to consult on the proposed scheme[19]. Likewise, there are regulations providing for the disclosure of more information generally about the running of occupational pension schemes; in the first instance, such disclosure is envisaged as being to the members themselves, but the relevant provisions also mention disclosure to independent trade unions recognised to any extent for the purposes of collective bargaining in relation to members and prospective members of the scheme in question[20].

14   *R v CAC, ex p BTP Tioxide Ltd* [1981] ICR 843, [1982] IRLR 60.
15   Trade Union and Labour Relations (Consolidation) Act 1992, ss. 188–192; this has now also been extended to elected worker representatives.
16   Health and Safety at Work etc. Act 1974, s. 2(3).
17   Ibid., s. 27; note that s. 28 imposes statutory restrictions on further publication of this information by the recipient officials.
18   Safety Representatives and Safety Committees Regulations 1977, S.I. 1977 No. 500, reg. 7; this contains grounds upon which an employer may refuse to disclose similar to those in the Trade Union and Labour Relations (Consolidation) Act 1992, s. 182, above. See also the Health & Safety Commission's Code of Practice on Safety Representatives (1978), para. 6. Again, there has been an extension to elected worker representatives: Health and Safety (Consultation with Employees) Regulations 1996 S.I. 1996 No. 1513.
19   Occupational Pension Schemes (Contracting-Out) Regulations 1996, S.I. 1996 No. 1172.
20   Occupational Pension Schemes (Disclosure of Information) Regulations 1996, S.I. 1996 No. 1655. The Pensions Act 1995, passed in reaction to the Maxwell scandal, has provisions for obligatory member trustees, but not surprisingly this is cast in terms of individual appointment, *not* in terms of any formal involvement of recognised trade unions.

Finally, a further category of compulsory disclosure was enacted in the case of transfers of business by the Transfers of Undertakings (Protection of Employment) Regulations 1981, considered separately in head 6, below.

5   SPECIAL REDUNDANCY PROCEDURES

The redundancy payments legislation gives to individuals rights to payments upon redundancy, but does not itself lay down any particular procedures for handling redundancies. However, pursuant to two EEC directives on collective redundancies[1], procedural requirements were established and are to be found in the Trade Union and Labour Relations (Consolidation) Act 1992, ss. 188–198, as amended by the Trade Union Reform and Employment Rights Act 1993, the Collective Redundancies and Transfer of Undertakings (Protection of Employment) (Amendment) Regulations 1995 and 1999[2]. In many industries, it appears that these provisions have had little effect due to more sophisticated approaches to necessary reductions in manpower, such as voluntary redundancies, redeployment and natural wastage[3]; in some 'problem' industries of greater labour fluctuations, such as the construction industry, the provisions are more relevant. There are two obligations laid upon the employer who is about to make employees redundant – first, to consult employee or trade union representatives and, second, to notify the Secretary of State.

i)   Consultation with employee or trade union representatives

It was enacted in the Employment Protection Act 1975 that where an employer proposes to dismiss as redundant[4] an employee of a class in respect of which he recognises an independent trade union, he must consult officials of that union, with a set time framework in the case of collective redundancies; these provisions are now contained in the Trade Union and Labour Relations (Consolidation) Act 1992, section 188. They were updated by the 1993 Act to take into account the 1992 amending Directive, but the whole basis of their enactment of the original 1975 Directive was severely shaken in enforcement proceedings brought by the EC Commission in *EC Commission v United Kingdom*[5]. The problem was the

1   Directives 75/129/EEC and 92/56/EEC (see Dolding (1992) 21 ILJ 310). The 1975 Directive was held not to be directly applicable in *Griffin v South West Water Services Ltd* [1995] IRLR 15, and so cannot be used as the basis of a separate legal action.
2   S.I. 1995 No. 2587 and S.I. 1999 No. 1925. On the latter, see Hall and Edwards 'Reforming the statutory redundancy consultation procedure' (1999) 28 ILJ 299.
3   Daniel and Stilgoe *The Impact of Employment Protection Laws* (Policy Studies Institute No. 577, June 1978), summarised [1978] Employment Gazette 658; Millward et al. *Workplace Industrial Relations in Transition* (1992) pp. 320–329. One interesting finding in the latter was that in 1990 compulsory redundancies were reported in 46% of workplaces without recognised unions that had made workforce reductions, compared with 17% where recognised unions were present: p. 324.
4   The definition of redundancy for these purposes in s. 195(1) was substituted by the Trade Union Reform and Employment Rights Act 1993, and now refers more simply and widely to 'dismissal for a reason not related to the individual concerned or for a number of reasons all of which are not so related'; under s. 195(2) there is a rebuttable presumption that a dismissal or proposed dismissal is for redundancy.
5   C-383/92: [1994] ECR I-2479, [1995] 1 CMLR 345, ECJ. Other infringements by the UK were found, but these had been dealt with by the 1993 Act, as well as taking the new Directive into account.

restriction of the consultation requirement to cases where there was a recognised union, whereas the Directive was held in that case to require far more general consultation with 'the workers' representatives'[6]. Given that this country does not have any mandatory system of works councils, this caused a problem as to *whom* to consult where there is no recognised union. The previous government's response came in the 1995 Regulations, which retained the possibility of consultation with a recognised union, but added the alternative route of consultation with elected employee representatives[7]. This system was subject to further refinement by the present government in the 1999 Regulations. As a combined result of the 1993 Act and the 1995 and 1999 Regulations, section 188 now requires the following.

Where an employer is proposing to dismiss as redundant 20 or more employees at one establishment within a period of 90 days or less, he must consult about the dismissals all the persons who are appropriate representatives of any of the employees who may be affected by the dismissals or measures taken in relation to them. Appropriate representatives are defined as (a) if the employees are of a description in respect of which an independent trade union is recognised by their employer, representatives of that union; or (b) in any other case employee representatives already appointed or elected who have authority from the affected employees in relation to the proposed dismissals, or such representatives elected specifically for these purposes[8]. It is specifically provided that existing elected representatives can be used if 'it is appropriate (having regard to the purposes for which they were elected) for the employer to consult them about dismissals proposed by him'[9]; taken together with other consultation requirements (especially on TUPE) and increasing advantages to be gained from workforce agreements (e.g. in relation to the Working Time Regulations and the new law on parental leave), this may argue strongly in favour of the employer having *standing* elected machinery for all of these purposes, even where no union is recognised.

The consultation must begin in good time[10], and in any event 90 days before the first dismissal takes effect (if the employer is proposing to dismiss 100 or

6   There is a political irony here, because the Conservative Government ended up defending the result of a Labour Government's pro-union policies; the aim of the restriction to recognised unions in 1975 was to concentrate industrial power in the latter's hands (see also the health and safety and pension legislation of that period). This of course backfired when the membership and influence of the unions declined dramatically, along with union recognition, so that the consultation requirements applied to fewer and fewer employees.

7   This was not purely defensive on the previous government's part, as they also viewed the need to change as an opportunity for some deregulation. Thus, the cut-off number was raised from 10 to 20 employees and the requirement still to consult under that number was dropped. These changes have not been reversed by the present government.

8   Trade Union and Labour Relations (Consolidation) Act 1992, s. 188 (1B), as substituted in 1999. The previous government's provisions had allowed the employer to choose to use directly elected representatives even if there was a recognised union, to allow the employer if desired to sideline the union; that has now been stopped by the current wording. Where elections are held specifically for this purpose, they must comply with rules ensuring fair elections, laid down in s. 188A.

9   Ibid., s. 196(1). They must be employed by the employer at the time when they are elected or appointed: s. 196(2).

10 Where an ad hoc election is being carried out, 'in good time' means as soon as reasonably practicable after the representatives are elected: s. 188(7A). If the employees fail to elect representatives within a reasonable time, the employer can give each affected employee the information required by law, but is absolved from the requirement to consult collectively: s. 188 (7B).

more within the 90 days), or at least 30 days beforehand otherwise. According to the statute, the consultation must include ways of avoiding the dismissals, reducing the numbers and mitigating the consequences and must be undertaken by the employer with a view to reaching agreement with the appropriate representatives. The case law also establishes that as a matter of general principle 'consultation' requires (a) consultation while the proposals are still at a formative stage, (b) adequate information, (c) adequate time in which to respond and (d) conscientious consideration of the responses to the consultation[11].

With regard to information, section 188(4) specifies that an employer must disclose in writing to the appropriate representatives (a) the reason for the proposals, (b) the numbers and descriptions of employees proposed to be dismissed, (c) the total number of such employees at the establishment, (d) the proposed method of selection, (e) the proposed method of carrying out the dismissals and (f) the proposed method of calculating any non-statutory redundancy payments to be made to those selected.

Four problems of definition have arisen under this section. The first is when it can be said that the employer is 'proposing' to make an employee redundant (as it is this that sets the wheels in motion); under the existing law, it appears that the word 'proposing' requires a certain amount of planning and resolution on the part of the employer, not just speculation:

'... a proposal to make redundant within the meaning of [section 188] connotes a state of mind directed to a planned or proposed course of events. The employer must have formed some view as to how many are to be dismissed, when this is to take place and how it is to be arranged. This goes beyond the mere contemplation of a possible event.'[12]

However, this use of the word 'proposing' has led to the argument that the UK provisions do not enact the original 1975 EC directive properly. The latter states that an employer should begin consultation when 'contemplating' collective redundancies, which may be construed as meaning *before* the employer has formed any definite views on the need for redundancies, whereas the domestic provision appears to apply only once that decision has been taken and therefore to apply principally to the question of *how* to deal with the proposed redundancies. This argument was accepted by Glidewell LJ in the Divisional Court in *R v British Coal Corpn and Secretary of State for Trade, ex p Vardy*[13] (the highly publicised decision declaring the previous government's original coal-mine closure programme to be unlawful), which was ironic because at the very time the 1993 Act was being enacted with provisions stated to be bringing the UK legislation into line with the new 1992 directive, that legislation was considered to be out of line in this

---

11   *R v British Coal Corpn and Secretary of State for Trade and Industry, ex p Price* [1994] IRLR 72, Div Ct (one of the 'pit closure' cases). Even if time limits are technically met, it may still be argued that in substance the whole exercise was a sham: *Transport and General Workers' Union v Ledbury Preserves (1928) Ltd* [1985] IRLR 412.

12   *APAC v Kirvin Ltd* [1978] IRLR 318 at 320 per Lord McDonald. *USDAW v Leancut Bacon Ltd* [1981] IRLR 295; *Hough v Leyland DAF Ltd* [1991] ICR 696, [1991] IRLR 194.

13   [1993] IRLR 104; the issue had been previously (understandably!) ducked in *Re Hartlebury Printers Ltd* [1992] ICR 559, [1992] IRLR 516. Another interesting facet of *ex p Vardy* is that it shows that a collective redundancy might be subject to challenge, not just under the employment legislation, but also by way of judicial review if there is a sufficient element of public law involved.

fundamental way with the original 1975 directive all along[14]. Subsequently, however, Blackburne J in *Griffin v South West Water Services Ltd*[15] was unimpressed with this argument and disagreed with the dicta of Glidewell LJ, and so the point remains open.

The second problem of definition is whether, in a case where a union is involved, it is 'recognised' in respect of the employees to be made redundant; this is considered in head 3, above.

The third problem concerns the nature of an 'establishment', for the purpose of applying the statutory time limits. The word appears in the Collective Redundancies Directive, but once again there is no statutory definition, even though the width of its construction could have an important effect on section 188 in cases where the employer operates at several locations; if each location is a separate 'establishment' and there are less than 20 redundancies at each, the requirements of the section will not apply, even if the overall number of redundancies is high. In *Barratt Developments (Bradford) Ltd v UCATT*[16] the EAT said that what constitutes an 'establishment' is a question for the industrial tribunal to decide, as an industrial jury using its common sense, on the particular facts of the case and upheld the tribunal's decision that 14 housebuilding sites administered from one central base in fact constituted one establishment. A similar decision was reached by the tribunal in *Clarks of Hove Ltd v Baker's Union*[17] where a firm employing 368 employees in their factory, bakery and 28 retail shops was held to constitute one establishment. It might be different, however, where one organisation is split into smaller parts which in fact have considerable autonomy, as for example in the case of one education authority in overall control of many different schools. However, the ECJ have stated that in interpreting the term the protective intent of the Directive must be kept in mind, and not frustrated by the technicalities of corporate structure[18]. The fourth problem is the converse of the third. Even where the 'establishment' has been discerned, it may still be necessary to decide who is the 'employer' and here there may be a problem for the concept of 'associated employers', so important elsewhere in employment law[19], is surprisingly *not* adopted by section 188 and the EAT has held that it will not unilaterally lift the veil of incorporation in this context. Thus, in *E Green & Son (Castings) Ltd v ASTMS*[20] three companies were making redundancies of 97, 36 and 24 employees respectively but the relevant consultation period was 30 days (not 90) since they were each separate employers even though (a) they were all subsidiaries of one holding company (and so would be associated employers in other contexts) and (b) they all operated from the same physical 'establishment'.

The sanction for failure to consult is a special device, the 'protective award'. This may be sought by employee representatives, the trade union or in any other

---

14 This had long been argued in *Harvey*, see E[2431]ff. The amendments in the 1993 Act requiring consultation as to ways of avoiding or minimising dismissals may now go some way towards mitigating this divergence between domestic and EC law, but are unlikely to be a complete answer, since they do not directly address the question of timing.
15 [1995] IRLR 15.
16 [1978] ICR 319, [1977] IRLR 403.
17 [1977] IRLR 167; the tribunal's decision was later affirmed by the Court of Appeal: [1978] ICR 1076, [1978] IRLR 366, CA.
18 *Rockfon A/S v Nielsen*: C-449/93 [1996] IRLR 168, ECJ. In particular, they held that a company in a group can still be an 'establishment' even if the power to make redundancies as a matter of policy lies elsewhere in the group.
19 See pp. 22-24, above.
20 [1984] ICR 352, [1984] IRLR 135.

case (including where no machinery at all has been set up) by any of the employees affected or dismissed. The matter is referred to a tribunal which, if it finds the complaint established, must make a declaration to that effect and may make a protective award, which is an order that the employer shall continue to pay wages to the employees concerned for a 'protected period'[1]. This period is within the tribunal's discretion, subject to a maximum of 90 days. The employee is entitled to a 'week's pay'[2] for each week of the protected period; if the employer fails to make any or all of the payments due for this period, the individual employee may complain within three months to a tribunal which may order payment. The employee may be disqualified from claiming under the protective award if he is fairly dismissed for a reason other than redundancy, unreasonably resigns during the period or unreasonably refuses suitable alternative employment[3].

The only guidance given to the tribunals by the statute on the way to apply a protective award is that it should be 'just and equitable in all the circumstances having regard to the seriousness of the employer's default'; this however could mean either a compensatory approach (looking at the employee's actual loss) or a punitive one (looking at the seriousness of the employer's default and its effect on industrial relations). In *Talke Fashions v Amalgamated Society of Textile Workers and Kindred Trades*[4] the EAT clearly preferred the compensatory approach, so that the tribunal should start by assessing the period of employment which the employee has lost through the employer not applying the statutory consultation time before dismissing, and then deduct any contractual payments referring to that time (e.g. any wages in lieu) and certain other payments such as accrued holiday money. This gives the minimum award, and any amount added on top because of the 'employer's default' should be because of the effect of that default in increasing hardship to the employee, not just as a punishment for an act of bad industrial relations. However, this distinction could be too subtle to apply in practice, as one tribunal pointed out[5], as well as arguably being a wrongful limitation on the wording of the subsection, and the EAT subsequently resiled from it, so that tribunals can take into account more general matters such as the potential disruption caused by unnotified redundancies[6] and the 'moral' responsibility of the employer, e.g. where he was acting upon wrong advice given by the Department of Employment[7]. Certainly increases or reductions in the protected period in some subsequent cases have fairly clearly been on a punitive basis, as has been recognised by the EAT in Scotland[8], so the position appears to be that the figure calculated on a compensatory basis is prima facie the period to be specified by the tribunal, but it is subject to variation (up to the statutory maxima) in the light of the seriousness of the employer's default. As a result, there may still be a protective award based upon the employer's default, even if

1   Trade Union and Labour Relations (Consolidation) Act 1992, ss. 189, 190. The period starts with the *proposed* date of the first dismissal, whether or not the *actual* date is different: *E Green & Son (Castings) Ltd v ASTMS*, above, applied in *TGWU v Ledbury Preserves (1928) Ltd* [1986] ICR 855, [1986] IRLR 492.
2   As defined in the Employment Rights Act 1996, Part XIV, Chap. II.
3   Trade Union and Labour Relations (Consolidation) Act 1992, s. 191; where there is an offer of alternative employment, the 'trial period' provisions are specially applied (see p. 538, below).
4   [1977] ICR 833, [1977] IRLR 309; *Barratt Developments (Bradford) Ltd v UCATT* [1978] ICR 319, [1977] IRLR 403.
5   *TGWU v Nationwide Haulage Ltd* [1978] IRLR 143, IT.
6   *TGWU v Gainsborough Distributors (UK) Ltd* [1978] IRLR 460.
7   *UCATT v H Rooke & Son Ltd* [1978] ICR 818, [1978] IRLR 204.
8   *APAC v Kirvin Ltd* [1978] IRLR 318.

the employees in question have suffered no pecuniary loss (e.g. through being found immediate alternative employment)[9].

ii) Notification to the Secretary of State

Where an employer proposes to dismiss as redundant 20 or more employees at one establishment within 30 days, he must give the Secretary of State written notice of the proposal at least 30 days before the first dismissal takes effect; where he proposes to dismiss 100 or more within 90 days, he must give 90 days' notice[10]. A copy of the notice must be sent to the appropriate representatives. If the employer fails to give this notice, the Secretary of State may prosecute the employer summarily (the maximum fine being level 5 on the standard scale)[11].

iii) The 'special circumstances' defence

It is expressly provided, in the case of both consultation and notification, that if there are special circumstances rendering it not reasonably practicable for an employer to comply with the statutory requirements, he need only take such steps towards compliance as are reasonably practicable[12]. The burden of proof is upon the employer to establish special circumstances, but if he can do so, and can show that he did what was reasonably practicable (which may in some cases be nothing), he has a good case that there should be *no* protective award, not just a reduction in it. The meaning of 'special circumstances' has been left to the tribunals and courts, and will be a question of fact in each case. The Court of Appeal in *Clarks of Hove Ltd v Bakers' Union*[13] held that the employer's insolvency and collapse were not in themselves special circumstances:

'... insolvency is, on its own, neither here nor there. It may be a special circumstance, it may not be a special circumstance. It will depend entirely on the cause of the insolvency whether the circumstance can be described as special or not. If, for example, a sudden disaster strikes a company, making it necessary to close the concern, then plainly that would be a matter which was capable of being a special circumstance; and that is so whether the disaster is physical or financial. If the insolvency however were merely due to a gradual run-down of the company, as it was in this case, then those are facts on which the industrial tribunal can come to the conclusion that the circumstances were not special. In other words, to be special the event must be something out of the ordinary, something uncommon ...[14].'

---

9   *Spillers-French (Holdings) Ltd v USDAW* [1980] ICR 31, [1979] IRLR 339, applied in *GKN Sankey Ltd v NSMM* [1980] ICR 148, [1980] IRLR 8.
10 Trade Union and Labour Relations (Consolidation) Act 1992, s. 193; the requirement of notice does not apply where less than 20 are dismissed.
11 Ibid., s. 194.
12 Ibid., ss. 188(7) and 193(7).
13 [1978] ICR 1076, [1978] IRLR 366, CA.
14 At 1085 and 369 respectively, per Geoffrey Lane LJ. Sudden financial deterioration following collapse of negotiations to sell the firm's shares to a third party was held to constitute a special circumstance in *USDAW v Leancut Bacon Ltd* [1981] IRLR 295; the shedding of labour normal on an insolvency was held not to in *GMB v Rankin and Harrison* [1992] IRLR 514.

Thus, although insolvency itself may not be special, the employer has been held to have a good defence where he carried on trading in the face of insolvency in the genuine hope that he would be able to sell the company as a going concern and so prevent redundancies, but had to appoint a receiver (without any consultation) when the last prospective purchaser disappeared[15]. In such a case, extensive consultation could be fatal to delicate negotiations, but on the other hand it may still be reasonable to expect *some* consultation and if that is the case the employer will not have shown that he did all that was reasonably practicable and so will remain liable[16]. The requirement of doing all that is reasonable puts a considerable onus on the employer to know and understand these legal requirements, so that in general a mistaken view of the law and its application to him will not be a 'special circumstance' unless it was a reasonable mistake[17], even if he was acting upon wrong advice, though in such a case the facts may support an argument for reduction of the protective award if the 'employer's default' is considered less[18].

The 1992 Directive sought to increase the protection for employees of transnational concerns who may be made redundant by decisions taken at higher levels than their immediate employer; this was put into effect in domestic law by the Trade Union Reform and Employment Rights Act 1993, which added to the 'special circumstances' defences a provision declaring that where the decision leading to the proposed dismissals is that of a person controlling the employer, a failure on the part of that person to provide information to the employer does *not* constitute special circumstances.

iv)   Protection of representatives

Where the 'appropriate representatives' are officials of a recognised trade union, then they will have the ordinary protection for such offices when taking part in union activities, and the ordinary right to time off work for these duties[19]. However, these provisions would not apply to the new category of elected employee representatives, and so the 1995 and 1999 Regulations enacted parallel provisions for them. Thus, an elected representative (or candidate for that office) has a statutory right not to be victimised (short of dismissal), dismissed or later selected for redundancy on the grounds of having performed or proposed to perform such duties, and similar protection is extended to employees participating in the election of representatives[20]. A representative or candidate also has the right to paid time off work in order to perform such duties or to undergo training[1].

6   CONSULTATION ON TRANSFERS OF UNDERTAKING

As in the case of obligatory consultation on redundancies considered in the previous head, the legal obligations to inform and consult trade unions in advance

15   *APAC v Kirvin Ltd* [1978] IRLR 318.
16   *Hamish Armour v ASTMS* [1979] IRLR 24; cf. *USDAW v Leancut Bacon Ltd*, n. 13 above.
17   *Joshua Wilson & Bros Ltd v USDAW* [1978] ICR 614, [1978] IRLR 120.
18   *UCATT v Rooke & Son Ltd* [1978] ICR 818, [1978] IRLR 204, applied in *Secretary of State for Employment v Helitron Ltd* [1980] ICR 523.
19   See ch. 10.
20   Employment Rights Act 1996, ss. 47, 103, 105(6).
1   Ibid., s. 61.

of certain transfers of business were enacted pursuant to an EEC directive, generally known as the Acquired Rights Directive[2]; this time, however, the enactment was done in the form of regulations, the Transfer of Undertakings (Protection of Employment) Regulations 1981[3], rather than by Act of Parliament. This caused some controversy at the time, inside and outside Parliament, and may not be the best way in which to introduce important new labour law provisions, particularly as the Regulations make little attempt to integrate the new provisions with certain existing ones and do not amend the existing statutes, thus leading to some duplication, though that is not the case in the present context since these consultation obligations were novel.

These regulations have caused major problems in interpretation, and in particular as to whether they enact the EC directive properly. As problems of application have arisen primarily in the context of continuity of employment and the statutory novation of contracts of employment, the question of the applicability of the regulations is considered in that context, below[4]. What is said there also applies here. For present purposes, it may be noted that, for the regulations to apply, there must be 'a relevant transfer', which may be affected by sale, or some other disposition as by operation of law[5]. This gives rise to their principal limitation in the context of union consultation, which is that they do *not* apply to the take-over of a business by the purchase of its shares, a limitation which does also appear in the Directive[6]. Also, there may be problems with the always-troublesome distinction between the sale of an 'undertaking' and a mere sale of assets.

If a projected transfer of undertakings does qualify as a 'relevant transfer', regulation 10 imposes duties to inform and consult and regulation 11 contains enforcement provisions similar in part to those applying to redundancy consultation (head 5, above), but in one crucial respect falling far short of them. However, it was the basic obligation to consult and inform that fell foul of EC law in *EC Commission v United Kingdom*[7], in the same way as the obligation to consult and inform on collective redundancies (above), through being confined to cases where there was a recognised trade union, whereas the Directive refers to workers or their representatives. Again, this has to be rectified by the Collective Redundancies and Transfer of Undertakings (Protection of Employment) (Amendment) Regulations 1995 and 1999[8]; the amended provisions largely mirror those that now apply to collective redundancies.

---

2   EEC Directive 77/187; see Hepple (1976) 5 ILJ 197 and (1977) 6 ILJ 106; the original draft of the directive was issued in 1974. Draft regulations were produced by the Labour government in 1978 but not proceeded with; the present regulations were introduced by the Conservative government, under pressure from the EEC Commission, with a declared lack of enthusiasm. The 1977 Directive has now been amended by Directive 98/50/EC.
3   S.I. 1981 No. 1794. See Hepple (1982) 11 ILJ 29, McMullen *Business Transfers and Employee Rights* and *Harvey*, Division F.
4   See p. 160, below.
5   Reg. 3(2). *Robert Seligman Corpn v Baker* [1983] ICR 770.
6   Art. 1.1 which applies the Directive to the transfer of an undertaking, business or part of a business to another employer as a result of a legal transfer or merger. The original draft directive of 1974 did apply to share takeovers. It is the case that the exclusion of such takeovers is not quite so drastic in the context of preservation of continuity of employment, since the corporate employer still exists unchanged (albeit under different control which may, in the longer term, have effects on the company's economic prospects, for better or for worse); in the present context, however, it is a serious limit on union rights to consultation.
7   Case C-382/92: [1994] ECR I-2435, [1995] 1 CMLR 345, ECJ.
8   S.I. 1995 No. 2587 and S.I. 1999 No. 1925.

i)   The duty to inform and consult

Long enough before a relevant transfer to enable the employer of any affected employees[9] to consult all their appropriate representatives, the employer must give those representatives information of (a) the fact that the relevant transfer is to take place, when, and the reasons for it, (b) the legal, economic and social implications for the affected employees, (c) the measures which he envisages he will take in relation to those employees in connection with the transfer and, (d) if the employer is the transferor, the measures which the transferee envisages he will be taking[10]. As with collective redundancies, the concept of appropriate representatives was materially widened by the 1995 Regulations to cover not just the officials of a recognised trade union, but also employee representatives directly elected, either ad hoc for this purpose[11] or having been elected for other purposes but being appropriate for this purpose too; as with collective redundancies, the 1999 Regulations removed the employer's choice of route, by providing that where a union is recognised in respect of affected employees, that is the proper channel. One possible problem relates to the timing. The regulation says that the information must be given 'long enough before a relevant transfer to enable consultations to take place', which is not further defined or qualified (contrast this with the provisions on collective redundancies); moreover, as has been pointed out[12], head (a) of the information to be given concerns the *fact* that the transfer is to take place, i.e. there need be no information or consultation at the stage of *proposals* for a transfer[13].

Where an employer of affected employees envisages that he will be 'taking measures' in relation to them in connection with the transfer, he must enter into consultations with the appropriate representatives with a view to seeking their agreement to measures to be taken, and in doing so must (a) consider any representations and (b) reply to them, giving reasons for any rejections[14]. If

9   An affected employee is defined as an employee of either the transferor or transferee who may be affected by the transfer or may be affected by measures taken in connection with it: reg. 10(1). This is a very wide definition, particularly as it also says that the employee does not have to be employed in the undertaking or part thereof to be transferred. As such, it seems open-ended, given that a transfer 'may' affect practically anyone in the two businesses in some way, which could cause problems of line drawing in businesses which recognise several unions (particularly if they know their Donne: no man is an island; any man's transfer diminishes me).

10   Reg. 10(2). In order to fulfil the transferor's obligation under (d) the transferee must give him the necessary information: reg. 10(3).

11   If elected ad hoc, the election must satisfy the requirements for a fair election set out in reg. 10A, as to numbers, constituencies, tenure of office, candidature, voting rights, secret voting and accurate counting.

12   Hepple (1982) 11 ILJ at p. 38.

13   Again this may be contrasted with the provisions on collective redundancies where the Trade Union and Labour Relations (Consolidation) Act 1992, s. 188 requires an employer 'proposing' to make redundancies to consult recognised unions; see p. 66, above. Reg. 10(8) provides that where the employer is going through the process of electing representatives, the employer complies with the time requirement if he acts as soon as reasonably practicable after the representatives are elected. If the employees fail to elect representatives within a reasonable time, the employer may give individual affected employees the information required by law, and is then absolved from collective consultation: reg. 10 (8A).

14   Regs. 10(5) and (6). In *IPCS v Secretary of State for Defence* [1987] IRLR 373 (decided under the Dockyard Services Act 1986 which adopted and applied the provisions of reg. 10), Millett J emphasised that although the obligation to give information applied to all four heads above, the obligation to consult only applies to head (c), the measures which are envisaged; his judgment gives guidance on the meaning of 'measures', which is not defined in the regulations.

there are special circumstances making it not reasonably practicable for an employer to inform or consult as required, he must take all steps as are reasonably practicable in the circumstances to comply; this means that an employer cannot say that, merely because full compliance was impossible, he did not need to do anything at all[15].

As in the case of consultation on impending collective redundancies (above), special legal protection is given to employee representatives from victimisation, dismissal and subsequent selection for redundancy, on the grounds of having fulfilled those functions; there is also a statutory right to time off work with pay for fulfilling them or for training.

ii) Enforcement provision

As in the case of a failure to consult on impending redundancies, a complaint of failure to comply with regulation 10 may be presented to a tribunal by the employee representatives, or the recognised trade union or, in any other case, by any affected employee[16]. The employer may raise the 'special circumstances' defence (i.e. that there were such circumstances making performance of the obligations not reasonably practicable *and* that he did all that was reasonably practicable in the circumstances), in which case the burden of proof is upon him[17]. If the tribunal finds the complaint well founded it must make a declaration to that effect and award compensation to affected employees.[18] The maximum amount was raised from four to 13 weeks' pay by the 1999 Regulations.[19]

7 FURTHER DEVELOPMENTS – TOWARDS WORKS COUNCILS?

As seen in this chapter and the preceding one, British industrial relations have been subject to major changes in the last two decades, and that has been reflected in some of the legal changes discussed above. The inception of the new statutory recognition laws may see the return of a level of collective negotiation in certain well-unionised industries which has been missing for some time. However, large parts of the economy are likely to remain untouched by it, but it may be that we are seeing the emergence of an alternative form of, at least, employee *involvement*

---

15 Reg. 10(7). This establishes a 'special circumstances' defence in similar terms to that applying to collective redundancies; see p. 69, above. Presumably the case law which has arisen in that context will be applied here.

16 Reg. 11(1). The complaint must be brought within three months of the date on which the transfer was completed (undefined): reg. 11(8); it may be brought *before* the transfer is effected: *BIFU v Barclays Bank plc* [1987] ICR 495; *South Durham Health Authority v UNISON* [1995] ICR 495, [1995] IRLR 407.

17 Reg. 11(2). If the complaint is against the transferor and he maintains that his reason for default was that the transferee had not provided him with the necessary information (see n. 10 above), he cannot raise the special circumstances defence unless he joins the transferee as a party to the proceedings: reg. 11(3).

18 Reg. 11(3). If it is not paid, the employee himself may complain to the tribunal within three months of the date of the order: reg. 11(5)–(8). Appeal on a point of law lies to the EAT: reg. 11(10).

19 Reg. 11(11). 'Week's pay' is calculated in accordance with the Employment Rights Act 1996, Part XIV, chap. II. Reg. 11(11) actually says that the award is of such sum 'as the tribunal considers just and equitable having regard to the seriousness of the failure of the employer to comply with his duty', so that the precedents on the similar wording governing protective awards under the Trade Union and Labour Relations (Consolidation) Act 1992, s. 189 (p. 68, above) should apply.

in decision-taking which, while falling significantly short of the old model of co-determination with recognised unions, could at least start to fill the void left in many areas by the demise of that old model and its replacement by ideas of 'human resource management', which a cynic might argue can be a euphemism for managerial discretion. The question is – are we seeing the beginnings of movements towards a consultation regime not dissimilar to the works council system that is common in much of the rest of the EU (to the extent that its existence is often implicitly assumed in certain employment-related EU Directives)?

We have seen the advent of consultation requirements (and their extension more recently to firms not recognising unions, through the concept of directly-elected employee representatives), largely driven by EU law requirements, which suggest a *via media* (or even Third Way?) of treating the workforce as possessing legal expectations of involvement, not just as a managerial resource[20]. Moreover, to these sticks (requiring consultation with elected representatives where there is no union recognition, in relation to collective redundancies, TUPE and health and safety) we have now seen added certain legal carrots. Thus, the Working Time Regulations 1998 lay down prima facie relatively strict rules on hours, night work and breaks, but then allow very major 'derogations' from them, in ways that can be highly advantageous to the employer[1]. In the case of most of them, the safeguard is that the derogation in question must be agreed; in the case of a non-unionised workplace, the mechanism established for this is the 'workforce agreement', i.e. a written agreement with elected employee representatives. A similar regime can be seen in relation to parental leave under the Maternity and Parental Leave Regulations 1999, where the 'default rules' on some of the principal administrative requirements for parental leave are to apply unless supplemented by a collective agreement or workforce agreement[2].

Does this mean that we are moving towards a works council system? The negative approach to this is that there are currently no legal requirements for them at domestic level. The only such requirements currently are at transnational level, under the European Works Council Directive[3]. This applies to a 'community scale undertaking', meaning one with at least 1,000 employees within the EU and at least 150 employees in each of at least two member states. Initially, the Directive did not apply in this country because of the previous government's opt-out, but the incoming New Labour government stated their intention to adopt it. Thus, a further Directive extended it to this country, and it was implemented as from January 2000 by the Transnational Information and Consultation of Employees Regulations 1999[4]. These complex Regulations largely follow the Directive and provide for an undertaking covered by them to set up a Special Negotiating Body, either of its own motion, or in response to a written request from at least 100 employees or their representatives in at least two member states. The purpose of this body is to negotiate on the establishment of a European Works Council

---

20   Current ideas of 'partnership at work' and the involvement of the workforce suffused the White Paper 'Fairness at Work' (Cm. 3968, 1998), especially chapter 2 'Modern business at work'. See generally Hyman 'The future of employee representation' (1997) 35 BJIR 309.

1   See p. 199, below.

2   See p. 345, below.

3   Council Directive 94/45; *Harvey* P [488]. See Bercusson *European Labour Law* (1996), ch. 19; Barnard *EC Employment Law* (1996), p. 422; Wedderburn 'Consultation and collective bargaining in Europe: success or ideology' (1997) 26 ILJ 1, at 21.

4   S.I. 1999 No. 3323.

(EWC) or, as a lesser form, an 'information and consultation procedure'[5]. It is primarily for the parties to agree the composition and procedure of the relevant body. If, however, the central management refuse to commence negotiations within six months of a request, or if negotiations are still fruitless after three years, the 'default' provision of Schedule 1 to the Regulations apply, i.e. there will be imposed a 'statutory EWC'[6]. These provisions lay down the basic rules for composition (between three and 30 members, with minimum numbers for each member state involved), appointment or election of UK members, conduct of ballots, the competence of the EWC[7], yearly information and consultation meetings on the progress of the business[8], exceptional information and consultation meetings[9] (where exceptional circumstances affect the employers' interests to a considerable extent, particularly in the event of relocations, closure of establishments or undertakings, or collective redundancies) and procedures. Provision is made for certain information not to be divulged by the central management where it would cause serious harm to the undertaking[10], and any disclosure by an individual representative of information given to him by the central management on the basis that it is to be held in confidence is declared to be a breach of statutory duty[11]. The usual series of employment protection laws (paid time off and protection from detriment or dismissal) are extended to members of the body in question. Disputes over procedural matters in setting up an EWC are heard by the CAC; complaints of failure to establish a EWC (or information and consultation procedure), or of failure to operate the system properly once it is set up are heard by the EAT[12]; employment protection disputes go to an employment tribunal in the ordinary way.

The likely impact of these Regulations has been a matter of some speculation. Their use may be limited by two factors. The first is that many UK supranationals have already been covered by the original Directive for some time because of their activities elsewhere in the EU; they could have set up an EWC only in relation to employees in other member states but in practice they have strongly

---

5   The central management and the special negotiating body are under a duty to 'negotiate in a spirit of co-operation with a view to reaching a written agreement': reg. 17(1). There is then a further statutory obligation to *work* in such a spirit once the relevant body is set up: reg. 19.

6   Reg. 18.

7   This is 'limited to information and consultation on the matters which concern the Community-scale undertaking or Community-scale group of undertakings as a whole or at least two of its establishments or group undertakings in different Member States: Sch. 1, para. 6(1).

8   This relates particularly to 'the structure, economic and financial situation, the probable development of the business and of production and sales, the situation and probable trend of employment, investments, and substantial changes concerning organisation, introduction of new working methods or production processes, transfers of production, mergers, cut-backs or closures of undertakings, establishments or important parts thereof, and collective redundancies': para. 7(2).

9   This may be done through a 'select committee' of the EWC, comprising no more than three members acting on its behalf: para. 2(6).

10   Reg. 24; the operation of this exception may be challenged before the CAC (this matter being similar to its longstanding jurisdiction over the disclosure of bargaining information, see above).

11   Reg. 23. Again, a declaration by the management that information is confidential may be challenged before the CAC. Further, the normal provisions of the Public Interest Disclosure Act 1998 on 'protected disclosures' apply.

12   Regs. 20, 21. The EAT may declare what steps are to be taken to remedy the default and issue a penalty notice on the employer, to pay a penalty up to £75,000 to the Secretary of State: reg. 22.

tended to include UK employees as a matter of good practice, and so have pre-empted the Regulations. The second is that in any event the Directive extending the EWC Directive to the UK allowed undertakings here (not already covered) until December 1999 to reach voluntary agreements on transnational information and consultation, in which case the Regulations do not apply; again, a significant number of these 'Article 13' agreements have been entered. TUC estimates of undertakings in the UK likely to be covered by the Regulations for the first time were 111 UK-based undertakings and between 35 and 140 non-UK-based[13].

Not surprisingly, there have been moves within the European Commission to build on these transnational provisions and move towards a European obligation to have consultative machinery at the member state level, i.e. to have a *domestic* works council requirement[14]. However, the approach of the UK government so far has been hostile, viewing this as a step too far and an unwarranted imposition on business.

On the other hand, we could be seeing more positive moves in such a direction in practice, if not by legal requirement. While the consultation obligations on collective redundancies and TUPE transfers concern potentially 'one-off' events, and so could be dealt with ad hoc if and when necessary, the health and safety consultation requirements are continuous and potentially involve day-to-day concerns. Add to this the potential advantages to the employer in involving the workforce in the implementation of the working time rules and the new laws on parental leave, and it can be argued that there is increasingly much to gain by an employer having *standing* consultative machinery, able to be used for all of these purposes[15] and, once established, for other more general purposes of involving the workforce. Where this does not now exist in the form of the recognition of trade unions (or where, for example, such a system still exists but only in relation to certain sectors of the workforce), the answer could be to have some sort of standing *elective* body representing the whole workforce, not a million miles away from what would elsewhere be called a works council.

---

13 TUC General Council Report 1998, p. 94, cited in the DTI Consultation Document 'Implementation in the UK of the EWC Directive' (URN 99/926, July 1999), Appendix 2.
14 Communication on worker information and communication COM (95) 547 final, considered in detail in Wedderburn, op. cit., n. 3, above.
15 There is unfortunately one technical problem with this – the collective redundancy and TUPE provisions permit the use of an *existing* elected body for the purpose of consultation (if it is appropriate), but the health and safety and working time provisions state that representatives must be elected for those specific purposes. A technically correct answer would be to ensure (in the case of existing consultative machinery) that *next* time worker representatives are elected it is made clear that their functions are to include these two specific areas.

Chapter 3

Contracts of employment (1): formation and content

I GENERAL

We have already seen that the relationship of employer and employee arises out of a contract. This however was not always so, for before the latter half of the last century the relationship was viewed more as one arising out of the 'status' of being a servant. Blackstone refers to master and servant as being one of the three great relationships in private life, along with husband and wife and parent and child[1], and the extensive legislation governing supply and conditions of employment, dating back to the Statute of Labourers 1351, was not finally abolished until 1875[2]. The movement towards contract proceeded throughout the last century and this century, becoming firmly established. In *Laws v London Chronicle*[3] Lord Evershed MR said:

> 'A contract of service is but an example of contracts in general, so that the general law of contract will be applicable.'

No sooner was this established beyond real doubt than the trend was arguably reversed. Since 1963, and particularly since the concept of unfair dismissal was introduced in 1971, the employment relationship has been increasingly overlaid with statutory criteria, rights and duties, to such an extent that it is certainly open to doubt whether we should still accept that contract law alone provides the underlying structure of employment law, or whether we should talk instead of a modern 'status' relationship of some sort or, at the least, of a sui generis Law of Employment which of necessity looks to contractual theories for guidance in

---

1   1 Bl Com 422.
2   See Wedderburn *The Worker and the Law* (3rd edn, 1986), p. 141.
3   [1959] 2 All ER 285, [1959] 1 WLR 698, CA at 287 and 700 respectively. This case demonstrates the purely contractual approach to summary dismissal, which can also be seen in the more colourful case of *Pepper v Webb* [1969] 2 All ER 216, [1969] 1 WLR 514, CA.

given areas[4]. Against that, it must be stressed that employment remains for the most part a voluntary relationship, and the content of most of the terms of employment remains to be negotiated by the parties, either individually or through the medium of collective industrial relations. The contract theory remains paramount and, if anything, of renewed importance, given the moves over the last two decades in many areas away from a collective model of wage and conditions determination, towards an emphasis on individual contracting; we therefore now have to consider the character of the contract, its formation and its content.

A contract is an agreement by which two or more persons agree to regulate their legal relationships recognised and, generally speaking, enforced by the law. Before the law will recognise an agreement as a contract certain essential conditions must be fulfilled. They are as follows:

i)   One party must agree expressly or implicitly to perform an undertaking and the other party must agree to accept such performance, that is to say, there must be offer and acceptance[5].

ii) The agreement must be supported by consideration or entered into according to certain prescribed forms.

iii) Both parties must be persons whom the law acknowledges as competent to enter contracts; they must have capacity.

iv) The objects of the contracts must be legal.

v)   Both parties must intend that the agreement shall give rise to a legally recognised obligation.

The first two principles serve to ensure that a contract is bilateral in nature, as opposed, for example, to a gift. The employment relationship is by its very nature bilateral, at its simplest work for wages[6], so much of the case law on this aspect of contract is of little practical importance. It is extensively dealt with in the contract textbooks which should be consulted as required. Form used to be of supreme importance in apprenticeship contracts whose impact has greatly declined, but it will be noted later that one of the major features of the modern legislation is a revived interest in form. Capacity needs brief consideration and legality in the field of employment law concerns principally the doctrine of restraint of trade, a relatively rare oasis where the courts over many decades have adopted an important stance based on public policy. It merits detailed treatment below, along with the way in which the general doctrine of illegality has more recently been imported into unfair dismissal law, occasionally doing it considerable violence. The question of 'intent to create legal relations' plays a major part in the sphere of collective agreements, where it is discussed, being largely responsible for the longstanding rule that collective agreements are not legally binding.

---

4   For general discussion, see Rideout 'The contract of employment' [1966] CLP 111; Khan-Freund 'A note on status and contract in British labour law' (1967) 30 MLR 635; Smith 'Is employment properly analysed in terms of a contract?' (1975) 6 NZULR 341; Napier 'Judicial attitudes towards the employment relationship' (1977) 6 ILJ 1; Kerr 'Contract doesn't live here any more?' (1984) 47 MLR 30; Honeyball 'Employment law and the primacy of contract' (1989) 18 ILJ 97. In particular, Professor Hepple argues that the statutory rights should be freed from their existing contractual basis, in order to avoid 'a multitude of common law snares': 'Restructuring employment rights' (1986) 15 ILJ 69.

5   An offer of employment 'subject to satisfactory references' means satisfactory subjectively to the employer, not an objective test of reasonably satisfactory references: *Wishart v National Association of Citizens' Advice Bureaux Ltd* [1990] ICR 794, [1990] IRLR 393, CA.

6   Even here, however, complications can arise in cases of partial performance by an employee, e.g. when taking part in industrial action short of a strike (such as a go-slow or refusal to perform certain duties) – is he still entitled to payment, and if so how much? See pp. 174-176, below.

One further significance of the contractual base is that certain tenets of contractual interpretation or modification (common law or statutory) may be argued by one party or the other to good effect. Thus, for example, in *Levett v Biotrace International plc*[7] a managing director benefiting from valuable share options was wrongfully dismissed and then told by the company that those options had lapsed under a clause in his employment contract providing for such lapse on termination of employment. However, the Court of Appeal interprets the clause as only applying to *lawful* termination (thus preserving their benefit for him), relying on the general contractual rule of construction that a party should not be able to take advantage of his own breach of contract. One uncertainty in relation to general principles here is whether the Unfair Contract Terms Act 1977 could even be relied on in an employment case. So far, this has been thought unlikely, but in *Brigden v American Express Bank Ltd*[8] Morland J held that the Act can apply, though he went on to find that a clause stating that an employee could be dismissed within the first two years without implementation of the disciplinary procedure was *not* an exclusion clause within s. 3 of the Act (with its requirement of reasonableness). Such a finding (that the Act applies) involves the rather artificial reasoning that the employee deals with the employer 'as consumer', but the answer to that is that that phrase is not a term of art, and that in fact the definition of it in section 12 is satisfied because the employee does not contract in the 'course of a business', whereas the employer does. Further developments are awaited here with interest, especially as to how a reasonableness test would be applied to terms of an employment contract.

2 CAPACITY

Although principles of law are designed to operate in normal circumstances on persons who are not subject to legal disabilities, there must be provisions relating to those who, because of their status or condition, require exceptional treatment. The principles of contract law which evolved to cover questions of capacity will apply to contracts of employment so that for example, employment by a foreign sovereign, a diplomatic agent or an enemy alien may be subject to special common law and statutory rules. Such cases, however, will be rare and are best dealt with elsewhere. It is of more importance to note that companies and partnerships do not lack capacity to enter into contract of employment, and to consider in more detail two classes of employee who are subject to special rules – Crown employees and minors.

i) Crown employees

Historically the Crown occupied a position of privilege in the law of contract in that it could not be sued in its own courts. This position has now been substantially amended[9], but the law relating to Crown employment is still distinct from ordinary employment law.

---

7   [1999] ICR 818, [1999] IRLR 375, CA.
8   [2000] IRLR 94, relying on Watson 'Employees and the Unfair Contract Terms Act' (1985) 14 ILJ 323.
9   Crown Proceedings Act 1947. Fredman and Morris 'The state as employer: is it unique?' (1990) 19 ILJ 142.

A contract of employment with the Crown is terminable without notice at the Crown's pleasure[10], and any term to the contrary is invalid[11] (unless there is some statutory restriction on the Crown's power to dismiss[12]). This proposition shows how far away from reality the law can stray, for civil servants are in practice renowned for the security of their employment. However, the theory is otherwise, and indeed was taken further at common law, for the earlier view was that the Crown employee in fact has no contract of employment *at all* (a point which was important in certain cases where the payment of arrears of remuneration was in issue)[13]. Other cases, however, have tended to assume that there *is* a contract of employment (albeit terminable at pleasure), and certainly the balance of authority is now in favour of the view[14]. This has been affirmed recently in cases exploring the borderline between private and public law remedies for Crown employees, the point being that if there is a contract of employment it is less likely (though not impossible) that the employee will be able to obtain a judicial review of an employment-related grievance. In *McClaren v Home Office*[15] it was held by the Court of Appeal that a prison officer was under a contract of employment and so could pursue private law remedies for an alleged breach of his contractual rights, and in *R v Lord Chancellor's Department, ex p Nangle*[16] the Divisional Court held that a civil servant's appointment was intended to, and did, create a contract of employment. However, even though there is a contract, its terms have always been variable unilaterally by the Minister of the Civil Service (in relation to the Home Civil Service) by virtue of the Civil Service Orders in Council, a point which came to the fore in 1984 when the government altered the terms of employment of employees at GCHQ to exclude union membership[17]. Moreover, the basis of civil service employment was subject to radical change in 1996, with each department or agency becoming responsible for setting its own terms and

10   *Dunn v R* [1896] 1 QB 116, CA.
11   *Denning v Secretary of State for India* (1920) 37 TLR 138; *Riordan v War Office* [1959] 3 All ER 552, [1959] 1 WLR 1046 (affd by the Court of Appeal: [1960] 3 All ER 774n, [1961] 1 WLR 210); cf. *Reilly v R* [1934] AC 176, PC.
12   *Gould v Stuart* [1896] AC 575, PC.
13   *Mulvenna v Admiralty* 1926 SC 842; *Lucas v Lucas* [1943] P 68, [1943] 2 All ER 110.
14   *Owners of SS Raphael v Brandy* [1911] AC 413, HL; *Sutton v A-G* (1923) 39 TLR 295; *Reilly v R* [1934] AC 176, PC; *A-G for Guyana v Nobrega* [1969] 3 All ER 1604, PC, *Kodeeswaran v A-G of Ceylon* [1970] AC 1111, PC.
15   [1990] ICR 824, [1990] IRLR 338, CA. In this case, a finding of a contract of employment was in the employee's favour since he was seeking contractual remedies, not judicial review. In the judgment of Woolf LJ there is a valuable summary of grounds on which a public employee can obtain judicial review (see p. 386, below); in *R v Secretary of State for the Home Department, ex p Benwell* [1984] ICR 723, [1985] IRLR 6 a prison officer was granted judicial review, but this was explained by Woolf LJ as a case where even though the relationship was contractual, there *still* arose a matter of public law.
16   [1991] ICR 743, [1991] IRLR 343. Here, ironically, it was the Crown arguing that there *was* a contract, in order to defeat the civil servant's claim for judicial review. This was successful. In the earlier case of *R v Civil Service Appeal Board, ex p Bruce* [1988] 3 All ER 686, [1988] ICR 649 the Divisional Court has said that there was nothing to *prevent* the Crown from entering a contract of employment, but *ex p Nangle* is a much stronger case, holding that it had.
17   Such orders are made under prerogative powers and are not contained in a statutory instrument. The fact that an order or decision is made under the prerogative does not mean that it is not subject to judicial review; however, it will only be so subject if the substance of the issue in question is 'justiciable', which was not so in the GCHQ case which concerned national security: *Council of Civil Service Unions v Minister for the Civil Service* [1985] ICR 14, [1985] IRLR 28, HL.

conditions of employment, which further emphasises the movement towards a more normal, contract-based model of employment.

Turning to the far more important question of the application of the modern statutory rights to Crown employees, the first point to notice is that the controversy over whether there is a contract of employment in existence is a sterile one in this context, for by virtue of the Employment Rights Act 1996, section 191 persons in Crown employment are to be treated as if in ordinary employment for the purpose of applying the statutory provisions to them. The important question is *which* statutory provisions are to apply to them. As the general rule is that an Act of Parliament does not bind the Crown unless it says so, this is a matter for the statute which provides[18] that all the major employment protection rights (including unfair dismissal) apply to Crown employees, except those relating to minimum notice periods and redundancy payments; in the case of the last right, civil servants are covered by more generous internal schemes[19]. The Trade Union Reform and Employment Rights Act 1993 extended most of the major employment protection rights to members of the armed forces, but the police are ineligible (except for those relating to written statements of terms of employment, minimum notice periods and redundancy payments)[20]. One general limitation is that a Minister of the Crown may issue a certificate that a certain type of work is required to be outside the scope of the statutory rights for reasons of national security[1]; this power was used in 1984 to support the instructions given by the government altering the terms of employment of civil servants at GCHQ to exclude union membership (referred to above), thus depriving anyone objecting to the ban of the right to complain to a tribunal.

Finally, there has been one further recent legislative development in a specialised area of Crown employment. The argument that Crown employees have no contract of employment might have been used to evade liability for unlawful industrial action since certain of the applicable torts pre-suppose the existence of such contracts (particularly the tort of inducement of breach of contract[2]); to cover this, there is now deemed to be a contract of employment between the Crown and a Crown employee for the purposes of the economic torts[3].

ii) Minors

The contractual capacity of a minor[4] rests upon a common law basis. It used to be modified and, in some directions, restricted by the Infants Relief Act 1874, but

18 Employment Rights Act 1996, s. 191(2). The Sex Discrimination Act 1975 and the Equal Pay Act 1970 apply to Crown employees, ss. 85 and 1(8) respectively; see *Department of the Environment v Fox* [1980] 1 All ER 58, [1979] ICR 736. See also the Race Relations Act 1976, s. 75, the Disability Discrimination Act 1995, s. 64, the National Minimum Wage Act 1998, s. 36 and the Working Time Regulations 1998, reg. 37. At the collective level, the provisions relating to enforcement of disclosure of information and the rules on union contributions, and procedures for handling redundancies do not apply to Crown employment: Trade Union and Labour Relations (Consolidation) Act 1992; s. 273.

19 Employment Rights Act 1996, s. 159.

20 Ibid., s. 200. The statutory exclusion also applies to prison officers: *Home Office v Robinson* [1982] ICR 31, [1981] IRLR 524.

1   Ibid., s. 193, Trade Union and Labour Relations (Consolidation) Act 1992, s. 275.

2   See p. 647, below.

3   This was introduced by the Employment Act 1988 and is now contained in the Trade Union and Labour Relations (Consolidation) Act 1992, s. 245.

4   See the Family Law Reform Act 1969, ss. 1 and 9, which reduced the age from 21 to 18.

that statute was repealed by the Minors' Contracts Act 1987[5] and so the common law rules now apply to all contracts, including those with which we are concerned, namely contracts of employment and apprenticeship. These are prima facie binding[6] and if they are, on the whole, for the minor's benefit at the time they are entered into, they will bind him. As Fry LJ said:

> 'The question is this – is the contract for the benefit of the [minor]? Not, is any one particular stipulation for the benefit of the [minor] … the court must look at the whole contract having regard to the circumstances of the case[7].'

The principle involved is not difficult to state or to understand, but its application has not been without difficulty[8]. It was laid down with great clarity by Lord Esher MR in *Corn v Matthews*[9]:

> 'It is impossible to frame a deed as between a master and apprentice in which some of the stipulations are not in favour of one and some in favour of the other. But if we find a stipulation in the deed which is of such a kind that it makes the whole contract an unfair one, then that makes the whole contract void.'

However, where a stipulation, though repugnant, does not make the whole contract unfair, and is severable from the rest, it may in fact be severed and the remainder of the contract, being for the minor's benefit, will bind him[10].

In assessing whether a contract is for the minor's benefit, courts have sometimes posed the question as to what would be the position if the offending clause were not in the contract at all – would the minor be able to enter into a contract of equal or greater benefit?[11] Another way of asking this would be – is the clause usual in contracts with minors of this particular type? Thus, although trade usage is only of evidential importance, a clause which is usual in a particular trade or industry will not generally be against the minor's benefit.

3   FORM

i)   Form generally

According to a doctrine peculiar to English law a contract must be under seal or based upon consideration. A promise gratuitously to perform services will not be actionable unless it is by deed. Subject to this, however, a contract of employment may be entered into orally at common law, and statute has not intervened to alter this general position. However, some particular contracts of employment or

---

5   The statute was based upon Law Comm No. 134, 'Law of Contract; Minors' Contracts'.
6   *Wood v Fenwick* (1842) 10 M & W 195; *De Francesco v Barnum* (1890) 45 Ch D 430.
7   *De Francesco v Barnum*, n. 4 above, at 439.
8   Contrast *Doyle v White City Stadium* [1935] 1 KB 110, CA with *Olsen v Corry and Gravesend Aviation Ltd* [1936] 3 All ER 241; see also *Chaplin v Leslie Frewin (Publishers) Ltd* [1966] Ch 71, [1965] 3 All ER 764, CA.
9   [1893] 1 QB 310, CA at 314. This dictum applies to minors generally, not just to apprentices: *Clements v London and North Western Rly Co* [1894] 2 QB 482, CA at 495 per A. L. Smith, LJ.
10   *Bromley v Smith* [1909] 2 KB 235.
11   *Bromley v Smith*, n. 10 above; *Doyle v White City Stadium* [1935] 1 KB 110, CA.

contracts relating to employment may have to be in writing. Thus, under Part II of the Employment Rights Act 1996, an employer and employee may agree for the former to make deductions from the latter's wages, provided that the agreement is either contained in a written contract (or in a contract whose effect has been notified to the employee in writing) or otherwise evidenced in writing signed by the employee prior to the making of the deductions[12]. Certain other provisions of the 1996 Act also require writing; thus under section 71 and the Maternity and Parental Leave Regulations 1999 a woman claiming to exercise her right to take maternity leave must inform her employer of her intention in writing if so requested by the employer, and under section 197 an employee on a fixed-term contract may agree in writing to exclude his rights to claim a redundancy payment (if the term is for two years or more). Similarly, an employee may consent in writing to work beyond the maximum 48 hours per week under the Working Time Regulations 1998.

The contracts of merchant seamen have long been regulated by statute[13]. The law here is now consolidated in the Merchant Shipping Act 1995 which applies to ships registered in the United Kingdom and covers matters such as engagement, discharge, discipline, trade disputes and disqualification. The justification for the special provisions arises from the nature of the merchant service[14]. Special attention is paid to the form of crew agreements. Each person employed as a seaman in a ship registered in the United Kingdom has to have a written agreement which has to be signed by him and by a person on behalf of his employers[15]. All the agreements with individual seamen must be collected together into one document, known as the crew agreement which must be in terms approved by the Department of Trade and Industry. This is not meant to be a standard form contract because different provisions and forms may be approved in different circumstances[16]. There is power vested in the Department to grant exemptions for specified types of ship or descriptions of seamen, and this can be done generally by regulation or in respect of individual employees or seamen where the Department is satisfied that there is adequate protection without a crew agreement. These provisions were originally enacted in the Merchant Shipping Act 1970 and replaced the old rules under the Merchant Shipping Act 1894 but in recognition of the growth of trade unions and collective agreements provide for greater flexibility. The details of permissible crew agreements are governed by regulations[17] for the legislation is basically enabling, leaving detailed regulation to subordinate legislation. There was, however, an intention to relax provisions of the old law; for example, it used to be necessary for an official known as a superintendent to be present both at a signing on and at discharge but the Pearson Report indicated that this was an unnecessary safeguard in modern conditions. The legislation itself determines a basic content of the contract of employment and in that sense is unusual. A group of sections deal with wages, aiming to ensure prompt payment, especially on discharge, and backed by punitive interest of 20%[18].

12 S. 13 see p. 213, below. There are exceptions in s. 14 and obviously certain statutory deductions (such as income tax under PAYE) do not need written consent.
13 See the Merchant Shipping Act 1894 and the Final Report of the Court of Inquiry under Lord Pearson (1967) Cmnd 3211, which led to the current legislation.
14 See the Pearson Report, cited in note 11 above.
15 Merchant Shipping Act 1995, s. 25.
16 Ibid., s. 25(3).
17 Ibid., Merchant Shipping (Crew Agreements, Lists of Crew and Discharge of Seamen) Regulations 1991, S.I. 1991 No. 2144.
18 Ss. 30–41.

ii)   Notice of terms of employment

Although English law is basically informal about the form of a contract of employment, Part I of the Employment Rights Act 1996 (first passed in 1963 as the Contracts of Employment Act) provides that an employee to whom the Act applies must be given written particulars of the salient terms of his employment. These provisions were amended and extended by the Trade Union Reform and Employment Rights Act 1993, in order to comply with an EC Directive on information concerning employment conditions[19], which the previous government were ready to agree to, for two reasons – (1) the existing law was already largely in compliance and (2) the extensions necessary (which stressed the need to give these written statements on an individual basis) were in line with their policy of encouraging more individual contracting, at the expense of collective negotiation of terms.

a)   The status of the written statement

The incontrovertible starting point is that the written ('section one') statement is *not* per se the contract of employment; it is, however evidence of the terms of the contract. This may seem a technical distinction (especially in a case where a longstanding statement appears to be the *only* tangible evidence), but it has the important consequence in law that it leaves the door open for an employee to argue in later proceedings that the statement was inaccurate as to the real terms on a given matter. The question then becomes how compelling the statement is to be as evidence. It is certainly not conclusive[20], but it is possible to point to earlier cases where courts showed themselves ready to incorporate terms from the written statement into the individual contract of employment, particularly where the statement appeared to have been accepted without protest for a reasonable period of time[1]. Later cases have, however, shown a tendency to treat the statement with more circumspection in circumstances where a major dispute has arisen as to the accuracy of a particular term, especially where 'acceptance without protest' is relied upon by the employer as showing the correctness of the statement. In *System Floors (UK) Ltd v Daniel*[2] Browne-Wilkinson J put the position thus:

> 'It seems to us, therefore, that in general the status of the statutory statement is this. It provides very strong prima facie evidence of what were the terms of the contract between the parties, but does not constitute a written contract between the parties. Nor are the statements of the terms finally conclusive: at most, they place a heavy burden on the employer to show that the actual terms of contract are different from those which he has set out in the statutory statement.'

19   Directive 91/533/EEC; see Clark and Hall 'The Cinderella Directive' (1992) 21 ILJ 106 and Kenner 'Statement or contract? – Some reflections on the EC Employee Information (Contract or Employment Relationship) Directive' (1999) 28 ILJ 205.

20   *Turriff Construction Ltd v Bryant* (1967) 2 ITR 292; *Parkes Classic Confectionery v Ashcroft* (1973) 8 ITR 43; see Dumville and Leighton 'From Statement to Contract' (1977) 6 ILJ 133.

1   *Camden Exhibition and Display Ltd v Lynott* [1966] 1 QB 555, [1965] 3 All ER 28, CA.

2   [1982] ICR 54, [1981] IRLR 475. This approach can also be seen in *Jones v Associated Tunnelling Co Ltd* [1981] IRLR 477 in the context of alterations to contractual terms, considered below.

This case concerned the less typical situation of the *employer* arguing that the statement did not properly reflect the contract; the burden is less heavy in the more typical case where it is the employee contesting the correctness of the statement, for as against him the statement will be (in Browne-Wilkinson J's words) 'no more than persuasive, though not conclusive, evidence'. It is therefore open for him to adduce hopefully more persuasive evidence that the real term was other than that contained in the employer's statement (e.g. evidence of what was said at the job interview, in letters of appointment, or even what was accepted in practice from the beginning of the employment). This can be seen from the subsequent decision of the Court of Appeal in *Robertson and Jackson v British Gas Corpn*[3] in which the above dicta by Browne-Wilkinson J were approved and the employee successfully challenged the accuracy of the section one statement on the basis that it did not reflect what was agreed at the commencement of employment on the bonus that was to be paid. At one stage, Ackner LJ seems to go further and say that the statement was not *even* evidence of the terms, but that must be taken in the light of the facts of the case, particularly the fact that the statement was not given until seven years after the commencement of the employment. In the more usual case, where the statement has been given at the time of or shortly after the commencement of employment and not dissented from, it certainly will be evidence, possibly compelling, for in practice these statements assume considerable importance in many employments.

One case that has caused some difficulty in this area is *Gascol Conversions Ltd v Mercer*[4] where the employer had sent written terms of employment to the employee who had signed them and a receipt which was attached; the Court of Appeal held that this constituted a written contract, governing inter alia the question of hours which was in dispute. The result of such a decision is that the written term in question is binding and not to be supplanted by evidence of extraneous matters or implied terms. However, this decision does not compromise the principles set out above, since it appears that the employee actually signed the written instrument as the new terms of his contract of employment, not just the attached receipt. It is common for section one statements to be signed for, but merely signing for receipt will *not* constitute a binding written contract, unlike in *Mercer's* case where the crucial extra step of signing *as the contract* was present. This view of *Mercer's* case (and the distinction between signing a contract and signing a receipt) has been accepted in the later cases[5]. It is thus possible for what would normally be a section one statement to be transformed into a formal written contract by the parties signing it as such, but if they are to do so it is doubly important that they should ensure that the terms are correct.

b) Requirements of the written statement

The obligation on an employer to give the section one statement arises whenever a person is taken on as an 'employee', thus excluding (as usual in statutory employment laws) the self-employed. Certain categories of employee are

---

3   [1983] ICR 351, [1983] IRLR 302, CA; note Leighton (1983) 12 ILJ 115. The case is also of particular interest on the incorporation of terms from collective agreements; see p. 114 , below.

4   [1974] ICR 420, [1974] IRLR 155, CA; cf. *Hawker Siddeley Power Engineering Ltd v Rump* [1979] IRLR 425. See Hepple (1974) 3 ILJ 164.

5   *System Floors (UK) Ltd v Daniel*, n. 20, above; *Robertson and Jackson v British Gas Corpn*, n. 3, above.

excluded; thus, this part of the Act does not apply to certain types of mariners,[6] employees working wholly outside Great Britain[7], or those employed for less than one month[8].

Wherever this part of the Act applies, the employer is given the period of two months from the beginning of the employment in question in which to deliver to his employee the necessary written statement[9], though in practice many employers will have the statement ready at the beginning, often as part of a 'starter pack' for new employees (along with other documents, such as a health and safety statement, disciplinary rules and company handbook). Where there is, subsequent to the giving of notice of particulars, a change in them the employer has one month in which to issue a statement of the change[10].

The initial notice must identify the parties and specify the date of commencement of employment and whether any employment with a previous employer is to count as part of the employee's continuous employment[11]. Section 1(4) then provides that certain particulars of the terms of employment must be stated (and if there are no agreed particulars under any of the heads that fact must be stated too)[12]. These particulars are – the scale or rate of remuneration; the intervals at which remuneration is to be paid; terms and conditions relating to hours of work (and possibly 'normal working hours'); any terms and conditions relating to holidays (including public holidays and holiday pay) with sufficient information to enable the entitlement to be calculated precisely, incapacity for work due to sickness or injury, and pensions and pension schemes; the length of notice which the employee is obliged to give and entitled to receive to determine the contract; the title of the job which the employee is employed to do[13]; how long the employment is to last if it is not permanent; the place of work; any collective agreements affecting terms and conditions; and, where the employee is to work outside the UK for more than a month, the period abroad, currency for remuneration, any additional remuneration or benefits, and any terms and conditions relating to his return to the UK. In addition section 3 provides that the employer must include a note specifying any disciplinary rules, how and to whom the employee may apply if dissatisfied with a disciplinary decision relating to him or if seeking redress of any grievance relating to his employment, and any

---

6   Ibid., s. 199.
7   This appears to be the case on general principles, in spite of the repeal of ibid, s 196 (by the Employment Relations Act 1999).
8   Ibid., s. 198.
9   Ibid., s. 1(2), as substituted by the 1993 Act.
10   Ibid., s 4; see below on changing the terms of employment.
11   This should now be viewed with caution by an employee, for a simple assurance of continuity of employment by a new employer (where such continuity is not preserved by a provision in the relevant statute) is not enough to safeguard continuity for the purpose of a later claim for a statutory right (especially a redundancy payment); *Secretary of State for Employment v Globe Elastic Thread Co Ltd* [1979] ICR 706, [1979] IRLR 327, HL, overruling *Evenden v Guildford City AFC Ltd* [1975] 3 All ER 269, [1975] ICR 367, CA; see p. 533, below.
12   Thus the obligation is to notify terms that exist, not to have a particular term in the first place: *Morley v Heritage plc* [1993] IRLR 400, CA (no term on accrued holiday pay).
13   This is not necessarily a full 'job description', but the employer should approach it with care, because the more specific the title is the less the employer will be able lawfully to demand flexibility on the part of the employee, a factor which could be of importance in a redundancy or unfair dismissal case; conversely, the wider the title, the more difficult it may be to establish that a dismissal is for redundancy. This one example of the job title (in addition to other clear examples such as job location clauses) shows how important it is for both employers and employees to treat contracts and/or written statements not as tedious bureaucracy, but rather as documents which may be decisive in actions before tribunals for modern statutory rights.

further steps in the employer's grievance procedure, though these requirements do not apply to any rules, procedures, etc., relating to health and safety at work. By an amendment made in 1989, the note of disciplinary and grievance provisions does not have to be given if, on the date when the employee's employment began, the number employed by the employer (and by any associated employer) was less than 20. Also under section 3 the note must state whether a contracting-out certificate is in force for the employment, for the purposes of the Pension Schemes Act 1993.

The principal change made in 1993 relates not to what has to be specified, but how it is to be notified to the employee. Previously, the employer was given a wide power to refer in the section 1 statement to other documentation, provided it was reasonably available to the employee. Thus, even on major terms such as pay, the statement could refer, for example, to a collective agreement. Increasingly, this technique was used where the firm produced a company handbook, to which frequent reference could be made[14]. However, that power of reference was restricted in 1993 and now only applies to (a) any particulars relating to sickness, sick pay or pensions, when reference may be made to some other document reasonably available, and (b) the length of notice, when reference may be made to the general law[15] or any relevant collective agreement[16]. Other than that (and the note on disciplinary and grievance procedures), the new rule is that the particulars required must be specifically included in a 'single document'[17]. Similarly, any changes must be notified specifically in a written statement, subject to the same exceptions. As stated above, this change was consistent with the previous government's stated policy to encourage the extension of individual contracting and flexibility in the setting of terms and conditions[18].

c) Enforcement

Contractual rights may of course be enforced by an ordinary common law action before the ordinary courts and so, for example, a claim that the employer should be paying more in wages under the contract may be tested by bringing an action for those wages in the county court, which may involve a determination by the court of the correct contractual term on wages, which in turn may involve a determination of the accuracy of the written statement on the question of wages. In addition to this, however, the Act provides for the *direct* enforcement of the requirement to give the written statement.

Under section 11 the method of direct enforcement of these provisions is by reference of the issue to an employment tribunal. Where either no statement has been given under sections 1 or 4 or a statement does not comply with those sections the employee may refer the matter, and where a statement has been

---

14 Company handbooks became increasingly popular with employers and ACAS have published advice on producing them (Advisory Booklet No. 9). However, there can be difficulties with the contractual status of different parts of such a handbook (see p. 117, below) and the new rules on written statements may make them less useful.

15 The legal minima are set out in the Employment Rights Act 1996, s. 86, see p. 368, below.

16 Ibid., s 2(2), (3).

17 Ibid., s. 2(4). There is a peculiarity in the new drafting. The old s. 5 used to state specifically that the need to give a statement did not apply if the employer instead gave a full written contract covering the relevant matters; no such provision now appears, so it must be assumed to be implied that such a written contract constitutes a 'written statement to the employee' under s. 1(1).

18 People, Jobs and Opportunity (Cm. 1810, 1992).

given but a dispute has arisen as to the particulars which ought to have been included or referred to in it so as to comply with the statutory provisions, either the employer or the employee may refer the matter. By section 12 the tribunal is given wide powers to determine what particulars ought to have been included, or whether any particulars which were included are to be confirmed, amended or substituted. These powers of the tribunal should be a considerable incentive for the employer to comply with the requirements of section 1 in the first place; if he does not do so, and a dispute later arises with his workforce over a particular term of employment (e.g. overtime arrangements) it would be possible for them to take him to a tribunal under section 11 and invite the tribunal to write into their statements the version of the term on overtime that *they* say they originally agreed – if they were successful that would in practice end the dispute in their favour[19].

However, two problems have arisen as to the construction of these powers. The first arises from the fact that they are declared to be only for the purpose of deciding what 'ought to have been included or referred to in the statement *so as to comply with the requirements of [these provisions]*'. This means that the tribunal may only declare what ought to have been included in the sense of what was agreed on these various enumerated matters between the parties; it cannot therefore go further and *interpret* any terms expressed in the written statement, for that would be to usurp the functions of the ordinary civil courts to whom the employee must turn for interpretation and enforcement of his contractual rights[20]. Thus in *Cuthbertson v AML Distributors*[1] the employee had not had any written statement of the terms of his notice and when he was dismissed the question arose as to what the length of his notice should have been. The tribunal could find no evidence of express or implied agreement between the parties on this matter, and therefore held that the term which ought to have been included on the question of notice was that it should have been governed by the residual common law requirement of 'reasonable notice'. The applicant employee had claimed that three months would have been reasonable, but the tribunal refused to quantify 'reasonable' as that would have been to interpret the contract, which was the province of the ordinary courts to which the employee would have to apply. The case of *Owens v Multilux Ltd*[2] in the NIRC may seem to go against this restricted view of the tribunal's jurisdiction, for there the court not only declared that the parties had agreed upon a salary of '£2500 net deductions' but also declared that this meant that the employer should pay the deductions other than those for income tax. The line here is of course a fine one, but the EAT clearly decided in favour of the restricted view in *Construction Industry Training Board v Leighton*[3] where the written

19   Note, however, that it is essential that there should be a dispute between the parties; it is an abuse of procedure to bring a s. 11 claim where there is no dispute, merely the parties wanting a ruling on a particular matter for some extrinsic purpose: *Baker v Superite Tools Ltd* [1986] ICR 189 (parties wanting a ruling as to whether the workers involved were employed or self-employed, for use in dealings with the Inland Revenue).

20   Unless the matter has arisen on termination of the employment, in which case a tribunal may have jurisdiction to determine a contract claim; see p. 433, below. This would now cover the case of *Cuthbertson* (see next note).

1   [1975] IRLR 228, IT.

2   [1974] IRLR 113; likewise, there are dubious dicta by Parker LJ in *Eagland v British Telecommunications plc* [1993] ICR 644, [1992] IRLR 323, CA that a tribunal would have power to *quantify* a 'reasonable notice' term.

3   [1978] IRLR 60. The decision in this case, and the rule that tribunals may not interpret statements, were approved by Stephenson LJ in *Mears v Safecar Security Ltd* [1982] IRLR 183, CA at 188, though certain dicta in the case no longer stand (see below).

statement had set out the salary terms for the employee but a dispute had arisen as to whether a salary increment mentioned in the terms was in fact payable to the employee. The tribunal decided that it was and so declared, but the EAT allowed the appeal. Kilner Brown J said:

'... the industrial tribunal allocated to themselves a jurisdiction which they did not have. They acted upon [s. 12(2)] which undoubtedly gives wide powers of amendment and substitution without giving proper consideration to the limitations imposed by [s. 11(2)]. An industrial tribunal can only embark upon an exercise of amendment or substitution of particulars where there is an omission to include or refer to a statutory requirement when setting out the terms of a contract of employment. Here the salary was set out in the contract. All that was unclear was whether the supplementary bonus for one year was already included in the expressed figure. In effect the industrial tribunal was exercising the power of the civil courts to declare what a contract meant or to rectify an error manifest in an otherwise binding contract. We are unanimously of the opinion that the words of the statute do not mean ... that the industrial tribunal could re-write or amend a binding contract which has one small area of misunderstanding between the parties'.

The second problem was potentially more far-reaching, for while it was clear on the wording of section 12 that a tribunal could determine a case where there was a partial or total *failure* by the employer to include the necessary terms in the statement, it was argued that it did not have jurisdiction where the employer had indeed given terms but the employee claimed that they were *inaccurate* (i.e. that they did not reflect what had actually been agreed)[4]. This very narrow view was supported by the ambiguous third sentence in the above dictum by Kilner Brown J in *Leighton's* case, and could be seen in the judgment of the EAT in *Brown v Stuart, Scott & Co Ltd*[5], though in each case the pronouncements were obiter. It is true that the wording of section 12 was not explicit on the point (though the use of words such as 'amend' and 'substitute' surely points in the direction of including claims that particulars are inaccurate) however it certainly seemed that the narrow view was contrary to Parliament's intention and an unnecessary restriction on the tribunals' jurisdiction. As originally drafted, the Employment Bill 1982 contained a provision which would have stated expressly that tribunals could hear complaints about particulars which had been included or referred to in statements, but this provision was removed as unnecessary when the position was rectified by the decision of the Court of Appeal in the important case of *Mears v Safecar Security Ltd*[6]. It is made clear in this case that a tribunal *does* have jurisdiction to hear complaints of inaccurate particulars. However, on its facts the case concerned the *failure* to give particulars[7] and in this context too the case is important for its clarification and extension of existing principles. Here, Stephenson LJ said that the complaint could be either (a) a complaint that the statement does not contain a term which had actually been agreed, or (b) a complaint that a term had not been included where in fact there had been no

4   See Gay [1980] CLJ 278 and Mogridge, 'Giving written particulars of employment – a valueless exercise?' (1981) NLJ 1250.
5   [1981] ICR 166.
6   [1982] 2 All ER 865, [1982] IRLR 183, CA. The case includes a detailed explanation by Stephenson LJ of the original drafting of ss. 11 and 12.
7   The particulars in question related to the payment (or non-payment) of sick pay; this aspect of the case is considered on p. 178, below.

express agreement. In the latter case, a tribunal must consider all the facts to determine what term should be implied[8], and normally there will be sufficient evidence for them to be able to do so (in particular, evidence of general working practices which are obvious at the latest by the end of the two-month period that the employer has in which to give the written statement). However, a further problem arose because the court went further and said obiter that the obligation upon the tribunal to declare the relevant particulars (on a complaint of failure to give them) applied even in the untypical case where there is no clear evidence at all, in which case the tribunal might ultimately be left to 'invent' them, on the basis of what would be reasonable and sensible terms in all the circumstances. However, the Court of Appeal subsequently disapproved strongly of that extreme position in *Eagland v British Telecommunications plc*[9], where it was reaffirmed that the tribunal's function is only to declare what has already been agreed in some way, not to impose upon the parties terms which have not been agreed. They adopted the distinction drawn by Wood P in the EAT in the case between 'mandatory' and 'non-mandatory' particulars[10]. In the case of the latter, if there is no evidence at all of any agreement, the tribunal should simply state that there is no term on the matter[11]. Mandatory terms cause more difficulty. They said that it is most unlikely that this problem will arise (an employment relationship with *nothing* ever said about pay?), but if it did a tribunal would have to look at what the law would normally include as the ordinary requirements of an employment relationship (the obvious example being the implication of a term of reasonable notice if there was no evidence of any agreement). However, Leggatt LJ in a short, concurring judgment stated what must eventually be the bottom line if no power of invention is allowed:

> 'If an essential term, such as a written statement must contain, has not been agreed, there will be no agreement.'

d)   Changing the terms of employment

We have already seen that section 4 states that changes in the relevant terms and conditions must be notified to the employee within one month. However, it is important to realise that section 4 only adds a procedural requirement – it does *not* give the employer any substantive right to alter the terms of employment simply by issuing an amending notice. Any such variation must first be lawful and effective under the ordinary law of employment contracts. There may be certain, untypical, cases where the employment contract itself is drafted to give the

---

8   The case is also important on this general question of the implication of terms into contracts of employment (see p. 108, below), for the approach of the Court of Appeal was not constrained by old contract law notions of the intent of the parties or business efficacy.

9   [1993] ICR 644, [1992] IRLR 323, CA.

10   [1990] ICR 248, [1990] IRLR 328. According to Parker LJ, giving the leading judgment in the Court of Appeal, mandatory terms (as the section stood pre-1993) are those relating to the parties, date of commencement, continuity of employment, rate of pay, intervals for payment, notice and job title; non-mandatory terms are those relating to hours of work, holidays, sickness/sick pay and pensions. Of the particulars added in 1993, those relating to termination of non-permanent employment, place of work and applicable collective agreements appear to be mandatory; the extra particulars relating to employment abroad appear to be split.

11   *Morley v Heritage plc* [1993] IRLR 400, CA.

employer a right of unilateral variation[12]. Less drastically, it may be that a particular 'variation' in fact falls within the managerial discretion to order changes[13], either because it is within an area of flexibility envisaged by the contract or because it falls within the scope of an implied term that the employee will adapt to necessary changes in what remains essentially the same job[14]. However, both of these possibilities show the basic problem here, that contracts are essentially static whereas work and work methods may change (sometimes rapidly), and the possibility may equally arise that the employer may wish to effect changes which are *not* envisaged by the contract. In such a case there has to be a legally effective variation; if this does not happen, an employee may insist upon adhering to the original contract and may bring a common law action to underline that adherence (e.g. by bringing an action in the county court for his wages, which are due by virtue of his being willing and able to continue performing his duties under the original, unamended contract)[15] or (in the case of a pay cut) proceedings before a tribunal on the basis that the change constitutes an unlawful 'deduction' from wages. In such a case, an employer who is insistent upon forcing through changes may have to grasp the nettle, dismiss those who still refuse to accept changes and take his chances before an employment tribunal by seeking to show that the dismissals were fair because of the business's need to alter working patterns[16].

From the employer's point of view, these uncertainties can be avoided if it can be shown that the employee in question in fact agreed to the proposed variation in the contract. How is that to be shown? Obviously the clearest case is where the employee has expressly agreed to the variation, either individually or collectively (through negotiations with his union). However, there remains a middle ground (especially where union representation is not involved), which is where the employer 'proposes' a variation simply by announcing it (possibly by reissuing an amended section one statement), thus putting the onus on the employee to *object*. If the employee does not object, that gives rise to the argument that he has impliedly assented to the variation. If such an argument were easily accepted,

12   The terms and conditions of employment of senior civil servants may be varied unilaterally by the government under the Civil Service Orders in Council; see p. 80, above. In an ordinary contract of employment, it would be an interesting question as to whether a term allowing unrestricted unilateral variation ('You are employed to do what I say, on any terms I may decide upon') could be held to be void for uncertainty; the Court of Appeal in *Wandsworth London Borough Council v D'Silva* [1998] IRLR 193 (obiter) recognised the possible contractual validity of such a clause, but stated that particularly clear language would be necessary to reserve such an unusual power to the employer, and courts should seek to avoid any unreasonable results of such a power.

13   As in the case of the introduction of a no-smoking policy in *Dryden v Greater Glasgow Health Board* [1992] IRLR 469, which was held not to be a breach of contract, so that the employee who left was not constructively dismissed.

14   This was the case with the computerisation of inland revenue procedures; this was held to be merely an updated version of the plaintiff tax officers' existing jobs (with which they were expected to cope), *not* a substantive variation of their terms of employment: *Cresswell v Board of Inland Revenue* [1984] ICR 508, [1984] IRLR 190; see p. 130, below.

15   As in *Burdett-Coutts v Hertfordshire County Council* [1984] IRLR 91 where dinner ladies who had refused to accept a unilateral decrease in their hours of work successfully sued their employer for arrears of wages due under their original contract.

16   This is one of the most difficult areas of unfair dismissal, for it is well established that dismissal because of refusal to accept a necessary business reorganisation can constitute dismissal for 'some other substantial reason' within the Employment Rights Act 1996, s. 98 (see p. 496, below and, again concerning dinner ladies and cost-cutting councils, *Gilham v Kent County Council (No 2)* [1985] ICR 233, [1985] IRLR 18, CA) but to take the final step and hold that that dismissal was *fair* is to give priority to the employer's business considerations over what the employee would normally expect to be his contractual rights (particularly the right not to have his contract altered except by agreement).

the contractual rights of an employee would mean little and so it was held in *Jones v Associated Tunnelling Co Ltd*[17] that the question of the correct interpretation to be placed on a lack of objection following a unilateral change in terms by the employer must be approached realistically; if the term in question is of immediate practical importance (e.g. a reduction in wages or alteration of working hours) and the employee fails to object, that may show implied assent on his part, but in the case of other terms of little immediate importance (e.g. as to sick pay or possible future changes in workplace) it may be expecting too much of an employee to make immediate objection (even if he understands the full significance of the changes) and so a tribunal in such a case should be slow to infer assent merely from lack of objection.

4   LEGALITY AND RESTRAINT OF TRADE

i)   The doctrine of illegality generally

All contracts having objects contrary to statute or common law, or which entail the passing of an illegal consideration, are void. So an agreement by which an employee purports to permit his employer to make deductions from his remuneration will be void unless there is compliance with the provisions of Part II of the Employment Rights Act 1996[18]. So too will a purported agreement to waive a breach of duty imposed by statute on an employer[19]. Sundry other forms of illegality may theoretically apply to contracts of employment as well as to contracts generally even if in practice they are less likely to do so. One which could arise directly in the context of employment is the rule that a contract of employment must not contain 'servile incidents', which may best be described as harsh terms showing a lack of mutuality, as where a cinema company obtained sole use of an actor's stage name[20] or where the defendant borrowed money from a money-lender on terms which made it impossible for him to change employment, deal with his possessions, change address, etc., without prior permission[1].

One particular application of notions of illegality has caused problems in the field of employment law. These problems arise when one of the parties (usually the employer) to a tribunal action concerning modern statutory rights such as redundancy payments or unfair dismissal argues that the contract of employment in question was in some sense illegal, usually because it contained some element of unlawful tax evasion (e.g. under-declaration of income payable under it, or the payment of non-declared extra amounts of income). If this is proved, it can lead to a decision that the contract itself is void and, as such a contract is necessary

---

17   [1981] IRLR 477.
18   *Kearney v Whitehaven Colliery Co* [1893] 1 QB 700, CA (case on the now-repealed Truck Acts); see p. 178, below.
19   *Baddeley v Earl of Granville* (1887) 19 QBD 423; for a strong case, see *Wheeler v New Merton Board Mills Ltd* [1933] 2 KB 669, CA.
20   *Hepworth Manufacturing Co v Ryott* [1920] 1 Ch 1, CA; however, some cinema contracts have validly imposed highly personal restraints on employees' diets, health, personal life etc., probably on the ground that they were in the interests of both parties; *Gaumont-British Picture Corpn v Alexander* [1936] 2 All ER 1686. A tie to pay back the cost of training is not illegal (*Strathclyde Regional Council v Neil* [1984] IRLR 11); indeed, the previous government expressed interest in extending such a system of self-financed training, backed by 'stay or pay' clauses: People, Jobs and Opportunity (Cm. 1810, 1992), see (1992) NLJ 358.
1   *Horwood v Millar's Timber and Trading Co Ltd* [1917] 1 KB 305, CA.

before an applicant can show that he was an 'employee' for the purpose of claiming his statutory rights, that the applicant's claim must be struck out[2]. The doctrine of illegality in the law of contract is a complicated subject at the best of times[3], but in the sphere of employment law can have particularly drastic effects by depriving tribunals of jurisdiction, even where the element of illegality might be incidental and (in the case of tax evasion) where the amount of money concerned is small. Moreover, it can lead to the problem, which arises generally under the doctrine of illegality in contract law, of one party to the contract (here usually the employer) benefiting from his own illegality, e.g. in a case where the evasion scheme was in fact initiated by the employer who later used it to try to defeat an employee's claim for unfair dismissal. The starting point here is that the general argument that the doctrine of illegality should not apply to contracts of employment (either at all, or at least to the extent of prejudicing statutory actions) on the grounds of employment law policy has clearly been disapproved by the EAT[4]. Thus, the doctrine is applicable and in a series of cases the tribunals have had to work out its effects. It may of course apply to forms of illegality other than tax evasion, for example in *Coral Leisure Group Ltd v Barnett*[5] where it was claimed that an ex-employee could not maintain an action for unfair dismissal because part of his job had entailed hiring prostitutes for the employer's clients, thus falling foul of the law on immoral contracts. In this sort of case it is easier to apply the basic common law distinction that contracts illegal in inception are void, but contracts which are legal in inception but later performed in an illegal manner may not be[6]. However, that distinction may be more difficult to apply to the more usual cases of tax evasion. The tendency has fortunately been to treat them as illegal only in performance, with the result that 'innocence' is a defence, and so in practice the determining factor has been whether the employee *knew* of the evasion being practised by the employer – if not, he can still claim his statutory rights[7]; moreover, it is clear that knowledge here means actual, subjective knowledge, so that it is an error of law for a tribunal to consider whether the

---

2   *Napier v National Business Agency Ltd* [1951] 2 All ER 264, CA; *Jennings v Westwood Engineering Ltd* [1975] IRLR 245; *Tomlinson v Dick Evans U Drive Ltd* [1978] ICR 639, [1978] IRLR 77.

3   See *Cheshire, Fifoot and Furmston* (13th edn, 1996) chs. 11 and 12.

4   *Newland v Simons and Willer (Hairdressers) Ltd* [1981] ICR 521, [1981] IRLR 359. It is of course possible for a statute to state expressly that contravention of its terms shall *not* make any resulting contract void for illegality (see, for example, the Company Securities (Insider Dealing) Act 1985, s. 8(3) and, in particular, the Social Security Contributions and Benefits Act 1992, s. 97 which covers industrial accidents in the course of illegal employments); it is unfortunate that the Employment Rights Act does not have such an exclusory provision.

5   [1981] ICR 503, [1981] IRLR 204.

6   In this case, the EAT held that the tribunal had jurisdiction to hear the claim. The ex-employee had not been taken on to hire prostitutes, and it was not part of his contract to do so (merely one of the ways in practice of discharging his functions); the contract was therefore not illegal in inception. Dicta in the case suggest that, because it was only illegal in performance, *therefore* it was not void, but it is submitted that the better view is that that means that it *may* not be void, and that the ground for the decision is that, given that the illegality was only in performance, that particular form of illegality (hiring prostitutes) was not sufficiently grave to justify invalidating the whole contract.

7   *Tomlinson v Dick Evans 'U' Drive Ltd*, no. 20, above; *Davidson v Pillay* [1979] IRLR 275: *McConnell v Bolik* [1979] IRLR 422 has an interesting twist in the story in that the case concerned non-declaration of income by the employee, so that the crucial question was the state of the *employer's* knowledge. The knowledge in question is as to the facts; lack of knowledge of the illegality of the transaction (i.e. a mistake of law) will not help the party: *Salvesen v Simons* [1994] ICR 409, [1994] IRLR 52.

employee ought to have realised what was happening[8]. The most difficult case here is *Corby v Morrison* where the primary ground for ruling out a claim for unfair dismissal by an ex-employee who had received £5 per week without deduction of income tax was that the contract of employment was illegal *in inception*, which renders the knowledge or otherwise of the employee irrelevant; the EAT did give as a secondary ground of judgment that, even if it was only illegal in performance, she knew what was going on and so was ruled out anyway. This second ground of judgment was emphasised in the explanation of the case subsequently in *Newland v Simons and Willer (Hairdressers) Ltd*[9], but the first ground was not disapproved. However, in *Hewcastle Catering Ltd v Ahmed*[10] the Court of Appeal clearly leaned towards treating tax evasion cases as illegality in performance, to which the doctrine should be applied sparingly. Beldam LJ stated that the modern law is that it applies only if in all the circumstances it would be an affront to the public conscience to allow the claim to proceed; further, the defence will not be allowed if the defendant employer's conduct in participating in the illegal contract is so much more reprehensible than the employee's conduct that it would be wrong to allow the employer to rely on it. This is an important case because of the facts – the employees were waiters at the employers' club who were involved in operating the employers' VAT fraud, *but* they did *not* derive any personal benefit from it. After the employers were caught (and the employees gave evidence against them), the employees were dismissed and the employers raised illegality as a defence. Had the court simply applied the existing test (did they *know* of it?) the defence would have succeeded, but on the two wider principles above the court was able to disallow it since (a) public policy did not demand its application and (b) the employers were clearly the more guilty. While this decision does not go as far as to say that an employee with knowledge (though possibly only an unwilling minion) *cannot* be debarred from an action if he made no personal gain, it did allow a decision to be taken much along those lines on the facts. Moreover, it may permit further developments towards what, it is submitted, would be the best solution (given that the doctrine has to apply at all), namely that any incidental tax evasion should only ever make the contract illegal in performance and that for the illegality then to make the contract void the employee must have known of *and benefited from* the evasion to such an *extent* (in comparison with the gain to the employer) that the court or tribunal has no option but to declare the whole contract void.

Finally three points might be noted. The first is that on general principles it is not every form of illegality that can render a contract void – the illegality must be sufficiently grave or of such a nature as to show (in the case of illegality through contravention of a statute) that the intention of the legislation is to affect contracts if necessary, not just to penalise the conduct in question in other ways[11]. It is this principle that prevents, for example, a lorry driver's contract of employment

---

8 *Corby v Morrison* [1980] ICR 564, [1980] IRLR 218; *Newland v Simons and Willer (Hairdressers) Ltd* [1981] IRLR 359.

9 See n. 8, above; the same judge presided over the EAT in both cases. *Newland's* case was clearly viewed as one of illegality in performance, and was remitted to the tribunal to make more precise findings of fact on the employee's knowledge of the evasion.

10 [1992] ICR 626, [1991] IRLR 473, CA.

11 The authority usually cited for this is the judgment of Devlin J in *St John Shipping Corpn v Joseph Rank Ltd* [1957] 1 QB 267, [1956] 3 All ER 683. One potentially controversial question now may be whether a contract to work hours in excess of the maxima in the Working Time Regulations could be argued to be illegal; this is probably *not* the intent of the Regulations (except to the extent of the excess?), and the results of so holding could be harsh and unpredictable for the employee.

being totally void as soon as he exceeds a speed limit. However, it cannot help an applicant before a tribunal in a case involving tax evasion, for it has so far been the approach of the courts (subject to any possible new emphasis on the respective moral blame worthiness of employee and employer, see above) that *any* element of tax evasion (even if concerning only small amounts, or only extra remuneration[12] on top of basic wages on which full tax may have been paid) is grave enough to activate the rules on illegality; likewise the tribunals have not accepted the argument that protection of tax revenue can be adequately left to the tax authorities and legislation and does not need to be reinforced by the striking down of contracts, though it has been accepted that employers may be deterred from making illegal payments and then trying to rely on them to defeat statutory claims by the power of a tribunal at the end of the day to transmit the evidence that they have received to the Inland Revenue[13]. The second point is that a slightly different approach to illegality was taken in the case of *Hyland v J H Barker (North West) Ltd*[14]. In this case the employee had taken illegal payments for a period of only four weeks (out of a total period of employment of 16 years); it was accepted that this did not render the whole contract void *but* that did not help the employee much since it transpired that those four weeks fell during his final year before dismissal and thus (as the contract was void for those four weeks) he could not show the year's continuous employment ending with the date of dismissal that was (then) required in order to bring proceedings for unfair dismissal. The case shows a possibly unfortunate combination of the restrictive rules on illegality and continuity of employment and also, more generally, the harsh effects of the doctrine of illegality in this field; it also leaves open the question as to how major and/or longstanding the illegality has to be to render the *whole* contract void (not just part of it, the timing of which could be entirely fortuitous). The third point is that, as a matter of statutory construction and policy, it has been held that the doctrine of illegality cannot be used to defeat a sex discrimination claim[15]; this would also apply to a racial discrimination claim and presumably, to an equal pay claim and a disability discrimination claim.

In addition to these general applications of the doctrine of illegality, much case law has been produced by one particular area of it, the area of restraint of trade. Indeed now that this has been held to apply to harsh and one-sided contractual conditions during employment as well as after it[16], it has probably made much of the law on servile incidents redundant. The classic restraint of trade clause in a contract of employment is where the employee agrees not to

---

12 If however the tax evasion applies only to extraneous payments (e.g. gifts) which are *not* part of contractual remuneration, the validity of the contract is not affected: *Annandale Engineering v Samson* [1994] IRLR 59.

13 A course advocated in *Corby v Morrison* and put into effect in *Newland v Simons and Willer (Hairdressers) Ltd* (n. 8, above). A similar device has been suggested to deter a person from claiming to be self-employed for tax purposes while working, but then turning round and claiming to have been in reality an employee all along when later dismissed and wanting to bring an action for unfair dismissal – he may end up with a tribunal finding in his favour outweighed by the hefty tax demand: *Young & Woods Ltd v West* [1980] IRLR 201, CA (see p. 15, above).

14 [1985] IRLR 403.

15 *Leighton v Michael* [1995] ICR 1091. This was approved by the Court of Appeal in *Hall v Woolston Hall Leisure Ltd* [2000] IRLR 578, [2000] NLJR 833, both as a matter of domestic law and in the light of the Equal Treatment Directive 76/207/EEC.

16 *Schroeder Music Publishing Co v Macaulay* [1974] 3 All ER 616, [1974] 1 WLR 1308, HL; *Clifford Davis Management Ltd v WEA Records Ltd* [1975] 1 All ER 237, [1975] 1 WLR 61, CA.

work in the same trade or not to solicit his employer's customers in a certain area for a certain period, after the termination of his employment with that employer. It is to the doctrine of restraint of trade, and the validity or otherwise of such an agreement, that we now turn.

ii)   The doctrine of restraint of trade

The doctrine of restraint of trade is a legal device to attempt to hold the balance between two competing factors – an employee's freedom to take employment as and when he wishes, and an employer's interest in preserving certain aspects of his business from disclosure or exploitation by an employee or, more usually, an ex-employee. Both factors are important, and indeed the law will protect the employer if necessary by the implication of a term of fidelity in the contract of employment thereby restraining the employee inter alia from divulging confidential information[17]. However, the employer may wish to go further and extract an express promise from the employee (a) not to disclose certain information and, more important, (b) not to place himself in a position in which he may do so, for example by not working for a competitor for a certain period of time within a certain area after leaving the employment.

> 'It is thus established that an employer can stipulate for protection against having his confidential information passed on to a rival in trade. But experience has shown that it is not satisfactory to have simply a covenant against disclosing confidential information. The reason is because it is so difficult to draw the line between information which is confidential and information which is not; and it is very difficult to prove a breach when the information is of such a character that a servant can carry it away in his head. The difficulties are such that the only practicable solution is to take a covenant from the servant by which he is not to go to work for a rival in trade. Such a covenant may well be held to be reasonable ...'[18]

The question then arises whether any given restraint clause is valid and enforceable against the ex-employee, or void. The modern law on restraint of trade is to be found in *Nordenfelt v Maxim Nordenfelt Guns and Ammunition Co*[19] and *Esso Petroleum Co Ltd v Harper's Garage (Stourport) Ltd*[20], a case on 'solus' agreements in the garage trade, in which the House of Lords reconsidered the whole doctrine. In the *Nordenfelt* case it was established that a restraint clause is to be considered void unless the party alleging its validity can prove that it is (a) reasonable as between the parties and (b) in the public interest. The two principal forms of agreement which have been subject to the doctrine are agreements by the vendor of a business not to compete with the purchaser of it, as in the *Nordenfelt* case, and by an employee not to act in a certain way after finishing the employment, and it has been clearly stated that it will be more difficult to establish the validity of a restraint clause in the latter case, with which we are primarily concerned here, for it concerns not a commercial transaction at arm's length, but rather a

17   This topic is discussed later in this chapter, under head 5.
18   *Littlewoods Organisation Ltd v Harris* [1978] 1 All ER 1026, CA at 1033 per Lord Denning MR.
19   [1894] AC 535, HL, as explained by a subsequent House of Lords in *Mason v Provident Clothing and Supply Co Ltd* [1913] AC 724, HL.
20   [1968] AC 269, [1967] 1 All ER 699, HL.

transaction, potentially between parties of different bargaining strengths, which could have a major effect on an individual's livelihood (future and present) to the disadvantage of himself and the public interest[1]. For present purposes, the decision in the *Esso Petroleum* case clarified the law in two major ways[2]. The first was to confirm that not all agreements which restrain a person's freedom of action are subject to the doctrine, for some are so accepted as normal incidents of particular businesses or transactions that they are not subject to challenge[3]. The test for deciding what is subject to the doctrine and what is not subject is not entirely clear, but what is important for present purposes is that the House of Lords said clearly that restraint clauses by employees in favour of employers are definitely subject to the doctrine. The second major effect of the case was to revive the ailing second limb of the rule in *Nordenfelt's* case, i.e., public interest. This had been so neglected as to have been virtually ignored[4], but this can no longer be so and indeed Lord Reid and Lord Hodson intimated[5] that certain past cases which were decided on the first limb, reasonableness as between the parties, might well have been better decided on the second limb. In the employment context this could be of some importance, as there might be certain forms of agreement as we shall see below, such as labour stabilisation agreements between employer and employer, which might be eminently reasonable as between the parties, but would now be subject to challenge on the wider ground of the public interest.

Thus, an employee might validly bind himself in a contract of employment as to his future activities, usually when he enters the contract, but also possibly during its currency[6] or at its termination, provided in the latter case that the agreement is genuinely referable to the contract of employment, and not just an after-thought 'in gross'[7]. Moreover, it is now established that a clause restraining certain activities by the employee *during* employment may be subject to challenge as well as one restricting activities upon termination of the employment; in *Schroeder Music Publishing Co v Macaulay*[8] an agreement whereby the plaintiff, a young and unknown songwriter, gave his exclusive services to the defendants for five years without any obligation on the latter to publish his works or provide him with any livelihood, and whereby the defendants could terminate or extend the contract at their election but the plaintiff could not, was held to be void as in restraint of trade. That was, however, an unusual case, and any more normal restraints during employment, e.g. not to work for competitors or not to disclose information, might well be held to be so common as to require no justification, under the *Esso Petroleum* case, and indeed certain standard ones would possibly be implied by operation of law even if not expressed[9].

1   See particularly *Herbert Morris Ltd v Saxelby* [1916] 1 AC 688, HL, per Lord Parker at 710 and Lord Shaw at 714.
2   See generally Cheshire, Fifoot and Furmston *Law of Contract* (13th edn, 1996), ch. 12.
3   Tied houses in the brewery trade are valid, whereas 'solus' agreements in the garage trade, not being so widely accepted, have been the subject of several legal cases.
4   'Their Lordships are not aware of any case in which a restraint, though reasonable in the interests of the parties, has been held unenforceable because it involved some injury to the public,' *A-G of Commonwealth of Australia v Adelaide Steamship Co Ltd* [1913] AC 781, PC, at 795 per Lord Parker. One exceptional case was *Wyatt v Kreglinger and Fernau* [1933] 1 KB 793, CA, followed by *Bull v Pitney-Bowes* [1966] 3 All ER 384, [1967] 1 WLR 273.
5   [1968] AC at 300 and 319, [1967] 1 All ER at 709 and 721.
6   *RS Components Ltd v Irwin* [1974] 1 All ER 41, [1973] ICR 535.
7   *Stenhouse Australia Ltd v Phillips* [1974] AC 391, [1974] 1 All ER 117, PC.
8   [1974] 3 All ER 616, [1974] 1 WLR 1308, HL, followed in *Clifford Davis Management Ltd v WEA Records Ltd* [1975] 1 All ER 237, [1975] 1 WLR 61, CA.
9   See head 5 of this chapter, under the duty of fidelity.

Given that restraint clauses in contracts of employment are amenable to challenge, the next relevant questions are: what interests warrant protection, how extensive can the restraint be if it is to be valid, and what remedies are available to the parties.

iii) Protectable interests

The clearest starting point is that an employer cannot simply restrain an ex-employee from competing with him in an ordinary manner; it must go far beyond that, and in the employment context this in practice means that the restraint must be necessary to protect either (a) trade secrets or (b) customer connections.

> 'I cannot find any case in which a covenant against competition by a servant or apprentice has as such ever been upheld by the court. Wherever such covenants have been upheld it has been on the grounds, not that the servant or apprentice would, by reason of his employment or training, obtain the skill or knowledge necessary to equip him as a possible competitor in the trade, *but* that he might obtain such personal knowledge of, and influence over, the customers of his employers, or such an acquaintance with his employer's trade secrets as would enable him, if competition were allowed, to take advantage of his employer's trade connection or utilise information confidentially obtained.'[10]

From this basic principle, certain important points arise. The first is that although 'trade secret' is difficult to define, it is an important concept and must be distinguished from the employee's own skill and general knowledge of the trade (albeit gained in the employer's service)[11], knowledge of general business methods and organisations[12], and information which lacks confidentiality (for example through having been published)[13], none of which merit lawful protection. The subject-matter must be something more in the nature of a secret process or formula[14] or the detailed design of a machine (albeit from parts the individual specifications of which are generally known)[15] and in modern circumstances may also cover highly confidential information of a non-technical or non-scientific nature (disclosure of which to a competitor could cause significant harm)[16] or detailed knowledge of the workings of a specialised business[17]. Particularly difficult questions may now arise in the computer and information technology industries, in deciding what remains confidential at the

10 *Herbert Morris Ltd v Saxelby* [1916] 1 AC 688, HL at 709 per Lord Parker. For a modern reaffirmation of this principle, see *Faccenda Chicken Ltd v Fowler* [1986] ICR 297, [1986] IRLR 69, CA.
11 *Herbert Morris Ltd v Saxelby*, n. 10 above; *Mason v Provident Clothing and Supply Co Ltd* [1913] AC 724, HL; *Faccenda Chicken Ltd v Fowler*, n. 8 above.
12 *Commercial Plastics Ltd v Vincent* [1965] 1 QB 623, [1964] 3 All ER 546, CA.
13 *Mustad v Dosen* [1963] 3 All ER 416, [1964] 1 WLR 109n, HL (though in fact decided in 1928).
14 *Haynes v Doman* [1899] 2 Ch 13, CA; *Forster & Sons Ltd v Suggett* (1918) 35 TLR 87; and see the detailed knowledge of current research carried on by the plaintiffs in *Commercial Plastics Ltd v Vincent* [1965] 1 QB 623, [1964] 3 All ER 546, CA.
15 *Haynes v Doman* [1899] 2 Ch 13, CA; *Forster & Sons Ltd v Suggett* (1918) 35 TLR 87; and see the detailed knowledge of current research carried on by the plaintiffs in *Commercial Plastics Ltd v Vincent* [1965] 1 QB 623, [1964] 3 All ER 546, CA.
16 *Lansing Linde Ltd v Kerr* [1991] ICR 428, [1991] IRLR 80, CA.
17 *Littlewoods Organisation Ltd v Harris* [1978] 1 All ER 1026, [1977] 1 WLR 1472, CA.

cutting edge and what is merely the (expert) employee's own knowledge, or indeed general knowledge in such a rapidly developing field.[18] The second point is that the phrase 'customer connections' is even more intangible; naturally, an employee in constant touch with customers may in certain circumstances attract a personal following, be they a solicitor's clerk[19], estate agent[20], bookmaker's assistant[1], or milkman[2]; sales representatives and canvassers might well be subject to valid restraints. Every case will depend heavily upon the facts, and in essence what must be shown is that there is a *real* possibility of *misuse* of the employee's knowledge of customers; if this is missing, for example because the employee's contact with the customers was insufficiently direct or influential, the restraint will be void[3]. However, once this elusive element is established, it may well be reasonable to restrain the ex-employee from soliciting not only his particular customers at the date of termination of employment, but also any other persons who were the employer's customers at any other time during the period of employment or some specified part thereof[4], though it will not generally be reasonable to restrain solicitation of persons who might become the employer's customers at some time after termination[5], as for example by a clause restraining a commercial traveller from soliciting anyone in the relevant trade in the area in which he used to travel for the employer, not limiting it to those who were the employer's customers, or from whom he had attempted to solicit custom for the employer[6]. The third point is that if the restraint clause cannot fairly be said to protect a trade secret or customer connection, the longstanding view has been that it should be void on the basis that it concerns no protectable interest known to the law, unless the court is to establish a new one. In *Kores Manufacturing Co v Kolok Manufacturing Co*[7], two neighbouring employers producing similar goods agreed that neither would employ anyone who had been employed by the other within the previous five years. As this mainly concerned labourers there was no question of trade secrets or customer connections, and the sole purpose of the agreement was to encourage a stable labour supply. The Court of Appeal held it to be void on the ground that it was, on its facts, unreasonable as between the parties[8], but it is submitted that conceptually the prime reason for invalidity should have been that it concerned no known protectable interest, and there are dicta in the judgment in support of this. This has, however, caused recent controversy and a change in the law, at least partially, because of moves by employers to prevent solicitation by leaving employees of *other employees*, especially in highly

---

18   *FSS Travel and Leisure Systems Ltd v Johnson* [1998] IRLR 382, CA.
19   *Fitch v Dewes* [1921] 2 AC 158, HL.
20   *Scorer v Seymour-Johns* [1966] 3 All ER 347, [1966] 1 WLR 1419, CA.
1   *S W Strange Ltd v Mann* [1965] 1 All ER 1069, [1965] 1 WLR 629.
2   *Home Counties Dairies Ltd v Skilton* [1970] 1 All ER 1227, [1970] 1 WLR 526, CA; *Dairy Crest Ltd v Pigott* [1989] ICR 92, CA.
3   *Bowler v Lovegrove* [1921] 1 Ch 642; *S W Strange Ltd v Mann* [1965] 1 All ER 1069, [1965] 1 WLR 629.
4   *G W Plowman & Son Ltd v Ash* [1964] 2 All ER 10, [1964] 1 WLR 568, CA, applied in *Home Counties Dairies Ltd v Skilton* [1970] 1 All ER 1227, [1970] 1 WLR 526, CA; *John Michael Design plc v Cooke* [1987] 2 All ER 332, [1987] ICR 445, CA.
5   *Konski v Peet* [1915] 1 Ch 530.
6   *Gledhow Autoparts Ltd v Delaney* [1965] 3 All ER 288, [1965] 1 WLR 1366, CA.
7   [1959] Ch 108, [1958] 2 All ER 65, CA.
8   This case is expressly mentioned by Lord Reid and Lord Hodson in *Esso Petroleum Ltd v Harper's Garage (Stourport) Ltd* [1968] AC 269, [1967] 1 All ER 699, HL as one which should have been decided on the other limb of the *Nordenfelt* test, public interest. It is interesting to note that the agreement was between employers; the existence of such contracts is difficult to discover.

competitive areas such as the City and/or in the case of highly marketable executives. At first, the traditional view was taken that such anti-solicitation clauses were not permitted. In *Hanover Insurance Bros Ltd v Schapiro*[9] certain standard clauses preventing solicitation of customers were enforced against the company's departing chairman and managing director, but a clause stating that they would not, within one year of leaving, solicit any *employees* to join them in their new venture was held to be unenforceable, the court giving its opinion that staff preservation was not a protectable interest. However, that was swiftly followed by an unreported Court of Appeal case, *Ingham v ABC Contract Services Ltd*[10] in which it was held that an employer does have a 'legitimate interest in maintaining a stable trained workforce in what is acknowledged to be a highly competitive business'. In the light of this, an injunction was granted in *Alliance Paper Group Ltd v Prestwich*[11] by a Chancery judge to enforce a covenant not to entice away certain employees, on the basis that the remarks on protectable interests in *Hanover* were obiter (the actual decision having been that the clause was too wide in any event), and that it was *Ingham* that was to be followed on this point. Likewise, when it went before the Court of Appeal again in *Dawnay, Day & Co Ltd v De Braconier d'Alphen*[12], where three Eurobond dealers broke away from their employer to join a similar competing venture, the court upheld the decision of Walker J to enforce (inter alia) covenants prohibiting for one year solicitation of certain other employees, again expressly on the basis of the employer's interest in maintaining a stable, trained workforce, within the bounds of reasonableness. Thus, this form of staff retention may now be seen as joining trade secrets and customer connections as a third protectable interest *but* with limits. It does not necessarily mean that *Koves v Kolok* is wrong, and simple attempts to stabilise non-key and non-specialist staff (i.e. just for administrative convenience) may still not be valid. The cases so far have concerned the solicitation of *senior* staff, in highly competitive industries subject to high turnover and 'head-hunting' of people with instantly marketable skills and knowledge.[13] It is possible that this legal development is confined to such cases, though with two caveats – there could also be arguments for a valid protectable interest in relation to a more junior employee if (i) that person, though junior, is a key employee in terms of skills, e.g. in computer technology,[14] or (ii) that person is a member of a whole *team* being enticed away by the departing employee.

iv)   The extent of the restraint

Once there is a legally protectable interest, the question which then arises concerns the extent to which the employer can bind the employee's future

9   [1994] IRLR 82, CA.
10   93/6609/F, CA.
11   [1996] IRLR 25.
12   [1997] IRLR 442, CA. This case was also notable for deciding that a joint venture had sufficient interest to protect. For extensive discussion of these cases, see *TSC Europe (UK) Ltd v Massey* [1999] IRLR 22.
13   In *Alliance Paper Group* the restraint related to company employees 'in a senior capacity' and in *Dawnay, Day* to directors or senior employees; in each case the court held that such phrasing was sufficiently precise to be enforceable, on the elephant principle, i.e. that you cannot define it but you know one when you see it. By contrast, in *Hanover* a non-solicitation clause applying to 'any employees' was too wide.
14   Readers of Joseph Heller's *Catch 22* will know that the whole Mediterranean theatre of war was in fact run by Ex-PFC Wintergreen, not the general staff.

conduct in order to protect that interest. Cases on this are as infinitely variable as are the facts upon which they are based, but certain important factors can be discerned. The terms of the restraint must be no more than is reasonably necessary to give the employer adequate protection[15], and in approaching this the court might first look at the type of business concerned to see how much protection it warrants[16]; in this context it might be significant if the business is either specialised in its product or service or localised in its area of operation. The position of the employee is also a matter for consideration. The closer his contacts with customers or prospective customers the easier it will be to justify a restraint[17]. Similarly the higher the employee is in the hierarchy of employees the easier it will be. Thus in *M and S Drapers v Reynolds*[18] where the restraint was imposed on a collector salesman, the court rejected the analogy with a managing director based on *Gilford Motor Co v Horne*[19] and held that in the light of its particular circumstances the restraint was unreasonable. It is nothing more than a question of fact for again, in *G W Plowman & Son Ltd v Ash*[20], a restraint on a sales representative was accepted as valid.

Given that the business merits some protection from an employee such as the one in question, the major factual problem is how wide the terms of the restraint may be in terms of geographical area and duration of time. There are no rules of law here; a 25-year world-wide restraint was valid in the context of the international armaments trade in the *Nordenfelt* case[1]; but a one-year restraint was held to be void in the context of the plastics industry in *Commercial Plastics Ltd v Vincent*[2] partly on the ground that it was unlimited in area. The only general rule is that the two factors of geographical area and duration of time tend to be complementary, in that the wider the geographical area, the shorter the period of time that might be considered reasonable, and vice versa as in *Fitch v Dewes*[3]

---

15   *Herbert Morris Ltd v Saxelby* [1916] 1 AC 688, HL; the longstanding test was reaffirmed by Millett J in *Allied Dunbar (Frank Weisinger) Ltd v Weisinger* [1988] IRLR 60, where he disapproved an attempt to replace it with a more flexible concept of 'proportionality' between the extent of the restraint and the benefit of the employer. For a good factual example, see *Scully UK Ltd v Lee* [1998] IRLR 259, CA.
16   The business in question must be that in which the employer is actually engaged, and not one in which he might be interested at some future date: *Bromley v Smith* [1909] 2 KB 235; however, it may be valid for the employer to protect the business carried out by its subsidiaries, provided the restraint does not go wider than that and apply to activities not covered by the group: *Stenhouse Australia Ltd v Phillips* [1974] AC 391, [1974] 1 All ER 117, PC at 404 and 125 respectively.
17   It was felt in *S W Strange Ltd v Mann* [1965] 1 All ER 1069, [1965] 1 WLR 629, that a bookmaker's clerk built up no real contact with clients as business was largely conducted on the telephone.
18   [1956] 3 All ER 814, [1957] 1 WLR 9, CA.
19   [1933] Ch 935, CA.
20   [1964] 2 All ER 10, [1964] 1 WLR 568, CA.
1   See also the permanent, worldwide restraint on a servant of the royal household, preventing disclosure of any personal information on the royal family in *A-G v Barker* [1990] 3 All ER 257, CA.
2   [1965] 1 QB 623, [1964] 3 All ER 546, CA; other grounds of invalidity were that the clause covered work in the whole field of PVC not just that part which was secret, and it applied to any employment not just research. On the importance of geographical area, see also *Greer v Sketchley Ltd* [1979] IRLR 445, CA, and *Marley Tile Co Ltd v Johnson* [1982] IRLR 75, CA. A longer period is more likely to be reasonable in the case of a non-solicitation of customers' clause than a non-competition clause: *Dentmaster (UK) Ltd v Kent* [1997] IRLR 636, CA (citing *Office Angels Ltd v Rainer-Thomas and O'Connor* [1991] IRLR 214, CA). The judgment of Slade LJ in *Office Angels* is now often cited as a good summary of the basic law.
3   [1921] 2 AC 158, HL.

where a restraint that a solicitor's clerk in Tamworth would *never* practice as such within seven miles of Tamworth Town Hall upon ceasing the employment was held to be valid in the light of the restricted area. Further than this, all that can be said is that the drafting of a restraint clause may require a delicate balance in order to protect the lawful interests of the employer whilst at the same time achieving no more protection than is reasonably necessary for that purpose in all the circumstances. After warning of the dangers of 'home-made' restraint clauses, Pearson LJ said in *Commercial Plastics v Vincent*[4]:

> 'It would seem that a good deal of legal "know-how" is required for the successful drafting of a restraint clause.'

v) Enforcement

In looking to see if a restraint agreement is valid and enforceable, the court is entitled to look at the realities and effect of any stipulation so that, for example, an employer may not disguise a restraint clause by providing that the employee is at liberty to solicit any customers but must pay a premium or commission for any of the employer's customers solicited[5]. Moreover, this point is reinforced by the fact that restraint of trade as a doctrine is not confined to bilateral contracts involving the party concerned[6], and for present purposes the significance of this is that two or more employers cannot evade the doctrine by agreeing between themselves to do that which if done between each one of them and his employees would be void. The facts of *Kores v Kolok*[7] are set out above under heading (iii); the indirect restraint there, which would clearly have been invalid if put directly into the contracts of employment of the individual employees affected, was held to be void, thus increasing the legal protection given to the employee. However, the question then arose whether the employee could himself challenge such an agreement, for the agreement in *Kores v Kolok* had in fact lasted for 23 years and was only finally challenged because one of the parties became dissatisfied with it. In *Eastham v Newcastle United Football Club Ltd*[8], a case concerning the 'retain and transfer' system whereby the restrictive agreement between the club and the Football Association and League could have a major effect on the livelihood of the individual players, Wilberforce J held that the individual does in fact have the right to challenge such an agreement even though he is not a party to it, and this was accepted as correct by Lord Upjohn in *Pharmaceutical Society of Great Britain v Dickson*[9].

If the restraint clause is void, it cannot be enforced by the employer, but there are two ways in which a court might be able to save a clause even if it is prima facie void. The first is that, although such a clause must normally be construed strictly, it may be the case that the potential invalidity arises from an ambiguity in the wording which, read one way, could mean that the restraint is too wide; if however, it is possible to read the clause realistically in the sense in which the parties

4   At 647 and 555 respectively; though cf. the possible qualification in section (v) post.
5   *Stenhouse Australia Ltd v Phillips* [1974] AC 391, [1974] 1 All ER 117, PC.
6   See e.g., *Nagle v Feilden* [1966] 2 QB 633, [1966] 1 All ER 689, CA, and *Edwards v SOGAT* [1971] Ch 354, [1970] 3 All ER 689, CA.
7   [1959] Ch 108, [1958] 2 All ER 65, CA; see also *Mineral Water Bottle Exchange and Trade Protection Society v Booth* (1887) 36 Ch D 465, CA.
8   [1964] Ch 413, [1963] 3 All ER 139, HC of A.
9   [1970] AC 403 at 433, [1968] 2 All ER 686 at 701, HL.

obviously meant it, and in that sense it is valid, the court may feel able so to validate it. In *Home Counties Dairies Ltd v Skilton*[10] the agreement was not to 'serve or sell milk or dairy products' and it was pointed out that taken literally this could stop the ex-employee from working in a grocer's shop as well as in the capacity of milkman, and was therefore void for being too wide, but the Court of Appeal held that the true meaning, in the light of the intention of the parties at the time of entering the agreement, was only to restrain future employment as a milkman, and as such the clause was valid. Likewise in *Marion White Ltd v Francis*[11] it was held that a clause restraining employment in the hairdressing business 'in any way' which could conceivably have prevented the ex-hairdresser from working as, for example, a receptionist or book-keeper, in fact was intended by the parties to refer only to actual hairdressing and as such was narrow enough to be valid. This power of construction was applied quite liberally by the majority of the Court of Appeal in *Littlewoods Organisation Ltd v Harris*[12] (in which Lord Denning MR suggested that the restraint clause in *Commercial Plastics Ltd v Vincent*[13] which the court had regretfully held to be too wide might have been validated in this way), but was treated much more circumspectly by a subsequent Court of Appeal in *J A Mont (UK) Ltd v Mills*[14] on the grounds that otherwise an employer would have little incentive to phrase covenants in appropriately restricted terms in the first place; clearly the matter is one of balance.

The second possible way to validate a potentially void clause is if the offending part may be severed, leaving the valid remainder capable of enforcement. The concept of severance is a difficult one best dealt with in detail elsewhere[15]. Suffice it to say that where a contract in restraint of trade contains some stipulations which are void and some which by themselves would be valid, it may be possible to sever the void ones and enforce the valid ones. However, the court will not rewrite the contract, and may only be prepared to sever where each stipulation is distinct in itself. In *Mason v Provident Clothing and Supply Co Ltd*[16] Lord Moulton said:

> 'It would in my opinion be pessimi exempli if when an employer had exacted a covenant deliberately framed in unreasonably wide terms, the courts were to come to his assistance and by applying their ingenuity and knowledge of the law, carve out of this void covenant the maximum of what he might validly have required.'

From this it has been argued that the courts should be less willing to sever in an employer-employee restraint case, but any such general principle was disapproved by the Court of Appeal in *T Lucas & Co Ltd v Mitchell*[17] where severance of words within a clause was allowed and the valid part of the restraint enforced.

10   [1970] 1 All ER 1227, [1970] 1 WLR 526, CA.
11   [1972] 3 All ER 857, [1972] 1 WLR 1423, CA.
12   [1978] 1 All ER 1026, CA.
13   [1965] 1 QB 623, [1964] 3 All ER 546, CA.
14   [1993] IRLR 172, CA.
15   Contrast *Attwood v Lamont* [1920] 3 KB 571, CA with *Goldsoll v Goldman* [1915] 1 Ch 292, CA.
16   [1913] AC 724 at 745, HL.
17   [1974] Ch 129, [1972] 3 All ER 689, CA; see also *Sadler v Imperial Life Assurance Co of Canada Ltd* [1988] IRLR 388 and *Scully UK Ltd v Lee* [1998] IRLR 259, CA. Severance was allowed with little difficulty in *Stenhouse Australia Ltd v Phillips* [1974] AC 391, [1974] 1 All ER 117, PC, where the relevant stipulations were not only separate in content but also expressed in separate clauses in the agreement, and in *Hinton & Higgs (UK) Ltd v Murphy*

If the restraint clause is held to be valid (either generally or via one of the above validation methods) it may be enforced against the employee, subject to the caveat that if the employer is in fact in breach of the contract of employment, for example by wrongfully dismissing the employee, he loses the benefit of any restraint clauses contained in it[18]. Provided this is not so, the employer may sue the employee for damages (and indeed either party may seek a declaration on the validity of the clause in question)[19]; in practice, however, the real importance of the action to the employer is that he may seek an injunction to restrain the employee from acting in breach of the clause, and in an urgent case may be granted an interlocutory injunction (provided he can show that he will suffer immediate loss, so that the 'balance of advantage' lies in his favour, within the principles in *American Cyanamid Co v Ethicon Ltd*[20]). Normally the court will not grant an injunction to enforce a contract of employment on the basis that it is a personal contract not amenable to such enforcement[1]; one longstanding exception to this, however, is the rule in *Lumley v Wagner*[2] that the courts will enforce a valid negative restraint clause, provided that to do so will not have the

[1989] IRLR 519, Ct of Sess. where the contract itself contained a clause inviting severance if any particular restriction was held to be too wide, though the validity of the latter point was later doubted in *Living Design (Home Improvements) Ltd v Davidson* [1994] IRLR 69, Ct of Sess. In *Marshall v NM Financial Management Ltd* [1997] IRLR 449, CA severance was allowed at the request of the *employee* in order for him to rely on a linked clause in his favour.

18 *General Billposting Co v Atkinson* [1909] AC 118, HL; *Spafax Ltd v Harrison* [1980] IRLR 442, CA; *Rex Stewart Jeffries Parker Ginsberg Ltd v Parker* [1988] IRLR 483, CA; *Briggs v Oates* [1990] ICR 473, [1990] IRLR 473. In *Rock Refrigeration Ltd v Jones* [1997] 1 All ER 1 [1996] IRLR 675, the Court of Appeal held that this still applies even if the employer has stated that the clause is to apply on termination 'however caused'; possibly significantly there are dicta in the case that they only so held because *bound* by *General Billposting*, not because they agreed with the principle. One open question is whether it would apply to a dismissal which was not a breach of contract by the employer (i.e. with proper notice, therefore not wrongful) but which was later held to have been *unfair* by an industrial tribunal; from a strictly contractual view, unfairness under the statute would have no effect on the restrictive covenants which would remain enforceable by the employer against the unfairly dismissed employee. It might be thought equally unjust that a (probably fair) dismissal for *redundancy* does not terminate a restraint clause, for here by definition the employer has no further need for the employee's skills, but the latter could still be restrained from using them to earn his living.

19 Even if the period of restraint is already over, provided the applicant can prove that he still has a worthwhile interest in pursuing it (e.g. where an employer has other employees who are subject to the same clause): *Marion White Ltd v Francis* [1972] 3 All ER 857, [1972] 1 WLR 1423, CA.

20 [1975] AC 396, [1975] 1 All ER 504, HL; there was disagreement in the Court of Appeal as to whether these principles apply to a restraint of trade case in *Fellowes & Son v Fisher* [1976] QB 122, [1975] 2 All ER 829, CA, the majority applying the 'balance of convenience' principle and Lord Denning MR declaring that the case came within an exception to the new rules, whereby the court could apply the old principles and look at the relative strength of each party's case; in *Lawrence David Ltd v Ashton* [1991] 1 All ER 385, [1989] ICR 123 the Court of Appeal affirmed that *American Cyanamid* normally does apply to restraint cases, but in *Lansing Linde Ltd v Kerr* [1991] ICR 428, [1991] IRLR 80, CA, an exception was established where full trial is not likely to occur quickly enough. The requirement of showing real harm (not just breach of a reasonable restraint) where the application is interlocutory was stressed by Lord Johnston in *Jack Allen (Sales & Service) Ltd v Smith* [1999] IRLR 19, OH.

1   *Whitwood Chemical Co v Hardman* [1891] 2 Ch 416; CA; cf. *Hill v CA Parsons & Co Ltd* [1972] Ch 305, [1971] 3 All ER 1345, CA. Section 236 of the Trade Union and Labour Relations (Consolidation) Act 1992 provides that no injunction may be granted compelling an employee to work. See ch. 7 on remedies for wrongful dismissal.

2   (1852) 1 De GM & G 604, 42 ER 687; see also *Warner Bros Pictures Inc v Nelson* [1937] 1 KB 209.

effect of specifically enforcing the actual contract. This will normally mean that an injunction *will* lie for breach of a restraint clause[3], but in an untypical case an injunction could be refused as in *Page One Records Ltd v Britton*[4] where the dismissed manager of a pop group, The Troggs, sought to enforce a clause in their agreement that they would not engage any other person or firm as manager during a five-year period and would not act as such themselves; Stamp J held that, as they had to have a manager in order to operate, to enforce the clause would be to force them to employ him, and so no injunction could be granted.

It can be seen from this discussion that restraint clauses are not simple, either in their framing or in their enforcement, especially as they tend to operate on an 'all or nothing' basis. It is probably this that has led to the search for other, more reliable, ways to safeguard the employer's confidences when an employee leaves the employment. One way currently attracting interest is the 'garden leave' clause, which operates on the basis of a very long notice requirement, during which the employee is paid in full (even though not actually working), but with an express obligation on the employee not to work for anyone else during the notice period. Such clauses may be more certain (though more expensive) than restraint clauses and are considered at p. 372, below.

5 TERMS OF THE CONTRACT OF EMPLOYMENT

i) Express terms

While the employer and employee are generally free to determine the content of the terms of employment, there are now legislative provisions in Part I of the Employment Rights Act 1996 requiring the employer to give written notice of certain basic terms. These provisions were considered above in head 3 of this chapter, where it was seen that while this notice does not itself constitute the contract it will be strong evidence as to its terms and indeed if it is signed by the employee it may be construed as the written contract, according to *Gascol Conversions Ltd v Mercer*[5]. For present purposes, the importance of these provisions is that they require that major terms be put down in writing and probably encourage the employer to give the employee an individual written contract of employment; as with all contracts, written terms are generally to be preferred for the certainty that they bring[6], and the legislation attempts to minimise the incidence of 'factory gate employment' where an employee was taken on without having the relevant terms settled, leaving potentially important matters to later decision by the courts. Certainty, however, can work both ways, and if the parties set something down in

---

3   Normally damages will not be considered a sufficient remedy instead; likewise, an injunction should not normally be refused on the ground that the defendant is willing to undertake not to use the trade secrets, etc. until final judgment: *Johnson & Bloy (Holdings) Ltd v Wolstenholme Rink plc* [1987] IRLR 499, CA (a case on the duty of confidentiality generally, but the principles should apply to a restraint of trade clause case).

4   [1967] 3 All ER 822, [1968] 1 WLR 157; *Warren v Mendy* [1989] ICR 525, [1989] IRLR 210, CA.

5   [1974] ICR 420, [1974] IRLR 155, CA; see p. 85, above.

6   For a particularly salutary example, see *Stubbes v Trower, Still & Keeling* [1987] IRLR 321, CA where solicitors, in offering articles, omitted to state expressly that the applicant had to pass the requisite examinations before beginning, and the Court of Appeal refused to find that there was an implied term to that effect on the facts; in the words of one commentator, you cannot always rely on common sense and implied terms to rectify a contractual oversight.

writing they should ensure that it is accurate, for once it is expressed there is less room for further extrinsic evidence as to their intentions. As an example of this, in *Nelson v BBC*[7] the contract stated that the employee could be required to work when and where the corporation demanded, but when the corporation closed down the Caribbean service in which he worked, they claimed that it was to be implied that he was only employed for the purposes of that one service and therefore that he was redundant; the tribunal and the EAT accepted this, but the Court of Appeal rejected it, since the express term was in unrestricted language, and as a basic principle of contract law it was impossible to imply a restriction of the kind that the tribunal had found. On the other hand, even in contract law there are exceptions to the rule against extrinsic evidence, particularly where a written contract does not completely cover all the matters upon which the parties had previously agreed. Thus, in *Tayside Regional Council v McIntosh*[8] a job advertisement for a vehicle mechanic stated that a clean driving licence was essential and this was restated at interview. When later the employee lost his licence and was dismissed, he pointed to the fact the written terms which he had been given upon appointment made no mention of a driving licence, but the Scottish EAT refused to accept that that meant there was no express term as to a licence. The basic distinction between these two case examples (out of many) is that in the latter extrinsic evidence was being properly used to amplify a written agreement which was incomplete, whereas in the former it was being used improperly to alter the meaning of an existing written term.

Two current uncertainties relating to express terms of contracts of employment are worth mentioning at this stage. The first is whether there is any requirement that an express contractual right for an employer (however clearly expressed) must be *exercised* reasonably. The traditional view is that there can be no such requirement; a contract is a contract, and if the employee agrees a term he must abide by it, even if its application by the employer seems harsh (e.g. where an employer activates an unrestricted mobility clause to require an employee to move hundreds of miles with little or no warning)[9]. However, recent case law has suggested a significant modification of that position and this is considered below at p. 109; if this trend continues, it will be of major importance and marks another departure of contracts of employment from orthodox contract law.

The second uncertainty concerns the extent to which an employer may use express terms to reserve to himself a right of unilateral variation. Flexibility in employment has been a nostrum of modern managerialism for some time now, and there will certainly be cases where an employer can lawfully claim to have carefully built in flexibility and an ability to change a particular term or, alternatively, that the matter has been so drafted as to remain non-contractual (so that change remains in the employer's discretion[10]). The question is whether a point could be reached where such phrasing became so unconscionable and vague as to be unenforceable; the contractual doctrine of uncertainty would be inappropriate in an employment context because it would render the whole contract void (to the employee's disadvantage), and so far this point has not had to be explored by

---

7   [1977] ICR 649, [1977] IRLR 148, CA; see the discussion of this case in *Cowen v Haden Ltd* [1983] ICR 1, [1982] IRLR 314, CA which shows the importance of the proper construction to be placed upon the express term in question.

8   [1982] IRLR 272.

9   *Rank Xerox Ltd v Churchill* [1988] IRLR 280.

10   *Airlie v City of Edinburgh District Council* [1996] IRLR 516, EAT (terms of a bonus scheme expressly subject to variation by employer after consultation with the workforce; no requirement of agreement before revision, provided consultation carried out).

the courts. The nearest that they have come is in *Wandsworth London Borough Council v D'Silva*[11] where, after upholding the employer's contention that a sickness absence policy in a code of practice remained non-contractual and so within the employer's power to change, Lord Woolf MR said obiter that, although a party to the contract could reserve a right of unilateral variation, it would take clear language to do it and a court should, in construing the contract, try to avoid a construction allowing a power of unilateral variation of significant employee rights which could produce an unreasonable result. Whether a court could go further in the case of an absolutely clearly drafted power of unilateral variation that was equally clearly inequitable in its result remains to be seen.

ii) The implication of terms

a) The process of implication

Even when the statutory provisions for written particulars are complied with, there will be areas left in a contract of employment where no terms are expressed, so that if a dispute arises in one of these areas the court or tribunal may have to have recourse to implied terms. The implication of terms is a concept of application to the whole law of contract, but in the context of employment it has evolved along more specialised lines. Starting from orthodox contract theory[12], the basis of implication is subjective, in that the court or tribunal should look at the likely intention of the parties at the time of contracting, and should not imply terms simply because they appear (objectively) reasonable when the case is viewed in hindsight[13]. The two classic tests for an implied term are (i) that it is necessary to give 'business efficacy' to the transaction as must have been intended by both parties[14], or (ii) that it is so obvious that it goes without saying, so that if an officious bystander had suggested that it be expressed the parties would have testily suppressed him with a common 'Oh, of course!'[15]. Moreover, it has been clearly stated that the presumption is against the adding to contracts of terms which the parties have not expressed, particularly if the term in question is of a novel nature[16]. This traditional view of implied terms has, however, been considerably modified in the case of contracts of employment where, particularly before the Contracts of Employment Act 1963, so many terms (often the basic ones) were not expressed and where the process of implication has been much used to fill in the details once it was clear that an employment relationship existed[17]. It has been modified in three main ways:

11 [1998] IRLR 193, CA.
12 See generally Cheshire, Fifoot and Furmston (13th edn, 1996) ch. 6.
13 *Reigate v Union Manufacturing Co (Ramsbottom) Ltd* [1918] 1 KB 592, CA at 605, per Scrutton LJ.
14 *The Moorcock* (1889) 14 PD 64, CA at 68 per Bowen LJ.
15 *Shirlaw v Southern Foundries Ltd* [1939] 2 KB 206, CA at 227 per McKinnon LJ; see *Spring v National Amalgamated Stevedores and Dockers Society* [1956] 2 All ER 221, [1956] 1 WLR 585.
16 *Luxor (Eastbourne) Ltd v Cooper* [1941] AC 108, HL at 137 per Lord Wright.
17 Certainty of terms is classically a prerequisite for a binding contract, but this too has been qualified almost to the point of extinction in contracts of employment; see *Powell v Braun* [1954] 1 All ER 484, [1954] 1 WLR 401, CA and *National Coal Board v Galley* [1958] 1 All ER 91, [1958] 1 WLR 16, CA. The problem is that the result of applying it would be to make the whole contract of employment void (regardless of how long the employee had actually been working for the employer), which is simply not an option in employment law.

1) *Inferred terms*   Although cases will of course arise where courts find implied terms on the above traditional grounds[18], there are also cases where they appear to have been more willing to imply terms because they appear reasonable in all the circumstances, rather than because of the supposed subjective intention of the parties, which, in the reality of a vague hiring, may have been non-existent. There is still a large role for the genuine factual implied term but in this context the court or tribunal may feel more ready to imply, or, more accurately perhaps, infer, a term because it seems reasonable in all the circumstances. This more objective approach can clearly be seen in the reasoning of the Court of Appeal in *Mears v Safecar Security Ltd*[19]. The case primarily concerns a complaint of failure to give the obligatory written statement of terms of employment, and the question of whether wages are to be paid during sickness[20], but (although certain rather extreme dicta that ultimately a tribunal may have to 'invent' a term were later disapproved[1]) it also contains important guidance on the implication of terms into contracts of employment, showing that in the case of such contracts the normal concepts of implied intention of the parties and business efficacy may have little part to play. Instead, a tribunal may have to take a broader approach and be ready to insert a reasonable term based on all the evidence of the relationship between the parties *and* what had happened in practice *since* the employment began (particularly where it is important that *some* term be included, e.g. whether or not such pay is payable, or where the employee could be made to work[2]). It is true that this case arose under the Employment Rights Act 1996, s. 11, and much of what is said about implying terms is inextricably linked to the court's approach to the tribunal's powers to declare or amend terms of employment under that section, but it is submitted that their approach to the implication of terms should be applicable to a common law action as well as a statutory one – it would be ridiculous if different principles were to apply depending on which forum the employee happened to choose; after all, on the facts of the case, the employee could just as easily have gone to the county court and *claimed* sick pay. The same approach can be seen in the later decision of the Court of Appeal in *Courtaulds Northern Spinning Ltd v Sibson*[3] where, in the context of the necessary implication into a contract of employment of a location/mobility clause (where the contract was silent on the matter, but the question was vital for deciding a point on constructive dismissal) Slade LJ said:

'... [I]n cases such as the present where it is essential to imply some term into the contract of employment as to place of work, the court does not have to be satisfied that the parties, if asked, would in fact have agreed the term before entering into the contract. The court merely has to be satisfied that the implied term is one which the parties would probably have agreed *if they were being reasonable*'. (emphasis added)

---

18   See eg *Ali v Christian Salvesen Food Services Ltd* [1997] ICR 25, [1997] IRLR 17, CA, where the question was whether it was possible to imply a term into an 'annualised hours' contract as to what was to happen to an employee leaving part of the way through the year, the parties having failed to cover the point expressly. The EAT thought it was, but the Court of Appeal held to the contrary and the loss lay where it fell.

19   [1982] 2 All ER 865, [1982] IRLR 183, CA.

20   See pp. 89-90, above and p. 178, below.

1   *Eagland v British Telecommunications plc* [1993] ICR 644, [1992] IRLR 323, CA.

2   See the facts of *Jones v Associated Tunnelling Co Ltd* [1981] IRLR 477.

3   [1988] ICR 451, [1988] IRLR 305, CA; the dictum cited is at 460 and 309, respectively.

2) *Imposed terms* The contract of employment has long been surrounded not only by terms implied or inferred from the facts of any given employment, but also by a quite distinct form of 'implied term', namely the term which will be imposed by the law on to most or all contracts of employment simply because the relationship of employment exists (except in so far as the parties are free to exclude it expressly and do so), which once again has little to do with any supposed intention of the parties. In *Lister v Romford Ice and Cold Storage Co Ltd*[4] Viscount Simonds said that the question whether there was an implied term that the employer would ensure that the employee was insured had little to do with the facts of a particular contract or any question of business efficacy, but depended instead on more general considerations relating to the very nature of contracts of employment. This approach is clearly seen in the following two dicta. In *Sterling Engineering Co Ltd v Patchett*[5] Lord Reid said:

'There are cases in which it has been said that the employer's right to inventions made by an employee in the course of his employment arises from an implied term in the contract of employment. Strictly speaking, I think that an implied term is something which, in the circumstances of a particular case, the law may read into the contract if the parties are silent, and it would be reasonable to do so; it is something over and above the ordinary incidents of the particular type of contract. If it were necessary in this case to find an implied term in that sense I should be in some difficulty. But the phrase "implied term" can be used to denote a term inherent in the nature of the contract which the Law will imply in every case unless the parties agree to vary or exclude it.'

In *Scally v Southern Health and Social Services Board*[6] Lord Bridge referred to the clear distinction between

'... the search for an implied term necessary to give business efficacy to a particular contract and the search, based on wider considerations, for a term which the law will imply as a necessary incident of a definable category of contractual relationship'.

In *Malik v BCCI SA (in liquidation)*[7] Lord Steyn referred to such terms as 'default rules' which are standardised terms which are incidents of all contracts of employment.

It is this form of 'implied term' that will be discussed below under the headings of Employer's Duties and Employee's Duties, and it could well be argued that the phrase 'implied term' should be discarded, and these duties viewed simply as incidents of the Law of Employment.

3) *Overriding terms* One of the most interesting recent developments in this area is the possible development of the concept of 'overriding terms' in a contract of employment, i.e. that certain terms may be so important that they will be applied

4   [1957] AC 555, [1957] 1 All ER 125, HL.
5   [1955] AC 534 at 547, [1955] 1 All ER 369 at 376, HL.
6   [1991] ICR 771, [1991] IRLR 522, HL; the decision in this case is considered at p. 127, below.
7   [1997] ICR 606, [1997] IRLR 462, HL; the decision in this case is considered at p. 125, below.

by the courts irrespective of the parties' intentions[8]. This would have the radical effect that they could even be used to qualify or attack clear express terms of the contract, something that in orthodox contract law no 'implied' term should be able to do. The prime candidate for beatification as an overriding term is the implied term of trust and respect[9] which, if applied widely, could be seen as having the effect that even where an employer has the contractual right to insist on something, he must do so *reasonably*. If not, the employee would be able to leave and claim constructive dismissal, through the employer's breach of that implied term. Perhaps the clearest example is an unrestricted mobility clause. Can the employer simply insist on the literal wording and require the employee to move his place of work from Norwich to Carlisle over a weekend and with no prior warning, or can the employee claim that that insistence (though technically within the employer's contractual power) is in breach of the term of trust and respect on the facts? Orthodox contract law is, of course, on the employer's side[10], but there have been developments. Where there is no express mobility clause and a court is having to imply one, there may be less problem in attaching implied conditions such as reasonable notice[11]. However, what may eventually prove to have been the crucial step was taken by the EAT in *United Bank Ltd v Akhtar*[12], where there was an express clause allowing the employer to move the employee to any branch in the UK. In spite of that, the EAT held that the employee could claim constructive dismissal when the employer ordered him to move from Leeds to Birmingham on only six days' notice and refused to grant his request for more time because of his personal circumstances. As well as finding an implied term of reasonable notice, the EAT held even more fundamentally that the employers' conduct in exercising their contractual rights was a fundamental breach of the implied term of trust and respect:

'... we take it as inherent that there may well be conduct which is either calculated or likely to destroy or seriously damage the relationship of trust and respect between employer and employee which a literal interpretation of the written words of the contract might appear to justify, and it is in this sense that we consider that in the field of employment law it is proper to imply an *overriding obligation* [of trust and respect] which is independent of, and in addition to, the literal interpretation of the actions which are permitted to the employer under the terms of the contract'[13]. (emphasis added)

8   This would mark them off from the above discussion of imposed terms, since the latter (as in the above dictum from Lord Reid) are conceived of applying 'unless the parties agree to vary or exclude them'; see also per Lord Steyn in *Malik v BCCI* (above). For an interesting argument that the courts should go even further and hold that the employment relationship gives rise to *fiduciary* duties (which could not be excluded), see Clarke 'Mutual trust and confidence, fiduciary relationships and the duty of disclosure (1999) 28 ILJ 348.

9   See p. 124, below.

10   This straightforward approach was applied as late as *Rank Xerox Ltd v Churchill* [1988] IRLR 280.

11   *Prestwick Circuits Ltd v McAndrew* [1990] IRLR 191, Ct of Sess.; however, the Court of Appeal had earlier declined to add any 'reasonable exercise' conditions to an implied mobility clause in *Courtaulds Northern Spinning Ltd v Sibson* [1988] IRLR 305, CA.

12   [1989] IRLR 507. See also *French v Barclays Bank plc* [1998] IRLR 646, CA where the termination of an interest free bridging loan to a relocated employee when it became too onerous was held to be in breach of the term of trust and respect, even though the granting of such a loan was clearly expressed to be discretionary.

13   At 512, per Knox J. There was an unreported tribunal decision in Cambridge in 1990 where an employee was dismissed for refusing to work 12 hours per day, seven days per week, for nine weeks; the employer had the power to require this under the strict terms

At first sight, the subsequent EAT decision in *White v Reflecting Roadstuds Ltd*[14] may appear to resile from *Akhtar*, for it was held that an employee who resigned after a transfer on to a lower-paid job which was permitted by the contract could not claim constructive dismissal. However, it is suggested that that was because the employee argued simply that a contractual right such as this must always be exercised reasonably; this was too much to accept and Wood P said that *Akhtar* does not establish any such sweeping principle. However, at the end of his judgment, he recognised that there was a problem with unconscionable action by an employer and offered the following solutions:

> 'As Knox J emphasised in *Akhtar* a purely "capricious" decision would not be within the express mobility clause. Likewise, in the present case if there were no reasonable or sufficient grounds for the view that Mr White required to be moved ... then there would be a breach of the clause. Secondly, it must be emphasised that as a result of the *Woods* decision[15] there is the *overriding implied term* as to the relationship of trust and respect between employer and employee and this is where communication is so important.'[16]
> (emphasis added)

The implication must therefore be that in a case such as this the employee may have a good argument if it is couched properly (in terms of the term of trust and respect, *not* simply as a general allegation of unreasonableness), and that *White* does not negate *Akhtar*.[17]

In addition to mobility and flexibility clauses, similar ideas of the use of the overriding term of trust and respect to qualify or restrain reliance by an employer on his strict contractual rights have been seen in relation to the imposition of disciplinary measures[18], the exercise of a power to suspend an employee[19] and (most strikingly of all) in the administration of employee pension funds[20].

The other principal candidate so far for an overriding term is the employer's obligation to take care for the employee's health and safety. The leading case, *Johnstone v Bloomsbury Health Authority*[1], shows very different approaches to the

---

of the contract, but the tribunal held that to do so was unreasonable, and the dismissal was unfair, on similar reasoning; see Earnshaw [1992] NLJ 1011.

14   [1991] ICR 733, [1991] IRLR 331.

15   I.e. *Woods v WM Car Services (Peterborough) Ltd* [1981] ICR 666, [1981] IRLR 347, the leading decision of Browne-Wilkinson P in the EAT on trust and respect; see p. 125 below.

16   At 742, 335.

17   In the unreported decision in *St Budeaux Royal British Legion Club v Cropper* (EAT 39/94) *Akhtar* was applied to hold that a flexibility clause applied in a 'high-handed and irresponsible manner' by the employer (when cutting hours) was a breach of the term of trust and respect.

18   The idea being that the exercise by an employer of his discretion under a disciplinary procedure must be subject to requirements of reasonableness and proportionality: *BBC v Beckett* [1983] IRLR 43; *Cawley v South Wales Electricity Board* [1985] IRLR 89.

19   *McClory v Post Office* [1992] ICR 758, [1993] IRLR 159. Previously, an express lay-off clause had been held to be subject to an implied limitation to a reasonable period in *Dakri & Co Ltd v Tiffen* [1981] ICR 256, [1981] IRLR 57, but a subsequent EAT had refused to follow this in *Kenneth MacRae Ltd v Dawson* [1984] IRLR 5.

20   *Imperial Group Pension Trust Ltd v Imperial Tobacco Ltd* [1991] ICR 524, [1991] IRLR 66 where Browne-Wilkinson V-C (applying his own previous decision in *Woods*, in n. 5 above) held that the black and white of pension fund deeds and rules should be impliedly subject to the limitation that they must be exercised in good faith and so as not to undermine the employees' trust and respect; see Nobles (1991) 20 ILJ 137.

1   [1991] ICR 269, [1991] IRLR 118, CA; see Dolding and Fawlk (1992) 55 MLR 562.

matter, which in turn shows well the conceptual difficulties yet to be addressed. This was the highly publicised case of the legal challenge to excessive hours by junior hospital doctors. The doctor plaintiff's contract stated a standard working week of 40 hours, but a further 48 hours on call, which was regularly required, sometimes up to 100 hours per week. He argued that this had a detrimental effect on his health[2] and was a breach of the employer's duty to take reasonable care for his health and safety. The proceedings in fact concerned an interlocutory application by the employers to have the claim struck out, as disclosing no cause of action. By a majority, the Court of Appeal allowed it to proceed. Leggett LJ, dissenting, applied orthodox contract law, stating that reliance on a clear express power could not make the employer in breach of an implied term (i.e. the traditional primacy of express terms; the doctor had signed the contract and must abide by its clear terms). The problem and fascination of the case is that the two majority judges differed in their reasoning. Browne-Wilkinson V-C took a middle path; he said that the extra 48 hours in question were an 'optional right' for the employers, not an absolute right and, while there must be no blatant conflict between an express term and an implied term, it was not improper to read in a term that, in exercising their *discretion* to call for further hours, the employers had to have regard to the employee's health and safety. However, possibly the more significant judgment for the future is that of Stuart-Smith LJ who held more simply that, although the contract gave the power to require work of up to 88 hours on average, that power had to be exercised subject to other contractual terms, in particular that relating to health and safety. The difference between the two majority judgments would be shown if a contract required a mandatory 88 hours, for Browne-Wilkinson V-C accepted that in that case that express term would have to be allowed to stand, whereas Stuart-Smith LJ would still have been prepared to make it subject to the requirement of health and safety[3].

b) Particular sources of terms

1) *Collective bargains* Although its use as the primary form of setting terms and conditions of employment has declined markedly in recent years[4], collective bargaining in the past was of central importance, and yet the precise legal effect of a collective bargain on the contracts of employment of employees potentially affected by it has always been a topic of some difficulty. The bargain is often classified as performing two functions – regulating the relationship between the bargainers, i.e. employers' association or employer and trade union, and settling

2   Let alone the prospects for a patient (treated in the hundredth hour) of a long and prosperous life.

3   The judge makes the significant point that even where the contract stipulates high hours, that still only gives the employer a *power* to call for them: 'There is no obligation to require the men to [work] for 88 hours in the week, and if by so doing he exposes him to foreseeable risk of injury he will be liable', at 277, 121.

4   'The decline in the extent of union recognition naturally fed through into a fall in the proportion of employees covered by collective bargaining. This had shrunk to 54 per cent in 1990 from 71 per cent six years earlier. As most employees outside the scope of the survey [ie. those employed by small firms] are almost certainly not covered, it is clear that only a minority of employees in the economy as a whole had their pay jointly determined by management and trade unions': Millward et al., 'Workplace industrial relations in transition' (the ED/ESRC/PSI/ACAS Survey) (1992) p. 102. We may be about to see at least some reversal of this trend under the statutory recognition procedure introduced by the Employment Relations Act 1999, see p. 54, above.

provisions (e.g. wage rates and hours) intended for the individual contracts of the employees who are covered. The collective bargain itself is generally not enforceable by the union or employer[5], and, as the individual is a third party not privy to the agreement, it will not generally be directly enforceable by an employee, particularly as the union is not viewed as acting as the employee's agent during negotiations[6]; in *Burton Group Ltd v Smith*[7] the EAT considered that any agency relationship must be capable of inference from the particular facts of the case and does not arise merely from the relationship of union and member. Thus, the employee will only be legally entitled to any parts of a collective bargain which in some way became terms of his individual contract of employment[8].

A term may be incorporated into a contract of employment from a collective bargain either expressly or impliedly. Express implication may come through the parties agreeing in writing that all or part of a particular collective bargain shall be binding upon them, as in *National Coal Board v Galley*[9]. In the past, this fitted in with the statutory requirements for written particulars in Part I of the Employment Rights Act 1996 (see above, under 'Form') which allowed the employer to refer the employee to some other document which the employee has reasonable opportunities of reading, and this 'other document' could well be the relevant parts of the current collective bargain. There may now be less scope for this approach, because the amendments to Part I by the Trade Union Reform and Employment Rights Act 1993 restrict the employer's right to refer to other documents (except in relation to sickness, pensions, and disciplinary notice guidance procedures); on the other hand, there is added to the list of matters to be notified in writing 'any collective agreements which directly affect the terms and conditions of the employment', which could be significant in any argument for the incorporation of terms other than those which now have to be given individually.

In *Marley v Forward Trust Group Ltd*[10] the EAT caused a considerable stir by holding that where a collective bargain was expressed to be binding in honour only, a contractual term purporting to incorporate a provision from the bargain was itself therefore of no legal effect; fortunately, this startling decision was quickly reversed by the Court of Appeal and orthodoxy re-established. However, some care may be needed with this form of incorporation (where it is still viable), for reference to a particular aspect of a collective bargain (e.g. sickness) does not necessarily incorporate other aspects of it (e.g. the right to lay off employees) which may need specific incorporation[11], and indeed the parties must be clear which particular collective agreement they are wishing to incorporate, which may not be as simple as it sounds where either there has been a series of agreements over a period of time or where there is, at any one time, more than

5   *Ford Motor Co Ltd v AUEFW* [1969] 2 QB 303, [1969] 2 All ER 481 (see Selwyn (1969) 32 MLR 377); Trade Union and Labour Relations (Consolidation) Act 1992, s. 179; see ch. 1, above; *National Coal Board v National Union of Mineworkers* [1986] ICR 736, [1986] IRLR 439.

6   *Holland v London Society of Compositors* (1924) 40 TLR 440; cf. *Edwards v Skyways Ltd* [1964] 1 All ER 494, [1964] 1 WLR 349.

7   [1977] IRLR 351.

8   *Hulland v William Sanders & Sons* [1945] KB 78, [1944] 2 All ER 568, CA.

9   [1958] 1 All ER 91, [1958] 1 WLR 16, CA.

10   [1986] ICR 115, [1986] IRLR 43, EAT; revsd [1986] ICR 891, [1986] IRLR 369, CA, applying *Robertson and Jackson v British Gas Corpn*, n. 4, below.

11   *Jewell v Neptune Concrete Ltd* [1975] IRLR 147, IT; *Cadoux v Central Regional Council* [1986] IRLR 131, Ct of Sess.; *Alexander v Standard Telephones and Cables Ltd (No 2)* [1991] IRLR 286.

one agreement possibly applicable; the latter possibility could well arise where there is both national and local bargaining within an industry, or where there has been a tendency over time to move the emphasis from national to local bargaining[12]. Moreover, in *Burroughs Machines Ltd v Timmoney*[13] the Court of Session, reversing the EAT, treated a contractual reference to a particular clause in a collective bargain as an independent term of the contract which merely relied on the clause for its exposition and definition, so that the employees continue to be bound by part of the clause that allowed the employer to lay them off in certain relevant circumstances, even though the employer had in fact left the employers' federation which was a party to the collective bargain. In this case the principle of the independent effect of a collective bargain term once incorporated worked to the employee's disadvantage. However, it is equally likely (if not more so) to work to the employer's disadvantage as can be seen from *Robertson and Jackson v British Gas Corpn*[14] where the Court of Appeal held that employees could still claim a bonus which had been incorporated into their contracts even though the collective agreement whence it had originally come had been unilaterally abrogated by the employer. The lesson is clear for an employer wishing to resile from the terms of a collective agreement – it may not be enough just to abrogate the agreement if in fact some of its provisions have been incorporated into individual contracts of employment; he may have to go further and show that those contracts have themselves also been varied (which will principally mean by consent, see p. 90, above) to exclude or amend the terms in question.

In the absence of express reference, a tribunal or court may be asked to incorporate a term of a collective bargain by implication, and this may raise difficulties, for if one thing is certain it is that implication is by no means automatic. On a structural level, it cannot be argued that an agreement is incorporated simply because the employer belongs to an employers' association that bargained for that agreement[15]. Further, it must be remembered that vague reliance upon implied terms from collective bargains (whether national or local) cannot oust or qualify clear express terms of a contract of employment covering the matters in question[16]. In *Young v Canadian Northern Rly Co*[17] an employee sued the company for wrongful dismissal on the basis that his dismissal for redundancy was not in accordance with the agreed seniority provisions in a collective bargain; he was not a member of the union, but claimed that the company's practice was to observe the terms of the agreement and apply them to all employees, whether or not members of the union. The Privy Council held for the company, refusing to incorporate the necessary collective terms into his contract of employment. They

---

12 This problem can be seen on the facts of *Gascol Conversions Ltd v Mercer* [1974] ICR 420, [1974] IRLR 155, CA (see p. 85, above). Site level bargaining was taken into account by the EAT in holding a site bonus to be contractually binding in *Donelan v Kerrby Constructions Ltd* [1983] ICR 237, [1983] IRLR 191, noted Freedland (1983) 12 ILJ 256.

13 [1977] IRLR 404.

14 [1983] ICR 351, [1983] IRLR 202, CA. See, to like effect, *Gibbons v Associated British Ports* [1985] IRLR 376. This was taken one stage further in *Whent v T Cartledge Ltd* [1997] IRLR 153 where employees could still claim a wage increase under a local authority collective agreement incorporated into their terms, even after their work was contracted out and they became employed by the private contractor (their incorporated term having been preserved because it was a TUPE transfer).

15 *Hamilton v Futura Floors Ltd* [1990] IRLR 478, OH. There is a similar rule in the law relating to recognition, see p. 53, above.

16 *Gascol Conversions Ltd v Mercer*, n. 12 above.

17 [1931] AC 83, PC; *Land v West Yorkshire Metropolitan County Council* [1979] IRLR 174 (reversed on other grounds: [1981] ICR 334, [1981] IRLR 87, CA).

said that he had not shown that the company's implementation of the collective bargain was due to contractual liability, that it was equally explicable on grounds of company policy, and that any remedy for breach, as in this case, was industrial and not legal. It may be argued that this is too strict an approach, making it too difficult to incorporate a collective bargain even in cases where there are no other clear, obvious terms in the contract of employment itself. All that can be said is that each case will depend on its own facts, and that one of the factors that may sway a court or tribunal is whether the clause of the bargain in question is really relevant to the individual circumstances of the employee claiming the benefit of it; if it concerns larger questions relating primarily to industrial relations, such as recognition of one or more unions[18], machinery for resolving collective disputes[19], or longer term policy planning on matters such as retraining or redundancy[20], the court or tribunal might decide that the clause is not to be incorporated into the contracts of the individuals concerned. On the other hand, if the correct inference is that it was envisaged that those conducting the bargaining would be binding those concerned in some relevant matters, the resulting clause might well be incorporated into the individual contracts and so binding, as with the 'no-strike' clause in *Rookes v Barnard*[1]. One of the strongest arguments in favour of incorporation would be custom and practice, evidenced by previous changes in the individual's contract in line with changes in the collective bargain; likewise, the collective bargain may itself be used as evidence of custom and practice within an industry where for some reason it becomes necessary to decide on such matters[2]. One point of difficulty is the position of the non-unionist. In *Singh v British Steel Corpn*[3] the employee resigned from the union which subsequently negotiated a new shift system which the employee did not want to work; he refused to work it and was dismissed. One of the questions in the case was whether the new union agreement could be considered to have been incorporated into his contract which would have thereby been modified and would have obliged him to work the new shift system. The tribunal held that it was not incorporated so he remained subject to his original contractual terms. The fact that he was no longer a member of the union obviously weighed heavily with the tribunal, and it will be recalled that in *Young v Canadian Northern Rly Co*, above, the employee was also a non-member and the fact that the employer in practice treated all employees alike was to little avail. To deny a non-unionist the

18   *Gallagher v Post Office* [1970] 3 All ER 712. Though cf *City and Hackney Health Authority v NUPE* [1985] IRLR 252, CA where it was thought arguable (on an interlocutory application) that a clause from a Whitley Council agreement concerning shop stewards *was* incorporated into a steward's individual contract of employment.
19   *National Coal Board v National Union of Mineworkers* [1986] ICR 736, [1986] IRLR 439; the judgment of Scott J is a useful affirmation of the principle.
20   *British Leyland UK Ltd v McQuilken* [1978] IRLR 245. In *Alexander v Standard Telephones and Cables Ltd (No 2)* [1991] IRLR 286 the court refused to incorporate a term in a collective bargain covering seniority in the redundancy procedure, though in *Anderson v Pringle of Scotland Ltd* [1998] IRLR 64 the Court of Session thought that it was at least arguable (in interlocutory proceedings) that a redundancy handling clause in a collective government had been incorporated (*Alexander* not cited). *Quaere* whether a term quantifying individuals' severance payments might be appropriate for incorporation.
1   [1964] AC 1129, [1964] 1 All ER 367, HL. No-strike clauses may now only be incorporated into individual contracts in restricted circumstances: Trade Union and Labour Relations (Consolidation) Act 1992, s. 180; they took on renewed topicality with the conclusion of 'single union' agreements by, in particular, the EETPU with employers in the so-called 'sunrise' industries, including inter alia no-strike agreements and pendulum arbitration.
2   *Howman & Son v Blyth* [1983] ICR 416, [1983] IRLR 139.
3   [1974] IRLR 131, IT.

rights (or, as in *Singh's* case, the obligations) under a collective bargain by not incorporating terms may perhaps seem just, but on the other hand, to say that *because* he was a non-member, therefore the term will not be incorporated would appear to be based principally on an agency theory (that the union always acts as agent of its members), which as seen above has been rejected in other contexts.

One final point to note is that the fact that incorporation of collective agreement terms is accomplished contractually may affect not just the incorporation itself, but also the *interpretation* of such terms. Although they may in practice have their origins in a loosely-drafted collective agreement, probably the result of compromise and horse-trading, once they are incorporated into a contract they take effect as contractual terms and are to be interpreted as such. In *Hooper v British Railways Board*[4] a sick pay term was incorporated into an employee's contract from an agreement of the Railway Staff Joint Council; the problem was that it was (according to the employers) badly drafted, did not reflect what the employers considered to be the actual basis of agreement and (when applied literally) produced arguably a bizarre result. The employers argued that the fact that the term came from a collective agreement should be taken into account when interpreting and applying it, and that the court should also look at the real intent of the employers at the time, and at how it had subsequently been applied in practice. The Court of Appeal, however, disagreed and held that it must be construed in the normal contractual way, ie objectively as it stood, and *not* by reference to any subsequent behaviour of the parties. The case, with its relatively strict contractual approach, shows that even though collective agreements are not themselves legally binding, the drafting of any clauses within them that may be incorporated into individual contracts (either expressly or by implication) should be approached with care.

2)   *Custom*   Trade usage or custom may have a role to play in filling a gap in the expressed terms of a contract of employment[5], or perhaps in the interpretation of a particular term (e.g. an incorporated clause in a collective bargain, as above[6]), as in the cases of *Sager v H Ridehalgh & Son Ltd*[7] (custom that the employer might deduct sums from weavers' wages for bad work held to be part of the individual weaver's contract) and *Marshall v English Electric Co Ltd*[8] (established practice of using suspension as a disciplinary measure held to be incorporated). To be thus accepted, a custom must be certain, general (e.g. in a trade or a particular area) and reasonable, but the legal basis for its incorporation into a contract of employment is not certain – is it automatically incorporated once it is certain, general and reasonable? Or does it have to be known to and, perhaps freely accepted by the employee? In *Marshall v English Electric Co Ltd* there was a division of opinion, Lord Goddard accepting automatic incorporation, but du Parcq LJ (dissenting) considering that mere operation is not enough, there being some

---

4   [1988] IRLR 517, CA.
5   Where this is the case, the Court of Appeal in *Mears v Safecar Security Ltd* [1982] IRLR 183, CA took a broad approach to the evidence that can be taken into account to imply the necessary term, in particular allowing evidence of actual working practices adopted or continued after the employment had commenced (following *Liverpool City Council v Irwin* [1977] AC 239, [1976] 2 All ER 39, HL and *Wilson v Maynard Shipbuilding Consultants AB* [1978] ICR 376, [1977] IRLR 491, CA); this could apply either to general evidence of trade custom, or to practices particularly applicable to the employee in question, or to both.
6   *Parry v Holst & Co Ltd* (1968) 3 ITR 317.
7   [1931] 1 Ch 310, CA.
8   [1945] 1 All ER 653, CA.

further element of acceptance necessary. *Meek v Port of London Authority*[9] is some authority in favour of a requirement of knowledge, but is a rather unusual case since it involved a change of employer and a custom (the payment by the employer of the employee's income tax if payable) which did not affect the employee when he commenced employment and had in fact been discontinued by the time the employee might be affected by it. It appears therefore that, although evidence of knowledge and acceptance might be most useful in establishing a binding custom, in some cases a custom might be applied without proof of them, and in particular in three instances:

i) Where the custom is so notorious that the court or tribunal may take judicial notice of it[10].

ii) Where it is so well established that the employee must be said to have accepted employment subject to it. In *Sagar v H Ridehalgh & Son Ltd* the practice of deductions from pay for bad work was widespread in Lancashire factories, and Lawrence LJ said[11]:

> 'I think that it is clear that the plaintiff accepted employment in the defendant's mill on the same terms as the other weavers employed at that mill ... Although I entirely agree with the [first instance judge] in finding it difficult to believe that the plaintiff did not know of the existence of the practice at the mill, I think that it is immaterial whether he knew or not, as I am satisfied that he accepted his employment on the same terms as to deductions for bad work as the other weavers at the mill.'

Much here may depend upon the certainty and generality of the custom, so that the mere fact that it has happened before in one firm may be insufficient[12]. Also there is the 'reasonableness' limb of the test which might be important[13].

iii) Where a practice grew up while the employee was in that employment and he impliedly accepted it (e.g. by accepting benefits under it). This might be a less certain area, for it should not cover unilateral practices, and might be subject to du Parcq LJ's caveat in *Marshall v English Electric Co Ltd* that mere continuance at work may not be enough for acceptance, for it might be caused by other factors such as fear of dismissal.

In the light of this uncertain legal position it is perhaps fortunate that the scope for custom in establishing terms of contracts of employment is much diminished in modern conditions, particularly in the light of the growing number of areas which are covered by statutory provisions or compulsory written terms, bearing in mind that the orthodox approach is that a 'custom' could not be used to overturn or alter a clear express term[14].

3)   *Works rules, company handbooks and policy statements*   An employer may lay down works or company rules, and it is possible that these may become, in whole or in part, terms of the contract of employment particularly if the employee expressly

9   [1918] 1 Ch 415.
10   *George v Davies* [1911] 2 KB 445.
11   [1931] 1 Ch 310 at 336, CA.
12   *Spencer Jones v Timmens Freeman* [1974] IRLR 325, IT; *Samways v Swan Hunter Shipbuilders Ltd* [1975] IRLR 190, IT.
13   *Hardwick v Leeds Area Health Authority* [1975] IRLR 319, IT.
14   Although the dividing line between unacceptable alteration and acceptable interpretation may be a thin one, see *McColl v Norman Insurance Co Ltd* (1969) 4 ITR 285.

agrees to abide by them or have some particular aspect of his employment governed by them, or if they are sufficiently brought to his notice when entering the employment. Also, some matters covered in a rule book may now be matters of which written notice must be given by statute, and so they may be strong evidence of the terms of employment by virtue of that (see above, under 'Form'). However, it is clear from *Secretary of State for Employment v ASLEF (No 2)*[15] that not all such rules will have contractual effect. Lord Denning MR said:

> 'Each man signs a form saying that he will abide by the rules, but these rules are in no way terms of the contract of employment. They are only instructions to a man as to how he is to do his work.'

The distinction between contractual and non-contractual rules is significant because if a rule is contractual, (a) it cannot be altered unilaterally by the employer, for that would require consensual variation in some form, and (b) the employee could, in the absence of such variation, insist upon continuing to work that rule and refuse to operate some other rule; if the rule is non-contractual, (a) it can be changed unilaterally by the employer for, being non-contractual, it remains in the sphere of managerial prerogative[16], and (b) if an employee refuses to operate the rule, or an alteration to it, he is refusing to obey a proper order and so at common law could be dismissed and under the statutes would quite possibly be fairly dismissed. Thus, the more the rules are considered to be contractual, the more restraints are placed upon the manager's prerogative, and where a rule is not expressly made contractual in some way a court or tribunal may have to make a difficult decision whether it is to be considered contractual by implication. A particularly good example (in an area which has plagued personnel managers in recent years) is *Dryden v Greater Glasgow Health Board*[17] where the employers introduced a no-smoking policy into the hospital and the employee, a heavy smoker, left and claimed constructive dismissal. Her claim failed because the EAT held that the no-smoking policy was in the realm of working rules and employer discretion, and so there was no breach of contract on which to base constructive dismissal:

> 'There can, in our view, be no doubt that an employer is entitled to make rules for the conduct of employees in their place of work, as he is entitled to give lawful orders, within the scope of the contract.'[18]

This long-standing law on 'works rules', itself rather an old-fashioned phrase, thus retains substantive significance and may be seen in two more current developments in managerial practice. The first is the modern tendency in medium and large firms to produce company handbooks; while these are in

---

15 [1972] 2 QB 455, [1972] 2 All ER 949, CA.
16 See, e.g. *Wandsworth London Borough Council v D'Silva* [1998] IRLR 193, CA where it was held that the council's sickness absence procedures were non-contractual and so could be lawfully altered by the council.
17 [1992] IRLR 469.
18 At 471, per Lord Coulsfield. The employee's second argument (if, as found, there was no contractual entitlement to smoke) was that the introduction of the policy was in breach of the implied term of trust and respect, but this failed on the facts since the employer had adopted a reasonable procedure for introducing it. One might be tempted, however, to the mischievous thought that formal approval for such a blatant exercise in managerial prerogative might have been more controversial had the case not concerned the politically correct matter of the current Jihad against smokers.

many ways a Good Thing (being readily available, relatively informal and much more of a guide to new employees) and are encouraged by ACAS[19], they could cause problems in that they may well mix together some matters that are formal contractual terms and others that are mere guidance or rules made within the managerial discretion, without any clear differentiation. The second development has been the increased use by employers of 'policies' of various kinds[20]. Again, these may or may not have contractual effect, though the cases so far have not accorded them great legal significance. In *Secretary of State for Scotland v Taylor*[1] prison officers tried to oppose a unilateral decrease in their retirement age by arguing that it was a breach of contract because it contravened their employer's equal opportunities policy which included a reference to age discrimination; the Scottish EAT held that the policy was part of the contract, but as a matter of construction further held that the parties could not have intended it to outlaw an otherwise lawful retirement provision in the contract. Perhaps more significantly, when in *Grant v South-West Trains Ltd*[2] an attempt was made to establish sexual orientation discrimination as a breach of contract (again because it appeared in the firm's equal opportunities policy) Curtis J held that the policy was not part of the contract at all; it was merely a statement of aims and aspirations. Given the prevalence of various forms of policies, circulars, codes of practice or (God forbid) mission statements, this distinction is likely to be troublesome for some time to come.

In dismissal law, however, the practical effect of these matters may be diminished by the fact that the modern law on unfair dismissal is not concerned with technical questions of breach of contract but rather with the overall merits of the dismissal, and in this context it is clear that, whilst breach of the rules (whether contractual or not) may well be important in any given case, it will only be *evidence*, not a determinative factor, and the existence of works rules will in no way preclude a tribunal from looking into the overall fairness of the employer's actions. Thus, for example, in *Laws Stores Ltd v Oliphant*[3] the disciplinary section of the works rules said that cases of gross misconduct (including the disregard of till procedures which was in question) would normally result in immediate dismissal, but the EAT held that such a provision (or even one more mandatory) could not limit a tribunal's jurisdiction and held the dismissal, on the facts of the particular case, to be unfair. This case is perhaps an example of the decline in the purely contractual approach to employment.

---

19 See p. 43, above.
20 See the code of practice on sickness absence in *Wandsworth London Borough Council v D'Silva*, n. 16, above.
1   [1997] IRLR 608, EAT, upheld by the House of Lords (where the incorporation point was not argued): [2000] IRLR 502.
2   [1998] IRLR 206, ECJ. One distinction with *Taylor* was that in the latter the employer's circular introducing the new equal opportunities policy had stated that it was being introduced into the employees' contracts of employment. There was no such evidence of contractual intent in *Grant*. Note that this *Grant* litigation was separate from and parallel to the main litigation which involved an ultimately unsuccessful argument before the ECJ that EC law on sex discrimination should also cover sexual orientation; see p. 239, below.
3   [1978] IRLR 251. An equally good example is the imposition of a disciplinary penalty by the employer – he may technically have had the contractual power to impose the penalty in question, but it is still open to the employee to argue that on the facts of the case it was excessive (thus, for example, justifying the employee in walking out and claiming constructive dismissal): *BBC v Beckett* [1983] IRLR 43; *Cawley v South Wales Electricity Board* [1985] IRLR 89.

iii)   Duties of the employer

a)   To pay wages

This obligation is so fundamental that the law relating to it is considered separately in chapter 4 below.

b)   To provide work

The general common law position has been that there is no obligation to provide work for the employee to do; there is only the obligation to pay the wages which may be due under the particular contract of employment concerned. The classic, if now rather nostalgic, statement of this rule was given by Asquith J in *Collier v Sunday Referee Publishing Co Ltd*[4]:

> 'Provided I pay my cook her wages regularly, she cannot complain if I choose to take any or all of my meals out.'

This means that in such a case the employer will not be in breach of contract by failing to provide work and so may, for example, normally give salary in lieu of notice[5]. However, the law recognised that in certain contracts the opportunity to work is of the essence, and so certain exceptions to the general rule evolved. In particular, it was held that there may be an obligation to provide work for an actor or singer where the publicity involved may be as important as the remuneration[6], for an employee paid on a piecework[7] or commission[8] basis where actual work is necessary for him to earn his living, and possibly for an employee engaged to fill a specific office (particularly of a professional nature)[9]. Outside such exceptional cases, however, the general rule applied, as can be seen in *Turner v Sawdon & Co*[10] where a salesman on a fixed term contract at a fixed salary was given no work to do but still paid his salary and it was held, distinguishing *Turner v Goldsmith*[11], that this was merely a contract to retain the employee so that the employer was not in breach of contract, in spite of the employee's assertions that denial of work would make him deteriorate as a salesman. However, some doubt was cast on this principle in *Langston v AUEW*[12] where an employee involved in an industrial dispute was suspended on full pay by his employer. To succeed in his claim

---

4   [1940] 2 KB 647 at 650, [1940] 4 All ER 234 at 236.
5   *Konski v Peet* [1915] 1 Ch 530. It is possible that in some cases, where the contract does not envisage dismissal with wages in lieu (either expressly or impliedly), such a dismissal will be a breach of contract *but* as damages have been paid in anticipation (by paying the wages due in the notice period) this will be a technical breach only and of little legal significance (except possibly where a restraint of trade clause is in issue): *Rex Stewart Jeffries Parker Ginsberg v Parker* [1988] IRLR 483, CA. See p. 370, below.
6   *Fechter v Montgomery* (1863) 33 Beav 22; *Bunning v Lyric Theatre* (1894) 71 LT 396; *Marbé v George Edwardes (Daly's Theatre) Ltd* [1928] 1 KB 269, CA; the obligation may be to provide not just work, but work of a particular kind or standard, e.g. a leading part in a play as in *Herbert Clayton and Jack Waller Ltd v Oliver* [1930] AC 209, HL.
7   *R v Welsh* (1853) 2 E & B 357; *Devonald v Rosser & Sons* [1906] 2 KB 728, CA.
8   *Turner v Goldsmith* [1891] 1 QB 544, CA; *Bauman v Hulton Press Ltd* [1952] 2 All ER 1121.
9   *Collier v Sunday Referee Publishing Co Ltd* [1940] 2 KB 647, [1940] 4 All ER 234.
10   [1901] 2 KB 653, CA. *Quaere* whether the position would be different if it was more urgent that the employee should keep in practice, as for example in the case of a surgeon.
11   [1891] 1 QB 544, CA.
12   [1974] 1 All ER 980, [1974] ICR 180, CA; see also *Breach v Epsylon Industries Ltd* [1976] ICR 316, [1976] IRLR 180; *Bosworth v Angus Jowett & Co Ltd* [1977] IRLR 374.

against the union involved under now repealed legislation[13] he had to show that the dispute had induced a breach of contract, and this would only have been so if he had a contractual right to be provided with work since the employers were continuing to pay his salary. The Court of Appeal thought that the duty to provide work might exist, and in a strong judgment Lord Denning MR said that the previous authorities such as *Collier v Sunday Referee Publishing Co Ltd* were out of date, that the courts now recognise a 'right to work' and that this was one application of it. However, it must be remembered that this decision was only at an interlocutory stage, so that the Court of Appeal had to decide only if there was an arguable case on this point – they then did not have to *decide* the point, and the judgments of the other two members of the court, Cairns and Stephenson LJJ, are much less emphatic on the point than that of the Master of the Rolls. The case was remitted to the National Industrial Relations Court which held in the employee's favour[14] but on much more restricted grounds than those explored by Lord Denning, for Sir John Donaldson P held that this case came within one of the existing exceptions to the old rule, since under the contract the employee was to be paid premium payments for night shifts and overtime, so that he came within the pieceworker exception in that denial of actual work meant denial of opportunity to earn the premium payments. Thus, in its result, the case is in fact compatible with the old common law rule and its established exceptions.

This question of whether and when there is a right to work (or more accurately, whether a contract requires the provision of work in addition to the payment of wages) has been dormant for many years, but was revived in an unusual context in *William Hill Organisation Ltd v Tucker*[15]. The case concerned an attempt by an employer to construct an implied 'garden leave clause'[16] from the terms of the employee's contract, quite simply because they had omitted to put an express clause in. The contract contained a long (six months') notice provision; when the employee left with only one month notice, the employers applied for an injunction restraining him from taking work elsewhere during the six-month period, on the basis that they were prepared to pay his wages *and* had a common law right to require him during that period to do no work for them or anyone else. The Court of Appeal held that that depended on whether his contract only required payment of wages (as the employers argued) *or* required the employers to provide him with work as well (in which case the employers would be in breach of contract and the employee could leave to take up other work); they thus revived the old controversy, and for good measure seemed to take an expansive view as to who can claim to have a sufficient interest in actually performing their work in order to claim that the contract is to be interpreted as requiring work to be provided, not just payment. Far from restricting it to theatrical or piecework/commission workers, they held that this employee, a senior 'spread betting' dealer with a betting organisation, *did* have a right to be provided with work; there was

13 Industrial Relations Act 1971, s. 96.
14 [1974] ICR 510, [1974] IRLR 182. It is made clear in the President's judgment that the employee had to work such shifts and hours as the employer stipulated, which made it easier to construe overtime as a contractual requirement; it is submitted, however, that purely voluntary overtime is not an essential part of a contract, and so failure to provide it should *not* be a breach of contract, and so not subject to the reasoning in *Langston's* case.
15 [1999] ICR 291, [1998] IRLR 313, CA.
16 A 'garden leave clause' is an alternative to a restraint of trade clause, whereby an employer puts an employee on to long notice with a provision that during that notice he can be sent home by the employer (to avoid damage to the employer's business) *but* cannot take any other work while still technically employed by that employer; see p. 372, below.

thus no inherent right for the employer to put him on garden leave[17], and so the employer's application for an injunction was refused. Factors leading to that conclusion were that the appointment was a specific and unique one, that the skills involved were those requiring constant practice and experience and that the contract contained certain provisions (as to obligations on the employee in carrying out his duties, training and an express power of suspension) which the court thought consistent with an obligation to provide work, provided that it was available. While the first point (a specific appointment) could point to a narrow future application of this case and some of the points on construction of the contract terms are, with respect, highly arguable, it is likely that most contention in any future cases will be over the second point – who will be considered to be in a job whose skills need constant honing and exercise, so as to come within a widened class of employees with some form of 'right to work'?

Two further points might be mentioned. The first is that this uncertain area of law will only be relevant where there is no express term covering the provision of work, and where such provision is important to either of the parties, they are advised to incorporate a clause in the contract putting the matter beyond doubt. The second is that this topic may be allied to the question of the continuation of wages during stoppages of work and for present purposes it might be noted that at common law suspension without pay will only be lawful if there is an express or implied term in the particular contract to that effect; that failure to provide work may constitute a lay-off, thus activating certain statutory provisions (principally concerned with redundancy – Employment Rights Act 1996, ss. 147–154); and that in the absence of continuing contractual payments the employee may be eligible for a statutory guarantee payment under the 1996 Act, ss. 28–35.

c)   To exercise care

This matter will normally relate to care for the employee's health and safety, and so is dealt with fully in chapter 12 below, for the employer's common law duty of care is one of the bases of the law relating to the compensation of an injured employee. However, five particular applications of it are important here. The first is that one of the commonly accepted aspects of this overall duty is that the employer must provide competent and safe fellow employees[18], for example to protect the employee from practical jokers; one effect of this is that there may be a positive common law obligation upon the employer to be rid of a potentially dangerous employee and this should be a good defence to an allegation of unfair dismissal by that employee, provided the necessary procedures are used in effecting the dismissal. The second is that the general duty of care may be construed as including an obligation upon the employer to pay attention to complaints from an employee that a particular appliance, method, etc. is unsafe and to act reasonably in dealing with matters of safety; if the employer does not do so, not only may the employee be justified in walking out and claiming, for the purposes of unfair dismissal, to have been constructively dismissed[19] but also

17   As Morritt LJ stated at the end of his judgment, the answer of course is for the employer to use an *express* garden leave clause wherever there might arguably be a right to work (more often now, in the light of this case?). Moreover, this case could also limit the hitherto widely assumed implied right of an employer to dismiss with wages in lieu; again, the preferred solution increasingly is an express wages in lieu clause in the contract; see p. 372, below.

18   *Wilsons and Clyde Coal Co Ltd v English* [1938] AC 57, HL; *Hudson v Ridge Manufacturing Co Ltd* [1957] 2 QB 348, [1957] 2 All ER 229.

19   *British Aircraft Corpn v Austin* [1978] IRLR 332; cf. *Lindsay v Dunlop Ltd* [1980] IRLR 93.

(since 1993) that dismissal may well be automatically unfair[20]. The third is that the employer may be under an obligation to indemnify the employee against expenses necessarily incurred in the course of his employment, which may include the cost of defending legal proceedings, though not where the fault was purely that of the employee and only collateral to the performance of his duties[1]; there is, however, no implied obligation to insure the employee's activities to any greater extent than is required by law[2]. The fourth is that the specialised duty of care will in general not extend to a duty to take care of the employee's belongings[3]; any possible liability for loss of the employee's goods would have to arise on ordinary principles of tort if there was evidence of particular proximity between the particular employer and employee, not just on the employment relationship per se, or possibly under the Workplace (Health, Safety and Welfare) Regulations 1992, reg. 23 which provides for 'suitable and sufficient accommodation' for clothing not worn during working hours[4]. The fifth concerns the application of a duty of care to the giving of references by an employer or ex-employer. There could, of course, be liability for a negligently written reference to the new employer[5], but the question arose whether the employee as the *subject* of the reference could sue in negligence, for breach of a duty of care. The House of Lords in *Spring v Guardian Assurance plc*[6] (reversing a more cautious decision by the Court of Appeal) held that there could be such a duty on the employer giving a reference; it lies both in tort (according to Lord Goff on a *Hedley Byrne* style assumption of responsibility, and according to Lords Lowry, Slynn and Woolf on the basis that this extension of liability is fair, just and reasonable, and concerning a sufficiently proximate relationship) and also in contract, based upon a breach of this implied term. This decision does not prevent the giving of a bad reference, only a negligently bad reference, and their lordships were not persuaded by the argument that to impose liability would deter people from writing references. One loose end in the case is whether there is any implied obligation on an (ex-) employer to *give* a reference; it has normally been thought that there is no such obligation, but in the speech of Lord Woolf there is a passage suggesting that in certain circumstances (where references are known to be an essential element of recruitment) it may be necessary to imply just such

20 Employment Rights Act 1996, s. 100, see p. 493, below.
1   *Burrows v Rhodes* [1899] 1 QB 816; *Re Famatina Development Corpn* [1914] 2 Ch 271, CA; *Gregory v Ford* [1951] 1 All ER 121.
2   *Lister v Romford Ice and Cold Storage Co Ltd* [1957] AC 555, [1957] 1 All ER 125, HL. Aliter where there is a legal obligation to insure: *Bernadone v Pall Mall Services Group Ltd* [1999] IRLR 617 (implied term that employee will have employer's liability insurance); upheld on appeal [2000] IRLR 487, CA.
3   *Deyong v Shenburn* [1946] KB 227, [1946] 1 All ER 226, CA; *Edwards v West Herts Group Hospital Management Committee* [1957] 1 All ER 541, [1957] 1 WLR 415, CA.
4   *McCarthy v Daily Mirror Newspapers Ltd* [1949] 1 All ER 801, CA (on the equivalent provision under the old Factories Acts).
5   Under the ordinary principles of *Hedley Byrne & Co Ltd v Heller & Partners Ltd* [1964] AC 465, [1963] 2 All ER 575, HL.
6   [1994] ICR 596, [1994] IRLR 460, HL. The decision was by 4–1, with Lord Keith dissenting. The majority held that a duty of care did exist on the facts, but this does not mean that an action will always succeed in such circumstances – the question of causation must also be established (did the employee fail to get new employment because of the negligent reference?); where the plaintiff was one of many applicants, that may be difficult to prove. Moreover, it was later held (adopting an approach found in defamation law) that a reference must be true, accurate and fair, not giving a misleading impression, *but* not always full and comprehensive: *Bartholomew v London Borough of Hackney* [1999] IRLR 246, CA.

an obligation[7]. As with the whole of the case, this could be seen against the factual background of the plaintiff seeking new employment under the LAUTRO rules (with their mandatory references), but equally both these remarks and the case itself are expressed in general terms, and so there could be further development of this point in future cases. On the other hand, Lord Slynn pointed out that it is open to the reference giver to state specifically the parameters within which the reference is given (and any limitations on his knowledge of the employee) or, ultimately, to rely on the *Hedley Byrne* aspect of the case to make his agreement to the employee to give the reference subject to an express disclaimer of liability.

d)   To treat the employee with respect

In modern employment law there has been a restatement of implied duties of mutual respect between employer and employee. In certain employments, particularly of a domestic nature, this may require positive courtesy[8] while in others it may mean treating each other with such a degree of consideration and tolerance as would allow the contract to be executed. This is, of course, a vague concept which will vary with the circumstances, and if there is a more concrete area of dispute in any given case questions of want of 'respect' will be of secondary importance[9]. However, an obligation upon the employer to treat the employee with respect and not to act in a manner likely to destroy or seriously damage the relationship of trust and confidence may be seen as a corollary of the employee's general duty of faithful service, as confirmed in *British Telecommunications plc v Ticehurst*[10]. Moreover, it is argued above[11] that there are developments suggesting not only that this is a well-established and much-used implied term, but that it is assuming an overriding nature, capable of qualifying the ability of an employer to rely on a literal application of his rights under a contract of employment.

The development of such a term is perhaps not so surprising, for the advent of the law on unfair dismissal has restricted the employer's prerogative to dismiss so that good personnel management has become an essential, not an optional extra. The overall requirement of fair dismissal procedures, for example, has meant that more notice has to be taken of the employee's viewpoint, and the employer is expected not just to assess conduct and issue warnings, but also to take more positive action to assist or train the employee to meet any required standards of competence or conduct. Moreover, in one important area of unfair dismissal law, the concept of an implied duty of respect has taken on definite significance; this is in the area of 'constructive dismissal'. This is discussed in detail in chapter 8 below, but the essence of it is that the employee can claim to be dismissed, even though he walks out, if he can show that the employer's conduct was such that he

---

7   At pp. 647, 481. In addition, the ECJ have held that if an employer *refuses* to give a reference to retaliation for a sex discrimination complaint made by the employee, that itself can constitute unlawful sex discrimination: *Coote v Granada Hospitality Ltd* C-185/97 [1998] IRLR 656, ECJ, applied in *Coote (No 2)* [1999] IRLR 452, EAT.
8   *Wilson v Racher* [1974] ICR 428, [1974] IRLR 114, CA.
9   As in *Donovan v Invicta Airways Ltd* [1970] 1 Lloyds Rep 486, CA.
10   [1992] ICR 383, [1992] IRLR 219, CA; see p. 146, below.
11   See p. 109, above.

was 'entitled' to do so[12]. In *Western Excavating (ECC) Ltd v Sharp*[13], a case which served to emphasise the underlying contractual nature of the employment relationship, the Court of Appeal held that this meant *contractually* entitled, i.e. where the employer's conduct went as far as to repudiate the whole contract; on the face of it, this narrowed the concept of constructive dismissal, for mere unreasonableness by the employer would not be enough per se, but the effect of this case has been considerably reduced by praying in aid the implied term of respect, for if there is such a term and the employer behaves unreasonably (i.e. with unacceptable disregard for the employee), the employer can be held to have broken the implied term, to have repudiated the contract, and therefore to have constructively dismissed the employee even within the narrower view taken in *Western Excavating (EEC) Ltd v Sharp*[14].

The implied term of trust and respect received the approval of the House of Lords in *Malik v BCCI SA*[15] where it formed the basis for an unusual claim at common law for 'stigma damages', the employees' argument being that they had had their future job prospects materially damaged (as ex-managers in the collapsed BCCI bank) by reason of the fraudulent conduct of the bank's operations, which had breached the term of trust and respect. Lord Steyn referred to the term as a 'sound development' which had met with widespread approval, and which had to be applied to a wide range of situations in order to strike a balance between the employer's interest in managing the business and the employee's interest in not being unfairly and improperly exploited[16].

e) To deal promptly and properly with grievances

In *W A Goold (Pearmak) Ltd v McConnell*[17] two salesmen whose commission-based pay had been hit by a change in sales methods, tried to raise this as a grievance; in the absence of a proper procedure[18] they tried to do so on several occasions in an

12 Employment Rights Act 1996, s. 95; a similar definition applies to redundancy claims – s. 136. For an application of similar ideas of a duty of trust and confidence in a common law claim, see *Bliss v South East Thames Regional Health Authority* [1987] ICR 700, [1985] IRLR 308, CA.
13 [1978] 1 All ER 713, [1978] ICR 221, CA.
14 There is an excellent explanation of this role for the implied term of respect in the judgment of Browne-Wilkinson J in the EAT in *Woods v WM Car Services (Peterborough) Ltd* [1981] ICR 666, [1981] IRLR 347 (approved by the Court of Appeal [1982] ICR 693, [1982] IRLR 413). See Elias 'Unravelling the concept of dismissal' (1978) 7 ILJ at 100–106. See also the modern case law set out at pp. 109-112, above, and in particular the extension of this term to the area of employees' pension rights in *Imperial Group Pension Trust Ltd v Imperial Tobacco Ltd* [1991] ICR 524, [1991] IRLR 66.
15 [1997] ICR 606, [1997] IRLR 462, HL; see Brodie 'The heart of the matter: mutual trust and confidence' (1996) 25 ILJ 121 (cited with approval in the case) and 'Beyond exchange: the new contract of employment' (1998) 27 ILJ 79. For the effect of the case on damages, see p. 393, below. The implied term was also used in the context of damages in *Clark v BET plc* [1997] IRLR 348, see p. 393, below.
16 The Northern Ireland Court of Appeal in *Brown v Merchant Ferries Ltd* [1998] IRLR 682 adopted Lord Steyn's formulation of the implied term which stressed that the test was an objective one, i.e. whether the employee could properly conclude that the employer was repudiating the contract, not whether the employer had intended so to act. It was also established in *Malik* that the repudiatory conduct does not in law have to be aimed directly at the employee.
17 [1995] IRLR 516.
18 As employees, they should have had a written note of the appropriate grievance procedure in their written ('section 1') statement of terms and conditions; see p. 86, above. This point was used by the EAT to demonstrate Parliament's intention that there should be proper such procedures, properly administered.

ad hoc manner with their manager and then with the new managing director, but with no results. When eventually they sought an interview with the company chairman and were refused they walked out. Upholding the tribunal decision that this was a constructive dismissal and unfair, the EAT held that it is an implied term in a contract of employment that employers will reasonably and promptly afford a reasonable opportunity to their employees to obtain redress of any grievances they may have. Moreover, this is a fundamental term, breach of which will be sufficiently serious to justify the employee in terminating the employment.

This declaration of a new (possibly overriding?) implied term is of particular significance for two reasons. First, it is a very good example of the use of implied terms set out above, as a way of the courts governing certain basic contents of the employment relationship and imposing certain standards of behaviour in employee relations. Secondly, although this point is not mentioned in the judgment of Morison J, the case could be seen as following on from at least two previous decisions in which failures to take up specific forms of complaints arising in the high-profile areas of health and safety[19] and sexual harassment[20] had been held to constitute fundamental breaches of contract for the purpose of establishing constructive dismissal when the complainant left. *Goold* in effect consolidates such disparate cases into one general principle and in doing so places new emphasis on the efficient administration of grievance procedures.

f)   To provide a reasonably suitable working environment

In *Waltons & Morse v Dorrington*[1] a non-smoking secretary in a solicitors' firm was moved into a room close to heavy smokers which she found a problem. Her complaints had only partial effects and eventually she was told to put up with the solution or leave. She left and claimed constructive dismissal, which was upheld by the EAT who held that it is now an implied term of all contracts of employment that the employer will provide and monitor for employees, so far as is reasonably practicable, a working *environment* which is reasonably suitable for the performance by them of their contractual duties. This term goes beyond the long-standing term of health and safety (above) (on the facts, for example it would probably have been too soon to show distinct health risks to her), and in formulating it (much more along 'welfare' lines) the EAT adopted much of the phraseology of the Health and Safety at Work etc. Act 1974, s. 2(2)(e) which provides that the employer must take reasonable care for 'the provision and maintenance of a working environment for his employees that is, so far as reasonably practicable, safe, without risks to health and adequate as regards facilities and arrangements for their welfare at work'. Moreover, although not mentioned in the judgment, this implied term is also consistent with (1) modern health and safety regulations, especially the Management of Health and Safety at Work Regulations 1999 with their emphasis on pro-active measures such as risk assessments in workplaces, and (2) the clear coverage of the 'working environment' (not just traditional health and safety) in Article 118A of the Treaty of Rome (now Art. 137), under which the Working Time Directive was validly passed, even though it does not concern health or safety directly[2]. This new implied term is potentially very wide and is likely to need much interpretation in the future case law on it.

---

19   *British Aircraft Corpn v Austin* [1978] IRLR 332.
20   *Bracebridge Engineering Ltd v Darby* [1990] IRLR 3.
1   [1997] IRLR 488.
2   See p. 199, below.

g) Further developments

As seen above, it is, of course, always open to the courts to extend the scope of these imposed duties on employers. In that context, three developments merit mention. The first is that in *Scally v Southern Health and Social Services Board*[3] the House of Lords upheld the finding of an implied term that the employer would *inform* the employee of valuable (but obscure) rights under his pension scheme; when the employer failed to do so and the employee lost those rights due to a time limitation, the employee could therefore sue the employer for breach of contract. Clearly, the facts of this case were unusual, but Lord Bridge drew a principle that there could be such an implied term where (a) the terms of the contract had not been negotiated individually, but resulted from negotiation with a representative body or were otherwise incorporated by reference, (b) the employee could only avail himself of a valuable right under the contract by taking certain action, and (c) the employee could not, in all the circumstances, reasonably be expected to be aware of the term unless it was brought to his attention. Obligations to inform or warn are common in modern health and safety law[4], and it is interesting to see this development in mainstream employment law (albeit in the specialised context of pensions), because the traditional approach was much more in the nature of caveat employee[5].

The second development is the possible extension of ideas of confidentiality in employment. There is a well-developed implied duty of confidence *on* an employee, but there may evolve an equal and opposite duty *towards* an employee. In *Dalgleish v Lothian and Borders Police Board*[6] an interdict was granted, preventing the employers from divulging employees' names and addresses to the Council who were chasing community charge defaulters, partly on the ground that this information was confidential, not in the public domain, and was held by the employers only for the purpose of the employer–employee relationship. Another sign of such ideas was the decision of the European Court of Human Rights in *Halford v United Kingdom*[7] that interception of telephone calls at work constituted a violation of the Convention rights to respect for private life and family life, home and correspondence. Arguments such as this are likely to multiply from October 2000 with the coming into force of the Human Rights Act 1998 (it is already in force in Scotland at the time of writing), backed by the Data Protection Act 1998. Thus, we are likely to see increased emphasis on an elementary right to privacy at work, an increasingly difficult area in an era of greatly increased communication (e.g. on e-mail and internet), and the drawing of difficult lines

---

3   [1991] ICR 771, [1991] IRLR 522, HL.
4   A good example is the decision of Waite J in *Pape v Cumbria County Council* [1992] 3 All ER 211 that there was a common law duty on the employer to warn cleaning staff of the danger of dermatitis from certain cleaning chemicals (*General Cleaning Contractors Ltd v Christmas* [1953] AC 180, [1953] 2 All ER 1110, HL applied).
5   In *Lister v Romford Ice and Cold Storage Co Ltd* [1957] AC 555, [1957] 1 All ER 125, HL there was no obligation on the employer to organise all matters of insurance and in *Reid v Rush & Tompkins Group plc* [1990] ICR 61, [1989] IRLR 265, CA it was held that the employer was under no duty to warn the employee of the risk of economic loss (through not insuring himself adequately when working abroad). It will be interesting to see if the latter decision stands, in the light of *Scally*. A relatively restrictive approach was taken in *University of Nottingham v Eyett* [1999] ICR 721, [1999] IRLR 87, Ch D where *Scally* was distinguished and it was held that an employer had no duty to tell an employee about to retire that his pension would be higher if he delayed slightly, when all the employee had asked was what his pension would be if he retired on a particular date.
6   [1991] IRLR 422, Ct of Sess.
7   [1997] IRLR 471, ECtHR.

between employee rights on the one hand and the employer's need for increasing control on the other hand, to prevent abuse by employees of these forms of communication which could make the employer vicariously liable, e.g. for defamation or harassment by the employee. If these developments continue, and as a result there evolves a general implied duty of confidence on an employer, one point of interest will be the extent to which (if at all) it continues to apply after termination of the employment, which has often proved a difficulty in the implied duty on the employee (see p. 136, below).

The third development concerns a modern trend in the employment of more senior employees of offering permanent health insurance ('PHI') as part of the remuneration package; paid for by the employer, this can offer major benefits to an employee who becomes permanently incapable of work through illness, but its relationship with ordinary sickness procedures and notice provisions has proved troublesome, especially where the PHI has been in the nature of an 'add-on' without thought as to its possible legal effects. In *Aspden v Webbs Poultry and Meat Group (Holdings) Ltd*[8] the plaintiff was a senior manager who was subject to the firm's PHI scheme for senior staff – if incapable of work for more than 26 weeks, he would be entitled to ¾ salary until death, retirement or ceasing to be an employee. However, on engagement he had been given a standard contract which did *not* take the separate PHI scheme into account and in the case of longterm illness provided for six months' sick pay and then for dismissal. When he became ill (after altercations with the firm over reorganisations) the employers, who suspected he might have been exaggerating his illness, exercised their contractual power of dismissal before he could qualify for the PHI benefits. The employee brought an action for wrongful dismissal; normally this would have been doomed to failure because of the terms of the contract, but Sedley J upheld the employee's claim that on the facts of the case there was an implied term that, save for summary dismissal for cause[9], the employer would not terminate the contract while he was incapacitated, so as to deprive him of the PHI benefits. The judge acknowledged that this was on the edge of permissibility for the use of implied terms, but was necessary because otherwise an unrestricted power to terminate would completely negate the working of the PHI scheme which clearly applied to the plaintiff but had been completely overlooked when his contract had been given to him. Although an adventurous decision, it has been followed by the Court of Session[10] and approved obiter in the Court of Appeal[11]; it marks yet a further move away from strict contract doctrine in the employment field.

8   [1996] IRLR 521. One interesting question is whether a wider principle could be extracted from this case, limiting the right to dismiss wherever (on the facts) there is an important condition precedent to the contract; for example, if an employee were taken on in order to bring certain lucrative business with him (but otherwise on a standard contract, including an ordinary notice provision), could it be argued that it is implied that he would not be dismissed under the notice provision for as long as that business stays with the employer?

9   This was expressed in *Aspden* to be the important protection that the employer needs in such a case; however, it now needs to be expanded to cover summary dismissal for cause *and* dismissal for bona fide redundancy, neither of which mean that the employer is trying to frustrate the PHI scheme, and so neither of which would be contrary to the implied term: *Hill v General Accident Fire and Life Assurance Corpn plc* [1998] IRLR 641, OH.

10   *Adin v Sedco Forex International Resources Ltd* [1997] IRLR 280, Ct of Sess.

11   *Brompton v AOC International Ltd* [1997] IRLR 639, CA. In *Villella v MFI Furniture Centres Ltd* [1999] IRLR 468 a similar argument succeeded again, this time where dismissal was used to try to avoid continuing with PHI payments already being made.

iv) Duties of the employee

a) Obedience

In the days before employment was explained in terms of a contract, the servant's duty of obedience was taken to be a natural element of employment and indeed if one delves far enough back it was accompanied by the master's right to discipline and perhaps chastise the erring servant. It is now explained as an aspect of the contract of employment that the employer may give and the employee should obey a lawful order, and indeed it has been argued that this should be taken a step further and viewed not as a duty of obedience, but rather as an example of co-operation. The term 'lawful' order is often used but in this context it means primarily an order which is reasonably within the ambit of the employment in question so that, once again, in any given dispute much or all will depend on the terms of the individual contract of employment, whether express or implied; the task of deciding what is the scope of the employment may be facilitated by the requirements in section 1 of the Employment Rights Act 1996 of written particulars of terms of employment, particularly of the title of the job which the employee is employed to do (section 1(4)(f)). Thus the employer cannot give orders outside the proper scope of the employment, for example orders of a 'personal' nature such as regulating the length of the employee's hair or his out of work activities (unless he can show some special considerations bringing such matters within the scope of employment, such as danger in having long hair when working machines). Also, this principle means that the employer cannot order the employee to change his contract, so that if it is clear that he is not contractually bound to be mobile or work overtime, it will not be 'lawful' to order him to work elsewhere[12] or put in hours above the basic[13].

Questions of obedience are naturally bound up with the law on dismissal, and at common law principally with the employer's right to dismiss summarily. In general, refusal to obey a proper order would usually justify summary dismissal and although such matters tend to change over time with different social attitudes this is still the basic position with regard to the common law action for wrongful dismissal. However, the statutory action for unfair dismissal is now far more important and the question of fairness depends upon all the factors in the case, not just whether the employee was technically in breach of contract[14]. In the light of this, although the employer may still dismiss summarily in cases of grave misconduct, a single act of disobedience may not necessarily render the dismissal fair, for although it would qualify as a reason concerning 'conduct' within section 98(2) of the Employment Rights Act 1996, the tribunal must go further and consider, under section 98(4), whether the employer acted reasonably in treating it as a sufficient reason for dismissal in all the circumstances of the particular case.

The duty of obedience at common law is subject to two particular qualifications. The first is that the employer may not order the employee to do something

---

12 *O'Brien v Associated Fire Alarms Ltd* [1969] 1 All ER 93, [1968] 1 WLR 1916, CA; *Courtaulds Northern Spinning Ltd v Sibson* [1988] ICR 451, [1988] IRLR 305, CA; cf. *Stevenson v Teesside Bridge and Engineering Ltd* [1971] 1 All ER 296 and *United Kingdom Atomic Energy Authority v Claydon* [1974] ICR 128.

13 *Pengilly v North Devon Farmers Ltd* [1973] IRLR 41, EAT.

14 *Farrant v Woodroffe School* [1998] ICR 184, [1998] IRLR 176, EAT.

illegal[15]; if he does so the employee is entitled to refuse to obey the order, and any purported summary dismissal will be wrongful, and of more importance, very likely to be held to be unfair, as in *Morrish v Henlys (Folkestone) Ltd*[16] where the employee was dismissed because he refused to falsify accounts. The second qualification is that the employer may not order the employee into danger; in *Ottoman Bank v Chakarian*[17] an employee was held to have been justified in disobeying an order to stay in Constantinople where he had previously been sentenced to death and was in danger of being apprehended a second time. However, it appears that for this exception to apply there must be immediate and personal danger so that in *Bouzourou v Ottoman Bank*[18], expectation merely of general hostility from the Turkish authorities was not enough to justify refusal of an order to work in Mersina; likewise with an unspecific fear of IRA activity if sent to work in Eire in *Walmsley v Udec Refrigeration Ltd*[19].

b)   Adaptation to new methods and techniques

As was pointed out earlier in this chapter when considering changes in the terms of employment, problems may arise from the fact that jobs change but contracts tend to be static. What is to happen if the employer introduces new working methods or techniques which the employee is unwilling to accept? In such a case, the employee may argue that the changes are sufficiently fundamental to fall outside the scope of his existing contract; if this is so, the employer must be able to show a consensual variation of the relevant terms before he can insist on the employee accepting the changes[20]. There is extensive case law on this point in the law on redundancy[1], where the courts have consistently given considerable latitude to employers to alter work practices without being held to have altered the job itself. A second possibility is that the employer may have envisaged the possibility of future changes and in the light of that either framed the contractual terms (particularly the job title/description) flexibly, or given himself express contractual authority to make the changes in question. However, the question remains what is to happen where neither of these solutions applies, i.e. where the changes are not fundamental enough to alter the job itself, but changes in methods or techniques are not expressly covered by the contract? Can the employee refuse to adapt?

It appears that in most cases he will not be able to refuse, for he will not be deemed to have a right to continue as he always had indefinitely. There is little case law directly on this point, but it is possible that if necessary the courts would develop an implied term of adaptation. Signs of this can be seen in the judgment of Walton J in *Cresswell v Board of Inland Revenue*[2]. In that case, inland revenue

---

15 *Gregory v Ford* [1951] 1 All ER 121. Semble there must be a clear order if the employer is to be in breach of this principle: *Buckoke v Greater London Council* [1970] 2 All ER 193 per Plowman J; affd by the Court of Appeal: [1971] 1 Ch 655, [1971] 2 All ER 254, CA.
16 [1973] 2 All ER 137, [1973] ICR 482.
17 [1930] AC 277, PC.
18 [1930] AC 271, PC.
19 [1972] IRLR 80, IT.
20 On variation, see p. 90, above. If no such variation is forthcoming, the employer may have to dismiss the objector employee and defend an unfair dismissal action on the ground that the dismissal was fair because of the business need to change; see p. 496, below.
1 See p. 527, below.
2 [1984] ICR 508, [1984] IRLR 190. Napier, 'Computerisation and employment rights' (1992) 21 ILJ 1.

officers and clerks refused to operate a new computerised system of PAYE administration when their employers could not guarantee that there would be no compulsory redundancies. They sought a declaration that their employers were in breach of contract in requiring them to operate the computers. It was held, however, that the change to computers was not sufficient to fall outside their contractual duties of tax gathering and that on the facts they were expected to adapt to the new methods:

'... there can really be no doubt as to the fact that an employee is expected to adapt himself to new methods and techniques introduced in the course of his employment'[3].

However, if such an implied term is to be developed, it should be noted that Walton J added a requirement of reasonableness, continuing the same passage as follows:

'Of course, in a proper case the employer must provide any necessary training or retraining. ... [I]t will, in all cases, be a question of pure fact as to whether the retraining involves the acquisition of such esoteric skills that it would not be reasonable to expect the employee to acquire them.'

Cresswell was a common law action, but this reasonableness approach would be particularly important in an unfair dismissal action where the employer, having introduced changes which were not sufficiently major to alter the contract of employment, insisted on the employee adopting the new methods but then dismissed him for incapability when he was unable so to adapt.

c)   The duty of care

An employee owes to his employer an implied duty of care in carrying out his job. The basic authority for this is usually said to be *Harmer v Cornelius*[4] even though that case actually concerned a representation that the employee possessed the necessary *skill* for the job, for in subsequent cases skill and care have been treated as roughly equivalent. This duty of care applies generally[5] and could cover, for example, care in using the employer's equipment. However, its principal legal significance arises where an employee in the course of his employment injures a third party or his goods. In these circumstances the employer may be sued for damages by the third party as being vicariously liable for the tort of the employee (see chapter 12, below). Once sued, however, the employer has a legal action against the employee for an *indemnity*, and this has caused some difficulty.

The employer's cause of action arises in two ways:
a)   He may sue the employee for breach of contract, for in incurring him in liability to pay damages the employee is in breach of his implied duty of care. The leading case on this is *Lister v Romford Ice and Cold Storage Co Ltd*[6] where it was clearly held that this implied duty exists, and the employer's insurers

---

3   At pp. 518 and 195, respectively.
4   (1858) 5 CBNS 236.
5   Theoretically breach of this duty could found an action for damages by the employer against the employee: this is most unlikely to happen, though there has been one modern example of it, on rather special facts: *Janata Bank v Ahmed* [1981] ICR 791, [1981] IRLR 457, CA.
6   [1957] AC 555, [1957] 1 All ER 125, HL.

were awarded an indemnity against the employee who had negligently run down a third party (his own father as it happened) who had sued the employer for damages. In the House of Lords, the employee attempted to mitigate this harsh application of the duty of care by saying that in modern employment law there is a further implied term that the employer will ensure that the employee is insured against liability such as this, but this was rejected by a majority of three to two.

b) He may sue the employee in tort, for where the employer has been held vicariously liable he and the negligent employee are in law joint tortfeasors, so that he may sue the employee for contribution or a full indemnity under the Civil Liability (Contribution) Act 1978; under this statute, the court may award such contribution as it thinks 'just and equitable having regard to the extent of [the employee's] responsibility for the damage'.

The decision in *Lister's* case caused some consternation and has been heavily criticised on the grounds that the principal rationalisation for vicarious liability is the practical one that it is the employer or his insurer who can afford to pay the damages and that a finding by a court that the employee was negligent may be just a means of fixing liability on to the employer or his insurers; on both of these grounds, a right of indemnity would be inconsistent[7]. Two ways round the decision in *Lister's* case have been suggested. The first was in *Harvey v R G O'Dell Ltd*[8] where McNair J held that the right of indemnity did not apply to an employee driving a vehicle in the course of his employment when such action was not work he was employed to do but was merely a special occasion on which the employee had assisted his employer by undertaking an unusual task; this, however, is to take a very refined view of what an employee is engaged to do. The second arises from the fact that at common law (before the new cause of action was added by statute in 1935) the rule was that there could be *no* contribution between joint tortfeasors[9]; there was, however, one longstanding exception to this where the party seeking contribution was wholly innocent[10] and only liable by some operation of law such as vicarious liability – *Lister's* case was an example of this exception, hence the common law indemnity. Thus, if some fault can be attributed to the employer who is seeking contribution, the case does not fall within the exception, but comes instead within the rule and so contribution cannot be claimed; such fault could arise, for example, if the employer had given the employee some task beyond his competence or had failed to give him proper instruction, as in *Jones v Manchester Corpn*[11] where an inexperienced doctor had caused physical injury to a patient who had sued the employing hospital board for damages, but when the board sought an indemnity from the doctor the Court of Appeal, by a majority, refused to allow it since the hospital had also been at fault in failing to provide adequate supervision for the doctor. The practical problem is that, even if one can circumvent the contractual action in this way, the court still has the discretion to apportion under the 1978 Act, and so an indemnity may still in the end be awarded against the employee, unless the court could be persuaded that it would not be 'just and equitable' to do so; 100% indemnities under the Act were awarded

---

7   Glanville Williams, 'Vicarious liability and the Master's indemnity' (1957) 20 MLR 220 and 437.
8   [1958] 2 QB 78, [1958] 1 All ER 657; criticised by Jolowicz: (1959) 22 MLR 71 and 189.
9   The rule in *Merryweather v Nixan* (1799) 8 Term Rep 186.
10 *Adamson v Jarvis* (1827) 4 Bing 66; *Pearson v Skelton* (1836) 1 M & W 504.
11 [1952] 2 QB 852, [1952] 2 All ER 125, CA.

against employees in *Ryan v Fildes*[12] , *Semtex Ltd v Gladstone*[13] , *Harvey v R G O'Dell Ltd*, supra and in *Lister's* case itself.

In the light of these problems, the effects of *Lister's* case were investigated by a committee of the then Ministry of Labour[14] which concluded that while legislation could alter the position, there was no urgency since in general employers would not seek indemnities because of the effect on industrial relations, and insurers (who were most likely to be interested, since when they pay the damages awarded against the employers they are 'subrogated' into their insured's shoes and can exercise their insured's rights in their own favour – it was an insurance company which brought the action in *Lister's* case, not the employers) have a 'gentleman's agreement' not to exercise these subrogated rights to indemnity against employees (in personal injury cases, where there is no willful misconduct or collusion). This remains the position and there has been no amending legislation. However, the rights against employees still exist in law (even if not generally exercised by employers or their insurers in practice) as can be seen from *Morris v Ford Motor Co Ltd*[15] where a third party who was neither the employer nor an insurance company, claimed to have acquired the important right of subrogation through a peculiar indemnity clause in a cleaning contract. The third party then sought to sue the negligent employee who had (indirectly) caused him to pay damages, but the Court of Appeal by a majority refused to allow it. There was no *express* subrogation clause in the cleaning contract, so Lord Denning MR disallowed an implied one on the grounds (a) that subrogation was an equitable concept and it would not be equitable to allow it in this case and (b) that no clause would be implied in the light of industrial realities, and James LJ also disallowed it on ground (b). However, this case does *not* remove the legal right to indemnity in the industrial sphere, for two reasons – first, it contains no assault on *Lister's* case, only upon the concept of subrogation which does not directly affect the actual right to indemnity; second, the majority could only decide the case this way because there was no express subrogation provision – if there had been it could not have been negated by an implied term to the contrary, so James LJ at least would presumably have had to decide the other way and that would have produced a majority in favour of the indemnity. The possibility of an indemnity being claimed from a negligent employee therefore continues to exist even if it is rarely enforced in practice. This raises two further points of interest – first, no concerted action has been taken by trade unions to secure insurance cover for employees (the term claimed in *Lister's* case), and second, it appears to be no-one's business or interest to clear up an area where the formal legal position is in no way in accordance with general assumptions or practice.

d) Good faith

An act which is inconsistent with the terms of the contract, express or implied, and which is injurious to the employer and his interest will amount to a breach of the duty of faithful service. Thus, a manager whose acts were injurious to the interests of the theatre he was employed to manage was held to have been rightly dismissed at common law[16], and conversely a court saved from attachment an employee who refused to produce material documents in his possession which

---

12   [1938] 3 All ER 517.
13   [1954] 2 All ER 206, [1954] 1 WLR 945.
14   See Gardiner (1959) 22 MLR 652.
15   [1973] QB 792, [1973] 2 All ER 1084, CA.
16   *Lacy v Osbaldiston* (1837) 8 C & P 80.

he held merely in his role of employee, for the court would not infer that he could produce the documents without violating the duty he owed to his employer[17]. In particular, an employee must not place himself in a position in which his own interests conflict with his duty to his employer[18]. The clash of interest and duty can be seen most clearly in the leading case, *Boston Deep Sea Fishing and Ice Co v Ansell*[19]. The defendant had been employed as managing director of the plaintiff company and he had contracted with a firm of shipbuilders for the supply of certain vessels and had taken from them a commission in respect of the transaction, of which his employers knew nothing. He also possessed shares in an ice-making and fish-carrying company which paid bonuses to those of its shareholders who, being owners of fishing vessels, used the company's ice or its services as a carrier. He was held to the strictest accountability but, apart from that, there was clearly a breach of his duty faithfully to serve, since the temptation to use the company's ice or its services as a carrier conflicted or might conflict with his duty to consider his employer's interests in preference to his own. It was held that he was properly dismissed, and he had to account to his employer for his profits. It is true that this case concerned a managing director and directors may be under a special fiduciary duty anyway[20], but the general principle may apply to any employee who misuses his employer's property in a way which shows breach of fidelity (for example by borrowing from the till when not allowed to do so: *Sinclair v Neighbour*[1]), or improperly exploits his position of employment in order to make a secret profit or gain. In *Reading v A-G*[2], Sergeant Reading who was stationed in Egypt agreed on a number of occasions to accompany lorries to certain destinations, his uniform guaranteeing that such lorries would avoid inspection by the police. These lorries contained illicit spirits and as a result of his services Reading secured almost £20,000. When the military authorities arrested him, they impounded the money and when he was released from prison he brought a petition of right claiming return of the money by the Crown. The House of Lords not surprisingly held against him, for he had misused his position in the service of the Crown and had to account for his profit.

Although secret profits and interests may have to be disclosed, and in certain circumstances an employee may have to inform his employer about matters in his knowledge which affect confidential interests of the employer[3], the duty of fidelity must not be taken too far. Except for the case of directors who are under a fiduciary duty[4], a contract of employment is not a contract uberrimae fidei requiring total

17 *Eccles & Co v Louisville and Nashville Railroad Co* [1912] 1 KB 135, CA.
18 *Pearce v Foster* (1886) 17 QBD 536, CA provides a good example; see generally Stephens 'An agent's duty to account' (1975) 28 CLP 39.
19 (1888) 39 Ch D 339, CA. Note that one of the main propositions established in this case, that at common law the employer may rely on misconduct unknown to him at the date of dismissal and only discovered subsequently in order to justify dismissal, does *not* apply to proceedings for unfair dismissal: *W Devis & Sons Ltd v Atkins* [1977] 3 All ER 40, [1977] ICR 662, HL.
20 *Cook v Deeks* [1916] 1 AC 554, PC; *Cranleigh Precision Engineering Ltd v Bryant* [1964] 3 All ER 289, [1965] 1 WLR 1293; *Industrial Development Consultants v Cooley* [1972] 2 All ER 162, [1972] 1 WLR 443; *Thomas Marshall (Exports) Ltd v Guinle* [1978] ICR 905, [1978] IRLR 174. The Companies Act 1985, s. 317 requires a director with an interest in a contract with the company to disclose that interest to the board of directors; for a newsworthy example, see *Guinness plc v Saunders* [1988] 2 All ER 940, [1988] 1 WLR 863, CA (non-disclosure leading to a constructive trust to repay £5.2m).
1   [1967] 2 QB 279, [1966] 3 All ER 988, CA.
2   [1951] AC 507, [1951] 1 All ER 617, HL.
3   *Cranleigh Precision Engineering Ltd v Bryant* [1964] 3 All ER 289, [1965] 1 WLR 1293.
4   *Regal (Hastings) Ltd v Gulliver* (1942) [1967] 2 AC 134n, [1942] 1 All ER 378, HL; *Horcal Ltd v Gatland* [1984] IRLR 288, CA.

and voluntary disclosure. Thus, an employee is not under a general duty to declare facts which may prove inimical to the employer, including his own misconduct[5] or unsavoury aspects of his own background[6]. However, this has always been subject to the qualification that he must not positively mislead the employer as to such matters[7], and in the important case of *Sybron Corpn v Rochem Ltd*[8] it was further (a) suggested that there may be a duty to disclose the employee's own misconduct which has been fraudulently concealed, and (b) held that there may be on the facts of the case a positive duty to disclose the misconduct of *other* employees (particularly in the case of an employee high in the company's hierarchy, with responsibility for those other employees) even if that involves of necessity disclosing his own misconduct[9].

From this general discussion of fidelity, we must now turn to four specific ways in which an employer might be in breach of his duty – by competition, misuse of confidential information, making his own inventions and failing to serve the employee in good faith.

1) *Competition* The courts will be most reluctant to impose restraints on a person's spare time and generally an employee's skills are his own (even if learned in the employer's time) so that normally there is no legal objection to an employee taking other employment in his spare time. The courts will, however, interfere in the untypical case where the use of the employee's skill and knowledge can be clearly shown to be harming the employer. This was the situation in the leading case of *Hivac Ltd v Park Royal Scientific Instruments Ltd*[10]. Certain employees of the plaintiff company worked in their spare time on a similar kind of highly specialised work for the defendant company, the two firms being in direct competition. There was no evidence that any of the employees (who were not parties to the action) had divulged any confidential information. It was found that the employees had agreed to do and had done work which they knew must harm their employers, that this was a breach of their duty of fidelity and that the defendant company would be restrained from employing them. The court made something of the fact that because of the abnormality of the times and the operation of an essential work order, the employees could not easily be dismissed, but it is doubtful how far this is relevant, as the principle remains that where the employee harms his employer the law may interfere:

'It would be most unfortunate if anything we said should place an undue restraint on the right of the workman, particularly a manual workman, to make use of his leisure for his profit. On the other hand, it would be deplorable if it were laid down that a workman could, consistently with his

---

5   *Bell v Lever Bros Ltd* [1932] AC 161, HL. Most of these cases involve attempts by an employer to recover golden handshakes given to employees who, after leaving, are discovered to have been defrauding the employer. For a recent affirmation of the general principles, see *Nottingham University v Fishel* [2000] IRLR 471

6   Note that a 'spent' conviction does not have to be disclosed anyway, under the Rehabilitation of Offenders Act 1974, s. 4 (for the application of this Act to unfair dismissal cases, see p. 481, below).

7   Hence the importance, on recruitment, of the employer asking the right questions (e.g. at an interview) so that the employee cannot simply refrain from volunteering information and obtain the employment sub silentio. Deliberate fraud in gaining employment will usually be a fair ground for dismissal: *City of Birmingham District Council v Beyer* [1978] 1 All ER 910, [1977] IRLR 211.

8   [1983] 2 All ER 707, [1983] IRLR 253, CA.

9   Applying *Swain v West (Butchers) Ltd* [1936] 3 All ER 261, CA.

10   [1946] Ch 169, [1946] 1 All ER 350, CA.

duty to his employer, knowingly, deliberately and secretly set himself to do in his spare time something which would inflict great harm on his master's business'[11].

There may, therefore, be cases where the courts will restrain competition, but even then it will only be during the course of employment, and will not apply to competition by an ex-employee[12]. If the employer wishes to fetter competition after the employee leaves him it will have to be by an express restraint clause (see above under head 4 – Legality and restraint of trade) and, as we have seen, even then the clause will only be valid if there is some definite element of trade secrets, customer connections or staff preservation to protect, for the courts will not allow a clause which is aimed simply at stifling competition[13].

If an employee engages in improper competition that may be a valid reason for dismissal, though as always in the realm of unfair dismissal the fact that it is a breach of contract is not conclusive (as it might have been at common law for wrongful dismissal) and the dismissal must still be fair in all the circumstances, including the procedure adopted[14]. If the employer finds that the employee is soliciting customers with a view to setting up in business when he leaves, that too may be a valid ground for pre-emptive dismissal, but once again the evidence of this will have to be clear, and may require reasonable investigation by the employer before this step is taken[15]; if the further elements of trade secrets or other confidential information being at risk are not present, however, merely planning to leave employment to work for a competitor or to set up in competition will probably not be a fair ground for dismissal[16].

2)   *Misuse or disclosure of confidential information*   During the course of his employment the employee is under an implied duty not to misuse confidential information belonging to his employer[17] and this is a duty which may continue to operate after the termination of his employment; however, it was pointed out by the Court of Appeal in what has for some time now been viewed as the leading modern case on the subject, *Faccenda Chicken Ltd v Fowler*[18], that there is a difference

---

11   Ibid., at 178 and 356 respectively per Lord Greene MR. This dictum was applied by the EAT to an unfair dismissal claim in *Nova Plastics Ltd v Frogatt* [1982] IRLR 146, reinforcing the requirement of definite harm to the employer before an ordinary employee can be said to be in breach of this duty.

12   *J A Mont (UK) Ltd v Mills* [1993] IRLR 172, CA. The combination of the duty on an *existing* employee not to compete and a long notice provision produces a 'garden leave clause', see p. 372, below.

13   *Herbert Morris Ltd v Saxelby* [1916] 1 AC 688, HL; *Faccenda Chicken Ltd v Fowler* [1986] IRLR 69, CA.

14   *Gibson v National Union of Dyers, Bleachers and Textile Workers* (1972) 7 ITR 324; *Golden Cross Hire Co Ltd v Lovell* [1979] IRLR 267.

15   *Hawkins v Prickett* [1976] IRLR 52, IT.

16   *Harris and Russell Ltd v Slingsby* [1973] 3 All ER 31, [1973] ICR 454; *Laughton and Hawley v Bapp Industrial Supplies Ltd* [1986] ICR 634, [1986] IRLR 245; cf. however *Marshall v Industrial Systems and Control Ltd* [1992] IRLR 294 where a managing director, proposing to leave, had suborned two other employees and approached customers (*Laughton* distinguished), and *Adamson v B & L Cleaning Services Ltd* [1995] IRLR 193 where the foreman of a contract cleaning firm tendered for a contract in competition with his employer prior to leaving to set up his own firm, and was fairly dismissed.

17   *Bents Brewery Co Ltd v Hogan* [1945] 2 All ER 570; see generally Bryan 'The employee and trade secrets law' (1977) 30 CLP 191.

18   [1986] ICR 297, [1986] IRLR 69, CA, noted Hepple [1986] 15 ILJ 183; applied in *Roger Bullivant Ltd v Ellis* [1987] ICR 464, [1987] IRLR 491, CA and *Johnson & Bloy (Holdings) Ltd v Wolstenholme Rink plc* [1987] IRLR 499, CA.

in the content and extent of the duty – in the case of an existing employee the obligation of confidentiality is wider (covering matters such as the employee's own particular skills and knowledge acquired generally during the employment) than in the case of an ex-employee whose obligations to his ex-employer are restricted to the kind of trade secrets or confidential customer connections that could be the subject of a valid restraint of trade clause[19]. To cover this latter case (of an ex-employee), in any employment where questions of confidentiality are at all likely to be material the employer is well advised to extract from the employee such an express restraint clause (or a garden leave clause) which is not only more certain, but which may in practice be more effective for, provided that it is valid, it will stop the ex-employee actually entering employment where he may be tempted to divulge confidential information, whereas the implied duty of fidelity could only be used to seek to prevent him from divulging such information once he is in the employment in question. An express clause is thus preferable, but if the employer omits to negotiate one or if there is an express clause which stops short of imposing any actual restraints on the employee, the courts will usually find an implied term as in *Robb v Green*[20] where a manager secretly copied out lists of his employer's customers, left the employment and set up in competition using the lists: the Court of Appeal upheld the injunction which had been granted restraining the ex-employee and Lord Esher MR said:

'I think that in a contract of service the Court must imply such a stipulation as I have mentioned (i.e., that the servant will act with good faith towards his master), because it is a thing which must necessarily have been in view of both parties when they entered into the contract. It is impossible to suppose that a master would have put a servant into a confidential position of this kind, unless he thought that the servant would be bound to use good faith towards him; or that the servant would not know, when he entered into this position, that the master would rely on his observance of good faith in the confidential relation between them.'

Thus, in *Sanders v Parry*[1] an assistant solicitor who set up independently, taking away from his employer one of the practice's main clients whose affairs he had looked after, was held to have broken his implied duty of good faith.

In general, the same rules will apply to this implied duty as apply to express restraint of trade clauses, and these are considered under head 4 of this chapter – Legality and restraint of trade; in particular, the duty will apply essentially to trade secrets and customer connections (those being recognised by the law as protectable interests, with increasingly the addition of staff preservation), there must be a genuine element of secrecy attached to the information in question, the duty will not apply to ordinary skills or knowledge gained during employment, and it will not be allowed in order simply to stifle bona fide competition. However, even though essentially the same principles apply, the express clause remains preferable, for it will normally restrain the ex-employee from entering certain

---

19   Thus in *Wallace Bogan & Co v Cove* [1997] IRLR 453, CA solicitors leaving their employer to set up their own firm played it 'by the book', doing nothing to infringe the higher duties before leaving; but *then* writing to clients of the old employer announcing the existence of the new firm. *Held* – no general restriction on this form of competition after employment, in the absence of a restraint of trade clause.

20   [1895] 2 QB 315, CA; the passage cited is at 317.

1   [1967] 2 All ER 803, [1967] 1 WLR 753. Contract on the facts *Wallace Bogan & Co v Cove*, n. 19 above.

forms of employment during a particular period, and so breach of it will readily be shown, whereas the implied duty allows other employment, only restraining the ex-employee from improper disclosure and this may be far more difficult to *prove*, particularly where there is no tangible evidence such as the deliberate copying out of plans or lists (as in *Robb v Green*)[2]. This problem arises because of the difficult borderline between the ordinary use of information and expertise, albeit gained in the previous employment, which is permissible[3], and the improper misuse of confidential information which may be restrainable; this may be further complicated if the ex-employee is using some information from each category, and the principle has been stated by Lord Denning in *Seager v Copydex Ltd*[4] thus:

'When the information is mixed, being partly public and partly private then the recipient must take special care to use only the material which is in the public domain. He should go to the public source to get it; or, at any rate, not be in a better position than if he had gone to the public source. He should not get a start over others by using the information which he received in confidence.'

The difficulties of applying such a principle to any particular set of facts, e.g. where a technical director has left his employer and gone to work for a competitor on similar work, are great, and in the light of this it may be the case in practice that although there is no legal requirement that the ex-employee should have carried the information away in some tangible (particularly written) form before the duty can be used to restrain him (and so in some cases evidence of deliberate solicitation of customers prior to leaving has been sufficient[5]), the presence of evidence of such conduct could be extremely persuasive and indeed in the lack of it the employer could have grave problems of proof. Considering this problem in *Printers and Finishers Ltd v Holloway*[6] Cross J said, in the context of the ex-employee's knowledge of the general workings of the employer's business:

'Recalling matters of this sort is, to my mind, quite unlike memorising a formula or list of customers or what was said (obviously in confidence) at a particular meeting. The employee might well not realise that the feature or expedient in question was in fact peculiar to his late employer's process and factory; but even if he did such knowledge is not readily separable from his general knowledge of the flock printing process and his acquired skill in manipulating a flock printing plant, and I do not think that there was anything improper in his putting his memory or particular features of his late employer's plant at the disposal of his new employer. The law will

---

2   If, however, it *is* the case that the employee leaves with written material containing confidential information, he may expect short shrift from a court, even if he argues that at least some of the information could have been carried away in his head: *Johnson & Bloy (Holdings) Ltd v Wolstenholme Rink plc* [1987] IRLR 499, CA, applying *Roger Bullivant Ltd v Ellis* [1987] ICR 464, [1987] IRLR 491, CA where Nouse LJ stated that it was still of great importance that the principle in *Robb v Green* should be steadfastly maintained.

3   *Spafax Ltd v Harrison* [1980] IRLR 442, CA; *Faccenda Chicken Ltd v Fowler*, n. 16 above.

4   [1967] 2 All ER 415 at 417, [1967] RPC 349 at 368, CA. This dictum refers particularly to the position of a third party, which is considered infra, but the principle is applicable to the ex-employee himself.

5   *Wessex Dairies Ltd v Smith* [1935] 2 KB 80, CA; *Thomas Marshall (Exports) Ltd v Guinle* [1978] ICR 905, [1978] IRLR 174, cf. *Hawkins v Prickett* [1976] IRLR 52, IT.

6   [1964] 3 All ER 731 at 736, [1965] 1 WLR 1 at 6.

defeat its own object if it seeks to enforce in this field standards which would be rejected by the ordinary man.'

The employer failed on this particular part of the case, essentially because his case was too vague (as in *Baker v Gibbons*[7]), and this is likely to be the case wherever the employer lacks compelling evidence such as deliberate subterfuge and compilation of information[8].

If an employee or ex-employee is misusing confidential information, what remedies are available to the employer? If the employee is still in employment, it might well be a good reason for dismissal which is likely to be held to be fair[9]. If he has already left employment, the employer may seek an injunction to restrain him from passing on information or damages for breach of the implied duty as in *Sanders v Parry*[10]. A complication might arise if the ex-employee passes on confidential information to a third party, for example a competitor with whom he has taken employment or a company which he has set up in order to take advantage of his illicit knowledge. This, however, has not proved a problem, for the original employer may sue that third party, seeking an injunction restraining him from taking advantage of the information either on the narrower ground of inducement to breach of contract[11] (particularly if the employee in question is still in employment with the original employer) or on the wider ground of breach of confidence. The exact basis and extent of this latter equitable concept are still arguable and some fundamental questions await a definite answer[12] (for example whether there is a breach if the recipient of the information is ignorant of its source or confidential nature, and if so, what the remedy should be). Whatever be the details and developments, however, it is capable of being a useful weapon against a third party in cases such as these, as a further ground for an injunction or damages[13], or, perhaps of more value, as a ground for ordering an account of profits[14] and delivery up or destruction of the material in question[15]. Thus, to

7   [1972] 2 All ER 759, [1972] 1 WLR 693.
8   This is as a matter of evidence; there is, however, no legal principle that an employee is free to use *anything* carried away only in his head: *Johnson & Bloy (Holdings) Ltd v Wolstenholme Rink plc* [1987] IRLR 499, CA, disapproving dicta in favour of such a principle by Scott J in *Balston Ltd v Headline Filters Ltd* [1987] FSR 330.
9   *Smith v Du Pont (UK) Ltd* [1976] IRLR 107, IT.
10 [1967] 2 All ER 803, [1967] 1 WLR 753. See Goulding, 'Springboard injunctions in employment law' (1995) 24 ILJ 152. In *Johnson & Bloy (Holdings) Ltd v Wolstenholme Rink plc* [1987] IRLR 499, CA it was held that a plaintiff employer in such a case should normally be entitled to an injunction – it is not enough for the defendant to offer an undertaking not to use the information to compete with the plaintiff (with the prospect only of damages if there is in fact unlawful competition).
11 *Bents Brewery Ltd v Hogan* [1945] 2 All ER 570; *Hivac v Park Royal Scientific Instruments Ltd* [1946] Ch 169, [1946] 1 All ER 350, CA. The injunction may even order the new employer not to proceed with contracts already entered into: *PSM International plc v Whitehouse* [1992] IRLR 279, CA.
12 On breach of confidence generally see *Saltman Engineering Co Ltd v Campbell Engineering Co Ltd* [1963] 3 All ER 413n, [1965] 65 RPC 203, CA; *Seager v Copydex Ltd* [1967] 2 All ER 415, [1967] RPC 349, CA; *Sun Printers Ltd v Westminster Press Ltd* [1982] IRLR 292, CA: Law Commission Report on Breach of Confidence, Law Comm. No. 110.
13 *Seager v Copydex Ltd (No 2)* [1969] 2 All ER 718, [1969] 1 WLR 809, CA. Causation must be proved: *Universal Thermosensors Ltd v Hibben* [1992] 3 All ER 257, [1992] 1 WLR 840.
14 *Peter Pan Manufacturing Corpn v Corsets Silhouette Ltd* [1963] 3 All ER 402, [1963] RPC 45. In a rather more sensational context, the possibility of an action for an account of profits through misuse of confidential information was mentioned as a further remedy for the government against Mr Peter Wright, author of *Spycatcher*, in the light of their failure to have it suppressed in other jurisdictions; no such proceedings were brought in the event.
15 *Industrial Furnaces Ltd v Reaves* [1970] RPC 605.

take a useful example from an Australian jurisdiction, in *Ansell Rubber Co v Allied Rubber Industries*[16] the plaintiff company made rubber gloves from machines whose parts and principles were known, but the actual construction of which was secret. One of their employees, A, left their employment and set up the defendant company using identical machines, and a fellow employee, G, remained in employment while helping A to do so. In the subsequent action, the court held (i) that the construction of a machine is capable of being a matter of confidence, albeit made from known components; (ii) that A was in breach of his contractual duty of fidelity through misuse of confidential information, G was likewise in breach for that reason and through improper competition while still employed, and the defendant company had received and misused confidential information and so was in breach of confidence; (iii) that the plaintiff company should be awarded damages against A and G, an account of profits against the defendant company and injunctions restraining any further use of the information and the machines.

One exception to the duty not to misuse or divulge confidential information arises where disclosure by the employee or ex-employee is in the public interest. This might arise where the employer is committing a criminal offence, but it might also go wider than this. The exception evolved at common law, but is now covered by statute.

i)   Common law   In *Initial Services Ltd v Putterill*[17] the ex-employee gave to a newspaper details of an unlawful price protection ring involving the employers (contrary to the Restrictive Trade Practices Act 1956) and of price rises attributed to Selective Employment Tax in order to disguise higher profits. The Court of Appeal held that this was capable of constituting proper disclosure in the public interest, and Lord Denning MR clearly envisaged that this exception went beyond crime and fraud and applied wherever disclosure was justified in the public interest. This principle was applied in *Fraser v Evans*[18] and *Hubbard v Vosper*[19] but was subject to restriction in *Beloff v Pressdram Ltd*[20] by Ungoed-Thomas J who thought that it only applied to the disclosure of 'misdeeds of a serious nature' by the employer. However, this restrictive view was later disapproved by the Court of Appeal in *Lion Laboratories Ltd v Evans*[1] where it was held that public interest disclosure could apply to a wide range of matters, of which 'iniquity' on the part of the employer was only one example. Moreover, disclosure in the public interest may be particularly justified where that disclosure is to a regulatory body with power of investigation and control of the employer's business[2]. This whole area became topical with increasing concern being expressed over attempts by certain

---

16   [1967] VR 37; the judgment of Gowans J contains an extensive review of the relevant British and American authorities on confidential information. For a more recent example, see *PSM International plc v Whitehouse* [1992] IRLR 279, CA.

17   [1968] 1 QB 396, [1967] 3 All ER 145, CA.

18   [1969] 1 QB 349, [1969] 1 All ER 8, CA.

19   [1972] 2 QB 84, [1972] 1 All ER 1023, CA.

20   [1973] 1 All ER 241 at 260. The earlier authorities would have restricted it to criminal acts or danger to the state: *Weld-Blundell v Stephens* [1920] AC 956, HL. Note that an employee may in certain circumstances be under a statutory duty to disclose certain material, e.g. under the Health and Safety at Work etc. Act 1974, ss. 27 and 28.

1   [1985] QB 526, [1984] 2 All ER 417, CA. This is an interesting case on the application of the public interest defence, containing inter alia a statement by Stephenson LJ that not all that is interesting to the public may be disclosed in the public interest, and a reminder that the press may have a private interest of their own in making disclosures, which may be a factor to be taken into account.

2   *Re a Company's Application* [1989] ICR 449, [1989] IRLR 477.

employers to prevent any form of disclosure by employees by the incorporation of 'gagging clauses' into their contracts, for example banning them from talking to the press about anything concerning their employment, and making it a disciplinary offence to do so[3]. Particular concern arose over the use of such clauses by the newly-independent trusts and other bodies in the NHS[4]. While at one level the incorporation of an express clause could be likened to the (lawful) use of a restraint of trade clause (rather than relying on the general implied term of confidentiality), the suspicion was quick to arise that these clauses were really intended to go further and prevent *any* disclosure or, as it has come to be known, whistle-blowing.

ii) Statute   Although the above common law will continue to apply by way of a defence to a civil action, concerns such as those above allied with certain moves (e.g. the Nolan Committee) towards more openness about standards in public life led to calls for more direct protection for the *individual* employee making disclosures in the public interest. This came about through a Private Member's Bill, backed by the government as a commitment in the White Paper 'Fairness at Work', which became the Public Interest Disclosure Act 1998[5]. This operates by way of additions to the Employment Rights Act 1996 to establish special protection from dismissal[6] or action short of dismissal[7] imposed because the worker[8] has made a 'protected disclosure'. This is the disclosure of information which, in the reasonable belief of the worker making the disclosure, tends to show a criminal offence, a failure to comply with a legal obligation, a miscarriage of justice, a health and safety danger, environmental damage, or deliberate concealment of any of these[9]. As with the wider view of the common law, this goes well beyond criminal offences and to that extent the protection is wide. However, the Act is also meant to strike a balance and not simply to allow the whistle-blower to go straight to the press on all occasions, especially where the press in question are waving chequebooks[10]. To that extent, it has advantages to an employer too in

3   Lewis 'Whistleblowers and job security' (1995) 58 MLR 208.
4   Vickers 'Whistleblowers and the NHS' (1995) NLJ 57. One such clause even prevented employees from contacting their MP without going through (protracted?) internal procedures. One irony is that, at the same time as concern was mounting about this practice, doctors were themselves being placed under a contractual *obligation* to blow the whistle on allegedly negligent colleagues (though not, of course, on the activities of the increasing legions of hospital administrators, a breed who have rapidly overtaken undertakers, farmers, estate agents and solicitors to top the list of public hate figures).
5   Lewis 'The Public Interest Disclosure Act 1998' (1998) 27 ILJ 325.
6   Employment Rights Act 1996, s. 103A; such a dismissal is automatically unfair, as is any later selection for redundancy for this reason; there is no qualifying period or upper age limit; the cap on the compensatory award for unfair dismissal has been removed completely in these cases and interim relief is available.
7   Ibid., s. 47B.
8   The 1998 Act adopts the wider definition of 'worker' in the Employment Rights Act 1996, s. 230(3), i.e. a person under a contract of employment *or* under any other contract to do or perform personally any work or services for another (other than a client or customer of any profession or business undertaking carried out by the person). For good measure, the new s. 43K specifically includes agency workers, homeworkers, work trainees and certain specified NHS staff who might not otherwise have qualified. Although the terminology of unfair dismissal is of course being used, the Act can go wider than the employment relationship because there is no requirement that the divulged information must show evildoing by the worker's employer (though of course in many cases that will be so).
9   Ibid., s. 43(B)(1). These matters may occur in the UK or abroad: s. 43B(2).
10   '[The Act] will encourage resolution of concerns through proper workplace procedures, but it will protect those who, in the last resort, have to go public': Fairness at Work (Cm. 3968, 1998), para. 3.3.

emphasising that disclosure is primarily and initially meant to be internal[11]. This is achieved by establishing the forms of disclosure that have the protected status, with four categories of disclosure to named persons, backed up by two categories of wider disclosure which are subject to much more stringent conditions. The four 'normal' categories are disclosure:

1) in good faith, to the employer or where the worker reasonably believes that the relevant failure relates solely or mainly to the conduct of another person or to any other matter for which another person has legal responsibility, to that person[12];
2) to a legal adviser, in the course of obtaining legal advice[13];
3) in good faith, to a Minister of the Crown (where the worker's employer is appointed by a Minister)[14];
4) to a person prescribed by order by the Secretary of State, where the worker reasonably believes that the relevant failure falls within the order and that the information disclosed (and any allegation contained in it) are substantially true[15].

Obviously, cases may well arise where one of these is not appropriate (particularly where the person to whom disclosure is primarily meant to be made is actually the culprit – in this context of course, the employer) and so the Act then establishes two longstops, where the worker is in effect allowed to 'go public':

1) 'disclosure in other cases';[16] – this applies where (a) the worker makes the disclosure in good faith, (b) he reasonably believes that the information disclosed (and any allegations contained in it) are substantially true, (c) he does not make the disclosure for personal gain, (d) any one of a series of conditions is met[17], and (e) in all the circumstances of the case, it is reasonable for him to make the disclosure[18];
2) 'disclosure of exceptionally serious failure'[19] – this applies where (a) the worker makes the disclosure in good faith, (b) he reasonably believes that the information disclosed (and any allegations contained in it) are

11 Although there is no obligation in the Act for an employer to have a formal whistle-blowing policy, this may well be advisable so that complaints/disclosures can be dealt with effectively in-house, thus avoiding the possibility of a protected disclosure to the press.
12 Ibid., s. 43C.
13 Ibid., s. 44D.
14 Ibid., s. 43E. See the Public Interest Disclosure (Prescribed Persons) Order 1999, S.I. 1999 No. 1549, *Harvey* R[1183].
15 Ibid., s. 43F.
16 Ibid., s. 43G.
17 The conditions are that (a) the worker reasonably believes that he will be subjected to a detriment by his employer if he makes the disclosure to him or to a prescribed person; or (b) that, where there is no prescribed person, the worker reasonably believes that it is likely that evidence relating to the relevant failure will be concealed or destroyed if he makes disclosure to his employer; or (c) that the worker has previously made a disclosure of substantially the same information to his employer or a prescribed person: s. 43F(2).
18 In deciding on reasonableness, regard is to be had to (a) the identity of the person (or tabloid?) to whom disclosure is made; (b) the seriousness of the relevant failure; (c) whether the failure is continuing or likely to occur in the future; (d) whether the disclosure is made in breach of a duty of confidentiality owed by the employer to any other person; (e) in a case of previous disclosure (under s 43G(2)(c), see previous footnote) any action which the employer or prescribed person has taken or might reasonably be expected to have taken as a result; and (f) in a case of previous disclosure to the employer, whether the worker complied with any disclosure procedure whose use by him was authorised by the employer: s. 43G(3). The final head shows the possible importance of a whistle-blowing policy in ensuring that disclosure follows the correct internal channels, rather than spilling out too easily into the public arena.
19 Ibid., s 43H.

substantially true, (c) he does not make the disclosure for purposes of personal gain, (d) the relevant failure is of an exceptionally serious nature (undefined) and (e) in all the circumstances of the case, it is reasonable for him to make the disclosure[20].

The question of gagging clauses is then dealt with directly and briefly by a provision which states that any provision in any agreement between a worker and his employer[1] (*including* a settlement of legal proceedings) is void in so far as it purports to preclude the worker from making a protected disclosure[2].

Finally, one possible further statutory development should be noted which would operate in the opposite direction, i.e. to *increase* the liability of an individual (possibly an employee) in relation to the use of information. The Law Commission have suggested that it should become a *criminal* offence (triable on indictment) knowingly to use or disclose a trade secret belonging to another without that other's consent[3]. Clearly this would need a carefully drafted public interest defence; the consultation paper came before the Public Interest Disclosure Act 1998 and so contained its own proposed draft of such a defence (including 'any use or disclosure of information which under the law of confidence would be justified on grounds of public interest'), but any developments in this area would now need to be consistent with the 1998 Act; of equal interest will be how it is eventually proposed to define 'trade secret', still a notorious area of difficulty in the civil context after a century of case law.

3) *The employee's inventions*   In the absence of an express term in the contract of employment, the common law position was that the employer was entitled to the benefit of inventions made by his employee if they were referable to the employment. Thus, in *British Syphon Co Ltd v Homewood*[4] the defendant discovered a new type of soda syphon and applied to patent it; he was employed by the plaintiffs as a chief technician to advise them generally on their business, but he had not been asked to make any new designs and there was no express agreement between them on the matter of inventions. Roxburgh J held that the plaintiffs were entitled to the benefit of the invention which had arisen out of the employment. This was a strong implied term at common law, usually explained on the basis of fidelity, and it would apply if the parties were silent or if an express term was void through being too wide; moreover, it would continue to apply even if the employee went ahead and patented the invention, for then it was held that he held the patent on trust for the employer[5]. It was even held that the employee might be under a continuing duty to do anything necessary to assist the employer to realise the patent[6]. Not every invention belonged to the employer, however,

---

20   In deciding on reasonableness, regard is to be had in particular to the identity of the person to whom the disclosure is made: s. 43H(2).

1   Whether or not a 'worker's contract' (under the extended definition in the Employment Rights Act 1996, s. 230(3)).

2   Ibid., s. 43J. A disclosure not protected under the Act would not come under this provision and so a gagging clause covering it would be valid *unless* a court were persuaded to strike it down at common law.

3   Misuse of Trade Secrets (Law Comm Consultation Paper No. 150, 1997). One other possibility raised in the paper is an offence of dishonest acquisition of trade secrets. See generally Colling 'Should the use and disclosure of trade secrets be criminalised?' (1998) 27 ILJ 147.

4   [1956] 2 All ER 897, [1956] 1 WLR 1190. See also *British Reinforced Concrete Engineering Co v Lind* (1917) 86 LJ Ch 486.

5   *Triplex Safety Glass Co Ltd v Scorah* [1938] Ch 211, [1937] 4 All ER 693.

6   *British Celanese Ltd v Moncrieff* [1948] Ch 564, [1948] 2 All ER 44, CA.

and much might depend on the nature of the invention and the position of the employee, but the employee was only really safe if the nature of the invention was clearly outside the employer's business interest[7]; however, if it was safely outside those interests, the fact that it was made during working hours or with the employer's materials would not deprive the employee of it[8] and indeed even an express term giving the benefit of *any* invention to the employer might be void as in restraint of trade[9]. Section 56(2) of the Patents Act 1949 appeared to mitigate this possibly harsh implied term by allowing the comptroller to apportion the benefits of an invention between employer and employee unless satisfied that one party was absolutely entitled, but this was construed restrictively by the House of Lords in *Sterling Engineering Co Ltd v Patchett*[10] so that it did not apply to the majority of employment cases where, by the operation of the implied term, the employer was already absolutely entitled to the invention. The whole area of patent law was overhauled, however, by the Patents Act 1977, and so the common law will now only apply (i) to inventions made before the commencement of the relevant parts of the Act[11]; (ii) where the Act does not apply, in particular where the employee was not 'mainly employed in the United Kingdom', but, under the conflict of laws rules, the matter remains generally governed by English law[12].

For present purposes, the modern legislation made two innovations – it sets out in section 39 when an invention will belong to the employer, and provides in sections 40 and 41 a scheme for compensating an employee inventor which is quite independent of contractual obligations. Now, therefore, most disputes as to employee inventions will be solved by a process of statutory interpretation, not by recourse to the common law rules. Section 39 provides that an invention belongs to the employee except in two specified instances when, for the purposes of the Act and all other purposes, it belongs to the employer; these are:

a)   if it was made *in the course of the normal duties of the employee* or in the course of duties falling *outside his normal duties, but specifically assigned to him*, and the circumstances in either case were such that an invention might reasonably be expected to result from the carrying out of his duties; or

b)   if the invention was made in the course of the duties of the employee and at the time of making the invention, because of the nature of his duties, he had a *special obligation to further the interests of the employer's undertaking*[13].

Unlike the common law position, this owes nothing to concepts of fidelity, and contentious points now are likely to be whether the invention was reasonably to be expected, and in what circumstances an employee is under the special obligation mentioned in paragraph (b) (a director under a fiduciary duty would presumably be covered, but the question is how far coverage will extend outside that special case)[14]. By section 42, any agreement purporting to diminish the employee's rights in an invention under section 39 is unenforceable to the extent that it does so diminish those rights.

Sections 40 and 41 provide in addition a statutory scheme for compensation for an inventor employee. Under this scheme, the employee may make a claim to

7   *Re Selz Ltd* (1953) 71 RPC 158.
8   *Mellor v Beardmore* (1927) 44 RPC 175.
9   *Electrolux Ltd v Hudson* [1977] FSR 312.
10   [1955] AC 534, [1955] 1 All ER 369, HL.
11   Patents Act 1977, s. 43(1); the 'appointed day' was 1 June 1978 – Patents Act 1977 (Commencement No. 2) Order 1978, S.I. 1978 No. 586.
12   Ibid., s. 43(2).
13   Author's italics.
14   For detailed discussion of these provisions, see the Commentary section in the *Encyclopedia of United Kingdom and European Patent Law* and Phillips 'Employee inventors and the new Patents Act' (1978) 7 ILJ 30; *Reiss Engineering Co Ltd v Harris* [1985] IRLR 232.

the Patents Court or the Patents Office within a year of the expiry of the patent for compensation in one of two circumstances:
a) where the invention belonged to the employer under section 39 and proved to be of 'outstanding benefit'[15] to that employer; or
b) where the invention belonged to the employee under section 39 and he assigned or exclusively leased it to the employer but received benefits from that contract which were 'inadequate in relation to the benefit derived by the employer from the patent'.

The court or comptroller is then empowered to award such compensation to the employee as will secure for him a 'fair share' of the actual or anticipated benefits derived from the patent. 'Fair share' is not defined, but section 41 lays down criteria to be considered. In the case of (a) above, these are:
i) the nature of the employee's duties, his remuneration and any other advantages from his employment or the invention;
ii) the employee's effort and skill in making the invention;
iii) the effort and skill of any third party involved;
iv) the significance of any contributions of the employer towards the invention (e.g. advice, facilities).

In the case of (b) above, they are:
i) any conditions in any licences granted under the Act in respect of the invention or the patent;
ii) any extent to which the invention was a joint project with a third party;
iii) any contributions by the employer (as in iv) above).

An order for compensation may be for a lump sum or for periodic payments or both[16]. Any agreement purporting to exclude the employee's right to statutory compensation is ineffective, but these provisions do not apply where the matter is already governed by a collective agreement[17].

The position with regard to copyright in material produced by an employee is governed by the Copyright, Designs and Patents Act 1988, section 11, which provides that, although the first owner of copyright is the author, 'where a literary, dramatic, musical or artistic work or a film is made by an employee in the course of his employment, his employer is the first owner of any copyright in the work subject to any agreement to the contrary'. This straightforward provision does not attempt any more ambitious scheme of recompensing employed authors, such as that seen above in the patents legislation, being content instead to leave the matter as essentially one for agreement between the parties. It substantially re-enacts the pre-existing law which was contained in the repealed Copyright Act 1956, section 4, whose effect can be seen from the case of *Stevenson, Jordan and Harrison Ltd v MacDonald and Evans*[18] where an accountant employed by the plaintiff company wrote a book on business management; part was based on public lectures given during his employment, part was composed while engaged on a particular assignment for the employer, and the rest was written after leaving the employment. The Court of Appeal held that the lectures were not given pursuant to his contract of employment, but that the second part (composed whilst on the assignment) was produced in the course of his employment, and so

---

15 'Outstanding' is not capable of definition and remains a question of fact in each case: *Memco-Med Ltd's Patent* [1992] RPC 403. It is a superlative term, not merely a comparative one, and so the burden of proof is a high one: *British Steel plc's Patent* [1992] RPC 117.
16 The first reported cases of applications by employees under s. 40 are set out and discussed in Wotherspoon 'Employee Inventions Revisited' (1993) 22 ILJ 119.
17 Patents Act 1977, s. 40(3).
18 [1952] 1 TLR 101, CA; see also *Beloff v Pressdram Ltd* [1973] 1 All ER 241.

the copyright in that part lay with the employer who could restrain publication of it.

4)   *Failure to serve the employer faithfully*   It has been seen above that the employee must obey proper orders of the employer and that there is a general duty of fidelity upon the employee. This does not give the employer an unrestricted prerogative and in general he will be bound by the terms of the contract of employment which he cannot change unilaterally. Thus, he cannot make the employee work overtime if it is purely voluntary or change the terms of employment (e.g. by making a day worker work nights where there is no such provision in the contract); to this extent the employee may stand upon the terms of the contract, and, if necessary, withdraw his goodwill, even if this has a disadvantageous effect on the employer's business. However, there may be cases where a lack of co-operation by the employee may be construed not as a lawful insistence upon observation of the contract, but instead as in fact collective industrial action aimed at prejudicing the employer's business. Although the employee may argue that this form of action (known, for example, as 'going slow', 'working to rule' or 'working to contract') is merely the insistence on the contractual minimum, it is clear that in some cases it can, in fact, be a *breach* of contract, in particular the implied duty to serve faithfully. The line between the two arguments can be a thin one, but it exists.

Strict adherence to contractual terms (on a collective level, as part of industrial action) was held capable of being a breach of contract by the Court of Appeal in *Secretary of State for Employment v ASLEF (No 2)*[19], though the reasoning of the three judges varied. However, the leading case is now *British Telecommunications plc v Ticehurst*[20] where a college manager took part in industrial action, first by way of a go-slow and work to contract, and then escalating to a rolling campaign of strikes. The question arose[1] whether this action was lawful under the contract and the Court of Appeal held that it was a breach of the implied term 'to serve the employer faithfully within the requirements of the contract'. Adopting that formulation from the judgment of Buckley LJ in the *ASLEF* case, Ralph Gibson LJ said:

'It is, in my judgment, necessary to imply such a term in the case of a manager who is given charge of the work of other employees and who therefore must necessarily be trusted to exercise her judgment and discretion in giving instructions to others and in supervising their work. Such a discretion, if the contract is to work properly, must be exercised faithfully in the interests of the employers.'

And later:

'The term is breached, in my judgment, when the employee does an act, or omits to do an act, which it would be within her contract and the discretion

---

19   [1972] 2 QB 455, [1972] 2 All ER 949, CA. The case concerned long-repealed provisions of the Industrial Relations Act 1971.
20   [1992] ICR 383, [1992] IRLR 219, CA.
1   Whether or not such action is a breach of contract is not particularly relevant in the context of unfair dismissal, since the special provisions on dismissal during industrial action (p. 635, below) apply to strikes 'or other industrial action', with the latter *not* depending on proof of breach of contract. However, this case concerned the equally vital question as to whether the employer can *refuse to pay* employees taking industrial action, where the question of breach is central; that aspect of the case is considered at p. 175, below.

allowed to her not to do, or to do, as the case may be, and the employee so acts or omits to do the act, not in the honest exercise of choice or discretion for the faithful performance of her work but in order to disrupt the employer's business or to cause the most inconvenience that can be caused[2].'

Although the case concerns a manager, it is suggested that the key to this is not managerial status but, much more generally, employee *discretion* in how to perform the work. It may be that, if a job was exhaustively defined in the contract, there could still be a work to contract that would not be in breach[3], *but* in modern conditions most jobs are not like that; in such circumstances, the decision in *Ticehurst* shows that such action is very likely to be a breach of the implied duty of faithful service in the contract.

Finally, it may be noted that in at least one area the employee may be under a positive obligation to co-operate with his employer, for under the Health and Safety at Work etc. Act 1974, section 7, there is a statutory duty upon every employee 'as regards any duty or requirement imposed on his employer or any other person by or under any of the relevant statutory provisions, to co-operate with him so far as is necessary to enable that duty or requirement to be performed or complied with'.

6   CONTINUITY OF EMPLOYMENT

i)   The concept of continuity and the treatment of part-time employees

The concept of 'continuous employment' is an important one in that many accruing rights, privately negotiated or statutory, depend upon it either for qualification for a particular right, or for computation of benefits to be received under it. Thus, various periods are laid down by statute for the purposes of qualification for written particulars of employment and minimum rights during notice, qualification for redundancy pay, computation of redundancy pay, qualification for protection from unfair dismissal, and qualification for various employment protection rights (particularly those relating to maternity). These matters are considered in detail elsewhere, but are mentioned to show the direct effect of the provisions that govern the question of continuity (now contained in sections 210–219 of the Employment Rights Act 1996). The scheme for computing continuous employment was altered by the Employment Act 1982 with the effects that (a) most qualifying periods are now expressed in months and years rather than weeks, which diminishes the former technical importance of the 'week' as the unit of account, and (b) the emphasis now is upon determining when the employment started[4] and ended, and then computing the period on a more straightforward calendar basis. The main aims of the change were to simplify record keeping and to avoid some of the stranger results of the previous week-base (under which, for example, part weeks counted as full weeks so that the 52

---

2   At 398, 225.

3   It could, of course, still constitute 'industrial action' for statutory purposes, see n. 1 above.

4   A person 'starts work' within s. 211 when his contract of employment begins, even if he does not actually take up his duties under the contract until some time later: *General of the Salvation Army v Dewsbury* [1984] ICR 498, [1984] IRLR 222.

weeks' qualifying period that used to be required in order to bring an unfair dismissal action could in some cases be satisfied where the employee had worked for 50 weeks plus a couple of odd days falling fortuitously in different weeks). Some of the case law on the old system is therefore no longer authoritative.

Four preliminary points should be noticed. The first is that continuity of employment means generally with one employer[5], and this has been construed widely to include continuity where the employee has changed department, job, seniority or even the terms of his contract of employment during the period, provided that he has remained with the same employer[6]. The second is that the Act governs which weeks count in computing a period of employment, and generally if a week does not count it will break continuity, so that the employee then loses his accrued period and must start again from scratch[7]; however, there is the qualification that certain weeks (particularly those spent on strike or, for the purpose of redundancy, abroad[8]) do not count, but at the same time are deemed not to break continuity, and thereby the position is effectively rendered neutral (the employee is not unduly penalised by losing all accrued continuity, but at the same time does not benefit because he cannot actually use the relevant period for any purpose of computation). The third is that there is a statutory presumption of continuity, unless the contrary is shown; thus, in cases of doubt (e.g. where there is a possibility that some relevant weeks may not count and so break continuity) the burden of proof is on the employer to show that the employee did *not* have the necessary continuity of employment[9].

The fourth, and much the most significant point is that this area underwent major change in February 1995 due to a conflict with EC law. In domestic law the concept of continuity had always been used to achieve the secondary, less obvious aim of excluding part-timers from employment protection rights such as redundancy and unfair dismissal. This was done by providing that a week did not count unless during it the employee actually worked (or normally worked) for 16 hours or more (or between eight and 16 hours after five years' service). Thus no matter how long the part-time employee worked, they never accumulated the necessary continuous period of employment for the major rights (e.g. two years in order to claim unfair dismissal) if they did not work the necessary hours. This

5   *Lee v Barry High Ltd* [1970] 3 All ER 1040, [1970] 1 WLR 1549, CA; *Harold Fielding Ltd v Mansi* [1974] 1 All ER 1035, [1974] ICR 347. It also means in relation to one contract of employment: *Lewis v Surrey County Council* [1988] AC 323, [1987] ICR 982, HL.

6   *Wood v York City Council* [1978] ICR 840, [1978] IRLR 228, CA; *Jennings v Salford Community Service Agency* [1981] ICR 399, [1981] IRLR 76; continuity is a purely statutory concept, exhaustively covered by the statutory provisions which are not to be qualified by courts or tribunals: *Carrington v Harwich Dock Co Ltd* [1998] IRLR 567 (applying Lord Denning MR's judgment in *Wood v York City Council* above and doubting the decision in *Roach v CSB (Moulds) Ltd* [1991] ICR 349, [1991] IRLR 200); *Sweeney v J & S Henderson Ltd* [1999] IRLR 306, EAT (going further and disapproving *Roach*).

7   S. 210(4). This significance of the 'week' survives the changes in the 1982 Act.

8   Ss. 216 and 215 respectively.

9   S. 210(5). The effect of the presumption was considered in *Nicoll v Nocorrode Ltd* [1981] ICR 348, [1981] IRLR 163 where the EAT held that where it is unclear whether an employee had worked the necessary number of qualifying weeks, the employee need only show that *some* weeks during the qualifying period count and the burden of proof then passes to the employer to prove that there were weeks that do not count and so break continuity. However, there is an exception – in *Secretary of State for Employment v Cohen* [1987] ICR 570, [1987] IRLR 169, the EAT held that the presumption does *not* apply to a 'transfer of business' case under s 218 (see below), though Scott J emphasised that although the burden of proving continuity through such a transfer lies on the employee, a tribunal should not apply an unrealistically high *standard* of proof.

was long-standing, deliberate policy and indeed at one time the previous government were proposing to increase the threshold to 20 hours per week, in order to carry further the deregulation of the part-time labour market[10]. However, the tide of EU law was running strongly in the opposite direction (towards extending rights to atypical employees). Although the Maastricht opt-out could be used to prevent any direct EC pressure for more such rights by employment law directives, the Government could not rule out the possibility of a challenge under already-applicable EC law, in particular that relating to equality of pay and treatment. This happened in *R v Secretary of State for Employment, ex p Equal Opportunities Commission*[11], in which the House of Lords held that (1) the EOC had locus standi to challenge the legality of the hours limits, (2) those limits were contrary to Article 119 and the Equal Pay Directive 75/117 (in relation to redundancy payments) and the Equal Treatment Directive 76/207 (in relation to unfair dismissal) and (3) in neither case was the discriminatory effect on women justified on the Government's assertions that such limitations were necessary socially and economically in order to promote the extension of part-time employment, in the absence of substantive *evidence* that deregulation had had that effect. This bombshell decision had certain loose ends[12] but the government soon realised that they could not sensibly hold any tenable line simply by amending the hours limits, and so by the Employment Protection (Part Time Employees) Regulations 1995[13] removed these limits altogether, as from 6 February 1995. Thus, the major statutory rights can now be claimed by part-timers; as will be seen below, this in turn has had serious long-term effects on the law relating to continuity of employment, though in the short term the primary battlefield is over the entertaining (or not) of back-dated claims by employees without the necessary weekly hours dismissed prior to February 1995 now wishing to bring actions for redundancy rights or unfair dismissal, not having done so initially because they assumed they would be ruled out. As the *EOC* case is a court decision determining the meaning of the EC provisions, it prima facie has full retrospective effect, but at the time of writing the courts are conducting a desperate rearguard action to prevent a flood of old cases, not by denying that retrospective effect, but by adopting a stringent approach to the domestic limitation periods[14].

10 'Building businesses … not barriers' (Cmnd 9794, 1986); it would appear that such a change would have removed employment protection rights at a stroke from a further 366,000 people: [1986] Employment Gazette 281.
11 [1995] 1 AC 1, [1994] ICR 317, HL; see Villiers and White (1995) 58 MLR 560.
12 As the redundancy restriction was contrary to Art. 119 itself, the decision applied directly in both public and private sectors; however, the House of Lords only held the unfair dismissal restriction to be contrary to the Equal Treatment Directive, which meant that apparently the decision could only be relied on directly in the public sector (under the principle of vertical effect of directives). Subsequently, however, the EAT held that the unfair dismissal restriction also fell under Art. 119 (*Mediguard Services Ltd v Thame* [1994] ICR 751, [1994] IRLR 504). Although this point is no longer relevant in cases arising since the 1995 Regulations came into force, it could still be material if retrospective claims were to be allowed.
13 S.I. 1995 No. 31.
14 *Biggs v Somerset County Council* [1996] ICR 364, [1996] IRLR 203, CA; *Setiya v East Yorkshire Health Authority* [1995] ICR 799, [1995] IRLR 348. This was possible because of the 'not reasonably practicable' test for extending the unfair dismissal time limit; it has subsequently been held that such an approach preventing backdating may not work in a sex discrimination claim where the test for extending the limit is whether it is 'just and equitable' to do so: *DPP v Marshall* [1998] ICR 518.

ii) Weeks which count

1)   '*Any week during the whole or part of which the employee's relations with the employer are governed by a contract of employment.*' (Employment Rights Act 1996, s. 212(1)).   As stated immediately above, this used to be a far more complex provision, linking continuity to the performance or normal performance of 16 hours work or more per week (or eight hours for more than five years). In that form, it required a very technical approach with much complex case law, often attempting to 'forgive' lapses in that normal hours requirement, and to count marginal hours, such as those spent on preparation work or breaks during employment. Moreover, there were several specific statutory provisions aimed at covering temporary breaks in work normally meeting the hours requirements. With the removal of these requirements in 1995, the result is a far simpler statutory provision, with the repeal of most of the special subsidiary rules. The emphasis now is on looking only at the continuing existence of the contractual relationship, and whether it covers the week(s) in question. Thus, in *Clifford v Devon County Council*[15] a dismissed employee was able to claim unfair dismissal even though for part of the two years prior to the claim she had only worked $7^1/_2$ hours per week and, most startlingly of all, in *Colley v Corkindale*[16] an employee working one $5^1/_2$ hour bar shift every *alternate* Friday was also allowed to bring an unfair dismissal action. Under the previous law the latter claim would have been doubly inadmissible, due to (i) the number of hours and (ii) the existence of the alternate weeks when no work was done or expected, which would have broken continuity anyway[17]. The test now is thus a far more general, less technical and (above all) contractual one than before. It is suggested therefore that the proper approach is to construe the new provision afresh, and to forget the substantial body of case law on the old provisions. That is not to say that the same result may not be reached in any given case. Thus, for example, there is still a requirement that the contract in question must be continuous, and so continuity might still be broken in a case of regular *but separate* contracts, as in *Hellyer Bros Ltd v McLeod*[18] where trawlermen were held not entitled to redundancy payments on the collapse of their part of the fishing industry, for although they had sailed for one particular owner for many years the court held that the proper construction was that they had been engaged on a series of separate crew agreements, each covering one voyage. Arguably this case would still be decided the same way now and so, although the continuity rules are now simpler, they still cannot be taken for granted. This was further emphasised in *Booth v United States of America*[19] where maintenance workers were put on to a series of fixed term contracts totalling more than two years, but with very deliberate two week gaps between each; their eventual claims for redundancy payments and unfair dismissal were disallowed for lack of continuity – the gaps broke normal

15   [1994] IRLR 628.
16   [1995] ICR 965.
17   Thus in *Lloyds Bank Ltd v Secretary of State for Employment* [1979] 2 All ER 573, [1979] ICR 258, an employee working one week on and one week off was *not* covered by the normal continuity rules, and only succeeded in the claim under the special 'saving' rule in s. 212(3)(b) by a strained interpretation which is now probably untenable (see below). This is a good example of the sort of technicality which hopefully should now arise less frequently.
18   [1987] 1 WLR 728, [1987] ICR 526, CA.
19   [1999] IRLR 16. This is a particularly harsh decision because, although the employees were formally 'terminated' and had to complete new application forms for the next contract (after a break which the employers insisted has to be for a minimum of two weeks – strangely), in fact when they returned they were given the same employee number and used the same tools and equipment, and even the same lockers. What a coincidence.

continuity, which (for technical reasons, see below) could not be covered by one of the 'deemed continuity' provisions, and the bottom line was expressed by Morison P as follows:

> 'If, by so arranging their affairs, an employer is lawfully able to employ people in such a manner that the employees cannot complain of unfair dismissal or seek a redundancy payment, that is a matter for him. The courts simply try and apply the law as it stands. It is for the legislators to close any loopholes that may be perceived to exist.'[20]

2) *A week during which there is no subsisting contract of employment, but which is covered by special statutory provisions*   In order to avoid unfortunate gaps or 'hiccoughs' in continuity, certain exceptions have always been specifically created by the legislation, and these are now contained in the Employment Rights Act 1996 section 212(3). When they were contained in the previous legislation[1], there was a problem of statutory construction because the headnote referred to 'Periods in which there is no contract of employment', but that phrase did not appear in the body of the provision. Earlier case law tended where necessary to ignore the question of whether or not the contract subsisted, and to apply the special provision (to preserve continuity) in cases where there *was* a continuing contract but it had some unfortunate hiatus or gap in it. However, in *Ford v Warwickshire County Council*[2] the House of Lords placed considerable emphasis on the requirement that there be no subsisting contract and so the decisions in those earlier cases have been dubious since then. Fortunately, the position is now simpler under the 1995 Regulations and the 1996 Consolidation – that marginal note now does not appear, but (a) the simplified format (with the removal of the hours requirements) means that section 212(1) applies where there *is* a subsisting contract and sub-section (3) therefore clearly applies only where there is *no* such contract (thus reinforcing the point in *Ford*) and (b) in any event there will be far less need now to try to squeeze cases within sub-section (3) in order to preserve continuity, since most of the hours-based complications of sub section (1) have been removed. Subject to that caveat, the three specific cases covered by sub-section (3) are now considered.

a)   Where the employee is incapable of work through sickness or illness (sub-s. (3)(a)). Incapable has been held to refer to the job in question and a temporary lighter job need not break continuity[3]. Absence from work does not normally, in default of express provision in the contract, terminate the contract[4]. If the contract has not been determined then the weeks of absence count under sub-section (1) anyway. This head is an extension stretching into the period after the contract has been determined[5]. It is limited to 26 weeks after a week counting under sub-section (1) and must be followed by a week so counting. Theoretically an employee could have a solitary week of employment followed by 26 weeks of illness and a further week of employment

---

20   At p. 18. There is nothing in the White Paper 'Fairness at Work' covering this matter. If it is allowed to continue, the moral of the story seems to be that the more cynical the manipulation of these rules, the more likely the employer is to win.
1   In the Employment Protection (Consolidation) Act 1978, Sch. 13, para. 9(1)(a)–(d).
2   [1983] ICR 273, [1983] IRLR 126, HL.
3   *Collins v Nats (Southend) Ltd* (1967) 2 ITR 423; *Donnelly v Kelvin International Services* [1992] IRLR 496.
4   For the law as to the payment of sick pay, see pp. 177–182, below.
5   There must be a causal link between the absence from work and the incapacity through sickness or injury: *Pearson v Kent County Council* [1993] IRLR 165, CA.

which would both maintain the continuity and permit a further 26 weeks of
absence through illness to count.

b)   Where the employee is absent from work on account of a 'temporary cessation
of work' (sub-s. (3)(b)); this has been in practice the most important special
case, but it is a phrase not without difficulty. No time-limit is laid down. The
phrase was considered by the House of Lords in *Fitzgerald v Hall, Russell & Co
Ltd*[6] where it was held that it refers to cessation of the *employee's* work for some
reason, so there is no requirement that the employer's business in which the
employee is engaged should have ceased. It was also held that each case
under this head must be looked at in the round and, if necessary, with
hindsight, to establish whether it was 'temporary' (the statute giving no
guidance on this). Thus, if both parties obviously envisaged that it would be
only temporary that would be cogent evidence, but the lack of it would not
mean that the arrangement would necessarily be construed to be permanent:

> 'The effect of that case is that the tribunal is enjoined to look at the
> matter as the historian of a completed chapter of events, and not as a
> journalist describing events as they occur from day to day. The
> importance of that is this, that things are seen, as they unfold, quite
> differently from the way in which they are seen when one looks back
> and considers the whole of the chapter in context. What at the time
> seems to be permanent may turn out to be temporary, and what at the
> time seems to be temporary may turn out to be permanent.'[7]

The essence of most successful cases is that the employee has been 'stood
off' in the sense that he was to be recalled later. The fact that a job is taken in
the period of cessation does not destroy the position[8], but it is plainly not
meant to cover the situation where an employee moves to a new employer,
fails to settle, and quickly moves back to his old job. It may cover situations
such as extra holiday periods taken as periods of absence with the employer's
agreement at the employee's expense, and, more particularly, periods when
the work-place is closed or no work is available[9] (which may arise through
many causes such as a natural calamity like a fire[10], or the disruption of
supplies of materials). In *Ford v Warwickshire County Council*[11] it was held to

---

6   [1970] AC 984, [1969] 3 All ER 1140, HL, approving *Hunter v Smith's Dock Ltd* [1968] 2 All
     ER 81, 3 ITR 198. 'Work' here means paid work; if that is missing, the paragraph may apply
     and it is not the tribunal's function to enquire into *why* the paid work is missing: *University
     of Aston in Birmingham v Malik* [1984] ICR 492. However, at the end of the day it must be
     the case that there is a 'cessation of work' available for the employee to do; if the work
     remains but for some reason he is not eligible to do it, the paragraph does not apply: *Bryne
     v Birmingham City District Council* [1987] ICR 519, [1987] IRLR 191, CA. It is that cessation
     that must then be 'temporary', not the employee's absence: *Flack v Kodak Ltd* [1986] ICR
     775, [1986] IRLR 255, CA. This can have the unfortunate effect that if the work remains
     available but the employer *refuses* at certain times to offer it to a particular employee (in
     order deliberately to break continuity, e.g. by insisting on gaps between fixed term
     contracts), then sub-s. (3)(b) cannot apply and the employee may be unable to claim
     statutory rights: *Booth v United States of America* [1999] IRLR 16.
7   *Bentley Engineering Co Ltd v Crown* [1976] ICR 225 at 228, [1976] IRLR 146 at 148; in this
     case, periods of two years and 21 months were held still to be temporary.
8   *Thompson v Bristol Channel Ship Repairers and Engineers Ltd* (1969) 4 ITR 262; affd 5 ITR 85,
     CA; *Bentley Engineering Co Ltd v Crown* [1976] ICR 225, [1976] IRLR 146.
9   *Hunter v Smith's Dock Ltd* [1968] 2 All ER 81, 3 ITR 198.
10   *Newsham v Dunlop Textiles Ltd (No 2)* (1969) 4 ITR 268.
11   [1983] ICR 273, [1983] IRLR 126, HL, overruling *Rashid v ILEA* [1977] ICR 157.

cover the case of a schoolteacher who had been employed on eight consecutive fixed term contracts for the academic year (September to July); thus, the periods of the summer vacations were held not to break continuity so that she could claim unfair dismissal and a redundancy payment when she did not receive a ninth contract. In interpreting the subsection, the House of Lords took a basically similar approach to that in their earlier decision in *Fitzgerald v Hall Russell Ltd* (above), holding that 'temporary' means 'transient' and adding that the application of subsection (3)(b) was not defeated either by the fact that the absences were easily foreseeable in advance or by the fact that the case concerned a series of fixed term contracts (rather than a series of contracts terminable by notice). The 'transience' requirement makes it clear that the principle in the case cannot be applied so widely as to give previously unheard of rights to genuinely casual/seasonal workers (who, for example, only work for three or four months of each year – there, the gaps would be anything but transient); however, the case may give food for thought to any employer seeking to avoid the application of employment laws by putting an employee on a series of short-term contracts, if it transpires that in fact the gaps are relatively short by comparison with the periods of work (provided that it remains the case that it is the *work* that is temporarily unavailable, not just the fact that it is not being done by that employee[12]). The application of hindsight and an overall view of events, permissible under this subsection, could easily work to the employer's disadvantage in such a case, though it must be remarked that the categorisation of transience as a matter of fact for the tribunal would make it difficult to give definite advice in advance in a marginal case on whether the sub-paragraph will apply[13], the lawyer being faced with the unanswerable question 'How long is short?'

In seeking to answer that question, two quite different approaches are possible. As stated above, *Fitzgerald v Hall Russell Ltd* sets out a 'broad brush' approach, looking at all the circumstances throughout the period of employment in order to see if any particular gap can be categorised as temporary. However, in *Ford v Warwickshire County Council*, Lord Diplock suggested a narrower 'mathematical' test of looking at whatever period is relevant to the claim in question[14] and, in the case of any gap during that time, comparing its length mathematically with the periods of work on either side of it to see if it was temporary. This latter approach could produce anomalies[15] and the matter was reconsidered by the Court of Appeal in *Flack v Kodak Ltd*[16] a case on very different facts from those in *Ford*. This case concerned a series of highly irregular work patterns over periods varying from three to 11 years (the employees having been laid off and taken back on again intermittently, depending on season and demand). The tribunal

12　See *Booth v United States of America*, n. 16, above.
13　See, for example, the facts in *Berwick Salmon Fisheries Co Ltd v Rutherford* [1991] IRLR 203 where salmon netters had been employed for 30 weeks on, 22 weeks off, until their final two seasons when they only worked for 23 weeks on, 29 weeks off.
14　For example, if the question arose as to entitlement to a redundancy payment, that period would be the last two years before the date of dismissal.
15　If in the relevant period, for example, the employee had a gap of eight weeks with periods in work of only two weeks on each side, that would not be 'temporary' on a straight mathematical comparison. If, however, that was because of short time in times of difficulties prior to his redundancy, and came as a series of late hiccoughs after years of unbroken service, the end result (no redundancy pay because not continuously employed for two years counting back from the date of dismissal) would be ludicrous.
16　[1986] ICR 775, [1986] IRLR 255, CA.

applied the mathematical approach (even to the extent of expressing the gaps as percentages of their surrounding periods in work) and found that in the case of each employee continuity was broken in the vital qualifying period for redundancy payments. However, the EAT and the Court of Appeal held that this was the wrong test to apply, that the 'broad brush' approach should be taken and that the matter should be remitted to another tribunal for reconsideration. The question is where this leaves the law. Although Lord Diplock's statements in *Ford* as to the mathematical test was said to be obiter, it is clear from later cases that that test has not been disapproved. In *Sillars v Charrington Fuels Ltd* the EAT[17] suggested that the mathematical test should apply to cases like *Ford* of regular gaps, and the broad-brush approach to cases like *Flack* of irregular gaps. Unfortunately, the matter was not fully resolved when the case went to the Court of Appeal[18] for it was there held that (the case being one of seasonal employment with long, regular gaps) the mathematical test was one which it was *open* to the industrial tribunal to have used. Although the distinction drawn by the EAT appears to have been thought too simplistic by the Court of Appeal, if one is looking for a rough rule of thumb it may not be a bad one, pending further authoritative guidance on the matter.

A lock-out is covered, and so are non-strikers laid off because a strike has disrupted production so that work is not available[19]. However, section 216(1) expressly provides that absence through strikes does not count (although, of course, by section 216(2) continuity is not broken by a strike), and so cannot be made to count by calling it a 'temporary cessation of work.' This, however was qualified in *Clarke Chapman-John v Walters*[20] where a period on strike was followed, in the employee's case, by a short period laid off pending a phased return to work; it was held by the NIRC that during that short period he was not on strike, so the predecessor of section 216(1) did not apply, and it could be construed as a 'temporary cessation of work', albeit the direct result of the actual strike.

c) Where the employee is absent from work in circumstances such that, by arrangement or custom, he is regarded as continuing in the employment of his employer for any purpose (subsection (3)(c)). Under this head any unique local practices are covered, and some potentially unfortunate breaks in continuity avoided. It appears that the agreement or custom must exist when the absence begins, not as an ex post facto afterthought[1], once this is

---

17   [1988] ICR 505, [1988] IRLR 180.
18   [1989] ICR 475, [1989] IRLR 152, CA. The mathematical approach was also applied to the facts of *Berwick Salmon Fisheries Co Ltd v Rutherford* [1991] IRLR 203, see n. 13, above.
19   *Macartney v Sir Robert MacAlpine & Sons Ltd* (1967) 2 ITR 399.
20   [1972] 1 All ER 614, [1972] ICR 83.
1   *Murray v Kelvin Electronics Ltd* (1967) 2 ITR 622; *Todd v Sun Ventilating Co Ltd* [1976] IRLR 4; cf. *Cann v Co-operative Retail Services Ltd* (1967) 2 ITR 649. 'Arrangement' requires some form of advanced discussion or agreement to the effect that the parties regard the employment as continuing; mere acquiescence or expectation that the employer would periodically lay the employees off is not enough: *Booth v United States of America* [1999] IRLR 16. An exception was created to the rule (that the arrangement or custom must already exist at the time of the absence) in *Ingram v Foxon* [1984] ICR 685, [1985] IRLR 5 where it was held that the subsection covered an agreement to reinstate on the understanding that continuity would be deemed to be unbroken, but this was disapproved in *Morris v Walsh Western UK Ltd* [1997] IRLR 562.

satisfied the cause of the absence appears to be immaterial – it could be something ad hoc, such as leave of absence for personal reasons[2] or a long-term agreement that the employer might keep the employee on a 'reserve-list' to be called upon when necessary[3]. In some previous cases, it was even applied to regularise peculiar work patterns, for example to an agreement whereby the employee does not work at all at certain times as in *Lloyds Bank Ltd v Secretary of State for Employment*[4] where an employee who worked one week on and one week off was held to have continuity of employment by virtue of sub-section (3)(c); a similar argument was put forward in *Corton House Ltd v Skipper*[5] (employee working 16 hours one week but only 12 hours the next) where it was unsuccessful (and *Lloyds Bank* distinguished) but only because the facts showed no 'agreement or custom'. Likewise, there have been cases[6] where the subparagraph was applied to the lending of an employee to a third party, even where it appeared that the employee was still being treated at least for some purposes as in the employment of the lender. In the light of remarks of the House of Lords in *Ford v Warwickshire County Council* (above) on the importance of the requirement that there should be *no* subsisting contract if the provision is to be applicable, it is likely that the decision in *Lloyds Bank* and the reasoning in *Corton House* can no longer stand. As pointed out above, this is reinforced by the wording of the continuity provisions substituted by the 1995 Regulations when removing the hours limitations. On the other hand, cases such as these will no longer need special coverage if it is clear that the employee's relations with his employer remained governed by a contract of employment throughout the relevant period, in which case the general principle in subsection (1) will apply, even in the case of an irregular work pattern[7]. Thus, in the case of a 'lent servant' there will now normally be continuity of employment under subsection (1) anyway, and subsection (3)(c) would only be necessary in the unusual case of that employee being entirely excluded from the lender's employment during the employment in question.

Note finally that there used to be a fourth heading to sub-s (3) relating to absence through pregnancy, but this became unnecessary under the new maternity rights provisions[8], and so was repealed by the Employment Relations Act 1999.

---

2   *Moore v James Clarkson & Co Ltd* (1970) 5 ITR 298; *Taylor v Triumph Motors* [1975] IRLR 369, IT.
3   *Puttick v John Wright & Sons (Blackwall) Ltd* [1972] ICR 457; *Normanton v Southalls (Birmingham) Ltd* [1975] IRLR 74, IT.
4   [1979] ICR 258, [1979] IRLR 41.
5   [1981] ICR 307, [1981] IRLR 78.
6   *Southern Electricity Board v Collins* [1970] 1 QB 83, [1969] 2 All ER 1166; *Price v Syd Long (Stockton) Ltd* [1976] IRLR 41, IT; *Wishart v National Coal Board* [1974] ICR 460.
7   See *Colley v Corkindale* [1995] ICR 965.
8   This is because the employee's contract is now deemed to subsist anyway, throughout the period of maternity leave.

iii)   Industrial disputes

The Act defines strikes and lock-outs in similar language[9]. A lock-out involves the closing of a place of employment, the suspension of work or the refusal by an employer to continue to employ any number of his employees. A strike involves cessation of work by a body of employees acting in combination, a concerted refusal to continue work. In the case of both strikes and lock-outs these actions must be in consequence of a dispute and in each case the aim of the action must be to coerce the employees or employers, as the case may be, to accept or not to accept terms or conditions of or affecting employment. Both definitions also expressly include similar action taken to aid other employers or employees in dispute.

If an employee is on strike during a week or any part thereof, that week does not count as a period of employment by virtue of section 216(1); however, a compromise is achieved by section 216(2) which provides that the employee's *continuity* of employment is not broken by a strike. The original legislation (Contracts of Employment Act 1963) made a distinction between lawful and unlawful strikes, in an attempt to curb the latter (principally 'unofficial' strikes) but these provisions were repealed in 1965. In the case of a lock-out section 216(3) provides that continuity is not broken by the fact that an employee is absent from work because of a lock-out, but the paragraph says nothing about whether such a period can *count*, so that that question must rely on whether the contract of employment subsists during the lockout[10]. If it does not, presumably the period will not count, though of course continuity will not be broken.

During the currency of a strike, the employer may in fact dismiss the employees, but this in itself will not affect continuity of employment for the following reasons – (i) section 216 makes no distinction between strikes where there are dismissals and those where there are not; (ii) the definition of 'employee' for the purposes of section 216, in section 230, includes an ex-employee; (iii) it was held in *Bloomfield v Springfield Hosiery Finishing Co Ltd*[11] that section 216 applies to persons who were employed at the *outset* of the strike, and that for present purposes the strike is to be considered as continuing as long as there is the possibility that normal employment will be resumed at the end of the dispute; this may mean in practice until the employer replaces the striking employees with others, closes down the department in question, or until the employees concerned find permanent employment elsewhere. Thus, if the striking employees are in fact re-engaged, their continuity will be safeguarded even if they were dismissed during the strike. Similar principles should apply to a lock-out.

As noticed above, a further extension of this is that if a striker is temporarily laid off at the end of a strike until the business picks up and there is work for him to do, that employee is not on strike during that period, but he may be considered to be absent on account of a temporary cessation of work under section 212[12], and so not only is his continuity safeguarded, but he may also count the period of lay-off.

9   Employment Rights Act 1996, s. 235. Note that these definitions are only for stated purposes; they do not apply to the unfair dismissal provisions relating to industrial action, see p. 635, below.
10   *E and J Davis Transport Ltd v Chattaway* [1972] ICR 267, 7 ITR 361.
11   [1972] 1 All ER 609, [1972] ICR 91.
12   *Clarke Chapman-John v Walters* [1972] 1 All ER 614, [1972] ICR 83; quaere whether this would apply if he was taken back into employment but then validly laid off under a contractual lay-off clause, in the light of the requirement that there be *no* subsisting contract if s. 213(2) is to apply (*Ford v Warwickshire County Council*, considered above).

iv)   Change of employment under the 1996 Act and the Transfer of Undertakings Regulations

a)   Continuity under the 1996 Act

Normally when an employee terminates his job with an employer and goes to work for another employer, his continuity ends and he must start to build up continuous service with the new employer from scratch[13]. However, there may be ways in which the continuity can be carried over, so that he is regarded as being employed by the new employer as from the date when he commenced employment with the old employer. The Employment Rights Act 1996, section 218 lays down six classes of case in which employment may be deemed to be continuous even though there is a change in employment. The six cases are as follows:

(i)   Where the trade of business or undertaking is itself transferred. Subsection (2) provides that continuity is unbroken; this is of general application, but particularly important in cases of redundancy. However, to be relied upon at all, the criteria for its application must be satisfied; one is that the employee in question must have been in the relevant employment 'at the time of the transfer' (which raises the problem of a gap in employment over the period of the transfer[14]), but the primary one is – was it a transfer of business, or merely the disposal of certain assets? If the latter, the provision does not apply, even if the employee goes with the asset, so that, for example, the sale of an operating factory may not come within subsection (2) if it is seen merely as the disposal of a surplus asset, particularly if the original employer carries on his business in other establishments[15]. In *Lloyds v Brassey*[16] Lord Denning MR said:

> 'The meaning of [this provision] was considered by the Divisional Court in *Kenmir Ltd v Frizzell*, where Widgery J said "In deciding whether a transaction amounted to the transfer of business, regard must be had to its substance rather than its form ... the vital consideration is whether the effect of the transaction was to put the transferee in possession of a going concern, the activities of which he could carry on without

---

13   *Lee v Barry High Ltd* [1970] 3 All ER 1040, [1970] 1 WLR 1549, CA.
14   This was for a long time complicated by the decision of the Court of Appeal in *Teesside Times Ltd v Drury* [1980] ICR 338, [1980] IRLR 72 which permitted a gap to count, but for three different reasons; in *Clark & Tokeley Ltd v Oakes* [1998] 4 All ER 353, [1998] IRLR 577, the Court of Appeal subsequently held that it is Stephenson LJ's judgment in *Teesside Times* that is to be applied, i.e. that there is no hard-and-fast rule, that a 'transfer' may well take place over an extended period of time, and that continuity will be preserved, provided that the employee was still in employment at the start of that process (a question of fact for the tribunal).
15   *Kenmir Ltd v Frizzell* (1968) 3 ITR 159; *Woodhouse v Peter Brotherhood Ltd* [1972] 2 QB 520, [1972] 3 All ER 91, CA; *Crompton v Truly Fair (International) Ltd* [1975] ICR 359, [1975] IRLR 250. There must be a legal transfer of sorts, it is not enough merely that de facto control has been given to someone else: *S I (Systems and Instrumentation) Ltd v Grist* [1983] ICR 788, [1983] IRLR 391. Continuity is preserved even if there is a gap between the two employments, provided that gap is related to the machinery of the transfer: *Macer v Abafast Ltd* [1990] ICR 234, [1990] IRLR 137. Note that the presumption of continuity in s. 210(5) does *not* apply to a 'transfer of business' case under s. 218: *Secretary of State for Employment v Cohen* [1987] ICR 570, [1987] IRLR 169.
16   [1969] 2 QB 98, [1969] 1 All ER 382, CA at 103 and 384, respectively.

interruption." I think that it is the right test. If the new owner takes over
the business as a going concern – so that the business remains the
same business but in different hands – and the employee keeps the
same job with the new owner … his period of employment is deemed
to continue without a break in the same job.'

This basic distinction between a transfer of business and a transfer of assets
was approved and applied by the House of Lords in *Melon v Hector Powe Ltd*[17]
to a case of the sale by the original employer of one of their two factories to
another employer in the same trade; in the circumstances it was held that
the tribunal had correctly decided that this was merely a transfer of assets,
not a transfer of business. However, certain forms of business may be sui
generis, and in *Lloyd v Brassey* the Court of Appeal held that in the case of
farming the essence of the business is the land itself, so that sale of the land
constitutes transfer of the business, not just the disposal of an asset; this idea
was applied by analogy to the transfer of the tenancy of a hotel in *Young v
Daniel Thwaites & Co*[18], but attempts to apply it more widely to other businesses
have failed[19]. The question whether there has been an actual transfer is to be
considered from the point of view of the dealings between the employers; if
their dealings do not disclose such a transfer subsection (2) does not apply
even if the employees carry on doing the same work and from *their* point of
view it appears to be a transfer. In *Woodhouse v Peter Brotherhood Ltd*[20] a factory
was sold and the new owner carried on using the same plant and equipment
and indeed completed the order for one of the old employer's contracts, but
it was held by the Court of Appeal that from the employer's point of view this
was no transfer, and it was irrelevant that from the employee's point of view
their 'working environment' had continued unchanged. One major factor
pointing towards a transfer might be the sale of goodwill[1] which was one of
the missing factors in the *Woodhouse* case. The term 'business' is defined in
section 235 as including a trade or profession and any activity carried on by a
body of persons, whether corporate or unincorporate[2]. It has been held to
cover the transfer of *part* of a business (for example where an employer
carries on business in place A and place B and sells off his whole business in
place A, as in *G D Ault (Isle of Wight) Ltd v Gregory*[3]), but only if that part is
genuinely severable (in its nature or location)[4] – if not, the transaction might
well be viewed as again merely the disposal of an asset.

---

17   [1981] ICR 43, [1980] IRLR 477, HL. Notice that in this case it was the *employees* who were
     arguing that there was no transfer of business, in order to be able to claim their redundancy
     rights from the original employer; this claim was upheld by the House of Lords. See to like
     effect *Ward v Haines Watts* [1983] ICR 231, [1983] IRLR 285 (concerning sale of the
     goodwill of a professional practice).
18   [1977] ICR 877.
19   *Port Talbot Engineering Co Ltd v Passmore* [1975] ICR 234, [1975] IRLR 156 (maintenance
     contracts); *Bumstead v John L Cars Ltd* (1967) 2 ITR 137 (petrol station).
20   [1972] 2 QB 520, [1972] 3 All ER 91, CA.
1   *H A Rencoule (Joiners and Shopfitters) Ltd v Hunt* (1967) 2 ITR 475; *Kenmir Ltd v Frizzell*
     [1968] 1 All ER 414, 3 ITR 159.
2   Explained by Diplock LJ in *Dallow Industrial Properties Ltd v Else* [1967] 2 QB 449, [1967]
     2 All ER 30 at 458 and 33, respectively.
3   (1967) 2 ITR 301.
4   *McCleod v John Rostron & Sons* (1972) 7 ITR 144; *Newlin Oil Co Ltd v Trafford* [1974] IRLR
     205, 9 ITR 324; *Gibson v Motortune Ltd* [1990] ICR 740.

(ii) Where an Act of Parliament causes one corporate body to replace another as employer: subsection (3).

(iii) Where the employer, not being corporate, dies and the personal representatives carry on the business: subsection (4)

(iv) Where the 'employer' is a partnership, personal representatives or trustees, and the composition of the body involved changes: subsection (5). This provision safeguards continuity when, for example, a partner retires and another is appointed. A more difficult case, however, arises where the partnership is dissolved but *one* of the partners carries on the business. On a narrow construction of subsection (5) it was held in *Harold Fielding Ltd v Mansi*[5] that this was not covered and so continuity was not preserved. The opposite conclusion was reached in the later cases of *Allen & Son v Coventry*[6] and *Jeetle v Elster*[7] but primarily on the alternative ground that, irrespective of subsection (5), such a change could constitute a 'transfer of business' under subsection (2); in each case the EAT criticised the reasoning on subsection (5) in *Mansi* but without actually overruling it.

(v) Where the employee is taken into the employment of an associated employer[8]: subsection (6).

(vi) Where an employee of the governors of a school maintained by a local education authority or that authority itself is taken into the employment of the governors of another such school or the authority: subsection (7).

b) Automatic transfer under the Transfer of Undertakings Regulations 1981

In addition to these provisions of the 1996 Act, there are extra rules which may apply to a change of employer by virtue of the Transfer of Undertakings (Protection of Employment) Regulations 1981[9]. These regulations (which are due to be updated at the time of writing, see below) were passed pursuant to an EC Directive[10] and contain provisions relating to union rights to information and consultation[11], the continuance of union recognition through a transfer[12] and the dismissal of employees as a consequence of a transfer[13]; they also have provisions relating to the continuance of contracts of employment through such a transfer of the employer's undertaking. Thus, regulation 5(1) states that a relevant transfer does not terminate contracts of employment, which are deemed to have been originally made between the employees and the transferee employer. In terms purely of protecting continuity of employment of employees who do in

---

5   [1974] 1 All ER 1035, [1974] ICR 347; *Wynne v Hair Control* [1978] ICR 870.
6   [1980] ICR 9, [1979] IRLR 399.
7   [1985] ICR 389, [1985] IRLR 227.
8   For the definition of associated employers, see pp. 22-24, above.
9   S.I. 1981 No. 1794. See Davies and Freedland *Transfer of Employment* (1982), Hepple (1982) 11 ILJ 29 and, particularly, McMullen *Business Transfers and Employee Rights* and 'Atypical transfer; atypical workers and atypical employment structures – a case for greater transparency in transfer of employment issues' (1996) 25 ILJ 286,'Takeovers, transfers and business re-organisations' (1992) 21 ILJ 15. The regulations are set out in *Harvey* R [181].
10 EEC Council Directive No. 77/187, known as the Acquired Rights Directive. The House of Lords held in *Litster v Forth Dry Dock and Engineering Co Ltd* [1989] ICR 341, [1989] IRLR 161 not only that the directive could be used as an aid to interpretation, but also that it justified the adoption of a broad and purposive construction of the regulations in order to effect the protective intent of the directive.
11 See pp. 70-73, above.
12 See p. 57, above.
13 See pp. 491-493, below.

fact end up working for the transferee, this actually adds little because the above provisions of the 1996 Act probably apply anyway. However, the regulations also contain the potentially radical concept of automatic transfer (whether or not the employees and/or the transferee want it). This has caused serious problems in recent years, due to a spate of ECJ decisions on the Directive, in the light of which the regulations must be construed; major uncertainties have arisen as to when the regulations apply, how far their effects go, who is covered by them and, most controversial politically, how they apply to the modern phenomenon of the contracting out of services to the private sector (a key policy of the previous government, not exactly reversed by the present government but given the more acceptable title of 'Best Value' in the public sector). For the purposes of relatively straightforward exposition, these are now considered separately, though of course any given case may concern several of them (*and* the provisions in the regulations on unfair dismissal, which are considered separately at p. 491, below).

1)   *Application of the regulations*   The regulations only apply to a 'relevant transfer', which is defined as a transfer 'from one person to another of an undertaking situated immediately before the transfer in the United Kingdom, or a part of one which is so situated'[14]. The transfer may be affected by sale, some other disposition or by operation of law[15], which means that one major limitation is that the regulations do not apply to a take-over of a business by the purchase of its shares[16]. An 'undertaking' is defined as including 'any trade or business' and was originally construed in a similar fashion to the 'transfer of business' provisions in the 1996 Act, namely as referring to a going concern, not just a sale of assets[17]. This was in line with older decisions on the Acquired Rights Directive, in particular that in *Spijkers v Gebroeders Benedik Abbattoir CV: 24/85*[18] which stressed the importance of the continuing viability of that which was transferred; that case arose in the context of the transfer of part of an undertaking where the emphasis on the transfer of significant parts of the going concern is of particular importance and so, although a relevant transfer is defined as including the transfer of *part* of a business it may still be necessary to apply a similar test of viability as a concern as under the old law, and so there may be little change there. Where, however, there has been potential for change and development is in the interpretation to be given to an 'undertaking', for in later cases on the Directive the ECJ have taken a broader approach to this, looking at whether there had been a transfer of some form of *economic unit* or a change of persons *operating* the undertaking, rather than more narrowly at the details of what tangible or intangible assets were transferred, or at

---

14   Reg. 3(1).
15   Reg. 3(2); *Robert Seligman Corpn v Baker* [1983] ICR 770. It may be effected by two or more transactions (see *Longden v Ferrari Ltd* [1994] ICR 443, [1994] IRLR 157) and it is declared that it may take place whether or not any property is transferred: reg. 3(4), as amended by the TURERA 1993.
16   This limitation is found in the Directive and continues to apply, even if being used deliberately by an employer in order to avoid the application of the Regulations: *Brookes v Borough Care Services* [1998] ICR 1198 [1998] IRLR 636. It is not of great significance for continuity of employment because in a take-over of this sort the employing company remains the same, albeit under new control. It is, of course, significant in relation to union consultation (see above).
17   *Premier Motors (Medway) Ltd v Total Oil Great Britain Ltd* [1984] ICR 58, [1983] IRLR 471; *BIFU v Barclays Bank plc* [1987] ICR 495.
18   [1986] ECR 1119, [1986] 2 CMLR 296, ECJ.

legal concepts of *ownership*[19]. *Spikjers* (above) is still widely cited, in the sense of determining whether some form of 'economic entity' has been transferred. While this is still not to look at the matter wholly through the eyes of the employees affected by it, it does suggest a wider application for the regulations; this has been particularly important in relation to tendering, and is further considered below. There used to be an important restriction written into the regulations, stating that they were not to apply to an undertaking not in the nature of a commercial venture. However, in the light of ECJ case law which showed that this restriction was inconsistent with the Directive[20], it was removed by the Trade Union Reform and Employment Rights Act 1993.

2)   *Effect on contracts – automatic transfer*   As we have seen, regulation 5(1) states that a relevant transfer does not terminate a contract of employment with the transferor, and has the effect that that contract operates after the transfer as if originally made between the employee and the transferee. Regulation 5(2) goes on to state that all the transferor's rights, powers, duties and liabilities under or in connection with the contract are transferred to the transferee[1]; the Directive gives member states the option of imposing joint liability on the transferee and the transferor, but the British government did not adopt that approach and it is not to be implied into the Regulations[2]. These transfer provisions are further underpinned by regulation 8 which makes any transfer-related dismissal unfair, unless for an 'economic, technical or organisational reason' (see p. 494, below).

---

19   This arose particularly in relation to the transfer of some form of business lease, with the employees going into the employment of the new lessee and being covered by the Directive: *Foreningen af Asbejdslederei i Danmark v Daddy's Dance Hall A/S*: 324/86 [1988] IRLR 315, ECJ; *Landsoganisationen i Danmark v Ny Molle Kro*: 287/86 [1989] ICR 330, [1989] IRLR 37, ECJ; *Berg v Besselsenn*: 144/87 [1990] ICR 396, [1989] IRLR 447, ECJ. A much-reported case showing such an approach in a more mainstream context is the *Christel Schmidt* case: C-392/92 [1994] ECR I-1311, [1995] 2 CMLR 331, ECJ; see p. 169, below. There can even be a relevant transfer between two companies in the same group: *Allen v Amalgamated Construction Ltd*: C-234/98 [2000] IRLR 119, ECJ.
20   In particular, *Dr Sophie Redmond Stichting v Bartol*: C-29/91 [1992] IRLR 366, ECJ where the Directive applied to the transfer of a franchise between two charities. In one way, however, the Regulations go beyond the Directive; this is in reg. 4 which gives protection to employees of an insolvent company that is subject to a rescue operation by way of 'hiving down' (see Davies and Fredland 'The effects of receivership upon employees of companies' (1980) 9 ILJ 95; McMullen, op. cit.; Collins 'Transfer of undertakings and insolvency' (1989) 18 ILJ 144; Pollard 'Insolvent companies and TUPE' (1996) 25 ILJ 191); the Directive does not extend to formal judicial liquidation proceedings: *Abels v Bedrijfsvereniging voor de Metaalindustrie en de Electrotechnische Industrie*: 135/83 [1985] ECR 469, [1987] 2 CMLR 406, ECJ.
1   Existing criminal liabilities of the transferor are not affected: reg. 5(4). The regime of transfer has been applied more widely than just to ordinary terms and conditions; it has been held to apply to a protective award for failure to consult on collective redundancies (*Kersy Foods Ltd v Creber* [2000] IRLR 10), the benefit of a restraint of trade clause which could be claimed by the transferee (*Morris Angel & Son Ltd v Hollande* [1993] ICR 71, [1993] IRLR 169, CA), liability for alleged sex discrimination (*DJM International Ltd v Nicholas* [1996] ICR 214, [1996] IRLR 76) and even liability for an industrial injury suffered by the employee while in the transferor's employment (*Bernadone v Pall Mall Services Group* [2000] IRLR 487, CA). Reg. 7 excludes occupational pensions; attempts were made to evade this by arguing that, although a transferee does not have to continue to operate an existing pension scheme, he is under an obligation (under art. 3(3) of the Directive) to provide something equivalent, but this was strongly disapproved by the EAT in *Walden Engineering Co Ltd v Warrener* [1993] 3 CMLR 179, [1993] ICR 967; this exclusion is not contrary to the Directive: *Adams v Lancashire County Council* [1997] IRLR 436, CA.
2   *Allan v Stirling District Council* [1995] ICR 1082, [1995] IRLR 301. Ct of Sess. approving *Ibex Trading Co Ltd v Walton* [1994] ICR 907, [1994] IRLR 564.

This form of automatic transfer (or statutory novation of the contract) goes beyond a mere matter of continuity of employment, which was probably safeguarded anyway, in two ways. The first is that, where the employees go with the business, not only is continuity preserved, but also their existing terms and conditions (and accrued rights, especially to redundancy payments[3]) are protected and the new employer takes them on subject to that, with a long-standing problem of when and how the transferee employer can lawfully change them (see below)[4]. The second is even more fundamental – the basic principle is that automatic transfer occurs on a relevant transfer *irrespective of the desires of the parties*. At common law, an employee could not be required to work for a particular employer without his consent[5]. That principle disappeared once the regulations applied[6]. Moreover, a purchaser of a business who, in earlier times, would have bought it without the staff (who would have been made redundant by the old employer), can now find that he is *deemed* to be their new employer, on their existing terms and responsible for any redundancy payments, based on their years of service with their old employer. Regulation 5(5) does give the employee a right to leave (and claim constructive dismissal) but it is restricted – it only applies if 'a substantial change is made in his working conditions to his detriment', and it is declared that the change in the identity of the employer is not per se such a substantial change (unless the employee can show real detriment because of it). Apart from that, the employees were as bound by automatic transfer as the transferee employer. Initially, this appeared to be very much in line with the intent of the Directive[7], but doubt was cast on that by the ECJ's decision in *Katsikas v Konstantinidis*[8] upholding the German equivalent of these regulations which allows an employee a right of objection to the transfer, avoiding automatic transfer of his contract; the view of the ECJ was that under the Directive it is for the member state to decide whether or not to legislate for automatic transfer. In the light of that case, a hurried amendment to the regulations was put into the Trade Union Reform and Employment Rights Act 1993 as it was going through Parliament. The new regulation 5(4A) states that there is not to be automatic transfer 'if the employee informs the transferor or the transferee that he objects to becoming employed by the transferee'[9]. However, regulation 5(4B) then goes on to state that where such objection is made 'the transfer of the undertaking ... shall operate so as to terminate his contract of employment with the transferor *but he shall not be treated, for any purpose, as having been dismissed by the transferor*'. The result of this bizarre amendment is that the employee has a theoretical right of

3   See p. 532, below, for the fundamental changes made to redundancy payments liability by the regulations.
4   This is especially so in the light of (a) the decision of the Court of Appeal in *Berriman v Delabole Slate Ltd* [1985] ICR 546, [1985] IRLR 305 that seeking to 'standardise' the newcomers' terms and conditions to those of the transferee's existing workforce is *not* within the 'economic, technical or organisational' defence and (b) the leading case of *Wilson v St Helens Borough Council* [1998] ICR 1141, [1998] IRLR 706 in the House of Lords on transfer-related variations.
5   *Nokes v Doncaster Amalgamated Collieries Ltd* [1940] AC 1014, [1940] 3 All ER 549, HL.
6   *Newns v British Airways plc* [1992] IRLR 575, CA. Paradoxically, in several of the leading cases it is the *employees* arguing that the regulations should *not* apply, because they want a break in their employment, so that they can cash in their accrued redundancy rights against the old employer and start afresh with the transferee; see, eg, *Whitewater Leisure Managment Ltd v Barnes* [2000] IRLR 456.
7   *Berg v Besselsen*, n. 19, above.
8   C-132, 138, 139/91: [1992] ECR I-6577, [1993] 1 CMLR 845, ECJ.
9   No particular form is laid down for objection, which may therefore be inferred from words or conduct: *Hay v George Hanson (Building Contractors) Ltd* [1996] IRLR 427, though notice the more cautious approach in *Senior Heat Treatment Ltd v Bell* [1997] IRLR 614.

objection but if he exercises it he may be left in a state of legal limbo, with no rights against the transferee (because there is no automatic transfer of his contract), but also no recourse against the transferor for any cause of action that requires him to have been 'dismissed' (because regulation 5(4B) deems there to have been no dismissal). The potential harshness of this situation led the Court of Appeal to add a major qualification, in a particularly purposive decision[10] holding that if an employee leaves by exercising his right to do so under regulation 5(5) (substantial detrimental changes being proposed/threatened by the transferee employer), then regulation 5 (4B) does *not* apply and the employee retains any remedies he may have against the transferor (which remain personal to that employer and do not pass to the transferee, because of regulation 5(4A)). This is a good example of both the complexity of these Regulations and the need occasionally for creative interpretation to avoid some of their more notable absurdities.

Following on from that point, recent domestic case law has shown two major difficulties for employers on a 'TUPE transfer' (to lapse into the jargon). The first is that if a transferee takes on employees whose existing terms of employment were made by reference to some extraneous factor affecting the transferor, the transferee will be bound by them, possibly with strange results. In *Whent v T Cartledge Ltd*[11] the transferee (the successful tenderer in a contracting-out case) took on employees whose terms on remuneration referred to collective bargains between the old employer and a recognised union, with the result that when wages were raised by the next such bargain the transferred employees successfully claimed the increase, even though by then in the employment of the transferee who was not concerned at all in the bargaining. In *Unicorn Consultancy Services Ltd v Westbrook*[12] transferred employees could claim from the transferee profit-related pay (PRP) due under their contracts, based on the *transferor's* profits and performance. This could be a serious problem – the case only involved an 'easy' version of this because the employees were claiming PRP that had already been earned by the time of the transfer. As the EAT noted, the real difficulty (yet to be faced in the cases) is the operation of such a PRP term in the *future*, after the transfer. On the *Whent* precedent, the transferee could be faced into the future with being liable to pay PRP on the transferor's profits, over which it has no control.

The second point of difficulty only compounds the first. In the straightforward world of domestic contract law, it would be possible for the transferee to take on the transferred employees on their existing terms and conditions and then to negotiate changes in the normal way. However, it has been held that the protection of the Directive (and hence the Regulations) is intended to be stronger than that, with the result that a transferee may *not* lawfully change the existing terms and conditions *if* the change is 'transfer-related', and that any attempt to do so will be void, even if for good consideration and with the ostensible agreement of the employees. This particular bombshell was dropped by the EAT in *Wilson v St Helens Borough Council*[13] (with the laconic comment that this may be 'surprising ... to English legal tradition'), with the result that employees who had agreed changes to their terms on a transfer for a buy-out payment could demand restoration of

10   *University of Oxford v Humphreys* [2000] IRLR 183, CA.
11   [1997] IRLR 153.
12   [2000] IRLR 80.
13   [1996] ICR 711, [1996] IRLR 320; this was based on long-overlooked dicta by the ECJ in *Foreningen of Arbejdsledere i Danmark v Daddy's Dance Hall A/S*: 324/86 [1988] IRLR 315, ECJ.

the original terms over a year later[14]. By the time that this case reached the House of Lords the basic principle seemed to be accepted, and the argument at that stage was over the circumstances in which the principle might be avoided (and a contractual change lawful)[15]. Two such circumstances were accepted – (i) where either transferor or transferee dismisses the employees and re-engages them on the new terms (this being effective because domestic law does not acknowledge the possibility of a dismissal being void, even under the Directive); (ii) where the transferee can break the claim of causation by showing that the changes were *not* 'transfer-related', i.e. that they were made for some other, independent reason such as a reorganisation of the whole workplace involving all employees (long-standing and transferred), in which case the ordinary rules of contract law apply. Category (i) is not as attractive as it seems, because it lays the employer open to unfair dismissal actions by the employees[16], compensation possibly reflecting the net loss incurred under the new terms and conditions[17]. Category (ii) can be fraught with problems of proof and timing (there being *no* rule of thumb that a change will not be transfer-related after a certain period from the transfer), and assumptions made by employers about their ability to impose or even negotiate changes after the transfer can sometimes be proved to have been entirely wrong[18].

3)   *Which employees are covered?*   In many cases it will be obvious which employees are covered by the regulations and the accompanying statutory protection, especially where a whole undertaking is transferred, with the whole existing workforce being kept on. However, problems have arisen in two areas. The first is where *part* of an undertaking is transferred, especially where it is a part of a complex organisation or group of companies; given that the remainder may be facing financial disaster, can an employee who worked for several or all parts of the organisation or group claim to be attached to the part transferred, and so 'jump ship' to the employment of the financially viable transferee/purchaser (at least for the purposes of bringing any redundancy or unfair dismissal claims

---

14   The mechanism used was a claim for unlawful deductions from wages under Part II of the Employment Rights Act 1996 (see p. 213, below), where the limitation period (in a case of continuing deductions) only flows from the last pay day, under the new terms, before the date of the proceedings. One unresolved point is a case like this is whether the employer can reclaim from the employees the amount paid to buy out the original terms, on the basis of failure of consideration.

15   [1998] ICR 1141, [1998] IRLR 706, HL; see McMullen (1998) 28 ILJ 76. The reasons for this subtle but significant change in emphasis were that (a) the case was consolidated with the appeal in *Meade and Baxendale v British Fuels Ltd* [1996] IRLR 541 where there had been a dismissal and re-engagement on new terms, not just a contractual variation, and (b) it became apparent that the dismissal tactic had in fact also been used in *Wilson* itself, a factor which had not been thought particularly significant at EAT level.

16   The employees can claim unfair dismissal from their old *contract*, even though still in the employment of the employer under the new contract, under the rule in *Hogg v Dover College* [1990] ICR 39: see p. 445, below.

17   *Cornwall County Care Ltd v Brightman* [1998] ICR 529, [1998] IRLR 228; the decision of the EAT was before that of the House of Lords in *Wilson*, trying to sort out the mess made in the meantime by the Court of Appeal, but the compensation point arguably remains good law.

18   In two cases, restraint of trade clauses negotiated into contracts by the transferee shortly after the transfer were held to be unenforceable because they were transfer-related and therefore void changes: *Crédit Suisse First Boston (Europe) Ltd v Padiachy* [1999] ICR 569, [1998] IRLR 504; *Crédit Suisse First Boston (Europe) Ltd v Lister* [1999] ICR 794, [1998] IRLR 700, CA. In the latter case, this was despite the employee having been paid £625,000 for the change in terms.

against the latter if not kept on)? In *Sunley Turriff Holdings Ltd v Thomson*[19] two companies (LC Ltd and LC Scotland Ltd) went into receivership and the latter was sold to Co X. The employee had been company secretary and chief accountant for both companies. Although his contract had been with LC Ltd, he had done substantial work for LC (Scotland) Ltd and so, when made redundant by the receivers the EAT held that he was able to claim that he was covered by the regulations and so technically taken on by Co X, against whom he could claim unfair dismissal. On the other hand, in *Michael Peters Ltd v Farnfield*[20] when receivers were called in to a group of a holding company and 25 subsidiaries, the EAT held that the chief executive of the group could not invoke the regulations and claim to go with the transfer when (only) four viable subsidiaries were sold to Co Y. In both cases, the court applied the test laid down by the ECJ in *Botzen v Rotterdamsche Droogdok Maatschappij BV*[1] , i.e. to look as a question of fact at 'to which part of the undertaking or business the employee was assigned' or allocated. It is clear from the first of the two EAT cases that this will not be resolved simply by looking at the technicalities of where the contract of employment lay. Other than that (which presumably must at least be a factor) this is a wide question of fact and degree with (so far) no attempt to lay down rules of thumb, such as at least x% of work being done for the part transferred, which could make advising on this point in advance of a transfer very difficult[2], especially as the EAT subsequently added that tribunals should be astute to ensure that protection of the individual (and the intent of the Directive and Regulations) should not be prejudiced by too formalistic an emphasis being placed on the intricacies of the corporate structure of the transferor organisation[3].

The second problem arose early in the convoluted history of the Regulations and involves a question of *when* the employee in question must have been in the transferor's employ. In order for these automatic transfer provisions to apply the employee must have been employed 'immediately before' the transfer of undertaking (reg. 5(3)); the question arose whether there can be a gap between the end of employment with the transferor and the transfer itself (e.g. over a weekend). Originally it was held that there could be[4], which could lead to a less technical application of the Regulations, though at the expense of considerable uncertainty (how long a gap was permissible?). However, in *Secretary of State for Employment v Spence*[5], the Court of Appeal overruled this approach and held that regulation 5 only applies to employees employed by the transferor at the precise moment of the transfer, so that a gap even of hours is fatal. This at least has the merit of certainty, important in itself in advising the parties to the transfer, but it

---

19   [1995] IRLR 184.
20   [1995] IRLR 190.
1   Case 186/83: [1985] ECR 519, [1986] 2 CMLR 50, ECJ. In *Michael Peters* it was held that the solution to this problem lies in applying this test, *not* in attempting to lift the veil of incorporation.
2   It may also reinforce the need, appreciated early on under these Regulations, to put indemnity clauses into business sales agreements to cover the possibility of unforeseen liabilities being placed on the transferee, contrary to the expectations of both parties.
3   *Duncan Web Offset (Maidstone) Ltd v Cooper* [1995] IRLR 633.
4   *Apex Leisure Hire v Barratt* [1984] ICR 452, [1984] IRLR 224; *Secretary of State for Employment v Anchor Hotel (Kippford) Ltd* [1985] ICR 724, [1985] IRLR 452.
5   [1986] ICR 651, [1986] IRLR 248, CA, applying *Wendeboe v LJ Music ApS*: 19/83 [1985] ECR 457, [1986] 1 CMLR 476, ECJ (a case on the Acquired Rights Directive). *Spence* was one of the cases where it was the employees who did *not* want reg. 5 to apply – they wanted to cash in their redundancy rights (in fact against the Secretary of State since their old employer was insolvent) and could do so only if their employment was not transferred to the new employer. However, by winning their case they appeared to worsen the position of employees in other cases who *do* wish to rely on the regulations.

did appear to give more scope to the purchaser/transferee who wishes to insist that the vendor/transferor dispense with the workforce before the transfer, if only marginally before (leaving the dispensed workers with rights only against the transferor who may in some cases be in a far weaker economic position than the transferee). However, this potentially major gap in the protection intended by the Regulations for employees in this position has now been rectified in two cases, not by overruling *Spence*, but rather by holding that in many cases the reasoning in that case does not go far enough. In *P Bork International A/S (in liquidation) v Foreningen af Arbejdsledere i Danmark*[6] the ECJ, construing the Acquired Rights Directive, held that if an employee is dismissed before the transfer and because of it, then Article 4(1) renders that dismissal ineffective; the result of this is that the employee is *deemed* still to be employed 'immediately before' the transfer, so that liabilities in respect of him *are* transferred to the transferee. The provisions of Article 4(1) appear in domestic law as regulation 8[7] which makes a dismissal because of the transfer automatically unfair unless it was for an 'economic, technical or organisational reason entailing changes in the workforce'. As the ECJ's decision in *Bork* produced a result contrary to that in *Spence*, the whole question had to be reconsidered as a matter of domestic law. This occurred in *Litster v Forth Dry Dock and Engineering Co Ltd*[8], where employees of the transferor company were dismissed only an hour before the transfer, but the transferee company denied that they were liable for any unfair dismissals because the employees were not employed 'immediately before the transfer' (thus leaving them to pursue any remedies only against the transferor company, which was in receivership). The House of Lords, applying *Bork*, held that regulation 5 did apply, so that the transferees were liable; *Spence* was upheld, in as much as it establishes that 'immediately before' means 'at the time of', *but* regulation 5(3) which contains that phrase must be read as if there were inserted the phrase 'or would have been so employed [immediately before the transfer] if he had not been unfairly dismissed in the circumstances described in regulation 8(1)'. The outcome of this decision is as follows – (i) the transferee cannot escape liability under regulation 5 merely by inducing the transferor to dismiss the employee shortly before the actual time of transfer, because that regulation is to be read subject to the unfair dismissal provisions of regulation 8; (ii) *Spence* is correct as an authority on the meaning of the phrase 'immediately before' *and* was correctly decided on its facts because in that case there *was* an 'economic ... reason' for the dismissal, so that regulation 8 did not apply; in most cases, however, that will not be so, regulation 8 will apply (in spite of any applicable gap between the dismissal and the time of transfer) and so for example – (iii) the cases of *Apex Leisure Hire* and *Anchor Hotel (Kippford) Ltd*[9] were correctly decided on their facts, but for the wrong reasons. As was pointed out in the House of Lords, this wide and purposive interpretation achieves the presumed intent of Parliament which

6   101/87: [1989] IRLR 41, ECJ.

7   See p. 491, below.

8   [1989] IRLR 161, HL; see Collins (1989) 18 ILJ 144. The wide and purposive interpretation of the regulations adopted in this case was justified (particularly by Lord Keith) on the grounds that the regulations were passed to implement the Directive and that the previous decision of the House of Lords in *Pickstone v Freemans plc* [1988] ICR 697, [1988] IRLR 357 permitted heavy reliance on the Directive (as construed in *Bork*) as an aid to interpretation. One possible problem was that Art. 4(1) renders a dismissal because of transfer *ineffective* whereas reg. 8 only renders it potentially *unfair*; however, this point is outflanked by the approach of the House of Lords in using a wide interpretation to imply wording into reg. 5(3), as set out below.

9   See n. 4, above.

was to give effect to the protective intent of the Directive, rather than to negative it (as the decision in *Spence*, standing alone, had been capable of doing).

4)   *Application to tendering and contracting out*[10]   It has been the policy of successive governments for several years now to encourage or even require bodies in the public sector to put out to tender certain services (such as catering or cleaning), on the basis that such services can be more efficiently and cheaply provided by the private sector. Similarly, large private concerns may decide to do so voluntarily, for similar reasons. When this happens, staff who previously performed these services in-house will often be taken on by the successful contractors, but it was always assumed that this was after a clean break with the old employer, so that (a) the contractor did not assume any responsibility for any accrued rights (in particular, accrued redundancy rights) and (b) he was free to take on only some of the old workforce and/or then to 'adjust' (i.e. diminish) their old terms and conditions, to reduce labour costs. Clearly, if the Regulations applied, neither of those assumptions would survive and the whole economic basis of contracting out would be called into question.

It initially seemed clear that under domestic law the Regulations could not apply, for two independent reasons. The first was the restriction that they did not apply to non-commercial undertakings. Thus in *Expro Services Ltd v Smith*[11] , where catering services were contracted out to a private company by the Ministry of Defence, it was held that the regulations did not apply (and so there was no continuity of employment for an employee who transferred to the private company and was later dismissed within the magic two years then required for an unfair dismissal claim), because the catering venture had not been a commercial venture when carried out by the Ministry. The second was that, in any event, the domestic courts took the view that merely giving out a contract or tender[12] could not constitute the 'transfer of an undertaking' because it fell short of a going business (even if the employees and certain premises or equipment went with it). Thus, in *Curling v Securicor Ltd*[13] the Home Office had contracted out services at a detention centre to Securicor, but when that contract came up for renewal it was awarded to another company; the employee stayed doing the same job and transferred to the employment of the other company, but it was held that regulation 5 did not apply because this mere change of contract did not constitute a transfer of undertaking.

This situation began to change when it became clear that the restriction to commercial undertakings was contrary to the Directive and so had to be removed by the Trade Union Reform and Employment Rights Act 1993[14] . At first, the then government maintained that the Regulations still would not apply to contracting

---

10   See McMullen (1994) 23 ILJ 230; Radford and Kerr 'Acquiring rights – losing power: a case study in ministerial resistance to the impact of EC law' (1997) 60 MLR 23.
11   [1991] ICR 577, [1991] IRLR 156.
12   This could happen in two ways – (1) the old employer A could change from performing the service in-house, and contract it out to private firm B (a 'first generation contracting-out') *or* (2) the old employer A could already have contracted it out to private firm B, but on the expiry of that contract retendered and awarded the new contract to private firm C (a 'second generation contracting-out'). Problems of continuity arise if a particular employee carries on doing the same job in the same place, but moves in the first case from A to B, and in the second case from B to C.
13   [1992] IRLR 549. This was another case where it was in fact the employees arguing that the regulations did *not* apply, because they were seeking (successfully) redundancy payments from Securicor.
14   See p. 161, above.

out because of the second reason above (no 'undertaking' transferred). However, the axe soon fell on that with the decision of the ECJ in *Rask v ISS Kantineservice A/ S*[15] that the Directive did apply where a large private company had contracted out the running of a staff canteen to a service company and an existing employee entered the latter's employment; the result was that when the service company changed one of her terms of employment she could claim the protection of the Danish legislation enacting the Directive[16]. Following on from this, it was held by the High Court in *Kenny v South Manchester College*[17] that effect must now be given to this wide approach in domestic law; thus, where prison education had been contracted out to a local authority but, as a result of re-tendering, was then contracted out to a college, the staff previously employed by the local authority on that work had to be taken on by the college, on the same terms and conditions. A similar conclusion was reached in *Wren v Eastbourne Borough Council*[18] where a mainstream example of a local authority being obliged to contract out its street cleaning and refuse collection functions led to the finding of a 'transfer of undertaking' when those functions were taken over by a private company. This approach was then taken further in three ways. First, in *Dines v Initial Health Care Services*[19] the Court of Appeal held that the inescapable logic (resisted, as a matter of policy, by the EAT in that case) was that the Regulations could apply to a subsequent re-tendering exercise; thus, where the original contract for the services (in that case, for hospital cleaning) by Co A ran out and the principal body retendered and Co B won the next contract, there was a transfer of undertaking from A to B (albeit in two stages – the handing back from A to the principal body and then the granting of the new contract to B); the effect was that employees of A were either notionally taken into the employment of B for the purposes of an unfair dismissal claim, or were actually taken on by B but with their existing terms and conditions protected. The counter argument, that all that had been 'transferred' was a contract, not an undertaking, was disapproved. Second, in *Isles of Scilly Council v Brintel Helicopters Ltd*[20] it was held that there was a transfer of undertaking where the firm to which airport support services had been contracted out went into administration and the council took these services back in-house, i.e. a contracting *back in*. Third, this broad approach to the contracting of services (and, more generally, to the defining of a transfer of undertaking by looking generally for the continuance of an economic entity or

15   C-209/91: [1993] IRLR 133, ECJ.
16   At least in *Rask* it concerned an employee who wanted to be there and whom the transferee wanted to employ; automatic transfer means that a firm contracting for a service would notionally have to take on *all* the employees currently doing the job (even those he had not planned on keeping), with all their accrued rights.
17   [1993] ICR 934, [1993] IRLR 265.
18   [1993] 3 CMLR 166, [1993] ICR 955. There was a transfer even though the council retained overall responsibility for the functions being performed; this point was emphasised in *Birch v Nuneaton and Bedworth Borough Council* [1995] IRLR 518 where there was a relevant transfer when the management of a leisure centre was contracted out, even though the council built into the contract remarkably detailed controls over its running.
19   [1995] ICR 11, [1994] IRLR 336, CA. In such a case, the potential problems are unlikely to be sorted out by the parties A and B amicably (e.g. through price adjustments and indemnity clauses) because they are commercial competitors and indeed, in an extreme case, may not even know who the other is. In fact, the application of the Regulations could give an opportunity for disappointed tenderer A to cause problems for the successful tenderer B – there are apocryphal stories of A's last act being to double their employees' wages, so that B has to take them on at those wage rates! Another possibility is that A could assign to that contract for the last phase of the contract all the employees he most wishes to lose.
20   [1995] ICR 249, [1995] IRLR 6.

activity with some sort of retained identity, rather than for more concrete matters such as the transfer of assets or equipment or good will) seemed to be taken to its logical conclusion by the decision of the ECJ in the *Christel Schmidt* case[1] that the Acquired Rights Directive applied where an employee who was the sole cleaner of a bank's premises was dismissed when that service function was contracted out to the firm that already provided it with other cleaning services; this was so in spite of the facts that (a) all that was concerned was a purely ancillary function (not part of the bank's principal business), (b) only one employee was involved and (c) there was no transfer whatever of any tangible assets. Intervening in the argument of the case, the British government had again tried to draw a distinction between the transfer of a business (or part thereof) and the mere entering of a contractual arrangement, but again this had fallen on deaf ears.

Those involved in contracting-out operations thus had to become accustomed to conducting them against the background of the Regulations, which were therefore giving considerable protection to the employees involved. Unfortunately, however, it could not be assumed that the Regulations would always apply, and the uncertainty caused by two subsequent ECJ cases (appearing to resile from the high point reached in *Christel Schmidt*) meant that this continued to be a troublesome area. *Rygard v Stø Mølle Akustik A/S*[2] caused some ripples by appearing to revive ideas that it may be only a contractual function that was being transferred, but it was on unusual facts and was later restrictively distinguished by the EAT and ECJ[3] and has had little effect. The case that did, however, cause most heartache even to TUPE-hardened employment lawyers was *Ayse Süzen*[4], in which the ECJ stated (helpfully) that a contracting-out may *or may not* be a relevant transfer, depending in many cases on whether assets and/or a significant part of the workforce were actually transferred by the commercial arrangement. Immediately after this decision the Court of Appeal held in *Betts v Brintel Helicopters Ltd*[5] that there was no relevant transfer (on a second generation contracting-out) where the new contractors for the supply of gas rigs had its own helicopters and facilities and deliberately declined to offer employment to any of the employees engaged on the service by the old contractor. A case such as this exposed the flaw in *Ayse Süzen* from the point of view of employee protection, namely that a cynical transferee could use it to make non-application of the Regulations a self-fulfilling prophecy by refusing to take on either assets or staff. This possibility has, however, been considerably lessened by the important case of *ECM (Vehicle Delivery Service) Ltd v Cox* where just such a tactic was used, again on a second generation contracting-out. The EAT[6] held that the Regulations did apply on two grounds that, they said, had not been before the ECJ in *Ayse Süzen* – (i) in a labour-intensive industry it may be relevant (as it was in *Christel Schmidt*) that the employee in question was 'dedicated' to the work that was being transferred (rather than

1   *Schmidt v Spar und Leihkasse der früheren Ämter Bordesholm, Kiel und Cronshagen*; C 392/92 [1994] ECR I-1311, [1995] 2 CMLR 331, ECJ.
2   C-48/94 [1996] ICR 333, [1996] IRLR 51, ECJ.
3   *BSG Property Services v Tuck* [1996] IRLR 134; *Allen v Amalgamated Construction Co Ltd*: C-234/98 [2000] IRLR 119, [2000] All ER (EC) 97, ECJ.
4   *Süzen v Zehnacker Gebäudereinigung GmbH Krankenhausservice*: C-13/95 [1997] ICR 662, [1997] IRLR 255, ECJ. A similar approach was taken subsequently by the ECJ in *Francisco Hernández Vidal SA v Gomez Perez*: C-127/96 [1999] IRLR 132, ECJ and *Sánchez Hidalgo v Asociación de Servicios Aser and Sociedad Cooperativa Minerva*: C-173/96 [1999] IRLR 136, ECJ, though (it has been argued) with more emphasis on the importance of the workforce itself as the 'economic entity' in a labour-intensive industry.
5   [1997] ICR 792, [1997] IRLR 361, CA.
6   [1998] ICR 631, [1998] IRLR 416.

merely being a member of staff of a large service company who, on the loss of one contract, will simply be moved on to the next one), which should point to there being a relevant transfer; (ii) in any event, as a matter of policy and purposive interpretation, a tribunal may wish to prevent an employer from deliberately using *Ayse Süzen* to avoid the Regulations. On appeal[7], point (i) was not in issue, and it may be that the EAT's view on it is of importance because arguably it goes to the heart of the economic realities of a transfer and whether the employee's continuing need of *that* job merits protection. On point (ii) the Court of Appeal dismissed the employer's appeal and held in a short judgment that *all* the circumstances of the transfer must be considered, *including* any intent to evade the Regulations, a point subsequently approved and applied in Scotland by the Inner House of the Court of Session[8]. At the time of writing, therefore, the protection given by the domestic courts is in advance of that suggested by the ECJ.

5)   *The new Acquired Rights Directive*   Council Directive 77/187 on which the Regulations are based is materially amended by Council Directive 98/50[9], and it is likely that early in the currency of this edition we shall have new Regulations reflecting the changes. In some ways, the new Directive is a disappointment, in particular because the 'new' definition of a relevant transfer merely seeks to codify the existing decisions of the ECJ without giving clearer guidance in contracting-out cases[10], and because the UK government's suggested way out of the *Wilson v St Helens* conundrum (i.e. that it should be lawful for the workforce *collectively* to agree post-transfer changes in terms) was only incorporated into the Directive in the restricted case where the employer is insolvent and it is necessary ensure the survival of the undertaking[11]. Changes in the Directive which are likely to feature in the new Regulations are a provision for joint and several liability on transferor and transferee employers[12], an obligation on a transferor to notify a transferee of rights and obligations to be transferred[13] and the inclusion of pension provisions[14], a matter of substantial complexity. One home-grown idea of considerable interest (given the excessive and frustrating complexity of this whole area) is that it should be possible to apply to a tribunal in advance for a declaration whether or not a proposed transaction would be a relevant transfer, applying the Regulations.

---

7   [1999] ICR 1162, [1999] IRLR 559, CA.
8   *Lightways (Contractors) Ltd v Associated Holdings Ltd* [2000] IRLR 247, Ct of Sess (contractor submitting a bid on the basis that TUPE applied was not allowed to insist later to the employees that it did not). One problem arising from *ECM* is that *Betts* (note 5 above) is not criticised, but appears to produce the opposite result on *very* similar facts (including an allegation that the refusal to take on the staff was a deliberate ploy). While each case is of course decided on its facts, it may be that *Betts* would probably be decided the other way today, and that the employees in *Betts* were extremely unlucky in the timing of their case.
9   See Davies, 'Amendments to the ARD' (1998) 27 ILJ 365. The government enacted a power to make TUPE Regulations (under the European Communities Act 1972, s. 2(2)) going beyond the requirements of the Directive: Employment Relations Act 1999, s. 38.
10   Directive 98/50, art. 1 substitutes new arts. 1–7 into the original Directive; this is the new art. 1(1).
11   Art. 4(2)(b).
12   Art. 3(1).
13   Art. 3(2).
14   Art. 3(4).

Chapter 4

Wages and hours

I INTRODUCTION

It will be seen in this chapter that the law has long had a role with regard to wages in providing certain forms of protection of the right to receive wages and in establishing rights to certain forms of income replacement, especially when ill. However, the prevailing political view of the last two decades has been that the law (i.e. the state) should *not* be involved in setting wage levels. Not only were moves within the EC to enter this area (e.g. by minimum wage rates or maximum hours) vigorously opposed by the previous government, but also they progressively dismantled those legal provisions that in the past did have an effect on wage setting. Mechanisms for imposing 'fair wages' requirements in state contracts were abolished, as were legal means of trying to enforce the 'going rate for the job'. Indeed, free market economics would doubt whether there was any such thing – the only rate is the rate that the market will bear, especially in times of declining collective bargaining and increasing individual bargaining. The only legally binding form of wage fixing in recent years was the wages councils, which operated in certain, very specific industries with little or no collective machinery. They remained, however, an anachronism under the new dispensation; initially the previous government curtailed their powers in 1986, and eventually abolished them in 1993, leaving only the Agricultural Wages Board which is set up under its own legislation.

The incoming New Labour government has been keen quick to stress its free market credentials and not to be seen to be going back to dated ideas of wages policies or wage restraint that caused so many problems for the Labour governments of the 1960s and 1970s. However, they were committed to two forms of statutory intervention strongly opposed by the previous government; those were a national minimum wage and compliance with the EC Working Time Directive, and both were enacted within the first two years of the government's term. While these provisions enact important minima and limitations, neither of them seek to determine the actual *levels* of wages or the hours of work required (or their organisation). For most purposes, therefore, wages and hours remain primarily a question for agreement and contract, not legal intervention. As such, they have in the past been primarily a matter for the ordinary courts, not the employment tribunals, in the case of disputes as to payability, amounts owed, etc.; this led in the past to an extremely unfortunate split in jurisdiction (e.g. a dismissed employee having to go to a tribunal for unfair dismissal, but to the county court for unpaid notice or holiday pay). We shall see, however, that there have been major inroads into this principle in recent years, by (1) the adoption of interpretations of Part II of the Employment Rights Act 1996 (originally the Wages Act 1986) which deserve a nomination for the Booker Prize for Fiction, in relation to what can constitute a 'deduction' from wages, and (2) at long last the granting to tribunals of jurisdiction to hear certain common law contractual claims (though unfortunately restricted to amounts owing on termination of employment).

2   THE RIGHT TO WAGES AT COMMON LAW

The obligation upon the employer to pay the wages which are due is a basic term of the contract of employment; details of the scale, rate or method of calculation of the remuneration should be given to the employee in writing[1], and he has a statutory right to receive an itemised pay statement upon payment of wages or salary[2]. However, it must be stressed that the details of the obligation upon the employer depend entirely upon the terms of the contract of employment, and there cannot be said to be any overall legal obligation to pay wages as such, since wages are not necessarily the consideration to be supplied by the employer for the work done or service rendered by the employee. Thus, at common law there can be a valid contract of employment, even though no set wages are payable, where the employee is to be rewarded by a commission[3], by fees, by the receipt of tips from customers[4] or by being given the *chance* to earn a salary[5]. Likewise, there will be no set wage or salary where the employee is paid on a piecework or hourly basis (with or without an agreed guaranteed minimum wage), though in such a case there may be an implied term that the employer shall provide a reasonable amount of work for the employee to do[6]. Moreover, in an extreme case it might be that the correct construction of the contract is that, in the circumstances, nothing is payable to the employee as in *Re Richmond Gate Property Co Ltd*[7] where the managing director of a company in liquidation had never had the question of his remuneration determined by the directors as required by the company's articles, and so Plowman J held that, in the circumstances, he was not entitled to receive anything for services rendered prior to the liquidation. Also, in certain older cases[8] it was held that an agreement which gives the employer the right to fix remuneration, gives him the right to give *no* remuneration. However, this is unlikely to be the case now, for where there is some reference to

1   ERA 1996, s. 1(4); on the significance of different forms of remuneration, see Freedland, 'The obligation to work and to pay for work' (1977) 30 CLP 175.
2   Ibid., s. 8.
3   *Phillips v Curling* (1847) 10 LTOS 245; *Clayton Newbury Ltd v Findlay* [1953] 2 All ER 826n, [1953] 1 WLR 1194n; *Bronester Ltd v Priddle* [1961] 3 All ER 471, [1961] 1 WLR 1294, CA.
4   *Pauley v Kenaldo Ltd* [1953] 1 All ER 226, [1953] 1 WLR 187.
5   *Gaumont-British Picture Corpn v Alexander* [1936] 2 All ER 1686.
6   See p. 109, above.
7   [1964] 3 All ER 936, [1965] 1 WLR 335.
8   *Taylor v Brewer* (1813) 1 M & S 290; *Roberts v Smith* (1859) 4 H & N 315. See, however, the explanation of these cases by Vaughan Williams LJ in *Loftus v Roberts* (1902) 18 TLR 532, CA.

remuneration, or some discernible understanding that there would be remuneration, or where the contract is just vague on the subject, the employee may be able to recover a reasonable sum on a quantum meruit basis, as in *Way v Latilla*[9] where the plaintiff, who had obtained gold mining concessions for the defendant (yielding a million-pound profit) on the vague understanding that the defendant would 'look after his interests', was held by the House of Lords to be entitled to £5,000 commission on a quantum meruit basis when the defendant refused to pay him anything. Likewise, in *Powell v Braun*[10] a secretary who had been offered an unspecified annual bonus (having regard to the firm's performance) in place of the usual increase in wages was held by the Court of Appeal to be entitled to a reasonable amount on a quantum meruit basis for the two years during which her employer had failed to pay any bonus at all, thus establishing that a quantum meruit action may be used to recover additional remuneration as well as ordinary wages or salary. Some of these stranger forms of renumeration (or, indeed, possible non-remuneration) may of course now have to be read subject to the national minimum wage legislation (below), but that only specifies a minimum *amount* that must eventually be payable and does *not* mean that these forms in themselves are illegal.

One theoretical problem concerning the common law right to wages has arisen where the employee does not complete the relevant obligation in the contract of employment. In strict theory it may be that *no* remuneration is payable (even on a quantum meruit action), as in the old case of *Cutter v Powell*[11] where a sailor who contracted for 30 guineas to act as second mate for a certain voyage died in the course of that voyage and his widow failed to recover any of the amount agreed upon, since the court held that partial performance of an entire obligation did not give rise to a right to any of the remuneration. This principle is most unlikely to apply to a case today, for most contracts are divisible, not entire, certainly to the extent of definite periods for payment of remuneration[12]. Even if this were not so, an employee could attempt to circumvent *Cutter v Powell* in several ways – first, by claiming that the employer had received substantial performance of the contract and so was not relieved from payment[13]; second, if complete performance was prevented by the employer, by bringing a quantum meruit action[14]; third, where the contract was frustrated[15], by claiming a just amount under the Law Reform (Frustrated Contracts) Act 1943, section 1(3); fourth, by claiming that his wages or salary are to be deemed to accrue from day to day (even though not so payable under the contract) under the Apportionment Act 1870, section 2 which thus apportions 'all rents, annuities, dividends and other periodic payments in the nature of income' – section 5 states that 'annuities' include 'salaries and pensions', and it appears that 'salaries' should be taken to include wages[16].

---

9   [1937] 3 All ER 759, HL. See also *Craven-Ellis v Canons Ltd* [1936] 2 KB 403, [1936] 2 All ER 1066, CA.

10   [1954] 1 All ER 484, [1954] 1 WLR 401, CA.

11   (1795) 6 Term Rep 320, followed in *Sinclair v Bowles* (1829) 9 B & C 92 and *Vigers v Cook* [1919] 2 KB 475, CA.

12   Details of the periods for payment must be given to the employee in writing: ERA 1996, s. 1(4).

13   *Hoenig v Isaacs* [1952] 2 All ER 176, CA; *H Dakin & Co Ltd v Lee* [1916] 1 KB 566, CA; *Bolton v Mahadeva* [1972] 2 All ER 1322, [1972] 1 WLR 1009, CA.

14   *Planché v Colburn* (1831) 5 C & P 58.

15   See p. 358, below.

16   *Moriarty v Regent's Garage Co Ltd* [1921] 1 KB 423 (reversed on other grounds: [1921] 2 KB 766, CA). See Matthews 'Salaries in the Apportionment Act 1870' (1982) 2 LS 302.

In addition to this theoretical problem, three points might be mentioned particularly about the employee's right at common law to be paid his wages. The first is that an action for wages due, brought in the ordinary courts, might be used not just as an individual's remedy but also as a way of testing the legal position in what is in essence a collective dispute between employer and workforce (possibly by the device of bringing an action by one named individual, which is viewed in reality as a test case affecting an entire class of employees). In *Burdett-Coutts v Hertfordshire County Council*[17] the county council purported to vary the terms of employment of school dinner ladies without their consent (indeed, in the face of their positive dissent); they continued to work under protest, accepting the lower wages under the new terms, but brought an action in the High Court claiming, inter alia, the payment of the arrears of wages that were due under the pre-existing terms of employment; the judge held that on the facts they had *not* impliedly accepted the employer's variation by continuing to work, and gave judgment for the arrears. The validity of such an action was accepted by the Court of Appeal in *Miller v Hamworthy Engineering Ltd*[18] (enforced short-time working, not covered by the terms of the contract and not agreed to by the employee or his union) and, more importantly, in the short but emphatic decision of the House of Lords in *Rigby v Ferodo Ltd*[19] (unilateral reduction in wages by the employer, not agreed to by the employee or his union). The point about such an action (or the threat of it) is that it may oblige the employer (who wishes still to force through the new terms) to dismiss the employees formally, and then have to defend an action for unfair dismissal[20].

However, this will only work if the employee is held to have been contractually in the right. This is because the second point is that in *Cresswell v Board of Inland Revenue*[1] Walton J held that where an employee refuses to perform duties that he is contractually obliged to perform, the simple principle 'no work, no pay' applies, so that an action for wages will then fail. Of course, such a principle begs the monumental question – what duties *is* the employee contractually obliged to perform? In fact, the case hinged on this question, and whether a requirement that the staff start to operate a newly computerised system had or had not altered the nature of the job[2]. The principle has acquired particular significance in a series of cases concerning deductions from wages due to industrial action – if the employee fails wholly or partly to carry out his duties, what can the employer do? An employee in breach of contract may be sued by the employer, but this is unlikely in practice; instead, the employer will wish to avoid paying some or all of the wages in the first place. If the employee fails to perform any of his duties (either through being on strike, or through only being willing to perform certain of his duties, which the employer refuses to allow, sending him home instead), then as in *Cresswell* the employer need not pay any wages. However, the position

---

17   [1984] IRLR 91. See also *Gibbons v Associated British Ports* [1985] IRLR 376.
18   [1986] ICR 846, [1986] IRLR 461, CA.
19   [1988] ICR 29, [1987] IRLR 516, HL.
20   As in *Gilham v Kent County Council (No 2)* [1985] ICR 233, [1985] IRLR 18, CA; see p. 496, below on the application of unfair dismissal laws to this class of case.
1   [1984] ICR 508, [1984] IRLR 190.
2   This aspect of the case is considered at p. 130, above and p. 497, below. One significance of applying such a general principle is that the employer has a freestanding right not to pay wages – it does not constitute a 'suspension' and so the employer does not have to comply with any contractual procedures that may exist before he can impose a suspension (so that *Gorse v Durham County Council* [1971] 2 All ER 666, [1971] 1 WLR 775 was distinguished in *Cresswell*).

becomes more complex when the employee is permitted by the employer to perform *part* of his duties.

Here, there are two possibilities. If the part not performed is discrete and quantifiable, it seems clear that the employer may refuse to pay the amount of wages representing that part. Thus, in *Royle v Trafford Borough Council*[3] where a teacher participating in industrial action refused to accept a further five pupils into his class but continued to teach his existing 31 pupils, the education authority were allowed to deduct $5/36$ths of his salary. Similar results were reached in *Sim v Rotherham Metropolitan Borough Council*[4] (amounts deducted from teachers' salaries representing their refusal to cover for absent colleagues as part of industrial action) and *Miles v Wakefield Metropolitan District Council*[5] (registrar normally working 37 hours per week refusing to perform marriage ceremonies in the three hours on a Saturday morning as part of industrial action; employer held correct to deduct $3/37$ths of his salary). However, there has been a significant divergence of view on the reasoning behind these deductions[6]; in *Sim* Scott J held that in such a case the employee could sue for his wages in full, but subject to the employer's right of equitable set-off of the amount representing the duties not performed (for which the employer could have sued the employee in separate proceedings). However, in *Miles* the House of Lords took the more fundamental approach that with regard to the three hours in question the employee had *no* right to the pay in the first place since he had failed to provide the consideration for his part of the contract, namely being ready and willing to work. In the case of a quantifiable failure to perform duties, these two approaches produce the same result, but the position becomes more difficult in the case of a more generalised and nebulous failure (e.g. as part of a general go-slow or withdrawal of goodwill). This could be particularly important if (a) the industrial action is 'guerilla' in nature[7], being aimed at inconveniencing the employer while at the same time allowing the employees still to earn most of their wages, (b) it involves employees who have some discretion in how they perform their work, and (c) they work in open premises from which the employer cannot simply lock them out. Under the above cases, the employer could counter the action by deducting a 'reasonable sum' (as in *Sim*) representing duties not carried out. However, two later Court of Appeal decisions (*Wiluszynski v London Borough of Tower Hamlets*[8] and *British Telecommunications plc v Ticehurst*[9]) have established that if the employer makes it *clear* that he will not accept the defective performance by the employees, he may lawfully refuse to pay anything *at all* (even if the employees have attended work and performed most of their duties). In *Wiluszynski* this was explained as following on from the reasoning in *Miles* (above), and the important decision in *Ticehurst* takes this further in two ways – (1) it links it in with an implied term that employees with a discretion how to perform their work will exercise that discretion so as to

3   [1984] IRLR 184.
4   [1986] ICR 897, [1986] IRLR 391.
5   [1987] ICR 368, [1987] IRLR 193, HL.
6   See the notes on *Sim* and *Miles* by McMullen (1988) 51 MLR 234 and Morris (1987) 16 ILJ 185.
7   This may now be more difficult to arrange lawfully because of the requirement of strike notice, introduced by the Trade Union Reform and Employment Rights Act 1993; see p. 671 below.
8   [1989] ICR 493, [1989] IRLR 259, CA; see also *MacPherson v London Borough of Lambeth* [1988] IRLR 470.
9   [1992] ICR 383, [1992] IRLR 219, CA.

advance the employer's business, not so as to frustrate it[10]; (2) it shows the efficacy of one particular employer tactic when faced with guerilla action, namely to give an ultimatum that the employees must work normally as from a certain date, otherwise the employer will refuse to pay at all as from that date. One final point on this area should be noted; if the employer permits imperfect performance by his employees in such a way as to suggest acquiescence in it, he may be held to have waived the employees' breach and so lost his right to deduct (whether partially or totally).[11]

The third point raises legal complications out of proportion to its commonplace nature. What is to happen if the employee is mistakenly overpaid? Can the employer recover the overpayment?[12] What if the employee has already spent the money? Can the employee simply keep quiet about it? Such problems could arise where payment is in cash, but may be more likely to arise now, with payment by direct debit more common. The starting point is that, in the ordinary law of restitution, payments made under a mistake of law are not generally recoverable, but those made under a mistake of fact are. Thus, the first point is to categorise the mistake. Simple inadvertent overpayment (whether by quill pen or computer) is likely to constitute a mistake of fact, thus giving the employer a prima facie right to recover. This was the case in *Avon County Council v Howlett*[13] where an employee off sick was inadvertently overpaid. The principal defence to the employer's action for repayment was estoppel by representation, in relation to the whole of the overpayment in spite of the admission by the employee that he had only spent *part* of the overpaid amount[14]. This defence succeeded. However, in the subsequent House of Lords decision in *Lipkin Gorman v Karpnale Ltd*[15] (not itself an overpayment of wages case), Lord Goff said that in future cases such as *Howlett* should be dealt with, not on grounds of estoppel, but on grounds of a general defence of 'change of position' in the law of restitution. He said that such a defence should now be evolved in case law and so is likely to be uncertain for some time. However, one relatively certain point is that such a defence would allow only that part of the overpayment actually spent innocently to become irrecoverable, rather than the defence of estoppel which would operate, potentially unfairly, on an all-or-nothing basis.

10　This aspect of the case is considered at p. 146, above; as pointed out there, most jobs today are likely to have some discretion in them, rather than being wholly governed by the contract; and so this case doubts the legality in most cases of any form of 'work-to-contract', 'work-to-rule' or 'withdrawal of goodwill'.

11　*Bond v CAV Ltd* [1983] IRLR 360 (employer's action in not insisting on the employee working on disputed machinery and allowing him to continue working on other machinery held to constitute waiver of the employee's breach).

12　On a technical level, a deduction to recover an overpayment is not an illegal deduction under the ERA 1996, Part II (p. 216, below) since it is covered by an exception in ibid., s. 14(1); however, that subsection does *not* give a positive right to recover and so the overall legality of recovery by the employer remains a common law matter, subject to the following rules.

13　[1983] 1 All ER 1073, [1983] IRLR 171, CA.

14　A peculiarity of the case, commented on adversely by Cumming-Bruce LJ, was that the evidence showed that the defendant had in fact spent *all* the overpayment before realising that he was not entitled to it. However, at the trial, counsel for the defence was instructed to proceed on the basis of only *part* expenditure, since the defendant's backers were using this as a test case, seeking to establish (for the purpose of others who had been overpaid) that even partial expenditure could defeat the employer's right to repayment.

15　[1991] 2 AC 548, [1992] 4 All ER 512, HL. Lord Goff is, of course, no stranger to the law of restitution. These important developments are fully considered in Burrows *The Law of Restitution* (1993) pp. 421–439.

All of this operates on the assumption that the employee has spent the money innocently. The one thing that he must not do is simply keep quiet about it if he does realise that he has been overpaid, because that can render him guilty of theft, by virtue of the Theft Act 1968, s. 5(4) which provides that:

'Where a person gets property by another's mistake, and is under an obligation to make restoration (in whole or in part) of the property or its proceeds or of the value thereof, then to the extent of that obligation the property or proceeds shall be regarded (as against him) as belonging to the person entitled to restoration, and an intention not to make restoration shall be regarded accordingly as an intention to deprive that person of the property or proceeds.'

The Court of Appeal held in *A-G's Reference (No. 1 of 1983)*[16] that this section (which does not actually create an offence, but rather supplies what might otherwise be the missing elements for a charge of theft under section 1) can apply to payment by direct debit of sorts as well as to payment in cash, and so provided the prosecution can prove dishonesty[17] the employee may be found guilty of theft through deliberately keeping the overpayment, though the Court of Appeal expressed some disquiet at the involvement of the criminal law in such cases which have the flavour predominantly of civil debt. However, there should only be criminal liability where the defendant deliberately kept it, or spent it *after* realising that he had been overpaid. If he had already spent it before so realising, then in civil law the employer would have lost his right to restitution according to the above cases and so section 5(4) ('... is under an obligation to make restoration ...') would not apply.

3   WAGES DURING SICKNESS AND STATUTORY SICK PAY

In most cases, questions of pay during sickness will be governed expressly by the contract of employment, some form of 'topping up' of state sickness benefits being now very common and usually clearly set out (e.g. as to how many weeks per year are payable, whether there is any waiting period before it is payable, whether there is a qualifying period for new employees, and at what rate it is payable, bearing in mind receipts from the state)[18]. However, there have been cases where the question of whether sick pay is payable has arisen where there has been no express agreement on the matter. The question then arises whether a term is to be implied covering sick pay and, as a matter of law, this has caused problems. Theoretically, the basis of the law here is the general common law tenet that the

---

16 [1985] QB 182, [1984] 3 All ER 369, CA, noted Hedley (1985) 14 ILJ 122 and Smith [1984] Crim LR 570. The Theft Act 1968, s. 5(4) made a definite change here, for under the pre-1968 law an employee keeping an overpayment was not guilty of theft: *Moynes v Coopper* [1956] 1 QB 439, [1956] 1 All ER 450.

17 Dishonesty is covered by *R v Ghosh* [1982] QB 1053, [1982] 2 All ER 689, CA, and is a question whether (a) the conduct in question is dishonest by the standards of ordinary people and (b) the defendant realised that it would be thought wrong by those standards. While this may often be obvious in one of these cases, there could be latitude for a defence of no dishonesty if, for example, the employee kept the overpayment because he was already owed money by the employer who was refusing to pay him it. A jury might be sympathetic.

18 See the statistics in the White Paper 'Income during initial sickness' (Cmnd. 7864, 1980) which introduced the idea of statutory sick pay.

employee's consideration for wages is 'service' (i.e. being ready and willing to serve), not the actual performance of work[19], and this could lead to the inference that, in the absence of anything to the contrary, wages should continue to be paid during sickness even though the employee is unable actually to perform his work. This view that there is a presumption that sick pay is payable was accepted by Pilcher J in *Orman v Saville Sportswear Ltd*[20] and was consistent with the judgment of the Court of Appeal in *Marrison v Bell*[1], as explained in later cases[2]. Such a presumption could be rebutted by factors such as payment on a piecework basis[3], a clear custom that nothing was offered or expected[4] or some form of notice by the employer that he would accept no, or restricted, liability to make any payments[5]. However, it was still arguable that it was putting matters too highly to say that there was a presumption, and fortunately the matter was clarified by the Court of Appeal in *Mears v Safecar Security Ltd*[6], an important case not only on sick pay but also on the jurisdiction of tribunals on complaints of failure to give any or proper particulars of the terms of employment[7] and on the whole question of the implication of terms into contracts of employment[8]. In this case it was clearly held that there is in law no presumption that sick pay is payable; if there is no express provision, a tribunal or court must look at all the facts of the case to determine the correct inference. Applying that approach, the Court of Appeal upheld the EAT's decision that nothing was payable on the facts of the case given that it was the employer's well-known practice not to pay, the applicant had been ill during the course of employment and had never asked for payment, and he had only brought his claim seven months after leaving employment, not really expecting to get anything. Stephenson LJ, giving the judgment of the court, did say that there might be a residual presumption that sick pay was payable in a case where there were no factors either way to guide the court on the correct term to be implied, but that this was inherently extremely unlikely to happen, since usually there will be some evidence at least of past custom and practice.

A clear contractual term covering sick pay entitlement is a good example of the benefits to be gained from a well drafted contract of employment[9], or proper

19   *Warburton v Co-operative Wholesale Society Ltd* [1917] 1 KB 663, CA; *Henthorn v CEGB* [1980] IRLR 361, CA; *Miles v Wakefield Metropolitan District Council* [1987] ICR 368, [1987] IRLR 193, HL; Elias 'The structure of the employment contract' [1982] CLP 95; cf. however, the different views expressed by Napier 'Aspects of the wage work bargain' [1984] CLJ 337.

20   [1960] 3 All ER 105, [1960] 1 WLR 1055.

1   [1939] 2 KB 187, [1939] 1 All ER 745, CA.

2   *Petrie v MacFisheries Ltd* [1940] 1 KB 258, [1939] 4 All ER 281, CA; *O'Grady v M Saper Ltd* [1940] 2 KB 469, [1940] 3 All ER 527, CA. The problem was that Scott LJ expressed his views on sick pay so strongly in *Marrison v Bell* that it was reported (in the law reports and the newspapers) as laying down a definite right to wages during sickness as a matter of law, leading to claims for it by people who could show little or no contractual backing for entitlement to it; this was rectified in the above two cases.

3   *Browning v Crumlin Valley Collieries Ltd* [1926] 1 KB 522; *Hancock v BSA Tools Ltd* [1939] 4 All ER 538.

4   *O'Grady v M Saper Ltd*, n. 2, above.

5   *Petrie v MacFisheries Ltd*, n. 2, above.

6   [1982] 2 All ER 865, [1982] IRLR 183, CA, applied by the EAT in *Howman & Son v Blyth* [1983] IRLR 139, where the implication of a term raised questions as to amount and duration of payment.

7   ERA 1996, Part I; see pp. 84-89, above. The case was brought before a tribunal under s. 11 to determine the correct contractual term; it was not a common law claim for actual payment.

8   See p. 107, above.

9   One complication in some recent cases has been the provision by the employer of permanent health insurance (PHI) on top of the normal sickness provisions in the contract, without really thinking through how the two are to fit together; see p. 128, above.

compliance with the obligation to give written notice of terms of employment. As stated above, such terms are common and, indeed, were for many years an important area for the improvement of terms and conditions by negotiation (e.g. by increasing payment rates and the entitlement per year, and decreasing or eliminating any qualifying periods), particularly in times of wage restraint (though with some evidence in the 1990s of retrenchment by employers and the worsening of sick pay terms in times of recession). Thus, except in the odd case unfortunately leaving sick pay as a matter to be implied (or not), it could have been said that there was little *law* on sick pay, merely a question of construction of individual contracts. However, that has not been the case since 1983 when there came into force the present scheme of statutory sick pay (SSP) under the Social Security and Housing Benefits Act 1982 (now Part XI of the Social Security Contributions and Benefits Act 1992)[10].

This scheme came into being pursuant to a White Paper[11] which showed that contractual sick pay terms are common and quantitatively more important than state national insurance benefits in the maintenance of income during short-term sickness[12], that such contractual schemes operated usually by taking into account amounts received from the state[13] and that most illness was in fact short-term[14]. From these findings, the government formed the view that the existing system was administratively inefficient – '... given that the great majority of claimants have available a second source of income from their employer, there is duplication of administrative machinery between employers and DSS in that evidence of incapacity has to be provided for both schemes and two sets of arrangements for the calculation and payment of income have to be maintained'[15].

The new scheme was therefore designed to prevent duplication in the large majority of claims – where an employee is sick, the employer must now by law pay an amount equivalent to what that employee would have received from the state. As originally enacted, SSP was payable for a maximum of *eight* weeks (either in one period of illness or cumulatively over several illnesses) in one tax year. However, the scheme was viewed as such a success by the government that the Social Security Act 1985 contained a major extension, so that the maximum entitlement is now *28* weeks (put on to a rolling basis, i.e. not tied now to the tax year); the overall

10 As amplified by the Statutory Sick Pay (General) Regulations 1982, S.I. 1982 No. 894, *Harvey* R [198].

11 Income during initial sickness (Cmnd. 7864, 1980). There was an attempt to bring a new scheme into operation in 1980–81 but it encountered much employer opposition at an early stage (leading to government concessions which, when viewed cumulatively, threatened to create a new system as complicated as that which it was intended to replace). This attempt was shelved and a year later the present scheme was enacted in the 1982 Act without any of the concessions previously made.

12 Contractual sick pay terms were relatively uncommon in 1948 at the inception of the National Insurance System, but by 1974 (the year used in the White Paper for statistical purposes) 80% of full-time male workers and 78% of full time female workers were covered by them; in the large majority of cases, employees qualified to claim sick pay either immediately upon becoming employed or at the most within six months.

13 In 1974, in the case of male workers for example, full pay without deduction was payable in only 11.5% of cases; full pay *less state benefits* was payable in 55% of cases; some other scheme operated in the remaining 33.5% of cases (e.g. topping state benefits up to 85% of full pay).

14 '... only a very small proportion of people who qualify for (state) benefit need to draw it for any length of time. No payment is made for the first three "waiting" days of incapacity; 60% of those who qualify for sickness benefit are back at work by the end of a fortnight, 80% within a month and 90% within six weeks. Yet the effort put in by DHSS in dealing with these short-term claims is considerable', White Paper, para. 3.

15 White Paper, para. 3.

effect of this is that now the employer is liable for the payment of all short-term sickness benefit due to one of his employees (with the principal function for the DSS now being the payment of long-term benefits such as incapacity benefit once the extended SSP entitlement has been exhausted in the case of a major illness or disability). Under the original scheme, the employer recouped the full amount of the money paid out as SSP, by deducting it from his National Insurance contributions. However, this position was gradually altered by the Statutory Sick Pay Acts 1991 and 1994, so that the current position is now that in most cases there is *no* recoupment, so that the employer actually *pays* the SSP; the only exception is that if in any income tax month the employer pays out SSP exceeding 13% of his liability to pay NI contributions in that month, he can recoup that excess[16]. This is a far cry from the original scheme under which the employer merely administered the payment of SSP.

Before looking at the details of the scheme, two important points must be noticed. First, the scheme does not in any way directly affect contractual sick pay terms which remain matters between the employer and the employee or his union. Thus, contractual sick pay is still to be paid on top of statutory sick pay if there is a contractual term to that effect; likewise, if an employer is not contractually obliged to pay sick pay, there is nothing in the new scheme to alter that – he will merely be obliged to discharge what was previously the function of the DSS to pay statutory sick pay. Second, the abolition of the separate claim for industrial injury benefit (for those injured at work or contracting a prescribed industrial disease)[17] should be seen in the light of this scheme for the administration of sick pay – employees are now eligible simply for sickness benefit when incapable of work whether or not they are injured in a work-related accident (or incapacitated by an industrial disease), and the SSP scheme will apply to any claim for such benefit by a person in employment.

Turning to the elements of the scheme, there is a legal obligation on all employers to pay statutory sick pay, with no contracting out by agreement with his employees[18]. There are three qualifying conditions for payment – (i) the day in respect of which payment is sought must form part of a 'period of incapacity for work', i.e. a period of four or more consecutive days (thus preserving the former rule that the claimant had to wait for three days before state sickness benefit was payable); any two periods of incapacity for work which are separated by not more than eight weeks are treated as one single period[19]; (ii) the day must fall within a 'period of entitlement', i.e. a period starting with the illness and ending with (a) the end of the illness, (b) the expiry of the maximum entitlement (formerly eight weeks, now 28 weeks), (c) the termination of the contract of employment, or (d) the 11th week before the expected date of confinement in the case of a pregnant employee[20]; (iii) the day must be a 'qualifying day', i.e. a day when the

---

16 Statutory Sick Pay Percentage Threshold Order 1995 S.I. 1995 No. 512. This may be a contributory reason for employers increasingly looking to make savings in their occupational sick pay schemes, which were established on the basis of the state also paying its share. There has also been said to be a danger that the removal of the recoupment may make employers more wary of taking on disabled employees, or those with a poor health record, though c.f. now the Disability Discrimination Act 1995.

17 See p, 708, below.

18 Social Security Contributions and Benefits Act 1992, s. 151. Statutory sick pay may not be paid in kind, or by provision of board, lodging, services or other facilities: Statutory Sick Pay (General) Regulations 1982, S.I. 1982 No. 894, reg. 8.

19 Ibid., s. 152. All days of the week are counted for this purpose.

20 Ibid., s. 153. An employer may not evade paying statutory sick pay by dismissing the employee in order to end the period of entitlement prematurely: S.I. 1982 No. 894, reg. 4.

employee would normally be required to work[1]. There are four main disqualifications[2] – (i) where the contract of employment is for a specific period of three months or less, (ii) where the employee has not yet started work, (iii) where the 28-week maximum entitlement is exhausted, and (iv) where at the time when the employee falls sick there is a trade dispute at his place of work; this last disqualification is the same as the well-known trade dispute disqualification from jobseeker's allowance, for it is provided that the employee can avoid it if he can prove that at no time on or before the date his sickness began did he participate in, or have a direct interest in, that trade dispute[3]. The amount of statutory sick pay which is payable after the first three days is fixed by the Act, subject to a power for the Secretary of State to increase the amount by statutory instrument[4].

The method by which a sick employee must notify that sickness to his employer is basically a matter for agreement, with residual provisions laid down by regulation[5]. In fact, it was in this sphere of the procedure for making a claim that developments had already obliged employers to consider making changes even before the introduction of the statutory sick pay scheme in 1983; this was because of the emphasis being placed on 'self certification'[6], i.e. allowing the employee to certify himself as incapable of work through illness without the need for a medical certificate, at least until the beginning of the second week of a period of sickness (thus avoiding the need for a doctor to certify short-term illness which is often of such a nature, e.g. the classic cold or 'flu, that such certification was of little practical value). One possible problem with self certification is how to prevent

---

1 Ibid., s. 154; see R (SSP) 1/85, para. 10 for a summary of the method of establishing qualifying days. This requirement is here to prevent a sick employee claiming payment in respect of a day on which he would not normally have worked anyway. Under s. 3(2), the definition of an employee's 'qualifying days' is primarily a matter for agreement between employer and employee, with detailed statutory rules in reg. 5 in default of such agreement.

2 Ibid., Sch. 11, para. 2. Also excluded are employees who are over retirement age, or pregnant (and past the eleventh week before the expected date of confinement).

3 Ibid., Sch. 11, para. 7; R (SSP) 1/86. The extensive case law in the jobseeker's allowance context (particularly on the concept of 'direct interest') will thus apply here too: see p. 547, below.

4 Ibid., s. 157. There used to be three rates of SSP (depending on normal earnings) but this was reduced to two in 1987 and then to one in 1994. At the time of writing it stands at £59.55 pw. To be eligible at all, the employee must earn over the lower limit for the payment of N.I. contributions; *quaere* whether this could be challenged under EC law as unlawful sex discrimination, contrary to the Equal Treatment Directive, as affecting more female employees than male. There used to be a requirement for the Secretary of State to review the SSP rates each year (though it stopped short of actual index-linking), but this was repealed by the Social Security Act 1986 and the upper (now the only) rate was pegged for several years.

5 S.I. 1982 No. 894, reg. 7.

6 The old system was that in order to claim state sickness benefits (after the three waiting days) the employee needed a medical certificate, which could then be used in a claim for contractual sick pay from his employer. In 1982 the DHSS went over to self-certification for the first week of illness for the purposes of claiming sickness benefit (S.I. 1982 No. 699). Theoretically this did not affect employers and contractual sick pay schemes (and it tended to be presented by the DHSS as merely a change in internal administrative procedure), but such was the inter-relationship between state and private schemes (as pointed out by the White Paper) that this immediately put pressure on employers to follow suit (especially as doctors are no longer obliged to give medical certificates until the second week of illness). Thus, self certification was a separate development from the introduction of statutory sick pay in 1983, but naturally in practice the two went hand in hand and constituted (along with the fusion of injury and sickness benefits) a major alteration to previous procedures.

abuse; it may well be that in most cases this will not be a significant problem[7], but in a case of persistent illnesses by one employee for periods of less than a week it may be necessary for the employer to investigate and ultimately even to treat it as a disciplinary matter[8], with deliberate fraud presumably a potentially fair ground for dismissal.

The last point to note about the SSP system is that, as stated above, it was viewed by the previous government (if not by employers who have to administer it) as a considerable success; this meant not only its major expansion by the Social Security Act 1985 but also the further possibility that it could be used as a model for other forms of income maintenance. The Social Security Bill 1986 as originally drafted was not only going to convert Family Income Supplement into Family Credit, but also make Family Credit payable through the employer in the same way as SSP. This second proposal was dropped because of employer opposition, *but* the Social Security Act 1986 as eventually passed did of course introduce the system of payment of maternity pay through the employer – Statutory Maternity Pay (SMP)[9]. The present government have now taken the matter further in the Tax Credits Act 1999 and extended payment through the employer to what were family credit and disability working allowance, and are now working families' tax credit and disabled person's tax credit.

The whole question of income maintenance during sickness or injury has thus been the subject of important developments, which should hopefully be properly reflected in well drafted contracts of employment, though in the nature of things there will still be cases which arise partly or wholly because contractual terms do not adequately reflect current law or actual working practices. Finally, the general point should be noted that receipt of any form of sick pay normally pre-supposes that the person claiming it is still in employment and there is of course the possibility of the sick employee being dismissed. The statutory scheme provides that an employer cannot evade paying statutory sick pay by dismissing the claimant employee[10], but does not go further and declare such a dismissal to be in law unfair. However, there is no reason why such a dismissal should not be unfair on general principles, as considered in chapter 8.

---

7   In fact, the experience of many employers has been that self certification actually *decreased* short term illness absences, due to the employee having to declare in writing that he had been incapable of work on each of the days on which he was away (rather than just being signed off for the week by his doctor). One possible administrative remedy for persistent absence is that if an employee has self certified himself four times within a year, an employer may refuse to pay SSP on the fifth occasion and refer him to the DSS for formal investigation and medical checks: *Employers' Guide to Statutory Sick Pay* (NI 227, DSS) paras. 92–95.

8   This would be aided by the approach of the EAT to persistent absence through illness in *International Sports Co Ltd v Thomson* [1980] IRLR 340.

9   See p. 339, below.

10   S.I. 1982 No. 894, reg. 4 states that where the contract of employment is brought to an end by the employer solely or mainly for the purpose of avoiding liability for statutory sick pay, the employer remains liable to pay it for as long as it would have been payable but for the dismissal. It would appear, however, that reg. 4 would not apply if the employer could claim successfully that the contract had been *frustrated* by virtue of the illness, because then it would have been brought to an end by law automatically, not by any action of the employer; in the light of the recent case law, there is still a distinct possibility that a contract could be frustrated by a serious illness, see p. 359, below.

4 WAGES DURING LAY-OFF OR SHORT TIME

i) Generally

Turning to the question of wages during a lay-off or short time, this too is likely to be covered in some way by a relevant contract or collective agreement, which might define or limit the employer's right to lay off, or provide a guaranteed minimum wage or minimum number of hours per week[11]. In the absence of some express provisions or definite custom, however, the common law position is unclear. The starting point is that, unless it consisted of a dismissal by the employer followed by re-engagement later[12], a lay-off would be a suspension without pay, and there is no general common law power to do this[13]. This approach would favour the continuance of wages, and indeed in *Devonald v Rosser & Sons*[14] the Court of Appeal held that the employer had no right to close down his work and fail to provide remunerative work for his pieceworkers simply because of a lack of profitable orders. However, in *Browning v Crumlin Valley Collieries*[15] Greer J held that there was an implied term that the employer could lay off without pay where the reason for the suspension (in that case closure of the colliery for necessary repairs) was outside his control. Moreover, although the employer's argument in *Devonald v Rosser & Sons* that there was a custom allowing lay-offs in the circumstances in question failed, there may well be cases where such a custom could be shown, particularly in an industry where lay offs are common and accepted (whatever be the usual common law position) and in such a case the court might well find suspension without pay impliedly allowed[16], thus at least bringing the law into line with the practical position. In *Puttick v John Wright & Sons (Blackwall) Ltd*[17] the NIRC held that where the employee had been available to do specific jobs for the same employer over a long period of time, being paid for the work done and then laid off until the next work was ready, the correct legal construction was that there existed an ordinary contract of employment for the whole of that period, including an implied term allowing the employer to lay him off without pay in the periods between available work. It is therefore difficult to state any particular common law rule, but this is of little significance, since most aspects of lay-offs will normally be covered (in a unionised industry) by a collective agreement (which may, for example, give a guaranteed minimum week, subject to safeguards for the employer who may be relieved from this obligation in the case of industrial action or events totally beyond his control, thus approximating to what may be the

11   See, e.g. *Powell Duffryn Wagon Co Ltd v House* [1974] ICR 123.
12   In which case continuity of employment is preserved if it is a 'temporary cessation of work': Employment Rights Act 1996, s. 212(3).
13   *Hanley v Pease & Partners Ltd* [1915] 1 KB 698; *Gorse v Durham County Council* [1971] 2 All ER 666, [1971] 1 WLR 775; *Neads v CAV Ltd* [1983] IRLR 360.
14   [1906] 2 KB 728, CA. See generally Freedland *The Contract of Employment* (1976), pp. 86–101.
15   [1926] 1 KB 522.
16   *Bird v British Celanese Ltd* [1945] KB 336, CA; *Marshall v English Electric Co Ltd* [1945] 1 All ER 653, CA.
17   [1972] ICR 457. The question whether on the facts there is a series of individual contracts or one global contract in such a case may cause difficulties; this has arisen in the context of trawlermen and the question whether they have continuity of employment between voyages; in *Hellyer Bros Ltd v McLeod* [1987] ICR 526, [1987] IRLR 232, CA it was held that there was not sufficient mutuality of obligations to establish a global contract (and so there was no continuity for redundancy payment purposes). However, in the present context it will not help the employee if the court finds a global contract but then proceeds to imply into it a lay-off clause.

common law position anyway) or by a statutory provision in the modern legislation. Such provisions affect lay-offs in four main ways – (i) by preserving continuity of employment[18]; (ii) by allowing an employee subject to lay-offs or short time (in certain circumstances) to treat himself as dismissed and apply for a redundancy payment[19]; (iii) by allowing an employee on short time or lay-off to claim jobseeker's allowance, even though technically the contract of employment subsists[20]; and (iv) by providing certain minimal statutory rights to lay-off pay, either generally or in relation to certain particular forms of lay-off[1]. It is this last category that must now be considered here, i.e. the general right to a guarantee payment and the specific right to pay if laid off for certain health and safety reasons.

ii) Guarantee payments

Where an employer is obliged to lay off employees, or is unable to provide them with work at a particular time, the salaried and weekly paid employees may not be affected in the short term, but those paid by the hour or by output (and those whose contracts provide for suspension without pay) may lose wages. To meet this situation, an obligation to make guarantee payments was introduced in 1975, and is now to be found in the Employment Rights Act 1996, sections 28–35. These provisions are a good example of the 'floor of rights' argument for providing statutory minima, for the amounts which may be received are meagre, but the principle is established, presumably in part to encourage the establishment and extension of more generous private schemes (e.g. to give a guaranteed minimum number of hours per week to hourly paid workers). This approach can be seen in two particular aspects of the statutory scheme. The first is that any contractual payments referable to the workless day are set off against the statutory right (often to the point of extinguishing it), *not* additional to it[2]. The second is that the Minister may make exemption orders, exempting from these provisions employers who are parties to a collective agreement or wages order which covers the question of guaranteed remuneration to his satisfaction[3].

To qualify for a guarantee payment, the employee must have been continuously employed under a contract of employment for the month ending with the last complete week before the workless day in question[4]. This may disqualify casual workers, as in *Mailway (Southern) Ltd v Willsher*[5] where the EAT held that a woman who was registered as a part-time packer with the employers who offered her

---

18   See n. 12, above.
19   Employment Rights Act 1996 1996, ss. 148; see p. 542, below.
20   See p. 544, below.
1   On the various statutory and contractual possibilities in this difficult area, see Szyszczak *Partial Unemployment: The Regulation of Short-time Working in Britain* (1990).
2   Employment Rights Act 1996, s. 32.
3   Ibid., s. 35; as at 1996, there were 26 such orders (see *Harvey* Q [659]).
4   Ibid., s. 29(1). Section 29(2) removes the right to a guarantee payment from casual workers who are employed either under a fixed term contract of three months or less, or under a contract to perform a specific task which is expected to last for three months or less; this exclusion does not apply if the worker is actually employed for *more* than three months.
5   [1978] ICR 511, [1978] IRLR 322; aliter where the employer may *oblige* the employee to attend work when he requires him, rather than just offering him work: *Miller v Harry Thornton (Lollies) Ltd* [1978] IRLR 430, IT. In relation to the decision in *Mailway*, note that the employee now does not have to work a minimum of 16 hours pw in order to have continuity of employment.

work as and when they needed her, and who on average worked more than 16 hours per week (though she had not in fact done so in the four weeks in question), was not eligible for a guarantee payment as this relationship was only a contract to pay for services rendered, not a contract of employment. If an employee is thus qualified he is entitled to a guarantee payment under section 28 when he is not provided with work by his employer on a day on which he would normally be required to work; the failure to provide work must be due to either (a) a diminution in the requirements of the employer's business for work of that kind, or (b) any other occurrence affecting the normal working of the employer's business in relation to that work (e.g. a power failure or natural disaster affecting the factory; it will not extend to extraneous matters such as factory holidays[6]). The requirement that the workless day be one on which he would normally be required to work means that this right cannot be used as a backdoor method to gain remuneration for days not in fact envisaged in the contract; for example, where a contract is only to work four days a week (possibly varied from an original five-day contract as an alternative to redundancy) an employee cannot claim a guarantee payment for the fifth day[7], nor can he claim one for days during an agreed annual shutdown of a factory[8].

The employee will lose his right to payment in three cases. The first is where the failure to provide work is in consequence of a strike, lockout or other industrial action involving his employer or an associated employer[9]. The second is where the employee refuses the offer of suitable alternative work for that day, which may be work outside his contract, provided it is suited to his skill, aptitude, etc[10]. The third is where the employee fails to comply with a reasonable attendance requirement, so that the employer can in certain circumstances hold his work force together, at least for part of the day, for example if he is still hoping that vital supplies will be delivered in time[11].

As stated above, the amount of the statutory guarantee payment is small, for although the principle is that the employee is to receive the number of working hours on that day multiplied by the 'guaranteed hourly rate' (as defined), this is all subject to a maximum of £16.10 per day at the time of writing, and any individual may only claim for a total of five workless days in any period of three months[12]. Where an employer fails to pay all or part of a guarantee payment, an employee may complain to a tribunal within three months of the last workless day (longer if the tribunal finds that it was not reasonably practicable to complain within that period), and if the tribunal upholds the claim it may order the employer to make the necessary payment[13].

---

6   *North v Pavleigh Ltd* [1977] IRLR 461, IT.
7   *Clemens v Richards Ltd* [1977] IRLR 332, IT; *Daley v Strathclyde Regional Council* [1977] IRLR 414, IT.
8   *York v Colledge Hosiery Co Ltd* [1978] IRLR 53, IT.
9   Employment Rights Act 1996, s. 29(3).
10 Ibid., s. 29(4); *Purdy v Willowbrook International Ltd* [1977] IRLR 388, IT.
11 Ibid., s. 29(5); *Meadows v Faithful Overalls Ltd* [1977] IRLR 330, IT.
12 Ibid., s. 30. This includes any such workless days in respect of which contractual remuneration has already been paid – the employee cannot claim five *further* days of guarantee pay if five or more days have already been paid for under the contract within the three-month period: *Cartwright v G Clancey Ltd* [1983] ICR 552, [1983] IRLR 355.
13 Ibid., s. 34.

iii) Suspension from work on medical grounds

Where an employee is suspended from work because of the operation of one of several specified health and safety provisions (e.g. where the employer has to close down his factory or that part of it where the employee works), he is entitled to be paid a 'week's pay' (as defined in the Employment Rights Act 1996, Part XIV, Chapter II) for each week of suspension, up to a maximum of 26 weeks[14]. It is thus more generous than the more general provisions on guarantee payments, because of the specialised nature of the reason for the suspension; the relevant health and safety provisions have been considerably shortened and simplified, so that they now only cover parts of the Control of Lead at Work Regulations 1980, the Ionising Radiations Regulations 1985 and the Control of Substances Hazardous to Health Regulations 1988. Two general points should be noted. The first is that these sections do not give the employer a positive right to suspend when one of these provisions applies; to suspend lawfully the employer must have contractual authority to do so, and only in such a case do these sections apply to give the employee a limited right to further payments. If there is no contractual right to suspend, the employee may have an ordinary contract action for his wages in full anyway, and indeed it is specially provided that any contractual payments received during the relevant period go towards discharging the employer's obligations under the statute, and vice versa[15]. The second point is that these provisions apply to suspension through the effect of the relevant health and safety legislation on the employer's undertaking, not on the health of the employee himself. Thus, if the employee is in fact incapable of work through disease or injury during the relevant time he cannot claim payment under section 64 for that period of incapacity[16]. It seems that this exclusion would even apply where the employee was ill because of the same health risk that caused the shut down (e.g. if he was suffering from lead poisoning after the factory had been closed because of contraventions of the relevant lead regulations), which may seem inequitable and could cause problems if ever there was added to the list of specified provisions a health and safety requirement which operated by reference to the individual employee and not to the nature of the undertaking (e.g. a regulation that no one with a particular skin disease should bake bread), for then the employee would have to be suspended but, on the strict wording of the Act, would be ineligible for section 64 payments because of his incapacity for work.

As well as the illness exclusion, an employee will also be disqualified from payment if he refuses suitable alternative work or fails to comply with a reasonable attendance requirement, as in the case of guarantee payments. Complaint lies to a tribunal within three months of the last day of suspension (longer if the tribunal finds that it was not reasonably practicable to complain within that period) and the tribunal may order the employer to make the relevant payment[17].

A further form of statutory protection requiring the continuation of wages through suspension, this time where it occurs on maternity grounds, was added by the Trade Union Reform and Employment Rights Act 1993. As this is an

---

14 Employment Rights Act 1996, ss. 64–65; the specified provisions may be in either statutes, regulations, or Codes of Practice issued under the Health and Safety at Work etc. Act 1974, s. 16.
15 Ibid., s. 69(3).
16 Ibid., s. 65(3).
17 Ibid., s. 70.

integral part of the new rules on maternity enacted by that statute, it is dealt with along with those rules in chapter 6.

5 CALCULATION OF NORMAL WORKING HOURS AND A WEEK'S PAY

The concepts of 'normal working hours' and 'a week's pay' are important in several contexts throughout modern industrial legislation. The principal significance of 'normal working hours' used to be in deciding whether an employee worked more than the magic 16 hours per week and so could claim statutory rights, but that hours limit has now been abandoned[18]. However, it is still necessary to know whether an employment has 'normal working hours' for the purpose of ascertaining what the 'week's pay' is and, in turn, it is necessary to know what the 'week's pay' is for the purpose of computing, inter alia, the amount of a redundancy payment, guarantee payment or basic award for unfair dismissal. Rather than being defined individually for the purpose of each statutory right where they are relevant, these two concepts are each covered for all statutory purposes in one place, namely sections 220–229 and 234 of the Employment Rights Act 1996. However, it must be added that these have always been difficult provisions and have required a considerable amount of statutory interpretation.

i) Normal working hours[19]

In many cases it will be obvious what an employee's normal working hours are, in the sense of the number of hours which the employee is *obliged* to work by his contract; there is no overall statutory definition of this, and it is essentially a matter of interpreting the contract. Thus, where the contract expressly states the number of hours this will usually be conclusive of the matter[20], and the employee should ensure that the contractual term correctly reflects the practical position, for he will be held to that term (e.g. for the purpose of calculation of a redundancy payment) even if in practice he works longer hours and regards himself as bound to work those longer hours, *unless* the facts in his case are such as to support an argument that the term of the contract relating to hours has actually been varied by the parties to include the longer hours[1]. This possibility apart, however, it will normally be to no avail that the employee in fact works longer hours than those stipulated in the contract. In *ITT Components (Europe) Group v Kolah*[2] a clerk was employed under a contract specifying 20 hours per week (at a time when the necessary minimum for qualification for an unfair dismissal claim was 21 hours per week), but she regularly worked a further three hours each week; the EAT, reversing the tribunal decision in her favour, held that this was not in itself a contract for 21 hours or more per week because of the express term for 20 hours, but remitted the case to the tribunal to discover what the correct interpretation of the contract should be, since the clerk had in fact been promoted to a supervisor

---

18 See p. 149, above.
19 See *Harvey* C2B.
20 *Gascol Conversions Ltd v Mercer* [1974] ICR 420, [1974] IRLR 155, CA; *Fewell v B & B Plastics Ltd* [1974] IRLR 154; *Lake v Essex County Council* [1979] ICR 577, [1979] IRLR 241, CA.
1   For a case in which it was held that there had been such a variation, see *Armstrong Whitworth Rolls Ltd v Mustard* [1971] 1 All ER 598, 9 KIR 279.
2   [1977] ICR 740, [1977] IRLR 53.

10 months before she was dismissed, and there was at least the possibility that the relevant contractual term might have been varied on the promotion (that being a question of fact for the tribunal to consider).

If there is no express term covering the normal working hours (in spite of the statutory obligation to give written particulars of this, under the Employment Rights Act 1996, section 1(4)), the tribunal must consider the facts and what happens in practice to decide what is the correct term to infer. This may be a difficult exercise where the employee has in fact been working fluctuating hours. In *Dean v Eastbourne Fishermen's and Boatmen's Protection Society Ltd*[3] a barman worked certain set sessions and at other times when requested to do so by his employer; this produced fluctuating hours, and as the set sessions amounted to less than the 21 hours per week at that time required for qualification for redundancy rights the tribunal rejected his claim for a redundancy payment when he was dismissed. However, the EAT allowed his appeal, holding that as the contract was silent on the matter, the tribunal had to infer the relevant term and in a case such as this, where that term was essentially to work the hours required of him, that meant looking at what happened in practice during a period before the dismissal. The appropriate period appears to be the period required to qualify for the particular right being claimed (e.g. two years for redundancy, one year for unfair dismissal or the major maternity right)[4]; in *Dean's* case the EAT held that as in the qualifying period of the last 104 weeks the employee had worked for more than 21 hours in 86 of those weeks the proper interpretation was that his normal working hours exceeded 21 per week and so he was eligible for a redundancy payment.

Whether 'normal working hours' are expressed in the contract or left to be inferred when the need arises, one overall consideration is that in general they will *not* include overtime. This proposition may help to simplify the question, for even if a contract of employment is not specific on the normal working hours (or, to put it another way, the minimum number of obligatory hours), it might well state that overtime is payable after a certain number of hours per week have been worked and where this is the case the Employment Rights Act 1996, section 234, provides that normal working hours shall be that number of hours to be worked before overtime becomes payable. Thus, in *Fox v C Wright (Farmers) Ltd*[5] an agricultural worker was employed under a contract which did not specify a minimum number of hours to be worked, and he often worked 50 or 60 hours per week as the job demanded; the contract did, however, provide that overtime was payable for hours worked in excess of 40 per week, and when he claimed a redundancy payment the EAT held that he was caught by this provision, and his normal working hours were therefore 40 (for the purposes of calculating the redundancy payment). Section 234 does, however, create an exception to this in a case where the contract sets a fixed number of obligatory hours which includes a number of hours in fact payable at overtime rates (e.g. an obligatory week of 40 hours, but with overtime rates payable from 35 hours). In such a case, the normal working hours will remain the obligatory figure even though that includes some overtime. The predecessor of this provision was considered by the Court of Appeal in *Tarmac Roadstone Holdings Ltd v Peacock*[6] where Lord Denning MR said that for

3   [1977] ICR 556, [1977] IRLR 143. See, to like effect, *Green v Roberts* [1992] IRLR 499.
4   *Larkin v Cambos Enterprises (Stretford) Ltd* [1978] ICR 1247.
5   [1978] ICR 98.
6   [1973] 2 All ER 485, [1973] ICR 273, CA, followed in *Lotus Cars Ltd v Sutcliffe* [1982] IRLR 381, CA.

overtime to be included under this exception it must be fully obligatory under the contract, in the sense that the employee must work it *and* the employer must provide it; it is not sufficient if the overtime is voluntary on both sides or if the employer is obliged to work it when requested but the employer is not obliged to provide it in any particular week. Thus this exception is restrictively construed (in line, it is submitted, with the clear wording of the provision), and so overtime will only be included in the normal working hours if it is clearly obligatory on both sides under the contract.

ii) A week's pay[7]

The rules governing the calculation of a weeks' pay for statutory purposes are laid down in Part XIV Chapter II of the Employment Rights Act 1996 (ss. 220 to 229). There are four different methods of calculation, depending upon the category into which the employee concerned falls; the first three cover cases where there are normal working hours (as defined above) but differing or specialised forms of payment for the work done during those hours, and the fourth covers the case where there are no discernible normal working hours. These are now considered in turn.

1) Where there are normal working hours and the remuneration does not vary with the amount of actual work done. This is the simplest case where, essentially, the employee is paid on a time basis, i.e. for the hours during which he is at work, and here the 'week's pay' is the amount payable under the contract of employment when the employee works throughout the normal hours of the week, the relevant contractual provision being that in force on the calculation date[8]. This may be simply the basic rate for a time worker, but not necessarily since it could include any further payments if they are paid on a regular basis, e.g. a night shift rate or a regular bonus[9].

2) Where there are normal working hours, but the remuneration varies with the amount of actual work done. This obviously covers pieceworkers, but also extends to persons basically on a time rate but eligible for variable bonuses or commission[10]. Here the 'week's pay' is the remuneration for the normal working hours payable at the *average hourly rate*, which is calculated by working out the total numbers of hours actually worked in a period of 12 calendar weeks preceding the calculation date, then the total amount of remuneration actually paid for those hours over that period (excluding any overtime premia paid), and then working out the average payment per hour[11].

3) Where there are normal working hours but they are to be worked at varying times and in varying amounts in different weeks. This category primarily covers employees working rotating shifts, where the pattern of work is set, but alternates from week to week, so that here it is necessary to average *both* the rate of remuneration *and* the number of hours worked in a week, once

---

7   See *Harvey* C2B(2).
8   Employment Rights Act 1996, s. 221(2); calculation dates vary with the particular statutory rights involved, and are laid down individually in ss. 225 and 226. This could cause injustice if, for example, the contractual term had been varied downwards by the calculation date (e.g. because of the firm's economic difficulties).
9   *A & B Marcusfield Ltd v Melhuish* [1977] IRLR 484. See the inclusion of a site bonus in *Donelan v Kerrby Constructions Ltd* [1983] ICR 237, [1983] IRLR 191.
10 Ibid., s. 221(4); *Jones v Shellabear Price Ltd* (1967) 2 ITR 36.
11 Ibid., s. 221(3).

again over a period of 12 calendar weeks preceding the calculation date. The 'week's pay' here is therefore the average weekly number of normal working hours payable at the average hourly rate[12].

4) Where there are no normal working hours. In this residual category, which would cover for example the case of a university lecturer, the tribunal must determine the 'week's pay' simply by calculating the amount of the average weekly remuneration received by the employee over the period of 12 calendar weeks preceding the calculation date[13]. This form of calculation could well be the most favourable for the employee since it looks at overall remuneration, and is not tied to concepts such as basic hours, so that, for example, in *Fox v C Wright (Farmers) Ltd*[14] the agricultural worker who regularly worked 50 to 60 hours per week was trying to argue that he had no normal hours in order to put the question of averaging at large, but the EAT held that as his contract provided for overtime rates to be paid after 40 hours' work per week, he was caught by section 234 (considered above) and so he was deemed to have normal working hours of 40 per week.

Those being the four categories of employee covered by the provisions, three general qualifications should be noticed:

a) The 12-week period referred to must consist of weeks during which the employee actually worked in order to earn some pay, and it is that earned pay which is used for the purpose of calculation even if in any given week he worked (and therefore earned) considerably less than usual for some reason; this leads to a possible gap in the legal coverage in the case where work is consistently run down in the 12 weeks (or more) immediately prior to dismissal – as long as the employee actually earned *something*, those weeks will be used for calculation purposes even if they are in fact untypical and decrease what would otherwise have been his statutory entitlement. This requirement of looking at the pay actually earned in any given calculation week excludes matters such as payment during rest days[15] and the payment of fall-back or guaranteed pay for periods when not actually working[16]. If, however, the period of 12 calendar weeks includes a week when *no* work is done to earn remuneration, the tribunal must ignore that week and take an earlier week instead to bring the number up to 12 again[17]. If the employee has not been employed long enough for calculation over 12 weeks, the tribunal must apply the above provisions as nearly as it can, looking at certain other factors, such as the remuneration of other persons in comparable employment, though if the employee has just joined the employer in question from another employer and his employment with both is deemed to be continuous, a period of employment with the previous employer can be taken into consideration if necessary[18].

b) The emphasis remains against the inclusion of overtime rates. As seen above, overtime other than fully obligatory and guaranteed overtime is not counted towards 'normal working hours' in the first place. However, for the purpose of calculating the 'average hourly rate' under categories (2) and (3) above the tribunal must look at the hours *actually worked* during the 12-week period,

12   Ibid., s. 222.
13   Ibid., s. 224.
14   Discussed above; see n. 6.
15   *Mole Mining Ltd v Jenkins* [1972] ICR 282.
16   *Adams v John Wright & Sons (Blackwall) Ltd* [1972] ICR 463.
17   Employment Rights Act 1996, s. 223(2). *Secretary of State for Employment v Crane* [1988] IRLR 238.
18   Ibid., ss. 228 and 229; on continuity of employment, see pp. 147-170, above.

and this may include some hours worked at overtime rates; where this is so, however section 223(3) provides that the amount of overtime premia earned is to be ignored when calculating the total remuneration for that period for the purpose of calculating the average; the employee therefore cannot take advantage of the overtime premia to increase the average, but this only applies to actual overtime, and does not disallow the inclusion of amounts under incentive or bonus schemes which may be built into the wage structure, for these are not to be treated as analogous to overtime[19].

c) The word used throughout the scheme is 'remuneration', but its definition has been left to the case law. It obviously includes wages and salaries, and has been held to include commission[20]; moreover, the tribunal must look at the realities of an employee's pay, which may be significant in the case of certain more complicated payment systems:

> 'It is not possible for an employer, as a matter of law, to represent that a worker who is paid £1 as remuneration for doing an hour's work is really paid 50p for an hour's work because the parties choose to specify that the rate shall be 50p an hour but one hour's work shall count as two hours' work in calculating pay[1].'

Contractually binding bonuses will be included, in whatever guise they are presented[2], and it is specifically provided that if such a bonus is only payable at a time outside the calculation period (e.g. once per year), it may be apportioned for calculation purposes in such manner as may be just, and taken into account accordingly[3]. In addition to such matters, an employee may in fact receive further indirect benefits which may cause more difficulty. He may, for example, receive an amount labelled 'expenses' which may be simply genuine reimbursement for money of his own actually expended, or may instead be a none-too-subtle form of giving increased remuneration. If the former, it is not to be included, but if the latter it may be brought into account according to the leading case of *S and U Stores Ltd v Wilkes*[4]; such an arrangement may sometimes raise a suspicion of tax evasion, but the general approach has been to ignore this, as being basically a matter for the Inland Revenue, not the industrial tribunals[5]. The case of *S and U Stores Ltd v Wilkes* also establishes that two other indirect benefits are *not* to be taken into account when quantifying remuneration; these are payments in kind, such as free accommodation or a firm's car, and payments from a person other than the employer. The latter means that a waiter cannot include cash tips in his remuneration for the purpose of calculating his 'week's pay', since these are discretionary payments by a third party[6]; this has however been held not to

---

19   *Ogden v Ardphalt Asphalt Ltd* [1977] ICR 604; the possible intricacies of bonus and overtime schemes in this context are well illustrated by *British Coal Corpn v Cheesbrough* [1990] ICR 317, [1990] IRLR 148, HL.

20   *Weevsmay Ltd v Kings* [1977] ICR 244.

1   *Mole Mining Ltd v Jenkins* [1972] ICR 282 at 284 per Sir John Brightman.

2   *Amalgamated Asphalte Companies Ltd v Dockrill* (1972) 7 ITR 198.

3   Employment Rights Act 1996, s. 229(2); *J & S Bickley Ltd v Washer* [1977] ICR 425.

4   [1974] 3 All ER 401, [1974] ICR 645.

5   *S and U Stores Ltd v Lee* [1969] 2 All ER 417, [1969] 1 WLR 626; cf. *Jennings v Westwood Engineering Ltd* [1975] IRLR 245, IT.

6   *Hall v Honeybay Caterers Ltd* (1967) 2 ITR 538; *Palmanor Ltd v Cedron* [1978] ICR 1008, [1978] IRLR 303. Note that tips not paid through the payroll also do not count as renumeration for the purposes of the national minimum wage.

apply to a fixed service charge shared out between the employees (through a tronc system or otherwise), since that is obligatory payment in fact payable by the employer[7]. Likewise, gratuities on credit cards or cheques paid out to waiters (under Inland Revenue pressure) directly through the employer as 'additional pay' may count as part of the week's pay[8].

6   STATUTORY REGULATION OF WAGES AND HOURS

i)   General

For many years the state, in pursuance of its economic policies, has sought to play a role in wage regulation though normally this has been done indirectly through extra-legal devices such as White Papers, social compacts/contracts or exhortation. Statutory regulation (outside wartime) has been rare. There have however, been incidents of legislative intervention to try to protect employees receiving inadequately low pay, though these have been on a specific basis applying to particular industries, persons or activities, as opposed to the new legislation on the national minimum wage which puts in place a general 'floor' right.

An early device relating to low pay was the establishment in 1909 of trades boards[9], later to become known as wages councils. These covered specific industries or trades where unionism was low, as were wages, and consisted of a statutory board (equal numbers of employers and workers, with independent members and chairman) charged with setting minimum wages and (later) other basic terms and conditions which were enforceable in the civil courts (and backed by criminal sanctions) through the administrative means of a wages inspectorate. Although the councils were supposed to be a temporary expedient (pending the growth of normal collective bargaining) they proved to be longlasting and their coverage spread[10], though of course they always remained the exception rather than the rule in industrial relations. With the election of a Conservative government in 1979 espousing laissez-faire free market economics, the wages council system fell into official disapproval, as being a statutory limitation on a free market in labour. Their powers were first curbed in the Wages Act 1986 (taking youth workers out of their jurisdiction and limiting them to setting basic rates) and they were finally abolished by the Trade Union Reform and Employment Rights Act 1993. The only survivor (and now the only example of a statutory minimum wage in a particular industry) was the Agricultural Wages Board which was set up under separate legislation[11]; although technically not a 'wages council' it operates in the same way and continues to set minimum wages, terms and

---

7   *Tsoukka v Potomac Restaurants Ltd* (1968) 3 ITR 259; *Keywest Club Ltd v Choudhury* [1988] IRLR 51.
8   *Nerva v RL & G Ltd* [1996] IRLR 461, CA (a case on the repealed Wages Councils legislation, but applying the same principle).
9   Trade Boards Act 1909; the first four boards covered the so-called 'sweated tracks' of trailoring, box-making, lace-making and chain-making.
10   The largest industries covered were retail, hotels and restaurants. In addition, there were certain rather more rarified examples, such as the ostrich feather and fancy hat council and the pin, hook and zip fasteners council. Shortly before their abolition, there were 24 councils covering 2.5 million workers.
11   Agricultural Wages Act 1948.

conditions for those employed in agriculture, horticulture and growing[12]. Revival of the wages council system generally has not figured in the plans of the present government.

A second form of low pay provision was the Fair Wages Resolution, a resolution of the House of Commons in 1891 (repeated in 1946) that employers receiving government contracts should be required to pay fair wages, i.e. the going rate for the job, in order to prevent undercutting by driving down wages[13]. Workers or their trade union could complain of breach of the Resolution to (initially) the Industrial Court (since 1976 the Central Arbitration Committee) which resolved the matter by arbitration, the result of which was legally binding on the employer. This was supplemented by other forms of unilateral arbitration on wages for either the resolution of disputes or for the maintenance of the going rate of pay. The former was particularly the case in wartime; that applying in the Second World War lasted until 1959, but on its abolition then the legislation[14] retained one form of it whereby a claim could be made to the Industrial Court that an employer was not observing the terms and conditions established in that industry. This eventually became embodied in Schedule 11 of the Employment Protection Act 1975, enforced by the Central Arbitration Committee. This 'Schedule 11 claim' procedure was widely used in the 1970s[15]; its primary aim was to attack pockets of low pay within an industry, though towards the end of that decade it was criticised as being used for other, less noble purposes because a Schedule 11 award was not subject to the then government's pay restraint policy. With the change of government in 1979 and the radical change in economic policy, these forms of statutory and quasi-statutory intervention quickly became viewed as anachronistic, for two reasons: (1) they pre-supposed the clear establishment by collective bargaining of comprehensive national terms and conditions across an industry, whereas that model was rapidly breaking down; and (2) in any event the Conservative economic orthodoxy of the time denied outright that there was any such thing as a 'fair' or 'going' rate for a job – the only rate for the job was increasingly to be that set by a deregulated market. Thus, Schedule 11 was repealed immediately, in the Employment Act 1980, and the Fair Wages Resolution was rescinded two years later[16]. Once again, restitution of specific provisions such as these has not been suggested by the present government, and indeed would be difficult if not impossible in the current flexible, devolved and localised labour market.

With regard to hours of work, these too have not been subject to wideranging statutory control in mainstream employment law. Of course, the movement to restrict maximum hours, especially in factories, was a major factor in nineteenth century social history and was eventually successful in a consistent series of factories statutes, aimed at improving what we would now call the health and safety of the workforce[17]. These provisions were, however, specific to certain places and/or

---

12 The previous government consulted on abolishing it, but to their surprise the farmer employers strongly favoured its retention. It is due for a further review during the currency of this edition, the result of which is uncertain because of the existence now of a national minimum wage.

13 Bercusson 'Fair Wages Resolution' (1978).

14 Terms and Conditions of Employment Act 1959.

15 ACAS Annual Reports show conciliation in 3,092 cases between 1976 and 1980, with 1,970 arbitration by the CAC.

16 The delay was due to the need for the government to denounce an International Labour Organisation Convention which underpinned the Resolution.

17 For an excellent description of this legislation, see Cornish and Clark 'Law and Society in England 1750–1950' (1989) chap 4.

industries and, although eventually extended to men, the initial thrust of them was to give extra protection to women and young persons. It was this that fed through into the modern factories legislation, and came increasingly under attack. In relation to women, the restrictions (e.g. on night working or overtime) were seen as unacceptably paternalistic and discriminatory (affecting questions of equal pay if women could not earn certain premium payments)[18] and they were repealed in the Sex Discrimination Act 1986. With regard to young persons, the restrictions were repealed as a deregulatory measure in the Employment Act 1989.

One unusual case where there are highly specific limitations on working hours is that of Sunday shop opening and betting. This was a highly contentious matter and, as part of the eventual political trade off, the legislation[19] creates a category of 'protected' workers who cannot be obliged to work on Sundays. Initially, this protection was only meant to be transitional, so that those already in employment when the change came in could not be forced to work on Sundays. However, due to pressure in Parliament, it was extended and so in fact enacts a legal regime covering Sunday working into the future too. It gives the right to opt out of Sunday working by giving three months' notice, and not to be prejudiced thereby; there is also provision for a protected shop or betting workers to opt back into Sunday working. Any provision in a contract which contravenes these rules is declared to be unenforceable.

Thus, in spite of a somewhat varied history, by 1997 and the change of government, statutory intervention in questions of wages and hours had been restricted to the setting of wages and conditions in agriculture and the specific rules on Sunday working in the retail and betting industries. That position has now been significantly altered by the National Minimum Wage Act 1998 (a New Labour election commitment) and the Working Time Regulations 1998 (an EC law requirement).

ii) The National Minimum Wage Act 1998

The advantages and disadvantages of a national minimum wage have been a controversial matter in this jurisdiction for some time; it is a device that is widely used in Europe and some states in the USA, and an early ILO Convention[20] encouraged such action by states. Its introduction was an election issue in 1997, and immediately on coming into office the present government established a Low Pay Commission, at first on an informal basis and then put on to a statutory footing by the legislation, to investigate and make recommendations. The government proceeded to pass the National Minimum Wage Act 1998 which operates in significant areas by giving regulation-making powers; when the Low

---

18   'Health and safety legislation: should we distinguish between men and women' (EOC, 1979).
19   The main controversy was over the Sunday Trading Act 1994, which gave rise to the provisions governing 'protected shop workers'. When Sunday betting was legalised by the Deregulation and Contracting Out Act 1994, similar provisions were inserted into the Betting, Gaming and Lotteries Act 1963. All of these protective provisions are now in the Employment Rights Act 1996, Pt. IV; the anti-victimisation or dismissal provisions are in ss. 45 and 101, see p. 496, below.
20   Convention No. 26 (1928) 'Minimum wage-fixing machinery'.

Pay Commission made its first report[1], its recommendations were incorporated into the National Minimum Wage Regulations 1999[2], which contain much of the detailed law – while obviously the most politically contentious question is the rate at which the minimum wage is set, the most difficult questions legally tend to be those of definition (what is pay? what can be disregarded? how to average? who is covered?) which are particularly acute in a piece of legislation intended to apply to employment across the board, in all its varieties.

The Act sets out a basic entitlement for any worker (working, or ordinarily working, in the United Kingdom under his contract) to be remunerated by his employer in any pay reference period at a rate not less than the national minimum wage fixed by regulations by the Secretary of State[3]. The ambit of this duty is deliberately broad through the use of the wide term 'workers' which covers employees and any other person under a contract (whether express or implied, written or not) whereby the individual undertakes to do or perform personally any work or services for another party to the contract whose status is not that of a client or customer of any profession or business undertaking carried on by the individual[4]. Any attempt to contract out of the protection of the legislation is void[5].

The rates set out for the national minimum wage in 1999 when the legislation came into force were:
1) £3.60 per hour generally[6];
2) £3.20 per hour for a worker of 22 or over who is in the first six months of employment with that employer[7];
3) £3.00 per hour for a worker aged 18 but under 22[8].

A worker under 18 does not qualify for the national minimum wage at all; nor does a worker under 26 employed under a contract of apprenticeship and in the

1   Cm. 3976, 1998. For the Commission's observations on other countries' legislation, see Cash 'Lessons from the international experience of statutory minimum wages' [1998] Labour Market Trends 463. Any further investigations are to be instigated by the Secretary of State; there is no obligation on the Commission to carry out periodic investigations, or to initiate them on its own initiative: National Minimum Wage Act 1998, s. 6. For the initial experience see the 2nd Report of the Law Pay Commission: Cm. 4571 (February 2000).
2   S.I. 1999 No. 584. For detailed guidance, see the DTI 'Guide to the National Minimum Wage' (1999). Simpson 'Implementing the national minimum wage' (1999) 28 ILJ 171.
3   National Minimum Wage Act 1998, s. 1. The pay reference period is a month or, in the case of a worker who is paid by reference to a period shorter than a month, that period: Reg. 10. This could cause problems with 'annualised hours' contracts.
4   S. 54; there are subsidiary provisions in ss. 34 and 35 to ensure (if necessary) that agency workers and home workers are covered. For the wide definition of 'worker' generally, see p. 24, above. Voluntary workers (e.g. for a charity or similar organisation) are specifically excluded: s. 44. At a late stage, under media pressure, au pairs and family workers were exempted: reg. 2(2)–(4).
5   S. 49. The Secretary of State has power to exclude or modify the right in relation to particular persons but, in response to concerns expressed about the width of this when the Bill war going through Parliament, it is specifically stated that this cannot be on the basis of specifying different areas, sectors of employment, sites of undertakings or occupations: ss. 3, 4. In the event, this power has been used in relation to workers of certain ages.
6   Reg. 11. Going up to £3.70 in 2000.
7   Reg. 13(2). The worker must not have been previously employed by that employer or an associated employer, and must be required to take part in accredited training on at least 26 days in the 6-month period.
8   Reg. 13(1). Going up to £3.20 in 2000.

first 12 months of his employment or who has not attained the age of 19[9]. A survey in Spring 1998 estimated that between 1.9m and 2.4m employees (i.e. between 8.4% and 10.4% of the workforce) earned below these projected levels of £3.60 (£3.00 for those aged 18–22), and that by commencement in April 1999 between 1.7m and 2.1m were likely to be affected[10]. This fits the Low Pay Commission's own estimate that about 2m employees should benefit, with a total recurring cost to industry of £2.4bn (0.6% of the national average wage bill); however, the government have been keen to argue that there should be significant offsetting savings to business in lower absenteeism and staff turnover costs, both of which tend to be higher in sectors of low pay[11].

In order to determine whether the legal minimum is being paid, it is of course necessary to work out the current hourly rate for the particular individual, which may be easier said than done where the contracting and/or pay arrangements are complex or flexible. The established formula is to take the total of renumeration for the reference period minus the total of reductions to be made, and divide it by the total hours worked in that period[12]. However, the question of 'total hours' is a potential stumbling block, and to try to cover this, the legislation divides work into four possible catgegories:

1) 'time work', i.e. work that is paid for by reference to the time worked (even if depending on the worker's output per hour)[13];

2) 'salaried hours work', i.e. where there are ascertainable basic hours in return for an annual salary, not varying with hours actually worked (except for any performance bonus)[14];

3) 'output work', i.e. work that is paid for wholly by reference to the number of pieces made or processed by the worker, or to some other measure of output (e.g. number or value of sales or transactions)[15];

4) 'unmeasured work', i.e. work not within the previous categories, in particular where there are no specified hours and the worker is required to work when needed or when work is available[16].

---

9   Reg. 12(1), (2). Being under a contract of apprenticeship includes being engaged in a Modern Apprenticeship. Workers participating in certain designated training or employment schemes also do not qualify: reg. 12(5).

10 Wilkinson 'Who are the low paid?' [1998] Labour Market Trends 617. Over half of those affected are women working part time; the percentage is highest in hotels and restaurants, with the highest actual numbers in wholesale and retail.

11 'The Low Pay Commission have confirmed the view taken by Government that sustainable economic growth and job creation cannot hinge on low pay alone. The rates introduced by these Regulations should encourage fairer competition by preventing undercutting based on unduly low wages and will reinforce companies which compete through quality, service and timeliness of delivery rather than just price and wage costs': Consultation Document URN: 98/885 (September 1998) Annex 5, para. 13. This argument primarily relates to competition with other *national* firms who are also subject to the minimum wage; international competition is another matter.

12 Reg. 14.

13 Reg. 3. In relation to time work, time spent while available for work and required to be available (e.g. on a stand-by arrangement at the employer's premises) is to count (Reg. 15(1)), which could be important where the employer has imposed a 'nil hours contract' in order to try to avoid payment in such circumstances. Time when the worker is absent from work does not count, and this is expressed to include rest breaks and industrial action: Reg. 15(5)–(7). Time spent on training counts: Reg. 19.

14 Reg. 4. This heading was added to the original draft Regulations, and gives rise to some of the most complex provisions in the Regulations.

15 Reg. 5.

16 Reg. 6.

Calculating the hours worked is simplest in the case of time work, where it is simply the number of hours actually worked in the relevant pay reference period. Likewise, there is a simple averaging process over the salary year in the case of salaried hours work *if* only the basic hours are worked. If, however, the salaried worker actually works more than this, a more complicated calculation is set out to take the extra hours into account[17]. More generalised problems are bound to arise with output work and unmeasured work because of the variability of the hours put in by the worker in discharging the duties. Prima facie, the measure here has to be the total number of hours *actually* worked in the reference period, but this could be administratively difficult where there are significant fluctuations, and so the Regulations permit the worker and employer to agree in writing what the worker's *normal* hours are likely to be, so determining what the 'ascertained hours' are to be for the pay reference period[18]. In the case of output work, this must be a 'fair estimate', bearing some relationship to the speed at which an average piece worker would work, and backed by records of actual hours kept by the worker. In the case of unmeasured work, it must be a 'realistic average' of the hours likely to be spent on the contractual duties. As will be seen below, this approach is similar to that in the Working Time Regulations, laying down default rules but placing major emphasis on fitting the requirements to individual jobs by agreement (though with the difference that in relation to working time the emphasis is largely on collective forms of agreement, whereas here it is on individual agreement). An employer may have much to gain in entering such agreements, especially where fluctuating or ungovernable work patterns may mean at times being technically in breach of the legislation, in the absence of agreed averages. One final point in ascertaining hours, possibly a problem with any of the four categories, is travelling time; this is dealt with specifically, the general rule being that work-related travelling (and necessary waiting times) are counted, but travelling from home to work is not[19].

The other variable which has to be calculated in order to determine whether the worker is being paid the legal minimum is of course the pay in the relevant reference period. The 'total of remuneration' is defined as all moneys paid by the employer to the worker in (or in respect of) that reference period, plus any permitted charge for living accommodation[20]. From this gross amount, there are then a series of reductions to be made[1], essentially in order to comply with the Low Pay Commission recommendation that (however the pay is calculated) it is components that comprise pay for standard working that are to count towards the national minimum wage, not premia or other additions for non-standard work.

17 Reg. 22; see the DTI Guide, paras. 155–172.
18 Regs. 24–29.
19 See the DTI Guide, para. 127.
20 Reg. 30. Benefits in kind are excluded (including exchangeable vouchers such as luncheon vouchers), as are (1) loans or advances of wages, (2) any pension or compensation for loss of office, (3) any tribunal award or settlement amount (other than for an amount contractually due), (4) any redundancy payment and (5) any amount under a suggestions scheme: Regs. 8 and 9.
1   These cover – (1) payment for work done in a previous reference period, (2) payment for time absent from work, (3) (crucially) overtime or shift premium, (4) special allowances (e.g. for dangerous work, antisocial hours or being on standby; however, performance or incentive payments *do* count), (5) tips or gratuities paid directly by customers and not through the payroll, (6) reimbursement of business expenses, (7) certain deductions which have been made by the employer (e.g. for purchase of tools, equipment or clothing), (8) certain payments by the worker to the employer (similar to the deductions in (7)) and (9) deductions for living accommodation in excess of £2.85 per day: Regs. 31–37.

The worker has a statutory right of access to the records which the employer must keep[2], In a case of non-compliance with the minimum, the individual worker is given a statutory entitlement under his contract to 'additional remuneration' representing the shortfall[3]. The legislation does not give any special procedure for recovery, and so this amount would have to be claimed in an ordinary breach of contract action (in the county court or, on termination, in a tribunal) or as an unlawful deduction for wages under Part II of the Employment Rights Act 1996; in any such proceedings there is a reversal of the burden of proof[4]. There is, however, in an interesting parallel with the old wages council system, an alternative form of enforcement which may be to an individual worker's advantage. The Secretary of State is given power to appoint minimum wage inspectors with wide powers to inspect records, require information and enter premises for these purposes[5]. If such an officer finds non-compliance with the minimum, he may serve an enforcement notice on the employer, requiring future compliance and the payment of arrears to the individual(s) concerned[6]. If the notice is not complied with, the inspector may bring proceedings for the arrears on behalf of the worker in a tribunal (under Part II of the 1996 Act) or by way of other civil proceedings[7] *and* may serve a penalty notice for a financial penalty equal to twice the hourly minimum rate (in respect of each underpaid worker) for each day of failure to comply[8]. Finally, the individual worker is given a right not to be subjected to any detriment by his employer because of any action taken by him or on his behalf under this legislation, because the employer has been prosecuted, or because he qualifies for the legal minimum[9]; in line with other areas of specialised protection in other contexts, a dismissal on these grounds is declared to be automatically unfair[10].

iii)   The Working Time Regulations 1998

The Working Time Regulations 1998[11], which came into force on 1 October 1998, enact the Working Time Directive (93/104/EC) and certain provisions of

---

2   S. 10; the worker may complain of failure to provide access to an employment tribunal (subject to the usual three month time limit) and if the complaint is upheld the tribunal must make a declaration to that effect and award compensation of 80 times the hourly amount of the minimum wage: s. 11. Details of the records to be kept are set out in Reg. 38, and because of employer pressure at draft stage they are much less onerous than as originally proposed.

3   S. 17.

4   S. 28. Refusal or wilful neglect to pay the national minimum wage is a criminal offence, punishable on summary conviction by a fine not exceeding level 5 on the standard scale: s. 31.

5   Ss. 13, 14.

6   S. 19. The employer may appeal against the notice to an employment tribunal, but only on certain enumerated grounds: ibid.

7   S. 20.

8   S. 21. Again, there is a right of appeal to a tribunal on enumerated grounds: s. 22.

9   S. 23. Complaint lies to an employment tribunal, subject to the same procedure as other classes of detriment (Employment Rights Act 1996, ss. 48 and 49): s. 24.

10   S. 25, adding the Employment Rights Act 1996, s. 104A. Adopting the usual 'package' approach, a subsequent redundancy on these grounds is also unfair, no qualifying period is required and the upper age limit does not apply. There is, however, no entitlement to higher levels of compensation.

11   S.I. 1998 No. 1833.

the Young Workers Directive (94/33/EC)[12], applying statutory limits or entitlements in four main areas – the 48 hours maximum working week, night working, rest breaks and paid annual holiday. The Working Time Directive had a complicated history, which has had important effects politically and in relation to the drafting of the eventual regulations[13]. The previous government took part in some of the negotiations on the Directive which eventually took on a much watered-down form, with major 'derogations' which a member state can adopt in order to lessen the effect of the main requirements. However, even in this form it turned out to be politically unacceptable to the previous government who refused to agree it, on the assumption that that meant that it could not be passed. However, the remaining member states proceeded to adopt it under Article 118 a (now Art. 137) of the Treaty of Rome, which permits the adoption of 'health and safety' directives by qualified majority voting. This meant that the UK government could neither block it nor use the then-existing opt-out; they instead brought proceedings in the ECJ to have the Directive annulled, arguing that working time was not a health and safety issue. This challenge was, however, eventually rejected by the ECJ[14] who took a broader approach to health and safety generally, pointing in particular to the phrasing of Article 118a itself which refers to 'improvements, especially in the *working environment*, as regards the health and safety of workers'; on this broader, 'welfare' approach, all elements of the Directive were upheld (except for one minor provision relating to Sunday normally being a rest day). The incoming New Labour government immediately made clear its intention to transpose the Directive willingly and, after a consultation exercise[15], produced the 1998 Regulations[16]. Although that willingness was in contrast to the attitude of their predecessors, the Regulations as drafted are in fact more notable for continuity of approach because they adopt in full all of the derogations negotiated by the previous government. The Regulations are in fact relatively short, largely adopting the 'copy out' technique of inplementation, so that (1) much of the wording comes from the Directive itself and (2) the Regulations are quite difficult to use because of the precision of drafting and the (logical but non-user-friendly) sequence of first setting out the obligations and only later the derogations that are adopted. To counteract this, and to give some practical guidance as to the *possible* interpretations and effects in the substantial number of grey areas, the government have issued DTI Regulatory Guidance[17] which aims

12   They do so in relation to young persons (i.e. between 15 and 18, and over school leaving age); in relation to children under that age, the Directive was transposed by the Children (Protection at Work) Regulations 1998, S.I. 1998 No. 276.
13   See Bercusson *European Labour Law* (1996), ch. 21.
14   *United Kingdom v EU Council:* C-84/94 [1997] ICR 443, [1997] IRLR 30, ECJ; see Fitzpatrick 'Straining the definition of health and safety?' (1997) 26 ILJ 115. The ECJ gave its decision on 12 November 1996 and the Directive came into force eleven days later; there was therefore a considerable period during which the UK was in breach. Not surprisingly, given our litigious nature and literal approach, the first case law on the subject concerned the legal position during this period of non-implementation. In *R v A-G for Northern Ireland, ex p Burns* [1999] IRLR 315 it was held that a private sector worker could bring a *Francovich* action against the government based on the non-implementation. In the public sector, the EAT at first held that a worker could rely directly on the Directive, but this was reversed by the Court of Appeal: *Gibson v East Riding of Yorkshire Council* [2000] IRLR 598.
15   DTI consultation document URN 98/645, April 1998.
16   The Regulations are set out at *Harvey* R[1072]. A useful source of discussion in the IDS Employment Law Supplement 'Working Time Regulations 1998' (October 1998); see also Barnard 'The Working Time Regulations 1998', (1999) 28 ILJ 61.
17   Available on www.dti.gov.uk/er. It was updated in 2000, but unfortunately in less detailed form.

to be easier to understand in its format; its use is recommended. It remains the case, however, that (as with the minimum wage provisions) this one set of Regulations is meant to apply to the whole diverse workforce, and so the areas of doubt and possible debate are widespread, and likely to remain so for some time. As in other areas of employment law, it may be necessary to adopt the approach that, on any given question of application, it may only be possible to advise or adopt a *possible* or *arguably tenable* interpretation or application, not *the* indisputably correct one.

a) Application

As with the minimum wage provisions, the Regulations use the wide definition of 'worker', as being an individual under a contract of employment *or* any other contract, whether express or implied, oral or written, whereby they undertake to do or perform personally any work or services for another party to the contract whose status is not that of a client or customer of any profession or business undertaking carried out by the individual[18]. The breadth of this approach is then immediately qualified by the first major exclusion (contained in the Directive) namely that three sectors of activity are excluded from the Regulations altogether – (a) air, rail, road, sea, inland waterway and lake transport[19], sea fishing and other work at sea, (b) the activities of doctors in training[20] and (c) activities of services such as the armed forces, police and civil protection services 'which inevitably conflict with the provisions of these Regulations'[1].

b) Agreements to vary or exclude

The various powers to vary or exclude the principal obligations (known in the Regulatory Guidance as 'flexibilities') are so important to these Regulations that it is necessary at the outset to set out the three forms of agreement specifically allowed by the drafting; in ascending order of potential protection for individual workers, these are.

individual agreement: in itself, this only applies in relation to opting out of the maximum 48 hours per week;

a 'relevant agreement': this is defined as a workforce agreement, any provision of a collective agreement which forms part of a contract between the worker and his employer, or any other agreement in writing which is legally enforceable as

---

18 Reg. 2(1); see p. 24, above. There are subsidiary provisions in Regs. 36 and 42 to ensure that agency workers and non-employed trainees are covered.

19 This is a major exception, especially as the Regulatory Guidance suggests that it applies not just to transport firms, but also to other firms which run their 'own account' transport operations (e.g. supermarkets). On the other hand, not all employees within a transport firm will be held to be covered as workers in that 'sector' (e.g. those loading or unloading vehicles).

20 The previous government were particularly concerned to have this exclusion written into the Directive; for the issues involved in lengthy trainee doctors' hours, see *Johnstone v Bloomsbury Health Authority* [1991] ICR 269, [1991] IRLR 118, CA, p. 111, above.

1   Reg. 18. There is a further exclusion in Reg. 19 of domestic service in a private household, which relates to maximum working hours, night work and pattern of work; this does not appear in the Directive but is justified as being part of the general exclusion of such activities from domestic health and safety law.

between the worker and his employer[2]. As this may include an individual agreement (provided in writing and legally binding, e.g. as part of a contract of employment), this format tends to be used for definitional issues (e.g. what may constitute working time), rather than outright exclusions;

a 'collective agreement or workforce agreement': this format, importing an obvious collective element of protection, is adopted for some of the major exclusions

Clearly, the most important development here is the introduction of the concept of the 'workforce agreement' which is meant to apply to workers who do not have any terms and conditions set by a collective bargain[3]. Such an agreement must be in writing, have a specified length of not more than five years, apply to either all the relevant members of the workforce or to all those in a particular group[4], and be signed by either the representatives of the workforce or group, or (if the employer employs 20 or fewer workers) either by such representatives or by the majority of the workers[5]. Where use is made of representatives, they must have been 'duly elected' and the Regulations provide the basic electoral rules that must be complied with[6]. There could be overlaps here with representatives elected for other consultative purposes, and this development could be seen as a further 'carrot' towards de facto works councils of sorts. There is, however, one possible trap because, although the point is not made expressly in the Regulations, the Regulatory guidance takes the view that, while dual (or more) use of the same representatives is possible, 'it would have to be made clear to those voting that the representatives were being elected for both purposes'. Thus, technically the use of *existing* consultative machinery for this further purpose might not be lawful (another similarity with the health and safety consultation requirements and difference from those applying to collective redundancies and TUPE). The answer in the longer term is to ensure that next time a consultative body is elected it is made express for what specific purposes the body is being constituted.

c)   Two principal exceptions

In addition to the excluded sectors, the Regulations adopt from the Directive's permissible derogations two broad exceptions which, while not applying across

2   Reg. 2(1).
3   To this extent, it follows the precedent of the Health and Safety (Consultation with Employees) Regulations 1998 which only allow consultation with directly elected worker representatives where there is *no* existing representation by a recognised union. This is achieved in these Regulations by defining the 'relevant members of the workforce' as 'all workers employed by a particular employer, *excluding* any worker whose terms and conditions of employment are provided for, *wholly or in part*, in a collective agreement': Sch. 1, para. 2 (emphasis added).
4   This is defined as a group undertaking a particular function, working at a particular workplace or belonging to a particular department or unit: ibid.
5   Sch. 1, para. 1(a)–(d); note that a worker disagreeing but in a minority is bound by the agreement. Before making an agreement available for signature, the employer must have provided all the affected workers with copies of the text and such guidance as they may reasonably require in order to understand it fully: para. 1(e).
6   The number of representatives is to be determined by the employer; candidates must be relevant members of the workforce or group; no eligible candidate must be unreasonably excluded from standing; all relevant members of the workforce or group must be entitled to vote, and able to vote for as many candidates as there are to be representatives; there must be secret voting (as far as is reasonably practicable) and the votes must be fairly and accurately counted: Sch. 1, para. 3.

the board, do apply to the majority of the rights and limitations. By virtue of Reg. 20 ('Unmeasured working time') the provisions on the 48-hour maximum week, the length of night working and daily/weekly rest and rest periods do not apply 'in relation to a worker where, on account of the specific characteristics of the activity in which he is engaged, the duration of his working time is not measured or predetermined or can be determined by the worker himself'. The interpretation of this extremely vague exception could prove to be crucial to the effectiveness or otherwise of the Regulations, since so many modern forms of flexible working have at least *some* element of unmeasured time, and discretion in working hours. How great that element needs to be proved to be highly controversial. A teacher, for example, will have set teaching hours, but may put in many hours over and above those in preparation and marking. On behalf of a broad construction, the original Regulatory Guidance[7] stressed that it is impossible to lay down comprehensively who is and is not covered. On the other hand, the examples given in the Regulation ('managing executives or other persons with autonomous decision-making powers', family workers and religious celebrants) are very narrow, and the Guidance suggested that only those with *complete* control over their hours would come within the exclusion[8]. This uncertainty caused problems, partly due to assumptions being made in certain sectors that this Regulation would apply (e.g. in law firms) which may or may not have been correct. In addition, employers nationally expressed their concerns over the uncertainty, with a result that (to the annoyance of the unions) the government amended the 1998 Regulations only a year later[9], to add a paragraph to Reg. 20 stating that where *part* of a worker's working time is measured or predetermined or cannot be determined by the worker himself, but the specific characteristics of the activity are such that, *without being required to do so* by the employer, he may also do work which is *not* measured or predetermined (or can be determined by the worker himself), then the provisions on the 48-hour week and night working only apply to the first part, i.e. the 'voluntary' part will not be subject to those provisions. What is to be the effect of this? One possibility is that it will simply legalise practices which were already assumed to be outside the Regulations (see the teacher and lawyer examples above). On the other hand, some employers may see it as extending the exception well down the management ladder from the managing executive. In an attempt to counter criticism of appearing to be saying different things to the TUC and the CBI about this amendment, the government said that the answers would be found in new guidance from the DTI, but when this appeared it was fairly anodyne and not of much help in the most marginal cases. Perhaps the key to the new paragraph is the meaning to be given to 'without being required to do so by the employer'. What if the pressure comes from the *amount* of work to be done, rather than any instructions? What if the unwritten *ethos* of the workplace is for long hours to be put in? What if promotion in practice depends on it, though without it being a formal requirement? One irony here is that if the directive and Regulations were supposed to help to counter our long-hours culture, this amendment may actually

---

7   Para. 2.2.2.
8   One interesting question is whether this is to be construed much more narrowly than the provisions in the minimum wage legislation on 'output workers' and 'non-hours workers'; homeworkers, for example might come under these 'pay' categories, but are a long way from managing executives.
9   Working Time Regulations 1999, S.I. 1999 No. 3372.

exempt just the sort of workers most in need of coverage. The guidance will only take us so far; the first court decisions are awaited with great interest.

The second principal exception is contained in Reg. 21 ('Other special cases') which again raises as many questions as it answers in relation to its likely breadth of interpretation. It states that the provisions on length of night working and daily/weekly rest and rest periods do not apply in relation to a worker:

'(a) where the worker's activities are such that his place of work and place of residence are distant from one another or his different places of work are distant from one another;

(b) where the worker is engaged in security and surveillance activities requiring a permanent presence in order to protect property and persons, as may be the case for security guards and caretakers or security firms;

(c) where the worker's activities involve the need for continuity of service or production, as may be the case in relation to—
(i) services relating to the reception, treatment or care provided by hospitals or similar establishments, residential institutions and prisons;
(ii) work at docks or airports;
(iii) press, radio, television, cinematographic production, postal and tele-communications services and civil protection services;
(iv) gas, water and electricity production, transmission and distribution, household refuse collection and incineration;
(v) industries in which work cannot be interrupted on technical grounds;
(vi) research and development activities;
(vii) agriculture;

(d) where there is a foreseeable surge of activity, as may be the case in relation to—
(i) agriculture;
(ii) tourism; and
(iii) postal services;

(e) where the worker's activities are affected by—
(i) an occurrence due to unusual and unforeseeable circumstances, beyond the control of the worker's employer;
(ii) exceptional events, the consequences of which could not have been avoided despite the exercise of all due care by the employer; or
(iii) an accident or the imminent risk of an accident.'

Once again, the original Regulatory Guidance was at pains to point out that it is the actual nature of the work that is to be considered and that the examples given are *only* examples. The bottom line was the statement (helpful?) that it is for the employer to take a view as to whether the conditions are satisfied for each individual worker's situation'[10]. The equal vagueness and potential significance of these categories mean that they are likely to be widely claimed and disputed.

---

10 Para. 2.2.3. The Guidance stated that head (e) relates essentially to emergency situations, and is not to be used on a routine basis.

d) Maximum weekly working time

A worker's working time, including overtime, is not to exceed an average of 48 hours for each seven days in any particular reference period[11]. The fact that this is an averaging process is fundamental, because it does not necessarily mean a maximum of 48 hours per week, and up to a point fluctuations can be accommodated. The question becomes over how long a period the averaging can be done, hence the importance of the 'reference period'. In the first instance this is stated to be 17 weeks[12], but where one of the 'Other special cases' in Reg. 21 (above) applies, this is increased to 26 weeks. Further, it can be raised by a collective or workforce agreement to a maximum of 52 weeks 'for objective or technical reasons or reasons concerning the organisation of work' (!), which could be highly advantageous to employers wanting variations in hours over certain prolonged seasons in the year[13]; protection for the worker lies in the collective nature of the necessary agreement

The 48-hour average maximum is then further subject to the most striking exception in the Regulations, namely that it does not apply *at all* to a worker who has agreed in writing with his employer that it should not apply in his case[14]; this individual agreement may be either for a specified period or indefinite, but a worker may terminate it by giving written notice (of a maximum of three months in the agreement or, in default of coverage in the agreement, of seven days). The *quid pro quo* for an exclusion agreement was originally an obligation on the employer to keep specified records of actual hours which were to be open to inspection by a Health and Safety Inspector; however, in another rapid volte-face, the Amendment Regulations in 1999 watered this down very considerably, so that now the only requirement is to keep a record of *who* has signed the opt-out[15]. One possible point of controversy not covered by the Regulations is what is to happen to the worker's wages if he or she does *not* opt out and their hours have to be reduced to meet the new 48-hour average? This will be primarily a matter of contract so that if, for example, the worker is paid at a fixed amount per hour the wage will have to go down pro rata to the new number of hours, whereas a worker paid a salary for work done (over however many hours it takes) would have a good argument for breach of contract if the employer reduced that salary (simply because of a new maximum on hours) without his or her consent. One possible complication could arise if most workers agreed to keep existing hours (and pay) but a particular individual refused to agree and insisted on the 48-hour

---

11 Reg. 4(1). Reg. 4(6), (7) set out the formula for calculating the average, and days of annual, sickness and maternity leave that are not to count. Note that where a worker works for more than one employer, the average applies to the aggregated hours; the Regulations are silent on what the employer(s) is or are to do in these circumstances, but the original Guidance para. 2.1.3 intimated that it is up to the employer to find out if a worker is working elsewhere and if necessary to adjust working arrangements accordingly; it did not say on *which* employer any primary responsibility to do so may rest. With regard to overall impact, in Summer 1998 29.8% of male full time employees and 11.6% of female full time employees worked more than 48 hours per week: [1998] Labour Market Trends 599.

12 Reg. 4(3); a relevant agreement can lay down *which* 17-week periods are to be used; failing that, the average must be met over '*any* period of 17 weeks in the course of his employment', which could be less advantageous for an employer with predictable variations in hours required.

13 Reg. 23(b).

14 Reg. 5(1).

15 Reg. 4(2), as amended.

maximum, suffering a pay cut in consequence – could he or she claim that this constituted a 'detriment' (for not entering an agreement) which is outlawed by the Regulations[16]? The original Guidance suggested that a purely pro rata wage reduction because of reduced working time should not be considered a 'detriment' but that any 'excessive' wage reduction might be[17].

e) Limits on night working

A night worker's normal hours of work in any reference period are not to exceed an average of eight hours in each 24 hours[18]. A 'night worker' is defined as a worker who normally works at least three hours of his daily working time during night time, or such proportion of his annual working time as may be specified in a collective agreement or workforce agreement[19]. As with maximum weekly hours, the averaging process is vital, and the reference period is 17 weeks; a relevant agreement can set out *which* succeeding 17-week periods are to be used, but in default it means *any* 17 weeks (i.e. a rolling period)[20]. There is, however, an exception to the averaging process where the night work involves 'special hazards or heavy physical or mental strain', in which case the limit is eight hours in *any* 24-hour period in which night work is done[1]. On the question of night work, much is left to be determined by agreement, and this goes beyond matters of definition because ultimately it is possible for the rules themselves to be modified or excluded completely by a collective agreement or workforce agreement[2], a particularly striking example of collective protection being thought sufficient.

Arguably, the night working provisions are most closely related to the health and safety provenance of the Regulations, and the Directive itself makes clear in its preamble the assumption on which this is based, one of the recitals being:

'Whereas research has shown that the human body is more sensitive at night to environmental disturbances and also to certain burdensome forms

16 Reg. 31, adding the Employment Rights Act 1996 s. 45A, see p. 496, below. This could raise complicated issues such as those arising in the context of detriment on union membership grounds in *Associated Newspapers Ltd v Wilson; Associated British Ports v Palmer* [1995] ICR 406, [1995] IRLR 258, HL; see p. 568, below. Would it be viewed as a 'detriment' by way of a pay cut, or just a natural inability to continue paying the higher wages of those agreeing to the longer hours?

17 Para. 1.4.

18 Reg. 6(1). Normal hours of work are to be calculated under the Employment Rights Act 1996, s. 234 where necessary: reg. 6(6); see p. 187, above. Other than that, overtime would not count.

19 Reg. 2(1). The original Guidance, para. 3.1.3 suggested that employers and workers may wish to clarify what constitutes 'normal' working in a collective or workforce agreement too. 'Night time' means a period set out in a relevant agreement, lasting at least seven hours and including the period between midnight and 5am; in default of agreement, it means 11pm to 6am: reg. 2(1). An employer could use this to push back the definition so that workers working late (e.g. up to 2am in a bar or night club) do *not* work the three hours in the period necessary to be a night worker.

20 Reg. 6(3). The formula for the average is set out in reg. 6(5).

1 Reg. 6(7); the actual circumstances in which this applies are left to be determined by a collective agreement or workforce agreement, or in a risk assessment required by the Management of Health and Safety at Work Regulations 1992. If neither of these avenues is used, there could be a health and safety breach by the employer, though the Regulations do not say so specifically.

2 Reg. 23(a). This is subject to the requirement of compensatory rest under reg. 24 (below), though on its wording (applying where 'a worker is ... required ... to work during a period which would otherwise be a rest period or rest break') it is more difficult to apply to night working than to the rules on rest breaks.

of work organisation and that long periods of night work can be detrimental to the health of workers and can endanger safety at the workplace'.

In the light of this, two further obligations are laid on employers of night workers, going beyond the regulation of hours. The first is that no adult worker is to be assigned to night work without at least an opportunity for a free health assessment (unless there is an existing such assessment still in operation), and each night worker must then have the opportunity of further assessments at regular intervals appropriate to his case[3]. A young worker must have the opportunity of such assessments (as to health *and capacity*) whenever assigned to work during the period from 10pm to 6am[4]. Secondly, the employer must transfer a night worker on to non-night work if a registered medical practitioner advises that he is suffering health problems related to night working and it is possible to transfer the worker to suitable work not at night[5]. Significantly, there are no permissible derogations to these duties.

f) Rest periods

An adult worker is entitled to the following rest periods:
(i)   a daily rest period of not less than eleven hours in each 24 hours work period[6];
(ii)   a weekly rest period of not less than 24 hours in each seven day work period[7];
(iii) a rest break of at least 20 minutes (subject to any longer time agreed in a collective agreement or workforce agreement) where daily working time is more than six hours[8].
In the case of young workers, these entitlements are increased to 12 hours daily rest, 48 hours weekly rest and a rest break of at least 30 minutes after four and a half hours work[9].

3   Reg. 7(1). This rather stark paragraph was considerably fleshed out by paras. 4.1.2 and 4.1.3 of the original Guidance which suggest that (i) while very few people will be unfit to work at night at all, there could be problems with diabetes, heart/circulatory disorders, stomach/intestinal disorders, sleep conditions, chest disorders and others requiring regular medication; (ii) the health assessment (undefined) could start with a screening questionnaire carried out by the employer, with professional opinion being involved in the interpreting of the questionnaire and any necessary follow-up action; (iii) while the Regulations are silent on how regularly to re-assess, a rule of thumb might be to administer the questionnaire annually.
4   Reg. 7(2); this does not apply where the work is 'of an exceptional nature' (undefined): reg. 7(4).
5   Reg. 7(6). If the health problems constituted a 'disability' within the Disability Discrimination Act 1995, this might be required in any event as a reasonable adjustment.
6   Reg. 10(1).
7   Reg. 11(1). The employer may vary this to two 24-hour rests or one 48-hour rest in a 14-day period: reg. 11(2). The relevant seven day period is to be laid down in a relevant agreement, or, in default of that, is to be a week beginning with Monday: reg. 11(6). The weekly rest period is not to include any daily rest period, 'except where this is justified by objective or technical reasons or reasons concerning the organisation of work': reg. 11(7).
8   Reg. 12(1)–(3). Whether such rest breaks are to be with pay is a matter of contract, as the Regulations are silent on the matter.
9   Regs. 10(2), 11(3), 12(4); the derogations applying to adult workers' rest periods do not apply to young workers, but there is a *force majeur* exception applying to them in reg. 27 (unforeseen or exceptional circumstances) in relation to daily rest and rest breaks).

As well as the normal derogations (including the ability to modify or exclude entirely all the adult entitlements by collective agreement or workforce agreement[10]), there are special provisions relating to daily and weekly rest periods in the case of shift workers being potentially in breach when changing shifts and, more generally, in the case of 'workers engaged in activities involving periods of work split up over the day, as may be the case for cleaning staff.'[11]

g) Compensatory rest

Although the derogations are of great importance to the overall scheme of the Regulations, there is one complication to some of them that could cause considerable difficulty in practice. This is that it is stated that where the application of any provision is excluded by Regulation 21 ('unmeasured working time') or 22 ('other special cases'), or is modified or excluded by a collective agreement or workforce agreement under Regulation 23(a) and a worker is accordingly required by his employer to work during a period which would otherwise be a rest period or rest break, the employer must wherever possible allow him to take an *equivalent period of compensatory rest*[12]. The original Guidance stated that an equivalent period of rest should be considered to be a period as long as that the worker was entitled to but not able to take, and that it should be provided within a reasonable time from when the entitlement to rest was modified (in the case of daily rest, this being within a couple of weeks; in the case of weekly rest, within a couple of months)[13]. This may help where there are regular fluctuations of work on a short cycle (so that rest breaks can be disapplied at the busy peaks and compensatory rest given during the slack periods) but this may not be possible where rest breaks are disapplied because of a sustained *season* of heavy work possibly lasting for several months (as may be envisaged, for example, in several of the 'special cases' set out in Regulation 21, e.g. a 'foreseeable surge of activity' in agriculture or tourism). In such cases there will be important questions of interpretation as to the meaning of 'wherever possible' and whether compensatory rest is legally acceptable if it only comes at the end of an extended season of consistent work. One other point of difficulty may be that the wording of the compensatory rest provision (as pointed out above) most naturally applies in the context of the various rest break provisions, but it also applies in the context of night working and even (in the case of the 'unmeasured working time' derogation) to the maximum 48-hour week, where it may be less easy to apply – what is the period spent working which would otherwise have been a rest period or break?[14]

---

10 Reg. 23(a).

11 Reg. 22.

12 Reg. 24(a). In exceptional cases where this is not possible for objective reasons, the employer must 'afford such protection as may be appropriate in order to safeguard the worker's health and safety': reg. 24(b); the original Guidance para. 6.2.4 stated that such cases will be rare and that this flexibility is not to be used on a routine basis. This raises a question of interpretation – are reg. 24(a) and (b) exhaustive, i.e. can (a) only be disapplied if (b) applies? *Or* can there be middle ground where it is not possible to give compensatory rest but for reasons which do not activate the requirements of (b)?

13 Para. 5.25.

14 Interestingly, compensatory rest did not appear in the notes on the 48-hour maximum week in the original Guidance, though it was specifically mentioned in relation to night work and rest breaks. Note also, in relation to the maximum week, that the compensatory rest provisions do not apply where the worker simply agrees individually that the maximum should apply to him or her under reg. 5.

h) Annual leave

Along with the 48-hour maximum working week, the aspect of the Regulations to which most publicity was given on their introduction was the entitlement to a statutory minimum period of paid leave in each leave year, set initially at three weeks (utilising a derogation in the Directive), but rising to four weeks as from November 1999[15]. The leave year is primarily left to be determined by a relevant agreement; in default of that, the general rule is that it runs from the date of commencement of employment[16], but of course that could be inconvenient for an employer who will normally wish to stipulate a standardised holiday year for all employees.

Given the existing contractual entitlements of most full time employees[17], it may seem that this new entitlement is hardly revolutionary, even after November 1999, but the provisions may bite in two particular ways:

(i)   This entitlement applies simply to 'workers', which may include certain casual or temporary workers previously without holiday rights by contract. Apart from 'worker' status, the only other key into the right is that the worker has been continuously employed for thirteen weeks[18]. This immediately raises the question whether an employer can deliberately break continuity with casual staff in order to avoid the paid holiday entitlement. The original draft Regulations adopted the normal continuity of employment provisions of the Employment Rights Act 1996, which are capable of negating some avoidance devices by employers, but after the consultation exercise the final version of the Regulations dropped that provision and now simply state that a worker has been continuously employed for 13 weeks if his relations with his employer have been governed by a contract during the whole or part of each of those weeks[19], thus permitting an employer to avoid the obligation by terminating employment for one or more complete weeks[20].

(ii) It is specifically provided that the statutory holiday period must be actually *taken*, in the sense that it may not (in whole or, particularly, in part) be either carried forward into the next holiday year or bought out by a payment in lieu (except on termination of employment)[1]. This is of course in line with the

---

15   Reg. 13. The worker is entitled to be paid a 'week's pay' for each week of leave, which is to be worked out by applying the Employment Rights Act 1996, ss. 221–224 (see p. 189, above): reg. 16. Contractual renumeration is offset against the statutory amount, and vice versa. Reg. 15 covers the case of a worker leaving part of the way through the holiday year.

16   Reg. 13. Where an employee joins part of the way through a leave year, he or she is entitled to a holiday period on a pro rata basis: reg. 13(5).

17   In summer 1998, 85% of permanent full-time staff already had 20 or more working days holiday per annum: Hours and Holidays 1998 (IDS Study No. 657).

18   Reg. 13(7). This will override any contractual term to the contrary, or any inconsistent use by an employer of the Protean category of 'casual'. In this context particularly, the wide definition of 'worker' should be remembered – even if the employer does not consider a casual to be an 'employee' (which itself may be legally dubious), the only relevant question is whether they qualify as a 'worker', which is more likely than not.

19   Reg. 13(8). The Regulations do not contain a definition of 'week'.

20   This is particularly so since the decision of the EAT in *Booth v United States of America* [1999] IRLR 16 that, even under the general continuity provisions of the 1996 Act, it is still open to an employer to avoid those provisions to the extent that the law permits it, i.e. there is no general power to strike down avoidance schemes.

1   Reg. 13(9). Subject to a relevant agreement, the general rules on the timing of holidays are that a worker may give notice of intention to take a certain period, of a length twice as long as the time to be taken off; equally, an employer may require a worker to take a particular period by similar notice, or may notify the worker of time that is not to be taken

health and safety provenance of the Regulations (i.e. that people should actually have the holiday period to rest, in spite of some evidence that holidays with the family can in some cases rate on the stress scale as highly as moving house, public speaking or Christmas!). It could, however, have an effect (especially with the full four-week minimum entitlement) in industries such as agriculture with a tradition of buying out holiday entitlements.

i) Pattern of work – the loose end

The Working Time Directive Article 13 contains the rather Delphic provision that member states are to take the measures necessary to:

'ensure that an employer who intends to organise work according to a certain pattern takes account of the general principle of adapting work to the worker, with a view, in particular, to alleviating monotonous work and work at a predetermined work-rate, depending on the type of activity, and of safety and health requirements, especially as regards breaks during working time'.

This is potentially a wide provision, arguably in line with the modern emphasis on the working *environment* generally. When, however, the government consulted on implementing the Directive they said that they thought the intention of Article 13 was 'unclear'[2] and that it appeared to replicate Article 6(2)(d) of the Health and Safety Framework Directive[3]. In the result, the only attempt at transposition in the Working Time Regulations is in Regulation 8, which picks up only on the specific point of rest breaks:

'Where the pattern according to which an employer organizes work is such as to put the health and safety of a worker employed by him at risk, in particular because the work is monotonous or the work rate is predetermined, the employer shall ensure that the worker is given adequate rest breaks.'[4]

This falls well short of any general obligation to fit the work to the worker; unless it can be argued that Article 13 is transposed in some other way (expressly or impliedly), it could be argued that there has been a failure to transpose, which might be relevant in independent proceedings (e.g. a civil action for damages for occupational stress), though there may be less scope for this now that it has been held that the Directive (or at least parts of it) does not have direct effect[5].

---

as holiday by notice of a length equal to that to be taken off: reg. 15. This gives the employer considerable ability to time holidays, either to bunch them (e.g. for annual shutdowns) or to spread them among employees to ensure continuity of production. Moreover, there is no magic to public or bank holidays, which are treated as any other day and so, where given, can count towards the statutory minimum.

2   URN: 98/645, para. 117.
3   Directive 89/391/EEC, see p. 762, below. Note however that Art. 6(2) was not specifically transposed in the enacting Management of Health and Safety at Work Regulations 1992, being left instead to be covered by the much more general (existing) provisions of the Health and Safety at Work etc Act 1974. Interestingly, it *was* specifically transposed when the Management Regulations were reissued in 1999 (S.I. 1999 No. 3242, reg. 4, Sch. 1).
4   The original Guidance, para. 6.1.3 merely stated that this may mean *regular* rest breaks.
5   *Gibson v East Riding of Yorkshire Council* [2000] IRLR 598, CA.

j) Enforcement

The way in which the Regulations effectively straddle employment law and health and safety law is particularly noticeable in the area of enforcement. The so-called 'limitations' relating to the 48-hour maximum working week, night working and patterns of work are enforceable under the Health and Safety system, with primary responsibility on the Health and Safety Executive[6]. Thus, the principal obligations in these areas are that the employer must 'take all *reasonable* steps' to ensure that the weekly maximum and the night working limit are observed. There is an obligation on employers to maintain records adequate to show compliance, and to keep them for two years[7].

On the other hand, the 'entitlements' to rest breaks and paid annual leave are enforceable by complaint by an individual worker to an employment tribunal which may make a declaration, award compensation (not subject to a maximum amount) and, where the complaint is of failure to pay holiday pay, order the employer to pay the amount due[8]. The individual worker is not given a statutory right to complain of breach of the maximum working week or night work (or pattern of work) provisions, but it is possible that breach of these obligations could be used *indirectly* by an individual in three ways – first, it could be used as evidence of unreasonable conduct by the employer in another form of claim, such as for constructive dismissal or in a personal injury action (e.g. for stress-related illness); secondly, it is possible that the Regulations could be held to support civil liability, so that in a case of non-compliance causing definable harm to the worker he or she could sue the employer for breach of statutory duty[9]; thirdly, in a highly purposive judgment in *Barber v RJB Mining (UK) Ltd*[10] Gage J held that it is an implied term of the contract of employment that the employer will comply with the maximum working week requirement, so that if an employee is made to work past the 48-hour average (without agreeing to do so) by an employer who assumes that this can 'only' be challenged by health and safety procedures, that employee may have a breach of contract action, or may even (according to the judge) calculate when he has done sufficient hours in that reference period to average 48 per week and then *stop* until the beginning of the

6   Reg. 28. It is an offence to fail to comply, carrying a fine on either summary conviction or conviction on indictment: reg. 29. The HSE (or local authority where that is the enforcing authority) must make adequate arrangements for enforcement (reg. 28(2)), but when the Regulations came into force the HSC made clear that they lacked the resources for proactive enforcement by inspector; it may be that enforcement turns out to be reactive, i.e. following on accidents or other notified events.

7   Reg. 9.

8   Reg. 30. The time limit is the usual three-month period, subject to the 'not reasonably practicable' power to extend: reg. 30(2). Complaint must be that the employer has 'refused' to permit the worker to exercise the right in question, not just that he has 'failed' to do so. This could be an important distinction, e.g. where the employer has *offered* to comply with the Regulations but the workforce have not wanted this because of the possible effect on pay – where is the employer 'refusal'?

9   This possibility was expressly envisaged in the government's consultation document URN: 98/645 at para. 184. Such liability would not be automatic under the Health and Safety at Work etc. Act 1974, s. 47(2) because the Regulations were passed under the European Communities Act 1972, not under the 1974 Act; it would therefore be necessary to prove Parliamentary intent that they should support civil liability in the usual way (see p. 728, below). Given this possibility, an employer might be advised to keep records for at least *three* years (the limitation period in personal injury actions) not just the statutory two years.

10   [1999] ICR 679, [1999] IRLR 308.

next reference period. Thus, there are several possibilities here that do not appear on the face of the Regulations.

Any provision in an agreement (whether or not a contract of employment) is void if it purports to exclude or limit the application of the Regulations or to preclude a person from bringing proceedings before an employment tribunal (subject to the usual exceptions for ACAS-conciliated (COT 3) settlements and compromise agreements)[11].

In line with most other recent protective legislation, it is provided that any dismissal because of refusal to comply with a breach of the Regulations, to forego a right or to sign a workforce agreement, or because of being or seeking to be a worker representative, is automatically unfair[12]; likewise, a worker has a right not to suffer a detriment (short of dismissal) for similar reasons[13].

7   PROTECTION OF WAGES

i)   The repeal of the Truck Acts and the effect on cashless pay

One of the longest standing pieces of social legislation in English law was the Truck Acts 1831–1940, designed and basically put into place early in the 19th century to protect the employee in his free enjoyment of his earnings[14]. They served two distinct purposes –

a)   the original Act of 1831 gave a legal right to payment in 'current coin of the realm', designed to prevent abuse of the then prevalent 'tommy shop' system whereby an employer might pay at least part of the employee's wages in tokens to be spent at the employer's own shop[15];

b)   the later legislation (particularly the Truck Act 1896) then placed restrictions on the making of deductions from wages, principally in respect of the provisions of goods and services by the employer, fines or bad workmanship; these were of great complexity, but in essence they usually provided that the deduction had to be authorised in writing and be fair and reasonable in the circumstances.

The principal limitation of the legislation was that it only applied to *manual* workers[16] (with certain limited extensions to shop assistants). Persons not covered were therefore left to their contractual rights on both payment methods and deductions[17]. It was recognised for years that the legislation was in need of, at the least, revision, and indeed the last major case on it showed just how unpredictable

---

11   Reg. 35.
12   Reg. 32, adding the Employment Rights Act 1996, s. 101A. Asserting a right under the Regulations is protected by s. 104 of the Act.
13   Reg. 31, adding the Employment Rights Act 1996, s. 45A.
14   For the details of this legislation, see the third edition of this book, at pp. 389–394. The archaic meaning of 'truck' was to exchange or barter; one of the few current usages is the phrase 'to have no truck' with something, in the sense of not wishing to have any dealings with it. The word 'truck' was not actually used in the wording of the legislation.
15   Such a system was not necessarily vicious, since the employer might have the benefit of discount buying, but obviously it was open to abuse.
16   This distinction caused great difficulties and a considerable amount of old case law; for a modern example of the problem, see *Brooker v Charrington Fuel Oils Ltd* [1981] IRLR 147, Co Ct.
17   On deduction, however, there was at least the statutory right to have deductions notified, as part of the statutory itemised pay statement under the Employment Rights Act 1996, s. 8.

and unreliable its coverage was[18]. However, the previous government became interested in the area not because of anything concerning deductions, but rather because of the first of the above two effects, that of the right to payment in cash. Britain had long lagged behind other western countries in the move towards cashless pay (i.e. pay by cheque or credit transfer)[19]. It is true that the strict requirement in the 1831 Act of current coin of the realm had been qualified by the Payment of Wages Act 1960 which permitted cashless pay with the employee's written agreement, but the problem was that that agreement could always be revoked by written notice and so a manual worker could re-invoke his rights under the Truck Act. Banks have of course been interested in extending cashless pay, and sometimes they and employers have offered cash incentives to go over to it; the problem with the 1960 Act was that any such agreement was *not* irrevocable. The government therefore decided to deregulate this area by the repeal of the Truck Acts and the Payment of Wages Act. However, to do so simpliciter would also remove all protection with regard to deductions and eventually this was thought to be too sweeping, particularly in the light of media coverage of certain cases of highly inequitable deduction clauses in employment contracts, particularly in certain areas of retailing[20]. The compromise was contained in Part I of the Wages Act 1986 which repealed the Truck legislation (and other related statutes)[1] but also enacted entirely new provisions giving at least partial protection in relation to deductions; the principal feature in favour of this scheme is that it applies to *all* employees, not just to manual workers; one criticism of it, however, is that (with the exception of certain extra protection for retail workers, considered below) the new provisions largely relate to the *mechanics* of making deductions (the principal requirement normally being the employee's written consent), rather than any concept of the substantive *fairness* or otherwise of the deductions – in this sense, they are not as interventionist as the old Truck Act provisions, and the question of the reason for the deduction in question is left largely as a matter of contract.

As seen above, however, the matter of deductions was (if not an afterthought) at least a subsidiary matter in the eyes of the government. The principal point was the removal of blockages to cashless pay, and this has been achieved. The repeal of the Truck Acts means that there is now no freestanding legal right to payment

18 In *Bristow v City Petroleum Ltd* [1988] ICR 165, [1987] IRLR 340 the House of Lords finally held that a deduction from a shop worker's wages in respect of a stock or till deficiency could be a 'fine' within the Truck Act 1896, s. 1, thereby resolving a conflict of opinion between different Divisional Courts on the issue. This final decision came too late to affect the decision to repeal the legislation.

19 In the early 1980s it was estimated that 50% of all workers in Britain and 78% of manual workers were still paid in cash. This compared with 20% of all workers in Holland and Sweden, 10% in France, 5% in West Germany and Canada and 1% in the USA. Approximately 400,000 workers in Britain were changing to cashless pay each year, but this was considered slow progress.

20 One area much in the news at the time was petrol stations, where contracts of employment often included a term requiring the attendant to refund out of his wages any stock or till deficiencies arising during his shift *whether through his default or not*, thus covering the motorist who deliberately drove off without payment. In *Bristow v City Petroleum Ltd*, n. 4, above, the deductions had averaged 17% of net pay over a period of five weeks but there was anecdotal evidence of far greater deductions in some cases, even to the extent of leaving little pay left after the deductions. See Goriely 'Arbitrary deductions from pay and the proposed repeal of the Truck Acts' (1983) 12 ILJ 236.

1 The Payment of Wages Act 1960, the Shop Clubs Act 1902, the Payment of Wages in Public-houses Prohibition Act 1883, the Checkweighing in Various Industries Act 1919 and various older statutes concerning coal-mines.

in cash and so an employer taking on a new employee (manual or otherwise) may lawfully make it a term of the contract that payment will be by cheque or credit transfer. However, it is important to note that the Wages Act did *not* give an employer a right to insist unilaterally on existing employees who were paid in cash changing to cashless pay. If there is a contractual term (express or implied from past conduct) for payment in cash, that may still only be varied by agreement[2]. The important point for the employer in such a case, however, is that if the employee does so agree that will be final since there is now no right to revert to cash.

The Wages Act 1986 was repealed by the Employment Rights Act 1996, and the provisions relating to deductions are now contained in Part II (ss. 13–27) of that Act.

ii) Deductions from wages

Section 13 provides that an employer shall not make deductions from the wages of a worker employed by him unless the deduction is (i) required or authorised by statute (e.g. PAYE, N.I. contributions or an attachment of earnings order), (ii) required or authorised by a provision in the contract of employment which has either been given to him or notified to him previously in writing, or (iii) agreed to by the employee in writing prior to the making of the deduction[3].

a) Application

From such humble beginnings, these provisions became subject to quite remarkable development, for one procedural reason which had little to do with their origins. Until 1994, we were afflicted with a split jurisdiction, so that in the past employment tribunals could not deal with common law matters such as non-payment of wages, which had to go to the ordinary courts (doubly annoying if, for example, the ex-employee was already bringing a tribunal action for unfair dismissal). However, a way round this was discovered – if an employee was complaining about a refusal to pay wages, holiday entitlements etc., could that be *called* a 'deduction'? If so, the employee could (on the assumption that there was no prior written consent) complain to a tribunal under the Wages Act for its 'recovery'. This reasoning has been largely successful, as can be seen from the very high number of 'Wages Act cases' brought in the last few years[4]; it operated

2   One difficult point would arise if an employer managed to negotiate a change to cashless pay with all but one or two of a large staff; would it be fair to dismiss them on the grounds of business need after taking all reasonable steps to persuade them to change? On dismissals and business need, see p. 496, above.

3   Section 15 has equivalent provisions concerning the making of payments by workers to employers, instead of operating by way of deduction. 'Worker' is defined widely in s. 230(3), as covering not only a person under a contract of service or apprenticeship, but also under a contract to do or perform personally work or services for another party (other than in a professional–client relationship). The requirement of *prior* written agreement means prior to the event causing the deduction, not just to the deduction itself: *Discount Tobacco and Confectionery Ltd v Williamson* [1993] ICR 371; *York City and District Travel Ltd v Smith* [1990] ICR 344, [1990] IRLR 213. To be relied on, a contractual provision must be notified to the employee individually, not just by a factory notice: *Kerr v Sweater Shop (Scotland) Ltd* [1996] IRLR 424.

4   In 1998, ACAS received 24,981 cases under Part II for individual conciliation, 71% of which settled or withdrawn: ACAS Annual Report 1998. In 1997/98 the tribunals received 15,660 applications under Part II, constituting 19% of total applications: Employment Tribunals Service Annual Report 1997/1998.

as a de facto transfer of certain common law, contractual claims to tribunals. It had been hoped that when an order was finally made by the government giving common law jurisdiction to tribunals, this would be in general terms, and would end the need to extend what is now Part II of the 1996 Act to perform a function it was probably not intended for. However, this simple hope has not come about, for two reasons – (1) the order[5] in fact only gives common law jurisdiction to tribunals in cases arising on or out of *termination* of employment, and so challenges to non-payment or under-payment of wages or other benefits *during* employment can still only be brought before a tribunal by squeezing them under Part II; (2) even on termination, it may still be tactically advantageous to the ex-employee to claim amounts not paid under Part II rather than directly under the order, since the latter is subject not only to a monetary limit (set relatively highly at £25,000) but also, and far more importantly, to an express power of counterclaim by the employer which can be avoided by claiming under Part II (leaving the employer to pursue any claim he may think he has through the ordinary courts, which in practice is highly unlikely to happen). Thus, claims under Part II are likely to continue at their present high level, and the reported cases show that such an action can be used as a relatively quick and certainly effective way of challenging an attempt by an employer to force through a unilateral variation of contractual terms[6].

As a matter of law, this development raised two questions of interpretation of the Act – what is a 'deduction' and what are 'wages'? On the first question, section 13(3) gives a broad definition[7] and certain cases have shown an equally broad approach, so that for example there can still be a deduction even if it is so large that it actually extinguishes the wage payment altogether[8], and the phasing out of a special bonus from a payment system was held to qualify as a deduction[9]. However, the crucial question was whether simple non-payment would qualify – on a straightforward application of section 13 it would, but it could also be argued as a matter of English that non-payment was different in kind from a deduction from wages paid. On the second question, section 27 gives a lengthy inclusive and exclusive definition[10], although not specifically covering one of the most

5   The Industrial Tribunals Extension of Jurisdiction (England and Wales) Order 1994, S.I. 1994 No. 1623; the Scottish order is S.I. 1994 No. 1624; see p. 433, below. A further point of difference is that Part II applies to the under category of 'worker' (including some self-employed) but the Extension Order only applies to 'employees' properly so called: *Robertson v Blackstone Franks Investment Management Ltd* [1998] IRLR 376, CA.

6   *Bruce v Wiggins Teape (Stationery) Ltd* [1994] IRLR 536 (withdrawal of shift bonus); *Morgan v West Glamorgan County Council* [1995] IRLR 68 (disciplinary salary cut in breach of contract); *Saavedra v Aceground Ltd* [1995] IRLR 198 (employer allocating part of waiters' tronc for tips to himself). In each case the employers' actions were held to be unlawful 'deductions'. See Miller (1995) 24 ILJ 162.

7   'Where the total amount of any wages that are paid on any occasion by an employer to any worker employed by him is less than the total amount of the wages that are properly payable by him to the worker on that occasion ...'

8   *Alsop v Star Vehicle Contracts Ltd* [1990] ICR 378, [1990] IRLR 83.

9   *McCree v Tower Hamlets London Borough Council* [1992] ICR 99, [1992] IRLR 56.

10   'Wages' means 'any sums payable to the worker by his employer in connection with his employment'; there are then six categories specifically included and five specifically excluded. The first included is 'any fee, bonus, commission, holiday pay or other emolument referable to his employment, whether payable under his contract or otherwise'. The last two words meant that the Act's procedure could be used to challenge non-payment of a *discretionary* or *ex gratia* payment, provided the making of such a payment was clearly anticipated: *Kent Management Services Ltd v Butterfield* [1992] ICR 272, [1992] IRLR 394. See also the recovery of commission by a self employed person in *Robertson v Blackstone Franks Investment Management Ltd* [1998] IRLR 376, CA. However, there must be a legal obligation of sorts to pay the amount in question: *New Century Cleaning Co Ltd v Church* [2000] IRLR 27, CA.

contentious areas, wages in lieu of notice on a dismissal; could such amounts, if kept by the employer, be recovered under the Act?

Both of these questions caused major disagreements between different divisions of the EAT, but the matter was largely settled by the decisions of the Court of Appeal and House of Lords in the leading case of *Delaney v Staples*[11]. The facts were refreshingly simple. The employee was dismissed, being owed £55.50 commission and holiday pay and £82 in lieu of notice. She claimed both of these amounts, not in the county court, but before a tribunal under the Wages Act. This neatly raised both of the above questions. The Court of Appeal held that the £55.50 could be recovered, because a simple non-payment such as this *does* qualify as a 'deduction', on a literal interpretation of section 13(3), and there was here no prior agreement. That point was not subject to further appeal and so remains governed by the Court of Appeal's decision. However, the matter of the £82 in lieu went on further appeal to the House of Lords and raised the second question – are payments in lieu of notice 'wages'? Here, the matter was resolved not primarily by the wording of the Act, but by a broader consideration of the nature of payments in lieu. Lord Browne-Wilkinson said that the essential characteristic of wages (at common law and under the Act) was as 'payments in respect of the rendering of services during the employment'. He then analysed 'wages in lieu' as covering four different possibilities[12]; in only one (where the employer formally gives the correct notice, pays during that period, but does not actually require the employee to work during it, e.g. in a 'garden leave' case) does the payment still constitute wages during employment, to which the Act could apply. In the case itself, the in lieu payment came into the much more common category of anticipatory *damages* for the employer's breach of contract in dismissing the employee instantly, without proper notice. It was therefore not 'wages' and so the non-payment could not be challenged before a tribunal. Thus, the end result is that non-payment of wages accrued during the employment can be subject to a statutory action under Part II before a tribunal, but in most cases non-payment of wages in lieu cannot be (though of course, as such a case by definition arises on termination, such amounts outstanding *can* now be claimed before a tribunal quite separately under the Transfer of Jurisdiction Order). One further class of case deserves mention. If it is the *employee* who is in breach of contract by leaving without giving his contractual notice, the employer may be very tempted to hang on to any final wages, holiday pay etc., still owing to that employee, as 'damages'. In the light of *Delaney's* reasoning and two earlier cases[13] this is likely to be unlawful in the absence of prior written consent. The moral is simple; if the employer wants a power to retain accrued wages in the event of the employee leaving in breach of his notice obligation (especially where the employer wants to be able to rely on that obligation, e.g. so as to have time to find a replacement) the employer should ensure that there is a clear written term to that effect in the employee's contract.

---

11   [1991] ICR 331, [1991] IRLR 112, CA; affd [1992] ICR 483, [1992] IRLR 191, HL. The previous EAT decisions now do not need to be considered.
12   These are set out at p. 369 below, in the discussion of dismissal by notice.
13   *Pename Ltd v Paterson* [1989] ICR 12, [1989] IRLR 195; *Chiltern House Ltd v Chambers* [1990] IRLR 88.

b) Exceptions

Section 14 contains a series of exceptions[14] : thus the provisions of section 13 do not apply to deductions in respect of –

a) overpayment of wages, or expenses;

b) disciplinary proceedings held by virtue of any statutory provision;

c) a statutory requirement to deduct from wages and pay over to a public authority;

d) payments agreed to by the worker which are to be made over by the employer to a third party;

e) a strike or other industrial action in which the worker took part; or

f) the satisfaction of a court or tribunal order requiring the worker to pay something to the employer.

The primary point to notice about these exceptions is that they do *not* establish an independent, unilateral right for the employer to make such deductions; they only state that deductions made on these grounds do not infringe the procedural requirements of section 13. In any given case, the question of the overall legality of a deduction may well depend on the contractual or other common law propriety of making it at all. If there is no contractual authority to make the deduction, the employee can sue for it in the county court in the normal way. However, the question again arose whether an action could be brought instead in a tribunal. At first that seemed possible, for in *Home Office v Ayres*[15] it was held that the exclusions in section 14 only apply to deductions *lawfully* made on the above grounds; it was therefore open to the employee to argue that the deduction (a) was unlawful at common law[16], (b) was therefore not covered by the relevant exclusion in section 14, and (c) was therefore recoverable under the Act, in the absence of prior written consent. However, this reasoning was later repudiated by the EAT in *Sunderland Polytechnic v Evans*[17] where it was held, by exercising the courts' new power to consider *Hansard*[18], that Parliament's intention was that section 14 and its exceptions were to be applied literally, leaving any question of the contractual lawfulness of the deduction in question to be fought over in the ordinary courts[19].

c) Retail employment

Due to the discussions prior to the introduction of the 1986 Act and concerns expressed as to certain inequitable deductions made in certain service industries, sections 17–22 of the 1996 Act impose a further limitation on deductions from

---

14 There is also an exception in s. 13(4) relating to errors of computation of wages, but this is to be construed narrowly: *Yemm v British Steel plc* [1994] IRLR 117; *Morgan v West Glamorgan County Council* [1995] IRLR 68.

15 [1992] ICR 175, [1992] IRLR 59.

16 The case itself concerned a deduction to recover an overpayment; the employers relied on s. 14 but the employee argued that there was no common law right to recover the amount because he had spent it innocently. The employee succeeded in a tribunal action.

17 [1993] ICR 392, [1993] IRLR 196, applied in *SIP Industrial Products Ltd v Swinn* [1994] ICR 473, [1994] IRLR 323.

18 *Pepper v Hart* [1993] AC 593, [1993] 1 All ER 42, HL.

19 The case itself concerned a deduction for taking part in industrial action (s. 14(5)), where this policy consideration is perhaps particularly strong; however, the reasoning should apply to all the heads of s. 14.

the wages of workers in retail employment[20]. Where such a deduction is made in respect of cash shortages or stock deficiencies, the maximum that may be deducted is 10% of the gross amount of wages for that particular pay day. While such an extra provision is to be welcomed, two further points should be noticed – (i) this limitation only applies to the *amount* deductible, not to the grounds for deduction, since there is still no requirement that those grounds be fair and reasonable[1]; (ii) there is nothing to stop the full amount of a contractually recoverable deficiency being carried forward over successive pay days until fully recovered, provided that only 10% is taken on each occasion and, indeed, section 22 states that the 10% rule does not apply to the final pay day if the employee's employment is terminated, when the whole of any outstanding deficiency could be set against the wages payable.

d) Remedies

A complaint that deductions have been made (or payments demanded) in contravention of section 13 may be presented to an employment tribunal within three months of the date of the last deduction or payment, or if that is not reasonably practicable within such further period as the tribunal thinks reasonable[2]. If the tribunal finds the complaint well-founded, it is to make a declaration to that effect and order the repayment of amounts improperly deducted[3]. Four final points should be noted on these provisions. The first is that section 205(2) states that '[t]he remedy of a worker in respect of any contravention of [sections 13 et seq] shall be by way of a complaint under section 23 *and not otherwise*'. At first sight, that may appear to rule out a common law action for wages (the traditional remedy to recover improper deductions). However, that is not so since, as pointed out above, all that the Act does is to apply to deductions from wages certain (albeit important) procedural requirements, particularly as to prior written agreement to the making of such deductions. There may well still be cases where the employee is objecting not just to the procedure adopted (which may have complied with section 13), but rather to the legality of making a deduction at all in those circumstances. In such a case the proper action for the employee remains a common law action in the county court[4]. The second point is that there is a measure of overlap between these provisions and the right in section 11 of the 1996 Act to bring tribunal proceedings against an employer for failing to give proper notification of deductions from wages in the statutory-required itemised pay statement[5]; section 26 provides that both actions can be brought, but that if that happens there is not to be double recovery of the deduction. The third point is that, in potentially an important

---

20 'Retail employment' is defined in s. 17(2), referring principally to the direct supply to the public or other individuals in a personal capacity of goods or services (including financial services).

1 It is therefore still lawful to incorporate a contractual term requiring the refunding of, for example, till deficiencies at a petrol station, even where those deficiencies are not the attendant's fault (as, for example, where caused by fraud by a customer).

2 S. 23. For the case law on the 'reasonably practicable' escape clause in the context of an unfair dismissal action, see p. 417, below.

3 Moreover, those amounts are *not* then to be treated as properly recoverable by further deductions (by whatever means) or by action in the ordinary courts, i.e. the employer loses the right to them altogether: s. 25, *Potter v Hunt Contracts Ltd* [1992] ICR 337, [1992] IRLR 108.

4 *Rickard v PB Glass Supplies Ltd* [1990] ICR 150, CA.

5 S. 8.

extension of the tribunal's powers under the Act, the EAT have held that even if the employer does have prior written consent to make a deduction on a particular ground, the employee can argue that the *amount* deducted was excessive and not justified by the written consent; this permits the tribunal to consider whether that particular deduction was sustainable in fact[6]. The fourth point is that special protection is given to an employee making a complaint under Part II. One problem always was that, although such a complaint is not subject to any qualifying period and so may be brought by a new employee, if such an employee did not have the necessary qualifying period for unfair dismissal he could be dismissed because of the complaint without protection. Now, however, the Employment Rights Act 1996 provides that if an employee is dismissed for asserting certain statutory rights (which include those under Part II), not only is that dismissal automatically unfair, but (crucially) the normal qualifying period does not apply[7].

8   RIGHTS ON THE EMPLOYER'S INSOLVENCY

Where an employer becomes bankrupt or insolvent, the general rule is that wages or salary due to an employee in respect of the four months before the bankruptcy or insolvency are a preferential debt, subject to a maximum of £800[8]. Beyond that, they constitute an unsecured debt. The Employment Protection Act 1975 introduced new measures to improve the position of the employee of a bankrupt employer in two ways; they are now in the Insolvency Act 1986 and Part XII of the Employment Rights Act 1996. First the Insolvency Act 1986, Sch. 6 provides that certain other amounts are to be treated as wages and so preferential debts. These are amounts owed by the employer in respect of a guarantee payment, remuneration during suspension on medical grounds, payment for time off for union duties, to attend ante-natal care and to look for other work and remuneration under a protective award[9]. Second, the Employment Rights Act 1996, section 182 gives the employee rights to claim certain amounts due to him from his employer from the Secretary of State instead, who is to pay them out of the National Insurance Fund[10]. The amounts in question are those relating to arrears of pay (up to a maximum of eight weeks), wages during the statutory minimum notice period[11], holiday pay (up to a maximum of six weeks), a basic

6   *Fairfield Ltd v Skinner* [1992] ICR 836, [1993] IRLR 4.
7   See p. 495, below. These provisions were introduced by the Trade Union Reform and Employment Rights Act 1993.
8   Insolvency Act 1986, s. 386, Sch. 6, para. 9; para. 10 covers holiday pay. Where the employer goes into administration or receivership and the employee is kept on, there may be a continuing liability on the administrator or receiver for 'qualifying liabilities' (wages, holiday pay, sick pay and pension contributions) *if* his contract is adopted by the administrator or receiver, and only from the *date* of adoption: Insolvency Act 1994. This Act (amending the 1986 Act) was rushed through Parliament to negative the effects of the decisions of the Court of Appeal and then the House of Lords in *Powdrill v Watson* [1995] 2 AC 394, [1995] 2 All ER 65, HL.
9   Ibid., Sch. 6, para. 13.
10   The Secretary of State may also make redundancy payments directly out of the Fund where he is satisfied that the employer is insolvent; Employment Rights Act 1996, s. 167.
11   Laid down in the ERA, s. 86. If for any reason wages during the notice period would not have been payable by the employer, they are not payable by the Secretary of State under s. 182; *Secretary of State for Employment v Wilson* [1978] ICR 200, [1977] IRLR 483; this imports the common law notion of mitigation of damage, so that if the ex-employee in fact earns money during what should have been his notice period, those earnings are

award for unfair dismissal and a reasonable sum to reimburse all or part of any fee paid by an apprentice or articled clerk; further, 'pay' is deemed to include any outstanding amounts by way of guarantee payment, remuneration during suspension on medical grounds, payment for statutory time off work or remuneration under a protective award. Where any of these sums is to be computed by reference to weekly pay (e.g. arrears of wages) the maximum amount that can be used for computation purposes at the time of writing is £230[12]. The employee may also request the Secretary of State to make up any contributions to his occupational pension scheme left unpaid due to his employer's insolvency. Any further sums outstanding can still be claimed by the employee as unsecured debts.

Where the Secretary of State makes one of the above payments to the employee, the rights and remedies which the employee had in the employer's bankruptcy in respect of that amount become vested in the Secretary of State[13]. However, the employee may still be the ultimate beneficiary from this statutory scheme (apart from gaining from its administrative convenience for him) for the amount which he can claim from the Secretary of State may be greater than that which the Secretary of State can then claim as a preferential debt in the bankruptcy, for two reasons. First, the amount claimable from the Secretary of State may be greater than the £800 maximum preferred debt for wages and salaries; second, certain items in respect of which the employee can claim from the Secretary of State are still not deemed to be preferred debts (e.g. the amount of a basic award for unfair dismissal). In the case of any such amounts, the Secretary of State must pay them to the employee, claim as much as possible as a preferred debt and then claim the balance simply as an unsecured debt; it is thus the National Insurance which bears the risk in such a case, not the individual employee.

---

deducted from the amount payable by the Secretary of State: *Secretary of State for Employment v Jobling* [1980] ICR 380. The major practical problem that arose was whether unemployment benefit received during what should have been the notice period should be deducted – application of the doctrine of mitigation would suggest that it should, but this would lead (in the case of an ex-employee becoming long-term unemployed) to the ex-employee's (then) one-year entitlement to unemployment benefit running out sooner than it would have done if he had received proper notice, without any recompense. After protracted litigation, the House of Lords finally held in *Westwood v Secretary of State for Employment* [1985] ICR 209, [1984] IRLR 209, HL, that the amount recoverable from the Secretary of State, though by a statutory right, represented damages for wrongful dismissal, so that the duty to mitigate applied, and this included deducting unemployment benefit (though they suggested a method of doing so that in fact recompensed the ex-employee). After this decision the position was altered to allow the employee to get the (net) s. 182 payment, but then receive what would otherwise have been his full entitlement to unemployment benefit (now jobseekers allowance).

12   This figure was substituted as from February 2000 and is subject to annual review under the Employment Relations Act 1999, s. 34. Applying the principle in *Westwood* (n. 11, above), the amount to be paid by the Secretary of State is the amount of the employee's *net* loss, so that from gross wages owed there is to be deducted the amounts normally payable as tax and N.I. contributions, and any mitigating amounts such as benefit received and/or any amounts earned elsewhere during the period in question: *Secretary of State for Employment v Cooper* [1987] ICR 766. However, for the purpose of applying the statutory maximum for a week's pay, the Secretary of State is correct to apply that maximum to the *gross* loss, and only then deduct the above amounts: *Morris v Secretary of State for Employment* [1985] ICR 522, [1985] IRLR 297; heads, the Secretary of State wins, tails... ?

13   Employment Rights Act 1996, s. 189.

Chapter 5

Discrimination in employment

I INTRODUCTION[1]

The common law placed no restrictions on an employer's freedom to decide whether to hire a particular individual, an approach deeply rooted in *laissez-faire* philosophy and encapsulated in the following dictum of Lord Davey in *Allen v Flood*[2]:

> 'an employer may refuse to employ [an individual] for the most mistaken, capricious, malicious or morally reprehensible motives that can be conceived, but [that individual] has no right of action against him'.

Thus, a refusal to employ on grounds of sex, race, marital status, disability or on any other ground was not unlawful[3], still less did the courts reveal any concern to enforce equality in the terms of employment. Indeed, in *Roberts v Hopwood*[4], Lord Atkinson in the House of Lords castigated the Poplar Council's policy of providing equal pay to men and women performing the same work as motivated by 'misguided principles of socialistic philanthropy'. The merest hint of a willingness to intervene in cases of sex discrimination on grounds of public policy can perhaps be discerned in the decision of the Court of Appeal in *Nagle v Feilden*[5], where it was held that the Jockey Club's 'arbitrary and capricious' refusal to grant a licence to a woman trainer infringed her 'right to work'. However, the 'right to work' principle is at best of dubious authority, and it is highly unlikely that the courts

1   See generally Townshend-Smith *Discrimination Law: Text, Cases and Materials* (1998); Fredman *Women and the Law* (1998); Donohue *Foundations of Employment Discrimination Law* (1997); McColgan *Just Wages for Women* (1997); Bourne and Whitmore *Anti-Discrimination Law in Britain* (1996); Dine and Watt (eds) *Discrimination Law: Concepts, Limitations and Justifications* (1996); McCrudden, Smith and Brown *Racial Justice at Work* (1991); O'Donovan and Szyszczak *Equality and Sex Discrimination Law* (1988).
2   [1898] AC 1 at 172.
3   See for example, *Weinberger v Inglis (No 2)* [1919] AC 606, HL; *Bebb v Law Society* [1914] 1 Ch 286, CA; *Short v Poole Corpn* [1926] Ch 66, CA.
4   [1925] AC 578, HL.
5   [1966] 2 QB 633, [1966] 1 All ER 689, CA; see p. 529, below.

would have been able (or indeed willing) to develop it into a broad principle capable of combating discrimination in employment generally.

Given the disinterest of the common law in tackling discrimination at work, it is to legislation that the victim of discrimination must look. The first legislative intervention, the Sex Disqualification (Removal) Act 1919, had a narrow scope, removing the restrictions on the employment of women in certain occupations and vocations (e.g. as civil servants or solicitors); crucially, it did not outlaw discrimination on grounds of sex in the appointment to those occupations or in the terms of employment. The Race Relations Act 1965 tackled discrimination in certain public places, and established the Race Relations Board, but it was a further three years before the Race Relations Act 1968 prohibited discrimination in employment on grounds of colour, race, ethnic or national origins. However, that Act relied for its enforcement on a combination of voluntary procedures and the institution of proceedings by the Race Relations Board, and was widely considered to have been a failure. The Equal Pay Act 1970[6] introduced a new right to equal terms and conditions for men and women in certain circumstances, but did not prohibit other forms of discrimination between the sexes, in particular discrimination at the point of hiring and in the provision of training. The turning point came with the enactment of the Sex Discrimination Act 1975, which introduced broad protection against direct and indirect discrimination in employment (and also in certain other specified areas such as education and the provision of goods and services) on the grounds of sex and marital status, with a right of complaint to a tribunal in employment cases; that Act also established the Equal Opportunities Commission (EOC) to oversee the operation of the legislation and to enforce it by bringing court proceedings or through the issue of non-discrimination notices. The Race Relations Act 1976 closely followed the provisions of the Sex Discrimination Act 1975, and established the Commission for Racial Equality (CRE) with powers similar to those of the Equal Opportunities Commission. As will be seen below, European law has had a profound impact on UK sex discrimination law, stretching it into areas which were not originally considered to fall within the scope of the domestic legislation, such as equal pay for work of equal value, benefits on death or retirement, and discrimination on grounds of gender reassignment. In recent years, strenuous efforts have been made to bring discrimination on grounds of sexual orientation within the scope of UK and/or European sex discrimination law, but so far to no avail.

While the legislation prohibiting discrimination on grounds of sex, marital status and race is now well-established, until recently there was scant protection against discrimination in employment on other grounds (with the notable exception of the statutory protection against discrimination on trade union grounds, considered below)[7]. However, after increasingly vociferous demands for legislative action, and no fewer than 14 abortive Private Members' Bills, the Disability Discrimination Act was introduced in 1995, the first piece of UK legislation to tackle discrimination against disabled people, which (inter alia) outlaws discrimination against disabled people in relation to employment, the provision of goods, facilities and services, and the sale and letting of property; the Act is considered below, at p. 309.

It remains the case that there is no legislation prohibiting age discrimination, despite widespread evidence that discrimination on grounds of age is endemic,

6   Commencement of the Act was delayed for five years to enable employers to remove discrimination in terms and conditions; the Act was heavily amended by the Sex Discrimination Act 1975, and both Acts came into force on the same date.
7   See p. 565, below.

particularly at the recruitment stage. In certain circumstances, however, age discrimination can constitute indirect sex discrimination (e.g. where an employer operates an age requirement which has an adverse impact on women)[8], and in *Nash v Mash/Roe Group*[9], an employment tribunal boldly disapplied the provisions in the Employment Rights Act 1996 which prevent employees over normal retirement age from claiming unfair dismissal or statutory redundancy payments[10], on the grounds that they indirectly discriminate against men (because more men than women work beyond 65) and are therefore contrary to Article 119 (now 141) of the EC Treaty. It is conceivable that an employee whose contract of employment includes an equal opportunities clause in which, inter alia, the employer undertakes not to discriminate on grounds of age may be able to claim a contractual right against age discrimination, but as a matter of construction such a clause is unlikely to be held to override an express contractual retirement policy[11], which of its very nature discriminates against people on grounds of age. Before the 1997 General Election, the Labour Party indicated that, if elected, it intended to legislate against age discrimination, but so far no such measure has been forthcoming. Instead, the Government has issued a Code of Practice on Age Diversity in Employment[12], which sets out a series of action points ('principles') for employers in six aspects of the employment cycle: recruitment, selection, promotion, training and development, redundancy and retirement. The action points include, for example, avoiding the use of age limits or age ranges in job advertisements, or using phrases which imply age restrictions, such as 'young graduates' or 'mature person'; using where possible a mixed age interviewing panel, and selecting on merit; ensuring that promotion opportunities are advertised through open competition; ensuring that age is not a barrier to training, and that all employees are aware of the training and development opportunities that are available and are encouraged to use them; using objective, job related criteria when considering candidates for redundancy, and making sure age is not a criterion (potentially very significant in an unfair dismissal claim based on unfair redundancy selection); and not seeing age as the sole criterion when operating early retirement schemes, and using flexible retirement schemes and phased retirement where possible. Laudable though these principles are, the main weakness in the Code is that it lacks any method of enforcement; it is entirely voluntary, issued on a non-statutory basis, and unlike other Codes of Practice in the employment field, there is no legal requirement on tribunals to take it into account where relevant. The early signs are that the Code has made little impact on age discrimination in the workplace[13]. The Government has undertaken to review the effectiveness of the Code in 2001, and it seems increasingly likely that the next edition of this book will contain a section on an Age Discrimination Act.

Another area not presently covered by legislation in Great Britain is discrimination on grounds of religion, although once again such conduct may constitute unlawful indirect discrimination on grounds of race or ethnic origin

---

8   See e.g. *Price v Civil Service Commission* [1977] IRLR 291, EAT.
9   [1998] IRLR 168.
10   Employment Rights Act 1996, ss. 109 and 156. See p. 459.
11   *Taylor v Secretary of State for Scotland* [2000] 3 All ER 90.
12   DfEE 1999; see Desmond [1999] 28 ILJ 186. The Code was preceded by a report: *Action on Age; Report of the Consultation on Age Discrimination in Employment* (DfEE, August 1998).
13   In September 1999, research conducted for the Employers Forum on Age found that 1 in 3 employers were completely unaware of the Code, and less than 1 in 10 intended to make any changes in the way they recruit and train.

under the Race Relations Act 1976[14]. There has however been 'fair employment' legislation prohibiting religious and political discrimination in Northern Ireland since 1976[15], and those measures provide a fascinating contrast with the other domestic anti-discrimination laws, not least in the use of the concept of 'fair participation'[16], and the imposition of requirements (backed by a range of civil, criminal and economic sanctions) in relation to registration, annual monitoring, three-yearly review, and mandatory affirmative action (linked to goals and timetables) to remedy under-representation. The fair employment provisions were consolidated and extended by the Northern Ireland Act 1998 and the Fair Employment and Treatment (Northern Ireland) Order[17]. Two of the reforms introduced in that process are worthy of special mention, not least because of their potential 'read across' implications for the rest of the United Kingdom[18]. First, the 1998 Act established the Equality Commission for Northern Ireland, replacing the Fair Employment Commission, the Equal Opportunities Commission for Northern Ireland, the Commission for Racial Equality for Northern Ireland and the Northern Ireland Disability Council[19]. Secondly, section 75 of the 1998 Act places a statutory duty on a public authority, in carrying out its functions relating to Northern Ireland, to have 'due regard to the need to promote equality of opportunity' in relation to religious belief, political opinion, racial group, gender, marital status, disability, and (most significantly) age, sexual orientation and persons with and without dependants. The duty thus extends well beyond the current scope of discrimination law in the United Kingdom. Public authorities were required to submit an 'equality scheme' to the Equality Commission for Northern Ireland within six months of the commencement of the provisions (on 1 January 2000) showing how they proposed to fulfil the duty to promote equality[20]. The extension of a duty to promote equality to public authorities in the rest of the United Kingdom is surely inevitable[1].

The main impetus behind the further extension and development of the UK law on discrimination in employment is likely to come from Europe. Article 13 of the EC treaty, as modified by the Treaty of Amsterdam, provides a legal basis for

14 See e.g. *Mandla v Dowell Lee* [1983] IRLR 209 HL; *Seide v Gillette Industries* [1980] IRLR 427, EAT.
15 The Fair Employment (Northern Ireland) Acts 1976 and 1989. The 1976 Act prohibited direct discrimination on grounds of religion or politics in public and private sector employment; the 1989 Act extended the coverage to indirect discrimination, and established the Fair Employment Commission, with powers which are considerably wider than those of the EOC or the CRE. For a comprehensive analysis of the 1989 Act, see Magill and Rose (eds) *Fair Employment Law in Northern Ireland: Debates and Issues*; McLaughlin and Quirk (eds) *Policy Aspects of Employment Equality in Northern Ireland*; McVey and Hutson (eds) *Public Views and Experiences of Fair Employment and Equality Issues in Northern Ireland* (SACHR, 1997).
16 See McCrudden (1992) 21 ILJ 170.
17 S.I. 1998 No. 3162. On the background to the new provisions, see *Employment Equality: Building for the Future*, Cm 3684 (1997), and the White Paper, *Partnership for Equality*, Cm 3890 (1998). See also Fitzpatrick (1999) 28 ILJ 336.
18 Hepple (1990) 10 OJLS 408.
19 Northern Ireland Act 1998, s. 73. The new Commission came into being on 1 October 1999.
20 Northern Ireland Act 1998, Sch. 9, para. 2.
1   Cf the Greater London Authority Act 1999, s.404, which imposes a duty on the Greater London Authority, Metropolitan Police Authority and London Fire and Emergency Planning Authority to 'have regard to the need (a) to promote equality of opportunity for all persons irrespective of their race, sex, disability, age, sexual orientation or religion; (b) to eliminate unlawful discrimination; and (c) to promote good relations between persons of different racial groups, religious beliefs and sexual orientation'.

community-wide action to combat discrimination on grounds of sex, racial or ethnic origin, religion or belief, disability, age or sexual orientation[2], and at the time of writing the Commission had proposed a three-part anti-discrimination package under Article 13, comprising two draft directives (a 'vertical' Race Directive combating discrimination on grounds of racial or ethnic origin in a wide range of areas, including employment, education, social security, cultural activities and access to goods and services[3], and a 'horizontal' Employment Directive dealing with discrimination in employment and occupation on all but one of the grounds covered by Article 13[4]), and a proposal for a six-year Action Programme to support and complement the implementation of the directives through the exchange of information and experience and the dissemination of best practice. The proposed Employment Directive is a framework directive which, if adopted, would require the UK Government to introduce measures prohibiting discrimination in employment (including self-employment) on grounds of religion or belief[5], age and sexual orientation, although the precise form and content of those measures is unclear[6]. As was noted in the Commission's proposal: 'The choice of a framework Directive reflects a desire to ensure flexibility for Member States in its implementation. The wording is sufficiently broad to accommodate the different circumstances of Member States, in particular their policy preferences and priorities'[7]. The introduction of measures under Article 13 requires unanimous acceptance by the Council of Ministers, and it seems likely that some of the provisions in the proposed Employment Directive will need to be diluted in order to ensure unanimity.

The other potential source of further developments in this area is the Human Rights Act 1998, which incorporates the European Convention on Human Rights into domestic law[8]. At first glance the Convention appears to have major significance for the law on discrimination in employment, as Article 14 provides that 'the enjoyment of the rights and freedoms set forth in this Convention shall be secured without discrimination on an any ground such as sex, race, colour, language, religion, political or other opinion, national or social origin, association with a national minority, property, birth or other status.' However, Article 14 does not confer a free-standing right not to be discriminated against; it merely confers a right not to be discriminated against in the enjoyment of the other rights and freedoms guaranteed by the Convention, and employment is not a Convention right. Certain types of employment discrimination can fall within the scope of the Convention, as was seen in *Smith and Grady v United Kingdom*[9], where the European Court of Human Rights held that the investigations into the sexuality

---

2   See Waddington (1999) 28 ILJ 133; (2000) 29 ILJ 176.

3   The Council of Ministers reached agreement on the Race Directive in June 2000; see p. 278 below.

4   The exception being discrimination on the ground of sex, which is already covered by Art. 141 and the associated Directives: see p. 227 below.

5   The measures on religion or belief would not need to apply in Northern Ireland.

6   Some modification of the existing anti-discrimination legislation would also be necessary, e.g. in relation to the definition of indirect discrimination, the express acknowledgement of harassment as a form of discrimination, and the right of associations and organisations to bring proceedings on behalf of individual complainants. See the discussion on the proposed Race Directive at p. 278 below.

7   Proposal for a Council Directive establishing a general framework for equal treatment in employment and occupation, COM(1999) 565 final, 25 November 1999.

8   See generally Hepple 'The Impact on Labour Law' in Markesinis (ed) *The Impact of the Human Rights Bill on English Law* (1998); Ewing 'The Human Rights Act and Labour Law' (1998) 27 ILJ 275; Palmer 'Human Rights: Implications for Labour Law' (2000) 59 CLJ 168.

9   [1999] IRLR 734, ECtHR. See p. 240 below.

of members of the British armed forces, and their subsequent discharge from the armed forces on the sole ground of their sexual orientation (pursuant to the Ministry of Defence's policy on homosexuals) constituted a violation of their right to respect for their private lives under Article 8 of the Convention[10]. The protection of freedom of religion under Article 9 is also of potential significance for the law on discrimination in employment, although previous attempts to challenge religious discrimination in employment as a violation of Article 9 have been unsuccessful[11]. In practice, it seems likely that the main impact of the incorporation of the Convention on the law on employment discrimination will stem from the duty placed on the domestic courts and tribunals, so far as possible, to interpret domestic legislation so as to accord with the Convention.

i)   The relationship between the Sex Discrimination Act 1975 and the Equal Pay Act 1970

The Sex Discrimination Act 1975 came into force in December 1975, along with the Equal Pay Act 1970. While the statutes are clearly complementary and wherever possible are to be construed 'so as to form a harmonious code'[12], it remains the case that they are mutually exclusive in their operation, so that an action must be brought under the correct statute[13]. The borderline is that the Equal Pay Act 1970 applies to contractual terms of employment, amenable to inclusion in the statutory 'equality clause', whereas the Sex Discrimination Act 1975 applies to discrimination on sexual grounds in matters outside the contract (such as recruitment, promotion and dismissal) and is thus much wider. The Race Relations Act 1976 was modelled on the Sex Discrimination Act 1975 (although it makes no distinction between pay and other aspects of employment), and cases decided under one Act will normally also be precedents for the other. The existence of two principal Acts concerning sex discrimination has given rise to complexity and confusion in this area, a situation exacerbated by the impact of EC law, and in particular Article 141 (ex Article 119) of the EC Treaty (discussed below). Although ostensibly concerned with equal pay, Article 141 (as explained and expanded by its supporting directives) is not confined to the terms of the Equal Pay Act 1970, and many of the cases decided by the European Court of Justice (ECJ) have concerned matters which, in English domestic law, would come under the heading of sex discrimination rather than equal pay. While European law has undoubtedly proved to be an extremely fertile source of developments in this area, it has added to the complexity of what was already an extremely complicated picture. As a result, the Equal Opportunities Commission has recommended the replacement of the two Acts by a single Sex Equality Act, incorporating European Community law and based on the principle of a

---

10   Art. 8 could also conceivably be used to challenge employers' dress and appearance rules; see p. 258 below.

11   See e.g. *Ahmad v Inner London Education Authority* [1978] 1 All ER 574, CA.

12   *Steel v UPOW* [1978] ICR 181 at 186, [1977] IRLR 288 at 290, per Phillips J; *Jenkins v Kingsgate (Clothing Productions) Ltd (No 2)* [1981] ICR 715, [1981] IRLR 388, EAT.

13   *Oliver v J P Malnick & Co (No 2)* [1984] ICR 458, IT is a good example. For an illustration of the difficulties raised by the distinction, see *Barclays Bank plc v James* [1990] ICR 333, [1990] IRLR 90; the case was subsequently settled on the understanding that the EAT's decision was wrong: [1990] IRLR 499.

fundamental right to equal treatment between men and women[14], but the Labour Government has indicated[15] that it does not believe that major legislative change is appropriate at this stage. The EOC has issued an Sex Discrimination Code of Practice[16] containing guidance on good employment practices for the elimination of sex and marriage discrimination and the promotion of equality of opportunity in employment, and a Code of Practice on Equal Pay[17].

ii) The impact of EC law[18]

EC law has had a profound impact on the development of the law on equal treatment. The principal measure is Article 141 (ex 119) of the EC Treaty, which provides that 'Each Member State shall ensure that the principle of equal pay for male and female workers for equal work or work of equal value is applied'[19]. In a series of landmark decisions[20], the ECJ has established that Article 119 (now 141) and its supporting directives (which extend the principle to pay and conditions and to work of equal value[1]) differs from the domestic law in several important respects, not least of which is that the definition of 'pay' under Community law is significantly wider than under domestic law. This is significant for three main reasons. The first is the supremacy of EC law over the national law of member states, which means that our domestic equality laws can be measured by the yardstick of Article 141 (ex 119) and the supporting directives. The principle of supremacy means that Article 141 (ex 119) prevails over any conflicting provisions of domestic law, in effect overriding them[2]; if domestic law fails properly to implement Community law, the European Commission can bring enforcement proceedings in the European Court in order to enforce compliance[3], and a person with sufficient standing can bring judicial review proceedings in the Divisional Court for the purpose of securing a declaration that UK primary legislation is incompatible with EC law. The significance of

14 *Equality in the 21st Century: A New Sex Equality Law for Britain* (EOC, 1998). The EOC also recommended, inter alia, the introduction of compulsory gender monitoring of the workforce, and of a legal duty on public authorities to work towards eliminating unlawful discrimination and to promote equality of opportunity.

15 The Government's response was heavily influenced by the Better Regulation Task Force's *Review of Anti-Discrimination Legislation in Great Britain* (May 1999).

16 S.I. 1985 No. 387.

17 S.I. 1997 No. 131.

18 See generally Barnard *European Employment Law* (2nd ed, 2000); Hervey and O'Keeffe *Sex Equality Law in the European Union* (1996); Ellis, *European Community Sex Equality Law* (1992); McCrudden (ed) *Women, Employment and European Equality Law* (1987).

19 Art. 119 only mentioned equal pay for *equal work*, not equal pay for *work of equal value*, but it was nevertheless held to cover work of equal value even before the amendment to the wording by the Amsterdam Treaty.

20 Beginning with *Macarthys Ltd v Smith* 129/79 [1980] ICR 672, [1980] IRLR 210, ECJ.

1 Directives 76/207/EEC (the Equal Treatment Directive) and 75/117/EEC (the Equal Pay Directive).

2 European Communities Act 1972, s. 2(1). See *Amministrazione delle Finanze dello Stato v Simmenthal SpA* [1978] ECR 629, ECJ.

3 As in Case 61/81 *EC Commission v United Kingdom* [1982] ICR 578, [1982] IRLR 333, where the ECJ held that the existing Equal Pay Act 1970 did not comply with the requirements of Equal Pay Directive 75/117 by allowing a woman to demand equal pay for work of equal value where there was no job evaluation scheme in force; this led to the introduction into domestic law in 1983 of the concept of equal pay for work of equal value (see p. 236, below). See also Case 165/82 *EC Commission v United Kingdom* [1984] ICR 192, [1984] IRLR 29, ECJ, concerning small firm and private household exceptions, discriminatory collective agreements and midwives.

judicial review in this area was graphically demonstrated in *R v Secretary of State for Employment, ex p EOC*[4], where the House of Lords, on an application for judicial review by the EOC, declared that the provisions of the Employment Protection (Consolidation) Act whereby part-time employees were subject to different qualifying conditions for unfair dismissal and statutory redundancy payments from those applicable to full-time employees were incompatible with EC law, as they indirectly discriminated against women; this led to the repeal of the offending provisions and the harmonisation of qualifying periods for full-time and part-time workers[5]. One of the most startling features of the decision in that case was the extent to which the court was prepared to question, and ultimately reject, the argument advanced on behalf of the UK Government that the qualifying period, although discriminatory, was justified for reasons of social policy[6]. The second reason is that Article 119 (now 141) has been held to have direct effect[7], in the sense that a complainant may rely upon it before a domestic court or employment tribunal[8], which must set aside any incompatible provision of domestic law to give effect to the supremacy of EC law; and the third reason is that the ECJ has held[9] that an individual who has suffered loss as a result of the failure of a member state to implement Community law fully may in certain circumstances sue the state for damages (a highly significant prospect in view of the continuing uncertainty over the requirements of Community law in this area).

While it is undoubtedly true that considerable steps forward have been taken by the use of EC law, this has been at the cost of equally considerable uncertainty, due in part to the case-by-case method of exploring the depths of Article 119 (now 141) and the supporting directives, which means that it is difficult to know how far the ECJ is likely to take the process (particularly as it tends to give narrow judgments only answering the specific questions asked, and only such of those questions as are necessary for the actual decision). Those seeking a detailed account should consult the specialist works on EC law; however, four problems are particularly worthy of mention here.

The first concerns the nature of a claim under Article 141 (ex 119), and in particular whether it gives rise to a separate, 'free-standing claim' which may be relied upon independently of any cause of action under domestic law. This is an important constitutional issue, but it also has very significant practical implications, particularly in relation to the time limits for bringing complaints under Article 141 (ex 119)[10]. On one view (sometimes referred to as the 'dualist' approach), the direct applicability of Article 141 (ex 119) means that it can confer entirely free-standing rights on individuals which may be enforced against employers in employment tribunals, so that a woman claiming equal pay may have two distinct

---

4   [1995] 1 AC 1, [1994] ICR 317 HL.
5   By the Employment Protection (Part-Time Employees) Regulations 1995, S.I. 1995 No. 31; see p. 458, below.
6   Compare the approach of the ECJ in *Nolte v Landesversicherungsanstalt Hannover* [1996] All ER (EC) 212, [1996] IRLR 225, and in *Megner v Innungskrankenkasse Vorderpfalz* [1996] All ER (EC) 212, [1996] IRLR 236, where the ECJ was content to accept the argument of the German Government that the measures in question were necessary to achieve the Government's social policy objectives, even in the apparent absence of any empirical evidence to support that case.
7   *Defrenne v SABENA (No 2)* [1976] ICR 547, [1976] ECR 455, ECJ.
8   *Secretary of State for Scotland v Wright and Hannah* [1991] IRLR 187, EAT; *Livingstone v Hepworth Refractories plc* [1992] ICR 287, [1992] IRLR 63, EAT.
9   In *Francovich v Italy* [1995] ICR 722, [1992] IRLR 84, ECJ; see p. 233, below.
10 A hugely important issue at the time of writing, in view of the many thousands of retrospective claims brought by part-time workers excluded from occupational pension schemes: see p. 301, below.

potential causes of action, one under the domestic law, the other under the Treaty. So, for example, in *Rankin v British Coal Corpn*[11], the EAT held that a woman made redundant in 1987 at the age of 61 had a directly enforceable right under Article 119 (now 141) to a redundancy payment equal to that which she would have received had she been a man, even though under the domestic law at that time women were not entitled to redundancy payments between the age of 60 and 65[12]; her claim for a redundancy payment was allowed to proceed, despite the fact that she did not bring proceedings until April 1990 (well outside the normal time limit for such claims in domestic law), because her claim was considered to be a free-standing claim under Article 119 (now 141) to which domestic time limits did not apply. Lord Coulsfield boldly stated:

'It is ... not now in dispute that a claim such as that made by the present appellant is a free-standing claim, and that Article 119 does not operate by amending or modifying the relevant domestic legislation, but confers an independent right upon persons who are entitled to rely on it[13].'

The alternative view (the 'monist' approach) is that Article 141 (ex 119) does not give rise to a separate, free-standing cause of action which has an existence apart from domestic law, but instead operates by disapplying any discriminatory provision in domestic legislation to the extent that it is incompatible with Community law. On this view, an employment tribunal, being a creature of statute, has no jurisdiction to entertain a claim for an infringement of rights under Community law outside the scope of the jurisdiction conferred by the domestic legislation, and claims before employment tribunals which invoke Article 141 (ex 119) may be subject to procedural conditions (including time limits) which are not less favourable than those applicable to similar actions of a domestic nature[14], unless those conditions are such as to make it impossible in practice to exercise the rights under Article 141 (ex 119)[15]. The prevailing view is that the monist approach is the correct one. In *Biggs v Somerset County Council*[16], a woman dismissed from her job as a part-time teacher in 1976, who lacked the necessary continuous service to complain of unfair dismissal at that time, brought an unfair

11 [1995] ICR 774, [1993] IRLR 69, EAT. See also *Secretary of State for Scotland v Wright* [1991] IRLR 187, EAT; *McKechnie v UBM Building Supplies (Southern) Ltd* [1991] ICR 710, [1991] IRLR 283, EAT.

12 The difference in the age limit for redundancy payments was removed by the Employment Act 1989 with effect from January 1990, but it was not until the ECJ decision in *Barber v Guardian Royal Exchange Assurance Group* [1991] 1 QB 344, [1990] ICR 616, that it became clear that discriminatory redundancy payments fell within the scope of Art. 119 (now 141); see p. 303, below.

13 [1993] IRLR 69, at p. 71. The EAT accepted that such claims must be subject to *some* time limit; on the facts, the time limit was held to run from the coming into force of the amending legislation in 1990 (that being the date upon which it could reasonably be said to be clear to any person affected that such a claim could properly be made), and the applicant's claim was therefore in time. See also *Methilhill Bowling Club v Hunter* [1995] ICR 793, [1995] IRLR 232, EAT, which probably represents the high water-mark of the 'free-standing claim' approach.

14 In the absence of any time limits in domestic or Community law which expressly apply to Art. 141.

15 *Rewe-Zentralfinanz GmbH v Landwirtschaftskammer für das Saarland* [1976] ECR 1989 ECJ; *Fisscher v Voorhuis Hengelo BV* [1995] ICR 635, [1994] IRLR 662, ECJ. In *Francovich v Italy* (above, n. 9), the ECJ said that the conditions for claiming reparation of loss laid down by national law 'may not be so framed as to make it virtually impossible or excessively difficult to obtain reparation'; see further p. 233, below.

16 [1996] ICR 364, [1996] IRLR 203, CA; affd [1995] ICR 811, [1995] IRLR 452, EAT.

dismissal complaint in June 1994 following the ruling in *R v Secretary of State for Employment, ex p EOC*. The EAT declined to follow the approach in *Rankin* based on the notion of a free-standing claim (Mummery J observing[17] that 'There is no Community right not to be unfairly dismissed'), and held that the applicant's claim was in fact a claim under the domestic unfair dismissal legislation (albeit with the offending qualifying conditions disapplied in order to comply with Community law), so that the normal three-month time limit for presenting a complaint applied[18]; as that period began to run from the date of the applicant's dismissal in 1976, her claim was out of time. Mummery J explained the relationship between domestic and Community law in the following terms:

> 'The imprecision in the expression "free-standing claims" has, in our view, created a misunderstanding. The claims are "free-standing" in the sense that they derive, ultimately, from a legal order recognised as superior in force to UK domestic law. It does not follow, however, that the two legal orders are independent or that Community rights are independent rights. Indeed, in most cases the reverse is the truth. Community law and domestic law are complementary. National law, not community law, confers the right not to be unfairly dismissed, setting the conditions on which the right may be enforced, the remedies available, and the appropriate procedures. Community law may operate to displace national law requirements, but unless national law is displaced, it is the duty of the tribunal to give effect to all the provisions of the statute from which it derives jurisdiction[19].'

The EAT controversially held that application of the domestic law time limits did not make it impossible in practice for the applicant to invoke her rights under Article 119 (now 141), as it would have been possible for her to present her unfair dismissal complaint to a tribunal in 1976, and to have argued at that time that the qualifying conditions then in force in UK domestic law which prima facie barred her claim were incompatible with EC law and should be disapplied. On appeal, the Court of Appeal upheld the EAT's decision[20], rejecting the argument that as the House of Lords did not declare the qualifying conditions to be indirectly discriminatory until March 1994, it was 'not reasonably practicable' for her to have brought her complaint within three months of her dismissal[1], on the grounds that there was no legal impediment which would have prevented her from arguing before a tribunal in 1976 that the restriction on claims by part-time workers was indirectly discriminatory and therefore contrary to Article 119 (now 141). Neill LJ acknowledged that, at that time, the fact that UK legislation might have to yield to Community law 'was fully appreciated only by a small

17   Ibid., at p. 458.
18   Subject to the usual extension for a further reasonable period if it was not reasonably practicable for the complaint to be presented within that time: see p. 417, below.
19   Ibid., at p. 460 (original emphasis). See also *Setiya v East Yorkshire Health Authority* [1995] ICR 799, [1995] IRLR 348, EAT, where Mummery J refused to allow an *appeal* out of time by a part-time employee whose unfair dismissal complaint was dismissed by a tribunal before the EOC decision on the grounds that he did not satisfy the qualifying conditions.
20   [1996] ICR 364, [1996] IRLR 203, CA. For further support for the monist approach, see *Barry v Midland Bank plc* [1998] IRLR 138, CA (affd [1999] ICR 859, [1999] IRLR 581, HL).
1   The Court of Appeal's interpretation of the words 'reasonably practicable' as being directed to some temporary impediment or hindrance, and confined to mistakes of fact rather than of law, appears to be narrower than the usual interpretation of those words in unfair dismissal cases; see p. 417, below.

number of people[2]', but he considered that 'it would be contrary to the principle of legal certainty to allow past transactions to be re-opened and limitation periods to be circumvented because the existing law at the relevant time had not yet been explained or had not been fully understood[3].' A similar approach was taken in *Staffordshire County Council v Barber*[4] where the Court of Appeal held that a part-time teacher who had brought a claim for a redundancy payment in 1992 which she subsequently withdrew[5] after receiving legal advice that she did not satisfy the qualifying conditions, was unable to make a fresh claim under Article 119 (now 141) for a redundancy payment or for compensation for unfair dismissal[6]; Neill LJ again emphasised that Article 119 does not confer any right to a redundancy payment or to compensation for unfair dismissal: '... the impact of Community law on claims brought before industrial tribunals is that Community law can be used to remove or circumvent barriers against or restrictions on a claim but that Community law does not create rights of action which have an existence apart from domestic law[7].'

The Court of Appeal's reluctance to sanction retrospective claims by part-time workers for unfair dismissal compensation and redundancy payments stretching back as far as 1976 was perhaps predictable in view of the thousands of similar claims which depended on the outcome of those cases[8]; the practical effect of the Court of Appeal's approach was that a significant proportion of the complaints brought by part-timers fell at the first hurdle.

The second problem is a general one in EC law, but of particular significance in this sphere given the broad terms in which Article 141 (ex 119) is drafted. What is the status of the two associated directives? The prevailing view is that a directive which is 'unconditional and sufficiently precise' can have vertical direct effect, i.e. it can be relied upon by individuals in the national courts and tribunals against the state or an 'organ of the state' (the reasoning being that as it is the state that should have put the directive properly into effect, which, ex hypothesi, has not been done, the state should not be allowed to rely on its own failure to implement the directive), but a directive does not have horizontal direct effect against individuals or non-state bodies (such as a private sector employer)[9]. This

2   Who, if indeed they exist, must surely be entitled to feel rather smug at their prescience.
3   At p. 207 (original emphasis); Neill LJ considered that the EOC case was merely declaratory of what the law had been since the primacy of Community law was first established by the European Communities Act 1972, s. 2. He also held for good measure that the claim had not been presented within a reasonable further period after the expiry of the time limit.
4   [1996] ICR 379, [1996] IRLR 209, CA. The appeal was heard on the same day as *Biggs* (above, n. 16); *Rankin* and *Methilhill* were not cited in either judgment, but the decisions in those cases must now be considered incorrect.
5   The Court of Appeal considered that the principles of cause of action or issue estoppel applied even though the applicant's claim was dismissed on withdrawal by the tribunal under r. 12(2)(c) of the Employment Tribunal Rules of Procedure (see now r. 13(2)(a)), rather than being rejected on its merits.
6   The principle of res judicata was held to apply to the applicant's unfair dismissal claim even though such a claim had not been advanced in the earlier proceedings, since the claim could have been litigated at that time.
7   At p. 212.
8   Cf. the decision of the ECJ in *Preston v Wolverhampton Healthcare NHS Trust* (C-78/98 [2000] IRLR 506), a test case on the exclusion of part-time workers from occupational pension schemes, where it was held that the six-month time limit on the presentation of claims under the Equal Pay Act does not contravene EC law; see p. 301 below.
9   The ECJ has stated that Directive 75/117 (the equal pay directive) does not extend Art. 119 (now 141) but is simply designed 'to facilitate the practical application' of the principle outlined in the Article, and 'in no way alters the content or scope of that principle as defined in the Treaty'. This suggests that Directive 75/117 has both vertical and horizontal direct effect: *Jenkins v Kingsgate (Clothing Productions) Ltd* [1981] ICR 592, ECJ.

view was accepted expressly in *Marshall v Southampton and South-West Hampshire Area Health Authority (Teaching)*[10] , where the ECJ decided that the compulsory retiring of a woman at an earlier age than a man in the same occupation (then lawful under English law) infringed the Equal Treatment Directive. That decision led to a major revision of the domestic law relating to compulsory retirement ages by the Sex Discrimination Act 1986, but while an employee in the public sector could rely on the Equal Treatment Directive to demand equal compulsory retirement ages even before that Act, an employee in the private sector could not. This, of course, raises the vexed question of just what counts as an 'organ of the state'? In *Foster v British Gas plc*[11] the ECJ ruled that Directive 76/207 could be relied upon against 'a body, whatever its legal form, which had been made responsible pursuant to a measure adopted by a public authority, for providing a public service under the control of that authority and had for that purpose special powers beyond those which resulted from the normal rules applicable in relations between individuals'; applying that ruling, the House of Lords subsequently held[12] that the nationalised British Gas Corporation was an organ of the state against which the directive could be directly relied upon by its employees to establish discrimination in compulsory retirement ages. In contrast, in *Doughty v Rolls Royce plc*[13] the Court of Appeal held that Rolls Royce was not an organ of the state (despite the fact that the state was the sole shareholder prior to its privatisation), as it had not been made responsible for providing a public service, nor was there any evidence that it had special powers.

The third problem is the extent to which EC law, and particularly the two directives, may be (or indeed should be) used as an aid to the interpretation of domestic legislation. The English courts have where possible attempted to construe domestic legislation in such a way as to accord with the requirements of EC law, if that can be done without distorting the meaning of the domestic legislation. One potential advantage of this approach is that it can enable a domestic court to give indirect effect to a directive in circumstances where the directive is not directly effective (e.g. because the complainant is not employed by an organ of the state). So, for example, in *Pickstone v Freemans plc*[14] , a case concerning the equal value provisions introduced into domestic law in 1983 in the wake of the ruling of the ECJ in *EC Commission v United Kingdom*[15] , the issue was whether the complainant was prevented from claiming equal pay for work of equal value by section 1(2)(c) of the Equal Pay Act 1970, which appeared to bar such a claim where any man was employed on like work or work rated as equivalent with the complainant. The Court of Appeal[16] , having held that the complainant could not bring her claim under English law because the wording of the section (which was unambiguous on its face) prevented her from doing so, held that she could bring a claim directly under Article 119 (now 141) instead; however, on further appeal the House of Lords approached the problem very differently[17] ,

10 152/84: [1986] ICR 335, [1986] IRLR 140, ECJ, noted Greenwood [1987] CLJ 9; Atkins (1986) 49 MLR 508. See also *Marshall (No 2)*, discussed at p. 270, below.
11 [1991] 1 QB 405, [1991] ICR 84, ECJ.
12 [1991] 2 AC 306, [1991] ICR 463, HL.
13 [1992] ICR 538, [1992] IRLR 126, CA. The Court of Appeal confirmed that the criteria formulated by the ECJ in *Foster* are cumulative, not alternative, requirements.
14 [1988] ICR 697, [1988] IRLR 357, HL; see also *Litster v Forth Dry Dock and Engineering Co Ltd* [1989] ICR 341, [1989] IRLR 161, HL.
15 See p. 279, below.
16 [1987] ICR 867, [1987] IRLR 218, CA.
17 Their Lordships declined to consider the correctness of the Court of Appeal's approach, since it was unnecessary to do so.

construing section 1(2)(c) purposively in order to bring it into line with Article 119 (now 141), even though it was necessary to adopt a strained interpretation of the ordinary literal meaning of the statute in order to achieve the desired result; as Lord Oliver put it, 'so to construe a provision which, on its face, is unambiguous involves a departure from a number of well-established rules of construction.' However, the purposive approach has its limits; the interpretation in *Pickstone* may have been strained, but their Lordships were careful to point out that the domestic statute was 'reasonably capable' of bearing the meaning given to it; the position is different where a provision of a domestic statute is unambiguously at variance with EC law. In *Duke v GEC Reliance Ltd*[18], the applicant sought to have section 6(4) of the Sex Discrimination Act 1975 (exclusion in respect of provisions in relation to death or retirement) reinterpreted in the light of *Marshall*'s case (above) so as to prohibit differential compulsory retirement ages[19]. Dismissing her appeal, the House of Lords pointed out that as s. 6(4) was in fact intended to preserve discriminatory retirement ages, it was not possible to construe the statute so as to give effect to the directive without distorting its meaning. Originally, there was some doubt as to whether the duty to construe domestic legislation so as to accord with a directive only arose where the domestic legislation was enacted to implement the directive; in *Pickstone*, it was clear that the English provision was meant to put into effect Article 119 (as interpreted by the ECJ in *EC Commission v United Kingdom*), whereas in *Duke* the relevant English provision had not been enacted in order to give effect to the Equal Treatment Directive, so that the interpretative nexus was missing. However, in *Marleasing SA v La Comercial Internacional de Alimentación SA*[20], the ECJ held that national courts are obliged to interpret national law as far as possible in the light of the wording and purpose of the directive in order to achieve the result sought by the directive, whether or not the national law in question pre-dates the relevant directive; that approach was subsequently approved by the House of Lords in *Webb v EMO Air Cargo (UK) Ltd*[1].

The fourth problem concerns the potential liability of member states for failure to implement Community law. In the landmark case of *Francovich v Italy*[2], the ECJ established the principle that 'a member state is obliged to make good the damage to individuals caused by a breach of Community law for which it is responsible', and held that an individual who has suffered loss as a result of the failure of a member state to take all the necessary steps to achieve the result required by a directive may in certain circumstances sue the state for damages under Community law. The possibility of a claim for damages against the state is of course of major significance for private sector employees, who (as seen above) have no remedy against their employer where the state has failed to implement a directive; it could also provide an alternative means of redress for employees who are unable to assert their rights against their employer under directly effective

---

18 [1988] ICR 339, [1988] IRLR 118, HL. See also *Finnegan v Clowney Youth Training Programme Ltd* [1990] ICR 462, [1990] IRLR 299, HL.

19 The applicant could not succeed otherwise, because (i) her claim arose before the commencement of the Sex Discrimination Act 1986 and so she could not invoke the amended English Law; (ii) unlike Mrs Marshall, she could not rely on the direct effect of the Equal Treatment Directive since she was not employed by an organ of the state (see above).

20 Case C-106/89: [1990] ECR I-4135, [1992] 1 CMLR 305. See Maltby (1993) 109 LQR 301; Greenwood [1992] CLJ 3.

1 [1992] 4 All ER 929, [1993] ICR 175, HL.

2 [1995] ICR 722, [1992] IRLR 84, ECJ. See Curtin (1992) 21 ILJ 74; Parker (1992) 108 LQR 180.

provisions of Community law because they are time-barred. After *Francovich*, there was considerable uncertainty over the circumstances in which a member state could be held liable in damages: for example, did the obligation to make reparation apply only where the provisions breached are not directly effective (as in *Francovich*), or could it be extended to provisions which could be relied upon directly by individuals in national courts? Would there be liability for incorrect implementation, or only for a total failure to implement? Was there a defence of good faith? In which court would an action for damages lie[3], and would it be subject to time limits? A number of these questions were subsequently answered in the joined cases of *Brasserie du Pêcheur SA v Germany* and *R v Secretary of State for Transport, ex p Factortame (No. 3)*[4], where the ECJ ruled that individuals suffering loss or injury as a result of breaches of Community law attributable to a member state are entitled to reparation where three conditions are satisfied: first, the rule of Community law infringed must be intended to confer rights upon individuals; secondly, the breach must be 'sufficiently serious'; and thirdly, there must be a direct causal link between the breach of the obligation resting on the state and the damage sustained by individuals. According to the ECJ, the decisive test for finding that a breach of Community law is 'sufficiently serious' is whether the member state concerned 'manifestly and gravely disregarded the limits on its discretion' in implementing the requirements of Community law[5]. The ECJ suggested that the factors which may be taken into consideration in determining whether a breach is sufficiently serious include the clarity and precision of the rule breached, the measure of discretion left by that rule to the national authorities, whether the infringement and the damage caused was intentional or involuntary, whether any error of law was excusable or inexcusable, the fact that the position taken by a Community institution may have contributed towards the omission, and the adoption or retention of national measures or practices contrary to Community law. The ECJ indicated that, on any view, a breach of Community law will be sufficiently serious 'if it has persisted despite a judgment finding the infringement in question to be established, or a preliminary ruling or settled case law of the Court on the matter from which it is clear that the conduct in question constituted an infringement', and confirmed that the liability of the state 'cannot be made conditional upon fault (intentional or negligent) on the part of the organ of the state responsible for the breach.' In *R v HM Treasury, ex p British Telecommunications plc*[6] (a case concerning the regulations introduced in the UK to implement the Public Utilities Procurement Directive[7]), the ECJ held that the same conditions apply where a member state has incorrectly transposed a directive into domestic law; although not an employment case, the ECJ's decision provides a very useful indication of the way in which the *Brasserie du Pecheur* test (and in particular the requirement that the state has 'manifestly and gravely disregarded the limits on the exercise of its powers') is likely to be interpreted in cases invoking Article 141 (ex 119) and the associated directives. On the facts, the ECJ held that while the regulations were in breach of the directive's provisions, the breach was not sufficiently serious to require the UK to

---

3   In *Secretary of State for Employment v Mann* [1997] ICR 209, the Court of Appeal considered that an employment tribunal has no jurisdiction to hear a *Francovich* claim, the appropriate forum being the High Court (or perhaps the County Court).
4   [1996] All ER (EC) 301, [1996] IRLR 267, ECJ.
5   This test is also used to determine the liability of Community institutions under Art. 215 of the Treaty of Rome: see *Bayerische HNL v EC Council and EC Commission* [1978] ECR 1209.
6   [1996] IRLR 300, ECJ.
7   [1996] IRLR 300, ECJ.

provide compensation for loss suffered as a result of the error, because the relevant Article of the directive was imprecisely worded and was 'reasonably capable of bearing ... the interpretation given to it by the UK in good faith and on the basis of arguments which were not entirely devoid of substance.' The UK's interpretation, which was shared by other member states, was not 'manifestly contrary' to the wording of the directive or to the objective pursued by it. Moreover, no guidance was available to the UK from the case law of the ECJ as to the interpretation of the provision at issue, nor did the Commission raise the matter when the regulations implementing the directive were adopted. This narrow interpretation of the *Brasserie du Pecheur* test inspires little confidence in the likely success of *Francovich* actions brought by employees hoping to recover damages from the UK Government to compensate them for their exclusion from occupational pension schemes or their inability to claim unfair dismissal compensation or redundancy payments from their employer.

Three further points arising from the *Brasserie du Pêcheur* case should also be noted: first, the ECJ held that the obligation of the state to make good the damage caused by breaches of Community law for which it is responsible applies even in the case of directly effective provisions[8], since 'the right of individuals to rely on the directly effective provisions of the Treaty before national courts is only a minimum guarantee and is not sufficient in itself to ensure the full and complete implementation of the Treaty'; secondly, where the stated conditions are satisfied, the state must make reparation for the consequences of the breach in accordance with the national laws on liability[9], provided that the conditions laid down by national law are not less favourable than those relating to similar domestic claims[10], or framed in such a way as in practice to make it impossible or excessively difficult to obtain reparation; and thirdly, the obligation to make reparation is not limited to damage sustained after the ECJ has made a ruling on the infringement in question (although once again, recovery is subject to the national law rules on retrospective claims).

It could be argued that in view of the continuing uncertainty over the relationship between domestic and Community law, and the obvious reluctance of the courts to impose retrospective liability on employers for acts which they had every reason to believe at the time were lawful, major changes in the law through ad hoc decisions of the ECJ and the domestic courts on the application of EC law should have prospective effect only. However, while the ECJ has accepted, in recognition of the principle of legal certainty, that in certain limited circumstances its decisions should only have prospective effect[11], the introduction of a general principle of prospective effect would require action at a political level (although in practice the strict application of domestic time-limits is likely to achieve a similar result, albeit by less politically controversial means).

8   A ruling which is potentially of great significance in view of the Court of Appeal's decision on retrospective claims in *Biggs v Somerset County Council* [1996] ICR 364, [1996] IRLR 203; see p. 229, above.

9   For example, on matters such as the forum for complaints, time limits, retrospective claims, calculation of damages, etc.

10   This obviously presents a difficulty where there is no similar domestic claim; in English law, the nearest equivalent claim is probably the tort of misfeasance in public office, but this is narrower in scope than the remedy envisaged by the ECJ, and the need to show intentional unlawful conduct arguably infringes the requirement that the conditions laid down by domestic law should not in practice make it impossible or excessively difficult to obtain reparation; significantly, the limitation period for a complaint of misfeasance in public office is six years (see n. 9, above).

11   As in *Barber v Guardian Royal Exchange Assurance Group* [1991] 1 QB 344, [1990] ICR 616, ECJ; see p. 303.

2 SEX DISCRIMINATION IN EMPLOYMENT

i) Application of the Sex Discrimination Act 1975

The aim of the Sex Discrimination Act 1975 is to prevent discrimination on the grounds of sex in several areas, including employment; although drafted in terms of women being the object of the discrimination, the Act is equally applicable to men[12] and also covers discrimination against a person on the ground of his or her marital status[13]. The parts which are relevant here apply to discrimination in 'employment' which is defined as employment under a contract of service or apprenticeship, or under a contract personally to execute any work or labour[14]; a person outside this definition may not claim the benefit of the relevant provision[15], except in the case of 'contract workers' (i.e. people working for A who have in fact been engaged by B and hired to A under a contract of supply of labour) who are included[16]. The Act prohibits discrimination at all stages of employment, whether in relation to the arrangements which the employer makes for selecting employees, the terms on which he offers employment, access to promotion, transfer, training or other benefits, or dismissal. However, once the employment has commenced any complaint relating to inequality in the terms and conditions of employment must be brought under the Equal Pay Act 1970, and not under the Sex Discrimination Act 1975[17]. The 1975 Act also gives a trade union member a right not to be discriminated against by the union on the ground of sex in matters of admission, expulsion and provision of union benefits, facilities, etc[18].

The Act specifies certain exclusions, some of which are particularly relevant to discrimination in employment. Thus, the application of the Act is modified in the case of the police, prison officers and ministers of religion[19], and cases where the alleged discrimination relates to the provision of services by the employer to the woman qua member of the public, rather than qua employee, are excluded[20]. On its introduction the Act contained a blanket immunity for the armed forces, but it was applied to them in 1995, albeit with an exemption for acts 'done for the purpose of ensuring the combat effectiveness of the armed forces'[1] (a dispensation which has been widely and controversially used in order to exclude women from certain sections of the armed forces). This more limited exemption was itself the subject of legal challenge in *Sirdar v Army Board*[2], where the ECJ held that the Royal Marines were not in breach of the Equal Treatment Directive by not engaging a woman as a cook, despite the seemingly tenuous connection between catering and combat effectiveness, on the grounds that their policy of 'inter-operability' meant that all members of the Marines had to be capable of

---

12 Sex Discrimination Act 1975, s. 2.
13 Ibid., s. 3. *Hurley v Mustoe* [1981] ICR 490, [1981] IRLR 208. It is not unlawful to discriminate against a single person on the ground of his or her marital status.
14 Ibid., s. 82(1). This is a deliberately extended definition, capable of taking in certain categories of the self-employed as well as employees: *Quinnen v Hovells* [1984] ICR 525, [1984] IRLR 227; *Gunning v Mirror Group Newspapers Ltd* [1986] 1 All ER 385, [1986] ICR 145, CA. The tribunal's jurisdiction is not dependent on the existence of an enforceable contract: *Leighton v Michael* [1996] IRLR 67, EAT.
15 *Knight v A-G* [1979] ICR 194, EAT.
16 Ibid., s. 9. *Rice v Fon-a-Car* [1980] ICR 133, EAT.
17 *Oliver v J P Malnick & Co (No. 2)* [1984] ICR 458, IT.
18 Ibid., s. 12. See Homans (1984) 13 ILJ 262.
19 Ibid., ss. 17–19.
20 Ibid., s. 6(7).
1   Ibid., s. 85(4), as substituted by S.I. 1994 No. 3276, with effect from 1 February 1995.
2   [2000] ICR 130, [2000] IRLR 47, ECJ.

serving as front-line commandos. The ECJ held that there is no general exception to the principle of equal treatment under Community law permitting the blanket exclusion of women from the armed forces, but that their exclusion from service in special combat units such as the Marines 'may' be justified under Article 2(2), provided the principle of proportionality is observed (i.e. that the exclusion is within the limits of what is appropriate and necessary in order to achieve the aim of protecting public security)[3].

There was previously an important (and extremely troublesome) exclusion for provisions in relation to death or retirement[4], which was considered necessary because discrimination in retirement provision (state and private) has historically been firmly entrenched, based on differential state pensionable ages. However, that exclusion became increasingly untenable in the light of the ECJ's rulings on the scope of Article 119 (now 141) and the associated directives, culminating in *Barber v Guardian Royal Exchange Assurance Group*[5], where the ECJ held that a pension paid under a contracted-out, private occupational pension scheme falls within the scope of Article 119 (now 141). The Government was therefore forced to reconsider the whole question of equality of treatment in pensions provision, and the Pensions Act 1995 introduced important new provisions requiring equal treatment in both membership of and rights under occupational pension schemes[6], repealing the existing exclusion in the sex discrimination and equal pay legislation for provisions in relation to death or retirement[7]. The issue is explored further below[8].

Two further exclusions may be relevant. The first is where questions of national security arise[9] and the second is where the discriminatory act is done under statutory authority[10]. The latter exclusion was significantly restricted by the Employment Act 1989. As originally enacted, section 51 of the Sex Discrimination Act 1975 gave a blanket exemption from liability for discriminatory acts which were necessary to comply with a statute or regulation in force before the passage of that Act. That provision was designed to avoid any conflict between the 1975 Act and the many, long-standing provisions in the Factories Act 1961 and other industrial safety legislation which gave special protection to women (e.g. by restricting night working or the number of hours that they could work in a factory). Many of the restrictions on women's employment had increasingly been seen as archaic and unnecessary, and most of the restrictions on the hours of work and

3 Article 2(2) of the Equal Treatment Directive permits a derogation from the principle of equal treatment in the case of occupational activities where the sex of the worker 'constitutes a determining factor'. See *Kreil v Bundesrepublik Deutschland* (C-285/98 (11 January 2000, unreported)), where the ECJ interpreted the derogation very narrowly.

4 Ibid., s. 6(4), as substituted by the Pensions Act 1995 s. 66(3). The equivalent exclusion in the Equal Pay Act 1970, s. 6(1A) and (2), was substituted by s. 66(1) of the 1995 Act.

5 [1991] 1 QB 344, [1990] ICR 616, ECJ.

6 Pensions Act 1995, ss. 62–66; see further, p. 308, below.

7 Ibid., s. 66(1), (3). Note however that s. 6(4) (as substituted by the 1995 Act) does not outlaw discrimination in relation to membership of, or rights under, an occupational scheme where such discrimination is not prohibited by the 1995 Act.

8 See p. 301, below.

9 Ibid., s. 52. The system whereby a minister could issue a conclusive certificate that national security was involved had to be discontinued (in the employment context) because of the decision of the ECJ in *Johnston v Chief Constable of the Royal Ulster Constabulary: 222/84* [1987] ICR 83, [1986] IRLR 263 that such a certificate was not conclusive in an action brought under the Equal Treatment Directive.

10 Ibid., s. 51, as substituted by the Employment Act 1989, s. 3(3). On the equivalent provision in the Race Relations Act 1976, see *Hampson v Department of Education and Science* [1990] IRLR 302, HL.

working conditions of women were removed by the Sex Discrimination Act 1986[11]. However, a number of restrictions remained in force, and in October 1986 the European Commission issued a reasoned opinion alleging that section 51 was inconsistent with the requirements of the Equal Treatment Directive 76/207/ EEC. In consequence the Employment Act 1989 narrowed the scope of the section 51 exemption[12], restricting it to discriminatory actions which are necessary to comply with a statutory provision concerning 'the protection of women' as regards pregnancy, maternity or other circumstances giving rise to risks specifically affecting women[13], and removed all remaining discriminatory provisions, such as the prohibition on the employment of women underground[14], other than those which could be justified on the basis of reproductive hazards[15]. Under the amended section 51 a discriminatory action will be lawful if it was 'necessary' in order to comply with a statutory requirement for the protection of women. In interpreting the word 'necessary' under the original section 51, the EAT in *Page v Freight Hire (Tank Haulage) Ltd*[16] was prepared to accept a broad measure of managerial prerogative, holding that an employer could defend his refusal to allow a woman to drive lorries containing dimethylformide (which could be harmful to women of child-bearing age) on the basis that this discriminatory action was 'reasonably necessary' to enable him to comply with his general duty under the Health and Safety at Work etc. Act 1974, s. 2[17].

Finally, one of the most controversial issues in discrimination law in recent years has been whether the prohibition of discrimination on the grounds of sex extends to discrimination on the grounds of sexual orientation. In *R v Ministry of Defence, ex p Smith*[18], an attempt was made to challenge the policy of the Ministry of Defence prohibiting homosexuals from serving in the armed forces as being a breach of the EC Equal Treatment Directive. The Court of Appeal declined to accept that the Directive had any application in such a case on the grounds that it is aimed at sex discrimination, not sexual orientation discrimination, and held that where an employer refuses to accept homosexuals of either sex, that is discrimination on grounds of sexual orientation, not on grounds of gender. On this narrow interpretation, the only situation in which sex discrimination law could apply to discrimination on grounds of sexual orientation would be if a gay man was treated less favourably than a lesbian, or vice versa[19]. However, in *P v S and Cornwall County Council*[20] the ECJ held that the dismissal of a transsexual who was proposing to undergo male to female gender reassignment did in fact

11   For further details, see the fourth edition of this book, ch. 11.
12   Employment Act 1989, s. 3(3). The 1989 Act went no further than was considered necessary to comply with European obligations, so that in areas other than employment and vocational training (the only areas covered by the directive) the exemption for discriminatory requirements which pre-date the 1975 Act still applies.
13   The list of restrictions which are still valid includes those on the employment of women in factories within four weeks of childbirth, the employment of women in work involving lead products, or exposure to ionising radiations, and the employment of women at sea or on aircraft during pregnancy: Employment Act 1989, s. 4.
14   The lifting of all restrictions on women working underground required the government to denounce ILO Convention 45 and Art. 8(4)(b) of the European Social Charter.
15   Exceptionally, s. 5 permits discrimination in connection with certain educational appointments, e.g. in Oxbridge women's colleges and religious schools.
16   [1981] ICR 299, [1981] IRLR 13.
17   See p. 744, below.
18   [1996] 1 All ER 257, [1996] IRLR 100, CA.
19   *Smith v Gardner Merchant Ltd* [1998] IRLR 510, CA.
20   [1996] All ER (EC) 397, [1996] IRLR 347, ECJ. See Wintemute (1997) 60 MLR 334; Skidmore (1987) 26 ILJ 51.

infringe the Equal Treatment Directive. It was argued on behalf of the employers in that case that as long as they would also have dismissed someone previously a woman who had undergone an operation to become a man, there was no discrimination on grounds of sex, but in a bold (and so it seemed at the time, potentially far-reaching) decision, the ECJ held that the principle of Community law that there should be 'no discrimination whatsoever on grounds of sex' was simply the expression of the fundamental Community law principle of equality, and that the scope of the Directive could not be confined to discrimination based on the fact that a person is of one or other sex, but also applied to discrimination arising from gender reassignment, the point being that 'such discrimination is based, essentially if not exclusively, on the sex of the person concerned.' In *Chessington World of Adventures Ltd v Reed*[1], the EAT in turn reinterpreted the Sex Discrimination Act, applying it to a case where the complainant had been discriminated against after declaring an intention to undergo gender reassignment, holding that where the reason for unfavourable treatment is sex-based, there is no requirement for the usual male/female comparison to be made. To formalise the position, the Government subsequently introduced regulations amending the Sex Discrimination Act to make it unlawful to treat a person less favourably because that person intends to undergo, is undergoing, or has undergone gender reassignment[2]. Where a person is absent from work as a result of undergoing gender reassignment, that person must not be treated less favourably than he would be if the absence was due to sickness or injury, or to some other cause such that, having regard to the circumstances, it is reasonable for him to be treated no less favourably[3].

After *P v S*, it was widely anticipated that the ECJ would hold that the Equal Treatment Directive also extended to discrimination on grounds of sexual orientation. However, in *Grant v South-West Trains*[4], the ECJ held that a female employee of a railway company had not been discriminated against because her lesbian partner had been denied travel concessions under a company policy, a condition of which restricted such concessions to workers living in a stable relationship with a person of the opposite sex. The Advocate-General's opinion was in her favour, but the ECJ dismissed her claim, holding that since the condition applied in the same way to male and female workers, it could not be regarded as constituting discrimination directly based on sex, since a male homosexual would also have been refused a travel concession for his male partner[5]. In the wake of the decision in *Grant*, the reference in *R v Secretary of State for Defence ex p Perkins*[6], which involved a challenge to the Ministry of Defence's policy prohibiting

---

1   [1997] IRLR 556, EAT.
2   Sex Discrimination Act 1975, s. 2A, added by the Sex Discrimination (Gender Reassignment) Regulations 1999, S.I. 1999 No. 1102. The new protection only applies to direct discrimination in employment and vocational training: ibid., s. 2A(1). Interestingly, in this context any discrimination in relation to pay falls to be dealt with under the Sex Discrimination Act, not the Equal Pay Act: s. 6(8). Note the specific genuine occupational qualifications relating to gender reassignment in ss. 7A and 7B.
3   Ibid., s. 2(3).
4   [1998] IRLR 206, ECJ.
5   Cf Wintemute, above n.20, at p. 347, who argues persuasively that sexual orientation discrimination is simultaneously discrimination based on sex, since if one applies the 'but for' test of direct discrimination laid down in *James v Eastleigh Borough Council* (see below), it is clear that the applicant would not have been treated in the same way 'but for' her sex, as the appropriate comparison would be the treatment accorded to a male employee with a female partner.
6   [1997] IRLR 297, QBD (referring the matter to the ECJ); (No 2) [1998] IRLR 508, QBD (withdrawing the reference).

homosexuals from serving in the armed forces, was withdrawn, on the basis that the ECJ had already settled the issue. In some respects *Perkins* was a far stronger case than *Grant,* as it involved the loss of a job, not just the loss of certain fringe benefits for a partner, and with hindsight it was perhaps unfortunate that it was *Grant* in which the ECJ was asked to rule on this important issue. In a further significant twist, in *Smith and Grady v United Kingdom*[7], the European Court of Human Rights held that the investigations conducted into the sexuality of two members of the British armed forces, one male and one female, and their subsequent discharge from the armed forces on the sole ground of their sexual orientation (pursuant to the Ministry of Defence's policy on homosexuals) constituted a violation of their right to respect for their private lives under Article 8 of the European Convention on Human Rights[8]. The UK Government had argued that the interference was justified under Article 8(2) as being 'necessary in a democratic society in the interests of national security ... for the prevention of disorder', because the presence of homosexuals within the armed forces would have a substantial and negative effect on morale and consequently on the fighting power and operational effectiveness of the armed forces, but the Court rejected the argument, observing that when the restrictions concern 'a most intimate aspect of an individual's private life', there must be 'particularly serious reasons' before such interference can be justified. The Court found that the perceived problems identified by the Ministry of Defence as a threat to the fighting power and operational effectiveness of the armed forces 'were founded solely upon the negative attitudes of heterosexual personnel towards those of homosexual orientation', and that 'these attitudes, even if sincerely felt by those who expressed them, ranged from stereotypical expressions of hostility to those of homosexual orientation, to vague expressions of unease about the presence of homosexual colleagues. To the extent that they represent a predisposed bias on the part of a heterosexual majority against a homosexual minority, these negative attitudes cannot, of themselves, be considered by the Court to amount to sufficient justification for the interference with the applicants' rights ... any more than similar negative attitudes towards those of a different race, origin or colour[9]'. This landmark decision will inevitably assume greater significance with the coming into force of the Human Rights Act 1998 incorporating the Convention into domestic law, not least because the Human Rights Act is directly enforceable against public authorities[10]. It also raises the intriguing possibility that the UK courts and tribunals may in due course be asked to reinterpret the Sex Discrimination Act as covering sexual orientation discrimination, in order to comply with their duty under the Human Rights Act to act in accordance with the Convention.

The other possible source of developments in this area is Article 13 of the EC Treaty[11], which provides a legal basis for Community legislation to combat

7   [1999] IRLR 734, ECtHR. Cf. the contemporaneous decision in *Lustig-Prean and Beckett v United Kingdom* (1999) 29 EHRR 548 to the same effect.

8   There was also held to be a violation of Article 13, in that they had no effective remedy before a national authority in relation to the violation of their right under Article 8.

9   Ibid., para. 90. In the wake of the ECHR decision, the Armed Forces Minister announced that the ban on homosexuals was to be replaced by a redrafted Code of Discipline covering inappropriate conduct generally, whether by heterosexuals or homosexuals.

10 See generally Hepple 'The Impact on Labour Law' in Markesinis (ed) *The Impact of the Human Rights Bill on English Law* (1998); Ewing 'The Human Rights Act and Labour Law' (1998) 27 ILJ 275; Palmer 'Human Rights: Implications for Labour Law' (2000) 59 CLJ 168.

11 See p. 224 above.

discrimination on grounds (inter alia) of sexual orientation. As seen in the introduction to this chapter, the Commission has published a draft Employment Directive 'establishing a general framework for equal treatment in employment and occupation' which would prohibit sexual orientation discrimination, but the prospect of achieving unanimity across the Community on the introduction of such legislation seems uncertain.

ii)   The meaning of 'discrimination'

a)   Direct discrimination

The Sex Discrimination Act 1975 covers both direct and indirect discrimination. Direct discrimination is defined in section 1(1)(a) as where the employer, on the ground of a woman's sex, treats her less favourably than he treats or would treat a man. The scope of section 1(1)(a) is wide, particularly as the House of Lords has made clear in the leading case of *James v Eastleigh Borough Council* [12] that in determining whether there as been direct discrimination the motive or purpose or intention of the alleged discriminator is irrelevant. In that case the applicant, a man of 61, complained that he had been discriminated against by the local authority because he had been charged 75p to swim in the municipal swimming baths, while his wife of the same age had been admitted free under the authority's policy of allowing free entry to those who had reached the state pensionable age of 65 for men and 60 for women. The Court of Appeal had held (distinguishing an earlier House of Lords decision to the effect that a subjective motive or intention to discriminate is not a condition of liability[13]) that there had not been less favourable treatment on the ground of sex because the reason for the concession was to benefit pensioners and not to discriminate against men. In the words of the Vice-Chancellor, Browne-Wilkinson VC: 'In my judgment there is a clear distinction between the ground or reason for which a person acts and his intention in so acting.' However, on further appeal the House of Lords overturned this decision, rejecting the subjective approach and instead affirming that the correct approach is an objective one: 'Would the complainant have received the same treatment but for his sex?' On the facts it was clear that the less favourable treatment would not have occurred but for the complainant's sex, and so there was direct discrimination. The fact that the council did not intend to discriminate against the applicant, and that its reason for adopting the policy of concessions to pensioners was an honourable one[14], was considered to be irrelevant.

It follows that a good motive on the part of the employer (e.g. a belief that the discriminatory action is in the applicant's own best interests) is no excuse for what is, on the wording, an act of discrimination[15], nor is the fact that the employer

12   [1990] ICR 554, [1990] IRLR 288, HL; reversing [1989] ICR 423, [1989] IRLR 318, CA.
13   *Birmingham City Council v Equal Opportunities Commission* [1989] AC 1155, [1989] IRLR 173, HL.
14   The case is a good illustration of the fact that, other than the GOQ's (genuine occupational qualifications – see p. 256 below), there is no 'justification' defence available in a complaint of direct discrimination.
15   *Peake v Automotive Products Ltd* [1977] IRLR 105 (reversed on other grounds, [1977] ICR 968, [1977] IRLR 365, CA); *Grieg v Community Industry* [1979] ICR 356, [1979] IRLR 158; *Din v Carrington Viyella Ltd* [1982] ICR 256, [1982] IRLR 281. While motive is not relevant when determining whether discrimination has occurred, it may be relevant when deciding the level of compensation to be awarded: *Chief Constable of the Greater Manchester Police v Hope* [1999] ICR 338, EAT.

has been pressurised to discriminate by a third party, e.g. a trade union, or the applicant's fellow employees[16]. Given that one of the aims of the legislation is to discourage the treatment of women or men *en masse* as capable of certain things and incapable of others, general stereotypical assumptions (e.g. that women cannot do heavy work or that men are not suited to secretarial work or to working in the caring professions) are likely to be held to be discriminatory, and an employer who acts on such assumptions may well contravene the statute[17].

For there to be a finding of direct discrimination the applicant must show that she has been treated 'less favourably' than a man on the grounds of her sex. Unlike the Equal Pay Act, which works on the basis of a comparison between the treatment of the applicant and that of a named comparator (or comparators), the Sex Discrimination Act is based on a comparison with a hypothetical comparator, and the comparison 'must be such that the relevant circumstances in the one case are the same, or not materially different, in the other'[18]. Differential treatment does not in itself amount to discrimination: 'If discrimination is to be established, it is necessary to show not merely that the sexes are treated differently, but that the treatment accorded to one is less favourable than the treatment accorded to the other'[19]. The need to show treatment which is less favourable, and not merely different, has been problematic, first, because it can give rise to the kind of tendentious 'separate but equal' arguments once used to justify racial segregation in the USA; and secondly, because it enables an employer to argue that because he treats his male and female employees equally badly, his treatment of one sex is no less favourable than his treatment of the other[20]. On the whole the courts have been robust in resisting such arguments, although not without the occasional unfortunate lapse. Indeed, in the first case under the 1975 Act to come before the Court of Appeal, *Peake v Automotive Products Ltd*[1], the Court was prepared to disregard differential treatment on the grounds that it was too minor. In that case, the employer allowed women to leave the factory five minutes before the men, in the interests of safety and to avoid women being caught in the rush to the gates. One of the men complained to a tribunal that this was unlawful discrimination against men. The EAT upheld his claim, but the Court of Appeal unanimously rejected it, on the grounds that the different treatment was in the interests of safety and good administration (in the words of Lord Denning MR: 'it is not discriminatory for mankind to treat womankind with the courtesy and chivalry which we have been taught to believe is right conduct in our society'), and that in any event the employer's action was harmless and could be disregarded under the de minimis principle. In the later case of *Ministry of Defence v Jeremiah*[2] the Court of Appeal reconsidered the approach taken in *Peake*. In that case it was held that requiring a man employed in an ordnance factory to perform dirty and unpleasant work making 'colour-bursting' shells when women

---

16   *R v Commission for Racial Equality, ex p Westminster City Council* [1985] ICR 827, [1985] IRLR 426, CA (a race relations case).
17   *Skyrail Oceanic Ltd v Coleman* [1981] ICR 864, [1981] IRLR 398, CA; *Horsey v Dyfed County Council* [1982] ICR 755, [1982] IRLR 395.
18   Sex Discrimination Act 1975, s. 5(3). This requirement has been especially problematic in cases involving pregnancy discrimination, where for obvious reasons it is not possible to make the necessary comparison. The point is discussed further below, at p. 347.
19   *Smith v Safeway plc* [1996] IRLR 456, CA, per Phillips J at p. 458.
20   An argument customarily referred to by the authors as the 'But I'm a bastard to everyone' defence.
1   [1977] ICR 968, [1977] IRLR 365, CA, restrictively interpreted by the EAT in *Grieg v Community Industry* n. 15, above.
2   [1979] 3 All ER 833, [1979] IRLR 436, CA.

working in the factory were excused from such work was less favourable treatment within the meaning of the Act, and therefore unlawful. Lord Denning MR stated that the approach to the definition of direct discrimination taken in *Peake* (i.e. exempting 'sensible administrative arrangements' in the interests of health or chivalry) was wrong and that the decision was only supportable on the alternative ground given (i.e. that on the facts the discrimination was too minor to be effective, under the de minimis principle). On the facts it was held that requiring only the men to do the work in question was unlawful, and the fact that they were paid extra to do it was irrelevant.

While the approach of the Court of Appeal in *Jeremiah v Ministry of Defence* showed a stronger adherence to the actual wording of the Act, it still seemed to allow some scope for the de minimis defence. In subsequent cases the courts have tended to take a more robust approach, particularly where the alleged less favourable treatment involves the denial of an opportunity afforded to persons of the opposite sex. In *Jeremiah*, Brightman LJ suggested that as differentiation is not necessarily discriminatory, a mere deprivation of choice might not of itself be unlawful[3]. However, in *Birmingham City Council, v Equal Opportunities Commission*[4] (a case involving access to grammar schools), the House of Lords held that in order to establish less favourable treatment on the grounds of sex, it is enough that members of one sex are deprived of a choice which is valued by them and which (even though others may take a different view) is a choice obviously valued on reasonable grounds by many others. A similarly broad approach to the concept of less favourable treatment was taken in *Gill v El Vino Co Ltd*[5], where the Court of Appeal held that it was unlawful for a wine bar to refuse to serve women at the bar. In that case Eveleigh LJ stated:

'I find it very difficult to invoke the maxim de minimis non curat lex in a situation where that which has been denied to the plaintiff is the very thing that Parliament seeks to provide, namely facilities and services on an equal basis[6].'

There is however an important caveat that needs to be entered, as the EAT held in *Burrett v West Birmingham Health Authority*[7] (a case involving dress and appearance rules) that the question of whether there is less favourable treatment is an objective one for the tribunal to decide; the fact that a complainant subjectively considers that she is being less favourably treated does not of itself establish that there is 'less favourable treatment' within the meaning of section 1(1)(a)[8]. A similar approach was taken in *Stewart v Cleveland Guest (Engineering) Ltd*[9], where the EAT refused to overturn the tribunal's finding that the employers had not discriminated against the complainant on grounds of sex by allowing male employees to display nude pin-ups in the workplace, even though they knew that the pictures were offensive to her. According to the EAT, there is room for disagreement as to what is or is not less favourable treatment, and the employment tribunal is best placed to make a decision on the facts of a particular

3   Ibid., at 840 and 440.
4   [1989] IRLR 173, HL.
5   [1983] IRLR 206, CA.
6   At 208.
7   [1994] IRLR 7, EAT. See p. 258, below.
8   Per Knox J, ibid., at p. 8. The House of Lords' decision in *R v Birmingham City Council, ex p EOC*, above, was not referred to in the judgment.
9   [1994] IRLR 440, EAT. See p. 260, below.

case. In subsequent cases involving alleged sexual harassment, the need to show less favourable treatment has been downplayed, and conduct which is 'gender-specific' has been held to constitute less favourable treatment on grounds of sex, without the need for a comparison[10].

Finally, it must be remembered that the complainant has to be able to show the necessary causal connection between the less favourable treatment and the sex or marital status of the complainant; if there is some other genuine reason for the less favourable treatment which is untainted by discrimination (e.g. the employer genuinely needs someone strong or experienced and the woman in question is weak or inexperienced), then that is not 'on the ground of her sex' and discrimination is not established. So for example, in *Bullock v Alice Ottley School*[11], the employers maintained a retirement age of 60 for teaching and domestic staff (who were primarily female) and 65 for gardeners and maintenance staff (who were all male). The applicant, a domestic worker who was retired at 60, complained that she had been treated less favourably because of her sex, but the Court of Appeal held that there was no direct discrimination on grounds of sex because there was no evidence that a man in the same job would have been treated any differently. Greater difficulties arise where the employer acts from mixed motives, not all of which constitute unlawful discrimination. It is clearly established that the unlawful motive need not be the sole reason for the employer's action. In *Owen and Briggs v James*[12], a race discrimination case, the Court of Appeal held that where there is more than one operating cause, it is enough if the unlawful motive is an 'important factor' in the employer's decision; in other words, the unlawful motive must be of sufficient weight in the decision-making process to be treated as a cause, but not necessarily the sole cause, of the act thus motivated[13].

b)   Indirect discrimination

Discrimination can, of course, take more subtle forms than the overt form envisaged above. In particular, it could take the form of a rule, policy, criterion or practice which, while not expressly mentioning sex or marital status, in practice puts those of one sex or marital status at a disadvantage because it has a disproportionate impact on the members of that group; for example, a requirement that applicants for a particular post be between 17 and 28, while gender-neutral on its face, may be held to discriminate indirectly against women because in practice many women would be unavailable for work between those ages because of family commitments[14]. Similarly, a rule that a candidate for a job should not have young children could be said to discriminate indirectly against married women in that it would tend to rule out large numbers of such persons[15]. On the other hand, it could be the case that the factor causing the discriminatory

---

10 See e.g. *British Telecommunications plc v Williams* [1997] IRLR 668, EAT. See p. 260.
11 [1993] ICR 138, [1992] IRLR 564, CA. The decision confirms that there is nothing unlawful about having different retirement ages for different jobs, provided there is no direct or indirect discrimination based on a prohibited ground.
12 [1982] ICR 618, [1982] IRLR 502, CA. Compare *Seide v Gillette Industries Ltd* [1980] IRLR 427, where the EAT suggested that the applicant must be able to show that the discrimination was the activating or the substantial cause. Both cases must now, of course, be considered in the light of the objective test laid down in *James v Eastleigh Borough Council*, above.
13 *Nagarajan v Agnew* [1995] ICR 520, [1994] IRLR 61, EAT.
14 *Price v Civil Service Commission* [1978] ICR 27, [1977] IRLR 291.
15 *Thorndyke v Bell Fruit (North Central) Ltd* [1979] IRLR 1, IT; *Hurley v Mustoe* [1981] ICR 490, [1981] IRLR 208, EAT.

effect is in fact necessary for the efficient performance of the job, and so a balance has to be struck so that legitimate business needs are not jeopardised, while at the same time recognising that the fact that the discrimination is indirect will often make it, if anything, more insidious. The statutory compromise is the concept of indirect discrimination enacted in section 1(1)(b), which applies when the following four conditions are satisfied:

i)   the employer has applied a requirement or condition which he also applies or would apply equally to a man;

ii)   the requirement or condition is such that the proportion of women who can comply with it is considerably smaller than the proportion of men who can comply with it;

iii) the requirement or condition cannot be shown to be justifiable irrespective of the sex of the person to whom it is applied; and

iv) it is to the complainant's detriment because she cannot comply with it.

In practice this subsection will operate by the complainant seeking to show i), ii) and iv) and, if she is successful, the burden then passing to the employer to argue justification under iii). The requirements are complex, and have given rise to a number of problems of interpretation.

The need for the complainant to show a specific 'requirement or condition' has been a major obstacle to a successful claim of indirect discrimination. In several of the earlier sex discrimination cases the EAT gave the phrase 'requirement or condition' a broad construction, holding that it was capable of including any kind of employment practice[16], but in *Perera v Civil Service Commission (No. 2)*[17] the equivalent provision in the Race Relations Act 1976 was interpreted far more narrowly by the Court of Appeal as meaning an absolute barrier or a 'must'. However, in *Falkirk Council v Whyte*[18], the Scottish EAT declined to apply this stricter test to a case under the Sex Discrimination Act involving selection criteria for a job which were stated to be 'desirable' rather than an absolute bar. The EAT held that the tribunal was entitled to give a liberal interpretation to the meaning of 'requirement or condition' under the Sex Discrimination Act, and to find on the facts that a criterion was a 'requirement or condition', even though it was only stated to be a desirable factor, where it was clear that it had been a decisive factor in the selection process. Significantly, the EAT further held that the race discrimination cases, and in particular *Perera*, would not be followed in the sex discrimination context if the case turned on whether a factor had to be an absolute bar for the post in question in order to become a 'requirement or condition'. It is submitted that the broader, purposive approach of the Scottish EAT is to be preferred. It removes an undesirable obstacle to a successful indirect discrimination claim, and also has the distinct advantage of being more closely aligned with European Community law, since it has become clear that under Article 119 (now 141), indirect discrimination can be established without the necessity for showing the application of a 'requirement or condition'. In *Enderby v Frenchay Health Authority*[19], the ECJ held that a prima facie case of sex discrimination arose under Article 119 (now 141) where statistics revealed an appreciable difference in pay between two jobs of equal value, one of which is carried out almost exclusively by women and the other predominantly by men,

---

16   *Clarke v Eley (IMI) Kynoch Ltd* [1983] ICR 165, [1982] IRLR 482; *Watches of Switzerland Ltd v Savell* [1983] IRLR 141; *Home Office v Holmes* [1984] ICR 678, [1984] IRLR 299.

17   *Perera v Civil Service Commission (No 2)* [1983] ICR 428, [1983] IRLR 166, CA; affirmed in *Meer v Tower Hamlets London Borough* [1988] IRLR 399, CA.

18   [1997] IRLR 560, EAT.

19   [1994] 1 All ER 495, [1994] ICR 112, ECJ.

shifting the burden of proof onto the employer to show an objective justification for the difference in pay. In that case, the comparison was between a group of predominantly female speech therapists who were receiving less pay than a group of predominantly male clinical psychologists and pharmacists, in circumstances where it was not possible to identify any requirement or condition applied by the employer which had an adverse impact on the former group. It was widely anticipated that the ECJ decision in *Enderby* would signal the end of the narrow approach in *Perera*, at least in sex discrimination cases. However, in *Bhudi v IMI Refiners Ltd* [20], the EAT held that, notwithstanding *Enderby*, it is still essential under section 1(1)(b) of the Sex Discrimination Act for the complainant to show that the employer has applied a requirement or condition. The explanation for this surprising ruling was that *Enderby* was said to be concerned with the EC provisions relating to equal pay, not equal treatment, where different considerations apply; and furthermore, that even if it is possible under EC law to establish indirect discrimination without having to show the application of a requirement or condition, it is not possible to construe section 1(1)(b) so as to accord with the EC position, since the wording of the statute does not allow such an interpretation[1]. It is submitted that the decision in *Bhudi* is unnecessarily narrow, and that the approach of the Scottish EAT in *Whyte* is to be preferred. Indeed, it could be argued that the very fact that the UK courts before *Perera* were prepared to give the words 'requirement or condition' a broader, more purposive interpretation undermines the argument of the EAT in *Bhudi* that it is not possible to construe section 1(1)(b) so as to accord with *Enderby*. In any event, the approach taken in *Bhudi* appears to be inconsistent with the EC Burden of Proof Directive[2], which defines indirect discrimination as covering any 'apparently neutral provision, criterion or practice'; the matter will therefore need to be reconsidered before the Directive is implemented in 2001[3].

In determining whether a 'considerably smaller' proportion can comply with the requirement or condition, the EAT have treated the selection of the appropriate pool of comparison as a question of fact for the tribunal[4], sometimes with unfortunate results. In *Kidd v DRG (UK) Ltd* [5], the complainant argued that a 'part-timers first' redundancy selection procedure was indirectly discriminatory on grounds of sex (because a greater proportion of women work part-time) and

20 [1994] ICR 307, [1994] IRLR 204, EAT. See also *Meade-Hill v British Council* [1995] IRLR 478, CA, where it was held that the inclusion of a contractual term (in that case, a mobility clause) imposing an obligation on a party to the contract constitutes the application of a requirement or condition, even if not invoked.

1 Cf *Webb v EMO Air Cargo (UK) Ltd* [1992] 4 All ER 929, [1993] ICR 175, where the House of Lords held that the UK courts should construe domestic legislation in any field covered by a Directive so as to accord with the interpretation of the Directive, as laid down by the ECJ, if that can be done without distorting the meaning of the domestic legislation.

2 Directive 97/80/EC.

3 The EOC has recommended that the definition of indirect discrimination in the Burden of Proof Directive (97/80/EC) should be adopted, modified to extend to 'policy' as well as 'provision, criterion or practice': *Equality in the 21st Century: A New Sex Equality Law for Britain* (EOC, 1998).

4 *Price v Civil Service Commission* [1978] ICR 27, [1977] IRLR 291; *Perera v Civil Service Commission (No 2)* [1982] ICR 350, [1982] IRLR 147, EAT.

5 [1985] ICR 405, [1985] IRLR 190. The decision has been widely criticised: see for example Byre *Indirect Discrimination*, EOC, 1987. The case demonstrates that the law on indirect discrimination can only work properly if the tribunal looks at what happens in practice (e.g. that most children are in fact still cared for by women, not by men); it founders if a tribunal looks instead at what might be considered desirable in the way of sex equality (e.g. men undertaking a greater degree of responsibility for looking after children).

marital status (because part-time workers are more likely to be married women with children), but the tribunal took as the pool for comparison those households where there are small children, and were not prepared to accept as a generalisation that in such households more women than men look after children, so that the claim of indirect discrimination failed. In *Jones v University of Manchester*[6], the university advertised a post of careers adviser as being for 'a graduate, preferably aged 27-35 years with a record of successful experience in an industrial, commercial or public service setting.' The complainant, although well qualified for the post, was not shortlisted, apparently due to the fact that she was aged 46 at the time, having obtained her degree as a mature student. The tribunal upheld her complaint that the age requirement indirectly discriminated on grounds of sex against women who were mature students, as statistics showed that the proportion of women graduates obtaining their degrees as mature students who could comply with the age requirement was considerably smaller than the proportion of male graduates. The EAT reversed the tribunal on this point, holding that the wrong pool for comparison had been used, and this view was upheld on further appeal. The Court of Appeal held that the appropriate pool for comparison was all men and women with the required qualifications for the job, not including the requirement complained of (i.e. all graduates with the required experience, not just those who had graduated as mature students), and warned of the dangers of allowing the pool for comparison to be sub-divided or altered in a way that might allow the outcome to be manipulated. As Ralph Gibson LJ put it, the legislation demands comparison of like with like, '... but that [does] not authorise an applicant to subdivide her sex. There would be many who could demonstrate disadvantage if they could elect their own parameters'[7].

Having established the appropriate pool for comparison, the next stage for the tribunal is to determine whether the proportion of women who 'can comply with' the requirement or condition is 'considerably smaller' than the proportion of men who can comply with it[8]. The EAT has held that 'can comply with' means 'can comply in practice with', so that it is not enough for an employer to argue that it was theoretically physically possible for a woman to comply with the requirement, if in practice it would be harder for her to do so than it would be for a man. Thus a requirement for a particular post that the applicant had to be between 17 and 28, which applied to both sexes, was held to be capable of being indirectly discriminatory because, although it was of course physically possible for a woman to comply, the tribunal accepted that a considerable number of women would be unable to apply when between those ages because of child-rearing commitments[9]. This practical approach is, it is suggested, in line with

6   [1993] ICR 474, [1993] IRLR 218, CA.

7   Ibid., at p. 224. See also *R v Secretary of State for Education, ex p Schaffter* [1987] IRLR 53, DC, where Schiemann J cautioned against reducing the size of the pool to a very small size, because there is 'very real risk that you have incorporated an act of discrimination into your definition' (at p. 56).

8   The Burden of Proof Directive (No. 97/80/EC) defines indirect discrimination in terms of disadvantage to a 'substantially higher proportion' of the members of one sex; the EOC has proposed that this definition should be adopted, but with the phrase 'substantially higher proportion' replaced by 'disproportionate number': *Equality in the 21st Century: A New Sex Equality Law for Britain* (EOC, 1998).

9   *Price v Civil Service Commission* [1978] ICR 27, [1977] IRLR 291, affirmed by the House of Lords in the important race relations case of *Mandla v Dowell Lee* [1983] ICR 385, [1983] IRLR 209. As the question is the proportion of women who can comply, not necessarily the number, over-elaborate statistical evidence may not be relevant: *Perera v Civil Service Commission (No 2)* [1982] ICR 350, [1982] IRLR 147; affd [1983] ICR 428 [1983] IRLR 166, CA.

the intent of the section. The crux of the definition is the need to show that a 'considerably smaller' proportion of women than men can comply with the requirement or condition. The EAT has held that what is or is not a 'considerably smaller' proportion is a matter for the employment tribunal, the words 'considerably smaller' being ordinary words in common usage[10]. In *R v Secretary of State for Education, ex p Schaffter*[11], Schiemann J explained the proper application of the test in the following terms:

'... The subsection would seem to indicate that what you should do is to establish: first, the proportion of all women who can comply with the requirement – I shall call this X per cent; secondly, the proportion of all men who can comply with the requirement – I shall call this Y per cent; thirdly, compare X and Y and determine whether one is considerably smaller than the other.'

In determining whether a 'considerably smaller' proportion of women can comply, a tribunal is entitled to take account of its own knowledge and experience[12], particularly in a traditionally male occupation where the number of women employed is so small as to make a purely statistical comparison unreliable. In *London Underground v Edwards (No 2)*[13], the applicant, a female train operator, complained that a change in the employer's rostering arrangements indirectly discriminated against her, because the proportion of female train operators who could comply with the new arrangements was considerably smaller than the proportion of male operators. The relevant statistics were that 100 per cent of the 2,023 of the male train operators could comply with the new arrangements, compared with 95.2 per cent (or 20 out of 21) of the 21 female train operators (the applicant being the only existing female train operator who could not comply)[14]. The Court of Appeal held that the tribunal was entitled to find that the change was indirectly discriminatory, even though statistically the percentage difference did not appear to be very great, because the tribunal was entitled to have regard to the comparatively small numbers of women involved, and to its common knowledge of the proportionately larger number of women than men with primary responsibility for the care of children[15].

10   *Staffordshire County Council v Black* [1995] IRLR 234, EAT.
11   [1987] IRLR 53, DC. This test was approved by the Court of Appeal in *Jones v University of Manchester* [1993] ICR 474, [1993] IRLR 218. See also *McCausland v Dungannon District Council* [1993] IRLR 583, a case under the Fair Employment (Northern Ireland) Act 1989, in which the Northern Ireland Court of Appeal held that a considerably smaller proportion of Catholics could comply with a condition of being an existing employee, where 1.5 per cent of all Catholics and 2.1 per cent of all Protestants were able to meet the condition. At first sight the difference between the two figures might appear to be insignificantly small, but when one is expressed as a percentage of the other, the proportion of Catholics who could comply was only 71 per cent of the other, which was held to be a considerably smaller proportion.
12   *Briggs v North Eastern Education and Library Board* [1990] IRLR 181, NICA. But cf. *Kidd v DRG (UK) Ltd*, above, where the EAT held that a tribunal may decline to act 'on generalised assumptions which it regards as too unsafe for acceptance' (e.g. in that case, that women's domestic responsibilities make it more difficult for them to work full-time).
13   [1998] IRLR 364, CA.
14   As the new arrangements only involved a change to existing terms and conditions, the Court of Appeal agreed that relevant pool for comparison was all the existing drivers.
15   Potter LJ noted that if only one other female operator had been unable to comply, that would immediately have put the percentage of women who could not comply up to 10 per cent.

While the above case demonstrates that statistics need to be treated with caution where the small numbers involved make statistical comparisons unreliable, it could be argued that where the quality of the statistical evidence is good, a tribunal should be prepared to find that a 'considerably smaller' proportion of women than men can comply where the difference in the compliance rates is statistically significant; on this view, the purpose of the requirement to show a 'considerable' disparity of impact is simply to ensure that any difference in compliance rates is in fact due to sex discrimination, rather than to chance. To date, the UK courts have declined to accept the argument that a disparity of impact will be 'considerable' if it is statistically significant, although in *R v Secretary of State for Employment, ex p Seymour-Smith (No. 2)*[16] the House of Lords acknowledged that the quality of the statistical information is relevant in determining what degree of disparate impact need be shown in order to establish indirect sex discrimination. In that case the applicants, who were dismissed from their employment in 1991, sought judicial review of the then two-year qualifying period for bringing an unfair dismissal complaint on the grounds that it indirectly discriminated against women, contrary to the Equal Treatment Directive. The House of Lords held, following a reference to the ECJ, that the statistical evidence for the period from 1985 to 1991 demonstrated that in 1991 the two-year qualifying period had a considerably greater adverse impact on women than on men, so as to amount to indirect discrimination contrary to Article 119 (now 141)[17]. Significantly, their Lordships held that a considerable disparity can be more readily established if the statistical evidence covers a long period and the figures show a persistent and relatively constant disparity[18]: 'In such a case a lesser statistical disparity may suffice to show that the disparity is considerable than if the statistics cover only a short period or if they present an uneven picture'[19]. You may think that this looks remarkably like a test of statistical significance; we could not possibly comment...

Some of the greatest difficulty has been experienced with the defence of justification, which often lies at the heart of an indirect discrimination case. Initially, a stringent view of the defence was taken. Phillips J held in *Steel v UPOW*[20] that generally there is a heavy onus on an employer asserting justification, and that in particular he must be able to show that the discriminatory requirement or condition in question was necessary for his business, not merely convenient. However, the strictness of this test was progressively watered down in a series of cases under the equivalent provision in the Race Relations Act 1976, in particular by the Court of Appeal in *Ojutiku v Manpower Services Commission*[1] where the necessity test was rejected in favour of an approach based on the existence of reasons which would be 'acceptable to right-thinking people as sound and tolerable

---

16 [2000] IRLR 263, HL (No. 2); see also [1999] IRLR 253, ECJ; [1997] IRLR 315, HL; [1995] ICR 889, [1995] IRLR 464, CA; [1994] IRLR 448, Div Ct.

17 Lord Nicholls, Lord Goff and Lord Jauncey, Lord Slynn and Lord Steyn disagreeing on this point. The ECJ had indicated that in its view the statistics for 1985 did not appear to show that a considerably smaller percentage of women than men was able to fulfil the two-year requirement: [1999] IRLR 253, at para. 64. On the facts, their Lordships held, by a 3:2 majority, that any adverse effect was in fact justified: see p. 251.

18 On this point their Lordships echoed the view of the ECJ that statistical evidence revealing 'a lesser but persistent and relatively constant disparity over a long period' could also be evidence of indirect sex discrimination: ibid., para. 61.

19 Per Lord Nicholls, at p. 270.

20 [1978] ICR 181, [1977] IRLR 288, followed in *Hurley v Mustoe* [1981] ICR 490, [1981] IRLR 208, EAT.

1 [1982] ICR 661, [1982] IRLR 418, CA. See *Singh v Rowntree MacKintosh Ltd* [1979] ICR 554, [1979] IRLR 199, EAT and *Panesar v Nestlé Co Ltd* [1980] ICR 144n, [1980] IRLR 64, CA.

reasons'[2]. It seemed for a time as though the tests of justification in sex and race discrimination cases had diverged as a result of the decision of the House of Lords in the equal pay case of *Rainey v Greater Glasgow Health Board*[3], where the stricter test of objective justification (laid down by the ECJ in *Bilka-Kaufhaus GmbH v Weber von Hartz*[4] as a defence to an action under Article 119 (now 141)) was applied by the House of Lords to the test of genuine material difference under section 1(3) of the Equal Pay Act 1970. In *Rainey*, Lord Keith stated that there was no material distinction in principle between the need to show 'objectively justified grounds' of difference in order to establish a defence under section 1(3) of the Equal Pay Act, and the need to justify a requirement or condition in a case of indirect discrimination under the Sex Discrimination Act, a comment which seemed to lend support to the argument that *Ojutiku* had been impliedly overruled by *Rainey*. However, in *Hampson v Department of Education and Science*[5], the Court of Appeal said that there was no significant difference between the test adopted by Stephenson LJ in *Ojutiku*[6] and that adopted by the House of Lords in *Rainey*, and ruled that whether a requirement or condition is justifiable requires an objective balance to be struck between the discriminatory effect of the requirement or condition and the reasonable needs of the person who applies it[7]. The test in *Hampson* was subsequently approved by the House of Lords in *Webb v EMO Air Cargo (UK) Ltd*[8]. It is submitted that this is the preferable view, for it would be unrealistic (and, on a more general level, undesirable) to expect courts or tribunals to apply a different standard in sex and race discrimination cases when the two statutes are in fact in pari materia on this point.

In *Cobb v Secretary of State for Employment*[9], Wood J explained the correct approach to the question of justification in the following terms:

'It was for the respondent to satisfy the Tribunal that the decisions which he took were objectively justified for economic, administrative or other reasons. It was for the Tribunal to decide what facts it found proved, and to carry out the balancing exercise involved, taking into account all the surrounding circumstances and giving due emphasis to the degree of discrimination caused against the object or aim to be achieved – the principle of proportionality ... we do not accept that the production of a mass of statistics, or of sociological or expert evidence is a necessity on these issues, nor do we accept that the absence of such evidence proves that the reasoning of the [respondent] is flawed ... a respondent is entitled to take a broad and rational view provided that it is based on logic, and is in the view of the Tribunal a tenable view. He is under no obligation to prove

---

2   Per Eveleigh LJ, at p. 421 (see also Kerr LJ to similar effect). Stephenson LJ preferred an approach based on the objective balancing of the discriminatory effect against the discriminator's need for it.

3   [1987] ICR 129, [1987] IRLR 26, HL: see p. 292, below.

4   170/84: [1987] ICR 110, [1986] IRLR 317, ECJ.

5   [1989] IRLR 69; overruled on other grounds, [1991] 1 AC 171, [1990] ICR 511, HL.

6   See n. 1 above. Balcombe LJ considered that neither Eveleigh LJ nor Kerr LJ in *Ojutiku* had indicated what they considered the test to be.

7   This test was approved by the Northern Ireland Court of Appeal in *Briggs v North Eastern Education and Library Board* [1990] IRLR 181, and by the EAT in *Greater Manchester Police Authority v Lea* [1990] IRLR 372.

8   [1992] 4 All ER 929, [1993] ICR 175, HL. Lord Keith stated expressly that the *Hampson* test must now be regarded as the appropriate one and as superseding that expressed by Eveleigh LJ in *Ojutiku*.

9   [1989] ICR 506, [1989] IRLR 464, EAT.

that there was no other way of achieving his object, however expensive and administratively complicated[10].'

Cobb involved a challenge to the eligibility criteria for admission to the Community Programme, a Government scheme which provided temporary employment for the long-term unemployed. In *R v Secretary of State for Employment, ex p Seymour-Smith (No. 2)*[11], which involved a challenge under Article 119 (now 141) to the legality of the two-year qualifying period for claiming unfair dismissal, the House of Lords held that the onus is on the member state to show (1) that the allegedly discriminatory rule reflects a legitimate aim of its social policy, (2) that this aim is unrelated to any discrimination based on sex, and (3) that the member state could reasonably consider that the means chosen were suitable for attaining that aim. It was also held that the test of justification applied in the lower courts was too stringent, and that governments should be afforded a broad measure of discretion in pursuing their social policy objectives (although generalised assumptions, lacking any actual foundation, would not be good enough)[12]. Significantly, however, the House of Lords held that if a government introduces a measure which proves to have a disparately adverse impact, it has a duty to take reasonable steps to monitor the working of that measure by reviewing the position periodically, because if the benefits hoped for do not materialise, the retention of such a measure may no longer be objectively justifiable[13]. There is no reason in principle why this duty to keep indirectly discriminatory policies and practices under periodic review should not also be applied to employers in both the public and private sector.

The question of justification is an issue of fact for the tribunal[14], with the result that a tribunal's decision on the matter will be difficult if not impossible to challenge provided it applies the correct tests[15]. This approach has been criticised for leading to an undesirable level of uncertainty and inconsistent decisions in this sensitive area[16], but it is very much in line with the 'anti-legalism' drive by the courts discussed in ch. 8. A good illustration of the potential for inconsistency may be seen by comparing two decisions of the EAT concerning refusal to allow a female employee to return to work part-time after maternity leave. In the first, *Home Office v Holmes*[17], the EAT upheld a tribunal decision that a refusal to allow a woman with children to transfer to part-time working constituted indirect sex discrimination (the 'requirement or condition' in question being the obligation

---

10   At 468.
11   Ibid., n. 16.
12   On the facts, the House of Lords held that the Secretary of State had discharged the burden of showing that the increase in the qualifying period in 1985, and its retention in 1991, were objectively justified.
13   Per Lord Nicholls, ibid., at p. 271. His Lordship also observed: 'The greater the disparity of impact, the greater the diligence which can reasonably be expected of the government'.
14   A point stressed by the House of Lords in the important race discrimination case of *Mandla v Dowell Lee* [1983] ICR 385, [1983] IRLR 209, HL.
15   In *University of Manchester v Jones* [1992] ICR 52 the EAT suggested that the exercise of a judicial discretion 'may be re-examined where irrelevant factors have been taken into consideration or where relevant considerations have been omitted in its exercise'. (The decision of the EAT was affirmed by the Court of Appeal: [1993] ICR 474, [1993] IRLR 218).
16   See in particular the remarks of Browne-Wilkinson J in *Clarke v Eley (IMI) Kynoch Ltd* [1983] ICR 165, [1982] IRLR 482.
17   [1984] ICR 678, [1984] IRLR 299. See also *London Underground Ltd v Edwards (No 2)* [1998] IRLR 364, CA, where the employer was unable to show that indirectly discriminatory rostering arrangements were justified.

to work full time) which, on the facts, was not justifiable. The potential effect of such a decision is considerable, particularly when allied to the woman's statutory right to return to work after maternity (the eventual outcome possibly being to leave full-time work and return to part-time work, at least where the employer cannot show good reason to refuse this)[18]. However, the case also demonstrates how difficult it can be to predict the outcome of indirect discrimination claims, for while the decision was hailed in the press as a major step forward in women's rights, in fact it was no such thing. At the end of his judgment, Waite P went out of his way to state that the decision was taken entirely on the particular facts of the case ('It is easy to imagine other instances, not strikingly different from hers, where the result would not be the same'), and the point was subsequently reinforced by the decision of the Scottish EAT in *Greater Glasgow Health Board v Carey*[19], where on facts very similar to those in *Holmes* it was held that a refusal to allow a return to work part-time after maternity leave was justified by considerations of administrative efficiency[20].

c)   Victimisation

The Sex Discrimination Act creates a third form of discrimination, victimisation, which applies where a person is subjected to less favourable treatment because he or she has brought proceedings or given evidence in proceedings against the discriminator under the Act or the Equal Pay Act 1970, or made allegations in good faith of breaches of one of these Acts[1]. However, to benefit from the statutory protection the applicant must show that the reason for the less favourable treatment is because he or she has done one of the protected acts. Until recently, the case law on victimisation required there to be some conscious motivation in the mind of the alleged discriminator which caused him to treat the complainant less favourably than other persons[2], but in *Nagarajan v London Regional Transport*[3], the House of Lords held that in complaints of victimisation under the Race Relations Act (and by analogy, under the Sex Discrimination Act) the motive of the alleged discriminator is irrelevant, and the question to be asked is the simple causative one, i.e. whether the complainant would have been treated in that way but for his race[4]. While the motive of the alleged discriminator is irrelevant, a claim of victimisation will still fail if the employer can show that he did not treat the complainant any less favourably than he would have treated a person who had not done one of the protected acts[5], and here it is important to note that in a

---

18   See p. 338, below. The Part-Time Workers Directive protects part-time workers from less favourable treatment by reason of their part-time status, but it does not give any right to insist on a transfer to part-time work. See p. 20 below.

19   [1987] IRLR 484.

20   For a further example of conflicting decisions on similar facts (this time in the context of part-timers–first redundancy selection procedures), compare *Clarke v Eley (IMI) Kynoch Ltd* [1983] ICR 165, [1982] IRLR 482 with *Kidd v DRG (UK) Ltd* [1985] ICR 405, [1985] IRLR 190. The decision in *Kidd* has been heavily criticised: see p. 246.

1   Sex Discrimination Act 1975, s. 4. For the comparable provision in the context of race discrimination, see the Race Relations Act 1976, s. 2.

2   See e.g. *Aziz v Trinity Street Taxis Ltd* [1988] ICR 534, [1988] IRLR 204, CA.

3   [1999] ICR 877, [1999] IRLR 572, HL, reversing the Court of Appeal.

4   This is the *James v Eastleigh Borough Council* test which applies in complaints of direct discrimination under section 1: see p. 241. Dicta to the contrary in *Aziz* (above, n. 2) were said to be incorrect. Cf the strong dissenting judgment of Lord Browne-Wilkinson, who said that he did not understand how one could victimise someone subconsciously.

5   On the identification of the appropriate comparator, see *Chief Constable of West Yorkshire v Khan* [2000] IRLR 324, CA, discussed below at p. 275.

related context, the House of Lords has held that it is not legitimate to infer less favourable treatment simply because the employer treats an employee unfairly[6].

The limits of the protection against victimisation under UK law were graphically demonstrated in two recent cases where the complaints were held to fall outside the domestic statutory provisions. In *Waters v Metropolitan Police Comr*[7], the employee alleged that she had been victimised by the employer for alleging sexual harassment by a work colleague. The Court of Appeal held that the protection against victimisation only applies where the alleged act is one for which the employer would be vicariously liable[8], and as the alleged harassment was not committed in the 'course of employment', the employer could not be held vicariously liable for it, and could not therefore be held to have victimised the complainant for making the allegations[9]. In *Nagarajan v Agnew*[10], a case under the Race Relations Act 1976, the EAT held that the protection against victimisation is limited to events occurring during the relevant employment, and does not cover the situation where an employer subjects a former employee to a detriment (in that case, the provision of an adverse reference) after the employment relationship has ended; there may however be a difference between the position under the Sex Discrimination Act and the Race Relations Act on this point, because in *Coote v Granada Hospitality Ltd*[11], the ECJ held that Article 6 of the Equal Treatment Directive requires member states to introduce measures protecting workers from discrimination after the employment relationship has ended, and in the resumed hearing[12], the EAT reinterpreted the 1975 Act as covering victimisation by an ex-employer. Unless the Race Relations Act is similarly reinterpreted[13], there will be a significant and undesirable divergence between the two Acts on this important point.

d) Positive discrimination[14]

The Sex Discrimination Act is based on a neutral or symmetrical model of equality. It gives each individual, male or female, the right not to be treated less favourably on grounds of his or her sex or marital status. As *James v Eastleigh Borough Council*[15] demonstrated, the fact that the defendant acted from a good or worthy motive is no defence to a complaint of unlawful discrimination. It follows that any preferential treatment aimed at redressing the historic disadvantage experienced by women will normally be illegal if it involves the less favourable treatment of a man. Such measures – generally referred to as 'positive discrimination' – must

6   *Zafar v Glasgow City Council* [1998] IRLR 36, HL. See p. 263 below.
7   [1997] IRLR 589, CA. See p. 267 below.
8   See further p. 265, below. Section 4(1)(d) of the Act only applies where the complainant has '... alleged that the discriminator or any other person has committed an act *which ... would amount to a contravention of this Act...*'.
9   The practical importance of the decision has arguably been reduced by the broad approach to vicarious liability taken in some recent cases: see p. 266.
10 [1995] ICR 520, [1994] IRLR 61, EAT. See also p. 244, above.
11 [1998] IRLR 656, ECJ.
12 *(No 2)* [1999] IRLR 452, EAT
13 The problem here being that the Court of Appeal has held (in *Post Office v Adekeye* [1997] ICR 110, [1997] IRLR 105) that the RRA does not apply to discrimination against an ex-employee: see p. 274.
14 See Fredman 'Reversing Discrimination' (1997) 113 LQR 575; Pitt 'Can Reverse Discrimination Be Justified?', in Hepple and Szyszczak (eds.) *Discrimination: the Limits of Law* (1992), ch. 16; McCrudden 'Rethinking positive action' (1986) 15 ILJ 219.
15 [1990] IRLR 288, HL. See also *Jepson and Dyas-Elliott v Labour Party* [1996] IRLR 116, IT (women-only shortlists unlawful).

be distinguished from measures which do not involve preferential treatment of one group but which are designed to promote a greater degree of equality of opportunity within the workplace (so-called 'positive action'). While positive discrimination will normally be unlawful, 'positive action' is not prohibited. The Code of Practice issued by the EOC suggests a number of such measures, including the introduction of a monitoring policy and the taking of positive steps to identify and remove potential barriers to the recruitment and advancement of women[16]. Other measures aimed at promoting equal opportunities which fall short of positive discrimination might include the development of policies and practices designed to assist disadvantaged groups (e.g. 'family-friendly' policies), encouraging applications from under-represented groups, and the setting of targets to reduce under-representation.

One exception to the prohibition on positive discrimination is section 47, which allows discrimination in favour of one sex in vocational training where it appears that in the previous 12 months there were no persons of that sex employed in the work in question in Great Britain, or an area within Great Britain, or the number was comparatively small[17]. Where such under-representation is established, it is not unlawful to provide women-only or men-only training facilities to help fit the under-represented sex for that work. There is also a special exemption targeted at those in special need of training because they have been out of full-time employment discharging domestic or family responsibilities[18]. This provision enables employers to run training courses targeted at women returning to work after maternity leave, irrespective of whether there is a general under-representation of women in that kind of work.

This may be one area in which UK law is not out of step with EC law, although the position is not entirely clear. In general terms, EC law adopts the same symmetrical approach to equality as English law. Article 2(4) of the Equal Treatment Directive provides that the Directive 'shall be without prejudice to measures to promote equal opportunity for men and women, in particular by removing existing inequalities which affect women's opportunities', but the ECJ has been reluctant to interpret this provision as legitimising positive discrimination. In *Kalanke v Freie Hansestadt Bremen*[19], the ECJ considered the legality of a so-called 'tie-break' provision in the relevant domestic provisions, whereby women who had the same qualifications as men for the same post were to be given priority in sectors where they were underrepresented. The ECJ held that national rules which guarantee women absolute and unconditional priority for appointment or promotion go beyond promoting equal opportunities and overstep the limits of the exception to the principle of equal treatment in Article 2(4)[20]; the exception was interpreted strictly, as permitting national measures relating to access to employment 'which give a specific advantage to women with a view to improving their ability to compete in the labour market and to pursue a career in an equal footing with men'. The decision in *Kalanke* was greeted with

16   EOC Code of Practice, paras. 37–40.
17   See Sacks 'Tackling Discrimination Positively', in Hepple and Szyszczak, op cit, n. 14. Employers are also permitted to target training on under-represented groups within their organisation: ibid., s. 48. There are parallel provisions in the Race Relations Act 1976, ss. 37 and 38.
18   Sex Discrimination Act 1975, s. 47(3).
19   [1996] ICR 314, [1995] IRLR 660, ECJ.
20   The ECJ held that the provisions in question fell outside this exception by substituting for equal opportunity 'the result which is only to be arrived at by providing such equality of opportunity.'

dismay (not least by the European Commission), and when the ECJ next had an opportunity to consider the issue, in *Marschall v Land Nordrhein-Westfalen*[1], there was a noticeable softening of the tone. That case also involved a tie-break provision giving women priority for promotion in the event of equal suitability, competence and professional performance, but with the crucial addition of a 'saving clause' whereby women were not to be given priority if reasons specific to an individual male candidate tilted the balance in his favour. The ECJ noted that even where male and female candidates are equally qualified, male candidates tend to be promoted because of prejudices and stereotypes concerning the role and capacities of women in working life, and the fear that women will interrupt their working lives more frequently, be less flexible in their working hours because of household and family duties, and be absent from work more frequently because of pregnancy or childbirth. The ECJ acknowledged that because of these factors, the mere fact that male and female candidates are equally qualified 'does not mean that they have the same chances', and held that although a national rule which guaranteed absolute and unconditional priority for women would not be lawful, a rule which counteracted the prejudicial effects of the attitudes and behaviour described above by giving preferential treatment to equally-qualified women candidates could be lawful if it provided 'a guarantee that the candidatures will be the subject of an objective assessment which will take account of all criteria specific to the individual candidates and will override the priority accorded to the female candidates where one or more of the criteria tilts the balance in favour of the male candidate' (all of which begs the question of what 'equally qualified' means in this context).

Finally, as a result of an amendment made by the Amsterdam Treaty, the EC Treaty now contains an express provision permitting positive measures aimed at promoting equality. Article 141(4) states: 'With a view to ensuring full equality in practice between men and women in working life, the principle of equal treatment shall not prevent any Member State from maintaining or adopting measures providing for specific advantages in order to make it easier for the under-represented sex to pursue a vocational activity or to prevent or compensate for disadvantages in professional careers.' It remains to be seen whether this provision will be interpreted more broadly by the ECJ than the existing derogation in Article 2(4) of the Equal Treatment Directive.

iii) Discrimination before employment

The first and perhaps most difficult stage at which a woman may encounter discrimination in employment is when she applies for a job. It is unlawful under section 6(1) for an employer to discriminate against a woman in the arrangements[2] he makes for the selection procedure, in the terms on which he offers her employment[3], or by refusing or deliberately omitting to offer her the

---

1   [1998] IRLR 39, ECJ. See also *Badeck's Application* [2000] IRLR 432, ECJ.
2   On the meaning of 'arrangements', see *Brennan v J H Dewhurst Ltd* [1984] ICR 52, [1983] IRLR 357 (biased interview).
3   Where the terms in question are amenable to inclusion in an 'equality clause', the claim should be under the Equal Pay Act 1970, not the Sex Discrimination Act – ibid., s. 8. On equal pay, see pp. 278-309, below.

employment[4]. Once again, a certain amount of realism is necessary in construing these provisions, so that for example it is not necessarily unlawful for an employer to ask a woman a question at an interview which would not be asked of a man (particularly questions about the suitability of a woman for a job where the employment of a man has been normal in the past); the issue is whether, by asking the question, the woman was treated less favourably on grounds of her sex than a man would be treated[5]. The law against discriminatory selection arrangements is indirectly strengthened by section 38, which makes it unlawful to publish or cause to be published a job advertisement which indicates or might reasonably be understood as indicating an intention to discriminate[6]. Only the Equal Opportunities Commission may bring proceedings against a publisher or advertiser under section 38[7]. At one time it was thought that a discriminatory advertisement qualified as an 'arrangement' for selection and therefore constituted unlawful discrimination under section 6(1), but the EAT has held that this is not so[8], and that only the statutory enforcement agencies can bring proceedings in respect of an advertisement which indicates an intention to discriminate. According to the EAT, it is necessary to distinguish between an intention to do an act of discrimination, and an act of discrimination; placing a discriminatory advertisement indicates an intention to do an act of discrimination, but it is not an act of discrimination in itself[9].

Section 7 creates a statutory exemption from liability for unlawful discrimination in selection for employment where being a man or a woman is a genuine occupational qualification (GOQ) for the job. The GOQ defence is an important exception to the normal rule that motive is irrelevant in cases of direct discrimination. It is designed to avoid some of the more obvious absurdities of complete equality, but it is important that the boundaries of the exception are not stretched too far, lest the protection against discrimination be undermined, and the EAT has held that section 7 lays down exhaustively the categories of job which come within the GOQ defence[10]. Thus, an employer can advertise for and appoint a man where the job calls for a man for physiological reasons (though this does not mean strength and stamina simpliciter), where a male actor is needed for a stage part, where a man is necessary to preserve decency or privacy (e.g. a lavatory attendant or possibly a tailor), where the job entails living in a private home in close contact with the employer (e.g. an old lady's companion)[11],

4   The Court of Appeal held in *Post Office v Adekeye (No 2)* (see n. 13 above) that the parallel provision in the Race Relations Act does not cover a dismissed employee seeking reinstatement on appeal, but the Sex Discrimination Act may need to be reinterpreted in order to comply with the Equal Treatment Directive on this point: see p. 253 above.

5   *Saunders v Richmond-upon-Thames London Borough Council* [1978] ICR 75, [1977] IRLR 362. The EOC's Code of Practice, para. 23, advises against asking questions about the candidate's marriage or family intentions.

6   It seems that this will include an advertisement which is indirectly discriminatory: *Commission for Racial Equality v Dutton* [1989] QB 783, [1989] IRLR 8, CA.

7   Sex Discrimination Act 1975, s. 72.

8   *Cardiff Women's Aid v Hartup* [1994] IRLR 390, EAT (a case under the equivalent provisions in the Race Relations Act 1976, s.4(1)(a)).

9   Quaere whether the outcome would have been different if the complainant had actually applied for and been refused the job in question?

10   *Grieg v Community Industry* [1979] ICR 356, [1979] IRLR 158, EAT. It could be argued that s. 7 is wider than the category of exclusions permitted by the Equal Treatment Directive, Art. 2(2).

11   There used to be a formal exemption in the case of domestic servants but this (along with the small firm exemption) was repealed by the Sex Discrimination Act 1986 in the wake of the decision of the ECJ in *EC Commission v United Kingdom*: Case 165/82 [1984] ICR 192, [1984] IRLR 29; the exemption for private homes is all that remains.

where the location is such that personal facilities can only reasonably be expected for men (the case of the proverbial lighthouse keeper), and where the work is in a men's hospital or prison and should not reasonably be done by a woman. Also included in the list are welfare or educational services which can 'most effectively be provided' by a man[12], jobs involving duties abroad in a country where those duties, by law or custom, are performed by men, and the employment of a man as half of a husband and wife team (e.g. chauffeur and housekeeper). The exemption will not apply if there are other employees who are capable of performing the duties in question and whom it would be reasonable for the employer to employ on those duties, provided they already[13] exist in sufficient numbers to meet the employer's likely requirements without undue inconvenience[14].

iv) Discrimination during employment

Under section 6(2) it is unlawful for an employer to discriminate against a woman during her employment in the way he affords or refuses to afford her access to opportunities for promotion, transfer or training[15], or to any other benefits, facilities[16] or services. It is also unlawful if he discriminates against her by subjecting her to any 'detriment'. It is clear from *Ministry of Defence v Jeremiah*[17] that 'detriment' is to be given its ordinary, common-sense meaning of being put under a disadvantage. This means that differentiation between sexes is not in itself unlawful discrimination, for there must be some element of disadvantage; it may also be possible for a tribunal or court to consider a claimed disadvantage to be so minor as to be disregarded on the de minimis principle, although as seen earlier the scope of the de minimis defence is probably very narrow[18]. Once there is a detriment, however, it will not be a defence for an employer to show that he takes the detriment into account by compensating those who experience it (e.g. where only men are obliged to do certain disagreeable work, but receive an extra payment in respect of it); there may still be unlawful discrimination even though special rates of pay are given for that work[19].

Two issues which have given rise to particular difficulty, and therefore warrant special attention, are dress and appearance rules, and sexual harassment.

---

12   This phrase also appears in the equivalent provision of the Race Relations Act, s. 5(2)(d); for its interpretation in that context, see *Tottenham Green Under Fives' Centre v Marshall* [1989] ICR 214, [1989] IRLR 147, EAT; *Tottenham Green Under Fives' Centre v Marshall (No 2)* [1991] ICR 320, [1991] IRLR 162, EAT; *Lambeth London Borough v Commission for Racial Equality* [1990] ICR 768, [1990] IRLR 231, CA.

13   See *Lasertop Ltd v Webster* [1997] IRLR 498, EAT.

14   Section 7(4); see *Etam plc v Rowan* [1989] IRLR 150 (employer could have employed male assistant in women's clothing shop because there were sufficient female assistants to preserve decency). See also *Wylie v Dee & Co (Menswear) Ltd* [1978] IRLR 103 (inside leg measurements).

15   This could occur in a redundancy situation where a new job is created but the employer refuses to transfer a person of a particular sex to it (subject to the genuine occupational qualification defence): *Timex Corpn v Hodgson* [1982] ICR 63, [1981] IRLR 530, EAT.

16   This refers to facilities which already exist: *Clymo v London Borough of Wandsworth* [1989] IRLR 241, EAT.

17   [1979] 3 All ER 833, [1979] IRLR 436, CA, disapproving the reasoning on this point in *Peake v Automotive Products Ltd* [1977] ICR 968, [1977] IRLR 365, CA – see p. 242, above.

18   See p. 243 above.

19   See *Ministry of Defence v Jeremiah*, n. 17 above.

a)   Dress and appearance rules

It is not uncommon for employers to impose rules on employees concerning their dress and appearance while at work. This may be done for operational reasons (e.g. in the interests of safety and hygiene), or simply because the employer is seeking to promote a particular corporate image which involves the employees wearing a uniform or observing restrictions on, for example, their hair-style or the wearing of jewellery. Such rules often impose different requirements on men and women, reflecting current perceptions of conventional appearance, yet it could be argued that under the test of direct discrimination approved by the House of Lords in *James v Eastleigh Borough Council*[20] , any such differentiation necessarily constitutes discrimination on the grounds of sex, because 'but for' a person's sex, the gender-specific appearance requirement would not have been applied[1] . Furthermore, the underlying rationale of the Sex Discrimination Act was to tackle discrimination which results from gender-stereotyping, yet arguably what is regarded as 'conventional' in terms of appearance is itself permeated by gender stereotyping, and therefore inherently sexually discriminatory.

The approach of the courts and tribunals to this issue has been to skirt around the problem by holding that there is no infringement of the Act where the employer imposes an appearance code which has different rules for men and women, as long as the code enforces a common principle of smartness or conventionality, and taken as a whole neither gender is treated less favourably. So, for example, in *Schmidt v Austicks Bookshops Ltd*[2] , the employer imposed a rule that women could not wear trousers at work and had to wear overalls, while men were not allowed to wear tee shirts. A female employee complained that the rule against trousers was unlawful under the Act, but the EAT held against her on the ground that the employer applied rules on clothing to all employees, although in the nature of things the rules were not the same given the difference between the sexes[3] . According to the EAT, an employer is entitled to a large measure of discretion in controlling the image of his establishment, including the appearance of the staff, especially where they come into contact with the public. The *Schmidt* approach was approved by the Court of Appeal in *Smith v Safeway plc*[4] . In that case, the employers' appearance code placed restrictions on hair length which applied to men only; women were allowed to have long hair provided it was tied back. The complainant was dismissed because he refused to cut off his pony-tail. The tribunal, following *Schmidt*, held that the treatment of the complainant was not less favourable than that which would have been accorded to a woman because the code, although different for men and women, enforced a common standard of smartness and conventionality, and taken as a whole it could not be said that either gender was treated less favourably. The EAT upheld the employee's appeal[5] , holding that since the employers' rules restricted only

---

20   [1990] IRLR 288, HL; see p. 241.
1   See Cunningham (1995) 24 ILJ 177; Wintemute (1997) 60 MLR 334.
2   [1978] ICR 85, [1977] IRLR 360, EAT.
3   See also *Burrett v West Birmingham Health Authority* [1994] IRLR 7, EAT, where it was held that a female nurse who was required to wear a cap as part of her uniform was not less favourably treated on grounds of sex than male nurses who were not required to wear a cap, since the requirement to wear a uniform applied equally to male and female nurses. Her honestly held belief that the requirement to wear a cap was demeaning was held not to be determinative of whether or not there was less favourable treatment (see p. 243, above).
4   [1996] IRLR 456, CA.
5   [1995] IRLR 132, EAT, Pill J dissenting.

the hair length of men, the treatment of the complainant was self-evidently less favourable, and that the employer's requirements with respect to hair style were capable of being applied to both men and women in such a way as to take account of convention (e.g. by allowing men to have a pony-tail), without placing a restriction on hair length for men only. The EAT also placed emphasis on the fact that, unlike other appearance requirements concerning uniform, hairstyle and jewellery, a restriction on hair length extends beyond working hours, and thereby affects individual choice detrimentally at all times (the implication being that such a restriction requires a stronger justification). However, the Court of Appeal overturned the EAT in favour of a more conventional interpretation of *Schmidt*. According to Phillips LJ, the starting point of the reasoning in *Schmidt*, which he considered to be 'plainly correct', was that it was necessary to show not merely that the sexes were treated differently, but that the treatment accorded to one was less favourable than the treatment accorded to the other; in his view, the most important element of the *Schmidt* approach was that, looking at the code as a whole, neither sex was to be treated less favourably as a result of its enforcement, and the tribunal's decision to that effect should therefore be upheld[6].

What is accepted as 'conventional' in relation to dress and appearance may however change with the passage of time, and employers may well be expected to modify their dress and appearance rules to reflect those changes. In *McConomy v Croft Inns Ltd*[7] , a case on discrimination in the provision of goods and services under Part III of the Act, it was held to be unlawfully discriminatory for a public house to refuse to serve a man for wearing earrings where there was no similar objection to women wearing earrings. The court stressed that while account must be taken of certain basic rules of human conduct, such as the ordinary rules of decency accepted in the community, which might permit or require different dress regulations as between men and women, in today's conditions it is not possible to say that the circumstances are different as between men and women as regards the wearing of personal jewellery or other items of personal adornment. The recent employment tribunal decisions in which dress codes prohibiting women from wearing trousers at work have been held to be discriminatory[8] may indicate that standards of what is 'conventional' in relation to appearance have shifted somewhat in the years since *Schmidt*, but the decision in *Smith v Safeway plc* suggests that the courts are not yet ready to accept as conventional a man who turns up for work wearing a pony-tail, let alone lipstick and high heels[9] .

b) Sexual harassment[10]

The Sex Discrimination Act does not expressly prohibit sexual harassment, but it is clear that sexual harassment may amount to unlawful sex discrimination

---

6   According to Phillips LJ, the fact that a restriction applied to permanent characteristics such as hair length or colour, and therefore extended beyond the workplace, was a factor to be taken into account in considering whether a code treats one sex less favourably than the other, but does not affect the test itself.

7   [1992] IRLR 561, NIHC.

8   See e.g. *Owen v Professional Golfers' Association* (January 2000, unreported), ET.

9   Cf Cunningham, op cit, p. 181. It remains to be seen what impact, if any, the incorporation the European Convention on Human Rights, and in particular Art. 8 (Right to respect for private and family life) by the Human Rights Act 1998 will have in this area. See p. 225 above.

10 See Dine and Watt 'Sexual Harassment: Moving Away From Discrimination' (1995) 58 MLR 343; European Commission Report 'The Protection of the Dignity of Men and Women at Work', OJ 97B (1992).

under the 1975 Act even though the complainant is unable to show that it has led to some employment-related detriment such as relocation or dismissal[11]. One of the main drawbacks in attempting to tackle sexual harassment through anti-discrimination law has been the need to show that the complainant has been less favourably treated than a man on the grounds of her sex. This may be hard to prove where the employer argues that there has been no disparate treatment because both male and female employees would have been treated alike[12]. In one of the early sexual harassment cases, *Porcelli v Strathclyde Regional Council*[13], the Court of Session held that a woman who had been subjected to persistent[14] personal insults, obscene language, suggestive remarks and unwanted physical contact by two male colleagues with the intention of forcing her to apply for a transfer had been less favourably treated on the ground of her sex than a man would have been treated. The Court held that if any material part of the unfavourable treatment to which a woman is subjected includes a significant sexual element to which a man would not be vulnerable, the treatment is on the grounds of her sex within the meaning of section 1(1)(a) of the 1975 Act[15]. The Court managed to overcome the problem of establishing less favourable treatment on the ground of sex by finding that while an equally disliked male colleague would have been subjected to equally unpleasant treatment, that treatment would not have been of a sexual nature[16], and it could therefore be said that the treatment of the complainant was different in a material respect from that which would have been inflicted on a male colleague.

Unfortunately, the tribunals have not always been so adept at avoiding the 'disparate treatment' trap. In *Stewart v Cleveland Guest (Engineering) Ltd*[17], the EAT refused to overturn the tribunal's finding that the employers had not discriminated against the complainant on the grounds of her sex by allowing male employees to display pin-ups of nude women in the workplace, even though they knew that the pictures were offensive to her. The tribunal had held that the display of pin-ups was 'neutral', in that a man might have found that sort of display just as offensive as the complainant did, and that as a result she had not succeeded in establishing that she had been treated less favourably than a man would have been treated[18]. The problem with this line of reasoning is that it fails to recognise that pin-ups of nude women are not gender-neutral, because women are more vulnerable to them than are men[19]. As McColgan has observed[20], the

11　*Wileman v Minilec Engineering Ltd* [1988] ICR 318, [1988] IRLR 144; *British Telecommunications plc v Williams* [1997] IRLR 668, EAT.

12　The 'But I'm a bastard to everyone' defence. See p. 242 above.

13　[1986] ICR 564, [1986] IRLR 134, Ct Sess (an unfortunately named case, since the acts complained of arose from the behaviour of male chauvinist *porcelli*).

14　This is not a necessary requirement, as a single act is capable of amounting to harassment: see below.

15　The Court of Session adopted the broad definition of 'detriment' from *Ministry of Defence v Jeremiah* (see n. 17, above) as meaning any conduct which places the applicant at a disadvantage.

16　Lord Grieve described the harassment of the complainant as a 'sexual sword' which 'had been unsheathed and used because the victim was a woman.'

17　[1994] IRLR 440, EAT; see p. 243, above. See also *Balgobin v London Borough of Tower Hamlets* [1987] IRLR 401, EAT.

18　The case is a good illustration of the fact that anti-discrimination legislation is an uncertain basis for the regulation of sexual harassment at work.

19　Cf. *Insitu Cleaning Co Ltd v Heads* [1995] IRLR 4, where the EAT refused to equate a remark by a man about a woman's breasts ('Hiya, big tits') with a remark by a woman about a bald head or a beard: 'One is sexual, the other is not' (per Morison J, p. 5).

20　McColgan (1995) 24 ILJ 181.

problem lies essentially in the necessity for a male comparator, and it is therefore to be welcomed that in *British Telecommunications plc v Williams*[1] the EAT held that in sexual harassment cases there is no necessity to look for a male comparator, and it is no defence to a complaint of sexual harassment that a person of the opposite sex would have been treated in the same way.

The other major difficulty in this area is in defining what sexual harassment actually is. There is no statutory definition, but the European Commission has issued a Recommendation and Code of Practice[2] which defines sexual harassment as 'unwanted conduct of a sexual nature, or other conduct based on sex affecting the dignity of women and men at work'. The Code of Practice states that such conduct is unacceptable if: (a) it is unwanted, unreasonable and offensive to the recipient; (b) a person's rejection of or submission to such conduct on the part of employers or workers (including superiors or colleagues) is used explicitly or implicitly as a basis for a decision affecting that person's access to training or employment, or their continued employment, promotion, salary or other employment decisions; and/or (c) such conduct creates an intimidating, hostile or humiliating work environment for the recipient. Although not legally binding on the UK courts and tribunals, this definition has been increasingly heavily relied upon in recent years[3].

In *Reed and Bull Information Systems Ltd v Stedman*[4], the EAT gave some useful guidance on the meaning of harassment and in particular what constitutes 'unwanted' conduct. The EAT stressed that the test of whether the conduct complained of amounts to sexual harassment is a subjective one[5]: 'The essential characteristic of sexual harassment is that it is words or conduct which are unwelcome to the recipient and it is for the recipient to decide for themselves what is acceptable to them and what they regard as offensive'[6]. A single act may be so clearly unwelcome as to be 'unwanted'[7], thus avoiding the argument that conduct cannot be said to be unwanted until it has been tried and rejected: 'A woman does not, for example, have to make it clear in advance that she does not want to be touched in a sexual manner.'[8]; at the other end of the scale, where a woman appears to be unduly sensitive to what might otherwise be regarded as unexceptional behaviour, the question becomes whether by words or conduct she has made it clear that she finds such conduct unwelcome: 'Provided that any reasonable person would understand her to be rejecting the conduct of which

1   Above, n. 11.
2   Commission Recommendation No. 92/131/EEC on the protection of the dignity of men and women at work.
3   See e.g. *Wadman v Carpenter Farrer Partnership* [1993] IRLR 374, EAT; *British Telecommunications plc v Williams*, above n. 11. The EOC has recommended that the Commission's definition should be incorporated into domestic law: *Equality in the 21st Century: A New Sex Equality Law for Britain* (EOC, 1998).
4   [1999] IRLR 299, EAT.
5   Compare *De Souza v Automobile Association* [1986] ICR 514, [1986] IRLR 103 (a case under the equivalent provisions of the Race Relations Act 1976), where the Court of Appeal suggested that the conduct must be such that 'a reasonable worker would or might take the view that he had been thereby disadvantaged in the circumstances in which he had thereafter to work'.
6   Per Morison J. See also *Wileman v Minilec Engineering Ltd* [1988] ICR 318, [1988] IRLR 144. Lack of intent is not a defence (although cf. the comment of Holland J in *Driskel v Peninsula Business Services Ltd* [2000] IRLR 151, EAT, that 'the understanding, motive and intention' of the alleged discriminator is one of the factors to be considered by the tribunal).
7   See e.g. *Insitu Cleaning Co Ltd v Heads*, above, n. 19; *Bracebridge Engineering Ltd v Darby* [1990] IRLR 3, EAT.
8   Per Morison J, ibid., n. 4.

she was complaining, continuation of the conduct would, generally, be regarded as harassment.[9] Where a number of specific incidents are alleged to constitute harassment, the tribunal should not carve up the case into a series of incidents and try to measure the harm in relation to each of them, but should instead consider the cumulative effect of such behaviour, lest it fall into the trap of 'ignoring the impact of the totality of successive incidents, individually trivial'[10]. Sexual harassment may well occur in circumstances where the victim is inhibited from making a complaint because of fear of the employment consequences (as in *Driskel v Peninsula Business Services Ltd*[11], where the complainant was told the evening before an interview for promotion that she had better turn up the following day 'in a short skirt and see-through blouse, showing plenty of cleavage'); the tribunal should therefore be slow to infer that the conduct was not unwelcome from the mere fact that the complainant does not complain or delays in making her complaint[12].

The subjective nature of the test for sexual harassment, with its emphasis on the effect of the action complained of on the complainant, is also highly relevant when considering the degree of injury to feelings that the complainant has suffered as a result of sexual harassment. The amount of compensation awarded will depend on the degree of detriment that the complainant is considered to have suffered, and the fact that the complainant's attitude to matters of sexual behaviour is such that she was unlikely to be very upset by conduct of an overtly sexual nature will have a direct bearing on the compensation awarded. So, for example, in *Snowball v Gardner Merchant Ltd*[13] the tribunal admitted evidence of the complainant's sexual exploits and that fact that she was in the habit of referring to her bed as a 'playpen', and in *Wileman v Minilec Engineering Ltd*[14] the tribunal took notice of the fact that the complainant sometimes wore what was described as provocative clothing to work. Significantly, however, the EAT held in that case that the complainant's willingness to pose for a national newspaper in a flimsy costume was not inconsistent with a finding that she had been sexually harassed by her employer: 'A person may be happy to accept the remarks of A or B in a sexual context, and wholly upset by similar remarks made by C'[15].

Finally, sexual harassment at the workplace will frequently give rise to the question of when an employer may be held liable for acts committed by their employees, or indeed by third parties such as customers of the employer. This is considered under vi) below.

v)   Discrimination in termination of employment

Under section 6(2) it is unlawful to discriminate against a woman by dismissing her, and this could give rise to a complaint to a tribunal of discrimination in the ordinary way, with the tribunal empowered to give compensation and make a recommendation, which could include reinstatement of the woman. However, it

9   Per Morison J, ibid.

10   *Driskel v Peninsula Business Services Ltd*, above, n. 6, at p. 154. ('That which in isolation may not amount to discriminatory detriment may become such if persisted in notwithstanding objection, vocal or apparent.' per Holland J, at p. 154).

11   Ibid.

12   *Wileman v Minilec Engineering Ltd*, above, n. 6.

13   [1987] ICR 719, [1987] IRLR 397

14   Above, n. 6.

15   Ibid., per Popplewell J.

is likely that in such a case the woman would also have a good claim for unfair dismissal[16] which has three advantages over the straight discrimination claim – the preliminary burden of proof in the unfair dismissal case is on the employer, there can be an order of reinstatement or re-engagement and, if the remedy is to be compensation, it will include a basic award. On the other hand, the discrimination claim has the distinct advantage that the one-year qualifying period for unfair dismissal does not apply, the tribunal is expressly empowered to award a sum for injury to feelings[17], and there is no upper limit on the compensation which can be awarded for discrimination[18]. It may therefore be wise for the dismissed woman to bring her complaint to the tribunal under both heads; if she does so, she cannot be doubly compensated, as the compensation for discrimination cannot take into account any head of loss already included in the compensation for unfair dismissal, and vice versa.

vi) Proving discrimination

Establishing the liability of an employer in a sex or race discrimination case can be extremely problematic. There is no statutory reversal of the burden of proof, so that prima facie the burden is on the applicant[19]. However, it has been recognised that proof can be extremely difficult in these cases, where frequently there will be little or no direct evidence of discrimination. In a series of cases[20], the EAT evolved a potentially useful approach which is that if the applicant shows less favourable treatment in circumstances consistent with discrimination, the tribunal may properly infer unlawful discrimination unless the respondent employer can satisfy it that there is an innocent explanation. This approach has now been sanctioned by the Court of Appeal[1], although care has been taken to affirm that there is no formal reversal of the burden of proof, which remains on the applicant[2], and the House of Lords has emphasised that the fact that an employee has been treated unfairly, and no satisfactory explanation has been given, does not make it proper to infer that there has been less favourable treatment on grounds of sex or race[3]. The relevant principles were restated in the following

16 A dismissal through an act of unlawful indirect discrimination is not automatically unfair in law, though in practice it is likely to be found unfair: *Clarke v Eley (IMI) Kynoch Ltd* [1983] ICR 165, [1982] IRLR 482, EAT.
17 See p. 269, below.
18 See p. 270, below.
19 *Oxford v Department of Health and Social Security* [1977] ICR 884, [1977] IRLR 225. It is, however, established that in a case of indirect discrimination the burden of proof on the question of justification is on the employer: *Steel v UPOW* [1978] ICR 181, [1977] IRLR 288.
20 *Moberley v Commonwealth Hall (University of London)* [1977] ICR 791, [1977] IRLR 176; *Khanna v Ministry of Defence* [1981] ICR 653, [1981] IRLR 331; *Chattopadhyay v Headmaster of Holloway School* [1982] ICR 132, [1981] IRLR 487.
1 *North West Thames Regional Health Authority v Noone* [1988] ICR 813, [1988] IRLR 195, CA; *West Midlands Passenger Transport Executive v Singh* [1988] ICR 614, [1988] IRLR 186, CA; *Baker v Cornwall County Council* [1990] ICR 452, [1990] IRLR 194, CA.
2 A point stressed by the EAT in *Barking and Dagenham London Borough Council v Camara* [1988] ICR 865, [1988] IRLR 373, and in *Carrington v Helix Lighting Ltd* [1990] ICR 125, [1990] IRLR 6. However, given the wide scope of the tribunals to draw inferences in the absence of reasonable explanation by the employer (and so, ultimately, to decide the case against the employer in the absence of such explanation), one wonders whether there is any significant difference (other than one of terminology) between the officially-stated position and a reversal of the burden of proof.
3 *Zafar v Glasgow City Council* [1998] IRLR 36, HL.

terms by Neill LJ in *King v Great Britain – China Centre*[4] (a case involving racial discrimination):

1) It is for the applicant who complains of racial discrimination to make out his or her case; if the applicant does not prove the case on the balance of probabilities he or she will fail.

2) It is important to bear in mind that it is unusual to find direct evidence of racial discrimination. Few employers will be prepared to admit such discrimination even to themselves. In some cases the discrimination will not be ill-intentioned but merely based on an assumption that 'he or she would not have fitted in'.

3) The outcome of the case will therefore usually depend on what inferences it is proper to draw from the primary facts found by the tribunal.

4) Though there will be some cases where, for example, the non-selection of the applicant for a post or for promotion is clearly not on racial grounds, a finding of discrimination and a finding of difference in race will often point to the possibility of racial discrimination. In such circumstances the tribunal will look to the employer for an explanation. If no explanation is then put forward, or if the tribunal considers the explanation to be inadequate or unsatisfactory, it will be legitimate[5] for the tribunal to infer that the discrimination was on racial grounds.

5) It is unnecessary and unhelpful to introduce the concept of a shifting evidential burden of proof. At the conclusion of all the evidence the tribunal should make findings as to the primary facts and draw such inferences as they consider proper from those facts. They should then reach a conclusion on the balance of probabilities, bearing in mind both the difficulties which face a person who complains of unlawful discrimination and the fact that it is for the complainant to prove his or her case.

One particularly difficult issue is the extent to which the tribunal may draw inferences of discrimination from statistical evidence, for example, that the employer's workforce is composed almost entirely of men[6]. On the one hand, the fact that in practice within a workplace men do one kind of work and women another will not per se contravene the statute, provided that the employer does not have a policy of never taking women on in the former occupation or men in the latter, even if they are capable of doing the job. Thus, for example, in *Noble v David Gold & Son Ltd*[7], the Court of Appeal found nothing discriminatory about the fact that in a packaging plant men in fact did the heavier tasks and women the lighter, even when the employer, faced with a fall-out of work, decided to run down the lighter side, which in practice meant making some of the women redundant. However, in the context of race discrimination the Court of Appeal has accepted that statistical evidence drawn from ethnic monitoring which reveals a discernible pattern in the treatment of a particular group to which the complainant belongs (e.g. a regular failure of members of the group to obtain promotion to particular jobs, or under-representation in such jobs) may justify

4   [1992] ICR 516, [1991] IRLR 513, CA.
5   But not mandatory: see *Zafar v Glasgow City Council*, above, n. 3.
6   The complainant may use the statutory 'Questions and Replies' procedure (Sex Discrimination Act 1975, s. 74; Race Relations Act 1976, s. 65) to obtain information from the employer; adverse inferences may be drawn from a failure to reply (s. 74(2)(b); s. 65(2)(b)). This procedure is in addition to the normal power of the tribunal to order discovery, on which see *Science Research Council v Nassé* [1979] ICR 921, [1979] IRLR 465, HL (discovery of confidential documents may be ordered, with suitable safeguards, where necessary to dispose fairly of the proceedings).
7   [1980] ICR 543, [1980] IRLR 252, CA.

the inference that 'the real reason for the treatment is a conscious or unconscious racial attitude which involves stereotyped assumptions about members of that group[8]'. In other words, statistical evidence, although not in itself conclusive, may be sufficient to raise an inference of discrimination which, in the absence of a satisfactory explanation by the employer, will be sufficient for the complainant to succeed on the balance of probabilities. This of course assumes that there is statistical evidence available, and here the problem for potential complainants is that there is no legal duty on employers to conduct gender or ethnic monitoring of the workforce[9]. The EOC has recommended that employers should be required to conduct gender monitoring on at least an annual basis, and to make the information obtained via monitoring available to employees, their representatives and the EOC[10], but that proposal has not been accepted by the Government.

In recognition of the difficulties often faced by complainants attempting to prove discrimination, and after an extremely long gestation period[11], all member states other than the UK adopted a Burden of Proof Directive[12] in December 1997; the UK Government subsequently acceded to the Directive in July 1998[13]. The main thrust of the directive is to shift the burden of proof onto the respondent in sex discrimination cases when the complainant establishes facts from which it may be presumed that there has been direct or indirect discrimination[14]. The implementation of the directive is unlikely to make very much difference in practice[15], given the existing approach of the UK courts and tribunals described above, but it is important symbolically. The main obstacle for complainants will still be the need to establish factual evidence of discrimination sufficient to shift the burden of proof onto the employer, which again serves to highlight the absence of a legal duty to monitor the workforce.

In at least one respect the complainant in a discrimination case receives some help from the statute, for section 41(1)[16] makes the employer vicariously liable for discrimination by the complainant's fellow employees in the course of their employment, whether or not done with the employer's knowledge or approval. This could be particularly important in a sexual harassment case where the harassment is coming from fellow employees rather than from a superior[17],

---

8 *West Midlands Passenger Transport Executive v Singh* [1988] ICR 614, [1988] IRLR 186, CA, per Balcombe LJ. In that case the Court of Appeal ordered discovery of statistics showing the ethnic origins of those who had applied for the post of inspector in the preceding two years, and those whose applications had been successful.

9 In *West Midlands Passenger Transport Executive v Singh*, ibid., the Court of Appeal held that discovery of statistics may not be ordered if the material is not readily to hand and it would be unreasonable to order it to be produced. See also *Carrington v Helix Lighting Ltd*, above, n. 2 (discovery is limited to the production of documents in being).

10 *Equality in the 21st Century: A New Sex Equality Law for Britain* (EOC, 1998). The CRE has proposed that ethnic monitoring should be made compulsory for all employers with more than 250 employees: *Reform of the Race Relations Act 1976* (CRE 1998).

11 A directive on the burden of proof in sex discrimination cases was first proposed by the European Commission in 1988.

12 Council Directive No. 97/80/EC 'on the burden of proof in cases of discrimination based on sex'.

13 Council Directive No. 98/52/EC. The UK Government is required to implement the directive by 22 July 2001.

14 The proposed Race Directive makes similar provision in relation to race discrimination cases; see p. 278 below.

15 Note however the definition of indirect discrimination in Art. 2(2) of the directive, which is broader than that contained in the SDA and RRA. See p. 246 above.

16 There are parallel provisions in the Race Relations Act 1976, s. 32 and the Disability Discrimination Act 1995, s. 58.

17 See, for example, *Porcelli v Strathclyde Regional Council* [1986] ICR 564, [1986] IRLR 134, Ct of Sess.

especially since an employee cannot be held directly liable under the employment-related provisions of the Act, which apply only to employers. However, the position is qualified by section 41(3), which provides a defence if the employer can prove that he took such steps as were reasonably practicable to prevent the fellow employees' conduct, and it has been held[18] that this defence is made out where it is shown that an employer (with no knowledge of the conduct) has maintained adequate supervision of the employees and publicised his policy of equal opportunities; in *Jones v Tower Boot Co Ltd*[19] (a case under the equivalent provisions of the Race Relations Act), the Court of Appeal explained the purpose of the 'reasonable steps' defence as exonerating a conscientious employer who has used his best endeavours to prevent harassment, and encouraging all employers to take the steps necessary to make the defence available in their own workplace.

The principal limitation on the vicarious liability of an employer in this context is the requirement that the person causing the disadvantage to the complainant was acting 'in the course of his employment'. In the earlier cases on this provision it was held that the statutory test of vicarious liability was the same as the common law test (i.e. whether the employee's act was merely an unauthorised or prohibited mode of doing an authorised act, as distinct from an act which was outside the sphere of what he was employed to do[20]). The problem with this approach, particularly in cases involving sexual or racial harassment, was that the worse an employee's acts, the less likely it was that he would be held to be acting in the course of his employment; indeed, taken to its logical conclusion it might even mean that no employer could ever be held responsible for such acts, as no employee is employed to harass other employees. It is therefore to be welcomed that the application of the common law test in this context was comprehensively rejected by the Court of Appeal in *Jones v Tower Boot Co Ltd*[1]. In that case, the complainant had been subjected to a number of extreme incidents of racial harassment by fellow employees, including being branded with a hot screwdriver, whipped across the legs and verbally abused. The EAT had overturned the tribunal's finding that the perpetrators were acting in the course of their employment, holding that the acts complained of could not 'by any stretch of the imagination' be described as an improper mode of performing authorised tasks. The Court of Appeal reversed the EAT's decision and held the employer liable; giving the principal judgment, Waite LJ held that a purposive approach should be taken to the statutory test, and that the words 'in the course of his employment' should be interpreted in the sense in which they are employed in everyday speech, unclouded by any parallels drawn from the common law of vicarious liability. This wide interpretation places heightened emphasis on the importance for the employer of being able to rely on the 'reasonable steps' defence, discussed above. In subsequent cases, the test has been interpreted as extending even to social activities occurring outside working hours, where those activities are work-related[2]; there are however limits, as was

---

18 *Balgobin v London Borough of Tower Hamlets* [1987] ICR 829, [1987] IRLR 401, EAT.
19 [1997] IRLR 168, CA.
20 See e.g. *Irving and Irving v Post Office* [1987] IRLR 289, CA (on the equivalent provision in the Race Relations Act 1976, s. 32).
1   Above, n. 19.
2   *Chief Constable of Lincolnshire Police v Stubbs* [1999] IRLR 81, EAT (police authority held liable for harassment of a female police officer while off-duty at a pub with her work colleagues, and while at a work-related leaving party).

shown in *Waters v Metropolian Police Comr*[3], where the Court of Appeal held that no tribunal applying the statutory test (as interpreted in *Tower Boot*) could find that an alleged sexual assault by a male police officer on a female officer was committed 'in the course of his employment', where both parties were off duty at the time, and the man was a visitor to her room.

Where the employer is held vicariously liable under section 41(1), the employee responsible for the discriminatory act may himself be held liable under section 42(1) for aiding the employer's breach[4]. By this convoluted process it is possible for an employee to be held liable for aiding and abetting his own acts, even though the statutory duty not to discriminate applies only to employers.

Until recently, it was assumed that employers could only be held liable for acts of sexual or racial harassment committed by themselves or their servants or agents, and not for harassment coming from a third party (e.g. a customer). However, in *Burton v De Vere Hotels*[5], the EAT held that an employer may be held *directly* liable for the acts of a third party in certain circumstances. In that case the complainants, who were both black, were employed as casual waitresses at a Round Table dinner at which Bernard Manning was the guest speaker. During his speech Mr Manning made a number of jokes about the sexual organs and sexual activities of black men, and used racially offensive language. Some of his remarks were directed at the complainants, and a number of the diners joined in the racial abuse. Both women brought complaints against the employer under the Race Relations Act. The tribunal dismissed their complaints on the grounds that, while they had undoubtedly suffered a detriment within the meaning of the Act, it was not the employer who had subjected them to it. The EAT allowed the appeal, holding that an employer 'subjects' an employee to the detriment of harassment if he causes or permits the harassment to occur, in circumstances in which he can control whether it happens or not. According to the EAT, the question for the tribunal is 'whether the event in question was something which was sufficiently under the control of the employer that he could, by the application of good employment practice, have prevented the harassment or reduced the extent of it. If such is their finding, then the employer has subjected the employee to the harassment'[6]. This principle has obvious implications for employers whose employees are at risk of racial or sexual harassment by customers or the general public; it could also be applied to make an employer directly liable for harassment by fellow employees which is *outside* the course of their employment (so that the employer would not be vicariously liable under the *Tower Boot* principle), where the employer is aware of the harassment, had power to control it, but took no adequate steps to prevent it[7].

---

3   [1997] IRLR 589, CA. See p. 253 above.
4   *Read v Tiverton District Council* [1977] IRLR 202; *Enterprise Glass Co Ltd v Miles* [1990] ICR 787, EAT; *AM v WC and SPV* [1999] IRLR 410, EAT. The employee remains liable even if the employer is able to make out the s. 41(3) defence: see s. 42(2). The intriguing result is that the employee who committed the acts in question can only be held liable for aiding and abetting the employer, who in turn is only liable through being vicariously liable for the employee's acts, and who may himself be able to make out a defence under s. 41(3). The law is truly a curious beast at times.
5   [1996] IRLR 596, EAT.
6   Ibid., per Smith J, at p. 600.
7   See e.g. *Chessington World of Adventures Ltd v Reed* [1997] IRLR 556, EAT.

vii) Remedies

An employee or ex-employee may bring to a tribunal a complaint of any of the above forms of discrimination in employment[8]; the time limit for the presentation of complaints is three months[9] beginning when the act complained of was done[10], or, in the case of a deliberate omission, when the person in question decided upon it[11], although the tribunal has a wide discretion to consider a complaint out of time if it considers that it is 'just and equitable' to do so[12]. Discrimination often takes the form of a continuing act extending over a period of time, in which case the time limit runs from the end of that period[13]. However, a continuing act of discrimination must be distinguished from a single act or event of discrimination which has continuing consequences, where the time limit runs from the act itself[14]. So, for example, in *Calder v James Findlay Corpn Ltd*[15], the employer's refusal to allow the complainant access to a mortgage subsidy scheme was held to be a continuing act of discrimination, entitling her to bring her complaint more than three months after the refusal. In contrast, in *Sougrin v Haringey Health Authority*[16], a case under the Race Relations Act, a grading decision was held by the Court of Appeal to be a single act with continuing consequences, not a continuing act of discrimination. The distinction can be extremely difficult to draw, especially where a single act of discrimination is repeated or reaffirmed on subsequent occasions[17]. A succession of specific instances of discrimination (e.g. a failure to re-grade over a number of years, or the reaffirmation of a refusal to allow an employee to job-share) may, however, indicate the existence of a discriminatory policy or regime (formal or informal), which can constitute a continuing act extending over a period[18].

8   Sex Discrimination Act 1975, s. 63. For a critique of the handling of sex discrimination cases by tribunals, see Alice Leonard *Judging Inequality* (1987, Cobden Trust, London).
9   Or six months for those serving in the armed forces, because of the need to follow the service redress procedures before making a complaint to a tribunal: ibid., s. 76(1)(b).
10   Ibid., s. 76(1). Where the act complained of is dismissal, the date of the dismissal for these purposes is not necessarily the same as the 'effective date of termination' for unfair dismissal purposes: *Lupetti v Wrens Old House Ltd* [1984] ICR 348 (under the Race Relations Act 1976); *Gloucester Working Men's Club and Institute v James* [1986] ICR 603; cf. *Adekeye v Post Office* [1993] ICR 464, [1993] IRLR 324, EAT, where the time limit was held to run from the rejection of an internal appeal, not from the date of dismissal.
11   Ibid., s. 76(6)(c). See *Swithland Motors plc v Clarke* [1994] ICR 231, [1994] IRLR 275, EAT ('decided' means 'decided at a time and in circumstances when he is in a position to implement that decision').
12   Ibid., s. 76(5). This is a much wider formulation than the usual 'reasonably practicable' escape clause: see *Hutchinson v Westward Television Ltd* [1977] ICR 279, [1977] IRLR 69, EAT; *Clarke v Hampshire Electro-Plating Co Ltd* [1992] ICR 312, [1991] IRLR 490, EAT; *Hawkins v Ball* [1996] IRLR 258, EAT; *British Coal Corpn v Keeble* [1997] IRLR 336, EAT; *DPP v Marshall* [1998] ICR 518, EAT.
13   Ibid., s. 76(6)(b).
14   See for example *Amies v Inner London Education Authority* [1977] 2 All ER 100, [1977] ICR 308, EAT (failure to appoint to a particular post held not to be a continuing act of discrimination).
15   [1989] ICR 157n, [1989] IRLR 55, EAT, approved by the House of Lords in *Barclays Bank plc v Kapur* [1991] ICR 208, [1991] IRLR 136 (under the Race Relations Act). See also *Littlewoods Organisation plc v Traynor* [1993] IRLR 154, EAT (failure to take promised remedial action in relation to a complaint of discrimination was a continuing act of discrimination by the employer).
16   [1992] ICR 650, [1992] IRLR 416, CA.
17   See e.g. *Rovenska v General Medical Council* [1997] IRLR 367, CA.
18   *Owusu v London Fire and Civil Defence Authority* [1995] IRLR 574, EAT (re-grading); *Cast v Croydon College* [1998] IRLR 318, CA (job-share).

If the tribunal finds the complaint well founded, it may make three orders – a declaration that the employee's rights have been infringed, an order for compensation and a recommendation that the employer take action suggested by the tribunal within a specified period in order to remove the discrimination[19]. The latter recommendation is just that; it is not a positive order and should not be framed as such[20], although the EOC has recommended that the tribunals should be given the power to order reinstatement, re-engagement, appointment or promotion, as appropriate[1]. If the employer fails to comply with a recommendation without reasonable justification, the complainant may go back to the tribunal which may award increased compensation if it considers it just and equitable to do so[2]. In such proceedings the tribunal must take a realistic approach and one of the main factors in deciding whether the employer had reasonable justification may be whether he has had sufficient time to put matters right, for the provisions relating to the recommendation clearly envisage the possibility of longer-term measures[3].

On the question of compensation, the tribunal is empowered to award it on the same basis as if the complainant had brought an action for damages in tort before an ordinary court, so that, as best as money can do it, the applicants must be put into the position they would have been in but for the unlawful conduct of the employer[4]. There is an express power to award damages for injury to feelings[5], difficult though this may be to quantify. An award for injury to feelings has been said to be 'almost inevitable' in a sex discrimination case[6], but this does not mean that it is automatic, as the applicant must still prove that some injury has been sustained[7]. The Court of Appeal has indicated that while damages for

19   Ibid., s. 65(1)(a), (b) and (c).
20   *Ministry of Defence v Jeremiah* [1978] ICR 984, [1978] IRLR 402; affd by CA: [1979] 3 All ER 833, [1979] IRLR 436. The recommendation may not include an increase of salary (*Prestcold Ltd v Irvine* [1981] ICR 777, [1981] IRLR 281, CA) or an instruction to appoint or promote the applicant to the next available vacancy, where he or she has not been appointed or promoted because of discrimination (*North West Thames Regional Health Authority v Noone (No 2)* [1988] ICR 813, [1988] IRLR 530, CA; *British Gas plc v Sharma* [1991] ICR 19, [1991] IRLR 101, EAT).
1   *Equality in the 21st Century: A New Sex Equality Law for Britain* (EOC, 1998).
2   Ibid., s. 65(3).
3   *Nelson v Tyne and Wear Passenger Transport Executive* [1978] ICR 1183.
4   Sex Discrimination Act 1975, s. 65(1)(b). See *Alexander v Home Office* [1988] ICR 685, [1988] IRLR 190, CA (under the Race Relations Act 1976) and *Ministry of Defence v Cannock* [1994] ICR 918, [1994] IRLR 509, EAT, which contain detailed guidance on the assessment of damages in discrimination cases.
5   Ibid., s. 66(4). The injury to feelings must arise directly from the sex discrimination, not from other, more remote, consequences: *Skyrail Oceanic Ltd v Coleman* [1981] ICR 864, [1981] IRLR 398, CA. The power to award damages for injury to feelings can include an award for psychological injury caused by the discrimination: *Sheriff v Klyne Tugs (Lowestoft) Ltd* [1999] IRLR 481, CA (under the parallel provisions in the Race Relations Act 1976, s. 57).
6   *Murray v Powertech (Scotland) Ltd* [1992] IRLR 257, EAT.
7   *Ministry of Defence v Cannock* [1994] ICR 918, [1994] IRLR 509, EAT. In *Cannock*, the EAT suggested that it will often be easy to prove injury, as no tribunal will take much persuading that the anger and distress caused by the discriminatory act has injured the applicant's feelings. In sexual harassment cases, the EAT has held that compensation must relate to the degree of detriment suffered; this has led to an uncomfortably close examination of the applicant's character and antecedents in some cases: see e.g. *Snowball v Gardner Merchant Ltd* [1987] IRLR 397; *Wileman v Minilec Engineering Ltd* [1988] IRLR 144, EAT.

injury to feelings in discrimination cases should not be minimal[8] (since this would tend to trivialise the issue and diminish respect for the law), the awards should be restrained, as to award sums which are generally felt to be excessive would do almost as much harm to the policy of the legislation as to make nominal awards[9]. In the earlier cases, awards for injury to feelings tended to be fairly small; however, in *Armitage, Marsden and HM Prison Service v Johnson*[10], a race discrimination case, the EAT upheld an award for injury to feelings of £21,000, holding that the award was not grossly or obviously out of line with the general range of awards in personal injury cases. Aggravated damages are available where, for example, the defendant has behaved in a high-handed, malicious, insulting or oppressive manner in committing the discriminatory act[11], but it has been held that a tribunal cannot award exemplary damages in sex and race discrimination cases[12].

Until recently, compensation under the Sex Discrimination Act was subject to two major limitations: first, it was subject to the same upper limit as the compensatory award for unfair dismissal[13]; and secondly, in a complaint of indirect discrimination under section 1(1)(b), compensation could only be awarded if the employer applied the requirement or condition with the *intention* of discriminating on the ground of sex (although the tribunal could still make a declaration and recommendation). However, as in so many other areas of UK sex discrimination law, EC law has made its mark in this area, and both these limitations have been removed. In *Marshall v Southampton and South-West Hampshire Area Health Authority (No. 2)*[14], the ECJ held that the upper limit on compensation infringed Article 6 of the Equal Treatment Directive, which requires the provision of adequate remedies which compensate the complainant in full for the loss and damage sustained as a result of the discrimination. This decision led to the removal of the upper limit in sex discrimination cases[15]; the limit in race discrimination cases was also subsequently abolished[16], bringing the two Acts into line once again. The effect of this change was demonstrated in dramatic fashion by the complaints brought against the Ministry of Defence by servicewomen

---

8   In *Sharifi v Strathclyde Regional Council* [1992] IRLR 259 (a race discrimination case), the EAT suggested an award of £500 was 'at or near the minimum'. In *Orlando v Didcot Power Station Sports and Social Club* [1996] IRLR 262, the EAT held that an award of £750 was not perversely low, despite the lifting of the upper limit on compensation.

9   *Alexander v Home Office* [1988] IRLR 190, CA.

10 [1997] IRLR 162, EAT. The EAT also upheld awards of £500 each against two prison officers personally. In *North West Thames Regional Health Authority v Noone* [1988] IRLR 195, the Court of Appeal stated that £3,000 was at the top end of the bracket that should be awarded for severe injury to feelings, but this was before the lifting of the upper limit on compensation in 1993.

11 *Alexander v Home Office*, above, n. 9; *Armitage, Marsden and HM Prison Service v Johnson*, above, n. 10; *Ministry of Defence v Meredith* [1995] IRLR 539, EAT.

12 *Deane v Ealing London Borough Council* [1993] ICR 329 [1993] IRLR 209, EAT, following the decision of the Court of Appeal in *Gibbons v South West Water Services Ltd* [1993] QB 507, [1993] 1 All ER 609. See also *Ministry of Defence v Meredith*, above, n.11.

13 See p. 505.

14 [1994] QB 126, [1993] ICR 893, ECJ.

15 Sex Discrimination and Equal Pay (Remedies) Regulations 1993, S.I. 1993 No. 2798. The regulations also empowered tribunals to award interest on compensation, in line with the ECJ's ruling in *Marshall*; see now the Employment Tribunals (Interest on Awards in Discrimination Cases) Regulations 1996, S.I. 1996 No. 2803.

16 Race Relations (Remedies) Act 1994.

dismissed on the grounds of pregnancy, where awards of compensation in excess of £300,000 were made in some cases[17]. The removal of the upper limit means that it may be preferable to challenge a discriminatory dismissal under the discrimination legislation rather than in a claim for unfair dismissal, although the normal rules concerning mitigation and discounting for future uncertainties will still apply[18].

The ruling in *Marshall* also brought into doubt the bar on the award of damages for unintentional indirect discrimination, long seen as a significant weakness in the domestic provisions. In *London Underground v Edwards*[19], the EAT managed to circumvent this bar by holding that an intention to discriminate could be inferred where the employer applied a requirement or condition with the knowledge of its unfavourable consequences for a woman, but in *MacMillan v Edinburgh Voluntary Organisations Council*[20], the EAT held that the provisions excluding compensation for unintentional indirect discrimination were unambiguous, and could not be construed to accord with the provisions of the Directive[1]. The uncertainty was subsequently resolved by the introduction of further regulations allowing the tribunal to award compensation for unintentional indirect discrimination where it is satisfied that the power to make a declaration and recommendation is not sufficient, and it is just and equitable to award compensation[2], thus bringing domestic law into line with the Directive.

In addition to the remedies available to the aggrieved employee, the Equal Opportunities Commission, set up under the Act[3], is empowered to take certain direct steps to secure compliance with the statute. In particular it may conduct a formal investigation into any alleged contraventions, which may result in the issue of a non-discrimination notice if it discovers breaches of the Act; such a notice requires the discontinuance of the act of discrimination or discriminatory practice in question, and it may contain requirements to be met by the employer, who has six weeks in which to appeal against it to a tribunal. If there is no appeal, or an appeal is dismissed, the notice becomes final, and any further contraventions of it may be restrained by injunction at the suit of the Commission[4]. There are also further, more specific powers given to the Commission to take action against

---

17 See *Ministry of Defence v Cannock* [1994] ICR 918, [1994] IRLR 509, EAT; *Ministry of Defence v Hunt* [1996] IRLR 139, EAT.

18 Ibid. See also *Ministry of Defence v Wheeler* [1998] IRLR 23, CA

19 [1995] ICR 574, [1995] IRLR 355, EAT; see also *J H Walker Ltd v Hussain* [1996] ICR 291, [1996] IRLR 11, EAT, a case under the Race Relations Act, where it was held that a person will be taken to have intended the unfavourable consequences to follow from his acts 'if he knew when he did them that those consequences would follow and if he wanted those consequences to follow' per Mummery J, at p.15.

20 [1995] IRLR 536, EAT.

1 The decision in *London Underground v Edwards* was not mentioned in the judgment. As a private sector employee, the complainant was unable to rely on the direct effect of the Directive.

2 S.I. 1996 No. 438. The parallel restriction in the Race Relations Act still applies: see p. 275.

3 Sacks 'The Equal Opportunities Commission – ten years on' (1986) 49 MLR 560.

4 Ibid., ss. 67–70. On the nature of an appeal against a non-discrimination notice, see *Commission for Racial Equality v Amari Plastics Ltd* [1982] ICR 304, [1982] IRLR 252, CA; if the formal investigation is not carried out in accordance with the stipulated procedure, any resulting non-discrimination notice is void: *Re Prestige Group plc, Commission for Racial Equality v Prestige Group plc* [1984] ICR 473, [1984] IRLR 166, HL. The EOC has recommended an extension of its powers to issue non-discrimination notices, and the introduction of a power to accept legally binding commitments as an alternative: *Equality in the 21st Century: A New Sex Equality Law for Britain* (EOC, 1998).

discriminatory advertisements[5], to seek an injunction to restrain 'persistent discrimination'. (i.e. where an employer appears likely to commit further unlawful acts within five years of receiving a non-discrimination notice, or being found liable for an act of unlawful discrimination[6]), and to give practical help to individuals to bring discrimination claims against their employers[7]. In recent years the EOC, in addition to supporting individual claimants before the courts and tribunals, has sought to make use of the machinery of judicial review in pursuance of its statutory duty to work towards the elimination of discrimination, with stunning results. In *Birmingham City Council v EOC*[8], the Commission successfully applied for judicial review to establish that the authority was in breach of its obligations under the 1975 Act in failing to provide as many grammar school places for girls as for boys. Initially the EOC's attempts to use judicial review to challenge the legality of domestic legislation under Community Law met with more limited success. In *R v Secretary of State for Social Security, ex p EOC*[9], the Commission unsuccessfully sought a declaration that the UK state pension scheme infringed EC Directive 79/7 (which establishes the principle of equal treatment in social security schemes) by requiring men to pay contributions for longer than women in order to qualify for the same state pension, the ECJ ruling that the unequal treatment was covered by the exception in Article 7(1) which allows member states to fix the state pensionable age[10]; however, in *R v Secretary of State for Employment, ex p EOC*[11], the House of Lords held that the EOC had locus standi to challenge by judicial review the legality under Community law of the legislative provisions which subjected part-time workers to different qualifying conditions for redundancy pay and compensation for unfair dismissal from those which applied to full-time employees[12] and, furthermore, that those qualifying thresholds were incompatible with Community law as they were indirectly discriminatory (the vast majority of part-time workers being women), and had not been shown to be objectively justified by reference to the extra costs to employers and the impact on the availability of part-time work[13]. This momentous ruling led to the repeal of the offending provisions, and the harmonisation of qualifying periods for full-time and part-time workers.

3   RACIAL DISCRIMINATION IN EMPLOYMENT

As seen in the introduction to this chapter, while race relations legislation in England and Wales dates back to 1965, the present provisions in the Race Relations Act 1976 are closely modelled on the Sex Discrimination Act 1975, and much of the discussion under head 2 above applies, mutatis mutandis, to racial discrimination as well. There are however some significant differences,

5   Ibid., s. 72.
6   Ibid., s. 71.
7   Ibid., s. 75.
8   [1989] AC 1155, [1989] IRLR 173, HL. This case is an important authority on the significance of a discriminatory motive or intent: see p. 241, above.
9   C-9/91: [1992] ICR 782, [1992] IRLR 376, ECJ.
10 The vexed question of discrimination in relation to pension schemes is considered more fully at p. 301.
11 [1995] 1 AC 1, [1994] ICR 317, HL. See p. 228, above
12 The Court of Appeal had held (by a majority, Dillon LJ dissenting) that the EOC lacked a sufficient interest to bring judicial review proceedings against the government or a minister for failure to fulfil obligations under Community law.
13 See p. 228, above.

some of which stem from the fact that the ECJ decisions on sex discrimination, which have required the reinterpretation (and in some cases the amendment) of the sex discrimination legislation, do not apply to race discrimination. So, for example, the Race Relations Act does not cover discrimination post-employment, and compensation for unintentional indirect discrimination is still unavailable. Moreover, unlike sex discrimination, the law on race discrimination is not bedevilled by separate legislation covering discrimination over pay and terms of employment, and other matters falling outside the contract: all complaints lie under the 1976 Act[14].

The 1976 Act prohibits discrimination on 'racial grounds', defined in section 3(1) as relating to colour, race, nationality, or ethnic or national origins. In *Mandla v Dowell Lee*[15], the complainant, a Sikh boy, was refused entrance to a private school unless he gave up wearing his turban and had his hair cut, a requirement which conflicted with his religion; the House of Lords held that Sikhs constitute an ethnic group within the meaning of the Act, Lord Fraser commenting that for a group to constitute an ethnic group it must regard itself, and be regarded by others, as a distinct community with a long shared history and a cultural tradition of its own. It is clearly established that Jews[16] and gypsies[17] constitute identifiable ethnic groups, but Rastafarians have been held not to, on the grounds that although they have certain identifiable characteristics, they have not established a separate identity by reference to their ethnic origins[18]. 'Nationality' in this context points to citizenship, and to the existence of a recognised state at the material time, but 'national origin' is a wider concept, turning on the existence of a nation at some point in time, established by reference to history and geography. Thus, in *Northern Joint Police Board v Power*[19], the issue was whether the applicant, who claimed that he had been rejected for a post of Chief Constable in Scotland because he was English, had been discriminated against on racial grounds. The tribunal held that there was no discrimination on grounds of nationality, as 'within the context of England, Scotland, Northern Ireland and Wales the proper approach to nationality is to categorise all of them as falling under the umbrella of British'; however, discrimination against an English person, or a Scot, was held to constitute discrimination on grounds of national origin, since it could not be in doubt that both England and Scotland were once separate nations[20].

The use of the expression 'on racial grounds' means that unlike the Sex Discrimination Act, which applies where discrimination is 'on the grounds of her sex', the 1976 Act can apply where a person suffers a detriment on the basis of *another* person's race, e.g. where a white person is dismissed for refusing to

---

14   See e.g. *Wakeman v Quick Corpn* [1999] IRLR 424, CA (complaint that Japanese managers working for a Japanese firm in the UK were being paid more than locally recruited managers; the complaint failed on the facts because the necessary causal link could not be established).

15   [1983] ICR 385, [1983] IRLR 209, HL. The decision shows how the 1976 Act can sometimes be used to outlaw discrimination on religious grounds, even though religious discrimination is not directly prohibited under the Act.

16   *Seide v Gillette Industries Ltd* [1980] IRLR 427, EAT.

17   *Commission for Racial Equality v Dutton* [1989] QB 783, [1989] 1 All ER 306, CA.

18   *Dawkins v Department of the Environment* [1993] IRLR 284, CA.

19   [1997] IRLR 610, EAT.

20   The same reasoning naturally applies to Wales and Ireland, although in *Gwynedd County Council v Jones* [1986] ICR 833, the EAT held that the 1976 Act does not apply to discrimination on the grounds of not being able to *speak* Welsh.

apply a colour bar. In *Weathersfield Ltd v Sargent*[1], the complainant resigned from her job with a vehicle hire firm after being told not to hire vehicles to black or asian prospective customers. The Court of Appeal held that she had been discriminated against on racial grounds, even though it was the race of the prospective customers that was at issue, and not her own race.

As seen above, the 1976 Act is almost identical to the Sex Discrimination Act 1975 in its scheme and its remedies. Thus, section 1(1) of the 1976 Act defines both direct and indirect discrimination in substantially the same terms as those in section 1(1) of the 1975 Act. Direct discrimination generally requires the making of a comparison with the treatment of a person not of that racial group, but as with sex discrimination[2], conduct which is 'race-specific' may be held to constitute less favourable treatment on racial grounds, without the need for a comparison[3]. Segregation on racial grounds is declared in section 1(2) to qualify automatically as 'less favourable treatment' for the purpose of direct discrimination (thus forestalling any 'separate but equal' arguments). In cases of indirect discrimination, the EAT has taken a narrower approach to the meaning of 'requirement or condition' under the 1976 Act than under the Sex Discrimination Act[4], but the approach to justification now seems to be the same[5], requiring an objective balance between the discriminatory effect of the requirement or condition and the reasonable needs of the employer[6]. Thus, in *Singh v Rowntree MacKintosh Ltd*[7] the employers operated a rule prohibiting the wearing of beards by employees in contact with the factory's products; this prima facie indirectly discriminated against Sikhs, but the EAT held that it was 'justifiable' within section 1(1)(b)(ii) in the interests of commercial hygiene. Discriminatory employment practices are defined in the same way as in the Sex Discrimination Act[8] (i.e. applying to selection, benefits, etc., during employment or dismissal or other detriment), although in one respect the scope of the protection under the 1976 Act is narrower than under the 1975 Act, as it does not extend to racial discrimination after the employment relationship has ended (e.g. where an employer provides a former employee with an adverse reference)[9]. Section 5 lays down certain exempted categories of employment where being a

1   [1999] IRLR 94, CA. The case also establishes the important point that a constructive dismissal is a detriment for the purposes of the anti-discrimination legislation. See also *Showboat Entertainment Centre Ltd v Owens* [1984] ICR 65, [1984] IRLR 7, EAT.
2   E.g. in complaints of sexual harassment: see p. 259.
3   *Sidhu v Aerospace Composite Technology* [1999] IRLR 683, EAT.
4   *Perera v Civil Service Commission (No 2)* [1983] ICR 428, [1983] IRLR 166, CA; affirmed in *Meer v Tower Hamlets London Borough* [1988] IRLR 399, CA. See p. 245 above.
5   *Hampson v Department of Education and Science* [1989] IRLR 69 CA, approved in *Webb v EMO Air Cargo (UK) Ltd* [1992] 4 All ER 929, [1993] ICR 175, HL. See p. 250 above.
6   For a case illustrating the difficulties which can sometimes arise in identifying the relevant pool for comparison under the RRA, see *Orphanos v Queen Mary College* [1985] IRLR 349, HL.
7   [1979] ICR 554, [1979] IRLR 199; *Bohun-Mitchell v Council of Legal Education* [1978] IRLR 525, IT; *Panesar v Nestlé Co Ltd* [1980] ICR 144n, [1980] IRLR 64, CA; *Kingston and Richmond Area Health Authority v Kaur* [1981] ICR 631, [1981] IRLR 337. The 'no turban' rule in a school in *Mandla v Dowell Lee* (above) was held not justifiable on the facts.
8   Race Relations Act 1976, s. 4. In *De Souza v Automobile Association* [1986] ICR 514, [1986] IRLR 103, CA, it was held that a racial insult by a fellow employee is not enough, by itself, to constitute a detriment within s. 4. Quaere whether such conduct might today be held to be 'race-specific' and therefore discriminatory per se? See n. 3 above.
9   *Nagarajan v Agnew* [1995] ICR 520, [1994] IRLR 61, EAT. See also *Post Office v Adekeye* [1997] ICR 110, [1997] IRLR 105, CA. In *Coote v Granada Hospitality Ltd (No 2)* [1999] IRLR 452, the EAT reinterpreted the Sex Discrimination Act as covering discrimination by an ex-employer in order to comply with a ruling of the ECJ: see p. 253 above. The CRE

member of a particular racial group is a 'genuine occupational qualification' for a job, e.g. where the holder of the job provides persons of that racial group with 'personal services promoting their welfare', and those services 'can most effectively be provided by persons of that racial group'[10], or where the job involves participation in a dramatic performance, working as an artist's or photographic model, or working in a bar or restaurant, where a person of a particular racial group is required 'for reasons of authenticity'[11]. The CRE has recommended that the latter exemption should be restricted to circumstances in which the employer can show that the employee's racial group is an essential, defining feature of the job[12].

Discrimination by way of victimisation on racial grounds is covered by section 2. The case law on victimisation under the 1976 Act has clarified several important points in recent years; thus in *Nagarajan v London Regional Transport*[13], the House of Lords held that in complaints of victimisation the motive of the alleged discriminator is irrelevant, the relevant question simply being whether the complainant would have been treated in that way but for his race; and in *Chief Constable of West Yorkshire v Khan*[14], the Court of Appeal held, in a victimisation complaint arising from the Chief Constable's refusal to provide a reference for an officer who had a claim of race discrimination outstanding, that the proper comparator was an officer who did not have a complaint outstanding, rather than an officer who had a complaint outstanding but not under the Race Relations Act. Had the decision been otherwise, it would have been a defence for the Chief Constable to claim that he would similarly have refused to provide a reference to another officer who was suing the police authority on some other ground.

Procedures and remedies in race discrimination cases are similar to those under the Sex Discrimination Act, but with the important difference that no compensation may be awarded for indirect discrimination under the Race Relations Act if the respondent proves that the discrimination was unintentional[15]. The practical impact of this restriction has to some extent been alleviated by the decision in *J H Walker Ltd v Hussain*[16], where the EAT held that a person will be taken to have intended the unfavourable consequences to follow from his acts 'if he knew when he did them that those consequences would follow and if he wanted those consequences to follow'[17]. Complainants in race discrimination cases may encounter the same difficulties in relation to proving

has recommended that the 1976 Act should be amended to provide protection to former employees who allege racial discrimination by a previous employer: *Reform of the Race Relations Act 1976* (CRE, 1998).

10 See *Tottenham Green Under Fives' Centre v Marshall* [1989] ICR 214, [1989] IRLR 147, EAT; *same v same (No. 2)* [1991] ICR 320, [1991] IRLR 162, EAT; *Lambeth London Borough v Commission for Racial Equality* [1990] ICR 768, [1990] IRLR 231, CA.

11 See Pitt 'Madam Butterfly and Miss Saigon: Reflections on Genuine Occupational Qualifications', in Dine and Watt (eds) *Discrimination Law: Concepts, Limitations and Justifications* (1996).

12 *Reform of the Race Relations Act 1976* (CRE, 1998).

13 [1999] IRLR 572, HL. See p. 252 above.

14 [2000] IRLR 324 (followed in *Brown v TNT Express Worldwide (UK) Ltd* [2000] 20 LS Gaz R 43, CA.

15 The restriction was removed in sex discrimination cases by S.I. 1996 No. 438: see p. 271 above. The CRE has recommended that compensation for unintentional indirect discrimination be made available under the 1976 Act: *Reform of the Race Relations Act 1976* (CRE, 1998).

16 [1996] ICR 291, [1996] IRLR 11, EAT.

17 Ibid., per Mummery J, at p. 15.

discrimination[18] and obtaining discovery of documents[19], and the criticisms made earlier in relation to sex discrimination cases apply with equal force here. The Commission for Racial Equality (CRE), set up under the 1976 Act, has similar powers to those of the EOC, in particular powers to conduct formal investigations[20], to issue and enforce non-discrimination notices[1], to take action against discriminatory advertisements[2] and persistent discrimination[3], and to help individuals to bring discrimination claims against their employers[4]. The CRE has produced a Code of Practice on racial equality in employment which came into force in 1984[5], setting out the relevant law and suggesting good employment practices on matters such as equal opportunity policies, recruitment (including the possible discriminatory effects of recruitment by word of mouth or through trade unions), cultural or religious needs, language training, the analysis and monitoring of the racial mix of the workforce[6] and positive action in training (the only area where this is legally permissible); the Code also considers the responsibilities of fellow employees, trade unions and employment agencies.

The CRE has a duty under section 43 of the Race Relations Act to keep the working of the Act under review and, if it thinks necessary, to make recommendations for amending it. To date, the CRE has carried out three reviews of the Act. The first, in 1985, elicited no response from government, while the second, in 1992, received a detailed response which rejected most of the proposals. In the third review, in 1998, the CRE recommended some 50 changes to the existing law[7], some of which built on the earlier proposals for reform of the law enforcement aspects of the 1976 Act, while others were aimed at establishing good equal opportunities practice within organisations. In particular, the CRE proposed the enactment of a broad right not to be discriminated against by public bodies (thereby extending the existing provisions, which only apply to discrimination in employment and training and the provision of goods, facilities

18 See p. 263, above. The fact that an alleged discriminator is related by marriage to people from one ethnic group does not justify an inference that he did not racially abuse a person from a different ethnic group: *Robson v IRC* [1998] IRLR 186, EAT.

19 See *Science Research Council v Nassé* [1979] ICR 921, [1979] IRLR 465, HL. In *West Midlands Passenger Transport Executive v Singh* [1988] ICR 614, [1988] IRLR 186, the Court of Appeal held that statistical material showing the numbers of white and non-white applicants for similar posts was logically probative of whether the employers had discriminated against the applicant on racial grounds, and was thus potentially subject to discovery. On discovery generally, see p. 264 above.

20 Such an investigation must stem from an existing belief that discrimination is taking place by a named person, who must be allowed to make representations: *Hillingdon London Borough Council v Commission for Racial Equality* [1982] AC 779, [1982] IRLR 424, HL; *Re Prestige Group plc* [1984] ICR 473, [1984] IRLR 166, HL.

1 Race Relations Act 1976, s. 58. The person against whom a notice is issued may appeal against it under s. 59; the complexity and time-consuming nature of the statutory appeal structure can be seen from *Commission for Racial Equality v Amari Plastics Ltd* [1982] ICR 304, [1982] IRLR 252, CA.

2 Ibid., ss. 29 and 63.

3 Ibid., s. 62.

4 Ibid., s. 66.

5 S.I. 1983 No. 1081. The text of the Code is set out in *Harvey* S[311].

6 The Code was taken into consideration in *West Midlands Passenger Transport Executive v Singh* (n. 19, above) as a factor in altering the previous judicial approach to ethnic monitoring (and the discovery of material relating thereto). In *Carrington v Helix Lighting Ltd* [1990] ICR 125, [1990] IRLR 6, the EAT indicated that failure to monitor as recommended by the Code may lead to an adverse inference being drawn by the tribunal.

7 *Reform of the Race Relations Act 1976* (CRE, 1998).

and services, to areas such as policing and the treatment of prisoners), and a positive duty on all public bodies to work for the elimination of racial discrimination and to promote equality of opportunity and good race relations. Other reforms proposed by the CRE included the adoption of a wider, less technical definition of indirect discrimination, extending the scope of the 1976 Act to cover office-holders and volunteers, empowering the CRE to enter into legally binding undertakings and to conduct formal investigations on its own initiative, clarifying the law on positive action, making ethnic monitoring compulsory for all employers with more than 250 employees, extending the power of employment tribunals to make recommendations on future conduct, and giving tribunals the power to consider group or class actions.

The case for reform of the Race Relations Act was given significant added impetus in February 1999 by the publication of the Stephen Lawrence Inquiry Report[8], which found clear evidence of institutional racism[9] within the Metropolitan Police, and accepted the CRE's submission that institutional racism is widespread in other institutions. One of the key recommendations of the Inquiry Report was that the full force of the race relations legislation should apply to all police officers, and that chief officers of police should be made vicariously liable for the acts and omissions of their officers relevant to that legislation[10]. In the wake of the Inquiry Report, the Government promised to respond with legislation, and in December 1999 it introduced the Race Relations (Amendment) Bill, bringing the activities of all public bodies (not just the police) within the scope of the Race Relations Act. As originally framed, the Bill fell a long way short of expectations. It did not include indirect discrimination or a positive duty to promote racial equality, nor did it implement the other reforms recommended by the CRE in its 1998 review, despite the fact that many of the CRE's proposals had been welcomed by the Home Secretary[11]. Following widespread criticism of its deficiencies, the Bill was amended during its passage through Parliament to cover indirect discrimination, and will place a positive duty on specified public authorities to 'make arrangements[12] to secure that [their] functions are carried out with due regard to the need (a) to eliminate unlawful racial discrimination; and (b) to promote equality of opportunity and good relations between persons of different racial groups.[13]' The criticism that the Bill fails to implement the other reforms recommended by the CRE remains valid, and in this respect the Bill must be regarded as a missed opportunity.

8 *The Stephen Lawrence Inquiry: Report of an Inquiry by Sir William Macpherson*, Cm 4262–I, 1999.
9 Defined in the Inquiry Report as: 'The collective failure of an organisation to provide an appropriate and professional service to people because of their colour, culture or ethnic origin. It can be seen or detected in processes, attitudes and behaviour which amount to discrimination through unwitting prejudice, ignorance, thoughtlessness and racist stereotyping which disadvantage minority ethnic people.'
10 Ibid., recommendation 11.
11 Response of the Home Secretary to the CRE's Third Review of the Race Relations Act, July 1999.
12 The Bill does not specify what types of 'arrangements' might be necessary to comply with this duty, but new s. 71(2) will give the Home Secretary a power to make regulations imposing specific duties on some or all public authorities 'for the purpose of ensuring the better performance' of the general duty; enforcement is by the CRE, which may serve a compliance notice (enforceable by a court order) if it is satisfied that a public authority has failed to comply with its statutory duty: ibid., new ss. 71D and 71E.
13 Race Relations Act 1976, s. 71(1), as substituted by the Race Relations (Amendment) Bill 2000. The duty to promote equality of opportunity between persons of different racial groups will not apply to public authorities carrying out immigration and nationality functions: ibid., new s. 71A. Those functions will also be exempt from the prohibition against discrimination on grounds of nationality and ethnic or national origin: ibid., new s. 19C.

Any further developments in this area are likely to come from Europe. As was seen in the introduction to this chapter, in June 2000 the Council of Ministers reached agreement on a Race Directive establishing for the first time a minimum standard of legal protection against racial discrimination across the European Union. The Directive, which was agreed under Article 13 of the EC Treaty[14], will make it unlawful to discriminate against people on grounds of racial or ethnic origin[15] in employment and training, and also in matters such as education, social protection and social security, 'social advantages' of an economic or cultural nature (e.g. concessionary travel, reduced prices at cultural events and subsidised school meals) and access to and the supply of goods and services[16]. Member states will have three years from the entry into force of the Directive in which to take the necessary steps to implement it[17]. Much of the content of the Directive as it concerns employment is already covered by UK law (this being one area where the UK is ahead of some other member states), but there are a number of areas where domestic law may need to be amended in order to implement the Directive fully; so, for example, the definition of indirect discrimination in Article 2 of the Directive[18] is arguably broader than the RRA definition; Article 3 of the Directive expressly states that harassment related to ethnic or racial origin which creates 'an intimidating, hostile, offensive or disturbing environment' constitutes discrimination; Article 5 permits positive action in the form of 'measures intended to prevent or compensate for disadvantages suffered by a group of persons of a particular racial or ethnic origin'; Article 7 enables associations and organisations to bring proceedings on behalf of individual complainants, with their approval; and Article 8 requires a shift in the burden of proof in civil cases from the complainant to the respondent once the complainant has established facts from which it may be presumed that there has been direct or indirect racial discrimination[19].

4   EQUAL PAY[20]

The Equal Pay Act 1970, as amended by the Sex Discrimination Act 1975, is aimed at preventing discrimination between men and women as regards terms

---

14   Art 13. of the EC Treaty, which was introduced by the Treaty of Amsterdam, confers a power on the Council to take action to combat discrimination based on sex, racial or ethnic origin, religion or belief, disability, age or sexual orientation: see p. 224.

15   The Directive does not prohibit discrimination on grounds of nationality, which is dealt with separately in Arts. 12 and 39 of the Treaty.

16   The proposed Action Programme 2001-2006 would allocate a budget of 100 million euros to fund practical action by member states to promote racial equality in the areas covered by the Race Directive and the proposed Employment Directive (e.g. through 'transnational cooperation' and the exchange of ideas and information).

17   At the time of writing, the Race Directive was expected to receive the formal approval of the Council of Ministers in the summer of 2000.

18   Art. 2 states that 'indirect discrimination shall be taken to occur where an apparently neutral provision, criterion or practice is liable to affect adversely a person or a group of persons of a particular racial or ethnic origin, unless that provision, criterion or practice is objectively justified by a legitimate aim which is unrelated to the racial or ethnic origin of a person or group of persons and the means of achieving that aim are appropriate and necessary.'

19   This mirrors the provisions on the burden of proof in sex discrimination cases under the Burden of Proof Directive (Council Directive 97/80/EC), which the UK is required to implement by 22 July 2001.

20   See McColgan Just Wages for Women (1997).

and conditions of employment. As such, it only applies to cases where a contractual relationship already exists between the complainant and his or her employer[1]; if a case arises concerning alleged discrimination in an area other than terms and conditions of employment (e.g. advertising vacancies, recruitment, refusal of employment or promotion), that will come under the Sex Discrimination Act 1975[2]. The 1970 Act, once passed, was held in abeyance for five years in order to give employers time to make necessary arrangements for compliance and it finally came into force on 29 December 1975. In its early years the Act led to a significant shift in relative pay levels as between men and women[3], but after it had been in operation for several years it became clear that it was subject to certain limitations which meant that it could go so far and no further. However, since the early 1980s the whole area has been revitalised by the impact of EC law, and in particular Article 119 (now 141) of the EC Treaty, which provided (before the Amsterdam Treaty modifications[4]) that each member state shall 'ensure and subsequently maintain the principle that men and women shall receive equal pay for equal work'. As explained earlier in this chapter[5], this is important for a number of reasons, not least that Article 119 (now 141) prevails over conflicting provisions of domestic law, and if domestic law is found wanting when measured against the yardstick of EC law, enforcement proceedings can be brought in the ECJ in order to enforce compliance. In Case 61/81 *EC Commission v United Kingdom*[6], the ECJ held that our existing Equal Pay Act 1970 did not comply with the treaty requirements by allowing a woman to demand equal pay for work of equal value. This led to the major amendments in 1983 instituting (by regulations) the 'equal value claim' which is considered below. More recently, the ECJ's broad interpretation of Article 119 (now 141), and in particular its landmark decision in *Barber v Guardian Royal Exchange Assurance Group*[7] that benefits under a contracted-out, private occupational pension scheme fall within the scope of the word 'pay' in Article 119 (now 141), led to the repeal of the exclusion in the 1970 Act for provisions made in connection with death or retirement, the enactment in the Pensions Act 1995 of a new right to equal treatment in occupational pension schemes, and the equalisation of state pensionable ages at 65[8]. Unusually, the ECJ held in *Barber* that its decision was not to operate retrospectively, so that Article 119 (now 141) could not be relied upon in order to claim entitlement to equal pension benefits for periods of service before the ruling in that case; however, the temporal limitation in *Barber* was held not to apply to the right to *join* a pension scheme[9], and the impact of Community law was graphically illustrated by the ECJ's decision in *Preston v Wolverhampton Healthcare NHS Trust*[10] (a test-case for some 60,000 part-time workers excluded from

---

1   The definition of 'employment' is wide enough to cover an independent contractor who executes work personally, as well as an employee: Equal Pay Act 1970, s. 1(8); for the cases on the similar provision in the Sex Discrimination Act 1975, see p. 236, above.
2   See p. 236.
3   By 1977, women's pay as a proportion of men's had risen to 75.5 per cent, compared with 63 per cent in 1970.
4   As modified in the Amsterdam Treaty, Art. 141 now expressly confers a right to equal pay for work of equal value: 'Each Member State shall ensure that the principle of equal pay for male and female workers for equal work *or work of equal value* is applied' (italics supplied).
5   See p. 227.
6   [1982] ICR 578, [1982] IRLR 333, ECJ.
7   [1991] 1 QB 344, [1990] ICR 616, ECJ. See p. 303, below.
8   See p. 308, below.
9   *Vroege v NCIV Instituut voor Volkshuisvesting BV* [1995] ICR 635, [1994] IRLR 651, ECJ.
10   Case C-78/98, [2000] IRLR 506. See p. 301 below.

occupational pension schemes) that workers unlawfully excluded from such schemes were in principle entitled to back-date their membership to 8 April 1976 (i.e. the date on which the ECJ first held that Article 119 (now 141) had direct effect).

While EC law has undeniably revitalised the domestic law on equal pay, the current position is far from satisfactory. The relevant principles and procedures are extremely complex and time-consuming (one well-known case involving a group of NHS speech therapists took 14 years to resolve[11]), yet the statistics indicate that the pay gap between men and women is stubbornly resistant to further reduction. Despite nearly 25 years of equal pay legislation, the average hourly pay of women full-time workers is still only 80 per cent of that of male full-time workers[12]. Reasons for the continuing disparity in pay levels include the disproportionate number of women in lower grades, and the fact that women are still heavily concentrated in employment sectors which have a high degree of gender-segregation and where pay levels are generally low[13]. The EOC has recommended a number of reforms to equal pay law, including the replacement of the existing Acts with a single Sex Equality Act, the introduction of compulsory gender monitoring of the workforce, a power for employment tribunals to hear group or representative actions and to make general findings of discrimination (rather than simply ruling on the individual case in hand), and a streamlining of procedures to make justice more speedy and straightforward, including time-limited hearings and greater use of preliminary hearings in equal value cases[14]. The Government has indicated its intention to consult on changes in the way equal pay cases are dealt with to make them clearer and simpler.

i)   The equality clause

Under section 1(1) of the Act, every woman's contract is deemed to include an 'equality clause' to the effect that i) if any term in her contract is less favourable than a similar term in a man's contract, that term is to be treated as modified so that it is not less favourable than the man's term, and ii) if her contract does not include a beneficial term which appears in a man's contract, her contract shall be treated as including that term[15]. For the equality clause to operate one of three tests must be satisfied; the woman must be employed either on 'like work' with a man 'in the same employment', or on 'work rated as equivalent' with a man in the same employment, or on 'work of equal value' to that of such a man. As there is no statutory reversal of the burden of proof[16], it will be for the applicant to show that

---

11   *The Guardian*, 8 May 2000, reporting a £12m settlement for 351 NHS staff, negotiated between the Department of Health and MSF union; the legal action in the case is discussed at p. 294 below.

12   *Equality in the 21st Century: A New Sex Equality Law for Britain* (EOC, 1998).

13   See '*Women's Incomes over a Lifetime*' (Cabinet Office, 2000).

14   Ibid., n. 12. The EOC has issued a *Code of Practice on Equal Pay* (1997) which aims to provide practical guidance and to recommend good practice to those with responsibility for, or an interest in, pay arrangements. The Code is admissible in evidence in proceedings under the Sex Discrimination Act or the Equal Pay Act, and must be taken into account by the tribunal where relevant.

15   Equal Pay Act 1970, s. 1(2); although framed in terms of women being at a disadvantage, these provisions apply equally if a man is at a disadvantage: s. 1(3). The effect of an equality clause was considered by the House of Lords in *Hayward v Cammell Laird Shipbuilders Ltd* [1988] ICR 464, [1988] IRLR 257, considered below.

16   Although note the potential impact here of the Burden of Proof Directive, discussed at p. 265.

her case falls within one of the three heads[17]. Where the applicant succeeds, a presumption will be raised that the difference in terms is due to sex discrimination, and her contract will be modified by the equality clause, unless the employer is able to rebut the presumption by showing that the difference in terms is genuinely due to some material factor other than the difference of sex between the applicant and her comparator, i.e. that the reason for the difference is not tainted by sex discrimination. The modification via the equality clause operates on a term-by-term basis. The tribunal is not empowered to act as a general wage-fixing body, deciding for example that the woman's work is worth 80 per cent of the value of the man's work and ordering any necessary wage adjustments accordingly. Neither is it possible to offset any disadvantageous terms in the applicant's contract by pointing to other terms in her contract which are more favourable that those enjoyed by her comparator, a point established in *Hayward v Cammell Laird Shipbuilders Ltd*[18], one of the first cases on the equal value provisions to come before the higher courts. Miss Hayward (supported by her union and the EOC) won on her substantive claim, but then the question arose as to what she was entitled to. She claimed the same basic rate of pay as her male comparator as a term of her contract under the equality clause, but the employers objected to this, pointing out that although her basic rate had been less, she had enjoyed other terms of employment (particularly as to sickness benefits, holidays and meal breaks) which were better than her comparator's, which offset the disadvantage on pay. Thus, if one took a 'term-by-term' approach she could succeed in her claim for the same basic pay, but if one took a broader, 'package' approach to her terms and conditions as a whole she would fail. The Court of Appeal opted for the package approach, but her appeal was allowed by the House of Lords which held, as a matter of construction of section 1(2), that the correct approach is to examine the two contracts term by term; she was therefore entitled to keep the benefit of those terms which were better than those of her comparator, while still being entitled to the equality of basic pay that she had sought all along[19], Lord Mackay LC adding for good measure that this approach is consistent with EC law[20].

a) Like work

This is defined in section 1(4) as work 'of the same or a broadly similar nature', such that any differences between the things the woman does and the things done by the male comparator 'are not of practical importance in relation to terms and conditions of employment'. Three points might be made on this definition. The first is that in deciding whether work is the same or broadly similar, the

---

17   Note, however, that in *Handels-og Kontorfunktionaerernes Forbund i Danmark v Dansk Arbejdsgiverforening (acting for Danfoss)*: 109/88 [1991] ICR 74, [1989] IRLR 532, the ECJ stated that by virtue of EC Directive 75/117, where a pay system is marked by a 'total lack of transparency' the burden of proof will be on the employer to show that the pay system was not discriminatory.

18   [1988] ICR 464, [1988] IRLR 257, HL (noted Napier (1988) NLJ 341), reversing [1987] ICR 682, [1987] IRLR 186, CA.

19   An obvious danger in this approach is the potential disruption of differentials in pay and conditions, particularly where the employer's payment system involves employees in choosing from a menu of fringe benefits. The scope to be given to the defence of 'genuine material factor' (below) could be crucial in such cases (see *Hayward*, per Lord Goff).

20   This was confirmed by the ECJ in *Barber*, above, n. 7.

tribunal should take a wide view. Thus in *Capper Pass Ltd v Lawton*[1] a female cook who prepared 10 to 20 lunches for directors was held to be employed on like work with two male assistant chefs who helped to provide many more meals at more times of the day in the works canteen, particularly as it was a generally similar type of work involved, with similar skill and knowledge required to do it. In deciding upon similarity or otherwise, the tribunal is not confined to the detailed physical processes performed by the employees in question, but may consider more general matters such as differences in responsibility (as in the case of two buyers, where the higher paid male buyer is in fact employed to buy more expensive goods, thereby incurring greater responsibility if he buys poor goods[2]), or the status of the complainant as a 'trainee'[3]. If matters such as these are taken into account in a bona fide grading scheme, under which the man and the women are genuinely on different grades, then the man and the woman will not be held to be on 'like work' and the woman will not be able to claim equality[4]. The second point is that in looking to see whether any differences are of practical importance the tribunal should take an equally broad approach, for the very concept of 'broadly similar' work necessarily implies differences in detail. However, these should not defeat a claim for equality unless they are such as the tribunal would expect in practice to be reflected in different terms and conditions of employment[5]. Also, section 1(4) itself states that in comparing work 'regard shall be had to the frequency or otherwise with which any such differences occur in practice as well as to the nature and extent of the differences'. Thus the tribunal must look at the duties actually performed, not those theoretically possible. In *Shields v Coomes (Holdings) Ltd*[6] a male counterhand at a betting shop was paid at a higher hourly rate than a female counterhand, the claimed difference being that the man was there partly as a deterrent to potential troublemakers; the Court of Appeal held that the woman was entitled to equal pay, since there was no evidence of the man in question being particularly skilled or specially trained for this extra function or of there in fact ever having been any particular trouble for him to deal with, so that any difference was in practice only one of sex and the tribunal, in finding for the employer, had paid too much attention to bare contractual obligations and too little to the practicalities. The third point is that the tribunal, in making its comparison, must look at the duties performed by the woman and the man, not at the time at which they are performed. In *Dugdale v Kraft Foods Ltd*[7] female quality control workers performed prima facie similar work to that done by male quality control workers, but the men were paid at a higher basic rate because they worked night shifts and certain Sundays. The tribunal thought that this was a material difference, but the EAT reversed this decision and remitted the case to another tribunal, which eventually awarded equal pay to a majority of the applicants in the case[8].

However, it must be remembered that the Act is aimed at securing treatment that is not less favourable than that given to a man in the circumstances, not at

1 [1977] ICR 83, [1976] IRLR 366.
2 *Eaton Ltd v Nuttall* [1977] ICR 272, [1977] IRLR 71.
3 *De Brito v Standard Chartered Bank Ltd* [1978] ICR 650, EAT.
4 *Capper Pass Ltd v Allan* [1980] ICR 194, [1980] IRLR 236, EAT.
5 *Capper Pass Ltd v Lawton* [1977] ICR 83 at 87H, [1976] IRLR 366 at 367.
6 [1978] ICR 1159, [1978] IRLR 263, CA; see also *Redland Roof Tiles v Harper* [1977] ICR 349, EAT.
7 [1977] ICR 48, [1976] IRLR 368. See also *Electrolux Ltd v Hutchinson* [1977] ICR 252, [1976] IRLR 410.
8 *Dugdale v Kraft Foods Ltd* [1977] IRLR 160, IT.

securing mathematical equality of pay packets at the end of the day, so that if men do in fact perform similar work but at anti-social hours, or in unfavourable conditions, this may amount to a material difference justifying the payment of extra remuneration (special premia for overtime, night working, Sunday shifts, etc.) provided that such premia genuinely reflect the extra inconvenience and are not so large that they are seen as simply a way of indirectly reintroducing a sex-based distinction:

'... this does not mean that men, or women, cannot be paid extra for working at night or at weekends, or at other inconvenient times; if the additional remuneration is justified by the inconvenience of the time at which it is done the claim [for equality] will not succeed. For, while every contract of employment is deemed to include an equality clause, it only has to take effect so that the terms of the woman's contract shall be treated as so modified as not to be less favourable than the man's. Thus the industrial tribunal – without falling into the error of setting itself up as a wage-fixing body – may adjust the woman's remuneration upon a claim by her so that it is at the same rate as the man's, discounting for the fact that he works at inconvenient hours, and she does not[9]'.

What has been said on this third point so far, however, assumes that there is a sex-based difference in the working patterns. Where, however, both men and women work at inconvenient times, there is no requirement that all those who work, e.g. at night, shall be paid the same basic rate as all those who work normal day shifts. Thus a woman who works days cannot use the principle (of disregarding the time of performing similar work) in order to claim equality with a man on a higher basic rate for working nights if in fact there are women working nights on that rate too, and the applicant herself would be entitled to that rate if she changed shifts[10].

Finally, it is implicit in what has already been said that a claim under this head should not be defeated simply on the grounds that the applicant and her comparator have different qualifications (although that may be give rise to a 'genuine material factor' defence: see below). However in *Angestelltenbetriebsrat der Wiener Gebietskrankenkasse v Wiener Gebietskrankenkasse*[11], the ECJ surprisingly held that for the purposes of Article 141 and the Equal Pay Directive, graduate psychologists employed as psychotherapists were not to be regarded as doing the 'same work' as trained doctors employed to do the same job, 'where the same activities are performed over a considerable length of time by persons the basis of whose qualification to exercise their profession is different'. The decision can perhaps be defended on its facts, on the grounds that the difference in the qualifications of the two groups probably meant that their level of performance was qualitatively different, but as a general proposition it is respectfully doubted.

b) Work rated as equivalent

A woman is to be regarded as being on work rated as equivalent to that of a man if it has been given an equal value with that of his (in terms of the demands made

9   *National Coal Board v Sherwin* [1978] ICR 700, at 740D, [1978] IRLR 122 at 124 per Phillips J (cf., on the facts, *Thomas v National Coal Board* [1987] ICR 757, [1987] IRLR 451, EAT).
10 *Kerr v Lister & Co Ltd* [1977] IRLR 259, EAT.
11 (Case C-309/97) [1999] IRLR 804, ECJ. See also *Glasgow City Council v Marshall* [2000] IRLR 272, HL.

on her under various headings such as effort, skill and decision) by a job evaluation scheme covering that employment[12]. The Act does not lay down detailed requirements for such a scheme[13], but it is in mandatory terms, so that where there has been such a study a tribunal should act upon its recommendations, even if the parties who drafted it are no longer happy with it[14]; once the scheme has been worked out, it will be binding for the purposes of the Act and may be relied on by the claimant, even if the employer has not in fact put it into effect[15]. However, to be binding the job evaluation scheme must be a valid scheme, in the sense that it must be non-discriminatory, objective and capable of impartial application:

> '... subsection (5) can only apply to what may be called a valid evaluation study. By that, we mean a study satisfying the test of being thorough in analysis and capable of impartial application. It should be possible by applying the study to arrive at the position of a particular employee at a particular point in a particular salary grade without taking other matters into account except those unconnected with the nature of the work ... One which does not satisfy that test, and requires the management to make a subjective judgment concerning the nature of the work before the employee can be fitted into the appropriate place in the appropriate salary grade, would seem to us not to be a valid study for the purposes of subsection (5)[16]'.

It may therefore be possible to challenge the validity of a scheme (indeed subsection (5) allows a tribunal to 'correct' a scheme which is based on different values for men and women, by looking to see if the work would have been rated equally but for that particular false premise). However, it should be noted that such a challenge might not in practice be of much assistance to the applicant for, having disposed of the scheme as it stood, she may not then rely on what she thinks the scheme should have provided, for no such different scheme ever existed and the tribunal may not undertake its own evaluation exercise under this head[17].

---

12   Equal Pay Act 1970, s. 1(5). In *Springboard Sunderland Trust v Robson* [1992] ICR 554, [1992] IRLR 261, the EAT held that where a job evaluation scheme operates by awarding points for different criteria, what matters is whether the woman and her comparator have been placed in the same grade under the scheme, and not the precise number of points awarded.

13   For some guidance on standard forms of schemes, see *Eaton Ltd v Nuttall* [1977] ICR 272 at 278, [1977] IRLR 71 at 74; also *ACAS Guide No. 1*.

14   *Greene v Broxtowe District Council* [1977] ICR 241, [1977] IRLR 34, EAT.

15   *O'Brien v Sim-Chem Ltd* [1980] ICR 573, [1980] IRLR 373, HL. For this principle to apply, however, the scheme must have been worked out and accepted as valid by the parties who had agreed to carry it out: *Arnold v Beecham Group Ltd* [1982] ICR 744, [1982] IRLR 307.

16   *Eaton Ltd v Nuttall* [1977] ICR 272 at 277H, [1977] IRLR 71 at 74. In *Bromley v H & J Quick Ltd* [1988] ICR 623, [1988] IRLR 249 the Court of Appeal held that, to be valid under s. 1(5) an employer-commissioned job evaluation must be 'analytical' in nature, i.e. based on the demands made on employees under various discrete headings, rather than on any job 'ranking' or 'felt fair' basis which would be too vague. Article 1 of the Equal Pay Directive (Directive 75/117/EEC) also has a requirement that an evaluation study must be fair, in the sense of being based on the same criteria for men and women, and so drawn up as to exclude any discrimination on the grounds of sex: see *Rummler v Dato-Druck GmbH*: 237/85 [1987] ICR 774, [1987] IRLR 32, ECJ.

17   *England v Bromley London Borough Council* [1978] ICR 1, EAT.

c) Work of equal value

The European Court of Justice ruled in Case 61/81 *EC Commission v United Kingdom*[18] that the existing equal pay laws did not comply with the requirement of the Equal Pay Directive[19] that a woman should be able to claim equal pay for work of equal value; this was only permitted under the existing laws if the employer had voluntarily undertaken some form of job evaluation (head *b*) above), so did not avail the majority of women in employments not subject to such a study. In order to comply with this judgment, the Government introduced by regulations[20] a right to equal pay for work of equal value[1], but subjected it to an exceptionally complicated, not to say tortuous procedure.

The change was achieved by an amendment to section 1 of the Equal Pay Act 1970, adding a third category of entitlement to equal pay, where a woman is employed on work which (though not being like work or work rated as equivalent)[2] 'is, in terms of the demands made on her (for instance under such headings as effort, skill and decision), of equal value to that of a man in the same employment'[3]. The immediate problem is that this takes the tribunals away from matters of relatively observable fact (Is the work the same or similar? Has the employer got a job evaluation study that applies to this woman?) and into the realm of assessment of value and the almost religious mysteries of job evaluation, for which arguably a tribunal as a judicial body is not particularly well suited. The compromise has been to keep the procedure judicial, but to make it heavily dependent in practice on the opinion of an independent expert, i.e. a person appointed by ACAS from a panel kept by them of persons knowledgeable in the techniques of job evaluation.

The equal value procedure has been highly controversial, not least because of the excessive delays which have bedevilled it since its introduction. In the first few years, the average time taken to resolve equal value cases was over $2^1/_2$ years, and some claims took far longer, particularly where the employer decided to fight the claim at each stage. It was widely thought that the decline in the number of equal pay complaints during the 1980s was (at least in part) a result of the length and complexity of the tribunal processes concerned[4], and some even went so far as to suggest that the system was designed to deter claims. By the early 1990s the case for a radical overhaul of the equal value procedures had become overwhelming. The President of the EAT described the procedures as in need

18   [1982] ICR 578, [1982] IRLR 333, ECJ.
19   Council Directive No. 75/117/EEC. Before the Amsterdam amendments, Art. 119 (now 141) did not expressly confer a right to equal pay for work of equal value: the only explicit reference to that head was in the Equal Pay Directive.
20   The Equal Pay (Amendment) Regulations 1983, S.I. 1983 No. 1794, amending the Equal Pay Act 1970, s. 1 and inserting new s. 2A, dealing with the main substantive changes.
1   Rubenstein *Equal Pay for Work of Equal Value* (1984); Hepple *Equal Pay and the Industrial Tribunals* (1984); Lester and Wainright *Equal Pay for Work of Equal Value: Law and Practice* (1984); McCrudden 'Equal pay for work of equal value' (1983) 12 ILJ 197 and (1984) 13 ILJ 50; Szyszczak 'Pay inequalities and equal value claims' (1985) 48 MLR 139; McCrudden (ed.) *Women, Employment and European Equality Law* (1987), ch. 7.
2   See on this requirement *Pickstone v Freemans plc* [1988] ICR 697, [1988] IRLR 357, HL, discussed under d) below.
3   In *Murphy v Bord Telecom Eireann*: 157/86 [1988] ICR 445, [1988] IRLR 267, ECJ the employer raised the astonishing defence in an equal value case that the women who were paid less than the male comparator could not claim equality because they were in fact engaged on work of *higher* value than his; this was held by the ECJ to be contrary to Art. 119 (now 141) and so, under EC law at least, a woman can claim equal pay for work that is at least of equal value to that of the male comparator.
4   ACAS Annual Report, 1992, p. 23; EOC Annual Report, 1991, p. 6.

of 'urgent review', and as giving rise 'to delays which are properly described as scandalous and amount to a denial of justice to women seeking remedy through the judicial process.[5]' In 1990, the EOC published a series of proposals for the reform of the equal pay laws[6], designed in part to tackle the inordinate delays in processing equal value cases. Most of the recommendations were not proceeded with, although some limited (and, it could be said, half-hearted) reforms were introduced in 1994, requiring independent experts to set a timetable for the production of reports, and preventing employers from raising the genuine material factor defence twice. After a further period of consultation[7], another series of reforms were introduced in 1996[8], reducing the role of the independent expert and restricting the circumstances in which employers can raise the 'genuine material factor' defence. However, despite these changes, the procedure in equal value claims is still extremely complex and prone to excessive delay, with even the less complicated cases taking an average of 20 months to decide (hence the EOC's recommendations for further reform, discussed above).

Turning to the detail of the equal value procedures[9], the initial emphasis in an equal value claim is, as usual, upon ACAS conciliation, but if that is not successful the first major stage is, in effect, a preliminary hearing in order to decide whether the case should be remitted to an expert for the compilation of a formal report. At this stage, a tribunal may dismiss the claim without considering it on its merits if it is satisfied that there are 'no reasonable grounds for determining that the work is of equal value', i.e. if it considers that the claim is so weak that it has no reasonable prospect of success[10]. One particular case is spelled out as having no reasonable prospect of success; this is where the employer has already undertaken a job evaluation study which shows that the man and woman in question are not performing work of equal value. Such a study will thus be a good defence to the employer, even if commissioned after the commencement of the proceedings[11], unless it was itself 'made on a system which discriminates on grounds of sex'[12]. The burden of proof will be on the employer to show that the existing job

5   *Aldridge v British Telecommunications plc* [1989] ICR 790, [1990] IRLR 10, per Wood J.

6   *Equal Pay for Men and Women: Strengthening the Acts* (EOC, 1990). The proposals included the automatic application of successful decisions to similarly placed employees, the removal of the initial requirement to show that the case has a reasonable chance of success, the appointment of full-time independent experts, and the removal of the bar on equal value claims where there is an existing job evaluation scheme.

7   *Resolving Employment Rights Disputes: Options for Reform* (1994).

8   S.I. 1996 No. 438.

9   The detailed rules are to be found in the Employment Tribunals (Constitution and Rules of Procedure) Regulations 1993, S.I. 1993 No. 2687, Sch. 2, as amended.

10 Equal Pay Act 1970, s. 2A. The tribunal should not dismiss the claim without giving the parties an opportunity to adduce their own evidence at a further hearing: *Wood v William Ball Ltd* [1999] IRLR 773, EAT. The EOC has recommended that the 'no reasonable grounds' defence should be abolished on the grounds that it 'allows traditional stereotypes and attitudes to go unchallenged': *Equality in the 21st Century: A New Sex Equality Law for Britain* (EOC, 1998).

11 *Dibro Ltd v Hore* [1990] ICR 370, [1990] IRLR 129, EAT. The tribunal may be unwilling to stay proceedings in order to allow such a study to come into operation: *Avon County Council v Foxall* [1989] ICR 407, [1989] IRLR 435, EAT.

12 This is defined in s. 2A(3) as a system under which 'a difference, or coincidence, between values set by that system on different demands under the same or different headings is not justifiable irrespective of the sex of the person on whom those demands are made'. This might be the case if more brownie points are given under the system for traditionally male attributes (e.g. strength) than for traditionally female attributes (e.g. dexterity), even though each attribute may be equally important in the job concerned. The study itself (to be valid under s. 1(5) and therefore under s. 2A) must be conducted on an analytical basis: *Bromley v H & J Quick Ltd*, n. 16, above.

evaluation study is untainted by sex discrimination[13]. Finally, the defence of 'genuine material factor' (considered below) may be raised at this preliminary stage[14], for it would be a waste of time and money to commission the report if the tribunal was then to rule out the claim on the basis of this particular defence. Originally, the employer was allowed two bites of this particular cherry, as the raising of the genuine material factor defence at the preliminary stage was expressly stated to be 'without prejudice' to further consideration of that defence after the expert had reported. However, the rules were changed in 1994 to avoid the possibility of the defence being raised twice[15], so that where the genuine material factor defence has been raised by the employer and considered by the tribunal at the preliminary hearing, the position now is that the employer will not be able to raise it a second time after the expert has reported.

If the claim is not rejected under the 'no reasonable grounds' defence, the tribunal must then decide whether to commission a report by an independent expert. Originally, the tribunal had no discretion whether or not to commission a report, even where the applicant's case was so strong (or so weak) that there seemed little point in doing so, but the procedure was amended in 1996 to give the tribunal such a discretion[16]. Where a report is commissioned, the tribunal must adjourn the proceedings pending receipt of it. The procedure for the expert to follow is set out[17] and in particular it requires him to listen to and consider representations from the parties; this could be an important stage for the parties, since their grounds of challenge once the report is written are restricted. He may also require the disclosure of evidence or documents, through application to the tribunal[18]. Job evaluation is an inexact science, with several different (though equally acceptable) approaches, but the Act does not require any particular method to be used[19], and in practice it is likely to be difficult to challenge the method in fact adopted. The original rules envisaged the report being submitted to the tribunal within six weeks, but in practice this timetable proved to be impossibly optimistic, with reports frequently taking over a year to be completed. In an effort to speed up the process, new rules were introduced in 1993 requiring the expert to notify the Secretary of State, within 14 days of his appointment or as soon as practicable thereafter, of the date by which he expects to send his report to the tribunal. If he is unable to fix the date he must explain the reasons why, and if there is any subsequent delay in the production of his report he must again notify the Secretary of State, giving his reasons, and must indicate the date by which he expects his report to be available. The tribunal may require him to submit a progress report, acting of its own volition or on the request of a party, and in cases of unjustifiable delay it may revoke the appointment and appoint another expert in his place[20].

13 *Bromley v H & J Quick Ltd*, ibid.
14 SI 1993/2687, r. 9 (2E); if the defence is made out at this stage, the tribunal must dismiss the claim without commissioning a report: *Reed Packaging Ltd v Boozer* [1988] ICR 391, [1988] IRLR 333.
15 S.I. 1994 No. 536.
16 S.I. 1996 No. 438. See *Wood v William Ball Ltd* [1999] IRLR 776, EAT.
17 SI 1993/2687, r. 8A.
18 SI 1993/2687, r. 4 (2A).
19 In *Leverton v Clwyd County Council* [1989] ICR 33, [1989] IRLR 28, HL, it was suggested that the independent expert has to carry out what is in effect an ad hoc job evaluation study, and assess the demands of the job on a qualitative rather than a quantitative basis. The EOC has recommended that the expert be required to draw up job descriptions of both the applicant's and comparator's jobs: *Equality in the 21st Century: A New Sex Equality Law for Britain* (EOC, 1998).
20 SI 1993/2687, r. 8A.

Once the report has been prepared and submitted, the tribunal convenes a resumed hearing. Its first function is to decide whether to accept the report; it may reject it if a) the expert has not followed the correct procedure, b) the conclusions are perverse (in the accepted sense) or c) the report is unsatisfactory for some other material reason. The importance of this stage must not be underestimated, for it is provided[1] that this is the only stage at which the parties may give evidence or question any witness on any matter of fact on which the expert's report is based. If the report is admitted, the tribunal proceeds to determine the case on the basis of the whole of the available evidence, of which the expert's report will be an important part[2]. The expert may be required to attend to be cross-examined; each party (though in practice this will mean the party against whom the expert has found) 'may, on giving reasonable notice of his intention to do so to the tribunal and to any other party to the claim, call one witness to give expert advice on the question on which the tribunal has required the expert to prepare a report' and this evidence is subject to cross-examination[3]. This is to prevent a situation where a party may claim to win on the basis of five experts to four.

Finally, while the criticisms of the equal value provisions are undoubtedly well-founded, it could be argued that the success or otherwise of those provisions cannot be measured entirely in terms of the number of successful tribunal applicants, for they act as a background to collective negotiations on the subject of pay and job comparisons, and the prospect of a tribunal application if negotiations fail may well influence the outcome of those negotiations. Just how significant that prospect is as a factor in pay negotiations is of course a matter of debate.

d)   The area of comparison

Unlike the Sex Discrimination Act, which works on the basis of a comparison between the treatment of the applicant and that of a hypothetical comparator, the Equal Pay Act is based on a comparison with a named comparator (or comparators). The general rule on the area of comparison in the Act is that the comparator must be 'in the same employment' as the applicant, in the sense that he is employed by her employer (or by an associated employer, as defined) at the same establishment, or at another establishment at which common terms and conditions of employment are observed, either generally or for employees of

---

1   SI 1993/2687, r. 9 (2C). In *Hayward v Cammell Laird Shipbuilders Ltd*, p. 281, above, the employers had not challenged the report at this stage and were ruled out when they tried to do so later; the tribunal emphasised that the employer must maintain a challenge at this stage, and may do so by commissioning his own study as evidence. There are two exceptional cases where matters of fact may be raised at a later stage (SI 1993/2687, r. 9 (2D)): i) where the employer raises the defence of genuine material factor; ii) where the expert's investigations have been frustrated by the failure of a party to comply with an order of disclosure under Rule 4 (so that the tribunal itself may proceed to consider questions of fact, possibly to the detriment of the party in breach of the disclosure order).
2   S. 2A(1). Recent cases have tended to play down the significance of the expert's report, emphasising that while it must be admitted in evidence, it is not conclusive of the question of equal value: *Tennants Textile Colours Ltd v Todd* [1989] IRLR 3, NICA; *Aldridge v British Telecommunications plc* [1989] ICR 790, [1990] IRLR 10, EAT.
3   SI 1993/2687, r. 9 (2B).

relevant classes[4]. In *Leverton v Clwyd County Council*[5], the House of Lords held that the requirement of common terms and conditions refers to the terms and conditions at the establishment at which the woman is employed and the establishment at which her comparator is employed, rather than to common terms and conditions as between the applicant and her comparator; in that case, the requirement was satisfied since both establishments were covered by the same collective agreement covering male and female employees of the employer, regardless of the establishment at which they worked[6]. 'Common terms and conditions' in this context means 'broadly similar' rather than 'the same'. In *British Coal Corpn v Smith*[7], some 1,286 women employed as canteen workers or cleaners at 47 different establishments claimed equal pay for work of equal value with 150 male comparators employed as clerical workers or surface mineworkers at 14 different establishments. The House of Lords held that the applicants were in the same employment as their comparators because the terms and conditions of the comparators were governed by national agreements which also applied (or would apply) to men of the same class employed at the applicant's establishment, even though local variations relating to incentive bonuses and entitlement to concessionary coal meant that the terms and conditions at different establishments for the same classes of worker were not the same. Lord Slynn interpreted the phrase 'common terms and conditions' purposively:

> 'The real question is what the legislation was seeking to achieve. Was it seeking to exclude a woman's claim unless, subject to de minimis exceptions, there was complete identity of terms and conditions for the comparator at his establishment and those which applied or would apply to a similar male worker at her establishment? Or was the legislation seeking to establish that the terms and conditions of the relevant class were sufficiently similar for a fair comparison to be made, subject always to the employer's right to establish a "material difference" defence .... If it was the former then the woman would fail at the first hurdle if there was any difference (other than a de minimis one) between the terms and conditions of the men at the various establishments, since she could not then show that the men were in the same employment as she was. The issue as to whether the differences were material so as to justify different treatment would then never arise. I do not consider that this can have been intended.'[8]

Provided she is able to overcome this hurdle, the complainant may choose the man with whom she wishes to be compared[9]; there is no express requirement

---

4   Equal Pay Act 1970, s. 1(6). There is no statutory definition of 'establishment'; for its construction in the context of redundancy consultation (where it is similarly not defined), see p. 67, above.
5   [1989] ICR 33, [1989] IRLR 28, HL. The case is a good illustration of the fact that, where there are common terms and conditions, there need be no male employees at the woman's establishment, and no women need be employed at the establishment where the male comparator works.
6   A situation described by Lord Bridge as the paradigm case.
7   [1996] IRLR 404, HL (reversing the Court of Appeal on this point).
8   Ibid., at p. 408.
9   *Ainsworth v Glass Tubes and Components Ltd* [1977] ICR 347, [1977] IRLR 74, EAT.

that the chosen comparator be 'fairly representative' of a group of workers[10], although the Court of Appeal has indicated that where the chosen comparator is from a separate establishment, it is implicit 'that the male comparator must be representative of the group or class to which he belongs[11]'. It is firmly established that an equal pay claim will not be undermined by the existence of a token male on the same terms and conditions as the complainant, as long as there is a man within the permitted area of comparison who is more favourably treated. At one time it seemed as if this basic principle was in danger of abrogation in an equal value claim; this was because the relevant provision, section 1(2)(c), states that it applies to work 'not being work in relation to which paragraph (a) [like work] or (b) [work rated as equivalent] above applies'. In *Pickstone v Freemans plc*[12] the question arose whether this prevented a woman doing job A from claiming equality of pay through work of equal value with a man doing job B if the employer simply pointed out that there were in fact other men doing job A, and so on 'like work'. This literal interpretation (which raised the possibility of an employer being able to avoid an equal value claim by employing a token male in an otherwise all-female workforce on job A) was upheld by the Court of Appeal[13] but disapproved on further appeal by the House of Lords, who held that an equal value claim can be brought in such circumstances – all that the wording in section 1(2)(c) means is that the chosen comparator must not be doing like work or work rated as equivalent; the existence of another male doing such work will be irrelevant.

The wording of the Equal Pay Act envisages a comparison between a man and a woman working together for the same employer (or an associated employer) at the same time. However, under European sex discrimination law the permitted comparison is wider ('in the same establishment or service, whether public or private')[14]. In *Macarthys Ltd v Smith*[15] the ECJ held, on a reference from the Court of Appeal, that a woman has the right under Article 119 (now 141) to compare her pay with that of her male predecessor in the same job, a decision which was subsequently applied by the Court of Appeal at the resumed hearing[16]; and more recently, in *Diocese of Hallam Trustee v Connaughton*[17] the EAT allowed a comparison to be made with a male successor. These two decisions represent a

10   *Thomas v National Coal Board* [1987] ICR 757, [1987] IRLR 451. In *McPherson v Rathgael Centre for Children and Young People and Northern Ireland Office (Training Schools Branch)* [1991] IRLR 206, the chosen comparator had been placed on a higher rate by mistake; the Northern Ireland Court of Appeal left open the question whether an anomalous comparator could be disregarded as inappropriate.

11   *British Coal Corpn v Smith; North Yorkshire County Council v Ratcliffe* [1994] ICR 810, [1994] IRLR 342, CA, per Balcombe LJ at p. 358 (reversed on other grounds; see n. 7, above).

12   [1988] ICR 697, [1988] IRLR 357, HL.

13   [1987] ICR 867, IRLR 218, CA. The Court of Appeal proceeded to consider the claim under Art. 119 (now 141) of the EC Treaty and upheld it independently on that ground (see p. 232). Thus, while the House of Lords disapproved of the Court of Appeal's narrow interpretation of English law, they in fact upheld the eventual decision, and found it unnecessary to pronounce upon the correctness or otherwise of the Court of Appeal's views on EC law.

14   *Defrenne v SABENA (No 2)* [1976] ECR 455, [1976] ICR 547..

15   [1979] 3 All ER 325, [1979] ICR 785, CA.

16   129/79: [1980] ICR 672, [1980] IRLR 210, ECJ; apld [1980] ICR 672, [1980] IRLR 210, CA. Note, however, that in such a case there may not be an order for equality (even under Art. 119 (now 141)) if there are genuine economic or other circumstances accounting for the difference in pay between the woman and her predecessor; i.e. there is under the article a defence for an employer analogous to the 'genuine material difference' defence to a claim under the Act: *Albion Shipping Agency v Arnold* [1982] ICR 22, [1981] IRLR 525.

17   [1996] IRLR 505, EAT.

fairly modest stretching of the boundaries of domestic law, but in *Scullard v Knowles*[18] the EAT took matters several steps further by overturning the decision of the tribunal not to permit the applicant, who was employed by a regional education advisory council, to compare herself with a man employed by a different regional advisory council, even though the two employers were not 'associated employers' within the meaning of the Act. There are however limits, as can be seen from *Lawrence v Regent Office Care Ltd*[19] , where the EAT refused to allow the applicant, a school catering assistant whose job was contracted out by a local authority to a private sector employer, to claim equal pay with staff still employed by the local authority whose work had already been rated as of equal value to hers, on the grounds that 'there is nothing about this case which would distinguish it from any other case where an applicant claimed equal pay with a comparator employed by another company, not necessarily even engaged in the same industry.' The decision underlines the point made earlier, that the function of the equal pay laws is not to act as a mechanism for the fixing of fair wages as such.

Finally, while the ability of an applicant in a equal pay case to choose her comparator may often work to her advantage (at least in raising an initial presumption of discrimination), there is a catch, because having chosen her comparator, she will not subsequently be able to argue that there are other factors (e.g. greater length of service) entitling her to terms which are *more* favourable than those of her comparator. In *Evesham v North Hertfordshire Health Authority*[19a] the applicant, a speech therapist, succeeded in establishing that she was employed on work of equal value with her named male comparator, a clinical psychologist, and was entitled to be placed on the pay scale for clinical psychologists. However, she had longer service than her comparator, and claimed that instead of being placed on the same point as him on his pay scale, she should be placed on that scale at a higher point, reflecting her additional years of service. The Court of Appeal rejected her claim, holding that the Equal Pay Act only requires equality of treatment by the employer of the applicant and the comparator whom she has chosen: 'were Mrs Evesham to enter, at the relevant date, the pay scale enjoyed by her comparator but at an incremental level higher than her comparator, the effect would be that from that date she received pay at a level in excess of that received by her comparator with whom she had established equal value, and commensurate with the pay scale of somebody with whom she had not established equal value.'

ii) Genuine material differences and factors

Even if there is a prima facie case of inequality, the applicant may still fail if the employer can show, on a balance of probabilities[20], that the difference in terms is

---

18 [1996] IRLR 344, EAT. The advisory councils were not 'associated employers' within the meaning of s. 1(6) because that definition only applies to companies, yet as Mummery J observed (at p. 346), under Article 141 no distinction is drawn between work carried out in the same establishment or service of limited companies and of other employers, whether incorporated or not.

19 [1999] IRLR 148, EAT. The case has been referred to the ECJ by the Court of Appeal [2000] IRLR 608.

19a [2000] IRLR 257, CA.

20 *National Vulcan Engineering Insurance Group Ltd v Wade* [1978] ICR 800, [1978] IRLR 225. This is consistent with EC law, which places the burden of proof on the employer where a pay system is marked by a 'total lack of transparency': *Handels-og Kontorfunktionaerernes Forbund i Danmark v Dansk Arbejdsgiverforening (acting for Danfoss)*: 109/88 [1991] ICR 74, [1989] IRLR 532.

genuinely due to a material factor which is not the difference of sex[1]. The most obvious examples of genuine material factors justifying differential treatment are personal differences between the applicant and her comparator, for example factors such as long service, superior qualifications, higher output or different geographical location[2], or where the man is on a higher grade under a bona fide, impartial grading scheme, so that, although in fact performing the same sort of work, he is rated more highly at doing it (e.g. he works more efficiently, or more reliably and so subject to less supervision)[3]. Unfortunately the precise formulation of the genuine material factor defence differs according to the category in which the applicant's claim falls. In cases of like work or work rated as equivalent, the employer must show that the genuine material factor is a *material difference* between the woman's case and the man's, whereas in equal value claims that requirement does not apply, and the employer need only show that the variation is genuinely due to a *material factor*. It appears that the aim of this exercise in inspired gobbledegook was to admit more matters by way of defence in equal value cases than were thought to be admissible under the existing material difference defence, and in particular to give full rein to arguments based on market forces and economic realities[4], but ironically the material difference defence was given such a wide interpretation by the House of Lords in *Rainey v Greater Glasgow Health Board*[5] that the gap between a 'material difference' and a 'material factor' has been substantially narrowed, if not entirely removed.

The issue in *Rainey* was whether a material difference under section 1(3) could relate to matters outside the personal equation, such as the operation of 'market forces'. The case concerned the expansion of a national health prosthetics department by the recruitment of prosthetists (all male, as it happened) from the private sector on their existing level of remuneration, which was higher than that paid to the existing national health service prosthetists (who were principally female and included the applicant). The applicant sought equal pay with one of the male entrants, who it was accepted was employed on like work with her. The employer's genuine material difference defence had seemed doomed to fail, as the Court of Appeal had previously held in *Clay Cross (Quarry Services) Ltd v Fletcher*[6] that the payment of higher wages to a male clerk than to a longer-serving female clerk on the basis that when his job was advertised he was the only suitable candidate and could only be induced to take the job by the offer of a higher salary than that already being paid to her, went outside the bounds of permissible personal differentials envisaged in section 1(3), and that any other conclusion could render the statute a dead letter by allowing employers simply to say that they paid the man more because he asked for more, or that they

1   Equal Pay Act 1970, s. 1(3), as substituted by the Equal Pay (Amendment) Regulations 1983, S.I. 1983 No. 1794. The employer must prove (i) that the variation is genuinely due to a material factor, and (ii) that this is not due to the difference of sex: *Financial Times Ltd v Byrne (No 2)* [1992] IRLR 163; see also *Barber v NCR (Manufacturing) Ltd* [1993] IRLR 95, EAT.

2   *Navy, Army and Air Force Institutes v Varley* [1977] ICR 11, [1976] IRLR 408, EAT.

3   *National Vulcan Engineering Insurance Group Ltd v Wade* [1978] ICR 800, [1978] IRLR 225, CA.

4   The distinction between material factors and material differences was introduced by the Equal Pay (Amendment) Regulations 1983, apparently to circumvent the decision in *Clay Cross (Quarry Services) Ltd v Fletcher* [1979] ICR 1, [1978] IRLR 361, CA, discussed below. See McCrudden (1983) 12 ILJ at 211.

5   [1987] ICR 129, [1987] IRLR 26, HL.

6   [1979] ICR 1, [1978] IRLR 361, CA; this case is also authority for the proposition that it is no defence for an act of unlawful discrimination to say that it was unintentional.

paid the woman less because she was willing to work for less. However, in *Rainey*[7], the House of Lords held that the genuine material difference defence under section 1(3) is not limited to personal differences, but is capable of extending to other objectively justified[8] grounds for the woman being paid less:

> 'In my opinion these statements [in *Fletcher*] are unduly restrictive of the proper interpretation of section 1(3). The difference must be "material", which I would construe as meaning "significant and relevant", and it must be between "her case and his". Consideration of a person's case must necessarily involve consideration of all the circumstances of that case. These may well go beyond what is not very happily described as "the personal equation", i.e. the personal qualities by way of skill, experience or training which the individual brings to the job. Some circumstances may on examination prove to be not significant or not relevant, but others may do so, though not relating to the personal qualities of the employee. In particular, where there is no question of intentional sex discrimination whether direct or indirect (and there is none here) a difference which is connected with economic factors affecting the efficient carrying on of the employer's business or other activity may well be relevant.'[9]

On the facts of the case, the House of Lords held that the applicant's case failed because there was objective justification for putting the male entrant on to a higher scale (given the need to expand the prosthetic service within a reasonable time), and for not raising the wages of the applicant and other existing prosthetists to that higher rate (since there were 'sound objectively justified administrative reasons' for maintaining their existing position within the overall Whitley Council scale). In so holding, the House of Lords adopted the 'objective justification' test for indirect discrimination under Article 119 (now 141) set out by the ECJ in *Bilka-Kaufhaus GmbH v Weber von Hartz*[10], where it was held that in determining whether there were any objectively justified grounds for the variation in pay, the court should consider whether the measures adopted by the employer:

> 'correspond to a real need on the part of the undertaking, are appropriate with a view to achieving the objectives pursued and are necessary to that end[11].'

While the decision on the facts in *Rainey* can perhaps be defended on the basis of the employer's need to recruit prosthetists against a specific labour market shortage, by breaching the 'personal equation' rule in such a comprehensive manner it was feared that the House of Lords might have opened something of a

---

7   Op. cit; the Scottish EAT and the Court of Session had distinguished *Fletcher* (though the grounds of distinction were difficult to see), but the House of Lords reconsidered the whole matter. The case is noted by McLean (1987) 46 CLJ 224, Schofield (1987) 50 MLR 379 and Townshend-Smith (1987) 16 ILJ 114.

8   Lord Keith, giving judgment, states that the test here is the same as that under the Sex Discrimination Act 1975, s. 1(1)(b)(ii) for the justification of a requirement or condition which indirectly discriminates against women.

9   At pp. 140 and 29, respectively, per Lord Keith.

10 170/84: [1987] ICR 110, [1986] IRLR 317, ECJ. The case is discussed further below.

11 In *Rainey*, Lord Keith added (at 143 and 30, respectively) that he considered that the ECJ's ruling 'would not exclude objectively justified grounds which are other than economic, such as administrative efficiency in a concern not engaged in commerce or business'.

Pandora's Box, particularly if the courts and tribunals were to accept too readily the sort of argument put forward in *Clay Cross*, i.e. that an employer was justified in paying a woman less because she was willing to work for less. The danger of such an approach is that it simply reinforces historic labour market inequalities in pay between men and women, and could render the equal pay laws a dead letter. In subsequent cases the courts have on the whole taken a cautious approach to market forces defences[12]. In *Enderby v Frenchay Health Authority*[13], the ECJ held, in a case under Article 119 (now 141), that 'the state of the employment market, which may lead an employer to increase the pay of a particular job in order to attract candidates, may constitute an objectively justified economic ground' for a difference in pay, but crucially also held that 'it is for the national court to determine, if necessary by applying the principle of proportionality, whether and to what extent the shortage of candidates for a job and the need to attract them by higher pay constitutes an objectively justified economic ground for the difference in pay between the jobs in question.' In other words, an employer will not be able to justify the whole of the difference in pay on the basis of market forces where only part of the difference in pay is attributable to that reason. In a further blow to the market forces defence, in *Ratcliffe v North Yorkshire County Council*[14], the House of Lords refused to accept that the imposition of a pay cut for a group of predominantly female school catering assistants to enable the employer to tender for work at a commercially competitive rate was due to a material factor which was not the difference of sex. In that case, the council had established a direct service organisation (DSO) for the provision of school meals following the introduction of compulsory competitive tendering, but its catering staff were forced to take a pay cut after it became apparent that the DSO was unable to compete for the school dinner contracts with commercial organisations, who employed only women, while continuing to pay the staff on their existing local government rates. The Court of Appeal held that the material factor which led to the lower rates of pay, the need to compete effectively with rival bidders, was genuinely due to the operation of market forces, and that those market forces were gender-neutral in the sense that they were unconnected with the difference of sex. However, the House of Lords upheld the appeal and restored the tribunal's decision that the material factor was in fact due to the difference of sex, in that the labour market for catering staff was almost exclusively female, whereas the council employees employed on work of equivalent value (roadsweepers, gardeners, refuse collectors and leisure attendants) were mostly men:

> 'Though conscious of the difficult problem facing the employers in seeking to compete with a rival tenderer, I am satisfied that to reduce the women's wages below that of their male comparators was the very kind of discrimination in relation to pay which the Act sought to remove[15].'

It could perhaps be concluded that where an employer pays one group of workers more, e.g. to combat a specific labour shortage, as in *Rainey*, the difference in pay

---

12   For an unfortunate lapse, see *Calder v Rowntree Mackintosh Confectionery Ltd* [1993] ICR 811, [1993] IRLR 212, CA.
13   [1994] ICR 112, [1993] IRLR 591, ECJ.
14   [1995] 3 All ER 597, [1995] ICR 883, HL.
15   Ibid., per Lord Slynn, p. 604. The fact that two men were employed on the same work at the same rate of pay as the applicants did not detract from this conclusion: 'It means no more than that the two men were underpaid compared with other men doing jobs rated as equivalent' (ibid., p. 603).

will be justifiable under section 1(3) provided the employer can demonstrate that the difference is genuinely gender-neutral; but where the difference in pay between two groups of employees is simply a reflection of historic inequalities in the labour market, e.g. where the work in question is sex-segregated, as in *Ratcliffe*, the employer will find it difficult to show that paying lower rates of pay to a predominantly female group of employees is genuinely gender-neutral.

As seen above, in *Rainey* the House of Lords held that in order to discharge the burden of proof under section 1(3), it is necessary for the employer to show that the difference in pay is objectively justified, applying the test laid down by the ECJ in the *Bilka-Kaufhaus* case. Until recently, it was believed that to make out a section 1(3) defence, an employer had to show an objective justification for a difference in pay in all cases. However, in *Strathclyde Regional Council v Wallace*[16] the House of Lords held that the requirement to show some objective justification for a variation in terms only arises where the factor which the employer is relying to explain the variation is itself directly or indirectly sexually discriminatory. Where there is no element of sex discrimination, 'the employer establishes [the section 1(3) defence] by identifying the factors which he alleges have caused the disparity, proving that those factors are genuine and proving further that they were causally relevant to the disparity in pay complained of'[17]. According to Lord Nicholls in *Glasgow City Council v Marshall*[18], the requirement that the factor be 'material' simply means that it must be significant and relevant in a causative sense, rather than in a justificatory sense. It follows that an employer who is able to show that a difference in pay is genuinely caused by a factor which is not itself tainted by direct or indirect sex discrimination (e.g. where there is an historic explanation for the variation[19], or where it resulted from a careless mistake[20]) is under no obligation to prove a 'good' reason for the pay disparity, even if it could not possibly be objectively justified.

The section 1(3) defence has given rise to particular difficulties in three areas. The first concerns the application of the section 1(3) defence to part-timers[1], an area of particular significance in the development of the law on equal pay because it was in cases involving part-timers that the legislation was reinterpreted to cover practices which indirectly discriminate against women. In the early cases it appeared to be established that the fact that a woman worked part-time was a genuine material difference, so that she could not claim equality of hourly pay rates with a man working full time, even if he was doing exactly the same work[2]. However, in *Jenkins v Kingsgate (Clothing Productions) Ltd (No 2)*[3], the EAT (following a reference to the ECJ) reinterpreted section 1(3), and held that the fact of being part-time can be a genuine material difference only if the

---

16 [1998] IRLR 146. HL.
17 Ibid., per Lord Browne-Wilkinson. Cases such as *Rainey*, *Enderby* and *Ratcliffe* can all be explained as cases where the factor relied upon was one which affected a considerably higher proportion of women than men, and which therefore required objective justification.
18 [2000] IRLR 272, HL.
19 As in *Marshall*, ibid., where the difference in pay between two groups of very similar gender composition (instructors and teachers) was due to different collective bargaining structures; significantly, the applicants had accepted that there was no sex discrimination.
20 See e.g. *Tyldesley v TML Plastics Ltd* [1996] IRLR 395, EAT.
1 Part-time workers now have a right to equal treatment under the Part-Time Workers Directive and the implementing Regulations (see p. 20) and are therefore less likely to need to argue indirect sex discrimination in the future.
2 *Handley v H Mona Ltd* [1979] ICR 147, [1978] IRLR 534.
3 [1981] ICR 715, [1981] IRLR 388, EAT

employer can show that the lower rate for part-timers is reasonably necessary to achieve some objective (probably economic) unrelated to sex. The overall effect of this was to introduce into equal pay law a concept of indirect discrimination akin to that in sex discrimination law, in that if the effect of the particular factor claimed to be the genuine material factor operates particularly harshly against women, it will only be permitted as a defence under section 1(3) if the employer can justify it objectively, on grounds other than sex.

Subsequent cases have graphically demonstrated the unwillingness of the courts to accept part-time working as a justification for indirect sex discrimination, unless some objective justification unrelated to any discrimination on grounds of sex can be shown. In *Bilka-Kaufhaus GmbH v Weber von Hartz*[4], the ECJ held that the exclusion of part-time workers from an occupational pension scheme is contrary to Article 119 (now 141) if the exclusion affects significantly more women than men, unless the employer can show that the exclusion is objectively justified on economic grounds relating to the management of the organisation[5]. In that case, the ECJ held that the exclusion of part-time workers from the pension scheme could in fact be justified by reference to the needs of the business, as it was the aim of the employer to employ as few part-time workers as possible. In *Rinner-Kühn v FWW Spezial-Gebäudereinigung GmbH & Co KG*[6], the ECJ adopted the same approach in holding that a provision in national legislation excluding part-timers from state sickness benefits was in breach of Article 119 (now 141), unless the member state could establish that the means selected corresponded to an objective necessary for its social policy and were appropriate and necessary to the attainment of that objective. The decision in *Rinner-Kuhn* was in turn applied by the House of Lords in the landmark case of *R v Secretary of State for Employment, ex p Equal Opportunities Commission*[7] to strike down the hours per week qualifying thresholds for redundancy pay and unfair dismissal compensation on the grounds that they indirectly discriminated against women and were therefore incompatible with European law. In that case, the Secretary of State had claimed that the discriminatory qualifying thresholds were objectively justified, as they were designed to reduce the costs to employers of employing part-time workers and therefore to bring about an increase in the availability of part-time work. However, while the House of Lords was prepared to accept that increasing the availability of part-time work was a necessary aim of social policy, it held that the Secretary of State had failed to establish an objective justification for the threshold provisions because it had not been shown that they were suitable and requisite for achieving that aim. Perhaps the most startling aspect of the decision was the unwillingness of the House of Lords to accept at face value the Secretary of State's assertion that the threshold provisions had actually resulted in greater availability of part-time work than would have been the case without them, and were therefore requisite to achieve the stated aim. Lord Keith described the evidence for the Secretary of

---

4   [1981] ICR 715, [1981] IRLR 388, ECJ. In *Kowalska v Freie und Hansestadt Hamburg* [1992] ICR 29, [1990] IRLR 447, ECJ, the *Bilka-Kaufhaus* test was applied to a collective agreement which excluded part-timers from severance payments; see also *Nimz v Freie und Hansestadt Hamburg* [1991] ECR I-297, [1991] IRLR 222, ECJ (seniority rules).
5   This test was subsequently adopted by the House of Lords in *Rainey* when construing the s. 1(3) defence: see p. 292, above.
6   171/88 [1989] ECR 2743, [1989] IRLR 493, ECJ. See also *Arbeiterwohlfahrt der Stadt Berlin eV v Bötel* [1992] 3 CMLR 446, [1992] IRLR 423, ECJ (legislative provisions limiting compensation available to part-timers for time off to undergo training).
7   [1995] 1 AC 1, [1994] ICR 317, HL. See further, p. 228, above.

State on this point as not containing 'anything capable of being regarded as factual evidence demonstrating the correctness of these views[8] .'

While part-time workers have undoubtedly been well-served by the decisions of the ECJ and the domestic courts over recent years, there have nonetheless been some cases where the courts have been prepared to accept the fact of part-time working as a justification for unequal treatment. In *Calder v Rowntree Mackintosh Confectionery Ltd*[9] , a woman employed part-time on an all-female 'twilight' shift claimed equal pay with a man employed on a predominantly male rotating shift (i.e. an alternating day and night shift) who received a 20 per cent shift premium. The employer's defence was that the shift premium reflected the inconvenience of being required to work rotating shifts, but the employers also conceded that there was an element in the premium of compensation for working anti-social hours, a factor which applied to both rotating and twilight shifts. The Court of Appeal upheld the tribunal's decision that the whole of the variation in pay was genuinely due to the fact that the man worked on a rotating shift. According to Balcombe LJ, 'The fact that some indeterminate part of the shift premium represented compensation for working unsocial hours does not necessarily preclude a finding that the payment of the shift premium was genuinely due to working rotating shifts; ... there is no logical impossibility in such a finding.'[10] The Court of Appeal considered that the transparency required by the *Danfoss*[11] case did not mean that the employers must explain precisely how the premium figure was achieved, but it could be argued that the inconsistency in the employers' explanation of the premium is just the type of issue which a requirement of transparency could be expected to address. In *Stadt Lengerich v Helmig*[12] , the ECJ considered whether it was discriminatory for an employer to pay overtime supplements only for hours worked in excess of the normal working hours for full-time employees, so that part-time employees (who were predominantly women) who worked in excess of their own normal working hours were not entitled to any overtime supplement unless their hours exceeded the normal working hours for full-time employees. The ECJ held that there is unequal treatment for the purposes of Article 119 (now 141) where full-time employees are paid more than part-time employees for the same number of hours worked, and that since on the facts the overall pay for full-time and part-time employees was the same for the same number of hours worked, there was no unequal treatment and therefore no discrimination, so that the question of objective justification did not arise. It is submitted that the decision is an unfortunate one, and that the overtime supplements should properly have been seen as compensation to employees for the disruption of having to work in excess of their own normal working hours, whether full-time or part-time. To require the part-timers to work considerably more than their normal working hours in order to earn the supplement was to disadvantage them and therefore indirectly to

---

8   Ibid., at p. 30. Note however the approach of the ECJ in *Nolte v Landesversicherungsanstalt Hannover* [1996] All ER (EC) 212, [1996] IRLR 225, and *Megner v Innungskrankenkasse Vorderpfalz* [1996] All ER (EC) 212, [1996] IRLR 236, where member states were said to have a 'broad margin of discretion' in exercising their competence to choose the measures capable of achieving their social and employment policy objectives.

9   [1993] ICR 811, [1993] IRLR 212, CA.

10   Ibid., at p. 214.

11   See above, p. 243.

12   [1996] ICR 35, [1995] IRLR 216, ECJ.

discriminate against women. At the very least, the court should have required the employer to provide an objective justification for the overtime rule[13].

The second area of difficulty concerns collective bargaining, and the extent to which an employer can argue that the separate bargaining processes for two groups of workers constitutes a genuine material factor which justifies a variation in terms between the two groups. On one view, as long as each bargaining process is in itself non-discriminatory, the different bargaining arrangements could be said to represent an objectively justified reason for the difference in outcome[14]; against that, however, it could be argued that the key issue is whether the difference in outcome between the two pay structures can *itself* be justified, so that the mere fact that pay is regulated by separate collective agreements will not of itself justify a difference[15]. The issue arose in stark form in *Enderby v Frenchay Health Authority*[16], where the applicant, one of a group of predominantly female speech therapists employed by the health authority, claimed that her work was of equal value with the predominantly male pharmacists and clinical psychologists, who were paid substantially more. The employer argued that the variation in pay was due to historical differences in the collective bargaining arrangements for the two groups, and that since those arrangements were not in themselves discriminatory, they constituted a genuine material factor which justified the difference. The EAT found for the employer[17], holding that if the factor causing the disparate impact has no taint of gender, there is nothing which requires justification. The Court of Appeal referred the matter to the ECJ[18], which held that the fact that the respective rates of pay of two jobs of equal value, one carried out almost exclusively by women and the other predominantly by men, were arrived at by collective bargaining processes which, although carried out by the same parties, were distinct and which, considered separately, were not in themselves discriminatory, is not sufficient objective justification for the difference in pay between those two jobs. The ECJ considered that if an employer could rely on the absence of discrimination within each of the collective bargaining processes taken separately as sufficient justification for the difference in pay, he could easily circumvent the principle of equal pay by using separate bargaining processes[19]. Under this approach, it is the *result* of the collective bargaining process which has to be justified by objective factors; the fact that the difference in pay arises from separate collective bargaining processes, while relevant[20], does not of

---

13   In his Opinion for the court, the Advocate-General considered (ibid., p. 219) that the restriction on the use of free time entailed in working overtime constituted an objective reason which might justify a difference in treatment between full-time and part-time workers, but arguably that reason applies with equal force to part-time workers, for whom working overtime may be just as disruptive as it is for full-time workers.

14   As was held in *Reed Packaging Ltd v Boozer* [1988] ICR 391, [1988] IRLR 333, EAT, where the genuine material factor defence was held to apply as the applicant and her comparator were employed under separate pay structures which were not in themselves discriminatory.

15   See *Barber v NCR (Manufacturing) Ltd* [1993] IRLR 95, where the EAT held that the fact that the difference in pay had arisen from collective bargaining did not constitute an objective factor which justified the result which had been produced.

16   [1994] ICR 112, [1993] IRLR 591, ECJ. The case is also an important authority on the need to establish a requirement or condition in cases of indirect discrimination (see p. 245), and on whether the whole or only part of a difference in pay need be objectively justified (see p. 294).

17   [1991] ICR 382, [1991] IRLR 44, EAT.

18   [1994] ICR 112, [1992] IRLR 15, CA.

19   [1994] ICR 112, [1993] IRLR 591, at p. 595.

20   See *Specialarbejderforbundet i Danmark v Dansk Industri, acting for Royal Copenhagen* [1996] ICR 51, [1995] IRLR 648, ECJ.

itself constitute an objective justification for that difference. Having said that, the House of Lords has recently confirmed[1] that the need for the results of separate bargaining processes to be objectively justified only arises where the difference in terms results from sex discrimination (for example, where there is evidence that the difference in bargaining processes has a disparate adverse impact on women and is therefore prima facie indirectly discriminatory[2]). If the separate bargaining structures do not impact disproportionately on one sex, there is no obligation on the employer to justify the disparity in the terms which result from that process[3].

The third area of difficulty under section 1(3) concerns the 'red circling' cases[4]. These arise where male employees are paid more than female employees on like or equally rated work because the pay of the men is protected, or 'red circled', because of some event in the past; examples of this would be where the man was injured and put permanently on to lighter work but at his previous higher wage, or where the man's job was down-graded but rather than being made redundant he was kept on at the lesser job but again at his previous higher wage. In both of these cases there may be women also doing the lighter or lesser work, but at the ordinary rate for that work, so that they are paid less. A genuine red circle case may well come within section 1(3) so that a woman cannot claim to be put on to the man's protected rate, as can be seen from the judgment of the EAT in *Charles Early and Marriott (Witney) Ltd v Smith and Ball*[5], but in the consolidated appeal in *Snoxell v Vauxhall Motors Ltd*[6] the EAT in fact held that the red circle argument failed, since it appeared that the existence of the men's protection was partly due to past discrimination on sexual grounds. Thus the important principle is that the tribunal should inquire into the original reason for the protection of the man's wages and should only accept the red circle as a genuine material factor if it had its origins in genuine factors other than any form of direct or indirect sexual discrimination. In *Methven v Cow Industrial Polymers Ltd*[7] the Court of Appeal emphasised that in 'red circling' cases the tribunals should not lose sight of the wording of the Act and accepted that three questions arise: i) was there a variation between the woman's contract and the man's? ii) was there a material difference (other than the difference of sex) between her case and his? iii) have the employers proved on the balance of probabilities that the variation in wages was due to the material difference (a matter of causation)? While it is clear that in an appropriate case red circling can provide a defence indefinitely[8], the EAT has stressed that even where a red circling agreement is genuine and reasonable at the time of its inception, its continuation indefinitely would be likely to cause bad feelings among those not thus protected, so that in the light of good industrial relations practice it might be expected that the employer would phase it out after a reasonable period, with the implication that if this is not done the employer might find after the expiry of such a period that

1   See *Glasgow City Council v Marshall* [2000] IRLR 272, HL.
2   An inference of discrimination can arise where 'significant' numbers of the disadvantaged group are female: see *British Road Services Ltd v Loughran* [1997] IRLR 92, NICA.
3   As in *Glasgow City Council v Marshall*, above.
4   Some care is needed, for 'red circle' must not be considered to be a term of art: *National Coal Board v Sherwin* [1978] ICR 700 at 706F, [1978] IRLR 122 at 125; *Methven v Cow Industrial Polymers Ltd* [1980] ICR 463, [1980] IRLR 289, CA, per Dunn LJ.
5   [1977] ICR 700, [1977] IRLR 123.
6   Ibid.
7   [1980] ICR 463, [1980] IRLR 289; *Ministry of Defence v Farthing* [1980] ICR 705, [1980] IRLR 402, CA; *Avon and Somerset Police Authority v Emery* [1981] ICR 229, EAT.
8   *Charles Early and Marriott (Witney) Ltd v Smith and Ball* [1977] ICR 700, [1977] IRLR 123.

he cannot use it as a defence to a claim for equal pay[9]. In *Benveniste v University of Southampton*[10], the Court of Appeal confirmed that this reasoning also applies in the reverse situation, i.e. where a person has been appointed on less favourable terms than normal because of temporary financial considerations. In that case the applicant had been appointed at a lower rate than would normally have been the case because of financial constraints then operating on the employer, but it was held that the employer could not use this as a defence under section 1(3) once those financial constraints had eased.

iii)   Remedies

A claim for equal pay may be brought before an employment tribunal[11]. On such a claim[12], the tribunal may declare the existence of the equality clause, to ensure treatment no less favourable. However, this is dependent upon a finding that there is like work/work rated as equivalent, or work of equal value; if that is not so, the tribunal has no jurisdiction to make any order, even if the women concerned are being poorly treated, and the gap in the remuneration between men and women is in no way commensurate to the difference in the work that they do: the Act does not enable a tribunal to act as a general wage-fixing body[13]. However, once there is a valid claim for equality, the applicant may be awarded arrears of pay or damages for contravention of the equality clause.

The Equal Pay Act contains two limitation periods which have been the source of much litigation. Section 2(4) states that a claim must be brought within six months of the end of employment; and section 2(5) places a limit of two years from the date of commencement of proceedings on any award of arrears of remuneration (i.e. back pay) or damages. Both limits have been challenged as incompatible with EC law. It is an accepted principle of EC law that in the absence of Community rules on the matter, it is for domestic legal systems to lay down procedural rules governing the enforcement of Community rights, provided they are not less favourable than those governing similar domestic actions (the principle of equivalence), and do not render the exercise of rights conferred by Community law virtually impossible or excessively difficult (the principle of effectiveness). In *Levez v T H Jennings (Harlow Pools) Ltd*[14], the ECJ held that the two-year limit on arrears of remuneration did not in itself infringe the principle of effectiveness (although on the facts that principle was held to have been infringed because the applicant had delayed bringing proceedings to enforce her right as a result of a deliberate misrepresentation by the employer); in relation to the principle of equivalence, the ECJ held that it was for the national courts to determine whether the rule in question was less favourable than the rules applying to similar domestic actions. When the case returned to the EAT[15], it was held that the two-year limit contravened the principle of equivalence, in that it was less favourable than the six-year limitation period governing similar claims

9   *Outlook Supplies Ltd v Parry* [1978] ICR 388, [1978] IRLR 12, EAT.
10   [1989] ICR 617, [1989] IRLR 122, CA.
11   Equal Pay Act 1970, s. 2.
12   In which the applicant may be assisted by the Equal Opportunities Commission if a question of principle is raised, or a complicated point is involved: Sex Discrimination Act 1975, s. 75.
13   *Maidment v Cooper & Co (Birmingham) Ltd* [1978] ICR 1094, [1978] IRLR 462.
14   [1999] IRLR 36, ECJ.
15   *Levez v T H Jennings (Harlow Pools) Ltd (No 2)* [1999] IRLR 764, EAT.

under domestic law (e.g. for breach of contract, unlawful deductions from wages under the Employment Rights Act 1996 or discrimination on grounds of race or disability). The EAT therefore disapplied the two-year limit as being incompatible with EC law, and held that the normal six-year time limit under the Limitation Act applies to claims under the Equal Pay Act.

In *Preston v Wolverhampton Healthcare NHS Trust*[16] (part of the litigation concerning the exclusion of part-time workers from occupational pension schemes, discussed below), the ECJ further clarified the position by holding that in relation to those excluded from occupational pension schemes, the two-year limit on the back-dating of membership infringes the principle of effectiveness, the implication being that workers unlawfully excluded from such schemes are in principle able to claim a right to back-date their membership to 8 April 1976 (i.e. the date of the *Defrenne* judgment[17] in which the ECJ first held that Article 119 (now 141) had direct effect)[18]. The ECJ also held that while the six-month time limit on the presentation of claims does *not* contravene the principle of effectiveness, the domestic rule that the six-month limitation period applies at the end of each contract of employment, even in cases where there has been a stable employment relationship resulting from a succession of separate short-term contracts in respect of the same employment, was incompatible with EC law because it made the enforcement of the right conferred by EC law excessively difficult.

iv) Death or retirement

As originally enacted, the Equal Pay Act contained a blanket exclusion for any provision made in connection with death or retirement[19], considered to be necessary because of the differential state pensionable age upon which many such provisions have traditionally been based. However, during the 1980s it became increasingly clear that the breadth of the exclusion in the domestic legislation was incompatible with EC law, in that while the differential state pensionable age itself was outside the scope of Article 119[20] (now 141), retirement benefits (and indeed retirement ages) which are based on the state pensionable age are not. As a result, the Government was forced to introduce legislation outlawing discrimination in provisions made in connection with retirement, initially in relation to promotion, transfer, training, demotion or dismissal[1], and later in the area of occupational pensions also[2]. The picture is a complex and

---

16   Case C-78/98, [2000] IRLR 506, ECJ. See also [1998] 1 All ER 528, HL. See p. 307 below.
17   *Defrenne v SABENA* [1976] ECR 455, [1976] ICR 547, ECJ.
18   See to like effect *Magorrian v Eastern Health and Social Services Board* [1998] IRLR 86, ECJ; the tribunal to which the matter was subsequently remitted disapplied the two-year rule and permitted membership to be back-dated to April 1976.
19   Equal Pay Act 1970, s. 6. There was an equivalent exclusion in the Sex Discrimination Act 1975, s. 6(4).
20   Article 7 of EEC Directive 79/7 on Social Security allows member states to exclude 'the determination of pensionable age for the purposes of granting old-age and retirement pensions' from the principle of equal treatment, but does not in terms extend to provisions which are tied to the state pensionable age. See *R v Secretary of State for Social Security, ex p Equal Opportunities Commission* [1992] ICR 782, [1992] IRLR 376, ECJ.
1   Sex Discrimination Act 1986, s. 2 (see p. 303, below)
2   Pensions Act 1995, ss. 62–66 (see p. 308, below).

difficult one, but the impact of EC law in this area has tended to crystallise around four main issues, of ascending practical importance.

The first concerns what might be considered the incidents, or 'perks', of retirement; in *Garland v British Rail Engineering Ltd* [3], the ECJ gave an early indication that the definition of 'pay' in Article 119 (now 141) was to be interpreted widely [4], and that the exclusion for death or retirement in the domestic legislation would have to be construed narrowly in order to comply with it. In *Garland*, the employer discriminated in the provision of travel concessions to retired employees by providing concessions for the families of male former employees but not for those of female former employees. The Court of Appeal applied the exclusion widely and held that it ruled out the complaint in English law; on further appeal, the House of Lords remitted the matter to the ECJ, which held that travel facilities accorded to employees after retirement are 'pay' within the meaning of Article 119 (now 141), and that the discrimination was therefore contrary to EC law. In the light of this, the House of Lords gave the exclusion a narrow construction in order to comply with EC law [5], and held that the travel concessions infringed English law since they were not directly the result of 'provisions in relation to death or retirement' [6].

The second issue which then arose was whether it was lawful for an employer to insist on discriminatory retirement ages (e.g. retiring a man at 65, but a woman at 60); it was clear that this widespread practice could be detrimental to a woman, both financially [7] and through premature loss of job satisfaction, but as it was directly linked to provisions in relation to retirement, it seemed fairly clear that it was lawful under English law [8]. However, the breakthrough here came in *Marshall v Southampton and South West Hampshire Area Health Authority (Teaching)* [9], where discriminatory compulsory retirement ages were held by the ECJ to be contrary to the Equal Treatment Directive. Significantly the ECJ rejected the argument that as differential retirement ages simply reflected the differential state pensionable age, they were covered by the exemption in the Social Security Directive [10], and held that the exclusion of social security matters from the scope of the Equal Treatment Directive must be interpreted strictly. The Equal Treatment Directive itself was held to be directly effective (i.e. giving rights directly enforceable in the national courts by a person such as Mrs Marshall), but the ECJ approved the prevailing theory that a directive (as opposed to an Article of the Treaty) can only have 'vertical' direct effect, i.e. only as against the state or one of its organs; this meant that the newly-won EC right to equal retirement ages only itself applied to

---

3   [1983] 2 AC 751, [1982] ICR 420, ECJ.
4   Art. 119 (now 141) provides that 'pay' means 'the ordinary basic or minimum wage or salary and any other consideration, whether in cash or in kind, which the worker receives, directly or indirectly, in respect of his employment from his employer.' *Garland* gave an early indication of the wide interpretation which the ECJ was prepared to give to the word 'pay'.
5   The extent to which the national courts and tribunals are required to interpret domestic legislation in the light of EC law is considered above at p. 232.
6   [1982] ICR 420, [1982] IRLR 257, HL. As there was no contractual entitlement to the benefits in question, the case came under the Sex Discrimination Act 1975.
7   In view of the likely difference between her earnings and her pension, and the fact that her pension entitlement might well depend on her final salary, so that by retiring five years earlier than a man, that salary could be substantially lower than it would have been five years later, with corresponding effect on her level of pension.
8   *Burton v British Railways Board (No 2)* [1982] ICR 329, [1982] IRLR 116, ECJ.
9   152/84 [1986] ICR 335, [1986] IRLR 140, ECJ.
10   Directive 79/7/EEC. See n. 20, above.

public sector employment[11]. This was clearly an untenable situation, and so *Marshall's* case led to an important legislative amendment in the Sex Discrimination Act 1986, section 2, which amended both the Equal Pay Act 1970 and the Sex Discrimination Act 1975 so that it became unlawful (in either public or private sector employment) to discriminate against a woman in provisions relating to retirement, in the area of promotion, transfer, training, demotion or dismissal; it is the last that is particularly important in a case like *Marshall*, as it renders illegal the compulsory retiring of a woman at an earlier age than a man in the same position[12].

The third issue is, however, that these developments did not appear to affect differential *pension* ages (the principal reason for the exclusion for death or retirement in the first place). In particular, it was thought that occupational pension schemes, which traditionally have tended to adopt the state differential pension ages of 65 for a man and 60 for a woman, were not amenable to challenge under EC law because the Social Security Directive expressly permits member states to continue to fix their own pension ages[13]. To that extent, *Marshall* and the 1986 Act appeared to have created an anomaly, by requiring equal retirement ages between men and women while still allowing pensions to be payable at different ages. However, this whole area was thrown into confusion by the ruling of the ECJ in the landmark case of *Barber v Guardian Royal Exchange Assurance Group*[14]. In that case Mr Barber had been made redundant at the age of 52, and complained that while a woman in those circumstances would have been entitled under the pension scheme in question to an immediate pension at 50, he would not be so entitled until he reached the age of 55 (a difference obviously based on the difference in the state pensionable ages). The ECJ ruled that benefits paid under a contracted-out, private occupational pension scheme fell within the definition of 'pay' in Article 119 (now 141), so that a differential entitlement as between men and women under such a scheme infringed Article 119, irrespective of the fact that the difference simply mirrored the state pension age[15]. Put simply, the effect of *Barber* was to require equalisation of benefits under contracted-out, private occupational pension schemes. However, the ECJ's decision raised as many questions as it answered, and it took a series of further references to the ECJ before the full implications of the decision were finally clarified. The uncertainty centred on two main areas, firstly, the scope of the *Barber* ruling (did other types of benefits and pension schemes also fall within the definition of 'pay' in Article 119?); and secondly, its practical implementation (did it require all benefits paid after the date of the judgment to be paid on an equal basis, or only those payable in respect of periods of service after that date? Did it require

11 The direct effect of directives is discussed above at p. 231.

12 It was also necessary to amend the Employment Protection (Consolidation) Act 1978 (see now the Employment Rights Act 1996, s. 109) to equalise the relevant ages in the 'normal retiring age' exclusion in complaints of unfair dismissal, see p. 459, below.

13 But cf. *Worringham v Lloyds Bank Ltd*: 69/80 [1981] ICR 558, [1981] IRLR 178, ECJ and [1982] ICR 299, [1982] IRLR 74, CA, where the ECJ held that Art. 119 (now 141) applied to a pension scheme under which the employer made extra pensions contributions for male employees under 25, on the basis that those additional sums were included in the calculation of gross salary and determined the calculation of other salary-related benefits, such as redundancy payments. Contrast *Newstead v Department of Transport*: 192/85 [1988] ICR 332, [1988] IRLR 66, ECJ.

14 Case C-262/88: [1991] 1 QB 344, [1990] ICR 616, ECJ

15 One of the ironies of *Barber* is that it overrode Social Security Directives 79/7 and 86/378, which required equal treatment in occupational pension schemes but permitted member states to defer the implementation until 1 January 1993; see p. 308, below.

the levelling up of benefits, or was it permissible for employers to equalise benefits by reducing the advantage of those previously favoured?). On the first point, it is now clear that the definition of 'pay' in Article 119 (now 141) covers all pension benefits paid to a worker by reason of the employment relationship[16], including those paid under a non-contracted-out occupational scheme[17], and also covers a survivor's pension provided by an occupational pension scheme[18]; it has also been established that Article 119 (now 141) may be relied upon by employees and their dependants against the trustees of a pension scheme[19]. However, Article 119 (now 141) does not apply to benefits which derive from additional voluntary contributions by employees[20], or to transfer benefits and capital-sum benefits[1] (the significant point here being that the ECJ has ruled that it is not a breach of Article 119 (now 141) for actuarial factors which vary according to sex[2] to be used in determining the employers' contribution rates and in calculating transfer values and capital lump sums[3]). A state pension is not 'pay' for the purposes of Article 119 (now 141), and a particularly difficult problem therefore arises where the payments made to an employee under an occupational pension scheme are reduced to take account of the amount of state pension which the employee is entitled to receive. In such a case, a choice has to be made between requiring formal equality under the scheme itself, irrespective of any entitlement to a state pension, and seeking to achieve overall substantive equality by taking entitlement to a state pension into account. This was the issue in *Roberts v Birds Eye Walls Ltd*[4], where the applicant, who had retired early on grounds of ill-health at the age of 57, complained that she had been discriminated against on the grounds of sex because the bridging pension which she received from her occupational pension scheme was reduced by £749 when she reached 60 (that being the amount of the state pension which it was assumed she would be receiving from that age), whereas a man taking early retirement at the same age as her would not have suffered any such reduction in entitlement until he reached the state pension age for men, i.e. 65. The EAT had held that the reduction in her bridging pension from the age of 60 was discriminatory, even though this gave rise to the seemingly absurd result that the achievement of 'equality' in her case meant that she would in fact be £749 per annum better off than her male comparator! However, the ECJ held that it is not contrary to Article 119 (now 141) for an employer to reduce the amount of a bridging pension to take account of the amount of the state pension which the employee will receive, even though, in the case of men and women

16 *Bestuur van het Algemeen Burgerlijk Pensioenfonds v Beune* [1994] ECR I-4471, [1995] IRLR 103, ECJ. In that case the ECJ also held that legislation which applies different rules for calculating the occupational pensions of married men and married women infringes Art. 119 (now 141).

17 *Coloroll Pension Trustees Ltd v Russell* [1995] ICR 179, [1994] IRLR 586, ECJ; see also *Moroni v Firma Collo GmbH* [1995] ICR 137, [1994] IRLR 130, ECJ.

18 *Ten Oever v Stichting Bedrijfspensioenfonds voor het Glazenwassers-en Schoonmaakbedrijf* [1995] ICR 74, [1993] IRLR 601, ECJ.

19 *Coloroll Pension Trustees Ltd v Russell,* ibid., n. 17. As the requirement of equal treatment takes precedence over the rules of the pension scheme, employers and trustees must do everything within their powers to ensure that the scheme complies with the principle of equal treatment, including where necessary having recourse to the national courts to amend the scheme.

20 Ibid.

1   Ibid.

2   For example, the actuarial assumption that women live longer than men and that their pensions are therefore more expensive to maintain.

3   *Neath v Hugh Steeper Ltd* [1995] ICR 158, [1994] IRLR 91, ECJ.

4   [1994] ICR 338, [1994] IRLR 29, ECJ.

aged between 60 and 65, the result is that a female employee will receive a smaller bridging pension than that paid to her male counterpart[5]. As the court observed, 'to maintain the amount for women at the same level as that which obtained before they received the state pension would give rise to unequal treatment to the detriment of men who do not receive the state pension until the age of 65.' The mechanism for ensuring overall equality of treatment (i.e. the deduction of the state pension from the bridging pension) was considered to be 'neutral', and therefore not discriminatory[6]. Taken at face value, the ECJ's decision could be seen as supporting the position that direct discrimination can be objectively justified under Community law (a view considered as little short of heresy by discrimination lawyers), but the court made no express ruling to that effect, and it is unlikely that it was intending to lay down any such general principle. Rather, the ECJ's decision is probably best seen as a pragmatic response to an untypical situation where the alleged discriminatory treatment is an attempt to achieve substantive equality by counteracting an existing inequality.

On the second point, in an attempt to restrict the impact of its ruling, the ECJ held in *Barber* that the decision was not to operate retrospectively, and that Article 119 (now 141) could not be relied upon in order to claim entitlement to a pension with effect from a date before the ruling in that case (i.e. 17 May 1990)[7], except in the case of those who had already initiated legal proceedings or raised an equivalent claim[8] under the applicable national law before that date. After much initial uncertainty over the scope of this temporal limitation, the ECJ has confirmed[9] that Article 119 (now 141) may only be relied upon in relation to benefits payable in respect of periods of service after the date of the *Barber* judgment; where a benefit is not linked to the length of actual service (as in the case of a lump-sum payment in the event of the employee's death-in-service), the principle of equal treatment applies where the operative event occurred after the date of that judgment[10]. On the vexed question of levelling-up versus levelling-down, the position is unfortunately very confusing: the ECJ has held that Article 119 (now 141) does not preclude the adoption of measures which implement the principle of equal treatment by reducing the advantages of the favoured class (i.e. by levelling-down), but that in relation to periods of employment between the date of the *Barber* judgment and the date on which the scheme adopted measures to achieve equal treatment, the equalisation of benefits

---

5 For good measure, the ECJ held that the employer was entitled to take account of the full state pension, even if the pension which the woman was in fact receiving was a widow's pension, or if she had exercised the married woman's option of paying reduced N.I. contributions in return for a reduced state pension.

6 Significantly, the ECJ stated that 'the principle of equal treatment laid down by Art. 119 ... presupposes that the men and women to whom it applies are in identical situations...', a requirement which, taken to its logical conclusion, would seem to undermine the application of Art. 119 (now 141) in cases of pregnancy discrimination; see p. 347, below.

7 This temporal limitation on the *Barber* ruling was subsequently endorsed in a Protocol to the Treaty on European Union (the Maastricht treaty).

8 In *Howard v Ministry of Defence* [1995] ICR 1074, [1995] IRLR 570, EAT, this was taken to mean that the dispute must have been raised before an independent third party with power to determine the matter (e.g. an arbitrator), and that merely asserting a claim would not be sufficient.

9 *Ten Oever v Stichting Bedrijfspensioenfonds voor het Glazenwassers-en Schoonmaakbedrijf*, ibid., n. 18; see also *Coloroll Pension Trustees Ltd v Russell*, ibid., n. 17.

10 *Coloroll Pension Trustees Ltd v Russell*, ibid., n. 17.

must be at the more favourable level (i.e. levelling-up)[11]; in relation to periods of employment before the *Barber* judgment, the ECJ has held that Community law imposes no obligation which would justify retroactive reduction of the advantages which women enjoyed[12]. So, to take the example of a scheme which, pre-*Barber*, assumed a pension age of 65 for men and 60 for women, this would mean that periods of service before the *Barber* judgment are unaffected, but that for the period between the date of the judgment and the date on which the scheme adopted measures to achieve equality, the pension rights of men would have to be calculated on the basis of a retirement age of 60. It seems that most occupational pension schemes have in fact equalised pension ages upwards, by raising the retirement age for women, and the ECJ has held that where the retirement age is raised, Article 119 (now 141) does not permit transitional measures designed to soften the blow for women adversely affected thereby as regards future periods of service[13].

Last but certainly not least is the important question of access to occupational pension schemes, and in particular the position of part-time workers denied access to such schemes. Section 6 of the Equal Pay Act, which excluded provisions made in connection with death or retirement from the scope of that Act, did not apply to access to occupational pension schemes[14], where a right of equal access was first introduced in 1975[15]. However, that right only prohibited direct discrimination between the sexes[16], and was therefore of no assistance to part-time workers who were indirectly discriminated against by being denied access to pension schemes. The turning-point came in *Bilka-Kaufhaus GmbH v Weber von Hartz*[17], where the ECJ held that the conditions for admission to an occupational pension scheme fall within the scope of Article 119 (now 141) (provided the benefits paid to employees under the scheme are paid in respect of employment), and that excluding part-timers from a pension scheme constitutes unlawful indirect discrimination if the exclusion affects a much greater proportion of women than men, unless the employer can show that the exclusion is objectively justified. This decision was reaffirmed in *Vroege v NCIV Institut voor Volkshuisvesting BV*[18], where the ECJ crucially held that the temporal limitation in the *Barber* judgment and the Protocol only applies to benefits under an occupational pension scheme, and does not apply to the right to join a pension scheme in the first place[19].

11   *Smith v Avdel Systems Ltd* [1995] ICR 596, [1994] IRLR 602, ECJ. That case also establishes that Art. 119 (now 141) precludes a scheme from retrospectively raising the retirement age for women in relation to the period between 17 May 1990 and the date of entry into force of the measures designed to achieve equal treatment, even if there are objectively justifiable considerations relating to the needs of the undertaking or of the scheme itself.

12   Ibid.

13   Ibid. See also *Van Den Akker v Stichting Shell Pensioenfonds* [1995] ICR 596, [1994] IRLR 616, ECJ.

14   Equal Pay Act 1970, s. 6(1A)(a), as amended by the Pensions Act 1995, s. 66(1).

15   Social Security Pensions Act 1975, s. 53(2) (see now the Pension Schemes Act 1993, s. 118).

16   Cf. s. 118(1) of the Pension Schemes Act 1993, which states: '... the equal access requirements in relation to an occupational pension scheme are that membership of the scheme is open to both men and women on terms which are the same as to age and length of service needed for becoming a member.'

17   [1987] ICR 110, [1986] IRLR 317, ECJ.

18   [1995] ICR 635, [1994] IRLR 651, ECJ.

19   Significantly, in *Dietz v Stichting Thuiszorg Rotterdam* [1996] IRLR 692, the ECJ ruled that a part-timer unlawfully excluded from a pension scheme can backdate beyond the *Barber* date in relation to both membership and benefits.

This ruling raised the fascinating prospect of part-time workers who had previously been excluded from an occupational pension scheme claiming the right to join a scheme retroactively, potentially as far back as 8 April 1976 (that being the date when the ECJ first ruled that Article 119 (now 141) had direct effect[20]). However, in *Fisscher v Voorhuis Hengelo BV*[1] , the ECJ held that there are two crucially important limitations on this right: first, a worker who claims the right to join a pension scheme retroactively cannot avoid paying the employee contributions for the period of membership in question, which is likely to be a major disincentive to bringing such a claim for many potential applicants; and secondly, the national (i.e. domestic) rules relating to time-limits for bringing actions under national law apply to workers asserting their right under Community law to join a pension scheme, provided that they are not less favourable than those which apply to similar actions under domestic law (the principle of equivalence), and that they do not render the exercise of rights conferred by Community law impossible in practice (the principle of effectiveness). In the wake of the *Vroege* and *Fisscher* judgments, some 60,000 part-time workers in both the public and private sectors commenced proceedings before tribunals claiming that they had been unlawfully excluded from membership of various occupational pension schemes. In a belated attempt at damage-limitation, the Government introduced regulations[2] prohibiting (as from 31 May 1995) all direct or indirect discrimination on grounds of sex regarding membership of any occupational pension scheme, requiring such claims to be brought within six months of the end of the employment in question, and limiting any backdated award to a maximum period of two years from the institution of proceedings (in effect applying the time-limits which apply to claims under the Equal Pay Act), but as those regulations did not have retrospective effect, they could not affect the many thousands of claims which had already been lodged before they came into force. As seen earlier, in *Preston v Wolverhampton Healthcare NHS Trust*[3] , the ECJ ruled on a series of carefully selected test cases on a variety of preliminary points arising out of those claims, holding that the two-year limit on the back-dating of membership of occupational pension schemes under the Equal Pay Act[4] infringes the principle of effectiveness, so that workers unlawfully excluded from such schemes are in principle able to claim a right to back-date their membership to 8 April 1976.

The issue of equal treatment in occupational pension schemes had been high on the agenda within the European Community for several years before the *Barber* judgment. In July 1986, the EC Council issued Directive 86/378 on the implementation of the principle of equal treatment for men and women in occupational social security schemes, with a deferred implementation date of 1 January 1993, and the Social Security Act 1989 contained a series of provisions

20 *Defrenne v SABENA* [1976] ECR 455, [1976] ICR 547, ECJ.
1   [1995] ICR 635, [1994] IRLR 662, ECJ.
2   The Occupational Pension Schemes (Equal Access to Membership) Amendment Regulations 1995, S.I. 1995 No. 1215. The regulations came into force on 31 May 1995, and apply to claims lodged on or after that date.
3   Case C-78/98, [2000] IRLR 506. The important ruling of the ECJ on the validity of the six-month time-limit on the presentation of claims is discussed at p. 301 above.
4   As modified by the Occupational Pension Schemes (Equal Access to Membership) Regulations 1976, S.I. 1976 No. 142, which, inter alia, provide that the only remedy under the 1970 Act for a failure to comply with the equal access requirements is a declaration that the employee is entitled to be admitted to the scheme, subject to a limitation period of two years before the date on which the proceedings were instituted (regs. 11 and 12).

designed to implement the requirements of the directive[5]. Article 9 of the directive appeared to allow member states to defer application of the principle of equal treatment in relation to differential pensionable ages in occupational pension schemes until equality in pensionable ages is achieved in statutory schemes, or is required by a further directive[6], and Schedule 5 of the 1989 Act contained an exemption to that effect[7]. However, before those provisions were brought into force they were overtaken by the decision of the ECJ in *Barber*[8], which went significantly further than the directive by holding that differential pensionable ages in occupational schemes are contrary to Article 119 (now 141), even if based on statutory schemes. In the light of *Barber* (and the subsequent ECJ decisions explaining and clarifying it), it was clear that further legislation was necessary, and this was introduced in the Pensions Act 1995 which, in addition to laying down a new regulatory regime for occupational pension schemes, equalising the state pension ages of men and women at 65 (from 2020), and abolishing Guaranteed Minimum Pensions[9], introduced new provisions requiring equal treatment in relation to membership of and rights under occupational pension schemes[10]. The new provisions echo those in the Equal Pay Act (and are to be construed as one with that Act[11]) by enacting that a statutory equal treatment rule (equivalent to an equality clause under the 1970 Act) is to be included in all occupational pension schemes, the effect of which is to require any term of a scheme which concerns access to or benefits[12] under the scheme, and which is less favourable to a woman than to a man, to be modified so as to be not less favourable, where the woman is employed on like work, work rated as equivalent or work of equal value with the man[13]. As with the Equal Pay Act, there is a defence if the trustees or managers of the scheme can prove that the difference in treatment is genuinely due to a material factor which is not the difference of sex[14]. The new provisions are however subject to two limitations: first, the requirement for equality in relation to the treatment of members of an occupational pension scheme applies only to pensionable service on or after 17 May 1990 (in line with the temporal limitation on the *Barber* judgment, discussed above)[15]; and secondly, the Act permits a variation in treatment as between a man

---

5   Social Security Act 1989, s. 23 and Sch. 5.

6   It was because Directive 86/378 appeared to allow an exception for the consequences of differences in state pensionable ages that the ECJ in *Barber* placed a limitation on the retrospective effect of its judgment, the point being that before that case it was reasonable for people to rely on the directive and to assume that Art. 119 (now 141) did not apply to differential pensionable ages in occupational pension schemes.

7   Ibid., para. 2(4).

8   See p. 303, above.

9   On these aspects of the Act, see Nobles (1996) 59 MLR 241.

10   Pensions Act 1995, ss. 62–66. The equal treatment provisions of the Act came into force on 1 January 1996, and are supplemented by the Occupational Pension Schemes (Equal Treatment) Regulations 1995, S.I. 1995 No. 3183. Paragraphs 5 and 6 of Sch. 5 to the 1989 Act (on unfair maternity and family leave provisions) came into force on 23 June 1994, and are adopted by s. 63(3) of the 1995 Act; the remainder of Sch. 5 would appear to be a dead letter.

11   Pensions Act 1995, s. 63(4).

12   Including benefits for dependants: ibid., s. 63(1).

13   Ibid., s. 62(1)–(3). The requirement of equal treatment also applies to any terms which confer a discretion on the trustees or managers of the scheme, or on any other person, and to the effect of the exercise of such a discretion: ibid., s. 62(5).

14   Ibid., s. 62(4).

15   Ibid., s. 63(6); as before, the temporal limitation does not apply to access to membership of a pension scheme: see p. 306, above.

and a woman where that variation consists of the application of actuarial factors[16] to the calculation of employers' contributions or the determination of benefits (an exception permitted by Directive 86/378 until July 1999)[17].

5   DISABILITY DISCRIMINATION IN EMPLOYMENT[18]

Statistics indicate that disabled people account for nearly a fifth of the working-age population in Great Britain, but for only about one eighth (or 12 per cent) of all people in employment. There are over 6.5 million people with a work-limiting long-term disability or health problem in Great Britain, but disabled people are only half as likely as non-disabled people to be in employment[19]. Disabled employees earn on average two-thirds of the wages of non-disabled employees[20], and are more likely to be employed in manual and unskilled occupations than are non-disabled employees[1]. To some extent this can be explained by the effect which a physical or mental impairment might have on a disabled person's capacity to perform the work in question, but there is also strong evidence to suggest that disabled people suffer systematic discrimination in relation to employment, often as a result of ill-informed, stereotypical assumptions on the part of employers about the impact of particular disabilities on the work-capacity of such employees and the difficulty of adapting working arrangements and premises to accommodate them[2]. Until recently there was no legislation tackling the problem of discrimination against disabled people in the workplace, successive governments having maintained (in what has become a familiar refrain) that the issue was most appropriately tackled by education and persuasion rather than by anti-discrimination legislation. However, following an intensive and well-organised campaign for the introduction of comprehensive civil rights legislation for disabled people, and no fewer than 14 abortive attempts to introduce Private Members' Bills on the subject, the Conservative Government introduced the Disability Discrimination Act 1995[3] (DDA), the first legislative attempt to tackle discrimination against disabled people. The DDA outlaws discrimination against disabled people in relation to employment, the provision of goods and services, and the sale and letting of property; it also requires schools, colleges, universities and LEAs to provide fuller information about their arrangements and facilities for disabled pupils and students, and it requires the Government to set a timetable for fully accessible public transport for disabled people.

In the area of employment, the DDA tries to strike a balance between the interests of disabled people (in terms of access to employment and equal

16   Within limits prescribed by regulations: see S.I. 1995 No. 3183.
17   Pensions Act 1995, s. 64(3); this exception may be repealed by regulations: ibid., s. 64(4).
18   See generally, Thomas *The New Law on Disability Discrimination* (Sweet & Maxwell, 1996), Doyle *Disability, Discrimination and Equal Opportunities* (Mansell, 1995). See also 'Monitoring the Disability Discrimination Act (DDA) 1995', (DfEE Research Series RR119, 1999).
19   Labour Force Survey, Summer 1999.
20   Martin, White and Meltzer *Disabled Adults: Services, Transport and Employment* (OPCS, 1989).
1   Prescott-Clarke *Employment and Handicap* (SCPR, 1990).
2   Honey, Meager and Williams *Employers' Attitudes towards People with Disabilities* (IMS, 1993).
3   The Act was heralded by a consultation document on *Government Measures to Tackle Discrimination Against Disabled People* (produced following the furore surrounding the 'talking-out' of the Civil Rights (Disabled Persons) Bill in 1994), and by a White Paper, *Ending discrimination against disabled people*, Cm. 2729, which was published on the same day as the Bill. The employment provisions of the DDA came into force on 2 December 1996.

treatment in the workplace, etc) and the interests of employers, by making it unlawful for an employer to discriminate against a disabled employee or job applicant by treating that person less favourably than he treats or would treat others for a reason relating to his or her disability, and by placing a duty on an employer to make reasonable adjustments to working arrangements and premises (by providing special equipment, altering working hours, arranging training, adapting premises, etc), in order to accommodate a disabled person who would otherwise be at a substantial disadvantage in comparison with non-disabled persons, while at the same time allowing an employer to claim that discrimination against a disabled person is justified in certain circumstances. The right not to be discriminated against is enforceable in an employment tribunal, as in the case of sex and race discrimination. The DDA repealed much of the Disabled Persons (Employment) Act 1944, including the system of voluntary registration of disabled persons, the requirement for those employing more than 20 employees to employ a quota of at least three per cent registered disabled employees (with preferential treatment for disabled candidates until the quota is met), and the designated employment scheme whereby certain occupations were reserved for disabled employees. The 1944 Act had been widely criticised for its ineffectiveness; the only sanction was criminal proceedings brought by the Secretary of State, and prosecutions were very rare, despite widespread evidence of non-compliance[4]; indeed, the number of people registered as disabled under the Act had fallen to such an extent (due at least in part to a fear of being discriminated against for carrying that label) that in practice it would not have been be possible for all employers to meet the three per cent quota anyway.

The DDA was given only a qualified welcome by disabled rights campaigners, on account of the perceived deficiencies in its provisions. In particular, concern was expressed at the narrowness of the definition of disability[5], the extent to which employers can claim that discrimination against disabled persons is justified, and the absence of a commission similar to the Equal Opportunities Commission and the Commission for Racial Equality with powers to investigate complaints, assist individuals in enforcing their legal rights or take enforcement action on its own account. By far the greatest criticism was levelled at the exemption of small businesses (originally, those employing fewer than 20 employees[6]) from the employment provisions of the Act[7], which was estimated to exclude 96 per cent of employers from the duty not to discriminate against disabled persons. Some of these criticisms have since been addressed. The Disability Rights Commission 1999 established a Disability Rights Commission, with powers similar to those of the EOC and CRE, and the small employer threshold was reduced from 20 to 15 in 1998[8], thereby extending the protection to a further 45,000 employers and 60,000 disabled employees[9]. Other criticisms have yet to be addressed, and the Disability Rights Task Force (created by the Government to examine the whole

4   There were only ever ten prosecutions, the last one in 1975.
5   Although the definition was broadened during the Act's passage through Parliament, it still does not cover some categories who might fall within a broader definition of disability, e.g. those with a reputation for disability.
6   Those employed by associated employers are not to be included in the calculation: *Hardie v CD Northern Ltd* [2000] ICR 207, EAT.
7   Disability Discrimination Act 1995, s. 7. The exclusion mirrored the 1944 Act, under which the duty to employ a three per cent quota of registered disabled employees only applied to firms employing 20 or more.
8   S.I. 1998 No. 2618. There was a statutory requirement to review the exclusion within four years of the provisions coming into force: s. 7(5).
9   DTI Regulatory Impact Assessment.

question of disability rights legislation) has recommended several more key reforms to the DDA's employment provisions, including the lowering of the small employer threshold to two[10], extending the scope of the provisions to cover, e.g. partnerships, police and prison officers, firefighters and the armed forces, restricting disability-related enquiries before the offer of a job is made, removing the justification defence in the case of the duty to make reasonable adjustments, and giving tribunals the power to order reinstatement or re-engagement where a disabled person is unlawfully dismissed, and the power to make recommendations regarding future conduct[11].

A noteable feature of the DDA is the extent to which it leaves many fundamental issues and concepts to be clarified and expanded upon by regulations, ministerial guidance and codes of practice. There are two principal sets of employment-related regulations[12], and the Secretary of State has issued Guidance on 'matters to be taken into account in determining questions relating to the definition of disability', and a Code of Practice 'for the elimination of discrimination in the field of employment against disabled persons or persons who have had a disability'. The Guidance and the Code of Practice are both admissible in evidence in proceedings before a tribunal, and must be taken into account where relevant. Some of the concepts and terminology used in the Act are borrowed from the sex and race discrimination legislation (e.g. 'less favourable treatment', 'any other detriment'), but the Court of Appeal has warned that a textual comparison between the disability discrimination legislation and the legislation relating to sex and race discrimination is not helpful, and may even be misleading:

'Contrary to what might be reasonably assumed, the exercise of interpretation is not facilitated by familiarity with the pre-existing legislation prohibiting discrimination in the field of employment (and elsewhere) on the grounds of sex (Sex Discrimination Act 1975) and race (Race Relations Act 1976). Indeed, it may be positively misleading to approach the 1995 Act with assumptions and concepts familiar from experience of the workings of the 1975 Act and the 1976 Act.[13]'

i) The meaning of 'disability'

The key to the Act's provisions is the definition of disability in section 1(1), which states that a person has a disability 'if he has a physical or mental impairment which has a substantial and long-term adverse effect on his ability to carry out normal day-to-day activities.' This definition has been described as a 'common-sense' definition which fits 'a generally acceptable perception of what disability means to employers, service providers, disabled people and the nation at large'[14]; however, it has also been criticised for being too narrow, and for adopting a medical as opposed to a social model of disability[15], by defining disability in

---

10 Or, at least, including those employed by associated employers in the calculation: see n. 6 above.
11 *From exclusion to inclusion*, Disability Rights Task Force, 1999
12 The Disability Discrimination (Meaning of Disability) Regulations 1996, S.I. 1996 No. 1455, and the Disability Discrimination (Employment) Regulations 1996, S.I. 1996 No. 1456.
13 *Clark v Novacold Ltd* [1999] IRLR 318, CA, per Mummery LJ, at para. 30.
14 Minister of State, *Hansard*, H.C., Standing Committee E, col. 73.
15 See e.g. Doyle (1996) ILJ, p. 1.

terms of impairments rather than focusing on the ways in which disabled people are disadvantaged by the organisation, structure and attitudes of the society in which they live and work.

The definition, which is fleshed out by regulations and guidance[16], has the following key elements[17]: i) there must be a 'physical or mental impairment'; these terms are not defined, but are intended to cover all forms of impairment, including sensory impairments. Mental illness only counts as a mental impairment if it is 'a clinically well-recognised illness'[18] (a requirement apparently designed to avoid 'the possibility of claims based on obscure conditions unrecognised by reputable clinicians'[19]), and a number of conditions are deemed not to be impairments for the purposes of the Act (e.g. dependency on alcohol, nicotine or other non-prescribed substance, pyromania, kleptomania, exhibitionism, voyeurism and hayfever[20]); ii) the impairment must have a 'substantial' effect[1]; this is not defined, although the intention is only to include impairments having an effect which is 'more than minor or trivial'[2]. The Guidance suggests that in determining whether the effect of an impairment is substantial, account should be taken of factors such as the time taken to carry out the activity (para. A2) and the way in which it is carried out (para. A3), in comparison with what might be expected if the person did not have the impairment[3]; iii) the impairment must have a 'long-term' effect; conditions which are only temporary, such as short-term illness, are not disabilities within the meaning of the Act. An impairment will be treated as having a long-term effect if it has lasted, or is likely to last, for at least 12 months, or if it is likely to last for the rest of a person's life (as in the case of a terminal illness)[4]. Where the impairment is intermittent or sporadic (e.g. epilepsy or multiple sclerosis), it will be treated as continuing to have a long-term adverse effect, even through periods of remission, if it is likely to recur[5]; iv) the impairment must have an adverse effect on a person's ability 'to carry out normal day-to-day activities'. Schedule 1 contains an exhaustive list[6] of activities which are to be treated as normal day-to-day activities for these purposes, namely: mobility; manual dexterity; physical co-ordination; continence; ability to lift, carry or otherwise move everyday objects; speech, hearing or eyesight; memory or ability to

---

16 The Disability Discrimination (Meaning of Disability) Regulations 1996, S.I. 1996 No. 1455, and 'Guidance on matters to be taken into account in determining questions relating to the meaning of disability' (1996).

17 The EAT gave useful guidance as to the correct approach to the question whether a person has a disability within the meaning of the Act in *Goodwin v Patent Office* [1999] IRLR 4.

18 Ibid., Sch. 1, para. 1(1). In the event of doubt as to whether a mental illness falls within the definition, the EAT suggested in *Goodwin v Patent Office*, above, that it would be advisable for the tribunal to consult the World Health Organisation's International Classification of Diseases.

19 Minister of State, *Hansard*, H.C., Standing Committee E, col. 104.

20 Disability Discrimination (Meaning of Disability) Regulations, above, n. 16, regs. 3 and 4.

1 Sch. 1, para. 3 provides that a severe disfigurement will be treated as an impairment having a substantial adverse effect; deliberately acquired disfigurements such as tattoos or decorative body piercing are excluded: Disability Discrimination (Meaning of Disability) Regulations, reg. 5.

2 *Goodwin v Patent Office*, above, n. 17.

3 The Guidance also advises that it may be appropriate to consider the cumulative effects of the impairment on a range of normal day-to-day activities (para. A4), and the cumulative effects of more than one impairment (para. A6).

4 Ibid., Sch. 1, para. 2(1). Cf *Greenwood v British Airways plc* [1999] IRLR 600, EAT.

5 Ibid., Sch. 1, para. 2(2).

6 Regulations may deem an impairment to affect a person's ability to carry out normal day-to-day activities, and vice versa: ibid., Sch. 1, para. 4(2).

concentrate, learn or understand; or the perception of the risk of physical danger. 'Normal day-to-day activities' are the activities of an ordinary average person, not a person with specialised skills or abilities[7]. In deciding whether an activity is a normal day-to-day activity, the Guidance states that account should be taken 'of how far it is normal for most people and carried out by most people on a daily or frequent or fairly regular basis' (para. C2). It follows that 'normal day-to-day activities' do not include work of any particular form, 'because no particular form of work is "normal" for most people' (para. C3)[8]. In *Goodwin v The Patent Office*[9], the EAT emphasised that the Act is concerned with the effect of an impairment on a person's *ability* to carry out activities:

> 'The fact that a person can carry out such activities does not mean that his ability to carry them out has not been impaired... In order to constitute an adverse effect, it is not the doing of the acts which is the focus of attention but rather the ability to do (or not to do) the acts... The focus of attention required by the Act is on the things that the applicant either cannot do or can only do with difficulty, rather than on the things that the person can do.'

In that case, the EAT also held that the tribunal should adopt a purposive approach to the interpretation of the definition, and should construe the language of the Act in a way which gives effect to the stated or presumed intention of Parliament, but with due regard to the ordinary and natural meaning of the words. One difficult practical issue for the tribunal is the weight to be placed on medical evidence. In *Kapadia v London Borough of Lambeth*[10], the EAT allowed the applicant's appeal against the decision of the tribunal that he was not disabled on the grounds that the tribunal had disregarded uncontradicted medical evidence from his own GP and consultant that he was disabled, preferring instead to rely on their own assessment of how he appeared when giving evidence; however, ultimately it remains a matter for the tribunal to determine whether the applicant has a disability within the meaning of the Act, and in *Vickary v British Telecommunications plc*[11], the EAT held that a tribunal makes an error of law if it relies too readily on medical opinion that the applicant has a disability.

A number of further points can be made in relation to the definition. First, the statutory protection extends to those who have had a disability in the past, even if they have made a full recovery and are no longer disabled[12]. This is in recognition of the fact that a person with a history of disability (e.g. a person with a history of mental illness) may continue to experience discrimination even when no longer disabled; it is a rare example of the Act adopting a more 'social' model of disability. Secondly, the effect of an impairment on normal day-to-day activities must be considered without taking into account any measures (e.g. medical treatment[13],

---

7   In *Vickary v British Telecommunications plc* [1999] IRLR 680, EAT, normal day-to-day activities were held to include making beds, doing housework, sewing and cutting with scissors, minor DIY tasks, filing nails, curling hair and ironing.

8   See e.g. *Quinlan v B & Q plc* (EAT 1386/97) (assistant at garden centre not disabled within the meaning of the Act because, although unable to lift heavy objects following heart surgery, he was capable of lifting everyday objects).

9   Above, n. 17.

10   [2000] IRLR 14, EAT.

11   Above, n. 7.

12   Ibid., s. 2.

13   This can include attendance at therapy or counselling sessions: *Kapadia v London Borough of Lambeth*, above, n. 10.

or the use of a prosthesis or other aid) which are being taken to treat or correct the impairment[14]; so for example, in the case of a person with diabetes which is controlled by medication, the Guidance states that whether or not the effect of the condition is substantial must be decided by reference to what the effects of the condition would be if that person were not taking his or her medication[15] (para. A13). Thirdly, a person suffering from a progressive condition, such as cancer, multiple sclerosis, muscular dystrophy or infection by HIV, will be deemed to fall within the definition of a disabled person from the point in time when that condition begins to have some, but not necessarily a substantial, adverse effect on that person's ability to carry out normal day-to-day activities, if the medical prognosis is that the condition is likely to result in an impairment which has a substantial adverse effect[16]. This is in recognition of the fact that a person who is diagnosed as suffering from a progressive condition may suffer discrimination as a result of that diagnosis well before the condition can be said to have a substantial adverse effect on that person's ability to carry out normal day-to-day activities. However, the protection only arises from the point when the condition begins to have some effect; it does not apply while the condition, although diagnosed, remains latent, and it could therefore be said to provide a positive incentive to discriminate before a person begins to manifest any symptoms. Neither does it provide any protection to a person diagnosed as having a genetic predisposition to a potentially disabling condition[17]. Finally, those registered as disabled persons under the Disabled Persons (Employment) Act 1944 are deemed to have a disability for the purposes of the DDA, regardless of whether they meet the Act's definition of a disabled person[18].

ii) The scope of the protection

Section 4 echoes the sex and race discrimination legislation by prohibiting discrimination against a disabled person in all aspects of employment[19]. It makes it unlawful for an employer to discriminate against a disabled applicant for employment in the arrangements which he makes for recruitment, in the terms on which employment is offered, or by refusing or deliberately omitting to offer employment[20]; it also makes it unlawful for an employer to discriminate against a disabled employee in relation to the terms of employment, the way he affords or

---

14 Ibid., Sch. 1, para. 6. This does not apply to those with impaired sight which is correctable by spectacles or contact lenses or some other prescribed method.

15 I.e. the tribunal must consider the 'deduced effects' of the impairment: *Goodwin v Post Office*, above, n. 17.

16 Ibid., Sch. 1, para. 8.

17 On the potential for genetic discrimination in employment, see the report of the Human Genetics Advisory Council 'The Implications of Genetic Testing for Employment' (HGAC, 1999).

18 DDA, s. 2. The provision only applies to those who were registered under the 1944 Act on 12 January 1995 and were still registered on 2 December 1996 (i.e. the date when the employment provisions of the DDA came into force); such persons are deemed to be disabled for three years from 2 December 1996.

19 The DDA uses the wider definition of employment used in the sex and race discrimination legislation, so the protection extends to employees and applicants for employment, including contract workers (s. 12), apprentices and self-employed workers who contract personally to do any work (s. 68(1)). Certain occupations (e.g. armed forces, police, prison officers and firefighters), are excluded: s. 64. Curiously, the Act does not apply to partners or prospective partners (cf. SDA, s. 11; RRA, s. 10).

20 Ibid., s. 4(1).

refuses to afford him opportunities for promotion, transfer, training or other benefit, or by dismissing him[1] or 'subjecting him to any other detriment'[2] (a phrase which has been interpreted in other contexts as covering any type of disadvantage)[3]. Section 11 of the 1995 Act makes special provision for discriminatory job advertisements, by providing that there will be a presumption of discrimination if a job advertisement[4] indicates (or might reasonably be taken to indicate) that the employer might discriminate against a disabled applicant[5]; however, this presumption only applies where a disabled person has applied for and not been offered the job in question, and the employer can rebut the presumption by showing that the failure to offer the job to that person was not related to his disability[6]. The Act contains no specific provisions dealing with pre-employment health screening, despite evidence that it is a common source of discrimination against disabled applicants, but it might be held to be unlawful for an employer to insist on a medical check for a disabled applicant if the same requirement is not applied to other, non-disabled applicants. The protection against dismissal operates alongside the existing law of unfair dismissal, but the two are not co-extensive because under the 1995 Act the employer is under a duty to make reasonable adjustments to arrangements and premises in order to overcome a disabled employee's disadvantage (see below), which may involve the employer in, for example, reallocating work or transferring the disabled employee to another vacancy. This duty is stricter than any obligation on an employer under the unfair dismissal legislation in the case of a dismissal for incapability or ill-health[7].

iii) The meaning of 'discrimination'

The definition of discrimination in section 5 of the DDA differs in several respects from that used in the sex and race discrimination legislation. In particular, the DDA does not draw a distinction between direct and indirect discrimination, it provides a defence of justification to less favourable treatment which would constitute direct discrimination under the sex and race discrimination legislation, and it does not prohibit positive discrimination in favour of disabled people.

a) Direct discrimination

Section 5(1)(a) provides that an employer discriminates against a disabled person 'if, for a reason which relates to the disabled person's disability, he treats him less favourably than he treats or would treat others to whom that reason does not or would not apply'. At first sight this looks very similar to the definition of discrimination which is used in the sex and race discrimination Acts; however,

---

1   A dismissal which is unlawful under the DDA is not automatically unfair under the Employment Rights Act: *H J Heinz Co Ltd v Kenrick* [2000] IRLR 144, EAT.
2   Ibid., s. 4(2).
3   See p. 257, above.
4   This includes every form of advertisement or notice, whether to the public or not: ibid., s. 11(3).
5   Ibid., s. 11(1). In contrast, the sex and race discrimination legislation makes it unlawful to publish a discriminatory job advertisement, and places enforcement of the restrictions on advertisements in the hands of the Equal Opportunities Commission and the Commission for Racial Equality: see p. 256, above.
6   Ibid., s. 11(2).
7   See ch. 8, below.

the DDA adopts a different comparator to that used in the other anti-discrimination legislation[8], and the employer has a defence if he can show that the treatment in question is justified (see below).

The scope of the protection offered by this section turns on two fundamentally important issues: first, the identification of the appropriate comparator when determining whether there has been 'less favourable treatment'; and secondly, the degree of knowledge of the complainant's disability required on the part of the employer. The first issue arose for consideration in *Clark v Novacold Ltd*[9], where the applicant was dismissed for long-term sickness absence following an accident at work. The EAT under Morison P identified two possible interpretations of this test: (i) to compare the treatment of the disabled person with the treatment of a person who was unable to fulfil all the requirements of the job, for a reason unrelated to disability (i.e. someone who had been absent from work for the same amount of time as the applicant, but for a reason other than disability); and (ii) to compare the treatment of the disabled person with the treatment of a person who was able to fulfil all the requirements of the job (i.e. someone who had not been absent from work at all, or who had the same absence record as the applicant when any disability-related absences were discounted). The EAT preferred (i), and held that the applicant had not been less favourably treated for a reason which related to his disability, because he was treated no differently than a person in similar circumstances who was not disabled would have been treated. In sharp contrast, in *British Sugar v Kirker*[10], the EAT held that the DDA does not require a like-for-like comparison, but 'simply requires the applicant to show that he was less favourably treated than other employees where the reason for the treatment, that is a reason related to his disability, does not apply to those other employees' (i.e. the straightforward causative test in (ii)); it was unnecessary to identify other employees with whom to compare the treatment of the disabled applicant, other than for the purpose of determining the causation question. On appeal, the Court of Appeal in *Clark v Novacold Ltd*[11] reversed the EAT's decision, and applied the causative approach: 'The test of less favourable treatment is based on the reason for the treatment of the disabled person and not on the fact of his disability. It does not turn on a like-for-like comparison of the treatment of the disabled person and of others in similar circumstances'.

Turning to the second issue, the degree of knowledge required on the part of the employer, in *O'Neill v Symm & Co Ltd*[12], the first EAT decision on the DDA provisions, the EAT held that the use of the words 'for a reason which relates to the disabled person's disability' means that that the employer must have knowledge of the employee's disability, or at least the material features of it, and not merely knowledge of one or other equivocal symptom. In that case, the employee was dismissed as a result of absences from work due to chronic fatigue syndrome. The EAT held that she had not been discriminated against for a reason which related to her disability, because her employers had no knowledge of her condition, and had dismissed her solely on the grounds of uncertified

---

8   In particular, the DDA does not include the requirement in s. 5(3) of the SDA and s. 3(4) of the RRA that when comparing the treatment of persons of different sex or different racial groups, the comparison must be such 'that the relevant circumstances in the one case are the same, or not materially different, in the other.'
9   [1998] IRLR 420, EAT.
10 [1998] IRLR 624, EAT. The earlier EAT decision in *Clark v Novacold Ltd* was not mentioned in the judgment.
11 [1999] IRLR 318, CA.
12 [1998] IRLR 233, EAT.

absence. However, in *H J Heinz Co Ltd v Kenrick*[13] the EAT disagreed with *O'Neill*, and held that it was not necessary for the employer to have knowledge of the disability in order to be said to have acted for a reason 'which relates' to the disability; according to the EAT, the reason may include a 'reason deriving from how the disability manifests itself even where there is no knowledge of the disability as such'. The EAT used the example of a postman who successfully conceals from the employer the fact that he has an artificial leg, and who is dismissed for making his rounds too slowly. If he can show that his slowness is attributable to his artificial leg, then according to the EAT he would have been treated less favourably than others 'to whom that reason does not apply' (i.e. others who do their rounds at an acceptable pace) for a reason which related to his disability, whether or not the employer knew before the dismissal that the reason for the slowness was that he was disabled.

The decision in *Heinz* is consistent with the approach of the Court of Appeal in *Clark v Novacold Ltd*[14], in that it applies an objective test of whether or not there is a causal connection between the less favourable treatment complained of and the applicant's disability, rather than a subjective test through the eyes of the employer: 'Unless the test is objective, there will be difficulties with credible and honest yet ignorant or obtuse employers who fail to recognise or acknowledge the obvious'[15]. The effect in practice is to place much greater emphasis on the question of justification, where absence of knowledge of the disability on the part of the employer may be highly material[16].

The employer has a defence to a complaint of direct discrimination if he can show that the less favourable treatment is justified[17]. The availability of a justification defence in complaints of direct discrimination is a recognition of the fact that a person's disability may have a bearing on their ability to do a job, but there is clearly a danger that if the defence is applied too widely, it could undermine the statutory protection. The Act states that treatment is justified if the reason for it 'is both material to the circumstances of the particular case[18] and substantial'[19]; this is amplified by the Code of Practice[20], which states that the reason must relate to the individual circumstances in question, and must not be trivial or minor, a test which has been judicially described as a 'very low threshold'[1]. In *Baynton v Saurus General Engineers Ltd*[2], the EAT held that in applying the test of justification the tribunal must carry out a balancing exercise between the interests of the disabled employee and the interests of the employer, but as the EAT subsequently observed in *Heinz*, in undertaking such an exercise the comparatively limited requirements of the justification test must be borne in mind.

13 [2000] IRLR 144, EAT.
14 Ibid., n. 11.
15 Ibid., n. 13, per Lindsay P, at p. 147.
16 Note that the employer's duty to make reasonable adjustments does not arise if the employer does not know and could not reasonably be expected to know that the person has a disability: DDA, s. 6(6).
17 Ibid., s. 5(1)(b).
18 The relevant circumstances include the circumstances of both the employer and the employee: *Baynton v Saurus General Engineers Ltd* [1999] IRLR 604, EAT.
19 Ibid., s. 5(3). Where an employer is under a duty to make a reasonable adjustment, but has failed without justification to comply with that duty, the employer cannot justify less favourable treatment of that person unless that treatment would have been justified even if the employer had made the adjustment: s. 5(5).
20 Code of Practice 'For the elimination of discrimination in the field of employment against disabled persons or persons who have had a disability', para. 4.6.
1 *H J Heinz Co Ltd v Kenrick*, above, n. 13, per Lindsay P, at p. 146.
2 Above, n. 18.

b) Failure to make a reasonable adjustment

Unlike the sex and race discrimination legislation, the DDA does not expressly prohibit indirect discrimination against a disabled person on the grounds of disability; instead, section 6 places a duty on the employer to make reasonable adjustments to his arrangements[3] (e.g. interview and selection procedures, job offers, contractual arrangements, working conditions and arrangements for redeployment[4]) or to any physical feature[5] of his premises[6] (e.g. doors which are too narrow for wheelchairs, lighting which is too dim for someone with restricted vision), where they place a disabled employee or a disabled applicant for employment at a 'substantial disadvantage' (not defined) in comparison with persons who are not disabled[7]. Failure to comply with the duty to make reasonable adjustments will constitute unlawful discrimination[8], unless the employer can show that his failure to comply is justified[9].

The duty to make adjustments does not arise if the employer does not know, and could not reasonably be expected to know, that the person has a disability which is likely to place him at a substantial disadvantage in comparison with non-disabled persons[10]. This raises the difficult question of just when an employer can be expected to draw an inference that an employee is disabled, and/or at a substantial disadvantage. In *Ridout v TC Group*[11], the applicant stated in her job application that she had photosensitive epilepsy controlled by medication, and was disabled. She was interviewed in a room which had bright fluorescent lighting. She entered the interview room wearing sunglasses around her neck (at 5 pm on a February afternoon) and remarked that she might be disadvantaged by the lighting. The interview proceeded, and she was not offered the job. She subsequently complained that the employers had failed to make a reasonable adjustment in respect of the physical arrangements for the interview. The EAT upheld the tribunal's decision that the applicant had not been unlawfully discriminated against on grounds of her disability. The EAT stated that tribunals should be careful not to impose on disabled people seeking employment a duty to give a long explanation as to the effects of their disability merely to cause the

3   As defined in s. 6(2), this applies to arrangements for determining to whom employment should be offered, and to any term, condition or arrangements on which employment, promotion, a transfer, training or any other benefit is offered or afforded. Although not expressly stated in the Act, the duty has been held to apply to the dismissal of a disabled employee: *Morse v Wiltshire County Council* [1998] IRLR 352, EAT.
4   *Kent County Council v Mingo* [2000] IRLR 90, EAT.
5   As defined in the Disability Discrimination (Employment) Regulations 1996, reg. 9.
6   The duty applies only to premises occupied by the employer; if the employer's premises are leased, the terms of the lease may be overriden if the landlord unreasonably withholds consent to the alterations, to enable the occupier to comply with the duty to make adjustments: ibid., s. 16.
7   The EAT provided useful guidance for a tribunal dealing with an alleged failure to make reasonable adjustments in *Morse v Wiltshire County Council*, above, n. 3.
8   A complaint of a failure to make a reasonable adjustment does not depend upon showing that there has been less favourable treatment: *Clark v Novacold Ltd* [1998] IRLR 420, EAT.
9   Ibid., s. 5(2). The test of justification is the same as applies in cases of direct discrimination: s. 5(4). The question of what steps were reasonable, and whether a failure was justified, is an objective test on which the tribunal should form its own view: *Morse v Wiltshire County Council*, above, n. 3.
10   Ibid., s. 6(6). In the case of a disabled applicant, the duty only applies in relation to a person who is, or has notified the employer that he may be, an applicant for the employment: s. 6(5).
11   [1998] IRLR 628, EAT. Quaere whether the decision in this case is affected by *H J Heinz & Co Ltd v Kenrick* [2000] IRLR 144, EAT (see p. 317 above).

employer to make adjustments which probably should have been made in the first place, but neither should an employer be required to ask a number of questions as to whether a disabled person feels disadvantaged, questions which would not have been asked of somebody who was able-bodied. On the facts, the EAT held that the tribunal was entitled to conclude that no reasonable employer would be expected to know, without being told in terms by the applicant, that the arrangements which the employer made for the interview might disadvantage the applicant, given that the applicant's form of epilepsy was rare. Whether the prospective employers should have taken any other steps as a result of what was said at the interview was said to be a matter of fact and evidence for the tribunal.

Section 6(3) contains a number of examples of steps which an employer might have to take to comply with this duty; they include: making adjustments to premises; reallocating duties to other employees; transferring a disabled employee to an existing vacancy; altering his working hours; assigning him to a different place of work; giving him time off during working hours for rehabilitation, assessment or treatment; arranging training; acquiring or modifying equipment; modifying instructions or reference manuals; modifying procedures for testing or assessment; and providing a reader or interpreter. In *Kenny v Hampshire Constabulary*[12], the EAT held that the duty to make reasonable adjustments to the employer's 'arrangements' only applies to job-related arrangements, and does not extend to a duty to provide a personal carer to assist with the personal needs of a disabled employee. The Act also lists five factors[13], embracing issues of cost, practicability and effectiveness, which must be taken into account in determining whether it is reasonable for an employer to have to take a particular step; they are i) the extent to which taking the step would prevent the effect in question; ii) the extent to which it is practicable for the employer to take the step; iii) the financial and other costs which would be incurred by the employer in taking the step and the extent to which taking it would disrupt any of his activities; iv) the extent of the employer's financial and other resources; v) the availability to the employer of financial or other assistance. The Act contains a power to put a financial ceiling on the cost of making adjustments[14], but this has not been exercised to date, with the result that the question of what is a reasonable cost for an employer to have to bear is left to the judgment of the employment tribunals[15] (with obvious implications for consistency of treatment).

iv) Remedies

The remedies available for unlawful disability discrimination are similar to those which apply in complaints of sex or race discrimination[16], as are the procedures. Complaints must be presented to an employment tribunal within three months of the act complained of[17], and if the tribunal finds the complaint well-founded, it may make a declaration that the employee's rights have been infringed, order

12 [1999] IRLR 76, EAT.
13 Ibid., s. 6(4).
14 Ibid., s. 6(9).
15 The Compliance Cost Assessment for the Act estimated an average cost of £200 per disabled employee for the 10 per cent of cases where a disabled employee is likely to require an adjustment.
16 See p. 268, above.
17 Ibid., s. 8(1) and Sch. 3, para. 3.

the employer to pay compensation, and/or recommend that the employer take action specified by the tribunal to remove the adverse effect of the discrimination[18]. If the employer fails without reasonable justification to comply with such a recommendation, the tribunal may make an increased award of compensation if it thinks it just and equitable to do so[19]. Compensation will be calculated on the same basis as an action for damages in tort, and may include compensation for injury to feelings[20]. A medical expert may be required if the parties are unable to agree the evidence. There is no upper limit on the amount of compensation which may be awarded under the Act. The highest award to date was in *British Sugar v Kirker*[1], where the applicant was awarded £103,146.

The remaining provisions concerning remedies (e.g. on contracting-out, protection against victimisation, questionnaires and vicarious liability) are very similar to those in the sex and race discrimination legislation[2]. Until recently, the most significant difference was unquestionably the absence of a Commission equivalent to the Equal Opportunities Commission or the Commission for Racial Equality[3], but that controversial omission was remedied by the Disability Rights Commission Act 1999[4], which established a Commission of that name with powers to investigate complaints of discrimination, assist individuals in bringing complaints before the courts and tribunals, and take strategic enforcement action on its own account. In an interesting innovation, the Commission is empowered to enter into a legally binding written agreement with a person it has reason to believe may have committed, or may be committing, an unlawful act[5], thus providing a less severe procedure than the usual alternatives of prosecution or formal investigation.

---

18   Ibid., s. 8(2).
19   Ibid., s. 8(5).
20   Ibid., s. 8(3) and (4). On assessment of compensation under the Sex Discrimination Act 1975, see p. 269, above. The normal tribunal procedures for fixing compensation are not well suited to DDA cases, which may hinge on disputed medical opinion, and the tribunal may need to have a directions hearing involving, amongst other things, an exchange of statements of case and any witness statements: *Buxton v Equinox Design Ltd* [1999] IRLR 158, EAT.
1   [1998] IRLR 624, EAT.
2   See p. 263 et seq, above.
3   The National Disability Council, established under s. 50 of the DDA, was only empowered to advise the Government on general issues relating to discrimination against disabled people.
4   The provisions of the Act establishing the DRC came into force on 6 August 1999: S.I. 1999 No. 2210.
5   Disability Rights Commission Act 1999, s. 5.

Chapter 6

Maternity and parental rights

I INTRODUCTION[1]

The new Labour Government came into office in May 1997 committed to a review of the existing law on maternity rights, and the introduction of new 'family-friendly' measures to help workers strike a balance between work and home[2]. The Employment Relations Act 1999 duly introduced a new framework of maternity rights, replacing the existing substantive provisions in the Employment Rights Act 1996 with a series of enabling powers which were subsequently fleshed out by supporting regulations in the form of the Maternity and Parental Leave etc (MPL etc) Regulations 1999[3].

That the existing law on maternity rights was long overdue for reform was not in doubt. The existing provisions had developed piecemeal since the Employment Protection Act 1975 first introduced three statutory rights relating to maternity – the right not to be unfairly dismissed because of pregnancy, the right to return to work after pregnancy or childbirth and the right to maternity pay. A fourth right, to time off work for ante-natal care, was introduced in the Employment Act 1980. The right to maternity pay was superseded in April 1987 by the statutory maternity pay (SMP) provisions, introduced in the Social Security Act 1986 and subsequently consolidated in the Social Security Contributions and Benefits Act 1992. The maternity provisions were notorious for their complexity, and were widely criticised, not least because it was possible for a minor, technical slip-up to cost the employee her rights. In one case, the provisions were memorably described as being 'of inordinate complexity exceeding the worst excesses of a taxing statute'[4]. The position was exacerbated

---

1   See McRae *Maternity Rights in Britain* (1991); Fredman *Women in Labour: Parenting Rights at Work* (1995); McColgan (2000) 29 ILJ 125; Conaghan (1993) 20 JLS 71.
2   *Fairness at Work* (Cm 3968, 1998), Chapter 5.
3   S.I. 1999 No. 3312. The MPL etc. Regulations came into force on 15 December 1999.
4   As was illustrated in *Lavery v Plessey Telecommunications Ltd* [1983] IRLR 180, EAT, per Browne-Wilkinson J, at p. 182. In *Lavery* the giving of five days' notice of intention to return to work after maternity leave instead of the seven then required robbed the employee of her right to return.

by the fact that the qualifications for the different rights differed in several important respects (e.g. there were different qualifying dates and notice requirements for the right to return and for SMP).

The whole area was the subject of major change in 1993 by the Trade Union Reform and Employment Rights Act, implementing the Pregnant Workers Directive[5]. The 1993 Act introduced a new right to 14 weeks' maternity leave, and gave improved protection against dismissal on grounds of pregnancy or childbirth, in both cases regardless of length of service[6]. It also introduced a right to be suspended from work on maternity grounds where continued employment would be unlawful or contrary to a Code of Practice. The 1993 Act provided an excellent opportunity for a thorough overhaul of the law in this area and the removal of unnecessary complexity, but unfortunately that opportunity was missed. The new provisions were simply overlaid onto the existing law, and it took a greater than usual degree of fortitude to attempt to unravel them. Some improvement flowed from the consolidation of employment rights in the Employment Rights Act 1996, but as a consolidating statute, that Act was bound to have only limited success in attempting to fashion the proverbial silk purse out of the raw materials. Nearly two decades after Browne-Wilkinson J uttered the remarks quoted above, Ward LJ was moved to state in the Court of Appeal[7] in a case on the interpretation of the provisions on maternity leave and the right to return to work (which by that stage had been in force since 1975), that 'it is surely not too much to ask of the legislature that those who have to grapple with this topic should not have to have a wet towel around their heads as the single most important aid to the understanding of their rights'[8].

As redrawn in the 1999 Act and the associated regulations, the new maternity provisions, while still complex, are undeniably an improvement on what went before. The notification requirements have been rationalised and simplified, as have some of the more cumbersome mechanisms (e.g. the old provisions on 'deemed dismissals'), and some notorious grey areas have been clarified, in particular the status of the contract of employment during maternity leave. As regards the other stated objective of the reforms, that of making employment law more 'family-friendly', the new measures have received only qualified approval. The extension of the right to 'ordinary' maternity leave from 14 to 18 weeks, and the reduction in the qualifying period for 'additional' maternity leave from two years to one, are modest improvements on the previous position. More significant is the introduction of the new right to parental leave for mothers and fathers, and the right to emergency leave ('time off for dependants'), implementing the Parental Leave Directive[9], but here again the new provisions have been the subject of criticism e.g. in relation to the restriction of the entitlement to parental leave to the parents of children born on or after 15 December 1999, the decision to restrict the taking of parental leave to the period up to the child's fifth birthday (under the Directive the Government could have allowed leave to be taken up to

---

5   EC Directive No. 92/85. The directive, which was agreed in October 1992, was brought forward as a health and safety measure under Article 118A of the Treaty of Rome, and as such required only qualified majority approval; the UK Government abstained in the vote on its adoption.

6   A right to pay during the 14-week maternity leave period was introduced via reforms to the SMP provisions.

7   *Halfpenny v IGC Medical Systems Ltd* [1999] IRLR 177, CA. See p. 337 below.

8   To which prescription both authors would probably wish to add a couple of aspirins or a large whisky, or quite possibly both.

9   EC Directive No. 96/34.

the age of eight), and the fact that there is no provision for any part of the leave to be paid.

The Government has claimed with some justification that, in addition to the above reforms, some of the measures introduced in other areas will assist parents in balancing work and family life, in particular the implementation of the Working Time Directive, which attacks the long-hours culture that can be so destructive to family life and gives workers the right to paid holidays, and the Part-Time Workers Directive, which indirectly benefits working mothers (many of whom work part-time) by prohibiting discrimination against part-time workers. Critics have however pointed to the lack of any enforceable right to transfer from full-time to part-time work in the regulations implementing the Directive. In practice, one of the most important factors for mothers and fathers seeking to find a satisfactory balance between work and family life is the availability of high quality, convenient and affordable childcare. It remains to be seen whether the Government's much-vaunted National Childcare Strategy, which aims to encourage the provision of good quality childcare, and the introduction of the Working Families Tax Credit, which provides financial support for working families to meet (inter alia) the cost of childcare, will be more successful than the previous Government-sponsored initiatives in this area.

Finally, it should be remembered that, as in other areas of the employment rights legislation, the statutory provisions outlined below represent a minimum entitlement which may in practice be replaced by more generous contractual schemes.

2   DISMISSAL AND DETRIMENT FOR FAMILY REASONS

All employees have the right not to be dismissed or subjected to any detriment by their employer for reasons connected with pregnancy or childbirth or for other specified family reasons, regardless of their age or length of service. Until 1993, the protection against dismissal on grounds of pregnancy or childbirth was seriously deficient, in that it only applied where the employee satisfied the normal qualifying period of continuous employment for unfair dismissal (which was still two years at that time). The effect of this was to exclude some 40 per cent of working women from the protection[10]. All was not lost, however, for a woman dismissed for pregnancy within two years of employment could complain that her dismissal was unlawful sex discrimination (such complaints not being subject to any qualifying period of continuous employment). In 1993, the protection against pregnancy dismissal was extended to all employees by the Trade Union Reform and Employment Rights Act 1993, implementing the Pregnant Workers Directive[11], with the result that a woman dismissed on grounds of pregnancy or childbirth within the first year of employment does not have to claim sex discrimination in order to obtain a remedy. There may however still be advantages in doing so, not least being the fact that compensation for sex discrimination is not subject to any upper limit. The significance of sex discrimination law in this area is considered below[12].

---

10   1989 Labour Force Survey, *Employment Gazette*, December 1990, p. 633. The problem was particularly acute for part-time workers (i.e. those working less than 16 hours per week) who at that time needed to work for five years in order to qualify.
11   EC Directive No. 92/85.
12   See p. 347.

The provisions on pregnancy dismissal were further amended by the Employment Relations Act 1999, which simplified the existing provisions, and extended the unfair dismissal protection to dismissal for other family reasons (including the fact that the employee took parental leave, or time off for dependants), as required by the Parental Leave Directive. The opportunity was also taken to introduce for the first time a parallel right not to suffer detriment short of dismissal for family reasons. Section 99 of the 1996 Act, which used to contain the substantive provisions on dismissal for pregnancy and childbirth, is now a framework provision conferring a power to make regulations concerning dismissal for family reasons, and the detailed provisions on dismissal and other detriment are to be found in the Maternity and Parental Leave Regulations[13].

i)   Dismissal for family reasons

Under the current provisions, as revised in 1999, a dismissal will be automatically unfair if the reason or principal reason for the dismissal[14] is connected with: i) the pregnancy of the employee[15]; ii) the fact that she has given birth to a child[16]; iii) her suspension from work on maternity grounds[17]; iv) the fact that she took, or sought to take, ordinary maternity leave, additional maternity leave, parental leave or time off for dependants; v) the fact that she availed herself of the benefits of ordinary maternity leave[18]; vi) the fact that she refused to sign a workforce agreement in relation to parental leave[19]; or vii) the fact that she performed (or proposed to perform) any functions or activities of a workforce representative (including standing as a candidate) for the purposes of the provisions on parental leave. Special rules apply in the case of redundancy. First, a dismissal will be unfair if the employee is made redundant and it is shown that she was selected for redundancy in preference to other comparable employees for one of the family reasons set out above[20]. Secondly, where a redundancy situation arises during the employee's ordinary or additional maternity leave which makes it impracticable for the employer to continue to employ her under her original contract of employment, the employee is entitled to be offered alternative employment with her employer (or with a successor, or an associated employer) where there is a suitable available vacancy, i.e. where the work to be done is of a kind which is suitable in relation to the employee, appropriate for her to do in

---

13   MPL etc. Regulations, reg. 20.
14   As in other unfair dismissal cases, it will be for the employer to show the reason for the dismissal. An employee dismissed while pregnant or during ordinary or additional maternity leave is entitled to a written statement of the reasons for dismissal, without requesting it, and regardless of her length of service: ibid., s. 92(4), as amended.
15   Before the 1993 Act, this was the only ground upon which a pregnancy dismissal could be held automatically unfair. As under the old provisions, the dismissal must be causally connected with the pregnancy: it is not sufficient that the employee was dismissed while pregnant: see, on the old law, *Del Monte Foods Ltd v Mundon* [1980] ICR 694, [1980] IRLR 224, EAT.
16   The protection under this head only applies during the employee's ordinary or additional maternity leave: MPL etc. Regulations, reg. 20(4).
17   I.e. under a relevant statutory requirement or relevant recommendation in a code of practice, as defined by s. 66(2) of the 1996 Act; see p. 341 below.
18   I.e. that during her ordinary maternity leave period, she availed herself of the benefit of any of the terms and conditions of her employment preserved under s. 71: MPL etc. Regulations, reg. 20(5), applying reg. 19(3).
19   See p. 345 below.
20   MPL etc. Regulations, reg. 20(2).

the circumstances, and on terms and conditions (including the capacity and place in which she is to be employed) not substantially less favourable to her than if she had continued to be employed under her previous contract[1]. If the employer has a suitable alternative vacancy available, but makes the employee redundant during ordinary or additional maternity leave without first offering it to her, the redundancy dismissal will be unfair[2]. If however there is no suitable alternative work available which could be offered to her, she will not be regarded as unfairly dismissed.

There are two further significant limitations on the protection against dismissal, both of which were originally introduced by the Employment Act 1980 in an attempt to redress what was seen by the Government of the day as an imbalance in the maternity leave provisions in favour of employees. First, if the employer is a small employer employing only five or fewer people (including the employee herself and any employee employed by an associated employer) at the time when her additional maternity leave ends, and the employer can prove that it is not reasonably practicable to permit her to return to her old job or to a similar job which is both suitable for her and appropriate for her to do in the circumstances, the employee will not be regarded as automatically unfairly dismissed when the employer does not allow her to return to work at the end of her maternity leave period[3]. Secondly, if the employer can prove that it is not reasonably practicable (for a reason other than redundancy) to permit the employee to return to her old job or to a similar job which is both suitable for her and appropriate for her to do in the circumstances, and an associated employer has offered her suitable alternative employment which she has accepted or unreasonably refused, then once again she will not be regarded as automatically unfairly dismissed when she is not allowed to return to work at the end of her maternity leave period[4]. Both these exceptions are a major limitation on the right to return to work after maternity leave; the only comfort given to an employee in this situation is that the burden of proof is placed squarely upon the employer to show (a) that it is not reasonably practicable to permit her to return in the normal way, and (b) that he or an associated employer has offered her alternative employment 'which is both suitable for her and appropriate for her to do in the circumstances'[5]. The concept of an offer of suitable alternative employment is well known in the law on redundancy[6] and there may be a tendency to apply redundancy precedents to this maternity leave provision (though the wording of the two provisions is not the same), but it is submitted that in construing the maternity provision a tribunal should consider it as very much the exception to the normal rule, for to allow it to apply too readily would be to jeopardise an important employment right.

Before the 1993 amendments, a pregnancy dismissal was not unfair where the employer could prove that the employee was incapable of doing her job properly

---

1   Ibid., reg. 10. The offer of alternative employment must be made before the end of her existing contract, and the new contract must take effect immediately on the ending of the previous contract.
2   Ibid., reg. 20(1)(b). If the employer offers her a suitable alternative vacancy and she unreasonably refuses it, she may lose her right to a redundancy payment. It was held under the old provisions that whether a vacancy is 'available' is a question of objective fact, not of reasonableness: *Community Task Force v Rimmer* [1986] ICR 491, EAT.
3   Ibid., reg. 20(6).
4   Ibid., reg. 20(7).
5   Ibid, reg. 20(8). The requirement in redundancy cases that the terms and conditions of the alternative employment be not substantially less favourable to her than if she had continued to be employed under her previous contract does not apply here.
6   See p. 536.

because of her pregnancy (e.g. where her job involved lifting)[7], or that she could not carry on working without contravening some statutory provision (e.g. the regulations prohibiting the exposure of pregnant women to ionising radiations or lead)[8]. Those exceptions no longer apply, but where the employee's continued employment would be unlawful or contrary to the recommendations of a code of practice, the employee may now be suspended from work on maternity grounds (see below), and a dismissal connected with such suspension will be unfair.

In the case law on the pre-1993 provisions, the words 'reason connected with pregnancy' were broadly construed. In *Brown v Stockton-on-Tees Borough Council*[9], the applicant, a care supervisor on a youth training scheme, was selected for redundancy on the basis that she was pregnant. The employers argued that they were justified in selecting the applicant for redundancy because otherwise they would have had to arrange a replacement for her during maternity leave. The EAT and the Court of Appeal held that this was not a case of dismissal 'for a reason connected with pregnancy', but was instead purely a redundancy situation[10]. However, in a judgment of some importance the House of Lords held that the dismissal fell within the section and was therefore unfair; the section was to be construed in its own terms, as 'part of social legislation passed for the specific protection of women and to put them on an equal footing with men', and it could not have been the intention of Parliament 'that an employer should be entitled to take advantage of a redundancy situation to weed out his pregnant employees' (per Lord Griffiths). As seen above, the redrafted provisions now expressly provide that selection for redundancy for family reasons will be automatically unfair, but the decision is arguably still important, for it shows that the courts will be prepared to interpret the provisions purposively where necessary in order to achieve the social policy objectives of the legislation.

ii)   Protection from detriment for family reasons

The statutory protection from detriment for family reasons was introduced in the Employment Relations Act 1999. Before that Act there was no explicit right not to suffer detriment for family reasons, although in practice detrimental treatment on grounds of pregnancy or childbirth will almost invariably constitute unlawful sex discrimination[11]. The new provisions bring the protection from detriment in line with the unfair dismissal protection, although there are some differences between the two.

Section 47C of the Employment Rights Act 1996 (as fleshed out by the Maternity and Parental Leave etc. Regulations 1999[12]) gives an employee the right not to be subjected to any detriment[13] (other than dismissal) by her employer for the reason that she: i) is pregnant; ii) has given birth to a child; iii) has been suspended from work on maternity grounds; iv) has taken, or sought to take, ordinary maternity leave, additional maternity leave, parental leave or time off for

---

7   See, for example, *Brear v Wright Hudson Ltd* [1977] IRLR 287.
8   The only exception was where the employer had failed to offer her a suitable available vacancy, in which case the dismissal was unfair.
9   [1988] ICR 410, [1988] IRLR 263, HL. See also *Clayton v Vigers* [1989] ICR 713, [1990] IRLR 177, EAT.
10   The argument on behalf of the employer being that cases of unfair redundancy selection were not subject to s. 99.
11   See p. 347 below.
12   MPL etc. Regulations, reg. 19.
13   This includes detriment by any act or by deliberate failure to act: ibid., reg. 19(1).

dependants; v) has availed herself of the benefits of ordinary maternity leave; vi) has refused to sign a workforce agreement in relation to parental leave; or vii) has performed (or proposed to perform) any functions or activities of a workforce representative (including standing as a candidate) for the purposes of the provisions on parental leave[14].

The remedy for an infringement of the right not to be subjected to a detriment for family reasons operates through the usual procedures in Part V of the Employment Rights Act for protection from suffering detriment in employment. Complaint lies to an employment tribunal, within three months of the act or deliberate failure to act complained of (or within a further reasonable period where not reasonably practicable)[15], and if the tribunal upholds the complaint it must make a declaration to that effect, and may award the employee such compensation as it considers just and equitable in all the circumstances[16].

3   ORDINARY MATERNITY LEAVE

All pregnant employees are entitled to at least 18 weeks' ordinary maternity leave, irrespective of length of service or hours of work, during which the contract of employment continues (unless either party expressly ends it, or it expires), and the employee is entitled 'to the benefit of the terms and conditions of employment which would have applied if she had not been absent'[17] (apart from remuneration, which is specifically excluded[18]). The right to ordinary maternity leave was first introduced by the Trade Union Reform and Employment Rights Act 1993, implementing the Parental Leave Directive. At the outset the entitlement was restricted to 14 weeks, but the ordinary maternity leave period was extended to 18 weeks by the Employment Relations Act 1999[19]. Employees with at least one year's continuous service[20] have a right to a much longer period of leave (now renamed 'additional maternity leave' to distinguish it from the shorter period of 'ordinary maternity leave') but for those who do not qualify for that right, and have no independent contractual right to maternity leave, the right to 18 weeks' ordinary maternity leave may be invaluable, particularly where the start of the ordinary maternity leave period can be delayed until just before childbirth, thereby allowing several months of leave after childbirth before having to return to work. The distinction between ordinary and additional maternity leave is important, because during ordinary maternity leave an employee has a statutory right to continue to benefit from all her normal terms and conditions of employment, except those providing for wages or salary (unless of course she has a contractual right to receive wages or salary during maternity leave). This means

14   For the detailed interpretation of these grounds, see the discussion of the parallel provisions concerning dismissal. As with dismissal, the protection for childbirth only applies where the detriment takes place during the employee's ordinary or additional maternity leave: ibid., reg. 19(5).

15   Employment Rights Act 1996, s. 48, as amended.

16   Ibid., s. 49, as amended.

17   Employment Rights Act 1996, s. 71(4), as amended by the Employment Relations Act 1999, Sch. 4.

18   Ibid., s. 71(5). Remuneration is defined for these purposes as 'sums payable to an employee by way of wages or salary': MPL etc. Regulations, reg. 9. On entitlement to pay during maternity leave, see p. 339, below.

19   The extended period applies to employees whose expected week of childbirth began on or after April 30, 2000.

20   The qualifying period for additional maternity leave was reduced from two years to one by the Employment Relations Act 1999.

that she is entitled to continue to benefit from any terms and conditions concerning, for example, the use of a company car or mobile phone, membership of clubs and societies, reimbursement of professional subscriptions and participation in employee share-ownership schemes. She is also entitled to any other benefits which would have accrued if she had been at work (e.g. holiday entitlement) as if she had been at work and not on maternity leave. The period of ordinary maternity leave counts towards her period of continuous employment for the purposes of qualifying for statutory employment rights, and because the contract continues throughout, the period also counts when assessing matters such as her seniority, pension rights and other similar rights which depend on length of service (e.g. contractual pay increments). In contrast, during additional maternity leave a woman is entitled to the benefit of a much narrower range of terms and conditions of employment, unless her contract provides otherwise. A woman who also enjoys a contractual right to ordinary maternity leave may not exercise the two rights separately, but may take advantage of whichever right is, in any particular respect, the more favourable[1].

i) Commencement and duration

Within certain limits, an employee is free to choose the date on which her ordinary maternity leave starts[2]. However, she cannot choose a start date earlier than the beginning of the eleventh week before the expected week of childbirth[3], and her maternity leave period will be *automatically* triggered by any day on which she is absent from work wholly or partly because of pregnancy after the beginning of the sixth week before the expected week of childbirth[4]. The thinking behind the latter provision is apparently to prevent a woman from delaying the start of her ordinary maternity leave until the last possible moment (thus ensuring the maximum amount of leave after childbirth) by taking sick leave instead of maternity leave, but it could have the unfortunate consequence of encouraging a woman to continue working during the latter stages of pregnancy, even though medically unfit to do so, in order to prevent her maternity leave period from being automatically triggered. This seems a strange way of giving effect to a Directive which is intended to protect the health and safety of pregnant women[5]. If childbirth occurs prematurely, the maternity leave period begins with the day of childbirth[6], and the employer must be notified of the birth as soon as is reasonably practicable.

Ordinary maternity leave normally lasts for a maximum of 18 weeks, but provision is also made for two weeks' 'compulsory maternity leave'[7], beginning with the day of childbirth, and if the compulsory maternity leave period extends

---

1   MPL etc. Regulations, reg. 21. This is commonly referred to as a 'composite' right. For the interpretation of this provision in relation to additional maternity leave, see p. 330 below.
2   Employment Rights Act 1996, s. 71(3), as amended. MPL etc. Regulations 1999, reg. 6.
3   MPL etc. Regulations, reg. 4(2)(b).
4   Ibid., reg. 6(1)(b). Absence from work due to time off for ante-natal care does not count. 'Childbirth' is defined as 'the birth of a living child or the birth of a child whether living or dead after 24 weeks of pregnancy': ibid., reg. 2; the same definition appears in the Employment Rights Act 1996, s. 235(1).
5   The employer can of course choose to disregard days of pregnancy-related illness if the employee wishes to defer the start of her maternity leave period.
6   MPL etc. Regulations, reg. 6(2).
7   It is an offence under the Factories Act 1961 to permit a woman to work in a factory within four weeks after the date of childbirth.

beyond the date on which ordinary maternity leave would have ended, the ordinary maternity leave period will be deemed to continue until the end of compulsory maternity leave[8]. The ordinary maternity leave period is also deemed to continue beyond the normal 18 weeks where the employee is prohibited by law from working, by reason of having recently given birth[9]. The Act does not specifically provide for a right to return to work at the end of the 18-week maternity leave period, but such a provision is unnecessary given that the contract of employment continues to exist throughout that period. An employee who wishes to return to work *before* the end of her ordinary maternity leave period may do so, on giving due notice to the employer[10], although she must still observe the compulsory maternity leave period. Dismissal during the ordinary maternity leave period brings that period to an end[11]. Such a dismissal will normally be automatically unfair[12], as will a dismissal at the end of ordinary maternity leave (e.g. where the employee is not given her job back) although special provision is made for redundancy during ordinary maternity leave[13], in that where a redundancy situation arises during the employee's ordinary maternity leave which makes it impracticable for the employer to continue to employ her under her original contract of employment, she is entitled to be offered alternative employment with her employer (or with a successor, or an associated employer) where there is a suitable available vacancy. Failure to offer such a vacancy will make the redundancy dismissal automatically unfair[14].

ii) Notice requirements

To take advantage of her right to ordinary maternity leave, the employee must satisfy certain notice requirements. These requirements, long criticised for their complexity, were simplified by the Employment Relations Act 1999 and the regulations issued thereunder. The employee is now required to notify her employer, at least 21 days before the date on which she intends her ordinary maternity leave to start[15]: i) that she is pregnant; ii) when the expected week of childbirth will be; and iii) the date on which she intends her ordinary maternity leave to start. If she gives birth before she has notified a date, or before the date she has notified, her maternity leave will start automatically on the date of childbirth, and she must notify her employer as soon as is reasonably practicable (in writing, if so requested) that she has given birth[16]. Until the 1999 reforms, notification of the fact of pregnancy and of the expected week of childbirth had

8   Employment Rights Act 1996, s. 72 (as amended) and MPL etc. Regulations, reg. 8. The requirement is compulsory on *both* sides, and an employer who infringes the prohibition is liable on summary conviction to a fine not exceeding level 2 on the standard scale; there is no provision for any sanction on the employee in such a case.
9   MPL etc. regulations, reg. 7(2).
10   Ibid., reg. 11. See p. 330 below.
11   Ibid., reg. 7(5).
12   Ibid., reg. 20. See p. 324 above.
13   MPL etc. Regulations, reg. 10. See p. 324 above. Similar provisions apply to redundancy during additional maternity leave; see p. 335 sbelow.
14   Ibid., reg. 20(1)(b).
15   Or as soon as reasonably practicable, where it is not reasonably practicable to give the notice 21 days before the intended start date. Cf. *Nu-Swift International Ltd v Mallinson* [1979] ICR 157, [1978] IRLR 537, decided under the old provisions, where it was suggested that a woman may only be allowed to use this exception if she did not know of the time limit and was not put on inquiry about it.
16   MPL etc. Regulations, reg. 4(4).

to be in writing, but this is no longer necessary. The employer is still entitled to ask for written notification of the intended start date of maternity leave[17], and may demand to see a medical certificate verifying the expected week of childbirth[18]. As seen above, a woman who wishes to return to work earlier than the end of her ordinary maternity leave period may do so, on giving the employer 21 days' notice of the date on which she intends to return[19]. If she attempts to return without giving the correct period of notice, the employer is entitled to postpone her return until 21 days have elapsed (although not to a date after the end of the ordinary maternity leave period)[20].

4   ADDITIONAL MATERNITY LEAVE

An employee who has at least one year's continuous employment with her employer is entitled to a period of additional maternity leave of up to 29 weeks after the date of childbirth, after which she is entitled to return to the same job, on terms and conditions no less favourable than if she had not been absent from work. The additional maternity leave period runs from the end of ordinary maternity leave[1] and continues until the end of the 29th week beginning with the week of childbirth[2]. Until the 1999 reforms, this entitlement was known as the 'right to return to work', but it was renamed additional maternity leave by the Employment Relations Act 1999 to distinguish it from ordinary and compulsory maternity leave.

As with ordinary maternity leave, the statutory right to additional maternity leave may be supplemented by more generous contractual arrangements. Where this is the case, the employee may not exercise the two rights separately, but may take advantage of whichever right is in any particular respect the more favourable[3]. However, this is not necessarily as generous as it may seem, as under the pre-1999 provisions the EAT held in *Bovey v Board of Governors of the Hospital for Sick Children*[4] that it does not allow the employee licence to carve out bits of each scheme in order to put together the most advantageous amalgam possible. In that case the employee, employed as a full-time grade 1 physiotherapist before taking maternity leave, told the employers that she wanted to return on a part-time basis only; the employers agreed, provided she returned on a lower grade. She did so, but later claimed that she should be employed as a part-timer at the grade 1 level, on the basis that she could use the contractual agreement to return part-time, but then rely on the statutory provisions that her terms of employment should be no less

17   Ibid., reg. 4(2).
18   Ibid., reg. 4(1)(b). There is no longer a requirement for an employee wishing to take additional maternity leave to inform the employer at this stage that she intends to exercise that right.
19   Ibid., reg. 11(1). Under the pre-1999 provisions, only seven days' notice of the intended date of early return was required.
20   Ibid., reg. 11(2), (3). If the employer has postponed the employee's return, the employer is under no obligation to pay her if she still insists on returning before that date: ibid., reg. 11(4).
1   Ibid., reg. 6(3).
2   Ibid., reg. 7(4).
3   Ibid., reg. 21(2). Some private contractual schemes are modelled for certain purposes on the State scheme, but here some care is needed, for if the State scheme is altered, that will not per se alter the private scheme, which must be changed independently by agreement and redrafting: CAC Award 82/7.
4   [1978] ICR 934, [1978] IRLR 241, EAT.

favourable in order to remain at the grade 1 level. The EAT dismissed this claim, on the grounds (inter alia) that the employee could not subdivide an essentially indivisible contractual arrangement and simply take out that part which was most favourable to her. In exercising a composite right, the employee must still comply with the statutory requirements, modified to give effect to any more favourable terms in her contract[5].

i) Qualification and notice requirements

In order to qualify for additional maternity leave, the employee must be entitled to ordinary maternity leave (see above), and she must have been continuously employed[6] for at least one year at the beginning of the 11th week before the expected week of childbirth[7]. Under the pre-1999 provisions, if the employee did not continue to be employed up to the 11th week before (e.g. if she resigned earlier in the pregnancy, or was dismissed), she lost her entitlement[8], although she did not have to be actually performing work up to that date as long as her contract still subsisted[9]. Premature resignation was therefore a major trap, being a sure way of losing the statutory right to return. The position appears to be the same under the redrafted provisions.

One of the most important changes introduced in 1999 was the relaxation of the notice requirements for additional maternity leave. Under the pre-1999 provisions, it was necessary for the employee to inform the employer, at least 21 days before her maternity leave commenced, that she intended to return to work after the end of her maternity leave. That requirement no longer applies, so that the notice requirements for additional maternity leave are satisfied if the employee has satisfied the notice requirements for ordinary maternity leave. The only difference is that, as before, the employer may seek confirmation *during* maternity leave of the employee's intention to return to work at the end of additional maternity leave (see below). The removal of the need to give notice of intention to return after maternity leave should help to reduce the risk of employees losing their right to maternity leave through failure to comply with technical notice requirements. That this was a very real danger under the old provisions was graphically demonstrated in *Nu-Swift International Ltd v Mallinson*[10] where the employee failed to give notice of her intention to return to work at the correct time because she could not make up her mind whether she wished to return to work or not. The EAT held that it had been reasonably practicable for her to give notice in time and therefore she had lost her right to return. Perhaps Mrs Mallinson was being too conscientious, for under the old provisions the employer had no recourse against an employee who gave notice saying that she

---

5 Note however the cases (discussed at p. 336 below) where an employee has been able to circumvent the statutory requirements altogether by relying on a wholly separate contractual right.

6 See ch. 3, above.

7 Ibid., reg. 5. Before the 1999 reforms, the qualifying period was two years.

8 *Mitchell v Royal British Legion Club* [1981] ICR 18, [1980] IRLR 425; *Williams & Co Ltd v Secretary of State for Employment* [1978] IRLR 235, IT. The tribunals were reluctant to interpret a statement by an employee that she did not intend to return to work as a resignation: *Hughes v Gwynedd Area Health Authority* [1978] ICR 161, [1977] IRLR 436.

9 *Satchwell Sunvic Ltd v Secretary of State for Employment* [1979] IRLR 455; *Secretary of State for Employment v Doulton Sanitaryware Ltd* [1981] ICR 477, [1981] IRLR 365, EAT.

10 [1979] ICR 157, [1978] IRLR 537.

intended to return to work but then changed her mind, or who gave notice while still undecided because she wanted to keep her options open. Indeed, pregnant employees were invariably advised to give notice that they intended to return to work, just as a matter of precaution. The removal of the need to give notice reflects the fact that, in practice, the giving and receiving of notice was an empty gesture which served only to trap the unwary or (as in Mrs Mallinson's case) the indecisive.

As a result of this uncertainty over whether in any particular case a notice of intention to return was worth a candle, in 1980 the government introduced an additional procedural requirement, in the shape of a right for an employer to seek written confirmation of the employee's intention to return. As originally enacted, the employer could write to the employee no earlier than 49 days after the expected week of confinement requesting written confirmation of her intention to return to work; failure to give the necessary confirmation within 14 days would lead to loss of the right to return. The present position, as modified in 1993, and again in 1999, is that the employer may write to the employee no earlier than 21 days before the end of the ordinary maternity leave period seeking confirmation in writing of the date of childbirth and whether the employee intends to return to work at the end of her additional maternity leave period[11]. The employee must reply within 21 days of receiving the letter. Failure to respond within the time-limit will no longer result in the loss of the right to return to work after maternity leave, but the employee will lose the benefit of the statutory protection against dismissal or detriment for family reasons[12]. This means that if the employer decides to take disciplinary action against her for not responding in time (e.g. by dismissing her) the dismissal will not be *automatically* unfair, but she will be able to claim before an employment tribunal that the dismissal was unfair on general principles[13]. Having said that, it remains true that the employer still has no recourse against an employee who confirms her intention of returning to work and then fails to do so[14].

One further, highly significant modification made in 1999 was the removal of the requirement to give the employer at least 21 days' written notice of the intended date of return to work. This final technical hurdle was a major obstacle at which many women fell[15]. To make matters worse, the requirement to give notice was held to be an absolute one, which meant that a failure to give the required notice disentitled the employee from returning to work at all[16]. There is no such requirement under the present provisions. The assumption is that an

---

11   MPL etc. Regulations, reg. 12(1). The employer's letter must include a written statement explaining how the employee may calculate the end of her additional maternity leave, and warning of the consequences of a failure to respond within the 21-day time limit; ibid., reg. 12(3).

12   Ibid., reg. 12(2).

13   Note that if the employer responds to the employee's failure to give notice more harshly than he would act in relation to other employees in comparable circumstances, the employee may have a claim for sex discrimination: see p. 347.

14   There is one possible (if disguised) disincentive to this course of action, in that if the employee states that she intends to return and the job is held open for her but then she decides that she does not wish to return after all, she may find that she is disqualified from receiving the jobseeker's allowance: Jobseekers Act 1995, s. 19(6)(d); see p. 552, below.

15   Although in a purposive interpretation of the old provisions, the Court of Appeal held in *Crees v Royal London Mutual Insurance Society Ltd; Greaves v Kwik Save Stores Ltd* [1998] IRLR 245, that once the employee had give notice of her intended date of return, her right to return crystallised, even if she was then unable through illness to return on the notified date: see p. 337 below.

16   See e.g. *Lavery v Plessey Telecommunications Ltd* [1983] ICR 534, [1983] IRLR 202, CA.

employee who takes additional maternity leave will be returning to work immediately after the end of that period, and if that is her intention she does not have to give notice of her intended date of return. She only need give notice to the employer to return to work if she wishes to return *before* the end of her additional maternity leave, in which case she must give at least 21 days' notice of the date on which she intends to return[17]. If she attempts to return early without giving the correct period of notice, then, as with ordinary maternity leave, the employer may postpone her return until 21 days' notice has been given, although not to a date later than the end of her additional maternity leave[18].

Under the pre-1999 provisions, the employer and the employee could postpone the return to work in certain circumstances: the employer could postpone the employee's return for up to four weeks, provided a reason was given for doing so and a new date for her return was specified; and the employee could postpone her return for up to four weeks where she was unable to return on the notified date due to illness, or where she was prevented from returning on that date because of an interruption of work due to industrial action or some other reason. There is no provision in the current regulations for either party to postpone the return to work. If an employee is unable to attend work at the end of additional maternity leave due to sickness, the normal sickness absence procedures under her contract of employment will apply. If the employer decides to dismiss her because of her inability to return to work, the employee will be able to claim that the dismissal was unfair on general principles, and if the employer responds more harshly to her sickness absence than he would to other employees in comparable circumstances, that could amount to sex discrimination.

ii) Rights during and after additional maternity leave

The basic position is that an employee who is entitled to ordinary maternity leave and who has completed one year's continuous service by the 11th week before the expected week of childbirth is entitled to a period of additional maternity leave which starts on the day after the last day of her ordinary maternity leave, and finishes at any time up to the end of the 29th week beginning with the week of childbirth[19] (so that when taken together with ordinary maternity leave, the total period of absence, if the ordinary maternity leave period starts 11 weeks before the expected week of childbirth, is approximately 40 weeks). The employee's contract of employment continues during her additional leave period (unless either party expressly ends it, or it expires), but during that period she is entitled to the benefit of a much narrower range of terms and conditions of employment than she enjoyed during her ordinary maternity leave, unless her contract provides otherwise. In the absence of an agreement to the contrary, she is entitled during the additional maternity leave period to the benefit of her employer's implied obligation to her of trust and confidence, and any terms and conditions of her employment relating to notice of termination by the employer, redundancy compensation, or disciplinary or grievance procedures; concomitantly, she is bound during that period by her implied obligation to her employer of good faith, and any terms and conditions of her employment relating to notice of

17 MPL etc. Regulations, reg. 11(1).
18 Ibid., reg. 11(2), (3). See n. 20 above.
19 Ibid., regs. 5, 6(3) and 7(4). Where the employee is dismissed during additional maternity leave, the period ends at the time of the dismissal. Such a dismissal will normally be automatically unfair: see p. 324.

termination by her, disclosure of confidential information, the acceptance of gifts or other benefits, or her participation in any other business[20].

An employee who takes additional maternity leave is generally entitled to return to the job in which she was employed before her absence, on terms and conditions as to remuneration not less favourable than those which would have applied to her had she not been absent from work, on other terms and conditions not less favourable than those which would have applied had she not been absent from work after the end of her ordinary maternity leave, and with her seniority, pension rights and other similar length-of-service rights as they would have been if the period of employment before the start of her additional maternity leave and after her return to work were continuous[1]. The effect of the latter provision is that while her continuity of employment for statutory purposes continues to accrue during additional maternity leave[2], the period of additional leave does not count in the computation of non-statutory rights (in the absence of any contractual provision to the contrary), which could be significant, for example in the operation of a 'last in first out' redundancy procedure[3]. This contrasts with ordinary maternity leave, which does count for the purpose of assessing such rights.

The right to return to the same job does not necessarily mean that a woman is entitled to go back into exactly the same job as before. The definition of 'job' for these purposes as 'the nature of the work which she is employed to do in accordance with her contract and the capacity and place in which she is so employed[4]' clearly implies that the employee does not have a right to return to exactly the same post doing exactly the same work in the same department or under the same person; it may be sufficient if the employer takes her on again in the same general kind of work, particularly if the work in question is subject to a comprehensive grading scheme with the employee being taken back at the same grade, and in such a case there may be certain necessary administrative changes in the organisation of the woman's work which she must accept and which are too minor to be capable of altering the nature of the job[5]. On the other hand, the tribunal will look at her overall position after maternity leave, and if for example there are any new and less favourable terms in her employment (for example affecting the security of her job) this may mean that the employer has not complied with his duty to allow her to return to the same job[6], even if in other respects her terms and conditions and the grade on which she is employed remain the same.

An employee who is not permitted to return to her old job at the end of additional maternity leave will normally be regarded as unfairly dismissed. However, the right to return is not absolute, for there are four situations in which the employee will not be entitled to return to her old job. The first is where there is some reason other than redundancy which makes it not reasonably practicable

20   Ibid., reg. 17.
1   Ibid., reg. 18(2), (5).
2   Under the old provisions there was an express provision to this effect in s. 212(2), but it was repealed by the 1999 Act because the contract of employment now continues through additional maternity leave in every case.
3   Note however the Social Security Act 1989, Sch. 5, para. 5, implementing EC Directive No. 86/378 on equal treatment in occupational social security schemes, which requires credit to be given for the period of paid maternity absence for the purposes of employment-related benefit schemes. These provisions were adopted by the Pensions Act 1995, s. 63(3): see p. 308, above.
4   MPL etc. Regulations, reg. 2.
5   *Edgell v Lloyd's Register of Shipping* [1977] IRLR 463, IT.
6   *McFadden v Greater Glasgow Passenger Transport Executive* [1977] IRLR 327, IT.

for the employer to permit her to return to her original job. In such a case, her entitlement is to return to another job which is both suitable for her and appropriate for her to do in the circumstances[7], and on terms and conditions no less favourable to her than if she had continued to be employed in her old job. Secondly, as with ordinary maternity leave, special provision is made for redundancy during additional maternity leave, in that where a redundancy situation arises during the employee's additional maternity leave which makes it impracticable for the employer to continue to employ her under her original contract of employment, the employee is entitled to be offered alternative employment with her employer (or with a successor, or an associated employer) where there is a suitable available vacancy[8]. Failure to offer such a vacancy will make the redundancy dismissal automatically unfair[9]. Thirdly, if it is not reasonably practicable for the employee to return to her old job, or to be offered a suitable alternative job, and the employer is a small employer employing no more than five people, the employee will not be regarded as unfairly dismissed if she is not permitted to return to work at the end of her additional maternity leave[10]. Finally, it is not unlawful for an employer to dismiss an employee during or after the end of maternity leave for a reason other than the fact that she has taken or availed herself of the benefits of maternity leave (or any of the other family reasons for which a dismissal will be automatically unfair[11]), unless of course the dismissal is unfair for some other reason. In all the above cases, however, the employer will need to take great care to ensure that there is no discrimination on grounds of sex or marital status (see below).

The most significant change to the provisions on additional maternity leave in the Employment Relations Act 1999 is that it is now made clear that the contract of employment continues throughout additional maternity leave. Under the old provisions, the right to return to work after maternity leave operated independently of the contract of employment. In most cases, it did not matter whether the employee's contract continued to exist during maternity absence: the statute gave her a right to return to work, irrespective of the status of her contract during maternity absence, provided she complied with the complex statutory notice requirements. If she was denied her right to return to work, whether by a total refusal to take her back or by being taken back on disadvantageous terms, she was *deemed* to have been dismissed on the 'notified date of return' (i.e. the date on which she intended to return to work). The provisions worked tolerably well where the employee complied to the letter with all the notice requirements, and was physically able to return to work on the notified date, but serious difficulties arose for the employee if she was not able to satisfy those requirements, in that she lost her statutory right to return (a problem exacerbated by the lack of any saving provision whereby minor or technical defaults could be overlooked). The problems were graphically illustrated by *Lavery v Plessey Telecommunications Ltd*[12] where the giving of five days' notice of intention to return (instead of the seven days then required) robbed the employee of her right to return, even though if she had understood the requirement she could in fact have given the required seven days' notice easily. The case contains strong criticism of the statutory

7   MPL etc. Regulations, reg. 18(2).
8   Ibid., reg. 10. See p. 329 above.
9   Ibid., reg. 20(1)(b).
10   Ibid., reg. 20(6). See p. 325 above.
11   See p. 323 above.
12   [1983] ICR 534, [1983] IRLR 202, CA.

provisions at that time, which were described as being 'of inordinate complexity exceeding the worst excesses of a taxing statute'[13].

One way in which an employee could avoid the strictness of the old statutory requirements was to argue that her contract of employment continued to subsist during her maternity absence, so that when the employer refused to permit her to return to work, she could bring an ordinary unfair dismissal action under section 95 of the 1996 Act, without having to base her complaint on a 'deemed' dismissal under the statutory provisions. The problem here, however, was that before the 1999 reforms, the status of the contract of employment during maternity absence was a matter on which the statute was silent, and success for the employee therefore turned on whether she could establish the existence of an express or (more usually) implied agreement with her employer that her contract continued to subsist throughout her maternity absence. So, for example, in *Lucas v Norton of London Ltd*[14], the employee was under the impression that her employer had agreed to her taking maternity leave, and she made no attempt to follow the statutory procedure. When she tried to return to work the employer would not let her do so, and she claimed unfair dismissal. The tribunal rejected her complaint since she had not complied with the statutory requirements, but the EAT held on appeal that she had been dismissed on ordinary principles – on the facts, her contract of employment had subsisted throughout her absence, and had only been terminated at the end of the leave through the employer's failure to allow her to return. She could thus claim unfair dismissal without having to rely on the complex statutory scheme.

Subsequent cases revealed a disturbing lack of judicial consensus on this matter. In *Hilton International Hotels (UK) Ltd v Kaissi*[15], the EAT held that the applicant was entitled to claim unfair dismissal on ordinary principles, even though she had no contractual right to return to work and had made no attempt to comply with the statutory notification procedures for the right to return, because her contract had continued to exist until it was brought to an end by the employers. Her failure to comply with the statutory requirements was held not to have terminated the contract automatically. Similarly, in *Lewis Woolf Griptight Ltd v Corfield*[16], the EAT held that the fact that the employee had claimed entitlement to SSP from her employer when she was unable to return to work after maternity absence, and that the employer had not demurred from that contention, was evidence of an intention to continue the contract, so that she had been dismissed when the employers treated her employment as terminated when she was unable to return to work after maternity leave due to illness. In contrast, in *Crouch v Kidsons Impey*[17], the EAT held (distinguishing *Kaissi*), that there was no presumption that the contract of employment continued during maternity absence, and that if the employee wished to rely on this contractual analysis there would need to be clear evidence of the continuance of her contract; and in *Halfpenny v IGC Medical Systems Ltd*[18], the EAT held that there was no dismissal

13   Per Browne-Wilkinson J, [1982] IRLR 180, EAT, at 182. His remarks were endorsed by the Court of Appeal, n. 12, above.
14   [1984] IRLR 86, EAT.
15   [1994] ICR 578, [1994] IRLR 270, EAT. See also *Institute of the Motor Industry v Harvey* [1992] ICR 470, [1992] IRLR 343, EAT (contract of employment likely to continue through maternity absence unless terminated by agreement, resignation or dismissal).
16   [1997] IRLR 432, EAT.
17   [1996] IRLR 79, EAT. See also *McPherson v Drumpark House* [1997] IRLR 277, EAT (no presumption that the contract continues during the payment of maternity pay).
18   [1998] IRLR 10, EAT.

when the employee failed to return to work after extended maternity leave due to ill health, as there was no evidence of an express or implied agreement to extend the employee's contract of employment beyond the end of maternity leave. The EAT held that when she failed to return to work on the notified date, her contract of employment came to an end not by any act of termination by the employer amounting to a dismissal, but by her own failure to exercise her statutory right to return. The EAT observed that: 'To find otherwise would be to render the respondent liable to the appellant for strictly complying with their statutory obligations. That cannot be right.'

The Court of Appeal had an opportunity to clarify the position in *Kwik Save Stores Ltd v Greaves; Crees v Royal London Mutual Insurance Society Ltd*[19], a joined appeal involving two employees who had complied with the statutory notice requirements but were unable to return to work at the end of their maternity leave due to illness. The Court of Appeal neatly avoided the issue of whether they had a *contractual* right to return by holding that they had completely and effectively exercised their *statutory* right to return by giving the appropriate notice of the notified date of return[20], so that the employers' refusal to allow them to return was a dismissal. The fact that they were prevented by illness from physically returning to work on the due date was therefore irrelevant, as was the question of their contractual status during maternity leave. Lord Woolf MR adopted a purposive interpretation of the provisions, observing that if the exercise of the right to return required physical attendance for work on the notified day of return, an employee who had given the appropriate notices would lose her right to return even if she was unable to return physically to work on the relevant day because she had been run over by the managing director on her way to work that morning, or because there had been a natural disaster, such as a flood or a blizzard, which prevented her from attending work. When *Halfpenny* subsequently came before the Court of Appeal, the Court was able to decide the appeal in the employee's favour simply by applying *Kwik Save*, although significantly the Court of Appeal referred to her contract as being 'suspended' during maternity leave, and as being 'revived' when she exercised her statutory right to return[1]. This begs the question what the outcome would have been if she had *not* complied with the statutory notice requirements, but had nevertheless claimed to have a separate contractual right to return to work....

While the practical significance of this issue has been greatly reduced as a result of the recent reforms, it remains the case that the employee's contract of employment only continues during maternity leave by virtue of the new provisions where the employee is *entitled* under those provisions to additional maternity leave, and that entitlement depends upon the employee having satisfied the notice requirements for ordinary maternity leave. It follows that where an employee does *not* comply with those (admittedly far less onerous) statutory requirements, the provisions which deem the contract to continue during additional maternity leave will be inapplicable, and the pre-1999 Act case law on whether the contract continues during maternity leave will still be highly relevant.

19   [1998] IRLR 245, CA. Significantly, in *Crees*, the employee's contract of employment expressly provided that if she failed to comply with the statutory notice provisions, she forfeited her right to return and her contract of employment would terminate at the end of the maternity pay period.
20   The requirement to give 21 days' notice of the intention to return no longer applies: see p. 331 above.
1   [1999] IRLR 177, CA. The Court of Appeal also held that the employers had discriminated against her on grounds of sex by dismissing her; see p. 347 below.

In addition to these intricacies, three further general points should be noted. The first point is that an employer (particularly in a small business) may need to take on a replacement to take the place of an employee on maternity leave. Such an employer is given qualified protection by section 106 which provides that if the employer informs the replacement in writing at the time of engagement that his or her employment will cease when the original employee returns to work, and then dismisses him or her in order to take that original employee back, that will constitute half a defence to an allegation of unfair dismissal in that it is deemed to be a substantial reason capable of justifying dismissal (within section 98), but the tribunal must still proceed to consider whether he acted reasonably in all the circumstances in actually dismissing the replacement, which may be difficult if there was a vacancy available elsewhere that the replacement might readily have filled. This provision was particularly important when the qualifying period for unfair dismissal was 26 weeks, for a replacement could well work for that long during the period of maternity leave and thus qualify to bring an unfair dismissal action; there was less need for it while the qualifying period was two years, but now that the qualifying period has been reduced to one year, it may assume a greater practical significance.

The second general point is that one major perceived deficiency of the statutory right to return is that it does not allow a woman to apply to return to work on *different* terms and conditions (e.g. on a part-time basis or with flexible working hours), yet for many women this may be the only way of reconciling the competing demands of work and family responsibilities, especially in view of the limited availability of affordable child care. However it is possible that the return-to-work provisions could be outflanked by the argument that a refusal to allow a woman previously in full-time employment to return to work part-time is indirect sex discrimination. This is what happened in *Home Office v Holmes*[2] where the woman used the return-to-work provisions to return full-time, but also claimed that the requirement to continue working full-time constituted unjustifiable indirect sex discrimination (in that compliance with it was particularly difficult for women with children). This argument succeeded in the case, which was widely reported in the press and said by the EOC to be a significant development. However, it does not stretch the imagination to suppose that there could be many circumstances in which a requirement to work full-time might be held to be justifiable[3] in economic terms, and the EAT's decision was based very much upon the facts of the particular case[4], as can be seen from the subsequent case of *Greater Glasgow Health Board v Carey*[5], where on similar facts it was held that the employer's refusal to allow a full-time health visitor to return on a part-time basis was indirectly discriminatory but was justified by the need for continuity of care by the same visitor.

The third general point is that in certain sectors (particularly local government, banks, computer companies, retail stores and oil companies) there have been

2   [1984] ICR 678, [1984] IRLR 299.
3   See p. 251, above.
4   It is important these days not to be too sanguine about cases as precedents; at its most basic, all that the EAT were doing was to say that in this case the tribunal were not manifestly wrong in holding that the requirement to work full time was a) discriminatory and b) unjustifiable on the facts before them.
5   [1987] IRLR 484. In coming to this conclusion, the EAT applied the obiter remarks in *Rainey v Greater Glasgow Health Board Eastern District* [1987] ICR 129, [1987] IRLR 26, HL that administrative efficiency, if sufficiently demonstrated, may be an important factor in the justification defence under the Sex Discrimination Act 1975, s. 1(1)(b)(ii); see p. 292, above.

significant moves towards allowing women employees to take far more substantial 'career breaks' in order to have a family – breaks of anything up to seven years are mentioned, and with the possibility of attending several days' training per year during the break in order to keep up with changes. For present purposes the main point to notice is that any such scheme can come about only by agreement and as a matter of contract; such breaks are not provided for in the statutory maternity leave scheme.

5 STATUTORY MATERNITY PAY

A pregnant employee who meets certain qualifying conditions based on her length of service and average earnings is entitled to receive statutory maternity pay (SMP) from her employer for up to 18 weeks, the first six weeks at nine-tenths of the employee's normal pay, and the remaining 12 weeks at a flat rate. The employer, in turn, is entitled to recover most of the amount paid out as SMP from the state, by deducting it from PAYE and National Insurance contributions. In effect, therefore, SMP can be seen as a state maternity benefit which is administered via employers. To understand how this convoluted state of affairs has come about, it is necessary to delve a little into the history of the current provisions.

Until April 1987 a pregnant employee leaving work to have a baby would normally qualify for the state maternity allowance, but on top of that she could qualify (if she had at least two years' service) for maternity pay from her employer; this latter was payable for the first six weeks of absence, at nine-tenths of her week's pay (less the amount of the maternity allowance and any remuneration paid by the employer under a contractual maternity scheme), and was payable whether or not the employee wished to return to work after her maternity absence, i.e. it was not dependent upon continuation in some form of the employment relationship. From the point of view of drafting this position was neat since the principal conditions for entitlement were the same as for maternity leave, so that the two major rights went hand in hand. However, the system was viewed as wasteful by the Government since it involved duplication of administrative effort by the State and the employer, and as the whole amount paid out as maternity pay could be recouped from the State-run Maternity Pay Fund, the employer was in reality simply performing a social security role.

The whole system was reformed in 1987 in order to require the employer to make all the payments, by the introduction of statutory maternity pay (SMP), payable at two levels depending on length of service, but with the employer able to recover the amount paid out by deducting it from national insurance contributions; the obvious model was statutory sick pay[6], introduced by the Government four years earlier for the same reasons of rationalisation and administrative ease (for the Government, that is, not for employers). The structure of the SMP scheme was very different from what had gone before, but the end result as far as most employees were concerned was very similar to the pre-1987 position, in that SMP was payable for up to 18 weeks at a lower rate (in effect replacing the state maternity allowance), but an employee with two years' continuous service was entitled to SMP at a higher rate of nine-tenths of her normal weekly earnings for the first six weeks (corresponding to the old maternity pay scheme).

6   See p. 177, above.

The SMP scheme was subject to major reforms in 1994 to bring it into line with the requirements of EC Directive 92/85 (the Pregnant Workers Directive), which provides for a minimum entitlement of 14 weeks' paid maternity leave for all pregnant employees[7], during which a woman is entitled to be paid an amount equivalent to the amount of state benefit she would receive if she were absent from work due to sickness. The Directive was implemented in the UK by equalising lower rate SMP with statutory sick pay, and granting all those entitled to SMP the right to receive it at the higher rate for the first six weeks. To meet the additional cost to the state of this enhanced entitlement, the amount of SMP which employers were able to recover was reduced to 92 per cent[8], albeit with special help for small employers[9], who are still able to recover the full amount[10]. The SMP provisions are currently to be found in Part XII of the Social Security Contributions and Benefits Act 1992, and the flesh is added to the bones by several sets of regulations[11].

i)   Qualification[12]

To qualify at all, the employee must satisfy a number of complex conditions: i) her earnings must have been at or above the lower earnings limit for the payment of National Insurance contributions (set at £67 per week for the tax year 2000/01)[13]; ii) she must have been employed by that employer[14] for a continuous period of at least 26 weeks ending with the 'qualifying week', a key piece of jargon which means the 15th week before the expected week of childbirth[15]; iii) she must give the employer medical evidence of the expected week of childbirth[16], and at least 21 days' notice of the date on which she intends to be absent from work and receiving SMP; iv) she must have reached the 11th week before the expected week of childbirth, or have recently given birth (although she does not need to remain in employment beyond the qualifying week); and v) she must have stopped work.

---

7   The Directive permits entitlement to pay during the maternity leave period to be made conditional on periods of previous employment of up to 12 months before the expected date of childbirth.

8   Statutory Maternity Pay (Compensation of Employers) and Miscellaneous Amendment Regulations 1994, S.I. 1994 No. 1882.

9   I.e. those whose gross N.I. contributions do not exceed £20,000 for the qualifying tax year.

10   Small employers are also entitled to deduct an additional five per cent of the SMP paid, to compensate for other costs: S.I. 1999 No. 363 (amending S.I. 1994 No. 1882).

11   Principally the Statutory Maternity Pay (General) Regulations 1986, S.I. 1986 No. 1960, as amended. Practical guidance is given in some detail (with worked examples) in the Employer's Guide to Statutory Maternity Pay (NI 257, DSS).

12   Social Security Contributions and Benefits Act 1992, s. 164.

13   The EAT has held that the application of the lower earnings limit as a qualifying condition for SMP is not contrary to Article 141 (ex 119) of the EC Treaty or the Pregnant Workers Directive: *Banks v Tesco Stores Ltd* [1999] ICR 1141, EAT.

14   A woman may not count her previous employment with another employer for these purposes; in this respect the system differs from that applying to statutory sick pay.

15   Compare the position with the right to additional maternity leave, where she must remain in employment up to the 11th week before the expected week of childbirth (see p. 331, above); the different qualifying dates for the two rights is still an unnecessary source of confusion.

16   This should normally be provided no later than the end of the third week of the maternity pay period. The employer cannot start paying SMP until the certificate has been received.

ii) The right to payment

If she can satisfy these conditions, the employee qualifies for SMP at the higher rate for six weeks, and thereafter at the lower rate for the remainder of the maternity pay period, subject to an overall maximum of 18 weeks. Once entitlement to SMP is established in the qualifying week, the employee is entitled to receive her full entitlement to 18 weeks' SMP, even if she leaves the employer's employment before her SMP was due to start. Alternatively, she may continue working right up to the date of childbirth, and still retain her full entitlement to 18 weeks' SMP. The lower rate of SMP is fixed by regulations (at the time of writing, it stands at £60.20 pw[17]). The higher rate of SMP is set at nine-tenths of her week's pay (averaged, if necessary, over the eight weeks prior to the qualifying week[18]). Payments of SMP must be offset against any contractual payments for the weeks in question (e.g. under a contractual maternity scheme) and vice versa. Under the pre-1994 provisions, an employee lost a week of her SMP entitlement for each week that she continued to work beyond the sixth week before the expected week of childbirth, but this rule no longer applies, and the maternity pay period will normally begin on the Sunday following the day on which the maternity leave period starts, whether or not this falls after the sixth week before the expected week of childbirth (thus removing the financial disincentive to working beyond the sixth week before). However, to ensure consistency with the maternity leave provisions, the maternity pay period is automatically triggered where a woman is absent from work wholly or partly because of pregnancy or childbirth after the sixth week before. The SMP period usually lasts for the full 18 weeks, but it is not payable for any week in which the employee does any work for her employer, and if she starts work for a new employer after childbirth, the entitlement to SMP stops completely.

An employee who does not qualify for SMP but who earns at least £30 per week on average[19] may be entitled to claim the state Maternity Allowance from the Benefits Agency. If her claim for Maternity Allowance is unsuccessful, she may be able to claim Income Support from the Benefits Agency, although this is not normally payable if she or her partner has savings of over £8000 or works for 16 or more hours a week; families in which one parent is working for 16 hours a week or more may be entitled to Working Families Tax Credit.

6 RISK ASSESSMENT AND SUSPENSION FROM WORK ON MATERNITY GROUNDS

All employers have a duty under the Management of Health and Safety at Work (MHSW) Regulations 1999 to assess the risks to health and safety to which their employees are exposed whilst they are at work[20]. In addition, as a result of an

17 Statutory Maternity Pay (General) Regulations 1986, S.I. 1986 No. 1960, reg. 6 (as amended with effect from April 2000).

18 Social Security Contributions and Benefits Act 1992, s. 166. If the employer subsequently grants a back-dated pay rise which affects that eight-week period, her earnings must be recalculated taking into account the arrears: S.I. 1996 No. 1335 (implementing *Gillespie*, see p. 351, below).

19 This applies to a woman whose expected date of childbirth falls on or after 20 August 2000. Before that date, entitlement to maternity allowance was conditional on earnings reaching the lower earnings level for N.I. contributions.

20 S.I. 1999 No. 3242 replacing S.I. 1992 No. 2051. The MHSW Regulations are discussed at p. 762 below.

amendment to the MHSW Regulations in 1994 (implementing the Pregnant Workers Directive[1]) employers of women of child-bearing age have a duty to carry out a further risk assessment where the work is of a kind which could involve a risk to the health and safety of a new or expectant mother[2], or to that of her baby, from any processes or working conditions, or from physical, biological or chemical agents[3]. Where that risk assessment identifies a risk to the health and safety of a new or expectant mother or her baby, the employer is under a duty in the first instance to take action to prevent her from being exposed to the risk by following the requirements of any relevant health and safety regulations (e.g. by removing the hazard or by providing protective clothing). If the risk cannot be avoided by such means, and it is not reasonable for the employer to alter the employee's working conditions or hours of work, or such an alteration would not avoid the risk, the employer must remove the employee from the risk by suspending her from work for as long as is necessary to avoid the risk[4]. An employer must also suspend an employee from work on maternity grounds where the employee is a new or expectant mother who works at night, and she has a certificate from a registered medical practitioner or registered midwife which shows that it is necessary for her health and safety that she should not be at work for any period of night work identified in the certificate[5].

Under the MHSW Regulations, the duty to take action by altering working conditions or hours of work, or by suspending an employee from work, does not arise until the employee has notified the employer in writing that she is pregnant, has given birth within the preceding six months or is breast-feeding[6], although even in the absence of written notification of pregnancy, an employer who fails to take reasonable action to protect an employee who is known to be pregnant or breast-feeding might well be in breach of the general duty to protect the health and safety of his employees. The duty to conduct a pregnancy risk assessment in the first place is triggered whenever the employer employs a woman of child-bearing age, and does not depend upon there being an employee who is pregnant[7].

The Trade Union Reform and Employment Rights Act 1993 introduced two new rights for employees suspended from work on maternity grounds[8], implementing the Pregnant Workers Directive[9]. First, before being suspended

1   EC Directive 92/85/EC.
2   Defined as employees who are pregnant, have given birth within the preceding six months or are breastfeeding.
3   MHSW Regulations, reg. 16(1). These are said to include the list of agents set out in Annexes I and II of the Pregnant Workers Directive.
4   MHSW Regulations, reg. 16(2), (3).
5   Ibid., reg. 17.
6   Ibid., reg. 18. If the employee has given the employer a medical certificate which arguably indicates that she is pregnant, but without expressly stating that fact, the burden may pass to the employer to show that there was no notification: *Day v T Pickles Farms Ltd* [1999] IRLR 217, EAT.
7   *Day v T Pickles Farms Ltd,* above. That case also established that an employer's failure to carry out such a risk assessment may amount to sex discrimination if a new or expectant mother can show that she has suffered a detriment. See p. 347 below.
8   See now the Employment Rights Act 1996, ss. 66-68. Suspension must be in consequence of a 'relevant requirement' or a recommendation in a Code of Practice issued or approved by the Health and Safety Commission under s. 16 of the Health and Safety at Work etc. Act 1974: s. 66(1). The Suspension from Work (on Maternity Grounds) Order, S.I. 1994 No. 2930, specifies reg. 17 of the MHSW Regulations as a relevant requirement for these purposes. Cf. also the Suspension from Work on Maternity Grounds (Merchant Shipping and Fishing Vessels) Order, S.I. 1998 No. 587.
9   EC Directive 92/85/EC. See p. 322, above.

from work on maternity grounds, an employee has the right to be offered suitable alternative employment by her employer where there is an available vacancy[10], with a right to complain to a tribunal if the employer fails to make such an offer[11]. The work must be suitable in relation to the employee, appropriate for her to do in the circumstances, and on terms and conditions which are not substantially less favourable than those under which she normally works[12]. Secondly, an employee who is suspended from work on maternity grounds has the right to be paid her normal remuneration by her employer during the period of suspension, unless she has unreasonably refused an offer of suitable alternative work for the period in question, in which case no remuneration is payable for the period during which the offer applies[13]; once again, there is a right of complaint to a tribunal that the employer has failed to pay the amount due[14], and where the tribunal finds the complaint well-founded it will order the employer to pay the unpaid remuneration to the employee.

7 TIME OFF FOR ANTE-NATAL CARE

A pregnant employee has a right not to be unreasonably refused time off during working hours to attend ante-natal care on the advice of a registered medical practitioner, registered midwife or registered health visitor[15], irrespective of her length of service. After the first visit, the employer may require the employee to produce a certificate from the doctor, midwife or health visitor confirming that she is pregnant, and an appointment card or other document showing that an appointment has been made[16], but for obvious reasons this is not necessary for the first visit. Ante-natal care is not defined in the Act, but it can include relaxation and parentcraft classes, as well as medical examinations, provided of course that the attendance is on the advice of a doctor, midwife or health visitor. The right to time off is not absolute: the Act states that an employee has the right not to be *unreasonably* refused time off, which implies that there may be circumstances where it would be reasonable for the employer to refuse time off; e.g. it might be reasonable for an employer to refuse time off to a part-time worker who could reasonably be expected to arrange her ante-natal care outside her working hours.

The employee is entitled to be paid at her normal rate of pay during the period of time off[17]. Complaint of unreasonable refusal to give time off, or of failure to pay wages during time off may be made to a tribunal within three months of the day of the appointment concerned (or within a further reasonable

---

10 Employment Rights Act 1996, s. 67(1).
11 Ibid., s. 70(4). The right of complaint is subject to the usual three-month time limit, calculated from the first day of suspension: ibid., s. 70(5); where the tribunal upholds the complaint it may make an award of compensation: s. 70(6).
12 See *British Airways (European Operations at Gatwick) Ltd v Moore and Botterill* [2000] IRLR 296, EAT, where an offer of ground work to two pregnant cabin crew workers failed the test because it did not include the flying allowances which they received while working as cabin crew.
13 Ibid., s. 68.
14 The time limit here is three months (or a further reasonable period where not reasonably practicable) from the day in respect of which the remuneration was not paid: s. 70(2).
15 Employment Rights Act 1996, s. 55.
16 Ibid., s. 55(2).
17 Employment Rights Act 1996, s. 56. See *Gregory v Tudsbury Ltd* [1982] IRLR 267, IT. The amount of pay will usually be calculated by dividing her week's pay by the number of normal working hours in a week.

period if the tribunal accepts that it was not reasonably practicable for the complaint to be presented within the three-month period)[18].

8 PARENTAL LEAVE

As seen in the introduction to this chapter, the Employment Relations Act 1999 introduced a new right to parental leave for male and female employees, implementing the Parental Leave Directive[19]. The detailed provisions on parental leave are contained in the Maternity and Parental Leave etc. (MPL) Regulations 1999[20], which set out who has a right to parental leave, and certain key elements which apply to everyone. Employers and employees are free to agree a detailed parental leave scheme, via a collective or workforce agreement, which will be valid provided it does not contradict any of the key elements in the regulations. The regulations also contain a set of 'default' provisions on parental leave, in the form of a 'model' scheme which will automatically come into operation unless the parties agree on their own scheme.

i) Entitlement to parental leave

The right to parental leave is available to an employee who has been continuously employed for at least one year, and who has, or expects to have, 'parental responsibility' for a child within the meaning of the Children Act 1989[1]. Such an employee is entitled to at least 13 weeks' parental leave in respect of each child, for the purpose of caring for that child[2]. If the employee works part time, the entitlement to leave is proportionate to the time for which the employee normally works[3], and if the leave is taken in shorter periods than the employee's normal working week, the individual periods of leave are aggregated together[4]. Employees have a right not to be dismissed or subjected to any detriment by their employer for taking or seeking to take parental leave[5].

The main controversies over the way in which the parental leave provisions have been implemented in the UK are that parental leave must generally be taken before the child's fifth birthday[6] (under the Directive the Government could have allowed leave to be taken up to the age of eight) and the leave may not be claimed in respect of a child born before 15 December 1999[7]. The latter

---

18 Ibid., s. 57. Dismissal or redundancy selection for taking time off for ante-natal care is likely to be automatically unfair under s. 99: see p. 323 above.

19 EC Directive No. 96/34. The Directive was extended to the UK by Directive No. 97/75.

20 MPL etc. Regulations, S.I. 1999 No. 3312. The parental leave provisions came into force on 15 December 1999 (the deadline by which member states were required to implement the Directive).

1 MPL etc. Regulations, reg. 13.

2 Ibid., reg. 14(1). In the case of multiple births, an employee is entitled to thirteen weeks' leave for each child.

3 Ibid., reg. 14(2).

4 Ibid., reg. 14(4).

5 Ibid., reg. 19, 20.

6 In the case of an adopted child, the leave may be taken up to the fifth anniversary of the date on which the child was placed for adoption, or the child's eighteenth birthday, whichever is the sooner; the parent of a child who is entitled to disability living allowance is allowed to take parental leave up to the date of the child's eighteenth birthday: ibid., reg. 15.

7 Ibid., reg. 13(3). An exception is made in the case of a child adopted by the employee, or placed with the employee for adoption, on or after that date.

restriction has been challenged by the TUC in judicial review proceedings as being in breach of the requirements of the Directive; the Divisional Court has referred the matter to the ECJ[8]. The other major bone of contention is that parental leave is unpaid, unless the employer agrees otherwise. In practice, this means that many employees who might wish to take some parental leave may simply be unable to do so because of the financial consequences.

During the period of parental leave, the employee remains in employment but, in the absence of an agreement to the contrary, is in the same position as an employee on additional maternity leave, i.e. the employee is only entitled to the benefit of the employer's implied obligation of trust and confidence, and any terms and conditions of employment relating to notice of termination by the employer, redundancy compensation, or disciplinary or grievance procedures. During that period the employee is bound by the implied obligation to the employer of good faith, and any terms and conditions of employment relating to notice of termination by the employee, disclosure of confidential information, the acceptance of gifts or other benefits, or the employee's participation in any other business[9]. As in the case of additional maternity leave, an employee who takes parental leave is entitled to return to work after parental leave to the job in which he or she was employed before taking leave, on terms and conditions not less favourable than those which would have been applicable to the employee had he or she not been absent[10]. If the period of leave is more than four weeks, or the leave is taken immediately after additional maternity leave, the employee is entitled to return to the old job or, if that is not reasonably practicable, to another job which is both suitable and appropriate for the employee in the circumstances.[11]

ii) Collective or workforce agreements

In line with the current political emphasis on 'partnership' in the workplace, the MPL etc. Regulations allow employers and employees to agree a detailed parental leave scheme via a collective or workforce agreement which is incorporated into the contracts of employment of individual employees[12]. Such a scheme may improve upon the entitlements set out in the regulations (e.g. by allowing parental leave after a child's fifth birthday, or for children born or adopted before 15 December 1999), but it may not contradict any of the key elements in the regulations (e.g. by imposing lower age limits, or a later birth or adoption date). The regulations contain a 'model' scheme which automatically comes into operation if the parties do not agree on their own scheme (see below). A 'workforce agreement' is defined for these purposes in similar terms to those used in the Working Time Regulations[13]. To be valid, a workforce agreement must (a) be in writing; (b) have effect for a specified period not exceeding five years; (c) apply to all the members of the workforce, or all the members of a particular group of workers who share a function, workplace or organisational unit (excluding those whose terms and conditions are provided for, wholly or in

---

8   Unreported, 5 June 2000, Div Ct.
9   Ibid., reg. 17.
10 Ibid., reg. 18.
11 Ibid., reg. 18(2).
12 Ibid., reg. 16. A 'collective agreement' is defined for these purposes as an agreement or arrangement made between one or more independent trade unions and one or more employers or employers' associations: ibid., reg. 2.
13 See p. 201, below.

part, by a collective agreement); and (d) be signed by all the elected workforce representatives (although if the employer employs 20 or fewer employees on the date when the agreement is first made available for signature, it is sufficient if the agreement is signed by a majority of the workforce). In addition, before the agreement is made available for signature, the employer must have provided all the employees to whom it was intended to apply with copies of the agreement, together with such guidance as they might reasonably require to help them understand it[14]. The MPL etc. Regulations set out the requirements for the election of workforce representatives[15], including matters such as candidature, entitlement to vote and the conduct of the ballot[16].

iii)   The model scheme

As seen above, the MPL etc. Regulations contain a model scheme[17] on parental leave which automatically comes into operation if the parties do not make their own collective or workforce agreement. The key elements of the model scheme are as follows: i) parental leave may not be taken in periods other than a week or multiple of a week (except in the case of a child entitled to disability living allowance); ii) an employee may not take more than four weeks' leave in respect of any individual child during a particular year; iii) the employee must give the employer at least 21 days' notice of the taking of parental leave, and its duration; iv) fathers wishing to take parental leave immediately after the baby is born must give the employer notice at least 21 days before the beginning of the expected week of childbirth; v) employees wishing to take parental leave immediately after the date of placement of an adopted child must give the employer notice at least 21 days before the beginning of the week in which placement is expected to occur, or as soon as reasonably practicable thereafter; vi) the employer may ask for reasonable evidence of the employee's entitlement to parental leave (e.g. evidence of the child's date of birth, or date of placement for adoption); vii) the employer may postpone a period of parental leave (other than leave on birth or adoption) where the employer considers that the operation of his business would be unduly disrupted if the employee took leave during the period identified in the notice; viii) leave may not be postponed for more than six months, and the employer must notify the employee of the postponement in writing within seven days of receiving the employee's notice, giving the reason for the postponement and specifying the dates on which the period of leave will begin and end.

9   TIME OFF FOR DEPENDANTS

In addition to the right to parental leave, the Employment Relations Act 1999 also introduced a right for employees to take a reasonable amount of unpaid time off to deal with incidents involving a 'dependant'[18]. Like the provisions on

14   MPL etc Regulations, Sch. 1.
15   Workforce representatives have a right not to be dismissed or subjected to any detriment by the employer for performing (or proposing to perform) any functions or activities as a workforce representative or a candidate for election as a workforce representative: see p. 324.
16   These requirements are similar to those which apply to the election of workforce representatives under the Working Time Regulations: see p. 201 above.
17   MPL etc Regulations, Sch. 2.
18   Employment Rights Act 1996, ss. 57A and 57B, added by the Employment Relations Act 1999.

parental leave, the provisions on time off for dependants are designed to implement the Parental Leave Directive, which gives a right to time off in family emergencies. The hope and expectation is that the new provisions will lead to a reduction in the number of employees taking odd days off sick in order to care for sick children or to cope when domestic arrangements (e.g. child-minding arrangements) go awry at short notice.

Although colourfully (and sometimes mischievously) portrayed in certain sections of the media as giving employees carte blanche to take time off whenever they wish to attend to the needs of leaking washing machines or sick poodles, the right to time off for dependants is in fact more limited than this. Under the new provisions, an employee has the right to be permitted to take a 'reasonable amount' of time off (not further defined or explained) during working hours: (a) to provide assistance when a dependant falls ill, gives birth, or is injured or assaulted; (b) to make arrangements for the provision of care for a dependant who is ill or injured; (c) when a dependant dies; (d) because of the unexpected disruption or termination of arrangements for the care of a dependant; or (e) to deal with an incident which involves a child of the employee and which occurs unexpectedly during school hours or other time when the child's school is responsible for the child[19]. A 'dependant' of an employee is defined for these purposes as a spouse, child, parent, or a person who lives in the same household as the employee, otherwise than as an employee, tenant, lodger or boarder[20]. For the purposes of heads (a) and (b) above, 'dependant' also includes a person who reasonably relies on the employee (i) for assistance on an occasion when the person falls ill or is injured or assaulted, or (ii) to make arrangements for the provision of care in the event of illness or injury; and for the purposes of head (d), it includes any person who reasonably relies on the employee to make arrangements for the provision of care. Where time off is taken under these provisions, the employee must tell the employer the reason for the absence as soon as reasonably practicable, and how long the employee expects to be absent from work.

A complaint that an employer has unreasonably refused time off under these provisions lies to an employment tribunal, within three months of the refusal, or within a further reasonable period where the tribunal is satisfied that it was not reasonably practicable for the complaint to be brought within that period[1]. Where the tribunal upholds the complaint, it must make a declaration to that effect, and may order the employer to pay compensation to the employee of such amount as the tribunal considers just and equitable in all the circumstances, having regard to the employer's default, and any loss suffered by the employee which is attributable to the matters complained of.

10 PREGNANCY, MATERNITY AND SEX DISCRIMINATION[2]

In the last 10 years or so, the law on maternity rights in the UK has been completely transformed by a series of landmark ECJ decisions in which it has been held that

---

19 Ibid., s. 57A(1).
20 Ibid., s. 57A(3).
1   Ibid., s. 57B. An employee also has a right not to be dismissed or subjected to any detriment by his or her employer for taking or seeking to take time off for dependants: MPL etc Regulations, regs. 19, 20.
2   See Fredman (1994) 110 LQR 106; Szyszczak (1996) 59 MLR 589; Wintemute (1998) 27 ILJ 23; Honeyball (2000) 29 ILJ 43.

adverse treatment of a woman on grounds of pregnancy or maternity can constitute unlawful direct[3] discrimination on grounds of sex. The possibility of challenging adverse treatment on grounds of pregnancy as sex discrimination was particularly attractive in the UK because of the gaps in the protection for pregnancy and maternity under the employment rights legislation: until 1993, the statutory protection against dismissal on grounds of pregnancy was significantly weakened by the requirement to satisfy the normal two-year qualifying period of continuous employment, and parallel protection against detriment short of dismissal for reasons of pregnancy was not introduced until December 1999. Since the 1993 reforms, the need to challenge a dismissal under sex discrimination law has been greatly reduced, although there may still be advantages in doing so, as sex discrimination claims are not subject to any upper limit on compensation.

Initially, there was some doubt as to whether adverse treatment on grounds of pregnancy fell within the scope of sex discrimination law *at all*. This might seem strange to those uninitiated in the mysteries of the Sex Discrimination Act 1975 – after all, one might be forgiven for thinking that adverse treatment on grounds of pregnancy must necessarily be sexually discriminatory, given the inescapable biological fact that men cannot become pregnant. The doubts arose because in determining whether a woman has been treated less favourably than a man on the ground of sex, the 1975 Act requires the comparison between the treatment of the applicant and that of a man to be such that the relevant circumstances in the one case 'are the same, or not materially different, in the other'[4], and so it seemed that in cases involving pregnancy the necessary comparison could not be made[5]. However, in *Hayes v Malleable Working Men's Club and Institute*[6], the EAT managed to avoid this conclusion by holding that the correct approach under the 1975 Act was to compare the treatment of a pregnant woman with that of a man in comparable circumstances (e.g. a man suffering from some temporary disability). While this 'sick man' approach was open to the objection that it treated pregnancy as analogous to illness, it did at least succeed in bringing pregnant women within the protection of the Sex Discrimination Act, which was crucially important at the time for those dismissed within the first two years of employment.

It soon became apparent that there was a further highly significant dimension to this issue, in the form of EC Directive 76/207 (the Equal Treatment Directive). In a series of cases, beginning with *Dekker v Stichting Vormingscentrum voor Jong Volwassenen (VJV- Centrum) Plus*[7], the ECJ held that less favourable treatment of a woman on account of her pregnancy constituted unlawful direct discrimination on the grounds of sex, contrary to the Equal Treatment Directive, irrespective of how a hypothetical male would have been treated in comparable circumstances. In *Dekker*, the employer refused to appoint the complainant on learning that she was pregnant (the reason being that under Dutch law the employer would have been required to pay Mrs Dekker her full salary while on maternity leave, but could not have recovered that amount from its insurers because her pregnancy was known at the time her appointment would have commenced). The ECJ ruled that as pregnancy is a condition unique to women, to refuse a woman employment on the ground of pregnancy constituted direct discrimination on grounds of sex, contrary to the Directive; this was held to be the case even though the refusal

3 Protection against indirect sex discrimination (e.g. in relation to a transfer to part-time work after maternity leave) is considered at p. 338 above.
4 Sex Discrimination Act 1975, s. 5(3).
5 *Turley v Allders Department Stores Ltd* [1980] ICR 66, [1980] IRLR 4, EAT.
6 [1985] ICR 703, [1985] IRLR 367.
7 Case 177/88: [1991] IRLR 27, ECJ.

of employment was on account of the adverse financial consequences to the employer of her absence due to pregnancy, as the refusal was still based on the fact of pregnancy itself. In *Handels-og Kontorfunktionaerernes Forbund i Danmark (for Hertz) v Dansk Arbejdsgiverforening (for Aldi Marked A/S)*[8], decided on the same day as *Dekker*, the ECJ held that the same principle applied to a dismissal on account of pregnancy, although on the facts the court held that a dismissal some 18 months after the end of maternity leave due to absence for prolonged post-natal illness would not be sexually discriminatory if a man absent from work due to illness for a similar period would have been treated in the same way.

The apparent conflict between domestic and Community law on this issue was first considered by the UK courts in *Webb v EMO Air Cargo (UK) Ltd*[9]. In that case the applicant, recruited to provide temporary cover for another employee who was about to take maternity leave, was dismissed when she discovered shortly after starting work that she too was pregnant. The industrial tribunal dismissed her claim that her dismissal constituted unlawful discrimination on grounds of sex under the 1975 Act, holding that the reason for her dismissal was her anticipated inability to carry out the primary task for which she had been recruited (i.e. to cover for an absent colleague) and that if a man recruited for the same purpose had told the employer that he needed to be absent for a similar period of time, he too would have been dismissed. The EAT and the Court of Appeal upheld the tribunal's decision, rejecting the argument that the fact that pregnancy is specific to women means that a dismissal for pregnancy must automatically be discriminatory, and applying the comparative approach by comparing the treatment of the pregnant applicant and the treatment which would have been accorded to a man in comparable circumstances (e.g. a man with a medical condition requiring him to be absent from work for a similar period of time). On appeal to the House of Lords, Lord Keith (giving the leading judgment) conceded that as child-bearing and the capacity for child-bearing are characteristics of the female sex, '… in general to dismiss a woman because she is pregnant or to refuse to employ a woman of child-bearing age because she may become pregnant is unlawful direct discrimination,' as it involves the application of a gender-based criterion[10]. However, he considered that on the facts the reason for the dismissal was not gender-based, since the applicant was dismissed not because she was pregnant but because of her unavailability for work at the critical period, and it was therefore appropriate to compare her treatment with that of a hypothetical man who would also be unavailable (for whatever reason) at the critical time[11]. As it was unclear whether under Community law the unavailability for work rather than the pregnancy would be regarded as being the real reason for dismissal, the House of Lords referred the case to the ECJ, which rejected the comparative approach, holding that under the Equal Treatment Directive the dismissal of an employee for pregnancy constitutes direct discrimination and is

8 C–179/88: [1992] ICR 332, [1991] IRLR 31, ECJ.
9 [1990] ICR 442, [1990] IRLR 124, EAT; affd [1992] ICR 445, [1992] IRLR 116, CA; [1993] ICR 175, [1993] IRLR 27, HL; refd [1994] ICR 770, [1994] IRLR 482, ECJ; revsd (No. 2) [1995] ICR 1021, [1995] IRLR 645, HL. The applicant was unable to complain under s. 99 because she lacked the necessary period of continuous employment.
10 Applying the 'but for' test approved by the House of Lords in *James v Eastleigh Borough Council* [1990] ICR 554, [1990] IRLR 288, HL, discussed at p. 241, above.
11 One obvious objection to this line of reasoning is that it could allow a gender-based dismissal to be disguised as gender-neutral, the point being that if the underlying reason for the woman's unavailability for work is her pregnancy, it is strongly arguable that the dismissal is in fact gender-based, as *but for her sex* she would not have been pregnant, and *but for her pregnancy* she would not have been unavailable for work.

therefore unlawful per se. Significantly, however, the ECJ's ruling indicated two possible limitations on the scope of the protection: first, the ECJ accepted that in the case of a dismissal for an illness attributable to pregnancy which manifests itself after maternity leave, it would be appropriate to adopt a comparative approach with the treatment of a sick man in analogous circumstances[12]; and secondly, the ECJ emphasised that Ms Webb had been engaged under a contract of employment of indefinite duration, the implication being that had she been engaged simply as a temporary replacement on a fixed-term contract, the outcome might have been different. When the case returned to the House of Lords, Lord Keith reinterpreted the 'more precise' test of unlawful discrimination under the 1975 Act so as to accord with the ECJ's ruling: 'It seems to me that the only way of doing so is to hold that, in a case where a woman is engaged for an indefinite period, the fact that the reason why she will be temporarily unavailable for work at a time when to her knowledge her services will be particularly required is pregnancy is a circumstance relevant to her case, being a circumstance which could not be present in the case of a hypothetical man[13].' As the applicant had been recruited for an unlimited term, her dismissal was unlawful under the 1975 Act. However, Lord Keith indicated that the outcome might have been different if the employment had been for a fixed period during the *whole* of which the employee would have been unavailable for work because of her pregnancy, commenting that if such a situation were not to be distinguished, 'the result would be likely to be perceived as unfair to employers and as tending to bring the law on sex discrimination into disrepute.' The legal basis for a distinction between indefinite and fixed-term contracts in such cases is, to say the least, obscure. Hard cases generally make bad law, and it is submitted that it would be most unfortunate if the reluctance of the House of Lords to accept the logical implications of the ECJ's ruling in *Webb* (i.e. that any adverse treatment of a woman on grounds of pregnancy is discriminatory per se) were to lead to the introduction of a type of justification defence, previously confined to cases of indirect discrimination[14].

In the cases since *Webb (No 2)*, the extent of the special protection from pregnancy discrimination has been clarified, and a robust approach has been taken. It is now well-established that any adverse treatment on grounds of pregnancy will be unlawful per se[15], albeit with a very narrow exception for those employed on fixed-term contracts, provided the necessary causal connection can be established. The EAT gave useful guidance on this latter point in *O'Neill v Governors of St Thomas More RCVA School*[16]. In that case, the complainant, a religious education teacher at a Roman Catholic school, was dismissed after becoming pregnant as a result of a relationship with a local Roman Catholic priest. The tribunal had held that the dismissal, although unfair, was not discriminatory, as pregnancy was not the predominant cause of the dismissal, but the EAT allowed

12   As in *Hertz*, above n. 8.
13   [1995] IRLR 645, at p. 647, HL.
14   In *Caruana v Manchester Airport plc* [1996] IRLR 378, the EAT confirmed held that any possible special rule for fixed-term contacts is restricted to cases where the employee would be unavailable for the *whole* of the term of the contract..
15   See e.g. *Mahlburg v Land Mecklenburg-Vorpommern* [2000] IRLR 276, ECJ (held to be unlawful to refuse a pregnant woman appointment to a post of unlimited duration on the grounds that a statutory prohibition on her employment because of her pregnancy prevented her from being employed in that post from the outset and for the duration of her pregnancy).
16   [1997] ICR 33, [1996] IRLR 372, EAT; see also *Shomer v B & R Residential Lettings Ltd* [1992] IRLR 317, CA; *P & O European Ferries (Dover) Ltd v Iverson* [1999] ICR 1088, EAT.

the complainant's appeal. According to Mummery J: 'The basic question is: what, out of the whole complex of facts before the tribunal, is the "effective and predominant" cause or the "real and efficient" cause of the act complained of?' He considered that the other factors surrounding the pregnancy which had led to her dismissal ('the paternity of the child, the publicity of that fact and the consequent untenability of the applicant's position as a religious education teacher') were all causally related to the fact that she was pregnant, and so it could be said, on an objective consideration of all the surrounding circumstances, that her pregnancy 'precipitated and permeated the decision to dismiss her'.

The 'special protection' is however subject to certain temporal limits, as the decision in *Hertz* showed. In *Handels-og Kontorfunktionaerernes Forbund i Danmark (for Larsson) v Dansk Handel & Service (for Fotex Supermarked A/S)*[17], the ECJ held that it was lawful for an employer to take into account periods of absence due to pregnancy-related illness outside the maternity leave period in calculating whether there are grounds for dismissal, provided a man with a similar record of sickness absence would also have been dismissed. To the extent that the decision in *Larsson* seemed to imply that an employer could take account of pregnancy-related absence before the beginning of maternity leave, it appeared to conflict with the basic principle established in *Dekker* and *Webb (No. 2)*, and it was no surprise that when the ECJ next had an opportunity to reconsider the matter, in *Brown v Rentokil Ltd*[18], it confirmed that when considering a dismissal for sickness absence, it is unlawful to take account of absences due to pregnancy-related illness that have occurred between the start of pregnancy and the start of maternity leave[19]. Indeed, in that case the ECJ took the rare step of expressly disapproving the distinction drawn in *Larsson* between absence for pregnancy-related illness during pregnancy and during maternity leave. After *Brown v Rentokil Ltd*, it is now possible to state with some assurance that the special protection against dismissal on grounds of pregnancy applies from the start of pregnancy to the end of maternity leave. Within that period, a dismissal (or other adverse treatment) for absence caused by pregnancy-related illness will be unlawful. After the end of maternity leave, the comparative approach applies, so that such treatment will only be unlawful if a man would have been treated more favourably in comparable circumstances (i.e. the sick man comparison applies)[20]. In making that comparison, however, it will be unlawful to take into account any period of pregnancy-related sickness absence occurring between the start of pregnancy and the end of maternity leave.

While the decisions in *Dekker* and *Webb (No. 2)* clarified the law in one area, they in turn gave rise to a further, related issue: if adverse treatment on grounds of pregnancy or maternity leave is unlawful, does this mean that a woman on maternity leave is entitled to claim the benefit of the terms and conditions of employment which she would have enjoyed if still at work? This issue first arose for consideration by the ECJ in *Gillespie v Northern Health and Social Services Board*[1],

---

17   [1997] IRLR 643, ECJ.
18   [1998] IRLR 445, ECJ.
19   The fact that her contract contained a term allowing the employer to dismiss after a stipulated number of weeks of absence was held to make no difference.
20   See e.g. *British Telecommunications plc v Roberts* [1996] IRLR 601, EAT (request to jobshare after maternity leave not covered by the special protection, but subject instead to the comparative approach).
1   [1996] All ER (EC) 284, [1996] IRLR 214, ECJ. The ECJ also held that where the amount of maternity pay is calculated on the basis of pay received before the maternity leave begins, a woman on maternity leave is entitled to the benefit of a pay-rise awarded during that period (including a retrospective award) when calculating her maternity pay: see p. 341, above.

where it was argued that a woman should be entitled to receive full pay during maternity leave, on the grounds that if the only reason she does not receive full pay is that she is on maternity leave, that must be direct discrimination on the grounds of sex contrary to Community law, since that reason can only affect women. In a decision which owed more to pragmatism than to logic, but which no doubt caused a huge collective sigh of relief amongst employers, the ECJ ruled that women taking maternity leave 'are in a special position which requires them to be afforded special protection, but which is not comparable either with that of a man or with that of a woman actually at work'; consequently it was not unlawful under Community law to pay women on maternity leave at a level which is less than their full pay for the period of the leave. The Court considered that it was for the national legislature to set the amount of maternity pay, provided this was not so low as to undermine the purpose of maternity leave. In subsequent cases on this issue, the ECJ has maintained a clear distinction between a woman's rights i) while she is pregnant and still working; ii) during maternity leave; and iii) following her return to work. While pregnant and still working, the *Dekker* principle applies, so that any adverse treatment on grounds of pregnancy will be unlawful per se[2]. During maternity leave, her rights are those set out in the Pregnant Workers Directive (unless enhanced under national law or by her contract of employment); she cannot compare herself with the position of a man or woman actually at work, nor is she entitled to compare herself with a man or woman absent from work on sick leave[3], or on holiday[4]. Following her return to work, however, the comparative approach applies.

While the basic principles are now tolerably clear (albeit thoroughly muddled conceptually), they can be difficult to apply in practice, particularly where the tricky issue of the pro-rata-ing of benefits in proportion to periods of absence arises. While the ECJ in *Gillespie* stepped back from the brink of accepting a right to full pay during maternity leave, this left open the question of whether an employee continues to build up entitlement to other contractual benefits (e.g. the accrual of holiday or pension entitlement or annual bonuses) during maternity leave, particularly where those benefits are not dependent on actual performance of work. Subsequent cases have established that it is permissible under Article 141 (ex 119) and the Equal Treatment Directive for entitlement to (or accrual of) such benefits to be limited to the minimum 14-week maternity leave period guaranteed under the Pregnant Workers Directive. In *Boyle v Equal Opportunities Commissions*[5], the applicant challenged several aspects of the EOC's maternity scheme, including a clause whereby annual holiday leave ceased to accrue during periods of supplementary contractual maternity leave after the end of the minimum 14-week leave period. The ECJ held that such a clause was not precluded by European law, since the period of contractual maternity leave

---

2   See e.g. *Handels-og Kontorfunktionaerernes Forbund i Danmark (for Pedersen) v Faellesforeningen for Danmarks Brugsforeninger (for Kwickly Skive)* [1999] IRLR 55, ECJ (held to be unlawful to pay a woman absent from work with a pregnancy-related illness *before* the start of maternity leave a lower level of sick pay than was paid to other employees).

3   *Boyle v Equal Opportunities Commission* [1998] IRLR 717, ECJ; see also *Todd v Eastern Health and Social Services Board; Gillespie v Northern Health and Social Services Board (No 2)* [1997] IRLR 410, NICA.

4   *Edwards v Derby City Council* [1999] ICR 114, EAT.

5   Above, n. 3.

was a special advantage available only to women, so the fact that annual leave ceased to accrue during that period could not amount to less favourable treatment of women[6]. The ECJ also held that a clause requiring the repayment of any contractual maternity pay over and above the level of SMP if a woman did not return to work after maternity leave was not unlawful (rejecting the comparison with a man or woman absent on sick leave, who would not have been required to repay sick pay on not returning to work), nor was a clause providing for the triggering of maternity leave where a woman absent on sick leave gave birth during such absence. A clause prohibiting an employee from taking sick leave during the minimum 14-week period unless she elected to return to work and terminate her maternity leave was held to be unlawful (although not so in relation to a period of supplementary maternity leave), as was a clause limiting the accrual of occupational pension rights during the minimum 14-week period to the period during which the woman received contractual or statutory maternity pay. In *Caisse Nationale d'Assurance Vieillesse des Travailleurs Salaries v Thibault*[7], the applicant was denied an annual performance assessment (and with it the possibility of qualifying for promotion) because the relevant collective agreement restricted such assessments to employees who had been present at work for at least six months in the relevant year, and she was unable to qualify because she had been away from work on maternity leave. She argued that to deny her the assessment was discriminatory, since if she had not taken maternity leave, she would have qualified for an assessment. In a brief (and unfortunately rather delphic) judgment which is difficult to reconcile with *Boyle*, the ECJ upheld her complaint, on the grounds that a woman who continues to be bound to her employer by an employment contract during maternity leave should not be deprived of the benefit of working conditions which apply to both men and women and which are a result of that relationship.

Finally, while most of the cases in this area have been brought by women, the question arises whether a man is able to complain that he has been discriminated against on grounds of sex through being denied benefits enjoyed by women in connection with pregnancy. The short answer to this is that such a claim is likely to fail. Section 2(2) of the Sex Discrimination Act provides that it is not unlawful for an employer to discriminate by affording 'special treatment' to women in connection with pregnancy or childbirth, and this is reinforced by Article 2(3) of the Equal Treatment Directive, which provides an exception to the principle of equal treatment for 'provisions concerning the protection of women, particularly as regards pregnancy and maternity'. In *Abdoulaye v Régie Nationale des Usines Renault SA*[8], a group of male employees claimed equal pay with women, who were entitled to receive a lump-sum maternity allowance while on maternity leave, in addition to their *full* pay. The applicants claimed that the refusal of the employers to pay an equivalent allowance to fathers was a breach of the principle of equal pay in Article 119 (now 141) of the EC Treaty. The ECJ reaffirmed the principle that the

---

6   This of course begs the question of whether the benefit in question is one which is awarded retrospectively as a reward for past service (in which case it may be reduced pro-rata for periods of maternity leave after the 14-week minimum) or merely depends on the employee being in current employment when the benefit is awarded: see *Lewen v Denda* [2000] IRLR 67, ECJ (a case on the Parental Leave Directive).

7   [1998] IRLR 399, ECJ.

8   [1999] IRLR 811, ECJ.

position of women on maternity leave is not comparable with that of men, and held that the principle of equal pay in Article 119 (now 141) does not preclude the payment of a lump-sum exclusively to female workers who take maternity leave, where that payment is designed to offset the occupational disadvantages which arise for them as a result of their being away from work.

Chapter 7

Contracts of employment (2): discharge at common law

I MODES OF TERMINATION OTHER THAN DISMISSAL

Certain common law and statutory rights depend upon an employee being dismissed, but there are certain ways in which employment may be terminated other than simply by dismissal. These are now considered, and one of the themes that runs through them is that they are founded on old common law principles established at a time when an employee had few rights and so the concept of continuity of employment was of little significance, but they are now heavily qualified (though not actually abrogated) by specialised statutory provisions aimed at mitigating their potentially harsh application to modern employment rights. One such provision is the Employment Rights Act 1996, section 136 which (along with s. 139) provides that, for the purposes of claiming redundancy payments, where an act of the employer or an event affecting the employer (including his death) has the effect of terminating the contract of employment by operation of law, that is deemed to be a termination by the employer (i.e. a dismissal) and is further deemed to be by reason of redundancy if that is the real reason behind the failure to continue employing the employee. This will go far towards safeguarding the employee's redundancy rights in most cases of death, dissolution or frustration. However, there remain areas not yet covered by ameliorating statutory provisions where the industrial lawyer (particularly when representing the employee) has to beware of the sudden emergence of arguments based on common law notions of discharge of employment which, if accepted, can do great harm to statutory rights; a good example is the effect of the doctrine of frustration on certain unfair dismissal actions.

i) Death or dissolution of the enterprise

At common law, death would bring the contract of employment to an end, whether it be the death of the employee[1] or the employer, as in *Farrow v Wilson*[2] where the

1   *Stubbs v Holywell Rly Co* (1867) LR 2 Exch 311; *Graves v Cohen* (1929) 46 TLR 121.
2   (1869) LR 4 CP 744.

personal representatives were held not to be liable to continue the engagement of the employee. The employee is discharged from further performance on the death of the employer, not through any breach of contract, but as the result of an implied condition that the continued existence of the parties is an essential of the contract. This position is now qualified by statute in three ways. First, if the business does not carry on after the employer's death, the termination of employment is deemed to be a dismissal for redundancy under the Employment Rights Act 1996, sections 136, 139, above, so the employee may claim a redundancy payment from the employer's personal representatives[3]. Second, if the deceased employer's business is carried on by his personal representatives and the employee continues to work for them there is deemed to be no termination for redundancy purposes[4], and his continuity of employment for general purposes is not broken[5]. Third, where it is the employee who dies, any pending proceedings of his before an employment tribunal may be instituted or continued by his personal representatives (or by other persons appointed by the tribunal if there are no personal representatives) and if he dies whilst under notice of dismissal he will be treated for the purposes of unfair dismissal and redundancy as if he had actually been dismissed[6].

In practice of course most employees will be employed by partnerships or companies which do not die, but they may be dissolved or wound up in certain ways, and the operation of these processes of law upon the contracts of employment concerned must now be considered.

In the case of a partnership, where a partners dies and there is a consequent dissolution of the partnership, the contract of employment will be discharged wherever it is one related to the personal conduct of the deceased person. In *Harvey v Tivoli (Manchester) Ltd*[7] the death of a member of a troupe of three music-hall artists was held to discharge the contract though he had been replaced, and the troupe was ready to appear. In *Phillips v Alhambra Palace Co*[8] one of the defendant partners had died after a contract had been entered into with the plaintiffs, who were also music-hall artists. In this case it was held that the obligation continued despite the death of the partner, for the obligation was not of a personal character and the partners, when they booked the artists to appear, were not individually known. In the first case the contract was with three specific persons – in the second case it was with a firm and the personal element was not paramount. A dissolution of a partnership on account of the retirement of a partner will operate as a wrongful dismissal at common law[9], but a continuance of employment under a firm containing some of the old partners will amount to a waiver of common law rights of action[10]. Under statute, even if the dissolution did not constitute a dismissal per se (which it almost certainly does) it would be deemed to be such for redundancy purposes under section 136 of the 1996 Act, above,

3   Employment Rights Act 1996, s. 206(3).
4   Ibid., s. 174. It must be shown on the acts that the personal representatives did renew the contract or re-engage the employee, but in practice the longer he continues to work for them the easier this will be to infer (in the absence of express agreement): *Ranger v Brown* [1978] ICR 603, EAT.
5   Ibid., s. 218(4).
6   Ibid., s. 206; Employment Tribunals Awards (Enforcement in case of Death) Regulations 1976, S.I. 1976 No. 663.
7   (1907) 23 TLR 592; *Tunstall v Condon* [1980] ICR 786.
8   [1901] 1 KB 59.
9   *Brace v Calder* [1895] 2 QB 253, CA; *Briggs v Oates* [1990] ICR 473, [1990] IRLR 472.
10   *Hobson v Cowley* (1858) 27 LJ Ex 205.

and where the employee continues in the reconstituted firm's employment his continuity of employment is safeguarded by section 218(5) of that Act.

In the case of a company, the legal position is complex[11]. The position seems to be as follows. An order of the court for a compulsory winding up of the company operates as notice of dismissal to its employees[12]. The effect of a voluntary winding up depends upon whether the business is to be carried on in some form (as for example where it has been taken over by another company); if it is to carry on *Midland Counties District Bank Ltd v Attwood*[13] decided that it does not operate as notice of dismissal, but if there is no intention of carrying on, then it may so operate, as in the case of a compulsory order[14]. The appointment of a receiver is a less drastic step than an immediate winding up, but once again the rules are complicated. The appointment of a receiver by the court terminates contracts of employment[15], but the appointment of a receiver out of court by the debenture holders, as agent for the company, does not have that effect[16], except perhaps in four cases:

a) where the receiver is appointed to act as agent for the creditors only, not for the company[17];
b) where the receiver sells the business, so that there is no continuation;
c) where the receiver enters a new contract of employment with the employee in question which is inconsistent with the existence of the old one;
d) where the continuation of the contract of employment is inconsistent with the appointment of the receiver because of the nature of the employment; this may be the case with a managing director, but is not necessarily so and will depend upon all the facts of the case[18].

The case law on these points is at times confusing, for though most of the cases envisage the effect of one of these events, if any, to be the giving of notice, some are capable of pointing to instant dismissal (as by operation of law) which, as has been pointed out[19], could jeopardise common law rights of the employee – though it might be noted that some of the cases concern managers on fixed term contracts, in whose case any termination (whether with or without notice) may constitute wrongful dismissal and so, for example, free the manager from any restraint of trade clause he may have signed which would otherwise have bound him[20].

11 See Freedland *The Contract of Employment* (1976), pp. 332–339; Graham 'The effect of liquidation on contracts of service' (1952) 15 MLR 48; Davies and Freedland 'The effects of receivership upon employees of companies' (1980) 9 ILJ 95; Pollard *Corporate Insolvency: Employment and Pension Rights* (2nd edn, 2000). Questions of continuity of employment may be covered separately by the Transfer of Undertakings (Protection of Employment) Regulations 1981, S.I. 1981 No. 1794; see p. 159, above.
12 *Re General Rolling Stock Co (Chapman's Case)* (1866) LR 1 Eq 346; *Re Oriental Bank Corpn Ltd (MacDowall's Case)* (1886) 32 Ch D 366.
13 [1905] 1 Ch 357.
14 *Fowler v Commercial Timber Co Ltd* [1930] 2 KB 1, CA: *Reigate v Union Manufacturing Co Ltd* [1918] 1 KB 592, CA; *Fox Bros (Clothes) Ltd v Bryant* [1979] ICR 64, [1978] IRLR 485, EAT.
15 *Reid v Explosives Co* (1887) 19 QBD 264, CA; *Re Foster Clark Ltd's Indenture Trusts* [1966] 1 All ER 43, [1966] 1 WLR 125; cf. *Pambakian v Brentford Nylons Ltd* [1978] ICR 665, EAT.
16 *Re Foster Clark Ltd's Indenture Trusts* [1966] 1 All ER 43, [1966] 1 WLR 125; *Re Mack Trucks (Britain) Ltd* [1967] 1 All ER 977, [1967] 1 WLR 780; *Nicoll v Cutts* [1985] BCLC 322, CA.
17 *Hopley Dodd v Highfield Motors (Derby) Ltd* (1969) 4 ITR 289.
18 On exceptions (b)–(d), see the cases cited in n. 16 above, and *Griffiths v Secretary of State for Social Services* [1974] QB 468, [1973] 3 All ER 1184.
19 *Re Patent Floor Cloth Co* (1872) 41 LJ Ch 476 at 477 per Bacon V-C.
20 *Measures Bros Ltd v Measures* [1910] 2 Ch 248, CA.

ii) Frustration of the contract

It is a general principle of the law of contract that a contract will be terminated automatically if it is frustrated[1], that is if a change of law or circumstances is such as to mean that the contract becomes impossible of performance or that performance of the contractual obligation would produce a result radically different from that which was originally undertaken in the contract. This doctrine of frustration applies to contracts of employment. Thus in *Morgan v Manser*[2] it was held that the calling-up for military service of a music-hall artist frustrated the contract which he had with his manager, and Streatfeild J formulated the test as follows:

'If there is an event or change of circumstances which is so fundamental as to be regarded by the law as striking at the root of the contract as a whole, and as going beyond what was contemplated by the parties and such that to hold the parties to the contract would be to bind them to terms which they would not have made had they contemplated that event or those circumstances, then the contract is frustrated by that event immediately and irrespective of the volition or the intention of the parties, or their knowledge as to that particular event, and this even though they have continued for a time to treat the contract as still subsisting.'

The effects of this doctrine on the contract of employment are threefold:

a) If the contract is frustrated it is terminated automatically, and immediately upon the happening of a frustrating event; there is no need, for example, for the employer to take any steps to terminate the contract or even to indicate that he regards it as terminated[3].

b) As a consequence of (a), there is no right to any back pay from the date of frustration until any other date (e.g. a date, if any, on which the employer indicated that he thought the contract had ended)[4]. However, any wages due up to the date of frustration may be claimed under the Law Reform (Frustrated Contracts) Act 1943, either under section 2(4) if the contract can be regarded as divisible and the employee has fully performed those severable parts before the date of frustration, or under section 1(3) if the wages concerned were not actually due at that date but it would be just in all the circumstances for the court to award a sum representing the work done up to that date.

c) If the contract of employment is frustrated, its termination is due to the operation of law, and not to dismissal (either at common law or under the Employment Rights Act 1996, ss. 95 or 136) which could have a serious effect on certain common law and statutory rights, particularly unfair dismissal, which may only be claimed if the employee is dismissed. However, where the frustrating event is one relating to the employer (e.g. his death or the

---

1 *Davis Contractors Ltd v Fareham UDC* [1956] AC 696, [1956] 2 All ER 145, HL. See Cheshire, Fifoot and Furmston *Law of Contract* (13th edn, 1996), ch. 20; Mogridge 'Frustration, employment contracts and statutory rights' [1982] NLJ 795.

2 [1948] 1 KB 184, [1947] 2 All ER 666; the passage cited is at 191 and 670 respectively.

3 *Marshall v Harland and Wolff Ltd* [1972] 2 All ER 715, [1972] ICR 101, disapproving suggestions to the contrary in *Thomas v John Drake & Co Ltd* (1971) 6 ITR 146; it is not necessary to be able to date the frustrating event precisely, which is particularly significant in the case of frustration through illness. See also *Egg Stores (Stamford Hill) Ltd v Leibovici* [1977] ICR 260, [1976] IRLR 376, EAT.

4 *Unger v Preston Corpn* [1942] 1 All ER 200.

destruction of his business), section 136(5) of the 1996 Act safeguards the employee's rights to a redundancy payment by deeming that termination to be a dismissal, and this will apply even if the event applies to both employer and employee (e.g. the passing of new legislation making the whole employment in question illegal), for it is enough that some of the effect is upon the employer[5].

For an event or circumstance to frustrate the contract of employment it must be exceptionally grave. Certain wartime factors have been held to have the effect of frustration, such as being called up or interned[6]. However, in practice the most important event is illness on the part of the employee, for if it is sufficiently grave to frustrate the contract the employee will lose any potential rights which he may have to claim unfair dismissal or redundancy (the latter because this is not an event befalling the employer, so not covered by the Employment Rights Act 1996, s. 136(5)). In *Poussard v Spiers*[7] an opera singer was ill during rehearsals for the opera for which she was engaged, and could not take part in the first four performances; this was held to frustrate the contract so that her employer was entitled to treat the contract as ended. This was also the case in *Condor v Barron Knights Ltd*[8] where the employee was physically unable to play with the pop group in question for seven nights per week through illness and this was held to be a frustration, particularly as the group could not operate on anything less than full time and could not reasonably operate with a part-time substitute. However, some care may be needed with certain theatrical cases, for a court or tribunal may be more ready to find frustration in the case of a short-term contract entered with a particular performance or set of performances in mind. It may be more difficult to establish in the case of a long standing employment of a permanent nature[9], particularly in view of the old common law principle that in general the consideration for wages is readiness and willingness to serve on the employee's part, not necessarily the performance of actual work[10]. As the question of frustration through illness is so important in the context of the statutory rights, it was reviewed by the NIRC in *Marshall v Harland and Wolff Ltd*[11] where Sir John Donaldson P laid down the following matters as factors which should be weighed by a tribunal in deciding whether a contract was frustrated:

a) the terms of the contract, including any provisions as to sick pay;

b) how long the employment was likely to last in the absence of sickness, for a temporary or specific hiring is more likely to be frustrated;

c) the nature of the employment, in particular whether the employee was in a 'key post' which had to be filled permanently if his absence was prolonged[12], or whether it was such that it could be held open for a considerable period[13];

---

5   *Fenerty v British Airports Authority* (1976) 11 ITR 1.
6   *Horlock v Beal* [1916] 1 AC 486, HL; *Marshall v Glanvill* [1917] 2 KB 87; *Morgan v Manser* [1948] 1 KB 184, [1947] 2 All ER 666; *Unger v Preston Corpn* [1942] 1 All ER 200. However, even something as potentially drastic as internment must have a substantial effect and not be merely transitory: *Nordman v Rayner and Sturges* (1916) 33 TLR 87.
7   (1876) 1 QBD 410; cf. *Bettini v Gye* (1876) 1 QBD 183, where a singer's illness incapacitated her for the rehearsals but not for any of the performances, and this was held *not* to be a frustration.
8   [1966] 1 WLR 87.
9   See e.g. *Storey v Fulham Steel Works Co* (1907) 24 TLR 89, CA.
10 *Warburton v Co-operative Wholesale Society Ltd* [1917] 1 KB 663, CA; *Henthorn v CEGB* [1980] IRLR 361, CA.
11 [1972] 2 All ER 715, [1972] ICR 101.
12 *Hebden v Forsey & Son* [1973] ICR 607, [1973] IRLR 344.
13 *Maxwell v Walter Howard Designs Ltd* [1975] IRLR 77, IT.

d) the nature of the illness, how long it has continued and the prospects of recovery; this may interact with (c) in that if there is no urgency for a replacement, a more distant prospect of recovery may keep the contract alive;

e) the period of past employment, for 'a relationship which is of long standing is not so easily destroyed as one which has but a short history'.

Tribunals have regularly followed these guidelines, but in *Egg Stores (Stamford Hill) Ltd v Leibovici*[14] the EAT pointed out that they raise a particular difficulty in the case of short-term periodic contracts of employment, which may be determined at short notice, for although the doctrine of frustration is necessary in longer-term contracts if it has become impossible for the employee to perform his part, in the case of the short-term contract the employer has the more ready remedy of dismissal on relatively short notice, which may be more appropriate in the circumstances than reliance upon frustration. In the light of this, although frustration has succeeded in such cases (and the EAT reaffirmed that where this is the case it operates automatically without the necessity of any steps being taken by the employer), in these cases more emphasis may be placed upon whether the employer has thought it right to dismiss the absent employee, for if he has not done so, the tribunal *might* infer that the reason was that he did not think that enough time had elapsed to make it a proper course to take, and that would be a strong inference against frustration. The EAT then said that a short-term periodic contract could be subject to an event (e.g. a crippling accident) so drastic that it was obvious that it was frustrated, but that in the more normal case of a lingering illness there are further matters to be taken into account along with those in *Marshall's* case; these are:

f) the risk to the employer of incurring obligations (in respect of redundancy payments and unfair dismissal) to an employee meant to be a replacement;

g) whether wages have continued to be paid;

h) the acts and statements of the employer in relation to the employment, in particular whether there has been a dismissal of sorts and if not, why not[15];

i) whether in all the circumstances a reasonable employer could be expected to wait any longer.

All of these factors must be weighed by the tribunal which will probably be loath to find frustration; if the contract is not frustrated and the employer is found to have dismissed the employee, a claim for unfair dismissal may proceed which must be decided in the normal way[16], and it has been stated that the tests laid down in *Marshall's* case are those for frustration, *not* those for deciding whether a dismissal for ill health is reasonable[17], though if the further factors in the *Egg Stores* case are applied, in particular factor (i) above, the two tests do begin to look somewhat similar[18].

At one point, the whole question of the application of the doctrine of frustration to contracts of employment was thrown into confusion by the decision of the EAT in *Harman v Flexible Lamps Ltd*[19] where it was held not only that the applicant's

---

14 [1977] ICR 260, [1976] IRLR 376, further discussed in *Hart v AR Marshall & Sons (Bulwell) Ltd* [1977] ICR 539, [1977] IRLR 51 and *Williams v Watsons Luxury Coaches Ltd* [1990] ICR 536, [1990] IRLR 164.

15 Emphasised in *Hart v A R Marshall & Sons (Bulwell) Ltd* [1977] ICR 539, [1977] IRLR 51.

16 See p. 475, below.

17 *Tan v Berry Bros and Rudd Ltd* [1974] ICR 586, [1974] IRLR 244.

18 *Egg Stores (Stamford Hill) Ltd v Leibovici* [1977] ICR 260 at 264G, [1976] IRLR 376 at 378 per Phillips J.

19 [1980] IRLR 418.

illness did not frustrate her contract on the facts, but further that the doctrine as a matter of law should only apply to long-term contracts not terminable by notice. However desirable such an approach may be as a matter of policy, the decision was fatally flawed as a precedent since it did not even cite either *Marshall v Harland and Wolff Ltd* or *Egg Stores (Stamford Hill) Ltd v Leibovici* (above), with both of which it was inconsistent. Not surprisingly, therefore, when the issue went to the Court of Appeal in *Notcutt v Universal Equipment Co (London) Ltd*[20] orthodoxy was re-established – it was accepted that Bristow J was correct to state in *Harman* that a court should be *cautious* about applying frustration to contracts easily terminable by notice (particularly if it is being used as a means of avoiding statutory rights), but to go further and suggest that the doctrine itself is not applicable was incorrect. In the case itself illness absence of eight months due to a coronary was held to have frustrated the contract of employment of an employee of 27 years service, who was entitled by law to 12 weeks' notice. The employee's claim was in fact a common law claim in the county court for sick pay (which in the event was not payable due to the frustration of the contract) but it is clear that the decision is also applicable to a statutory action, particularly an action for unfair dismissal. While the court did state that defences of frustration should be treated carefully[1], it must be accepted that the decision does leave considerable scope for frustration in sickness cases – 12 weeks was not an unduly long notice period, and the dominant factor in the case appears to be that the illness led immediately to total and lasting incapacity for work, which is not going to be a rare occurrence in cases of major illness or accident. In such an event, however, the position may now be complicated by a modern tendency in some employments to offer (as part of enhanced terms and conditions) 'permanent health insurance' covering generously employees who are permanently unable to work – in such a case, could this factor be used to defeat an argument for frustration, on the basis that the illness was fully covered by the contract and so not an *unforeseen* frustrating event?[2] If so, could the argument eventually be taken even further and applied to an employment covered by an *ordinary* sick pay term, at least where it is relatively generous and envisages a long period off work while still receiving pay?

Varying views as to the proper approach to be taken to frustration can also be seen in the other major area for its potential application to employment contracts, the effect of imprisonment of the employee. Here the complicating factor is not whether the contract is terminable on short notice, but rather whether imprisonment constitutes 'self induced frustration', for it is usually said that the frustrating event must not be self induced[3]. In *Hare v Murphy Bros Ltd*[4] the Court of Appeal held that a contract of employment was automatically terminated when

---

20   [1986] ICR 414, [1986] IRLR 218, CA, followed in *F C Shepherd & Co Ltd v Jerrom* [1986] ICR 802, [1986] IRLR 358, CA.

1   Further, it was accepted by Mustill LJ in *F C Shepherd & Co Ltd v Jerrom* (above) that the existence of a disciplinary procedure covering the event in question (in that case, imprisonment) might be a factor against finding frustration.

2   This argument was accepted in *Villella v MFI Furniture Centres Ltd* [1999] IRLR 468. For the effect of such permanent health insurance schemes or the giving of notice to persons subject to them, see p. 128, above.

3   *Bank Line Ltd v Arthur Capel & Co* [1919] AC 435 at 452, HL per Lord Sumner; *Denmark Productions Ltd v Boscobel Productions Ltd* [1969] 1 QB 699, [1968] 3 All ER 513, at 736, CA and 533 respectively, per Harman LJ. It is for the party relying on frustration to prove it, but for the other party to prove that it was self-induced (if that be their allegation): *Joseph Constantine SS Line Ltd v Imperial Smelting Corpn Ltd* [1942] AC 154, [1941] 2 All ER 165, HL.

4   [1974] 3 All ER 940, [1974] ICR 603, CA.

the employee was sentenced to twelve months' imprisonment for an assault unconnected with his employment. Lord Denning clearly said that the contract was frustrated and that it was not a case of self induction for the frustrating event was the imposition of the sentence (even though that was of course originally caused by the criminal behaviour). The problem was, however, that the other two judgments were not unequivocally in agreement with this approach, and a major disagreement arose between different EATs as to whether the doctrine of frustration should apply to imprisonment cases. In one sense the end result might be much the same since even if frustration does not apply and an unfair dismissal action proceeds, it is likely that the dismissal of an employee who has received an immediate and substantial term of imprisonment will be fair, provided it is sensibly handled by the employer[5]. However, it remains of considerable interest legally whether the employer can go further and stop an unfair dismissal action dead in its tracks in such a case by pleading frustration. A finding of frustration through imprisonment was upheld in *Harrington v Kent County Council*[6] (even though the employee's sentence was under appeal, which was ultimately successful), and was assumed to be possible (though not proved on the facts) in *Chakki v United Yeast Co Ltd*[7]; to the contrary, however, it was held in *Norris v Southampton City Council*[8] that a contract of employment is *not* frustrated by imprisonment, as a matter of law. The point was eventually resolved by the Court of Appeal in *F C Shepherd & Co Ltd v Jerrom*[9] which concerned an unfair dismissal action by an apprentice who lost his employment when sentenced to borstal training for offences of violence halfway through his apprenticeship. The EAT[10] held that imprisonment can frustrate a contract of employment, that *Hare v Murphy Bros Ltd* (above) does support that proposition and that *Norris* is wrong. However, they upheld the industrial tribunal's decision that there was no frustration here on rather novel grounds – seeking to restrict the operation of the doctrine, Waite P added the gloss that where, as here, the contract contained a prescribed termination procedure covering the event in question (in this case, incorporated from a national joint agreement governing apprenticeship) that event cannot be an *unforeseen* eventuality and so cannot be a frustrating event. However, this interesting and positive gloss was disapproved by the Court of Appeal who allowed the employer's appeal and held the doctrine to be applicable to cases of imprisonment simpliciter. That left one remaining problem – was not this frustration self-induced? Further, was it not the case that frustration must not be the fault of *either* party?[11] This was resolved in two ways – Balcombe LJ accepted Lord Denning MR's view in *Hare v Murphy Bros Ltd* that the frustrating event was actually the imposition of the sentence, not the misconduct by the employee, but Lawton and Mustill LJJ took a more fundamental approach – that, properly understood, the rule against self-induction only meant that neither party could

5   *Kingston v British Railways Board* [1984] ICR 781, [1984] IRLR 146, CA.
6   [1980] IRLR 353, EAT.
7   [1982] 2 All ER 446, [1982] ICR 140, EAT.
8   [1982] ICR 177 [1982] IRLR 141. The decision in this case involved a strained reading of *Hare v Murphy Bros Ltd*, n. 4, above and, arguably, entirely misplaced reliance on *London Transport Executive v Clarke* [1981] ICR 355, [1981] IRLR 166, CA, p. 453 below, which concerned a case of clear repudiation of contract, not frustration.
9   [1986] ICR 802, [1986] IRLR 358, CA.
10 [1985] ICR 552, [1985] IRLR 275. The case was newsworthy when decided by the EAT; the idea of a boy sent to borstal for offences of violence receiving compensation of £7,000 for being refused his job back was not treated sympathetically in the tabloid press.
11 See, in a commercial context, *Paal Wilson & Co A/S v Partenreederei Hannah Blumenthal* [1983] 1 AC 854, [1983] 1 All ER 34, HL.

rely on his *own* misconduct to establish a defence of frustration. As the employer was relying on the *employee's* fault here, that requirement was satisfied and frustration could succeed; to hold otherwise would allow a party at fault to benefit from his own misdeeds, which would not be tolerated. As with *Notcutt's* case in the context of sickness, this decision of the Court of Appeal resolved an unfortunate division of opinion on frustration, and did so by applying a fairly straightforward and orthodox approach again. It leaves one (possibly unanswerable) question – how long does the sentence of imprisonment have to be in order to justify a finding of frustration? This presumably remains a question of fact for the tribunal or court.

iii)   Expiry of fixed term contracts

There used to be a presumption that a general hiring (i.e. one with no fixed duration) was a hiring for a year, the significance of this being that it guaranteed agricultural labourers employment through all four seasons. This, however, no longer has any place in employment law, and a general hiring now is regarded as a hiring for an indefinite period, determinable by reasonable notice[12]. However, the employer and employee may agree that a contract shall be for a fixed period only (possibly for a probationary period) and at common law that contract terminates automatically at the expiry of the period[13]. Now, however, fixed term contracts have acquired particular significance in the context of statutory rights in two ways:

a)   an employee under a fixed term contract may agree in writing to renounce his rights to claim a redundancy payment (if the contract is for two years or more)[14]; there used to be a similar power to renounce unfair dismissal rights (if the contract was for one year or more) but this was repealed by the Employment Relations Act 1999;

b)   expiry of a fixed term contract without renewal is deemed to be a dismissal for unfair dismissal and redundancy purposes[15].

For the purposes of both of these provisions, it is important to know what a 'fixed term contract' actually is, for there is no statutory definition. In *BBC v Ioannou*[16] the Court of Appeal had to decide this in the context of (a) above; the contract in question was for a fixed period, but with a provision for termination by three months' notice, and this was held not to be a 'fixed term contract', so that the purported written surrender of redundancy and unfair dismissal rights was ineffective. Termination by notice was held to be inconsistent with a fixed term contract, which had to be for that term and not terminable during it. In this case the Court of Appeal were attempting to safeguard the position of those on fixed term contracts by ensuring that only those *genuinely* on such contracts could sign away their rights. When, however, this reasoning was applied to (b) above it had potentially dire results for the employee[17], for it meant that if the employer put

---

12   *De Stempel v Dunkels* [1938] 1 All ER 238, CA; *Richardson v Koefod* [1969] 3 All ER 1264, [1969] 1 WLR 1812, CA.

13   *R v Secretary of State for Social Services, ex p Khan* [1973] 2 All ER 104, [1973] 1 WLR 187, CA. See also *Brown v Knowsley Borough Council* [1986] IRLR 102 (contract expressed to be subject to continued external funding held to terminate automatically when that funding ceased).

14   Employment Rights Act 1996, s. 197(3)-(5); *Kingston-upon-Hull City Council v Mountain* [1999] ICR 715.

15   Ibid., ss. 95 and 136.

16   [1975] 2 All ER 999, [1975] ICR 267, CA.

17   See Hepple and Napier 'Temporary workers and the law' (1978) 7 ILJ 84.

him on a contract which was ostensibly for a fixed term but used the ploy of inserting a notice provision of sorts, the employer could then have argued that, under *BBC v Ioannou*, that was *not* a fixed term contract, and so when it expired that was *not* the expiry of a fixed term contract under the Employment Rights Act 1996, sections 95(1)(b) and 136(1)(b) and so, as it would not qualify as an ordinary dismissal under section 95(1)(a) and 136(1)(a), there would have been no 'dismissal' and so no possible claims for unfair dismissal or redundancy. This was argued by an employer in *Dixon v BBC*[18], but in that case the Court of Appeal recognised the absurdity that would arise from this application of *BBC v Ioannou* and so, not wishing to establish two different definitions for 'fixed term' depending on whether the case concerned (a) or (b) above, they reversed as per incuriam that part of *BBC v Ioannou* which dealt with the definition of 'fixed term', and held that a contract for a set period remains a fixed term contract for statutory purposes even if it also contains a provision for termination by notice during its currency. Thus *Dixon v BBC* is now the ruling case, and so the employer cannot use this simple device to rule out the employee's action, but must instead accept that when a fixed term contract expires (whether or not there is a notice provision in it), that is a 'dismissal' under sections 95 and 136 and, in an unfair dismissal case, be prepared to justify his reasons for not renewing the contract[19]. However, there is a gain to the employer in that, contrary to what was said in *BBC v Ioannou*, he can put a notice provision into a fixed term contract for two years or more and still validly require the employee to sign away his rights to claim a redundancy payment.

One further point of definition to notice is that a fixed term contract is one which is to expire on a definable *date*, not on the happening of a particular event or the completion of a particular task at some time in the future[20]. There is therefore the possibility of such a 'purpose contract' terminating automatically without there being a dismissal in law, which could, of course, materially prejudice statutory rights[1]. If, however, the event or completion in question (e.g. the end of a particular course in a short term teaching contract) can in fact be dated with reasonable precision, that should be treated as sufficient for the existence of a fixed term contract; if it were otherwise, it might be easy for an employer to avoid the statutory definition of dismissal by putting the contract in the *form* of an engagement pending a particular event, even if the date of that event could be discerned. Further, it may be significant for future developments that the Fixed Term Worker Directive 1999/70/EC (yet to be transposed into domestic law at the time of writing) adopts a wider definition, namely 'where the end of the employment contract or relationship is determined by objective conditions such as reaching a specific date, completing a specific task, or the occurrence of a specific event'.

iv) Mutual consent

As with other contracts, a contract of employment may in general be terminated by the mutual agreement of the employer and employee so to do (just as they may

18   [1979] ICR 281, [1979] IRLR 114, CA.

19   *Terry v East Sussex County Council* [1977] 1 All ER 567, [1976] ICR 536, approved by the Court of Appeal in *Fay v North Yorkshire County Council* [1986] ICR 133, [1985] IRLR 247, CA.

20   *Wiltshire County Council v NATFHE* [1980] ICR 455, [1980] IRLR 198, CA.

1   *Brown v Knowsley Borough Council*, n. 13, above, is an extreme example of this.

agree to vary the agreed terms of the contract during its operation, provided that the variation is voluntary and without undue pressure on the employee[2]). Thus in *S W Strange Ltd v Mann*[3] the defendant was employed as the plaintiff company's manager under a contract which included a restraint clause, restricting his post-employment activities. After certain disagreements the parties agreed that the defendant should cease to be manager and instead take over the running of only one department. When he was eventually dismissed, the plaintiff tried to enforce the restraint clause, but the court held for the defendant on the ground, inter alia, that the original contract had been terminated by mutual consent, and the new contract which was entered did not contain the relevant clause. As with other common law concepts, however, 'mutual consent' gained renewed significance with the advent of the new statutory rights, often dependent upon continuity of the employment, and the fact of dismissal. While the concept of mutual consent in fact worked in the employee's favour in *Strange Ltd v Mann*, it would be more likely to jeopardise an employee's statutory rights if found too readily, for it could break continuity and provide the employer with an argument that there had in fact been no dismissal, only a voluntary parting of the ways. In *McAlwane v Boughton Estates*[4] an employee was given notice to terminate his employment on 19 April, but during the notice period he asked if he could leave on 12 April. The employer agreed, and, when the employee claimed a redundancy payment and unfair dismissal, argued that there was no dismissal because the contract had been terminated by mutual consent on 12 April. The NIRC rejected this argument, holding that this merely constituted an agreed variation of the notice period, so that the employee was still dismissed by the employer. Sir John Donaldson P said:

'We would further suggest that it would be a very rare case indeed in which it could properly be found that the employer and the employee had got together and, notwithstanding that there was a current notice of termination of the employment, agreed mutually to terminate the contract, particularly when one realises the financial consequences to the employee involved in such an agreement. We do not say that such arrangement cannot arise; we merely say that, viewed in a real life situation, it would seem to be a possibility which might appeal to a lawyer more than to a personnel manager[5] .'

This decision, and this dictum in particular, was applied by the Court of Appeal (by a majority) in *Lees v Arthur Greaves Ltd*[6] where, on similar facts, it was once again held that there was no termination by mutual consent.

Mutual consent will therefore be difficult to establish, particularly in a statutory context; this is particularly so in an unfair dismissal action, for the Employment Rights Act 1996, section 95(2) provides that where an employee under notice gives his employer notice that he wishes to leave before the expiry of the employer's notice, the employee is deemed still to have been dismissed by the employer for unfair dismissal purposes. The applicants in *McAlwane* and *Lees*

2   *Marriott v Oxford and District Co-operative Society Ltd (No 2)* [1970] 1 QB 186, [1969] 3 All ER 1126, CA.
3   [1965] 1 All ER 1069, [1965] 1 WLR 629; cf. *Cowey v Liberian Operations Ltd* [1966] 2 Lloyd's Rep 45.
4   [1973] 2 All ER 299, [1973] ICR 470.
5   [1973] 2 All ER 299 at 302, [1973] ICR 470 at 473.
6   [1974] 2 All ER 393, [1974] ICR 501, CA. See also *Glacier Metal Co Ltd v Dyer* [1974] 3 All ER 21, [1974] IRLR 189.

could not rely upon the equivalent provisions in the legislation at the time[7] since they then required *written* notice by the employee, and this had not been given. The requirement of writing was deleted for unfair dismissal purposes by the Employment Protection Act 1975, but not for redundancy purposes where it is still required[8]. However, termination by mutual consent does remain a possibility as can be seen from *Lipton Ltd v Marlborough*[9] where an employee, faced with the loss of his job on a reorganisation, began to look for other employment, but was hindered by his contract which required him to give six months' notice and contained a restraint of trade clause. During negotiations he requested that he be released from his contract immediately and the employer agreed. When he later claimed unfair dismissal the tribunal found that he had been constructively dismissed (on the basis that the employer intended to phase out his job), but the EAT allowed the employer's appeal and held that this was a termination by mutual agreement, not a dismissal, Bristow J stating:

> 'The whole difference between termination by mutual agreement in this context and constructive dismissal is that in the first case the employee says "Please may I go?" and the employer says "Yes". In the second case the employee says "You have treated me in such a way that I'm going without a by-your-leave".'

Such a case will, however, remain a rarity (either in the specific context of a cross-notice to end employment or more generally) and the fact that the employee did not object to his own dismissal (e.g. on an agreed redundancy) will not normally prevent it from still being a dismissal[10]; the usual narrow approach was reaffirmed by the EAT in *Tracey v Zest Equipment Co Ltd*[11] where termination of employment following a failure to return on time from holiday (when the employee, who had been late back before, had agreed beforehand that his employment would be terminated in the event of lateness) was held not to have been terminated by mutual consent, but rather to have been repudiatory conduct leading to dismissal, thus allowing the tribunal to consider the substantive question of fairness.

As against that, termination by mutual consent was subsequently found by the Court of Appeal in *Birch v University of Liverpool*[12] in the case of two academics taking early retirement under a scheme adopted by universities and their relevant unions. The facts were exceptional in that the scheme required a high degree of mutual agreement and clearly envisaged that statutory redundancy payments (which the two applicants were now claiming) would *not* be payable on top; the case does, however, show an important potential application of the idea of mutual consent in modern circumstances particularly where, as Ackner LJ pointed out, the employer calls for resignations well in advance of decreases in the workforce, there is no compulsion and the employer offers financial inducements well in

---

7   Industrial Relations Act 1971, s. 23(3) (later the Trade Union and Labour Relations Act 1974, Sch. 1, para. 5(3)) and the Redundancy Payments Act 1965, s. 4(2).

8   ERA 1996, s. 136(3).

9   [1979] IRLR 179.

10 *Burton, Allton and Johnson Ltd v Peck* [1975] ICR 193, [1975] IRLR 87; cf. however *Birch v University of Liverpool* [1985] ICR 470, [1985] IRLR 165, CA, below.

11 [1982] ICR 481, [1982] IRLR 268. The case is in line with the restrictive approach taken at the same time to the analogous area of 'constructive resignation' or 'self dismissal', as seen in *London Transport Executive v Clarke* [1981] ICR 355, [1981] IRLR 166, CA (see below) which is cited in the judgment of the EAT.

12 [1985] ICR 470, [1985] IRLR 165, CA, distinguishing *Burton, Allton & Johnson Ltd v Peck*, n. 12 above; noted Freedland (1985) 14 ILJ 243.

excess of what would be payable under the ordinary redundancy payments scheme. The decision in *Birch* was taken one step further by the EAT in *Scott v Coalite Fuels and Chemicals Ltd*[13] where it was held that there was mutual termination where employees took voluntary early retirement while already under notice of dismissal for redundancy. While such a decision may make good industrial sense in a case where early retirement (with a lump-sum payment, but a reduced weekly pension) is negotiated as an *alternative* to redundancy, it does call into question the dictum of Sir John Donaldson cited at the beginning of this section that mutual termination during a current notice period would only be found in 'a very rare case indeed'. Perhaps cases involving genuine early retirement schemes should be treated as sui generis.

2   DISMISSAL BY NOTICE

Most contracts of employment may be terminated by either party giving the necessary notice of termination. The period of notice may be agreed expressly by the parties[14] and, more unusually, the parties may agree to restrict the reasons behind the giving of notice[15]. More usually, however, the right to give notice will not be so restricted and only the mechanics of the period to be given will be laid down. If there is no such express provision, and no term can be ascertained from custom or trade usage[16], the law will read into a contract of employment that it is terminable upon 'reasonable notice'. It may then be a litigious matter to quantify what is reasonable; as this is a matter of construction of the contract it has in the past been within the jurisdiction of the civil courts, but it could now be raised in proceedings before tribunals, under their common law jurisdiction on termination of employment[17]. There are many reported cases on this question of quantification and all that can be said is that each case must depend upon its own facts such as the position of the employee within the firm, his or her professional standing and, in some cases, the intervals for payment[18]. To be effective (since it has such a drastic effect) the notice must be definite and explicit. Thus in *Morris v Bailey*[19] it was held that a notice of termination given to the plaintiff's union but not to him personally was not effective to dismiss him, even though most of his contract of employment (including the notice provisions) consisted of terms

13   [1988] ICR 355, [1988] IRLR 131 (see also *Logan Salton v Durham County Council* [1989] IRLR 99, where an employee under threat of disciplinary proceedings negotiated severance terms and was held to them). It remains the case, however, that there will still be a dismissal (even if in form there appears to be mutual agreement) if either (a) all that the employee has done is to volunteer to be dismissed for redundancy, or (b) there has been pressure put on the employee to agree to go (see p. 451, below).
14   Written particulars of the notice period should be given to the employee within two months of commencement: Employment Rights Act, s. 1(4)(e).
15   *McClelland v Northern Ireland General Health Services Board* [1957] 2 All ER 129, [1957] 1 WLR 594, HL. It has been held that there is an *implied* restriction on giving notice to a long-term sick employee where there is a permanent health insurance scheme in operation under the contract; see p. 128, above.
16   *George v Davies* [1911] 2 KB 445.
17   See p. 433, below.
18   Thus in *Grundy v Sun Printing and Publishing Association* (1916) 33 TLR 77, CA, an editor was entitled to 12 months' notice, but in *Fox-Bourne v Vernon & Co Ltd* (1894) 10 TLR 647 another editor was only entitled to six months. For a more modern example of this process of quantification, see *Hill v CA Parsons & Co Ltd* [1972] Ch 305, [1971] 3 All ER 1345, CA.
19   [1969] 2 Lloyd's Rep 215, CA.

incorporated from the union's collective agreement. Moreover, the details of the notice that is to be given must be made known to the employee, so that a mere warning of impending dismissal (e.g. for redundancy) will not constitute notice[20]. However, once an effective notice has been given by one of the parties, he may not withdraw it unilaterally, and so withdrawal of the notice may only be by mutual consent[1].

Under the common law of employment, the availability to the employer of dismissal by notice could in practice negate what rights an employee might have; for example, an employee might be justified in refusing to obey an order which was illegal or outside the scope of his employment and the employer could not summarily dismiss him for that refusal, but there was nothing to stop the employer from giving him notice because of the incident, since a dismissal on proper notice was lawful regardless of the motive behind it. If the notice period was only a matter of days or even hours, that could be a powerful threat to the employee. This position is now heavily overlaid by the statutory provisions as to redundancy and unfair dismissal (particularly as the latter entails scrutiny of the merits of the dismissal, not just its technical correctness), but the question of notice was first affected by statute in the Contracts of Employment Act 1963[2] which attempted to alter the common law in two ways – first, by gearing the period of notice to the length of continuous service, not simply to the status of the employee; second, by safeguarding certain employee rights during the period of notice. The present provisions relating to these two points will now be considered.

The common law rules proved to be inadequate in that they made no distinction for the long-serving employee. Thus an employee on a weekly contract would only be entitled to a week's notice whether he worked for his employer for one week or forty years. Large scale redundancies emphasised this defect, and certain minimum notice periods are now laid down by statute. Under the Employment Rights Act 1996, section 86, the minimum notice period for an employee with under two years continuous employment[3] is one week; where there is over two years' continuous employment, the employee is entitled to one week's notice for each year up to a maximum of 12 weeks. As for the employee, the statutory minimum which he must give to terminate his employment is one week if he has been employed for four weeks or more. The section states that it does not affect the right of either party to terminate the contract through the other party's conduct, and does not prevent either party from waiving his right to notice on any particular occasion[4]. Sub-section (3) also states that the section does not prevent a party from accepting a payment in lieu of notice[5]. 'Wages in lieu' is a common

20 *Morton Sundour Fabrics Ltd v Shaw* (1966) 2 ITR 84; *Pritchard-Rhodes Ltd v Boon and Milton* [1979] IRLR 19; *International Computers Ltd v Kennedy* [1981] IRLR 28; *Doble v Firestone Tyre and Rubber Co Ltd* [1981] IRLR 300; *Haseltine Lake & Co v Dowler* [1981] ICR 222, [1981] IRLR 25. This is particularly important in the context of the giving of counter-notice by an employee, for the purposes of redundancy law; see p. 521, below.

1 *Riordan v War Office* [1959] 3 All ER 552, [1959] 1 WLR 1059 (affd [1960] 3 All ER 774n, [1961] 1 WLR 210, CA); *Harris and Russell Ltd v Slingsby* [1973] 3 All ER 31, [1973] ICR 454.

2 Later the Contracts of Employment Act 1972, and now to be found in the Employment Rights Act 1996, ss. 86–91.

3 The right to the minimum of one week does not apply to a casual worker taken on to perform a specific task for less than three months: Employment Rights Act 1996, s. 86(5).

4 Waiver of notice includes waiver of any right to payment for the notice period (especially in a voluntary severance case): *Trotter v Forth Ports Authority* [1991] IRLR 419, Ct of Sess; *Baldwin v British Coal Corpn* [1995] IRLR 139.

5 *Staffordshire County Council v Secretary of State for Employment* [1987] ICR 956, [1988] IRLR 3 (reversed on other grounds, [1989] ICR 664, [1989] IRLR 117, CA).

phenomenon, whereby the employer gives the employee the wages which he would have earned during the notice period, and instructs him not to work out the notice period, so that the employer is rid of him immediately. This is perfectly lawful if both parties agree to it, and this is as far as the subsection goes. One contentious point, however, is whether the employer has a *right* to give wages in lieu if the employee wishes to work out the notice period. The old tenet of employment law that the employer's only obligation is to provide wages, not work, suggested that dismissal with wages in lieu would be lawful[6], except in one of the exceptional cases where work also had to be provided[7]. However, the more modern approach has been to look more closely at *how* the dismissal is effected. The renewed interest in this point is not because of its direct effect on wrongful dismissal (since, even if the dismissal is wrongful, the prima facie measure of damages, the wages themselves, have already been paid[8]), but rather because of four incidental matters which may be affected – (1) whether the protection against unlawful deductions in Part II of the Employment Rights Act 1996 applies to any non-payment of the wages[9]; (2) what is the effective date of termination of the dismissal[10]; (3) whether any restraint of trade clause in the contract survives the termination[11]; (4) whether an employee deprived of the qualifying period for unfair dismissal by a instant dismissal just before reaching it can claim loss of compensation for unfair dismissal in a wrongful dismissal action[12]. In *Delaney v Staples*[13], the leading case on deductions from wages, Lord Browne-Wilkinson analysed the law on dismissal with wages in lieu; adopting his classification, the position in relation to the above matters appears to be as follows.

(i)   The employer gives the employee proper notice, but then tells him that he need not work it out; in such a case (including a 'garden leave' case) the dismissal is lawful, with advance payment of 'wages', the effective date of termination is the end of the notice period, and any restraint clause may continue to apply.

(ii)   The contract itself provides for termination by notice *or* by wages in lieu; here, the dismissal is lawful, the payment is not 'wages' for the purposes of Part II of the 1996 Act (because not paid under a subsisting contract of employment), the effective date of termination is the date the wages in lieu

---

6   *Konski v Peet* [1915] 1 Ch 530.

7   See p. 120, above. This point was particularly taken up (in the context of garden leave) in *William Hill Organisation Ltd v Tucker* [1998] IRLR 313, CA which showed a broader approach to who can claim an interest in having the work itself provided.

8   Though it can still affect whether the nature of the employee's right is damages or *debt* (in which case there is no obligation to mitigate loss, and so earnings in new employment need not be taken into account): *Gregory v Wallace* [1998] IRLR 387, CA.

9   If it does, the ex-employee may challenge any non-payment (total or partial) of the wages in lieu before an employment tribunal, instead of before the ordinary courts; see p. 213, above.

10 See p. 453, below. This is relevant because (a) by that date the employee must have the necessary qualifying service and (b) the three-month time limit for claiming unfair dismissal flows from that date. It is thus in the employer's interest to have the EDT early, i.e. when the employment actually ends, not the (later) date on which notice would notionally have expired.

11 If the dismissal is wrongful, the restraint clause falls; see p. 104, above.

12 See p. 393, below; if there is an express wages in lieu clause, the instant termination is not wrongful and so no damages can be claimed, even though the employee has still lost the unfair dismissal rights: *Morran v Glasgow Council of Tenants' Associations* [1998] IRLR 67, Ct of Sess.

13 [1992] ICR 483, [1992] IRLR 191, HL.

are given (*not* the end of the period of notice) and any restraint clause may continue to apply[14].

(iii) At the end of the employment, the employer and employee agree ad hoc that it will end forthwith, on the payment of the sum in lieu; the results here are as in (ii), it being a lawful variation of the normal notice term.

(iv) The employer summarily dismisses the employee, without his agreement, but tenders a payment in lieu of notice; here, the employer is in breach of contract and so the dismissal is wrongful, which means that the payment is *damages*, not 'wages' (but they extinguish any *claim* for damages), the effective date of termination remains the date of the summary dismissal and payment in lieu, *but* any restraint of trade clause now becomes invalid because of the wrongful dismissal.

From this analysis, it can be seen that the employer now has much to gain from putting into the contract of employment a term expressly permitting dismissal with wages in lieu, since it provides the optimum position of a lawful dismissal, no challenge to the payment in tribunal proceedings, an early effective date of termination and the preservation of any restraint of trade clause. From the employee's point of view, the existence of an express payment in lieu clause is both advantageous and disadvantageous. On the positive side, as the dismissal is lawful, the employee may claim any unpaid wages in lieu as a debt due under the contract, not as damages for breach of it; this means that the employee is not under a duty to mitigate his loss, which may be of particular importance for a highly paid employee on long notice, who has obtained new employment during what would have been the notice period but who does *not* have to bring those new (equally high?) earnings into account, and so may receive and retain both sums of money in full[15]. On the negative side, however, the fact that the payment in lieu is contractual means that the amount paid is taxable in the employee's hands, since it cannot be construed as 'damages' and hence not subject to income tax (as remains the case with a non-contractual payment, under head (iv) above).[16]

In addition to laying down minimum periods of notice, the legislation also safeguards certain employee rights during the period of notice[17], though it should be noted that these provisions do not apply where the notice to be given by the employer under the contract is more than a week longer than the statutory minimum as laid down in section 86[18]. These provisions differ slightly, depending upon whether or not the employee who is under notice works 'normal working hours'. The construction of that phrase is therefore important, and essentially the test is whether the contract of employment lays down a certain or minimum

---

14 *Rex Stewart Jeffries Parker Ginsberg Ltd v Parker* [1988] IRLR 483, CA, explaining the earlier decision in *Dixon v Stenor Ltd* [1973] ICR 157, [1973] IRLR 28.

15 *Abrahams v Performing Right Society* [1995] ICR 1028, [1995] IRLR 486, CA. This case also contains some extremely dubious dicta, to the effect that even if the dismissal had been unlawful (i.e. under category (iv)) there would still have been no duty to mitigate; this is contrary to established principle (on mitigation, see p. 394, below), contrary to the speech of Lord Browne-Wilkinson in *Delaney v Staples* (n. 13 above, at pp. 493, 194), contrary to dicta in the earlier House of Lords case of *Westwood v Secretary of State for Employment* [1985] ICR 209, [1984] IRLR 209 where mitigation was in issue (see particularly per Lord Bridge at pp. 219, 211), and best tactfully forgotten. It was discretely ignored subsequently in *Gregory v Wallace* [1998] IRLR 387, CA. According to *Cerberus Software Ltd v Rowley* [1999] IRLR 690 where there is an in lieu clause but the employer refuses to pay under it, the employee can sue either in debt *or* for breach of the in lieu clause, and in *neither* case does mitigation apply.

16 *EMI Group Electronics Ltd v Coldicott* [1999] IRLR 630, [1999] STC 803, CA.

17 Employment Rights Act 1996, ss. 87-91.

18 Ibid., s. 87(4).

number of hours which the employee must work; if so, he works 'normal working hours'. Prima facie this might be expected to be exclusive of overtime, but under section 234(3) of the 1996 Act some overtime may count if it is included in the number of hours which the employee must work (e.g. if he is contractually bound to work forty hours per week, and overtime rates begin to be payable after 37 hours, then that is still normal working hours of 40 per week); to qualify under this extension, however, the overtime must be compulsory in the sense of being obligatory for the employee and guaranteed by the employer[19]. Where the employee works normal working hours and actually works during the notice period he will be contractually entitled to the correct payment without assistance from the legislation but section 88(1) ensures that he continues to be paid at the relevant rate for any periods when (a) he is ready and willing to work but the employer has no work for him, (b) he is incapable of work through sickness or injury, or (c) he is away on proper holiday; it is provided[20] that where the employee draws sickness or industrial injury benefit that is to be taken into account in computing the employer's liability to him, since otherwise he might be doubly entitled, through drawing the benefit and receiving full pay from the employer. Where the employee does not work normal working hours, the employer must pay him a week's pay (calculated in accordance with Part XIV of the 1996 Act[1]) for each week of the period of notice, provided that he is ready and willing to do work of a reasonable nature and amount to earn it; once again, the employee is specifically entitled to payment during absence through sickness or injury, or whilst on proper holiday. The legislation contains three main qualifications upon these rights to payment:

a) the employee is not entitled to be paid during time off which he has requested (including time off governed by statute[2]);

b) if the employee breaks the contract during the period of notice and is justifiably summarily dismissed, he is not entitled to further payment as from that dismissal;

c) if it is the employee who has given notice and he goes on strike during the notice period, he is not entitled to payment under these provisions at all; where it is the employer who has given notice this qualification does not apply, so that the employee will be contractually entitled to payment for that part of the notice period when he was not on strike[3].

If an employer fails to give the statutory notice, the rights laid down in these provisions are to be taken into account in assessing damages, and it is further provided that if the employer breaks the contract of employment during the period of notice (e.g. by wrongfully terminating it summarily) the benefits that

---

19 See, in the context of the *computation* of the number of normal working hours *Tarmac Roadstone Holdings Ltd v Peacock* [1973] 2 All ER 485, [1973] ICR 273, CA, applied to the present context of the *definition* of normal working hours in *Fox v C Wright (Farmers) Ltd* [1978] ICR 98. The questions of 'normal working hours' and what constitutes 'a week's pay' are discussed at p. 187, above.

20 Employment Rights Act 1996, s. 90. The rationale behind this was queried by Dillon LJ in *Notcutt v Universal Equipment Co (London) Ltd* [1986] ICR 414, [1986] IRLR 218, CA, since it may mean paying sick pay during notice to an employee not normally entitled to it; however, as the court held that the contract was frustrated by the sickness the matter did not arise.

1 This calculation is considered at p. 189, above.

2 Employment Rights Act 1996, Part VI; Trade Union and Labour Relations (Consolidation) Act 1992 ss. 168, 170.

3 For the effect on redundancy entitlements of a strike during the notice period, see the 1996 Act, ss. 140 and 143.

the employee will receive anyway under these provisions are to go towards mitigating any damages payable to the employee[4].

One final point to notice on the common law doctrine of notice is that it has increasingly been used by employers to safeguard trade secrets or (in businesses which are highly reliant on skilled employees) to prevent head-hunting by other firms, by the incorporation into sensitive contracts of employment of 'garden leave' clauses. These provide for long periods of notice on either side, during which the employee will be remunerated in full but not necessarily required to work. Thus, an employee wishing to leave may be required to give, say, six months' or a year's notice during which (provided the employer pays him his full entitlement to wages and benefits) he continues to be subject to the implied term not to compete or breach confidence[5], or even to an express term to like effect. Compared with the traditional restraint of trade clause[6], this is expensive *but* it is probably more reliable since restraint clauses are notoriously difficult to draft and enforce. In an appropriate case, a garden leave clause may be enforced by injunction[7], but it must be remembered that ultimately an injunction is a discretionary remedy and may be refused by a court if it appears that the clause is unconscionable as, for example, if there is little or no chance of the employer suffering actual damage if the employee does take up a particular new job (albeit in breach of the clause)[8]. Moreover, the efficacy of garden leave clauses generally may now be subject to some limitation because of the decision of the Court of Appeal in *William Hill Organisation Ltd v Tucker*[9]; the ratio of the case is that a court will not *imply* a garden leave clause in any case where it is arguable that the employee has an interest in doing the work not just receiving payment[10], and to this extent it is unexceptionable (merely stressing the advantage of an express term) but at the end of the judgment Morritt LJ said obiter that it should not be too readily assumed that a garden leave clause will succeed where a restraint clause might fail; he said that:

> 'if injunctive relief was sought then it had to be justified on similar grounds to those necessary to the validity of the employee's covenant in restraint of trade. The court should be careful not to grant interlocutory relief to enforce a garden leave clause to any greater extent than would be covered by a justifiable covenant in restraint of trade previously entered into by an employee'.

4   Employment Rights Act 1996, s. 91(5).
5   See p. 136, above.
6   See p. 96, above. It is possible to have both a garden leave clause and (then) a restraint of trade clause in a contract, though a court would need to consider the reasonableness of them taken together: *Crédit Suisse Asset Management Ltd v Armstrong* [1996] ICR 882, [1996] IRLR 450, CA.
7   *Evening Standard Co Ltd v Henderson* [1987] ICR 588, [1987] IRLR 64, CA (clause requiring a year's notice enforced to prevent a newspaper production manager from taking up employment during that time with a new newspaper venture, the employers undertaking to pay in full during the year); *Euro Brokers Ltd v Rabey* [1995] IRLR 206 (six-month garden leave clause enforced against a money broker wishing to move to a competitor firm); see Freedland (1989) 18 ILJ 112 and Gouldring 'Injunctions and contracts of employment: the *Evening Standard* doctrine' (1990) 19 ILJ 98.
8   *Provident Financial Group plc v Hayward* [1989] ICR 160, [1989] IRLR 84, CA (injunction to restrain financial director from taking up new employment towards the end of a long notice period refused because there was little evidence of any actual detriment to the employers).
9   [1998] IRLR 313, CA.
10   For this aspect of the case, see p. 121, above.

This may mean that in future there may be more emphasis on the *extent* of the garden leave, what interests it is protecting, and a tougher line on severing or reducing an unreasonably wide clause[11]. Further developments in this area will be important.

3 DISMISSAL FOR CAUSE

At common law an employer may dismiss an employee summarily (i.e. without notice) if he has sufficient cause to do so. In old cases, from the nineteenth century and before, this was viewed as a natural and necessary aspect of the relationship between master and man, and the servant's duty of obedience. The judgment of Parke B in *Callo v Brouncker*[12] was treated for many years as laying down set rules on summary dismissal which, he said, could be for moral misconduct (pecuniary or otherwise), wilful disobedience or habitual neglect. However, with the move in the nineteenth century towards viewing employment in a contractual light, the emphasis changed so that the right to dismiss summarily became explicable on the ground that the conduct of the employee was such that it showed a repudiation by him of the contract of employment which the employer then accepted and treated as terminating the contract immediately[13]. In *Laws v London Chronicle (Indicator Newspapers) Ltd*[14], Lord Evershed MR said:

'... the proper conclusion ... is that, since a contract of service is but an example of contracts in general, so that the general law of contract will be applicable, it follows that the question must be – if summary dismissal is claimed to be justifiable – whether the conduct complained of is such as to show the servant to have disregarded the essential conditions of the contract of service.'

This will apply as a general principle, not just to the particular categories listed by Parke B, but to any context in which the employee's conduct is sufficiently grave as to be repudiatory, so that, for example, an employee may be summarily dismissed for going on strike[15]. The principal effect of this contractual approach is that every case must be viewed on its own facts to determine whether the conduct in question was grave enough, and the question is not to be solved by searching for absolute rules covering each particular context (with the result that decided cases may be of little or no assistance). Thus:

---

11 For example, in *GFI Group Inc v Eaglestone* [1994] IRLR 119 on over-long garden leave clause was saved by being reduced in length by the court (and then enforced for that shorter period), but this is just what a court will *not* normally do with a restraint clause which usually has to stand or fall as originally drafted.
12 (1831) 4 C & P 518.
13 *Boston Deep Sea Fishing and Ice Co v Ansell* (1888) 39 Ch D 339, CA, particularly per Bowen LJ at 364–5; *Laws v London Chronicle (Indicator Newspapers) Ltd* [1959] 2 All ER 285, [1959] 1 WLR 698, CA; *Pepper v Webb* [1969] 2 All ER 216, [1969] 1 WLR 514, CA.
14 [1959] 2 All ER 285 at 287, [1959] 1 WLR 698 at 700.
15 *Simmons v Hoover Ltd* [1977] 1 All ER 775, [1977] ICR 61, not following the distinction between those strikes with and those without strike notice drawn in *Morgan v Fry* [1968] 2 QB 710, [1968] 3 All ER 452, CA; the common law position on strikes is now considerably affected by statute.

'... the true question is whether the acts and conduct of the party evince an intention no longer to be bound by the contract[16].'

'... in every case the question of repudiation must depend on the character of the contract, the number and weight of the wrongful acts or assertions, the intentions indicated by such acts and words, the deliberation or otherwise with which they are committed or uttered and on the general circumstances of the case[17].'

Much will therefore depend upon the context and the nature of the reason, so that for example, a relatively minor instance of dishonesty may warrant summary dismissal, particularly if the employee's job involves dealing with money[18], whereas mere negligence may in most cases be amenable only to dismissal by notice and a summary dismissal may be wrongful[19], unless there are other particular factors, such as endangering life by neglect[20]. Also, while an employer may not be justified in dismissing summarily for a single 'offence', a previous history of similar transgressions, even if not as serious as the one leading to dismissal, may be important evidence in the employer's favour[1]. Any particular case should also be viewed with a certain amount of realism, so that in *Jupiter General Insurance Co Ltd v Shroff*[2] the Privy Council said:

'Their Lordships would be very loath to assent to the view that a single outbreak of bad temper, accompanied, it may be, by regrettable language, is sufficient ground for dismissal. Sir John Beaumont CJ [in the court below] was stating a proposition of mere good sense when he observed that in such cases we must apply the standard of men and not angels and remember that men are apt to show temper when reprimanded.'

The court went on to make two observations which might be borne in mind. The first was that summary dismissal is a strong measure justified only in exceptional circumstances; the second was that the test to be applied in determining whether a dismissal was justified must vary with the nature of the business and the position held by the employee and that decisions in other cases are of little value. This variable approach can also be seen more recently in *Neary v Dean of Westminster*[3] where ideas taken from the modern law on the implied term of trust and respect were also introduced, looking at whether the employee's conduct was such as to undermine completely that element of the employment relationship. In the light of all these factors (and particularly the number of old or very old cases on

16   *Freeth v Burr* (1874) LR 9 CP 208 at 213, per Lord Coleridge CJ, applied by the House of Lords in *General Billposting Co Ltd v Atkinson* [1909] AC 118, HL.
17   *Re Rubel Bronze and Metal Co and Vos* [1918] 1 KB 315 at 322 per McCardie J.
18   *Sinclair v Neighbour* [1967] 2 QB 279, [1966] 3 All ER 988, CA.
19   See e.g. *Gould v Webb* (1855) 4 E & B 933.
20   It has been held, however, that the court should look primarily at the negligent act, and not at the consequences which flowed from it, as the latter could be too harsh and involve too much hindsight: *Savage v British India Steam Navigation Co Ltd* (1930) 46 TLR 294.
1   See e.g. *Clouston & Co Ltd v Corry* [1906] AC 122, PC (intoxication); *Pepper v Webb* [1969] 2 All ER 216, [1969] 1 WLR 514, CA (unsatisfactory work), discussed in *Wilson v Racher* [1974] ICR 428 [1974] IRLR 114, CA.
2   [1937] 3 All ER 67, PC.
3   [1999] IRLR 288 (Lord Jauncey, sitting as a Special Commissioner for the Visitor to Westminster Abbey).

the subject), another important factor may be changing attitudes, modes of organisation or *mores* in general. Thus in *Wilson v Racher*[4], Edmund Davies LJ said:

'Reported decisions provide useful, but only general guides, each case turning upon its own facts. Many of the decisions which are customarily cited in these cases date from the last century and may be wholly out of accord with the current social conditions. What would today be regarded as almost an attitude of Czar-serf, which is to be found in some of the older cases where a dismissed employee failed to recover damages would, I venture to think, be decided differently today.'

A good example of responsiveness to new needs is the decision in *Denco Ltd v Joinson*[5] that almost any form of deliberate computer misuse during employment will justify summary dismissal.

The advent of the modern statutory rights for employees has of course had an effect on summary dismissal, but usually indirectly, since the presence or absence of notice is a procedural matter and as such only of paramount importance in a common law action for wrongful dismissal; the statutory action for unfair dismissal requires an examination of the substantive fairness of the dismissal, and so any question of the presence or absence of notice will be of secondary importance. Under the legislation, the employer is not deprived of his right to dismiss summarily, and the continuance of this common law concept is clearly envisaged in the Employment Rights Act 1996, section 86(6) (rights to minimum periods of notice not to affect cases where summary termination is justified) and the ACAS Code of Practice, 'Disciplinary and grievance procedures'[6]. However, the existence of the unfair dismissal legislation is likely to make employers more wary of dismissing summarily and may perhaps make them more likely to punish misconduct by action short of dismissal (e.g. suspension) or by dismissal by notice after exhausting a set procedure of warnings and a hearing; this might particularly be the case where the ground for dismissal is incompetence or negligence. The absence of notice would not per se make the dismissal unfair[7], but might sway the tribunal against the employer on the question whether he acted reasonably. Also, the employer might be mindful of paragraph 9(xi) of the Code of Practice which states that a disciplinary procedure should 'ensure that, except for gross misconduct, no employees are dismissed for a first breach of conduct' – this applies to *any* dismissal, whether with or without notice, and shows that the modern emphasis is generally against hasty action on dismissal, even if summary dismissal may still be justified in certain extreme cases. Moreover, the advent of the unfair dismissal action has placed new emphasis on *procedures* and so an employer might be advised to exercise his rights to dismiss summarily in the light of modern personnel management techniques, in particular the desirability of such matters as laying down in the company's rules what conduct may warrant summary dismissal, ensuring that the decision to dismiss is taken at a reasonably high level (certainly higher than immediate superiors), and providing for an appeal structure[8].

4   [1974] ICR 428, [1974] IRLR 114, CA.
5   [1991] ICR 172, [1991] IRLR 63; see Napier 'Computerisation and Employment Rights' (1992) 21 ILJ 1.
6   Particularly para. 7.
7   *Treganowan v Robert Knee & Co Ltd* [1975] ICR 405, [1975] IRLR 247; *BSC Sports and Social Club v Morgan* [1987] IRLR 391. See the discussion of the different bases for wrongful and unfair dismissal in the judgment of Judge Clark in *Farrant v Woodroffe School* [1998] ICR 184, [1998] IRLR 176.
8   Code of Practice paras. 7, 9(vii) and 9(xiv) respectively.

The common law on dismissal for cause is thus heavily qualified by statute and the modern statutory provisions owe little to the existing common law rules. For example, at common law a dismissal would be lawful if the employer acted on reason A which was quite inadequate, but later found out about reason B which could in fact justify dismissal[9], but under the unfair dismissal legislation the relevant reason is the one upon which the employer acted at the time of dismissal, and not anything that he only discovered later[10]. Moreover, at common law there was no obligation upon the employer to give his reasons, but under the Employment Rights Act 1996, section 92, an employee with one year's continuous service has a statutory right to be provided with a written statement giving particulars of the reasons for his dismissal[11].

4   WRONGFUL DISMISSAL

i)   Meaning

As can be seen from the discussion above, the common law on dismissal looks basically at form, not at substance so that, except in the case of a purported dismissal for cause, the concept of wrongful dismissal is essentially procedural and largely dependent upon the actual terms of the contract in question. Thus, if a contract is for a fixed term, or expressly stated to be terminable only in certain ways[12], and it is terminated before the term expires or in an improper way, that may be a wrongful dismissal. More typical, however, is the case where the employer dismissed the employee with no or inadequate notice, or purported to dismiss him for cause where the facts did not justify such action. This common law action for wrongful dismissal must therefore be kept separate from the statutory action for unfair dismissal which entails an examination of the substantive merits of the dismissal. For many years, there was also a formal split of forum, with a unfair dismissal claim going to an employment tribunal, but a wrongful dismissal claim having to go to the ordinary civil courts; since 1994, however, tribunals have been given jurisdiction over contractual claims on termination of employment[13], and so can hear a claim for wrongful dismissal (up to the statutory limit of £25,000).

ii)   Remedies

a)   The rule against enforcement

While the idea of wrongful dismissal is explicable on a contractual basis (i.e. that the employer has repudiated the contract by his actions), it is when one comes to

---

9   *Boston Deep Sea Fishing and Ice Co v Ansell* (1888) 39 Ch D 339, CA; *Cyril Leonard & Co v Simo Securities Trust Ltd* [1971] 3 All ER 1313, [1972] 1 WLR 80, CA.

10   *W Devis & Sons Ltd v Atkins* [1977] AC 931, [1977] 3 All ER 40, HL.

11   See p. 431, below.

12   This is rare in practice: *McClelland v Northern Ireland General Health Services Board* [1957] 2 All ER 129, [1957] 1 WLR 594, HL is an unusual example. In modern circumstances, it might arise if an employer agreed to a contractually binding 'no compulsory redundancy' deal; any redundancy dismissal during its currency would then be wrongful and arguably the damages should not be restricted (as is usual) to wages for the notice period, but should be for the rest of the period of the agreement, subject to mitigation and a discount for the possibility of lawful dismissal (i.e. on non-redundancy grounds) during that period.

13   Employment Tribunals (Extension of Jurisdiction) Orders 1994 (one order applying to England and Wales, another to Scotland); see p. 433, below.

the nature of the remedies open to the dismissed employee that the inadequacies of contract theory and, as a consequence, the practical ineffectiveness of the common law become obvious[14]. The starting point is the general principle that the courts will not enforce a contract of employment, either directly by specific performance or indirectly by injunction or any other means[15], the principal explanation being that the contract is of a personal nature, not amenable to enforcement. Thus, in *De Francesco v Barnum*[16] Fry LJ said:

'I should be very unwilling to extend decisions the effect of which is to compel persons who are not desirous of maintaining continuous personal relations with one another to continue those personal relations. I think the courts are bound to be jealous lest they should turn contracts of service into contracts of slavery; and ... I should lean against the extension of the doctrine of specific performance and injunction in such a manner.'

Moreover, this is now enshrined in statute as far as such an order against an employee is concerned, for the Trade Union and Labour Relations (Consolidation) Act 1992, section 236 provides that no court shall issue an order compelling an employee to do any work or attend at any place for the doing of any work. This sentiment has been applied by the courts equally to cases where the order is sought against the employer, who may not be made to continue employing a particular individual, and so at common law there has never been any general remedy of reinstatement. If an employee is wrongfully dismissed the general rule is that his remedy lies in damages[17].

Such a rule (of automatic termination) may, or may not, make practical sense but it is difficult to explain in contractual terms, for in contract law a repudiation is usually of no effect unless accepted by the innocent party – '... an unaccepted repudiation is a thing writ in water and of no value to anybody'[18] – and so in theory an employee faced with wrongful dismissal should be entitled to refuse to accept this repudiation and insist on carrying on in the employment. This, however, used not to be the prevailing view and it was said that contracts of employment form an exceptional category in which the employee has no choice but to accept the repudiation and sue for damages, so that the employer's repudiation automatically terminates the contract[19]. Thus, for example in *Sanders v Ernest A Neale Ltd*[20] Sir John Donaldson P said:

'The obvious, and indeed the only, explanation is that the repudiation of a contract of employment is an exception to the general rule. It terminates the contract without the necessity for acceptance by the injured party.'

14 For an analysis of the difficult case law on remedies and possible developments, see Ewing 'Remedies for breach of the contract of employment' [1993] CLJ 405.
15 *Whitwood Chemical Co v Hardman* [1891] 2 Ch 416, CA. For a peculiar application of this on the facts (employee not seeking to continue his contract per se, but rather to continue to exercise his contractual rights as a shop steward in spite of being suspended), see *City and Hackney Health Authority v NUPE* [1985] IRLR 252, CA.
16 (1890) 45 Ch D 430 at 438.
17 Or, in an appropriate case, a quantum meruit action: *Planché v Colburn* (1831) 8 Bing 14.
18 *Howard v Pickford Tool Co Ltd* [1951] 1 KB 417 at 421, CA, per Asquith LJ. See *White and Carter (Councils) Ltd v McGregor* [1962] AC 413, [1961] 3 All ER 1178, HL.
19 *Denmark Productions Ltd v Boscobel Productions Ltd* [1969] 1 QB 699, [1968] 3 All ER 513, CA.
20 [1974] 3 All ER 327 at 333, [1974] ICR 565 at 571.

In *Vine v National Dock Labour Board*[1] a dismissal was held to be invalid on the peculiar facts of the case (considered below), but Viscount Kilmuir LC was at pains to point out that

'This is an entirely different situation from the ordinary master and servant case; there, if a master wrongfully dismisses the servant, either summarily or by insufficient notice, the employment is effectively terminated, albeit in breach of contract'

and he approved the decision of Jenkins LJ in the Court of Appeal[2] that

'... in the ordinary case of master and servant the repudiation or the wrongful dismissal puts an end to the contract, and the contract having been wrongfully put an end to a claim for damages arises. It is necessarily a claim for damages and nothing more. The nature of the bargain is such that it can be nothing more.'

On the other hand, this doctrine of automatic (or 'unilateral') termination was doubted in cases such as *Decro-Wall International SA v Practitioners in Marketing Ltd*[3], *Hill v CA Parsons & Co Ltd*[4] and *CH Giles & Co Ltd v Morris*[5]. This counter argument is that the rule against enforcement is not a rule of law, but only a question of fact (albeit frequently-recurring fact) in that in nearly all cases the basis of mutual confidence has been destroyed and it would be futile to keep the employment relationship in being. More recently this alternative doctrine of elective (or 'acceptance') termination has gained ground, with the result that in some cases it can be argued that the employee did not accept the employer's repudiation of the contract (although in most cases in practice such acceptance will be easy to infer). This can be seen in the judgment of Megarry V-C in *Thomas Marshall (Exports) Ltd v Guinle*[6], in the majority decision of the Court of Appeal in *Gunton v Richmond-upon-Thames London Borough Council*[7] and in the judgment of Hodgson J in *Dietman v Brent London Borough Council*[8]. In practice the difference in common law claims between the automatic and elective theories may not be great, for in *Gunton's* case the majority, having clearly decided in favour of the latter, went on to stress (a) that in most cases the employee will have no option in reality but to accept the employer's repudiation and seek a remedy in damages[9],

1   [1957] AC 488 at 500, [1956] 3 All ER 939 at 944, HL.
2   [1956] 1 QB 658 at 674, [1956] 1 All ER 1 at 8, CA.
3   [1971] 2 All ER 216, [1971] 1 WLR 361, CA, per Salmon and Sachs LJJ; aliter per Buckley LJ. The majority judgments are cogently criticised by Sir John Donaldson P in *Sanders v Ernest A Neale Ltd* [1974] 3 All ER 327, [1974] ICR 565.
4   [1972] Ch 305, [1971] 3 All ER 1345, CA, per Lord Denning MR and Sachs LJ. The more traditional view that there is a rule of law against enforcement is well set out in Stamp LJ's dissenting judgment at 322 and 1357 respectively.
5   [1972] 1 All ER 960 at 970, [1972] 1 WLR 307 at 318, per Megarry J.
6   [1978] 3 All ER 193, [1978] ICR 905.
7   [1980] ICR 755, [1980] IRLR 321, CA, per Buckley and Brightman LJJ. Shaw LJ dissented on the reasoning, adopting the automatic approach, but concurred in the result on the facts. The later decision of the Court of Appeal in *London Transport Executive v Clarke* [1981] ICR 355, [1981] IRLR 166, CA, though of fundamental importance on the statutory definition of dismissal, was ambiguous on this point of theory.
8   [1987] ICR 737, [1987] IRLR 259; upheld on appeal [1988] IRLR 299, CA.
9   See e.g. *Dietman v Brent London Borough Council* (n. 8, above) where the acceptance theory was applied, but the court found acceptance established on the facts fairly readily. In *Delaney v Staples* [1992] ICR 483, [1992] IRLR 191, at 489, 193, HL, Lord Browne-

and (b) that the rule of practice against specific enforcement of contracts of employment remains strong and may operate independently of the elective theory so that while, for some purposes[10], an employee may wish to argue that he did not accept the employer's repudiation, he will not normally be allowed to do so in order to claim specific performance (directly or indirectly). These severe limitations on the elective theory can be seen in *Gunton*'s case where the theory was invoked to attack the validity of a dismissal which had omitted proper observance of a contractually-binding disciplinary procedure, the plaintiff claiming that he never accepted this repudiation by the employer; to that extent it succeeded, but given that the employer could have dismissed lawfully by going through the procedure properly the court held that the normal rule on damages for wrongful dismissal applied and all that the plaintiff was entitled to was his wages until the date on which a proper dismissal could have been achieved after exhaustion of the procedure. The plaintiff thus succeeded in invalidating the original dismissal, but only obtained a short stay of execution and a few weeks' extra pay (representing the time it would have taken to exhaust the procedure). He certainly did not get his job back, though the elective theory would in theory help to allow room for an untypical case where a court might be persuaded to enforce a contract of employment (where the usual factors against enforcement do not apply) as in *Hill v CA Parsons & Co Ltd*, which is considered below. Moreover, swings continue to swing and roundabouts to turn; in *R v East Berkshire Health Authority, ex p Walsh*[11] in the Court of Appeal May LJ stated unequivocally that he preferred the dissenting judgment of Shaw LJ in *Gunton* and the automatic view, and Sir John Donaldson MR was clearly not ecstatic about the overruling by the majority in *Gunton* of his own previous decision in *Sanders v Ernest A Neale Ltd*[12], and in *Boyo v Lambeth London Borough Council*[13] the Court of Appeal applied the ratio of *Gunton* (to allow wages for a short extra period that it would have taken the employer to go through the contractual disciplinary procedure properly), but stated their unease at doing so, making it clear that they had grave doubts about the reasoning of the majority in that case.

The question of which theory (elective or automatic) is to be preferred remains at best undecided; in the context of common law claims it has the same intellectual fascination as the question as to how many angels may dance on the head of a pin and (except perhaps in a case where some collateral or incidental matter relies

---

Wilkinson spoke of an unequivocal instant (wrongful) dismissal being 'effective to put an end to the employment *relationship*, whether or not it unilaterally discharges the contract of employment'. Moreover, in *Marsh v National Autistic Society* [1993] ICR 453 it was held that, even if the elective theory is applied, the demise of the employment relationship will mean that the employee may not sue in debt for continuing wages, but will be confined to the (restricted) action for damages.

10 See e.g. the continued existence of the contractual term restricting the employee's activities during employment in *Thomas Marshall (Exports) Ltd v Guinle* (n. 6, above) in spite of the employee's wrongful resignation, the desire in *CH Giles & Co Ltd v Morris* (n. 5, above) to put the plaintiff into employment in the first place, if only so that his remedies would be better when then dismissed, and the (unsuccessful) attempt to enforce a shop steward's contractual right to enter the employer's premises in spite of being under suspension in *City and Hackney Health Authority v NUPE* [1985] IRLR 252, CA. More recently, there have been attempts to seek specific enforcement of contracts of employment in order to insist on disciplinary procedures being properly applied – see p. 389, below.

11 [1984] ICR 743, [1984] IRLR 278, CA.

12 N. 20, above.

13 [1994] ICR 727, [1995] IRLR 50, CA. Appearing in person, the employee (who was on a month's notice) had initially argued that, as he had not accepted the employer's repudiation, he was entitled to his wages up to the year 2000(!).

upon the technical continued existence of the contract) about as much practical relevance.

However, when one turns to the possible impact of these theories on statutory rights on dismissal, the picture becomes much more complicated, and in fact it is in the statutory context (usually of unfair dismissal) that most of the active dispute has arisen. One problem is that if the automatic theory is applied to the statutory definition of dismissal[14] it can support the idea of 'self dismissal', i.e. that if an employee misbehaves sufficiently badly he can be said to have repudiated his contract of employment, thus automatically terminating it; if this is so, there is no 'dismissal' by the employer and so the tribunal is denied jurisdiction to hear a claim of unfair dismissal. The elective theory in fact fits the statutory definition of dismissal much better, for if acceptance of a repudiation is required the termination of the misbehaving employee's contract is brought about by the employer's acceptance of the repudiation and *is* thus 'dismissal' by the employer[15]; on the other hand if the *employer* repudiates the contract, termination is brought about by the employee's acceptance, but this is specifically covered by statute which deems it to be a 'constructive dismissal'[16]. The *elective* theory is thus important for the actual definition of dismissal. However the second problem is that equal difficulties arise if one applies it to the *date* of dismissal. It is important to know precisely the date for the purpose of applying the stringent time limits in the statute (particularly the limitation period for starting an unfair dismissal action of three months from the 'effective date of termination'[17]), but if an employee could claim that he had in fact refused to accept the employer's repudiation he could argue that the time limit either never started to run or, at least, started to run at some time significantly later than the wording of the statutory definition of 'effective date of termination' would suggest. In the interests of certainty, therefore, it is important that the *automatic* theory be applied to questions of limitation.

One commentator has made a strong case for adopting this differential approach in the statutory context[18], and this now seems to be the position in practice – in *London Transport Executive v Clarke*[19] the Court of Appeal by a majority disapproved of the idea of 'self dismissal', applying the elective theory, whereas in *Brown v Southall and Knight*[20] and *Robert Cort & Son Ltd v Charman*[1] the EAT rejected arguments based upon that theory when determining the effective date of termination, preferring instead an automatic termination approach based on (a) the wording of the statutory definition of effective date of termination and (b) the need for certainty on this vital concept. As long as this practical compromise is maintained, the position now seems to be satisfactory, but if there were in the future any real danger of the reintroduction of the sort of uncertainty that existed prior to this case law (and which may still exist in the case of a common law claim), the time would surely be ripe for legislative clarification.

---

14 Contained in the Employment Rights Act, 1996, s. 95 (in relation to unfair dismissal) and s. 136 (in relation to redundancy).
15 Within ss. 95(1)(a) and 136(1)(a).
16 Within ss. 95(1)(c) and 136(1)(c); see p. 447, below.
17 See pp. 417-422, below.
18 J. McMullen in his very useful article 'A synthesis of the mode of termination of contracts of employment' [1982] CLJ 110.
19 [1981] ICR 355, [1981] IRLR 166, CA.
20 [1980] ICR 617, [1980] IRLR 130.
1 [1981] ICR 816, [1981] IRLR 437, approved by the Court of Appeal in *Stapp v Shaftesbury Society* [1982] IRLR 326, CA.

Returning to the common law position, and accepting that there is at least a rule of practice (if not an absolute rule of law) against enforcing contracts of employment in most cases, we must now consider certain establishment exceptions.

b)   Exceptions to the rule against enforcement

1)   *A negative restraint clause*   Where the employee has agreed in the contract not to do certain things (e.g. not to perform for any other theatre owner during the currency of the contract, or not to work for a competitor within a certain period after leaving the employment[2]), the court will hold him to his promise and enforce that negative stipulation (even if it would not enforce the positive obligations in the contract)[3]. It is immaterial that this may indirectly persuade the employee to remain in the employment (i.e. that it may have indirectly a positive effect), but on the other hand it is well established that the clause must be bona fide, in particular that it must not be in reality a positive obligation merely expressed in a negative way[4]. Moreover, an injunction will not be granted if the practical effect would be to compel the employee to perform his side of the contract or starve (e.g. where the stipulation is that he will not take *any* employment for a period after leaving the employment)[5].

2)   *Where the dismissal is a nullity*   In certain restricted cases, a dismissed employee may be able to invoke certain administrative law remedies to argue that his dismissal was invalid; if this is accepted, the legal result is that there was no effective dismissal, and so the contract of employment will be indirectly enforced. The two principal bases for challenge are that the dismissal was contrary to the rules of natural justice or was in some way ultra vires[6]. There has been considerable case law on this question, though in the modern case law the emphasis has switched to consideration of how this confusing area of law fits in with the procedure for claiming judicial review under RSC Order 53. In turn, this has coincided with increased interest in this area of employment law since it is well appreciated now that in unfair dismissal cases tribunals hardly ever order reinstatement or re-engagement; thus any remedy that may in fact *keep the employee in employment* such as this may well be worth pursuing, certainly in cases arising in the public sector. The following attempt[7] at explanation

2   See pp. 96-105, 'Legality and Restraint of Trade', above.
3   *Lumley v Wagner* (1852) 1 De GM & G 604.
4   *Davis v Foreman* [1894] 3 Ch 654; *Warner Bros Pictures Inc v Nelson* [1937] 1 KB 209, [1936] 3 All ER 160.
5   *Rely-a-Bell Burglar and Fire Alarm Co Ltd v Eisler* [1926] Ch 609; *Warner Bros Pictures Inc v Nelson* [1937] 1 KB 209, [1936] 3 All ER 160; *Page One Records Ltd v Britton* [1967] 3 All ER 822, [1968] 1 WLR 157; *Warren v Mendy* [1989] ICR 525, [1989] IRLR 210, CA.
6   Ganz 'Public law principles applicable to dismissal from employment' (1967) 30 MLR 288; Freedland *The Contract of Employment* (1976) pp. 278–292; Davidson 'Judicial review of decisions to dismiss' (1984) 35 NILQ 121 (written before the decision in *ex p Walsh*, below); Fredman and Lee 'Natural justice for employees' (1986) 15 ILJ 15; Ewing and Grubb 'The emergence of a new labour injunction?' (1987) 16 ILJ 145; Fredman and Morris 'Public or private? State employees and judicial review' (1991) 107 LQR 298; Sedley 'Public law and contractual entitlement' (1994) 23 ILJ 201; Laws 'Public law and employment law: abuse of power' [1997] PL 455; Freedland (1990) 19 ILJ 199, (1991) 20 ILJ 72; Carty (1991) 54 MLR 129. Presumably other public law grounds of challenge such as perversity would be applicable, though less likely to succeed, see *R v Hertfordshire County Council, ex p NUPE* [1985] IRLR 258, CA.
7   Humility is, it is said, a virtue. Any over-confident lawyer wishing to learn it should consider the case law that follows in some depth. He or she is likely to come away from it feeling at best chastened and at worst an ursus mentis parvae.

proceeds by examining first the older case law and then the more recent case law on Order 53. It is tempting to think of the former as establishing the principles and the latter as determining the remedy but, as will be seen, that would be an oversimplification.

The older case law In *Ridge v Baldwin*[8] a chief constable who was dismissed without a proper opportunity to be heard in his own defence was granted a declaration that the decision to dismiss him was a nullity as it was in breach of natural justice[9]. Remedies such as this are familiar in the context of expulsion from a trade union and indeed if a dismissal involved jeopardising trade union rights (as in *Taylor v National Union of Seamen*[10] where dismissal as branch secretary disqualified the individual from later standing for office in the union) the safer course is to rely upon the denial of those rights, not the dismissal. However, in the ordinary case of dismissal the application of these remedies has been confused and illogical. In *Malloch v Aberdeen Corpn*[11] Lord Wilberforce said:

> 'A comparative list in which persons have been held entitled or not entitled to a hearing, or to observation of rules of natural justice, according to the master and servant test, looks illogical and even bizarre. A specialist surgeon is denied protection which is given to a hospital doctor; a University professor, as a servant, has been denied the right to be heard, a dock labourer and an undergraduate have been granted it[12].'

This confusion arises because if one thing is certain in this area it is that these remedies are not available in 'ordinary master and servant cases'. Thus, in *Ridge v Baldwin* Lord Reid said[13]:

> 'The law regarding master and servant is not in doubt. There cannot be specific performance of a contract of service and the master can terminate his contract with the servant at any time and for any reason or for none[14]. But if he does so in a manner not warranted by the contract he must pay damages for breach of contract. So the question in a pure case of master and servant does not at all depend on whether the master has heard the

---

8   [1964] AC 40, [1963] 2 All ER 66, HL; applied in *Chief Constable of the North Wales Police v Evans* [1982] 3 All ER 141, [1982] 1 WLR 1155, HL.
9   One possible limitation on the effectiveness of natural justice (even if locus standi can be shown) may be the decision in *R v Chief Constable of the Thames Valley Police, ex p Cotton* [1990] IRLR 344, CA, that in order to succeed the applicant employee must show not just a breach of the procedural requirements of natural justice, but also *actual prejudice* caused to him; if this allows a defence that in fact it made no difference to the outcome it is inconsistent with developments in unfair dismissal law where just that defence (to procedural failure) was disapproved by the House of Lords in *Polkey v A E Dayton (Services) Ltd* [1988] ICR 142, [1987] IRLR 503, see p. 443, below.
10   [1967] 1 All ER 767, [1967] 1 WLR 532; *Stevenson v United Road Transport Union* [1977] 2 All ER 941, [1977] ICR 893, CA.
11   [1971] 2 All ER 1278 at 1294, [1971] 1 WLR 1578 at 1595, HL; *Jones v Lee and Guilding* [1980] ICR 310, [1980] IRLR 67, CA.
12   See *Barber v Manchester Regional Hospital Board* [1958] 1 All ER 322, [1958] 1 WLR 181; *Palmer v Inverness Hospitals Board* 1963 SC 311; *Vidyodaya University of Ceylon v Silva* [1964] 3 All ER 865, [1965] 1 WLR 77, PC; *Vine v National Dock Labour Board* [1957] AC 488, [1956] 3 All ER 939, HL; *Glynn v Keele University* [1971] 2 All ER 89, [1971] 1 WLR 487.
13   [1964] AC 40 at 65, [1963] 2 All ER 66 at 71, HL.
14   The case was decided before the introduction of the unfair dismissal provisions in the Industrial Relations Act 1971.

servant in his own defence; it depends on whether the facts emerging at the trial prove breach of contract.'

The problem therefore becomes to determine how to distinguish between ordinary master and servant cases and those rare cases in which the remedies may be invoked. In *Ridge v Baldwin*[15] Lord Reid envisaged the doctrine of natural justice as applicable to an 'office-holder' who could only be dismissed for some measure of cause, and in *Malloch v Aberdeen Corpn*, where a Scottish teacher whose employment was heavily qualified by statute was held by a majority of the House of Lords to have been entitled to a hearing before dismissal, Lord Wilberforce said[16]:

> 'One may accept that if there are relationships in which all requirements of the observance of rules of natural justice are excluded … , these must be confined to what have been called "pure master and servant cases", which I take to mean cases in which there is no element of *public employment or service*, no support by *statute*, nothing in the nature of an *office or a status* which is capable of protection. If any of these elements exist, then, in my opinion, whatever the terminology used, and even though in some inter partes aspects the relationship may be called that of master and servant, there may be essential procedural requirements to be observed, and failure to observe them may result in a dismissal being declared to be void.'

It is submitted that this is one of the clearest statements of the position in the older cases, but even here the difficulties are numerous, for although his Lordship talks of 'any' of these elements existing, it is clear that they are not necessarily enough by themselves; for example, many employees are in 'public employment' but at too lowly a level to claim protection[17]. This means that there will be some need for additional 'status', as in the third element mentioned, but it is this very 'status' that is the elusive factor. Moreover, the question arises whether an office holder in purely private, commercial employment (e.g. a company secretary) would be able to challenge his dismissal in this way – in theory there is no reason why not, but so far the cases have all been in the context of public employment of sorts, except in *Stevenson v United Road Transport Union*[18] where the dismissed employee was employed by a trade union as an officer of that union.

The position is little clearer when one turns from questions of natural justice to a challenge on the basis of the dismissal being ultra vires. In *McClelland v*

15 [1964] AC 40, [1963] 2 All ER 66, HL.
16 [1971] 2 All ER 1278 at 1294, [1971] 1 WLR 1578 at 1595, italics added. Lord Morris (dissenting) took a narrower view of the application of the remedies to employment cases, as he had done in his decision in *Vidyodaya University of Ceylon v Silva* [1964] 3 All ER 865, [1965] 1 WLR 77, PC, but in his speech in *Malloch's* case Lord Wilberforce doubted the correctness of that case on this point (see 1295 and 1596 respectively).
17 See, e.g., *Forbes v Johnston* [1971] NZLR 117. The point is taken up in the case law on Order 53, below. In *R v BBC, ex p Lavelle* [1983] ICR 99, [1982] IRLR 404, Woolf J suggested that *any* employment protected by procedural rules before dismissal might have the necessary office-holding status; this would have had enormous repercussions since most permanent employments these days would come into that category, with disciplinary rules written into their terms of employment. This idea has not been taken any further in the subsequent case law (see e.g. the narrow approach to 'office' in *R v Hertfordshire County Council, ex p NUPE* [1985] IRLR 258, CA).
18 [1977] 2 All ER 941, [1977] ICR 893, CA; cf. *Taylor v National Union of Seamen* [1967] 1 All ER 767, [1967] 1 WLR 532.

Northern Ireland General Health Services Board[19] the House of Lords appear to have held by a majority that a dismissal for a reason other than one expressly permitted in the particular contract of employment in question was ultra vires in the sense of not being allowed under the contract. Normally, however, such a dismissal would only give rise to an action for damages for wrongful dismissal[20], and if that case is correct the reasoning can only apply where the contract is particularly explicit on the permissible reasons for dismissal. More normally, a challenge on the basis of ultra vires will be based upon a statutory scheme or requirement governing the employment, as in *Vine v National Dock Labour Board*[1] where a registered dock worker employed by the Board (under the now-repealed statutory scheme designed to dispense with casual labour on the docks) was dismissed for refusing a valid order, but his dismissal was effected by a committee which, on the true construction of the statutory scheme, did not have power to do so. The House of Lords held the dismissal to be ultra vires, and gave a declaration that it was a nullity. Viscount Kilmuir LC stressed that the existence of the special statutory scheme took the employee out of the 'ordinary master–servant' category[2]:

'Here, the removal of the plaintiff's name from the register being in law a nullity, he continued to have the right to be treated as a registered dockworker with all the benefits which, by statute, that status conferred on him. It is therefore right that, with the background of this scheme, the court should declare his rights.'

Challenge on the basis of ultra vires has, however, been restrictively construed, and will not apply simply because the employment in question is in some way governed by statute; even if it has a 'strong statutory flavour' it may still be deemed to be an ordinary master-servant case[3], and in *Francis v Municipal Councillors of Kuala Lumpur*[4] Lord Morris said that relief could only be given in such cases if there were 'special circumstances'; in *Vine's* case, those circumstances were the all-embracing nature of the statutory scheme and the fact that the employee could not work as a docker *at all* if dismissed from the Board's employment.

Thus, the cases where a dismissal has been successfully challenged as a nullity have been uncommon in the past, and the principles upon which they have succeeded are uncertain, though usually revolving round some sort of elusive office-holding status. Theoretically that has been no great hardship for we now have the laws relating to unfair dismissal, where matters of natural justice[5] and compliance with internal disciplinary procedures may be important, if only indirectly. However, the practical position may be slightly different with, as stated above, renewed interest generally in common law and/or administrative law

19   [1957] 2 All ER 129, [1957] 1 WLR 594, HL.
20   For the more normal treatment of dismissal from a 'permanent and pensionable' employment see *Clark v Independent Broadcasting Corpn* [1974] 2 NZLR 587.
1   [1957] AC 488, [1956] 3 All ER 939, HL; *Taylor v Furness, Withy & Co Ltd* [1969] 1 Lloyd's Rep 324, 6 KIR 488.
2   [1957] AC 488 at 500, [1956] 3 All ER 939 at 944.
3   *Barber v Manchester Regional Hospital Board* [1958] 1 All ER 322, [1958] 1 WLR 181.
4   [1962] 3 All ER 633, [1962] 1 WLR 1411, PC.
5   Ideas derived from natural justice permeate the Code of Practice No. 1 'Disciplinary practice and procedure in employment', particularly paras. 10(e), (f), (g), and 11. Also, there have been cases where rules of natural justice have been applied directly when considering procedural unfairness; see, e.g., *Ayanlowo v IRC* [1975] IRLR 253; CA; *Khanum v Mid-Glamorgan Area Health Authority* [1979] ICR 40, [1978] IRLR 215; cf. *Slater v Leicestershire Health Authority* [1989] IRLR 16, CA.

remedies for dismissed employees, given the low instance of reinstatement by tribunals and, in some cases, the desire to use the vehicle of an individual challenge in order to prevent or deter abuse of disciplinary procedures by the employer[6]. We can now turn to the later case law but here we find procedural complications.

The problem of Order 53　　Order 53 was introduced into the Rules of the Supreme Court in 1977 in order to simplify procedure, so that now there can be one application for 'judicial review' which can lead, if successful, to the granting of any one of the appropriate remedies (certiorari, mandamus, prohibition, declaration, injunction or, possibly, damages). It contains an anti-technicality rule in Order 53, rule 9(5) whereby an application under the Order can, if it transpires that that is the wrong procedure, be deemed to have been commenced instead by writ, and proceed accordingly. Essentially it was a liberalising reform though it does import certain restrictions (especially a time limit) and, more important here, has led to a position in which the division between 'public law' and 'private law' is thrown into higher relief than previously[7]. This has happened through a series of House of Lords cases[8] in which their Lordships have been concerned to establish the proper relationship between the new public law remedy in Order 53 and ordinary private law claims, so that hopefully the Order will be neither abused nor so construed as to restrict unduly (or even prejudice) genuine private law claims. The position basically is that application is to be made under Order 53 if, but only if, the subject matter of the complaint relates to public law (as that is in the process of being defined). Thus, tests have been evolving as to when the *Order 53 remedy* is available but the problem in the employment law field is that those tests may not be exactly the same as the principles that evolved under the previous case law as to when *some sort of remedy* should be given by the courts to a dismissed employee (usually in the past by way of a declaration or injunction); in other words, the older principles and the new remedy may not be co-terminous.

　　The leading case is *R v East Berkshire Health Authority, ex p Walsh*[9] in which a senior nursing officer (employed under a contract which pursuant to regulations and with the approval of the Secretary of State incorporated terms and conditions jointly agreed for the health service) sought to challenge his dismissal on the grounds of breach of natural justice (through not being given a proper hearing) and ultra vires (having been dismissed, he argued, by an official who did not have the power to do so under the relevant contractual term). He applied for judicial review under Order 53, seeking an order of certiorari to quash the dismissal; he

---

6　See p. 389, below.

7　This distinction may now have yet more significance with the enactment of the Human Rights Act 1998; see Morris 'The Human Rights Act and the public/private divide' (1998) 27 ILJ 293.

8　*O'Reilly v Mackman* [1983] 2 AC 237, [1982] 3 All ER 1124, HL; *Cocks v Thanet District Council* [1983] 2 AC 286, [1982] 3 All ER 1135, HL; *Davy v Spelthorne Borough Council* [1984] AC 262, [1983] 3 All ER 278, HL; *Wandsworth London Borough Council v Winder* [1985] AC 461, [1984] 3 All ER 976; *Roy v Kensington, Chelsea and Westminster Family Practitioner Committee* [1992] 1 All ER 705, [1992] IRLR 233, HL. For an interesting application in the employment context, see *Doyle v Northumbria Probation Committee* [1991] 4 All ER 294, [1992] ICR 121. A different, less technical, approach applies in Scotland: *West v Secretary of State for Scotland* [1992] IRLR 399, Ct of Sess.

9　[1984] ICR 743, [1984] IRLR 278, CA, noted Cripps [1984] CLJ 214, Collins (1984) 13 ILJ 174; *R v Derbyshire County Council, ex p Noble* [1990] ICR 808, [1990] IRLR 332, CA. Where the applicant is a civil servant, an application for judicial review can raise fundamental questions as to the contractual position for Crown servants, see p. 80, above and in particular *R v Lord Chancellor's Department, ex p Nangle* [1991] ICR 743, [1991] IRLR 343.

was successful at first instance but the Court of Appeal unanimously rejected the application. They held that the dismissal did not raise the sort of issues of public law necessary under Order 53 to attract the remedy of certiorari. What is the basis for such a decision? The one thing that is clear is that the fact that the applicant was employed by a public body of sorts is *not* enough without more to attract public law remedies; if it were otherwise a substantial proportion of the workforce would be able to seek remedies on dismissal from the Divisional Court, thus potentially outflanking the employment tribunal system which, according to the Court of Appeal, is a far more appropriate forum for the sort of issues that arise on dismissal. The relevant distinction must therefore lie elsewhere. As seen above, in the older case law the courts tended to look at *the status of the applicant*. In *ex p Walsh* however the court clearly looked instead at *the nature of his complaint* – did it raise matters categorisable as public law? It is true that Mr Walsh's contract was made by reference to regulatory provisions and subject (ultimately) to sanctioning by the Secretary of State. However, he was not complaining that his contract had not been made in accordance with the correct statutory procedures; his complaint was in essence quite simply that, having been properly made, his contract had then been *broken* by the Health Authority by the manner of his dismissal. Breach of contract, said the Court of Appeal, remains a matter of private law (even when the employment is in the public sector with some measure of public control):

> 'The ordinary employer is free to act in breach of his contracts of employment and if he does so his employee will acquire certain private law rights and remedies in damages for wrongful dismissal, an order for reinstatement or re-engagement and so on. Parliament can underpin the position of public authority employees by directly restricting the freedom of the public authority to dismiss, thus giving the employee "public law" rights and at least making him a potential candidate for administrative law remedies. Alternatively, it can require the authority to contract with its employees on specified terms with a view to the employee acquiring "private law" rights under the terms of the contract of employment. If the authority fails or refuses thus to create "private law" rights for the employee, the employee will have "public law" rights to compel compliance, the remedy being mandamus requiring the authority so to contract or a declaration that the employee had those rights. If, however, the authority gives the employee the required protection, a breach of that contract is not a matter of "public law" and gives rise to no administrative law remedies[10].'

> 'The only remedies sought by Mr. Walsh arise solely out of his contract of employment with them as opposed to any public duty imposed upon the Health Authority[11].'

Thus the requirements for Order 53 were not satisfied. In the subsequent case of *McClaren v Home Office*[12] the doyen of modern administrative law, Woolf LJ, developed this approach into four principles which constitute valuable guidance in this maze.

10   Per Sir John Donaldson MR at 752 and 281, respectively.
11   Per Purchas LJ at 769 and 288, respectively.
12   [1990] ICR 824, [1990] IRLR 338, CA. The case is primarily of importance as a statement of the contractual status of civil servants, see p. 80, above. The following passage is merely a precis; Woolf LJ's erudite judgment deserves reading as a whole.

(i) In relation to a personal claim against the employer, an employee of a public body is normally in exactly the same situation as other employees and can bring proceedings in the ordinary way for damages, a declaration or an injunction (except in relation to the Crown).[13]

(ii) An employee of a public body can seek judicial review and obtain a remedy which would not be available to an employee in the private sector where there exists some disciplinary or other body established under the prerogative or by statute to which the employer or employee is entitled or required to refer disputes affecting their relationship.

(iii) In addition, if an employee of a public body is adversely affected by a decision of general application by his employer, he can be entitled to challenge that decision by way of judicial review on grounds that it is flawed.

(iv) Judicial review will *not* be available where disciplinary procedures are of a purely domestic nature, albeit that their decisions might affect the public.

At first sight, it may appear that what the Court of Appeal were doing in these cases was to lay down new principles to replace those in the older case law as to when any form of remedy is to be given, and to do so restrictively in an attempt to minimise the use of administrative law remedies and have dismissal cases dealt with before the proper forum of employment tribunals (a strong and patent policy factor). However, the position is not so simple because there is a further stage. As explained above, under Order 53, rule 9(5) an action wrongly commenced under the Order can be transformed at the court's discretion into an action begun by writ. In *ex p Walsh*, the employee applied for this to be done but that application was refused by the Court of Appeal on procedural grounds. Thus although *ex p Walsh* is the leading case on Order 53 and dismissal cases, it does not answer the further question – if rule 9(5) is applied (or indeed if an action is commenced by writ in the first place seeking a declaration or injunction on the grounds of breach of natural justice or ultra vires), what principles are *then* to apply to determine whether relief should be given? Here it seems that the principles in the older cases still apply, and we are back to the status of the employee. As Purchas LJ put it:

'It is important to remember that the three categories of employment described by Lord Reid in *Ridge v Baldwin* and referred to in *Malloch v Aberdeen Corpn* were directed to the question of the right to be heard and not to the procedural question [i.e. under Order 53] which is central to the instant appeal. ... It is important, in my judgment, to distinguish the two concepts involved. The first is the well-debated problem as to whether or not an obligation to obey the rules of natural justice in master and servant cases encapsulated in the expression "audi alteram partem" is imported into a contract of employment. The second is whether that invokes of necessity the supervisory powers of the court[14].'

To sum up, an application under Order 53 to challenge a dismissal will only be successful if the nature of the applicant's complaint is such as to raise issues of public law and *ex p Walsh*, the leading case, establishes that a complaint that is essentially one of breach of contract by the employer is *not* categorisable as a

13 In the case itself a prison officer was seeking to sue the Home Office for *breach of contract*; it was therefore the Home Office who were arguing that his remedies properly lay in judicial review (for which his application would have been out of time). The restrictive approach to Ord. 53 thus worked in the employee's favour on the facts.

14 At 768 at 287, respectively.

matter of public law. Even if Order 53 is inapplicable, a court may in its discretion treat the application as if begun by writ for a declaration or injunction (or indeed the applicant may have proceeded in that manner in the first place). In such a case the court may still have jurisdiction to intervene (even though this leads to the logically unsatisfactory position of applying public law concepts such as breach of natural justice or ultra vires in cases to which ex hypothesi the principal public law procedure of Order 53 is not applicable). Moreover, the grounds for interfering appear to be wider, for the test to be applied is *not* that contained in *ex p Walsh* of the nature of the complaint (i.e. the criterion for coming under Order 53), but rather the old test based upon the status of the employee. The older case law on this (considered above) tended to look for something in the nature of, or analogous to, 'officeholding' and, while it stands independently of the recent case law on Order 53, the tenor of the latter suggests that here too a restrictive approach is likely to be taken, for fear of opening the way for a multitude of cases (especially from the public sector) being brought before the ordinary courts which, in the opinion of the Court of Appeal in *ex p Walsh*, should be dealt with instead by employment tribunals[15].

3)   *The decision in Hill v CA Parsons & Co Ltd*[16]   In this case, the plaintiff refused to join a union which had negotiated a closed shop with his employers, who therefore gave him one month's notice of dismissal. He had been employed by them for 35 years as a chartered engineer, and had two years to go to retirement, so that the dismissal would affect his pension rights; moreover, the unfair dismissal legislation was due to come into force within six months of the dismissal. The plaintiff sued the employers for wrongful dismissal and claimed an interim injunction restraining them for treating the notice as terminating his employment. This could be construed as enforcing the contract of employment, but the Court of Appeal by a majority (Lord Denning MR and Sachs LJ, Stamp LJ dissenting) granted the interim injunction. The imminence of the new legislation was obviously a strong background factor (and hence the finding that proper notice would have been at least six months for a man in his position), but to find in the plaintiff's favour the majority had to go against the normal rule against enforcement (the application of which was the basis of Stamp LJ's dissent). To do so they held that that rule is not a fixed rule of law, but a question of fact which therefore permits exceptions in cases where the usual reasons against enforcement do not apply, in particular where there is continued confidence between the parties (as in this case, where both the parties wanted to continue the employment and the pressure to terminate it came from the trade union[17]). Further, Lord Denning said that in this case damages were not an adequate remedy, so it was right that an injunction should be granted, on the principle 'ubi jus ibi remedium'[18] which would allow the court to 'step over the trip-wires of previous cases and to bring the law into accord with the needs of today'. It may certainly be argued that

---

15   The Scottish courts have shown a consistently strict view on the matter, not allowing judicial review of what are essentially contractual matters: *West v Secretary of State for Scotland* [1992] IRLR 399, Ct of Sess. In *Blair v Lochaber District Council* [1995] IRLR 135 the Court of Session refused review to a chief executive allegedly suspended contrary to the authority's own rules, which was held to remain essentially a contractual matter. Distinguishing *Malloch*, above (itself a Scottish decision, but now apparently out of favour) it was held that even if the older case law had to be considered, the chief executive here did *not* have the necessary 'status' as an office holder. If he did not, who does?

16   [1972] Ch 305, [1971] 3 All ER 1345, CA; noted [1972A] CLJ 49, (1972) 35 MLR 310.

17   This view of the facts was disputed by Stamp LJ.

18   'Where there is a right, there is a remedy', but in this context perhaps best translated as 'where there is a will, there is a way'.

justice was done to the plaintiff in this case, but it left many questions open which would have had to have been solved had this area of law not been effectively superseded by the new unfair dismissal action, particularly as the case cast doubt on the general principle discussed above that when an employer repudiates a contract of employment, that automatically terminates the contract and the employee must accept the repudiation and sue for damages; this raised the problem of what circumstances would put a case into the category in which the employer's repudiation might not have this automatic effect, and opened the way for rather refined arguments based on the concept of repudiation which at times, it is submitted, could stray a long way from the realities of employment[19]. In the event, the case did not lead to a radical reappraisal of enforcement of contracts of employment at common law, and was restrictively construed in subsequent cases as a rare case on its facts, relying upon the continued existence of mutual confidence between the parties, which is unlikely to be so in many cases[20]. However, the case is a decision of the Court of Appeal and at least shows that there may be *some* scope for enforcement of the contract as a remedy at common law.

More recently, interest has been rekindled to some extent in the possibility of such a common law remedy – in *Irani v Southampton and South West Hampshire Health Authority*[1] Warner J applied *Hill v C A Parsons & Co Ltd* to grant an injunction restraining a dismissal in breach of quasi-statutory disciplinary procedures; a similar result was reached by Mervyn Davies J in *Wadcock v London Borough of Brent*[2] and by Morland J in *Robb v London Borough of Hammersmith and Fulham*[3] in the case of contractually-binding disciplinary procedures; in *Powell v London Borough of Brent*[4] the Court of Appeal granted an interlocutory injunction restraining the employers from depriving the employee of a promotion for which she had successfully applied; in *Hughes v London Borough of Southwark*[5] Taylor J granted an interlocutory injunction restraining the employers from insisting on the employees taking on work which the latter argued was not within their contractual obligations; in *Anderson v Pringle of Scotland Ltd*[6] Lord Prosser granted

19   See, e.g., *Shields Furniture Ltd v Goff* [1973] 2 All ER 653, [1973] ICR 187, NIRC.
20   *GKN (Cwmbran) Ltd v Lloyd* [1972] ICR 214; *Sanders v Ernest A Neale Ltd* [1974] 3 All ER 327, [1974] ICR 565; *Chappell v Times Newspapers Ltd* [1975] 2 All ER 233, [1975] ICR 145, CA; *City and Hackney Health Authority v NUPE* [1985] IRLR 252, CA. In *GKN (Cwmbran) Ltd v Lloyd* Sir John Donaldson P suggested (at 221) that a further material factor in *Hill v CA Parsons & Co Ltd* was that the actual dismissal had not taken place, so that the court was restraining a proposed dismissal, not putting an employee back into employment after he had been effectively dismissed. This point was also stressed by Lord Prosser in the Court of Session in *Anderson v Pringle of Scotland Ltd* [1998] IRLR 64.
1   [1985] ICR 590, [1985] IRLR 203.
2   [1990] IRLR 223.
3   [1991] ICR 514, [1991] IRLR 72.
4   [1988] ICR 176, [1987] IRLR 466, CA; after the plaintiff's successful application for the senior post, one of the unsuccessful applicants claimed that the council's equal opportunity policy had been infringed and so the council purported to negate the promotion and readvertise the post.
5   [1988] IRLR 55. In *Ali v London Borough of Southwark* [1988] ICR 567, [1988] IRLR 100 a challenge to threatened disciplinary proceedings that the plaintiff said would be irregular failed on two grounds: (a) no continued mutual confidence; (b) the court will not normally step in in advance to restrain *pending* disciplinary proceedings (applying the similar rule in trade union cases, in *Longley v National Union of Journalists* [1987] IRLR 109, CA, see p. 595, below).
6   [1998] IRLR 64, OH. Lord Prosser stated that 'such exceptional cases as there have been give no very clear picture of the criteria for intervention', but justified his order on the grounds that (a) there was no evidence of loss of trust in the employee (this being a redundancy case) and (b) court intervention was possible *before* the dismissal was due to take place.

an interim interdict to restrain a redundancy dismissal in breach of a LIFO redundancy agreement which was assumed to be part of the employee's individual contract and in *Peace v City of Edinburgh Council*[7] Lord Penrose restrained the disciplining (*short* of dismissal) of the employee under a new procedure which he argued he had not consented to as part of his contract. In these cases, the basis of the court's power to intervene is clearly seen as the (argued) continued existence of mutual confidence between the parties[8]. However, the point remains that these are *not* ordinary, everyday dismissal cases (indeed, *Powell*, *Hughes* and *Peace* are not dismissal cases at all) and while they may point to interesting and useful developments in the use (or threatened use) of the common law to restrain employer misuses of contractually-binding disciplinary procedures[9], it would be premature to consider them as showing a resurgence of common law actions aimed at preserving employment in wrongful dismissal cases generally, particularly as it is equally possible to point to recent decisions refusing similar relief for traditional reasons[10]. There is, however, one procedural innovation which might have some influence here. What is now Part 24 of the Civil Procedure Rules (originally order 14A of the Rules of the Supreme Court) was introduced to allow a court to determine any question of law or construction of any document at any stage in the proceedings where it appears to the court that (a) such question is suitable for determination without a full trial of the action and (b) such determination will finally determine the entire cause or matter or any claim or issue therein. This de facto power to issue a declaration of the meaning of, for example, a contract of employment, was used by Chadwick J in *Jones v Gwent County Council*[11] to declare that a letter of dismissal was not validly issued within the contract and, on that basis, to grant injunctions restraining the employers from acting on it. Technically, this power does not 'enforce' the contract of employment, but if its use became more widespread the question would have to be faced as to whether it constituted unacceptable back-door enforcement.

c) Damages for wrongful dismissal

The remedies for wrongful dismissal are limited not only by the rule against enforcement, but also by the restricted measure of damages recoverable in many cases. The restriction arises once again from the doctrine of notice, for if an employer wrongfully dismisses an employee who should have had, say, two weeks' notice, what has the employee in fact lost? He cannot be said to have lost his long

---

7 [1999] IRLR 417, OH. Here it was important that it was a breach of contract *during* employment that was being restrained, and that both parties were assuming that the contract was to continue.

8 This means either no loss of confidence on the facts or, possibly, that any such loss by the employer is on irrational grounds, and so rectifiable. In *Hughes*, Taylor J said that mutual confidence should not be considered to have gone merely because the employer and employee are in genuine dispute as to the construction or application of certain contractual terms or duties. Note, however, that in *Robb* Morland J took a slightly different approach saying that, while continued trust and confidence is important where the employee is trying to get his job back, if (as in that case) the employee was only interested in securing use of the disciplinary procedure in order to air his grievances the test should be whether a court order would actually be workable.

9 Similar proceedings can be seen in *Deitman v Brent London Borough Council* [1988] IRLR 299, CA.

10 *Alexander v Standard Telephones and Cables plc* [1990] ICR 291, [1990] IRLR 55; *Jakeman v South West Thames Regional Health Authority and London Ambulance Service* [1990] IRLR 62; *Wishart v NACAB Ltd* [1990] ICR 794, [1990] IRLR 383, CA.

11 [1992] IRLR 521.

term livelihood, for at common law he could have been dismissed at any time merely by being given two weeks' notice. Thus, all that he has lost is his two weeks' notice, and so his measure of damage is restricted to his pay during that period[12]. This is backed by the general principle that, in a damages action, the employers must be assumed to have discharged their contractual duties towards the employee in the way least onerous to them, which will usually mean assuming that they would have ended the contract in any event, as quickly as they could lawfully have done so (usually by giving notice)[13] Basically, therefore, a wrongfully dismissed employee is entitled to damages equal to his wages or salary during his notice period[14]. Moreover, the common law was always wary of giving further damages under other heads. Thus in *Addis v Gramophone Co Ltd*[15] an employee who was paid at a fixed salary plus commission was wrongfully dismissed and claimed damages under the following heads – (i) salary for the six-month notice period, (ii) reasonable commission for a six-month period, (iii) damages for the humiliating manner of dismissal, (iv) damages for loss of reputation leading to future difficulty in obtaining employment. The House of Lords held by a majority that only heads (i) and (ii) were recoverable. Also, the law only looked at the definite contractual liabilities of the employer in assessing damages, not at what the employee might in fact have received (e.g. a discretionary bonus which he might have received during the notice period). In *Lavarack v Woods of Colchester Ltd*[16] an employee who was wrongfully dismissed had been on a five year contract with a fixed salary subject to periodic discretionary bonuses. After he had been dismissed (but during the period for which the contract should have continued) the employers discontinued the bonus scheme and increased the wages of their staff. The Court of Appeal held by a majority that the increase in wages should not be taken into account when assessing the damages, since the only fully contractual obligation upon the employers was to pay the fixed salary and anything on top of that was discretionary (whether a bonus or an increase in wages). Lord Denning MR, dissenting, took the wider view that the dismissed employee was

12 A gloss here is that if a contractually binding disciplinary procedure has been breached, a court may look at when the contract could *lawfully* have been terminated, awarding damages for a short period representing the time necessary to have operated the procedure properly and *then* the notice period: *Gunton v Richmond-upon-Thames London Borough Council* [1980] ICR 755, [1980] IRLR 321, CA; *Boyo v Lambeth London Borough Council* [1994] ICR 727, [1995] IRLR 50, CA. However, a court or tribunal cannot go farther and speculate on the *chances* of the employee having been kept on if the proper procedure had gone in his favour: *Focsa Services (UK) Ltd v Birkett* [1996] IRLR 325; *Janciuk v Winerite Ltd* [1998] IRLR 63, EAT.

13 This principle, taken from the majority decision in *Laverack v Woods of Colchester Ltd* [1967] 1 QB 278, [1966] 3 All ER 683, CA (below), was applied strongly in *Janciuk v Winerite Ltd* (above) and *Morran v Glasgow Council of Tenants' Associations* [1998] IRLR 67, Ct of Sess.

14 Recent Australian case law departing from this harsh rule and allowing general damages in such cases is considered in Ewing 'Remedies for breach of the contract of employment' [1993] CLJ 405, at 428.

15 [1909] AC 488, HL, reaffirmed in *Bliss v South East Thames Regional Health Authority* [1987] ICR 700, [1985] IRLR 308, CA. See *Alexander v Standard Telephones and Cables Ltd (No 2)* [1991] IRLR 286. The employee's remedy lies in damages; he may not sue instead in debt for continuing wages into the future: *Marsh v National Autistic Society* [1993] ICR 453.

16 [1967] 1 QB 278, [1966] 3 All ER 683, CA; *Bold v Brough, Nicholson and Hall Ltd* [1963] 3 All ER 849, [1964] 1 WLR 201. Damages for loss of rights under a share option scheme were refused because of a literal interpretation of the scheme's rules in *Micklefield v SAC Technology Ltd* [1991] 1 All ER 275, [1990] IRLR 218.

entitled to recover all that he would *in fact* have earned but for the employers' breach of contract.

To this harsh general rule on damages, there are exceptions. The *first* is that where the contract of employment is for a fixed term, not terminable by notice, the damages recoverable are the amount which the employee would have earned under the contract during the remainder of the term, after the wrongful dismissal (subject to mitigation, which is considered below). The *second* is that certain untypical contracts of employment may be construed as envisaging a greater reward for the employee than the bare wage or salary, so that damages in respect of this further loss can be recovered in addition. Thus in *Marbé v George Edwardes (Daly's Theatres) Ltd*[17] an American actress wishing to establish her reputation in London contracted to play a particular part for the defendant, who undertook to give her full publicity. When she was wrongfully denied the chance to play the part, the Court of Appeal held that she could recover the salary due to her for the period of the contract *plus* an amount representing loss of reputation. The extent of this exception outside the theatre is uncertain (quaere, e.g., whether it would apply to any case where the courts found that there was a contractual obligation to provide the employee with actual work, not simply to pay wages[18]), but one case which is at least analogous is *Dunk v George Waller & Son Ltd*[19] where the plaintiff, an apprentice, was wrongfully dismissed during the four year term in question and was held entitled to his net loss of wages for the rest of the term plus an amount representing loss of tuition and training and diminution of future prospects. One possible variant of this may be where the extra 'benefit' that the employee expects under the contract is so important that the court will imply a term that the employer will not use the normal power to dismiss by notice so as to deprive the employee of that benefit. This has arisen in the 'PI cases', where a long-term sick employee is deprived of major financial benefits under a permanent health insurance scheme, provided by the employer, though the employer dismissing him by notice before he can qualify under the scheme[20]. In such cases, courts have impliedly restricted the power to give notice in sickness absences where the result would be deprivation of PHI rights. Thus, a dismissal (otherwise lawful under the contractual notice provision) may become wrongful, with the prospect opening up of *general* damages for loss of those rights. An open question then becomes whether the PHI cases could be extended to other analogous contexts, for example where an employee is taken on specifically in order to bring with him particular trade, contacts or contracts to the new employer; could it be argued that it is an implied term that he will not be dismissed (other than for gross misconduct) as long as the employer retains that trade, etc., so that general damages for wrongful dismissal could be awarded for any such dismissal?[1]

A third exceptional case has been suggested for some time. This may arise where the employer breaks the contract of employment by dismissing the

---

17 [1928] 1 KB 269, CA. See also *Herbert Clayton and Jack Waller Ltd v Oliver* [1930] AC 209, HL; *Withers v General Theatre Corpn Ltd* [1933] 2 KB 536, CA.

18 See pp. 120-121, above.

19 [1970] 2 QB 163, [1970] 2 All ER 630. Quaere whether the reasoning in this case applies only to apprenticeship, or might be applicable to any contract of employment envisaging vocational training or retraining.

20 *Aspden v Webbs Poultry and Meat Group (Holdings) Ltd* [1996] IRLR 521; *Adin v Sedco Forex International Resources Ltd* [1997] IRLR 280, Ct of Sess; see p. 128, above.

1 General damages could cause particular problems of quantification in a context such as this; a court or tribunal would have to fix some sort of 'multiplier' to assess the likely period of loss, but without the highly developed 'tariff' system available to perform a similar task in personal injury cases.

employee with no or short notice, thereby depriving him of his statutory rights (especially the right to claim unfair dismissal) by advancing the effective date of dismissal to *within* the qualifying period[2]. In such a case, the employee would be debarred from claiming unfair dismissal (if that were the right in question) but may be able to bring an action in the ordinary courts for *wrongful* dismissal claiming extra damages representing the loss to him of his potential statutory rights[3]. This would seem to be a practical answer to the possible problem of an employer being able to rely on the relatively rigid rules on dates of termination and qualifying periods through deliberate breach of contract on his own part, and an award of damages on this basis was finally permitted by the EAT in *Raspin v United News Shops Ltd*[4] where a summary dismissal three weeks short of the unfair dismissal qualifying period was held to have been wrongful *and* in breach of a contractually binding disciplinary procedure, proper exhaustion of which would have taken long enough to have allowed the employee to reach the qualifying period.

The fourth exception arises from a potentially significant application of the modern term of trust and respect[5] to the area of damages. In *Clark v BET plc*[6], a wrongful dismissal claim by a highly paid chief executive on a three-year fixed-term contract, liability was conceded but a major question arose as to quantification of damages because the executive had been heavily reliant for much of his pay package on salary increases and bonuses which, while regularly paid in the past, remained discretionary. On a strict approach (typified by the *Laverack* case considered above and the principle that the employer should normally be assumed to have discharged the contract in the way least onerous to himself) the executive would not have been awarded anything for these heads, because technically the employer could have decided to give *nothing* for the remainder of the contract. However, Walker J avoided that harsh result by looking at what the employers were likely to have paid out (given the firm's known performance over the relevant period) if they had continued to exercise their discretion *in good faith*. Although only at first instance, this is clearly an important decision in any case where significant elements of remuneration are discretionary, and it does show a significant departure from the straight *Laverack* approach. However, it is a second development that might show the most radical developments, involving a reappraisal of the most fundamental limitations of all, namely those to be found in *Addis v Gramophone Co Ltd* (above) itself, though at the time of writing its implications are uncertain. In *Malik v BCCI SA (in liquidation)*[7] ex-employees of the failed BCCI bank claimed damages in respect of injury to their reputation and future employment prospects caused by the bank conducting a dishonest or corrupt business. The House of Lords upheld this claim on the grounds that the conduct of the employer was a serious breach of the implied term of trust and

---

2   This is consistent with the better view of the meaning of 'effective date of termination', that it occurs when the dismissal in practice takes effect (see p. 454, below); this remains so even where the dismissal is in breach of contract (and even if that breach is deliberate): *Stapp v Shaftesbury Society* [1982] IRLR 326, CA.

3   *Robert Cort & Son Ltd v Charman* [1981] ICR 816, [1981] IRLR 437, per Browne-Wilkinson J, approved by the Court of Appeal in *Stapp v Shaftesbury Society*, n. 2, above. This analysis does not work if there is a *express* payment in lieu of notice clause in the contract, because then the instant dismissal is not wrongful: *Morran v Glasgow Council of Tenants' Associations* [1998] IRLR 67, Ct of Sess.

4   [1999] IRLR 9.

5   See p. 124, above.

6   [1997] IRLR 348.

7   [1997] ICR 606, [1997] IRLR 462, HL; see McMullen (1997) 26 ILJ 245.

respect (to the evolution of which they gave their clear support[8]). *Addis* was subject to considerable scrutiny by Lords Nicholls and Steyn, giving the principal judgments, and was side-stepped partly on the basis that it principally concerned a claim for injury to feelings caused by the wrongful dismissal whereas the claim in *Malik* was clearly for future financial loss caused by the employer's conduct, and partly on the basis that *Addis* was decided well before the development of the term of trust and respect which now occupies a central position in employment law. This new genus of 'stigma damages' caused much interest and, once again, seemed to open up a vista into general damages for wrongful dismissal, even though (a) the case was *not* in fact one of wrongful dismissal but one of breach of contract during employment, and (b) both law lords ended their speeches with warnings that the facts in *Malik* were extreme and that in many, more ordinary cases there could be severe problems of causation, remoteness and mitigation[9]. Thus, the case poses the question – a claimant's Pandora's Box or an interesting decision on unusual facts? The argument that *Malik* is *not* meant to allow damages for injury to feelings was accepted by the Court of Appeal in *French v Barclays Bank plc*[10], a common law damages claim involving breach of trust and respect where a head of claim relating to stress and anxiety caused by the breach was disallowed. This was consistent, however, with the view that stigma damages for financial loss would now be claimable, including in a wrongful *dismissal* case, but that view is questionable now in the light of the decision of the Court of Appeal in *Johnson v Unisys Ltd*[11]. This is a difficult case on rather unusual facts, since the employee (who had suffered from work-induced stress prior to being summarily dismissed) had already succeeded in an unfair dismissal action, and then brought a substantial claim for damages for wrongful dismissal, alleging that as a result of it he had suffered a nervous breakdown and was unable to work (thus arguably covering both injured feelings *and* future financial loss, through admittedly not in the usual 'stigma' manner). Ruling this claim out, the Court of Appeal held that *Malik* had not seriously doubted *Addis* (referred to by Lord Woolf MR as 'a cornerstone of the law of master and servant'); using certain specific aspects of the judgments of Lords Nicholls and Steyn, and pointing to certain inconsistencies, the court held that *Addis* was simply distinguished in *Malik on its facts*, because it concerned *dismissal*, whereas *Malik* concerned breach of contract *during employment*. On this analysis (arguably regrettably formalistic), stigma damages (for future financial loss) would only be recoverable for breach during employment, and *Addis* would continue to rule them out in a wrongful dismissal case *even if* for future financial loss. Whether this very restrictive line will continue to be held will be an important factor in this area of damages law.

Once the prima facie amount of damages has been ascertained, it is subject to reduction in three ways:

1) *Mitigation* The employee is under a duty to mitigate his loss, and in the context of the contract of employment this will mean essentially finding another job. This will be particularly important in the case of the wrongful termination of a fixed term contract which had several years to run, but will apply generally to all wrongful

---

8   They added that the trust-destroying conduct did not have to be aimed at the individual, and that it was not necessary that that individual became aware of the conduct while still an employee.

9   The claim did indeed finally fail on its facts: *BCCI SA (in liquidation) v Ali* [1999] IRLR 226.

10   [1998] IRLR 646, CA.

11   [1999] ICR 809, [1999] IRLR 90, CA.

dismissals[12] . What constitutes reasonable steps to mitigate will be a question of fact in each case, but two general points might be made. The first is that the courts apply a realistic standard, so that the dismissed employee is not expected to take any job immediately, irrespective of his former position; thus, he may be allowed a certain time to look around for a position of equal status before resorting to lesser employment, and it may not be reasonable to expect him to take another post inside the firm that dismissed him, if that is offered, particularly if it involves a reduction in status[13] . The second is that matters other than another job could constitute mitigation, but before allowing them as such (with the resultant decrease in the amount of damages to be paid by the defendant employer) the court should be satisfied that they are not too remote to be taken into consideration. In *Lavarack v Woods of Colchester Ltd*, the facts of which are given above, the employee was debarred by the contract of employment from engaging in, or holding shares in, any other business during his employment. After his dismissal, he became employed by M Ltd (purchasing half of its stock) and invested in V Ltd. The defendant employers claimed that the profits on these investments should be taken into account to mitigate his damages; the Court of Appeal held that the profits from his shares in M Ltd were to be taken into account, since his dismissal had left him free to *partake* in M Ltd and thereby increase the value of those shares, but the profits from his shares in V Ltd were not to be taken into account, since these were too remote, and the mere fact that he could not have invested while in the defendant's employment was not enough to alter that.

2) *Taxation*   The general rule on the taxation of damages, laid down by the House of Lords in *British Transport Commission v Gourley*[14] , is that where a head of damage is based on an estimate of lost wages, the court should make allowance for the tax that would have been paid, and so deduct that figure and award the damages net of tax. This applies to damages for wrongful dismissal. However, the basis for the rule is that the amount awarded as damages is not taxable in the plaintiff's hands, and at the time of *Gourley* this was generally the case. Now, however, under the Income and Corporation Taxes Act 1988, sections 148 and 188 such 'post-cessation receipts' are taxed to the extent that they exceed £30,000. The end result is that the rule in *Gourley*'s case applies to the first £30,000 of damages for wrongful dismissal, which must be awarded net of tax, but not to any amount over and above that, which must be awarded gross (and will then be taxed by the Inland Revenue)[15] .

12   If the dismissal is not wrongful, the employee may sue for unpaid wages for the notice period in an action for debt, to which the obligation to mitigate does not apply: *Abrahams v Performing Right Society Ltd* [1995] ICR 1028, [1995] IRLR 486, CA; dicta in this case suggesting that the obligation does not apply even where dismissal is wrongful must be considered to be wrong; see p. 370 n. 15, above.

13   *Yetton v Eastwoods Froy Ltd* [1966] 3 All ER 353, [1967] 1 WLR 104; *Shindler v Northern Raincoat Co Ltd* [1960] 2 All ER 239, [1960] 1 WLR 1038.

14   [1956] AC 185, [1955] 3 All ER 796, HL.

15   *Parsons v BNM Laboratories Ltd* [1964] 1 QB 95, [1963] 2 All ER 658, CA. The tax position must be considered realistically, taking into account any tax rebates due to the employee being unemployed after the dismissal: *Hartley v Sandholme Iron Co Ltd* [1975] QB 600, [1974] 3 All ER 475 (a personal injury case). See also *Bold v Brough, Nicholson and Hall Ltd* [1963] 3 All ER 849, [1964] 1 WLR 201, *Basnett v J & A Jackson Ltd* [1976] ICR 63, [1976] IRLR 154 and *Shove v Downs Surgical plc* [1984] ICR 532, [1984] IRLR 17; Harvey A5A(1); Powell 'The taxation of payments received on termination of employment' (1981) 10 ILJ 239; Bishop and Kay 'Taxation and damages: the rule of Gourley's case' (1987) 104 LQR 211. This is, of course, all on the assumption that the amount recovered by the plaintiff is *damages*; if it is simply a debt under the contract (e.g. a payment in lieu under an *express* 'in lieu' clause in the contract), it is taxable in the hands of the plaintiff anyway: *EMI Group Electronics Ltd v Coldicott* [1999] IRLR 630, [1999] STC 803, CA.

3) *Deduction of other benefits received*   Where a person is unable to work and claims damages because of that, it is likely that he will receive benefits from various sources during the period out of employment; the question then arises whether the amount of those benefits should be deducted from the damages which the defendant must pay. This is obviously of great importance in personal injury claims, where it is well established that insurance payments provided by the plaintiff's own foresight and payment of the premia are not deductible[16], whereas most social security benefits are now (since the Social Security Act 1989) recoverable in full by the state through the system of civil recoupment[17]. Outside those areas, however, the position is less clear, particularly since the decision of the House of Lords in *Parry v Cleaver*[18] which showed a modern tendency not to deduct benefits[19] and concentrated on public policy and overall fairness rather than the older, more technical test for deductibility, such as remoteness, whether the benefit was received as of right and whether the plaintiff had contributed to the scheme providing the benefit. The problem is that the case itself only concerned a contributory police disablement fund and indeed their Lordships declined to consider the deductibility of other benefits (such as those more relevant to the dismissed employee)[20], so that any effect that this case may have on other benefits must be by implication. While in some respects courts subsequently have taken a more straightforward view of quantifying the plaintiff's actual loss[1], the approach in *Parry v Cleaver* was strongly reaffirmed by the House of Lords in *Smoker v London Fire and Civil Defence Authority*[2] where it was held in a personal injury case that private pension benefits were not to be deducted from the plaintiff's damages for loss of earnings and this was applied directly to an action for wrongful dismissal in *Hopkins v Norcros plc*[3]. As the law stands at present, with regard to other benefits particularly applicable to wrongful dismissal cases, it appears that contractual payments by the employer such as sick pay are deductible (even if provided under an insurance policy maintained by the employer)[4], that jobseekers allowance (previously unemployment benefit) received by the dismissed employee during the

---

16   *Bradburn v Great Western Rly Co* (1874) LR 10 Exch 1.

17   Social Security (Recovery of Benefit) Act 1997; see p. 722, below. This new recoupment system does *not* apply to damages for wrongful dismissal.

18   [1970] AC 1, [1969] 1 All ER 555, HL. See generally on this question Lewis 'Deducting collateral benefits from damages: principle and policy' (1998) 18 LS 15, and 'The overlap between damages for personal injury and work related benefits' (1998) 27 ILJ 1.

19   See also *Daish v Wauton* [1972] 2 QB 262, [1972] 1 All ER 25, CA.

20   See [1970] AC 1 at 19 and 39, [1969] 1 All ER 555 at 562 and 579 per Lord Reid and Lord Wilberforce.

1   *Dews v National Coal Board* [1987] ICR 602, [1987] IRLR 330, HL; *Hodgson v Trapp* [1989] AC 807, [1988] 3 All ER 870, HL.

2   [1991] ICR 449, [1991] IRLR 271, HL, see also *Longden v British Coal Corpn* [1998] 1 All ER 289, [1998] ICR 26, HL.

3   [1994] ICR 11, [1994] IRLR 18, CA; this meant on the facts of the case that the wrongfully dismissed company chairman received £99,604 twice, once from the pension fund and once as damages for lost income. The judge at first instance had pointed out that provision could be made expressly either in an employment contract or in the rules of a pension scheme to prevent such double recovery.

4   *Hussain v New Taplow Paper Mills Ltd* [1988] ICR 259, [1988] IRLR 167, HL. In an industrial injury case, one way to prevent the employer (by paying sick pay) effectively subsidising the tortfeasor is to provide in the sick pay clause that, in the event of the injured employee later recovering damages from a third party, amounts paid to the employee as sick pay are refundable to the employer; this should enable damages to be awarded to the employee in full, without deduction of sick pay. Such clauses are used, for example, in agricultural, railway and police contracts.

period by which the damages are calculated is deductible[5], and after considerable doubt over a long period the Court of Appeal held that the same rule of deductibility applies to supplementary benefit (now income support)[6]. The other major benefit which might be relevant is a redundancy payment and while there was some authority in earlier cases[7] against deductibility (on the basis that the payment is due on dismissal anyway, whether or not the dismissal is wrongful) the Court of Appeal have held that such a payment *is* deductible, except possibly in a rare case where it can be shown that the employee would have been made redundant anyway[8].

iii) Wrongful dismissal and unfair dismissal

The obvious contrast between the two is that the statutory action for unfair dismissal involves an enquiry into the overall merits of the dismissal whereas the common law action for wrongful dismissal looks basically to the *form* of the dismissal (except in cases where the employer purported to dismiss summarily for cause and the employee alleges that he gave no such cause). Thus, at common law an employer could dismiss for any reason provided he gave the correct length of notice (or wages in lieu thereof), but for the purposes of unfair dismissal this previously all-important question of notice is of evidential value only, if that, and the fact that proper notice was given will certainly not mean that the dismissal is necessarily fair. Thus, although a dismissal could be both wrongful and unfair, it could also easily be one but not the other. Fundamental concepts, such as the meaning of 'dismissal', can vary from one to the other and so for example a finding that an employee was unfairly dismissed will not necessarily put him at an advantage if he wishes later, in some other context, to claim that the dismissal was also wrongful[9]. Also, the separate principles of compensation operate independently[10] and indeed in theory the primary remedy for unfair dismissal is reinstatement of re-engagement, a remedy which, as seen above, the common law would only countenance in highly unusual cases.

---

5   *Parsons v BNM Laboratories Ltd* [1964] 1 QB 95, [1963] 2 All ER 658, CA: *Foxley v Olton* [1965] 2 QB 306, [1964] 3 All ER 248; *Cheeseman v Bowater UK Paper Mills Ltd* [1971] 3 All ER 513, [1971] 1 WLR 1773, CA. In *Nabi v British Leyland (UK) Ltd* [1980] 1 All ER 667, CA, the Court of Appeal applied the *Parsons* case, but thought that the rule was due for reconsideration. However, the House of Lords applied *Parsons* without demur in *Westwood v Secretary of State for Employment* [1985] ICR 209, [1984] IRLR 209, HL.
6   *Lincoln v Hayman* [1982] 2 All ER 819, [1982] 1 WLR 488, CA (a personal injury case).
7   *Yorkshire Engineering and Welding Co Ltd v Burnham* [1973] 3 All ER 1176, [1974] ICR 77; *Millington v TH Goodwin & Sons Ltd* [1975] ICR 104, [1974] IRLR 379; *Basnett v J and A Jackson Ltd* [1976] ICR 63, [1976] IRLR 154. In each of these cases the decision of Arnold J in *Stocks v Magna Merchants Ltd* [1973] 2 All ER 329, [1973] ICR 530 that a redundancy payment should be deducted was not followed.
8   *Colledge v Bass Mitchells & Butlers Ltd* [1988] ICR 125, [1988] IRLR 163, CA (another personal injury case, where the judge at first instance had made a finding of fact that it was unlikely that the plaintiff would have been made redundant but for the accident).
9   *Turner v London Transport Executive* [1977] ICR 952, [1977] IRLR 441, CA. There is certainly no question of issue estoppel as such as between the unfair and wrongful dismissal actions, but on the other hand there are cases where a finding of fact by a tribunal has been treated as res judicata in later civil proceedings: *Green v Hampshire County Council* [1979] ICR 861; *Automatic Switching Ltd v Brunet* [1986] ICR 542, EAT.
10   *Norton Tool Co Ltd v Tewson* [1973] 1 All ER 183, [1972] ICR 501; *Everwear Candlewick Ltd v Isaac* [1974] 3 All ER 24, [1974] ICR 525; there is, however, a duty to mitigate loss as at common law, imposed specifically by the provisions relating to the compensatory award: Employment Rights Act 1996, s. 123(4).

There used to be a further difference in the appropriate forum. In *Treganowen v Robert Knee & Co Ltd*[11] an employee was dismissed without notice because of a personality clash between her and her colleagues for which she was to blame; the tribunal held that this reason rendered the dismissal fair, but considered that she should not have been dismissed summarily, but should instead have received six weeks' pay in lieu of notice, though they did not have jurisdiction to award this sum. The employee appealed claiming that they did have jurisdiction since the lack of notice was capable of making the dismissal unfair. The EAT dismissed the appeal, clearly holding that, while lack of notice could possibly be of evidential value in deciding some of the points necessary for an unfair dismissal action, it could not per se make a dismissal unfair that was otherwise fair, since it only gave rise to an action for *wrongful* dismissal which had to be brought in the ordinary courts, not before a tribunal at that time. While this case remains an instructive one on the distinction between the two actions, the forum point has been altered by the Employment Tribunals Extension of Jurisdiction Orders 1994[12] which give tribunals the power to hear claims for breach of contract on termination of employment (up to a maximum of £25,000) and at long last have rid us of the previous, very unfortunate, split jurisdiction.

iv) The residual importance of wrongful dismissal

The common law doctrine of notice meant that wrongful dismissal was only a theoretical remedy for a large number of employees, since they were on relatively short notice, so that even if such an employee went to the trouble and expense of bringing a common law action, his damages would be small, since they were so rigidly tied to the amount of wages during the notice period. The statutory action for unfair dismissal, whilst not abolishing wrongful dismissal, is now far more important in practice, with its easier procedure, the possibility (at least in theory) of reinstatement or re-engagement and the more liberal and realistic approach to compensation. On the other hand, there may still be some untypical cases where wrongful dismissal is still important. One class of case would be where the employee does not qualify for the statutory action, in particular where he is in an excluded category or where he lacks the necessary period of continuous service; indeed, in the latter case it has been held that if he falls short of that qualifying period because of the action of the employer in wrongfully dismissing him, he may claim loss of statutory rights as a head of damage in a common law wrongful dismissal action[13]. The most important case, however, would be that of a highly paid employee either on a fixed term contract or entitled to a substantial period of notice, for the compensation for unfair dismissal is subject to statutory maxima[14] which, though perhaps adequate for many employees (certainly when compared to the small amounts recoverable by them for wrongful dismissal), may be a real restriction in the case of the high earner who, if dismissed unfairly *and* wrongfully,

---

11 [1975] ICR 405, [1975] IRLR 247, applied in *BSC Sports and Social Club v Morgan* [1987] IRLR 391.
12 S.I. 1994 No. 1623 in England and Wales; S.I. 1994 No. 1624 in Scotland; see below.
13 See p. 393, above.
14 At the time of writing, the maximum basic award is £6,900; the maximum compensatory was for many years kept at a low level, *not* keeping up with inflation, so that as late as 1999 it was only £12,000. It has now been raised to £50,000 (see p. 505, below), but that could still be a low ceiling in the case of a very high earner.

may have more to gain by an action for wrongful dismissal which is not subject to the statutory maxima. Such an action continues to be governed by the law as set out above, but for most practical purposes a modern dismissal case is likely to proceed on the statutory basis and be subject to the separate body of law on unfair dismissal, to which we must now turn.

Chapter 8

The law and procedure of unfair dismissal

'If we are not careful, we shall find the industrial tribunals bent down under the weight of the law books or, what is worse, asleep under them. Let principles be reported, but not particular instances.'[1]

'We must not strive to create a body of judge-made law supplementing the law as laid down in the Employment Protection (Consolidation) Act 1978. The Act itself provides quite enough law in all conscience ...'[2]

'This is a Tribunal which, rightly in our view, preferred to drink at the pure waters of the section rather than allow itself to be diverted into the channels created by judicial decisions ... in other cases in different circumstances.'[3]

'Deciding these cases is the job of industrial tribunals and when they have not erred in law neither the appeal tribunal nor [the Court of Appeal] should disturb this decision unless one can say in effect: "My goodness, that must be wrong"[4].'

'... [T]he only truth lies in learning to free ourselves from insane passion for the truth[5].'

I   EMPLOYMENT TRIBUNALS AND THE EMPLOYMENT APPEAL TRIBUNAL

The large majority of all employment and industrial relations litigation is handled by employment tribunals, which from inauspicious beginnings under the

1   *Walls Meat Co Ltd v Khan* [1979] ICR 52 at 57, [1978] IRLR 499 at 501, CA per Lord Denning MR.
2   *Kearney & Trecker Marwin Ltd v Varndell* [1983] IRLR 335 at 340, CA per Eveleigh LJ.
3   *Siggs & Chapman (Contractors) Ltd v Knight* [1984] IRLR 83 at 85, per Waite P.
4   *Neale v Hereford and Worcester County Council* [1986] ICR 471 at 483, [1986] IRLR 168 at 173, per May LJ.
5   Umberto Eco *The Name of the Rose* (Picador, 1984) p. 491.

Industrial Training Act 1964 have expanded to assume wide new jurisdictions under the modern employment legislation and in 1994 were at last given common law jurisdiction over breach of contract claims, at least on termination of employment[6]. They started life as 'industrial tribunals' but were renamed 'employment tribunals' in 1998[7], for no apparently compelling reason. As 'industrial juries' they are designed to provide a means of speedy resolution of industrial cases which will often turn very heavily upon their particular facts, and the Donovan Report in 1968[8] referred to their potential advantages as being ease of access, informality, speed and inexpensiveness. Rules of procedure (including pre-trial procedures, such as the simplified pleadings) are drafted with this aim in mind, and the tribunals have wide powers to decide most cases in a common sense way, having regard to 'good industrial practice'. The paradox here, however, is that while the tribunals' procedure may be simplified, the law which they have to apply is often of great complexity and hence the major controversy over how 'legalistic' the proceedings and decisions of tribunals should be. Simple, common sense access to quick justice may be a worthy aim, but there is still a lot of hard law which must be complied with in most of the statutory actions.

This controversy over legalism will be one of the major themes throughout this chapter; it is viewed in many quarters as little less than a disease infecting the tribunal system[9] and, while views in the courts have varied over time (at times involving a clear difference of opinion between the EAT and the Court of Appeal), the modern approach has come down strongly in favour of the anti-legalism camp, with the Employment Rights (Dispute Resolution) Act 1998 making at least piecemeal attempts at reform. The aim of this part of the chapter is to look briefly at the constitution of tribunals and the EAT (and at certain proposals for reform) and then to consider the assault on legalism, suggesting that the problem is not quite as one-dimensional as some would suggest and that perhaps at present the see-saw is a little too far down at one end.

i)   Employment tribunals

Tribunals sit in most local centres of population, under the auspices in England and Wales of 20 local offices, all under the control of the Central Office of Employment Tribunals (COET) in London, and in Scotland three local offices under the control of the COET in Glasgow. Since 1997 the general administration of the whole system is undertaken by an executive agency, the Employment Tribunals Service. A tribunal consists of three people, a legally-qualified chairman and two lay members, one from a panel kept by the Secretary of State in

---

6   See p. 433, below.
7   Employment Rights (Dispute Resolution) Act 1998, s 1. The Industrial Tribunals Act 1996 was renamed the Employment Tribunals Act 1996. All references to these bodies pre-1998 (in cases and legislation) will of course be to 'industrial tribunals'.
8   Royal Commission on Trade Unions and Employers Associations (1968) Cmnd. 3623.
9   See, e.g. ACAS Annual Report 1983, paras. 5.8–5.10 and Annual Report 1984, pp. 63–66. The most obvious manifestation of legalism is the involvement of lawyers at tribunals (and indeed before, e.g. at conciliation), but the application of the phrase goes much deeper, calling into question the very role of the law, the appellate courts and any concept of precedent in the resolution of industrial law cases. For a refutation of the current anti-legalism arguments, see Leslie 'Legalism in industrial tribunals?' [1985] Employment Gazette 357, and in particular the strong defence of the tribunal system in MacMillan 'Employment tribunals: philosophies and practicalities' (1999) 28 ILJ 33.

consultation with employers' organisations and one from a panel kept in consultation with employees' associations. The theory is that, although expressly appointed from each side of industry, the lay members are to act as independent members of the bench, not in a partisan manner, and so they are full members of the tribunal which decides its cases if necessary by a majority (even in the unusual case of the chairman being in the minority)[10]. One of the principal functions of the side members is to use their industrial experience to help the tribunal to come to a sensible and practicable decision; however, this approach must not be taken too far, and the Court of Appeal has warned that knowledge of the industrial background and industrial common sense (though of great importance in many cases) may *not* be used to take a decision directly against the plain meaning of a statutory provision, even if the side members consider the end result of applying that plain meaning to be unfair or ridiculous[11].

The Trade Union Reform and Employment Rights Act 1993 amended these provisions as to the composition of a tribunal by establishing a class of case to be heard by a chairman alone; this was partly to deal with withdrawn or non-contested cases, but it also covered Wages Act cases, applications for interim relief and the common law proceedings that may now be heard by a tribunal, *unless* they raise matters of fact or law such that they should be heard by a full tribunal. This process was taken further by the Employment Rights (Dispute Resolution) Act 1998 which extended the categories of chairman-alone hearings (covering, for example, guarantee payments and redundancy payments and cases involving union subscriptions) against the background of a significant increase in tribunal applications[12]. That Act also provided for the appointment of 'legal officers' to assist the tribunal, in particular by dealing with certain preliminary or interlocutory matters.

The tribunal is administered by a clerk who is a full-time official. The applicant may conduct his case before the tribunal in person or be represented by any other person (sometimes a lawyer, sometimes a trade union official, and the respondent employer may often be represented by a member of the firm's personnel or legal staff[13]); there is no legal aid for representation, and little sign

---

10 Note however that in *Smith v Secretary of State for Trade and Industry* [2000] IRLR 6 Morison P suggested that when the Secretary of State (who appoints the tribunals) is a party to proceedings, the tribunal may not be 'independent' (as required by the Human Rights Act 1998 when it comes into force). This is a matter which will have to be faced.

11 *British Coal Corpn v Cheesbrough* [1988] ICR 769, [1988] IRLR 351, CA.

12 Applications rose sharply from 34,697 in 1990/91 to 71,821 in 1992/93; they peaked at 108,827 in 1995/96, fell back slightly to 80,435 in 1997/8, then rose again to 91,913 in 1998/99 and 103,937 in 1999/2000. Ironically, the changes in the 1998 Act came at a time when the EAT was strongly asserting the desirability of hearings by a full tribunal: *Sutcliffe v Big C's Marina Ltd* [1998] IRLR 428, *Sogbetun v London Borough of Hackney* [1998] ICR 1264, [1998] IRLR 676, EAT.

13 Dickens et al. *Dismissed: a Study of Unfair Dismissal and the Industrial Tribunal System* (1985) found that 23 per cent of applicants had legal representation, 22 per cent had trade union representation and 9 per cent had some other form of representation; 41 per cent of employers had legal representation, 52 per cent had internal company representation and 5 per cent were represented by an employers' association. The Genn Report (The Effectiveness of Representation at Tribunals; Report to the Lord Chancellor, 1989) found broadly the same, with 28 per cent of applicants having legal representation, 16 per cent trade union representation and 18 per cent some other form of representation; 42 per cent of employers had legal representation, 49 per cent internal company representation and 8 per cent employers' association representation. The report has a wealth of information on the effects of representation; see Mullen (1990) 53 MLR 230 and Genn 'Tribunals and Informal Justice' (1993) 56 MLR 393. See also Banerji, Smart & Stevens 'Unfair dismissal cases in 1985–6 – impact on parties' [1990] Employment Gazette 547; Tremlett and Banerji *1992 Survey of Industrial Tribunal Applications* (1994).

of it coming, though a dismissed employee may be eligible to obtain free preliminary advice from a solicitor, and may also be able to turn to his trade union or to the CAB.

Costs are not usually awarded; previously there was an exception where one of the parties acted in a frivolous or vexatious way, and this was widened in 1980 to the present rule[14] whereby an order for costs may be made if a party, in bringing or conducting the proceedings, has acted frivolously, vexatiously *or otherwise unreasonably*[15]. However, this is still far from being an automatic (or indeed ordinary) costs rule and actual orders remain rare[16]; the change in 1980 was probably essentially cosmetic, given complaints by employers that the previous rule encouraged hopeless applications and gave even such hopeless cases a 'nuisance value' (leading, so the argument goes, to too many cases being settled for a certain sum of money to buy off the applicant, regardless of the merit of the claim). This nuisance value remains in spite of the present rule on costs, and it must always be remembered that it is one thing to obtain an order for costs, another thing to enforce it (particularly against an unemployed ex-employee). Apart from specific rules, such as that on costs, the tribunals have wide powers to determine their own procedure by virtue of the Rules of Procedure laid down in regulations[17], which are considered below.

ii)   The Employment Appeal Tribunal

Appeal from a tribunal decision lies to the Employment Appeal Tribunal, a body set up under the Employment Protection Act 1975[18] in much the same form as the National Industrial Relations Court which existed under the Industrial Relations Act 1971. The EAT, a superior court of record, consists of a High Court judge and either two or, more unusually, four lay members, once again giving equal representation to both sides of industry, though once again the members should not act in a partisan manner and the decision of the EAT is by simple majority, if necessary[19]. Where a tribunal has consisted of a chairman sitting alone (as now permitted since the Trade Union Reform and Employment Rights Act 1993), an appeal may be heard by the judge alone. The constitution of the EAT is laid down in the Employment Tribunals Act 1996, which expressly gives it the powers of the High Court *and* those of the employment tribunals[20]. Its procedure

14   Rule 12 – see n. 13, below. Where an applicant is represented by his trade union, any costs awarded against him may take into account that union's means: *Beynon v Scadden* [1999] IRLR 700 (going against earlier authority).

15   This refers to acting unreasonably in bringing or defending the proceedings, *not* to acting unreasonably at the time of the dismissal; thus, costs are not to be used to penalise a party (especially the employer) at that stage: *Davidson v John Calder (Publishers) Ltd* [1985] ICR 143, [1985] IRLR 97, EAT.

16   For example, in 1993–94 costs orders were made in only 177 cases: [1994] Employment Gazette 371.

17   Employment Tribunals (Constitution and Rules of Procedure) Regulations 1993 S.I. 1993 No. 2687, *Harvey* R[540] (in Scotland, S.I. 1993 No. 2688, *Harvey* R[622]). Rule 9 in particular gives a wide discretion: *Dean v Islamic Foundation* [1983] ICR 36, [1982] IRLR 290, CA.

18   Now the Employment Tribunals Act 1996 Part II.

19   This has caused some debate, particularly after the case of *Nethermere (St Neots) Ltd v Gardiner* [1983] ICR 319, [1983] IRLR 103 (extending rights to homeworkers), the argument being that if appeal to the EAT is so stringently confined to a point of law, then should there be two non-lawyers with the power to outvote a High Court judge? The point made about side members in employment tribunals above (p. 403) also applies to side members in the EAT.

20   Ss. 28, 33.

is contained in the EAT Rules laid down in regulations[1]. As in the case of tribunal proceedings, the parties may be represented by anyone and costs are not normally awarded, unless the EAT considers that the appeal was 'unnecessary, improper or vexatious' or there was 'unreasonable delay or other unreasonable conduct in bringing or conducting the proceedings'[2].

The most important point about the appeal to the EAT is that it is an appeal on a point of law *only* (except on an appeal from a decision of the Certification Officer on the registration or certification as independent of a union, where appeal may be on law or fact)[3]; this is a deliberate policy to minimise appeals. The practical significance of this is that the parties must ensure that they argue the facts properly and fully before the tribunal, for if they do not and they lose on the facts (e.g. by not calling all the relevant evidence or by not presenting it sufficiently persuasively) they may not take the matter to the EAT for a second chance. To appeal to the EAT, the party must be able to show that the tribunal were wrong in law. It has been authoritatively stated in *British Telecommunications plc v Sheridan*[4] by the Court of Appeal that this means one of two things – either (a) an ex facie error of law or (b) that the tribunal's decision was perverse. There had been said to be a third category, i.e. where the tribunal misunderstood or misapplied the facts[5], but that was specifically disapproved in *Sheridan*, since it would have permitted the EAT to allow an appeal simply by taking a different view of the facts[6]. The judicial approach to perversity has undergone considerable changes in the last ten years and these are considered below, for it is suggested that the present restricted approach is an integral part of the attack on legalism. In addition to such policy considerations, perversity appeals also face another problem; it is now well established that a tribunal must not simply substitute its own view of what would have been reasonable in the circumstances for that of the employer, but must consider (in an unfair dismissal case) whether dismissal was an option which *a* reasonable employer might have chosen, even if others might not (the 'range of reasonable responses' test, see p. 469, below). Thus, if a tribunal's decision on reasonableness is to be challenged as perverse the appellant has, in effect, a double hurdle – he must show that *no* reasonable tribunal could possibly have come to the conclusion that *a* reasonable employer could have decided to dismiss (where the appellant is the employee) or that *no* reasonable employer could have decided to dismiss (where the appellant is the employer).

Appeal on a point of law is thus tightly circumscribed and the point has been made repeatedly that the EAT must exercise considerable self-restraint in cases where it disagrees profoundly with the decision of the tribunal on the facts but where there is no definable error of law; in such a case it must not interfere[7].

1   S.I. 1993 No. 2854, *Harvey* R[714]. These rules are supplemented by the EAT *Practice Direction* (effective 15 April 1996), set out in *Harvey* at T[1761].
2   Rule 34. *Ravelin v Bournemouth Borough Council* (1986) Times, 19 July, CA.
3   TULR(C)A 1992, s. 9. The EAT will not hear appeals where the dispute has in fact been resolved, even if one or both of the parties wish to have a particular point resolved as a matter of principle: *IMI Yorkshire Imperial Ltd v Olender* [1982] ICR 69. Likewise if there is no real dispute between the parties, who want a ruling for some extraneous purpose: *Baker v Superite Tools Ltd* [1986] ICR 189.
4   [1990] IRLR 27, CA.
5   *Watling v William Bird & Son Contractors Ltd* (1976) 11 ITR 70, per Philips J.
6   Note, however, that if there can be said to be *no* evidence to support a particular finding of fact, that is an error of law under head (a).
7   *Retarded Children's Aid Society Ltd v Day* [1978] ICR 437, [1978] IRLR 128, CA; *Martin v Glynwed Distribution Ltd* [1983] ICR 511, [1983] IRLR 198, CA; *O'Kelly v Trusthouse Forte plc* [1983] ICR 728, [1983] IRLR 369, CA; *Spook Erection v Thackray* [1984] IRLR 116, Ct of

Likewise, there have been repeated warnings by the Court of Appeal to appellants and, more particularly, their legal advisers, that points of fact are not to be dressed up in the garb of points of law in order to bring an appeal[8].

Three further points about the EAT are worth noting. The first is that it will be most reluctant to admit fresh evidence unless, exceptionally, the existence of the fresh evidence could not have been reasonably known of or foreseen (akin to the 'reasonable diligence' test applied generally by the Court of Appeal)[9]; this rule is not to be circumvented by remitting the case to the tribunal for a re-hearing including the otherwise inadmissible evidence[10]. This reinforces the point made above that it is essential that all relevant evidence is placed before the tribunal at the hearing. The second point is that, although the EAT is empowered on appeal to substitute its own decision for that of the tribunal if it allows the appeal[11], if the decision on appeal entails the finding of further facts or the reconsideration of certain existing facts the proper course will normally be to remit the case to the tribunal for further consideration in the light of the EAT's decision[12]. The third point is that as a matter of precedent the EAT is not bound by a previous decision of its own[13]. Thus there have been many instances, in cases raising bona fide matters of law, of a later EAT decision altering the direction of an area of law away from previous authorities. However, there have also been in the past instances of a division of the EAT simply producing a decision inconsistent with previous authority. In a court as busy as the EAT this has sometimes merely been a case of the left hand not knowing what the right is doing, but equally there have been cases where previous authority has been suddenly departed from simply because that particular division of the EAT disagreed with the previous case law[14]. This has caused problems of uncertainty

---

Sess. The decision of the EAT in *Woods v WM Car Services (Peterborough) Ltd* [1981] ICR 666, [1981] IRLR 347 (upheld on appeal: [1982] ICR 693, [1982] IRLR 413, CA) is a good example of the necessary self denial; see also the judgment of Mummery P in *Stewart v Cleveland Guest (Engineering) Ltd* [1996] ICR 535, [1994] IRLR 440. This will be particularly so in matters of procedure which fall primarily within the discretion of the tribunal chairman: *Dietmann v London Borough of Brent* [1987] IRLR 146, CA.

8 See, for example, *Hollister v NFU* [1979] ICR 542, [1979] IRLR 238, CA; *Thomas and Betts Manufacturing Ltd v Harding* [1980] IRLR 255, CA.

9 *Borden (UK) Ltd v Potter* [1986] ICR 647 (overruling the previous 'reasonable explanation' test in *Bagga v Heavy Electricals (India) Ltd* [1972] ICR 118); for an example of the application of this test (and the further requirement that the new evidence would have an important influence on the outcome of the case) see *Wileman v Minilec Engineering Ltd* [1988] ICR 318, [1988] IRLR 144. Similarly, the EAT will not normally allow a party to argue a point of law not taken at the tribunal, unless it is a point that the tribunal should have considered on its own motion: *Langston v Cranfield University* [1998] IRLR 172.

10 *Kingston v British Railways Board* [1984] ICR 781, [1984] IRLR 146, CA.

11 Employment Tribunals Act 1996, s. 33.

12 *O'Kelly v Trusthouse Forte plc* [1983] ICR 728, [1983] IRLR 369, CA.

13 *Secretary of State for Trade and Industry v Cook* [1997] ICR 288, [1997] IRLR 150.

14 A prime example was the decision of Kilner Brown J in *Norris v Southampton City Council* [1982] ICR 177, [1982] IRLR 141 that, contrary to previous authority, a contract of employment *cannot* be rendered void for frustration if the employee is imprisoned. The judgment contains this passage: 'None of this makes the task of Chairmen of Industrial Tribunals any easier. All that we can say by way of comfort is that where there are conflicting decisions of the EAT an Industrial Tribunal may prefer the two decisions previously promulgated and no one would criticise them if they did.' Fortunately, the position has now been set straight, and orthodoxy re-established by the Court of Appeal in *F C Shepherd & Co Ltd v Jerrom* [1986] ICR 802, [1986] IRLR 358, CA, see p. 296, above. For a further example, see *Barking and Dagenham London Borough v Camara* [1988] ICR 865, [1988] IRLR 373, where the EAT under Wood P disapproved and declined to apply the approach to the burden of proof in discrimination cases established by previous EATs in two cases in 1981.

in the past (a point commented on particularly in previous editions of this book), for while flexibility on points of fact may be desirable, it must not be forgotten that employment law has to be applied initially by industrial relations practitioners (in unions and in management) who do look for certainty, at least on points of law that concern them. It is suggested therefore that, in this area, ready departure from established case law may be a luxury that should not be afforded. Fortunately, however, most of the outstanding examples of blatant differences of opinion on major points of law have been resolved over the past few years[15] and the problem now seems to be much less.

iii) The attack on legalism

As stated above, the attack on the perceived problem of over-legalism in the industrial tribunals has been a major feature of modern employment law. It explains certain procedural changes, for example the consistent statements from the Court of Appeal that tribunals do *not* now have to give their reasons as exhaustively (as to fact and law) as a normal court would; presumably the policy behind this is to discourage the losing side's lawyers from poring over the written reasons looking for any technical slip or omission in order to mount an appeal[16]. Further, the Rules of Procedure were altered in 1985 to allow a tribunal to give its reasons in summary form only, in the first instance[17]; where this is done, either party may still require full reasons for the purpose of mounting an appeal, but the onus is upon them to do so. Another procedural example was the institution in 1985 of a special procedure in cases involving appeals on the grounds of perversity (the most suspect ground from the modern point of view, since it can come closest to trying to get the EAT simply to *review* the tribunal's decision on the facts); this was extended in 1997, so that now all cases are to be listed for a short preliminary hearing in order to weed out cases which do not appear to the EAT to raise any genuine point of law[18].

These procedural changes are important in themselves but the principal attacks have come on three substantive fronts – the classification of as many issues as possible as 'ultimately questions of fact for the [employment] tribunal to decide'[19], the disapproval of the previous practice of appellate courts laying down guidelines for tribunals to follow in frequently-recurring instances, and finally (as, arguably, an integral part of the first two) a consistently narrow approach to what can constitute a 'perverse' decision on the facts by a tribunal. The first two of these will now be considered separately (though of course they do tend to run into one another). Looking first at the classification as fact aspect, examples of this abound and will be found throughout this chapter. The following examples

---

15 Two remaining examples are the important practical question of what is the effective date of termination (for unfair dismissal purposes) of a dismissal with wages in lieu of notice (see p. 454, below) and whether the range of reasonable responses test for an unfair dismissal is right or not (see p. 473, below).

16 See p. 429, below. Not only does this mean that tribunal decisions are not to be upset on narrow grounds, but also there is the potentially even more significant point that, given that the reasons do not have to be exhaustive, the EAT and Court of Appeal will *not* draw the inference that because the tribunal omitted to mention a particular fact or argument, therefore they must have overlooked it; this could make an appeal on perversity difficult to maintain.

17 Employment Tribunals (Constitution and Rules of Procedure) Regulations 1993, S.I. 1993 No. 2687, r. 10; *Harvey* R[561].

18 EAT Guidance Notes (Preliminary Hearing/Directions) [1997] IRLR 618.

19 If it moves classify it.

of matters classified as pure questions of fact will suffice for present purposes (and illustrate the breadth of the modern approach which is not confined to major areas of unfair dismissal law): whether a contract is a contract of employment or a contract for services[20]; whether an employer's conduct is bad enough to constitute a constructive dismissal[1]; whether an employee resigned or was forced to do so[2]; contributory fault[3]; whether it was reasonably practicable to present an unfair dismissal claim in time[4]; when discovery is to be ordered[5]; what is 'reasonable' time off work[6]; whether a requirement that indirectly discriminates against women is justifiable[7]. A stir was caused here by the decision of the House of Lords in *Davies v Presbyterian Church of Wales*[8] where Lord Templeman stated that the matter before the court (whether a Methodist minister was an employee) was a question of law, so that the tribunal's decision was reviewable on appeal. However, this dictum in the event has not led to any major change of direction, and was restrictively construed by Slade LJ in *Hellyer Bros Ltd v McLeod*[9], as being confined to cases where the decision on employment status depends wholly on the interpretation of documents. It would therefore take a considerably more unambiguous decision of the House of Lords than *Davies* to reverse the current trend.

Where a matter is clearly classified as one of fact, the losing party cannot appeal on the ground that the tribunal misdirected itself in law, and so will probably be thrown back on the ground that the tribunal's decision was perverse. It is here that the narrow approach to perversity comes in (with the corresponding warnings to the EAT not to reverse a tribunal decision merely because they think it wrong on the facts). In *RSPB v Croucher*[10] Waite P went as far as to call cases of perversity 'exceptional' and said:

> 'We have to remind ourselves of our duty and our functions as an appellate tribunal. We have to remember that it is our duty loyally to follow findings of fact by an industrial tribunal which has enjoyed the advantages, which can never be ours, of having seen witnesses, sensed the atmosphere prevailing in a particular work-place, gauged the qualities of the different personalities, weighed the impact of their effect each upon the other; and that cases must

---

20   *O'Kelly v Trusthouse Forte plc* [1983] ICR 728, [1983] IRLR 369, CA; *Nethermere (St Neots) Ltd v Gardiner* [1984] ICR 612, [1984] IRLR 240, CA. Presumably the *tests* to be applied remain a question of law, but that may mean little here since arguably there are *no* clear tests as to the existence of a contract of employment, see p. 10, above.

1   *Pedersen v Camden London Borough Council* [1981] ICR 674, [1981] IRLR 173, CA; *Woods v WM Car Services (Peterborough) Ltd* [1982] ICR 693, [1982] IRLR 413, CA; see p. 447, below.

2   *Martin v Glynwed Distribution Ltd* [1983] ICR 511, [1983] IRLR 198, CA.

3   *Hollier v Plysu Ltd* [1983] IRLR 260, CA; see p. 514, below.

4   *Palmer v Southend-on-Sea Borough Council* [1984] ICR 372, [1984] IRLR 119, CA; see p. 417, below.

5   *Medallion Holidays Ltd v Birch* [1985] ICR 578 [1985] IRLR 406, disapproving *British Library v Palyza* [1984] ICR 504, [1984] IRLR 306, which had held that a tribunal's decision on procedure was fully reviewable on appeal. See also *Dietmann v London Borough of Brent* [1987] IRLR 146, CA on appeals on procedural matters generally.

6   *Thomas Scott & Sons (Bakers) Ltd v Allen* [1983] IRLR 329, CA.

7   *Home Office v Holmes* [1984] ICR 678, [1984] IRLR 299; *Greater Glasgow Health Board v Carey* [1987] IRLR 484, EAT.

8   [1986] ICR 280, [1986] IRLR 194, HL.

9   [1987] ICR 526, [1987] IRLR 232, CA. This explanation was later approved in *Lee Ting Sang v Chung Chi-Keung* [1990] ICR 409, [1990] IRLR 236, PC and *Clifford v Union of Democratic Mineworkers* [1991] IRLR 518, CA.

10   [1984] ICR 604, [1984] IRLR 425; the passage cited is at 609 and 428, respectively.

be very rare indeed where we take upon ourselves to reach the conclusion that a tribunal has arrived at a result not tenable by any reasonable tribunal properly directed in law.'

This narrow approach to perversity was approved by the Court of Appeal in *Neale v Hereford and Worcester County Council*[11] where May LJ said that an appellate court should only reverse a tribunal's decision if it could be said 'My goodness, that must be wrong'[12]. Indeed, even this well-known explanation was thought possibly too liberal in *Piggott Bros & Co Ltd v Jackson*[13] by Lord Donaldson MR who thought that it might tempt an interventionist EAT into the forbidden land of fact. However, his preferred solution (that perversity could normally only be shown by an error of law or a total lack of evidence) was arguably capable of removing perversity as a separate heading. Subsequently, Wood P in the EAT in *East Berkshire Health Authority v Matadeen*[14] complained that *Piggott* was causing difficulties in appeals, and sought to lean back towards the *Neale* approach, stating that the EAT could interfere if the members[15] were satisfied that the tribunal decision was not a permissible option, or was one which offended reason, or was one which no reasonable tribunal could have reached, or was so clearly wrong that it could not stand. This formulation would leave perversity as a freestanding ground, but how it will eventually fare in the Court of Appeal remains to be seen.

It is not being argued here that the whole movement towards classification as fact is ill-founded, and the policy reasons behind the desire to 'return decision making to the tribunals' can easily be appreciated. What is suggested, however, is that this process has in the past been taken too far and has in certain cases been extended into areas more properly categorisable as matters of law, particularly areas of statutory interpretation, which could lead to major uncertainties as to the ground rules that are to be applied by the tribunals. The clearest example of this occurs under the Trade Union and Labour Relations (Consolidation) Act 1992, section 238 which (after an initial eight-week period) removes the jurisdiction of a tribunal where an employee is dismissed for taking part in 'a strike or other industrial action' unless, inter alia, others taking part were not dismissed (i.e. there has been victimisation). The phrase 'other industrial action' is not defined in the Act and one might have expected it to be a matter of statutory interpretation as to how the phrase is to be applied to the various forms that industrial action can take, i.e. a question of law on which the EAT should pronounce. However, the Court of Appeal held that what constitutes 'other industrial action' is a question of *fact* for the tribunal[16]. Thus, a tribunal in Manchester might decide one day that, in a strike-dismissal case, taking part in a ban on voluntary overtime *was*

---

11   [1986] ICR 471, [1986] IRLR 168, CA; moreover it was held in *Campion v Hamworthy Engineering Ltd* [1987] ICR 966, CA that if a case goes to the Court of Appeal on perversity, that court's function is to apply the *Neale* test to the tribunal's decision, *not* to consider whether the EAT's decision on the point was correct.

12   This is known in some quarters as the 'Biggles test' (see (1987) 16 ILJ 213) due to a flippant remark in the *Harvey* bulletin that although this statement is entirely consistent with the modern approach, its phraseology may appear over-reliant on the writings of Captain W. E. Johns ('Gosh' said Biggles as a shell ripped off his right leg).

13   [1992] ICR 85, [1991] IRLR 309, CA.

14   [1992] ICR 723, [1992] IRLR 336.

15   One strong argument by Wood P is that the lay members are there to contribute their industrial expertise, and are capable of applying such tests of perversity 'when viewed against appropriate industrial experience and practice'.

16   *Coates v Modern Methods and Materials Ltd* [1982] ICR 763, [1982] IRLR 318, CA; see p. 640, below.

industrial action, while the next day a tribunal in Leeds in a similar case might decide that such a ban was *not* industrial action, with the result that the bar on jurisdiction in section 238 would apply in one case but not in the other; however, the point would then be that, as it is a question of fact, *both* tribunals would be right and (except in the 'exceptional' case of a finding of perversity on appeal) both decisions would be upheld[17]. What is the lawyer to say if asked, for example, by an employee client whether he will be able to claim unfair dismissal if he takes part in a voluntary overtime ban and is dismissed (naively expecting there to be an answer to his question)? This particular problem under section 238 occurred in *Naylor v Orton and Smith Ltd*[18] and was subject to strong criticism by Browne-Wilkinson P:

> '... [A] decision to impose an immediate overtime ban could reasonably be considered as not constituting taking industrial action, as the Industrial Tribunal held: it could also reasonably be considered to constitute industrial action. Since both views are reasonable, we cannot interfere with the Industrial Tribunal decision. ... Whether such employees have a claim for unfair dismissal will depend on whether or not the Industrial Tribunal they chance to come before takes the view that they were taking part in industrial action. ... In our view it is not in the best interests of orderly industrial relations that such severe consequences to both employers and employees should depend on which of two, equally correct but diametrically opposite, views is subsequently adopted by the Industrial Tribunal before which the case may come.'

However, in the light of the later case law, the voice of this particularly learned President of the EAT has been as one crying in the wilderness, for subsequently the possibility of this sort of major inconsistency has been said to be an inherent, if unfortunate, aspect of the flexibility of the tribunal system[19], a price which has to be paid. Part of that price is that it might be difficult, if not impossible to bring a case before a tribunal or, indeed, an appeal to the EAT in order to set a clear precedent, in the nature of a 'test case' (e.g. where there are likely to be several or indeed many other employees in a similar position); likewise, cases which are reported and seem to mark a significant development in the law should be treated with caution for the same reason – to take one example, the case of *Home Office v Holmes*[20] which was widely reported in the press (and greeted enthusiastically by the EOC) as a major breakthrough allowing women to claim to work part-time

---

17   To paraphrase a character from N.F. Simpson's play *A Resounding Tinkle* – isn't the world wonderful, and if it had all been totally different, that would have been pretty wonderful too.

18   [1983] IRLR 233; the passage cited is at 237. Remarks about the length of tribunal members' feet might also have been appropriate.

19   See, e.g. *Kidd v DRG (UK) Ltd* [1985] ICR 405, [1985] IRLR 190, at 417 and 196 respectively, per Waite P, and *Gilham v Kent County Council (No 2)* [1985] ICR 233, [1985] IRLR 8, CA at 240 and 22, respectively, per Griffiths LJ ('endemic in a system where there is no appeal on fact') and pp. 244 and 23, per Dillon LJ ('inherent in the system which Parliament has set up'). In the latter case it was clearly held that the fact (put forward by the appellant) that two other tribunals had previously reached the opposite conclusion in very similar cases (concerning councils effecting cuts by altering dinner ladies' contracts) was *no* basis for an argument that the tribunal's decision was perverse. For a further example, contrast the end results of two cases of dismissals arising during the miners' strike – *McLaren v National Coal Board* [1988] ICR 370, [1988] IRLR 215, CA and *Dillett v National Coal Board* [1988] ICR 218, CA.

20   [1984] ICR 678, [1984] IRLR 299; see p. 251, above.

through the use of the concept of indirect sex discrimination is, when looked at in the light of this modern approach, nothing of the sort, as in fact Waite P was at pains to point out at the end of his judgment, and indeed subsequently in *Greater Glasgow Health Board v Carey*[1] the EAT held in a similar case that although there might be indirect discrimination, it was justified on the facts and so the claim failed; a sobering example is set by another 'breakthrough', that in *Clarke v Eley (IMI) Kynoch Ltd*[2] that operating a 'part-timers first' rule on redundancy may constitute indirect sex discrimination, for in the subsequent case of *Kidd v DRG (UK) Ltd*[3] the EAT upheld a tribunal decision entirely to the contrary.

Turning now to the other major limb of the attack on legalism, the discouragement of judicial guidelines, a similar picture emerges but here, if anything, the law has seen more definable swings. During the 1970s, under the NIRC and in the early days of the EAT (especially under the presidency of Phillips J), a need was perceived to put some flesh on to the bare bones of the new statutory provisions on unfair dismissal – after all, a statute that simply says that a tribunal is to look at how reasonably an employer behaved in the light of equity and the substantial merits of the case, or that an employee who is a union officer has a right to reasonable time off, is not immediately self-explanatory. Moreover, in the law on unfair dismissal, it soon became obvious that the overall test of fairness was having to be applied by tribunals in many cases to frequently-recurring fact situations (e.g. suspected theft, long-term illness, business reorganisation), so that some consistency of approach was needed in order to avoid a completely 'palm tree justice' approach. The answer was for the appellate court to lay down judicial guidelines for the tribunals on major aspects of unfair dismissal law. These were not rules of law, so that it was never the case that failure to apply a relevant guideline was automatically an appealable error of law[4]. However, if a tribunal did apply such a guideline its decision would probably not be upset on appeal. Moreover, this approach fitted in well with the then prevailing views on when a tribunal decision should be held to be perverse. A much wider approach was taken in this time of judicial activism, and in particular a decision that was thought to be 'contrary to good industrial practice' by all three members of the EAT (the two wingmen taking that decision in the light of their industrial experience) was likely to be held to be perverse[5]; 'good industrial practice' in many instances was to be found in the existing and often-applied guidelines. This gave the appellate court a considerable supervisory jurisdiction and had the merit of a desirable amount of certainty; however the other, less desirable effect was the growth of a formidable body of precedent on unfair dismissal law, a proliferation of appeals, what was seen to be an unnecessarily high level of legalism, and the danger of turning employment law into a heavy case-law subject (especially with the large scale reporting of the cases in the specialist law reports). These negative factors, along with the general feeling that the tribunals' discretion was being unduly restricted and real decision-making being taken away from them contrary to Parliament's intention, led to a major attack on judicial

---

1   [1987] IRLR 484.
2   [1983] ICR 165, [1982] IRLR 482; see p. 490, below.
3   [1985] ICR 405, [1985] IRLR 190. Once again, what is the lawyer to say if an employer seeks his advice, asking 'Is it lawful to make redundancies on a part-timers-first basis?'
4   See *Jowett v Earl of Bradford (No 2)* [1978] ICR 431 at 436, per Bristow J.
5   This approach was summarised by Phillips P writing extra-judicially in 'Some notes on the Employment Appeal Tribunal' (1978) 7 ILJ 137, p. 140. For a rare subsequent application of this approach, see the judgment of Nolan J in *Payne v Spook Erection Ltd* [1984] IRLR 219.

guidelines by the Court of Appeal, principally in *Bailey v BP Oil (Kent Refinery) Ltd*[6] in which Lawton LJ said:

'Each case must depend on its own facts. In our judgment it is unwise for this Court or the Employment Appeal Tribunal to set out guidelines, and wrong to make rules and establish presumptions for Industrial Tribunals to follow or to take into account when applying [the statutory test of fairness].'

The implication of this (i.e. that there is *no* value in guidelines) was contested by the EAT under the presidency of Browne-Wilkinson J who, while accepting the argument that judicial intervention had gone too far[7], considered the position taken by the Court of Appeal to be an over-reaction and tried to take a middle course. This consisted of continuing to develop guidelines but with more circumspection and with more stress on their evidential value only; *Williams v Compair Maxam Ltd*[8] is the best example of this, with its comprehensive re-examination of the circumstances in which a redundancy dismissal (normally fair) can become unfair on general principles. However, the approach of the Court of Appeal continued unaltered[9] and with the change of presidency in 1983 it soon became clear that under Waite P the EAT itself would apply the law as laid down by the Court of Appeal, and enthusiastically rather than reluctantly[10], an approach also adopted by his successor, Popplewell P[11]. Indeed, whereas it was possible to argue that what the Court of Appeal was saying initially on the question of guidelines was 'so far and no further'[12], the approach particularly of Waite P was to call into question even well established guidelines and cases which for years have been considered central to the developing law on unfair dismissal[13].

As in the case of classification as fact, the narrow approach to what can constitute perversity aided this approach materially, for under this approach not only would it not be a ground for perversity that the tribunal failed to apply an established guideline, but ironically the only certain ground for perversity would be that a tribunal felt itself *bound* to follow a guideline rather than applying a more general

---

6   [1980] ICR 642, [1980] IRLR 287, CA; the passage cited is at 648 and 289 respectively. See also *Thomas and Betts Manufacturing Ltd v Harding* [1980] IRLR 255, CA and *UCATT v Brain* [1981] ICR 542, [1981] IRLR 224, CA. One problem is that, as Browne-Wilkinson P pointed out in *Grundy (Teddington) Ltd v Plummer* [1983] ICR 367, [1983] IRLR 98, the Court of Appeal at the time on at least two occasions specifically approved existing guidelines laid down by the EAT: *W Weddel & Co Ltd v Tepper* [1980] ICR 286, [1980] IRLR 96, CA and *W & J Wass Ltd v Binns* [1982] ICR 486, [1982] IRLR 283, CA (though the latter case was later overruled by the House of Lords, see p. 469, below).

7   See the Hon Mr Justice Browne-Wilkinson, 'The role of the EAT in the 1980s' (1982) 11 ILJ 69.

8   [1982] ICR 156, [1982] IRLR 83. See also *Grundy (Teddington) Ltd v Plummer*, in n. 1, above.

9   *Varndell v Kearney & Trecker Marwin Ltd* [1983] ICR 683, [1983] IRLR 335, CA; see the dictum cited at the beginning of this chapter on the primacy of the wording of the statute.

10 Sir John Waite 'Lawyers and laymen as judges in industry' (1986) 15 ILJ 32.

11 Sir Oliver Popplewell 'Random thoughts from the President's chair' (1987) 16 ILJ 209; at p. 213 he states, 'So far as the present EAT is concerned, we have striven continuously to discourage the constant or indeed any citing of authorities wherever that is possible'.

12 It would, for example, be almost impossible to apply any kind of rational rules now as to the assessment of compensation for unfair dismissal, without applying the categories of loss set out in the central case of *Norton Tool Co Ltd v Tewson* [1972] ICR 501, [1972] IRLR 86, see p. 508, below.

13 See particularly *Anandarajah v Lord Chancellor's Department* [1984] IRLR 131, EAT.

test based upon the wider wording of the statute[14]. It is of course true that a tribunal might choose to apply existing and well-applied guideline authority, and hopefully in many instances would continue to do so. The uncertainty inherent in this modern approach arose from the fact that a *failure* to follow the commonly accepted pattern in frequently recurring cases would *not* be an appealable error of law. Perhaps fortunately, the pendulum received a healthy pull back towards the centre under the presidency of Wood P who, from the beginning of his term, showed himself more sympathetic to the constructive use of guideline authority[15], and (as will be seen throughout the parts of this book dealing with individual employment law) handed down a series of lucid and highly useful judgments on approaches or procedures to be adopted when dealing with frequently-occurring employment problems, in what may be considered a particularly fruitful period in the EAT's short history. His successors, Mummery P and Morison P, have continued this more active approach, which has been emphasised by the sudden increase during this time of cases in which the EAT has had to consider complex questions of EC law and its effect on domestic employment legislation (which certainly cannot be shunted off into limbo by being called a matter of fact, and on which detailed guidance to tribunals has been essential). Moreover, the novel approach of appointing a specialist employment lawyer directly to the EAT (in the person of Judge Clark) has had an effect in producing judgments reassessing and re-evaluating certain longstanding rules or guidelines in the light of modern employment conditions. However, it remains the case that in general the use of guidelines today has to be not only constructive, but also circumspect, and we have not necessarily heard the last word[16].

To reiterate the point made above about the first line of attack on legalism, the argument here is *not* that a drive to decrease legalism and formalism in industrial tribunals is misconceived, especially given the widespread criticism of over-legalism from *both* sides of industry. The point that is being made is that it is possible to take the attack too far and produce a situation of equal but opposite imbalance, in which the disadvantages of rampant uncertainty and difficulty (if not impossibility) of advising in advance of problems outweigh the advantages of what is perceived to be desirable non-legalism[17]. The clarion call to return decision making to the tribunals and keep the lawyers out[18] may be superficially of great attraction to practitioners of industrial relations, but one may wonder whether

---

14   *Rolls-Royce Motors Ltd v Dewhurst* [1985] ICR 869, [1985] IRLR 184, EAT.

15   Sir John Wood, 'The EAT as it enters the 1990s' (1990) 19 ILJ 133; note particularly his approving references to (now) Lord Browne-Wilkinson's presidency and his remarks on perversity and the role of the EAT's industrial members.

16   A very different Court of Appeal approach can be seen in *Kwik Save Stores v Greaves; Crees v Royal London Mutual Insurance Society Ltd* [1998] ICR 848, [1998] IRLR 245, CA where the law relating to the return to work of an employee after maternity leave was subjected to fundamental (and surprising) revision, purely as a matter of statutory interpretation in a very interventionist judgment. However, that was in the context of our previous, fearsomely complex, maternity laws; in the wider context of unfair dismissal it may be that that court would still be more 'hands off'.

17   One argument might be that if non-legalism is the dominant aim, the best way to achieve it would be to do away with the whole tribunal system and replace it with a system of compulsory arbitration in dismissal cases; see heading (iv) below. For a strong refutation of this view, see MacMillan 'Employment tribunals: philosophies and practicalities' (1999) 28 ILJ 33, and see to the contrary Clark 'Adversarial and investigative approaches to the arbitral resolution of dismissal disputes (1999) 28 ILJ 319.

18   'The first thing we do, let's kill all the lawyers' (*Henry VI, Part 2,* IV ii) is merely an exaggerated form of such a sentiment.

the attraction would be as great if the corresponding disadvantages were properly explained, particularly the disadvantage of not being able to get a relatively simple answer to a simple question from a lawyer consulted on the legality or otherwise of a projected course of action; if taken to its logical conclusion, the only answer to most questions, given an extreme anti-legalism approach, would be that it would depend on the reaction of the particular tribunal on the day in question. A danger of this would be that if employers were convinced that tribunals operated in an unpredictable, or even random, manner[19], unfair dismissal law could lose much of its normative value as an instrument for the promotion of fair employment practices, in that employers might take the view that there was little point in trying to act in a way that could predictably be judged as good industrial relations practice, and that they might as well simply proceed in any way that seemed most expedient in the circumstances and hope, if challenged, to strike lucky with a sympathetic tribunal.

Given that there is a serious problem over the balance to be struck between flexibility and informality on the one hand and certainty and normative effect on the other, one possible way out of the log-jam was perceived at one stage to be the updating and, more importantly, the expansion of the original ACAS Code of Practice No. 1 on disciplinary practice and procedures[20]. The idea was that such a code would be a more far-reaching document giving guidance on the handling, not just of dismissals generally, but of dismissals and disciplinary proceedings concerning some of the more common problems encountered in practice. After much work, ACAS produced a draft code which, while giving guidance largely gleaned from the decided cases, could have been relied on as a *distillation* of that case law, without reference to a battery of law reports (and, arguably, without the need for it to be supplemented by further case law). The middle ground could have been reoccupied without falling into the trap of over-legalism. However, when the draft code was submitted to the then Secretary of State for Employment, Lord Young, he refused to approve it[1]. The basis for this deeply regrettable decision was largely that the code was thought to be too long and detailed ('aimed primarily at lawyers and personnel managers in larger firms') and would be difficult for a small firm to apply[2]; the irony here is that it is precisely these small firms, without professional personnel staff, who could be said to be most in need of straightforward guidelines (indeed, check-lists) on the various problems likely to be encountered in practice which could lead to a dismissal, and although the draft code as a whole was quite long, the individual chapters were not and any complications were largely the result of the legal complications inevitably arising in such a diverse area. The Secretary of State invited ACAS to redraft the code and resubmit it. Instead of doing so, they used much of the material to produce

19   In such matters, objective fact may be less important than received opinion; an example of this is the resilience of the myth that employers are guilty until proved innocent in tribunal proceedings, in which they stand little chance of success, whereas in practice for years the employee applicant has had a less than evens chance of success before a tribunal.

20   See p. 436, below. See, e.g., the support given to this idea by Sir John Waite, op. cit., n. 10 above.

1   See p. 44, above. The text of the Secretary of State's letter to the Chairman of ACAS setting out his reason is in [1987] Employment Gazette 150.

2   Other reasons related to the danger of the code itself giving rise to case law on its interpretation (leading to frequent need for revision) and the criticism that the code mixed up substantive law with general advice so that it was difficult to tell what was actually obligatory. It is interesting to note that the latter criticism was made of the codes of practice on the closed shop and on picketing, which were produced by the previous government.

an advisory handbook 'Discipline at Work' which covers rules and procedures, counselling, disciplinary interviews, disciplinary action and appeals; in addition, it gives guidance on the substantive areas of criminal charges, absence, substandard work, ill health and failure to return from leave, and contains checklists, precedents and the text of the Code of Practice. As this is not formally a code of practice, it does not have to be considered by a tribunal, but on the other hand there is no reason why it could not be put to a tribunal by either party as evidence of good practice or otherwise. It should certainly be read and borne in mind by students and practitioners of this subject, particularly as it gives a good flavour and overview of many of the detailed legal rules that follow in this chapter.

iv) Suggested reforms

Partly due to concerns about over-legalism, real or perceived, suggestions for reform of the industrial tribunal system have been put forward with some frequency. Three in particular are mentioned here. The first is that there has been a long-standing argument that unfair dismissal cases should be dealt with by arbitration rather than through tribunals. As the legislation is drafted, it seems to be assumed that arbitration should be at least a viable alternative, since by virtue of section 110 of the Employment Rights Act 1996 the parties to a dismissal procedure agreement (e.g. as part of a collective agreement) may apply to the Secretary of State to 'contract out' of unfair dismissal law (i.e. that any dismissals will be dealt with *solely* under the procedure, with no right to apply to a tribunal). In the event, however, only the electrical contracting industry has taken advantage of this procedure, which has fallen into disuse[3]. It has always been arguable that more use could be made of contracting out, particularly in large industries with sophisticated disciplinary procedures, often culminating in ACAS-organised arbitration[4], and the case has been made for a large-scale transfer of functions[5].

The second significant set of suggestions were contained in the Justice Report 'Industrial Tribunals' (1987) which is highly recommended reading on this subject. The committee which produced the report saw considerable scope for reforms to the present tribunal system; these included the following: (1) wider selection of side members to be more representative; (2) increased training for both chairmen and side members; (3) specialised training for those who are to sit on sex discrimination and race relations cases[6]; (4) the appointment of 'tribunal officers' whose task it would be to investigate cases at a preliminary stage and isolate the issues to be tried if and when a case came before the tribunal

---

3 Two reasons are put forward for this: (1) an over-rigid approach by the DE (as it was), insisting that any exempt procedure should mirror unfair dismissal law closely, and (2) simple ignorance today of the possibility of contracting out.

4 If there is no contracting out order, a dismissed employee can go through the whole internal procedure and, if he loses, then go to a tribunal (provided he submitted his claim within the three-month limitation period). In practice, however, when this happens, the tribunal usually comes to the same conclusion as the arbitrator.

5 Rideout, 'Unfair dismissal – tribunal or arbitration' (1986) 15 ILJ 84.

6 This would have to be handled carefully – the report argues that these cases are special in that frequently there will be no *direct* evidence of discrimination and so the issue will be as to the inferences that should properly be drawn; on the other hand, if badly handled a recommendation such as this might appear to be a sophisticated form of jury knobbling.

itself[7]; (5) the transfer of most common law claims on the contract of employment from the ordinary courts to the tribunals[8]; (6) the transfer of the tribunals' current jurisdiction over cases between a member and his trade union to the ordinary courts or the Certification Officer; (7) the encouragement of collective contracting out (above); (8) the laying down of guidelines by ACAS in regularly reviewed codes of practice[9] and (9) a power to award interest on tribunal awards, which should be made easier to enforce.

The report then goes on to consider a more radical set of reforms, involving a complete restructuring[10]. Their suggested system would be two-tier: (i) a lower tier of tribunals hearing the bulk of cases with increased reliance on preliminary investigation to sift the facts (by the tribunal officer suggested above) and an improved inquisitorial procedure aimed at lessening the need for legal representation[11]; (ii) a reconstituted EAT sitting as an Industrial Court with appellate jurisdiction from the lower tier on points of law, but also original jurisdiction to hear cases assigned to it because they involve either points of law, complex facts or importance as test cases. In contrast to the improved inquisitorial function of the lower tier, the Industrial Court would have improved representation before it (with legal aid), relying on a more traditional adversarial approach, though staffed by a more specialised judiciary and more highly trained side members.

The third set of suggestions came in late 1994 with the publication of the long-promised Green Paper on the future of the tribunals[12]. Given some urgency by the doubling of the number of cases registered before tribunals in four years[13] with little sign of any slow down, the paper was generally less wide ranging than the Justice Report and more concerned with procedural reforms aimed at cost-reducing efficiencies, such as easier disposal of weak or unpursued cases, extending the scope of compromise agreements, more chairman-only hearings and improved liaison with ACAS. However, two ideas were floated that are of greater interest in principle. The first was the possibility of placing more emphasis

---

7   This would be in addition to ACAS conciliation, and would *not* be done by ACAS; the officer would produce a written dossier for the tribunal, and would increase the inquisitional function of the system generally. In a successful case, the officer could investigate the possibility of re-employment. This suggestion goes much further than the 'legal officers' appointable under the Employment Rights (Dispute Resolution) Act 1998.

8   Such a transfer occurred in 1994, but unfortunately only in relation to claims arising on termination of employment. The case for going further and having full 'labour courts' is made by Wedderburn 'The social charter in Britain – labour law and labour courts' (1991) 54 MLR 1, especially at pp. 25ff.

9   This proposal is of interest in the light of the discussion under heading iii) above. Discussing the modern anti-legalistic approach, the report states (at p. 53), 'The result of this reduction of the appellate function and the abandonment of guidelines has been to devalue the EAT. It has in effect condoned a great degree of inconsistency between tribunals hearing similar cases in different parts of the country. Little practical guidance can now be obtained from EAT decisions by industrial relations practitioners who wish to avoid facing an industrial tribunal'.

10   Appendix 1 to the report contains comparative material on the approach to labour courts taken in certain foreign jurisdictions.

11   This suggestion is of course the very reverse of the well-known statement of the EAT on the desirability of normally following usual court procedures and rules of evidence in tribunal cases: *Aberdeen Steak Houses Group plc v Ibrahim* [1988] ICR 550, [1988] IRLR 420, see p. 428, below.

12   Resolving employment rights disputes – options for reform (Cm. 2707, 1994); see Cockburn (1995) 24 ILJ 285 he refers to the Green Paper as a 'pot pourri of ideas that the authors have assembled and put under various subject headings', i.e. with little internal coherence.

13   See p. 403, n. 12, above

on the exhaustion by an employee of internal procedures within the firm or organisation before going to a tribunal; the second was the re-emergence of the voluntary arbitration option, as a binding (and cheaper) alternative to tribunal proceedings, with the clear understanding that the arbitrator would not primarily be applying unfair dismissal law as applied by the tribunals, but would instead be applying the parties' own rules and expectations, as reflected in the terms of reference[14]. The previous government stated their intent to proceed with most of the Green Paper proposals; on the change of government in 1997, this was one of the first areas to show the likely continuity of approach by the new government which, after a further consultation exercise, produced and passed the Employment Rights (Dispute Resolution) Act 1998 (their first legislation in the area) which (i) renamed the tribunals 'employment tribunals', (ii) increased the incidence of determinations without full hearings or by chairman alone, (iii) introduced legal officers to deal with preliminary issues, (iv) broadened the rules on compromise agreements, (v) placed penalties on employees seeking unfair dismissal awards without first going through internal procedures, and (vi) gave the statutory basis for the ACAS arbitration alternative in unfair dismissal cases[15]. Conceptually it is this last development which is the most fundamental, though at the time of writing the eventual take-up rate is unforeseeable.

2 PROCEDURE

The rules of procedure have been deliberately simplified in tribunal and EAT cases[16], particularly as regards pre-trial matters such as pleadings, which are on simplified standard forms and administered through the tribunal offices. The detailed rules of procedure are considered in full elsewhere[17], but certain of the more important aspects are considered now in outline.

i) Time limits

As in the case of actions to enforce other employment protection rights such as guarantee payments, payment during suspension on medical grounds, and time off work[18], an action for unfair dismissal is subject to a fairly stringent three month time limit, i.e. the action must be commenced within three months of the effective date of termination[19]. The aim is obviously to promote speedy trial of

---

14 In this context, the Green Paper draws heavily on Lewis & Clark *Employment rights, industrial tribunals and arbitration: the case for alternative dispute resolution* (Institute of Employment Rights, 1993).

15 See p. 434, below.

16 Tribunal procedure is governed by the Employment Tribunals (Constitution and Rules of Procedure) Regulations 1993, S.I. 1993 No. 2687 (in Scotland S.I. 1993 No. 2688); see *Harvey* R[540] and [622].

17 *Harvey* Div. T.

18 An action for a redundancy payment is subject to a six month limit which operates in a different way – Employment Rights Act 1996, s. 164(1).

19 Ibid., s. 111(2); see *Harvey* T[186]. Sub-s. (3) allows a complaint to be presented before the effective date of termination provided that the complainant is under notice at the time; this includes notice given by the employee himself where he resigns but claims constructive dismissal: *Presley v Llanelli Borough Council* [1979] ICR 419, [1979] IRLR 381. The earlier 28-day period had proved to be too short and gave rise to problems for the NIRC. The difficulty for the non-unionised worker, not fully aware of his rights, is considerable – see, e.g., the discussion in *Crown Agents v Lawal* [1979] ICR 103, [1978]

the matter, but an absolute rule could cause hardship, so in each statutory provision which is modelled on the unfair dismissal one there is a qualification in this form: '... or within such further period as the tribunal considers reasonable in a case where it is satisfied that it was not reasonably practicable for the complaint to be presented before the end of the period of three months.' There are three leading cases on the construction of the 'not reasonably practicable' exception; the first is the decision of the Court of Appeal in *Dedman v British Building and Engineering Appliances Ltd* [20] that the test is whether the applicant had just cause or excuse for not complying with the limit. Ignorance of his rights (or knowledge of his rights but ignorance of the time limit) will not normally be sufficient (particularly as unfair dismissal has now been with us for some time, and a dismissed employee has various sources of information and advice, for example posters and leaflets at employment offices); the applicant will have to show some further factor:

> '... does total ignorance of his rights inevitably mean that it was impracticable for him to present his complaint in time? In my opinion, no. It would be necessary to pay regard to his circumstances and the course of events. What were his opportunities for finding out that he had rights? Did he take them? If not, why not? Was he misled or deceived? Should there prove to be an acceptable explanation of his continuing ignorance of the existence of his rights, it would not be appropriate to disregard it, relying on the maxim "ignorance of the law is no excuse". The word "practicable" is there to moderate the severity of the maxim and to require an examination of the circumstances of his ignorance. But what if, as here, a complainant knows he has rights but does not know that there is a time limit? Ordinarily, I would not expect him to be able to rely on such ignorance as making it impracticable to present his claim in time. Unless he can show a specific and acceptable explanation for not acting within [three months] he will be out of court[1].'

Secondly, in *Walls Meat Co Ltd v Khan*[2] the applicant knew of his rights and of the three months limit, but mistakenly thought that his unfair dismissal claim would be covered by the same procedure and heard by the same tribunal as his concurrent claim for unemployment benefit; he did not discover his mistake until the three month period had elapsed, but the Court of Appeal allowed him to bring his claim, on the basis that his genuine mistake constituted just cause or excuse. However, Lord Denning MR (in addition to stressing that the application

IRLR 542. In this context, 'presented' means actually received; *House v Emerson Electric Industrial Controls* [1980] ICR 795; *Post Office v Moore* [1981] ICR 623. On the posting of an application, see *St Basil's Centre v McCrossan* [1992] ICR 140, [1991] IRLR 455 and *Birmingham Midshires Building Society v Horton* [1991] ICR 648, EAT.

20   [1974] 1 All ER 520; [1974] ICR 53, CA. When *Dedman* was decided, the relevant wording was 'not practicable'; however, that was construed in such a way that the addition of 'reasonably' in 1974 was held not to alter the test: *Times Newspapers Ltd v O'Regan* [1977] IRLR 101. The phrase 'reasonably practicable' was criticised by Waite P as too imprecise (*Croydon Health Authority v Jaufurally* [1986] ICR 4); he thought that Parliament should either spell out the exceptions or leave the whole matter in the discretion of the tribunal, to extend time simply if it was 'fair' to do so. Similar sentiments were expressed by the Master of the Rolls in *London International College Ltd v Sen* [1993] IRLR 333, CA.

1   Ibid., at 528 and 64 respectively, per Scarman LJ.

2   [1979] ICR 52, [1978] IRLR 499, CA.

of the test lies very much within the discretion of the tribunal) said that tribunals should be 'fairly strict' in enforcing the time limit, and so wherever possible the dismissed employee should ensure that an application goes in within the period – it may not be enough to say that he thought it better to wait the outcome of some other event before applying (e.g. the decision of a court in a pending criminal action against him, on the ground of which he was dismissed[3]). The applicant will not be in any better position if he seeks the help of a 'skilled adviser' (such as a lawyer, trade union official or the Citizens' Advice Bureau[4]), for if that adviser makes a mistake as to the time limit, or omits to advise him about it (even where the adviser was primarily being consulted on another matter[5] such as defending a pending criminal action, as in the above example), the applicant may not use that mistake or omission as a ground for seeking an extension of time:

'But what is the position if he goes to skilled advisers and they make a mistake? The English court has taken the view that the man must abide by their mistake. There was a case where a man was dismissed and went to his trade association for advice. They acted on his behalf. They calculated the three months wrongly and posted the complaint two or three days late. It was held that it was "practicable" for it to have been posted in time. He was not entitled to the benefit of the escape clause: see *Hammond v Haigh Castle & Co Ltd*[6]. I think that was right. If a man engages skilled advisers to act for him – and they mistake the time limit and present it too late – he is out. His remedy is against them[7].'

The third leading case is *Palmer v Southend-on-Sea Borough Council*[8] which sets the previous case law into the context of the modern approach to unfair dismissal law by stressing that the application of the exemption is essentially a question of fact. The Court of Appeal did consider the test to be applied and May LJ suggested that the question is whether it was 'reasonably feasible' to have presented the

---

3   *Norgett v Luton Industrial Co-operative Society Ltd* [1976] ICR 442, [1976] IRLR 306; *Porter v Bandridge Ltd* [1978] ICR 943, [1978] IRLR 271, CA; *Walls Meat Co Ltd v Khan*, n. 2, above, at 56 and 501 respectively, per Lord Denning MR.
4   *Riley v Tesco Stores Ltd* [1980] ICR 323, [1980] IRLR 103, CA. However, reliance on bad advice from a tribunal official *may* be acceptable: *Rybak v Jean Sorelle Ltd* [1991] ICR 127, [1991] IRLR 153; even if a solicitor has also been consulted: *London International College v Sen* [1993] IRLR 333, CA.
5   *Norgett v Luton Industrial Co-operative Society Ltd*, n. 3, above; cf. *Union Cartage Co Ltd v Blunden* [1977] ICR 420, [1977] IRLR 139, though the approach in this case was doubted by Lord Denning MR in *Walls Meat Co Ltd v Khan*, n. 19, above and the approach in *Norgett*'s case preferred by the Court of Appeal in *Riley v Tesco Stores Ltd*, n. 4, above. Confusion between the employee and the adviser as to who was to make the application will not be enough: *Dowty Aerospace Gloucester Ltd v Ballinger* (1993) Times, 5 March, EAT.
6   [1973] ICR 148, [1973] IRLR 91, NIRC.
7   *Dedman's* case, n. 20, above, at 526 and 61 respectively, per Lord Denning, MR; *Croydon Health Authority v Jaufurally* [1986] ICR 4. The logic of this was doubted obiter by Sir Thomas Bingham MR in *London International College v Sen* [1993] IRLR 333, CA, but it was accepted as an established approach.
8   [1984] ICR 372, [1984] IRLR 119, CA. The judgment of the court, given by May LJ, contains a particularly full and useful review of the previous authorities. The factual nature of the apparent 'rules' on this point was again stressed by the Court of Appeal in *London International College v Sen*, n. 4, above. A generally more liberal approach was taken in a case of illness towards the end of the 3 month period in *Schultz v Esso Petroleum Co Ltd* [1999] 3 All ER 338, [1999] IRLR 488, CA.

claim in time[9]. Having said that, however, it was stated clearly that it is for the industrial tribunal to decide as a matter of fact (with little chance of a successful appeal) and so, in line with the modern approach, the most that can be said of the previous case law is that it suggests 'factors' which a tribunal may decide to take into account when applying the test:

> 'Dependent upon the circumstances of the particular case, an industrial tribunal may wish to consider the manner in which and reason for which the employee was dismissed, including the extent to which, if at all, the employer's conciliatory appeals machinery has been used. It will no doubt investigate what was the substantial cause of the employee's failure to comply with the statutory time limit; whether he had been physically prevented from complying with the limitation period for instance by illness or a postal strike, or something similar. It may be relevant for the industrial tribunal to investigate whether at the time when he was dismissed and if not then when thereafter, he knew that he had the right to complain that he had been unfairly dismissed; in some cases the tribunal may have to consider whether there has been any misrepresentation about any relevant matter by the employer to the employee. It will frequently be necessary for it to know whether the employee was being advised at any material time and, if so, by whom; of the extent of the adviser's knowledge of the facts of the employee's case; and of the nature of any advice which they may have given to him. In any event it will probably be relevant in most cases for the industrial tribunal to ask itself whether there had been any substantial fault on the part of the employee or his adviser which has led to the failure to comply with the statutory time limit. Any list of *possible relevant considerations*, however, cannot be exhaustive and, as we have stressed, at the end of the day *the matter is one of fact for the industrial tribunal* taking all the circumstances of the given case into account.'[10]

In addition to these general principles, three particular problems deserve mention. The first arises where the dismissed employee does not put in his complaint within three months because he spends that time trying to regain his job through the firm's internal appeal structure, not wishing to jeopardise that procedure by also making a tribunal application. This problem was potentially more acute when the time limit was 28 days[11], but could still arise with the present three month limit, for if the ex-employee uses the internal appeal and *fails* it is well established that the effective date of termination (from which the three months run) is the date of the initial dismissal, *not* the date of the rejection of the appeal[12]. In such circumstances, the dismissed employee is best advised to put

---

9   The desire for an alternative formulation was prompted by a feeling that to construe the phrase 'reasonably practicable' in the sense simply of 'reasonable' was too wide, but that to construe it as meaning 'reasonably capable of being done' (as in the factory legislation) would be too restrictive. 'Feasibility' was thought to express a middle way; note, however, that in other contexts the Court of Appeal have held that courts or tribunals should *not* place glosses on to the plain wording of the statute.

10   At 385 and 125 respectively, per May LJ (italics added).

11   Under the Industrial Relations Act 1971.

12   *J Sainsbury Ltd v Savage* [1981] ICR 1, [1980] IRLR 109, CA, approved in *West Midlands Co-operative Society v Tipton* [1986] ICR 192, [1986] IRLR 112, HL. In *Batchelor v British Railways Board* [1987] IRLR 136, CA it was held that it is irrelevant that the dismissal was in breach of a contractually-binding procedure – that cannot be relied on to advance the date of termination (to within the three-month period).

in his application to safeguard his position, if only to make an immediate request to the tribunal to postpone any proceedings pending the outcome of the internal appeal. What is to happen, however, if he does not do so? In *Crown Agents for Overseas Governments and Administration v Lawal*[13] the EAT expressed the opinion that the exhaustion of internal remedies should in most cases be a good reason for a tribunal to allow an extension of time. However confusion was caused by the subsequent EAT decision in *Bodha v Hampshire Area Health Authority*[14] saying precisely the opposite, i.e. that there should be *no* extension. The facts of *Palmer v Southend-on-Sea Borough Council* (considered above) raised this very point and the Court of Appeal stated unequivocally that *Bodha* was to be preferred, thus settling the matter[15]. This may be seen as a very unfortunate decision on two grounds, first that it makes it more difficult to integrate internal and external forms of challenging a dismissal, and second that the law should encourage such internal appeals, just as it encourages other forms of voluntary settlement without recourse to a tribunal (such as ACAS conciliation and compromise agreements); this decision provides no such encouragement[16].

The second particular problem arises where the employee does not learn of a material fact until more than three months after the date of the dismissal. In *Churchill v A Yeates & Sons Ltd*[17] the employee was dismissed ostensibly for redundancy, but more than three months later discovered that someone had been taken on to do his job, thus raising the inference that the redundancy was in fact a sham and his dismissal may have been unfair. The EAT held that the tribunal was acting properly in extending the time limit. This decision was later approved by the Court of Appeal in *Machine Tool Industry Research Association v Simpson*[18], where a similar decision was taken. Again, the case concerned a 'sham redundancy' and it is possible that that is the only area in which this principle is likely to apply in practice (though its importance in that area should not be underestimated[19]).

The third particular problem has been of particular concern in recent years, and arises where there has been a change in the law through a court decision, in

---

13 [1979] ICR 103, [1978] IRLR 542.
14 [1982] ICR 200. This was a good example of the confusion that can be caused when one EAT simply declines to follow the decision of a previous EAT (see p. 406, above). In his judgment Browne-Wilkinson P said that there ought to be amending legislation specially providing that time should not run until after the exhaustion of an internal appeal, but there has been no sign of this happening, even under the Employment Rights (Dispute Resolution) Act 1998 which in other ways tried to emphasise the importance of going through internal procedures.
15 This was even applied where an internal procedure resulted in an offer of re-engagement which was then dishonoured: *London Underground Ltd v Noel* [2000] ICR 109, [1999] IRLR 621, CA.
16 It is of course arguable that the law should not encourage (by extending time limits) attempts to regain employment by the organisation of industrial action to put direct pressure on the employee; after all, one of the aims of the unfair dismissal legislation was to lessen the incidence of strikes over dismissals. However, that rationale does *not* apply to the use of internal grievance procedures.
17 [1983] ICR 380, [1983] IRLR 187.
18 [1988] ICR 558, [1988] IRLR 212, CA. The Court of Appeal added the gloss that in such a case the tribunal does not have to decide on the truth of the alleged further facts – it is sufficient (for the purposes of extending the time limit, to establish jurisdiction) to show their effect on the applicant's state of belief.
19 Many employers, particularly in small business, seem to assume that redundancy means getting rid of X and not replacing him *for about six months*; there is no legal validity for the latter, even if in practice there may be something to it as a rule of thumb. This case may have some effect in attacking at least *blatant* attempts to misapply the rules on redundancy.

particular where a long-standing assumption or rule of domestic law has been successfully challenged under EC law and 'disapplied'. Can employees who thought that they had no cause of action when dismissed prior to that court decision now seek to bring an unfair dismissal case? This happened in particular with the ruling in *R v Secretary of State for Employment, ex p EOC*[20] by the House of Lords that the old 16 hours pw qualification was contrary to EC sex equality requirements. This raised the potential for a flood of cases by employees under that limit who had been dismissed before that decision. However, the courts (faced with that prospect) have taken a stringent view, (a) applying the domestic limit even where the claim is at least partly under EC law, (b) holding that there was technically nothing to have stopped the employee challenging the old qualification prior to the *EOC* case, and (c) refusing to exercise the power to extend the period because what was involved in these cases was an error of *law* by the employee, not the sort of error of fact that could lead to a finding that it had not been reasonably practicable to present the claim at the time of the actual dismissal[1].

ii)   Originating procedure[2]

An applicant to a tribunal claiming, for example, unfair dismissal commences his action, not by writ, but by submitting an 'originating application' to the appropriate local tribunal office in England, or to the COET in Scotland. This application, usually made in standard form on document IT1[3], requires the applicant to state certain particulars about himself, the relief he is claiming, and, in an unfair dismissal case, the reasons for which he says he was dismissed and what remedy he is seeking. The application is then sent to the respondent employer who should enter an appearance within 21 days of receiving the application; the employer does so by completing standard form IT3 which asks, inter alia, whether the employer intends to resist the claim, whether he accepts that the applicant was dismissed and on what grounds he intends to defend the case. Failure to enter an appearance means that the employer will not be allowed to take part in the hearing, though he can apply for the 21 days to be extended[4]. It is at this stage, if not before, that the employer should consult his lawyers if the case is going to be contentious for, although he is not absolutely bound by what he puts on form IT3, he may weaken his case if the grounds put down in it are not fully consistent with the way in which he wishes to defend the case before the

---

20   [1994] ICR 317, [1994] IRLR 176, HL; see p. 149, above.
1   *Biggs v Somerset County Council* [1996] ICR 364, [1996] IRLR 203, CA (in which the applicant, who had worked 14 hours p.w. had tried to claim unfair dismissal based on the termination of her employment in 1976). Definitive rulings by the ECJ are awaited as to whether this UK domestic approach is consistent with EC law. In the meantime, it has been need that the *Biggs* decision does *not* apply to the backdating of a sex discrimination claim where the power to extend the time limit is differently worded ('just and equitable'): *British Coal Corpn v Keeble* [1997] IRLR 336, EAT.
2   See *Harvey* T[268] ff.
3   Use of the form IT1 is not mandatory; a letter may be sufficient to constitute an originating application provided that it is clear that that is the intention: *Smith v Automobile Proprietary Ltd* [1973] ICR 306, 8 ITR 247; *Alex Munro (Butchers) Ltd v Nicol* [1988] IRLR 49. Whether it is the standard form or a letter, the application should contain the basic information required by r. 1(1), though an incomplete application may be accepted and then cured by the power to amend: *Dodd v British Telecom plc* [1988] ICR 116, [1988] IRLR 16.
4   Rules of Procedure, rules 3(2) and 15.

tribunal. Likewise, the applicant should make sure that he raises all the allegations and various causes of action that he wants considering because, on ordinary principles of issue estoppel[5], the eventual tribunal decision will finally decide the points raised *and* all *others* that could with reasonable diligence have been raised at the same time[6].

In preparation for a tribunal hearing, either side may request of the other further and better particulars of the matters raised in the pleadings and discovery of documents. If a party refuses a request, the other party may refer the question to the tribunal which may order further particulars or discovery[7]. The question of discovery of documents may be sensitive where the documents in question are of a confidential nature and, although there are provisions for safeguarding confidentiality and holding hearings in private[8], the courts have held in the context of discrimination cases that discovery of confidential documents such as references and personal files should only be granted subject to restrictive conditions[9], and the EAT have held that this should also apply in unfair dismissal cases[10].

iii) Conciliation and settlement[11]

As often seen elsewhere in industrial law, emphasis is placed upon reaching agreed settlements. To this end, copies of all application documentation are sent to the ACAS conciliation officers[12] who are under a statutory duty to attempt to conciliate at the request of either party or, in the absence of such a request, where the officer considers that he could act with a reasonable prospect of success[13]; in doing so, the officer should have regard to the desirability of the parties using established grievance procedures. In unfair dismissal cases, the legislation states that the conciliation officer should seek to promote reinstatement or re-engagement on terms which seem to him to be equitable, and only seek to promote agreement on compensation where the applicant does not wish to have his job back, or where it would not be practicable; in practice

---

5   *Henderson v Henderson* (1843) 3 Hare 100: 'The plea of res judicata applies ... not only to points on which the court was actually required by the parties to form an opinion and pronounce a judgment, but to every point which properly belonged to the subject of litigation and which the parties, exercising reasonable diligence, might have brought forward at the time', per Sir James Wigram V-C, at 114.

6   *Divine-Bortey v Brent London Borough Council* [1998] ICR 886, [1998] IRLR 525, CA; *Hancock v Doncaster Metropolitan Borough Council* [1998] ICR 900; *Sheriff v Klyne Tugs (Lowestoft) Ltd* [1999] IRLR 481, CA. These are relatively stringent applications of the rule in *Henderson*, given that tribunals in other contexts are supposed to be inquisitorial in nature.

7   Ibid., r. 4(1); *West Midlands Passenger Transport Executive v Singh* [1988] ICR 614, [1988] IRLR 186, CA. Important guidance on discovery was given by Wood P in *Byrne v Financial Times Ltd* [1991] IRLR 417. By virtue of r. 3(2)(b) an employer may make an application for further and better particulars even before entering an appearance, a tactic that could be used to try to scare off a weak claim.

8   Ibid., r. 8(3); matters conveyed to the conciliation officer are confidential: Employment Tribunals Act 1996, s. 18(7).

9   *Science Research Council v Nassé* [1979] 3 All ER 673, [1979] IRLR 465, HL; *West Midlands Passenger Transport Executive v Singh* (n. 20, above).

10   *Crown Agents v Lawal* [1979] ICR 103, [1978] IRLR 542.

11   See *Harvey* T[676] and [726].

12   In 1998, 72 per cent of applications notified to conciliation officers in this way were settled or withdrawn without proceeding to a hearing: ACAS Annual Report 1998.

13   Employment Tribunals Act 1996, s. 18(2); see *Individual Employment Rights – ACAS Conciliation between Individuals and Employers* (ACAS).

however this hardly even happens and compensation is the only realistic remedy pursued. Any information or statement communicated to a conciliation officer during the course of conciliation is not admissible in evidence at a subsequent tribunal hearing without the consent of the person who communicated it[14].

It is important that the parties, particularly the applicant, should understand the significance of statutory conciliation. If they reach an agreed settlement they may submit it to the tribunal for promulgation as a formal decision which will bring an end to the case.[15] However, the agreement may still be binding without this formal step if it is reached after the involvement of the conciliation officer, for in such a case (usually resulting in the officer recording the agreement on form COT 3) the legislation provides that the agreement is an exception to the rule that the parties cannot by contract or agreement exclude the right to bring a case before a tribunal and so the applicant cannot then go back on the agreement and renew his tribunal application[16]. This drastic effect can place ACAS officers in a difficult position – the emphasis is upon reaching settlements, but where are justice and fairness to fit in? Here there is a major divergence between the law and the practice. Case law (largely brought by applicants with second thoughts wishing to evade their agreements to settle) has given ACAS a very wide discretion here; in particular, the House of Lords has held that a conciliation officer does not have to investigate the 'fairness' of an agreement that is simply presented to him after being worked out between the parties[17] and, more generally, the EAT has held that there is no legal obligation on a conciliation officer to explain his legal rights to an applicant before he agrees to settle[18]. However, it is clear from the following passages (among many) that that is not how ACAS see their functions in practice:

> 'During 1984 the Service pointed out to a number of commentators and interested organisations that, for the purposes of providing a valid conciliation settlement, a conciliation officer cannot simply rubber stamp or verify an existing agreement which either or both parties regard as binding. Officers endeavour to ensure that the parties, particularly the individual employees concerned, are making decisions on a properly informed basis concerning their rights, the options open to them and the implications of their decision. This necessitates private discussions with employees or their representatives which can result in changes being made to previous agreements'[19].

14 Ibid., s. 18(7).
15 Rules of Procedure, rule 13(2)(b).
16 Employment Rights Act 1996, s. 203(2)(e); *Moore v Duport Furniture Products Ltd* [1982] ICR 84, [1982] IRLR 31, HL. An agreement is also binding if signed by the employee's adviser (e.g. a CAB adviser): *Freeman v Sovereign Chicken Ltd* [1991[ICR 853, [1991] IRLR 408. There is no legal requirement that an agreement be recorded in writing – an oral agreement is binding if it is reached through ACAS: *Gilbert v Kembridge Fibres Ltd* [1984] ICR 188, [1984] IRLR 52. An attempt to have an agreement declared invalid through economic duress failed in *Hennessy v Craigmyle & Co Ltd* [1986] ICR 461, [1986] IRLR 300, CA. Ultimately, there is an equitable power to set aside an unconscionable agreement: *BCCI SA v Ali* [2000] IRLR 398, CA.
17 *Moore v Duport Furniture Products Ltd*, n. 16, above. The Justice report *Industrial Tribunals* (1987) para. 2.28 points out that one view is that ACAS may be *too* impartial, in that any existing imbalance between employer and employee is perpetuated, not ameliorated, by a neutral stance in conciliation.
18 *Slack v Greenham (Plant Hire) Ltd* [1983] ICR 617, [1983] IRLR 271, EAT.
19 ACAS Annual Report 1984, p. 63.

'... [A]n important part of the conciliation officer's work in trying to promote a settlement is to ensure that both sides are adequately informed, and fully understand the range of options open to them and the consequences of the different decisions they may take[20].'

ACAS found particular difficulty with this balancing act when faced with a steep rise in the late 1980s of cases being referred to them for rubber-stamping of an existing agreement where there had not even been a complaint presented to a tribunal ('non-IT1 cases'). As a result of this, they decided on a policy of only exceptionally dealing with such cases, which by 1992 had produced a radical decrease in their number[1].

The point remains, however, that while ACAS officers may (commendably) take this more positive view of their role generally, if for any reason (except possibly mala fides) a conciliation officer does not take this approach (particularly by omitting to offer relevant advice to an applicant) that will *not* be a good ground for challenging the validity of the agreement to settle, once the fact of agreement and the involvement of ACAS have been shown.

If a settlement is reached without the involvement of ACAS, the position was originally that it was not binding on the parties because of the rule that the employee may not contract out of the protection of the legislation; it was therefore always possible for the employee to pocket the money on offer and still proceed to bring an action, although in such a case a tribunal finding in his favour might decide it was not just and equitable to award any compensation[2]. However, the law here was materially altered by the Trade Union Reform and Employment Rights Act 1993 which introduced the concept of a legally binding 'compromise agreement' *without* the involvement of ACAS (presumably to take the place of what used to be the 'non-IT1 cases', above). Such an agreement became legally binding if (a) it is in writing, (b) it relates to the particular proceedings, (c) the employee received independent advice as to the terms and effect of the proposed agreement and in particular its effect on his ability to pursue his rights before a tribunal, (d) the adviser was professionally insured, (e) the agreement identifies the adviser and (f) it states that these statutory conditions regulating compromise agreements are satisfied. Originally, the independent advice (the crux of the employee's protection) had to be from a qualified lawyer, but this was widened in an attempt to increase the use of compromise agreements yet further by the Employment Rights (Dispute Resolution) Act 1998, and so now the advice can come from a qualified lawyer, an authorised trade union official, an authorised advice centre worker, or any other person specified by order of the Secretary of State (though to date no such order has been made). This regime applies not only to the settlement of unfair dismissal actions, but also to other statutory actions under the Employment Rights Act 1996 and under the Sex Discrimination Act 1975, the Race Relations Act 1976, the Trade Union and Labour Relations (Consolidation) Act 1992, the Disability Discrimination Act 1995, the National Minimum Wage Act 1998 and the Working Time Regulations 1998. Common law claims arising on termination, which may now be brought before a tribunal, are subject to a general ability to settle (as in the county court) without the above safeguards. Compromise agreements, after a relatively slow start, have now become

---

20   *Individual Employment Rights – ACAS Conciliation between Individuals and Employers*, n. 20, above.

1   See p. 40, above for the figures and a statement of the current policy.

2   *Courage Take Home Trade Ltd v Keys* [1986] ICR 874, [1986] IRLR 427. For the deductibility of ex gratia payments from compensation, see p. 509, below.

part of the landscape, but they received a warning as to possible overuse from the EAT in *Lunt v Merseyside TEC Ltd* [3] where it was pointed out that the reference in the legislation to 'particular proceedings' being compromised means that one of these agreements cannot be used for an 'all claims settlement'; it can be used to settle multiple claims, but these must be specified in the agreement. COT 3 settlements can be used on an 'all claims' basis, provided that all the claims in question are ones in respect of which ACAS have conciliatory jurisdiction.

iv)   Pre-hearing reviews

In a further attempt to keep to a minimum the number of cases actually going before a tribunal, there was introduced in 1980 a further stage (if conciliation fails). This was the pre-hearing assessment, whereby a tribunal could (at the request of one of the parties, or of its own motion) hold a preliminary review of a case on the basis of the pleadings and written and oral submissions by the parties (but without witnesses). The aim was not actually to strike out cases which are unlikely to succeed, but it was provided that if the tribunal indicated that in its opinion an application was unlikely to succeed, or that any particular contention of either of the parties has no reasonable prospect of success, that the party in question (if he continued with the case) could be at risk under the rule on costs (considered above). The figures suggest that this procedure could be effective; for example, in 1990–91 73 per cent of those applicants who had been given a 'costs warning' at a pre-hearing assessment settled or withdrew their applications, and of the 21 applicants who proceeded to a tribunal hearing in spite of a costs warning, 18 failed (with seven actual orders for costs).

However, in other ways the picture was much less encouraging. Firstly, the take-up rate declined substantially, from a peak of 3,555 assessments in 1983 to only 196 in 1992–93. Secondly, concern was expressed by ACAS that even when the number was high the assessment procedure could also have a 'backlash' effect in making ordinary conciliation more difficult (and making an employee *less* likely to settle if an employer in fact failed to secure a costs warning in an assessment) [4]. Thirdly, the Justice Report [5] considered that on the whole the assessment procedure had not been a success and should be repealed.

However, far from going for repeal, the previous government decided to try to strengthen the procedure. The result is the present replacement for assessments, the pre-hearing review (PHR). The statutory basis for this was laid by the Trade Union Reform and Employment Rights Act 1993 and the procedure is contained in rule 7 of the Employment Tribunal Rules of Procedure. As with the previous procedure, either party may apply for a review or the tribunal may hold one of its own motion, and if (on consideration of the originating application and notice of appearance, and any written or oral representation) the tribunal considers that a party's contentions have 'no reasonable chance of success' it may make a costs warning [6]. However, the novelty of this procedure is that in addition the

---

3   [1999] ICR 17.
4   ACAS Annual Report 1984, p. 67. For the experience of assessments in their early years, see Wallace and Clifton 'Pre-hearing assessments in unfair dismissal cases' [1985] Employment Gazette 65 and Smith 'Operation of the pre-hearing assessment procedure in England and Wales and Scotland' [1985] Employment Gazette 182.
5   *Industrial Tribunals* (1987), para. 2.34.
6   Members who sit on a PHR may not then sit on any eventual hearing: r. 7(9). Although theoretically there is a right of appeal from a PHR ruling, such an appeal is very unlikely to succeed: *Mackie v John Holt Vintners Ltd* [1982] ICR 146, [1982] IRLR 236, EAT.

tribunal may make an order requiring that that party pay a deposit of up to £150 as a condition of continuing with the application or response. If the party continues, loses and has an award of costs made against him, the deposit goes towards those costs; further, the fact of the deposit having been ordered is itself a factor in deciding whether to make a costs order[7].

v) Procedure at the tribunal hearing

Exceptionally, the tribunal may wish to consider certain points relating to jurisdiction (territorial or otherwise) as a preliminary issue[8]. Normally, however, the case will be set down for one hearing, though the standard practice is to hear the parties first on the question of liability, only going on to arguments over remedies once there is a finding in favour of the applicant[9]. The tribunal has power to postpone the hearing if other proceedings relating to the dismissal are pending elsewhere (e.g. in the High Court or Crown Court); the decision whether to postpone is in the discretion of the tribunal chairman and his decision will not usually be altered on appeal (in the absence of a clear error of law)[10], though a decision to postpone may be particularly appropriate where identical issues are likely to arise in parallel court proceedings (e.g. for wrongful dismissal), especially as there is a danger of a tribunal decision raising an issue estoppel in any subsequent court proceedings[11]. Each side has the right to call witnesses, give evidence, cross examine witnesses called by the other side and address the tribunal at the conclusion[12]. In unfair dismissal cases, the respondent employer will usually present his case first, as he bears the burden of proving that the dismissal was not unfair; if however the employer disputes that there was ever a dismissal (e.g. in a constructive dismissal case) it will be for the employee to begin and argue that he was in fact dismissed[13].

Although it is for the parties to conduct their own case, as in an ordinary court, the tribunal chairman may take steps to ensure that a party's case is considered fully if he is not represented, which may mean that the chairman adopts a more

---

7   Rule 12(7).
8   There is a specific power to do so in r. 6, but its desirability has been the subject of disagreement within the EAT; at the time of writing, the latest guidance is from Morison P, generally discouraging the practice, which is viewed as often a false economy giving rise to problems on appeal, and being particularly hostile to any practice of having preliminary points considered by a chairman alone: *Sutcliffe v Big C's Marina Ltd* [1998] ICR 913, [1998] IRLR 428.
9   Such a 'split hearing' may encourage a settlement on remedies if there is a finding of unfairness. However, if such a procedure is to be adopted, the tribunal must make this clear at the beginning and state how the evidence is to be called: *Iggesund Converters v Lewis* [1984] ICR 544, [1984] IRLR 431. Tribunals should not normally entertain a submission of no case to answer half way through the case: *Ellis v Ministry of Defence* [1985] ICR 257, EAT.
10 *Carter v Credit Change Ltd* [1979] ICR 908, [1979] IRLR 361, CA.
11 *First Castle Electronics Ltd v West* [1989] ICR 72; *Warnock v Scarborough Football Club* [1989] ICR 489; *Bowater plc v Charlwood* [1991] ICR 798, [1991] IRLR 340. On issue estoppel, see *Green v Hampshire County Council* [1979] ICR 861; *O'Laoire v Jackel International Ltd (No 2)* [1991] ICR 718, [1991] IRLR 170, CA.
12 Rule 9(2).
13 The burden of proof may assume substantive importance at the end of the case – if the tribunal is genuinely stuck on a point of fact it may resort to the burden of proof to resolve it, though with the caveat that this approach should *not* be resorted to over-hastily, where the tribunal is merely having difficulty in making up its mind: *Morris v London Iron and Steel Co Ltd* [1987] ICR 855, [1987] IRLR 182, CA.

'inquisitorial' role. The extent to which such a role should be adopted by the tribunal generally has been the subject of mixed messages in recent cases. On the one hand, there are EAT decisions saying that a tribunal should if necessary consult the ACAS Code of Practice on its own initiative[14], and that there are certain rules of unfair dismissal laws (e.g. on redundancy selection) that are so well accepted that they should automatically be considered by a tribunal even if not specifically raised by a party, especially if unrepresented[15]. On the other hand, in more procedural contexts, the emphasis has been placed more strongly on the responsibility on the parties themselves to raise and argue all relevant points; if they do not, then (a) it will not be a ground of appeal that the tribunal did not decide on an issue not specifically relied on[16], and (b) any later attempt to raise such a point in separate proceedings is likely to be struck out on the grounds of issue estoppel and res judicata[17].

The proceedings are usually marked by a greater degree of informality than in an ordinary court[18] and the Rules specifically state that a tribunal is not bound by 'any enactment or rule of law relating to the admissibility of evidence in proceedings before the courts of law'[19]; thus, for example, in a case concerning dismissal for suspected crime a tribunal may hear evidence that would be inadmissible in a criminal trial, such as hearsay, complaints, previous convictions and even improperly obtained confession evidence[20]. However, this emphasis on informality is subject to at least two caveats. First, with regard to the wider discretion on evidence, this only works one way – a tribunal may receive evidence otherwise inadmissible but may *not* exclude evidence which would normally be admissible (as being relevant and probative)[1]. Secondly, this whole question has been considered by Wood P in *Aberdeen Steak Houses Group plc v Ibrahim*[2], in terms which suggest that in practice there should normally be less informality than rule 8 would at first sight allow. The principal point made is that too much informality may be counter-productive and too loose a procedure may lead to perceived unfairness. Normal laws of procedure and evidence do not have to be followed slavishly, but on the other hand Wood P points out that those laws (unlike the laws and usages of Gormenghast) do not exist just for the sake of it, or merely because things have always been done that way[3] – they are there so that both sides know the rules of the game and are less likely to be ambushed. Thus, the present guidance of the EAT is that normally it should be for the parties to run their own

14 *Lock v Cardiff Rly Co Ltd* [1998] IRLR 358.

15 *Langston v Cranfield University* [1998] IRLR 172.

16 *Mensah v East Hertfordshire NHS Trust* [1998] IRLR 531, CA; for the position where it is the employer who has not raised all necessary points before the tribunal, see *Church v West Lancashire NHS Trust (No 2)* [1999] ICR 586, [1998] IRLR 492.

17 *Divine-Bortey v Brent London Borough Council* [1998] ICR 886, [1998] IRLR 525, CA; *Hancock v Doncaster Metropolitan Borough Council* [1998] ICR 900; *Sheriff v Klyne Tugs (Lowestoft) Ltd* [1999] IRLR 481, CA; see p. 423, above.

18 Rule 9(1) states that 'the tribunal shall so far as appears to it appropriate seek to avoid formality in its proceedings ...'.

19 Rule 9(1), making express (as from 1980) what had already been established in the case law: *Coral Squash Clubs Ltd v Matthews* [1979] ICR 607, [1979] IRLR 390, EAT.

20 *Morley's of Brixton Ltd v Minott* [1982] ICR 444, [1982] IRLR 270; *Dhaliwal v British Airways Board* [1985] ICR 513, EAT.

1 *Rosedale Mouldings Ltd v Sibley* [1980] ICR 816, [1980] IRLR 387; this was doubted in *Snowball v Gardner Merchant Ltd* [1987] ICR 719, [1987] IRLR 397, but that case was in turn doubted subsequently in *Aberdeen Steak Houses Group plc v Ibrahim*, n. 10, below, and so *Rosedale* appears to be still good law.

2 [1988] ICR 550, [1988] IRLR 420.

3 Even in Norfolk.

cases, call witnesses and ensure that all relevant evidence is adduced[4]; the party opening the case should call all his evidence and then close his case, leaving the field to the other side and the normal rules of cross-examination should apply; although normally-inadmissible evidence may be admitted, it should be remembered that there is usually good reason for not admitting it, which may mean here treating it with caution. The case may be seen as a useful statement of desirable practice but, on the other hand, (a) it sits oddly alongside the usual criticism that tribunals are already *too* legalistic, and (b) it raises the question as to whether these are 'guidelines' to be followed by tribunals and, if so, whether it will be an appealable error of law for a tribunal to depart from them without good reason.

At the conclusion of the case the tribunal gives its decision (either immediately or in reserved form). However, although there is a mandatory requirement to give reasons[5], this area has seen two important developments (one legislative, one judicial) as part of the current campaign to curb 'legalism' in tribunal procedure. The first is that in 1985 what is now rule 10 was amended to allow a tribunal to give its reasons *in summary form only*; however, full reasons must be given in four cases – (a) in cases concerning equal pay, sex discrimination or race discrimination; (b) where a party requests full reasons orally at the hearing; (c) where a party submits a written request for full reasons within 21 days of the document recording the summary reasons being sent to the parties or (d) where the tribunal considers that summary form would not sufficiently explain the grounds for its decision, Thus by virtue of (b) and (c) a party still has a right to full reasons, which is of course important for a party wishing to appeal to the EAT. The second development was a reconsideration by the Court of Appeal of what is meant by 'reasons' in the first place; in particular, how detailed they need to be. As noted above, reasons have to be given and they will form the basis for any appeal[6]. However, in a series of cases[7] the Court of Appeal stressed that there is no obligation on the tribunal to set out the facts in full with the arguments put for both sides and a closely reasoned conclusion; the fact that many tribunal decisions are in this form does not mean that it is obligatory and, indeed, merely to point out that a particular fact or argument is not expressly referred to in the reasons will not be sufficient to show that the tribunal's decision was perverse. As a way of discouraging appeals, this approach is possibly something of a blunt instrument and the EAT subsequently qualified it, at least to the extent of (a) holding that where there is a conflict of fact on a particular issue the tribunal should make that clear in its decision and state which version of the facts is believed[8] and (b) stating that a case may be remitted to the tribunal if the EAT is unable to see from the reasons *why* the tribunal reached its decision[9]. The latter point can also be

---

4   This includes the normal rule that if a party specifically states that he will not be calling particular evidence, he should normally be bound by that statement.
5   Rule 10(3), *Guest v Alpine Soft Drinks Ltd* [1982] ICR 110, EAT,
6   *Owen and Briggs v James* [1982] ICR 618, [1982] IRLR 502, CA. In the light of the more restrictive approach adopted by the Court of Appeal (n. 7, below), however, the tribunal chairman's note of evidence may assume more significance, especially in an appeal on the grounds of perversity: *Martin v Glynwed Distribution Ltd* [1983] ICR 511, [1983] IRLR 198, CA.
7   *UCATT v Brain* [1981] ICR 542, [1981] IRLR 224, CA; *Martin v Glynwed Distribution Ltd*, n. 7, above; *Varndell v Kearney & Trecker Marwin Ltd* [1983] ICR 683, [1983] IRLR 335, CA; *Morris v London Iron and Steel Co Ltd*, n. 13, above.
8   *Levy v Marrable & Co Ltd* [1984] ICR 583.
9   *Yusuf v Aberplace Ltd* [1984] ICR 850.

seen in a subsequent Court of Appeal decision[10] in which (i) the court (though purporting to apply the previous case law) upheld the EAT's decision to allow an appeal on the basis of inadequate reasons, and (ii) Bingham LJ stated that tribunals should outline their factual conclusions and reasoning at least sufficiently for the parties and an appellate court to see why the decision went that way and whether any point of law is involved. However, it may take more than one decision to swing the pendulum back in this area.

The reasons, in either summary or full form, are put into writing, signed by the chairman, transmitted to the central office for entering in the Register and sent to the parties. Until a decision is entered in the Register, the tribunal has the same inherent power as a court to alter any mistakes in it, though this power is to be used sparingly and after giving the parties the opportunity to be heard further[11]. An order by a tribunal for monetary compensation is enforceable by county court order[12].

vi)   Review and appeal[13]

Under rule 11 of the Rules of Procedure, a party to a tribunal hearing may apply to have the decision reviewed on certain grounds. This procedure is appropriate, rather than an appeal, where an error of law *or fact* is discovered soon after the decision. The party must make his application within 14 days of the decision being sent to the parties (unless he actually makes it at the end of the hearing), and it must be in writing stating grounds for requesting a review *and* the reasons why that party says that the tribunal decision was wrong[14]. The application is considered by the chairman of the tribunal that heard the case, who may refuse it on the ground that he considers it has no reasonable chance of success. If it is not refused, it is heard by that tribunal (or another if it is not practicable to remit it to the same one) which may vary or revoke its decision, or order a re-hearing before a different tribunal. The grounds for review set out in rule 11 are (a) that the decision was wrong through an error made by the tribunal staff, (b) that a party did not receive notice of the proceedings leading to the decision, (c) that the decision was made in the absence of a party entitled to be heard, (d) that new evidence has become available which could not reasonably have been known of or foreseen at the time of the hearing, or (e) that the interests of justice require such a review. If a party wishes to rely on (c) he will have to show good cause for his

10   *Meek v City of Birmingham District Council* [1987] IRLR 250, CA. Bingham LJ (at 251) also suggested that it was highly desirable that the tribunal 'should give guidance to employers and trade unions as to practices which should or should not be adopted', which appears to be doubly heretical in the light of the prevailing views on guidelines.

11   *Hanks v Ace High Productions Ltd* [1978] ICR 1155, [1979] IRLR 32, doubting the reasoning (though not the decision) in *Jowett v Earl of Bradford* [1977] 2 All ER 33, [1977] ICR 342. A tribunal should not use this power to go back on primary findings of fact and change the whole basis of its decision: *Lamont v Fry's Metals Ltd* [1985] ICR 566, [1985] IRLR 470, CA. Unfortunately, however, in the latter case the Court of Appeal only assumed (without deciding) that there is a power to amend an oral decision; some doubt was expressed about that power in *Spring Grove Service Group plc v Hickinbottom* [1990] ICR 111 by the EAT, and the matter remains in need of an authoritative ruling.

12   Employment Tribunals Act 1996, s. 15.

13   See *Harvey* T[1111] and [1401].

14   *Drakard & Sons Ltd v Wilton* [1977] ICR 642. The decision of the EAT in *Ladup Ltd v Barnes* [1982] ICR 107, [1982] IRLR 7 to use the power of review to alter a decision in the light of subsequent events is open to criticism as (a) an extension of the true purpose of a review and (b) possibly introducing a large measure of uncertainty.

failure to attend[15], and likewise under (d) he will have to show that the new evidence could have an important bearing on the decision and is genuinely 'new', not just something which could have been adduced at the hearing by the use of due diligence[16]. Moreover, ground (e) has not been construed so as to short-circuit the other grounds (particularly (d)), since it is also in the 'interests of justice' that tribunal decisions should be as final as possible once handed down[17].

A tribunal decision is subject to appeal on a point of law to the EAT. The appeal must be instituted by serving on the EAT a notice of appeal together with a copy of the decision or order within 42 days of the date on which the decision was sent to the appellant[18]; the EAT has power to extend this period, though the appellant must show cause why this should be done[19]. The notice of appeal is served on the respondent who must make his reply if he intends to contend the issue and may at this stage cross-appeal. Interlocutory matters may be raised before the hearing and a preliminary hearing will be held in order to establish that there is a genuine point of law involved in the appeal[20]. At the hearing, fresh evidence will only rarely be heard and the EAT will rely primarily upon the written decision of the tribunal and, if necessary, upon the chairman's notes made at the tribunal hearing. The decision of the EAT is by simple majority, if necessary, and it is expressly given all the powers of an employment tribunal to make relevant orders to dispose of the case, or it may decide to remit the whole matter to the same or another tribunal for a rehearing[1]; the EAT may be particularly disposed to remit the case if there are, in the light of its decision, further factual matters to consider before coming to a final conclusion[2]. The EAT has power to review its own decisions once given[3], and on points of law appeal then lies to the Court of Appeal and then to the House of Lords.

vii) Statements of reasons for dismissal

One further point of procedure to be noticed in the context of an unfair dismissal action is that under the Employment Rights Act 1996, section 92 an employee with one year's qualifying service who is under notice or who has been dismissed has a right to be provided by the employer (within 14 days of making the request) with a written statement of reasons for his dismissal; there was no such common law right. If the employer unreasonably fails to give such a statement, the ex-

15 *Morris v Griffiths* [1977] ICR 153, EAT.
16 *Flint v Eastern Electricity Board* [1975] ICR 395, [1975] IRLR 277.
17 Ibid., at 404 and 281 respectively per Phillips J; *General Council of British Shipping v Deria* [1985] ICR 198; *Ironside Ray & Vials v Lindsay* [1994] ICR 384, [1994] IRLR 318.
18 EAT Rules 1993, r. 3. Note that if separate decisions are given on liability and remedy, the 42-day period flows from *each*, not just from the date of the later decision.
19 Appeals out of time are governed by the EAT *Practice Direction* (dated 15 April 1996; see *Harvey* T [1761]) and the guidelines laid down in *United Arab Emirates v Abdelghafar* [1995] ICR 65, approved in *Aziz v Bethnal Green City Challenge Co Ltd* [2000] IRLR 111, CA.
20 EAT Guidance Notes (Preliminary Hearing/Directions) [1997] IRLR 618.
1 Employment Tribunals Act 1996, s. 35. *Dobie v Burns International Security Services (UK) Ltd* [1984] ICR 812, [1984] IRLR 329, CA.
2 *Askew v Victoria Sporting Club Ltd* [1976] ICR 302. However, a case should not be remitted in order to hear evidence that was in fact available but not given at the original hearing: *Kingston v British Railways Board* [1984] ICR 781, [1984] IRLR 146, CA.
3 EAT Rules 1993, r. 33; this power should not normally be used to challenge rulings of law in the decision, where the proper recourse is to an appeal, not to a review: *Blockleys plc v Miller* [1992] ICR 749.

employee may complain to the tribunal on that ground (or on the ground that a statement given under this section is inadequate or untrue[4]) and the tribunal has powers (a) to make a declaration as to what it finds were the employee's real reasons for the dismissal, and (b) to award the employee two weeks' pay. A small but important change was made to the wording by the Trade Union Reform and Employment Rights Act 1993. Previously, an employer was liable if he *refused* to give a statement, and this led to case law on the subtle difference between refusal and mere failure. However, the wording was altered in 1993 to extend to *failure* to provide the statement, and so that previous case law is no longer applicable[5]. However, it remains the case that, once 'failure' has been shown the tribunal must still go on to consider whether that failure was 'unreasonable'; the most important type of case raising this point is where the employer refuses to give a statement because he denies that there was a dismissal *at all* (e.g. where the employee walked out and now wants to claim constructive dismissal, which is contested by the employer) – where the employer can show that he reasonably believed that there was no dismissal, a tribunal will probably hold his failure to have been reasonable and so not contrary to the section[6].

The section does not say how detailed the statement has to be, but at the least it must be such that anyone reading it can tell on its face why the employee was dismissed; thus in *Horsley, Smith and Sherry Ltd v Dutton*[7] it was held by the EAT that it is not enough to refer *solely* to reasons given in earlier conversations or separate documents; however, in the subsequent case of *Kent County Council v Gilham*[8] the Court of Appeal narrowed the scope of that decision by holding that there was compliance with the section where the employer replied to the ex-employee's request by referring to reasons set out in two previous letters, copies of which were attached to the reply.

The procedural significance of section 92 is that, by sub-section (5), a written statement provided under the section is expressly made admissible in subsequent proceedings; a section 92 request may therefore be a useful 'first shot' for an ex-employee claiming unfair dismissal and the respondent employer might be advised to seek legal advice upon receipt of it in any case likely to be difficult to defend for, although he will not be absolutely bound by what he says in the written statement (in the sense of only being able to rely on points of law raised in it), any basic inconsistency between the terms of the statement and his defence as actually put forward before the tribunal could seriously weaken his case.

4   *Harvard Securities plc v Younghusband* [1990] IRLR 17, EAT.
5   One further change in the 1993 Act is that where an employee is dismissed while she is pregnant (or after childbirth but in circumstances in which her maternity leave period is ended by dismissal), she is entitled to a s. 92 statement (a) without having to request it and (b) whether or not she has the one-year qualifying period: s. 92(4). This is part of the increased protection given by the 1993 Act against pregnancy dismissal.
6   *Broomsgrove v Eagle Alexander Ltd* [1981] IRLR 127, stressing the objective nature of the test; in the slightly earlier case of *Brown v Stuart Scott & Co* [1981] ICR 166 the EAT had put it in terms of whether the employer had a 'conscientious' and bona fide belief that there was no dismissal (though stressing that the tribunal must first decide whether there had in fact been a dismissal). The objective view in *Broomsgrove* is more consistent with the requirement of 'unreasonable' failure.
7   [1977] ICR 594, [1977] IRLR 172. Where, however, the document or letter to which reference is made was explicit as to the reasons, there may be a 'refusal' but it may in the circumstances be a *reasonable* refusal: *Marchant v Earley Town Council* [1979] ICR 891, [1979] IRLR 311. It is not enough for the employer to rely on the fact that he has entered an appearance to the ex-employee's unfair dismissal application stating the grounds for dismissal; s. 92 assumes some form of independent documentation directly to the ex-employee: *Rowan v Machinery Installations (South Wales) Ltd* [1981] ICR 386, [1981] IRLR 122.
8   [1985] ICR 227, [1985] IRLR 16, CA.

viii) Contract claims

One of the long-standing criticisms of the tribunal system has been that tribunals could not deal with common law claims for breach of contract, which had to go to the county court. In practice, such cases could be heard if they could be squeezed under the 'deductions' rules in the Wages Act 1986 (now Part II of the Employment Rights Act 1996), but that was less than satisfactory and so eventually the Government exercised its long-standing power[9] to extend common law jurisdiction to tribunals. This was done in the two Employment Tribunals Extension of Jurisdiction Orders of 1994[10], with effect from July 1994. The first point to notice is that such contract claims can only be brought before a tribunal if they arise or are outstanding on the *termination* of the employee's employment. While it is to be welcomed that a tribunal can now, for example, deal with a claim for notice pay or holiday pay outstanding at the same time as hearing an unfair dismissal action, it is unfortunate that, due to this limitation, they cannot hear a claim for amounts alleged to be outstanding *during* the employment, at least directly under the Orders. Certain common law claims are excluded[11], and the claim must be brought within three months of termination (subject to the usual 'not reasonably practicable' power to extend). The procedure for bringing such a claim is the same as that (above) for statutory claims, but two peculiarities must be noted – (i) the Orders specifically give the employer a right of counter-claim (within six weeks of receiving the originating application for the employee's claim, subject again to the power of extension); (ii) the employee's claim is subject to a statutory maximum of £25,000 in respect of any one contract (regardless of the number of claims brought on it). As this maximum is relatively high (half the new limit of £50,000 for the compensatory award for unfair dismissal, and indeed twice that award when it previously stood at only £12,000) it has given scope (when both breach of contract and unfair dismissal are being claimed) for the employee's representatives to seek to bring as much of the immediate loss as possible under the heading of the contract claim, thus freeing the compensatory award to reflect future loss more fully, at least in the case of a higher earner, for example on a longer notice period.

Although these orders are an important development and the first full year's figures show a consistently high take-up rate[12], there may still be many cases where employees and their representatives continue to use the 'deduction' provisions of Part II of the 1996 Act instead for two reasons: (i) because in any case arising during employment that remains the only way to challenge breaches of contract before a tribunal rather than a court; (ii) even where a case arises on

---

9   Previously contained in the Employment Protection (Consolidation) Act 1978, s. 131 (hence references to these as 'section 131 orders'), but now contained in the Employment Tribunals Act 1996, s. 3.

10 The England and Wales Order is S.I. 1994 No. 1623; the Scotland Order is S.I. 1994 No. 1624. See *Harvey* R[778], [788].

11 Art 5 excludes claims relating to the employee's living accommodation, intellectual property, confidence and restraint of trade. The Employment Tribunals Act 1996, s. 3 excludes claims for damages for personal injuries.

12 The two different sets of tribunal figures show clearly that a contract claim is frequently *added* to another primary claim (especially unfair dismissal); according to the Employment Tribunal Service figures for 1998/99 (which only count *applications* to tribunals, under the heading of the primary claim) there were 7,724 cases where the primary claim was for breach of contract (10% of total applications), but according to ACAS figures for 1998 (which count *all* claims, including multiple claims in one application) there were 23,578 claims for breach of contract (21% of total claims).

termination, the action under Part II may be used to avoid the possibility of a counter-claim under the Orders.

ix)   ACAS arbitration in unfair dismissal cases

Voluntary arbitration organised through ACAS has always been available, though (in common with arbitration generally) its incidence has been declining. Moreover, it is not a true *alternative* solution, since an employee failing at this arbitration stage still has the right to bring a claim before a tribunal. For some time now, ideas have been mooted of producing a special statutory scheme that would indeed act as a true alternative to the tribunal system[13]. Faced with the steep rise in tribunal applications, the previous government looked with favour on this idea[14] and the present government proceeded with it by giving the necessary powers in the Employment Rights (Dispute Resolution) Act 1998[15], permitting ACAS to produce a scheme for the approval of the Secretary of State. There has, however, been serious 'slippage' in its production, largely due to the large amount of legislation on employment matters ahead of it in the queue for DTI attention. It was originally scheduled for April 1999, but by the time of writing (March 2000) had been put back to mid or late 2000.

Views vary considerably as to its desirability[16], partly depending on one's views of whether tribunals are too legalistic, because it can be argued that it is meant to produce a form of alternative dispute resolution which was the original aim of the tribunals themselves. The scheme as suggested by ACAS at the time of writing would work as follows. The parties would have to agree to use the arbitration alternative, and sign a COT 3 or compromise to that effect, thus giving up *totally* their rights to go to a tribunal. ACAS would then organise for the case to be heard by a single arbitrator (from a panel already appointed for that purpose). The parties would submit written statements of case and the hearing would take place locally. Legal representation would be discouraged, and the hearing would be relatively informal, with no prolonged cross-examination and a relatively inquisitorial role for the arbitrator. The result would be an award by the arbitrator, issued through ACAS, with the arbitrators having all the remedies powers of a tribunal. In line (controversially) with ordinary arbitrations, there would be *no* appeal (only certain, restricted grounds of challenge for procedural irregularity under the Arbitration Act 1996). The advantages of the scheme would be speed (the aim being to have the hearing within two months of the reference to ACAS), less expense, more informality, relative confidentiality and a greater possibility of re-employment. The disadvantages would be its finality (for the party losing), a more 'basic' approach to disputed facts, reliance on a single-member forum and the fact that *only* an unfair dismissal claim could be heard (with any other allegations, e.g. of discrimination, having to go to a tribunal). The lack of an appeal may certainly cause employers to be nervous of it, particularly with the raising of the maximum compensatory award from £12,000 to £50,000, which

13   Particularly influential was Lewis and Clark *Employment Rights Industrial Tribunals and Arbitration: the Case for Alternative Dispute Resolution* (Institute of Employment Rights, 1993).

14   Green Paper 'Resolving employment rights disputes: options for reform' (Cm. 2707).

15   Adding new ss. 212A and 212B to the Trade Union and Labour Relations (Consolidation) Act 1992.

16   Contrast to hostile view of a Regional Chairman of Tribunals in MacMillan 'Employment tribunals – philosophies and practicalities' (1999) 28 ILJ 33 with the view of one of the scheme's original proponents in Clark 'Adversarial and investigative approaches to the arbitral resolution of dismissal disputes' (1999) 28 ILJ 319.

would be in the arbitrator's 'gift'. All of this has meant that ACAS have had a major problem in trying to guess the likely take-up rate (in order to be able to cope with it), and that remains the great uncertainty.

In addition, there is one other uncertainty, of a more principled nature. What *standard* would an arbitrator apply when judging the fairness of a dismissal? The aim would be to have a less legalistic forum, not dependent on the citation and use of legal authority, from which it would follow that the arbitrator (often not legally trained) would tend to apply what is sometimes described as an 'industrial relations' or 'felt-fair' standard, possibly reflecting the standards and assumptions of the parties themselves in that particular industry. Some lawyers would therefore fear double standards, with the tribunals continuing to apply a more legally refined standard based on case precedents. On the other hand, (a) this issue may in practice be lessened by the expected heavy reliance of arbitrators on ACAS publications (in particular, the Code of Practice on Discipline and Grievances and the handbook 'Discipline at Work') which to an extent distil the wisdom of the case law, and (b) arguably double standards are nothing new and were inherent in the system as it was first set up 30 years ago, when the assumption was that *most* cases would be dealt with by internal procedures (often including voluntary arbitration), with tribunals operating only as long-stops. In this context, as in so many others, the final start-up and initial experience of this novel scheme are awaited with great interest, though its success cannot be confidently predicted.

3 CODES OF PRACTICE AND DISCIPLINARY PROCEDURES

i) The Code of Practice as a legal device

Increasing use has been made of codes of practice in modern industrial law in an attempt to apply necessarily vague general principles to the wide variety of industrial practices. In the area of discipline and dismissal this is particularly so for three reasons. First, it has long been established in unfair dismissal law that there is a distinct head of 'procedural unfairness', so that a dismissal for a substantive reason which is prima facie fair may still be unfair if the wrong procedure was adopted[17]; this therefore puts emphasis upon determining what is the *right* procedure. Second, tribunals are consistently encouraged to reach their decisions in the light of 'good industrial relations practice' which up to a point is amenable to distillation into codes of practice. Third, the advent of the modern legislation has led to increased formalisation and legalisation of many aspects of employment, including questions of discipline and the procedures leading up to dismissal[18], in which previously there was little law involved; now however there is a considerable body of law involved, and codes of practice have figured largely in this intervention. What then is the legal status of a code of practice? It is not law in itself, though it has to be issued by ACAS in accordance with a set procedure[19]. Thus contravention of one of its provisions by someone

---

17   *Earl v Slater and Wheeler (Airlyne) Ltd* [1973] 1 All ER 145, [1972] ICR 508, NIRC, approved by the House of Lords in *W Devis & Sons Ltd v Atkins* [1977] ICR 662, [1977] IRLR 314, HL.

18   Questions of discipline are intertwined with the law on dismissal, for dismissal may be seen as the ultimate form of disciplining, and the procedures for each may to a large extent be the same; therefore much of what follows is applicable to both.

19   Trade Union and Labour Relations (Consolidation) Act 1992, s. 200; under s. 203 the Secretary of State may also issue codes of practice, after consultation with ACAS; this power has been exercised in the politically controversial areas of picketing and balloting.

does not render that person directly liable to any form of proceedings (by way of enforcement or otherwise); however, it is expressly provided[20] that it is admissible in evidence before a tribunal (or the CAC) and, further, that if any of its provisions are relevant to the proceedings in question 'it shall be taken into account in determining that question'. As with the Highway Code, a person ignores it at his peril, particularly if that person is an employer wishing to dismiss an employee without risking a finding of unfair dismissal. Compliance with code provisions on matters of discipline and dismissal will therefore be most material to an employer's claim that he acted reasonably and fairly although, as the code does not have the force of law, failure to comply with it will not make the action in question automatically unfair[1], for there may be good reasons for not complying on the facts of a particular case[2]. The EAT have recently reaffirmed the continuing importance of the code, stating that it may be part of the tribunal's inquisitorial function to consult it wherever relevant, even if it is not specifically referred to by the parties[3].

The provisions relevant to discipline and dismissal were introduced in the highly influential ACAS Code of Practice No. 1 *Disciplinary Practice and Procedures in Employment* and many employers now have definite rules and procedures (often in works rules or handbooks) drafted in the light of the code's recommendations. The code itself (reissued in expanded form in 2000) places great emphasis on involvement of employees and their representatives in the drafting of procedures covering grievances, discipline and appeal structures. Union agreement is not essential in order to have an effective disciplinary procedure, for such matters lie in the first place within the management's responsibilities[4] and in any event only a minority of employees are now union members or covered by any form of collective bargaining. However, the fact that the procedure is an agreed one will greatly add to its authority, and to the authority which may be exercised by the management when they take action clearly in accordance with the agreed rules; tribunals will naturally tend to pay great attention to an agreed procedure as a question of fact and evidence[5]. Where there are set rules on discipline, grievances and appeals (whether agreed or not) the employer must give the employee written notice of them within two months of the commencement of his employment[6]. For the guidance of employers when drawing up rules and procedures, the code makes the following general points:

'Disciplinary procedures should not be viewed primarily as a means of imposing sanctions. Rather they should be seen as a way of helping and encouraging improvement amongst employees whose conduct or standard of work is unsatisfactory.'

'When drawing up rules the aim should be to specify clearly and concisely those necessary for the efficient and safe performance of work and for the maintenance of satisfactory relations within the workforce and between

---

20 Ibid., s. 207; a COP produced by the Secretary of State is also admissible in court proceedings.
1   *Lewis Shops Group v Wiggins* [1973] ICR 335, [1973] IRLR 205.
2   *Retarded Children's Aid Society Ltd v Day* [1978] ICR 437, [1978] IRLR, 128, CA.
3   *Lock v Cardiff Rly Co Ltd* [1998] IRLR 358.
4   Code of Practice para. 4.
5   *Securicor Ltd v Smith* [1989] IRLR 356, CA.
6   Employment Rights Act 1996, s. 3, see p. 86, above.

employees and management. Rules ... should not be so general as to be meaningless.'

ii) Disciplinary measures

Although certain forms of disciplinary action may still lie entirely within the managerial prerogative (e.g. transferring a general labourer to a different job or refusing to give a discretionary bonus), many other forms will impinge upon the rights and expectations of the disciplined employee (e.g. fines, suspension, demotion) and so the crucial point about lawful disciplinary measures is that the employer must have the power to impose them, and normally this will involve having the contractual authority (express or implied) to do so. If the employer goes outside this authority the employee may in theory maintain a common law action (e.g. to recover the amount of a fine unlawfully deducted)[7]; of much greater significance in modern employment law is the possibility that the wrongly disciplined employee may walk out and claim to have been constructively dismissed, for the purpose of bringing an unfair dismissal action. Thus, although some managers remain suspicious of setting down their disciplinary powers in writing on the basis that it restricts managerial prerogative, the modern tendency is to put down in written form the company's policy on discipline (which will of course vary from industry to industry) and the procedures to be adopted, which may then form part of the employment contract either expressly or by implication. A leading survey referred to a 'massive spread of formal disciplinary and dismissal procedures across British industry and commerce' in the 1970s as a 'remarkable development in British industrial relations'. Their findings in 1990 showed that 97 per cent of establishments recognising a union operated a disciplinary and dismissal procedure and (perhaps even more significantly) so did 83 per cent of those not recognising a union; 93 per cent of procedures were written, 74 per cent provided for union representation of employees and 65 per cent were jointly agreed[8]. On the other hand, *compliance* with procedures may sometimes be a different matter and a DTI survey in 1998 found that when one looked at cases actually brought to tribunals (itself arguably a sign of failure of the system) they were characterised by a relatively high incidence of lack of procedures or failure to operate them[9]; one reason for this was that the small firm sector produces a disproportionate number of tribunal cases, and that sector was particularly covered by the survey (which also found evidence of continued widespread reliance on informality and flexibility, especially in smaller firms, i.e. still viewing formal disciplinary procedures only as a last resort).

Turning to the detailed provisions of the ACAS Code, the primary suggestion is that where a disciplinary procedure is established it should be clear and unambiguous so that the individual employee may know what is expected of him; in particular, he should be made aware of the likely consequences of breaking

---

7   *Gorse v Durham County Council* [1971] 2 All ER 666, [1971] 1 WLR 775. In the example given, there may also be a statutory action under the Employment Rights Act 1996, s. 13.

8   Millward et al. 'Workplace industrial relations in transition' (the ED/ESRC/PSI/ACAS Survey) (1992), ch. 6. A similar pattern was found in the preliminary results of the 1998 exercise: Cully et al. The 1998 Workplace Employee Relations Survey: the First Findings (ESRC/ACAS/PSI, 1998; URN 98/934).

9   Earnshaw, Goodman, Harrison & Marchington 'Industrial Tribunals, Workplace Disciplinary Procedures and Employment Practice' (DTI Employment Relations Research Paper, 1998); see Edwards (1998) 27 ILJ 362.

the rules and the type of conduct which may warrant summary dismissal[10]. Although it is therefore desirable to lay down the major forms of unacceptable conduct in the circumstances of the particular industry involved, and the likely consequences of each form, the list should not necessarily be exhaustive otherwise novel forms of transgression could be construed as permissible (in the sense of not attracting a valid penalty).

A system of warnings (considered below) may be an integral part of a disciplinary system (as well as leading up to a dismissal), but if warnings are ignored and the misconduct repeated the employer, in a case not warranting dismissal, may wish to impose a lesser sanction. Fines or deductions must be permissible under the contract of employment if they are to be valid, and must also comply with the requirements of Part II of the Employment Rights Act 1996[11]. Suspension with pay will usually be lawful[12], and may be the proper step to take for a brief period while a serious allegation against the employee is under investigation[13]; for any longer period however it is tantamount to a holiday and the more obviously punitive sanction is suspension *without* pay. It is here, however, that the question whether the employer has contractual authority to act becomes particularly vital for, in the absence of express or implied incorporation into the contract, there is *no* common law power to suspend without pay, for this would contravene the employer's basic obligation to pay wages[14]. Thus, as in the case of lay-offs, the employer is clearly allowed to suspend without pay only where he incorporates a clause to that effect in the contract, either directly or via the works rules or a collective agreement. Other discipline may take forms such as reprimands, temporary withdrawal of privileges or demotion or transfer; once again these are in theory only lawful if allowed by the contract though the practical position, particularly in the case of demotion or transfer, may be that even if the legality is dubious the employer may go ahead and then, if the employee walks out and claims constructive dismissal, accept that there was a dismissal but argue that it was fair because of the urgent need to remove the employee from his previous position. These are, however, all matters which are amenable to inclusion in a contract of employment in the first place (possibly via a set disciplinary code for the firm) and so an employer who finds himself unable to take certain disciplinary action (or the subject of an unfair dismissal action for doing so) may have only himself to blame for the lack of foresight.

---

10   COP, para. 7; a statement that an employee is 'liable to' dismissal for particular misconduct is probably strong enough: *Procter v British Gypsum Ltd* [1992] IRLR 7. If the rules are ambiguous as to the seriousness of a particular matter but then the employer dismisses for the *first* breach (i.e. without warning), a tribunal may well consider that unfair: *Trusthouse Forte (Catering) Ltd v Adonis* [1984] IRLR 382. On the other hand, however, the fact that particular conduct is absolutely banned by the rules and stated to warrant mandatory dismissal does not mean that such a dismissal will automatically be fair, for the rules cannot oust the jurisdiction of the tribunal to look into the overall merits: *Laws Stores Ltd v Oliphant* [1978] IRLR 251; *Ladbroke Racing Ltd v Arnott* [1983] IRLR 154, Ct of Sess; *Taylor v Parsons, Peebles NEI Bruce Peebles Ltd* [1981] IRLR 119. This may cause problems in striking a reasonable balance between certainty and flexibility; see p. 480, below.
11   See p. 213, above.
12   Except perhaps in cases where the employee claims a right actually to work, not just to be paid wages: *Langston v AUEW* [1974] 1 All ER 980, [1974] ICR 180, CA; see p. 120, above. This category of case might expand in the light of *William Hill Organisation Ltd v Tucker* [1998] IRLR 313, CA, which emphasis the advantage to an employer of having an express power to suspend with pay.
13   COP, para. 13.
14   *Hanley v Pease & Partners Ltd* [1915] 1 KB 698; *Bird v British Celanese Ltd* [1945] KB 336, [1945] 1 All ER 488, CA; See p. 183, above.

The Code of Practice, paragraph 9, should be considered when drafting a disciplinary procedure, for it states that such procedures should:

i) be in writing;
ii) specify to whom they apply;
iii) be non-discriminatory;
iv) provide for matters to be dealt with quickly;
v) address the issue of confidentiality;
vi) indicate the disciplinary actions which may be taken;
vii) specify the levels of management which have the authority to take the various forms of disciplinary action (ensuring that immediate superiors do not normally have the power to dismiss without reference to senior management);
viii) provide for employees to be informed of the complaints against them and any relevant evidence before any hearing and to be given an opportunity to state their case before decisions are reached;
ix) inform workers of their statutory, and any other, right to be accompanied;
x) ensure that, except for gross misconduct, no employee is dismissed for a first breach of discipline;
xi) ensure that disciplinary action is not taken until the case has been fully investigated;
xii) ensure that employees are given an explanation for any penalty imposed;
xiii) provide a right of appeal – normally to a higher level of management – and specify the procedure to be followed.

iii) Warnings and hearings

A system of warnings has become an integral part of modern employment procedures, particularly where there is a possibility of dismissal. Warnings may seem particularly appropriate to cases of misconduct by the employee, but the general requirement for them has also been applied to cases of lack of capacity (such as inefficiency, bad workmanship and incompetence)[15] and, in line with the principle that discipline should be constructive as well as punitive, a warning to the employee should not just point out the unsatisfactory conduct but may also be expected to specify any required improvements. Many employers will have a definite warning procedure built into their disciplinary code (which may be in the firm's rules or jointly agreed with a trade union), and may operate on a 'rule of thumb' basis such as 'one oral and two written'; there is no magic in a particular combination, but paragraph 15 of the code does lay down this general advice:

'Supervisors or managers will often give *informal* oral warnings for the purpose of improving matters when employees commit minor infringements of the established standards of conduct and performance. However, where the facts of a case appear to call for disciplinary action, other than summary dismissal, a *formal* procedure should be followed. The type of procedure will vary depending on the circumstances of the organisation. A typical procedure would normally incorporate the following stages:

Stage 1: Oral warning – In the case of minor offences the employee should be given a *formal* oral warning. Employees should be advised of the reason

15 *Winterhalter Gastronom Ltd v Webb* [1973] ICR 245, [1973] IRLR 120, NIRC.

for the warning, that it constitutes the first stage of the disciplinary procedure and of their right of appeal. A note of the oral warning should be kept but should be disregarded for disciplinary purposes after a specified period (e.g. six months) subject to satisfactory conduct and performance.

Stage 2: Written warning – If the offence is regarded as more serious, or if a further offence occurs within the currency of a prior warning, the employee should be given a formal written warning giving details of the complaint, the improvement required, the timescale allowed for improvement and the right of appeal. The warning should also inform the employee that action under stage three of this procedure may be considered if there is no satisfactory improvement. A copy of the written warning should be kept on file but should be disregarded for disciplinary purposes after a specified period (e.g. 12 months) subject to satisfactory conduct and performance.

Stage 3: Final written warning – Where there is a failure to improve during the currency of a prior warning, or where the offence is sufficiently serious, the employee should normally be given a final written warning. This should give details of the complaint, warn the employee that failure to improve may lead to dismissal or to some other action short of dismissal and refer to the right of appeal. The final written warning should be kept on file but should be disregarded for disciplinary purposes after a specified period (e.g. 12 months).

Stage 4: Dismissal or suspension – If the employee's conduct or performance still fails to improve the final step might be disciplinary transfer, disciplinary suspension without pay, demotion, loss of seniority, loss of increment (provided these penalties are allowed for in the contract of employment) or dismissal. The decision to dismiss should only be taken by the appropriate senior manager and the employee should be informed as soon as reasonably practicable of the reasons for the dismissal, the date on which employment will terminate, the appropriate period of notice (or pay in lieu of notice) and information on the right of appeal including how to make the appeal and to whom'.

Further to this general statement, three particular points should be noticed. First, the existence of a warning system places emphasis upon writing and the keeping of detailed personnel records by the employer[16] who must be able, if necessary, to provide documentary proof of previous warnings; this leads, for example, to the practices of giving written confirmation even of an 'oral' warning, and of requiring the employee's signature of acknowledged receipt of a warning. This may lead to an increased personnel function within a firm, but is inevitable with the modern movement towards increased legalisation. Second, the employer's system should include some time limit on warnings, so that after a set period they lapse[17]. Third, a warning should be reasonably specific, identifying the precise ground of complaint by the employer. One consequence of this is that a warning

---

16   COP, para. 28. The warning should usually be given to the employee personally; giving it to his trade union may not be enough: *W Brooks & Son v Skinner* [1984] IRLR 379, EAT.

17   A firm's disciplinary procedure may permit an appeal against a warning; a warning which is under appeal may be considered by an employer when dismissing, but the fact that the appeal has not yet been heard should also be taken into account: *Tower Hamlets Health Authority v Anthony* [1989] ICR 656, [1989] IRLR 394, CA.

on ground A (e.g. swearing) should not be used as a step in the procedure to dismiss on ground B (e.g. bad workmanship), so that one employee may be subject to more than one series of warnings concurrently if he is deficient in different respects; this must be viewed realistically, however, and there may come a point when a multitude of warnings on different matters add up overall to reasonable grounds to dismiss, particularly if some of the grounds are not dissimilar, and the employer may genuinely issue one final warning on generally unsatisfactory conduct[18].

The presence or absence of warnings may be a most important factor in determining the fairness or otherwise of a dismissal, though as always on matters of procedure it is not necessarily conclusive. Thus there may be circumstances in which lack of a warning is reasonable; summary dismissal for gross misconduct is still permissible[19], and a warning might also be dispensed with where the employee has made it clear that he does not intend to 'improve' (e.g. where he is at odds with the company's policy)[20], where his incapability is so bad as to be irredeemable or where (as in the case of senior management) the employee already knows exactly what is required of him, so that a warning would be irrelevant[1].

In addition to warnings, the employee who is in danger of dismissal should normally be allowed a hearing of sorts, which may be built into the firm's disciplinary procedures, or be arranged ad hoc. This may perform two functions, first to ascertain the true facts of the incident in question and second to allow the employee to make representations on the question whether he ought on those facts to be dismissed (when he may wish to refute the charges against him, or accept them but put forward matters such as length of service or previous good conduct in mitigation); where these two functions are separated (e.g. where the second is considered by a higher level of management), the employee should normally be given a proper opportunity to be heard at each stage[2].

It will usually be of the essence of a fair hearing that the employee must be made aware of the charges against him[3] (unless they are obvious[4]), but the precise form of the required hearing will vary with the circumstances and the emphasis is on the overall failures of the procedure adopted, rather than any rigidly prescribed format[5]. Although the basic requirement of a hearing is akin to the rules of natural justice (which are sometimes prayed in aid in such cases), it must be remembered that these are *not* court proceedings, and so there is no

18   *Auguste Noel Ltd v Curtis* [1990] ICR 604, [1990] IRLR 326 is a particularly strong case on this point. One innovation in the draft ACAS code on discipline and dismissal (which the Secretary of State refused to accept – p. 44, above) was the concept of a 'first and final' warning, to apply to cases of serious misconduct just falling short of warranting dismissal; this would have provided more flexibility, with a half-way house between instant dismissal and exhaustion of the full warning system. The idea was finally taken up in the 2000 revision of the code and is implicit in the warnings system (see above).

19   See p. 373, above.

20   *Retarded Children's Aid Society Ltd v Day* [1978] ICR 437, [1978] IRLR 128, CA.

1   *James v Waltham Holy Cross UDC* [1973] ICR 398, [1973] IRLR 202.

2   *Budgen & Co v Thomas* [1976] ICR 344, [1976] IRLR 174; *Tesco (Holdings) Ltd v Hill* [1977] IRLR 63. It is normally for the employer to take the initiative in operating the procedure; it is not enough to say that the employee could have used the *grievance* procedure: *Clarke v Trimoco Motor Group Ltd* [1993] ICR 237, [1993] IRLR 148, EAT.

3   *Louies v Coventry Hood and Seating Co Ltd* [1990] ICR 54, [1990] IRLR 324; *Spink v Express Foods Group Ltd* [1990] IRLR 320, EAT.

4   *Fuller v Lloyds Bank plc* [1991] IRLR 336, EAT.

5   There is, however, a very useful summary of the key points normally expected of a fair hearing in the judgment of Wood P in *Clark v Civil Aviation Authority* [1991] IRLR 412, at 415.

inalienable right to appear in person[6], to receive witness statements[7], or to be allowed to cross examine 'witnesses'[8]. On the other hand, a fair hearing procedure (in whatever form) should normally give the employee a reasonable opportunity to hear the allegations against him and to attempt to refute them[9]. However, the analogy with the rules of natural justice must not be exaggerated, especially in the difficult area of potential bias, for it may not always be practicable to expect a complete separation of powers between the person dismissing and the person holding the disciplinary hearing (or appeal), since they may both be ordinary line managers; as long as there is substantive fairness in the internal procedure (and such procedures are, of course, to be encouraged), it is not to be attached with rules of natural justice on bias which evolved in different contexts[10]. Where the employee is to attend a formal hearing, he should normally be allowed to be represented if he so wishes (by a trade union representative or a fellow employee); this has always been good practice, but in addition the Employment Relations Act 1999, ss 10–13 now give a statutory right to be accompanied at a disciplinary hearing[11] by a trade union official or another of the employer's workers; that person is to be permitted to address the hearing (but not answer questions on behalf of the worker[12]) and to confer with him or her during the hearing, and is to be given paid time off work for the purpose[13]. If the chosen companion is not available at the time proposed for the hearing, the employer must postpone it to an alternative time proposed by the worker (provided it is reasonable and falls within the next five working days). Complaint of breach of this right lies to an employment tribunal (subject to the usual three-month time limitation provisions), which may order compensation of up to two weeks' pay.

In addition to a hearing, most disciplinary procedures in other than small firms will include some form of appeal from an adverse decision; this is suggested

6   *Ayanlowo v IRC* [1975] IRLR 253, CA. Moreover, it has been emphasised that the rules of natural justice do not constitute an independent head of challenge to the fairness of a dismissal in this context: *Slater v Leicestershire Health Authority* [1989] IRLR 16, CA.

7   *Hussain v Elonex plc* [1999] IRLR 420, CA; on the facts, the tribunal had taken the view that the employee had been made sufficiently aware of the allegations in other ways.

8   *Khanum v Mid-Glamorgan Area Health Authority* [1979] ICR 40, [1978] IRLR 215. There may, in particular, be cases where an informant wishes to remain anonymous for fear of reprisals; Wood P laid down guidance on how to deal with the situation in *Linfood Cash and Carry Ltd v Thomson* [1989] ICR 518, [1989] IRLR 235, EAT.

9   *Bentley Engineering Co Ltd v Mistry* [1979] ICR 47, [1978] IRLR 437. For subsequent examples of findings of unfair dismissal based on breach of natural justice (in these cases, the rule on potential bias) see *Moyes v Hylton Castle Working Men's Social Club and Institute Ltd* [1986] IRLR 482 and *Campion v Hamworthy Engineering Ltd* [1987] ICR 966, CA; cf. however *Slater v Leicestershire Health Authority*, n. 7 above.

10 *Rowe v Radio Rentals Ltd* [1982] IRLR 177, where the (unsuccessful) ground of challenge was that the person hearing the appeal had been told of the facts beforehand by the person who dismissed the employee, and the latter person had been present at the appeal hearing; *R v Chief Constable of South Wales, ex p Thornhill* [1987] IRLR 313, CA. However, wherever possible (especially in a large organisation), it is highly desirable to have separate levels of management dealing with the different stages: *Sartor v P&O European Ferries (Felixstowe) Ltd* [1992] IRLR 271, CA; *Byrne v BOC Ltd* [1992] IRLR 505, EAT.

11 This means a hearing that could result in a formal warning, the taking of some other action or the confirmation of either: Employment Relations Act 1999, s. 13(4). Note that this right also applies to grievance hearings 'which concern the performance of a duty by an employer in relation to the worker': s. 13(5).

12 The wide definition of 'worker' is used in relation to this right, which is itself extended to cover agency workers and home workers: ibid., s. 13(1)–(3).

13 Ibid., s. 10(6), (7). Section 12 extends the usual package of employment protection measures (concerning detriment and dismissal) to both the worker relying on this right and the chosen companion (when in that employer's employment).

by the Code of Practice, paragraph 9(xiii) (set out above) and may take many forms, from a simple further hearing by a more senior manager up to a formal appeal hearing by a joint management–union committee or even ACAS-organised arbitration. The importance of such an appeal as an integral part of the internal procedure (lack or denial of which may per se make the dismissal unfair) has been recognised by the House of Lords[14]; this has been emphasised even further subsequently by the evolution of the rule that a bad initial dismissal may be 'cured' by a fair appeal, *provided* that the appeal takes the form of a full re-hearing of the facts (rather than just a review of the initial decision)[15].

As in the case of a warning, a hearing and appeal may well be expected in most cases, but lack of them will not necessarily make a dismissal unfair. There may be definite classes of case where it is highly arguable that a hearing would have been inappropriate, such as where the employee clearly refuses to accept the employer's legitimate requirements, where the employee's conduct 'is of such a nature that, whatever the explanation, his continued employment is not in the interests of the business'[16] (particularly where the employment in question is of a delicate or sensitive nature[17]) or where the employee is already being investigated by the police with a view to criminal charges being brought[18]. More generally, however, this is clearly an area where views may differ, and indeed we have seen definite changes of judicial approach to the whole question of fair procedure over the years. In the seventies (in the infancy of the unfair dismissal law) great emphasis was placed on proper procedures, but this was then perceived to have gone too far and a reaction set in, from two directions – first, through a generally more relaxed approach to procedural requirements beginning with the decision of the Court of Appeal in *Hollister v NFU*[19], taking the view that a lapse in procedure (such as failure to give a hearing) is merely one factor to take into account and, secondly and more specifically, through the evolution and widespread application of the rule in *British Labour Pump Co Ltd v Byrne*[20] that an element of procedural unfairness (such as the lack of a hearing) may be 'forgiven' if the employer could show that even if the proper procedure had been carried out it would have made no difference. The potential inroad of the *Byrne* principle into any general requirement of a hearing hardly needed to be spelled out. That is why its overruling in the leading House of Lords decision in *Polkey v A E Dayton Services Ltd*[1] was of such great importance, and led to a general swing back of the pendulum, with more emphasis again being placed on procedure in general, and hearings in particular. The court emphasised that the task of a tribunal is to assess the reasonableness of what the employer actually did at the time, not what he might have done, and that the question whether at the end of the day the

14 *West Midlands Co-operative Society Ltd v Tipton* [1986] ICR 192, [1986] IRLR 112, HL.
15 *Whitbread & Co plc v Mills* [1988] ICR 776, [1988] IRLR 501; *Clark v Civil Aviation Authority* [1991] IRLR 412; approved by the Court of Appeal in *Sartor v P&O European Ferries (Felixstowe) Ltd*, n. 10, above. In *Post Office v Marney* [1990] IRLR 170 an EAT held a fair initial decision cures a bad appeal, sed quaere whether this goes against *Tipton*, n. 14, above.
16 *James v Waltham Holy Cross UDC* [1973] ICR 398, [1973] IRLR 202.
17 *Alidair Ltd v Taylor* [1978] ICR 445, [1978] IRLR 82, CA.
18 *Carr v Alexander Russell Ltd* [1979] ICR 469n, [1976] IRLR 220, applied in *Parker v Clifford Dunn Ltd* [1979] ICR 463, [1979] IRLR 56, EAT.
19 [1979] ICR 542, [1979] IRLR 238, CA.
20 [1979] ICR 347, [1979] IRLR 94, EAT.
1 [1988] ICR 142, [1987] IRLR 503, HL; see p. 399, below and Collins (1990) 19 ILJ 39. Arguably, however, the later interpretation of *Polkey* in *Duffy v Yeomans Ltd* [1995] ICR 1, [1994] IRLR 642, CA has within it certain unfortunate echoes of *Byrne*; see p. 488, below.

employee actually suffered injustice goes only to compensation, *not* to liability. The case of *McLaren v National Coal Board*² is a good example of the result of once again taking procedures seriously. The employee was accused of assaulting a working miner during the strike; normally the matter would have been investigated by the local manager but in the circumstances this was thought to be impracticable and so it was left to the police and the court – once the employee was convicted, he was automatically dismissed without a hearing. The tribunal held that this was fair given the surrounding circumstances of industrial warfare, but the Court of Appeal held that it was unfair, Sir John Donaldson MR stating:

> '[N]o amount of heat in industrial warfare can justify failing to give an employee an opportunity of giving an explanation. ... You have the position that acceptable reasons for dismissing may change in a varying industrial situation, but *the standards of fairness never change. They are immutable but are applied in a different situation.*' (Emphasis added.)

The pendulum may therefore be on its way at least partially back; there will still be cases where lack of a hearing is explained sufficiently to the tribunal's satisfaction to produce a finding of fair dismissal, and it remains ultimately a matter of fact for the tribunal³. However, in entertaining an employer's case that it was reasonable to dispense with a hearing a tribunal might do well to bear in mind the words of Megarry V-C in *John v Rees*⁴:

> '[T]he path of the law is strewn with examples of open and shut cases which, somehow, were not; of unanswerable charges which, in the event, were completely answered; of inexplicable conduct which was fully explained; of fixed and unalterable determinations that, by discussion, suffered a change. Nor are those with any knowledge of human nature who pause to think for a moment likely to underestimate the feelings of resentment of those who find that a decision against them has been made without their being afforded any opportunity to influence the course of events.'

4   THE DEFINITION OF DISMISSAL AND THE DATE OF TERMINATION

i)   Dismissal

The existence of a dismissal is a vital jurisdictional factor in the laws relating to unfair dismissal and redundancy. In most cases it is obvious that there has been a dismissal, but in cases of doubt the onus is upon the applicant to prove that he is dismissed; if he fails to do so, he cannot proceed with his claim. In particular, a tribunal will have no jurisdiction to hear the claim if the true construction of the facts is that the termination of employment was brought about by some factor

2   [1988] ICR 370, [1988] IRLR 215, CA; the passage cited is at pp. 377 and 218.
3   This can be seen from the decision of a differently constituted Court of Appeal in *Dillett v National Coal Board* [1988] ICR 218, where on facts similar to those in *McLaren* they confirmed a decision that a dismissal without a hearing in the middle of the miners strike was *fair*, but largely on the ground that that had been the view of the tribunal on the particular facts of the case and it was not open to an appellate court to reverse them (see p. 410, above).
4   [1970] Ch 345 at 402, [1969] 2 All ER 274 at 309.

other than dismissal (e.g. frustration or mutual consent)[5] or that the employee resigned (see below). Dismissal is therefore a central concept in this area of law and has not been without its problems[6].

a) The definition of dismissal [7]

Dismissal is defined for the purposes of unfair dismissal and redundancy in sections 95 and 136 respectively of the Employment Rights Act 1996. These definitions are similar and envisage dismissal arising in one of three situations:

a) where the contract is terminated by the employer either with or without notice;
b) where a fixed term contract expires without being renewed;
c) where the *employee* terminates the contract, with or without notice, in circumstances such that he is *entitled* to terminate it without notice by reason of the employer's conduct.

Category (a) covers the usual case of dismissal, where the employer clearly dispenses with the employee's services either summarily or by giving him notice (or by giving him wages in lieu thereof). As it means the termination of a particular contract, there can be a category (a) dismissal (and hence a claim for unfair dismissal) even though the employee is still working for the same employer under a new contract (which may be particularly useful for the employee where the employer has unilaterally insisted on radically different terms of employment, sufficient to constitute a 'new' contract, rather than just a modification of the existing one)[8]. It has also been held to cover cases where at first sight the employee appears to have resigned, but evidence then clearly establishes that the resignation was procured by the employer either by fraud[9], pressure[10] or ultimatum ('resign or be sacked')[11]; this has been done by concentrating, as a matter of fact, on the question – who *really* terminated the employment. This question may also be of importance where there is an ambiguous or hot-headed 'resignation'; while an employer may rely on a clear statement by the employee, there may be an onus on him to investigate further if there are special factors or circumstances leading up to the employee's actions, and failure to do so may mean that what eventually occurred was actually a dismissal and in all likelihood

---

5   For modes of termination other than dismissal, see pp. 355-367, above.
6   See Elias 'Unravelling the concept of dismissal' (1978) 7 ILJ 16 and 100.
7   See *Harvey* D[201].
8   This is the rule in *Hogg v Dover College* [1990] ICR 39 which, while only likely to apply on strong facts (of a major change in terms imposed by the employer on a reluctant workforce), was affirmed and applied in *Alcan Extrusions v Yates* [1996] IRLR 327. Its importance is that, unlike constructive dismissal (the usual possibility in a case of unilateral change by the employer), the employees can claim unfair dismissal while keeping their jobs.
9   *Makin v Grews Motors (Bridport) Ltd* (1986) Times, 18 April, CA.
10   *Caledonian Mining Co Ltd v Bassett* [1987] ICR 425, [1987] IRLR 165, applying *Martin v Glynwed Distribution Ltd* [1983] ICR 511, [1983] IRLR 198, CA; *Hellyer Bros Ltd v Atkinson* [1992] IRLR 540, EAT.
11   *East Sussex County Council v Walker* (1972) 7 ITR 280; *Martin* (n. 10, above). However, these cases must be carefully distinguished from – (i) cases where the employer has merely indicated a general intention to dismiss at some time in the future (e.g. on a planned future factory closure): *Haseltine Lake & Co Ltd v Dowler* [1981] ICR 222, [1981] IRLR 25; *International Computers Ltd v Kennedy* [1981] IRLR 28, (ii) cases where an employee under threat of dismissal reaches acceptable terms on which to leave (see p. 381, n. 4, below). These will be ordinary resignations.

an unfair dismissal[12]. One point of historical importance to note (explaining certain older cases) is that at one time the tribunals and courts sought to extend this head of dismissal to cover matters now covered by category (c) (i.e. constructive dismissal), because that category (c) for redundancy purposes used to be more narrowly drafted[13], and for unfair dismissal purposes was not expressly included in the legislation until 1974[14]; thus in certain cases category (a) was stretched to cover applicants who would otherwise have fallen outside the legislation for one of these reasons, but there is now no need for this stretching and so such cases should not necessarily be viewed as good law in this context, since the type of dismissal in question should now be considered under category (c)[15].

Where under category (a) an employee is given notice of dismissal, he may wish to leave his job before expiry of that notice (e.g. where, being about to be made redundant, he finds another job which he wishes to start immediately). In such circumstances he would normally be in a difficult position for if he gave notice to leave he might be construed as having resigned or terminated the employment by mutual consent with his employer[16]; in either case there would be no dismissal and so he would lose his unfair dismissal and redundancy rights. To avoid this pitfall, the legislation includes the concept of 'early notice'[17], so that if, during the currency of the employer's notice, the employee gives counter-notice to terminate the employment at an earlier date he may leave and still be taken to have been dismissed by the employer. It must be noted here, however, that the provisions relating to early notice for redundancy purposes are narrower than those for unfair dismissal purposes in two ways – (i) the employee must give his counter-notice in writing, and (ii) the counter-notice must be given during the *obligatory* period of the employer's notice (i.e. the period which the employer must by law give, either under the individual contract, or by virtue of the minimum notice requirements[18], whichever is the longer). These requirements used to exist for unfair dismissal purposes also, but were removed by the Employment Protection Act 1975.

Category (b) exists to safeguard the position of employees under fixed term contracts (other than those under contracts for two years or more who have validly

---

12   *Kwik Fit (GB) Ltd v Lineham* [1992] ICR 183, [1992] IRLR 156. One problem is, of course, that in such extreme circumstances the language used tends not to be that contained in s. 95; more often a tribunal will have to decide instead whether telling the employer where to insert the job, in graphic anatomical detail, constitutes an unambiguous resignation.

13   For category (c) to apply, the employee had to leave *without* notice (Redundancy Payments Act 1965, s. 3(1)(c), now repealed): *Marriott v Oxford and District Co-operative Society Ltd (No 2)* [1970] 1 QB 186, [1969] 3 All ER 1126, CA.

14   See the Industrial Relations Act 1971, s. 23(2), in force between 1971 and 1974; the NIRC filled this gap by construing category (a) as extending to constructive dismissals for unfair dismissal purposes in *Sutcliffe v Hawker Siddeley Aviation Ltd* [1973] ICR 560, [1973] IRLR 304, NIRC.

15   See the explanation of *Marriott*'s case by Lord Denning MR in *Western Excavating (ECC) Ltd v Sharp* [1978] ICR 221 at 227, [1978] IRLR 27 at 29, CA.

16   See p. 364, above, under 'Mutual consent'.

17   Employment Rights Act 1996, ss. 95(2) and 136(3). The counter-notice given by the employee may be of any length; it does not have to be of the length required by his contract (or even the statutory minimum of one week under s. 86): *Ready Case Ltd v Jackson* [1981] IRLR 312; quaere what if it was only a few hours, or even minutes? The employer must have given *actual* notice for these provisions to apply; it is not enough that he has made some general statement of a possible future dismissal: see p. 368, n. 20, above.

18   Ibid., s. 86.

signed away their redundancy rights[19]). Expiry without renewal is deemed to be a dismissal, so that in an unfair dismissal action, the employer will have to show that the reason for failure to renew was a fair one[20]. The meaning of 'fixed term contract' is considered above[1].

b) Constructive dismissal

While categories (a) and (b) have not been without difficulties, it is category (c) which has been most contentious. This sets out the statutory definition of 'constructive dismissal' which, as seen above, was always in the redundancy payments legislation and was read into the unfair dismissal provisions[2] before being expressly included in 1974. Constructive dismissal occurs where, although it is the employee who appears to terminate the employment by walking out, it can be said that the real reason for termination was in some way the prior conduct of the employer; it is necessary in order to avoid the employer being able to force or goad the employee to leave his employment and then say that the employee in fact resigned and so was not dismissed. When it is established, it means that for statutory purposes the contract is terminated by the employer and so, for example, there is no continuing obligation on the employee to exhaust established grievance procedures – he may simply leave and make an immediate claim for unfair dismissal[3]. This is clearly the most contentious kind of dismissal, for there is no express act of dismissal by the employer. It must be remembered, however, that a constructive dismissal is *not* necessarily unfair and so a tribunal, even if it finds in the employee's favour on constructive dismissal, must still go on to consider fairness in the ordinary way; in many cases there will be little argument on this and the dismissal will, in the nature of things, be unfair, but this is not automatically so and there may be cases where, even though the employee had technically the right to walk out, the employer may be able to show that it was fair to act as he did[4].

The key element of the definition of constructive dismissal is that the employee must have been *entitled* to leave without notice because of the employer's conduct. What does 'entitled' mean? There were two possible interpretations of this crucial word – first that the employee could leave when the employer's behaviour towards him was so unreasonable that he could not be expected to stay, and second that the employer's conduct had to be so grave that it constituted a repudiatory breach of the contract of employment, i.e. that the employee was *contractually* entitled to leave. Clearly the second is a narrower approach, and it was argued that the first was more in line with the overall approach in unfair dismissal cases of looking at the reasonableness of the employer's conduct. Following a period of uncertainty,

---

19 Employment Rights Act 1996, s. 197 (3)–(5).
20 *Terry v East Sussex County Council* [1976] ICR 536, [1976] IRLR 332, approved by the Court of Appeal in *Fay v North Yorkshire County Council* [1986] ICR 133, [1985] IRLR 247.
1 P. 363, above, under 'Expiry of fixed term contracts'.
2 *Sutcliffe v Hawker Siddeley Aviation Ltd* [1973] ICR 560, [1973] IRLR 304, NIRC.
3 *Seligman and Latz Ltd v McHugh* [1979] IRLR 130. There is an interesting overlap here with the law on jobseeker's allowance – if the employee leaves 'voluntarily without just cause' he can be disqualified for benefit for up to 26 weeks (see p. 551, below); if, however, he had enough reason to leave for the purposes of establishing constructive dismissal, he should normally be able to show 'just cause', and so he can leave the employment and validly claim benefit.
4 *Savoia v Chiltern Herb Farms Ltd* [1982] IRLR 166, CA. Note, however, the unenthusiastic approach taken to this distinction by the EAT in *Cawley v South Wales Electricity Board* [1985] IRLR 89 where it was said that in a case where the two stages (constructive dismissal and then fairness under s. 98) raise the same issues a constructive dismissal should almost invariably be held to be unfair; sed quaere.

with conflicting decisions, the Court of Appeal held in *Western Excavating (ECC) Ltd v Sharp*[5] that the contractual approach is the correct one, Lord Denning MR defining it as follows:

> 'If the employer is guilty of conduct which is a significant breach going to the root of the contract of employment, or which shows that the employer no longer intends to be bound by one or more of the essential terms of the contract, then the employee is entitled to treat himself as discharged from any further performance. If he does so, then he terminates the contract by reason of the employer's conduct. He is constructively dismissed. The employee is entitled in those circumstances to leave at the instant without giving any notice at all or, alternatively, he may give notice and say that he is leaving at the end of the notice. But the conduct must in either case be sufficiently serious to entitle him to leave at once.'

Thus, in a constructive dismissal case the tribunal is looking primarily for conduct by the employer[6] which is clearly a breach of one of the terms of the contract, and sufficiently important to be repudiatory on the part of the employer[7]. Certain examples may be fairly obvious, such as a refusal to pay wages[8], an unjustified demotion or suspension[9], failure to follow a contractually binding disciplinary procedure[10], unilateral alteration of job content without contractual authority[11], or insistence upon an unlawful or illegal order or the imposition of

---

5   [1978] ICR 221, [1978] IRLR 27, CA; the passage cited is at 226 and 29 respectively; *Courtaulds Northern Spinning Ltd v Sibson* [1988] ICR 451, [1988] IRLR 305, CA.

6   Conduct by an immediate superior (e.g. a supervisor) may be enough to justify walking out, even if the employer later argues that that superior did not actually have the power to dismiss: *Hilton Industrial Hotels (UK) Ltd v Protopapa* [1990] IRLR 316.

7   It has been held by the Court of Appeal that the question of whether a particular breach of contract is sufficient to be repudiatory (for the purpose of establishing constructive dismissal) is one of mixed fact and law, so that the EAT should rarely interfere with a tribunal's decision on this point, provided there was some evidence on which to base that decision: *Pedersen v Camden London Borough Council* [1981] ICR 674, [1981] IRLR 173, CA. In *Dutton & Clark Ltd v Daly* [1985] ICR 780, [1985] IRLR 363 the EAT went further and held that the range of reasonable responses test (p. 469, below) should be applied by the tribunal when deciding this question, but it is arguable that ultimately this is inconsistent with the contractual test in *Western Excavating*. Although the test is contractual, seriously unreasonable conduct by the employer may be powerful *evidence* of breach of contract (in particular, the implied term of trust and respect): *Brown v Merchant Ferries Ltd* [1998] IRLR 682, NICA.

8   Even this major term is not sacrosanct, however, as every case must be considered on its facts; even a failure to pay wages might not be repudiatory in exceptional circumstances: *Adams v Charles Zub Associates Ltd* [1978] IRLR 551. Further, there is no implied term of an annual wage rise, so failure to give one will not necessarily amount to repudiatory conduct by the employer: *Murco Petroleum Ltd v Forge* [1987] ICR 282, [1987] IRLR 50; likewise, there is no implied term that there will never be a pay decrease: *White v Reflecting Roadstuds Ltd* [1991] ICR 733, [1991] IRLR 331; on the other hand, the Court of Appeal held in *Cantor Fitzgerald International v Callaghan* [1999] ICR 639, [1999] IRLR 234 (a common law action, but on the same point) that failure to pay any element of remuneration, however minor, will usually be repudiatory. For detailed consideration of matters held to be repudiatory in the past, see *Harvey* D[425].

9   *McNeill v Charles Crimm (Electrical Construction) Ltd* [1984] IRLR 179, EAT.

10   *Post Office v Strange* [1981] IRLR 515, EAT.

11   *Millbrook Furnishing Industries Ltd v McIntosh* [1981] IRLR 309; where the alteration is only temporary and for pressing business need, it *may* be arguable that it is not enough to be repudiatory, but such an argument failed in the *Millbrook* case. The practical answer for the employer is to incorporate a flexibility clause in the contract in the first place.

a penalty disproportionate to the offence[12]. It may however go wider than this, for the breach in question may be of an implied term as well as an express one, and therefore it is important to be able to say exactly which term it is claimed that the employer broke, and whether any such term ever actually existed in the contract[13]. The question of definition of contractual terms, considered in chapter 3 above, has thus been given renewed significance.

The contractual test as laid down in *Western Excavating (ECC) Ltd v Sharp* appears to be much narrower and more precise than the 'reasonableness' test, and at first seemed to be a significant restriction on constructive dismissal. However this has not been so, principally for two reasons. The first is that the Court of Appeal, while firmly basing the law upon ideas of contract, did not mean to impose a rigid test and envisaged some flexibility in its application; this can be seen particularly in the judgment of Lawton LJ:

'... I do not find it either necessary or advisable to express any opinion as to what principles of law operate to bring a contract of employment to an end by reason of an employer's conduct. Sensible persons have no difficulty in recognising such conduct when they hear about it. ... Lay members of the industrial tribunals ... do not spend all their time in court and when out of court they may use, and certainly will hear, short words and terse phrases which describe clearly the kind of employer of whom an employee is entitled without notice to rid himself. This is what [constructive dismissal] is all about; and what is required for the application of this provision is a large measure of common sense[14].'

The second, and more far-reaching, reason is that in subsequent cases, the EAT has shown itself ready to read into contracts of employment a new term obliging the employer to treat the employee with trust and respect (though this has been variously expressed)[15]. To a large extent this development has outflanked the

---

12   *BBC v Beckett* [1983] IRLR 43; *Cawley v South Wales Electricity Board* [1985] IRLR 89; this class of case is more interesting, for here the employer may technically have the contractual power to impose the penalty in question, but semble must still act in accordance with some sort of proportionality which is presumably implied into the contractual disciplinary rules; these cases are considered at p. 109, above.

13   A good example is *Dryden v Greater Glasgow Health Board* [1992] IRLR 469 (no implied term allowing smoking); it was also held there that if a change of practice is lawful under the contract (there, the imposition of a no-smoking policy) the fact that it bears more heavily on one employee than on others is *not* a ground for constructive dismissal.

14   At 229 and 30 respectively. Generally speaking, the test is objective, in that the employer's conduct does *not* have to be intentional or in bad faith before it may be repudiatory: *Post Office v Roberts* [1980] IRLR 347. In line with this, 'seriously unreasonable' conduct can be *evidence* of contractual breach: *Brown v Merchant Ferries Ltd* [1998] IRLR 682, NICA. However, one class of case has imported a potentially subjective test – in *Frank Wright & Co (Holdings) Ltd v Punch* [1980] IRLR 217 it was held that where there is a genuine dispute as to the meaning of a contractual term and the employer insists on implementing his genuine (but possibly mistaken) version of it, that it *not* a repudiatory breach (even if he is later proved to have been wrong). This principle has backing from the normal law of commercial contracts (see *Woodar Investment Development Ltd v Wimpey Construction (UK) Ltd* [1980] 1 All ER 571, [1980] 1 WLR 277, HL) but its application to the specialised area of constructive dismissal could have an unfortunately restrictive effect (see the strong criticisms in *Harvey*, D[486] ff); it was treated with caution in *Financial Techniques (Planning Services) Ltd v Hughes* [1981] IRLR 32, CA, but mentioned with approval obiter by Sir John Donaldson MR in *Bridgen v Lancashire County Council* [1987] IRLR 58, CA, and so the point remains unresolved.

15   See p. 124, above.

more purely contractual approach of the Court of Appeal in *Western Excavating (ECC) Ltd v Sharp*, so that harsh and unreasonable conduct by the employer might be construed by the tribunal as breach of this implied term of mutual respect, giving rise (where the conduct is serious enough) to a constructive dismissal. Thus, in the outcome, the contractual approach may differ little from a simple 'reasonableness' approach[16], and indeed a tribunal or court may now be impatient with an excessively contractual or technical argument by an employer which is aimed at frustrating the protective policy behind constructive dismissal[17]. However, there remain two main qualifications. The first is that if the 'conduct' in question consists simply of the employer exercising one of his definite contractual rights (e.g. to make the employee move from site to site, where there is a mobility clause in the contract), the employee who refuses to comply *should* not, under the contractual approach, be able to claim constructive dismissal for there has been no breach of contract; however, it is argued elsewhere[18] that this may be changing, with the development by the courts of possible *overriding* implied terms, particularly that of trust and respect, which may impose limits on the *way* in which even express terms are applied and in so doing increase the scope for constructive dismissal. The second is that a particularly contractual approach has been taken by the Court of Appeal to the question of *anticipatory* breach by the employer; this is unlikely to occur often in practice but if it does (e.g. by an employer announcing that he intends to implement unilateral changes of terms and conditions at some time in the future) it has been held that the employer may retract his intended repudiation as long as he does so before the employee has unequivocally accepted it and terminated the contract in anticipation[19].

Although the theory behind constructive dismissal is that it is the employer who terminates the contract for statutory purposes, in practice it will usually be the employee who takes the final step by resigning and walking out, thus showing that he has accepted the employer's repudiation as concluding the contract. If the employee does not take such action, or does so after a delay, there is the danger (particularly in cases where the employer's conduct consists of a unilateral proposal to change the terms of employment) of this being construed as an agreement by the employee to a variation in the contract; if this is so there is no constructive dismissal, even if the employee later resigns. To avoid this danger, the employee should make up his mind quickly whether to leave[20], or, if his economic circumstances are such that he feels he has to continue working for a short period following the conduct in question, he should let it be known that he

---

16   See *British Aircraft Corpn v Austin* [1978] IRLR 332 at 334, per Phillips J.
17   In *Greenaway Harrison Ltd v Wiles* [1994] IRLR 380 an employer, trying to force through a change of terms (normally giving rise to a constructive dismissal) in fact threatened to give the employees proper notice of dismissal in doing so. He contested their claim for constructive dismissal on the basis that he had acted *lawfully* under the contract, but the EAT refused to accept that and found for the employees, largely as a matter of policy.
18   See p. 109, above.
19   *Norwest Holst Group Administration Ltd v Harrison* [1985] ICR 668, [1985] IRLR 240, CA.
20   *Western Excavating (ECC) Ltd v Sharp* [1978] ICR 221, [1978] IRLR 27 at 226 and 29 respectively per Lord Denning MR; *Land and Wilson v West Yorkshire Metropolitan County Council* [1981] ICR 334, [1981] IRLR 87, CA. Note, however, that even if the employee must be taken to have consented to previous repudiations by the employer, it may be possible to rely on the *fact* of those repudiations having occurred as evidence of overall breach of the general implied term of trust and respect: *Lewis v Motorworld Garages Ltd* [1986] ICR 157, [1985] IRLR 465, CA. One problem is that if the employee leaves without another job to go to, he may face a disqualification of up to 26 weeks for jobseeker's allowance (see p. 551, below); if that happens he should appeal, arguing that he had 'just cause' because of his position in employment law and the need to protect his legal rights.

does not agree to that conduct and is working under protest. The courts and tribunals have taken a realistic view of this[1], but of course the employee cannot work under protest indefinitely and is expected to decide what his final response is to be within a reasonable period. This is because it remains the legal position that the employee must be able to show that he left *in response to* the employer's conduct (i.e. the causal link must be shown). However, this itself is to be viewed realistically (given the employee's difficult position), and so it has been held that (1) there can still be a constructive dismissal if the employee waits to leave until he has found another job to go to[2], and (2) as a matter of law there is no absolute requirement on the employee to tell the employer the real reason for leaving (given that the worse the employer's behaviour, the less likely the employee may be to want to dispute the position before getting out)[3].

c) Resignation by the employee

An employee may resign from his employment for any reason or none; if there is a reason and it is connected with the employer's conduct he may argue that he has been constructively dismissed, but otherwise he may not claim unfair dismissal or a redundancy payment for there is no dismissal[4]. An express resignation may be by unambiguous wording or, if the wording is ambiguous, by a combination of wording and circumstances from which a reasonable employer would understand the employee to be resigning[5]. However, the concept of resignation has caused problems when attempts have been made to apply it in circumstances other than those of express resignation by the employee, usually in order to deprive the tribunals of the jurisdiction to assess the merits in an unfair dismissal action by establishing that there was no dismissal in the first place.

---

1   *Marriott v Oxford and District Co-operative Society Ltd (No 2)* [1970] 1 QB 186, [1969] 3 All ER 1126, CA; *Shields Furniture Ltd v Goff* [1973] 2 All ER 653, [1973] ICR 187; *Sheet Metal Components Ltd v Plumridge* [1974] ICR 373, [1974] IRLR 86; *W E Cox Toner (International) Ltd v Crook* [1981] ICR 823, [1981] IRLR 443. See too, in the context of *wrongful* dismissal, *Bliss v South East Thames Regional Health Authority* [1987] ICR 700, [1985] IRLR 308, CA.

2   *Jones v F Sirl & Son (Furnishers) Ltd* [1997] IRLR 493; *Waltons and Morse v Dorrington* [1997] IRLR 488, EAT.

3   *Weatherfield Ltd v Sargent* [1999] IRLR 94, CA, overruling on this point *Holland v Glendale Industries Ltd* [1998] ICR 493. Failure to make clear the reason for leaving when that might reasonably be expected could cast doubt on the genuineness of that reason, but only as a question of factual causation, not as a matter of law.

4   Also a resignation under threat of dismissal may constitute a dismissal (see p. 446, above), unless the parties reach a mutually satisfactory agreement of terms (usually monetary) upon which the employee agrees to go; in that case it is a genuine resignation in spite of the previous threats – compare *Sheffield v Oxford Controls Co Ltd* [1979] ICR 396, [1979] IRLR 133 with *Thames Television Ltd v Wallis* [1979] IRLR 136. If the employer has already given the employee notice and the employee resigns during that period by giving counter-notice, he may still be 'dismissed' by virtue of ss. 95(2) and 136(3) (see p. 446, above).

5   *BG Gale Ltd v Gilbert* [1978] ICR 1149, [1978] IRLR 453; *Sothern v Franks Charlesly & Co* [1981] IRLR 278, CA. There may, however, be problems with a 'hotheaded' resignation which the employee seeks to retract almost immediately – theoretically a retraction would need the consent of the employer, but there have been cases where it has been said that a tribunal should take a broader, more common sense approach to whether the employee must be taken to have unequivocally resigned (even if, for example, the wording at the time left little to the imagination!): *Barclay v City of Glasgow District Council* [1983] IRLR 313; *Martin v Yeoman Aggregates Ltd* [1983] ICR 314, [1983] IRLR 49; *Sovereign House Security Services Ltd v Savage* [1989] IRLR 115, CA; *Kwik-Fit (GB) Ltd v Lineham* [1992] ICR 183, [1992] IRLR 156, EAT.

Such problems have arisen in two principal ways. The first occurs where the employee simply walks out or where, as in *British Leyland (UK) Ltd v Ashraf*[6] the employee is allowed a definite period of leave from which he does not return on time. It is arguable that there needs to be a concept of 'resignation by conduct' to cover the first of these examples (i.e. where the employee never returns), but the problem with the second example was that it was tied in frequently with rather more spurious arguments on mutual termination or termination by agreement, for in such cases the employer may have allowed the leave on terms that 'if you do not return on time, your employment will terminate'; when the employee arrived back late, he was then told that his contract had ended automatically, without the need for a dismissal. This argument by the employer succeeded in *Ashraf*'s case, but its wider implications soon became obvious and a very different approach was taken. *Ashraf*'s case was first distinguished by the EAT[7], and finally overruled by the Court of Appeal in *Igbo v Johnson Matthey Chemicals Ltd*[8], on the ground that such an agreement for automatic termination (on failure to return from leave of absence) was void for contravening the Employment Rights Act 1996, section 203 which invalidates any agreement (whether in a contract of employment or not) which 'purports ... to exclude or limit the operation of any provision of this Act ...'[9] – this agreement limited the operation of sections 95 and 98 which give the right to claim unfair dismissal. The advantage from the employee's point of view of this reasoning is that even if he signs such an agreement in full knowledge of what he is signing (e.g. because the employer will only grant leave if he does so), the agreement will still be of no legal effect under the anti-contracting-out provisions of the section.

The second way in which problems arose had a far greater potential for driving the proverbial horse-drawn transport through the unfair dismissal legislation. This was the idea (known variously as 'constructive resignation' or 'self-dismissal') that in some cases the employee may commit such a grave breach of contract that he must be considered to have resigned by his own act[10]. Once again, this meant that there was no dismissal, and so no action for unfair dismissal. Moreover, such an agreement might arise not only from unusual or drastic facts, but could also possibly be set up by an employer phrasing a final warning in terms that 'if this happens again, you will be considered as having dismissed yourself'. The employer succeeded in showing self-dismissal in *Gannon v Firth*[11] where the employees (pursuant to a dispute) walked out without informing the management and leaving the plant in a dangerous state; the EAT held that this repudiatory conduct terminated their employment, they had not been dismissed, and so they could not claim unfair dismissal. This was a short decision, citing no authority, but was followed in subsequent cases[12]. Fortunately the position has been clarified by

6   [1978] ICR 979, [1978] IRLR 330. For termination by mutual consent generally, see pp. 364-367, above.
7   *Midland Electric Manufacturing Co Ltd v Kanji* [1980] IRLR 185; *Tracey v Zest Equipment Co Ltd* [1982] ICR 481, [1982] IRLR 268.
8   [1986] ICR 505, [1986] IRLR 215, CA.
9   See *Harvey* Q[827].
10 The theoretical basis for this in contract law can be found in the previously current idea that contracts of employment formed an exception to the normal rule that a repudiation is only effective when accepted by the innocent party; thus, on this 'automatic termination' theory (see p. 377, above) the contract was in fact ended by the *employee's repudiation of it*, which did not need any further action on the part of the employer and do did not constitute a 'dismissal'.
11 [1976] IRLR 415.
12 Particularly *Smith v Avana Bakeries Ltd* [1979] IRLR 423 and *Kallinos v London Electric Wire* [1980] IRLR 11.

the Court of Appeal in *London Transport Executive v Clarke*[13] which concerned the taking of unauthorised leave by an employee in the knowledge that if he did so his name would be 'removed from the books'. When he returned the employers refused to take him back and he claimed unfair dismissal. The majority of the Court of Appeal (Templeman and Dunn LJJ) held that he had in fact been dismissed, applied the 'elective theory'[14] to repudiation of contracts of employment so that the employment was terminated by the employer's acceptance of the employee's repudiation, and overruled *Gannon v Firth* and the cases that had followed it; Lord Denning MR, dissenting, would have continued to apply the concept of self-dismissal, but the majority decision is clearly against it. Employers should not, however, throw up their hands in despair at this decision, for it was always arguable that the concept of self-dismissal was not particularly necessary anyway – if the employee's conduct was so drastic as to have been clearly repudiatory, then in most cases a tribunal is going to find his dismissal fair anyway (as was the ultimate conclusion of the Court of Appeal in *Clark*'s case, unanimously). The advantage of the majority's decision is that at least the fairness of the employer's conduct can be tested in such cases, rather than the employee's (possibly weak) claim being ruled out altogether on the jurisdictional point that technically there had been no dismissal[15].

ii) The date of termination[16]

In the law relating to unfair dismissal and redundancy it is necessary for several reasons[17] to know when the employment ended; for unfair dismissal purposes this is known as the 'effective date of termination' and for redundancy purposes the 'relevant date'. The principal rules relating to these dates are found in the Employment Rights Act 1996, sections 97 and 145, and are as follows:

a) Where the contract is terminated by notice (whether given by the employer or employee) – the date that the notice expires (whether or not the notice was of proper length)[18].

b) Where the contract is terminated without notice – the date on which the termination takes effect[19].

c) Where a fixed term contract expires without renewal – the date of expiry.

d) Where the employee under notice gives counter-notice to terminate the employment sooner – the date of expiry of the counter-notice.

These rules are relatively straightforward, except in the case of head (b) above, which unfortunately has attracted a difference of judicial opinion on one of its most important applications. It is clear that (b) applies to summary dismissals,

---

13 [1981] ICR 355, [1981] IRLR 166, CA.

14 See p. 378, above.

15 Presumably there is now also the secondary ground that if the purported self-dismissal came from an agreement that 'if you do that again, you will be deemed to have dismissed yourself', that agreement itself will be void under s. 203 (applying *Igbo v Johnson Matthey Chemicals Ltd*, n. 8, above).

16 See *Harvey* D[704].

17 E.g. for calculating the period of continuous employment (for calculation and possibly for qualification purposes) and for determining the date from which the three and six month limitation periods run.

18 *TBA Industrial Products Ltd v Morland* [1982] ICR 686, [1982] IRLR 331, CA.

19 This may even mean a precise *time* on the date in question: *Octavius Atkinson & Sons Ltd v Morris* [1989] ICR 431, [1989] IRLR 158, CA.

and in *Stapp v Shaftesbury Society*[20] the Court of Appeal affirmed that the simple rule that the date of termination is the date of the summary dismissal applies even if (i) that summary dismissal is affected while the employee is already under ordinary notice and (ii) the effect of the summary dismissal bringing the date of termination forward is to deprive the employee of the qualifying period for unfair dismissal which he would otherwise have attained. However, summary dismissal is only one aspect.

Far more common as a form of dismissal in practice is dismissal with wages in lieu of notice whereby the employer is rid of the employee immediately (particularly vital where the employee under notice would otherwise have access at work to the firm's computers or confidential information) but with payment of what the employee would have earned had he worked out his notice period. What is to be the date of termination – the date when the notice would have expired (i.e. under (a) above) or the date when the employee in fact leaves, albeit with a payment in lieu (i.e. under (b) above)? This could be particularly material on the question of whether a claim is brought in time, especially when the notice period is several weeks (e.g. from which date does the three month limit for bringing an unfair dismissal action run?), and could also affect whether the employee has satisfied the qualifying period for the right in question. The interests of certainty would be best served by simply opting for the date when the employee actually leaves (i.e. treating it as under (b) above, as if a summary dismissal), and this was for several years thought to be the case, after the decision of the Court of Appeal in *Dedman v British Building and Engineering Appliances Ltd*[1]. However, confusion was caused by the decision of the EAT in *Adams v GKN Sankey Ltd*[2] where it was suggested that the date of termination depends on the true construction to be placed on the dismissal – if it was expressed as a dismissal by notice (but with the employee not actually required to work out that notice), the date of termination should be the date of expiry of the notice; if however, it was expressed as an instant dismissal (but with the payment of wages in lieu of notice as, in effect, compensation for wrongful dismissal), the date of termination should be the date the employee left. This distinction seems a thin one on which to base such an important concept as the date of termination and in practice may, one suspects, owe more to fortune than reality in its application. It certainly means that letters of dismissal should be drafted carefully, from the employer's point of view.

This 'construction' approach can also be seen in *Chapman v Letheby and Christopher Ltd*[3] where it was stated that the mere fact that a dismissal was stated to be with payment in lieu did not mean that it constituted an instant dismissal, and

---

20   [1982] IRLR 326, CA. It was suggested by the Court that if the employee loses his statutory rights because of the summary dismissal, he should bring an action for *wrongful dismissal* claiming loss of statutory rights as a head of damage; see p. 393, above. The fact that the summary dismissal was in breach of a contractually binding disciplinary procedure which would have taken some time to go through properly *cannot* be used to advance what is otherwise under the section the effective date of termination: *Batchelor v British Railways Board* [1987] IRLR 136, CA.

1   [1974] 1 All ER 520, [1974] ICR 53, CA, the leading case on the extension of time limits for commencing tribunal actions.

2   [1980] IRLR 416.

3   [1981] IRLR 440; the facts in the case were distinctly ambiguous, showing the difficulties that this 'construction' approach can cause, though the EAT did say that ultimately any ambiguity should be construed against the employer, who should have drafted the letter of dismissal more carefully. *Quaere* – how would this apply to an oral dismissal with wages in lieu where no-one can remember exactly what was said?

that the effect of the dismissal depended on the construction which would be placed on it by an ordinary, reasonable employee. However, in *Robert Cort & Son Ltd v Charman*[4] the EAT reverted to the straightforward *Dedman* view, stressing (i) the proper interpretation of the wording of section 97 and (ii) the need for absolute certainty on the effective date of termination, especially in the context of limitation periods (though the case itself concerned the question whether the employee had served the necessary qualifying period for an unfair dismissal action). This left the law in an uncertain state. The question was canvassed before the Court of Appeal in *Stapp v Shaftesbury Society*[5], but that case concerned a different aspect of dismissal without notice (considered above)[6]. However, Stephenson LJ, giving the principal judgment, did allude to the present problem at two stages; at one point he expressly approved of the statement of Browne-Wilkinson J in *Chapman v Letheby and Christopher Ltd* that any ambiguity in a dismissal notice should be construed against the employer (though without commenting on the construction approach generally), but later said

> 'But the effect of summary dismissal in fixing the effective date of termination cannot be questioned. The case of *Cort* is a very recent application of what was laid down by this court some years ago in the case which it followed, *Dedman v British Building and Engineering Appliances Ltd.*'

The judgment in *Stapp*, is therefore at best ambiguous and subsequently in *Leech v Preston Borough Council*[7] the EAT pointed out that the well-worn phrase 'wages in lieu of notice' has two distinct meanings[8] and applied the 'construction' approach in *Adams* and *Chapman*. That must now be considered to be the correct approach, since it is consistent with the explanation of dismissal with wages in lieu generally by Lord Browne-Wilkinson in the leading case on deductions from wages, *Delaney v Staples*[9]; he in fact isolated *four* possible forms of such a dismissal[10], but they include the two principal forms alluded to in *Leech* and as, in his judgment, he explained that they operate on different grounds, it is reasonable to conclude that the EDT will be different, as the majority of the case law suggests.

Four further points should be noted. The first is that where the employee is dismissed by being given less notice than the employer is obliged to give him by

4   [1981] ICR 816, [1981] IRLR 437 (*Chapman v Letheby and Christopher Ltd* not referred to). The principal significance of the EAT's emphasis on the statutory interpretation of s. 97 was that it enabled them to dispose of the employee's subtle arguments based on contractual ideas of repudiation and acceptance (see p. 378, above); hopefully this case is authority that the 'elective' theory of repudiation does *not* apply for the purpose of fixing the date of termination for statutory purposes, so that an employee cannot push forward that date for some unspecified time simply by arguing that he never in fact accepted the employer's repudiation.

5   [1982] IRLR 326.

6   The case was principally argued on the point whether an employer could avoid statutory rights by wrongfully dismissing the employee (and after having given him proper notice at that). It was, however, a case of dismissal with wages in lieu (in effect, though not in the usual way), for he had been given notice, then when summarily dismissed during the notice period was told that he would in fact be paid for the whole of the rest of what should have been his notice period.

7   [1985] ICR 192, [1985] IRLR 337; *Cort*'s case is not cited in the judgment.

8   The 'grammatically accurate sense of compensation for summary dismissal without notice' or the 'more colloquial sense of payment to someone who is excused or prohibited from attending the workplace during the notice period'.

9   [1992] ICR 483, [1992] IRLR 191, HL.

10 These are set out at p. 369, above, along with the suggested EDTs, in the light of this discussion.

statute[11], the date of termination is deemed to be the date it would have been had that statutory minimum been given, for certain purposes. Those purposes are computation of the qualifying period for claiming unfair dismissal and demanding a written statement of reasons for dismissal, calculation of the basic award for unfair dismissal, computation of the two year qualifying period for a redundancy payment and calculation of the period of continuous employment by which such a payment is determined[12]. The second point is that if the employee has been dismissed, the fact that he is actively pursuing an appeal under the firm's grievance procedure does *not* mean that the date of termination is extended to the completion of that appeal process[13]; moreover this is likely to be of most significance when deciding when the three-month time limit for an unfair dismissal action begins to run and the Court of Appeal have affirmed that the fact of pursuing an internal appeal will *not* be a good reason to extend the three months' period in the tribunal's discretion[14], thus making it doubly important for the employee to ensure that his application for unfair dismissal is lodged in time, even if his internal appeal is still pending. The third point is that sections 97 and 145 do not state what the date of termination is to be in a case of constructive dismissal; it has been held that the EDT is the date of acceptance of the employer's repudiation of the contract, which will normally mean the date when the employee walks out, but it has also been held that an employee cannot use this argument to prolong the EDT past the date the employment *actually* ended[15]. The fourth, final, and perhaps most fundamental point on the EDT is that ultimately it is for the employer to get it right, so that any ambiguity is likely to be construed in the employee's favour[16]. In particular, there is in general no doctrine of *constructive* notice of dismissal, so that a dismissal by letter will only take effect when it is actually received by the employee, even if that is later than expected by the employer (who will thus often be well advised to communicate the dismissal

11   ERA 1996, s. 86. The employee can only claim an extension by the period of his *statutory* entitlement, not by the period of any more generous notice entitlement agreed in his contract: *Fox Maintenance Ltd v Jackson* [1978] ICR 110, [1977] IRLR 306. Note, however, that s. 86(6) preserves the employer's right to dismiss summarily for gross misconduct, and so if an employer does so justifiably there can be *no* extension under the statute: *Lanton Leisure Ltd v White and Gibson* [1987] IRLR 119, EAT.

12   Ibid., ss. 97(2) and 145(5). The statutory extension is for these purposes *only*, it is not of general application: *Slater v John Swain & Son Ltd* [1981] ICR 554, [1981] IRLR 303; *Secretary of State for Employment v Cameron Iron Works* [1988] ICR 297 (revsd on other grounds [1989] ICR 664, [1989] IRLR 117, CA). In particular, note that it does *not* apply for the purposes of the three/six month limitation periods for bringing tribunal proceedings.

13   *J Sainsbury Ltd v Savage* [1981] ICR 1, [1980] IRLR 109, CA. If however, the appeal is successful there is no break in continuity, as the appeal decision applies as from the date of the original dismissal: *Howgate v Fane Acoustics Ltd* [1981] IRLR 161, EAT.

14   *Palmer v Southend-on-Sea Borough Council* [1984] ICR 372, [1984] IRLR 119, CA; see p. 353, above.

15   Contrast *G W Stephens & Son v Fish* [1989] ICR 324 with *BMK Ltd v Logue* [1993] ICR 601. Note, however, that there was introduced in 1982 an extension of time for certain purposes (akin to those in n. 12 above) in the case of a consecutive dismissal, the extension period being the amount of notice that should have been given under s. 86 if it had been the employer who was terminating the employment: s. 97(4).

16   *Widdicombe v Longcombe Software Ltd* [1998] ICR 710 (ambiguous correspondence between employer and absent employee; EDT fixed as the date of the final, clearest letter, which came within the limitation period).

directly to the employee, or at the very least to use registered or recorded post so that the date of service can be ascertained)[17].

5 UNFAIR DISMISSAL

Just under half the cases heard by tribunals each year concern claims of unfair dismissal. As is immediately obvious, such a claim is a much more realistic action to bring in most cases than the common law action for wrongful dismissal, and since its inception in 1971[18] this branch of industrial law has given rise to an enormous amount of case law. It is therefore particularly important in this context to bear in mind the dictum of Lord Denning MR cited at the beginning of this chapter and to appreciate that the only way to cope successfully with the intimidating case law is to concentrate on those cases which establish principles, points of interpretation or (at least when they are in fashion) general guidelines for the tribunals, and consider the rest as mere illustrations, interesting though they may be. One simple truth, so easy to overlook when surrounded by industrial law reports, is that unfair dismissal is *not* primarily a case-law subject – primacy must remain with the relevant wording of the statute. Further, the statute in most contexts puts matters into the discretion of the tribunals (and expressly gives a restricted right of appeal to the EAT, on points of law only) and so, although for the sake of exposition the following discussion will look at the law under certain headings and will concentrate on the evolving rules relating to certain categories of dismissal of practical importance, it must be remembered that in many instances the seeming rules of law under discussion may only be guidelines to the factors to be taken into consideration by the tribunal in deciding upon what is usually the central issue in an unfair dismissal case, namely whether the employer's conduct in the dismissal was reasonable.

i) The right and the exclusions[19]

Subject to certain exclusions, the Employment Rights Act 1996, section 94 gives to every employee the right not to be unfairly dismissed. There are two principal qualifications for this right: first, the employee must have been 'dismissed' (a concept which is considered in head 4 above) and second, on the effective date of termination the employee must have been continuously employed by his employer for the necessary qualifying period, now one year (unless dismissed for

---

17 *McMaster v Manchester Airport plc* [1998] IRLR 112 (sick employee not receiving dismissal letter on the expected day of delivery because on a day trip to France; limitation period only flowed from the day of his return).

18 The provisions relating to unfair dismissal were first enacted in the Industrial Relations Act 1971; they were re-enacted in the first Schedule to the Trade Union and Labour Relations Act 1974, amended by the Employment Protection Act 1975, and then consolidated, first in the Employment Protection (Consolidation) Act 1978 and then in the Employment Rights Act 1996. The scheme of the provisions follows ILO Recommendation 119 (1963); revised ILO standards on dismissal worked out subsequently have not been adopted; see (1984) 13 ILJ 130. For detailed consideration of this branch of law, see *Harvey* Division D, to which more detailed references are made below; also Dickens et al. *Dismissed* (1983), Collins 'The meaning of job security' (1991) 20 ILJ 227 and, for a fundamental critique of the existing law, Collins *Justice in Dismissal* (1992) and Pitt 'Justice in dismissal – a reply to Hugh Collins (1993) 22 ILJ 251.

19 See *Harvey* D[24] ff.

a reason stated specifically not to require such qualifying service, such as one relating to membership or non-membership of a trade union, maternity, health and safety complaints, assertion of statutory rights or acting as an employee trustee of a pension scheme or as an elected employee representative). Initially this period was six months, but it was raised by the previous government, first to a year in 1979 and then to two years in 1985[20]. The imposition of any such period had two aims. A long-term aim was to exclude (indirectly) part-timers from the right to claim unfair dismissal; this happened because in order to count time worked towards the required period of continuous employment at all, the employee had to work more than 16 hours per week (or more than eight hours per week for five years). The second aim under the previous government, in line with its free market and deregulatory economic policy, was to lessen what have been perceived to be the adverse effects of employment law on business and the creation of jobs[1]; this aim was particularly important with regard to the significant lengthening of the period. This however was controversial; although it is the case that a qualifying period has the bona fide effect of allowing an employer to operate a fairly lengthy trial period for a new employee and assess suitability without having to face an unfair dismissal application, it was argued that the very long period of two years was operated more as a blanket initial immunity, and in recent years there was at least anecdotal evidence of some employers cynically using that immunity (particularly in areas of high labour turnover) by taking employees on for only 18 months or thereabouts and then dismissing them as a matter of policy.

Both of these aims of the qualifying period have been subject to attack under EC law. The exclusion of part-timers no longer works because the 16 hour rule (and eight hours for five years rule) had to be removed[2] in order to comply with the ruling of the House of Lords in *R v Secretary of State for Employment, ex p EOC*[3] that those hours limitations had a disproportionate effect on female employees and so constituted indirect sex discrimination (contrary to Art. 119 and the Equal Treatment Directive) which was not justified by the Government's arguments on economic necessity. Thus, an employee with two years' continuous employment could claim unfair dismissal regardless of their hours of work[4]. However, the matter did not rest there, for the next stage was to attack the two-year qualifying period *itself* as sexually discriminatory (thus negativing the second aim). This was done in *R v Secretary of State for Employment, ex p Seymour-Smith*[5] in which the application for a declaration that the increase of the qualifying period in 1985 to two years was contrary to the Equal Treatment Directive was granted by the Court of Appeal; at further appeal, the House of Lords remitted the question to the ECJ which gave an exceptionally Delphic reply[6]. When the House of Lords reconsidered the case in the light of this, they finally held that the 1985 increase

20   Unfair Dismissal (Variation of Qualifying Period) Order 1985, S.I. 1985 No. 782.
1   Lifting the Burden (Cmnd. 951, 1985), ch. 5.
2   Employment Protection (Part-time Employees) Regulations 1995, S.I. 1995 No. 31.
3   [1994] ICR 317, [1994] IRLR 176, HL. This seemed to open the floodgates to many backdated claims (under EC law, not under the prospective-only regulations) by employees who had not claimed unfair dismissal at the time because they worked too few hours. However, at the time of writing the courts are trying hard to prevent this happening by applying a very stringent approach to the three-month limitation period: *Biggs v Somerset County Council* [1996] ICR 364, [1996] IRLR 203, CA (where the applicant sought unsuccessfully to claim that she had been unfairly dismissed in 1976!); *Setiya v East Yorkshire Health Authority* [1995] ICR 799, [1995] IRLR 348 (refusal of late appeal to EAT).
4   In *Colley v Corkindale* [1995] ICR 965 an employee working one $5^1/_2$ hour bar shift every other Friday was able to claim unfair dismissal.
5   [1995] ICR 889, [1995] IRLR 464, CA.
6   C-167/97 [1999] ICR 447, [1999] IRLR 253, ECJ.

was *not* discriminatory (three Lords holding that any adverse effect was justified and two that there was no significant adverse effect in the first place)[7]. By this time, however, the present government had lowered the period to *one year* in any event legislatively[8], a far more satisfactory method of reform. The one year period applies to a dismissal occurring on or after 1 June 1999 and, given that the challenge in *R v Secretary of State for Employment, ex p Seymour-Smith* failed, we have been spared any problems of backdating.

The right to bring an action is also subject to certain general exceptions, so that the following employees are excluded:

a) *An employee who is over the retirement age on the effective date of termination* Section 109 excludes an employee who:

> '... on or before the effective date of termination ... has attained –
> (a) in a case where –
>> (i) in the undertaking in which the employee was employed there was a normal retiring age for an employee holding the position held by the employee, and
>> (ii) the age was the same whether the employee holding that position was a man or a woman,
>> that normal retiring age, and
> (b) in any other case, the age of sixty five.'

This formulation was substituted as from November 1987 by the Sex Discrimination Act 1986; the previous wording had allowed two forms of sex discrimination – first, there could be different contractual retiring ages for men and women, and secondly the 'fall back' in (b) was 65 for a man and 60 for a woman. Enforced retirement of a woman at an earlier age than a man could adversely affect her rights (especially pension rights when based on her *final* salary), and was held by the ECJ to be contrary to Directive 76/207/ EEC in *Marshall v Southampton and South West Hampshire Area Health Authority (Teaching)*[9], leading to the substitution of the present formulation.

The subsection thus creates two ages, the normal retiring age of the job (provided that it is sexually neutral) and the 'statutory' retiring age of 65, and on the wording as it was originally cast it was generally understood that attainment of the latter excluded reliance on the former, so that if the normal retiring age for a job was 70 and the employee was dismissed when 68, he could not claim unfair dismissal because he had already reached the statutory age of 65. However, the House of Lords in *Nothman v Barnet London Borough*[10] held by a majority of 3–2, in an exercise in statutory interpretation astonishing to many people (including Lord Diplock in the minority), that that is not the correct interpretation of the section, for the majority decision was that the section does not create one test with two hurdles for the employee to clear, but instead creates two separate hurdles, one applying where there *is* a normal retiring age for the job and the other (the statutory 65) only applying if there

---

7   [2000] IRLR 263, HL.
8   Unfair Dismissal and Statement of Reasons for Dismissal (Variation of Qualifying Period) Order 1999, S.I. 1999 No. 1436.
9   152/84: [1986] ICR 335, [1986] IRLR 140, ECJ; *Beets-Proper v F Van Lanschot Bankiers NV*: 262/84 [1986] ICR 706, ECJ.
10 [1979] ICR 111, [1979] IRLR 35, HL; for the continuing story of Miss Nothman, see [1980] IRLR 65, CA.

is *no* such normal retiring age. Thus Miss Nothman, a teacher subject to a contractual retiring age of 65, was able to claim unfair dismissal when sacked at the age of 61, as she had not reached her 'normal retiring age'; the fact that she was over 60 was irrelevant, since that statutory retiring age (as it then stood) was not applicable to her. Thus, if there *is* a normal retiring age the tribunal must look at that; it is only if there is no such retiring age that it can apply the statutory 65 as the exclusory age. This is now made clearer in the present statutory wording ('... (b) *in any other case*, the age of sixty five.')

It may therefore be essential to decide whether in any given case there is a normal retiring age and, if so, what it is. This caused considerable problems over a series of cases, but is now governed by two House of Lords decisions. In *Waite v Government Communications Headquarters*[11] the House was faced with the problem of a discrepancy between what the contract said about retirement and what was argued to be the practical position of employees frequently being allowed to work past the contractual age. The decision was that the contractual age is presumed to be the normal retiring age, but that this presumption can be displaced by evidence that in practice persons in the position of the employee in question[12] have a reasonable expectation of working past the contractual age to some further age, which can then be considered as the normal retiring age. On the other hand, if the evidence only shows that employees regularly work past the contractual age to a variety of ad hoc ages, then there is *no* normal retiring age and so the statutory age of 65 applies. This was put clearly by Lord Fraser:

'The proper test ... is to ascertain what would be the reasonable expectation or understanding of the employees holding that position at the relevant time. The contractual retiring age will prima facie be the normal, but it may be displaced by evidence that it is regularly departed from in practice. The evidence may show that the contractual retiring age has been superseded by some definite higher age, and, if so, that will have become the normal retiring age. Or the evidence may show merely that the contractual retiring age has been abandoned and that employees retire at a variety of higher ages. In that case there will be no normal retiring age and the statutory alternatives of 65 for a man and 60 for a woman will apply[13].'

The application of these principles can be seen in *Hughes v DHSS*[14]; this was a case where the Civil Service conditions of employment stated 60 as the

11 [1983] ICR 653, [1983] IRLR 341, HL, noted McMullen (1984) 13 ILJ 57; previous case law in the EAT and Court of Appeal is now redundant: *Mauldon v British Telecommunications plc* [1987] ICR 450. Several of those cases had arisen in the same context as *Waite*, i.e. the policy of the Civil Service of a gradual reduction of the retirement age.

12 One problem with the idea of looking at the expectations of the *class* of employee is that if an employer gives a personal assurance to keep one employee on after his contractual retirement age that will not be sufficient since there is no class involved: *Age Concern Scotland v Hines* [1983] IRLR 477, EAT.

13 At 662 and 344 respectively. 'Abandoned' here merely refers to the existence of sufficient evidence to show significant departure from the contractual age: *Secretary of State for Scotland v Meikle* [1986] IRLR 208; statistical evidence may be important here: *Whittle v Manpower Services Commission* [1987] IRLR 441, EAT.

14 [1985] ICR 419, [1985] IRLR 263, HL, applied in *Highlands and Islands Development Board v MacGillivray* [1986] IRLR 210, Ct of Sess, *Whittle v Manpower Services Commission* (above), *Brooks v British Telecommunications plc* [1992] ICR 414, [1992] IRLR 66, CA and *Barber v Thames Television plc* [1992] ICR 661, [1992] IRLR 410, CA. A further point established in

retirement age, but the practice was to allow employees (subject to conditions) to remain until 65. However, the applicants in question, having worked past 60, were caught by a change in departmental policy lowering the actual retirement age to 60. When they were compulsorily retired they claimed unfair dismissal but the House of Lords held that they fell within the exclusion – their 'reasonable expectation' may have been initially to work until 65, but by the date of their dismissal (which is the relevant time at which to apply the *Waite* principles) that expectation must have changed with the well publicised change of departmental policy, which was thus effective to change the 'normal retiring age' within section 109. There have been moves to attack the age limitation under EC law (given the lack of any actual or prospective age discrimination legislation[15]); in *Nash v Mash/Roe Group Ltd*[16] an adventurous tribunal held that the age limitation is contrary to EC sex discrimination law (impacting disproportionately on men, who tend to work on past retiring age more often than women, and not being subjectively justified) and so is to be disapplied. Further developments here are awaited with interest, to say the least.

b) *Two miscellaneous categories of excluded persons* – share fishermen and the police[17].

c) *An employee governed by a dismissal procedures agreement designated by the Secretary of State's order as operating in substitution for the statutory scheme*[18].

d) *An employee whose dismissal was for the purpose of safeguarding national security.*[19]

The Employment Relations Act 1999 made two important changes to the exceptions to the right to claim unfair dismissal. First, it repealed the provisions in the Employment Rights Act 1996, s. 197 which used to permit an employer to put into a fixed-term contract of one year or more a clause excluding unfair dismissal rights on termination. There had been longstanding criticisms of this power, on the basis of abuse by employers (especially by the device of putting employees on to successive such contracts, possibly over a long period of time), and the government decided to abolish it altogether. Secondly, the 1999 Act also

---

this case is that Lord Fraser's reference in *Waite* to the 'group' of employees holding the 'position' held by the applicant is covered by the statutory definition of 'position' in s. 235, i.e. as pertaining to 'his status as an employee, the nature of his work and his terms and conditions of employment.' There can still be a normal retiring age where occasional, specific exceptions are made to it: *Barclays Bank plc v O'Brien* [1994] ICR 865, [1994] IRLR 580, CA; this case contains a very useful summary of the applicable principles by Peter Gibson LJ.

15 All that the present government has done so far is to publish a draft code of practice on age diversity in employment, but this is in very anodyne terms. It does, however, point out that by 2010 almost 40% of the workforce will be aged 45 or over, with only 17% in the 16–24 group, and there has been some discussion that if a voluntary approach does not work there could be legislation in the future.

16 [1998] IRLR 168, IT.

17 Ibid., ss. 199 and 200 respectively. On the meaning of 'share fisherman', see *Goodeve v Gilsons* [1985] ICR 401, CA. Employment protection legislation was in the main extended to the armed forces by the Trade Union Reform and Employment Rights Act 1993.

18 Ibid., s 110. So far only one industry (electrical contracting) has opted for this form of collective contracting out. In some industries, ACAS arbitration on a voluntary basis could be resorted to under a firm's own procedures. As, however, they are not formally within s. 110 a dismissed employee could go to arbitration and *then* (if unsuccessful) claim unfair dismissal. In practice this is unlikely to happen, but it can – see, e.g., *Cawley v South Wales Electricity Board* [1985] IRLR 89, EAT.

19 Employment Tribunals Act 1996, s. 10. Note that this is an ad hoc security power; the long term national security exclusion used in the GCHQ case was contained in the Employment Rights Act 1996 s. 193, which was substantially narrowed by the Employment Relations Act 1999, Sch. 8.

repealed s. 196 of the 1996 Act, which used to disapply most of the rights in the latter (including unfair dismissal) where 'under the employee's contract of employment he ordinarily works outside Great Britain'. There was considerable case law on this wording[20], which tended to help a British employee sent temporarily to work abroad, but equally tended to prejudice a foreign employee temporarily working in Britain, as was seen particularly in *Carver v Saudi Arabian Airlines*[1]. When the Employment Relations Bill was before the House of Lords, a modest amendment to make this area fairer to foreign employees was proposed, but the government minister undertook (a withdrawal of the amendment) to consider the matter. In fact, when the matter returned to the Lords the government suggested a far more radical solution, namely to repeal s. 196 altogether. By now, the real impetus behind this was the need to comply with the Posted Workers Directive 96/71/EC which requires workers sent to work in another member state to have the same rights as workers in that state. Removal of the territorial bars in s. 196 was perceived to be one way of doing this, and so this was done. What is to replace it? The government simply said that the matter would now be satisfactorily covered by the well-known rules of private international law (!), and a DTI press release said that the normal provisions of the Brussels and Rome Conventions should be used. However, it is possible that this was a serious mistake, because while these rules and provisions are capable of governing the proper law of, and jurisdiction in relation to, a *contract* (such as a contract of employment) it is arguable that they cannot govern the position in relation to a purely statutory right such as unfair dismissal[2]. If this is correct, what the government have done is to create a *hole* in the 1996 Act, so that we have a statute giving rights *without* the necessary statutory provisions on territorial jurisdiction[3]. The result would be that it would become a matter of statutory interpretation (not private international law) as to what was intended with regard to jurisdiction. Looking at the Parliamentary debate (which was short, on a very late amendment) the only clue is that the government stated that an employee should only be able to use a British tribunal if there was a 'proper connection with the UK'[4]. What this means will have to be explored judicially; in the meantime, the position in particular of employees of British companies working abroad or sent to work abroad remains uncertain.

---

20   The leading cases were *Wilson v Maynard Shipbuilding Consultants AB* [1978] ICR 376, [1977] IRLR 491, CA; *Todd v British Midland Airways Ltd* [1978] ICR 959, [1978] IRLR 370, CA and *Janata Bank v Ahmed* [1981] ICR 791, [1981] IRLR 457, CA.

1   [1999] IRLR 370, [1999] 3 All ER 61, CA.

2   There is no implied contractual right not to be unfairly dismissed: *Focsa Services (UK) Ltd v Birkett* [1996] IRLR 325, EAT.

3   Contrast this with the far more sensible amendments to the discrimination legislation in the Equal Opportunities (Employment Legislation) (International Limits) Regulations 1999, S.I. 1999 No. 3163 (again seeking compliance with the Posted Workers Directive) which simply removed the wording 'or mainly' from the exclusion of employees working 'wholly or mainly outside Great Britain'. There may now be disputes over what is meant by 'wholly' outside GB (e.g. what level of involvement within GB could be ignored as de minimis), but at least we still have a statutory provision here to apply.

4   HL Official Report, 8 July 1999, col. 1089.

ii) What is an unfair dismissal?

Once the employee has proved that he was dismissed (if that is a live issue in the case) the burden of proof then passes on to the employer, under section 98 of the 1996 Act, to show two things:

1. what was the reason for the dismissal (or the principal reason if more than one);
2. that it fell within one of the enumerated categories of prima facie fair dismissals, namely that the reason was
   a) related to the capability or qualifications of the employee for performing his work,
   b) related to the conduct of the employee,
   c) that the employee was redundant,
   d) that the employee could not continue to work in that position without contravention of a legislative provision[5],
   e) 'some other substantial reason of a kind such as to justify the dismissal'.

It is then for the tribunal to decide whether in the circumstances (having regard to equity and the substantial merits of the case) the employer acted reasonably in treating that reason as a sufficient reason for dismissing the employee (section 98(4)).

This basic structure of an unfair dismissal action should be borne in mind (except in cases where the statute expressly provides that a certain type of dismissal shall be automatically fair or unfair), and the significance of the burden of proof being upon the employer is that if he fails to satisfy the tribunal at either of the first two stages the dismissal will be held to be unfair. The previous government altered section 98 in the Employment Act 1980 in two ways – first, by expressly requiring the tribunal to take into account all the circumstances (including the size and administrative resources of the employer's undertaking); second, by removing from the employer the burden of proof on the overall question of reasonableness, equity and substantial merits, which is now made a matter for the tribunal. It is doubtful whether the first did more than enact the existing practical position, for the matters mentioned were ones which the EAT had already taken into account in decided cases[6]. Likewise, it is arguable whether the second has a major impact (other than a possible psychological impact which *may* in some cases reduce the nuisance value of an unfair dismissal claim and make employers less ready to settle); it does not remove the more important burdens of proof of *facts* on the employer under the first two elements of the action, and in practice this third element was already very much the province of the tribunal's discretion anyway. Moreover, it will only rarely be the case that the evidence is so evenly balanced that the claim can only ultimately be determined by the application of a burden of proof. With these two alterations in mind, we must now look at these three stages of the unfair dismissal action.

---

5   E.g. where an employee employed wholly or principally to drive a vehicle is disqualified and there is no alternative work for him: *Appleyard v F M Smith (Hull) Ltd* [1972] IRLR 19, IT; *Fearn v Tayford Motor Co* [1975] IRLR 336, IT. The tribunal must still go on to consider whether the dismissal was reasonable under s. 98(4), as this is not an automatically fair reason for dismissal: *Sandhu v DES* [1978] IRLR 208. A mistaken belief by the employer that he cannot lawfully continue to employ the employee does not come under this heading, but may qualify as 'some other substantial reason': *Bouchaala v Trust House Forte Hotels Ltd* [1980] ICR 721, [1980] IRLR 382, EAT.

6   *MacKellar v Bolton* [1979] IRLR 59; *Royal Naval School v Hughes* [1979] IRLR 383.

a) Stage one: the reason[7]

The first stage is that the employer must show what the real reason was for the dismissal[8]; if he clearly relies upon one particular reason and the tribunal disbelieves him, the finding should be one of unfair dismissal and he should not normally be allowed to try to rely upon an entirely different reason either at the tribunal hearing (without applying for leave to amend his defence) or on appeal[9]. However, tribunal proceedings are not meant to be as formal as High Court proceedings, and it must be accepted that, in the light of the complexity of certain of these areas of law, the employer may not always initially put the correct legal interpretation on the factors determining his decision to dismiss[10]. The general approach has therefore been that the tribunal's task is to discover the reason actually motivating the employer at the time of the dismissal. In *Abernethy v Mott, Hay and Anderson*[11], Cairns LJ said:

> 'A reason for the dismissal of an employee is a set of facts known to the employer, or it may be of beliefs held by him, which cause him to dismiss the employee. If at the time of his dismissal the employer gives a reason for it, that is no doubt evidence, at any rate as against him, as to the real reason, but it does not necessarily constitute the real reason. He may knowingly give a reason different from the real reason out of kindness or because he might have difficulty in proving the facts that actually led him to dismiss; or he may describe his reasons wrongly through some mistake of language or of law.'

Thus a wrong label given by the employer is not fatal to his case and, further, it is clear from the cases that the approach here is basically subjective particularly in cases where it is a *belief* on the part of the employer which led him to dismiss. The obvious example here is a belief that the employee is guilty of a crime (see below, under 'conduct'), for in such cases, as with other 'belief' cases, it has been consistently held that what the employer is required to prove is his genuine belief, *not* that his belief was factually correct[12]. However, in the nature of things

---

7   See *Harvey* D[801].
8   The burden of proof is on the employer; if he leads evidence supporting his contention that he dismissed for reason A, that may cast an evidential burden on the employee to adduce some evidence to doubt reason A and/or suggest reason B; if he does so, the legal burden of proof remains with the employer at the end of the day: *Maund v Penwith District Council* [1984] ICR 143, [1984] IRLR 24, CA. If dismissal is with notice, it may be necessary to look at the reason(s) operating both at the giving and expiry of the notice: *Parkinson v March Consulting Ltd* [1998] ICR 276, [1997] IRLR 308, CA; *West Kent College v Richardson* [1999] ICR 511, EAT.
9   *Nelson v BBC* [1977] ICR 649, [1977] IRLR 148, CA. This is certainly so on appeal as *Nelson* shows, if only because it is contrary to natural justice to decide an appeal on a ground that was not fully argued before the tribunal; a similar rule applies before the tribunal itself, but here a change of label may be permissible where the employee is in fact given a proper opportunity to refute the new ground: *Murphy v Epsom College* [1985] ICR 80, [1984] IRLR 271, CA; *Hotson v Wisbech Conservative Club* [1984] ICR 859, [1984] IRLR 422; *Burkett v Pendletons (Sweets) Ltd* [1992] ICR 407. Likewise, if the employer fails to establish the reason put forward, the tribunal should not cast around to try to find some other dismissible reason: *Adams v Derby City Council* [1985] IRLR 163, EAT.
10   'Redundancy' for example may cover a multitude of sins in layman's use, but in law it has a precise and restricted meaning.
11   [1974] ICR 323, [1974] IRLR 213, CA; the passage cited was approved by the House of Lords in *W Devis & Sons Ltd v Atkins* [1977] ICR 662, [1977] IRLR 314, HL. For an example of wrong labelling, see *Hannan v TNT–IPEC (UK) Ltd* [1986] IRLR 165, EAT.
12   *Trust House Forte Leisure Ltd v Aquilar* [1976] IRLR 251.

the approach cannot be totally subjective, for the employer has to *prove* that he held the belief in question and so in practice will have to go on to adduce some supporting evidence of the facts upon which he based his belief (even though it does not have to amount to clear proof of the correctness of that belief), otherwise there is the danger that the tribunal will not believe him.

At the heart of the matter of labelling lies a question of balance. It is clearly important in practice that a relatively lax approach should be taken to the label applied by the employer. On the other hand, too lax an approach could leave too much leeway for an employer to operate a 'shotgun' defence – to make multiple allegations, under different headings, against the employee and hope that one or two are accepted by the tribunal. A major step towards preventing improper use of such tactics was taken by the House of Lords in *Smith v City of Glasgow District Council*[13]. The employer put forward a mixture of reasons for dismissal, relating to incompetence and misconduct, crystallised into three substantive allegations; the tribunal found that one of them had not been made out but proceeded to find the dismissal generally fair. This reasoning was disapproved by the House of Lords, since what appeared to be an integral part of the reason for dismissal had not been proved (or, at least, proved to have been the subject of reasonable belief by the employer). This case does *not* mean that an employer cannot plead several reasons and win; it does mean, however, that if one of several reasons put forward collapses the employer must go further and show that the collapsed reason was not, or did not form a significant part of, the principal reason for the dismissal (i.e. that the remaining reasons were more important and justified the dismissal by themselves); according to the House of Lords, that had not been shown on the facts of this case. Clearly, the more reasons the employer loads into the shotgun (and the more he eventually fails to prove), the more difficult this will be to establish.

Two further points on this first stage of the action should also be noticed. The first is that the House of Lords held in *W Devis & Sons Ltd v Atkins*[14] that the employer can only rely on the facts as known to him at the date of dismissal; contrary to the position in a common law action for wrongful dismissal[15] therefore, the employer cannot rely upon subsequently discovered misconduct (as in a case where there is a dubious dismissal for inefficiency, following which the employer checks the books and finds clear evidence of embezzlement by the ex-employee – there must still be a finding of unfair dismissal in such a case, though the subsequently discovered misconduct may be relevant on the question of compensation, see below).

There is one major qualification to this fundamental rule. Where an initial decision to dismiss is subject to an internal appeal, further evidence may come to light during the course of the appeal and it has been held that the tribunal can look at this (it being unrealistic to do otherwise) *provided* that the new evidence

---

13   [1987] ICR 796, [1987] IRLR 326, HL, noted [1988] CLJ 21.
14   [1977] ICR 662, [1977] IRLR 314, HL. Date of dismissal here means the effective date of termination, so that if the facts change between the giving and the expiry of notice (e.g. a redundancy situation is affected by the receipt of a new order during that period), the tribunal should look at the facts as known at the expiry date: *Stacey v Babcock Power Ltd* [1986] ICR 221, [1986] IRLR 3. Thus, further evidence coming to light during the notice period can be taken into account: *Alboni v Ind Coope Retail Ltd* [1998] IRLR 131, CA (employer's reasonable conduct looking for an alternative to dismissal during the notice period taken into account); *White v South London Transport Ltd* [1998] ICR 293 (further medical evidence during notice period backed up the original ill health dismissal).
15   *Boston Deep Sea Fishing and Ice Co v Ansell* (1888) 39 Ch D 339, CA.

relates to the original ground of dismissal[16]. However, this must not be taken too far and it has been held that (a) this exception does not allow an employer to use evidence from the appeal to set up an entirely new ground for dismissal[17] and (b) it does not render admissible evidence of matters occurring after the conclusion of the appeal[18]. The series of EAT decisions that established these principles were eventually strongly affirmed by the House of Lords in *West Midland Co-operative Society Ltd v Tipton*[19], where the approach was taken that internal appeal procedures are an integral part of the dismissal procedure and so should be taken into account; to do so does *not* offend the principle in *Devis & Sons Ltd v Atkins*. Indeed, the *Tipton* case takes matters one stage further and holds that a *refusal* by an employer to allow an internal appeal may itself be evidence of unfairness.

The second point is that section 107 of the 1996 Act provides that in determining the reason for dismissal the tribunal may *not* take into account any industrial pressure (whether by strike or lesser action) which was exercised on the employer in order to procure the dismissal, or which was such that it was foreseeably likely to lead to dismissal[20]. This might apply where action was taken by a union or group of fellow employees against an employee who had refused to join in a strike, and if the employer sacks him solely because of the pressure, section 107 leads to the artificial position before the tribunal that the only reason for dismissal has to be ignored. The employer will then be found to have dismissed the employee unfairly, no reason having been shown, and, unless there was unreasonable conduct or undue obstinacy on the employee's part during the dispute, the employer may have to pay full compensation[1]. Where, however, the pressure was exercised on the employer because of the non-membership of a union of the applicant, it is now provided that an action may be brought against the union (or other person exercising the pressure) either by the employer or by the applicant himself and the union or other person may be ordered to pay some or all of the compensation awarded to the applicant[2]. These provisions supplement s. 107 without replacing it.

b) Stage two: prima facie fair grounds

The second stage of the action is that the employer must prove that the reason for the dismissal fits into one of the enumerated categories. These are considered below, but it should be noted here that the final residual category, 'some other substantial reason justifying dismissal', is deliberately wide and not to be restricted by being construed ejusdem generis with the previous categories[3]. Dismissal of a replacement for a woman temporarily absent on maternity leave (or for a person subject to compulsory medical suspension[4]) is expressly stated to be for a

---

16   *National Heart and Chest Hospitals v Nambiar* [1981] ICR 441, [1981] IRLR 196; *Sillifant v Powell Duffryn Timber Ltd* [1983] IRLR 91.
17   *Monie v Coral Racing Ltd* [1981] ICR 109, [1980] IRLR 464, CA.
18   *Greenall Whitley plc v Carr* [1985] ICR 451, [1985] IRLR 289.
19   [1986] ICR 192, [1986] IRLR 112, HL.
20   *Ford Motor Co Ltd v Hudson* [1978] ICR 482, [1978] IRLR 66, EAT.
1   *Hazell Offsets Ltd v Luckett* [1977] IRLR 430; *British United Trawlers (Grimsby) Ltd v Carr* [1977] ICR 622; *Colwyn Borough Council v Dutton* [1980] IRLR 420. Although it is easiest to imagine this section applying to normal industrial disputes, it could also possibly apply to a case of pressure from a workforce to dismiss an AIDS sufferer.
2   TULR(C)A 1992, s. 160.
3   *RS Components Ltd v Irwin* [1973] ICR 535, [1973] IRLR 239. See *Harvey* D[1854].
4   Under the ERA 1996, s. 64.

substantial reason (provided the replacement was told of the temporary nature of the job when engaged)[5], as is a dismissal because of a transfer of the employer's undertaking (see p. 491, below), but other than that all that can be said is that the question of what can be a substantial reason is an open one in respect of which the onus is clearly upon the employer to satisfy the tribunal on the facts of the particular case; the wider it is construed by the tribunals, the wider ostensibly is the area of management prerogative[6], though of course any particular dismissal still has to be shown to be fair, even if for a substantial reason[7]. It has been held in the past to cover a range of miscellaneous reasons including an employer's mistaken belief that he had other fair grounds on which to dismiss,[8] dismissal at the behest of an important customer[9], personality clashes[10], sexual orientation[11] and the dismissal of the spouse of a person already dismissed where they were engaged as a pair[12]; as will be seen at p. 496, below, it has been particularly important in cases of dismissals following necessary business reorganisations.

c) Stage three: fairness[13]

The third stage is that the tribunal must consider under section 98(4) whether the employer acted reasonably in actually 'activating' the reason in question and dismissing the employee; this demonstrates clearly that it is not enough to show that the employer had a reason which would normally justify dismissal – it has to be shown that, in all the circumstances of the case, it actually justified the particular dismissal in question. Unlike a wrongful dismissal action, this is not a technical exercise, looking at the parties' contractual entitlements and rights, but instead entails examination of the *substance* of the dismissal and consideration of the wider circumstances such as the employer's business needs (e.g. in a case of inefficiency or ineptitude by the employee) and any factors in mitigation of the employee's default, such as long service, lack of prior grounds for complaint and

5   Ibid., s. 106. This is of less importance now that the qualifying period is two years.
6   Bowers and Clark 'Unfair dismissal and managerial prerogative: a study of "other substantial reason"' (1981) 10 ILJ 34.
7   *Gilham v Kent County Council (No 2)* [1985] ICR 233, [1985] IRLR 18, CA. A defence of some other substantial reason requires the tribunal 'to consider the reason established by the employer and decide whether it falls within the category of reason which could justify the dismissal of *an* employee – not *that* employee, but *an* employee – holding the position which that employee held': *Dobie v Burns International Security Services (UK) Ltd* [1984] IRLR 329 at 331, CA per Sir John Donaldson MR; the next stage is to consider whether the dismissal of *that* employee was fair on the facts, within s. 98(4).
8   *Taylor v Co-operative Retail Services Ltd* [1981] ICR 172, [1981] IRLR 1; affd [1982] ICR 600, [1982] IRLR 354, CA (mistaken belief that employer obliged to dismiss under a closed shop agreement); *Bouchaala v Trust House Forte Hotels Ltd* [1980] ICR 721, [1980] IRLR 382 (mistaken belief that continued employment would contravene a statutory enactment).
9   *Scott Packing and Warehousing Ltd v Paterson* [1978] IRLR 166; *Grootcon (UK) Ltd v Keld* [1984] IRLR 302; *Dobie v Burns International Security Services (UK) Ltd* [1984] ICR 812, [1984] IRLR 329, CA. As with pressure from co-workers (s. 107, n. 20 above) this could be relevant in the dismissal of an AIDS sufferer; on such a dismissal generally, see Napier, 'AIDS, discrimination and employment law' (1989) 18 ILJ 84 and Watt, 'HIV, discrimination, unfair dismissal and pressure to dismiss' (1992) 21 ILJ 280.
10 *Treganowan v Robert Knee & Co Ltd* [1975] ICR 405, [1975] IRLR 247.
11 *Boychuk v H K Symons Holdings Ltd* [1977] IRLR 395 (the 'Lesbians Ignite' case); *Saunders v Scottish National Camps Association Ltd* [1980] IRLR 174; affd briefly by the Ct of Sess [1981] IRLR 277 (dismissal of homosexual from employment in children's camp).
12 *Kelman v Oram* [1983] IRLR 432 (dismissal of publican's wife after (unfair) dismissal of publican).
13 See *Harvey* D[952].

the possibilities of improvement. While the burden of proof on this overall question of fairness is technically neutral, the House of Lords in *Smith v City of Glasgow District Council*[14] approved the view of the Court of Session below that it remains logical to expect the employer to prove that the reason in question has been established – it cannot be reasonable to treat that reason as sufficient to justify dismissal unless the employer has shown either that it is true or that he believed it to be true. Although other factors (such as procedural considerations) may have to be considered, this emphasis on isolating the real reason(s) for dismissal may mean that in many cases the issue of overall fairness will tend to merge with the question of establishing the reason (on which the employer does still bear the burden of proof).

In applying the test of fairness, the tribunal must consider the reasonableness of the employer's conduct, *not* the injustice (or lack of it) done to the employee. This fundamental principle was reaffirmed by the House of Lords in *Polkey v AE Dayton Services Ltd*[15], probably the most important decision on unfair dismissal since *W Devis & Sons Ltd v Atkins*[16] ten years earlier. An employee dismissed without warning for redundancy and sent home immediately had his claim for unfair dismissal turned down by the tribunal because they found that proper consultation would not have made any difference, i.e. they looked at the eventual lack of injustice to the employee. The House of Lords clearly held this to be wrong and remitted the case to another tribunal, who were to apply the correct test of looking at the reasonableness of the employer's conduct in deciding not to consult or warn; the question of the amount of injustice done to the employee should only be relevant at the later stages of assessing compensation. This reasonableness test in section 98(4) has two overall effects. The first is that it is primarily responsible for giving the tribunals their wide discretion to reach just and equitable decisions in the light of 'good industrial practice' (the relevant wording in section 98(4) being 'in accordance with equity and the substantial merits of the case'); in the exercise of this discretion the tribunals have considerable freedom of action and in general the EAT will be reluctant to interfere with their decisions on such matters. The second effect is that it is the existence of section 98(4) which has led to the importance attached to the concept of 'procedural unfairness', i.e. the possibility that a dismissal may be unfair if an unfair procedure is adopted by the employer (e.g. no warnings, lack of a hearing), even if there is prima facie a good substantive reason for the dismissal. This concept, not to be found expressly stated in the legislation, was developed at an early stage in the history of the action[17] and remains a significant element in it. It has been subject to definable fluctuations in the amount of emphasis to be placed on it. After being a dominant factor in unfair dismissal law during most of the 1970s, it suffered a definite wane in the later years of that decade for two reasons – (i) a generally less enthusiastic attitude by the Court of Appeal, seen most clearly in *Hollister v NFU*[18] with a tendency to view procedural matters as

14   [1987] ICR 796, [1987] IRLR 326, HL; *Post Office (Counters) Ltd v Heavey* [1990] ICR 1, [1989] IRLR 513, EAT.
15   [1988] ICR 142, [1987] IRLR 503, HL.
16   See p. 465, n. 14, above.
17   *Earl v Slater and Wheeler (Airlyne) Ltd* [1973] 1 All ER 145, [1972] ICR 508, approved by the House of Lords in *W Devis & Sons Ltd v Atkins* [1977] ICR 662, [1977] IRLR 314, HL. The procedural steps necessary in most dismissals are considered at pp. 437-444, above.
18   [1979] ICR 542, [1979] IRLR 238, CA; *Retarded Children's Aid Society v Day* [1978] ICR 437, [1978] IRLR 128, CA; *Bailey v BP Oil (Kent Refinery) Ltd* [1980] ICR 642, [1980] IRLR 287, CA. See Elias, 'Fairness in unfair dismissal: trends and tensions' (1981) 10 ILJ 201.

merely one of the background factors; (ii) the evolution and widespread application of the rule in *British Labour Pump Co Ltd v Byrne*[19], to the effect that even if the employer failed to use the proper procedure on dismissal, it would still be fair if he could prove on a balance of probabilities that even if he had gone through the proper procedure the employee would still have been dismissed (and that dismissal would then have been fair) – i.e. a lapse by the employer could be forgiven if with hindsight it made no difference. However, we saw a swing back of the pendulum with the decision of the House of Lords in *Polkey v A E Dayton Services Ltd*[20] in which *Byrne*'s case was overruled[1] for two reasons – (i) it is inconsistent with *W Devis & Sons Ltd v Atkins*[2] since the tribunal should be considering what the employer actually did at the date of dismissal (and with his state of knowledge then), not what he might have done with hindsight; (ii) more significantly, the *Byrne* approach was based on consideration of the (lack of) injustice to the employee, not the reasonableness of the employer's actions and, as we have seen above, that is a fundamentally flawed approach. In addition, the case of *Polkey* also shows a generally more favourable approach to procedural unfairness[3]; Lord Mackay LC said that a lapse of procedure will not automatically make a dismissal unfair and accepted that (taking the facts of the case) a redundancy dismissal without consultation or warning might still be fair, *but* that would only be so if the employer could show that the decision not to consult or warn was a positive decision taken reasonably in the circumstances at the time, not justified merely as an ex post facto afterthought once the deed had been done[4]. We have seen, therefore, the reinstating of procedural fairness, not just as *a* factor, but as one of *the* factors that are likely to dominate an unfair dismissal action, even if realistically we are unlikely to see it return in full to its heyday in the early years of the unfair dismissal jurisdiction.

d) The correct approach: the 'range of reasonable responses' test

One aspect of section 98(4) has caused considerable disagreement in the cases; that is whether the approach of the tribunal should be subjective or objective. To any lawyer versed in criminal law or tort, the concept of 'reasonableness' is clearly objective, and in earlier cases on section 98(4) the approach was indeed objective, viewing the tribunal as an 'industrial jury' with full powers to review the employer's conduct from their standpoint and decide, in the light of standard industrial

---

19   [1979] ICR 347, [1979] IRLR 94; see p. 442, above.

20   N. 15, above. In his speech, Lord Mackay LC, giving the judgment of the court, relied heavily on the strong criticisms of *Byrne*'s case by Browne-Wilkinson P in *Sillifant v Powell Duffryn Timber Ltd* [1983] IRLR 91.

1   Also overruled is *W & J Wass Ltd v Binns* [1982] ICR 486, [1982] IRLR 283 in which the Court of Appeal had approved *Byrne*'s case, and 'all decisions supporting it'.

2   See p. 465, n. 14, above.

3   See also the post-*Polkey* decisions in *McLaren v National Coal Board* [1988] ICR 370, [1988] IRLR 215, CA; *Whitbread & Co plc v Mills* [1988] ICR 776, [1988] IRLR 501; *Spink v Express Foods Group Ltd* [1990] IRLR 320; *Stocker v Lancashire County Council* [1992] IRLR 75, CA; and Collins 'Procedural fairness after *Polkey*' (1990) 19 ILJ 39.

4   The formulation of this exception caused problems. Lord Bridge in *Polkey* said that it should only apply where the employer had *actually* (subjectively) considered the matter at the time of dismissal and concluded that consultation would be useless. However, in *Duffy v Yeomans & Partners Ltd* [1995] ICR 1, [1994] IRLR 642 the Court of Appeal applied Lord Mackay's view that it can apply where the employer *could reasonably have* so concluded. This could be seen as capable of reviving at least parts of *Byrne*'s case and the 'it made no difference' defence, if not quite as purely retrospectively as in *Byrne*. See Wynn (1995) 24 ILJ 272.

practice (hence the lay membership), whether on the facts they would have dismissed[5]. Some later cases, however, adopted the view that the approach should be subjective (at least in part) particularly in cases where the employer's belief in a set of facts at the time of dismissal is important, so that the employer's own view that he acted reasonably should have some effect[6]. Thus in *Alidair Ltd v Taylor*[7], where an airline pilot's instant dismissal after damaging an aircraft in a faulty landing was held to be fair, Lord Denning MR said,

> '... it must be remembered that [section 98] contemplated a subjective test. The tribunal have to consider the employer's reason and the employer's state of mind. If the company honestly believed on reasonable grounds that this pilot was lacking in proper capability to fly aircraft on behalf of the company, that was a good and sufficient reason for the company to determine the employment then and there. ... They clearly had no further confidence in him. He could not be trusted to fly their aircraft on their behalf. That being their honest belief on reasonable grounds, they were entitled to dismiss him. They acted reasonably in treating it as a sufficient reason for dismissing him.'

Reinforcing this, his Lordship then said,

> 'If a man is dismissed for stealing, as long as the employer honestly believed it on reasonable grounds, that is enough to justify dismissal. It is not necessary for the employer to prove that he was in fact stealing. Whenever a man is dismissed for incapacity or incompetence it is sufficient that the employer honestly believes on reasonable grounds that the man is incapable or incompetent. It is not necessary for the employer to prove that he is in fact incapable or incompetent.'

However, the approach cannot be totally subjective (otherwise the tribunal's discretion would be minimal when faced by an employer unshaken in his assertion that he thought he had acted reasonably), as can be seen from the above references to belief *on reasonable grounds*. Moreover, some later cases reaffirmed an objective element:

> '... the industrial tribunal, while using its own collective wisdom, is to apply the standard of the reasonable employer; that is to say, the fairness or unfairness of the dismissal is to be judged ... by the objective standard of the way in which a reasonable employer in those circumstances, in that line of business, would have behaved[8].'

Thus the correct position must lie in a combined approach, namely that the tribunal must have to gauge the employer's conduct by *some* objective yardstick, but at the same time take into account the honest beliefs of the employer where

5   *Bessenden Properties Ltd v Corness* [1977] ICR 821n, [1974] IRLR 338, CA.
6   *Ferodo Ltd v Barnes* [1976] ICR 439, [1976] IRLR 302; *Post Office v Mughal* [1977] ICR 763, [1977] IRLR 178.
7   [1978] ICR 445, [1978] IRLR 82, CA; the passages cited are at 450–451 and 84–85 respectively; *Vickers Ltd v Smith* [1977] IRLR 11. Cf. *ILEA v Lloyd* [1981] IRLR 394, CA.
8   *Watling & Co Ltd v Richardson* [1978] ICR 1049, [1978] IRLR 255 at 1056 and 257 respectively, per Phillips J, explaining *Vickers Ltd v Smith* (n. 7, above); see also *Mitchell v Old Hall Exchange Club Ltd* [1978] IRLR 160.

they are relevant. It may seem unsatisfactory not to be able to give a clear answer to what appears to be a fundamental question – subjective or objective? – but in practice it may in most cases be an empty question in the light of two aspects of section 98 which *are* clear and which may be seen as embodying elements of objectivity and subjectivity respectively:

1) It is clear that, in all but the most blatant and obvious case of misconduct or incapability, the employer must have made a proper investigation of the grounds of his complaint against the employee and come to proper, tenable conclusions if he is to convince the tribunal that he had reasonable grounds for any belief which he is putting forward as a reason for the dismissal. Thus in a suspected theft case the employer must show reasonable investigations, reasonably allowing him to point the finger of accusation at the employee. Moreover, the requirement of reasonable investigation means that an employer cannot rely upon his own ignorance at the time of dismissal of a particular point in the employee's favour if a reasonable investigation would have revealed it, i.e. the tribunal may look at the facts of which the employer knew *or ought to have known*[9]. To this extent at least, the test is objective as can be seen from the formula 'belief on reasonable grounds', and if the employer can show these reasonable grounds he may be in a strong position[10]. The test cannot be wholly objective, however, as can be seen from the second point.

2) If the tribunal could adopt an entirely objective approach, there would be nothing to stop them looking at the facts of every case *de novo* and simply applying their own view of those facts, deciding whether they would have done what the employer did in the circumstances. However, the courts have consistently held that this is what a tribunal must *not* do[11]. Instead, they have to look at what the employer in fact did and decide whether that was a course of action which a reasonable employer could have taken in those circumstances (applying the standard of the reasonable employer as envisaged in the wording of section 98(4) itself). This becomes of particular significance in a case where in the circumstances the employer had several courses of action open to him, all of which were potentially what a reasonable employer might do, e.g. where the misconduct was such that he could dismiss, suspend without pay or fine and he chose to dismiss, or where in a redundancy case he could dispense with A or B or C and he chose A. In such a case, the tribunal should not consider which course they would have taken and decide whether the dismissal was fair or not in accordance with that (e.g. holding dismissal unfair if they would on balance have decided upon suspension, or holding the dismissal of A unfair if on balance they would have dismissed C). Instead, they should decide whether the course of action in fact chosen was one which a reasonable employer *could* have decided upon, i.e. whether the employer acted *within the area of discretion covered by what would have been reasonable in the circumstances*. Thus in *Trust House Forte Leisure Ltd v Aquila*[12], Phillips J said,

---

9   *St Anne's Board Mill Co Ltd v Brien* [1973] ICR 444, [1973] IRLR 309, approved by the House of Lords in *W Devis & Sons Ltd v Atkins* [1977] ICR 662, [1977] IRLR 314, HL.
10 *Post Office v Mughal* [1977] ICR 763, [1977] IRLR 178.
11 *Trust House Forte Hotels Ltd v Murphy* [1977] IRLR 186; *Meridian Ltd v Gomersall* [1977] ICR 597, [1977] IRLR 425; *Mansfield Hosiery Mills Ltd v Bromley* [1977] IRLR 301; *Watling & Co Ltd v Richardson* [1978] ICR 1049, [1978] IRLR 255.
12 [1976] IRLR 251 at 254.

'... when the management is confronted with a decision to dismiss an employee in particular circumstances there may well be cases where reasonable managements might take either of two decisions: to dismiss or not to dismiss. It does not necessarily mean if they decide to dismiss that they have acted unfairly because they are plenty of situations in which more than one view is possible.'

In *Watling & Co Ltd v Richardson*[13] the same judge, using the redundancy example given above as a warning to tribunals not simply to apply their own views, said,

'It has to be recognised that there are circumstances where more than one course of action may be reasonable ... In such cases ... if an industrial tribunal equates its view of what itself would have done with what a reasonable employer would have done, it may mean that an employer will be found to have dismissed an employee unfairly although in the circumstances many perfectly good and fair employers would have done as that employer did.'

Indeed the development of this 'range of reasonable responses' approach has been a major feature of unfair dismissal law and has had the effect of broadening the area of managerial discretion – it does not apply a test entirely subjective to the respondent employer, but it does enjoin the tribunals to look at the matter from an employer standpoint generally (albeit that of a reasonable employer). This approach was approved by the Court of Appeal in *British Leyland (UK) Ltd v Swift*[14], where Lord Denning MR said

'The correct test is: was it reasonable for the employer to dismiss him? If no reasonable employer would have dismissed him, then the dismissal was unfair. But if a reasonable employer might reasonably have dismissed him, then the dismissal was fair. It must be remembered that in all these cases there is a band of reasonableness, within which one employer might reasonably take one view; another quite reasonably take a different view ... if it was quite reasonable to dismiss him, then the dismissal must be upheld as fair: even though some other employers may not have dismissed him.'

The 'range of reasonable responses' approach has been universally accepted for years and was particularly well set out by Browne-Wilkinson P in *Iceland Frozen Foods Ltd v Jones*[15] as follows:

'... [T]he correct approach for the Industrial Tribunal to adopt in answering the question posed by [section 98(4) of the 1996 Act] is as follows: (1) the

13   N. 1, above, at 1056 and 258 respectively; *Grundy (Teddington) Ltd v Willis* [1976] ICR 323, [1976] IRLR 118.
14   [1981] IRLR 91, CA. The principle was well expounded by the EAT in *Rolls-Royce Ltd v Walpole* [1980] IRLR 343 and *British Gas plc v McCarrick* [1991] IRLR 305, CA is a strong decision reaffirming it.
15   [1982] IRLR 439 at 442. The EAT was at pains to point out that this did not mean (as may have appeared from *Vickers Ltd v Smith* [1977] IRLR 11) that a dismissal could only be unfair if *perverse* (i.e. no reasonable employer could possibly have decided to dismiss); the test is not as stringent as that. In a case depending on the credibility of a witness, the question is whether the employer could reasonably believe him, *not* whether the tribunal does: *Linfood Cash and Carry Ltd v Thomson* [1989] ICR 518, [1989] IRLR 235, EAT.

starting point should always be the words of [section 98] themselves; (2) in applying the section an Industrial Tribunal must consider the reasonableness of the employer's conduct, not simply whether they (the members of the Industrial Tribunal) consider the dismissal to be fair; (3) in judging the reasonableness of the employer's conduct an Industrial Tribunal must not substitute its decision as to what was the right course to adopt for that of the employer; (4) in many (though not all) cases there is a band of reasonable responses to the employee's conduct within which one employer might reasonably take one view, another quite reasonably take another; (5) the function of the Industrial Tribunal, as an industrial jury, is to determine whether in the particular circumstances of each case the decision to dismiss the employee fell within the band of reasonable responses which a reasonable employer might have adopted. If the dismissal falls within the band the dismissal is fair; if the dismissal falls outside the band it is unfair.'

However, a bombshell was dropped in late 1999 by the EAT under Morison P (in one of his final judgments in that court) in *Haddon v Van den Bergh Foods Ltd*[16], where they stated that in their opinion the range of reasonable responses test is *wrong* (being said to be an unhelpful 'mantra', along with the general point that a tribunal should not substitute its own view for that of the employer). This revisionism was based on the argument that the 'range' test makes it too difficult for an employee to succeed in a misconduct case, and that it is too close to the administrative law concept of perversity (see note 15). However, the reasoning in the case is, with respect, fragile because (a) its treatment of the strong authorities in favour of the test is little short of cavalier, (b) its reliance on *Kent County Council v Gilham*[17] to attack these authorities is arguably misplaced because *Gilham* has never been a mainstream case on this point, and (c) the strong reaffirmation of the test in *British Gas plc v McCarrick*[18] is not cited, let alone distinguished. On these grounds, an EAT under Lindsay P subsequently criticised *Haddon* in *Midland Bank plc v Madden*,[19] holding that it was not open to the previous EAT to disapprove of the range test, quite simply on grounds of binding precedent. *Haddon* therefore seems to have had little effect, but a Court of Appeal decision is now highly desirable to settle the point.

iii) Particular cases

Having considered the basis of an unfair dismissal action generally, in the light of the above trilogy of House of Lords decisions in *Smith v City of Glasgow District Council, West Midlands Co-operative Society Ltd v Tipton* and *Polkey v A E Dayton Services Ltd*, we can now turn to eight particular cases of practical importance. The first three (capability, conduct and redundancy) are the major headings contained in section 98(2), the fourth (dismissal on a transfer of undertaking) has been

16 [1999] ICR 1150, [1999] IRLR 672. The tribunal had held that the test forced them to find fair the dismissal of a employee who had been invited to a drinks party to celebrate 15 years good service, who was then summarily dismissed for not returning for the last 1½ hours of his shift because he had been drinking! Arguably, the EAT could just have reversed this on ordinary grounds of perversity.
17 [1985] ICR 227, [1985] IRLR 16, CA.
18 See note 14 above. Also ignored is *Gair v Bevan Harris Ltd* [1983] IRLR 368 in the Inner House of the Court of Session, also approving the range test.
19 [2000] IRLR 288. In the meantime, the Scottish EAT had approved of *Haddon* in a short judgment in *Wilson v Ethicon Ltd* [2000] IRLR 4.

added by Regulations; the fifth and sixth (dismissals for making health and safety complaints and for asserting statutory rights) were added by the Trade Union Reform and Employment Rights Act 1993; the seventh concerns special protection added by subsequent legislation; the eighth (changing business needs and reorganisation) is not specifically covered by statute but is treated separately because of its practical significance and because it involves a complicated interaction of laws relating to unfair dismissal, redundancy, construction of contracts of employment and variation of such contracts. The other heads of unfair dismissal (maternity dismissal, trade union reasons and dismissal while taking part in industrial action) are treated separately in the context in which they arise elsewhere in the book (in chs. 6, 10 and 11); they tend to be subject to more specialised rules, though some of the general principles discussed here lie behind them.

The following discussion of these headings (cross-referred to *Harvey* for further, exhaustive consideration) is, however, subject to the major caveat discussed at pp. 407-415, above, that the modern approach is to treat the accumulation of case law in these areas circumspectly and to deprecate over-reliance on previous authorities (however venerable) if that either over-complicates the issue before the tribunal, or leads the tribunal to stray from the clear wording of the statute. Put shortly, precedents in this area are, to adapt Noël Coward's saying on wit, to be taken like caviar, not like marmalade.

a) Capability or qualifications[20]

The first category of prima facie fair dismissals in section 98(2) is where the reason for dismissal is related to the capability or qualifications of the employee for performing his work. 'Capability' is defined in section 98(3) as capability assessed by reference to skill, aptitude, health or any other physical or mental quality, and 'qualifications' as any degree, diploma or other academic, technical or professional qualification relevant to the employee's position[1]. Lack of capability is of course the more important of these two categories, though the EAT have said that it should be viewed relatively narrowly as applying principally to cases where the employee is *incapable* of satisfactory work[2]; where the employee is capable of it, but refuses to exercise his ability, skills, etc., that should preferably be viewed as a case of misconduct, with the result that the employer should apply his warnings procedure more strictly and with more emphasis on the disciplinary aspect[3].

In the realm of dismissal for incapability, it is important that the employer's business should not have to suffer, to the detriment of all concerned, through the ineptitude or inefficiency of a particular employee. However, it is also important that the employee whose work is causing dissatisfaction should be treated fairly. The question for the tribunal is whether the employer has satisfied them that he genuinely believed on reasonable grounds that the employee was incapable[4]. The requirement of reasonable grounds means that the employer

---

20 See *Harvey* D[1101] and Q[722]n. Practical advice on handling cases of absence (medical and otherwise) is given in the ACAS advisory handbook *Discipline at Work* ch. 9; sub-standard work is covered in ch. 10.
1 *Blue Star Ship Management Ltd v Williams* [1978] ICR 770, [1979] IRLR 16.
2 *Sutton and Gates (Luton) Ltd v Boxall* [1979] ICR 67, [1978] IRLR 486.
3 *Littlewoods Organisation Ltd v Egenti* [1976] ICR 516, [1976] IRLR 334.
4 *Alidair Ltd v Taylor* [1978] ICR 445, [1978] IRLR 82, CA.

should make a proper and full investigation into the facts of the case, and give careful consideration to the decision to dismiss[5]; amongst other things, this consideration may include as a factor whether the employee was given proper training for the job, adequate supervision and, where appropriate, proper support from the employer. Also, it is well established that this area is amenable to the application of a warnings procedure[6], though the emphasis may be different from that in misconduct cases, for here the constructive side of a warning may be more important, not only pointing out the employer's ground for complaint but also instructing the employee how to improve and giving him reasonable time in which to do so. Of course, warnings are not essential in every case, and may perhaps be irrelevant where it is clear that the employee is completely incapable of improvement or where he already clearly knows that is expected of him[7]. That apart, however, the importance of a fair procedure in this area should not be underestimated, and lack of it (particularly if it leads to inadequate investigation by the employer) may make dismissal of an incompetent employee unfair (though it may still be open to the employer to argue that there should be little or no compensation where there was wilful default on the part of the employee, such as failure or refusal to improve[8]). One of the ways in which the ACAS Code of Practice on Disciplinary and Grievance Procedures was expanded in 2000 was by the inclusion (in paras. 21–23) of guidance on sub-standard work, which adopts and simplifies very much the results of this case law.

One particular aspect of incapability which has given rise to much litigation is where the employee is incapable of performing his work due to prolonged and/ or frequent illness. Three preliminary points may be made on this subject. The first is that an exceptionally severe and incapacitating illness could have the effect of frustrating the contract of employment, in which case there would be no dismissal and so no action could be brought; frustration is considered elsewhere[9], and in general it should not be found readily by a tribunal because of its drastic effect on the employee's rights. The tests for a frustrating illness are therefore stringent, and are not the tests to be applied to the separate question whether a dismissal for illness was fair[10]. The second point is that many employees are covered by contractual sick pay schemes which will provide for payment during sickness up to a maximum period. A sick employee in most cases will expect to remain 'employed' during an illness at least until the sick pay period elapses. There is, however, no necessary link-up in law between the sick pay period and the question of dismissal for illness for (a) a contractual sick pay term only covers payment while still employed and, although it would not normally be reasonable to dismiss before the end of the sick pay period, there may be cases where the employer's business needs are so urgent that dismissal (and replacement) *during* that period could be reasonable; (b) on the other hand, it is not necessarily fair

5 *Cook v Thomas Linnell & Sons Ltd* [1977] ICR 770, [1977] IRLR 132.
6 *Winterhalter Gastronom Ltd v Webb* [1973] ICR 245, [1973] IRLR 120, NIRC.
7 *James v Waltham Holy Cross UDC* [1973] ICR 398, [1973] IRLR 202.
8 *Sutton and Gates (Luton) Ltd v Boxall* [1979] ICR 67, [1978] IRLR 486, explaining *Kraft Foods Ltd v Fox* [1978] ICR 311, [1977] IRLR 431.
9 Pp. 358-363. The applicability of the doctrine of frustration in this context was reaffirmed by the Court of Appeal in *Notcutt v Universal Equipment Co (London) Ltd* [1986] ICR 414, [1986] IRLR 218.
10 *Tan v Berry Bros and Rudd Ltd* [1974] ICR 586, [1974] IRLR 244, NIRC.

to apply a policy of dismissing automatically once the sick pay period expires[11]. Thus, the two matters are conceptually separate. The third point is that if the medical cause of the absence is likely to be long term and have a significant effect on the employee's life, the employer may now have to consider whether it could constitute a 'disability' within the Disability Discrimination Act 1995, in which case the following unfair dismissal law considerations may have to be supplemented by others under that Act, in particular any reasonable adjustments that might have to be made to help the employee to return.[12]

Subject to these three points, it is well established by leading cases such as *East Lindsey District Council v Daubney*[13] that the approach of the tribunal in assessing the reasonableness of the employer's decision to dismiss should be to consider whether it was reasonable to expect the employer to wait any longer before dismissing, in the light of such factors as the nature of the illness, the actual and potential length of the absence, the circumstances of the individual employee, the urgency of the need to fill the employee's job and the size and nature of the employer's undertaking. The procedural steps to be taken by the employer will vary widely according to the facts of the case but, although a 'warning' as such is hardly appropriate, in most cases the employer will be expected to consult the employee and discuss the nature of his illness and his future prospects, bearing in mind the employer's need to have the work done[14]. The employer may also be expected to make such investigations as are necessary to establish the true facts of the case, which may mean taking further medical advice on the nature of the illness. It has been stressed by the EAT that the eventual decision whether to dismiss remains a managerial one, not a medical one[15], but in the nature of things the employer may reasonably have to rely heavily upon a medical prognosis (even if it later turns out to have been wrong). Even if the employee is likely to be away for a considerable period and his position needs to be filled, the employer may still be expected to consider the possibility of alternative (perhaps lighter)

11   *Hardwick v Leeds Area Health Authority* [1975] IRLR 319. For a later confirmation of this point, on rather unusual facts, see *Smiths Industries Aerospace and Defence Systems Ltd v Brookes* [1986] IRLR 434. In addition, it may be necessary also to consider the rules on statutory sick pay, discussed at pp. 179-182, above, which may have an indirect effect particularly if there was evidence that one of the reasons behind the dismissal was the avoidance of payment of sick pay. It is increasingly possible that to dismiss before exhausting sick pay, even if fair on the facts, might be viewed as breach of contract in a common law action, on analogy with the 'PHI cases', see p. 128, above.

12   For disability discrimination law, see p. 309, above.

13   [1977] ICR 566, [1977] IRLR 181. This long-standing approach was reaffirmed (and said to be in line with the leading case on procedure generally, *Polkey v A E Dayton Services Ltd* [1988] ICR 142, [1987] IRLR 503, HL) in *A Links & Co Ltd v Rose* [1991] IRLR 353, Ct of Sess.

14   *Spencer v Paragon Wallpapers Ltd* [1977] ICR 301, [1976] IRLR 373. There may however be special factors, perhaps in the nature of the job itself, rendering consultation unnecessary: *Leonard v Fergus and Haynes Civil Engineering Ltd* [1979] IRLR 235; *Taylorplan Catering (Scotland) Ltd v McInally* [1980] IRLR 53. Note also that persistent absenteeism through a series of unrelated medical complaints (often impossible to verify medically) may in fact be more amenable to treatment as misconduct (with warnings and a final decision) than under the illness principles in *Spencer* and *Lindsey: International Sports Co Ltd v Thomson* [1980] IRLR 340; *Lynock v Cereal Packaging Ltd* [1988] ICR 670, [1988] IRLR 510; this may be particularly so under the current system of *self*-certification for the first week of sickness.

15   *East Lindsey District Council v Daubney* [1977] ICR 566, [1977] IRLR 181. The managerial role would be particularly important in the case of an employee either with, or suspected of being with, AIDS, and faced by reaction from fellow employees and/or customers; some practical (and educative) advice has been given in the joint DE/HSE booklet *AIDS and Employment*.

work for the employee instead of dismissal; this may particularly be the case where the employer is a large concern, though even then it probably stops short of an obligation to create an entirely new job for that employee[16]. Once again, one of the changes in the ACAS Code of Practice on Disciplinary and Grievance Procedures in 2000 was the addition of a section (paras. 19 and 20) giving guidance on absence handling, drawing heavily on the case law.

It has been argued that these rules may have to be applied even more circumspectly and sympathetically if the incapacity was in fact the fault of the employer in the first place (most obviously in the case of a work accident to the employee), but the EAT have ruled that there is no such principle; in such a case, the only question at issue remains the fairness of the employer's handling of the situation, however it arose[17].

It will be clear from the above that the obtaining of reliable medical evidence on the sick employee is of great importance. Medical confidentiality could be a problem since the employer may not simply demand a report from the employee's own doctor. He may of course invite the employee to allow such a report to be compiled and released to him; if the employee agrees, that covers the matter of confidentiality. However, there is now the further complication that the Access to Medical Reports Act 1988 gives the employee a right to see such a report by his own doctor (provided he follows the prescribed procedure) in advance of its disclosure to the employer and, further, a right to object to part or all of it and, ultimately, to refuse to allow it to be disclosed (though of course in the latter, extreme, case there would be nothing to stop the employer drawing his own adverse inferences from the refusal and so in practice this may not be a realistic option). However, the Act is limited to reports compiled by the employee's *own* doctor, and so does not apply to a report compiled by an in-house company doctor, or an independent doctor nominated by the employer[18]. This factor now gives even more importance to the incorporation of a term into contracts of employment (as is now commonly done) that specifically gives the employer the right to require the employee to undertake a medical examination by a doctor nominated by the employer, with the results divulged to the employer. If there is no such term, the employer may only *request* such an examination.

The above discussion of illness has primarily envisaged physical illness as the incapacitating factor. Similar principles apply to mental illness, though in such a case it may be that the problem is more delicate and requires an even more understanding approach by the employer (particularly if he hired the employee knowing of his actual or potential condition). If, however, the employee actively concealed a mental condition when applying for the job, that may be a good reason for dismissal when the employer finds out (depending perhaps on the nature of the job) for that would not be primarily a dismissal for illness but rather

---

16 *Merseyside and North Wales Electricity Board v Taylor* [1975] ICR 185, [1975] IRLR 60.
17 *London Fire and Civil Defence Authority v Betty* [1994] IRLR 384; the EAT said that any matters relating to the responsibility for the incapacity are to be left to a civil action for damages.
18 This limitation is achieved indirectly by the drafting of the definition of 'medical report' in s. 2(1), as 'a report ... prepared by a medical practitioner who is or has been responsible for the clinical care of the individual.' Section 3 states that the employer must have the consent of the employee before requesting the report in the first place; s. 7 contains exceptions where the doctor may withhold parts of the report if disclosure could cause the employee serious physical or medical harm. On the Act generally, see Pitt (1988) 17 ILJ 239.

for misconduct, as in other cases where an employee is taken on in some way under false pretences[19].

b)   Conduct[20]

As seen above[1], dismissal for misconduct was an important concept at common law, primarily in the context of wrongful dismissal where the main factor was whether the misconduct was so bad that it repudiated the whole contract and so justified summary dismissal. In the modern context of unfair dismissal, dismissal for misconduct is obviously important (as one of the principal heads of prima facie fair dismissals) but it operates on a much broader base than at common law, so that the misconduct may or may not be dealt with by summary dismissal. The reason for this is that the tribunals can now look into the substantive fairness of any dismissal for misconduct, whereas at common law if an employer wished to be rid of an employee guilty of some lesser form of misconduct than that which would justify summary dismissal, he could just dismiss him with notice and, provided that notice was of the proper length, there could be no legal redress for the employee. Thus, the legal rules relating to the modern and the common law approaches to misconduct are different, so that many dismissals which at common law were unexceptionable can now be challenged as unfair; likewise, a dismissal could be wrongful at common law (because the conduct was not grave enough to warrant the summary dismissal which was inflicted upon the employee) but a tribunal might still hold that in the circumstances it was fair[2]. On the other hand, there will remain a practical relationship between the modern and the common law actions in that certain major heads of misconduct accepted as justifying summary dismissal at common law will remain major categories of fair dismissals, for example failure to obey proper and lawful orders[3], breach of confidence by the employee by unfairly competing with the employer or prejudicing confidentiality necessary to his business[4] and computer misuse by the employee[5]. One further influence of the common law could arise in the case of an employee who consistently plays practical jokes or is inclined to show physical aggression, for in such a case there is a common law duty upon the employer to take reasonable care for the safety of that employee's *fellow* employees[6], which may ultimately require his dismissal.

These overlaps apart, misconduct in the modern statutory context fits into the overall pattern of unfair dismissal law in being essentially a matter of assessing

---

19   *O'Brien v Prudential Assurance Co Ltd* [1979] IRLR 140. Likewise, fraudulent use of a sick note might be good grounds for dismissal for misconduct: *Hutchinson v Enfield Rolling Mills Ltd* [1981] IRLR 318, EAT.

20   See *Harvey* D[1351] and Q[722]n. Practical advice on handling disciplinary matters is given in the ACAS advisory handbook *Discipline at Work* chs. 3–7; criminal offences by employees are covered in ch. 8.

1   Pp. 373-376, above.

2   *Treganowen v Robert Knee & Co Ltd* [1975] ICR 405, [1975] IRLR 247.

3   As at common law, the employee may refuse to obey an unlawful order: *Morrish v Henlys (Folkestone) Ltd* [1973] ICR 482, [1973] IRLR 61, NIRC.

4   *Mansard Precision Engineering Co Ltd v Taylor* [1978] ICR 44; *Golden Cross Hire Co Ltd v Lovell* [1979] IRLR 267; *Nova Plastic Ltd v Frogatt* [1982] IRLR 146, EAT.

5   *Denco Ltd v Joinson* [1991] ICR 172, [1991] IRLR 63, EAT.

6   *Hudson v Ridge Manufacturing Co Ltd* [1957] 2 QB 348, [1957] 2 All ER 229; see p. 653, below. Various statutory duties upon the employer to ensure compliance with safety regulations and the use of safety devices may be an important factor in the dismissal of an employee who consistently acts to the peril of himself and other employees.

the reasonableness of the employer's reaction to it in all the varied circumstances of the case, including any extraneous matters such as length of service and previous good conduct which may act in mitigation of the offence; it is a particularly wide category of dismissal, ranging from gross misconduct (still justifying summary dismissal) such as theft, violence, wilful refusal to obey an order and gross negligence, down to lesser matters such as swearing and poor timekeeping which may only become serious if committed regularly. Faced with this wide diversity, there is sometimes an unfortunate tendency to attempt to over-classify, as if for example the many decided cases established a 'law on fighting at work'; while collecting together all the cases on one kind of misconduct may have some value, it must be stressed that that value is restricted to attempting to point out certain factors which *may* be important in certain of the more typical cases. Further than that, these matters remain clearly within the factual jurisdiction of the tribunals. Swearing is a good example of this, for there are ample cases on it but it remains purely a question of fact whether a particular incident merited dismissal, usually depending on factors such as the nature and place of the employment, the effect upon the recipient, whether it was gratuitous or provoked and any previous incidents; thus, for example, words used to a fellow employee in the course of work on a building site could give rise to different considerations if used to a customer by an assistant at a perfume counter.

Except in cases of dismissal for a single act of gross misconduct, this area of dismissal is a prime one for the application of a warnings system (and in most cases for the granting of a hearing to allow the employee to put forward either his view of the facts, or mitigating circumstances having a bearing upon the question whether to dismiss[7]). A series of warnings may be particularly important in cases of persistent minor misconduct where it is primarily the fact of repetition which may eventually justify dismissal. Moreover, the emphasis in the warnings in this context will normally be disciplinary and so the employer should ensure that they are given in accordance with any procedure laid down in the employee's contract or in the works rules; to this end, it is usually advisable for such terms or rules to lay down any types of misconduct which are particularly relevant to the job in question and the likely consequences of transgressions. Some employers may feel that by laying down such rules they are fettering their discretion, but this should not be the case for in general disciplinary rules, if properly phrased, need not be viewed as exhaustive (and so the employee cannot claim that he cannot be disciplined because what he did does not fall neatly within a particular category in the rules[8]); moreover, the employer stands to gain, for if he wishes to treat as particularly heinous (in his circumstances) something which normally would not be viewed as serious (such as smoking at work or drinking at lunch time), he is well advised to say so in his rules – if not he may have difficulty

---

7   The importance of following proper procedures in misconduct cases was given a welcome reaffirmation by the Court of Appeal in *McLaren v National Coal Board* [1988] ICR 370, [1988] IRLR 215 (dismissal without any form of hearing unfair, even though it was impossible to operate the normal procedures in the middle of the miners' strike); cf. however the different decision on the facts in *Dillett v National Coal Board* [1988] ICR 218, CA (a pre-*Polkey* case).

8   *Distillers Co (Bottling Services) Ltd v Gardner* [1982] IRLR 47; *Macari v Celtic Football & Athletic Co Ltd* [1999] IRLR 787, Ct of Sess. An ambiguous approach by an employer (e.g. when setting out disciplinary rules) may however render a dismissal for a *first* breach of a particular rule unfair: *Trusthouse Forte (Catering) Ltd v Adonis* [1984] IRLR 382, EAT.

showing that a dismissal is fair when the subject matter of it would not normally be viewed as a dismissable offence in other contexts[9].

The major conceptual problem here is in trying to achieve the right balance between certainty and flexibility. On the one hand, it is said to be an important principle that people committing like offences should be treated alike (equality is equity), which argues in favour of a consistent application of disciplinary rules, regardless of who the culprit is[10]. On the other hand it is said that the key to unfair dismissal is flexibility by the employer, judging each case on its merits and not simply adopting a 'tariff' approach to misconduct based upon rigid disciplinary rules[11]. In as much as the latter point means the matters of *mitigation* should be considered in each individual case (e.g. length of service, previous work record) it is consistent with a more certain approach to the offence itself (as in the former point) and so one possible approach (particularly in a larger organisation) is that the employer should *start* by considering from the personnel records whether there have been any similar previous incidents and how they were dealt with, before going on to consider the specific facts and any mitigation in the instant case[12]. One thing that can be stated with some confidence, however, is that tribunals should be wary of simple 'disparity' arguments by applicants because, as any lawyer knows, few cases are so similar as to be directly comparable, particularly when the element of mitigation is taken into account[13].

Suspension pending fuller investigation by the employer may be appropriate in serious cases (provided the employer has contractual authority to do so); the Code of Practice[14] states that normally this should be with pay and only for a brief period and so in reality the employer may not be expected to do so for any great length of time and may reasonably have to take the decision to dismiss once he has had time to make reasonable investigations, even if other eventualities such as a criminal trial of the employee are still pending[15]; indeed, any greater delay before the employer takes decisive action could conceivably make the eventual dismissal unfair[16]. As well as the application of warnings and hearings, dismissal for misconduct is also a prime area for the application of the principle that the function of the tribunal is to decide upon the reasonableness of the action taken by the employer, not simply to substitute their views for his; in a case as heavily dependent upon its facts as a misconduct case, there may well be a considerable area of discretion in which several solutions might have been reasonable and as long as dismissal was within that area the employer is not to be penalised for choosing it in preference to any lesser measure[17].

The type of misconduct case which has caused most concern is the case where the employee has committed a criminal offence, particularly (though not necessarily) theft. Proved theft from the employer will usually be a clear ground

9   *Dairy Produce Packers Ltd v Beverstock* [1981] IRLR 265. One example might be particularly high standards of hygiene in food processing establishments.
10 *Post Office v Fennell* [1981] IRLR 221, CA.
11 *Taylor v Parsons Peebles NEI Bruce Peebles Ltd* [1981] IRLR 119; *Hadjioannous v Coral Casinos Ltd* [1981] IRLR 352, EAT.
12 *Procter v British Gypsum Ltd* [1992] IRLR 7; *Harrow London Borough v Cunningham* [1996] IRLR 256.
13 *Paul v East Surrey District Health Authority* [1995] IRLR 305, CA.
14 Para. 13.
15 *Conway v Matthew Wright & Nephew Ltd* [1977] IRLR 89, EAT.
16 Cf. *Refund Rentals Ltd v McDermott* [1977] IRLR 59.
17 *Trust House Forte Leisure Ltd v Aquilar* [1976] IRLR 251; *Trust House Forte Hotels Ltd v Murphy* [1977] IRLR 186. See p. 469, above.

for dismissal (regardless of the amount taken)[18] as will wilful concealment of previous convictions when applying for a job[19] unless the conviction is 'spent' within the meaning of the Rehabilitation of Offenders Act 1974, in which case the employee is not obliged to disclose it and a dismissal because of it will be unfair[20]. The problems arise in cases where there is only a *suspicion* that the employee has committed an offence, for the employer may feel that he ought to dismiss the employee immediately even though it may be some time before a criminal case can be brought against the employee (which may of course result in his eventual acquittal). Where the criminal offence arose outside the employment (e.g. theft from another person or the commission of a sexual or drug offence outside working hours), the employer should not normally dismiss before the employee has been found guilty[1] and even then should only do so if on the facts (looking at the nature of the offence, the type of job and the potential effects on customers and fellow employees) the commission of that offence renders the employee unsuitable for the job in question[2]. The Code of Practice, paragraph 18 puts it thus:

> 'Criminal offences outside employment. These should not be treated as automatic reasons for dismissal regardless of whether the offence has any relevance to the duties of the individual as an employee. The main considerations should be whether the offence is one that makes the individual unsuitable for his or her type of work or unacceptable to other employees. In all cases, employers, having considered the facts, will need to consider whether the conduct is sufficiently serious to warrant instituting the disciplinary procedure. Employees should not be dismissed solely because a charge against them is pending or because they are absent through having been remanded in custody.'

One possible complicating factor, yet to be elaborated upon, is the suggestion that, in a case of misconduct away from work, it may be reasonable to expect a *large* employer at least to consider whether there was any other employment to which the employee could be transferred, rather than being dismissed[3]. The idea of alternative work is, of course, well known in capability and redundancy cases, but could be difficult to apply here.

18   *Murphy*'s case, n. 17, above.
19   *Torr v British Railways Board* [1977] ICR 785, [1977] IRLR 184, EAT.
20   *Property Guards Ltd v Taylor* [1982] IRLR 175. Certain categories of persons, primarily professional or connected with law enforcement, are excluded: Rehabilitation of Offenders Act 1974 (Exceptions) Order 1975, S.I. 1975 No. 1023. *Harvey* R[40].
1   *Securicor Guarding Ltd v R* [1994] IRLR 633. In the contrary case, where a criminal conviction comes *before* an internal disciplinary hearing, it will normally be reasonable for the employer to rely on the court's finding of guilt (including where the employee has pleaded), without going behind that finding, even where the employee still maintains his innocence: *P v Nottinghamshire County Council* [1992] ICR 706, [1992] IRLR 362, CA; *Secretary of State for Scotland v Campbell* [1992] IRLR 263, EAT.
2   See *Nottinghamshire County Council v Bowly* [1978] IRLR 252; *Norfolk County Council v Bernard* [1979] IRLR 220; *Moore v C & A Modes* [1981] IRLR 71; *Mathewson v RB Wilson Dental Laboratory Ltd* [1988] IRLR 512. 'Conduct means actions of such a nature, whether done in the course of employment or outwith it, that reflects in some way on the employer – employee relationship': *Thomson v Alloa Motor Co* [1983] IRLR 403 at 404, per Lord McDonald.
3   *P v Nottinghamshire County Council*, n. 6 above. If the employer does look for other work before dismissing, however, that is *not* to be used by the employee as an argument that the misconduct could not have been too serious: *Hamilton v Argyll and Clyde Health Board* [1993] IRLR 99, EAT.

Where the crime arises within the employment (the obvious example being theft of the employer's property) the employer's need to dismiss may appear to him to be more urgent, but at the same time the employee under suspicion must not be treated arbitrarily. The position as it has evolved (particularly since the decision of the EAT in *British Home Stores Ltd v Burchell*[4], approved by the Court of Appeal in *W Weddel & Co Ltd v Tepper*[5] and fully in line with the current, post-*Polkey* approach[6]) is that the employer may dismiss if he has a genuine belief in the employee's guilt, which is based upon reasonable grounds; he does not have to be able to *prove* the employee's guilt and so provided the employer has his genuine belief it is irrelevant if the employee is later acquitted of the offence (or indeed if the police decline to bring charges)[7]. Thus it is not the function of the tribunal to try the criminal action against the employee and the employer certainly does not have to prove guilt beyond reasonable doubt – the enquiry is a much more general one than that[8], looking into the bona fides and reasonableness of the employer's claimed belief. The reasonableness of his belief will depend primarily upon whether the employer made a reasonable investigation to establish the facts and drew tenable conclusions from the results.

What constitutes a reasonable investigation will of course vary with the circumstances, so that in the case of red-handed theft with little attempt at explanation, the requirement may not be onerous. In less obvious cases, the employer should make a careful inquiry[9], allowing the employee to be heard in his own defence, but there is a major qualification on this for the EAT have suggested that where the employee's actions are being actively investigated by the police with a view to criminal proceedings it may be improper for the employer to hold a full investigation of his own and to expect the employee to explain his

4   [1980] ICR 303n, [1978] IRLR 379; see also *Ferodo Ltd v Barnes* [1976] ICR 439, [1976] IRLR 302; *Alidair Ltd v Taylor* [1978] ICR 445, [1978] IRLR 82, CA, at 451 and 85, respectively, per Lord Denning MR. The requirement is of actual belief, not just suspicion. However, a well-founded belief in the employee's *intent* to commit the offence may suffice, if he has been found out before committing it: *British Railways Board v Jackson* [1994] IRLR 235, CA. The principles in *British Home Stores Ltd v Burchell* apply to all forms of misconduct, not just to dishonesty cases: *Distillers Co (Bottling Services) Ltd v Gardner* [1982] IRLR 47; they were reaffirmed in *ILEA v Gravett* [1988] IRLR 497 and *Whitbread & Co plc v Mills* [1988] ICR 776, [1988] IRLR 501.

5   [1980] ICR 286, [1980] IRLR 96, CA. See, however, the very untypical criticisms of *British Home Stores v Burchell* in *Wilson v Ethicon Ltd* [2000] IRLR 4.

6   [1980] ICR 286, [1980] IRLR 96, CA. See, however, the very untypical criticisms of *British Home Stores v Burchell* in *Wilson v Ethicon Ltd* [2000] IRLR 4.

7   *Da Costa v Optolis* [1977] IRLR 178; *Harris (Ipswich) Ltd v Harrison* [1978] ICR 1256, [1978] IRLR 382. A difficult case might arise if an employee, having been (fairly) dismissed for theft, was later proved to have been innocent and brought defamation proceedings against the employer. Presumably the defence of justification would not be available and so the employer would have to rely on the protean defence of qualified privilege. For an example of findings of fair dismissal after acquittals by a criminal court, see *Dhaliwal v British Airways Board* [1985] ICR 513, EAT.

8   The strict rules of criminal evidence do not apply so that, for example, evidence of previous dishonesty is admissible, and indeed may be highly relevant: *Docherty v Reddy* [1977] ICR 365; *Coral Squash Clubs Ltd v Matthews* [1979] ICR 607, [1979] IRLR 390.

9   This is another area in which to stress the importance of the overruling by the House of Lords in *Polkey v A E Dayton Services Ltd* [1988] ICR 142, [1987] IRLR 503 of *British Labour Pump Co Ltd v Byrne* [1979] ICR 347, [1979] IRLR 94 and all cases supporting the rule that used to be contained in it, namely that a lapse in procedure could be forgiven if, with hindsight, it actually made no difference; see p. 469, above. On hearings generally, see p. 439, above.

conduct[10]. However, on at least one occasion[11], the EAT have suggested that in such a case the employer might at least give the employee an opportunity to make representations particularly on the question whether the employer ought to go as far as to dismiss (which may involve matters in mitigation, such as long and satisfactory service); in many cases, the employer might in fact gain from doing so, for he will be seen to be acting in the spirit of a fair procedure and also any failure by the employee to put forward his point of view might be held against him. When carrying out his investigation, the involvement of the police may be important for if they give to the employer definite information about their findings that may go far towards confirming the employer's suspicions[12]; on the other hand, the mere fact of police investigation may not be sufficient in itself to constitute reasonable grounds for a belief in guilt and likewise an employer should not simply 'delegate' the matter to the police and the courts (e.g. deciding not to investigate for himself, but merely to await the outcome of the court case, dismissing automatically if the employee is found guilty)[13].

The employer must therefore have a genuine belief in the employee's guilt based upon such investigations as were reasonable in the circumstances; primarily the belief must relate to the guilt of the particular individual though it has been held by the Court of Appeal that if the employer can only narrow it down to one of two employees, but he genuinely believes it must be one or other of them, it may be reasonable to dismiss *both*, which seems distinctly hard on the innocent one[14]. Once the employer has the necessary belief, he will normally be acting reasonably in dismissing in the standard case of theft (in the absence of exceptionally strong mitigating factors of which he knew or ought to have known). It should be noted, however, that there have been suggestions that, as in the other misconduct cases, it depends upon the facts of the case whether the offence is grave enough to warrant dismissal; in particular, it has been suggested that minor participation in theft, or theft from someone other than the employer (e.g. from a fellow employee) *might* not warrant dismissal in some cases[15], though it remains clear that theft from the employer himself will be a good ground for dismissal in almost all cases.

---

10 *Carr v Alexander Russell Ltd* [1979] ICR 469n, [1976] IRLR 220; *Conway v Matthew Wright & Nephew Ltd* [1977] IRLR 89; *Tesco (Holdings) Ltd v Hill* [1977] IRLR 63; *Parker v Clifford Dunn Ltd* [1979] ICR 463, [1979] IRLR 56. If the employee chooses to remain silent because of impending criminal charges, it may still be reasonable for the employer to dismiss on the basis of other evidence available: *Harris v Courage (Eastern) Ltd* [1981] ICR 496, [1981] IRLR 153.

11 *Harris (Ipswich) Ltd v Harrison* [1978] ICR 1256, [1978] IRLR 382.

12 As in *Carr's* case and *Parker's* case, n. 15, above. However, actual police presence at an internal disciplinary hearing may well be held to render it invalid because of the pressure put on the employee: *Read v Phoenix Preservation Ltd* [1985] ICR 164, [1985] IRLR 93.

13 *McLaren v National Coal Board* [1988] ICR 370, [1988] IRLR 215, CA. It will, however, normally be reasonable for the employer to rely on the *fact* of conviction when making his decision, see p. 481, n. 1, above.

14 *Monie v Coral Racing Ltd* [1981] ICR 109, [1980] IRLR 464, CA. This decision was applied to a case of suspected *negligence* by one of two fitters in *McPhie v Wimpey Waste Management Ltd* [1981] IRLR 316 and to a case of incapability in *Whitbread & Co plc v Thomas* [1988] ICR 135, [1988] IRLR 43. In *Parr v Whitbread & Co plc* [1990] ICR 427, [1990] IRLR 39 it was applied to one of four; the case contains useful guidance from Wood P.

15 *Johnson Matthey Metals Ltd v Harding* [1978] IRLR 248, EAT.

c)   Redundancy[16]

The conceptual problem with redundancy in this context is that it is a dismissal which is at the same time ostensibly fair (in that the employer has no option but to dismiss) and unfair (in that the employee has done no wrong). The basic approach has therefore been to make it subject to a separate code (now Part XI of the 1996 Act, governing the statutory rights to redundancy payments), but to acknowledge that in some redundancy cases the employer may still be said to have acted unfairly, especially procedurally. With this background in mind we must look at the detailed rules.

Redundancy is a prima facie fair ground for dismissal. The employer must establish that redundancy was the principal reason for dismissal, since the statutory presumption of redundancy for the purposes of the redundancy payments scheme[17] is not applicable in an unfair dismissal claim[18]; once he has done so, a tribunal may not look behind that reason and consider whether the employer really was obliged to make employees redundant and if so whose fault it was – that economic decision remains with the employer[19], and if he succeeds in showing it as the principal reason his primary liability will only be to make the statutory redundancy payments. In a simple redundancy case, for example upon a properly conducted liquidation[20], that will be the appropriate action to bring, but it is also possible for a dismissed employee to claim both a redundancy payment and unfair dismissal[1], since a redundancy dismissal is only prima facie fair and may become unfair either under special statutory provisions, or under the general test of reasonableness contained in section 98(4).

A redundancy dismissal is deemed to be unfair by a combination now of section 153 of the Trade Union and Labour Relations (Consolidation) Act 1992 and section 105 of the Employment Rights Act 1996 if the employee can show that the circumstances producing the redundancy applied equally to other comparable employees[2] in the same undertaking who were not dismissed, and the applicant employee was chosen for dismissal because of union membership or activities, or non-membership[3] or for an 'inadmissible reason' (i.e. contrary to the special protection against dismissal because of pregnancy or childbirth, making health and safety complaints, asserting statutory rights, being a protected shopworker, acting as an employee representative or pension fund trustee, or exercising rights to the national minimum wage or under the Working Time Regulations or the protection given to whistleblowers). The aim of these provisions is to prevent an employer from using the more subtle technique of getting rid of perceived troublemakers or difficult cases by a later redundancy selection (an immediate dismissal on any of these grounds now being declared automatically unfair, see below).

There used to be a second ground of statutory unfair redundancy dismissal, which was where the dismissal was in breach of a collectively agreed redundancy

---

16   See *Harvey* D[1602], Q[722]n.
17   Employment Rights Act 1996, s. 170(2).
18   *Midland Foot Comfort Centre Ltd v Richmond* [1973] 2 All ER 294, [1973] IRLR 141.
19   *Moon v Homeworthy Furniture (Northern) Ltd* [1977] ICR 117, [1976] IRLR 298; *James W Cook & Co (Wivenhoe) Ltd v Tipper* [1990] ICR 716, [1990] IRLR 386, CA.
20   *Fox Bros (Clothes) Ltd v Bryant* [1979] ICR 64, [1978] IRLR 485.
1   Though he cannot receive double compensation: Employment Rights Act 1996, s. 122(4).
2   *Powers v A Clarke & Co (Smethwick) Ltd* [1981] IRLR 483.
3   This head of unfair dismissal generally is considered at p. 586, below.

procedure (or arrangement)[4]. The aim of this long-standing provision was to give statutory backing to such procedures. However, by 1994 the previous government took the view that it was out of line with their current thinking (being an element of the collective co-determination model of industrial relations that they had spent years dismantling); traditionally, such procedures had been heavily based on LIFO (last-in-first-out) which was seen by unions as, at least, the less unfair way of selecting employees[5]. However, in times of recession and declining union influence and recognition, many managers were seeking to move away from LIFO and towards far more rigorous procedures of selection on merit and ability, regardless of length of service. Redundancy procedures were thus being radically altered or scrapped altogether (at a time when large numbers of redundancies were having to be made, and when selection on merit was seen as an essential aid to business survival)[6] and so the decision was taken to repeal the statutory protection for redundancy procedures altogether[7]. The present government have shown no intention to reinstate it.

This removal of collectively-based safeguards in redundancy cases has placed even more emphasis on what has been the most important development in this branch of unfair dismissal law, namely that (in addition to any special statutory provisions) an employee may claim that his dismissal for redundancy was unfair *generally*, i.e. that, under section 98(4), the employer's conduct was unreasonable having regard to equity and the substantial merits of the case. This significant widening of the approach to redundancy cases was originally approved by the Court of Appeal in *Bessenden Properties Ltd v Corness*[8] and remains as important head of unfair dismissal, primarily because of the greater compensation available than the amount recoverable as a simple redundancy payment. This widening allows a tribunal some discretion to review the overall fairness of the dismissal and has led in the cases to the evolution of three general requirements upon an employer who is about to make an employee redundant[9]. The first is that he must not select that employee unfairly; blatant unfairness may be challenged in this way, but in many cases it will be difficult to establish for many different factors may be involved and so questions such as efficiency and suitability of the employee may arguably be just as reasonably relied upon as a general LIFO principle. The second is that the employer should make reasonable efforts where practicable to look for alternative employment within the firm (or possibly within the group to which the firm belongs[10]), though tribunals should not expect unrealistic efforts

---

4   This used to be contained in the EP(C)A 1978, s. 59(1)(b); for its interpretation in the case law, see the fifth edition of this book, at pp. 371–372.

5   In 1990 length of service as the criterion was found in 70 per cent of workplaces with a recognised union but in only 35 per cent of workplaces without such recognition: Millward et al. *Workplace Industrial Relations in Transition* (1992), p. 325. The survey also found that, where redundancy procedures still existed, there was no evidence of LIFO becoming less common.

6   This was commented on particularly in the ACAS Annual Reports 1991, p. 16 and 1992, p. 12.

7   Deregulation and Contracting Out Act 1994, s. 36.

8   [1977] ICR 821n, [1974] IRLR 338, CA.

9   These three requirements are now so well established that they should automatically be considered by a tribunal in an unfair redundancy case, even if not specifically raised by an applicant (e.g. where he or she is a litigant in person): *Langston v Cranfield University* [1998] IRLR 172, EAT.

10 *Vokes Ltd v Bear* [1974] ICR 1, [1973] IRLR 363; *Modern Injection Moulds Ltd v Price* [1976] ICR 370, [1976] IRLR 172. However, a requirement to look within the group, not just within the firm itself, was looked on with disfavour by the Scottish EAT in *Barratt Construction Ltd v Dalrymple* [1984] IRLR 385, and by the English EAT in *MDH Ltd v Sussex* [1986] IRLR 123, EAT.

to be made in what may be difficult circumstances[11]. The third is that, as a rule, the employer should consult the employee and give him reasonable warning of impending redundancy[12]; this requirement has been said to increase in importance the more the employer moves away from easily applied criteria for selection such as LIFO, towards more judgemental criteria based on work performance and company need[13]. On a general level, its importance has been strengthened by the renewed emphasis on procedure in *Polkey* (below), itself a redundancy dismissal case, in the light of which it has been subsequently said by the EAT that 'the importance of such consultation cannot be over-emphasised'[14].

These guidelines were reaffirmed and recast by the EAT in *Williams v Compair Maxam Ltd*[15], giving additional emphasis to two further criteria. The first is that where the employer recognises a union the necessary consultations will normally of course be with that union, and where this is the case the employer should give as much warning as possible of the impending redundancies, seek to agree criteria for selection with the union, review the eventual selection with the union to consider whether it is in accordance with those criteria and consider union representations on selection. This point will now have to be expanded to include the case where there is no recognised union but, because of the new rules requiring consultation with employee representatives[16], there are collective redundancies requiring by law such consultation; lack of it may affect the fairness of any eventual individual redundancies. One major point of difficulty is whether there has to be *double* consultation, i.e. with both union or employee representatives and individual employee. In *Walls Meat Co Ltd v Selby*[17] the Court of Appeal declined to lay down any principle requiring such two-stage consultation; on the other hand, Balcombe LJ did say that in a particular case good industrial practice might require it. The court did uphold a tribunal decision of unfair dismissal based on failure to consult the individual as well as the union,

11   *British United Shoe Machinery Co Ltd v Clarke* [1978] ICR 70, [1977] IRLR 297. In *Thomas and Betts Manufacturing Ltd v Harding* [1980] IRLR 255, CA, it was said that s. 98 is so wide that this may mean looking for other jobs for A to do, even if that means dismissing B instead (if B has less seniority than A), i.e. a 'bumping' redundancy (though cf the problems with this concept, p. 526, below); once again, however, the Scottish EAT has been unwilling to apply this wider approach: *Green v A&I Fraser (Wholesale Fish Merchants) Ltd* [1985] IRLR 55. Note that statutory preference (in finding other work) is given to (a) women on maternity leave when made redundant (Maternity and Parental Leave etc. Regulations 1999, S.I. 1999 No. 3312, reg. 10) and (b) disabled employees, where the employer is making reasonable adjustments (Disability Discrimination Act 1995, s. 6(3)(c); *Kent County Council v Mingo* [2000] IRLR 90).

12   *Clarkson International Tools Ltd v Short* [1973] ICR 191, [1973] IRLR 90; *Kelly v Upholstery and Cabinet Works (Amesbury) Ltd* [1977] IRLR 91; *British United Shoe Machinery Co Ltd v Clarke* [1978] ICR 70, [1977] IRLR 297; cf. *Atkinson v George Lindsay & Co* [1980] IRLR 196, Ct of Sess. The importance of this factor was reaffirmed by the EAT in *Freud v Bentalls Ltd* [1983] ICR 77, [1982] IRLR 443 and *Holden v Bradville Ltd* [1985] IRLR 483. The requirement is for warning *and* consultation, not just one: *Rowell v Hubbard Group Services* [1995] IRLR 195, EAT.

13   *Graham v ABF Ltd* [1986] IRLR 90; *Ferguson v Prestwick Circuits Ltd* [1992] IRLR 266. Small size of an enterprise may affect the level of consultation, but cannot excuse total lack of it: *De Grasse v Stockwell Tools Ltd* [1992] IRLR 269, EAT.

14   *Dyke v Hereford and Worcester County Council* [1989] ICR 800 at 807 per Wood J. A particularly useful summary of the consultation requirements is to be found in the judgment of Judge Clark in *Mugford v Midland Bank plc* [1997] ICR 399, [1997] IRLR 208.

15   [1982] ICR 156, [1982] IRLR 83.

16   See p. 64, above.

17   [1989] ICR 601, CA.

and other cases have assumed the need to involve the individual as well[18]. This will therefore be a matter heavily dependent on the circumstances of a particular case, with much discretion given to a tribunal, and resulting uncertainly for an employer in knowing whether he has done enough to resist an individual challenge of unfair dismissal. The second is that when working out criteria for selection (whether or not with union agreement) the emphasis must be on criteria which leave as little as possible to subjective assessments by the people making the selection, but rather are capable of being objectively applied on the basis of matters such as length of service, experience and efficiency[19].

The reaction to *Williams v Compair Maxam Ltd* has been mixed. It initially fared badly in the Scottish courts with the Scottish EAT showing itself unwilling to apply it to redundancies in smaller firms, especially when they are not unionised[20], and the Court of Session in *Buchanan v Tilcon Ltd*[1] taking a broader, less specific approach to redundancy cases, assuming that it will be relatively easy for an employer to show a redundancy dismissal to have been fair generally, once he has shown compliance with the specific statutory requirements. The English EAT, however, applied it[2], but subject to the qualification that this is an area in which it is particularly important that the tribunal should apply the 'range of reasonable responses' test[3] and not simply impose its own view as to how its members might have handled the redundancy[4]. There used to be a further qualification that even where the employer failed to carry out normal procedures, such a lapse could be forgiven if with hindsight it made no difference to the eventual result; this proposition was contained in a number of cases applying what was known generally as the rule in *British Labour Pump Co Ltd v Byrne*[5], but as we have seen several times already that rule was comprehensively disapproved by the House of Lords in *Polkey v A E Dayton Services Ltd*[6]. That case was itself, of course, an unfair redundancy case. Curiously, *Williams v Compair Maxam Ltd* was not specifically approved but, although Lord Mackay LC did not hold that a breach of normal procedure would invariably make a dismissal unfair, the overall effect of *Polkey* in reinstating procedural fairness as a central factor must be taken as backing for *Williams*. This was certainly the tenor of subsequent reported cases[7], a point of some significance given the generally high level of unfair redundancy claims in recent years, especially during times of recession.

---

18   In *Huddersfield Parcels Ltd v Sykes* [1981] IRLR 115 it was held that union consultation was not enough if the employee himself is left in the dark, and the general guidance on handling redundancies by Wood P in *Dyke v Hereford and Worcester County Council* [1989] ICR 800 assumes that, at least in most cases, consultation will be with both; *Rolls-Royce Motor Cars Ltd v Price* [1993] IRLR 203 is to like effect.

19   Thus, in *Williams v Compair Maxam Ltd* the redundancy was held to be unfair, partly on the ground that the criteria established by the employer (that those retained would be those 'who, in the opinion of the managers concerned, would be able to keep the company viable') lacked the necessary objectivity.

20   *Meikle v McPhail (Charleston Arms)* [1983] IRLR 351; *A Simpson & Son (Motors) v Reid and Findlater* [1983] IRLR 401; *Gray v Shetland Norse Preserving Co Ltd* [1985] IRLR 53.

1   [1983] IRLR 417, Ct of Sess.

2   *Grundy (Teddington) Ltd v Plummer* [1983] ICR 367, [1983] IRLR 98.

3   See p. 469, above.

4   *Grundy (Teddington) Ltd v Willis* [1976] ICR 323, [1976] IRLR 118; *Watling & Co Ltd v Richardson* [1978] ICR 1049, [1978] IRLR 255.

5   [1979] ICR 347, [1979] IRLR 94; see p. 469, above.

6   [1988] ICR 142, [1987] IRLR 503, HL.

7   *Walls Meat Co Ltd v Selby* [1989] ICR 601, CA; *Dyke v Hereford and Worcester County Council* [1989] ICR 800; *Ferguson v Prestwick Circuits Ltd* [1992] IRLR 266; *De Grasse v Stockwell Tools Ltd* [1992] IRLR 269; *Rolls-Royce Motor Cars Ltd v Price* [1993] IRLR 203, EAT.

However, possibly as a reaction to that high level of claims, two later Court of Appeal decisions have shown yet another potential change in emphasis, placing qualifications on findings of unfairness, and demonstrating again the volatility of this area of law. The first qualification concerns those cases where the normal procedures can reasonably be dispensed with. As stated above, *Polkey* does not require slavish adherence to procedures in cases where they could have no effect. The tendency was to look to Lord Bridge's speech for the exceptional case[8], which he described as being where the employer (subjectively) thought reasonably *at the time* that to go through the usual procedures would be meaningless; in such a case, the dismissal could still be fair. However, in *Duffy v Yeomans & Partners Ltd*[9] the Court of Appeal held that the proper description of the exception is that given by Lord Mackay LC, i.e. an objective test of whether the employer *could reasonably have concluded* at the time that to go through the usual procedures would be meaningless. This is more than semantics because the latter, objective, test could (if applied too loosely) come to bear an unfortunate resemblance to the old 'but it made no difference' test in *Byrne*'s case, which was disapproved in *Polkey*. There is a difference in principle (under *Duffy* the tribunal must still look at the date of dismissal, whereas *Byrne* allowed the unrestrained use of hindsight), but it is a point that may need careful handling by the tribunals.

The second qualification poses an even more fundamental question – given that (a) a tribunal cannot rule upon the business need for the redundancy, (b) it is therefore confined to judging the fairness of the *handling* of the situation by the employer, and (c) the modern tendency has been to replace more simple LIFO-based criteria with more complex and judgmental assessments of skill and worth (often on a points-scoring, 'brownie points', system), how closely should a tribunal investigate the fairness of the *application* of such a system? Should it just look at the general fairness of the system set up by the employer, or should it (as the applicant will probably want) investigate in detail the scoring of *all* the employees involved, in order to decide whether the applicant had been wrongly scored or harshly treated, and so unfairly selected? One point of procedure which may act as the focus for this whole question is the power of the tribunal to order discovery; if the employee chosen has been given his score, but the employer has refused to divulge the scores of the others under consideration, should a tribunal accede to that employee's request for an order for discovery of that further information (without which a detailed analysis of the application of the employer's selection scheme probably cannot be made in practice)? In *Eaton Ltd v King*[10] a selected employee was not given the scores of others not selected; moreover, at the tribunal hearing the only employer witness was the plant manager who had *reviewed* all the employee assessments but had not carried them out and could not say why any particular scores had been awarded. In spite of this, the Scottish EAT held that the dismissal was not unfair, commenting that all that the employer has to prove is that the method of selection was fair, and was generally applied reasonably by the responsible manager(s); moreover effective consultation did not require the divulging of information on other employees. In itself, this case could merely have been an example of the more trenchant

---

8   See *Robertson v Magnet Ltd* [1993] IRLR 512, EAT.
9   [1995] ICR 1, [1994] IRLR 642, CA; see Wynn (1995) 24 ILJ 272.
10 [1995] IRLR 75 (revsd on other grounds by the Court of Session: sub nom *King v Eaton Ltd* [1996] IRLR 199).

approach normally taken by the Scottish courts to redundancy dismissal cases[11].
However, the same approach was taken (and the case approved) subsequently by
the Court of Appeal in *British Aerospace plc v Green*[12], where an order for discovery
was refused and, on the substantive point at issue, Waite LJ summed up the view
of the whole court as follows:

> 'Employment law recognises, pragmatically, that an over-minute
> investigation of the selection process by the tribunal members may run the
> risk of defeating the purpose which the tribunals were called into being to
> discharge – namely, a swift, informal disposal of disputes arising from
> redundancy in the workplace. So in general the employer who sets up a
> system of selection which can reasonably be described as fair and applies it
> without any overt sign of conduct which mars its fairness will have done all
> that the law requires of him'[13].

It must be said at the outset that there was indeed a 'pragmatic' reason for refusing
discovery in this case because of its very scale – it involved the making redundant
(following the cancellation of a fighter contract) of 530 employees out of a
workforce of approximately 7,000. However, only one judge (Stuart-Smith LJ)
made any reference to the court's approach being restricted to mass redundancy
cases, and the two other judgments are in broad terms, which are capable of
causing severe problems because their premise is a denial that redundancy
selection operates on a comparative and competitive basis at all:

> 'Documents relating to retained employees are not likely to be relevant in
> any but the most exceptional circumstances. The question for the industrial
> tribunal, which must be determined separately for each applicant, is
> whether the applicant was unfairly dismissed, *not whether some other employee
> could have been fairly dismissed*'.[14]

This cannot, with respect, be correct; given that X redundancies have to be made
(which cannot be challenged) and that an inherently competitive points-scoring
system has been put into place to effect that, any consideration of the fairness of
selecting employee A *must* involve their comparison with those not chosen, and
whether the criteria have been properly applied; however distasteful it may be, a
challenge to the fairness of selecting A must include within it at least an implied
assertion that B or C should have been chosen instead. *British Aerospace* denies
this completely. Moreover, only two months later the EAT in *FDR Ltd v Holloway*[15]
effectively ignored *British Aerospace* and upheld an order for discovery of information
on employees not selected[16], stating that this was essential in order to dispose of

---

11   See above, p. 487. In particular, the EAT relied on the decision of the Court of Session in
     Buchanan v Tilcon Ltd [1983] IRLR 417.
12   [1995] ICR 1006, [1995] IRLR 433, CA.
13   At p. 434.
14   At p. 438, per Millett LJ (emphasis added).
15   [1995] IRLR 400. Quantitatively the case is at the opposite end of the scale, involving the
     making redundant of one employee out of eight.
16   On the question of discovery, the case is distinguishable – in *British Aerospace* the employees
     wanted the information to see if there were any faults in the selection, and this was
     disallowed on the ordinary principle of discovery that the court will not allow it for a
     'fishing expedition'; in *FDR* the EAT held that 'an issue' had already arisen (to which
     discovery could be attached) because the employee's suspicions were aroused by the
     retention of an employee with less service and a poorer record. In spite of this, it must be

the issue of whether the selection criteria had been applied fairly, and that a tribunal was *not* to take at face value an employer's assertion that it had all been done properly. These decisions are, quite simply, conflicting and in spite of the pure argument of precedent that the decision of the Court of Appeal should always apply it would be dangerous for an employer to assume that simple reliance could be placed on that decision in order to refuse disclosure of other scores as a matter of course. The Scottish EAT in *John Brown Engineering Ltd v Brown*[17] upheld a tribunal decision of unfair dismissal where the employers had refused to divulge scores (either to individuals or their representatives), stating that such a refusal may make individual consultation worthless, and the Court of Session in *King v Eaton Ltd (No 2)*[18] (the remedies stage of the original decision) simply stated in passing that 'the general reasons for trying to avoid that kind of enquiry [i.e. into individual scores] do not seem to us to be absolute'. As far as one can gather, the general approach in the tribunals has been to continue to order discovery of other employees' scores where appropriate, though it must be accepted that there is a problem of law here because of the uncompromising language in *British Aerospace*, which may eventually have to be referred to the House of Lords (for further guidance to follow on from that given in *Polkey*).

In addition to these general developments, there has been another, quite different, specific development which might add a further layer of complexity to redundancy cases. This was the decision of the EAT in *Clarke v Eley (IMI) Kynoch Ltd*[19] that a woman who is unjustifiably prejudiced on the grounds of sex by a selection procedure for redundancy may complain of indirect discrimination under the Sex Discrimination Act 1975[20]. In that case, the EAT held that a selection procedure based on part-timers going first was unlawful sexual discrimination (even though it was a procedure jointly agreed with a union and, under the unfair dismissal rules *alone*, probably fair), because of the predominance of women in part-time work. Thus, a redundancy selection may now have to be judged according to the sex discrimination legislation as well as the unfair dismissal provisions; if unlawful under the former, it will probably be unfair under the latter (even if ostensibly in line with the ordinary rules on fair and unfair redundancies). However, the volatility and indeed unpredictability of this area of law (particularly when allied to the modern approach of treating almost everything as a question of fact) is shown by the subsequent decision of the EAT

---

said that the EAT's treatment of *British Aerospace* is on the cavalier side of brusque – the judgment is short, citing hardly anything of the Court of Appeal judgments, and dismissing their ratio decidendi as 'certain observations' which had been 'misread' by counsel for the employers. Lord Denning himself could hardly have done better.

Where a recognised trade union is involved, it may be able instead to seek the information required on a collective level, under the TULR(C)A, s. 181, since the CAC have held that redundancy selection methods may remain in the sphere of collective bargaining, for the purpose of disclosure of bargaining information: see p. 60, n. 8, above.

17   [1997] IRLR 90; analytically, the case is less than helpful, because all it does is to rehearse the arguments for both sides and then decide it as a question of fact; arguably it is the actual *decision* that is significant.

18   [1998] IRLR 686; see particularly para. 21.

19   [1983] ICR 165, [1982] IRLR 482.

20   See p. 244, above.

in *Kidd v DRG (UK) Ltd*[1] upholding, on similar facts, a decision of an industrial tribunal that the dismissing as redundant of part-timers first was *not* unlawful discrimination (on the grounds of either sex or marital status) and that even if it was it was justified. However, even if *Clarke* is now thought generally applicable the effect in practice on redundancy might not be as disruptive as at first sight, for two reasons. Firstly, in the course of his judgment, Browne-Wilkinson J took pains to point out that, while 'part-timers first' may be of dubious legality (unless the company can clearly show justification), an ordinary application of LIFO will not be held to constitute unlawful sex discrimination; even if it may have some discriminatory effect (in that women often have been employed for shorter periods than men), that effect is too limited to be unlawful and in any event (as was pointed out by Wood P in *Brook v London Borough of Haringey*[2]) would readily be held to be justifiable in the light of the hitherto widespread acceptance of LIFO in industrial relations[3]. Secondly, a simple 'part-timers first' policy may now come within the Part Time Worker Directive anyway, in which case under the implementing Regulations there would be an obligation on the employer to justify it, presumably on grounds similar to those required by sex discrimination law.

d)   Dismissal on a transfer of undertaking[4]

A further head of unfair dismissal (arising where a business is transferred from one employer to another) was added by the Transfer of Undertakings (Protection of Employment) Regulations 1981[5], reg. 8, which states that the dismissal of any employee of the transferor or transferee on the transfer of an undertaking (whether before or after the transfer) is automatically unfair if the reason or principal reason for the dismissal was the transfer (or some reason connected with it). This can apply either where dismissal is due to the actual transfer taking place, or to the likelihood of an imminent transfer (e.g. where the undertaking is being 'slimmed down' with a view to a sale), as long as the causal link can be shown[6]. However, regulation 8(2) goes on to provide a defence to the employer if the dismissal was for an 'economic, technical or organisational reason entailing

1   [1985] ICR 405, [1985] IRLR 190. Waite J stressed the flexibility (a euphemism for unpredictability?) of the concept of indirect discrimination (see p. 410, above) and added, 'It would be unwise and unsafe, therefore, for anyone with a taste of drawing generalised conclusions to set the decision in the present case beside, for example, ... the earlier decision of the appeal tribunal in *Clarke v Eley (IMI) Kynock Ltd* for the sake of deriving supposed differences of principle from the fact that in apparently similar contexts they have arrived at opposite results. Any difference follows only from the application by the tribunals in those cases of flexible criteria to the varied circumstances confronting them' (at 417 and 196, respectively).
2   [1992] IRLR 478, EAT.
3   In the case itself, the (part) LIFO arrangement which was being challenged as discriminatory had been agreed by employer, union and ACAS. On the other hand, the case does perhaps show that if, in difficult times, employers (and unions) fall back on 'tried and tested' solutions, that may negate any advances made in other contexts towards greater equal opportunities.
4   See *Harvey* D[2201], R[188]; McMullen *Business Transfers and Employee Rights* ch. 6; Collins, 'Dismissals on transfers of a business' (1986) 15 ILJ 244; McMullen 'Takeovers, transfers and business reorganisations' (1992) 21 ILJ 15. The fundamental (and always difficult) question of when the regulations apply *at all* is considered at p. 160, above.
5   S.I. 1981 No. 1794, *Harvey* R[181].
6   *Morris v John Grose Group Ltd* [1998] ICR 655, [1998] IRLR 499, following on this point *Harrison Bowden Ltd v Bowden* [1994] ICR 186 and disapproving the narrower view in *Ibex Trading Co Ltd v Walton* [1994] ICR 907, [1994] IRLR 564, EAT.

changes in the workforce of either the transferor or the transferee'; this is a defence in as much as the dismissal is then deemed to be for a 'substantial reason' (within section 98(1)), but the employer must then go on to show that he acted reasonably in dismissing (within section 98(4))[7]. The potential effect of this, greatly to the transferee employer's disadvantage, was disclosed by the decision of the Court of Appeal in *Berriman v Delabole Slate Ltd*[8] that 'changes in the workforce' in the defence means changes in the composition of the workforce; mere changes in the terms and conditions of the workforce are not enough. On the other hand, if there are actual changes to the jobs of those transferred (e.g. as part of a reorganisation, but with a knock-on effect on terms and conditions) it was subsequently held in *Crawford v Swinton Insurance Brokers Ltd*[9] that that *can* constitute a 'change in the workforce' and so give rise to the regulation 8(2) ('ETO') defence. Clearly, there could be a thin line between these two outcomes, with allegations by the employees that the job changes were a sham, aimed at avoiding the regulations. If, however, a transferee employer falls on the wrong side of the line, he will face the problem that if he buys the undertaking wishing to keep the existing workforce (or, indeed, simply *having* to take them because of the provisions in regulation 5 on automatic transfer of contracts), but then proceeds to alter their terms and conditions (for example to bring them into line with terms and conditions in the establishments that he already runs), the workforce could walk out, claim constructive dismissal and the defence in regulation 8(2) would *not* apply. The boomerang effect of this could have been that, far from *protecting* the employment of those in the transferred undertaking, it put the emphasis on the transferee employer making it a condition of purchase that the transferor dismisses the workforce as redundant before the sale, in an attempt to ensure that the transferee did not 'inherit' them at all[10]. However, as pointed out at p. 166 above, this form of evasion has been effectively countered by the decision of the House of Lords in *Litster v Forth Dry Dock and Engineering Co Ltd*[11]. The end result is a considerable level of legal protection through the

---

7   *McGrath v Rank Leisure Ltd* [1985] ICR 527, [1985] IRLR 323. Where the r. 8(2) defence works in a redundancy context, the tribunal should go on to decide on fairness on the ordinary principles of unfair redundancy selection (above): *Warner v Adnet Ltd* [1998] IRLR 394, CA. In *Whitehouse v Chas A Blatchford & Sons Ltd* [1999] IRLR 492 the Court of Appeal held (contrary to previous understanding) that a dismissal must be *either* because of transfer (Reg. 8(1)) *or* because of an ETO reason (r. 8(2)); according to *Kerry Foods Ltd v Creber* [2000] IRLR 10 this means that if there is an ETO reason but the dismissal is then found unfair, liability for it remains on the transferor.

8   [1985] ICR 546, [1985] IRLR 305, CA, noted McMullen (1986) 49 MLR 524.

9   [1990] ICR 85, [1990] IRLR 42, EAT.

10   This appeared possible in the light of the decision in *Secretary of State for Employment v Spence* [1986] ICR 651, [1986] IRLR 248, CA that the continuity of employment provisions only apply to those in employment with the transferor at the moment of transfer.

11   [1989] ICR 341, [1989] IRLR 161, HL, applying the decision of the ECJ in *P Bork International A/S (in liquidation) v Foreningen af Arbejdsledere i Danmark*: 101/87 [1989] IRLR 41, to the effect that the continuity provisions in reg. 5 must be read subject to these provisions in reg. 8, so that if a dismissal is contrary to the latter the employee is to be deemed still in the transferor's employment at the time of transfer, for the purposes of reg. 5. According to the Scottish EAT in *Anderson v Dalkeith Engineering Ltd* [1985] ICR 66, [1984] IRLR 429 the transferor employer may have the reg. 8(2) defence ('economic, technical or organisational' reasons), if he shows that he was obliged to sack the workforce by the intending purchaser as a condition of sale; however, this was not followed by the English EAT in *Wheeler v Patel* [1987] ICR 631, [1987] IRLR 211 for two reasons – 1) it did too much violence to the employee's rights under reg. 8(1); 2) 'economic' was to be read *ejusdem generis* with 'technical' and 'organisational', so that the reason must relate to the conduct of the business itself, not just its attractiveness to a buyer; this decision was

actual transfer for employees covered by the Regulations, and their existing terms and conditions. Indeed, that protection was taken further by the decision of the EAT in *Wilson v St Helens Borough Council*[12] that any transfer-related change of terms of employment by the transferee employer is *void*, even if (as a matter of ordinary contract law) freely agreed to by the employees and for good consideration (e.g. a lump sum buy out of some of the old terms). This bombshell decision led to much inventiveness in ways to escape the conundrum that it posed for employers trying to rationalise terms and conditions after the transfer. One such way involved construction of regulation 8 indirectly – on appeal, *Wilson* became joined with another case[13] where the tactic had been adopted of firing the staff and re-hiring them on the new terms; was this effective? It was argued for the employees that it was not, but that involved arguing that regulation 8 meant (in order to apply the Acquired Rights Directive properly) that a dismissal in breach of it was *invalid*. This approach was adopted by the Court of Appeal[14] but was arguably too radical an approach for ordinary domestic employment law and, when the two cases were finally heard by the House of Lords,[15] an element of orthodoxy was reasserted – in a 'fire and re-hire' case, the dismissals are effective, and the staff are taken back on by the transferee employer on the *new* terms. However, the disadvantage to the employer is that in such a case the staff, though still in his employment, could claim unfair dismissal from their previous contracts; indeed, on one occasion the EAT said that compensation for unfair dismissal could amount to the 'price' of the change of terms.[16] In the unfair dismissal action, regulation 8(1) would of course apply and, on the facts and in the light of its interpretation above, regulation 8(2) would be unlikely to afford a defence where the only employer motive was a transfer-related rationalisation of terms. As spelled out by the House of Lords, the only way out of the conundrum other than the fire and re-fire tactic (with the danger of unfair dismissal actions) is to break the causal link between the transfer and the change of terms (e.g. where it can be shown that wider changes were being made anyway to all employees' jobs and terms), so that the initial *Wilson* invalidity does not apply.

e) Health and safety protection

In order to comply with the Framework Directive on the introduction of measures to encourage improvements in the safety and health of workers at work[17], the

---

subsequently followed by the Scottish EAT (rather than *Anderson*) in *Gateway Hotels Ltd v Stewart* [1988] IRLR 287. There is nothing in the decision of the House of Lords in *Litster* to contradict this later interpretation of the defence; indeed, it is entirely in line with their Lordships' views in that case as to the interpretation of the Regulations generally.

12 [1996] ICR 711, [1996] IRLR 320; see p. 163, above.
13 *Meade and Baxendale v British Fuels Ltd* [1996] IRLR 541.
14 [1998] ICR 387, [1997] IRLR 505, CA.
15 Sub nom *British Fuels Ltd v Baxendale; Wilson v St Helens Borough Council* [1998] ICR 1141, [1998] IRLR 706, HL.
16 *Cornwall County Care Ltd v Brightman* [1998] ICR 529 [1998] IRLR 228, decided before the House of Lords gave judgment in *Wilson*, and having to struggle with the solution proposed by the Court of Appeal (the invalid dismissal), which the EAT considered unworkable; the EAT's view was then cited with approval by the House of Lords in *Wilson*.
17 Directive 89/391/EEC; most of the requirements of this Directive were put into domestic law by the Management of Health and Safety at Work Regulations 1992, with effect from 1 January 1993; see p. 762, below. However, the Directive also contains (in Arts. 7.2, 8.4, 8.5 and 11.4) directions to member states requiring protection for workers and workers' representatives from detrimental treatment and rights to take direct action to counter imminent dangers.

Trade Union Reform and Employment Rights Act 1993 inserted what is now section 100 of the Employment Rights Act 1996. This makes a dismissal automatically unfair if the reason (or, if more than one, the principal reason) was that the employee:

1) having been designated by the employer to carry out health and safety functions, carries out or proposed to carry out such activities;
2) being a safety representative or member of a safety committee, performed or proposed to perform such functions, or acted as an elected worker representative of employee safety (or took part in an election for such position)[18];
3) (where there was no representative or committee, or it was not reasonably practicable to raise the matter with them) brought to his employer's attention, by reasonable means, harmful or potentially harmful circumstances;
4) left the place of work, or refused to return to it, in circumstances of danger which he reasonably believed to be serious or imminent and which he could not reasonably have been expected to avert[19]; or
5) in such circumstances, took or proposed to take appropriate steps to protect himself or others from the danger[20].

In addition to the automatic unfairness, extra protection is achieved in the following ways:

1) the normal qualifying period and age limit do not apply;
2) any selection for redundancy because of the above factors is automatically unfair;[1]
3) the normal exclusions of tribunal jurisdiction in cases of dismissal while taking part in industrial action do not apply[2];
4) interim relief is available[3];
5) in addition to these unfair dismissal provisions, section 44 of the 1996 Act gives an employee a right not to have action *short of* dismissal taken against him on the above grounds, and a right to complain to a tribunal of any such detrimental treatment[4].

---

18 See p. 759, below. To have this protection, the safety representative must have been acting within the scope of his responsibilities or jurisdiction: *Shillito v Van Leer (UK) Ltd* [1997] IRLR 495 (a case under the parallel provisions of s. 44 on victimisation short of dismissal on these grounds); once that is the case, the protection is wide covering the exercise of the functions *and* the manner of doing so: *Goodwin v Cabletel UK Ltd* [1998] ICR 112, [1997] IRLR 665, EAT.

19 The danger in question can cover threats from another employee, not just for machinery or chemicals: *Harvest Press Ltd v McCaffrey* [1999] IRLR 778, EAT.

20 Whether steps were appropriate must be judged by reference to all the circumstances, including the employee's state of knowledge, and the facilities and advice available to him: s. 100(2). The special protection in 5) does not apply if the employer shows that it was so negligent for the employee to take those steps that a reasonable employer might have dismissed him for taking them: s. 100(3). This derogation is specifically permitted by Art. 8(3) of the Directive. The reference to danger to 'others' primarily means other employees *but* it has been held that it an apply more widely, e.g. to customers or members of the public: *Masiak v City Restaurants (UK) Ltd* [1999] IRLR 780, EAT.

1 This protection is neutral; it does not put the representative/complainant into a *better* position in redundancy selection: *Smiths Industries Aerospace and Defence Systems v Rawlings* [1996] IRLR 656, EAT.

2 For those exclusions, see p. 635, below.

3 For interim relief see p. 580, below.

4 This is closely modelled on the remedy for action short of dismissal taken on union or non-union grounds, see p. 576, below.

While an employee dismissed for making health and safety complaints had some protection previously under the ordinary unfair dismissal law, it was patchy[5]. These provisions are therefore an important step forward. Unlike most of unfair dismissal law, they are the product of an EC directive and this may mark them apart for two reasons: 1) arguments may arise that they in fact do not go far enough to meet the standards required by the directive (in which case an applicant may try to claim rights directly under the directive, if not covered by the new domestic provisions); 2) in any event, in the light of the purposive interpretation to be given to domestic provisions enacting EC directives[6], it may be necessary for a tribunal considering a claim under this new law to keep an eye on the wording and intent of the directive as a guide to interpretation[7]. One further point to note is that a person making health and safety complaints in a more public arena may now also have protection under the Public Interest Disclosure Act 1998, as a protected 'whistleblower'.[8]

f) Assertion of statutory rights

The Trade Union Reform and Employment Rights Act 1993 inserted a new provision (now section 104 of the Employment Rights Act 1996) making a dismissal automatically unfair if the reason (or principal reason) for it was that the employee had brought proceedings against the employer to enforce a 'relevant statutory right' or had alleged infringement by the employer of such a right[9]; this does not apply if the dismissal was because of an allegation that was false and not made in good faith. The following rights are laid down as 'relevant statutory rights':

1) any right conferred by the 1996 Act, for which the remedy is by way of a complaint to an employment tribunal;
2) the right to notice laid down in section 86 of the 1996 Act;
3) the rights conferred by the Trade Union and Labour Relations (Consolidation) Act 1992 relating to deductions from pay, union activities and time off;
4) the rights conferred by the Working Time Regulations 1998.

As with health and safety complaints (above), any redundancy selection because of such assertion of statutory rights is made automatically unfair and the normal qualifying period and age limit do not apply. The latter point may be particularly significant where the alleged breach relates to the provisions on unlawful deductions (originally in the Wages Act 1986 and now in Part II of the 1996 Act), since that protection has no qualifying period, but in the past the exercise of the employee's rights under it was always dangerous if that employee lacked the qualifying period for ordinary unfair dismissal.

---

5   An employee without the necessary continuous employment was unprotected, unless he could show that the dismissal was for trade union reasons; however, a health and safety complaint taken up on an individual basis was unlikely to qualify as 'union activities': *Chant v Aquaboats Ltd* [1978] 3 All ER 102, [1978] ICR 643, EAT.

6   *Litster v Forth Dry Dock and Engineering Co Ltd* [1989] ICR 341, [1989] IRLR 161, HL.

7   Smith, Goddard and Randall *Health and Safety – the New Legal Framework* (1993) ch. 15.

8   See p. 141, above.

9   There are two gaps in the protection, due to this emphasis on the employee having complained of infringement – (1) if the employer has allowed the right in question (e.g. to time off for public duties), but then dismisses (before the qualifying period is served) because tired of having to allow it, that is not within the statutory protection; (2) it is not enough that on the facts the employee *could* have brought a complaint: *Mennell v Newell & Wright (Transport Contractors) Ltd* [1997] IRLR 519, CA.

g)   Further specific protection

We have seen recently the addition to the long-standing general rules on unfair dismissal of several specific categories of special protection to meet particular concerns. As seen above, the Trade Union Reform and Employment Rights Act 1993 gave such protection to health and safety representatives/complainants and to those asserting their statutory rights. In addition, there is now special coverage for (1) protected shop workers and betting workers, who may not be dismissed for refusing to work on Sundays[10], (2) employees appointed as member-nominated trustees of their pension fund, under the Pensions Act 1995, who may not be dismissed for exercising their functions as such[11], (3) employees elected (or seeking election) as employee representatives for the purposes of consultation over collective redundancies or transfers of undertakings, who may not be dismissed for performing, or proposing to perform, any such functions or activities[12], and (4) employees exercising rights under the Working Time Regulations 1998, the Public Interest Disclosure Act 1998, the National Minimum Wage Act 1998 or the Tax Credits Act 1999 who may not be dismissed for any such reason[13]. In each case, there is also protection from victimisation short of dismissal.

The form of the special protection is becoming familiar (in effect now being adopted 'off the peg' by the draftsman) – a dismissal on these grounds is automatically unfair, as is any later selection for redundancy; the normal qualifying period for unfair dismissal does not apply, and neither does the normal age limit. In the cases of pension trustees, employee representatives and complaints by whistleblowers or under the Working Time Regulations there are further provisions making interim relief available. The need for the extra protection for employee representatives is presumably strengthened by the fact that it is backed by EC Directives, which could give rise to arguments that any lesser provision failed to enact those Directives fully; with this background, there is a further protective provision in their case, namely that (as in the case of health and safety representatives/complainants and working time complainants who are also covered by EC Directives) the normal exclusions of tribunal jurisdiction in cases of dismissal while taking part in unofficial or official industrial action do not apply, so that the employer cannot use those immunities as a cover for getting rid selectively of elected representatives.

h)   Changing business needs and re-organisation[14]

Although cases where employees are dismissed consequent upon a reorganisation are not treated separately in the legislation, they are worth special consideration since they form one particular head of 'some other substantial reason' which has evolved through the cases and which demonstrates how difficult it is to draw the line between fairness and unfairness where there is a clear conflict between the

---

10   Employment Rights Act 1996, s. 101; for the status of protected shop or betting workers, see p. 194, above.
11   Ibid, s. 102.
12   Collective Redundancies and Transfer of Undertakings (Protection of Employment) (Amendment) Regulations 1995, S.I. 1995 No. 2587, reg. 14; for the election of representatives, see p. 65, above.
13   Employment Rights Act 1996, ss. 101A, 103A, 104A, 104B respectively.
14   See *Harvey* D [1854].

employer's legitimate business interests and the employee's contractual rights. The problem arises where the employer wishes to re-organise his operation in such a way that there will have to be changes in the employee's job, or in the way he carries it out (e.g. changes relating to hours, shifts, wages, job content or location); the employee's contract, however, is static and so prima facie he can insist upon continued performance of it as it stands. To achieve a sensible balance, the employer must somehow be allowed to make changes necessary for the efficiency (and in an extreme case the survival) of the enterprise[15], but in ordinary contract law he may not make unilateral alterations to existing contracts of employment. If he attempts to do so the employee has a common law action for breach of contract[16] and, more significantly, may under the legislation walk out because of it and claim to have been constructively dismissed through the employer's breach[17]; alternatively, the employer may dismiss the employee who refuses to change by giving him proper notice, which is lawful at common law but is of course a dismissal for statutory purposes and so either way the employer lays himself open to an unfair dismissal claim. From the decided cases, it appears that there are three possibilities in such a case:

1) It may be that the proposed changes are such that, on a proper construction, they fall within the permissible range of managerial discretion to organise the work[18] or indeed within the proper ambit of the contractual job description for that employee anyway. This will be particularly so if the changes are minor or of an administrative nature, if they can be construed merely as an up-dating of essentially the same job (seen in the light possibly of an implied term of the contract that the employee will adapt to new methods and techniques reasonably required of him[19]), or if the job description in fact covers jobs A and B but the employee, used to doing only A in practice, refuses to do B instead, for it is the contractual term which counts, not any particular practice which evolved, and so a skilfully drafted contractual job description could perhaps anticipate and cover subsequent re-organisations. If this is the case, the changes are not sufficiently major to constitute a breach of contract and so if the employee still refuses to accept them and is dismissed, that will be a dismissal for refusal to obey a lawful order and so probably fair; likewise, if the employee walks out because of such changes, it will not

---

15   This has been recognised in the context of redundancy law: *Chapman v Goonvean and Rostowrack China Clay Co Ltd* [1973] 1 All ER 218, [1973] ICR 50; *Johnson v Nottinghamshire Combined Policy Authority* [1974] ICR 170, [1974] IRLR 20, CA; *Lesney Products & Co Ltd v Nolan* [1977] ICR 235, [1977] IRLR 77, CA.

16   This can take the form of an action for wages due under the old contract, on the old terms, and can be an effective tactic: *Burdett-Coutts v Hertfordshire County Council* [1984] IRLR 91 (concerning unilateral changes to dinner ladies' terms and conditions, a fruitful source of important case law in the mid-1980s); *Rigby v Ferodo Ltd* [1988] ICR 29, [1987] IRLR 516, HL; see p. 174, above. Unless the employer can show a variation of contract, assented to by the employee, he will lose the common law action, and will then have to force the issue by dismissing those who refuse to accept the changes and taking his chances in an unfair dismissal action (discussed below).

17   *Greenaway Harrison Ltd v Wiles* [1994] IRLR 380, EAT.

18   See p. 119, above.

19   *Cresswell v Board of Inland Revenue* [1984] ICR 508, [1984] IRLR 190 (computerisation of PAYE system still within the ambit of the existing contracts of those operating the system, who were expected to adapt); see p. 130, above.

constitute constructive dismissal. He will therefore not receive a redundancy payment or compensation for unfair dismissal[20].

2) If the changes are more major and would actually cause a decrease in the employee's work, that may constitute redundancy within the definition in the Employment Rights Act 1996, section 139[1]. If so, the dismissed employee may be eligible for a redundancy payment but, as redundancy is a prima facie fair ground for dismissal, he may not be able to claim unfair dismissal[2] (unless the redundancy was itself unfair – see (c) 'Redundancy', above). This solution (probably highly acceptable to the employer) is more likely to occur now, with the emphasis of the Court of Appeal in *Murphy v Epsom College*[3] on looking at the 'kind of work' that the dismissed employee was employed to do; if on the reorganisation it can be said that the kind of work changed and the employee was incapable of performing the new kind of work, then he may be dismissed as redundant even though a new employee (skilled in the new kind of work) is taken on to replace him, i.e. where there is *no* net loss in the number of employees required at the end of the day.

3) If the changes are major but do not produce in law a redundancy (e.g. where the work is undiminished but the hours and remuneration have to change), it is well established that the re-organisation *can* constitute 'some other substantial reason' within section 98(1), in which case there will be no redundancy payment and the employee may not be able to succeed in a claim for unfair dismissal[4]. This is the type of case which causes most problems, for to reach that result the tribunal in effect has to give precedence to the employer's business needs over the employee's normal contractual and statutory rights, and allow the employer to insist upon a unilateral variation of the contract without incurring a finding of unfair dismissal[5]. It is the section 98(4) concept of reasonableness which holds the balance – given that the re-organisation is a substantial reason which *can* justify dismissal, was the dismissal of the recalcitrant employee *in fact* justified on the facts of the particular case? The tribunal is therefore looking at the reasonableness of the employer's handling of the change, and in essence looking to see whether

20 *George Wimpey & Co Ltd v Cooper* [1977] IRLR 205; *Glitz v Watford Electric Co Ltd* [1979] IRLR 89. In the latter case the EAT pointed out that in a small firm or unit the job descriptions may necessarily be more vague, allowing the employer to expect greater flexibility and adaptability from his employees.

1 See p. 524, below.

2 *Wilson v Underhill House School Ltd* [1977] IRLR 475; *Robinson v British Island Airways Ltd* [1978] ICR 304, [1977] IRLR 477, EAT.

3 [1985] ICR 80, [1984] IRLR 271, CA (dismissal of plumber held to be for redundancy where a modern heating system installed and a heating engineer appointed to replace him). The case also shows that an employer can run *both* redundancy *and*, in the alternative, some other substantial reason (through reorganisation) as defences, provided both are properly considered at the tribunal hearing.

4 *RS Components Ltd v Irwin* [1973] ICR 535, [1973] IRLR 239; *Wilson's* Case and *Robinson's* case, n. 2 above; *Hollister v National Farmers' Union* [1979] ICR 542, [1979] IRLR 238, CA; *Genower v Ealing, Hammersmith and Hounslow Area Health Authority* [1980] IRLR 297; *Farrant v Woodroffe School* [1998] ICR 184, [1998] IRLR 176. Cf., however, *Labour Party v Oakley* [1988] ICR 403, [1988] IRLR 34, CA where the reorganisation was shown on the facts to be a pretext for dismissing someone they had already decided to dispense with.

5 The existence of a 'dismissal' will normally be clear, through either (a) an express dismissal by the employer of the refusenik, (b) a constructive dismissal if the employee leaves, or (c) an application of the rule that a unilateral change can be so fundamental as the constitute termination of the old contract by the employer, even where the employee in fact carries on working (under, in effect, a new contract), as in *Hogg v Dover College* [1990] ICR 39, affirmed in *Alcan Extrusions Ltd v Yates* [1996] IRLR 327, EAT.

the time had come when the employer had no further option but to dismiss the employee in order to put into effect the necessary changes. In doing so, the tribunal may have to consider three questions –

a) Was the re-organisation necessary? Although it is not for the tribunal to decide how the employer ought to run his business and the employer's genuine belief in the necessity for changes is likely to be paramount, a tribunal may expect the employer to lead evidence showing why he thought change necessary and how he reached the particular decisions in question[6]. In one of the original cases, *Ellis v Brighton Co-operative Society Ltd*[7], the EAT seemed to assume that in order to justify eventual dismissals for non-compliance, the changes had to be so vital that if they were not put into effect the whole business would be brought to a standstill, but this was held by the Court of Appeal to be too restrictive in *Hollister v National Farmers' Union*[8] where it was said that it is sufficient if there is a good, sound business reason for the re-organisation. This approach leaves a great deal in the employer's discretion, and indeed the area of business reorganisations has produced many findings of fair dismissal. In *Evans v Elemeta Holdings Ltd*[9] the EAT appeared to move in the direction of redressing this imbalance by concentrating more upon examining the changes imposed by the employer and considering whether it was *reasonable for the employee to reject them* (the case itself concerning major changes to overtime obligations, disadvantageous to the employee). However, in the event this case did not lead to a significant development in this area, for it did not decide what was to happen in the most difficult class of case, i.e. where it was reasonable for the employee to reject the changes because of their effect on his livelihood, but equally it was reasonable for the employer to insist upon them because of the needs of his business; the fact that one party was acting reasonably does *not* mean that the other was therefore acting unreasonably. On those grounds, a differently constituted EAT soon afterwards refused to follow *Evans* in *Chubb Fire Security Ltd v Harper*[10]. In that case, a middle way of sorts was suggested, namely that a tribunal might consider whether the employer had acted reasonably in deciding that the advantages of the reorganisation to him outweighed the disadvantages to the employee. This is an interesting approach but it was stressed subsequently that this is only a *factor* (not a test) for a tribunal to consider when deciding whether the dismissal was fair within section 98(4) (as being within the range of reasonable responses that an employer faced with the employee's

---

6   *Banerjee v City and East London Area Health Authority* [1979] IRLR 147; *Ladbroke Courage Holidays Ltd v Asten* [1981] IRLR 59; in *Orr v Vaughan* [1981] IRLR 63 it was said that, while business reorganisations are basically for the employer to decide upon, the tribunal must be satisfied that, at the least, the employer came to his decision on reasonable information reasonably acquired.

7   [1976] IRLR 419.

8   [1979] ICR 542, [1979] IRLR 238; *Bowater Containers Ltd v McCormack* [1980] IRLR 50. Outside pressure for change, e.g. from customers or insurers, may be a relevant factor, but the employer must still establish that he handled the pressure reasonably; *Scott Packing and Warehousing Ltd v Paterson* [1978] IRLR 166; *Dobie v Burns International Security Services (UK) Ltd* [1984] ICR 812, [1984] IRLR 329, CA.

9   [1982] ICR 323, [1982] IRLR 143.

10   [1983] IRLR 311; applied in *Catamaran Cruisers Ltd v Williams* [1994] IRLR 386.

refusal to change might have adopted)[11]; this is ultimately the test and its application, here as elsewhere, is a question of fact for the tribunal, as the Court of Appeal has emphasised[12].

b)   Given the re-organisation plan, was it necessary to insist upon changing the employee's job in order to put that plan into effect? In many cases, the answer may simply be 'Yes', particularly where the employee is in a key position. It may be, however, that if only one or two employees are holding out, and their concurrence is not absolutely vital, the employer may be expected to consider any minor alterations to his plan which might accommodate those employees without frustrating the re-organisation[13].

c)   Was there sufficient consultation? Consultation with the employee and perhaps his union has been seen in the past as one of the major requirements of a fair dismissal in these cases and it is clear that if the employer does negotiate a re-organisation with the relevant union or with the majority of the employees and one employee still holds out, that agreement will considerably strengthen his hand if he then dismisses that employee. Thus, it has been said by the EAT that there must be proper consultation, not just the presentation of a fait accompli or ultimatum[14], and that the employer should consider any counterproposals put forward by the employee, and should bear in mind the position of the individual employee, which may not be done if he treats all cases as one, for example by just consulting a weak union or staff association[15]. However, in *Hollister v National Farmers' Union*[16] the Court of Appeal held that too much emphasis had been placed upon consultation in past cases, to the point that the EAT was in danger of putting a gloss upon the simple reasonableness test in section 98(4)– consultation is only one of the factors to be considered when looking at the circumstances of the case, and so lack of it (as in that case, where the changes were just announced to the employee) is not necessarily fatal to the employer's case. It is likely, however, that (if and when the matter is tested again) there will be a move back towards more emphasis on consultation in this area in the light of the decision of the House of Lords in *Polkey v A E Dayton Services Ltd*[17], which concerned consultation in the context of redundancy dismissals, but in the subsequent case law has taken on wider significance.

Thus, to recap, the employer who wishes to re-organise parts of his business should first attempt to gain the agreement of the affected employees to variations

---

11   *Richmond Precision Engineering Ltd v Pearce* [1985] IRLR 179. One point in this case had to be rectified subsequently, for it was suggested that the test is the reasonableness of the employer's *offer*; in fact, the correct test (under s. 98) is the reasonableness of the decision to *dismiss* because of the employee's *refusal* of the offer: *St John of God (Care Services) Ltd v Brooks* [1992] ICR 715, [1992] IRLR 546. Further factors to consider may include how many other employees had accepted the changes and the attitude of any trade union involved: *Caramaran Cruisers Ltd v Williams* [1994] IRLR 386. The existence of a financial inducement to 'buy out' the old terms may also be relevant.
12   *Gilham v Kent County Council (No 2)* [1985] ICR 233, [1985] IRLR 18, CA.
13   *Martin v Automobile Proprietary Ltd* [1979] IRLR 64.
14   *Ellis v Brighton Co-operative Society Ltd* [1976] IRLR 419.
15   *Martin v Automobile Proprietary Ltd* [1979] IRLR 64. Presumably this would require some form of individual consultation in the case of a non-unionist.
16   N. 8, above.
17   [1988] ICR 142, [1987] IRLR 503, HL; see p. 487, above.

in their contractual terms. If this is not forthcoming but the changes are still necessary, he may order unilaterally such changes as are permissible within the scope of the contracts of employment (and the amount of managerial discretion left to him under their terms); if an employee refuses to accept this category of change he may be dismissed for disobedience. Alternatively, if the changes alter the kind of work required and lead to a definite diminution in the requirements for the kind of work that the employee was engaged to perform, then the employee may be made redundant (with a redundancy payment but, provided a proper procedure was adopted, no compensation for unfair dismissal). However, if the case falls outside these two possibilities (i.e. where there is no redundancy, but the changes are major enough to involve definite variations of contract) the employer should usually follow some consultative procedure (depending on the facts of the case), but if an employee still refuses to change he may dismiss him, or insist upon the changes and be prepared to concede that that employee was constructively dismissed if he still refuses and walks out; in either event, he can then argue that the dismissal (actual or constructive[18]) was fair in the light of the necessity for change, the need to alter the employee's job within the scheme of the reorganisation and the consultative procedure which he adopted. However, it must be remembered in these cases that a finding of fairness jeopardises what would normally be the employee's contractual and statutory rights, and so should not be arrived at lightly.

iv) Remedies for unfair dismissal

The statutory rules governing remedies for unfair dismissal were altered by the Employment Protection Act 1975 which split compensation into a basic award and a compensatory award, and sought to strengthen the provisions relating to the direct remedies of reinstatement and re-engagement in an attempt to make them the primary remedies in practice as well as in theory; the figures have consistently shown that this aim has not been achieved[19], and so compensation remains the prime remedy in most cases. The rules governing remedies are contained in sections 111-132 of the Employment Rights Act 1996. In addition, now that dismissal for trade union reasons is covered by the Trade Union and Labour Relations (Consolidation) Act 1992, there are special provisions in sections 161-166 of that Act relating to 'interim relief' which may serve to keep a contract of employment subsisting while a complaint in such cases is considered; such interim relief was extended by the Trade Union Reform and Employment Rights Act 1993 to the new head of dismissal for health and safety reasons and then to cases involving pension trustees, employee representatives, working time complaints and whistleblowers, and so equivalent provisions now appear in the 1992 and 1996 Acts. The normal remedies are now considered in turn, along with the important concepts of contributory fault and mitigation, either of which

---

18 The fact that a dismissal is constructive does not automatically mean that it is unfair: see p. 447, n. 4, above, and particularly *Savoia v Chiltern Herb Farms Ltd* [1982] IRLR 166, CA.

19 In 1998/99 32,632 unfair dismissal cases were disposed of (out of a total of 74,006 in all jurisdictions). Of these, 21,448 (66 per cent) were settled without a hearing, either by an ACAS conciliated settlement (13,033) or by some other form of withdrawal (8,415). Of the 11,184 cases actually heard by a tribunal, 3,246 were upheld, a success rate of 29% (down from 40% the previous year); the success rate in all jurisdictions was 39%. The lowest success rate was in 1981 when it was only 23%. So much for received employer wisdom, still occasionally heard, that tribunals are Marxist conspiracies.

may decrease an award of compensation. As elsewhere in unfair dismissal law, it must be remembered that, although case law may be important in filling out the legislative bones (particularly in the area of the compensatory award), it is the wording of the statute which remains of paramount importance and the majority of cases are merely illustrations of the application of that wording.

a)   Reinstatement and re-engagement[20]

If a tribunal finds that a dismissal was unfair, it then proceeds to hear the parties on the question of remedies and by virtue of section 112 it must explain to the complainant the possible orders for reinstatement and re-engagement and ask whether he wishes the tribunal to make such an order.[1] An order for reinstatement means that the employer must take him back into his job; as he is in effect treated as not having been dismissed this means that he is entitled to any benefits he might reasonably have expected to receive during his period of dismissal, principally back pay (including any *improvement* of terms and conditions which he would have received during that period had he not been dismissed, but deducting any amounts actually received from the employer by way of wages in lieu or ex gratia payments, or from any employment during that period with another employer[2]); further, any other rights and privileges such as seniority and pension rights must be restored to him, and the tribunal must specify the date upon which reinstatement is to take effect. An order for re-engagement means that the employee must be taken back on by the employer (or by a successor or an associated employer[3]) in 'employment comparable to that from which he was dismissed or other suitable employment' on terms which are, so far as reasonably practicable, as favourable as if he had been reinstated; this too carries rights to back pay and preservation of accrued interests, and here the tribunal must specify not only the effective date of the order but also the identity of the re-engaging employer, the nature of the employment and the rate of remuneration. In the case of either kind of order, the employee's continuity of employment is preserved and the time between dismissal and re-employment counts as a period of employment[4].

In a case where an employee expresses a desire for reinstatement or re-engagement, section 116 lays down a definite procedure to which the tribunal must adhere[5]. The tribunal must first decide whether to make an order for

---

20   See *Harvey* D[2371]. Dickens, Hart, Jones and Weeks 'Re-employment of unfairly dismissed workers: the lost remedy' (1981) 10 ILJ 160; Williams and Lewis 'The aftermath of tribunal reinstatement and re-engagement', DE Research Paper No. 23 (1981).
1   The mandatory nature of this wording is not what it seems; a tribunal decision will *not* be rendered void by a failure to comply with this requirement: *Cowley v Manson Timber Ltd* [1995] ICR 367, [1995] IRLR 153, CA.
2   Employment Rights Act 1996, s. 114.
3   Defined ibid., s. 231; see p. 22, above. A tribunal should stick to the wording of the statute and make orders for either reinstatement or re-engagement, not just make an order that the employer should *offer* to re-employ: *Lilley Construction Ltd v Dunn* [1984] IRLR 483. An order may not be made to re-employ on significantly better terms: *Rank Xerox (UK) Ltd v Stryczek* [1995] IRLR 568.
4   Employment Protection (Continuity of Employment) Regulations 1996, S.I. 1996 No. 3147, *Harvey* R[1034]. These regulations apply where either there has been an application to a tribunal, or an agreed re-employment after the involvement of an ACAS conciliation officer or through a compromise agreement; thus an employee negotiating re-employment is advised to do so through ACAS or by a formal compromise agreement, otherwise there may be a break in continuity even if the employer had voluntarily taken the employee back: *Morris v Walsh Western UK Ltd* [1997] IRLR 562, EAT.
5   *Pirelli General Cable Works Ltd v Murray* [1979] IRLR 190, EAT.

reinstatement and only if it decides not to do so should it go on to consider whether to order re-engagement and, if so, on what terms. In both exercises, it must take into account (a) the expressed wishes of the complainant, (b) whether it is *practicable* for the employer to comply with an order for reinstatement or re-engagement and (c) whether the complainant caused or contributed to his dismissal and if so whether it would be just to make an order[6]. An employer who does not wish to take the dismissed employee back may therefore at this stage make representations on grounds (b) and (c) and, although (c) is important in ruling out important remedies for a 'rogue', it is (b) and the question of practicability which is likely to be the most pressing. It is for the employer to show impracticability, and as this is such an important matter he must discharge that onus properly – it is not enough for the tribunal to take a lax approach and decide that perhaps it would not be 'expedient' to put the employee back into employment[7]. Impracticability is a question of fact in each case, but may arise from inability to perform the work, unsuitability for it, definite opposition to his return among the workforce (either collectively or individually)[8], inability to take him back without having to dismiss another employee[9], continued breakdown of trust and confidence between the parties[10] or through an intervening factor arising since the dismissal such as redundancy or potential overmanning (though in such a case the tribunal should be satisfied that it is genuine)[11]. In *Enessy Co SA v Minoprio*[12] the Scottish EAT stated obiter that practicability may depend inter alia upon the size of the employer and that reinstatement into a small concern where a close personal relationship has to exist should only be ordered in exceptional cases; this may be a factor, particularly in domestic or quasi-domestic employment as in that case itself, but it is submitted that this approach should not be applied too widely, for as a principle it could come to bear an unfortunate resemblance to the old common law rules against enforcement of contracts of employment[13].

If an order for reinstatement or re-engagement is made and the employee is taken back but the employer does not comply fully with the terms of the order, the employee may complain under section 117 to the tribunal[14] which is to order

---

6   Lewis 'Interpretation of "practicable" and "just" in relation to re-employment in unfair dismissal cases' (1982) 45 MLR 384. Contributory conduct here is the same in content as contributory fault in a compensation case (see below): *Boots Co plc v Lees-Collier* [1986] ICR 728, [1986] IRLR 485, EAT.

7   *Qualcast (Wolverhampton) Ltd v Ross* [1979] ICR 386, [1979] IRLR 98, EAT.

8   *Coleman v Magnet Joinery Ltd* [1975] ICR 46, [1974] IRLR 343, CA; *Langston v AUEW (No 2)* [1974] ICR 510, [1974] IRLR 182; *Meridian Ltd v Gomersall* [1977] ICR 597, [1977] IRLR 425.

9   *Freemans plc v Flynn* [1984] ICR 874, [1984] IRLR 486, EAT.

10   *Wood Group Heavy Industrial Turbines Ltd v Crossan* [1998] IRLR 680, EAT.

11   *Cold Drawn Tubes Ltd v Middleton* [1992] ICR 318, [1992] IRLR 160, EAT.

12   [1978] IRLR 489. As pointed out in the DE Working Paper No. 23 (n. 13, above) a further problem is that, in fact many firms in Britain could claim to be 'small' for this purpose, and in many of them trade union representation will be weak.

13   See p. 376, above.

14   One problem is whether s. 117 can be relied upon where an employer uses more subtle tactics, e.g. taking the employee back but subtly victimising him; also, where the employer takes the employee back on normally, but then *later* changes the terms of his employment (e.g. by downgrading him), that would have to be the subject of a separate unfair dismissal action. The tribunal decision in *Nensi v Vinola (Knitwear) Manufacturing Co Ltd* [1978] IRLR 297, IT that a re-employed employee fell between two stools in such a case is per incuriam since his continuity should in fact have been preserved by the 1996 Regulations (n. 4, above), so that he had the necessary qualifying period and so should have been allowed his separate unfair dismissal action.

such compensation as it thinks fit having regard to the loss caused to the employee by the employer's actions. The more common form of complaint, however, will be that the employer has not complied with the order *at all* and has refused to take the employee back. In this case, section 117(3) provides that the tribunal shall make an award of compensation in the normal way instead[15] *and* an award of 'additional compensation' of between 26 and 52 weeks' pay. A 'week's pay' is subject to the same maximum as that in force at the time for the ordinary basic award[16] and, as the additional compensation is not expressly limited to compensation for loss actually suffered by the employee because of the employer's refusal to comply, it can include a punitive element[17].

Once again, it is a defence to the granting of the additional compensation if the employer can satisfy the tribunal that it was not practicable to comply with the order; this may seem a strange provision as it allows the employer a second opportunity to plead impracticability. In *Timex Corpn v Thomson*[18] Browne-Wilkinson P held that the test effectively was the same (the latter stage *not* being confined to matters arising since the date of the order), so that it was possible for a tribunal merely to 'have regard' to practicability at the first stage and, if necessary, make the order on a fairly speculative basis and leave it to the employer to raise impracticability as a defence at this second stage if it did not work out in practice. This approach was generally approved by the Court of Appeal in *Port of London Authority v Payne*[19] where it was said that, although a determination of sorts has to be made at the first stage, that will be 'of necessity provisional' and without prejudice to a fuller consideration of practicability at the second stage if necessary, with the burden of proof clearly on the employer (though only to show impracticability, not absolute impossibility). Finally, it should be noted that the statute provides that the fact that the employer has hired a replacement for the dismissed employee is not to be taken into account when deciding upon impracticability (at either stage at which it may arise) unless the employer can show that it was not practicable for him to arrange for the work to be done without engaging a permanent replacement, or (at the first stage, when deciding whether to make an order) that he only engaged the replacement after a reasonable period without hearing from the dismissed employee, and then had to do so in order that the work could be done[20].

In the light of these detailed legal rules (and the elevation of reinstatement/re-engagement into an 'order' in 1975) it is surprising that it is ordered in so few cases. Research has shown a patchy picture (even in geographical terms) with many reasons being accepted by tribunals for not making an order and, indeed,

15 If the tribunal finds that the employee himself unreasonably prevented the order being complied with, that is to be considered as failure to mitigate his loss, with a view to decreasing the award of compensation: Employment Rights Act 1996, s. 117(8).

16 As from February 2000, the figure is £230, giving a maximum additional award of £11,960. For the calculation of a week's pay, see p. 189, above.

17 *George v Beecham Group* [1977] IRLR 43; IT; *Morganite Electrical Carbon Ltd v Donne* [1988] ICR 18, [1987] IRLR 363, EAT.

18 [1981] IRLR 522, applied in *Freemans plc v Flynn* [1984] ICR 874, [1984] IRLR 486 and *Boots Co plc v Lees-Collier* [1986] ICR 728, [1986] IRLR 485.

19 [1994] ICR 555, [1994] IRLR 9, CA, reversing the decision of the EAT which had been inconsistent with *Timex*. The case itself held the record for a tribunal hearing, having lasted 189 days.

20 Ibid., s. 116(5), (6).

considerable reluctance among ex-employees to press for one[1]. Overall, it has been suggested that, in spite of the term 'order' being used, the emphasis before tribunals is still to look for an element of *agreement* on the part of the employer to re-employ and, in the absence of that, to be very wary about going further. This may be in line with general ideas of good industrial relations practice (i.e. looking to see what the likely long-term effects are of an order), but it must have a severely depressing effect on prospects for re-employment[2]. If this is correct, it casts doubt on whether any alterations in the law could have much effect on what is basically a question of attitude (given the failure of the redrafting in 1975 to increase the incidence of re-employment, as it was clearly meant to do). However, certain reforms have been suggested[3], including enacting a special statutory action for victimisation after re-employment[4], the use of trial periods (at present restricted to redundancy cases), the abolition of 'practicability' as a criterion for the making of an order (leaving 'impracticability' as a defence for an employer on a complaint of failure to comply with an order) and, perhaps the most interesting, extending the application of interim relief to any case where an employee wants reinstatement[5].

b) Compensation

The scheme of the present provisions on compensation is that the employee is eligible for a 'basic award' which is calculated mechanically in the same way as a redundancy payment and so rewards long service, and a 'compensatory award' which aims to put a realistic figure upon the employee's actual loss. The maximum for the basic award is determined by the maximum amount for a 'week's pay' for this purpose, and the compensatory award is subject to a maximum set figure in the statute[6]. This latter figure was allowed to fall behind inflation for much of the 1980s and 1990s, so that by 1999 it still stood at only £12,000, which had a depressing effect on unfair dismissal compensation[7], and caused problems when the equivalent maximum was removed from discrimination cases, so that it was in an applicant's interests to seek to bring a dismissal case as a discrimination claim whenever possible. The present government at first proposed in the White Paper Fairness at Work to remove the limit altogether, but were prevailed upon only to raise it instead; this was done in the Employment Relations Act 1999 which increased it to £50,000, and at the same time instituted a system for raising all the

---

1   Williams and Lewis 'The aftermath of tribunal reinstatement and re-engagement' DE Research Paper No. 23 (1981). There is also a suggestion that increased legal representation (and hence less of an inquisitorial approach by the tribunal) may have a depressing effect on the incidence of re-employment. For the experience of ACAS on the factors leading to low levels of re-employment, see the ACAS Annual Report 1983, para. 5.11.

2   It certainly means that ideas of practicability are not tied to the physical existence of a job for the applicant to do.

3   Research Paper No. 23, pp. 40–41.

4   See n. 14, above.

5   There is a precedent of sorts here in the extension of interim relief by the Employment Act 1982 to employees being dismissed for non-membership of a union, pursuant to a closed shop agreement, where the previous government clearly wanted the remedy of reinstatement to be effective; for interim relief, see p. 580, below.

6   As from February 2000 the maximum for a week's pay is £230 pw, giving a maximum basic award of £6,900.

7   Given that the figure stood at £6,250 in 1980, by the late 1990s inflation alone should have raised it to £30,000–40,000. The latter figure was suggested by the CBI and IPD in their responses to Fairness at Work.

award limits each September in line with the retail prices index. One earlier, but also significant reform in this area was that tribunals were eventually given the power to award interest on their awards[8].

1) *The basic award*[9]. The calculation method for this is similar to that for a redundancy payment; it is dependent upon the length of the employee's continuous employment as at the effective date of termination, and under section 119 the employee is to receive one and a half week's pay for each year of employment over the age of 41, one week's pay for each year between 22 and 41 and half a week's pay for each year under the age of 22; a maximum of 20 years may be counted and, as stated above, the maximum week's pay for this purpose is limited to a fixed amount, subject to review; special provisions apportion the amount claimable where dismissal takes place in the employee's retirement year. The basic award is subject to reduction (a) by the amount of any redundancy payment received (either under the Act or by virtue of a private scheme)[10], (b) where the tribunal finds that there was contributory fault on the part of the employee[11] (see below), (c) where the ex-employee has refused an offer of, in effect, reinstatement[12] and (d) where the employer has made an ex gratia payment meant to offset or extinguish all legal rights (in as much as that amount may be set off against both basic and compensatory awards, if large enough)[13].

The basic award used to be subject to a minimum of two weeks' pay, but this was abolished by the Employment Act 1980, which also extended the idea of contributory fault to cover any conduct by the employee prior to the dismissal (not just conduct known to the employer and contributing positively to the decision to dismiss). A combination of these two reforms to the basic award ensured that an employee who is unfairly dismissed on ground A (e.g. unsatisfactory work) but who is later discovered to have been dismissable on ground B (e.g. concealed fraud, only coming to light after he left) cannot now claim the minimum basic award of two weeks; the reforms were in response to fears expressed by the House of Lords in *W Devis & Sons Ltd v Atkins*[14] that the minimum basic award could be a 'rogue's charter' in such cases.

As will be seen below, there is now a minimum basic award (£3,100 at the time of writing) where an employee is unfairly dismissed for being or not being a union member; these provisions were extended in 1993 to the new ground of dismissal for health and safety reasons, and subsequently to the unfair dismissal of pension trustees, elected employee representatives, or complainants under the working time provisions.

2) *The compensatory award*[15]. Various aspects of the compensatory award can cause problems of quantification, and it is part of the tribunal's function to ensure that the

8   Employment Tribunals (Interest) Order 1990, S.I. 1990 No. 479, *Harvey* R[459].
9   See *Harvey* D[2503].
10   Ibid., s. 122(4); any excess over the amount of the basic award (which is thereby extinguished) is deducted from the compensatory award: s. 123(7).
11   Ibid., s. 122(2).
12   Ibid., s. 122(1).
13   *Chelsea Football Club and Athletic Co Ltd v Heath* [1981] ICR 323, [1981] IRLR 73, EAT.
14   [1977] ICR 662, [1977] IRLR 314, HL; see p. 465, above.
15   See *Harvey* D[2524]; on the calculation of compensation generally, see Upex *Termination of Employment* (3rd edn, 1991), Collins 'The just and equitable compensatory award' (1991) 20 ILJ 201, Hough and Spowart-Taylor 'Liability, compensation and justice in unfair dismissal' (1996) 25 ILJ 308 and Crump, Pugsley and Ashtiany 'Butterworths Compensation Calculations (1999).

relevant heads of compensation are considered[16]. However, since this award is meant to constitute realistic recompense and as such has to be approached from first principles in each case, the onus lies primarily upon the employee to adduce evidence of his losses[17]; the tribunal should not speculate unduly, but on the other hand the EAT has pointed out that only a realistic standard should be expected of the employee (who may have difficulty gaining certain evidence, even with the aid of discovery against the employer) and the tribunal should not hide behind the burden of proof where major problems of quantification arise[18].

The basis of the compensatory award is contained in section 123(1) which provides that:

'... the amount of the compensatory award shall be such amount as the tribunal considers just and equitable in all the circumstances having regard to the loss sustained by the complainant in consequence of the dismissal in so far as that loss is attributable to action taken by the employer.'

In a potentially important and expansive decision, the Inner House of the Court of Session held in *Leonard v Strathclyde Buses Ltd*[19] that this statutory language is to be applied as it stands, and is not to have grafted on to it common law tests such as whether damage claimed was foreseeable or too remote; thus, when an unfairly dismissed employee had to sell back 6,000 company shares on leaving at the current price of £1.70, only to see them rise to £5.85 some months later (on a take-over), it was held that it was 'just and equitable' to award the difference on the facts, and that this was not to be defeated by technical arguments on remoteness of damage taken from other areas of the law. Such an expansive approach (leaving much in the discretion of the tribunal) may be particularly important with the raising of the statutory limit to £50,000. On the other hand, it must also be remembered that ultimately the aim of an award is to reimburse the employee, not to punish the employer[20], and this principle can have certain overall effects. In particular, it means that if the employee has in fact lost nothing, he is entitled to no compensatory award (only the basic award) and this may be held to be the case where it is clear that it would have made no difference even if he had not been unfairly dismissed; for example in a redundancy dismissal where it is held to have been unfair through lack of consultation but it is clear that he would have been made redundant anyway, or in an incapacity or misconduct case where the dismissal was unfair because the proper procedure was not followed but it is clear that the employee would have been dismissed in any event[1]. In such a case it has long been clear that there may be a nil compensatory award, or a very

---

16 *Tidman v Aveling Marshall Ltd* [1977] ICR 506, [1977] IRLR 218.
17 *Adda International Ltd v Curcio* [1976] ICR 407, [1976] IRLR 425; *Lifeguard Assurance Ltd v Zadrozny* [1977] IRLR 56; *Smith, Kline and French Laboratories Ltd v Coates* [1977] IRLR 220.
18 *Barley v Amey Roadstone Corpn Ltd (No 2)* [1978] ICR 190, [1977] IRLR 299.
19 [1998] IRLR 693, Ct of Sess; *Balmoral Group Ltd v Rae* (2000) Times, 25 January, EAT.
20 *Clarkson International Tools Ltd v Short* [1973] ICR 191, [1973] IRLR 90; *Lifeguard Assurance Ltd v Zadrozny* [1977] IRLR 56. It was said in *Townson v Northgate Group Ltd* [1981] IRLR 382 that the tribunal could look at *how unfair* the dismissal was when assessing compensation but this was later disapproved in *Morris v Acco Ltd* [1985] ICR 306.
1 *Clarkson International Tools Ltd v Short* [1973] ICR 191, [1973] IRLR 90; *British United Shoe Machinery Co Ltd v Clarke* [1978] ICR 70, [1977] IRLR 297; *Barley v Amey Roadstone Corpn Ltd (No 2)* [1978] ICR 190, [1977] IRLR 299; *Clyde Pipeworks Ltd v Foster* [1978] IRLR 313; *Brittains Arborfield Ltd v Van Uden* [1977] ICR 211.

limited one (for example where in a case of lack of redundancy consultation it appears that proper consultation would have lasted for four weeks but then the employee would have been dismissed; in such a case the compensatory award may only reflect four weeks' loss of wages).

As we have already seen (p. 469, above) the decision of the House of Lords in *Polkey v A E Dayton Services Ltd* [2] means that it is *not* now open to a tribunal to find a dismissal substantively fair merely because with hindsight a procedural lapse in fact made no difference, but on the other hand that decision does accept (and, indeed, emphasise) the important point being made here, namely that the injustice (or lack of it) to the employee at the end of the day *is* to be taken into account in fixing compensation, and that approach has been applied strongly in the post-*Polkey* case law [3]. This may mean that the tribunals have to be more pro-active on this point, investigating the likelihood of continued employment, and if necessary making a percentage estimate of that likelihood (known in the jargon as the 'Polkey reduction') [4].

Moreover, an employee may be said to have lost nothing if his conduct is such that it is not just and equitable to give any compensatory award, in spite of the finding of unfairness. This would be the case for example where the employer unfairly dismissed the employee on a weak ground (e.g. incapability) but then later found out about a cast-iron ground for dismissal (e.g. embezzlement) which the employee had kept hidden from him. In such a case, the House of Lords held in *W Devis & Sons Ltd v Atkins* [5] that that subsequently discovered reason could not affect the fairness of the dismissal, or activate the provisions on contributory fault, for both of these matters have to be judged according to the employer's knowledge at the time of the dismissals; it could, however, justify the tribunal making a nil or nominal compensatory award on the ground of justice and equity, quite independently of any question of contributory fault [6].

Given such general considerations, tribunals have to have a system of dividing up possible heads of loss, and this is well established, principally following the early NIRC case *Norton Tool Co Ltd v Tewson* [7] which also established that the tribunal should set out in their judgment the relevant heads of compensation and the

2   [1988] ICR 142, [1987] IRLR 503, HL.
3   See particularly *Mining Supplies (Longwall) Ltd v Baker* [1988] ICR 676, [1988] IRLR 417; *Slaughter v C Brewer & Sons Ltd* [1990] ICR 730, [1990] IRLR 426; *Red Bank Manufacturing Co Ltd v Meadows* [1992] ICR 204, [1992] IRLR 209; *Campbell v Dunoon and Cowal Housing Association Ltd* [1993] IRLR 496, Ct of Sess; *Britool Ltd v Roberts* [1993] IRLR 481; *Rao v Civil Aviation Authority* [1994] ICR 495, [1994] IRLR 240, CA.
4   *Dunlop Ltd v Farrell* [1993] ICR 885; *Wolesley Centers Ltd v Simmons* [1994] ICR 503; *Fisher v California Cake & Cookie Ltd* [1997] IRLR 212. The EAT have suggested two glosses to this rule, where the tribunal should not consider future likelihoods – (i) where the unfairness comes from a defect of substance (e.g. improper selection criteria) rather than of procedure: *Steel Stockholders (Birmingham) Ltd v Kirkwood* [1993] IRLR 515 (criticised by the Court of Appeal in *O'Dea v ISC Chemicals Ltd* [1996] ICR 222, [1995] IRLR 599, but reaffirmed by the Inner House of the Court of Session in *King v Eaton (No 2)* [1998] IRLR 686); (ii) where the unfairness comes from positive steps taken by the employer (e.g. wrong application of criteria), rather than a sin of omission: *Boulton & Paul Ltd v Arnold* [1994] IRLR 532. Arguably, both of these are unfortunate complications in an already difficult area.
5   [1977] ICR 662, [1977] IRLR 314, HL.
6   Ibid., at 680 and 319 respectively, per Lord Dilhorne. This point was reaffirmed by the Court of Appeal in *Tele-Trading Ltd v Jenkins* [1990] IRLR 430.
7   [1973] 1 All ER 183, [1972] ICR 501. For a criticism of this whole approach, see Collins (1991) 20 ILJ 201. It is possible that the raising of the statutory limit to £50,000 will lead to more fought cases on compensation, and future case law reconsidering the existing rules, which have evolved against the background of much lower limits.

amounts awarded under each, not just one global sum[8]. The emphasis is very clearly upon pecuniary loss, and the following are the major heads:

1) *Loss up to the date of hearing.* This head requires a relatively simple mathematical calculation of the employee's actual loss of income during the period between the dismissal and the hearing; it is aimed at realistic compensation, so, as in the case of future loss (below), the relevant figure is his previous weekly take-home pay (net of tax and national insurance contributions) which may include matters such as overtime and tips which may *not* be counted under the stricter rules for calculating a 'week's pay' for the purpose of the basic award[9]. From this amount which the employee would have earned but for the dismissal the tribunal must deduct any sums earned in alternative employment during the period, or indeed in self employment[10]. There is however one qualification – where the employee earns money during what should have been his notice period, that amount will normally *not* be deducted from the compensation ordered under this head; this is in contravention of the requirement of mitigation, but is justified on the basis of good industrial relations practice[11]. A problem then arose that there were attempts to extend the qualification to cases where the employer had dismissed with wages in lieu of notice; if this amount too could be disregarded, the employer would end up paying for the notice period twice and the problem was that this would be a material disincentive to the making of voluntary payments to dismissed employees, whereas it is clearly within the policy of the statute to try to encourage settlements of disputes without going to a tribunal. Moreover, if voluntary payments of wages in lieu were disregarded, could it logically be argued that ex gratia payments *generally* should not? Once again, this could have had a serious effect on settlements. Fortunately, the position was rectified by the important decision of the Court of Appeal in *Addison v Babcock FATA Ltd*[12] – non-deductibility may apply to earnings during the notice period from elsewhere, but it does *not* apply

8   See also *Adda International Ltd v Curcio* [1976] ICR 407, [1976] IRLR 425, EAT.

9   *Brownson v Hire Service Shops Ltd* [1978] ICR 517, [1978] IRLR 73; *Palmanor Ltd v Cedron* [1978] ICR 1008, [1978] IRLR 303. Tax matters should not be considered in too great detail by the tribunal which may, for example, ignore minor tax rebates: *MBS Ltd v Calo* [1983] ICR 459, [1983] IRLR 189. If there is a dispute as to what is the correct amount of wage payable at the date of dismissal, that must be resolved by the tribunal which is deciding upon compensation: *Kinzley v Minories Finance Ltd* [1988] ICR 113, [1987] IRLR 490, EAT.

10   *Ging v Ellward (Lancs) Ltd* (1978) [1991] ICR 222n; *Lee v IPC Business Press Ltd* [1984] ICR 306. This remains the case, even if the employee obtains new, permanent employment at *higher* pay, which eats into the compensation: *Dench v Flynn & Partners* [1998] IRLR 653, CA, disapproving on this point *Whelan v Richardson* [1998] IRLR 114.

11   *TBA Industrial Products Ltd v Locke* [1984] ICR 228, [1984] IRLR 48 (disapproving a contrary decision in *Tradewinds Airways Ltd v Fletcher* [1981] IRLR 272 and reverting to the original rule as laid down in *Norton Tool Co Ltd v Tewson* (above)), approved in *Addison v Babcock FATA Ltd*, n. 3 below. The word 'normally' is used in the text because there is an exception – if in what should have been the notice period the ex-employee in fact earns a considerable sum, it may not be in the interests of good industrial relations practice to disregard that fact and award some or all of the wages for the period against the ex-employer: *Isleworth Studios Ltd v Rickard* [1988] ICR 432, [1988] IRLR 137 (ex-employee setting up in business and making £10,000 *more* than he would have earned in the remaining 29 weeks of his fixed-term contract; *held* the money made in the new business *was* to be taken into account as mitigation). The drawing of this particular line could be very difficult; it serves to show that the rule in *TBA Industrial Products* is an exception to normal principles.

12   [1987] ICR 805, [1987] IRLR 173, CA, overruling *Finnie v Top Hat Frozen Foods* [1985] ICR 433, [1985] IRLR 365, EAT.

where the ex-employer has properly discharged the contract by paying wages in lieu of notice – there, the normal principle of mitigation applies and the employer is permitted to set that payment off against the compensation otherwise payable under this head; the employer will therefore *not* lose out by having to pay twice by reason of attempting to settle the case by, inter alia, the payment of wages in lieu. Moreover, it is clear that this principle applies to ex gratia payments generally[13] – again, the employer will normally[14] be given credit for such payments and be able to set them off against any compensation awarded later[15].

As well as salary, wages and other monetary receipts, the employee can claim compensation for past (and future) loss of other benefits such as a company car, a low interest mortgage or loan, free or cheap accommodation and other fringe benefits such as medical insurance and school fees; also, section 123(2) expressly includes any expenses reasonably incurred as a result of the dismissal (for example expenses incurred in seeking other employment) though this does not include the expense of bringing the unfair dismissal action itself.

2)   *Future loss.* In contrast to the relative certainties of the first head, compensation for future loss may require the tribunal to perform a highly speculative exercise. The actual loss per week may be easy to quantify (either where the ex-employee has not obtained other employment, or has done so at a lower wage) and it may include the extra matters and perks mentioned above, but the tribunal has to fix a 'multiplier' (as in personal injury cases) of a number of weeks, months or even years during which this loss might continue[16]; the state of the local labour market and conditions in the industry concerned will be factors, but there will be other discounting factors, such as the possibilities that the employee might have resigned in the future anyway, moved from the area, had a child, etc. Also, the principle mentioned above that the employee will not be compensated if he has in fact suffered no loss must be borne in mind, so that if he would probably have lost his employment in the near future anyway (e.g. through impending redundancies) he may

---

13   *Horizon Holidays Ltd v Grassi* [1987] ICR 851, [1987] IRLR 371, EAT.

14   Once again the word 'normally' is used because there is an exception – if an ex gratia payment is made on dismissal which would have been made to the employee *anyway* even if no unfair dismissal had taken place (e.g. where a redundancy dismissal is unfair for lack of warning, but the facts show that the same ex gratia payment would have been made even if proper warning had been given), then it may be argued that that particular payment should *not* be taken into account as mitigation: *Roadchef Ltd v Hastings* [1988] IRLR 142; one complication in *Addison* was that there was (in addition to the payment in lieu) an ex gratia payment which was not taken into account, but it was for this reason.

15   Though even here the employer may lose out, for if the eventual amount of compensation is going to be over the statutory maximum, it has been held that the tribunal must deduct the ex gratia payment and *then* apply the maximum to what is left, which means that the employer may end up paying in total *more* than the statutory maximum: *McCarthy v BICC plc* [1985] IRLR 94; for the order of making deductions, see p. 517, below. Thus the employer must be careful with ex gratia payments and, certainly in the case of higher earners, might be better advised to seek a binding *settlement* (either under the aegis of ACAS or under the new rules on binding compromise agreements) rather than attempting a simple pay-off.

16   See, e.g., *Cartiers Superfoods Ltd v Laws* [1978] IRLR 315. This must be viewed in the context of that individual claimant so that if his personal circumstances render new employment more difficult, the compensation may reflect that: *Fougère v Phoenix Motor Co Ltd* [1976] ICR 495, [1976] IRLR 259; *Gilham v Kent County Council (No 3)* [1986] ICR 52, [1986] IRLR 56, EAT.

only be compensated in respect of that short extra period of likely employment[17]. The number of factors in any particular case may thus be considerable and so, although as in other aspects of compensation the tribunal should explain in its decision how it arrived at the multiplier it used[18], this is not an exercise in precision and so that multiplier may be one general approximation of several different factors and, unless very clearly misguided, will not usually be altered by the EAT. In the past, even rough calculations could soon reach the low statutory maximum, rendering further precision unnecessary, but the raising of that maximum to £50,000 may well mean much more argument on exact calculation, in order to maximise compensation within (and up to) that limit, especially in cases of higher earners and/or likely long-term unemployment; in the large majority of cases, however, this will not be so and the multiplier will be relatively modest[19].

3) *Loss of accrued rights.* When an employee is dismissed and takes other employment, he loses any statutory (or other) rights against the dismissing employer which depend upon continuous service (e.g. redundancy and the employment protection rights) and must begin to accrue new rights against his new employer. This head of loss established in *Norton Tool Co Ltd v Tewson*, was meant to reflect that disadvantage and initially caused some problems. Now, however, the major loss (of accrued redundancy rights) is in effect taken into account by the institution of the basic award and so any further compensation under this head will be less, though the EAT held in *Daley v A E Dorsett (Almar Dolls) Ltd*[20] that the right to the longer notice that accrues with service is itself valuable (particularly in times of economic recession) so that, independently of the power that a tribunal now has to award common law damages for loss of wages during the notice period, it is open to it to make an award including an amount reflecting the employee's loss of accrued statutory rights to longer notice[1].

4) *Loss due to the manner of dismissal.* The compensatory award is clearly tied to pecuniary loss and so, as at common law[2], no amount may be awarded for loss of dignity, anguish, etc., simpliciter; an amount may only be granted under this head if the manner of dismissal can be said to affect the employee's

---

17 *Young's of Gosport Ltd v Kendell* [1977] ICR 907, [1977] IRLR 433.
18 *Qualcast (Wolverhampton) Ltd v Ross* [1979] ICR 386, [1979] IRLR 98. There is *no* 'conventional sum' of between 6 and 12 months – the period is to be determined by the tribunal in the light of all the evidence, subject only to the statutory maximum amount that can be awarded: *Morganite Electrical Carbon Ltd v Donne* [1988] ICR 18, [1987] IRLR 363 (impossible to say that an award covering 82 weeks was excessive).
19 In 1998/99 the medium award was £2,388. However, 15% of awards were for over £9,000 and it is possible that the raising of the maximum to £50,000 will significantly alter the profile of awards, with the tribunal being a more attractive forum for higher paid employees (especially when the £25,000 maximum for a common law claim on termination is added in).
20 [1982] ICR 1, [1981] IRLR 385. Compensation may also reflect the loss of any *extra* redundancy rights that the ex-employee may have had under this contract over and above his ordinary statutory entitlement: *Lee v IPC Business Press Ltd* [1984] ICR 306.
1 The EAT quantified this amount as half the wages for the statutory minimum of eight weeks' notice to which he was entitled. However, in the subsequent case of *S H Muffett Ltd v Head* [1987] ICR 1, [1986] IRLR 488 the EAT thought that in most cases it would be more appropriate merely to award a nominal sum of £100 under this head.
2 *Addis v Gramophone Co Ltd* [1909] AC 488, HL; *Bliss v South East Thames Regional Health Authority* [1987] ICR 700, [1985] IRLR 308, CA; see p. 391, above.

future employment prospects, e.g. by blackening his name in the industry or in some way rendering him unfit for immediate re-employment[3].

5) *Loss of pension rights.* Where the dismissed employee cannot find new employment, or can or may find new employment to which he cannot transfer his existing pension rights, this head of compensation may produce a considerable sum. It is, however, perhaps the most complicated head of all and the EAT have stressed that the tribunal should adopt a broad approach so that actuarial evidence, though of considerable help (bearing in mind that the claimant must adduce evidence of loss), is not conclusive. Once again the tribunal is aiming for a realistic, if approximate, estimate of actual loss so that if no loss is sustained overall, nothing is payable under this head; this might occur if the employee has to take, or opts for[4], a deferred pension from his existing entitlement and can build up a suitable further entitlement from new employment, or if he moves to employment with a better pension scheme (e.g. from a contributory to a non-contributory scheme), or if he can simply transfer his pension. In *Copson v Eversure Accessories Ltd*[5] the NIRC said that there is no one correct way to quantify loss of pension rights, but isolated two types of loss – (a) loss of present pension position and (b) loss of future pension opportunity (i.e. the opportunity, had he not been dismissed, to improve his pension position during further service with that employer). Except in cases where the employee is close to retiring age (where the better approach may be to capitalise the cost of an annuity to produce a sum equal to the likely pension, discounting if for accelerated payment), the starting point for both (a) and (b) will be the contributions already paid to the scheme. The employee may have received back his own contributions, but can also claim (except in cases of transfer or deferment) credit for his legitimate interest in the contributions paid by the employer (plus interest thereon) which may be viewed as an adjunct to his salary[6]. As well as being the primary measure for the detriment to his present pension loss, lack of the employer's future contributions will be a guide to any future loss when compared with the position under any actual or likely pension scheme in new employment; the factors to be taken into account here may be numerous. Having arrived at a prima facie figure for loss, however, it is incorrect for the tribunal just to apply that for the number of years left to retirement age, because account must be taken of many contingencies, such as future resignation, future dismissal, early death, possible tax advantages and the fact that any capital sum is being paid sooner than normal. This discounting process is achieved by the fixing of the tribunal of a multiplier to take all of these factors into account[7]; this may considerably decrease the possible compensation under

---

3   *Norton Tool Co Ltd v Tewson*, n. 7, above; *Vaughan v Weighpack Ltd* [1974] ICR 261, [1974] IRLR 105; *Brittains Arborfield Ltd v Van Uden* [1977] ICR 211, EAT.

4   Where there is an option the choice lies with the employee, who is not to be penalised by the tribunal if he opts not to take the deferred pension: *Sturdy Finance Ltd v Bardsley* [1979] ICR 249, [1979] IRLR 65. Deferment of pension has been the normal position in the pension scheme since the Social Security Pensions Act 1975, though the amended pensions regime since 1986 puts more emphasis on personal, 'portable' pensions which may go with the person and the present government's intentions in relation to 'stakeholder pensions' remain in line with this, in which case there will be less of a problem of quantification under this head.

5   [1974] ICR 636, [1974] IRLR 247, NIRC.

6   *Copson's case*; *Hill v Sabco Houseware (UK) Ltd* [1977] ICR 888; *Smith, Kline and French Laboratories Ltd v Coates* [1977] IRLR 220; *Sturdy Finance Ltd v Bardsley* [1979] ICR 249, [1979] IRLR 65.

7   *Powermatic Ltd v Bull* [1977] ICR 469, [1977] IRLR 144, EAT.

this head and inevitably imports an element of uncertainty. In an attempt to lessen the uncertainty generally, a committee of tribunal chairmen in conjunction with the Government Actuary's Department has produced a report suggesting methods of quantifying loss of pension rights; it contains examples of cases which might be likely to arise in practice, and certain basic actuarial material[8]. It is not necessarily determinative, though in the sea of actuarial uncertainty it may appear to a tribunal to be the only lifeline[9], and it may prove difficult to introduce independent actuarial evidence based on different calculation methods[10]. The large amounts of money involved in the loss of pension position (just on moving jobs, let alone on being dismissed) are yet another reason for amazement that the levels of compensation awards in practice are so low (see n. 19, above); perhaps one reason is that in the past the low level of the statutory maximum on the compensatory award has had a depressing effect on arguing this head of loss – it may need expensive actuarial evidence, which was hardly worthwhile if any eventual claim was to be severely restricted by the maximum. Now that the limit has been raised to £50,000, we may expect more effort to be put into proving pension loss.

One final point may be noted about the compensatory award. What is the position if the employee has received unemployment benefit (now jobseeker's allowance) or income support prior to the date of the hearing? Before 1977, this was treated in the same way as receipt of income from another source during that period, and so was deductible. However, that meant that the employer was paying less compensation through a 'subsidy' from the state. Under the Employment Protection (Recoupment of Jobseeker's Allowance and Income Support) Regulations 1996[11], the position now is that the tribunal is not to deduct the amount representing jobseeker's allowance or income support paid up to the date of the hearing, but instead must instruct the employer not to pay immediately that amount of the compensation it has awarded which represents loss of income during the period (i.e. head 1 above, called in the Regulations the 'prescribed element'). The Department of Trade and Industry will then serve upon the employer a recoupment notice (or a notice that no such notice will in fact be served) which requires him to pay back to them from the prescribed element the amount representing jobseeker's allowance or income support paid to the claimant prior to the hearing; after this has been done, the remainder of the prescribed element may be paid to the successful claimant. Thus the Department obliges the employer to repay to them amounts made payable by them because of the unfair dismissal and the claimant still only receives what he has in fact lost. If no jobseeker's allowance or income support was in fact claimed during the period,

---

8 *Industrial Tribunals: Compensation of Loss of Pension Rights* (HMSO, 1991).

9 Its predecessor (by the GAD itself) was relied on in *Manpower Ltd v Hearne* [1983] ICR 567, [1983] IRLR 281 and *Mono Pumps Ltd v Froggatt* [1987] IRLR 368. However, the EAT in *Bingham v Hobourn Engineering Ltd* [1992] IRLR 298 pointed out that a tribunal is not bound to follow it.

10 See the views of the EAT on this point in *Tradewinds Airways Ltd v Fletcher* [1981] IRLR 272. While a tribunal will properly not expect an employee to come armed with complex actuarial evidence, it is surely another matter actually to exclude it if the employee wishes to put it forward, especially where pension loss is a major factor.

11 S.I. 1996 No. 2349, *Harvey* R[1007], replacing the original 1977 Regulations. *Mason v Wimpey Waste Management Ltd* [1982] IRLR 454. The Regulations do not apply to the settlement of an unfair dismissal action, so such a settlement may well take into account the state benefits in fact received, and those benefits will not be recoverable by the state. This may be an inducement to the employer to settle, since he may end up paying less.

the Regulations do not apply. Thus, the tribunal is relieved of the task of deducting benefits from the award (in return for the administrative chore of explaining the procedure to the parties) and, moreover, need not take the possibility of further receipt of benefit into account when deciding upon future loss (head 2 above) either, for where compensation is awarded based on future loss for a set period of X weeks, months or years, the claimant is disqualified from receiving benefit during that period.

3) *Contributory fault*[12]. If a tribunal, having found in the claimant's favour on liability, considers that the dismissal was to any extent caused or contributed to by any action of the complainant, it must reduce both the basic award and the compensatory award by such proportion as it considers just and equitable[13]. The 'action' of the claimant must constitute blameworthy conduct in some way (so that it will not apply to proper and lawful activity on his part, such as refusing to obey an improper or unlawful order[14]) and this provision is aimed at giving the tribunal discretion to reach a just solution when both parties have been to blame[15], as in the case of contributory negligence in a tort action. Contributory fault constitutes a separate stage in the enquiry, once the tribunal has put a figure on the compensation, and should be explained by the tribunal as such[16]. In *Maris v Rotherham Corpn*[17] the NIRC said that the tribunal should approach this question in a broad common sense manner, looking at all the circumstances of the case and the employee's overall conduct (even if the actual ground of unfairness is a narrow, technical one); a slight change in the wording in 1975 strengthened this view[18]. The actual figure thus lies predominantly within the tribunal's discretion and may be difficult to challenge on appeal, provided that it has been properly considered at the hearing[19].

Where the ground for dismissal was misconduct, but the dismissal is held to have been unfair (e.g. because of lack of warnings or a hearing) in spite of evidence of actual misconduct, that may be a clear case for reduction of compensation.

12   See *Harvey* D[2707].
13   Employment Rights Act 1996, ss. 122(2) and 123(6) ; by a combination of the Employment Acts 1980 and 1982 the contributory fault provision in the case of the basic award was widened to cover *any* conduct before the dismissal making it just and equitable to decrease that award; the reason for this is discussed below. The procedure to be adopted (especially in a 'split' hearing) is considered by the EAT in *Iggesund Converters Ltd v Lewis* [1984] ICR 544, [1984] IRLR 431 at 552 and 435, respectively. There is no requirement that the basic and compensatory awards have to be reduced by the same percentage once contributory fault is found: *Charles Robertson (Developments) Ltd v White* [1995] ICR 349 (reviewing the previous, inconsistent case law); *Optikinetics Ltd v Whooley* [1999] ICR 984.
14   *Morrish v Henlys (Folkestone) Ltd* [1973] ICR 482, [1973] IRLR 61, approved by the Court of Appeal in *Nelson v BBC (No 2)* [1980] ICR 110, [1979] IRLR 346, CA.
15   The matter must be looked at between employer and employee, *not* involving the actions of third parties (e.g. other employees at fault): *Parker Foundry Ltd v Slack* [1992] ICR 302, [1992] IRLR 11, CA. Contributory fault can be applied even if the dismissal was constructive for, looking at the history of the matter, the employee may have been partly responsible for the employer taking the actual repudiatory action: *Garner v Grange Furnishing Ltd* [1977] IRLR 206; *Morrison v ATGWU* [1989] IRLR 361, NICA; *Polentarutti v Autokraft Ltd* [1991] ICR 757, [1991] IRLR 457 (not following *Holroyd v Gravure Cylinders Ltd* [1984] IRLR 259). 'Fault' on the part of the employee can include fault on the part of his agent, e.g. his solicitor: *Allen v Hammett* [1982] ICR 227, [1982] IRLR 89.
16   *Nudds v W and JB Eastwood Ltd* [1978] ICR 171.
17   [1974] ICR 435, [1974] IRLR 147.
18   *Brown v Rolls-Royce (1971) Ltd* (1977) 12 ITR 382 at 386, per Phillips J. There must still be a causal link between the conduct and the dismissal: *Hutchinson v Enfield Rolling Mills Ltd* [1981] IRLR 318, at least in the case of the compensatory award, though that link has been deliberately loosened in the case of the basic award (see n. 5, above).
19   *Sutcliffe and Eaton Ltd v Pinney* [1977] IRLR 349; *Hollier v Plysu Ltd* [1983] IRLR 260, CA.

Indeed, in *W Devis & Sons Ltd v Atkins*[20] Lord Dilhorne, disapproving earlier dicta that there may be a limit on the amount of reduction (e.g. 80 per cent maximum reduction), held that there is nothing inconsistent in finding unfairness but then using contributory fault in an extreme case to reduce compensation to nil or a merely nominal amount. The position, however, is more difficult in the case of a dismissal for incapacity, for can an employee's unfortunate incapacity ever be considered to be 'fault' on his part? In *Kraft Foods Ltd v Fox*[1] the EAT held that it could not, but in the subsequent case of *Moncur v International Paint Co Ltd*[2] it was explained that that was too sweeping a proposition and that the *Kraft* case envisaged the sort of incapability that was entirely outside the employee's control; even there, the EAT in *Moncur's* case doubted whether it was an absolute rule that such incapability could *never* amount to contributory fault and a reduction in such circumstances was approved subsequently in *Finnie v Top Hat Frozen Foods*[3]. In *Slaughter v C Brewer & Sons Ltd*[4] a different tack was taken; the EAT said that a reduction of contributory fault would be rare in an incapability case *but* if it was clear that, even if the employee had been treated fairly, the employment would have had to end shortly, then compensation can be reduced accordingly under the general 'just and equitable' basis to the compensatory award, thus achieving much the same result. One matter that is well established is that where the incapability is in any way within the employee's control (e.g. where he is negligent, lazy or unwilling to improve), that can clearly be contributory fault and indeed, according to the case of *Sutton and Gates (Luton) Ltd v Boxall*[5] (where a similar view was taken of the *Kraft* case) it may warrant a sizeable reduction.

A particular problem with contributory fault arose where the employer unfairly dismisses on one ground but then subsequently discovers other grounds which would certainly have justified dismissal. The House of Lords in *W Devis & Sons Ltd v Atkins*[6] held that in such a case the subsequently discovered misconduct cannot alter the finding of unfairness under section 57(3) *and* cannot be used as contributory fault for, being unknown at the time of dismissal, it could not have 'caused or contributed to' the dismissal. In such a case, however, justice could be done by giving a nil award under the general 'just and equitable' basis for compensation, *but* in that particular case the House of Lords were applying the old law on compensation which operated *before* the basic award was introduced in 1975. Once that award was introduced, the problem arose that a tribunal could not impose a nil basic award because the calculation is mathematical (not based on what is just and equitable) and it could only be reduced by contributory fault, which did not include subsequently discovered misconduct. Thus, in such a case, the employee whose dishonesty only came to light after being unfairly dismissed for laziness might still get a nil compensatory award but remain eligible for a basic award. Lord Diplock called this a 'rogue's charter' and in the

20 [1977] ICR 662, [1977] IRLR 314, HL, disapproving in this context dicta in *Kemp v Shipton Automation Ltd* [1976] ICR 514, [1976] IRLR 305 and *Trend v Chiltern Hunt Ltd* [1977] ICR 612, [1977] IRLR 66. See *Marley Homecare Ltd v Dutton* [1981] IRLR 380 and *Chaplin v H J Rawlinson Ltd* [1991] ICR 553.
1   [1978] ICR 311, [1977] IRLR 431.
2   [1978] IRLR 223; *Brown's Cycles Ltd v Brindley* [1978] ICR 467.
3   [1985] ICR 433, [1985] IRLR 365 (overruled later on other grounds in *Addison v Babcock FATA Ltd* [1987] ICR 805, [1987] IRLR 173, CA).
4   [1990] ICR 730, [1990] IRLR 426.
5   [1979] ICR 67, [1978] IRLR 486.
6   N. 20, above.

Employment Act 1980 the previous government took steps to prevent it, in two ways. First, the statutory minimum basic award of two weeks' pay was abolished; secondly, the tribunals were given a wider power to decrease (and possibly extinguish) a basic award where the conduct of the complainant before the dismissal was such that it would be just and equitable to reduce the award. This is wider than the previous rule on contributory fault per se (which still applies to the compensatory award) in that it does not require a definite causal link between the conduct and the dismissal[7]. Thus, the undisclosed rogue may now be awarded no compensation at all.

4) *Mitigation.* Under section 123(4), the dismissed employee must take the same reasonable steps to mitigate his losses as he would have to at common law[8]; these might include answering job advertisements and going to the local job centre, though of course it might not be reasonable in the circumstances to expect him to take any job that occurs. Refusal of an offer of reinstatement by the same employer can constitute failure to mitigate[9], but failure to use the company's appeal procedure once dismissed probably will not[10]; it may be reasonable in certain circumstances to leave one industry altogether and retrain for another, even if that necessarily means a longer period without work[11]. If the employee unreasonably refuses to mitigate, that can lead to a reduction in his compensatory award[12], though (on general principles) the onus lies upon the employer to prove failure to mitigate[13].

These general principles may now be subject to two legislative developments. First, the Employment Rights (Dispute Resolution) Act 1998 introduced a form of statutory mitigation, in that an employee who fails to use an available appeal procedure to challenge his dismissal can have his compensation reduced by the tribunal by up to two weeks' pay[14]. Secondly, the raising of the statutory limit on the compensatory award to £50,000 may lead to more arguments by respondent employers on failure to mitigate, as part of a generally greater emphasis on calculating compensation.

7   Employment Rights Act 1996, s. 122(2).
8   See p. 394, above.
9   *Sweetlove v Redbridge and Waltham Forest Area Health Authority* [1979] ICR 477, [1979] IRLR 195; *Gallear v J F Watson & Son Ltd* [1979] IRLR 306; cf. *Tiptools Ltd v Curtis* [1973] IRLR 276, where the offer of re-engagement included demotion.
10   *Seligman and Latz Ltd v McHugh* [1979] IRLR 130; cf. *Hoover Ltd v Forde* [1980] ICR 239. The rule was approved (and *Hoover* not followed) in *William Muir (Bond 9) Ltd v Lamb* [1985] IRLR 95. This is now subject to the Employment Rights Act 1996, s. 127A, see below.
11   *Sealey v Avon Aluminium Co Ltd* [1978] IRLR 285, IT.
12   By taking it into account when fixing the multiplier: *Smith, Kline and French Laboratories Ltd v Coates* [1977] IRLR 220; *Peara v Enderlin Ltd* [1979] ICR 804. Note that the basic award is *not* subject to mitigation (except in the special case where the employee unreasonably refuses an offer of re-employment: s. 122(1)), so that if the dismissed employee obtains new employment immediately he may get little or no compensatory award, but he remains eligible for the basic award (reflecting his loss of accrued employment rights).
13   *Bessenden Properties Ltd v Corness* [1977] ICR 821n, [1974] IRLR 338, CA; *Fyfe v Scientific Furnishings Ltd* [1989] ICR 648, [1989] IRLR 331 (disapproving statements to the contrary in *Scottish and Newcastle Breweries plc v Halliday* [1986] ICR 577, [1986] IRLR 291.
14   Employment Rights Act 1996, s. 127A, added by the 1998 Act; likewise, up to two weeks pay can be added if the employer prevents the employee from using an applicable appeal procedure.

5) *The order of deductions*. In complex cases, where there may be several deductions to be made from an award of compensation (e.g. for mitigatory amounts, contributory fault, a *Polkey* reduction and, of course, the statutory limit) a longstanding problem has been the order in which such deductions are to be made. This sounds very technical, but in practice can make a difference of thousands of pounds to the eventual award. It becomes particularly acute where the mitigatory amount in question is an ex gratia payment by the employer who, of course, wants to get full benefit of it when compensation is awarded. This however will only happen if that amount is deducted last (i.e. after the award has been subjected to all the other necessary adjustments). After years worth of confusing and often inconsistent case law, the EAT reviewed the whole question in *Digital Equipment Co Ltd v Clements (No 2)*[15] and produced a definitive order of deductions, *starting* with mitigatory amounts including ex gratia payments (thus meaning that an employer may *not* get the full benefit of such a payment[16]). When the case was appealed to the Court of Appeal[17], a complication was introduced – on the facts of the case the ex gratia payment was in fact a non-statutory (i.e. more generous) redundancy payment and the court held that Parliament's intent[18] was that such payments were to be encouraged by being set off in full (subject only to the statutory limit), which could only be done by deducting them later. To that extent they allowed the employers' appeal; however, it is submitted that most of the reasoning of the EAT stands, subject only to this one qualification. On that basis, the order of deduction is –

(i)   any mitigatory amounts (from the ex-employer or new employment) *other than* a non-statutory redundancy payment exceeding the statutory amount;
(ii)   any *Polkey* reduction;
(iii)   any contributory fault;
(iv)   any non-statutory redundancy payment;
(v)   the statutory limit, if applicable.

It is to be hoped that order has now been introduced into this complex area (and also that the statutory limit will now be less of a complication in many cases, after being raised from £12,000 to £50,000).

---

15   [1997] ICR 237, [1997] IRLR 140. The case concerned a *Polkey* reduction of 50% and an ex gratia payment of £20,685, against a total loss of £43,136. If the *Polkey* reduction was taken off first, eventual compensation was £883. If the ex gratia payment was taken off first eventual compensation was £11,225 (reduced to the then maximum of £11,000). The EAT held for the latter approach.

16   A simple ex gratia pay-off (or attempt thereat) has thus always been inadvisable – it cannot be legally binding (Employment Rights Act 1996 s. 203(1) which invalidates any attempt to contract out of the Act); finality can only be achieved by an ACAS (COT 3) settlement or a compromise agreement (s. 203(2)–(4)).

17   [1998] ICR 258, [1998] IRLR 134, CA, awarding compensation of £883.

18   As evidenced by the Employment Rights Act 1996 s. 123(7) which provides that any redundancy payment (statutory or otherwise) exceeding the basic award is to be set off then against the compensatory award.

Chapter 9

Redundancy rights and benefits for unemployment

I   INTRODUCTION

Questions of redundancy figure largely in the news in times of recession, and this was reflected, for example, in the case load of ACAS in the 1990s. Compulsory redundancy leads to significant problems in employment law, and the question of the fairness of a redundancy dismissal has already been considered in chapter 8 above. However, research has shown[1] that, even in recessionary times with the strong emphasis on 'down sizing'[2], compulsory redundancy is *not* the first option chosen and that other methods of reduction or reorganisation of the workforce are usually considered more desirable, including natural wastage, redeployment, early retirement and voluntary redundancy. Compulsory redundancy tends to be more common in the private sector, particularly where there is no recognised trade union[3]. Although therefore the majority of workforce reductions will be done in ways which, by and large, do not involve litigation (actual or potential) in employment law and will normally be dealt with by agreement (either long standing or ad hoc), it is now necessary to consider the redundancy rights of those not so dealt with. In addition, this chapter also considers the rules relating to what is now the jobseeker's allowance (replacing unemployment benefit); although this usually comes under the heading of social security law, it does have significant overlaps with employment law, and it is an area about which the employment lawyer should have some knowledge in order to give all-round advice (just as a lawyer advising on personal injuries needs to know the social security background of the various forms of sickness and injury benefits).

---

1   Millward et al. 'Workplace industrial relations in transition' (the ED/ESRC/PSI/ACAS Survey) (1992), ch. 9. The results of the 1998 Workplace Employee Relations Survey were not available at the time of writing.
2   Large sections of British management no longer communicate in English.
3   In 1990, compulsory redundancies were reported by 30 per cent of all establishments; this consisted of 52 per cent in private manufacturing and 35 per cent in private services, but only 4 per cent in the public sector. Overall, compulsory redundancies were reported in 46 per cent of workplaces without recognised unions, compared with 17 per cent where recognised unions were present: op. cit., pp. 321, 324.

2   REDUNDANCY PAYMENTS

i)   The redundancy payments scheme

The scheme requiring employers to make compulsory payments to redundant employees was introduced by the Redundancy Payments Act 1965; this Act was repealed and the relevant provisions are now found in Part XI of the Employment Rights Act 1996. A first basic point to make about the scheme is that it is entirely separate from the dismissed employee's right to claim benefit; in one of the early cases on the 1965 Act Lord Denning MR said:

> '... As I read the Act, a worker of long standing is now recognised as having an accrued right in his job, and his right gains in value with the years. So much so that, if the job is shut down, he is entitled to compensation for loss of the job ... It is not unemployment pay. I repeat "not". Even if he gets another job straightaway, he nevertheless is entitled to full redundancy payment. It is, in a real sense, compensation for long service[4].'

There has been some controversy over the overall purpose of the legislation; ideas of increasing mobility of labour, giving greater job security, reducing the number of strikes over redundancies and rewarding long service have been advanced, but none are complete answers and all are open to doubt[5]. Moreover, one major criticism from a legal point of view is that the legislation is arguably far too complicated for its modest aims, particularly as it is subject to a relatively low maximum payment and in practice yields on average much lower amounts than that[6]. The argument that the whole scheme is itself redundant is now supported by the existence of compulsory consultation procedures in cases of impending redundancy[7] and the redundancy aspects of the law on unfair dismissal (which of course did not exist in 1965), which is now a more important claim than one for straightforward redundancy pay. On the other hand many employers now have private redundancy schemes[8], often more generous than the legislative scheme, and it may be that it was the legislation which gave the spur to these improved schemes, while retaining some residual importance in ensuring that an employee who is not subject to such a scheme at least receives *something* if he is fairly dismissed because of economic conditions outside the control of himself or his employer.

In order to claim a redundancy payment, the ex-employee must have been 'dismissed', and that dismissal must have been 'by reason of redundancy'. The

---

4   *Lloyd v Brassey* [1969] 2 QB 98 at 102, [1969] 1 All ER 382 at 383, CA. Thus, receipt of a redundancy payment does not disentitle a person from jobseeker's allowance.

5   See Fryer 'The Myths of the Redundancy Payments Act' (1973) 2 ILJ 1. The standard works on the subject are Grunfeld *The Law of Redundancy* (2nd edn, 1980) and Bourn *Redundancy Law and Practice* (1983).

6   As from February 2000 the maximum amount is £6,900. This level was *not* subject to increase in the Employment Relations Act 1999 (in spite of the major increase in the limit on the compensatory award for unfair dismissal from £12,000 to £50,000).

7   See pp. 64-70, above.

8   Also, certain specific redundancy schemes have been established by statute in the public sector, e.g. the steelworkers' redundancy scheme, that relating to British shipbuilders and the scheme for dock workers, following the abolition of the national dock labour scheme; the scheme relating to the coal mining industry was of considerable importance in a time of contraction, but has been discontinued.

statutory definition of dismissal has already been considered[9], but three particular points may be noted. The first is that dismissal may not be necessary in certain cases if there has been instead a lay-off or short-time working; this matter is considered below. The second is that 'dismissal' cannot be stretched to include failure to employ in the first place. Thus in *North East Coast Shiprepairers Ltd v Secretary of State for Employment*[10] it was argued that an apprentice was redundant for statutory purposes when he could not be taken on by the employer as a journeyman fitter at the end of his contract of apprenticeship, because there was no such work available. The EAT held, however, that there was no dismissal, only a refusal to employ him in a different capacity upon the proper termination of the previous contract. The third point is that the legislation attempts to safeguard the position of an employee under notice of dismissal who wishes to leave early (e.g. to take up other employment). The Employment Rights Act 1996, section 136(3) provides that he is still deemed to have been dismissed if he leaves during the obligatory period of the employer's notice and gives written[11] counter-notice of his intention to do so during that period. If, however, the employer has good reason to want him to stay for the full period and gives him a further written notice to that effect, but the employee still leaves early, he will only be eligible for a payment if the tribunal thinks it just and equitable that he should receive some or all of his entitlement, after considering the strength of the employer's reasons for wanting to prolong the employment and the employee's reasons for wanting to leave early[12]. One major restriction on these provisions is that the employee's counter-notice is only effective if given during the 'obligatory' period of the employer's notice; this means the amount of time which, by statute[13] or under the individual contract of employment, the employer *has* to give to terminate the contract and so if the employer is generous and in fact gives longer notice than in law he has to, the employee must wait until he is within the obligatory period before giving the counter-notice, otherwise that counter-notice is invalid and he may be deemed to have resigned on his own initiative, not to have been dismissed[14]. This is a potential trap for the employee who, under longer notice than he is contractually entitled to, finds a new job and needs to leave immediately to take it up, thus not being able to rely on section 136(3) if still outside the

---

9   Pp. 444-453, above. See *Harvey* E[401]. As seen at pp. 364-367, above, termination of contract by mutual consent will rarely be found in employment law, for it robs tribunals of jurisdiction; however, one application of it is particularly important here, namely a finding of mutual termination (not dismissal) on a voluntary early retirement/severance on satisfactory terms; in such a case, the volunteer *cannot* claim a redundancy payment as well: *Birch v University of Liverpool* [1985] ICR 470, [1985] IRLR 165, CA; *Scott v Coalite Fuels and Chemicals Ltd* [1988] ICR 355, [1988] IRLR 131, EAT.
10   [1978] ICR 755, [1978] IRLR 149.
11   In s. 95(2), the equivalent provision for unfair dismissal purposes, there is no longer the requirement of writing; before the requirement was dropped it caused problems in cases where there was no notice in writing and the employer then contended that termination of the contract was in fact due to mutual agreement, not dismissal: *Lees v Arthur Greaves (Lees) Ltd* [1974] 2 All ER 393, [1974] ICR 501, CA; *McAlwane v Boughton Estates Ltd* [1973] 2 All ER 299, [1973] ICR 470. There appears to be no good reason why the requirement should remain in the redundancy provision.
12   Employment Rights Act 1996, s. 142.
13   Ibid., s. 86.
14   *Armit v McLaughlin* (1965) 1 ITR 280; *Pritchard-Rhodes Ltd v Boon and Milton* [1979] IRLR 19; *Doble v Firestone Tyre and Rubber Co Ltd* [1981] IRLR 300, EAT.

obligatory period. However, the EAT have suggested[15] a possible way round in one class of case; this is where the employee *requests* that he be allowed to leave early and the employer *agrees*. This is not a section 136(3)case (which is where the employee serves formal notice of his *intention* to leave early) and so can be construed on wider principles; in particular, it may be construed as a consensual variation of the employer's original notice, meaning that the employee leaves at the earlier date, is still 'dismissed' by the employer, and can claim his redundancy payment. However, it must be remembered (a) that the employer must still have given *actual notice* in the first place (not just made vague statements about future job losses)[16], and (b) that this alternative approach only works if there is definite agreement between employer and employee – if the employee wants to (or has to) act unilaterally he must still comply with section 136(3) and beware the 'obligatory period' trap.

A dismissed employee may present a claim for a redundancy payment to an employment tribunal within six months of the 'relevant date' of dismissal, though the tribunal may also hear the claim if presented during the six months following that period if it appears just and equitable to do so, having regard to the employee's reasons for failing to comply with the normal time limit[17]. In such proceedings, one crucial factor is that there is in section 163(2) a statutory presumption that the dismissal was for redundancy, so that the burden of proof is upon the *employer* to prove on a balance of probabilities, that the dismissal was for some other reason[18]. This leads to one problem of at least theoretical importance to which there is no definite answer, and that is – is the test to be applied subjective (what the employer *thought* was the dominant reason for dismissal) or objective (what the overall facts suggest)? The problem arises where there was on the facts prima facie a 'redundancy situation', but the employer states that he genuinely believed at the time that some other ground existed (e.g. incompetence, suspected dishonesty) and that he was acting on that ground in dismissing; does that discharge his burden of proof and defeat the claim, or should the tribunal look at the facts objectively? The majority decision of the Court of Appeal in *Hindle v Percival Boats*

---

15   *CPS Recruitment Ltd v Bowen* [1982] IRLR 54, approving *Tunnel Holdings Ltd v Woolf* [1976] ICR 387.

16   Thus certain previous cases such as *Pritchard-Rhodes Ltd v Boon and Milton* (n. 14 above) remain good law and are reconcilable with *Bowen*'s case on the ground that the employer had not actually given notice, and so there was no notice there to be varied by agreement. On the requirement of notice, see p. 367, above.

17   Ibid., s. 164; 'relevant date' is defined in s. 145 as (a) the date the employer's notice takes effect, (b) the date the dismissal takes effect, if no notice is given, (c) the date of expiry of a fixed term contract, (d) the 'relevant date' (as already defined) of the last contract where there has been one or more trial periods, or (e) the date of expiry of the employee's notice where he has given valid early notice under s. 136(3). Where, however, any notice given (including the case where no notice is given) is shorter than the legal minimum which is required by s. 86, the relevant date may be deemed to be the later date of the notional expiry of that legal minimum period, for three purposes – the calculation of the two years' qualifying period, the computation of the length of service for calculation of the payment and the determination of the relevant statutory maximum on a 'week's pay' for calculation purposes (i.e. where that maximum has been raised by regulations between the dismissal and the claim). The purpose of this complicated provision is to prevent an employer gaining an advantage in these three areas by wrongfully dismissing the employee with short or no notice.

18   He may then have to prove that that other reason, if accepted by the tribunal, was fair, if unfair dismissal is also being claimed. However, the presumption of redundancy will *not* apply to the latter claim: *Midland Foot Comfort Centre Ltd v Richmond* [1973] 2 All ER 294, [1973] ICR 219. For a relatively rare example of a case being decided by recourse to the statutory presumption, see *Willcox v Hastings* [1987] IRLR 298, CA.

Ltd [19] has been said to be clear authority in favour of the subjective approach and indeed Sachs LJ said:

'... once the tribunal is satisfied that the ground put forward by the employer is genuine and is the one to which the dismissal is mainly attributable the onus is discharged – and it ceases to be in point that the ground was unwise or based on a mistaken view of facts[20] .'

However, Lord Denning MR's dissent (on the decision and on this point) is a strong one, clearly favouring an entirely objective test[1] and the third judgment, that of Widgery LJ, is less than clear on the point, for although he expresses agreement with Sachs LJ, he states that he finds the distinction between objective and subjective tests neither helpful nor conclusive, and later says:

'... the lesson of the *MacLaughlan* case in my opinion is that the tribunal must not accept the explanation put forward by the employer however honestly, without looking at the whole of the evidence to see if it positively established that the dismissal was not mainly due to a diminution in the requirement of the business for employees on work of a particular kind[2] .'

However, even if a general subjective test can be constructed from this case, it is certainly not an unqualified one, and in practice the following qualifications may make the gap between it and an objective approach unimportant in many cases – first, the tribunal clearly does not have to take the employer's word at face value and may look behind it, at the very least to confirm that it is supported by facts (per Widgery LJ, supra); second, the tribunal may look behind it to ensure that the employer has not 'misdirected' himself [3] or used the wrong label[4] in calling it redundancy; third, in reorganisation cases (which can prove some of the most difficult) the tribunal can clearly investigate whether it is a genuine reorganisation and not just a cover for redundancies[5] ; fourth, in any case where the tribunal is left in real doubt as to the truth of the employer's assertions (especially if they are at variance with some of the facts) the statutory presumption can decide the case in the employee's favour. There may however remain cases where none of these qualifications apply, where an employer who is faced with a diminution of work still genuinely thinks (without misdirecting himself) that he is dismissing for a reason other than redundancy, and it is submitted that in such a case the approach of the tribunal should remain subjective[6] , particularly as the employer may now

---

19 [1969] 1 All ER 836, [1969] 1 WLR 174, CA.
20 At 842 and 182 respectively.
1   Approving the decision of the Court of Session in *MacLaughlan v Alexander Paterson Ltd* (1968) 3 ITR 251; see also his Lordship's judgment in *Mumford v Boulton and Paul (Steel Construction) Ltd* (1971) 6 ITR 76, CA.
2   At 848 and 188 respectively.
3   Per Widgery LJ at 847E and 187G respectively.
4   On analogy with the unfair dismissal case of *Abernethy v Mott, Hay and Anderson* [1974] ICR 323, [1974] IRLR 213, CA, see p. 464, above; this may be a particular danger in this area, since the word 'redundancy' in common usage in industry may mean much more than its restricted legal meaning.
5   *Johnson v Nottinghamshire Combined Police Authority* [1974] 1 All ER 1082, [1974] ICR 170, CA.
6   Drawing an analogy with the requirements in unfair dismissal that the tribunal must look for the reason actually acting upon the employer's mind at the date of dismissal: *W Devis & Sons Ltd v Atkins* [1977] 3 All ER 40, [1977] ICR 662, HL.

have to go further (where both redundancy and unfair dismissal are claimed) and show that that subjective reason is fair; it must be admitted though that *Hindle v Percival Boats Ltd*[7] is not clear authority for this view.

ii)   The definition of redundancy[8]

As stated above, the word 'redundancy' can mean different things to different people and in different contexts. For the purposes of the statutory scheme, however, it is defined in section 139, and this definition is exhaustive[9]. An employee is dismissed by reason of redundancy if the dismissal is attributable wholly or mainly to—

'a)   the fact that his employer has ceased, or intends to cease (i) to carry on the business for the purposes of which the employee was employed by him, or (ii) to carry on that business in the place where the employee was so employed, or

b)   the fact that the requirements of that business (i) for employees to carry out work of a particular kind, or (ii) for employees to carry out work of a particular kind in the place where the employee was employed by the employer have ceased or diminished or are expected to cease to diminish.'

This definition applies in two principal cases – where the whole business closes down and where the business carries on (in some cases actually expanding) but its requirements for the services of people such as the applicant cease or diminish. In either case, this can happen either generally or just in the place where the applicant was employed to work. These major elements will now be considered.

a)   Closure of the business

This type of case is usually easy from the legal point (though it may be particularly appropriate for the compulsory consultation procedures which are discussed in chapter 2). Some problems may arise, however, in defining the 'business' and the 'employer', although 'business' is widely defined in section 235 as including a trade or profession or any activity[10] carried on by a body of persons, whether corporate or unincorporate. Moreover if the business is a company which has

---

7   See n. 19, above.
8   See *Harvey* E[601].
9   *Hindle v Percival Boats Ltd* [1969] 1 All ER 836, [1969] 1 WLR 174, CA (Lord Denning MR dissenting). Per Widgery LJ at 847 and 187 respectively; 'It is not the policy of this Act to reward long service and good conduct as such, but only to compensate an employee who is dismissed for redundancy as defined in [section 139]'. The function of the tribunal is to apply the statutory definition to the facts, *not* to seek to look behind the facts and assess the rights and wrongs of the employer's decision to make the redundancy: *Moon v Homeworthy Furniture (Northern) Ltd* [1977] ICR 117, [1976] IRLR 298; *AUT v Newcastle-upon-Tyne University* [1987] ICR 317, [1988] IRLR 10; *James W Cook & Co (Wivenhoe) Ltd v Tipper* [1990] ICR 716, [1990] IRLR 386, CA; this is subject to the point made above, in the context of re-organisation, that the tribunal may look into the reasons at least to the extent of being satisfied that they are genuine and not just a sham.
10   *Dallow Industrial Properties Ltd v Else* [1967] 2 QB 449, [1967] 2 All ER 30.

other associated companies[11] and the economic factors in question affect that group as a whole or some other part of it, that too can be taken into account to satisfy the definition. It is also established that it is not necessary to show that the employer was the legal owner of the 'business' in question, only that that person was generally in control of it prior to its closure. Thus, when a sub-postmistress gave up the business of the sub-post office upon her retirement it could not be argued that the 'business' was that carried on by the Post Office (which of course had not ceased), and so her ex-employee was able to claim a redundancy payment[12].

b) Diminished requirements for employees to do work of a particular kind

Section 139 is designed to cover the case where the business remains (or even expands), but the employee's particular function disappears; the obvious case of this would occur when the function is automated or, on the same principle, if the work is given instead to independent contractors[13] or if work previously done by two employees is amalgamated and done by one, the other being dismissed.[14]

The question whether there has been a diminution in the requirements for employees to do work of a particular kind has caused problems for years. To decide whether an individual employee comes within this wording, two tests evolved – the factual test (i.e. has the work he or she was actually doing gone?) and the contract test (has all the work that he or she *could* be required to do under the contract gone?). It was the latter that gained ground more recently[15], based on two decidedly ambiguous Court of Appeal decisions[16], which could have the effect of making it more difficult to establish redundancy where the contractual obligations were drafted to include a level of flexibility. However, on this point we have seen a major change of approach. This began with the judgment of Judge Clark in *Safeway Stores plc v Burrell*[17] which went back to the pure wording of the section and held that both the factual and contractual tests are wrong, and unnecessary glosses on that wording. It was pointed out that the wording considers the need for employees (plural), not that particular employee, and so what matters is whether a redundancy situation has arisen and whether he or she has lost employment because of it. Shortly afterwards another division of the EAT in

---

11 Defined in s. 231: '… any two employers are to be treated as associated if one is a company of which the other (directly or indirectly) has control, or if both are companies of which a third person (directly or indirectly) has control …'. See pp. 22-24, above.
12 *Thomas v Jones* [1978] ICR 274, EAT.
13 *Bromby & Hoare Ltd v Evans* [1972] ICR 113, 12 KIR 160, *Amos v Max-Arc Ltd* [1973] ICR 46, [1973] IRLR 285. Contracting out of services or activities has been a dominant theme in modern employment relations: 'The 1998 Workplace Employee Relations Survey – First Findings' (DTI/ACAS/ESRC/PSI; URN/98/934) p. 7. Where the employee takes a job knowing that the work is subject to steady decline so that his employment can only be temporary, there may still be a redundancy when he is eventually dismissed: *Nottinghamshire County Council v Lee* [1980] ICR 635, [1980] IRLR 284, CA; this case must cast doubt on the correctness of the EAT's decision in *O'Hare v Rotaprint Ltd* [1980] ICR 94, [1980] IRLR 47.
14 *Sutton v Revlon Overseas Corpn* [1973] IRLR 173; *Carry All Motors Ltd v Pennington* [1980] ICR 806, [1980] IRLR 455. The fact that the total amount of work to be done remains constant is irrelevant; there is a redundancy provided the number of employees required to do it has diminished: *McCrea v Cullen & Davison Ltd* [1988] IRLR 30, NICA.
15 *Cowen v Haden Ltd* [1983] ICR 1, [1982] IRLR 314, CA; *Pink v White* [1985] IRLR 489.
16 *Nelson v BBC* [1977] ICR 649, [1977] IRLR 148, CA and *Nelson v BBC (No 2)* [1980] ICR 110, [1979] IRLR 346, CA.
17 [1997] ICR 523, [1997] IRLR 200, EAT.

Church v West Lancashire NHS Trust[18] disagreed strongly, but when the matter went to the House of Lords in *Murray v Foyle Meats Ltd*[19] it was *Safeway Stores* that was unequivocally approved. Giving the principal speech, Lord Irvine LC said:

> '... the language of [s. 139(1)(b)] is in my view simplicity itself. It asks two questions of fact. The first is whether one or other of various states of economic affairs exists. In this case the relevant one is whether the requirements of the business for employees to carry out work of a particular kind have diminished. The second question is whether the dismissal is attributable, wholly or mainly to that state of affairs. This is a question of causation. In the present case, the Tribunal found as a fact that the requirements of the business for employees to work in the slaughter house had diminished. Secondly, they found that that state of affairs had led to the appellants being dismissed. That, in my opinion, is the end of the matter. This conclusion is in accordance with the analysis of the statutory provisions by Judge Peter Clark in *Safeway Stores plc v Burrell* and I need to say no more than that I entirely agree with his admirably clear reasoning and conclusions'.

He went on to disapprove of the cases said to establish the contract test, and for good measure Lord Clyde giving the other speech castigated both previous tests as unnecessary.

This reinterpretation is very welcome and of great importance generally. However, it arose in the two EAT cases in a specialised and difficult area, known as a 'bumping' redundancy. This occurs where, for example, within a department employee A's job disappears, but A (thought to be a good worker) is retained and given B's job, with B being dismissed instead. Is B redundant? Under the old tests, B's job is still there, and so he is not redundant, but under the new approach there is a diminution in employees (plural) required by the employer and B's dismissal is causally linked ('attributable') to it, and so now B is indeed redundant. Given the curious agendas behind some of these cases this is in fact usually to the *employer's* advantage, redundancy often being the easier and cheaper option, whereas the employee may want *not* to be redundant, in order to open up an unfair dismissal action. Arguably, this is why the EAT in *Church* were so against this development especially when allied to what they saw as an objectionable *way* of bumping by the employer, namely sacking all employees and 'inviting' them to reapply for the jobs left (where, the EAT feared, there would be too much scope for subjective choice and favouritism by the management). However, *Church* must now be considered wrong, and in a bumping case there now will normally be a redundancy. However, it may be that this will have the effect of increasing the importance of an unfair dismissal challenge based on the methods and procedures used to effect the eventual shedding of labour[20]. This may be the real answer to the problems faced in *Church*.

There remains, however, one further element of the definition of redundancy which is not affected by *Murray* (not being relevant on the facts of the case, and so

---

18   [1998] ICR 423, [1998] IRLR 4.
19   [1999] ICR 827, [1999] IRLR 562, HL. Arguably, the broader approach in this case brings the definition more into line with that now used in the Trade Union and Labour Relations (Consolidation) Act 1992 s. 195 (on collective redundancies), i.e. 'dismissal for a reason not related to the individual concerned or for a number of reasons all of which are not so related'.
20   For unfair redundancy, see p. 484, above.

are addressed). This is the question of what is meant by 'work of a particular kind', a particularly crucial concept where for example, the numbers involved remain much the same but the *skills* required change. There is much case law on this, and the law clearly looks at the *work function* of the employee within the organisation, not necessarily at his particular job at the time, still less at any particular job title. Thus the job may change over time in its organisation (and thereby, in some cases, in its suitability for, and attractiveness to a particular employee) but, as long as the function remains, an employee who is dismissed for refusing to accept the changes (or who walks out because of them and then claims constructive dismissal under section 136(1)(c)) is *not* 'redundant'. In *Chapman v Goonvean and Rostowrack China Clay Co Ltd*[1] ten employees were provided with free transport to work; when three were made redundant during a trade recession the transport became uneconomic and the employer discontinued it for the remaining seven who, though offered continued employment with the employer, gave in their notice, left the employment and claimed redundancy payments. The Court of Appeal held that they were not redundant since the work that they performed had not ceased or diminished (the employer had shown that the seven were replaced by other employees taken on to do their work); the only change was in the organisation and attractiveness of the jobs for the time being. The facts of this case concern a relatively incidental aspect of employment, but the principle goes further and can apply to changes in the job structure itself, for there is no definite right to have employment continued indefinitely on the same terms and the courts and tribunals have ensured that an employer can take necessary steps to increase the efficiency of his enterprise without being liable to make redundancy payments unless there is a genuine diminution in the work function in question. In *Johnson v Nottinghamshire Combined Police Authority*[2] two clerks, whose work had been reorganised from a five-day week to a shift system operating over six days per week to increase overall efficiency, refused to accept this and claimed redundancy pay (in spite of the fact that they had been replaced by two new employees), but this was refused by the Court of Appeal on the ground that the kind of work remained the same and so the reorganisation was not due to redundancy:

> 'It is settled ... that an employer is entitled to reorganise his business so as to improve its efficiency and, in doing so, to propose to his staff a change in the terms and conditions of their employment; and to dispense with their services if they do not agree. Such a change does not automatically give the staff a right to redundancy payments. It only does so if the change in the terms and conditions is due to a redundancy situation[3].'

A similar result was achieved in *Lesney Products Ltd v Nolan*[4] where the work of machine setters was altered from a day shift and a night shift to a double day shift

1   [1973] 2 All ER 1063, [1973] ICR 310, CA, overruling *Dutton v CH Bailey Ltd* [1968] 2 Lloyd's Rep 122, 3 ITR 355; see also *Arnold v Thomas Harrington Ltd* [1969] 1 QB 312, [1967] 2 All ER 866.
2   [1974] 1 All ER 1082, [1974] ICR 170, CA.
3   Per Lord Denning MR at 1084 and 176 respectively; the phrase 'redundancy situation' is clarified in his Lordship's judgment in *Lesney Products Ltd v Nolan* (n. 3). The last two sentences in the dictum are important, for they make it clear that there *could* be a redundancy in certain circumstances; the EAT reaffirmed that there is no rule of law that a change of hours or shifts cannot produce a redundancy – it remains ultimately a question of fact for the tribunal: *MacFisheries Ltd v Findlay* [1985] ICR 160, EAT.
4   [1977] ICR 235, [1977] IRLR 77, CA.

system, with a consequent decrease in overtime payments; when six of the setters refused to work the new system and claimed redundancy payments, the Court of Appeal held against them since the amount of work to be done remained constant, though reorganised on to a daytime basis (the undoubted overall 'redundancy situation' having been dealt with by the company by discontinuing the night shift worked by another class of employees who were not parties to the action). Moreover, this principle is not restricted to alterations in the structure or pattern of working hours and conditions, but may also apply to necessary changes in the discharging of the employee's function, for, as long as that function remains the same overall, the employer may introduce new methods and technology to increase the efficiency of the function and if the employee is either unwilling or unable to adapt to them, he may be dismissed without being redundant[5].

It can be seen from the above discussion that, under this head of redundancy, much will depend on the difficult question of fact – how radical does a change in the job, or the reorganisation of it, have to be before it can be said that the function itself has changed? To put it in the language of section 139 – what *is* work of that 'particular kind'? If the change is great enough to turn it into work of a different kind, then the employee who is unwilling or unable to perform the new function can claim that he is redundant since his old function has disappeared[6]. In the earlier cases, this was not easy since the courts and tribunals in general took a fairly wide view of what constitutes one type of work (thus allowing the employer more scope for reorganisation without having to make redundancy payments); thus the function of 'barmaid' remained the same, even when an older style public house was transformed into a 'road house' requiring barmaids with certain attributes which no amount of retraining could possibly have produced in the original incumbent[7], and the function of 'boatbuilder' remained the same even though the boatyard went over to fibreglass boats instead of the wooden ones which the dismissed employee was by long practice used to making[8]. Such questions may raise difficult borderline cases[9], and the approach in the later case of *Murphy v Epsom College*[10] shows a narrower approach to 'kind of work' and emphasises that if that changes there may be a redundancy even if the redundant employee is immediately replaced by someone else skilled in the new kind of work (i.e. where there is no net decrease in the workforce). In that case the college's heating system was modernised, calling for new skills to maintain it. One of the existing two plumbers said that he was unwilling/unable to perform all the necessary new functions; he was dismissed and replaced with a heating technician. The Court of Appeal upheld the tribunal's decision that the dismissed employee was redundant since the employer's need for *plumbers* was reduced from two to one on the reorganisation (with its corresponding requirement for a heating technician instead).

5   *North Riding Garages Ltd v Butterwick* [1967] 2 QB 56, [1967] 1 All ER 644; *Hindle v Percival Boats Ltd* [1969] 1 All ER 836, [1969] 1 WLR 174, CA. It is argued above that the courts might be willing to apply in such cases an implied term of reasonable adaptation to new methods and techniques, see p. 130, above and *Cresswell v Board of Inland Revenue* [1984] 2 All ER 713, [1984] ICR 508.

6   *Robinson v British Island Airways Ltd* [1978] ICR 304, [1977] IRLR 477, a case where the employee was arguing that he was *not* redundant, in order to claim the more generous remedies for unfair dismissal. A redundancy can arise from a change in specialisms within an overall job: *BBC v Farnworth* [1998] ICR 1116, EAT.

7   *Vaux and Associated Breweries Ltd v Ward* (1968) 3 ITR 385.

8   *Hindle v Percival Boats Ltd* [1969] 1 All ER 836, [1969] 1 WLR 174, CA.

9   See, e.g., *European Chefs (Catering) Ltd v Currell* (1971) 6 ITR 37.

10 [1985] ICR 80, [1984] IRLR 271, CA.

This whole problem flows from the emphasis in section 139 on the overall work function and not the particulars of the job as organised at the material time; it has been argued that this should not be so, as it puts the financial risk of a particular job becoming uneconomic upon the employee, rather than upon the employer[11]. However, the courts have consistently adopted the view that this legislation is not meant to be a brake upon necessary reorganisation, and it can be argued that the hasher result of this may be mitigated by two factors: first, it has been stated by the courts that a bogus reorganisation is not to be used by an employer as a cover for dismissals which are in fact due to redundancy[12]; second, since 1971 it has been possible for an employee dismissed because of changing work patterns (or resigning because of them and claiming constructive dismissal) to bring an action for unfair dismissal against the employer if he thinks he has been harshly treated over the change or reorganisation (or if he has grounds to doubt the bona fides of the employer's actions), and this action may lead to more generous remedies (especially since the major increase in the compensation limit in the Employment Relations Act 1999), so that in many cases it may be in the employee's favour *not* to be in law redundant, since that would prima facie be a *fair* ground for dismissal[13]. Therefore there can easily arise (especially in reorganisation cases) the topsy turvy situation of the employee (wanting more than the statutory redundancy payment) arguing that his dismissal was *not* for redundancy and the employer (happy to keep the labour-related cost of the reorganisation down to statutory redundancy payments) arguing that it was, as indeed was the case in *Murphy v Epsom College*[14]. Thus, the narrower approach to 'kind of work' in that case, with its easier finding of redundancy, paradoxically may operate *against* the employee's wider interests.[15]

c) 'in the place where the employee was so employed'

Both of the above heads of redundancy envisage the relevant economic factors producing effects either generally or only in the place where the employee worked. It may therefore be vital to know what that 'place' is. It could cover the whole of the United Kingdom or be as small an area as one part of one city[16]. The problem often arises in cases where the employer orders the employee to move to a new workplace, for example if the company wishes to close down a factory in Ipswich, telling its employees there to work in its other factory in Norwich. The approach generally adopted here in the past has been that the question of law involved is whether the employer has *contractual* authority to give the order to move, so that 'in the place where the employee was so employed' means in the

11 See Freedland, (1977) 6 ILJ 237.
12 *Johnson v Nottinghamshire Combined Police Authority* (n. 1, above) at 1087 and 179 respectively, per Stephenson LJ.
13 Employment Rights Act 1996, s. 98(2)(c); see n. 5, above.
14 See n. 10, above. This kind of prevented logic can also occur in TUPE cases (p. 159, above) with the employees arguing that they have *no* TUPE protection, in order to cash in their redundancy rights against the transferor employers and start afresh with the transferee employer.
15 Though it is not necessarily so simple – even if the employee succeeds in showing (in an unfair dismissal case arising from a reorganisation) that he was *not* dismissed for redundancy, but rather for refusing to agree to changes insisted upon by the employer, contrary to his contractual rights, there is still the danger that the tribunal might hold the dismissal *fair*, as for 'some other substantial reason' (see p. 496, above). In such a case he would receive *neither* a redundancy payment *nor* unfair dismissal compensation.
16 *Rowbotham v Arthur Lee & Sons Ltd* [1975] ICR 109, [1974] IRLR 377; *Air Canada v Lee* [1978] ICR 1202, [1978] IRLR 392, EAT.

place where he could be obliged to work under the terms of his contract of employment, not simply where he had in fact been working prior to the order to move[17]. If the contract envisages working in the new location (e.g. in the example used, a term that the employee would work anywhere in East Anglia), then the employee who refuses is dismissed for failure to comply (even if he had in fact been working solely in Ipswich for years); if the contract does not envisage this (i.e. Ipswich only), then the employee has prima facie a redundancy claim based upon the closure of the Ipswich factory.

Questions have therefore often arisen as to the construction of the individual's contract of employment. The contract may contain an express term[18] which will usually dispose of the matter as the traditional view is that a clear express term should not normally be subject to extension or restriction by any claimed implied term[19]. If there is no such express term the tribunal must consider whether a term should be implied in the contract[20] by looking at all the relevant evidence. In *O'Brien v Associated Fire Alarms Ltd*[1] two electricians worked for a company at its Liverpool office, working exclusively in that city (although the company operated throughout the United Kingdom and the Liverpool office controlled the whole of the north west); when the company's business in Liverpool diminished and they were asked to work in Cumberland, they refused because it would have meant working away from home and they were dismissed. Their claims for redundancy payments were upheld by the Court of Appeal on the basis that, there being no relevant express term in their contracts, there was no implied term obliging them to work outside daily travelling distance from their homes, particularly as they had never been called upon to do so before and there was no clear evidence of any implied agreement to do so[2]. However, in *Stevenson v Teesside Bridge and Engineering Ltd 0*[3] a steel erector who refused to move to another site when work on the existing site (which was close to his home) finished was not entitled to a redundancy payment since travelling from site to site was found by the Divisional Court to be an integral part of that trade (which there was evidence he had accepted when interviewed for the post) and the contract of employment, though not containing an express mobility clause, was held to envisage such mobility through terms relating to travelling and subsistence allowances, and the transfer of contracts. However, this whole contractual approach had long been criticised in the leading practitioner work[4], which argued that a practical and

---

17 *Sutcliffe v Hawker Siddeley Aviation Ltd* [1973] ICR 560, [1973] IRLR 304, NIRC; *Rank Xerox Ltd v Churchill* [1988] IRLR 280, EAT.

18 As for example in *Sutcliffe v Hawker Siddeley Aviation Ltd* (supra) and *United Kingdom Atomic Energy Authority v Claydon* [1974] ICR 128, [1974] IRLR 6. If the employer wishes to rely on a mobility clause, he should do so clearly, and not as an afterthought: *Curling v Securicor Ltd* [1992] IRLR 549, EAT.

19 *Nelson v BBC* [1977] ICR 649, [1977] IRLR 148, CA. However, recent cases have shown movement towards a concept of *overriding* implied terms (especially the term of trust and respect), see p. 124, above; it is possible that this development (if it continues) could spread into redundancy law.

20 *GEC Telecommunications Ltd v McAllister* [1975] IRLR 346. For the implication of terms into contracts of employment, see p. 107, above.

1 [1969] 1 All ER 93, [1968] 1 WLR 1916, CA; *Mumford v Boulton and Paul (Steel Construction) Ltd* (1970) 5 ITR 222; *Managers (Holborn) Ltd v Hohne* [1977] IRLR 230, EAT.

2 While each case must depend on its facts, it is likely that a term that an employee may be required to work *within* reasonable daily travel will be easy to imply where the contract is silent on the matter: *Courtaulds Northern Spinning Ltd v Sibson* [1988] ICR 451, [1988] IRLR 305, CA.

3 [1971] 1 All ER 296, 10 KIR 53.

4 *Harvey* E[657]ff.

geographical test (where was the employee *actually* working?) would fit better the purpose and intent of the legislation. The EAT in *Bass Leisure Ltd v Thomas*[5] agreed with that approach, held that the authority in favour of the contractual approach was only persuasive, and applied a geographical test. Thus, an employee whose work at a Coventry depot had ceased with its closure *was* redundant, even though the employers had a contractual right (which they had sought to exercise) to require her to work at another depot 20 miles away, where she did not wish to work. In this particular case, the geographical approach was in the employee's favour, but this is an area ripe for boomerang effects of decisions, and the overall result of this approach (if generally followed) is that it may make it easier for an employer to make an employee redundant (a prima facie fair ground of dismissal) at one location, even where there is a mobility clause in the contract. This could be significant where an employer wants to close down one whole location (where perhaps productivity and labour relations have not been good), dispense with the workforce there and build up production elsewhere by taking on new staff. Something of this sort occurred in *High Table Ltd v Horst*[6] where waitresses dismissed by a service company when the client no longer wanted their work were held to be redundant, in spite of a mobility clause in their contracts. The Court of Appeal approved *Bass Leisure*, on the basis that a factual approach to the actual place of work will normally resolve the question, subject to the caveat that if the employee has in fact been mobile it may well be necessary to consider the terms of the contract (as in the older case law considered above). Thus, their approach is an amalgam, though with a normal bias towards the factual/ geographical test, applied by the good sense of the tribunal. Two points are worth noting: (i) the court seemed to view this decision as pro-employee (i.e. redundancy rights are not to be prejudiced by the inclusion of a mobility clause), but as seen above it will often be in the employer's interests to establish a redundancy (and indeed, the end result of the case was to allow the *employers'* appeal); (ii) the employer may now have the best of both worlds with a mobility clause, in that if he tries to enforce it and the employee refuses to go, the latter is potentially subject to fair dismissal through disobedience to a lawful order, whereas if the work dries up in one area but the employer decides *not* to enforce the mobility clause and simply dismisses those working that, the result may well be a simple redundancy (which is *not* defeated by the existence of the clause).

There is however (whatever the test) one further factor that may cloud the issue; as will be seen below, a redundant employee may be under an obligation to accept suitable alternative work if it is offered by the employer[7] and it is possible that although an employee may have a right to refuse to transfer elsewhere (as in *O'Brien*'s case, or if the geographical test is widely applied), in certain cases where the distance is not great the offer to work at the new location may constitute an offer of suitable alternative work which the employee would be advised to accept.

---

5   [1994] IRLR 104.
6   [1998] ICR 409, [1997] IRLR 513, CA.
7   Employment Rights Act 1996, s. 141.

iii)   The right to payment

a)   Qualification: transfer of business or undertaking

In order to qualify for a redundancy payment, the dismissed employee must have been continuously employed for at least two years on the 'relevant date'[8]. Continuity of employment is considered in detail in chapter 3 above; one particular point needs to be added to the general discussion there, relating to continuity through a transfer of business or undertaking. This is now covered by the general rules under (now) the 1996 Act and also by special rules under regulations; as these unfortunately apply independently of each other, it is necessary to consider them separately.

Transfers of business under the 1996 Act. Continuity of employment through a transfer of business (where the employee in fact remains with that business) is preserved by section 218 of the 1996 Act[9], so that if the employee is later made redundant by the new employer he can count his time with the old employer for the purposes of qualification for and computation of a redundancy payment. These provisions related solely to questions of continuity of employment and did not prejudice the general common law rule that an employee could not be made to change employer without his consent[10]. Further, these longstanding provisions meant that if the transferor employer sold the business to the transferee who did *not* keep on the workforce, it was clear that the *transferor* employer, dismissing the workforce on the transfer, was liable for the redundancy payments.

Transfers of undertaking under the Regulations. The above position has however been materially complicated by the provisions of the Transfer of Undertakings (Protection of Employment) Regulations 1981[11] which apply where there has been a 'transfer of undertaking'. It is particularly unfortunate in this context that these changes were enacted by extraneous regulations, rather than by amendments to the existing provisions of the legislation, for the position is subject to a separate set of legislative provisions, on the assumption that there is a 'transfer of undertaking'[12]. On that assumption, the continuity of employment of those transferring to the employ of the transferee is preserved by regulation 5. To this extent, the regulation is in most cases otiose since (assuming it also to be a 'transfer of business') this will be the case anyway under section 218. However, regulation 5 goes considerably further, for it states that a relevant transfer *automatically* transfers the employee's contract of employment from the transferor employer to the transferee employer[13]. This means

---

8   Ibid., s 155, for the 'relevant date' see p. 522, above.
9   Provided that there is a genuine transfer of business, and not just the sale of one of its assets – see p. 142, above; *Melon v Hector Powe Ltd* [1981] ICR 43, [1980] IRLR 477, HL.
10   *Nokes v Doncaster Amalgamated Collieries Ltd* [1940] AC 1014, [1940] 3 All ER 549, HL.
11   S.I. 1981 No. 1794, see *Harvey* R[181]; McMullen *Business Transfers*. The effects of these regulations are considered above at pp. 70-73 (union rights to consultation), pp. 159-170 (continuity of employment) and pp. 490-493 (unfair dismissal).
12   For the meaning of this phrase (and 'relevant transfer'), see p. 160, above.
13   This was irrespective of the wishes of the parties (*Newns v British Airways plc* [1992] IRLR 575, CA) and meant that the old common law rule in *Nokes* (n. 10, above) no longer applied to a case covered by the regulations. However, serious confusion was caused by the decision of the ECJ in *Katsikas v Konstantinidis* C-132/91: [1993] IRLR 179 that Directive 77/187/EEC does not *oblige* member states to legislate for automatic transfer against the employee's wishes. In the light of this, the Trade Union Reform and Employment Rights Act 1993 added a right to object to transfer, but for reasons given above (p. 162) it appears that this may be an empty right for many employees, and so automatic transfer will continue to be the norm.

that the employee's previous right to claim a redundancy payment from the transferor is no longer applicable and, contrary to previous accepted practice, if the transferee does *not* take the workforce on he may still find that it is he, not the transferor, who has to pay the redundancy payments[14]. Regulation 5 applies wherever an employee is employed by the transferor employer 'immediately before' the transfer. It used to be the case that the regulation could be avoided relatively easily by the device of the transferee requiring the transferor to dismiss the workforce at some point before the transfer; this was possible because in *Secretary of State for Employment v Spence*[15] the Court of Appeal held that 'immediately before' meant 'at the time of' the transfer, so that an employee dismissed before that time (possibly by only a few hours) could not claim the protection of regulation 5, i.e. *any* gap was fatal (leaving the employee to pursue his remedies, including a redundancy payment, against the original employer who might well be insolvent). However, as pointed out at p. 166 above, this position changed radically in the light of two decisions – that of the ECJ in *P Bork International A/S (in liquidation) v Foreningen of Arbejdsledere i Danmark*[16] on the meaning of Directive 77/187/EEC on which the regulations are based, and that of the House of Lords in *Litster v Forth Dry Dock and Engineering Co Ltd*[17] which followed and applied the decision of the ECJ. The end result is that if the transferor dismisses the employee because of the transfer (e.g. at the transferee's request) and that dismissal is unfair under regulation 8 (which it will be unless it comes within the 'economic, technical or organisational reasons' defence in regulation 8(2))[18], then for the purposes of regulation 5 the employee will be *deemed* to have been still employed by the transferor immediately before the transfer, so that automatic transfer of his contract to the transferee *will* apply. Prior dismissal will therefore no longer be effective in itself in most cases.

The inapplicability of estoppel. Normally questions of continuity (for qualification and computation purposes) will be solved by applying the provisions of Part XIV of the 1996 Act or the regulations but one judicial gloss was added in the case of a change from one employer to another where there has been *no* 'transfer of business' or 'transfer of undertaking' (so that the above provisions do not apply). In such a case, there is normally a break in continuity, but the Court of Appeal held in *Evenden v Guildford City AFC Ltd*[19] that where at the time of the change the new employer gave the employee an assurance that he would regard the employment as unbroken, so that time with the previous employer would count for redundancy purposes, the new employer should not be allowed to go back on that later and claim that continuity was in fact broken by the change. This meant that the presumption of continuity, now contained in section 210(5), was not rebutted and so the whole period could be counted; this principle was accepted by the whole court and Lord Denning MR (with the support of Browne LJ) added the further ground that such conduct by the new employer gives rise to a promissory estoppel[20] in the employee's favour.

---

14 As in *Premier Motors (Medway) Ltd v Total Oil Great Britain Ltd* [1984] ICR 58, [1983] IRLR 471 in which Browne-Wilkinson P made it clear that the position now is the reverse of the old law, a fact that had not been realised when the parties negotiated the transfer deal.
15 [1986] ICR 651, [1986] IRLR 248, CA.
16 101/87: [1989] IRLR 41, ECJ.
17 [1989] ICR 341, [1989] IRLR 161, HL.
18 See p. 491, above.
19 [1975] 3 All ER 269, [1975] ICR 367; *Rastill v Automatic Refreshment Services Ltd* [1978] ICR 289, EAT.
20 *Central London Property Trust Ltd v High Trees House Ltd* [1947] KB 130, [1956] 1 All ER 256.

However, in the case of *Secretary of State for Employment v Globe Elastic Thread Co Ltd*[1], a case primarily concerned with the (now repealed) redundancy rebate aspect of this problem, the House of Lords overruled *Evenden*'s case and held that questions of continuity through a change of employment are governed by the statutory provisions alone; thus if continuity is not preserved by a statutory provision such as that relating to a 'transfer of business' or the regulations on transfers of undertakings, it is broken by the change of employment and any agreement to the contrary between the parties at the time of the change can only be viewed, if at all, as a separate contract (with a view to which the transferred employee would be advised to demand a formal written agreement[2]).

b) Exclusions

The following classes of employees are excluded from the redundancy payments scheme:
a) persons under 20[3] or past normal retiring age (or, if there is no such age, 65)[4];
b) employees with less than two years' continuous employment[5];
c) employees dismissed for misconduct (see below);
d) redundant employees refusing suitable alternative employment (see below);
e) employees under a fixed term contract for two years or more, who have renounced their redundancy rights in writing[6];
f) share fishermen[7], employees of foreign governments[8], civil servants and certain public officials[9];
g) classes of employees specifically excluded by order of the Secretary of State, where a collective agreement covers the question of redundancy[10].

c) Computation of a redundancy payment[11]

The procedure for calculating a payment is contained in section 162; it is calculated by reference to the period of whole years, ending with the relevant date, during which the employee has been continuously employed. He then receives (a) one and a half week's pay for each year in which the employee was over 41 years old; (b) one week's pay for each year not covered by (a) but in which

---

1   [1979] 2 All ER 1077, [1979] IRLR 327, HL.
2   Though even this would not help if, for example, the employee was dismissed by his new employer before serving the qualifying period for unfair dismissal.
3   Employment Rights Act 1996, s. 211(2).
4   Ibid., s. 156, this provision had to be amended by the Employment Act 1989 to equalise the provision as between the sexes.
5   Ibid., s. 155.
6   Ibid., s. 197(3), on the meaning of 'fixed term contract' see *Dixon v BBC* [1979] 2 All ER 112, [1979] ICR 281, CA, pp. 363–364, above. This power to exclude redundancy rights was unaffected by the repeal by the Employment Relations Act 1999 of the parallel power covering unfair dismissal rights; it can operate harshly where there is a series of contracts – normally the question will be whether the *original* contract satisfies s. 197(3) (and is then extended), but the exclusion may also apply where the *final* contract satisfies the section, as in *Kingston-upon-Hull City Council v Mountain* [1999] ICR 715, EAT.
7   Ibid., s. 199(2).
8   Ibid., s. 160.
9   Ibid., s. 159.
10 Ibid., s. 157.
11 See *Harvey* E[2201] and Department of Employment Booklet No. 16 *Redundancy Payments* which contains a 'ready reckoner'.

he was over 22 years old; (c) half a week's pay for each other year (over the age of 18). The maximum number of years which may be counted is 20, and a 'week's pay' is calculated in accordance with Part XIV Chap II of the 1996 Act, subject to a statutory maximum figure for computation purposes[12].

It will be recalled that an employee who has reached the normal retiring age (if any) or 65 before the relevant date is not entitled to a redundancy payment. Where the relevant date falls in the last year of normal working life the payment will be reduced by the fraction $^x/_{12}$ where x is the number of months from the last birthday to the relevant date; the claimant keeps the remaining fraction, so that if he is made redundant at the end of the third month after the last birthday before the normal retiring age (or 64) he is entitled to $^9/_{12}$ of the payment, at the end of the ninth month $^3/_{12}$ and so on[13].

d) Procedure for claiming a redundancy payment

A claim for a payment is subject to a prima facie time limitation of six months from the relevant date, in that the employee will lose his entitlement unless during that period the payment has been agreed and paid or the employee has made a claim in writing to the employer, or has referred the question to an industrial tribunal (either directly, or indirectly through making a complaint of unfair dismissal)[14]. However, the employee is given a further six month period in which to submit a claim, but in such a case the awarding of a payment is put into the discretion of the tribunal, which must have regard to whether an award would be 'just and equitable' in the light of the employee's reason for failure to claim during the first six months[15].

The claim in writing to the employer does not have to be in any particular form, the test being that it must be such that the employer could reasonably appreciate the employee's intention to claim[16]; however, it has been held that it must be submitted during the six month period *beginning with* the relevant date, so that a claim submitted earlier than the date of termination of employment is invalid[17], which seems to be an unnecessary complication capable of amounting to a trap for an unwary employee.

---

12 As from February 2000, £230 per week, yielding a maximum payment of £6,900. For the purpose of calculation, actual pay as at the 'relevant date' is used, even if there is a later pay rise back dated to before that date: *Leyland Vehicles Ltd v Reston* [1981] ICR 403, [1981] IRLR 19. Statutory redundancy payments are exempt from income tax: Income and Corporation Tax Act 1988, s. 579; non-statutory (i.e. contractual) redundancy payments are treated in the same way up to the usual ceiling of £30,000, as a matter of concession, and this has been extended to payments made to buy out a contractual right to enhanced redundancy payments: *Mairs v Haughey* [1994] 1 AC 303, [1993] IRLR 551, HL; the Inland Revenue statement of practice on this matter was reissued (SP 1/94, see [1994] NLJ 599) to take *Mairs* into consideration.

13 Employment Rights Act 1996, s. 162(4); *Slater v John Swain & Son Ltd* [1981] ICR 554, [1981] IRLR 303. For the position where the employee is entitled to a pension upon dismissal, see s. 158 and the Redundancy Payments Pensions Regulations 1965, S.I. 1965 No. 1932, *Harvey* R[15].

14 Ibid., s. 164(1). Semble provided the employee has taken one of these steps (and so safeguarded his entitlement) he may still dispute the amount of the payment even after the expiry of the six months: *Bentley Engineering Co Ltd v Miller* [1976] ICR 225, [1976] IRLR 146.

15 Ibid., s. 164(2).

16 *Price v Smithfield and Zwanenberg Group Ltd* [1978] ICR 93, [1978] IRLR 80, EAT.

17 *Watts v Rubery Owen Conveyancer Ltd* [1977] ICR 429, [1977] IRLR 112; *Pritchard-Rhodes Ltd v Boon and Milton* [1979] IRLR 19, EAT.

When an employer voluntarily gives the payment to which an employee is entitled, he must give a written statement to the employee showing how the amount has been calculated[18]; the consequences of failure are, first, that the employer may be fined and, second, that he may in fact have to pay the sum again in a proper manner, particularly if, for example, he just gives the employee one unspecified lump sum upon termination with a vague indication that it is meant to include something for redundancy[19].

Finally, two points should be noted about the potential role of the Secretary of State. The first is that he has a right to appear in any redundancy proceedings before a tribunal[20] (because of his interest as guardian of the National Insurance Fund). The second is that if the employer either refuses to pay after the employee has taken all reasonable steps (short of legal proceedings) to recover payment, or is insolvent, the employee may apply to the Secretary of State for payment of the amount directly out of the National Insurance Fund; when such a payment is made, the Secretary of State may exercise the employee's rights against the employer to attempt to recover the amount for the fund[1].

iv)   Special provisions

a)   Offers of alternative employment[2]

If the employer makes an offer to an employee before the termination of his contract of employment to renew the contract or re-engage him on suitable alternative work[3], two consequences may flow. The first is that if the employee accepts that renewal or re-engagement (and there is either no gap, or a gap of less than four weeks between the contracts), there is in law no 'dismissal' at the end of the first contract[4] (subject to the rules on trial periods, considered below). The second is that if the employee unreasonably refuses to accept the offer he is disqualified from claiming a redundancy payment[5].

Cases of 'renewal' are not likely to cause many problems, for the word means renewal on the *same* terms (including possibly cases where any differences are negligible)[6]. 'Re-engagement' may prove more difficult, for this envisages the new terms differing from the old ones, and raises two questions – first, was the alternative employment on offer suitable; second, was the employee's refusal of it reasonable? In theory, the tribunal should start with the first question which entails consideration of the nature of the new employment in relation to the employee's skills and abilities. In many cases the offer will be of a similar type of employment, and it has been said that the mere offer of the same salary may not

18   Ibid., s. 165. This can be done by using the final page of form RP 1.
19   It depends on the facts: *Barnsley Metropolitan Borough Council v Prest* [1996] ICR 85.
20   Employment Tribunals (Constitution and Rules of Procedure) Regulations 1993, r. 8(6).
1   Employment Rights Act 1996, s. 166.
2   See *Harvey* E[1501].
3   In *SI (Systems and Instrumentation) Ltd v Grist* [1983] ICR 788, [1983] IRLR 391 the EAT stated obiter that on the strict wording of the subsection, there is a distinction between 'renewal' (which automatically operates to deem there to have been no dismissal) and 're-engagement' (which only so operates if in pursuance of a formal offer, whether in writing or not, made before the end of the first contract).
4   Ibid., s. 138(1).
5   Ibid., s. 141. In addition he may find himself disqualified for benefit for up to 26 weeks for neglecting, without good cause, to avail himself of a reasonable opportunity of employment: Jobseekers Act 1995, s. 19(6).
6   *Devonald v J D Insulating Co Ltd* [1972] ICR 209, NIRC.

be enough if the job is totally different[7]. However, this is not an invariable rule, and an offer of a completely different job may on the facts be suitable, even for a skilled employee, particularly if it is part of a larger, generally beneficial scheme, and particularly if it is of a temporary nature[8]. Naturally questions of pay may loom large, and difficulties may arise. Opportunities to earn overtime make a comparison of basic rates unreal, but on the other hand overtime may not be certain; the same problem applies to future prospects which might soon recoup and perhaps surpass an initial drop in earnings. Thus, the tribunal must take a realistic view of the question of pay[9], while at the same time accepting that the matter may be complicated by relevant changes in status and promotion prospects consequent upon acceptance of the new employment[10]. Two further matters which might be material are the expected duration of the new employment and its location. If the new employment is likely to last only for a short time, it has nevertheless been held that it may be suitable provided that it is full-time and regular during that time[11]. Once again, however, this is not a definite rule, for potential duration could be material in some cases, for example where the redundant employee, fearing a general recession in that particular industry if he stays in it, has found another job in another industry, particularly if he is approaching retirement age when employment for his last few years is not easy to find anywhere[12]. The fact that the employment on offer is in a different location, necessitating a move of home or increased travelling, does not necessarily render it unsuitable; obviously this is very much a question of fact, but it is an important qualification on the employee's right, discussed above, not to be required to move to a new locality not covered by his contract of employment – he can insist upon that right and refuse an *order* to move, but if in fact the *offer* of work elsewhere is considered 'suitable' by a tribunal, he may still lose his redundancy payment.

The second question, the reasonableness of a refusal, requires consideration of a wider range of different factors, looking at the matter more subjectively from the point of view of the employee who may have certain pressing reasons of a personal nature which make it reasonable to refuse what appears at first sight to be suitable alternative work (e.g. health problems, family commitments); in addition, the employee may have personal objections to the job offered (e.g. perceived lack of status), even though under the first test the job is objectively 'suitable'[13]. This means that even where several employees of the same type are made redundant (where possibly one general offer of the same type of alternative work is made to them collectively by the employer)[14], a tribunal must look into the particular circumstances of each individual employee before disqualifying

7   The judgment of Lord Parker CJ in *Taylor v Kent County Council* [1969] 2 QB 560, [1969] 2 All ER 1080 is often cited on this point, as to whether the offer is of 'employment which is substantially equivalent to the employment which has ceased'. However, this is not part of the statutory wording, and ultimately the question is one of fact for the tribunal: *Standard Telephones and Cables Ltd v Yates* [1981] IRLR 21, EAT.

8   *Dutton v Hawker Siddeley Aviation Ltd* [1978] ICR 1057, [1978] IRLR 390, EAT.

9   *Kennedy v Werneth Ring Mills Ltd* [1977] ICR 206, EAT.

10 *Harris v E Turner & Sons (Joinery) Ltd* [1973] ICR 31, NIRC; *Kane v Raine & Co Ltd* [1974] ICR 300, NIRC.

11 *Morganite Crucible Ltd v Street* [1972] 2 All ER 411, [1972] ICR 110, NIRC.

12 *Thomas Wragg & Sons v Wood* [1976] ICR 313, [1976] IRLR 145; *Paton Calvert & Co Ltd v Westerside* [1979] IRLR 108; cf. *James and Jones v NCB* (1969) 4 ITR 70.

13 *Cambridge and District Co-operative Society Ltd v Ruse* [1993] IRLR 156, EAT.

14 *McCreadie v Thomson and MacIntyre (Patternmakers) Ltd* [1971] 2 All ER 1135, [1971] 1 WLR 1193, HL; cf. *E & J Davis Transport Ltd v Chattaway* [1972] ICR 267, NIRC.

anyone for refusal[15]. The factors which may arise under this second question may be even more various than those under the first, so that the one overall point about the law relating to suitable alternative employment is that each case is heavily dependent upon its own facts, with the results that the tribunal has a wide discretion to use its common sense, precedents from decided cases are of little use[16] and the EAT will only reverse a decision if it is clear that the tribunal completely misdirected itself[17]. Moreover, although the questions of suitability and reasonableness of refusal are in theory separate, they may often be run together in practice in the process of reaching a fair and common sense decision, particularly as it is well established that the employer bears the burden of proof on *both* questions[18].

The above discussion has tended to assume that the employee has either unequivocally accepted or refused the offer. However, it may be the case that he is unsure about the new employment because it differs from the old employment in material ways, but wishes to give it a try. To improve the position of such a person, there is now a statutory 'trial period' of four weeks from the end of the old employment[19]; if during that period the employee terminates the contract for any reason or the employer terminates it for a reason connected with the change of employment, the employee is treated as having been dismissed at the date of termination of the old contract, and for the reason or reasons prevalent at that date, and so may still bring redundancy proceedings on that basis. In the ordinary case where the employee is dismissed by the employer, but with the offer of other employment, this means that he has the next four weeks in which to make up his mind, without prejudice to his rights[20]. However, one problem has arisen in the case of 'constructive dismissal' within section 136(1)(c), i.e. where the employer, instead of dismissing the employee, says that he is not prepared to carry on employing him in his present capacity, but expects him to change to something different. In this case, the employee could leave and claim to have been constructively dismissed. What happens, however, if the employee is unsure whether to do so and in fact carries on with the employer, performing the new work on a trial basis and only resigns at a later date having decided that he does not like it? In such circumstances it was held (in cases decided before

---

15   *John Fowler (Don Foundry) Ltd v Parkin* [1975] IRLR 89.

16   In *Spencer and Griffin v Gloucestershire County Council* [1985] IRLR 393, CA, the EAT had stated as a principle that an employee could not reasonably object on the grounds that the quality of the work was not up to his or her standards, the setting of standards being a matter for the employer (the case concerned the dismissal of school cleaners and the offer to re-engage them on new, inferior contracts which would diminish the standard of cleaning). The Court of Appeal reversed this decision, holding that there is no room for any such principle and that reasonableness remains a question of fact for the tribunal.

17   *Collier v Smith's Dock Co Ltd* (1969) 4 ITR 338.

18   *Jones v Aston Cabinets Co Ltd* [1973] ICR 292. In an appeal against a benefit disqualification (n. 5, above), however, the burden lies principally on the employee to show unsuitability and/or good cause for refusal: R(U) 26/52.

19   Employment Rights Act 1996, s. 138(2); the trial period may be longer than four weeks if there is a written agreement to that effect, and there may be more than one trial period, in which case the same rules apply with necessary modifications. The four weeks of the trial period are to be applied on a simple calendar basis; the period cannot be extended merely because there was no work available for part of the time (e.g. because of a Christmas closure): *Benton v Sanderson Kayser Ltd* [1989] ICR 136, [1989] IRLR 19, CA.

20   If all that has happened is that the employee (already under notice) has agreed to work on temporarily, e.g. to finish a job, and is then dismissed, that remains an ordinary dismissal for redundancy, without the need to invoke those specialised provisions: *Mowlem Northern Ltd v Watson* [1990] ICR 751, [1990] IRLR 500, EAT.

the Employment Protection Act 1975 introduced the statutory trial period) that mere continuance at work did not show acceptance of the new terms and that the employee dismissed under section 136(1)(c) had, in effect, a 'common law trial period' of an agreed or reasonable length during which he would still decide that he did not like the new work, leave and still claim to have been constructively dismissed[1]. With the introduction of the statutory trial period, the question arose whether it replaced the common law period, or supplemented it (the practical point being that this period could be *longer* than the statutory four weeks – if a constructively dismissed employee left the new job more than four weeks after the change, could he still claim to be within the common law's 'reasonable period' instead?). The EAT have clearly held that the common law period is *not* abrogated and that the statutory period is in addition[2]. Thus, where the employee is dismissed in the ordinary way it is just a question of applying the statutory period, but where he claims to have been constructively dismissed he may claim to have a period at common law to decide whether to take on the new work (either an agreed period or, in the absence of agreement, a period which is 'reasonable' in all the circumstances), plus a further statutory four-week period (if he decides to try the new work) during which his right to leave and claim constructive dismissal is still protected:

'This is an improvement in the position of the employee who is dismissed in [ordinary dismissal] circumstances. It is also an improvement in the protection of the employee in [constructive dismissal] circumstances. He has a period X in which to make up his mind. If his decision is not to take the new job, he is treated as dismissed at the moment he brings period X to an end by leaving the new job. If his decision is to take the new job and he brings period X to an end by making a new contract or renewing the old one with variations he then has the further trial period created by [section 138] in which to make up his mind, before losing his right to say, "You dismissed me by repudiating the old contract" ... So he has his common law period X protection plus his statutory trial period protection[3].'

In practice, the addition of four weeks may be of little significance; it is the fact that, in constructive dismissal cases, the common law trial period may be *longer* than four weeks which may be crucial in a particular case.

b) The effects of misconduct and industrial action[4]

Although an employee may be prima facie redundant, it may be the case that he has also misconducted himself (whether by going on strike or otherwise) so that the employer would in fact be justified in dismissing him summarily because of that misconduct. In such a case, section 140 provides that he shall lose his entitlement to a redundancy payment *provided* that the employer dismisses him either (a) without notice, (b) with shorter notice than he is entitled to, or (c) with his full notice which must include a statement in writing that the employer

1 *Marriott v Oxford and District Co-operative Society Ltd (No 2)* [1970] 1 QB 186, [1969] 3 All ER 1126, CA; *Shields Furniture Ltd v Goff* [1973] 2 All ER 653, [1973] ICR 187; *Sheet Metal Components Ltd v Plumridge* [1974] ICR 373, [1974] IRLR 86, NIRC.
2 *Air Canada v Lee* [1978] ICR 1202, [1978] IRLR 392; *Turvey v C W Cheyney & Son Ltd* [1979] ICR 341, [1979] IRLR 105.
3 *Turvey v C W Cheyney & Son Ltd* at 346 and 108 respectively.
4 See *Harvey* E[1251], [1401].

would have been entitled, had he wished, to dismiss without notice (this last possibility being referred to in the cases as 'special notice'). This subsection has caused problems in its interpretation, particularly as it is clear that, if the employer dismisses for cause, that is *not* a dismissal for redundancy anyway, so in theory there is no need in such a case for section 140 in order to disentitle the employee. Two principal interpretations have been put forward. The first, following on from this basic point, is that section 140 is meant to apply where the employee is dismissed for redundancy, but in circumstances where the employer could have dismissed for cause (and makes this known to the employee, either impliedly by giving no or short notice, or expressly by giving special notice). The second is that the subsection applies to dismissals for cause, in order to add the procedural rider that the employer must have given no, short or special notice if he is to rely on 'cause' to rebut the presumption of redundancy. There is still no clear decision as to which view is right; the most important case so far, *Sanders v Ernest A Neale Ltd*[5], clearly leans towards the first view, though at the same time stressing the importance of the procedural requirement of special notice:

'We agree ... that neither section [now section 140(1) and (3), discussed below] has any application if the dismissal is neither wholly nor mainly attributable to redundancy ... It seems therefore that, subject to [section 140(3)], a man who is dismissed solely on account of redundancy may lose his right to a redundancy payment if, by reason of the employee's conduct, his employer was actually entitled to dismiss him without notice.

Sir Diarmid Conroy [in *Essen v Vanden Plas (England) Ltd*[6]] says he finds it difficult to understand why [section 140] provides for a special notice to be given to the employee if he is allowed to work out his notice and what sanction there is for not giving the notice. We suggest that the answer to the first question is that Parliament thought that an employer should not be allowed to resist a claim for a redundancy payment upon the ground that the employee could have been dismissed without notice, unless the employee was warned of the facts upon which this defence is based at the time of the dismissal ... The answer to the second question is that if the employee is dismissed wholly or mainly on account of redundancy and receives full notice of dismissal, the employer cannot rely on [section 140] unless he has given a notice complying with [section 140(1)(c)]. This is not an insignificant sanction.'

This dual approach can also be seen in the judgment of the EAT in *Simmons v Hoover Ltd*[7]:

'Certain matters can be stated with a fair amount of confidence:

(1) [section 140] operates only by way of exclusion and, accordingly, has no effect in the case of an applicant who is not prima facie entitled to a redundancy payment, e.g. where, although there is a redundancy situation, his dismissal is not attributable wholly or mainly to redundancy but to some other cause such as misconduct; (2) the requirements of [section 140(1)(a), (b) or (c)] are presumably designed to ensure that the employee is put on

5   [1974] 3 All ER 327, [1974] ICR 565, at 336 and 574 respectively.
6   (1966) 1 ITR 186.
7   [1977] ICR 61, [1977] 1 All ER 775 at 79 and 787 respectively.

notice that he is being dismissed otherwise than in the ordinary course of the contract'; (3) a failure to serve such a notice under (a), (b) or (c) prevents the employer from relying on [section 140] …'

Whichever is the preferable interpretation in theory, the practical point is that an employer is advised to safeguard his position by giving no short or special notice when dismissing an unsatisfactory employee for redundancy or, ex abundanti cautela, even when dismissing him for misconduct in circumstances where he may claim to have been redundant.

The exclusory effect of section 140, however it is construed, is subject to two main qualifications, found in that section. The first is that under subsection (2), where an employee under notice of dismissal for redundancy is in fact dismissed during the obligatory period[8] of that notice because of misconduct, the complete exclusion does not apply and a tribunal has discretion to award all or only part of the payment to which he would otherwise have been entitled. This is a wide discretion, not likely to be altered on appeal unless the tribunal has clearly made an error in principle in exercising it[9].

The second qualification applies where the misconduct in question is the participation in a strike. This is classed as misconduct, entitling the employer to dismiss without notice, and so the exclusion in section 140(1) is applicable[10]. However, subsection (2) provides that where the strike and dismissal take place during the obligatory period of an existing notice of dismissal for redundancy the exclusion does not apply, and so the employee may still seek a redundancy payment, subject to the employer's statutory right to serve a written notice of extension on the employee requiring him to work extra days after the expiry of the notice, equivalent to the number of days lost due to the strike[11]; if he fails to comply with such a notice, he loses his right to claim. Thus, the position of the redundant employee on strike during his notice period is safeguarded, but only if he is within the scheme of section 140(2). In *Simmons v Hoover Ltd*[12] the unusual situation arose where the employee was already on strike when he was dismissed for redundancy (i.e. the opposite of the facts envisaged by section 140(2)); the EAT held that this fell outside the wording of the section, so that the employee remained disqualified under subsection (1) and could not claim a redundancy payment. Finally on industrial action, it should be noted that there is no concept of 'self-induced redundancy' (operating to disqualify an employee); thus, even if the employee is a member of a group which has precipitated redundancies by continued industrial action, he will remain entitled to payment unless and until he is clearly disqualified in some way under the legislation:

'The court would like to take this opportunity of exorcising the ghost of self-induced redundancy. It can certainly occur, but as such it has no legal significance … the mere fact that the employee's action created the redundancy situation does not disentitle them to a redundancy payment. The entitlement depends upon the words of the statute and there is no

---

8   Defined in s. 136(4), see p. 521, above.
9   *Lignacite Products Ltd v Krollman* [1979] IRLR 22.
10   *Simmons v Hoover Ltd* [1977] ICR 61, [1977] 1 All ER 775. Notice that the exclusion also applies, indirectly, to the case where an employee walks out because of a lock-out: s. 143.
11   Employment Rights Act 1996, s. 143.
12   N. 10, above.

room for any general consideration of whether it is equitable that the employee should receive a payment[13].'

c) Lay off and short time[14]

An ordinary claim for redundancy depends upon the existence of a 'dismissal'. In some cases of shortage of work, however, the employer may not dismiss, but instead may lay off the employee who has no work to do or put him on to short time. If he has no contractual right to do so, this may constitute constructive dismissal so that the employee may walk out and still claim his rights[15]. However, where the employer *has* such a contractual right this will not apply[16] and if the employee, short of money, walks out that will prima facie be a resignation not a dismissal, to the prejudice of his rights. To protect such a person, the legislation contains complicated provisions allowing the employee to claim a payment, though it is emphasised that to take advantage of these provisions the employee must qualify strictly under their wording – it is not necessarily enough to say that he was 'laid off' in common parlance. For statutory purposes, an employee is 'laid off' during any week when he receives no remuneration under this contract, and is on 'short time' if he receives during the week in question less than half his normal week's pay[17]; thus, if he receives more than half (e.g. under a guaranteed minimum wage clause in his contract) he is not within the statutory scheme[18]. These definitions will be primarily applicable to piece-work employees, but are not restricted to this class[19]. The employee may claim a redundancy payment where he has been laid off or on short time (as defined) for a period of four consecutive weeks, or for a total of six weeks in a 13-week period; the procedure is that he must give written notice to the employer of his intention to claim a redundancy payment by virtue of the lay off or short time (within four weeks of the end of either of the specified periods) and must terminate his employment by giving the amount of notice required of him under his contract[20]. The employer may contest the claim by giving the employee a written counter-notice within seven days of receiving the employee's notice and by seeking to show that it could reasonably be expected (as the date of the employee's notice) that within four

---

13 *Sanders v Ernest A Neale Ltd* [1974] 3 All ER 327, [1974] ICR 565 at 335 and 573 respectively.

14 See *Harvey* E[1901].

15 *Powell Duffryn Wagon Co Ltd v House* [1974] ICR 123; *Jewell v Neptune Concrete Ltd* [1975] IRLR 147, IT; *Kenneth McRae & Co Ltd v Dawson* [1984] IRLR 5. This may be an important argument if for some reason the employee cannot rely on the statutory procedure about to be described (e.g. if he fails to comply with the detailed requirements); he can try to prove that there was *no* contractual right to lay off, so that he was constructively dismissed, on ordinary principles.

16 This conclusion was avoided in *A Dakri & Co Ltd v Tiffen* [1981] ICR 256, [1981] IRLR 57 by arguing that even an express lay-off term is subject to an implied term that any lay-off would only last for a reasonable period (so that if it lasted longer an employee could still leave and claim constructive dismissal). This reasoning was disapproved in *Kenneth McRae & Co Ltd v Dawson* (n. 15, above) but surfaced again in *McClory v Post Office* [1992] ICR 758, [1993] IRLR 159 (in the context of a disciplinary suspension) and it can be seen to be consistent with other recent moves towards giving the implied term of trust and respect overriding effect, see p. 124, above.

17 Employment Rights Act 1996, s. 147. An employee is not on short time if he refuses work that is offered (e.g. because he thinks it too poorly paid): *Spinpress Ltd v Turner* [1986] ICR 433.

18 *Powell Duffryn Wagon Co Ltd v House*, n. 15, above, at 126.

19 *Hulse v Perry* [1975] IRLR 181, IT; *Powell Duffryn Wagon Co Ltd v House*, n. 15 above; cf. *Hanson v Wood* (1967) 3 ITR 46.

20 Employment Rights Act 1996, s. 148. Note the time limit on giving notice: s. 150.

weeks the employee would enter a period of at least 13 weeks without any lay offs or short time[1]; this question is then decided by the industrial tribunal. The period of work without lay offs or short time refers to work of the same type as that previously performed by the employee; this provision is not to be confused with the separate provisions on offers of alternative work of a different kind[2]. Finally, the legislation provides that if the lay off or short time in question is caused by a strike or lockout in *any* industry *anywhere*, these special provisions do not apply[3].

3   JOBSEEKER'S ALLOWANCE

i)   **Background**

Compulsory insurance against ill health and unemployment became law in this country for the first time in 1911 as a result of the National Insurance Act of that year[4]. That Act, limited in scope to certain specified industries, was enlarged and consolidated and eventually overtaken by the Beveridge reforms in the 1946 legislation setting up the modern Welfare State, as from 1948. Unemployment benefit became one of the central benefits. It was a contributory benefit, paid on flat rate scales for the first year of unemployment; if the claimant's needs (especially due to a family) were greater, it could be topped up with the means-tested income support. This system came under review by the Government in 1994, along with the question of benefits for the long-term sick and incapable. The latter resulted in the Social Security (Incapacity for Work) Act 1994 which sought to tighten entitlement to the (largely non-means-tested) benefits for sickness[5]. The second phase of these changes was the Jobseekers Act 1995. Like the 1994 Act which produced the unified incapacity benefit, this Act enacts a unified jobseeker's allowance in place of unemployment benefit and income support[6]. The Government said that it was necessary to produce a more 'modern' form of benefit, to do more to help people back into work, but it is clear that the opportunity was being taken to restrict expenditure on the benefit and also to tighten certain conditions of entitlement, especially the measures that a claimant must take to try to find work; the grafting on to this system of the New Deal (for unemployed people aged 18–24, and for those over that age unemployed for two years) with its possibility of subsidised employment is a further example of this process. The fear of fraud and over-reliance on welfare has always been a strong political consideration in this area.

1   Ibid., s. 152; if the tribunal finds with hindsight that the employee was in fact laid off or on short time during the whole four weeks following the date of the notice, that is conclusively deemed to decide the case against the employer on this point – s. 152(2).
2   *Neepsend Steel and Tool Corpn Ltd v Vaughan* [1972] 3 All ER 725, [1972] ICR 278.
3   Ibid., s. 154.
4   For the historical development, see Cornish and Clark *Law and Society in England 1750–1950* (1989), pp. 447–472.
5   See p. 719, below. The aim was to move substantial numbers off sickness-related benefit; if, however, those people (as was likely) were deemed capable of work but unable to find any, they would become claimants of unemployment benefit and/or income support, thus placing more strain on the system at that point, unless further economies could be made there too.
6   The changes were proposed in the White Paper 'Jobseeker's Allowance' (Cm. 2687, 1994). On the policy behind the benefit, see Bryson 'The Jobseeker's Allowance: help or hindrance to the unemployed' (1995) 24 ILJ 204. Income Support remains a fall-back benefit for those not available for employment.

There is in fact a strong sense of déjà vu in this new benefit. Not only are many of the more justiciable rules (i.e. the ones most likely to produce appeals to appeal tribunals, which will be emphasised below) taken almost wholesale from the old unemployment benefit law, but also it was necessary to re-enact large parts of the complex income support rules. This is because the 1995 Act creates two forms of allowance – the contributions-based allowance (the equivalent of the old unemployment benefit *but* now payable only for six months) and the income-based allowance, which is income support under a new name. However, this should not be viewed merely as old wine in new bottles, since there are important changes in emphasis (along with incapacity benefit) to move from the old-style national insurance benefits (based on contributions and entitlements) towards means-tested benefits; one version of this is that it concentrates help where it is needed, but another is simply that it cuts down on cost (especially for example, where the claimant has a working partner whose income must be taken into account where the benefit is means tested). Moreover, even the residue of the 'entitlement' benefit (the contributions-based allowance) is redefined in many ways on to the income support model, very deliberately. In some ways this was overdue. The old unemployment benefit was creaking in modern conditions because it was largely based on 1948 employment conditions, i.e. of full-time work or complete lack of work; it therefore caused problems with the modern tendency towards more diverse patterns of partial employment[7]. The new allowance addresses this, for example by setting hours limits for 'remunerative work' and allowing earning up to a limit (subject to deduction of those earnings from benefit)[8], and by further trying to encourage claimants to ease themselves back into full work by taking on part-time employment by the new back-to-work bonus system. These ideas are more akin to the old income support system, but this in itself further emphasises the point made above about the movement towards means testing.

ii) Entitlement to jobseeker's allowance

In order to qualify for the allowance a claimant must[9]:

a) be available for employment[10];

b) have entered into a jobseeker's agreement;

---

7   For example, unemployment benefit was a daily benefit, still based on a six-day working week; it therefore needed special rules (very much the exception in 1948 but heavily relied on more recently) to deal with other patterns of work or temporary lay-offs. The notorious 'full extent normal' rules were examples of this and caused serious problems of application (see the fifth edition of this book, at p. 433). Most such rules (on which there were large numbers of reported Commissioners' Decisions) have been abolished completely, and their complexity will not be missed.

8   The other principal benefit here is of course working families' tax credit, replacing family credit which had been viewed as the 'flagship' of the major 1986 social security reforms, again because of its emphasis on encouraging people back into work.

9   Jobseekers Act 1995, s. 1.

10 The claimant must be willing and able to take up immediately any employed earner's employment, normally of at least 40 hours p.w.: s. 6; Jobseeker's Allowance Regulations 1996, SI 1996/207, reg. 6. A claimant can place restrictions on the work he will accept, but only where they mean he has a reasonable chance of employment; these restrictions may be to his normal occupation (on his previous terms) for up to 13 weeks; after six months, no restriction as to the acceptable level of pay is permitted: regs. 7, 8, 9, 16.

c) be actively seeking employment[11];
d) satisfy either the contribution or income requirements;
e) not be engaged in remunerative work[12];
f) be capable of work[13];
g) not be receiving relevant education;
h) be under pensionable age;
i) be in Great Britain.

If these eligibility tests are satisfied, the claimant may receive, first, the contributions-based allowance for up to 26 weeks (subject to the normal three waiting days) if he satisfied the normal contributions conditions[14]. The amount is fixed by regulations (with lower amounts for those under 25); unlike the old unemployment benefit, a person can remain eligible while doing part-time work (up to 16 hours pw), but the amounts earned must be declared and deducted from the allowance (subject to a disregard of the first £5, or £10 for a couple, and the possibility of those earnings giving rise to a back-to-work bonus)[15]. Secondly, and quite independently, there is the income-based allowance. This is what the claimant is entitled to after 26 weeks, *and* can be claimed during that first period to top up the flat rate contributions-based allowance where the claimant has higher recognised needs (especially for a family and/or a mortgage). This part is income support under a new name, with the existing panoply of rules on the person's 'applicable amount' (for the claimant, spouse, children, and special premia for age or disability), the calculation of income, and the rules on capital stating that the claimant is ineligible if their capital exceeds £8,000, and that capital of between £3,000 and £8,000 is deemed to give 'notional income'[16]. Again any income from work (up to the permitted hours) is deducted from the applicable amount to give the entitlement.

Three innovations in the Jobseekers Act 1995 should be noted. The first is the introduction of the jobseeker's agreement which a claimant will be expected to enter with an employment officer. This will set out the claimant's availability and the steps to be taken in seeking work; failure to comply will result in a benefit

---

11 The claimant must take those reasonable steps which give him the best prospects of securing employment; following on from a general tightening of this requirement in 1989, the legislation sets out the details of what may be expected in any given case: s. 8; regs. 18–22. These may of course link in to the jobseeker's agreement, the power to give the claimant directions (below), and to any special rules relating to persons under the New Deal programme.

12 'Remunerative work' for these purposes means work for less than 16 hours p.w. (or, in the case of the claimant's partner, 24 hours p.w.): reg. 51. Regs. 52 and 53 have special rules covering those either deemed to be in remunerative work, or deemed not to be. This is a good example of the point made above about the adoption of the income support style of drafting.

13 Capability of work is now governed generally by the 'own work' and, more significantly, the 'all work' tests now applying to incapacity benefit: Jobseekers Act 1995, Sch. 1 para. 2; see p. 719, below.

14 These are that the claimant has (a) actually paid contributions in one of the previous two tax years giving an 'earnings factor' of at least 25 times that year's lower earnings limit, and (b) actually paid, or been credited with, in the two previous tax years contributions yielding an earnings factor of at least 50 times those years' lower earnings factor: s. 2.

15 Section 4(1). In the case of a retired claimant, income from an occupational pension is deducted to the extent that it exceeds £50 p.w.: reg. 81.

16 Section 3. These rules are not set out here, being more purely social security provisions; they are covered in detail in the annual editions of Bonner et al. *Non-Means Tested Benefits* and Mesher and Wood *Income Related Benefits*.

sanction, though the claimant is given a right of appeal[17]. The second is the back-to-work bonus. As an incentive to take on part-time work (in order to keep a foothold in the employment market) it is provided that, although the income from that work is deducted from the benefit at the time, it can give rise to a stored 'credit' of half the amount earned, which can be paid to the claimant in a lump sum when he finds full-time work and goes off benefit, up to a maximum of £1,000[18]. The third innovation is an incentive (in the form of an N.I. contributions reduction for a maximum of a year) for an employer to hire a person who has been in receipt of the allowance or its predecessor continuously for two years or more[19].

It is necessary now to look at the areas of the new allowance which are most justiciable, i.e. most likely to arise on an appeal to an appeal tribunal. These concern the important questions of disqualification of a claimant. Although much of the substance of the allowance (above) is taken from income support law, these next questions are taken almost entirely from the old unemployment benefit law, and so the existing case law on them continues to be applicable.

iii) Disqualification

Even if a claimant is prima facie entitled to benefit, he might be disqualified in certain circumstances which must now be briefly considered. The trade dispute disqualification is 'permanent' in the sense that it lasts for as long as the dispute does; the other disqualifications are 'temporary', lasting for maximum periods of two, four or 26 weeks.

a) The trade dispute disqualification

As this topic would be likely to be of some sensitivity, particularly if the rights and wrongs of a dispute had to be evaluated, the solution has been to disallow unemployment benefit altogether during the currency of the stoppage of work[20], this being analogous to the exclusion of claims for unfair dismissal when the termination arose out of a strike or lockout[1]. For the disqualification to apply, the loss of employment must arise out of a trade dispute at the claimant's place of work. 'Trade dispute' is defined as it used to be for the purpose of statutory immunity from tort liability in the Trade Disputes Act 1906, and as such it is capable of a wide definition which is ironic, for while a wide construction in the context of tort immunities is beneficial to the employee, in this context it can be most disadvantageous to him since it extends the ambit of the disqualification[2]. The disqualification lasts throughout the dispute, but it may cease even during the dispute in one of four ways:

17   Section 9; regs. 31–45. Further, an employment officer may give a 'jobseeker's direction' to the claimant in writing, specifying further steps to be taken by him: s. 19(10). The sanction is two week's loss of benefit, or four weeks if repeated: reg. 69.
18   Section 26; Social Security (Back to Work Bonus) Regulations 1996, SI 1996/193. This has been criticised on the basis that, although the lump sum bonus will be helpful, the time of greatest need is while still unemployed (at which time there is *no* provision for retention of part of the part-time income, other than the minimal £5/£10 disregard): Bryson, op. cit., n. 6, above, at p. 207.
19   Section 27; Employer's Contributions Reimbursement Regulations 1996, SI 1996/195.
20   Jobseekers Act 1995, s. 14. For the history of the trade dispute disqualification; see the Donovan Report (Cmnd. 3623, 1968) pp. 246–256.
1   Trade Union and Labour Relations (Consolidation) Act 1992, ss. 237, 238; see p. 635, below.
2   R(U) 5/87.

1. If the employee becomes bona fide employed elsewhere; if he then loses that other employment he may escape the disqualification even if the original dispute is still continuing. To come within this exception the employee must actually take up other employment – it is not enough that he has resigned his employment with the original employer without another job, no matter how genuine the resignation may be (though in such a case it now appears that the employee may seek to rely on the 'proviso', that he is no longer directly interested in the dispute, see 4, below). The phrase '*bona fide* employed' could be ambiguous, and could have ruled out the taking up of temporary employment, but it has been held[3] that bona fide means genuine employment not taken up merely to escape the section 14 disqualification; it could therefore cover temporary employment.

2. If the employee's employment has been terminated by reason of redundancy[4]; this qualification was inserted by the Social Security Act 1986 in order to deal with the harshness of the decision in *Cartlidge v Chief Adjudication Officer*[5] where a miner who had already volunteered for redundancy before the miners' strike and who was made redundant during it was prevented from working because of the strike prior to his dismissal; this activated what is now section 14 and the Court of Appeal reluctantly upheld the Commissioners' decision that he was disqualified for the whole length of the strike, despite the bona fides of his dismissal for redundancy eight months before the end of it.

3. If the employee has bona fide resumed employment with his employer but has subsequently left for a reason other than a trade dispute; again, this qualification was inserted by the Social Security Act 1986 in order to mitigate the effects of the disqualification on those genuinely losing employment for other reasons, especially during a protracted dispute.

4. If the employee can prove that he is not directly interested in the dispute. This qualification (usually referred to as the 'proviso' to section 14, because of the way it used to be drafted) used to be more harsh in two ways, for the employee used to have to prove in addition (i) that he was not participating in the dispute, and (ii) that neither he nor others in his occupation were participating in or financing the dispute. The latter limb was repealed by the Employment Protection Act 1975 and the former disappeared when the section was redrafted by the Social Security Act 1986. However, the breadth of the remaining 'direct interest' limb should not be underestimated, for it makes clear that the disqualification applies not only to those taking an active part, but also to those who have lost their employment through the dispute but also stand to *gain* from the outcome. The crucial question therefore is how strict the nexus of gain must be between the dispute and the claimant. Clearly many people could be 'interested', in that a settlement concerning one group of workers could well have a ripple effect throughout a plant or industry. The necessary restriction is to be found in the requirement of *direct* interest. In R(U) 13/71, the Commissioner said,

> 'I think that a claimant should not be regarded as having a direct interest in another's dispute ... unless there is a close association between the

---

3   R(U) 6/74, where the new work was to do a particular job of dismantling certain machinery, which was obviously finite.

4   This means redundancy as defined by the Employment Rights Act 1996, s. 139; there is no requirement that a redundancy payment must actually be payable.

5   [1986] QB 360, [1986] ICR 256, CA.

two occupations concerned, and the outcome of the dispute is likely to affect the claimant, not at a number of removes, but virtually automatically, without further intervening contingencies.'

This dictum, applied by the Court of Session in *Watt v Lord Advocate* [6], means that groups of workers other than those on strike, who are laid off, will only be disqualified if the settlement of the dispute would have a virtually automatic effect on their own terms and conditions[7] (e.g. by some direct form of linkage); it is not enough that in practice the settlement may have an indirect effect through a further round of negotiations, however strong that effect might be[8]. At one end of the scale is the case of direct linkage of the wages of those on strike and those laid off (by contract or by collective agreement), in which case the disqualification will apply; at the other end is the case where a settlement in favour of those on strike will be used in further negotiations to attempt a similar settlement for those laid off, in which case the disqualification will not apply. The difficulty arises in the middle ground, where there is no formal direct linkage, but the employers' practice will almost inevitably mean that the settlement for those on strike will be applied to those laid off. This arose in *Presho v Insurance Officer*[9], where the Court of Appeal took a narrow approach and held that this was not direct interest, but this was reversed by the House of Lords, Lord Brandon stating that, in line with *Watt v Lord Advocate*, there are two conditions for the disqualification to apply:

'The first condition is that, whatever may be the outcome of the trade dispute, it will be applied by the common employers not only to the group of workers belonging to the one union participating in the dispute, but also the other groups of workers belonging to the other unions concerned. The second condition is that this application of the outcome of the dispute "across the board", as it has been aptly described, should come about automatically as a result of one or other of three things: first, a collective agreement which is legally binding; or, secondly, a collective agreement which is not legally binding; or, thirdly, established industrial custom and practice at the place of work concerned.'

It is the third of these that extends the disqualification to the middle ground in question, that explains why the House of Lords reversed the decision of the Court of Appeal, and that meant that the claimant was in fact disqualified.

As stated above, the disqualification lasts throughout the dispute; normally it will be obvious when the dispute (and so the disqualification) ends; but it could cause problems, particularly in a case where the employer in fact closed down the factory or subsidiary in question, or dispensed totally with the existing workforce (replacing some or all with new workers), never taking the employee back on – is that the end of the dispute, or could it be said that the dispute never

---

6   1979 SC 120, 1979 SLT 137, on appeal from R(U) 6/78.
7   R(U) 8/80; this case also shows that the trade dispute does not have to be successful before the disqualification applies – it is enough if the employee would have benefited directly had the dispute led to a successful conclusion.
8   R(U) 5/79.
9   [1984] ICR 463, [1984] IRLR 74, HL; the passage cited is at 471 and 77 respectively. See Troup (1985) 14 ILJ 112.

ended and that the disqualification continues? This latter possibility would be highly disadvantageous to the employees concerned and was avoided in R(U) 15/80 by a finding that the eventual closure was primarily due to the financial collapse of the firm, not wholly due to the dispute; in such a case it can be said that, from the date of the closure, another cause operates and the disqualification ends. However, leaving the matter purely as one of causation would be unsatisfactory, for there would be still the possibility that a closure or widespread dismissal could be considered wholly due to the dispute, and so open-ended. Fortunately, this is now less likely since another approach is possible because of a change in the interpretation of the proviso (above). It had been held in R(U) 4/79 that the proviso could not apply once disqualification had been imposed – in other words, it could only be used to prevent disqualification arising in the first place and could not be relied on where the claimant argued that there had been a change of circumstances which meant that he was *no longer* (participating or) directly interested in the dispute[10]. However, that view was disapproved in R(U) 5/86[11], so that now the proviso *can* apply to end a disqualification because of a change of circumstances. Such a change could come about through the closure of the factory or the irrevocable dismissal of the workforce and so, as pointed out in the important decision in R(U) 1/87[12], the proviso applies *as from that date* to end the dispute, since the employees are no longer directly interested in the dispute. Further, it would appear from this decision that the same applies if, during the dispute, the employee resigns (even without having another job to go to), subject again to the qualification that the resignation must be intended to be a final termination of that employment relationship and not just a tactical move during the currency of the dispute.

The trade dispute disqualification applies to both the contributions-based allowance and the income-based allowance, but it is provided that the latter can be claimed in respect of the striker's family[13]. Moreover, the Government have placed further restrictions on striking employees in two ways:

(i) there is to be deducted from the dependants' entitlement to the income-based allowance a 'prescribed sum' (set currently at £27)[14] which, though not stating so expressly, was introduced to represent notional strike pay (the stated aim having been to encourage unions to make strike payments, at least to the extent of making up this shortfall)[15];

---

10 The case concerned a fireman taking part in a dispute who resigned in December and took up other work in January; it was held that he was not entitled to benefit between December and January since he was already disqualified under the section and he did not cease to be so under the proviso when he resigned.
11 This was the decision that was appealed to the Court of Appeal in *Cartlidge v Chief Adjudication Officer*, in n. 5, above, but this particular point was not in issue on the appeal.
12 28 employees withdrew their labour over rates of pay and were locked out and dismissed; $3^1/_2$ months later, 13 (not including the claimant) were re-engaged and work restarted. *Held* as it was clear with hindsight that the dismissal of the claimant was not a manoeuvre in the dispute but was intended to be an irrevocable end to his employment, the proviso applied as from the date of dismissal, and so the claimant was *not* disqualified for the next three and a half months.
13 Jobseekers Act 1995, s. 15.
14 Ibid., s. 15(2)(d); Jobseeker's Allowance Regulations 1996, reg. 172.
15 The origin of this measure can be traced to the steel strike of 1979, but it assumed particular importance and prominence during the miners' strike of 1984/5 (see Mesher 'Social security in the coal dispute' (1985) 14 ILJ 191); an attempt was made by the NUM to circumvent it on the grounds that they were not able to make payments of strike pay but (not surprisingly given the clear wording of the statute) this failed: *R v Chief Adjudication Officer, ex p Bland* (1985) Times, 6 February, DC.

(ii) tax law has been altered to prevent the payment of tax rebates to persons on strike[16].

b) Temporary disqualification

We have already seen that the new jobseeker's agreement and employment officer's power of direction are backed by disqualification sanctions of two or four weeks for failure to comply[17]. In addition, there are three other, principal grounds for disqualification which have existed for many years under the old unemployment benefit law and will continue to give rise to many of the appeals in this area; they each provide interesting parallels or comparisons with mainstream employment law. They are as follows:

1. Where the claimant lost his employment through misconduct[18]. This is a potential area for controversy, for in effect the employment officer must evaluate the blameworthiness of the dismissed employee with a view to disqualifying him. The misconduct in question must be causally connected to the dismissal, but it could in an appropriate case arise from factors outside the actual employment, e.g. conviction of a criminal offence. Outside that principle, however, this is a wide question of fact. If the employee had just cause for leaving, e.g. through a breach of contract by his employer, that will not bring disqualification, and it has been held that misconduct in this context means 'conduct which is causally but not necessarily directly connected with employment, and having regard to the relationship of employer and employee and the rights and duties of both, can fairly be described as blameworthy, reprehensible and wrong'[19]. With the advent of the action for unfair dismissal, there is now far more likelihood of there being judicial consideration of the merits of any particular dismissal, and so, in order to avoid seemingly conflicting decisions, any decision by an industrial tribunal on the fairness or otherwise of a dismissal is likely in practice to be followed by the Agency officer or appeal body on the question of disqualification, provided the actual question of misconduct was considered, although it is not binding[20] and it must be remembered that in any given case the employment tribunal may have had to consider wider aspects of the case with no immediate relevance to unemployment benefit disqualification such as procedural unfairness and contributory fault.

---

16 Finance Act 1981, s. 29, S.I. 1982 No. 66; see now the Income and Corporation Taxes Act 1988, s. 204.

17 Jobseekers Act 1995, s. 19(5). The subsection also covers failure to take up or attend a training scheme placement, or giving up such a placement, or losing it through misconduct. Each of these is subject to a 'good cause' defence. Factors to be taken into account in such a defence are set out in the Jobseeker's Allowance Regulations 1996, regs. 72 and 73.

18 Ibid., s. 19(6)(a). Use of the phrase 'lost his employment' means that this head can cover dismissal, voluntary leaving or resignation as an alternative to impending dismissal (R(U) 17/64; R(U) 2/76).

19 R(U) 2/77. Note, however, that if it is alleged that the misconduct consisted of refusing to obey an order, and the evidence shows that several employees did likewise because of a disagreement with the employer, that should probably be dealt with as a trade dispute case under s. 14, *not* as individual misconduct under s. 19.

20 R(U) 2/74; R(U) 4/78. This approach was reaffirmed in R(U) 3/79, though it was pointed out that for present purposes the state authorities are *not* concerned with dismissal as a matter between employer and employee, and so should be wary of using terms such as 'proper dismissal' or 'unfair dismissal'.

2. Where the claimant voluntarily gives up his employment without just cause[1].
Thus, the employee who resigns of his own accord will be disqualified unless
he can show that he had just cause (a matter which might also be important
if the employee is claiming to have been constructively dismissed for the
purpose of an unfair dismissal claim), and unless there was some material
deterioration in the job or some pressing personal factor operating this may
be hard to show, particularly if he left without any job to go to; this can be seen
from the following dictum from a Commissioner:

> 'An examination of the decisions on the topic leads me to think that in
> general it is only where circumstances are such that a person has virtually
> no alternative but to leave voluntarily that he will be found to have had
> just cause for doing so, rather as a person who throws his baggage
> overboard to make room in the lifeboat can claim on his baggage
> insurance[2].'

This is one further example of the premise that benefit is paid for involuntary
unemployment, an approach clearly seen in the approach to this
disqualification of the Court of Appeal in *Crewe v Social Security Comr*[3] where
the test was said to be whether leaving the employment was right and
reasonable from the point of view of the national insurance fund which has
to bear the burden of the employee's decision, *not* whether it was reasonable
or convenient as between employer and employee or generally in the interests
of the community; this disqualification was thus seen as primarily a protection
for the fund. While such an approach may be logical, it could have practical
drawbacks in discouraging voluntary severance schemes (considered below).
Faced with the large numbers of redundancies to be made in the mining
industry on a voluntary basis, the previous government altered the position
by the Social Security Act 1985, which inserted a new provision[4] which
provides that a person who has been dismissed by his employer by reason of
redundancy (within the meaning of section 139 of the Employment Rights
Act 1996) after volunteering or agreeing so to be dismissed or to leave without
dismissal is not to be treated as having left his employment voluntarily.

Thus, provided the statutory definition of redundancy is satisfied[5], the
decision in *Crewe* will no longer apply. One further practical problem now
addressed specifically concerned the person who took a job, found it
unsuitable and left. That person could be disqualified for benefit for
voluntarily leaving, in spite of the fact that it was in the public interest for
unemployed people to try to take up employment offers. As part of the general
changes under the Social Security Act 1989, a 'trial period' was enacted;

---

1 Section 19(6)(b).
2 R(U) 4/87, para. 9, per Commissioner Monroe.
3 [1982] 2 All ER 745, [1982] IRLR 295, CA, where a teacher who took early retirement in
line with a local authority scheme to decrease the number of teachers (thus acting in
accordance with the wishes of his employer and arguably in the wider interests of the
community) was held to have left his employment without just cause and so was disqualified
under s. 19.
4 Now the Jobseeker's Allowance Regulations 1996, reg. 71; this covers the case where
employer and employee mutually agree severance, as well as where the employee is
formally 'dismissed' for redundancy: R(U) 3/91.
5 Note that it does not say that a redundancy payment has been made; there may be
technical reasons why the employee is not eligible for a payment, but he may still be
'redundant' within s. 139, and this is what matters.

thus, a person who has been unemployed for over thirteen weeks may take a job on trial and, if he leaves between the beginning of the fifth week and the end of the twelfth week in that job, he is not to be disqualified for voluntarily leaving[6].

3. Where the claimant without good cause refuses or fails to apply for or avail himself of a suitable job[7]. Once a vacancy has been notified to the unemployed claimant, he is expected to take reasonable steps to obtain it and, if offered it, should accept it. As seen above, this is closely tied in with the primary requirement that the claimant must be available for and actively seeking work. Just as those provisions were tightened up by the Social Security Act 1989, so there were also major amendments here, introducing a more complex scheme. Previously, there was a simple test as to whether the job offered was 'suitable', with questions such as the length of time a person could wait before lowering his sights and taking lesser work than before left as questions of fact and judgement. However, the drafting substituted in 1989 removes references to suitability and instead states that *any* failure to avail will trigger disqualification *unless* the claimant can prove 'good cause' for his failure. Criteria are then laid down[8] for deciding on good cause, including any condition or personal circumstances indicating serious harm to health or excessive physical and mental stress, any religious or conscientious belief, any responsibility for another member of the household, travelling time (more than an hour each way) and unreasonably high expenses in taking the job. The effect that taking up the employment may have on the claimant's income or that of his household is not a relevant factor[9]. On the crucial question of the time a newly-unemployed person can spend looking only for a job of similar status, there is now a maximum 'permitted period' of 13 weeks[10].

If one of the above temporary disqualifications applies, how long is it to last? The maximum period stood for many years at six weeks, but then was raised by the previous government, first to 13 weeks in 1986, and then to 26 weeks, in 1988. This radical increase has given greater importance to considering the appropriate length of disqualification, particularly as a person so disqualified is only eligible for a reduced version of the income-based allowance, and then only if certain tightly defined conditions of particular hardship apply to their case[11]. In the past, the standard practice has been for the Agency officer (having decided to apply one of the disqualifications) to apply the maximum period in many cases, leaving it for an aggrieved claimant to appeal to an Appeal Tribunal against such an award. Although officers have now been instructed not to do so and there is evidence of them using their discretion more often to give more consideration to length of disqualification when making their decisions, it remains the case

---

6   Section 20(3); reg. 74.
7   Section 19(6)(c),(d); this list covers not just failing to apply, but also refusal to accept or neglecting to avail himself of a reasonable opportunity.
8   Jobseeker's Allowance Regulations 1996, reg. 72(2). Note that s. 20(1) continues the old provision that a claimant does not have to accept a job which is vacant due to a trade dispute, i.e. he cannot be required to act as a strike breaker.
9   Reg. 72(6); thus the claimant cannot argue that, overall, he was better off on benefit.
10 Regs. 16, 72(5); it could be less than 13 weeks, in which case relevant factors are again laid down in reg. 16. Once the period has expired, the claimant is subject to the rule that the level of pay is not good cause: s. 19(9). There used to be a rule that the claimant could refuse a job in his trade but at below trade rates of pay (i.e. that he could not be used as cheap labour) but this was repealed.
11 Regs. 140–146.

that the increase of the maximum period to 26 weeks has increased the importance of the right of appeal in disqualification cases. On appeal, the tribunal may consider the length of disqualification imposed and alter it where appropriate; indeed, it has been held that failure to give such consideration (or to give reasons for the eventual decision) is an error of law, giving rise to further appeal to the Commissioner[12]. Within a figure as high as 26 weeks, there is therefore considerable scope for arguments in mitigation (even where the claimant/ appellant accepts that *some* disqualification is merited). However, there is unfortunately little guidance as yet from the Commissioners as to how the adjudicating authorities are to exercise their powers; apart from stating that the discretion is to be exercised judicially, they have been content to leave it as a question of fact for the particular tribunal[13] (an approach that was easier to apply when the maximum period was only six weeks). In a misconduct case, this will mean considering how bad the misconduct was and any factors in mitigation[14]. In a case of voluntary leaving, it will mean considering *how much* cause the claimant had to leave (accepting that it was not sufficient to constitute 'just' cause) and how responsibly (or otherwise) he acted in giving up his existing job. An interesting, relatively liberal, example of this can be seen in R(U) 4/87 where a civil servant gave up his job to seek work as a social worker helping the mentally handicapped; because of the decision of the Court of Appeal in *Crewe v Social Security Comr*[15] this could not be considered just cause and so the voluntary leaving disqualification applied *but* in the light of the public interest involved in having people volunteer for such work the Commissioner held that a period of only one week's disqualification was appropriate.

iv) Four overlaps with termination of employment

Although the law relating to jobseeker's allowance is contained in the social security legislation, it is important for an industrial lawyer to have a knowledge of it, because it may be an important background factor in certain areas of employment law, particularly termination of employment. Four particular points of overlap between the allowance and employment law might be borne in mind, the first two relating to major statutory rights and the last two to informal, ad hoc severance agreements.

The first point is that the relationship between benefits and compensation for unfair dismissal[16] is formalised in regulations, so that the state may recover from the employer who unfairly dismissed the claimant the amount of allowance paid to the claimant in the period up to the tribunal hearing[17], and the claimant is

12 R(U) 4/87.
13 While this may be admirable from the point of view of flexibility and, dare one say it, anti-legalism, there may be certain areas where at least basic *principles* should be set out; for example, if the claimant was dismissed for taking home certain work items of minimal value (viewed as 'perks' by most of the workers there, i.e. a classic 'gleaning' case), should the tribunal take the view that 'theft is theft' and apply the maximum, or take into account that this was a very minor example of theft and apply only a few weeks' disqualification?
14 There may be a further overlap with unfair dismissal concepts here, e.g. whether the claimant had already been warned by his employer.
15 N. 3, above.
16 For the relationship between a *finding* of fair and unfair dismissal and eligibility for benefit, see p. 550, n. 20, above.
17 Employment Protection (Recoupment of Jobseekers' Allowance and Income Support) Regulations 1996, S.I. 1996 No. 2349; see p. 513, above.

disqualified from claiming benefit for the period in respect of which compensation is ordered by the tribunal to cover loss of future wages[18].

The second point is that it is well established that receipt of a statutory redundancy payment does not disentitle the redundant employee from claiming jobseeker's allowance, the point being that although in practice the receipt of the payment will help the ex-employee financially for a certain period into the future, it is calculated by reference to *past* service and so does not disentitle the claimant from future claims for benefit[19].

The third point is that, as seen above, the rules relating to employees volunteering for or accepting early severance of sorts were possibly a disincentive to such schemes before 1985, because of the decision of the Court of Appeal in *Crewe v Social Security Comr*[20] that such a volunteer could be disqualified on the ground of having left his employment without just cause. However, such schemes comprise a much used form of shedding labour without the need to make compulsory redundancies, and the overruling of *Crewe* by the Social Security Act 1985 has already been considered.

Potentially more drastic is the fourth overlap which arises where the employee leaves employment with some form of lump sum (other than a statutory redundancy payment), once again a not-uncommon occurrence when firms are wishing to shed labour by agreement. Once again, there were major changes here in 1989. The old provision used to disqualify an employee leaving employment with a payment 'in lieu of notice or the remuneration which he would have received ... had his employment not been terminated'. Thus, someone leaving with wages in lieu of notice was ineligible for benefit for the notice period. However, it was held in *R v National Insurance Comr, ex p Stratton*[1] that it was necessary to look at the dominant nature of the payment and that if (as in that case) that nature was a reward for *past* services, it was analogous to a redundancy payment and so *not* caught by the provision. This gave considerable scope for avoidance of the regulation, either by the description given to the terminal payment, or by disguising it in some form of overall, unspecific 'severance pay', not uncommon in negotiated redundancies[2]. To counter this, the law was completely redrafted to produce a scheme which is far more difficult to avoid, and this was carried over into the Jobseeker's Allowance Regulations 1996. It is complicated, and works in four stages.

1) Regulation 98(1) states that the claimant's earnings are deemed to include 'any compensation payment'.

2) 'Compensation payment' is then defined in regulation 98(3) as *any* payment made *in respect of* the termination of the employment, *unless* it comes within one of several specific exceptions, the most important of which are (i) any remuneration or emolument which accrued in the period before the

---

18 The amount ordered is considered to be 'earnings' for the period in question: Jobseeker's Allowance Regulations 1996, reg. 98(1)(f).

19 Reg. 98(2); R(U) 6/73, approved by the Court of Appeal in *Stratton*'s case (n. 1, below). This is in line with Lord Denning's view in the early redundancy case of *Lloyd v Brassey* [1969] 2 QB 98, [1969] 1 All ER 382, CA (p. 520, above) that a redundancy payment is not meant to be a glorified form of unemployment benefit.

20 [1982] 2 All ER 745, [1982] IRLR 295, CA.

1 [1979] 2 All ER 278, [1979] ICR 290, CA.

2 See R(U) 1/80, R(U) 2/80 and R(U) 4/80, in each of which the element of past service avoided the regulation; cf. R(U) 7/80 where the payment mentioned the obligatory consultation period for collective redundancies and payment in lieu thereof, and so that payment was caught.

termination[3], (ii) holiday pay, (iii) a refund of pension contributions, (iv) maternity or sick pay, (v) employment expenses, (vi) an occupational pension or (vii) a statutory redundancy payment. If the payment cannot be shown to be under one of these exceptions (which concentrate primarily on money already earned or a *statutory* redundancy payment), it is likely to be caught, as it will be very difficult to show that a terminal payment (of whatever kind) was not made 'in respect of' the termination.

3) Once the payment is caught, regulation 94(6) notionally spreads the payment over the period ending (a) where the employer represents that it (or part of it) was paid in lieu of notice of termination or on account of early termination of a fixed term contract, on the 'expiry date'; (b) where it is paid in lieu of statutory consultation on collective redundancies[4], on the date that consultation period would have ended; (c) in any other case, on the 'standard date'.

4) Regulation 94(8) then defines this verbiage. The 'expiry date' means the date on which the notice applicable to that person (by contract, statute or custom, whichever is the longer) would have expired, or the expiry date of a fixed term contract. The (fall-back) 'standard date', if all else fails, means the earlier of (a) the expiry date (!) or (b) a period worked out mathematically by dividing the amount of the terminal payment by the maximum 'week's pay' for statutory purposes[5].

The end result of this tortured drafting is that in nearly all cases now where an employee leaves with a terminal payment which includes any element[6] of payment not falling within the above exemptions for already earned pay or statutory redundancy payments, that payment will be deemed to be their earnings for the period in question, which will normally disentitle them to the allowance. Moreover, the ineligibility will normally be for the contractual notice period, whether the actual payment is the same as, more than or less than what would actually have been earned in that period[7].

A good example of this post-1989 regime is provided by R(U) 5/92, where a long-standing employee was made redundant, being given only two weeks' notice, though contractually entitled to 12 weeks. He received a terminal payment of £20,400, made up of a statutory redundancy payment, accrued wages, holiday pay and £14,229 'severance payment', calculated entirely by reference to past years of service. The first three were clearly exempt and the argument was over the severance payment. The Commissioner held that it was a payment 'in respect of the termination of the employment' and so constituted 'compensation' which was *not* within one of the exempt categories. The claimant was therefore disentitled for the 'ineligible period' which, on these facts, was until the 'expiry date', i.e. the end of 10 weeks of notice that he had not had. Arguments by the claimant's representative that the overall nature of the payment should be considered were dismissed on the ground that these new provisions must be construed as they

---

3 This does not include a contractual or negotiated redundancy/severance payment, even though it is *calculated* by past service, because such a payment is not 'remuneration': R(U) 5/92 see below.

4 See p. 67, above.

5 One saving grace is that no ineligible period, however calculated, can last for more than 52 weeks: reg. 94(7).

6 R(U) 1/94.

7 It may now be necessary to *sever* the payment into its component parts, rather than looking as its dominant characteristic: C(U)88/90. If *any* element is not exempt (as will usually be the case), it is 'compensation' and so is caught.

stand and that *ex p Stratton* and the other previous case law 'concerned the previous and very different version of [the regulations] and do not seem to me to be of assistance in relation to the meaning of "compensation" in the new provisions'.

Chapter 10

The law on trade unions

1 INTRODUCTION[1]

The legal history of trade unions is one of long periods of their treatment as illegal or potentially illegal either under particular statutes or by virtue of certain general common law tenets, particularly restraint of trade and criminal conspiracy. The removal of these threats and the repeal of the old master and servant legislation in the last quarter of the nineteenth century was a major step forward, but then the spectre was raised of unions being readily sued in the civil courts through the development of the industrial torts, until the granting of immunities to unions and their members by the Trade Disputes Act 1906. Even in the twentieth century, legislative intervention was necessary to reverse certain court decisions which could have had far-reaching consequences for what trade unionists see as their proper purposes. Legal regulation of the external activities of trade unions and the question of the proper limits of union-organised industrial action is considered in chapter 11; in this chapter we examine the legal regulation of the internal workings of trade unions.

For much of the last hundred years the stance of the law towards union internal affairs has principally been one of non-intervention, in line with the approach taken to the internal affairs of voluntary associations generally. The courts at common law assumed jurisdiction to interpret and enforce union rules, and the judges showed themselves vigilant in the protection of the rights of individual union members, particularly where livelihoods were at risk. However, with the exception of the Industrial Relations Act 1971, which proved to be a spectacular failure and a traumatic experience for all concerned, until the 1980s there had been no systematic attempt to regulate the internal workings of trade unions by legislation. The period since 1980 has seen a dramatic transformation in the legal regulation of internal union affairs, and as a result of the legislation of that

---

1   The standard works on trade union law are Morris and Archer *Trade Unions, Employers and the Law* (2nd edn, 1993) and Kidner *Trade Union Law* (2nd edn, 1983). See also Thomas *The Trade Union Acts 1992 and 1993* (1994). For background reading, see Millward, Bryson and Forth *All Change at Work? British Employee Relations 1980-1998* (2000).

period the internal workings of a trade union are now subjected to an unprecedented degree of statutory control covering almost every aspect of union activity. This has come about largely through the enactment of new rights for union members in relation to matters such as expulsion, discipline and the use of union funds, and the imposition of legally enforceable balloting requirements. Some of these reforms did little more than extend the good practice of some trade unions to all unions, and over a period of time have come to be accepted by the union movement (e.g. the balloting requirements for union elections and the requirement of a ballot before industrial action); others (e.g. the controls on access to membership and the imposition of discipline) are widely seen as striking a lethal blow at the status of unions as voluntary associations, by undermining the very foundations of collective responsibility and self-determination upon which trade unions have traditionally been based.

At the root of the problem in applying the law to trade unions and their activities is the inherent conflict which exists between the individual and the collective interest[2], and the different natural standpoints of unionists and lawyers. The lawyer's natural sympathy often lies with an individual, particularly when opposed by a large body (of whatever sort) more powerful than him; when, however, that body is a trade union, the unionist may see nothing inherently sinister or dangerous about such an organisation – indeed, it is its very size and collective power that has historically been his only protection against the infinitely greater economic power of his employer. The collective aspect can thus become dominant, and a certain (or even a large) amount of individualism may have to be sacrificed in order to maintain that collective power. Thus, for example, where a union member is improperly expelled (e.g. in breach of the rules, or in defiance of the rules of natural justice) and brings an action against the union, that one action may be seen entirely differently by the lawyer and the unionist; one man's persecuted individual is another man's threat to the collective security of the union. This divergence is most clearly seen in cases concerned with the rights of individuals (particularly members) *vis-à-vis* the union and in that context it may pose difficult questions as to how union rules are to be interpreted and applied (considered below). It has also been seen in other areas, e.g. the application of the TUC's internal rules and procedures for the resolution of inter-union disputes over membership. From the collective standpoint, such procedures may be considered necessary and desirable to avoid fragmentation of bargaining units and discourage competition between unions for members; but from the standpoint of an individual denied access to membership of a trade union, those procedures may appear to be an unwarranted interference with his freedom to belong to the union of his choice.

Not surprisingly, where the courts have been faced with cases involving a clash between the collective interests of the union and the individual interests of a member, greater emphasis has tended to be placed upon the individual aspect, particularly in cases involving expulsion and discipline where the decision is likely to have a major impact on individual rights. However, in certain cases concerning more general questions as to the functioning and vires of unions, the courts have shown more appreciation of the collective side of the equation[3]. In *Goring v British Actors Equity Association*[4] one of the plaintiff's arguments was

---

2   See Kidner, 'The individual and collective interest in trade union law' (1975) 5 ILJ 90.
3   See *Cheall v APEX* [1983] ICR 398, [1983] IRLR 215, HL (considered below at p. 625), which provides a good example of this in a decision of the House of Lords.
4   [1987] IRLR 122, Ch D at 125.

that a union instruction (that no member should work in South Africa) that he was challenging conflicted with the objects of the union which included the head 'to maintain the professional rights and liberties of its members individually and collectively', the point being that the instruction, in his submission, interfered with members' individual rights; dismissing this argument, Browne-Wilkinson V-C said:

'The essence of a trade union activity is that members are bound to act collectively to achieve the objects of the majority. Such collective action must necessarily impair the individual rights of some members ... [The objects clause in question] expresses objects. It enables the union to protect individuals as well as collective interests; it does not mean that the union can only do such things as are in the interests of all members both individually and collectively.'

In *Iwanuszezak v GMBATU* [5] the plaintiff union member had been adversely affected by an agreement negotiated by his union with his employer, which altered shift arrangements to the benefit of most employees, but to his detriment; he attempted to sue the union for breach of membership contract and negligence but his action was struck out at first instance and, in upholding that decision in the Court of Appeal, Lloyd LJ said:

'The judge put the matter well when he said that it is the primary function of a union to look after the collective interests of its members. Of course, it also looks after individual members in all sorts of different ways. But where the collective interests of the union conflict with the interests of an individual member, it only makes sense, as the judge said, that the collective interests of the members as a whole should prevail.'

While the courts at common law have therefore shown themselves able to recognise the collective interest, and even on occasion to uphold it at the expense of the interests of individuals, the stance of the Conservative Government in its legislative stranglehold on internal union affairs during the 1980s and 1990s was increasingly one of almost total subordination of the collective interest and the adoption of a highly individualist model of trade unionism. Thus, for example, the restrictions on union expulsions and exclusions introduced by the Trade Union Reform and Employment Rights Act 1993 have removed from a union the freedom to determine its own membership, and the tight controls on union discipline introduced by the Employment Act 1988 effectively allow the interests of individual members to override the interests of the membership as a whole in the observance of collective decisions reached in accordance with the rules. Given the historic tussles throughout much of the nineteenth century between the courts and Parliament over the legality of trade unions and their activities, there is a certain irony in the fact that in the latter years of the twentieth century the courts arguably showed a greater readiness to uphold the collective interest than did the legislature.

---

5   [1988] IRLR 219, CA; the passage cited is at 220. See also, in an entirely different context, *Weaver v NATFHE* [1988] ICR 599 where the EAT upheld a union policy not to assist a member to make a complaint which might jeopardise the job of another member, even where that refusal of assistance might constitute racial discrimination.

2   DEFINITION, LISTING AND LEGAL STATUS

i)   Definition

A trade union is defined in the Trade Union and Labour Relations (Consolidation) Act 1992, s. 1 as an organisation which consists wholly or mainly of workers of one or more descriptions and whose principal purposes include the regulation of relations between workers of that description or those descriptions and employers or employers' associations[6]; the definition also extends to organisations which consist of constituent or affiliated trade unions, or the representatives of such organisations. This definition contains three elements: first, there must be an 'organisation', whether temporary or permanent, which indicates that there must be some degree of formal structure as opposed to a casual grouping of workers[7]; secondly, the organisation must be composed wholly or mainly of workers[8] or their trade unions or federations[9]; and thirdly, the principal purposes of the organisation must include industrial relations with employers or their associations[10]. In *Midland Cold Storage v Turner*[11], a joint shop stewards' committee was held not to satisfy this requirement because it had not itself entered into negotiations with employers, but had merely acted as a pressure group, seeking to influence the decisions of the dock workers' unions on the taking of industrial action. In contrast, in *British Association of Advisers and Lecturers in Physical Education v National Union of Teachers*[12], a professional association whose objects clause stated that it 'shall be concerned with the professional interests of its members' was held to be a trade union, although to describe industrial relations as one of its principal purposes might seem on the facts to be stretching several points.

ii)   Listing

The procedure for listing trade unions and employers' associations under the Trade Union and Labour Relations (Consolidation) Act 1992, s. 2 and s. 123 is more of a formality than registration was under the Trade Union Act 1871 or the Industrial Relations Act 1971. Under the former Act, there were certain legal

6   An employers' association is similarly defined in s. 122 as an organisation which consists wholly or mainly of employers or individual owners of undertakings and which has among its principal purposes the regulation of relations between employers and workers or trade unions: see e.g. *Greig v Insole* [1978] 3 All ER 449, [1978] 1 WLR 302; this definition also extends to federations of employers' associations.

7   *Frost v Clarke & Smith Manufacturing Co Ltd* [1973] IRLR 216; *Weeks v National Amalgamated Stevedores and Dockers' Union* (1940) 67 Ll L Rep 282; *Midland Cold Storage v Turner* [1972] ICR 230.

8   'Worker' is defined for these purposes as including those working or seeking to work under contracts of employment and those who contract personally to perform work or services for another, but excluding contracts with professional clients (see e.g. *Carter v Law Society* [1973] ICR 113): Trade Union and Labour Relations (Consolidation) Act 1992, s. 296(1). There are specific exclusions for members of the armed forces (ibid) and the police service (ibid., s. 280).

9   Ibid, s. 1(b). This covers union federations such as the International Transport Workers' Federation: see e.g. *Camellia Tanker Ltd SA v ITWF* [1976] ICR 274, [1976] IRLR 190, CA.

10   There is an exception in the case of union federations, where the definition is satisfied if the organisation's principal purposes include the regulation of relations between its constituent or affiliated organisations: ibid., s. 1(b).

11   [1972] ICR 230.

12   [1986] IRLR 497, CA.

requirements as to rules which the union had to have, and under the latter Act registration was the keystone to much of the rest of the legislation (which in turn meant that the TUC's tactic of non-registration was extremely effective). Now, however, listing (as it is called) is much more mechanical. The operation is carried out by the Certification Officer[13] who maintains a list (open to the public) of unions and employers' associations[14]. Any unlisted organisation may apply in prescribed form to be listed; if listing is refused, the organisation may appeal to the EAT (on both fact and law)[15]. An organisation also has a right to be removed from the list if it wishes. In deciding whether to list an organisation, the Certification Officer has two functions: i) to decide whether it in fact qualifies as a trade union or employers' association, under the definitions considered in head 1 above; ii) to ensure that its name is not the same as that of an existing listed organisation, or misleadingly similar. Entry on the list is itself declared to be evidence that the organisation in fact is a trade union or employers' association (and the organisation may request a certificate from the Certification Officer to the effect that it is on the list)[16]. There are two principal advantages for a trade union in being listed. The first is that it gains certain tax exemptions with regard to its provident benefits funds[17], the second is that listing is a precondition for the far more important step of gaining a certificate of independence[18], which is the key which unlocks the door to most of the statutory union rights contained in the modern legislation.

iii) The legal status of a trade union

Except during the brief currency of the Industrial Relations Act 1971, trade unions have never been bodies corporate, and indeed under the present legislation are forbidden to be so[19]. In law, a trade union is an unincorporated association, a collection of individuals bound together by the contract of membership with no separate legal personality. However, trade unions are invested with some of the most important attributes of legal personality by statute, including the power to make contracts, to sue and be sued and to be prosecuted for criminal offences. A trade union can therefore be seen as a curious hybrid falling somewhere between an unincorporated association and a body corporate – a 'quasi-corporate' body. Until the landmark case of *Taff Vale Rly Co v ASRS*[20] it was

---

13 See p. 46.
14 Trade Union and Labour Relations (Consolidation) Act 1992, s. 2 and s. 123. At the end of 1998, there were 224 trade unions and 106 employers' associations on the list: *Annual Report of the Certification Officer*, 1998.
15 Trade Union and Labour Relations (Consolidation) Act 1992, ss. 9 and 126.
16 Ibid., s. 2(4) and s. 123(4). The fact of being listed is not a necessary precondition of claiming to be a trade union or employers' association (see e.g. the attempt of the ICC and TCCB to claim the status of employers' associations in *Greig v Insole* [1978] 3 All ER 449, [1978] 1 WLR 302), but it may be useful evidence.
17 Income and Corporation Taxes Act 1988, s. 467.
18 Trade Union and Labour Relations (Consolidation) Act 1992, s. 6; see p. 47, above.
19 Trade Union and Labour Relations (Consolidation) Act 1992, s. 10; a professional organisation which is a 'special register body' as defined in s. 117 (e.g. the British Medical Association) is permitted to have corporate status. An employers' association may be incorporated or unincorporated: s. 127.
20 [1901] AC 426. Not all doubts were cleared away by the case; for example it was not established until the decision of the House of Lords in *Bonsor v Musicians' Union* [1956] AC 104, [1955] 3 All ER 518, HL, that a member could be awarded damages against the union.

thought that a trade union could not be sued because it had no legal personality. In that case the House of Lords held that, whatever the precise juristic basis, a union was a creature known to the law and could therefore be sued. The prospect of union funds (including benefit funds) being taken in satisfaction of judgment led to the enactment in 1906[1] of the blanket immunity for trade unions in tort, but this immunity was in turn removed by the Employment Act 1982[2]. The legal status of a trade union is now governed by section 10 of the Trade Union and Labour Relations (Consolidation) Act 1992, which provides that although a union is not a body corporate and is not to be treated as if it were a body corporate[3], it is capable of making contracts and of suing or being sued in its own name (in any cause of action), and furthermore that criminal proceedings may be brought against the union itself. All property belonging to the union must be vested in trustees[4] in trust for the union and that property may be attached for the satisfaction of any judgment, order or award in the same way as if the union were a body corporate. This vesting in trustees was important during the miners' strike of 1984/5, for when fines imposed on the NUM for contempt of court were not paid and sequestration was ordered, an application was successfully made to the court to have the union's trustees removed and a receiver appointed in their place, who thus gained control of the union's property[5]. These steps were taken under the general law (though applying it to hitherto unchartered territory), but the position is now covered by statute[6].

Section 11 of the 1992 Act contains a provision which historically was of great significance when passed[7], for it removed from unions the threat of being found to be illegal (directly or indirectly) on the basis of constituting a restraint of trade. This provision (extended in its present form in one important way) now declares that the purposes of a trade union are not, by reason only that they are in restraint of trade, to be regarded as unlawful so as a) to make any union member liable to criminal proceedings for conspiracy[8] or otherwise, or b) to make any agreement or trust void or voidable. This protection is now also given to the union's rules, which are not to be regarded as unlawful or unenforceable by reason only that they are in restraint of trade. This extension of the protection

---

1   Trade Disputes Act 1906, s. 4.
2   S. 15(1), repealing the Trade Union and Labour Relations Act 1974, s. 14; see p. 696, below.
3   On a literal interpretation of s. 10 it has been held that a union cannot sue for libel in its own name, as it lacks sufficient legal personality: *EETPU v Times Newspapers Ltd* [1980] QB 585, [1980] 1 All ER 1097. This formulation also gives rise to the argument that the doctrine of ultra vires should not now apply to trade unions: Wedderburn (1985) 14 ILJ 127, commenting on the case of *Taylor v NUM (Derbyshire Area)* [1985] IRLR 99, in which the doctrine was applied; Clayton and Tomlinson 'Vicarious liability and trade unions' [1985] NLJ 361.
4   Ibid., s. 12(1). S. 129 applies similar provisions to an unincorporated employers' association.
5   *Clarke v Heathfield* [1985] ICR 203, CA; the action showed that the concentration of property-holding power in the hands of the trustees gave the union a vulnerability of which the Emperor Caligula would have been envious ('Would that the Roman people had but one neck').
6   See p. 612, below.
7   Trade Union Act 1871, ss. 2 and 3; s. 128 of the 1992 Act gives similar protection to the purposes and rules of an unincorporated employers' association. For an example of the application of this section, see *Goring v British Actors Equity Association* [1987] IRLR 122, Ch D.
8   Possible liability for conspiracy on more general grounds (where the object of the conspiracy is not itself unlawful) is excluded in the criminal context by the Criminal Law Act 1977, s. 1(1) and in the tortious context by s. 219 of the 1992 Act.

was given in the light of certain views expressed in *Edwards v SOGAT*[9], where the Court of Appeal asserted a jurisdiction to supervise the content of union rules, not just to secure their proper enforcement. Sachs LJ based this power on restraint of trade arguing that if a rule was capricious and oppressive it might not be made pursuant to the proper purposes of the union and so not be validated by the predecessor to section 11[10]. This view is no longer tenable in the light of the extended wording, though it should be noted that that does not necessarily mean the end of the possible legal development contained in *Edwards v SOGAT*, for Lord Denning MR's approach was wider, being based on general public policy and a 'right to work', not tied to restraint of trade; if this approach is correct, it is not nullified by section 11.

Legal liabilities of unions markedly increased during the 1980s. As already stated, the general tort immunity was removed in 1982, with special statutory rules on when a union is to be liable for the acts of its officers and members (substantially modified in 1990), and statutory maximum amounts of damages recoverable; these matters are considered in chapter 11, below. Also, a union may now be made a party to unfair dismissal proceedings (either at the suit of the employee applicant or the employer respondent) where it is alleged that it put pressure on the employer to dismiss the employee because of non-membership, and may be ordered to pay some or all of the compensation (see p. 580, below).

3 FREEDOM OF ASSOCIATION[11]

Trade unions can only exist where individuals are free to combine together in associations. This freedom to associate was granted in Britain as long ago as 1824 with the repeal of the Combination Acts[12], which had made it unlawful for workers to combine together in trade unions. At common law, therefore, individuals were free to form and join trade unions[13]. However, the common law did not grant positive *rights* of association, enforceable against others, so that at common law there was no protection against discriminatory action by an employer on grounds of union membership, whether in the form of a refusal to hire, dismissal or some other action aimed at discouraging union membership; neither did the common law give any enforceable right *not* to associate to non-union members seeking to work in a closed shop; and, with one possible exception[14], there was no common law right to insist on being admitted to a trade union of one's choice: admission to a union presupposed the willingness of that union to admit the applicant into membership. As Lord Diplock put it in *Cheall v APEX*[15]:

9 [1971] Ch 354, [1970] 3 All ER 689, CA; see head 4, below.
10 In spite of the rejection of this argument by the House of Lords in *Faramus v Film Artistes' Association* [1964] AC 925, [1964] 1 All ER 25, HL. For an interesting illustration of the effect of the restraint of trade doctrine in a case where s. 11 did not apply, see *Boddington v Lawton* [1994] ICR 478, Ch D.
11 See, generally, Von Prondzynski *Freedom of Association and Industrial Relations* (1987), Wedderburn 'Freedom of association and philosophies of labour law' (1989) 18 ILJ 1.
12 Combination Laws Repeal Act 1824. Repeal of the legal restrictions on union activities did not come until much later – see chapter 11.
13 With the exception of the police (Police Act 1964, s. 47) and those working in the intelligence services, who are restricted from joining trade unions by contract.
14 Lord Denning's 'right to work' principle: see p. 599, below.
15 [1983] ICR 398, [1983] IRLR 215, HL.

'My Lords, freedom of association can only be mutual; there can be no right of an individual to associate with other individuals who are not willing to associate with him ...'

Such positive rights to associate as there are in English law have been granted by statute, not in the form of a broad and general right to associate, but instead through the enactment of a complex set of measures (now contained in Part III of the Trade Union and Labour Relations (Consolidation) Act 1992), giving specific protection to those who are refused employment, discriminated against or dismissed for union reasons, and controlling admission to and expulsion from trade unions. The approach in English law has therefore been to build a collective right to associate 'out of the bricks of certain individual employment rights'[16]. These rights exist against the backdrop of an array of international treaties and conventions guaranteeing the principle of freedom of association (albeit in varying degrees), including Article 11 of the European Convention on Human Rights and Fundamental Freedoms, Article 5 of the European Social Charter, and ILO Conventions No. 87 (on Freedom of Association and Protection of the Right to Organise) and No. 98 (on the Right to Organise and Bargain Collectively)[17]. For many years there has been a lively debate over the extent to which the UK law on freedom of association complies with these international standards, fuelled by a number of cases in which the fragility of the right to associate has been graphically demonstrated, for example, the ban in 1984 on union membership at the Government Communications Headquarters (GCHQ), on grounds of national security[18] and more recently, the controversial ruling of the House of Lords in *Associated Newspapers Ltd v Wilson; Associated British Ports v Palmer*[19] that the statutory protection against discrimination for union reasons only applied to positive actions, and not to failures to act (i.e. omissions).

The election of a new Labour Government in 1997 has given new impetus to the debate over freedom of association in the UK. The Employment Relations Act 1999[20] introduced important new measures tackling the blacklisting of trade unionists and reversing (at least in part) the House of Lords' decision in *Wilson* and *Palmer*; and the Human Rights Act 1998 has given the issue an entirely new dimension by incorporating into English law the European Convention on Human Rights, Article 11 of which states:

'(1) Everyone has the right to freedom of peaceful assembly and to freedom of association with others, including the right to form and to join trade unions for the protection of his interests.

(2) No restrictions shall be placed on the exercise of these rights other than such as are prescribed by law and are necessary in a democratic society in the interests of national security or public safety, for the prevention of disorder or crime, for the protection of health or morals or for the protection of the rights and freedoms of others ...'.

16   Wedderburn (1976) 39 MLR 168.
17   See generally Ewing *Britain and the ILO* (2nd ed 1994); Morris, 'Freedom of Association and the Interests of the State' in Ewing, Gearty and Hepple (eds) *Human Rights and Labour Law: Essays for Paul O'Higgins* (1994).
18   *Council of Civil Service Unions v Minister for the Civil Service* [1985] ICR 14, [1985] IRLR 28, HL. See Morris [1985] Public Law 177. The ban was eventually lifted by the new Labour Government in 1998.
19   [1995] ICR 406, [1995] IRLR 258, HL; see p. 568 below.
20   See Ewing 'Freedom of Association and the Employment Relations Act 1999' (1999) 28 ILJ 283.

Opinions differ as to the likely impact of the Human Rights Act 1998 on freedom of association in the UK[1]. On the evidence of the judgments of the European Court and Commission to date under Article 11, there is little cause for optimism that the incorporation of the Convention will lead to a strengthening of the collective right to associate[2]; indeed, individuals seeking to assert a right to dissociate have on the whole had far greater success under Article 11 than have trade unions[3], hence Ewing's comment that 'the contribution of Article 11 to date has been disappointing, failing to deliver any meaningful protection for trade union activities, while being used as an instrument for undermining trade union security[4].' Yet as Palmer has observed[5], the 'pivotal issue' will be the attitude of the English judiciary to the Convention rights, and particularly whether the domestic courts are prepared to draw on the broader, more pro-union rights established in the European Social Charter and ILO Conventions No. 87 and 98 in developing their own jurisprudence under Article 11.

The approach taken in this section will be, first, to examine the legal protection enjoyed by union members against dismissal or other discrimination by employers on the grounds of their union membership or activities, including the right not to be refused employment on grounds of trade union membership; secondly, to examine the circumstances where union officials and members may claim time off work for their trade union duties and activities, and, finally, to consider the legal protection of the right to dissociate, with particular reference to the closed shop. The controversial controls on union admissions and expulsions are considered below under head 5, in the context of the other statutory controls on internal union affairs.

i) The right to associate

a) Refusal of employment on grounds of union membership

Union members have for many years enjoyed protection within employment against dismissal and discriminatory action short of dismissal (e.g. demotion, blocking promotion, etc.) for union reasons. However, until 1990 the law offered no redress to a union member who was refused employment on those grounds. That omission was rectified (at least in part) by the Employment Act 1990[6], which made it unlawful to refuse a person employment on grounds related to union membership[7]. It is generally accepted that the previous Government's primary aim in introducing these measures was to attack the practice of the pre-entry closed shop, not to provide additional protection for union members (indeed, the Green Paper in which the proposals originally saw the light of day made no mention of extra protection for union members)[8], but in the event the

---

1   See Hepple 'The Impact on Labour Law' in Markesinis (ed) *The Impact of the Human Rights Bill on English Law* (1998); Ewing 'The Human Rights Act and Labour Law' (1998) 27 ILJ 275; Palmer 'Human Rights: Implications for Labour Law' (2000) 59 CLJ 168.
2   See e.g. *Council of Civil Service Unions v United Kingdom* (1987) 10 EHRR 269.
3   *Young, James and Webster v United Kingdom* [1981] IRLR 408, ECtHR.
4   Ewing, op cit, n. 1, p. 279.
5   Palmer, op cit, n. 1, p. 196 et seq.
6   Employment Act 1990, s. 1. The measures are now contained in the Trade Union and Labour Relations (Consolidation) Act 1992, s. 137.
7   This includes a situation where a person is refused employment because he is unwilling to accept a requirement not to join or to cease to be a union member: s. 137(1)(b).
8   *Removing Barriers to Employment* (Cm. 655, 1989).

protection was extended to union members and non-members alike. 'Refusal of employment' is defined very widely[9], and includes a refusal or 'deliberate omission' to entertain and process an application or to offer employment to the applicant (simple oversight will not be enough), causing the applicant to withdraw or cease to pursue his application, and making an offer of employment 'the terms of which are such as no reasonable employer who wished to fill the post would offer, and which is not accepted'. It will normally be for the applicant to prove that the refusal of employment was on grounds related to union membership and not for some other reason (e.g. inferior qualifications or experience), but in certain specific circumstances a refusal of employment will be deemed to be unlawful; in particular, where a job advertisement is published which indicates (or might reasonably be understood as indicating) that a particular job is only open to union members or to non-union members, a person who does not satisfy that requirement and who applies unsuccessfully for that job will be conclusively presumed to have been refused employment unlawfully, whatever the employer's reason for not appointing[10].

There is an important limitation on the protection afforded by this right, in that it only covers refusal of employment on grounds of union *membership*; it does not expressly cover an applicant who is refused employment because of his or her past union *activities*. It therefore compares unfavourably with the protection against discrimination within employment, where dismissal and detriment for taking part in union activities is specifically prohibited[11]. If membership of a union means no more than the mere possession of a union membership card, the statutory protection against refusal of employment on grounds of union membership would be narrow indeed. Significantly, however, in *Harrison v Kent County Council*[12], the first reported case on the new provisions, the EAT refused to draw a rigid distinction between membership of a trade union and taking part in union activities, holding that if a person was refused employment because he was a trade union activist or because of his union activities, it was open to a tribunal to conclude that he was refused employment because he was a member of a union. This broad, purposive interpretation of section 137 mirrors the approach taken in an earlier case involving dismissal for union membership[13], where the EAT held that union membership must necessarily imply some degree of participation in union activities; however, the House of Lords has since denied the existence of any general principle that a reference to union membership includes union activities[14], and the correctness of the decision in *Harrison* must therefore be in some doubt.

9   Trade Union and Labour Relations (Consolidation) Act 1992, s. 137(5).

10   Ibid., s. 137(3). A refusal of employment will also be deemed unlawful where it is in pursuance of a union-labour-supply arrangement and the applicant is not a member of the relevant union (s. 137(4)), and where the applicant rejects a job offer because he is unable or unwilling to accept or comply with conditions attached to it concerning union membership (s. 137(6)).

11   See p. 567 et seq, below.

12   [1995] ICR 434, EAT.

13   *Discount Tobacco and Confectionery Ltd v Armitage* [1995] ICR 431n, [1990] IRLR 15, EAT (a case involving dismissal for union membership under s. 152; see p. 575, below).

14   *Associated Newspapers Ltd v Wilson; Associated British Ports v Palmer* [1995] ICR 406, [1995] IRLR 258, HL (a case involving action short of dismissal under s. 146; see p. 576, below). The House of Lords was however prepared to accept that the decision in *Discount Tobacco* was correct on its facts. See also *Speciality Care plc v Pachela* [1996] IRLR 248, EAT, considered at p. 576, below.

Complaints of a breach of this right lie to an employment tribunal[15], which may make a declaration, order the employer to pay compensation (up to the limit of the compensatory award for unfair dismissal)[16] and/or recommend that the respondent take remedial action 'for the purpose of obviating or reducing the adverse effect on the complainant of any conduct to which the complaint relates'[17].

While the introduction in 1990 of the right not to be refused employment on grounds of union membership went some way towards plugging the gaps in the protection of the right to associate, it did not tackle the controversial practice of compiling 'blacklists' of union officials or members. The practice of blacklisting in the UK has been criticised on more than one occasion by the International Labour Organisation[18], and although the Government has acknowledged that there is no evidence that blacklisting is still widespread, section 3 of the Employment Relations Act 1999 confers a power on the Secretary of State to make regulations[19] prohibiting the compilation of lists[20] which contain details of trade union members or persons who have taken part in trade union activities, and which are compiled 'with a view to being used by employers or employment agencies for the purposes of discrimination in relation to recruitment or in relation to the treatment of workers'[1]. Regulations may also be made prohibiting the use, sale or supply of such lists[2]. Enforcement of the anti-blacklisting provisions may be through the employment tribunals and EAT, with the possibility of criminal sanctions[3].

b) Detriment short of dismissal on trade union grounds

Under section 146 of the Trade Union and Labour Relations (Consolidation) Act 1992[4], an employee has a right not to be subjected to any detriment as an individual by his employer, whether by an act or a deliberate failure to act, for the purpose of (a) preventing or deterring him from being or seeking to become a member of an independent trade union, or penalising him for doing so; (b) preventing or deterring him from taking part in the activities of an independent trade union at an appropriate time, or penalising him for doing so; or (c) compelling him to be or become a member of a trade union[5].

---

15 Trade Union and Labour Relations (Consolidation) Act 1992, s. 137(2). Complaints must be brought within three months of the conduct complained of, subject to the usual extension where not reasonably practicable: ibid., s. 139(1).

16 Compensation is assessed on the same basis as an award of damages in tort for breach of statutory duty, and may include an amount for injury to feelings: ibid., s. 140(2).

17 For the interpretation of this formula in the context of complaints of sex and race discrimination, see p. 269, above. Failure to comply with such an order without reasonable justification may lead to an increased award of compensation, but still subject to the statutory maximum: ibid., s. 140(3).

18 See e.g. ILO, 287th Report of the Freedom of Association Committee (1992), para. 267.

19 At the time of writing, no regulations had yet been made under these provisions.

20 'List' is defined widely to mean 'any index or other set of items whether recorded electronically or by any other means': Employment Relations Act 1999, s. 3(5).

1 Ibid., s. 3(1).

2 Ibid., s. 3(2).

3 Ibid., s. 3(3).

4 As amended by the Employment Relations Act 1999, s. 2 and Sch. 2. Note the analogous protection in Part V of the Employment Rights Act 1996 for e.g. health and safety representatives and pension scheme trustees.

5 Before the Employment Act 1980 altered it, limb (c) was confined to action compelling the employee to join a *non-independent* trade union (such as the employer's 'house' union). The removal of this wording in 1980 altered its meaning completely, so that it

Until recently, the protection only applied where an employer took '*action short of dismissal*' against an employee for one of the prohibited purposes. It had long been thought to be established beyond doubt that 'action' in this context included an omission to act, such as a block on promotion or a refusal to extend a pay increase to the members of a particular union[6] (a view which appeared to be confirmed by the statute, which provides an extended definition of 'act' and 'action' as including an omission, 'unless the context otherwise requires'[7]). However, in *Associated Newspapers Ltd v Wilson; Associated British Ports v Palmer*[8], the House of Lords surprisingly held[9] that, for reasons of legislative history, the statutory definition of 'action' as including an omission did not apply to the protection against 'action short of dismissal' on trade union grounds. The facts of the two cases were very similar; in both, the employers had offered a substantial pay increase to those employees who agreed to give up their right to have their terms and conditions negotiated through collective bargaining and sign individual contracts instead. Those who did not sign the new contracts did not get the pay increase. The only significant difference between the two was that in *Palmer,* the employees who refused to sign personal contracts had the option of continuing to be represented by their union, whereas in *Wilson* the employers had terminated the collective agreement and derecognised the union. The House of Lords held that, as the employers' failure to extend the pay increases to those who refused to sign individual contracts was an omission, it did not constitute 'action' within the meaning of the section.

Although the decision on this point has now been reversed by the Employment Relations Act 1999, their Lordships' intricate reasoning is worth exploring, for it illustrates just how fragile collective rights can sometimes be in the hands of the judiciary. The gist of the argument was as follows[10]. The extended statutory definition of 'action' only applies 'except so far as the context otherwise requires'[11], and it was impossible to include the words 'omit' or 'omission' into the crucial phrase 'the right not to have action ... taken against him' without substantial recasting and the introduction of additional words[12]. To solve this grammatical difficulty it was permissible to look at the legislative history of the provisions on action short of dismissal, to see whether the extended definition of 'action' was intended to apply in that context. Prior to the 1978 Consolidation Act, the provisions on action short of dismissal were contained in the Employment

---

now applies wherever there is managerial pressure to join any union; as this is most likely to occur where there is a closed shop, this aspect of s. 146 is considered separately at p. 586, below.

6   *National Coal Board v Ridgway* [1987] ICR 641, [1987] IRLR 80, CA. This was so even where the employer was under no obligation to do the act in question, as in *Ridgway*. See also *Carlson v Post Office* [1981] ICR 343, [1981] IRLR 158, EAT (refusal of a parking space).

7   Trade Union and Labour Relations (Consolidation) Act 1992, s. 298; this definition was formerly located in the Employment Protection (Consolidation) Act 1978, s. 153(1), with some minor differences in wording.

8   [1995] ICR 406, [1995] IRLR 258, HL, overruling the Court of Appeal in *National Coal Board v Ridgway*, n. 6 above. See Simpson (1995) 24 ILJ 235.

9   By a 3:2 majority (reversing the Court of Appeal), Lord Keith and Lord Browne-Wilkinson agreeing with Lord Bridge on this point; Lord Lloyd and Lord Slynn dissented, preferring a more purposive interpretation of the provisions.

10 The facts arose before the enactment of the Trade Union and Labour Relations (Consolidation) Act 1992, and the references in the judgments are therefore to the pre-1992 law as contained in the Employment Protection (Consolidation) Act 1978.

11 Employment Protection (Consolidation) Act 1978, s. 153(1); see n. 7, above.

12 Lord Lloyd and Lord Slynn, dissenting on this point, considered that the words of the Act were clear and unambiguous and should be given effect according to their meaning.

Protection Act 1975, which did *not* contain an extended definition of 'action'. If the extended definition were now to be applied to the provisions on action short of dismissal, that would have meant that the 1978 Consolidation Act would have altered the pre-existing law, in a way that neither the draftsman nor Parliament could have intended[13] (the convention being that Consolidation Acts merely restate the law, and do not alter it in substance). It followed that the right of an employee not to have action short of dismissal taken against him could not properly be construed as including an omission to act.

The effect of the decision (which has been described as 'a brilliant example of grammatical pedantry' and a 'singular triumph of the clever mind at the expense of the big picture'[14]) was to restrict the statutory protection against victimisation on trade union grounds to positive acts, such as the imposition of a financial penalty. In view of the fact that the victimisation of union members is in practice very likely to involve the withholding of some benefit which is conferred on other employees, the effect of the decision in *Wilson* and *Palmer* was to render the statutory protection against action short of dismissal almost worthless. Indeed, Lord Browne-Wilkinson acknowledged that the conclusion 'leaves an undesirable lacuna in the legislation protecting employees against victimisation'[15]. As seen above, the ruling in *Wilson* and *Palmer* on this point was subsequently reversed by the Employment Relations Act 1999, which amended section 146 so that it now applies where an employee is 'subjected to any detriment' by his employer, whether by an act or a deliberate failure to act (i.e. a deliberate omission). However, as will be seen below, it seems very likely that the decision *on the facts* in *Wilson* and *Palmer* would probably still be the same even after the redrafting of section 146 by the 1999 Act.

Turning to the rest of section 146, to fall foul of the statutory protection the employee must be subjected to a detriment 'as an individual', and the act or omission must take place 'for the purpose of' preventing or deterring union membership or participation in union activities, etc. The first of these requirements is designed to ensure that the protection cannot be used to claim what are essentially collective rights. Action taken by the employer against a trade union (e.g. derecognition of the union, or the withdrawal of union facilities) may well have an indirect adverse effect on union members, but it is unlikely to constitute a detriment to them as individuals within the scope of the statutory protection unless it affects them personally, otherwise than merely as union members or officials (e.g. through their pay packets)[16]. Derecognition of an individual shop steward will however constitute action taken against that person as an individual, even though it may not directly affect him as an employee[17]. In

---

13   The history of the provisions on action short of dismissal was seen as supporting this interpretation, as in their original form in the Industrial Relations Act 1971, s. 5, they included a specific provision covering omissions, and if the draftsman of the 1975 Act had intended to achieve the same legislative consequences, he would have used the same language or language substantially to the like effect.

14   Ewing (1999) 28 ILJ 283, at 287.

15   Ibid, at p. 264.

16   *National Coal Board v Ridgway* [1987] ICR 641, [1987] IRLR 80, CA. See also *Cheall v Vauxhall Motors Ltd* [1979] IRLR 253, where the employer's refusal to allow union representation in disciplinary proceedings was held to be action taken against individual employees. Although *Ridgway* was overruled by the House of Lords in *Associated Newspapers Ltd v Wilson; Associated British Ports v Palmer* (above, n. 8) on other grounds, the reasoning of the Court of Appeal on this point would appear still to be valid.

17   *F W Farnsworth Ltd v McCoid* [1999] ICR 1047, CA, upholding the EAT decision on this point: [1998] IRLR 362.

the context of dismissal for union membership or activities, it has been held that the protection does not apply where action is taken by the employer in retaliation for activities by the union generally, unless those affected were singled out for attention because of their own trade union membership or activities[18]; it is unclear whether the same reasoning would be applied in a case involving detriment short of dismissal.

Once an employee has established that he was subjected to some detriment short of dismissal 'as an individual', it then falls to the employer under section 148 to show the purpose for which he acted or failed to act[19]. One of the main controversies in this area is whether it is appropriate to equate the employer's *purpose* with the *effect* of the action complained of. In *Gallacher v Department of Transport*[20], the employee, a civil servant who for several years had spent most of his time on trade union duties, was advised by his career development officer that in order to gain promotion he would need to acquire greater line management experience, which would necessitate a sharp reduction in his union activities. The industrial tribunal held that this recommendation was intended to deter him from continuing with his union activities, and that the employers had therefore taken action short of dismissal against him for the purpose of deterring him from taking part in trade union activities. However, the Court of Appeal, upholding the EAT, held that the tribunal had misconstrued the meaning of the word 'purpose', by failing to distinguish between purpose and effect. According to Neill LJ, in this context the phrase 'for the purpose of' 'connotes an object which the employer desires or seeks to achieve'; on the facts, the employers' purpose was to ensure that only those with sufficient management experience were promoted, not to deter the employee from continuing with his union activities.

The same issue also arose in stark form in *Associated Newspapers Ltd v Wilson; Associated British Ports v Palmer*[1]. The principal issue in the lower courts was whether the purpose of the employers' actions in offering a pay rise only to those employees who agreed to sign personal contracts was to deter employees from continuing to be union members or to penalise them for doing so, or was instead to achieve a smooth transition from collective bargaining to individual contracting, and to achieve greater flexibility. The EAT in *Wilson*[2] held that the employer's actions did not constitute action short of dismissal against those refusing to agree to the new arrangements, because the purpose of those actions was to achieve greater flexibility. On appeal[3], the Court of Appeal reversed the EAT, holding that there had in fact been a breach of the section, in that the purpose of the employers' actions, in offering what Dillon LJ described as a 'douceur' to those who accepted personal contracts while withholding it from those who were not prepared to do so, was to persuade the employees to give up their right to union representation, and that this constituted action short of dismissal which deterred them from being union members and penalised them for their union membership if they refused to agree to the new arrangements. As seen above, the main ground on

---

18   *Carrington v Therm-A-Stor Ltd* [1983] ICR 208, [1983] IRLR 78, CA; the decision has been heavily criticised, and rightly so.
19   Trade Union and Labour Relations (Consolidation) Act 1992, s. 148(1).
20   [1994] IRLR 231, CA.
1   Ibid, n. 8.
2   [1992] ICR 681, [1992] IRLR 440, EAT; followed in *Associated British Ports v Palmer* [1993] ICR 101, [1993] IRLR 63, EAT.
3   [1994] ICR 97, [1993] IRLR 336, CA (the appeal was heard together with the appeal in *Palmer*, which was also reversed).

which the House of Lords allowed the employers' appeal was that the statutory protection against action short of dismissal did not extend to omissions; however their Lordships also considered the lawfulness of the employers' purpose, and held, reversing the Court of Appeal, that as the employers' purpose in *Wilson* was to end collective bargaining, and in *Palmer* to achieve greater flexibility, there was no unlawful purpose within the meaning of section 146. According to Lord Slynn, there was no evidence '… that the employers' purpose in paying a salary differential was to prevent or deter union membership, even if derecognition in itself might make the union less attractive to members or to potential members[4].' This part of the House of Lords' decision is unaffected by the recent redrafting of section 146 to include deliberate omissions, so that on the face of it an employer is still able to offer a payment to employees to encourage them to sign individual contracts. However, section 17 of the Employment Relations Act 1999 gives the Secretary of State a power to make regulations about cases where a worker is subjected to a detriment by his employer or dismissed 'on the grounds that he refuses to enter into a contract which includes terms which differ from the terms of a collective agreement which applies to him'[5]. At first sight this seems wide enough to cover the situation in *Wilson* and *Palmer*, but it is expressly provided that certain forms of conduct (including the payment of higher wages, bonuses or the provision of benefits in kind to other workers employed by the same employer) will *not* constitute a detriment within the meaning of section 146, so long as the workers receiving those enhanced payments or benefits are not contractually inhibited from being trade union members, and the payments or benefits are contractual in nature and 'reasonably relate to services provided by the worker under that contract'[6].

There is yet another reason why the outcome in *Wilson* and *Palmer* would probably still be the same even after the 1999 reforms. In the aftermath of the Court of Appeal decision (which was widely seen as threatening the trend towards individual contracting by preventing employers from offering a sweetener to those agreeing to give up collective bargaining), the Conservative Government rushed through an eleventh-hour amendment to section 148 in the Trade Union Reform and Employment Rights Bill (then at Third Reading stage in the House of Lords) seeking to reverse the effect of the Court of Appeal's ruling[7]. By virtue of the amended section 148, where in a complaint under section 146 'there is evidence that the employer's purpose was to further a change in his relationship with all or any class[8] of his employees', the tribunal must regard that as the purpose for which the employer acted or failed to act, even if there is also evidence that the employer's purpose was an unlawful one of preventing or deterring

---

4   Ibid, n. 8, at p. 265. See also Lord Lloyd, at p. 266, on the importance of distinguishing between the *purposes* and the *consequences* of derecognition.

5   At the time of writing no regulations had been made under s. 17. In Committee, the minister suggested that a worker could be regarded as having been subjected to a detriment for refusing to give up the terms of a collective agreement where there was a block on promotion, the withholding of discretionary benefits or the allocation to less favourable duties or locations (*Hansard*, Standing Committee E, 18 March 1999, col. 478).

6   Employment Relations Act 1999, s. 17(4) (an Opposition amendment in the House of Lords).

7   Trade Union Reform and Employment Rights Act 1993, s. 13, amending the Trade Union and Labour Relations (Consolidation) Act 1992, s. 148.

8   Defined as 'those employed at a particular place of work, those employees of a particular grade, category or description or those of a particular grade, category or description employed at a particular place of work': ibid., s. 148(5).

union membership within section 146, unless the tribunal considers that no reasonable employer would have so acted or failed to act, having regard to that former purpose. This amendment, heavily criticised upon its introduction for undermining the protection afforded to union members against attempts by employers to discourage union membership[9], was surprisingly left untouched by the Employment Relations Act 1999.

As seen earlier, the statutory protection of union members arises where an employee is subjected to any detriment for the purpose of (a) preventing or deterring him from being or seeking to become a union member, or (b) preventing or deterring him from taking part in union activities, or penalising him for doing so. To take limb (b) first, it is clear that to be protected, the activities in question must be those of a trade union, in the sense of having a genuine trade union connection rather than just being the type of activity which one might expect a union to engage in. Thus, protected activities would include taking part in union meetings[10], consulting a shop steward or union official[11] and attempting to recruit new members or form a workplace union group[12] (particularly if the employee concerned is himself a shop steward or union officer). However, it would not include actions on an individual basis without any union involvement, as in *Chant v Aquaboats Ltd*[13] where the EAT held that the applicant's actions, in personally complaining about woodworking machinery which did not comply with safety standards and organising a petition of other employees to support the claim, did not qualify as trade union activities and so were not protected.

The section only protects activities which take place during the employment in question, not to previous activities in other employments, so that if the employer takes action against an individual (e.g. by transferring him to a non-sensitive area) on finding out about his record of union activity in a previous employment, that person may not complain under section 146. So, for example, in *City of Birmingham District Council v Beyer*[14], a case on the analogous provisions concerning dismissal for union activities, a well-known union activist gained employment with the council by using a false name, and was subsequently dismissed because of the deceit; the EAT held that the employee could not benefit from the statutory protection, because it did not extend to pre-employment activities. However, the protection does apply where action is taken to prevent or deter an employee from engaging in union activity within the current employment[15], and it may well be difficult for an employer in such a case to persuade the tribunal that he was

9   See e.g. ILO, 294th Report of the Freedom of Association Committee, para. 162.
10 *Miller v Rafique* [1975] IRLR 70, IT; this may apply to attendance at a meeting which is critical of the union: *British Airways Engine Overhaul Ltd v Francis* [1981] ICR 278, [1981] IRLR 9, EAT.
11 *Marley Tile Co Ltd v Shaw* [1978] ICR 828, [1978] IRLR 238, EAT (reversed by the Court of Appeal on other grounds: [1980] ICR 72, [1980] IRLR 25).
12 *Brennan v Ellward (Lancs) Ltd* [1976] IRLR 378, EAT; *Lyon and Scherk v St James Press Ltd* [1976] ICR 413, [1976] IRLR 215, EAT; *Dixon and Shaw v West Ella Developments Ltd* [1978] ICR 856, [1978] IRLR 151, EAT.
13 [1978] 3 All ER 102, [1978] ICR 643, EAT (an unfair dismissal case); *Gardner v Peeks Retail Ltd* [1975] IRLR 244, IT; *Drew v St Edmundsbury Borough Council* [1980] ICR 513, [1980] IRLR 459, EAT.
14 [1978] 1 All ER 910, [1977] IRLR 211, EAT. See Evans and Lewis, 'Anti-union discrimination: practice, law and policy' (1987) 16 ILJ 88.
15 *Fitzpatrick v British Railways Board* [1992] ICR 221, [1991] IRLR 376, CA.

entirely motivated by the employee's previous conduct and not by fears that it might be repeated in the present employment[16].

The principal limitation on limb (b) (preventing or deterring union activities), which attempts to hold a balance between the employee's rights and the employer's business interests, is that to be protected the union activities must take place at an 'appropriate time'. This is defined in section 146(2) as either outside the employee's working hours or during his working hours but with the agreement or consent of the employer. 'Working hours' are defined as time when the employee is contractually obliged to be at work, which has been construed as meaning when he is actually performing work, so that when an employee takes part in activities during a tea break or lunch break that will be an 'appropriate time', even if he is still on the premises and being paid by the employer during the break[17]. One potentially contentious area is whether the employer has in fact consented to an activity where it takes place during working hours. The case of *Robb v Leon Motor Services Ltd*[18] showed a fairly rigorous approach to the issue, in the employer's favour. The employee, a shop steward, was transferred to a department where he was no longer in contact with other employees (i.e. 'neutralised') because of his over-enthusiastic pursuit of union activities in working hours. The union was not recognised and there was no express agreement allowing union activities during working hours, but the employee's written statement of terms of employment stated that he would be permitted to take part in union activities 'at the appropriate time', though without defining it. The EAT dismissed the employee's claim under what is now section 146, holding that there was not the necessary agreement or consent to his union activities (the written term being too vague to be construed as such). In contrast, in *Bass Taverns Ltd v Burgess*[19], the employee, a pub manager who was also a shop steward of the National Association of Licensed House Managers, was regularly permitted by the company to make presentations on behalf of the union at induction courses for new employees. On one occasion he made some remarks which were highly critical of the company, and which led to his demotion; he resigned and claimed constructive dismissal, arguing that his dismissal was for taking part in union activities at an appropriate time, and was therefore automatically unfair under section 152. The Court of Appeal held that the employer's consent to his participation should not be considered as subject to an implied limitation that nothing critical of the company would be said, so that, despite his remarks, he was still taking part in trade union activities at an appropriate time, and his claim therefore succeeded.

It is however clear from later cases that consent does not have to be express (and also that recognition is not a prerequisite), though in practice an express agreement is more certain, and it may well be easier to imply consent from a course of conduct if the union is in fact recognised. This possibility of implied

---

16 As seen above, a *refusal* of employment on grounds of previous union activity is unlikely to be covered by the Act.

17 *Post Office v UPOW* [1974] 1 All ER 229, [1974] ICR 378, HL; *Zucker v Astrid Jewels Ltd* [1978] ICR 1088, [1978] IRLR 385, EAT.

18 [1978] ICR 506, [1978] IRLR 26, EAT.

19 [1995] IRLR 596, CA. Cf. the suggestion in the case that the activities might fall outside the protection of s. 152 if the employee indulged in malicious, untruthful or irrelevant invective; see also *Shillito v Van Leer (UK) Ltd* [1997] IRLR 495, EAT (on the analogous provisions on victimisation for health and safety reasons).

consent was accepted by the Court of Appeal in *Marley Tile Co Ltd v Shaw*[20], but the case also shows that consent will not be readily implied merely from the employer's silence (particularly on an ad hoc basis, where it is being argued that on one particular occasion the employee proposed to do something during working hours and the employer did not strenuously object), and that implied consent is still not easy to establish where the union member is not accredited by the employer, or the union is not recognised. On the other hand, where the union presence is accepted by the employer it is possible that, even in the absence of express agreement, consent might be implied over a period of time on the basis of established workplace practice or good industrial relations practice. To this extent the onus is placed upon the employer, if he wishes to prevent extraneous activities during working hours (and so preserve his right to stop them), to state expressly that he does not agree or consent (either by notice or in contracts).

Three further points should be noticed on the question of appropriate time. The first is whether an employer can revoke his consent on any given occasion, especially if he has only given it indirectly, by implication; it is strongly arguable that the purpose of the section would be defeated if the employer was allowed to revoke on an ad hoc basis, though unfortunately the section does not contain provisions directly preventing it. Such revocation, if allowed, would certainly make the right in section 146(1)(b) highly uncertain and ultimately of little value. The second point is that if an activity is taking place at an appropriate time, the protection given to it by the section could be seen to presuppose some provision of material facilities by the employer (or, at least, no unreasonable withholding of them), if only to the extent of noticeboards or room for a meeting. However, once again the section is not specific on this question[1]. Finally, it seems clear that taking industrial action will rarely (if ever) constitute taking part in union activities at an appropriate time within the meaning of section 146, not least because it is unlikely to be an activity undertaken outside working hours or with the employer's consent; in *Brennan v Ellward (Lancs) Ltd*[2] Phillips J stated that the section: '... cannot extend to the activities of employees in suddenly downing tools and leaving the premises in order to consult their union officials elsewhere, and wherever they may happen to be.' The EAT has however held that the preliminary planning and organisation of industrial action can constitute taking part in union activities for the purposes of the protection against dismissal for union reasons[3].

Turning to limb (a) (preventing or deterring union membership), two particular issues have been especially problematic: the first concerns the possible application of section 146 to cases of inter-union rivalry, such as in *National Coal Board v Ridgway*[4]. That case arose in the aftermath of the miners' strike, and the breakaway of the UDM from the NUM. A pay rise was negotiated with the UDM but rejected by the NUM, and at the colliery in question the rise was paid to UDM members but not to NUM members. Two of the latter complained to an industrial

---

20   [1980] ICR 72, [1980] IRLR 25, CA; *Zucker v Astrid Jewels Ltd*, n. 17, above. In *Marley's* case the Court of Appeal upheld the EAT on the possibility of implied consent, but reversed their decision on the facts, holding that no consent could be inferred in the circumstances.

1   The statutory right to use the employer's premises for the purposes of a workplace ballot was repealed by the 1993 Act.

2   [1976] IRLR 378, EAT; see also *Drew v St Edmundsbury Borough Council* [1980] ICR 513, [1980] IRLR 459, EAT.

3   *Britool Ltd v Roberts* [1993] IRLR 481, EAT. See p. 579, below.

4   [1987] ICR 641, [1987] IRLR 80, CA, reversing [1986] IRLR 379, EAT; see Simpson (1987) 50 MLR 639.

tribunal that this constituted action short of dismissal taken against them as individuals by their employer, for the purpose of preventing or deterring them from being members of an independent trade union, or penalising them for doing so. The tribunal found for the applicants, but in allowing the appeal the EAT seemed concerned that the section should not apply to large-scale collective disputes such as this. It was accepted that the withholding of the pay rise from NUM members was 'action'[5] which 'penalised' them for their membership; however, the EAT found against the applicants on the grounds (i) that the employers' action was not taken against them as individuals, but against the union itself; and (ii) the section only outlawed action to prevent an employee being a member of any trade union whatsoever, not to prevent membership of a *particular* union (here, the NUM). The EAT's finding on the second point appeared to gain support from the differences in the wording within section 146, and in particular the fact that whereas limbs (a) and (b) refer to preventing or deterring membership or activities 'of an independent trade union', limb (c) specifically refers to compelling membership 'of any trade union or of a particular trade union or of one of a number of trade unions.'

However, on further appeal the Court of Appeal allowed the applicants' appeal and held that the section applied. Both of the above grounds were disapproved: there was action taken against them as individuals because the action against the union also affected them as individuals through their pay packets[6], and on its proper construction, the protection in the section applied to penalising membership of a particular union as well as membership of unions generally[7]. The court therefore accepted the possible application of the section to inter-union disputes which lead to differential treatment by the employer.

The second issue arising from limb (a) concerns the scope of the protection of union membership, and in particular whether the right to be a trade union member means anything more than simply having a right to possess a membership card. In *Discount Tobacco and Confectionery Ltd v Armitage*[8] (a case on the parallel provisions on dismissal for union membership), the EAT declined to draw a sharp distinction between membership of a union and making use of the essential services of a union[9]. In that case, the employee was dismissed after invoking the assistance of a union representative in a matter concerning her terms of employment. The EAT upheld the finding of the industrial tribunal that she had been dismissed by reason of her union membership, Knox J stating that: 'In our judgment, the activities of a trade union officer in negotiating and elucidating terms of employment is, to use a prayer book expression, the outward and visible manifestation of trade union membership. It is an incident of union membership which is, if not the primary one, at any rate a very important one and we see no genuine distinction between membership of a union, on the one hand, and

---

5   The decision of the Court of Appeal was subsequently overruled by the House of Lords on this point in *Associated Newspapers Ltd v Wilson; Associated British Ports v Palmer*, see p. 568, above.

6   See p. 569, above.

7   Although *Ridgway* was subsequently overruled on other grounds (see n. 5), the reasoning of the Court of Appeal on this point would appear still to be valid.

8   [1995] ICR 431n, [1990] IRLR 15, EAT.

9   *Discount Tobacco* was followed in *Harrison v Kent County Council* [1995] ICR 434, where the EAT held that it was open to a tribunal to conclude that a person who was refused employment because he was a trade union activist or because of his union activities was refused employment because he was a member of a union within the meaning of s. 137(1); see p. 566, above.

making use of the essential services of a union, on the other.' However, in *Associated Newspapers Ltd v Wilson; Associated British Ports v Palmer*[10], the House of Lords held[11] that while the decision in *Discount Tobacco* might have been correct on its facts, it did not establish any general principle that membership of a union and making use of the union's services are in some way to be equated. The statutory protection of union membership was intended to protect union membership as such (i.e. the right to associate as members of an independent union), and in their Lordships' opinion there was no justification for reading in the words 'or making use of the essential services of the union', and still less justification for regarding trade union membership and the use of trade union services as the same thing[12]. It could be argued that this narrow interpretation would reduce the protection of union membership under limb (a) almost to vanishing point[13], as employers are in practice more likely to object to the consequences of union membership rather than to the mere fact of membership. It certainly makes the scope of the protection of union activities under limb (b) of crucial importance as far as freedom of association is concerned.

If an employee is subjected to a detriment in contravention of section 146, he may complain to a tribunal within three months of the act or failure to act (or within such further period as the tribunal thinks reasonable if it was not reasonably practicable for the complaint to be presented within three months)[14]. In such a complaint, the onus is upon the employer to show the purpose for which he acted or failed to act[15]. If the tribunal finds the complaint justified, it must make a declaration to that effect and may order such compensation as it thinks just and equitable[16]; the section states that the tribunal is to have regard to the infringement of the employee's rights under section 146 and to any loss sustained by the employee, in particular any expenses incurred by him and any loss of benefits which he might reasonably have expected but for the employer's act or

---

10 See p. 568, above.

11 The comments of the House of Lords on this point were strictly speaking obiter, as the main ground of the decision was that the statutory protection only applies to actions, not to omissions.

12 See Lord Lloyd at p. 266. Cf. Lord Slynn, at p. 265, taking a somewhat broader view. The ruling of the House of Lords on this point places the correctness of the decision in *Harrison v Kent County Council* (see p. 566) in some doubt; however, in *Specialty Care plc v Pachela* [1996] IRLR 248, the EAT re-examined the status of *Discount Tobacco* in the light of *Wilson* and *Palmer*, and held that it was still open to an industrial tribunal to hold that employees who were dismissed for engaging the assistance of their union in a protest over a change in working hours were dismissed on grounds of union membership. In such a complaint, the tribunal must find as a fact '… whether or not the principal reason for dismissal related to the applicant's trade union membership not only by reference to whether he or she had simply joined a union, but also by reference to whether the introduction of union membership into the employment relationship had led the employer to dismiss the employee. Tribunals should answer that question robustly, based on their findings as to what really caused the dismissal in the mind of the employer.'

13 Per Knox J in *Discount Tobacco*, at p. 16.

14 Ibid., s. 147. In *British Airways Board v Clark* [1982] IRLR 238 it was held by the EAT that where the disciplinary action complained of was only effective after exhaustion of the employer's disciplinary procedure (including an appeal), time only began to run (for computing the three-month period) from the date when the employee was finally informed of the failure of his appeal. Where the act or failure to act is part of a series of similar acts or failures, time runs from the last of them; where a single action has a continuing effect, time will run from the initial act: *Adlam v Salisbury and Wells Theological College* [1985] ICR 786, EAT.

15 Ibid., s. 148(1).

16 Ibid., s. 149(2).

failure to act. In *Brassington v Cauldon Wholesale Ltd*[17] the EAT held that, while the remedy is compensatory rather than penal, the tribunal is not restricted to the employee's pecuniary loss, and may award compensation over and above such pecuniary loss for any non-pecuniary injury such as stress and anxiety caused to the employee and deprivation of benefits which might have come from trade union membership; it is, however, for the employee to establish that he has suffered the type of injury for which he seeks compensation. Section 148(2) states that in determining a complaint the tribunal shall not take into account any pressure exerted upon the employer (by industrial action or the threat of it) by a union[18], which may mean that the employer is placed in a difficult position, particularly in the case of an inter-union dispute. However, if the pressure is exercised by the union in order to compel the employee to be or become a union member the union may be joined as a party to the action[19].

c) Dissmissal on trade union grounds[20]

In parallel with the previous provisions, section 152 of the Trade Union and Labour Relations (Consolidation) Act 1992 provides that a dismissal will be *automatically unfair* if the reason for it (or, if more than one, the principal reason) was that the employee (a) was, or proposed to become, a member of an independent trade union, or (b) had taken part, or proposed to take part, in the activities of an independent trade union at an appropriate time, or (c) was not a member of any trade union, or of a particular trade union, or of one of a number of particular trade unions, or had refused, or proposed to refuse, to become or remain a member. The section was subject to major amendment by the Employment Acts 1980, 1982 and 1988, and as it now stands it is a curious hybrid, for heads (a) and (b) are there to protect union members in their membership and activities, whereas head (c) serves the totally different purpose of protecting *non*-union members, and is therefore considered below in the context of the closed shop. A dismissal for redundancy will be deemed to be unfair under section 153 of the 1992 Act if it is shown that the circumstances producing the redundancy applied equally to other comparable employees in the same undertaking who were not dismissed[1], and the employee was selected for dismissal for any of the above reasons.

Apart from rendering a dismissal automatically unfair, the other significant difference (leaving aside for the moment the question of remedies, considered below) between a dismissal for union reasons and an ordinary unfair dismissal action is that the normal requirements as to the qualifying period of continuous employment and the restrictions on those who have reached retiring age do not

---

17   [1978] ICR 405, [1977] IRLR 479, EAT. In *Cleveland Ambulance NHS Trust v Blane* [1997] IRLR 332, the EAT confirmed that compensation for insult or injury to feelings may be awarded under this head.

18   A similar provision in the Employment Rights Act 1996, s. 107 applies to unfair dismissal complaints; see p. 466, above.

19   Trade Union and Labour Relations (Consolidation) Act 1992, s. 150. Similar provisions apply in the case of dismissal for union reasons: see s. 160. The joinder provisions are considered at p. 580, below.

20   See *Harvey* N, 5C.

1   In making the comparison with the position of other employees, anything that the employee did or had a right to do as a trade union official must be left out of account, lest the purpose of the section be defeated: *O'Dea v ISC Chemicals Ltd* [1995] IRLR 599, CA.

apply in this context[2]. Establishing that a dismissal or a redundancy selection is on trade union grounds can give rise to considerable evidential problems, particularly where the employer claims that there was some other reason (e.g. misconduct) for the dismissal. As in other unfair dismissal cases, it will normally be for the employer to show what the reason for the dismissal was[3]; however, where an employee lacks the necessary one year's continuous employment, the burden of proving that he was dismissed on trade union grounds (and can therefore bring his case) lies with him[4]. It is clear that an employer does not have to be motivated by malice or a deliberate desire to be rid of a trade union activist in order to fall foul of these provisions[5], and the EAT has emphasised that the scope of the factual enquiry into the reason for the dismissal should not be restricted[6].

The provisions in heads (a) and (b) are substantially the same as those in section 146 which protect the employee from detriment short of dismissal for trade union membership or activities, so that cases on the one section (e.g. on the meaning of 'activities of a trade union' and 'appropriate time') apply mutatis mutandis to the other. Two further points should be noted here. First, as in the case of detriment short of dismissal, the protection for those dismissed for taking part in union activities only applies to activities during the employment in question, and does not extend to an employee who is dismissed because of participation in union activities before the employment began[7]. However, in *Fitzpatrick v British Railways Board*[8], the Court of Appeal held that an employee with a reputation as a union activist in her previous employment who was dismissed not because of anything she had done in her present employment but because the employer feared that she might become a disruptive influence at some time in the future was still protected, because a dismissal will be unfair if the reason for it was that the employee was *proposing* to take part in trade union activities. Secondly, although one might be forgiven for thinking that participation in industrial action is a classic example of taking part in trade union activities, and therefore protected under section 152, the EAT has said, obiter, that taking part in industrial action does not count as taking part in the activities of a trade union for present purposes, and that the two situations are mutually exclusive[9]. This was said to be because the legislation makes separate provision for those dismissed while taking part in industrial action[10], so that if an employee is dismissed while

2 Trade Union and Labour Relations (Consolidation) Act 1992, s. 154.
3 *Maund v Penwith District Council* [1984] ICR 143, [1994] IRLR 24, CA. The usual test applies, i.e. the reason for dismissal is the set of facts known to the employer or the set of beliefs held by him which causes him to dismiss (see p. 464, above); the 'but for' test which applies in sex and race discrimination cases does not apply in this context: *CGB Publishing v Killey* [1993] IRLR 520, EAT.
4 *Smith v Hayle Town Council* [1978] ICR 996, [1978] IRLR 413, CA; once he has done so, the burden of proof in the actual unfair dismissal hearing goes back to the employer: *Shannon v Michelin (Belfast) Ltd* [1981] IRLR 505, NICA.
5 *Dundon v GPT Ltd* [1995] IRLR 403, EAT.
6 See *Driver v Cleveland Structural Engineering Co Ltd* [1994] ICR 372, [1994] IRLR 636, EAT, where the employer's failure to select the applicant, a former shop steward, for alternative employment in a redundancy situation was held to be legally relevant in determining whether he was unfairly dismissed on account of his trade union activities under s. 152.
7 *City of Birmingham District Council v Beyer* [1978] 1 All ER 910, [1977] IRLR 211, EAT (discussed at p. 572, above).
8 [1991] IRLR 376, CA.
9 *Drew v St Edmundsbury Borough Council* [1980] ICR 513, [1980] IRLR 459, EAT.
10 Trade Union and Labour Relations (Consolidation) Act 1992, ss. 237 - 238A; see p. 635, below.

on strike, his complaint will be determined under the special rules which apply in such a case, and not under section 152. It is arguable that there are circumstances[11] where a tribunal might have to consider whether an employee dismissed during industrial action was dismissed for taking part in trade union activities within the meaning of section 152; however, the issue is of limited practical importance, because even if participation in industrial action could in principle constitute an activity of a trade union, it will rarely, if ever, be undertaken at an 'appropriate time', as it is unlikely to be an activity undertaken outside working hours or with the employer's consent[12]. Significantly, the EAT has held that participating in the preliminary planning and organisation of industrial action can amount to taking part in trade union activities within the meaning of section 152[13].

Turning to remedies, there are some significant differences between the remedies available in cases of dismissal for trade union reasons and in most other unfair dismissal cases. Where a dismissal is unfair by virtue of being for trade union reasons the amount of compensation is likely to be higher, because provision is made for a minimum basic award of £3,100 in such cases[14]. Until recently, an employee unfairly dismissed for trade union reasons was entitled to a 'special award' of compensation, on top of the normal basic and compensatory awards, where the employee requested the tribunal to make an order for reinstatement or re-engagement. The special award was however abolished by the Employment Relations Act 1999, and replaced by the additional award. Unlike the additional award, which can only be made where the employer fails to comply with an order of reinstatement or re-engagement, the special award was not conditional on the tribunal actually *making* such an order, and the amount of the special award was likely to be much higher than the additional award[15]. As in other unfair dismissal cases, compensation awarded in cases of dismissal for trade union reasons may be reduced where there is contributory fault, although it is specifically provided that failure on the part of the employee to comply with a requirement (whether or not contractual) to join or not to join a union, or not to take part in union activities, is not to be regarded as 'fault' for these purposes[16].

The increased levels of compensation originally introduced by the Employment Act 1982 were part of the attack on the closed shop[17] (the idea

---

11   For example, where the employer has sacked or re-engaged some but not all of the strikers, and the dismissal is neither automatically unfair for taking protected industrial action, nor outside the jurisdiction of the tribunal because the industrial action is unofficial.

12   *Britool Ltd v Roberts* [1993] IRLR 481, EAT. One example of industrial action which could conceivably be held to be at an 'appropriate time' is a ban on voluntary (i.e. non-contractual) overtime.

13   Ibid.

14   Trade Union and Labour Relations (Consolidation) Act 1992, s. 156. In common with most other statutory compensation limits, the minimum basic award is subject to indexation under the Employment Relations Act 1999, s.34. For the other special cases in which a minimum basic award will be made, see p. 506.

15   At the time it was abolished, the amount of the special award where the tribunal did *not* order reinstatement or re-engagement was 104 weeks' pay (subject to a minimum of £14,500 and a maximum of £29,000); if such an order was made but not complied with, the special award was 152 weeks' pay (subject to a minimum of £21,800, but with no maximum). The maximum additional award is only £11,960: see p. 504.

16   Trade Union and Labour Relations (Consolidation) Act 1992, s. 155. In determining whether there has been contributory fault the tribunal is entitled to take into account the employee's conduct *leading up* to the dismissal, although clearly it must disregard the conduct which in fact led to the dismissal: *TGWU v Howard* [1992] ICR 106, [1992] IRLR 170, EAT.

17   See p. 586, below.

being to make an unfair dismissal because of a closed shop very expensive in order to have a deterrent effect), but the drafting of the 1982 Act was such that the increased compensation was extended to *all* employees dismissed for union reasons, and not confined to those dismissed for *non-membership*. Clearly it was no part of the previous Government's intention to put greater liabilities onto *employers* in closed shop cases, however much it wanted to improve the lot of those dismissed for refusing to become union members. The solution adopted[18] was to allow the employer or the dismissed employee to request the tribunal to join a trade union or other person as a party to the tribunal proceedings where it is claimed that a) the employer was induced to dismiss the complainant by industrial pressure exercised by that third party (whether by strike or otherwise), and b) that pressure was exercised because the complainant was not a union member[19]. Any award of compensation in those proceedings may then be made wholly or partly against the union or other person joined in the proceedings, as the tribunal considers just and equitable, instead of against the employer. As first introduced in 1980, the joinder provisions only allowed the *employer* to join the union, but the present position is that the *employee* can also join the union (as, in effect, a second defendant) and in practice may be more likely to do so than the employer (who may be more inclined to pay up and hope to forget the whole matter).

Finally on remedies, sections 161–166 of the 1992 Act make special provision for 'interim relief' pending a hearing where an employee complains that he has been unfairly dismissed for trade union reasons. The aim of interim relief is to secure the position of the employee pending the hearing by seeking to ensure that he remains in employment until the tribunal is able to hear the unfair dismissal complaint. Originally introduced to protect those dismissed for their union membership or activities, interim relief was extended by the Employment Act 1982 to a person who is dismissed for not being a union member, thus allowing it as a remedy in closed shop dismissal cases[20]. An application for interim relief must be presented to a tribunal within seven days of the effective date of termination[1], and where the complaint is of dismissal for union membership or activities it must be backed by a certificate from an official of the union concerned[2] stating a) that the applicant is a member of the union (or proposed to become one) and b) that in the official's opinion there are reasonable grounds for supposing that the dismissal was for union reasons. The tribunal must hear the application as soon as practicable, although the employer must be given at least seven days' notice of the hearing[3]. If the tribunal thinks it likely[4] that the employee's complaint will be upheld at the full hearing, it must ask the employer

---

18   See now the Trade Union and Labour Relations (Consolidation) Act 1992, s. 160; similar provisions apply in the context of detriment short of dismissal: s. 150.

19   Such a request must be granted if made before the hearing but thereafter the tribunal has a discretion to refuse it, save that no such request may be made after the tribunal has made a declaration that the complaint is well-founded: s. 160(2).

20   Interim relief has subsequently been made available in certain other unfair dismissal complaints: see the Employment Rights Act 1996, s. 128(1).

1   On which, see p. 453, above.

2   The official must be authorised by the union to act for this purpose: s. 161(4). If the authority of the official is challenged, it will be for the union to prove that the official was authorised to sign the certificate: *Sulemany v Habib Bank* [1983] ICR 60, EAT. For obvious reasons there is no requirement of a certificate where an application for interim relief is made in a case of dismissal for non-membership.

3   Trade Union and Labour Relations (Consolidation) Act 1992, s. 162.

4   I.e. the applicant must have a 'pretty good' chance of success, per Slynn J, *Taplin v C Shippam Ltd* [1978] ICR 1068, [1978] IRLR 450, EAT.

if he is willing to reinstate or re-engage the employee pending the hearing. If so, the tribunal will make an order to that effect; if not, the tribunal will make an order for the continuation of the employee's contract pending the full hearing[5]. This is an order that the contract shall continue until the hearing, but only for the stated purposes of pay or any other benefits, seniority, pension rights and other similar matters, and continuity of employment[6]; the order must specify the amount to be paid, which will be the amount which the employee could reasonably have been expected to earn (had he not been dismissed) in the period between the date of the dismissal and the date of determination of the complaint[7]. Any payments received from the employer under the contract or by way of damages for breach of contract must be taken into account. The crucial point however is that other obligations under the contract, in particular the employee's duty to work, do not continue in force, which means that there is a very strong incentive for the employer to agree to re-employ the employee pending the hearing. If the employer fails to comply with the order, the applicant may complain to the tribunal which, in a case where the failure consists of non-payment of wages as specified in the order, will determine the amount owed under the order or, in the case of some other failure (e.g. failure to comply with an order for reinstatement or re-engagement), will order the employer to pay such compensation as it considers just and equitable[8].

ii)   Time off work

The Trade Union and Labour Relations (Consolidation) Act 1992 gives special rights in sections 168–173 to reasonable time off work for trade union duties and trade union activities. The first of these is with pay, the second without (unless there is a contractual agreement to pay), and so there is a crucial difference between a union duty and a mere activity, as this decides whether the employer must pay. The statutory provisions are supplemented by the ACAS Code of Practice No. 3 on *Time Off for Trade Union Duties and Activities*[9], which recommends the negotiation of specific agreements on the question between employers and unions, to take into account the particular features of each industry, and to provide clear guidelines against which applications for time off can be determined, thereby avoiding misunderstanding, facilitating better planning and ensuring fair and reasonable treatment[10].

a)   Trade union duties

An employer is obliged by section 168 to allow an employee of his who is an official of an independent, recognised trade union to have a reasonable amount

---

5   Trade Union and Labour Relations (Consolidation) Act 1992, s. 163. If the offer is one of re-engagement in another job, the tribunal must ask the employee whether he is willing to accept that job on the terms and conditions specified; if the employee unreasonably refuses the offer the tribunal will make no order: s. 163(5).
6   Trade Union and Labour Relations (Consolidation) Act 1992, s. 164(1).
7   Trade Union and Labour Relations (Consolidation) Act 1992, s. 164(3).
8   Trade Union and Labour Relations (Consolidation) Act 1992, s. 166. There is no statutory limit on the amount which may be awarded under this section.
9   S.I. 1991 No. 968. The Code is admissible in evidence and is to be taken into account when deciding what time off would be reasonable: s. 168(3). The Code was revised in 1991 to take account of the Employment Act 1989.
10 COP No. 3, para. 33. The Code is set out in *Harvey* S [101].

of paid time off during working hours[11] for the purposes of carrying on official duties concerned with i) negotiations with his employer over matters falling within section 178(2) (which defines the subject-matter of collective bargaining) in relation to which the union is recognised by the employer, or ii) the performance of functions which the employer has agreed to the union performing on behalf of his employees; an official is also entitled to reasonable paid time off for undergoing training in aspects of industrial relations which is relevant to the above duties and approved by the TUC or his union[12]. 'Official' is defined as covering union officers and shop stewards elected or appointed under the union rules[13].

Before 1989, the right to time off for trade union duties was much wider than it is today. A trade union official was entitled to reasonable paid time off for duties concerned with industrial relations between his employer (and any associated employer) and their employees, and for industrial relations training relevant to those duties, and the phrase 'concerned with industrial relations' was broadly interpreted[14]. The right was not restricted to actual negotiations with the employer, or to matters in respect of which the employer recognised the union; it was enough if the duties for which time off was claimed were sufficiently proximate to industrial relations between the employees and their employer[15], and the union in question was recognised by the employer to any extent for the purposes of collective bargaining, even if the recognition was partial so that the union was not recognised in relation to the matters for which time off was claimed. However, the right to time off for union duties was significantly narrowed by the Employment Act 1989, which limited the proper subject matter for time off to duties 'concerned with negotiations'[16] with the employer, and to matters in respect of which the union is recognised by the employer (unless the employer has agreed to the union performing functions on behalf of his employees), and restricted time off for industrial relations training to training which is relevant to the above duties. Thus for the first time the scope of recognition became important in determining the *extent* of the right to time off, not just the eligibility of a particular union official to claim it[17].

The ACAS Code of Practice gives guidance on proper purposes for time off under the existing law, and offers a number of examples of trade union duties

---

11   See n.3, below for a possible challenge to this restriction.
12   There are two stages in a claim to this right: i) is the activity one envisaged by the Act and COP?; ii) if it is, is it reasonable to give time off in all the circumstances? In *Ministry of Defence v Crook and Irving* [1982] IRLR 488, the EAT suggested that the question of reasonableness is to be approached by applying the 'range of reasonable responses' test evolved in the context of unfair dismissal (see p. 469, below), but this view is not universally accepted. Note that employee trustees (who may well be union officials) also have a right to paid time off to perform their duties or undergo relevant training: Pensions Act 1995, s. 42.
13   Trade Union and Labour Relations (Consolidation) Act 1992, s. 119.
14   See, for example, *Sood v GEC Elliott Process Automation Ltd* [1980] ICR 1, [1979] IRLR 416, EAT; *British Bakeries (Northern) Ltd v Adlington* [1989] ICR 438, [1989] IRLR 218, CA.
15   This was ultimately a question of fact for the tribunal: *British Bakeries (Northern) Ltd v Adlington* supra.
16   The right is not necessarily restricted to actual negotiations with the employer: see *London Ambulance Service v Charlton* [1992] ICR 773, [1992] IRLR 510, EAT, where attendance at a union district co-ordinating committee to prepare for negotiations with the employer was held to fall within the scope of the section because on the facts there was sufficient nexus between the duty in question and negotiations with the employer.
17   As in the law relating to disclosure of bargaining information, where the extent of recognition is crucial in determining what information has to be disclosed. See p. 59, above.

for which reasonable time off should be allowed, including duties concerned with terms and conditions of employment (e.g. pay or hours of work), recruitment and selection policies, redundancy and dismissal arrangements, job grading and job evaluation, flexible working practices, disciplinary procedures and arrangements, matters of trade union membership, facilities for union officials, collective bargaining machinery, grievance procedures and other procedures for consultation and communication (paragraph 12). The Code also emphasises that the duties must be connected with or related to negotiations or the performance of agreed functions in time as well as in subject-matter, and suggests that reasonable time off may be sought to prepare for negotiations, inform members of progress, explain outcomes to members and prepare for meetings with the employer about matters for which the union has only representational rights (paragraph 13). The Code is also concerned with the question of time off for relevant training, suggesting that employers should consider releasing employees for initial basic training in industrial relations duties as soon as possible after their election or appointment, and subsequently for further training covering special responsibilities and changing circumstances (paragraph 18). The Code makes two other general points which might be noted. The first is that it suggests that the management should consider making available to officials material support such as accommodation for meetings, telephones, noticeboards and possibly even office space, the irony here being that a small union should only claim such things after it has been certified as independent, since if it obtains them beforehand, that might be a factor working against 'independence'[18]. The second point is that where an official is not himself engaged in industrial action being taken by his constituents, but he is still representing them, he should be allowed time off in the normal way to exercise that function[19].

Time off under this section is with pay[20]. According to the 1992 Act, the employee is entitled to be paid the amount which he would normally have received during the time off in question, as if he had worked his normal hours (or, where his remuneration varies with the amount of work done, on the basis of an average of his hourly earnings for that work)[1]. This causes few problems where paid time off is claimed for duties which take place at a time when the employee would normally have been at work; the position is however more problematic where the employee is a shift worker or part-time worker, and the duties in question are carried out at a time when the employee would not otherwise have been at work. In one case, the EAT held that as the right is to paid time off 'during his working hours', an employee who undertook trade union duties outside his working hours had no right under the 1992 Act to paid time off or to payment in lieu[2]. However, it seems that this approach may be in conflict with the EC law on equal pay, because the ECJ has held[3] that it may be unlawful indirect sex discrimination

18 Trade Union and Labour Relations (Consolidation) Act 1992, s. 5. See p. 47, above.
19 COP No. 3, para. 39.
20 It appeared to be self-evident from the section that once it was established that there was a 'duty' and that the time off requested was 'reasonable', the official was automatically entitled to be paid; this was accepted by the EAT in *Beecham Group Ltd v Beal (No 2)* [1983] IRLR 317, but in *Thomas Scott & Sons (Bakers) Ltd v Allen* [1983] IRLR 329, CA, May LJ seems to assume that there may be cases where it is reasonable to allow the time off, but not reasonable to pay the official for it; sed quaere. See Fitzpatrick (1983) 12 ILJ 258.
1 Trade Union and Labour Relations (Consolidation) Act 1992, s. 169.
2 *Hairsine v Kingston upon Hull City Council* [1992] ICR 212, [1992] IRLR 211, EAT.
3 *Arbeiterwohlfahrt der Stadt Berlin v Botel* [1992] IRLR 423, ECJ. On equal pay generally, see p. 278.

not to pay a part-time female worker for the total number of hours spent on trade union duties (including those outside her normal working hours) in circumstances where a full-time male worker would have been paid for all the hours spent undertaking those duties. Such an outcome hinges upon whether the time off in question is for 'work' within the meaning of Article 141. It is clear from the ECJ decisions that time off to attend the employer's staff council, or to undergo training necessary for performing staff council functions, does constitute 'work' for the purposes of Article 141[4], and after some initial uncertainty[5] the EAT has confirmed[6] that attendance at a union-organised health and safety training course also constitutes 'work', because it is 'by reason of the existence of an employment relationship'[7]: 'Attending a training course organised by a recognised trade union is still related to the employment relationship and is safeguarding staff interests which is ultimately beneficial to the employer.' Significantly, the EAT rejected the employer's argument that only paying part-time workers for their contractual working hours was not indirectly discriminatory because it was objectively justified: 'The issue is whether part-time workers (predominantly female) engaged on a full-time course should receive full-time pay. There cannot, it seems to us, be a justifiable policy or aim which maintains the inequality.'

It may be that, pursuant to the exhortation in the Code or otherwise, the employer has agreed to allow certain paid time off, in which case the employee may have a contractual right to his pay during the relevant times (in which case, the pay would be computed according to the contractual terms). Any such contractual remuneration which is received goes towards discharging (or extinguishing) the statutory liability, and vice versa[8].

b) Trade union activities

An employee is entitled under the Trade Union and Labour Relations (Consolidation) Act 1992, s. 170, to reasonable time off during working hours to take part in any activities of an independent trade union to which he belongs and which is recognised by his employer in respect of employees such as him. In *Luce v Bexley London Borough Council*[9], the EAT interpreted this right narrowly, holding that time off may only be claimed for union activities that are in some way connected with the employment relationship between the employer, the employee and the union. In that case the employee, a member of the National Union of Teachers, was refused unpaid time off to attend a TUC lobby of Parliament in protest against the Education Reform Bill. The EAT held that the industrial tribunal was entitled to take the view on the facts that as the lobby was

---

4   Ibid. See also *Kuratorium fur Dialyse Und Nierentransplantation v Lewark* [1996] IRLR 637, where the ECJ considered the scope of the justification defence.

5   See *Manor Bakeries v Nazir* [1996] IRLR 604, where the EAT, distinguishing *Botel*, held that attendance at a trade union annual conference was not 'work'.

6   *Davies v Neath Port Talbot County Borough Council* [1999] ICR 1132, [1999] IRLR 769. The EAT acknowledged that the effect of their judgment was that s. 169(2) 'is in conflict with Art. 119' (now Art. 141).

7   Ibid., per Morison J. Arguably, it would have been open to the EAT in *Davies* to distinguish *Nazir* on the basis that while attendance at a union health and safety training course is 'work' because it is 'by reason of the existence of an employment relationship', attendance at a union's annual conference is not 'work' because it lacks sufficient nexus with the employment relationship; however, the EAT held that the decision in *Nazir* 'should not be followed'.

8   Trade Union and Labour Relations (Consolidation) Act 1992, s. 169(4).

9   [1990] ICR 591, [1990] IRLR 422, EAT.

intended to convey only political or ideological objections to the proposed legislation, attendance at it could not be regarded as a trade union activity within the meaning of the section. The ACAS Code of Practice suggests in paragraphs 21 and 22 that the right should extend to activities such as attending workplace meetings to discuss and vote on the outcome of negotiations with the employer, meeting full-time officials to discuss issues relevant to the workplace, and voting in industrial action ballots and union elections (paragraph 21). Where the member is acting as a representative of the union, the activities may also include taking part in branch, area or regional meetings of the union, attending meetings of official policy making bodies such as the executive committee or annual conference, and attending meetings with full-time officials to discuss issues relevant to the workplace (paragraph 22). The section specifically excludes activities which themselves consist of industrial action, whether or not in contemplation or furtherance of a trade dispute. Time off for 'activities' under section 170 is without pay (in the absence of any contractual term to the contrary) and it has been held that what constitutes 'reasonable' time off may include a consideration of how much time off has already been given to the employee on previous occasions[10].

c) Remedies for breach by the employer

Where an employer has failed to permit an employee to take time off in accordance with the statutory provisions, the employee may make a complaint to a tribunal within three months of the date when the failure occurred (or a longer period if the tribunal is satisfied that it was not reasonably practicable to complain within that period). A union official may also complain if the employer has failed to pay him for the time necessary to perform his duties under section 168, in which case the tribunal may order payment of the amount due to him. The EAT has held that in order for a trade union official to show that the employer has failed to permit him to take time off in order to carry out union duties, the request for time off must have come to the notice of the employer's appropriate representative, and it must be established that they have either refused it, ignored it or, in some other way, knowing of it, simply failed to deal with it[11]. In the case of a complaint of failure to permit time off, the tribunal, if it finds it justified, must grant a declaration to that effect and may in addition award such compensation as it thinks just and equitable, having regard to the employer's default and any loss sustained by the employee attributable to the failure to permit time off[12]. If this is considered analogous to the similar provision on compensation for detriment short of dismissal on trade union grounds[13], it will mean that it will not be viewed as a penal fine on the employer, but at the same time the tribunal will not be limited to awarding compensation only for pecuniary loss and will be able to include an amount for non-pecuniary matters such as interference with the employee's rights and desires to participate in the activities in question. It has been decided by the EAT, however, that the tribunal's powers are only those of awarding a declaration and compensation, which are both essentially ex post facto; the tribunal cannot go further and lay down conditions upon which time off shall be allowed in future, and in particular it cannot rewrite any contractual

---

10   *Wignall v British Gas Corpn* [1984] ICR 716, [1984] IRLR 493, EAT.
11   *Ryford Ltd v Drinkwater* [1996] IRLR 16, EAT.
12   Trade Union and Labour Relations (Consolidation) Act 1992, s. 172(2).
13   Ibid., s. 149(2), as explained by the EAT in *Brassington v Cauldon Wholesale Ltd* [1978] ICR 405, [1977] IRLR 479; see p. 576, above.

terms which already exist on the question, even if it has decided that the operation of those terms in the past has not constituted 'reasonable' time off[14]. In *Ryford Ltd v Drinkwater*[15], the EAT confirmed that an employee does not lose the right to receive compensation by taking time off without permission.

iii)   The right to dissociate and the closed shop[16]

a)   Protection of individual non-members

While the right to associate has been protected since 1974 through the statutory controls on dismissal and action (now detriment) short of dismissal for trade union reasons, and more recently by the statutory protection against refusal of employment, the protection afforded in English law to those not wishing to associate together with others has been less secure. When the Donovan Commission in 1968 examined the relationship between the right to associate and the right to dissociate it concluded that the one did not necessarily entail the other, since the latter was 'designed to frustrate the development of collective bargaining, which it is public policy to promote', whereas no such objection applied to the former[17]. For much of the following decade this reasoning was applied to justify the greater protection afforded by the law to the positive right. The reason why this conceptual riddle has historically been so important is, of course, the long-standing tradition in British industrial relations of the closed shop, defined by McCarthy as 'a situation in which employees come to realise that a particular job is only to be obtained or retained if they become and remain members of one of a specified number of trade unions'[18]. Unlike in certain other jurisdictions where it has long been subject to detailed control or regulation, in Britain the law until comparatively recently adopted a studiously non-interventionist stance on the closed shop, a reflection perhaps of the philosophy of collective laissez-faire which dominated our labour law for much of the twentieth century. However, in the period after the 1979 General Election the political climate became increasingly hostile towards the closed shop, and this was reflected in legislation which, while not rendering the closed shop unlawful per se, made it increasingly difficult for employers and trade unions to enforce a closed shop agreement or arrangement within the law. As a consequence the importance of the closed shop as a social institution declined drastically during the 1980s[19], and there were many notable examples of employers terminating long-standing closed shop agreements (e.g. at British Gas, British Telecom and British Rail), without significant opposition from the unions. This startling turn-around came about in a series of stages, and in order to understand the present

14   *Corner v Buckinghamshire County Council* [1978] ICR 836, [1978] IRLR 320, EAT.
15   See above, n. 11.
16   See Davies and Freedland *Kahn-Freund's Labour and the Law* (3rd edn, 1983) pp. 236–270; Millward, Bryson and Forth *All Change at Work? British Employee Relations 1980-1998* (2000).
17   *Royal Commission on Trade Unions and Employers' Associations* (Cmnd. 3623, 1968), para. 599.
18   *The Closed Shop in Britain* (1964).
19   In 1984, it was estimated that some 3.5 to 3.7 million employees were covered by closed shop arrangements: Millward and Stephens *British Workplace Industrial Relations 1980–1984* (1986); by the time of the follow-up survey, the estimated figure had fallen to somewhere between 0.3 and 0.5 million: Millward, Stephens, Smart and Hawes *Workplace Industrial Relations in Transition* (1992). The most dramatic fall was in the nationalised industries, from 80 per cent of workplaces with manual closed shops in 1984 to less than 1 per cent in 1990.

position it is necessary to trace those stages, starting with the highpoint of legal protection for the closed shop under the Labour Governments of the 1970s.

Before the change of Government in 1979 the principal legal significance of a closed shop (or 'union membership') agreement lay in the field of unfair dismissal; the relevant law supported the enforcement of the closed shop by providing that a dismissal for non-membership of an independent trade union would be automatically *fair* where there was a union membership agreement in operation which applied to the dismissed employee, unless the employee had a religious objection to union membership, or a genuine objection on reasonable grounds to being a member of a union, in which case the dismissal was deemed automatically *unfair*[20]. The second ground of objection was removed by the Trade Union and Labour Relations (Amendment) Act 1976, leaving religious objection as the only basis for exemption. The Trade Union and Labour Relations Act 1974 had also introduced a statutory right not to be excluded or expelled from trade union membership by way of arbitrary or unreasonable discrimination; however, this too was repealed in 1976, leaving any legal remedies back in the hands of the uncertain common law. As a quid pro quo for the retreat in the 1976 Act, the TUC set up an Independent Review Committee[1] (in consultation with ACAS and the Secretary of State for Employment) to investigate complaints of improper or unreasonable expulsion and exclusion from unions, but the IRC only had jurisdiction a) where the union was affiliated to the TUC and b) where there was a closed shop in operation.

Thus, between 1974 and 1980 (and particularly after 1976) the closed shop was well established, with little legal protection for employees who did not wish to be union members, other than under the TUC's own voluntary procedure. The legislation of this period was subsequently challenged before the European Court of Human Rights in *Young, James and Webster v United Kingdom*[2] where the dismissal of three railway workers because of a closed shop was held to have violated Article 11 of the European Convention on Human Rights, which contains the right to freedom of association and to join a trade union[3]. The case was not a total denunciation of the closed shop – the latter was not declared illegal per se, and the court did not uphold the existence of a negative right to dissociate as strong as the positive right to associate contained in the wording of Article 11[4]. The case was decided on its facts, chief among which were that a) the employees had already been in employment when the closed shop agreement came into force, and b) there was already a very high level of union membership without invoking the full rigour of a closed shop; the Court considered that the threat of dismissal for non-membership, involving a loss of livelihood, was 'a most serious form of compulsion' which struck at 'the very substance of the freedom' guaranteed by Article 11. On the facts, interference with the employees' limited negative right was not 'necessary in a democratic society' and so the justification defence in Article 11(2) did not apply[5]. If the legal effects of the ruling at that

---

20 The same rules applied mutatis mutandis to the protection against action short of dismissal.
1   The Donovan Report ((1968) Cmnd. 3623) had recommended the establishment of such a body, though not necessarily by the TUC: para. 631. See Ewing and Rees 'The TUC Independent Review Committee and the closed shop' (1981) 10 ILJ 84.
2   [1981] IRLR 408, ECtHR; see Forde 'The "closed shop" case' (1982) 11 ILJ 1.
3   See p. 564, above.
4   Although see *Sigurjonsson v Iceland* (1993) 16 EHRR 462, ECtHR.
5   Compare *Sibson v United Kingdom* (1993) 17 EHRR 193, ECtHR, where the Court, distinguishing *Young, James and Webster*, held that the employer's actions in exercising his contractual right to relocate the employee because he had resigned from the union did not violate Article 11, because there was no question of the employee losing his job.

time were difficult to assess[6], the political effect was of course to give further backing to the incoming Conservative Government, who had promised in their 1979 election manifesto to take steps to reform the closed shop.

The Employment Act 1980 did not represent a frontal assault on the closed shop. Rather, it introduced a series of what were called 'crucial but limited reforms', in an attempt to strike a balance between the collective interest of the union and its members in maintaining a closed shop, and the individual interests of those who did not wish to join. It sought to achieve this balance, first, by introducing a new right not to be unreasonably expelled or excluded from a union where a closed shop was in operation; secondly, by extending the permissible grounds for non-membership to include those who had a genuine objection on the grounds of conscience or deeply-held personal conviction, those already in employment before the closed shop agreement took effect[7], and those who had obtained a declaration of unreasonable expulsion or exclusion from the union; and thirdly, by introducing a balloting requirement for the establishment of a new closed shop, and providing that a dismissal for non-membership in a new closed shop would be automatically unfair unless that closed shop had been approved in a secret ballot by not less than 80 per cent of those entitled to vote[8]. The Employment Act 1982 took matters several stages further, adding to the categories of exempted employees, and introducing a requirement for the periodic review of existing closed shops by making it automatically unfair to dismiss an employee for non-membership where the closed shop agreement had not been approved within the previous five years in a secret ballot of the employees covered by it; again, the majority required for approval was very high: 80 per cent of those entitled to vote, or 85 per cent of those actually voting. The 1982 Act also introduced a minimum basic award and a 'special' award in cases of dismissal for trade union reasons (thereby increasing substantially the compensation which could be awarded against the employer or, through the joinder provisions, the union or other third party which had pressurised the employer to dismiss), and introduced a scheme to compensate all those who lost their employment without remedy during the period 1974–1980 because of the existing legislation on the closed shop[9].

After the Employment Act 1982, the law relating to dismissal for non-membership of a trade union was left in a state of considerable complexity. The combined effect of the 1980 and 1982 Acts was to make it difficult to establish a legally effective closed shop, and arguably even more difficult to enforce it (given the width of the individual exemptions, particularly that relating to conscientious objection). The position was that dismissal for non-membership was prima facie unfair, but would be fair if there was an approved closed shop agreement in operation and the complainant was dismissed because he was not a member of a closed shop union, *unless* he fell into one of the categories of exempted employees, in which case the dismissal would again be unfair. However, in 1987 the

---

6   The Convention had not yet been incorporated into English law: see p. 564.
7   The existence of this reform in the Employment Act 1980 allowed the Conservative Government (defending the previous Labour Government's legislation before the European Court of Human Rights in the *Young* case) to argue that even if that previous legislation had been contrary to Art. 11, their new legislation met the most serious objection raised by the court on the facts of the case, i.e. that the employees had already been in employment with British Rail when the closed shop agreement was concluded.
8   See Lewis and Simpson 'Disorganising industrial relations' (1982) 11 ILJ at pp. 239–244.
9   Ewing and Rees 'Closed shop dismissals 1974–1980: a study of the retroactive compensation scheme' (1988) 12 ILJ 148.

Conservative Government decided to take the further step of removing all legal protection from a closed shop[10], and so most of this complexity was in turn swept away by the Employment Act 1988, which removed all legal protection from action taken by an employer to enforce a closed shop against existing employees. This was achieved simply by removing the balloting provisions and the exempted categories, so that a dismissal for non-membership was rendered automatically unfair in *all* cases if the reason (or principal reason) was that the employee 'was not a member of any trade union, or of a particular trade union, or of one of a number of particular trade unions, or had refused or proposed to refuse to become or remain a member[11].' Similarly, all protection for discriminatory action short of dismissal against non-members was removed[12]. Thus, any dismissal or detriment short of dismissal whose purpose is the establishment or maintenance of a closed shop agreement is now per se unfair or unlawful, and the protection against dismissal or discrimination enjoyed by non-members is co-extensive with that enjoyed by union members.

While the 1988 Act removed the ability of an employer to enforce a closed shop against existing employees (the 'post-entry' closed shop), it remained lawful for an employer to discriminate against non-union members at the point of hiring, and thus to operate a pre-entry closed shop. That final loophole was, however, closed by the Employment Act 1990[13], which introduced a right not to be refused employment on grounds of union membership or non-membership[14]. It is still technically correct to say that the closed shop has not been 'outlawed', in that a closed shop agreement or arrangement is not illegal or proscribed as such. However, the reforms which were introduced by the 1988 and 1990 Acts have made it legally very difficult for an employer to enforce a closed shop against existing or prospective employees[15]. The current position in English law is therefore that, whether or not the right to dissociate is properly seen as the logical corollary of the right to associate, both rights are accorded equal respect.

b) Other measures restricting the closed shop

In addition to the above measures restricting the enforcement of a closed shop against individual employees, there are a series of further measures restricting its enforcement against employers and third parties through contract compliance or by industrial pressure. Thus, the Employment Act 1982 introduced measures designed to render illegal the practice of encouraging closed shops by making it a condition of contracts or tenders that the contractor or tenderer must use employees who are union members (whether generally, or of a particular trade union). Any such term in a contract is void and any person who refuses to contract or to accept tenders on such grounds may be liable in tort for breach of statutory

---

10 Green Paper, *Trade Unions and Their Members* (February 1987).

11 See now the Trade Union and Labour Relations (Consolidation) Act 1992, s. 152(1)(c). It will also be an automatically unfair dismissal to select an employee for redundancy because of his non-membership if other employees holding similar positions were equally affected and have not been dismissed: s. 153.

12 See now the Trade Union and Labour Relations (Consolidation) Act 1992, s. 146(1)(c).

13 White Paper, *Employment for the 1990s* (Cm. 540, 1988) para. 2.23; Green Paper, *Removing Barriers to Employment* (Cm. 655, 1989).

14 See now the Trade Union and Labour Relations (Consolidation) Act 1992, s. 137.

15 Ironically, the protection of non-union members appeared to have been significantly weakened by the House of Lords' ruling in *Wilson* and *Palmer* that s. 146 of the 1992 Act only applied to actions, not omissions, but the decision on that point has now been reversed by the Employment Relations Act 1999: see p. 568, above.

duty to anyone adversely affected by his actions[16]. Moreover, that Act provided that if any other person (in practice a union) exerts industrial pressure in order to secure a union-labour-only clause in a contract or to induce an unlawful refusal to contract or tender on the ground of the employment of non-union labour, the usual immunities from suit in tort are expressly withdrawn from that industrial pressure[17], so that the union may be sued for an injunction or damages. The political impetus behind these complicated provisions appears to have come from the insistence on union-labour-only contracts by some Labour-controlled local authorities[18].

This process was taken an important stage further by the Employment Act 1988, which removed the immunity from suit in tort from any industrial action taken because a particular employer is employing, has employed or might employ a non-union member, or is failing, has failed or might fail to discriminate against such a non-union member[19]. This is aimed principally at the situation where an employer is unwilling to establish or (more likely?) continue with a closed shop agreement and the union seeks to bring industrial pressure to bear to require him to do so; any person affected by that industrial action (directly or indirectly) may, if he has been injured tortiously by it, sue the union for an injunction and for damages without the union having its normal trade dispute immunity.

4   UNION RULES AND JUDICIAL INTERVENTION

Traditionally the main source of legal control of internal union affairs has been through the union's rule book, which is both the constitution of the union, defining and delimiting the powers enjoyed by the union, its officers and officials, and also the basis of the contract of membership which exists between the union and its members. In recent years the significance of union rules as a source of control of union activity has tended to be overshadowed by the legislative activity in this area, with a plethora of statutory provisions striking ever deeper into the structure and organisation of institutions which were previously regarded as autonomous. Those statutory provisions are considered below, but the common law on union rules and judicial intervention is still of importance, first, because common law actions may still have considerable impact (as was seen particularly in the miners' strike of 1984/5), and secondly, because the statutory provisions for the most part build upon the common law foundation rather than replacing it.

16   See now the Trade Union and Labour Relations (Consolidation) Act 1992, ss. 144, 145; s. 145 also applies to refusals to contract or tender on the ground that the contractor or tenderer uses union labour. Sections 186 and 187 impose similar restrictions on such refusals where the aim is to oblige the contractor or tenderer to recognise or consult with a particular trade union (see p. 58, above). It seems that only the term is void, not the whole contract, so that where such a contract has in fact been entered into the contractor may insist on performing (and being paid for) his part of the contract but ignore the void clause.

17   See now the Trade Union and Labour Relations (Consolidation) Act 1992, s. 222(3). For the statutory immunities, see pp. 645-680, below.

18   Lewis and Simpson, 'Disorganising industrial relations' (1982) 11 ILJ at pp. 227. One practical problem in a claim for wrongful refusal to contract on the ground of union membership would be in proving that that was in fact the real ground for the refusal, when the plaintiff's was only one of many tenders.

19   See now the Trade Union and Labour Relations (Consolidation) Act 1992, s. 222(1), (2), discussed at p. 669, below.

i) Union rules

The union's rule book may be of crucial importance in the legal regulation of the relationship between the union and its members (or its constituent parts). As originally drafted the Trade Union and Labour Relations Act 1974, s. 6 laid down certain matters which had to be specified in the rules (e.g. eligibility for benefits, procedures for alteration of rules, election of officers and disciplinary procedures)[20]. This section was, however, repealed in toto by the Trade Union and Labour Relations (Amendment) Act 1976, so that now (with very few exceptions) the question of the drafting of rules is left entirely to the union itself, and the statutory controls on union activity operate outside the rule book rather than through it. The exceptions are i) the implication into all contracts of trade union membership of a right to terminate membership on giving reasonable notice and complying with any reasonable conditions[1]; ii) the compulsory provisions on the appointment and removal of auditors[2]; and iii) the requirement that a union's political fund and political ballot rules comply with the relevant statutory provisions[3].

While union rules have a vital role as the union's constitution, regulating the union's powers and duties towards its members, they may not in practice be drafted with the clarity of a legal or parliamentary document, particularly as many rules may be of long standing and may have been subject to periodic amendments[4]. The approach of the courts to the construction of union rules has not been consistent. On the one hand, primarily in the context of rules setting out the general running and constitution of the union, the courts have recognised that they should not expect legal precision and so may have to take a broad approach to construction, looking for the general intent and purpose of the provisions in question[5]; this approach may allow a court to take into account the customs and practices of the union which have evolved to supplement the bare rules (provided that any given custom or practice is not contrary to an express rule, in which case the rule must prevail). So, for example, in *Heatons Transport (St Helens) Ltd v TGWU*[6], the question of the scope of the authority of a shop steward in a particular union was considered by the House of Lords in the light of

---

20 As recommended by the Donovan Report ((1968) Cmnd. 3623), paras. 648–657 and 698–699.

1 Trade Union and Labour Relations (Consolidation) Act 1992, s. 69.

2 Ibid., s. 35; see p. 614, below.

3 Ibid., s. 71 (political fund rules) and s. 74 (political ballot rules); see p. 617, below.

4 See the confusion caused by failure specifically to include in union rules the terms of the Bridlington agreement (p. 625, below): *Spring v NASDS* [1956] 2 All ER 221, [1956] 1 WLR 585 and *Rothwell v APEX* [1976] ICR 211, [1975] IRLR 375.

5 Though cf. the application of ordinary rules of construction by Lord Dilhorne in *British Actors' Equity Association v Goring* [1978] ICR 791, HL. The potential conflict between these two approaches was considered by Vinelott J in *Taylor v NUM (Derbyshire Area)* [1985] IRLR 99, Ch D and by Warner J in *Jacques v AUEW (Engineering Section)* [1987] 1 All ER 621, [1986] ICR 683, Ch D; in each case the judge, though purporting to synthesise the two approaches, in fact applied the wider approach in *Heatons Transport*. One caveat, however, appears in *Burnley, Nelson, Rossendale and District Textile Workers' Union v Amalgamated Textile Workers' Union* [1987] ICR 69, [1986] IRLR 298, QBD where it was held that a court may not invent missing union rules.

6 [1972] 3 All ER 101, [1972] ICR 308, HL. The case concerned an action against a union under the Industrial Relations Act 1971. Where questions as to the vicarious liability of a union in tort arise, the position is now governed by statute (s. 20, see p. 696, below). Where the section does not apply, however, the common law rules on vicarious liability as laid down by the House of Lords will still apply; see, e.g. *Taylor v NUM (Derbyshire Area)* [1985] IRLR 99.

customary arrangements, the union's rules being unclear on that point. On the other hand, where the rules may have a direct effect on a member's individual rights (e.g. in cases of disciplining or expulsion), the courts have tended to take a strict view of the rule under which a union is acting, particularly in closed shop situations where the link between union membership and access to work enables the union to exercise power over its members' livelihoods, such that it might be considered inappropriate to treat the union simply as the voluntary association which is theory it is. Lord Denning MR in particular carried this proposition further and stated in several cases that, although the law had treated membership as a contract (this then providing the basis for legal intervention; see below), that is a fiction and in fact union rules more closely resemble a 'legislative code' governing the individual members; and denial or removal of a members' rights must therefore fall strictly within the powers contained in the rules:

> 'Trade unions are not above the law, but subject to it. Their rules are said to be a contract between the members and the union. So be it … But the rules are in reality more than a contract. They are a legislative code laid down by the council of the union to be obeyed by the members. This code should be subject to control by the courts just as much as a code laid down by Parliament itself[7].'

ii) Judicial intervention

In general the courts seek to intervene as little as possible in the internal affairs of purely voluntary bodies[8], however, judges have taken the view, particularly since the decision of the Court of Appeal in *Lee v Showmen's Guild of Great Britain*[9], that the law has a significant role to play in protecting the rights of members of trade unions, particularly where denial of those rights could adversely affect individuals' livelihoods. As will be seen below, the greatly increased statutory protection for individual union members since 1980, particularly the enactment of the right not to be excluded or expelled from union membership and the right not to be unjustifiably disciplined, has meant that the common law has lost some of its practical significance. However, the common law will still be relevant in cases where the statutory rights do not apply, e.g. where the reason for the expulsion or other form of disciplining does not fall within the prohibited grounds set out in the 1992 Act; in such a case the member's rights will only lie, if at all, at common law. Moreover, there may be cases where the statutory actions are available, but some tactical advantage may be gained by bringing common law proceedings instead; such proceedings may be brought for speed[10], or in order to obtain declaratory or injunctive relief, particularly where what is at stake is not just the position of one individual member, but rather the government of the

---

7   *Breen v AEU* [1971] 2 QB 175, [1971] 1 All ER 1148, CA at 190 and 1154 respectively, per Lord Denning MR. See also *Bonsor v Musicians' Union* [1954] Ch 479, [1954] 1 All ER 822, CA; *Enderby Town Football Club Ltd v Football Association Ltd* [1971] Ch 591, [1971] 1 All ER 215, CA.

8   *Edwards v Halliwell* [1950] 2 All ER 1064, CA.

9   [1952] 2 QB 329, [1952] 1 All ER 1175, CA.

10   Significantly, the Employment Relations Act 1999, s. 29, conferred jurisdiction on the Certification Officer to hear complaints about certain alleged breaches of trade union rules, along with the power to make declarations and issue enforcement orders, as an alternative to the courts: Trade Union and Labour Relations (Consolidation) Act 1992, s. 108A-C. See p. 47.

union itself. This was a particular feature of the unprecedented amount of litigation arising from the miners' strike of 1984/5, most of which was brought by groups of working miners using the long-established common law principles[11]. Some new principles were established and some reaffirmed (e.g. the clear decision that action taken by a union in defiance of a court order is ipso facto void[12]), but it could be argued that the principal significance of that litigation lay not so much in the establishment of new principles, but rather in the demonstration of a greater readiness on the part of union members to have recourse to the courts to enforce their rights under the union's rules and to restrain what they saw as abuses of power by the leadership. Having said that, the Commissioner for the Rights of Trade Union Members (CROTUM), established under the Employment Act 1988 to assist union members in bringing legal proceedings against their union, was not exactly deluged with applications from union members for assistance in bringing complaints of alleged breaches of union rules[13].

Judicial intervention has principally been based on two grounds – the power of the courts to secure compliance with the union rules, and their insistence upon observation by the union of the rules of natural justice. The first ground, enforcement of the rules, rests upon the theory of the contract of membership, with every member having a contractual right to have the terms of that contract (i.e. the rules) observed[14], so that an aggrieved member may seek to restrain unlawful action by the union by declaration or injunction and may, in a suitable case, be awarded damages[15]. This power of intervention might be invoked in larger-scale internal disputes between different factions within a union, in which case the court may have to pronounce upon matters going to the very heart of the union's constitution[16]. More usually, the plaintiff will be an individual, or smaller group, claiming that certain material[17] irregularities are being committed by the union leadership, for example, in relation to the holding of meetings[18], the use of committees[19], rights of appeal from decisions[20], the treatment of union officers[1], the expenditure of funds[2], the alteration of union rules[3], the holding

---

11 See Ewing 'The strike, the courts and the rule book' (1985) 14 ILJ 160.
12 See *Clarke v Chadburn* [1985] 1 All ER 211, [1984] IRLR 350, where a purported alteration to the NUM's disciplinary rules voted on in defiance of a court order was held to be void.
13 In 1997/98 the CROTUM received a total of 94 formal applications for assistance, of which 68 concerned a claimed failure to observe the rules; assistance was granted in 6 such cases: Annual Report, 1997–1998. The CROTUM was abolished by the Employment Relations Act 1999; see p. 46.
14 *Lee v Showmen's Guild*, n. 9, above.
15 *Bonsor v Musicians' Union* [1956] AC 104, [1955] 3 All ER 518, HL.
16 See, e.g., *British Actors' Equity Association v Goring* [1978] ICR 791, HL, and *Douglas v Graphical Paper and Media Union* [1995] IRLR 426.
17 *Brown v AUEW* [1976] ICR 147.
18 *MacLelland v NUJ* [1975] ICR 116.
19 *Abbott v Sullivan* [1952] 1 KB 189, [1952] 1 All ER 226, CA; *Leary v National Union of Vehicle Builders* [1971] Ch 34, [1970] 2 All ER 713.
20 *Hiles v Amalgamated Society of Woodworkers* [1968] Ch 440, [1967] 3 All ER 70; *Braithwaite v EETU* [1969] 2 All ER 859, CA; *Loosley v NUT* [1988] IRLR 157, CA.
1 *Taylor v NUS* [1967] 1 All ER 767, [1967] 1 WLR 532; *Stevenson v United Road Transport Union* [1977] 2 All ER 941, [1977] ICR 893, CA; see Kidner 'The right to be a candidate for union office' (1973) 2 ILJ 65.
2 *Drake v Morgan* [1978] ICR 56; *Thomas v NUM (South Wales Area)* [1985] 2 All ER 1, [1985] IRLR 136.
3 *Clarke v Chadburn* [1985] 1 All ER 211, [1984] IRLR 350; *Taylor and Foulstone v NUM (Yorkshire Area)* [1984] IRLR 445.

of union elections[4] and the calling and running of strike or other industrial action[5]. In the litigation arising out of the 1984/5 miners' strike, the court's rulings on the illegality under the NUM's rules of calling a national strike without a ballot were of crucial significance, for it meant that working miners did not have to join a strike called in breach of the rules, and the expenditure of union funds on the strike could be restrained[6]. However, the most vital area from the point of view of protection of the individual has been that of disciplining and expulsion[7]; this was particularly important where there was a closed shop in operation, as loss of a union card could mean loss of a job, but a member may have important interests in remaining within the union even where his livelihood is not at stake. Expulsion[8] will therefore be closely scrutinised by a court and must be fully in accordance with the relevant rules of the union. There is no inherent common law power to expel and the courts will not readily construe one from a vague rule[9], and thus there must normally be (a) an express power to expel and (b) strict adherence to any necessary procedure which is laid down by the rules[10]. Such adherence (or lack of it) is a question of fact, and in some cases it will be a simple matter to enquire whether the action taken by the union was within the ambit of the power conferred by the rules. In more complicated cases, however, the courts have extended their power to intervene by claiming jurisdiction, where necessary, to interpret the union's rules. Thus, if it is the construction put upon the rule in question by the union which has led to the expulsion of the member, he may challenge the correctness of that construction, for that is a matter of law within the jurisdiction of the court[11].

Traditionally, the courts have been very reluctant to imply terms into union rule-books, especially in relation to discipline. However, in *McVitae v UNISON*[12] it was held that the courts can as a matter of principle imply a power by a union to discipline a member where there are compelling circumstances to justify it, although the power to imply a disciplinary power should be exercised with care in view of the potentially serious consequences for the reputation and livelihood of the union member. In that case, the plaintiffs were former members of NALGO against whom disciplinary proceedings in relation to alleged sexist and racist

---

4   *Brown v AUEW*, n. 17, above; *Douglas v Graphical Paper and Media Union*, n. 16, above.

5   *Taylor v NUM (Derbyshire Area)* [1984] IRLR 440; *Taylor and Foulstone v NUM (Yorkshire Area)* n. 3, above.

6   *Taylor and Foulstone v NUM (Yorkshire Area)* n. 3, above. That case was of great importance as it was defiance of its order not to call the strike official that led to a fine for contempt of court which, when not paid, led to sequestration and receivership (*Clarke v Heathfield* [1985] ICR 203, CA).

7   *Porter v NUJ* [1980] IRLR 404, HL. On discipline and expulsion rules, see Gennard, Gregory and Dunn 'Throwing the book: trade union rules on admission, discipline and expulsion' [1980] Employment Gazette 591.

8   One class of case does not come under the normal rules on expulsion; this is where the member was improperly admitted in the first place, so that his membership is ultra vires and when his name is removed he is not 'expelled': *Faramus v Film Artistes' Association* [1964] AC 925, [1964] 1 All ER 25, HL; *Martin v Scottish TGWU* [1952] 1 All ER 691, 1952 SC 92, HL.

9   *Kelly v NATSOPA* (1915) 31 TLR 632, CA; *Luby v Warwickshire Miners' Association* [1912] 2 Ch 371; *Abbott v Sullivan* [1952] 1 KB 189, [1952] 1 All ER 226, CA.

10 See. e.g., *Bonsor v Musicians' Union* [1954] Ch 479, [1954] 1 All ER 822, CA; *Hiles v Amalgamated Society of Woodworkers* [1968] Ch 440, [1967] 3 All ER 70.

11 *Lee v Showmen's Guild of Great Britain* [1952] 2 QB 329, [1952] 1 All ER 1175, CA, particularly at 344 and 1182, respectively, per Denning LJ, and 350 and 1185 per Romer LJ. This power of interpretation applies to all rules, but may be particularly important in an expulsion case.

12 [1996] IRLR 33.

acts were pending at the time when NALGO merged with NUPE and COHSE to form UNISON. Charges were subsequently brought against the plaintiffs under the UNISON rules, but those rules did not contain any express power allowing UNISON to take disciplinary action against members in relation to conduct prior to the amalgamation. In a landmark decision, Harrison J held that UNISON did have the power to take disciplinary action against the plaintiffs, notwithstanding that there was no express rule to that effect in its rule-book. He considered that the circumstances warranted implying a term empowering UNISON to discipline its members for conduct prior to the amalgamation, where the conduct in question was contrary both to the rules of the former and the present union; there was no evidence that the parties had intended that there should be a complete amnesty for conduct before the inception of the new union, and common sense suggested that this would not have been the intention.

Four particular problems deserve special mention. The first arises if the rule in question is cast in subjective terms ('conduct prejudicial to the union in the opinion of the executive') for while the courts do have a wide jurisdiction, they should not simply act as appeal bodies on acts and matters properly left within the discretion of the domestic tribunal in question; in *Lee v Showmen's Guild of Great Britain* Romer LJ stated[13] that it would require clear language to establish that the rules meant that a question was to lie entirely within the discretion of the union or one of its organs, but even so subjective rules may be more difficult to challenge[14] and may require the plaintiff to show mala fides or that the decision is so wrong that no reasonable tribunal acting bona fides could have reached it[15].

The second problem is whether the plaintiff must have exhausted all possible internal remedies (particularly any appeals provided for in the rules) before resorting to the courts; in some cases, such internal measures may bring about a more effective settlement than escalation of the dispute by the service of writs, and in some of the older cases a definite requirement of exhaustion of internal remedies can be found[16]. However, the modern approach is that to be found in the judgment of Goff J in *Leigh v NUR*[17], where he said that even an express clause in the rules that the plaintiff must exhaust his internal remedies cannot oust the jurisdiction of the court[18], but in such a case the court will tend to apply the clause unless the plaintiff shows good cause why it should not (an approach which recognises the importance of resolving disputes through agreed procedures[19]); where there is no such express provision, the court will more readily hear the case without exhaustion, but still has a discretion to require

---

13   Ibid., at 349 and 1185 respectively; a hostile judicial approach to such clauses may be supported by the principle that it is contrary to public policy to allow the jurisdiction of the courts to be ousted.

14   *Kelly v NATSOPA* (1915) 31 TLR 632, CA; *Wolstenholme v Amalgamated Musicians' Union* [1920] 2 Ch 388. If, however, Lord Denning's views in *Edwards v SOGAT* (p. 600, below) were ever to be accepted, a vague and subjective rule might be in danger of being declared invalid.

15   *Lee v Showmen's Guild of Great Britain* at 339 and 1178, respectively, per Somervell LJ; *Esterman v NALGO* [1974] ICR 625.

16   *White v Kuzych* [1951] AC 585, [1951] 2 All ER 435, PC.

17   [1970] Ch 326, [1969] 3 All ER 1249; *Lawlor v UPOW* [1965] Ch 712, [1965] 1 All ER 353; *Radford v NATSOPA* [1972] ICR 484; *Partington v NALGO* [1981] IRLR 537, Ct of Sess.

18   *Scott v Avery* (1856) 5 HL Cas 811. This principle could invalidate other restrictions on legal action, such as a clause requiring union consent before such an action is brought: *Enderby Town Football Club Ltd v Football Association Ltd* [1971] Ch 591, [1971] 1 All ER 215, CA.

19   A point acknowledged by Ralph Gibson LJ in *Longley v NUJ* [1987] IRLR 109, CA.

exhaustion if that seems appropriate on the facts of the case[20]. One potential problem for a member pursuing internal procedures is that of delay, particularly where those procedures involve several stages. That issue is now addressed by statute, for the Trade Union and Labour Relations (Consolidation) Act 1992, section 63, provides that where a member applies to his union to have some matter determined and six months have elapsed since then without any such determination, a court is to ignore any union rule requiring the exhaustion of internal remedies (or indeed any court practice to that effect) when deciding whether to hear the case[1]. However, section 64(6) states that this six-month rule is without prejudice to any rule of law by which a court could ignore any such union rule already, and so a plaintiff could still try to invoke the principles of *Leigh v NUR* (above) in order to bring court proceedings before the expiration of six months. One problem here is whether a plaintiff may bring an action to prevent impending proceedings by his union (e.g. disciplinary or expulsion proceedings); there have been cases where a court has been persuaded to intervene in advance, on the basis that no reasonable tribunal acting bona fides could possibly find against the plaintiff[2], but it is clear from the later decision of the Court of Appeal in *Longley v NUJ*[3] that such cases are highly exceptional. Normally, therefore, the court will expect the plaintiff to proceed at least with the original internal hearing against him, so that there is a substantive decision of sorts before the court on whose validity it can pronounce.

The third problem is one of terminology. The phrase 'ultra vires' is used frequently in these cases, but it appears to have two meanings – it is widely used to describe an act which is, quite simply, contrary to the union's rules (e.g. an act of the executive which is beyond their powers as defined by the rules), but it is also sometimes given a narrower meaning (more in line with company law) of an act which is outside the *objects* of the union itself. The use of 'ultra vires' as a synonym for breach of contract, while terminologically incorrect, is at least coherent in conceptual terms; however, the second meaning presents a greater difficulty, because it is doubtful whether the ultra vires doctrine (in this narrow sense) can be applied to trade unions *at all*. There are two main reasons for this view: first, under the present law a union does not have to have an objects clause, so any argument on this narrower ground would depend on being able to discern 'objects' from the rule book as it stands; secondly, the Trade Union and Labour Relations (Consolidation) Act 1992, s. 10, states that a trade union is not and '*shall not be treated as if it were* a body corporate …', and so it can be argued that the application to a trade union, which is an unincorporated association, of a doctrine developed by the courts to restrict the activities of companies, which are artificial

---

20   The Certification Officer has the power to refuse to accept an application concerning a breach of the rules unless satisfied that all reasonable steps have been taken to use any internal complaints procedures to resolve the dispute: Trade Union and Labour Relations (Consolidation) Act 1992, s. 108B(1).

1   If the court is satisfied that the delay is attributable to the plaintiff's unreasonable conduct, it may extend the six-month period: s. 63(4). Rules on internal remedies include rules requiring or permitting some form of conciliation or arbitration machinery.

2   *Esterman v NALGO* [1974] ICR 625 is the prime example; see also *Partington v NALGO*, n. 17, above. Such actions were also seen during the miners' strike, restraining threatened disciplinary action against working miners either because the disciplinary rules had not been validly adopted (*Clarke v Chadburn* [1985] 1 All ER 211, [1984] IRLR 350; *Taylor and Foulstone v NUM (Yorkshire Area)* [1984] IRLR 445), or because the strike was not official because it had been called in defiance of the rules (*Taylor v NUM (Derbyshire Area)* [1984] IRLR 440).

3   [1987] IRLR 109, CA.

legal persons with limited capacity, is inappropriate[4]. Be that as it may, these two separate meanings can be seen in *Hopkins v National Union of Seamen*[5] in which a resolution by the union executive to raise a levy on members to support the NUM in the miners' strike was held to be 'ultra vires' (in the wider sense) since the executive did not, on a proper construction of the rules, have the right to raise such a levy; however, the expenditure by the executive of amounts from existing union funds on aid to the NUM was held not to be 'ultra vires' (in the narrow sense), since the union rules set out its objects as 'To improve the conditions and protect the interests of all members of the union' and it was quite arguable that giving aid to the NUM would help to achieve those objects (e.g. by ensuring a high supply of coal, to be transported in ships employing NUS members)[6]. Thus, the levy was restrained by injunction but the expenditure was not.

The fourth problem concerns the possible application of the rule in *Foss v Harbottle*[7] to an action by a union member against his union and its executive. In company law, a member who wishes to bring an action to remedy an alleged wrong done to the company may be met with the rule in *Foss v Harbottle* that a) the proper plaintiff in such a case is the company itself, not an individual member; and b) that if the alleged wrong is something which might be ratified by a simple majority vote of the members, no individual member may maintain an action in respect of that matter, the logic being that if the majority decide to ratify the wrong, there is nothing left to complain of, whereas if the majority do not ratify the wrong, there is then no reason why the company itself should not sue. The company law rule is, however, subject to a number of exceptions; for example, it does not apply where the complainant's action is based on an infringement of his personal rights, nor to an ultra vires act, since such an act cannot lawfully be later ratified. The rule has in the past been applied to trade unions, on account of their quasi-corporate status[8], and the courts have declined to interfere in internal union affairs to remedy some minor or insignificant breach of the rules which causes no substantial injustice[9]. In practice, however, the court may readily be able to find that one of the exceptions to the rule applies; so, for example, in *Wise v Union of Shop, Distributive and Allied Workers*[10], a case involving a challenge by two union members to a decision of the union executive relating to the election of union officers, Chadwick J held that as the source of the union executive's powers was the contract between all of the members embodied in the rules of the union, each union member had a contractual right to complain of a breach of the rules which was individual to that member, and so the rule in *Foss v Harbottle* had no application; and in *Taylor v NUM (Derbyshire Area*[11], Vinelott J granted an injunction

---

4   The case is put convincingly by Wedderburn (1985) 14 ILJ 127. Crucially, in the period between 1901 and 1971 unions were widely regarded as 'quasi-corporations', hence the argument that they were subject to the ultra vires doctrine: see for example *Cotter v NUS* [1929] 2 Ch 58, CA; however, the enactment in 1974 of the formula now contained in s. 10 could be said to have closed off that particular line of reasoning.
5   [1985] ICR 268, [1985] IRLR 157.
6   Similarly, it was held that the expenditure was not ultra vires merely because the miners' strike had been held by the courts to be unofficial; the legality of the expenditure was to be judged by references to the NUS's objects, not the NUM's rule book.
7   (1843) 2 Hare 461.
8   *Cotter v NUS* [1929] 2 Ch 58, CA; *Hodgson v NALGO* [1972] 1 All ER 15, [1972] 1 WLR 130. See n. 4, above.
9   See e.g. *Brown v Amalgamated Union of Engineering Workers* [1976] ICR 147 (election irregularities).
10 [1996] ICR 691, [1996] IRLR 609, Ch D.
11 [1985] IRLR 99.

restraining further expenditure on an improperly called strike[12], on the grounds that, being ultra vires, the misapplication of funds could not be ratified by a majority of the union's members. Ultimately, however, the practical point remains that an action by a member on behalf of the union may be less certain to produce results than an action based upon infringement of his personal rights since, at the end of the day, a judge might decide (as Vinelott J eventually did in *Taylor*[13]) that he will not interfere in the internal workings of the union if it appears that to do so would serve no useful purpose:

'... [I]t does not matter much whether the rule [in *Foss v Harbottle*] is held to apply to unions or not. The courts are in principle reluctant to intervene in the internal affairs of any association, corporate or unincorporate. If they do intervene, they take the view that the affairs of the association should generally be conducted in accordance with the will of the majority, and they will decline to interfere if the order sought can be overturned by a simple majority of the members. You can please yourself whether you call that the rule in *Foss v Harbottle* or not[14].'

The second ground for judicial intervention at common law has been through enforcement of the procedural requirements of natural justice; the detailed requirements are fully discussed elsewhere[15], but may be summed up in brief as absence of bias (actual or potential), the right to a hearing and the maxim nemo judex in sua causa (i.e. no one person should act as both 'prosecutor' and 'judge'). In the nature of things, the rules against potential bias may have to be applied realistically in union cases, particularly in a dispute which has divided the union, making it difficult to find a tribunal which could not possibly be biased in any way[16]. However, there remains a clear rule against actual bias[17], and in an expulsion case the requirement of a genuine and unprejudiced hearing may be particularly strong[18], though once again the actual procedure need not follow a set legalistic pattern (other than that laid down in the rules), as long as it is fair; so for example,

---

12   Applying *Howden v Yorkshire Miners' Association* [1903] 1 KB 308, CA; upheld [1905] AC 256, HL.

13   Vinelott J refused to make an order requiring the union officers to repay the £1.7m already spent in breach of their fiduciary duty to the union, on the grounds (at p. 108) that a majority of the members may have decided in the future not to seek repayment from the officers (who had acted throughout in good faith), so that the court order would have been unnecessary. However, this sits rather oddly alongside the holding that, as the officers' action was ultra vires, it could not be ratified; once again, this may beg the question of what is meant by 'ultra vires' in this context (above).

14   Perrins *Trade Union Law* (1985) p. 97.

15   De Smith, Woolf and Jowell *Judicial Review of Administrative Action* (1995); Elias and Ewing *Trade Union Democracy, Members' Rights and the Law* (1987), pp. 212–226.

16   *Maclean v Workers' Union* [1929] 1 Ch 602 per Maugham J. See also the decision in *Rowe v Radio Rentals Ltd* [1982] IRLR 177, EAT in the analogous context of dismissal from employment.

17   *Taylor v NUS* [1967] 1 All ER 767, [1967] 1 WLR 532; *Losinska v CPSA* [1976] ICR 473, CA; *Roebuck v NUM* [1977] ICR 573; *Roebuck v NUM (No 2)* [1978] ICR 676. Cf., however, the decision in *Hamlet v GMBATU* [1987] ICR 150, [1986] IRLR 293, Ch D that there is no immutable rule of natural justice that a person sitting on a union body at first instance cannot sit on appeal, particularly where the rules allow for such double appearance (although note that this was not an expulsion case).

18   *Annamunthodo v Oilfield Workers' Trade Union* [1961] AC 945, [1961] 3 All ER 621, PC; *Losinksa v CPSA* [1976] ICR 473, CA.

there is no inalienable right to legal representation[19], though the member should be given proper notification of the charges against him and be given a proper opportunity to refute them[20]. It used to be a moot point whether the rules of natural justice could be expressly excluded in a union's rules (e.g. a rule specifically disentitling a member to a hearing), but the weight of modern authority is against any such power to exclude[1].

Thus it can be seen that, even before the legislative onslaught of the last two decades, the courts at common law had succeeded in evolving two considerable bases for their interventionist jurisdiction, in order to regulate to some extent the internal affairs of a union:

> 'It is through insisting on a strict observance of the union's own rules and of the elementary rules of decency which bear the ancient name of "natural justice" that the courts can and do make up for the lack of a statutory guarantee of an equal opportunity to participate in the making of union decisions[2].'

However, in at least two respects the extent of this jurisdiction is uncertain. The first problem is whether the protective rules on expulsion can apply to refusal of membership in the first place. The second is whether the courts have jurisdiction over the substance of union rules, so as to be able to strike down harsh and oppressive rules. The first problem arises because, although the courts may enforce the contract of membership in an expulsion of someone already a member, that cannot apply to exclusion of an applicant for membership, for by definition there is at that stage no contract of membership to enforce. In the absence of legislation[3], there appeared to be little that the law could do about this. However, in *Nagle v Feilden*[4] Lord Denning MR put forward a legally recognised 'right to work' as a possible legal basis for protecting an applicant excluded from membership for arbitrary or capricious reasons; the extent of this development remains uncertain, partly because the case did not concern a trade union, a point which brings us on to the second problem. Can a court go beyond the simple interpretation of union rules as they stand, and actually strike down a rule which the court sees as causing an injustice to a member? The orthodox view was that the court could not query the substance of the rule[5]; if any doctrine of law is capable of doing so, it is that of restraint of trade[6], and in a non-union case such as *Nagle v Feilden* that is feasible. However, the purposes of a trade union have

---

19   *Enderby Town Football Club Ltd v Football Association Ltd* [1971] Ch 591, [1971] 1 All ER 215, CA. See also *Pett v Greyhound Racing Association* [1969] 1 QB 125, [1968] 2 All ER 545, CA; and *Maynard v Osmond* [1977] QB 240, [1977] 1 All ER 64, CA.
20   *Stevenson v United Road Transport Union* [1977] 2 All ER 941, [1977] ICR 893, CA.
1   *Faramus v Film Artistes' Association* [1964] AC 925, [1964] 1 All ER 25, HL, particularly per Lords Evershed and Pearce; *Enderby Town Football Club Ltd v Football Association Ltd* (n. 19, above); *Breen v AEU* [1971] 2 QB 175, [1971] 1 All ER 1148, CA.
2   Kahn-Freund *Labour and the Law* (2nd edn, 1977) p. 224.
3   Exclusion from a union is now covered by the Trade Union and Labour Relations (Consolidation) Act 1992, s. 174; see p. 601, below. Note also that the sex, race and disability discrimination legislation outlaws certain reasons for exclusion (see ch. 5).
4   [1966] 2 QB 633, [1966] 1 All ER 689, CA; the case is discussed at p. 221, above.
5   *Faramus v Film Artistes' Association* [1964] AC 925, [1964] 1 All ER 25, HL.
6   Which can be prayed in aid by a person not party to the actual agreement (*Eastham v Newcastle United Football Club Ltd* [1964] Ch 413, [1963] 3 All ER 139, HC; *Greig v Insole* [1978] 3 All ER 449, [1978] 1 WLR 302) and so could be used by a person not yet a member of an association, but wishing to join (as in *Nagle v Fielden*). For restraint of trade, see ch. 3, above.

been immune from the restraint of trade doctrine since the Trade Union Act 1871 and so a challenge to a restrictive union rule seemed to be impossible on that ground[7]. Nevertheless, in *Edwards v SOGAT*[8] the majority of the Court of Appeal considered that an automatic expulsion rule was invalid; Sachs LJ considered that it was in restraint of trade and not covered by the immunity in the 1871 Act (since it was not a 'proper' purpose for a union), but Lord Denning MR flew higher, striking it down on the basis that it was ultra vires and void since it interfered with the right to work. This approach, which is essentially one based upon concepts of public policy, can be seen again in his Lordship's judgment in *Enderby Town Football Club Ltd v Football Association Ltd*[9], where he asserted a wide jurisdiction in the courts to control the rules of unions and other important associations on the basis that they form 'legislative codes' which must be subject to notions of public policy. The approach of Sachs LJ in *Edwards v SOGAT* is no longer tenable (if it ever was)[10] since the immunity from the restraint of trade doctrine now contained in section 11 of the Trade Union and Labour Relations (Consolidation) Act 1992, applies both to trade union purposes *and* rules. The approach of Lord Denning, however, is not so easily disposed of[11], and leads to considerable uncertainty as to the extent of a court's power to intervene.

5 STATUTORY CONTROL OF INTERNAL UNION AFFAIRS

The period between 1980 and 1997 saw a radical transformation in the law relating to internal union affairs, as a result of a series of legislative interventions of the profoundest significance. The statutory provisions were introduced in several stages, as part of the Conservative government's 'step-by-step' reform of trade union law. The Employment Acts 1980 and 1982 were largely concerned with external activities of trade unions rather than their internal workings, but the 1980 Act reintroduced a statutory right not to be unreasonably excluded or expelled from membership where a closed shop was in operation, and, in the days before balloting was compulsory, offered at least the carrot of state funding for union ballots by establishing a scheme (administered by the Certification Officer) whereby an independent trade union could apply for reimbursement of expenses incurred in holding a secret postal ballot for certain purposes; the 1982 Act laid down the circumstances where a union would be held liable in tort for the actions of its officers and members. The Trade Union Act 1984 represented a significant turning-point, for it was markedly more interventionist in the internal affairs of trade unions, the main theme of the Act being to 'give unions back to their members' by imposing minimum standards of democracy, including ballots for high union office, for political funds, and before industrial action (albeit indirectly, by removing the statutory immunities against liability in tort where such a ballot had not been held). Four years later, the Employment Act 1988 went

7   *Faramus v Film Artistes' Association*, n. 5, above.
8   [1971] Ch 354, [1970] 3 All ER 689, CA; the case actually concerned the quantification of damages, the validity of the rule in question only arising indirectly; Megaw LJ came to the same decision as Lord Denning MR and Sachs LJ but without adopting their reasoning on this point.
9   [1971] Ch 591, [1971] 1 All ER 215, CA, at 606 and 219, respectively.
10 It appeared directly to contradict the decision on this point by the House of Lords in *Faramus v Film Artistes' Association*, n. 5, above.
11 It was applied to an automatic expulsion rule by Plowman J in *Radford v NATSOPA* [1972] ICR 484.

considerably further, tightening up the rules on balloting for union office, giving members rights to be balloted before being called out on industrial action and to challenge certain perceived misuses of union funds, and introducing a new right not to be unjustifiably disciplined. That Act also established the office of the Commissioner for the Rights of Trade Union Members (CROTUM) to assist union members in taking legal action to enforce statutory rights against their union. The relentless pace continued with the Employment Act 1990, which although mainly concerned with external activities, greatly extended the range of circumstances where a union could be held responsible in tort for the actions of its officers and members[12], and extended the powers of the CROTUM to include action by union members to enforce union rules. Just when most commentators were beginning to think that this seemingly inexorable legislative steamroller had reached a halt, the Trade Union Reform and Employment Rights Act 1993 introduced a broad right not to be excluded or expelled from a trade union (no longer restricted to closed shop situations, unlike the provisions in the 1980 Act which it replaced), required periodic renewal of check-off arrangements for collecting union subscriptions, increased control over union financial affairs, and phased out the provisions entitling unions to claim state reimbursement of the cost of holding ballots[13].

Many of these reforms, while generating acute controversy upon their introduction, have over time gained a large measure of acceptance within the trade union movement (albeit a grudging acceptance in certain quarters); others, and in particular the controls over admission, discipline and expulsion, are still bitterly resented by many as undermining the status of trade unions as voluntary associations and as threatening the very principle of trade unionism itself. Any faint hopes there might have been within the union movement that a change of government would lead to a widespread relaxation of the legislative stranglehold on internal union affairs were dashed by the publication of the White Paper, *Fairness at Work*[14], in 1998. There have however been a few modest reforms, in particular the relaxation of the strike ballot provisions (considered in ch. 11) and the abolition of the need to obtain periodic renewal of the employer's authorisation to deduct union subscriptions[15], and these have been widely welcomed by the union movement.

i) Exclusion or expulsion

As seen above at head 4, the courts were able to develop a range of techniques at common law to protect the interests of individual union members in cases of discipline and expulsion, by requiring a rigid adherence to the rules and procedures laid down in the union's rule book, and by the imposition of standards of procedural fairness. However, these common law controls could be considered as deficient in certain respects, not least in the fact that they do not provide any satisfactory mechanism for the control of exclusions. The Industrial Relations Act 1971 sought to impose statutory controls on admission to and expulsion from

---

12   See p. 696, below.
13   Trade Union Reform and Employment Rights Act 1993, s. 7. Take-up under the scheme was initially slow owing to a TUC boycott (only £72,496 was paid out in 1984), but at its peak in 1992 the scheme was costing the state in excess of £4.25m per year, hence the decision to phase it out, over a three year period from April 1993; it ceased to operate altogether on 1 April 1996.
14   Cm. 3968, 1998.
15   See p. 613 below.

unions[16], with restrictions on the exclusion of appropriately qualified workers from membership by 'arbitrary or unreasonable discrimination', and on 'unfair or unreasonable disciplinary action'. These provisions were carried over into the Trade Union and Labour Relations Act 1974, s. 5, by a reluctant minority Labour Government, but were repealed in 1976 in a political compromise which involved the TUC in forming an Independent Review Committee to consider cases of expulsion and exclusion in a closed shop situation. The Employment Act 1980 reintroduced a statutory action against a union for a person expelled or refused membership, in the form of a right not to be unreasonably excluded or expelled from membership; it bore a resemblance to the action previously contained in the 1974 Act, but with the important difference that the protection only applied where a closed shop agreement was in operation. The justification for imposing *some* controls on union admissions and expulsions in a closed shop, where the possession of a union card may determine a worker's ability to pursue his trade, is self-evident, but rather than attempting to define the circumstances in which an exclusion or expulsion would be justifiable, the approach taken in the 1980 Act was to leave it to the tribunal (as the industrial jury) to decide whether or not the trade union had acted reasonably or unreasonably 'in accordance with equity and the substantial merits of the case'.

With the tightening of the statutory controls on the ability of employers to enforce a closed shop against both existing and prospective employees, the justification for the continued retention of measures controlling access to union membership could be said to have receded. However, the previous Government's view, as expressed in the Green Paper, *Industrial Relations in the 1990s*[17], was that individuals should not only have the right to decide whether or not to belong to a trade union, but should also have the right to join the union of their choice. Accordingly, the Trade Union Reform and Employment Rights Act 1993 repealed the measures on unreasonable expulsion and exclusion dating from the 1980 Act, and replaced them with a new, more general right not to be excluded or expelled from a union[18]. Two highly significant features of the current provisions should be noted: first, unlike the pre-1993 laws, the statutory controls on expulsion and exclusion are not restricted to those seeking to work in closed shop employment, but apply generally; and secondly, the former approach whereby exclusions and expulsions fell to be judged by the tribunal against a broad test of reasonableness has been abandoned; instead, the present law provides for a limited number of circumstances where a union will be permitted to control access to or retention of membership. Thus, the exclusion or expulsion of an individual is permitted if (and only if):

(a) he does not satisfy, or no longer satisfies, an 'enforceable membership requirement' contained in the rules of the union;

(b) he does not qualify, or no longer qualifies, for membership of the union by reason of the union operating only in a particular geographical area;

(c) where the union is a single-employer union[19], he is not, or is no longer employed by that employer;

16   Industrial Relations Act 1971, s. 65.
17   Cm. 1602, 1991.
18   Trade Union and Labour Relations (Consolidation) Act 1992, ss. 174–177, as substituted by s. 14 of the 1993 Act. 'Exclusion' from a union refers to a refusal to admit into membership, not to suspension of the privileges of membership: *NACODS v Gluchowski* [1996] IRLR 252, EAT.
19   This includes associated employers.

(d) the exclusion or expulsion is entirely[20] attributable to his conduct.

Paragraphs (a) and (d) are undoubtedly the key elements in the new provisions. An 'enforceable membership requirement' is defined[1] as one which restricts membership *solely* by reference to one or more of the following criteria: (a) employment in a specified trade, industry or profession; (b) occupational description (including grade, level or category of appointment); or (c) possession of specified trade, industrial or professional qualifications or work experience. It follows that a union may deny access to those who are not eligible for membership under its rules, but it may only exclude or expel a person falling *within* one of those categories where that expulsion or exclusion is entirely attributable to that person's conduct. Subsection (4) then states that certain types of conduct must be disregarded, viz., being or ceasing to be (or having been or ceased to be) (i) a member of another trade union, (ii) employed by a particular employer or at a particular place, or (iii) a member of a political party; and conduct of the type which is protected from the imposition of discipline by virtue of the controls on unjustifiable discipline in section 65 (considered below). So, for example, it would appear that a union will be entitled to refuse membership to an applicant who is in arrears with subscriptions or under discipline with another union, but may not refuse membership simply because that person previously belonged to another union, or had failed to participate in industrial action while a member of that union.

A person who claims to have been excluded or expelled in contravention of the section may present a complaint to an employment tribunal within six months of the expulsion or exclusion, or within a further reasonable period if the tribunal considers that it was not reasonably practicable to present the complaint within six months[2]. If the tribunal finds the complaint well-founded it must make a declaration to that effect[3], but no award of compensation will be made at that stage. A person who has obtained a declaration from a tribunal may claim compensation[4], but here the action becomes more complicated, for the procedure he must follow varies depending on whether the union has in fact admitted (or readmitted) him pursuant to the declaration. The applicant must wait for at least four weeks after the date of the declaration (to give the union an opportunity to admit or readmit), but then he has until six months after the date of the declaration to present a claim for an award of compensation. If he has been admitted or readmitted by the time of the application, complaint lies to a tribunal (with appeal on law to the EAT); if not, complaint lies directly to the EAT, which becomes, in effect, a court of first instance for this purpose. In both cases the amount of compensation will be such as is considered just and equitable in all the circumstances, subject to a maximum amount which is tied to the aggregate

---

20　This may cause problems where there is arguably more than one reason for the expulsion or exclusion; in other contexts it is normally sufficient to show that the prohibited reason is the 'principal' reason (see e.g., s. 152, p. 577, above).

1　Trade Union and Labour Relations (Consolidation) Act 1992, s. 174(3).

2　Ibid., s. 175. The 'escape clause' in the limitation period is similar to that applying to an unfair dismissal claim, and so would be subject to the case law in that context; see p. 417, above.

3　Ibid., s. 176(1). There is an appeal to the EAT on a point of law: s. 291, as amended by the Trade Union Reform and Employment Rights Act 1993, Sch. 8, para. 87. Under the repealed provisions there was an appeal on law *and* fact.

4　Ibid., s. 176(2).

of the maximum basic and compensatory awards for unfair dismissal[5], and in the case of an award by the EAT, a minimum of £5,300.

These provisions add up to an extremely tight strait-jacket on union admissions and expulsions, particularly as there is no residual test of reasonableness where an exclusion or expulsion falls outside the permitted categories. The acknowledged target of the current provisions were the principles developed by the TUC to regulate inter-union disputes over membership (the Bridlington Principles, considered below), reflecting the previous Government's view that the freedom of an individual worker to belong to the union of his choice should not be constrained by arrangements reached between unions over their respective spheres of influence. Under the pre-1993 provisions it was never clearly established whether an expulsion of a union member because of a decision of the TUC Disputes Committee under the Bridlington Principles would, in general, be held to be reasonable or unreasonable (although the Code of Practice on Closed Shop Agreements and Arrangements, revoked in 1991, stated that this might be a good reason not to admit). However, at common law the House of Lords in *Cheall v APEX*[6] held that the Bridlington Principles were not contrary to public policy, and that it was not unlawful for a union to expel a member pursuant to a rule allowing expulsion in order to comply with a decision of the TUC Disputes Committee. Lord Diplock in that case adopted a stance supportive of union autonomy over access to membership, stating that 'there can be no right of an individual associate with other individuals who are not willing to associate with him'; the enactment of just such a right in the 1993 Act reflected a very different view of the meaning and dictates of freedom of association. Significantly, the right of a majority of union members not to associate with another was affirmed by the European Commission on Human Rights in *Cheall v United Kingdom*[7], but while the Commission decided that the right of association under Article 11 of the Convention does not create a right to join a trade union of one's choice in all circumstances, it also emphasised that a trade union's right to choose its members was not absolute, and that 'for the right to join a union to be effective the state must protect the individual against any abuse of a dominant position by trade unions'. A challenge to the statutory provisions on exclusion and expulsion under the Human Rights Act 1998 remains a possibility, but the emphasis in other cases decided under the Convention[8] on the individual rather than the collective aspect of freedom of association gives little cause for optimism that such a challenge would succeed[9].

Finally, concern was expressed on the introduction of the present rules in 1993 that the undermining of the Bridlington Principles could lead to fragmentation of union representation and have a destabilising effect on collective bargaining, particularly with regard to single-union deals. On one analysis there is no necessary reason why this should be so, since the law only

5   As from 1 February 2000, £56,900. Compensation may be reduced on account of contributory fault: s. 176(5); on contributory fault under the pre-1993 provisions (which were identical on this point) see *Howard v NGA* [1985] ICR 101, [1984] IRLR 489, CA and for an example of this procedure generally see *Day v SOGAT 1982* [1986] ICR 640, EAT. There is no express duty to mitigate loss, unlike under the pre-1993 provisions.

6   [1983] ICR 398, [1983] IRLR 215, HL; see p. 625, below. The statutory action was not available in this case because there was no closed shop in operation.

7   (1986) 8 EHRR 74; (1985) 42 DR 178, EComHR.

8   See e.g. *Young, James and Webster v United Kingdom* (1981) 4 EHRR 38, ECtHR, discussed at p. 587, above.

9   See Ewing, 'The Human Rights Act and Labour Law' (1998) 27 ILJ 275; Palmer, 'Human Rights: Implications for Labour Law' (2000) 59 CLJ 168.

gives workers a right to join a union of their choice: it places no obligation on an employer to recognise that union. However, it is not difficult to envisage circumstances where a disaffected group of union members might leave the recognised union to join a non-recognised union, which might itself then press hard for recognition, with potentially harmful consequences for industrial relations.

ii) Unjustifiable disciplining

The Trade Union and Labour Relations (Consolidation) Act 1992, section 64[10], gives a trade union member a statutory right not to be unjustifiably disciplined by his union. This provision was introduced in the aftermath of the miners' strike of 1984/5, with the particular aim of protecting dissentient members who refused to go along with the majority view within the union (e.g. by refusing to comply with a strike call), and 'whistle-blowers' who allege wrongdoing by the union, or its officers or representatives. It is important to appreciate at the outset that while the generalised nature of the exposition of the right (in particular the use of the term 'unjustifiable') implies some evaluative process, the tribunal here has no wide discretion to determine whether the conduct in question is or is not unjustifiable; instead, subsection (2) lists the kinds of disciplining covered by the section and, crucially, section 65 lists exhaustively the circumstances in which any of those forms of disciplining will be considered 'unjustifiable' within the meaning of the Act. The question whether the imposition of discipline is or is not unjustifiable is therefore purely a matter of statutory interpretation[11].

Under subsection (2), the following forms of discipline are covered by the section: (a) expulsion from the union or a branch or section of the union; (b) a fine; (c) the treatment of sums paid by way of subscriptions or otherwise as not having been paid or paid for a different purpose; (d) deprivation of some or all of the benefits, services or facilities normally enjoyed by union members; (e) encouraging or advising another union not to accept the individual in question as a member; or (f) subjecting the individual to 'any other detriment'[12]. Any determination[13] by the union to impose such discipline will be 'unjustifiable' if the reason (or one of the reasons) for it being imposed is conduct falling within section 65; as originally enacted, the section listed the following as conduct for which the imposition of discipline would be unjustifiable: (a) failure to participate in or support any strike or other industrial action[14] (whether by his union or by

---

10 As amended by the Trade Union Reform and Employment Rights Act 1993, s. 16. The provisions derive from the Employment Act 1988, s. 3.

11 On the prospects of a successful challenge to these provisions under the Human Rights Act 1998, see the text at n. 8 above.

12 Detriment' is not defined; in *NALGO v Killorn and Simm* [1991] ICR 1, [1990] IRLR 464, the EAT held that suspension from membership necessarily implies deprivation of the benefits, etc., of membership, and that naming a member on a list of strike-breakers could constitute a detriment. For the interpretation of 'detriment' in sex and race discrimination cases, see p. 257, above.

13 This means a final decision rather than a provisional or conditional recommendation: *TGWU v Webber* [1990] ICR 711, [1990] IRLR 462, EAT.

14 This is undoubtedly the most controversial aspect of this right, since it gives a union member a right not to participate in industrial action even where a strike ballot has been properly held. It has therefore been dubbed (accurately, if rather predictably) a 'scabs' charter'. See *Knowles v Fire Brigades Union* [1996] IRLR 617, CA, where Neill LJ held that the question of what is 'industrial action' in this context is a mixed question of fact and law.

others) or the expression of opposition or lack of support for such action; (b) failure to contravene (for purposes connected with a strike or other industrial action) any requirement of his contract of employment or any other agreement with his employer; (c) making any assertion that the union, its officers, representatives or trustees have broken the union's rules or the law[15]; (d) encouraging or assisting someone else to act as in (b) or (c) above; (e) contravening any requirement imposed by or in consequence of a determination by the union that is itself an infringement of individual rights under the section. As if this were not enough, the Trade Union Reform and Employment Rights Act 1993 added a further five categories to the list of conduct protected from discipline: (f) failure to agree to the deduction of membership subscriptions from wages; (g) resigning (or proposing to resign) from the union or from another union, or becoming, refusing to become or being a member of another union; (h) working (or proposing to work) with others who are not members of the union or who are or are not members of another union; (i) working (or proposing to work) for an employer who employs non-union labour; (j) requiring the union to fulfil any of its duties to its members under the 1992 Act (e.g. requesting a copy of the scrutineer's report on a ballot). A union member is also protected against being disciplined for consulting or seeking the advice or assistance of the Certification Officer, and for proposing to engage in any of the above conduct or doing anything preparatory or incidental to such conduct[16].

The specified conduct does not have to be the sole or even the main reason for the imposition of discipline by the union in order to be immune, and the only circumstance where conduct listed above falls outside the statutory protection is where the union can show that it would have disciplined the member for that conduct anyway, whether or not it fell within the section.

An individual member who considers that he has been unjustifiably disciplined may complain to an employment tribunal which, if it finds the complaint well-founded, must make a declaration to that effect[17]. The complaint must be made within three months of the date of the infringement; this is subject to the usual escape clause allowing a complaint to be made out of time where it was not reasonably practicable to bring it in time[18], but unusually the tribunal may also allow a complaint out of time where the delay is wholly or partly attributable to the applicant's reasonable efforts to appeal against the disciplinary decision or to have it reconsidered or reviewed, e.g. by pursuing the union's internal grievance procedures. This is a rare but nevertheless welcome endorsement of the desirability of resolving disputes through domestic procedures, and avoids the risk of a tribunal holding that a delay occasioned by the pursuit of an internal appeal may not be a good reason for extending the statutory limitation period[19].

---

15   Protection under this head does not apply if the accusation was false to the individual's knowledge, or he was acting otherwise in bad faith, and he has been disciplined on that ground alone: s. 65(6). There is no requirement that he has reasonable grounds for believing that the allegation is true.

16   Trade Union and Labour Relations (Consolidation) Act 1992, s. 65(3), (4), as amended by the Employment Relations Act 1999, Sch 9.

17   Trade Union and Labour Relations (Consolidation) Act 1992, s. 66(1), (3). Appeal lies to the EAT on a question of law: ibid., s. 291(2).

18   Ibid., s. 66(2). For the application of the escape clause in the context of unfair dismissal claims, see p. 417, above.

19   Contrast *Palmer v Southend-on-Sea Borough Council* [1984] ICR 372, [1984] IRLR 119, CA (an unfair dismissal case): see p. 419. In *NALGO v Killorn and Simm* [1991] ICR 1, [1990] IRLR 464, the EAT held that a letter to the union questioning the imposition of discipline may be sufficient for the limitation period to be extended.

Adopting a similar (though not identical) procedure to that in a successful complaint of exclusion or expulsion (above), section 67 goes on to provide that an individual who has obtained a declaration that his complaint is well-founded may seek the further remedies of compensation from the union and/or the return of any fine, etc., paid by him. Such a further claim cannot be made until four weeks after the date of the tribunal declaration[20], thereby giving the union time to make amends. If by that time the union has rescinded the disciplinary decision in question and has taken all steps necessary[1] to reverse anything done in pursuance of it, complaint lies to the employment tribunal, but if not, it lies directly to the EAT (once again, as under section 176, giving that appellate body original jurisdiction)[2]. Compensation will be what the tribunal considers just and equitable in the circumstances[3], again subject to a maximum amount tied to the maximum sum of the basic and compensatory awards for unfair dismissal (at the time of writing, £56,900), and, in the case of an award by the EAT, a minimum of £5,300[4].

In enacting these provisions, the statute had to deal with two major overlaps. First, it is made clear in section 64(5) that the existence of the right not to be unjustifiably disciplined is without prejudice to any existing common law rights, and so there may still be cases where for some reason it is advantageous for a member to rely on such rights, based on the rules and the contract of membership described above. Secondly, given that the relevant forms of discipline set out above include expulsion, there is a potential overlap with the provisions on expulsion in section 174; before the changes to that section by the Trade Union Reform and Employment Rights Act 1993, the position was that in the event of an overlap the complaint lay under section 176, not under section 66, but if the exclusion or expulsion infringed the right not to be unjustifiably disciplined, it was deemed unreasonable under section 176. After that Act the position is simplified, in that once a complaint relating to an expulsion is declared to be well-founded under either section, no complaint in respect of that expulsion may be brought under the other section.

iii) Elections for union office[5]

It has always been possible for an individual union member to seek legal redress if he alleges that elections for union office have been conducted otherwise than

---

20   Ibid., s. 67(3); the claim must also be made within six months of the date of the declaration; the escape clause does not apply here.

1   This includes steps which the applicant could have taken himself, such as telling his employer to resume the check-off of his membership subscriptions: *NALGO v Courtney-Dunn* [1991] ICR 784, [1992] IRLR 114, EAT.

2   Ibid., s. 67(2).

3   See *Bradley v NALGO* [1991] ICR 359, [1991] IRLR 159, where the EAT held that compensation for injury to feelings under this head may only be awarded where that injury is caused by the act of discipline itself.

4   Ibid., s. 67(5), (8). By virtue of s. 67(6), (7), the normal principles of mitigation and contributory fault apply.

5   See Kidner 'Trade union democracy: election of trade union officers' (1984) 13 ILJ 193; *Harvey* M [951]. The genesis of these provisions can be seen in the Green Paper *Democracy in Trade Unions* (Cmnd 8778, 1983).

in accordance with the rules of the union[6]; this, however, restricted the role of the law to securing compliance with those rules as laid down through the internal constitutional workings of the union. Since the Trade Union Act 1984 there has been a separate statutory duty on a trade union to ensure that elections are held for certain major union offices, and that certain irreducible minimum requirements are observed in the conduct of those elections, irrespective of what a union's rules say on the matter[7]. While the mischief at which the election requirements were aimed was the spectre of the unrepresentative union 'baron' elected for life, it soon became clear that many of the prominent figures in the union movement to whom such a description was intended to apply were not affected by the original provisions, which only applied to *voting* members of the union's executive committee; hence the widening of the balloting requirement by the Employment Act 1988 to cover the president, general secretary and all members of the union executive, voting and non-voting.

Section 46 of the Trade Union and Labour Relations (Consolidation) Act 1992 imposes a duty on every trade union to ensure that certain officers are elected by a ballot which satisfies the Act[8], and that they stand for re-election at least once every five years. As seen above, the class of officers caught by the section was originally restricted to those who were voting members of the union's executive (defined as the 'principal committee of the union exercising executive functions, by whatever name it is called'). Whether any particular member of the union's executive was a voting member depended on the rules of the particular union in question, and it was not always the case that the major personalities associated with a union in fact had the necessary vote[9]. Even if he had, there was nothing to stop the union changing its rules (by the necessary constitutional means) to divest him of it and to avoid the application of the section to his office[10]. In the light of these points, the law was considerably tightened in the 'we'll-get-Scargill-this-time' amendments in the Employment Act 1988, whereby the election requirements were extended to all members of the executive (whether voting or not) and, in any event, to all union presidents and general secretaries[11]. 'Member of the executive' is broadly defined to include ex officio members and de facto members ('those who under the rules or practice of the union may attend and speak at some or all of the meetings of the executive'), although the net does not extend to those who attend the executive for the

---

6   A notable example (resolved by the union itself, to pre-empt any possible legal challenge) was the re-running of the election for the post of general secretary of the TGWU in 1985, after allegations of irregularities in the original balloting. Complaint could also be made that an election has not been held at all (contrary to the rules), as in *Taylor and Foulstone v NUM (Yorkshire Area)* [1984] IRLR 445.

7   Thus, the Trade Union and Labour Relations (Consolidation) Act 1992, s. 46(6) states that any term of employment in a union employee's contract (e.g. giving him permanent tenure of office under the rules) may be disregarded if to enforce it would prevent the union from complying with the Act. Curiously, however (as pointed out by Kidner, op. cit., at p. 197) there is no general statement that the Act's provisions are to prevail over a union rule; in one sense this is obvious, but a difficult question could arise if a member sought to enforce a rule by a common law action which the union had breached in order to comply with the Act.

8   It is expressly provided that no ballot need be held at an uncontested election: Trade Union and Labour Relations (Consolidation) Act 1992, s. 53.

9   Kidner, op. cit., at p. 197 states that the general secretaries of the TGWU, NALGO, NUT, NUR, NGA, USDAW, ASTMS and NUM did not have the necessary vote.

10 Such a rule change was carried out, for example, by the NUM in 1985 to remove their president's vote.

11 Trade Union and Labour Relations (Consolidation) Act 1992, s. 46(2)–(5).

purpose of providing factual information or technical or professional advice (e.g. union legal officers, accountants, research officers, etc.).

There are a set of complex exemptions: thus, a 'federated trade union' (i.e. a union which is purely a federation of other unions and has no individual members) is exempt[12], as is a new union in the first year of its existence[13]. There is also a dispensation for a person holding the office of president or general secretary in an honorary capacity[14], and a 'pensioners' charter' allowing a long-standing union employee to continue in office without re-election (where that is permitted by the union rules) until his impending retirement[15]. Attempts were made during the passage of the 1988 Act to obtain an exemption for non-voting general secretaries appointed following public advertisement, who are in effect administrators responsible for implementing rather than determining policy (one analogy might be with a local authority chief executive), but no exemption was made.

The Act also provides that no member may be unreasonably excluded from standing as a candidate for office (although it is permissible to exclude all the members of a particular class from standing, as long as that class does not consist solely of those which the union chooses to exclude)[16], and no candidate may be required directly or indirectly to belong to a political party[17].

The procedural requirements to be satisfied in order for an election to be valid under the Act are extremely detailed: (a) all members of the union must have an equal entitlement to vote[18], except where entitlement to vote is restricted to a class of members under the rules (i.e. voting may be restricted to certain constituencies, whether defined by trade or occupation or geographical area, provided all members of those constituencies have a vote); (b) the voting must be by marking a numbered voting paper, sent and returned by post, and as far as reasonably practicable, without any direct cost to the voter[19]; (c) voting must be without any interference or constraint by the union or any of its members, officials or employees and, as far as reasonably practicable, in secret; (d) votes must be counted by one or more 'independent persons' appointed by the union[20]; and

12   Ibid., s. 118(6). This is not such a statement of the blindingly obvious as it might appear, for the strike ballot provisions do not contain such an exemption, and it has been held that a purely federal union which took industrial action without a ballot (because it had no members to ballot) was still in breach of the Act and therefore lost its immunities: *Shipping Co Uniform Inc v ITWF* [1985] ICR 245, [1985] IRLR 71.
13   Ibid., s. 57.
14   Ibid., s. 46(4); this limited exception only applies to non-voting members who are not employees of the union and who cannot hold office for more than 13 months.
15   Ibid., s. 58.
16   See *Ecclestone v National Union of Journalists* [1999] IRLR 166, where an attempt by the union to exclude from candidature those in whom the union's NEC had no confidence was held to infringe this proviso.
17   Ibid., s. 47; there is nothing to prevent a union from *excluding* members of a particular political party from standing (e.g. the Communist party), but a positive requirement to *be* a member of a political party will be invalid.
18   Ibid., s. 50; a union may validly exclude members out of work, those in arrears, apprentices (or trainees, students or new members) and any overseas members: ibid., ss. 50(2), 60. By analogy with the strike ballot provisions, inadvertent failure to supply a ballot paper will probably not be regarded as a denial of a person's entitlement to vote: see *British Railways Board v NUR* [1989] ICR 678, [1989] IRLR 349, CA (p. 674, below).
19   Ibid., s. 51. The union can satisfy this requirement by supplying a pre-paid envelope: *Paul v NALGO* [1987] IRLR 43, CO.
20   Ibid., s. 51A, inserted by the Trade Union Reform and Employment Rights Act 1993, s. 2. This can either be the independent scrutineer, or some other competent person whose independence in relation to the union or the election cannot reasonably be called into question.

(e) the result of the election must be determined solely by counting the number of votes cast directly for each candidate. This final requirement is aimed at such practices as the block vote and voting through an electoral college; it is not infringed by an electoral rule which interprets the result of the ballot (e.g. a rule which provides that only a certain number of members from any one area may serve on the executive)[1].

Until 1988 a union could opt for a workplace election ballot where it was satisfied that such a ballot was equally capable of meeting the statutory requirements in relation to secrecy, etc. However, in line with the previous Government's growing conviction that postal ballots provide the best security against manipulation and malpractice[2], the Employment Act 1988 introduced a mandatory requirement of a fully postal ballot. To facilitate the balloting process, a union is required to compile, maintain and keep up to date a register of the names and addresses of its members, possibly by computer[3]. In addition, the Employment Act 1988 introduced two further requirements on elections for union office. The first is that each candidate must be given an opportunity to prepare an election address, and have it produced and distributed by the union[4]. The second is that the union must appoint an independent scrutineer to oversee the election, to supervise the production, distribution and return of ballot papers, and to prepare a report on the ballot, certifying that it was properly carried out[5]; the union must not publish the result of the election until that report is received, and must then publicise the report to the members[6]. To ensure that members are left in no doubt as to the identity of the scrutineer, the union must take steps to notify them of his identity before he begins his duties (e.g. through a notice in the union newsletter) and the voting papers must state his name[7].

The remedy for failure on the part of a union to comply with the statutory election requirements is placed in the hands of a union member[8], who may

---

1   *R v Certification Officer, ex p EPEA* [1990] ICR 682, [1990] IRLR 398, HL.
2   See the Green Paper, *Trade Unions and their Members* (1987). Cf., however, the conclusions of Undy and Martin that 'no single system of voting maximises turn-out and secrecy and minimises the opportunity for malpractice': *Ballots and Trade Union Democracy* (1984).
3   Ibid., s. 24. A member can request in writing that an address other than his home address (e.g. his work address) be used. The register is to be kept open to inspection by individual members: ibid., s. 24(3); and a copy must be made available to the election scrutineer: ibid., s. 49. Complaint by a member of a breach of this duty lies to the Certification Officer or to the High Court, either of which may make a declaration and, where appropriate, an enforcement order: ibid., ss. 25, 26, as amended by the Employment Relations Act 1999, Sch. 6.
4   Ibid., s. 48. The union may impose a word-limit of 100 words and restrict the use of graphics, etc. The election address must be in the candidate's own words, but this does not prevent a candidate from choosing someone else's words written on his behalf: Certification Officer, D/1–2/94.
5   Ibid., s. 49. To be qualified to act as an independent scrutineer a person must come within a list of approved persons designated by the Secretary of State: see the Trade Union Ballots and Elections (Independent Scrutineer Qualifications) Order 1993, S.I. 1993 No. 1909, which specifies solicitors, chartered accountants, the Electoral Reform Society, the Industrial Society and Unity Security Balloting Services.
6   Ibid., s. 52.
7   Ibid., ss. 49(5), 51(2). These requirements were added by the Employment Act 1990 following accusations of ballot-rigging in the TGWU elections in early 1990, and apparent confusion over the identity of the independent scrutineer appointed to oversee that election.
8   Ibid., s. 54(2). This apparently includes retired members with no entitlement to vote: *Re SOGAT 1982* (Certification Officer, D/3/90; D/2/91; D/3–4/94). Where the complaint relates to an election that has been held, there is a limitation period of one year from the date of the election: s. 54(3).

complain either to the Certification Officer or to the High Court (or in Scotland, the Court of Session), seeking a declaration that the union is in breach of the requirements. The member may choose which route to adopt; application to the Certification Officer will of course be cheaper and easier, and probably effective[9]. Until recently, the main difference between the two procedures was that unlike the court, the Certification Officer was unable to make an enforcement order requiring the union to take certain specified steps in order to remedy its failure to comply with the Act (e.g. ordering the union to hold an election). However, as part of the general enhancement of the Certification Officer's role by the Employment Relations Act 1999, he now has substantially the same powers to make an enforcement order as the court[10]. Under the pre-1999 provisions it was expressly stated that an application to the Certification Officer did not prevent the applicant from making a subsequent application to the court in respect of the same complaint[11], but the revised provisions rule out any such possibility[12]. Where an enforcement order has been made, it can if necessary be enforced by any person who is a member of the union at the time the enforcement proceedings are begun and who was also a member at the time when the enforcement order was originally made[13]. As the Act does not lay down any special procedures in the case of breach of an enforcement order, the form of enforcement in question would be to bring proceedings against the union for contempt of court.

iv) Ballots before industrial action

As will be seen in the next chapter, strike ballots have been a requirement of lawful industrial action since the enactment of the Trade Union Act 1984, but the peculiarity of that Act (which was otherwise concerned with 'giving unions back to their members') was that it contained no mechanism whereby an individual union member could take legal action to restrain his union from calling for industrial action without first holding a ballot. It merely rendered that industrial action actionable at the suit of an *employer*, by removing the statutory immunities from suit in tort from industrial action not supported by a ballot. That omission was subsequently remedied by the Employment Act 1988, which introduced a statutory cause of action for a union member aggrieved at being

---

9 The Certification Officer issued 12 decisions under these provisions in 1998, a larger number than in most recent years: *Annual Report of the Certification Officer*, 1998, para. 8.5 et seq.

10 Ibid., s. 55, as amended by the Employment Relations Act 1999, Sch. 6. See p. 47. An enforcement order made by the Certification Officer may be enforced in the same way as an order of the court: ibid., s. 55(9). There is a right of appeal to the EAT on any question of law arising in proceedings before or arising from any decision of the Certification Officer under this head: ibid., s. 56A.

11 This was held to be so even if the original application had yet to be determined: *Lenahan v UCATT* [1991] ICR 378, [1991] IRLR 78.

12 Ibid., ss. 55(10), 56(8). It is however possible for a *different* person to make an application to the Certification Officer in relation to an alleged failure which was previously the subject of a complaint to the court, and vice versa, and on any such application the Certification Officer or the court, as the case may be, is to have due regard to any declaration, order, observations or reasons made regarding that failure which are brought to its notice: ibid., ss. 55(10), 56(8).

13 Ibid., ss. 55(5C), 56(6). Note that the requirement of contemporary membership does not apply to enforcement by a person who was a candidate in the election.

called out without a proper ballot[14]. Section 62 of the Trade Union and Labour Relations (Consolidation) Act 1992, now states that a member who claims 'that members of the union, including himself, are likely to be or have been induced by the union to take part or to continue to take part in industrial action[15] which does not have the support of a ballot' may apply to the High Court[16]; if that court is satisfied that the complaint is established, it may make such order as it considers appropriate to require the union to cease the inducement and stop the industrial action. The section only applies to industrial action which is official ('induced by the union'), in the sense that it is taken to have been authorised or endorsed by the union under the rules which determine the vicarious liability of a trade union in tort[17]. The balloting requirements are largely the same as those which apply for the purposes of tortious liability and the statutory immunities[18], and it is specifically provided that the same ballot may fulfil both requirements, so that there is no need for two ballots[19]. The Code of Practice on industrial action balloting, considered in the next chapter in the context of the tortious liability of a union, gives guidance on the statutory balloting requirements.

v)   Union funds

As seen at head 4 above, union members have the right at common law to ensure that their union's funds are applied in accordance with the rules, as was graphically demonstrated by the legal actions brought by union members during the miners' strike of 1984/5, where an application was successfully made to the court by union members to have the union's trustees removed and a receiver appointed in their place[20]. Those steps were taken under the general law (though applying it to hitherto uncharted territory), but the government of the day considered that the procedures for the removal of trustees were too slow and uncertain[1], and a statutory remedy against union trustees for the unlawful use of union property was therefore introduced in the Employment Act 1988. Now contained in the Trade Union and Labour Relations (Consolidation) Act 1992, section 16, this provides that where trustees have so carried out their functions (or propose to do so) as to 'cause or permit an unlawful application of the union's property' a

---

14   The member may, of course, have a common law action based upon the union rules relating to strike ballots. The statutory right does not affect such an action, but it may be preferable since it applies standards for ballots across the board and operates independently of the union's rules.

15   'Industrial action' is defined in s. 62(6) as 'a strike or other industrial action by persons employed under contracts of employment'. 'Strike' and 'other industrial action' are not further defined in this context, although 'strike' is defined in s. 246 as 'any concerted stoppage of work', for the purposes of Part V of the 1992 Act (Industrial Action); for their interpretation in the context of the dismissal of those taking part in industrial action, see p. 640, below.

16   But not, it should be noted, the Certification Officer; compare p. 611.

17   Trade Union and Labour Relations (Consolidation) Act 1992, s.62(5). The rules governing vicarious liability of a union are contained in s. 20. See p. 696, below.

18   Ibid., ss. 226–234A. These are considered at p. 671, below. Note however that a failure to give notice of the ballot or a sample voting paper to the employer under s. 226A, or to inform the employer of the result of the ballot under s. 231A, will not be actionable by a union member under s. 62.

19   Ibid., s. 62(9).

20   *Clarke v Heathfield* [1985] ICR 203, CA.

1   Green Paper *Trade Unions and their Members* (1987), ch. 3.

member may apply to the High Court for relief[2]; if the complaint is well founded, the court may make such order as it considers appropriate, and in particular it may (a) order the trustees to take action necessary to protect or recover the property, (b) appoint a receiver of the union's property and (c) remove one or more of the trustees[3]. The principal problem with this statutory action is that the word 'unlawful' is not defined (in particular, it is unclear whether it includes the use of union funds in support of industrial action unprotected by the statutory immunities), and so the section as it stands is open-ended, and in need of judicial interpretation.

The Employment Act 1988 introduced a further right in relation to union property, now contained in the Trade Union and Labour Relations (Consolidation) Act 1992, section 15, which applies where union property is applied for the purpose of paying any individual's fines (for an offence or for contempt of court), or indemnifying him for fines which have been or may be imposed on him. Such use of union property is declared to be unlawful[4] and the property is further declared to be recoverable from the individual by the union. The crucial provision is then section 15(3), which permits an aggrieved member, who considers the union's failure to recover the property to be unreasonable, to apply to the High Court which may make an order authorising the member to bring or continue proceedings for such recovery on the union's behalf and at the union's expense[5].

vi) Union subscriptions

Traditionally, most trade union members have paid their union subscription under a check-off system, whereby the amount of the subscription is deducted from their wages by the employer and passed on to the union. Since the Employment Act 1988, union members have had a right to require employers to stop deducting union subscriptions from wages immediately upon receiving notice that the individual has terminated his union membership[6]. However, the law concerning the operation of the check-off was controversially amended by the Trade Union Reform and Employment Rights Act 1993, which introduced a requirement for the employer to obtain a worker's renewed authorisation for the deduction of union subscriptions in writing at least every three years, and also required the employer to give at least one month's written advance notice to the worker of any increase in the amount of the subscription. On their introduction

2 The existence of this statutory action is without prejudice to any other remedies available against the trustees in respect of breach of trust: s. 16(6).
3 Ibid., s. 16(3). In a case where the trustees have applied (or propose to apply) union property in contravention of a court order, the court *must* remove all the trustees, except any trustee who satisfies the court that there is a good reason for allowing him to remain a trustee: s. 16(4).
4 This provision adds to the common law, for the position there was less certain; it appeared that an agreement by a union to indemnify members for any fines incurred *in future* was void but that a decision to indemnify for a fine already imposed was lawful, if within the rules: *Drake v Morgan* [1978] ICR 56; *Thomas v NUM (South Wales Area)* [1985] ICR 886, [1985] IRLR 136. Any such existing illegality (and any other actions against the trustees) is expressly preserved by s. 15(6), but the blanket illegality under the section will normally be a better ground of challenge.
5 Thereby avoiding any problems under *Foss v Harbottle* (1843) 2 Hare 461, p. 597, above.
6 A right which parallels the longer-standing right to require immediate discontinuance of deductions of the political levy: see p. 621, below.

these new requirements generated considerable controversy, particularly the need for periodic renewal of the authorisation, which was seen in certain quarters as a thinly-veiled attempt to encourage workers to terminate their union membership. As had been promised, the incoming Labour government removed these two requirements in 1998[7], but not before many trade unions had decided to abandon the check-off system and to collect subscriptions directly from their members by means of direct debit, the result being that many employers lost an extremely useful means of monitoring the level of union membership within their organisation. Needless to say, this was not a consequence which was intended (or, presumably, foreseen) by the authors of the 1993 Act. The current position, therefore, is that an employer must obtain a worker's written authorisation before making any subscription deductions, and that authorisation may be withdrawn by the worker at any time, but once given, the authorisation will remain valid unless and until it is withdrawn. It is expressly stated that a worker's authorisation of the making of subscription deductions does not give rise to any obligation on the part of the employer to continue the check-off arrangements[8].

A worker who believes that his employer has contravened these requirements has a right of complaint to an employment tribunal, which if it upholds the complaint must make an declaration to that effect and order the employer to repay any amount improperly deducted[9].

vii)   Union accounts

Every trade union (other than a federated trade union consisting wholly or mainly of representatives of constituent organisations) is subject to four principal requirements relating to financial matters under the Trade Union and Labour Relations (Consolidation) Act 1992, whether or not it is listed. First, under section 28, the union must keep proper accounting records with respect to its transactions, assets and liabilities (i.e. records which 'give a true and fair view of the state of the affairs of the trade union and explain its transactions'), and establish and maintain a satisfactory system of control of accounting records, cash holdings, and receipts and remittances. This may be done at either branch or union level. Following reforms introduced by the Employment Act 1988, these accounting records must be kept available for inspection for a period of six years after their preparation[10], and a union member has the right to inspect them, on request, provided he was a member for at least part of the period covered by the records he seeks to inspect[11]. If that qualification is met, he is entitled to inspect the records where they are normally kept, at a reasonable hour and paying only reasonable administrative expenses. Perhaps most importantly, the member is

---

7   Deregulation (Deduction from Pay of Union Subscriptions) Order 1998, S.I. 1998 No. 1529, substituting the Trade Union and Labour Relations (Consolidation) Act 1992, s. 68. There is a nice irony in the fact that this reform was achieved by the use of regulation-making powers contained in the previous government's Deregulation and Contracting Out Act 1994.

8   Ibid., s. 68(4). This is, of course, significant in view of the practice of some employers to use the threat to end check-off arrangements as a means of bringing pressure to bear on a union in a trade dispute.

9   Ibid., s. 68A, inserted by the Trade Union Reform and Employment Rights Act 1993, s. 15.

10   Ibid., s. 29.

11   Ibid., s. 30.

entitled to be accompanied by an accountant[12] (provided the latter gives any assurance of confidentiality reasonably required by the union) and to take copies. Arrangements for inspection must be made within 28 days of the member's request. A person who claims that a union has failed to comply with his request may apply to the High Court or the Certification Officer[13] for an order to ensure compliance[14], and any order made by the Certification Officer may be enforced in the same way as an order of the court[15]; it is an offence for a union to fail to keep its accounting records available for inspection[16].

Secondly, under section 32, the union must send to the Certification Officer an annual return relating to its affairs and containing audited accounts[17]. These returns are to be kept open to public inspection by the Certification Officer, and must also be provided by the union on request to any person free or on payment of a reasonable charge. The Trade Union Reform and Employment Rights Act 1993 introduced the additional requirement that the annual return must contain information about the salary and benefits paid to the union's president, general secretary and each member of the executive, and a statement of the number of names on the register and how many of those are not accompanied by an address[18].

Thirdly, under section 32A, inserted by the 1993 Act, a union must take all reasonable steps to secure that within eight weeks of sending its annual return to the Certification Officer, every member of the union is provided with a written statement giving details of the union's income and expenditure for the period in question, how much of that income came from membership subscriptions, the total income and expenditure on the political fund during that period, details of the salary and benefits of its leaders, and the full report of the auditors on the accounts contained in the annual return. The statement must also contain the lengthy statement set out in the Act which describes the steps which may be taken by any member concerned about possible irregularity in the conduct of the union's financial affairs.

Finally, under section 38, every trade union which maintains a members' superannuation scheme[19] must arrange to have it examined by an actuary at least once every five years, with a copy of the actuary's report sent to the Certification Officer.

12 Defined as a person who, at the time of inspection, is eligible for appointment as a company auditor under s. 25 of the Companies Act 1989. The right to be accompanied by an accountant had, in fact, already been established at common law during the miners' strike (in *Taylor v NUM (Derbyshire Area)* [1985] IRLR 65, Ch D), but only where the member himself had a right of access under the rules: *Hughes v TGWU* [1985] IRLR 382.

13 Under the new powers introduced by the Employment Relations Act 1999, Sch. 6; see p. 47.

14 Trade Union and Labour Relations (Consolidation) Act 1992, s. 31, as amended by the Employment Relations Act 1999, Sch. 6. An application to the court precludes a subsequent application by the same person to the Certification Officer in relation to that failure, and vice versa: Trade Union and Labour Relations (Consolidation) Act 1992, s. 31(6), (7).

15 Ibid., s. 31(5). There is a right of appeal to the EAT on any question of law arising in proceedings before or arising from any decision of the Certification Officer under this head: ibid, s. 45D.

16 Ibid., s. 45(1).

17 There is a one-year exemption for newly formed unions: ibid., s. 43(1).

18 Trade Union and Labour Relations (Consolidation) Act 1992, s. 32(3), as amended by the Trade Union Reform and Employment Rights Act 1993, s. 8.

19 As at the end of 1998, only 12 unions maintained such schemes: *Annual Report of the Certification Officer*, 1998, Appendix 6.

If a union refuses or wilfully neglects to comply with any of these requirements, it renders itself and any officers charged with the relevant duties[20] liable to summary criminal proceedings under section 45. The Trade Union Reform and Employment Rights Act 1993 introduced sweeping (not to say draconian) new powers for the Certification Officer to investigate union financial affairs, including the power to require a union to produce documents relating to its financial affairs, and to appoint inspectors to conduct an investigation where there appears to have been some financial impropriety, backed up by criminal sanctions in the event of a failure to co-operate[1]. These new powers were introduced in the wake of the unsuccessful prosecution of the National Union of Mineworkers in 1990 over an alleged failure to keep proper accounting records and other alleged irregularities in the conduct of the union's financial affairs during and after the miners' strike of 1984/5[2]. The charges, brought by the Certification Officer, were dismissed following rulings by the stipendiary magistrate that certain 'crucial prosecution evidence'[3] was inadmissible, and the episode was cited by the government of the day[4] as an illustration of the limitations of the Certification Officer's powers in relation to trade union finances and the prosecution of offences under the Act, and the inadequacy of the existing legislative arrangements. The 1993 Act also extended the range of offences under section 45 to include, inter alia, the destruction, mutilation or falsification of a document relating to a union's financial affairs, or making or being privy to the making of a false entry in such a document, unless the official or agent concerned 'proves that he had no intention to conceal the financial affairs of the trade union or to defeat the law'.[5] It is also an offence if a person fraudulently parts with, alters or deletes anything in any such document, or is privy to such conduct, or knowingly or recklessly provides or makes an explanation or statement in purported compliance with the duty to co-operate which is false in a material particular. The penalties for the commission of certain of these offences include imprisonment for a term not exceeding six months[6]. Finally, any person convicted of an offence under section 45 is *automatically* disqualified from being the president or general secretary of a union, or a member of the union' executive, for a period of five or ten years, depending on the gravity of the offence[7]. Interestingly, under the Company Directors' Disqualification Act 1986, the court generally has a discretion whether or not to disqualify company directors (except in the case of unfit directors

---

20   It is a defence for an officer to prove that he believed on reasonable grounds that some other person was discharging the relevant duty. The phrase 'wilfully neglects' is a curious one to a criminal lawyer; it presumably means 'knowingly fails' and does not include negligence or simple inadvertence.

1   Trade Union and Labour Relations (Consolidation) Act 1992, ss. 37A-E, inserted by the Trade Union Reform and Employment Rights Act 1993, s. 10. The report of any such investigation is to be published by the Certification Officer and the expenses of an investigation may be recovered from a person convicted on a prosecution instigated as a result of the investigation.

2   See *The Lightman Report on the NUM* (1990); Lightman 'A trade union in chains: Scargill unbound – the legal constraints of receivership and sequestration' (1987) 40 CLP 25.

3   *Annual Report of the Certification Officer*, 1991, p. 8. The crucial evidence in question was the report by Gavin Lightman, ibid., which was commissioned by the NUM.

4   In the Green Paper *Industrial Relations in the 1990s* (Cm. 1602, 1991).

5   Trade Union and Labour Relations (Consolidation) Act 1992, s. 45(7).

6   Ibid., s. 45A.

7   Ibid., s. 45B. A member who claims that his union has failed to comply with the duty to disqualify offenders may apply to the Certification Officer or to the court for a declaration and, where appropriate, an order requiring the union to remedy its failure to comply: s. 45C, as amended by the Employment Relations Act 1999, Sch. 6.

of insolvent companies, where there is a discretion over the length of the disqualification), whereas here the disqualification is automatic.

6 POLITICAL FUNDS[8]

The political activities of trade unions, particularly the giving of financial support to the nascent Labour party out of general union funds, received a major set-back in 1910 when the House of Lords held in *ASRS v Osborne*[9] that such activities were ultra vires the union's statutory objects[10]. Following this decision, the unions looked to Parliament to provide them with the means of lawfully carrying on such activities, while at the same time safeguarding the political independence of individual members. The solution was found in the Trade Union Act 1913, which permitted a union to spend money on political purposes ('political objects') where its members had voted to approve those objects and the establishment of a separate political fund into which the members could contribute through the political levy, and out of which any such expenditure could be made. Detailed rules were laid down safeguarding the position of those who wished to 'contract out' of the political levy. Those detailed rules were subject to major revision by the Trade Union Act 1984[11], which extended the definition of political objects (so that more payments now have to come out of the political fund), added further rules as to the running of political funds, strengthened the procedural requirements for ballots and, most important of all, provided that a political fund must be reballoted at least once every 10 years to determine whether the membership wish to retain it. As the previous law only required an initial ballot, many funds had not been balloted on for many years; the Act provided that any fund passed more than nine years before the commencement date (31 March 1985) was deemed to have been passed nine years before that date, which meant that unions with long-standing political funds had one year from the commencement date in which to reballot. Not surprisingly, political differences over this reballoting requirement were intense. The Conservative Government of the day argued that this move was simply part of its declared policy of returning decision-making in unions to the membership, that political funds were retained largely through apathy and that the frequently very high percentage of union members contributing (98 per cent of the membership of the TGWU in 1983 was a figure often quoted) was unrepresentative of members' real political views, in particular in the light of the number of union members not voting Labour in the 1983 General Election with its landslide Conservative victory. The opposition view was that this was a partisan political move by the Conservative Government to bankrupt the Labour party by cutting it off from its most important source of finance (particularly unfair as it was not accompanied by parallel restrictions on business financing of the Conservative party). This seemed to be a particularly potent threat to the Labour party, since in fact (contrary to much of the

---

8   On political funds generally, see Ewing 'Trade union political fund rules' (1980) 9 ILJ 137. At the end of 1998, 38 unions maintained political funds; the total number of members contributing to political funds in 1997 was 4.7m. The total income of political funds in 1997 was £16.0m and the total expenditure £18.2m; at the end of the year, total political fund assets stood at £13.1m: *Annual Report of the Certification Officer*, 1998, Appendix 8.
9   [1910] AC 87, HL.
10 A strict view of ultra vires is not possible now, for the definition of a trade union in s. 1 of the 1992 Act only lays down the principal objects, and so is not exhaustive.
11 Ewing 'Trade union political funds: the 1913 Act revised' (1984) 13 ILJ 227.

propaganda) the contribution rate in many of the key unions at that time was quite low[12] – and if those who were already contracted out of the political levy took the further step of voting against having a fund at all, it seemed likely that several of the major funds would disappear[13]. If, however, that was a major aim of the reballoting requirement, it failed spectacularly because, following a very well-organised campaign of publicity and persuasion by the union movement and the Labour party, the necessary reballots went uniformly in favour of the retention of the political funds, even in unions with only a minority of members contributing. Political funds have thus been a source of considerable political interest over the years[14], but one highly contentious facet which remains unaltered is the old chestnut of whether those who wish to contribute should be required to 'contract in' or those who do not wish to contribute should be required to 'contract out' (the difference being, as has been said, where the burden of apathy lies). Contracting out remains the position, partly because of a TUC undertaking to the Government in 1984 to run the system fairly[15], and in recent years attention has shifted away from the narrow debate over contracting-in versus contracting-out to the much more fundamental issue of the funding of political parties generally.

Turning to the detailed rules on political funds, now contained in Part I of the Trade Union and Labour Relations (Consolidation) Act 1992, the basic position is that union funds may not be applied (directly or indirectly) in furtherance of 'political objects' unless those objects have been approved by a majority of the members voting in a ballot (i.e. the members must have passed a 'political resolution'), and the union must also have adopted certain rules (political fund rules) which have been approved by the Certification Officer[16]. A union member who claims that his union has applied funds in furtherance of political objects without having a valid political resolution in force, or without having adopted valid political fund rules, may apply to the Certification Officer, who may make a declaration and, if he thinks it just in the circumstances, an enforcement order requiring the union to remedy the breach[17].

This, of course, begs the fundamental question, what are 'political objects'? The definition of political objects was significantly altered and extended by the

---

12 Ewing, op. cit., at p. 242, points out that in 1982, 10 unions had political funds to which less than 50 per cent of the membership contributed, including the Blastfurnacemen (48 per cent), SOGAT (44 per cent), NGA (42 per cent), ASTMS (30 per cent) and ACTT (7 per cent).

13 This would have had wider implications than the loss of income to the Labour party, for if a union does not have (or loses in a reballot) a political fund, it may not spend money on anything defined as 'political' at all (since it has no fund out of which to finance it and, by definition, its general funds may not be used); thus, for example, if a union in the health service did not have a political fund it could still campaign on the basis of 'save the NHS', but not (even supposing it were minded to do so) on the basis of 'save the NHS by voting Labour'; see e.g. *Paul and Fraser v NALGO* [1987] IRLR 413, Ch D.

14 The rules on ballots were further altered by the Employment Act 1988 (which introduced a requirement of postal ballots and independent scrutiny) and the Trade Union Reform and Employment Rights Act 1993.

15 (1984) 13 ILJ 125.

16 Trade Union and Labour Relations (Consolidation) Act 1992, s. 71.

17 Ibid., s. 72A, inserted by the Employment Relations Act 1999, Sch. 6. An order made by the Certification Officer under this section may be enforced in the same way as an order of the court; ibid, s. 72A(9); such an order can be enforced by any person who is a member of the union and was a member at the time the enforcement order was originally made: ibid, s. 72A(8). There is an appeal on a point of law from the Certification Officer to the EAT: s.95.

Trade Union Act 1984, and is now contained in the Trade Union and Labour Relations (Consolidation) Act 1992, section 72, which refers to the 'expenditure of money:

(a) on any contribution[18] to the funds of, or on the payment of expenses incurred directly or indirectly by, a political party;

(b) on the provision of any service or property[19] for use by or on behalf of any political party;

(c) in connection with the registration of electors, the candidature of any person[20], the selection of any candidate or the holding of any ballot by the union in connection with any election to a political office[1];

(d) on the maintenance[2] of any holder of a political office;

(e) on the holding of any conference or meeting[3] by or on behalf of a political party or of any other meeting the main purpose of which is the transaction of business in connection with a political party;

(f) on the production, publication or distribution of any literature, documents, film, sound recording or advertisement the main purpose of which is to persuade people to vote for a political party or candidate or to persuade them not to vote for a political party or candidate.'

The post-1984 definition is considerably wider than the previous one[4], particularly in head (f) above, which now extends to negative persuasion. One direct consequence of the redefinition is that union campaigns critical of Government policy are now likely to fall within the scope of political objects and have to be financed out of the political fund, particularly where they take place in the run up to national or local elections. In *Paul and Fraser v NALGO*[5], the union mounted a major campaign against Government spending cuts and the effect of privatisation on the public services in the run-up to the 1987 election. The union had no political fund, and so the campaign was financed out of general funds. Browne-Wilkinson V-C held that this expenditure was caught by head (f), as the main purpose of the campaign was to persuade people not to vote for the Conservative party. He considered that a campaign to change Government policy would not be caught by the section, whereas a campaign to change the Government would be; however, this is clearly a very difficult distinction to draw, particularly at election

---

18 This includes affiliation fees to a political party and any loans made to it: Trade Union and Labour Relations (Consolidation) Act 1992, s. 72(4).

19 One major subject of litigation under the pre-1984 definition of political objects was the provision by a consortium of unions of new London premises for the Labour party; in spite of the unions' arguments that this was merely the acquisition by them of commercial assets, it was held to be of a political nature so that the large amounts concerned could not be taken from the unions' general funds: *Richards v NUM* [1981] IRLR 247, CO; *ASTMS v Parkin* [1984] ICR 127, [1983] IRLR 448, EAT. This is now made express.

20 This includes the payment of expenses incurred by union employees assisting candidates for election to public office: Certification Officer, Decision CO/1913/13.

1 'Political office' is the key concept here; it means the office of MP, MEP, member of a local authority or any position within a political party: ibid., s. 72(4). 'Candidate' includes a prospective candidate.

2 'Maintenance' here is to be construed widely. In *ASTMS v Parkin*, n. 19, above, its use in the previous definition was held to cover money donated to provide research facilities for the leader of the opposition.

3 Including the payment of expenses incurred by delegates in attending any such conference or meeting: ibid., s. 72(2). In *Richards v NUM* [1981] IRLR 247, it was even held to cover payment for a brass band at a political lobby.

4 See Ewing, op. cit., at pp. 235–239. As the post-1984 definition involved such a comprehensive reformulation, it is submitted that the old case law on the previous definition is of little assistance, except to the limited extent already noted.

5 [1987] IRLR 413, Ch D.

time, and as a result of that decision a number of trade unions (including NALGO and the Association of University Teachers) voted to establish political funds for the first time to preserve their ability to campaign on policy issues affecting their members during election campaigns.

As seen above, before a political fund can be established the union must hold a ballot in which a political resolution is passed approving the furtherance of political objects, and since 1984 there has been a further requirement of periodic reballoting every ten years at least[6]. Such ballots must be in accordance with union rules approved for this purpose by the Certification Officer[7]. The rules must comply with a detailed set of requirements which are similar to those which apply in union elections. Thus, the union must appoint an independent scrutineer to oversee and report on the ballot (ss. 75 and 78); all members must be entitled to vote (s. 76); and voting must be secret, by the marking of a numbered ballot paper (i.e. no ballots by show of hands), free from interference or constraint and without direct cost to the voter. As in the case of elections for union office, the balloting must be entirely postal, with ballot papers distributed and returned by post (s. 77), the alternative of workplace ballots having been removed by the Employment Act 1988. A union member who claims that his union has taken a ballot (or is proposing to do so) otherwise than in accordance with rules approved by the Certification Officer may apply either to the Certification Officer or to the High Court for a declaration to that effect[8]; in such an application, similar rules (as to procedure and the power to make enforcement orders) apply here as apply to a complaint of failure to comply with the statutory requirements for elections to union office[9].

Where a union has passed a political resolution in a ballot of the membership, it must also adopt a set of political fund rules[10] providing (a) that payments in furtherance of political objects shall be paid out of a separate 'political fund'; (b) that any member who does not wish to contribute to that fund shall be exempt if he gives notice in the prescribed form to 'contract out'[11]; (c) that a member who is exempt from making contributions shall not be excluded from any benefits of the union or placed at a disadvantage as compared with other members of the union (except in relation to control or management of the political fund itself)[12]; and (d) that contribution to the political fund shall not be made a condition of admission to the union. A member who claims that there has been a breach of the political fund rules (e.g. that the union has made payments in furtherance of political objects out of general funds instead of the political fund) may complain to the Certification Officer who may, after hearing the parties and making such

---

6   State funding was available until April 1996 in respect of political fund reballots but, by virtue of a somewhat mean exception, not in respect of a ballot on whether a political fund should be established in the first place; see p. 601, above.

7   Trade Union and Labour Relations (Consolidation) Act 1992, s. 74. Fresh approval is required before each ballot, even where the rules have been approved previously. The Certification Officer has model rules on balloting which may be adopted by a union.

8   Trade Union and Labour Relations (Consolidation) Act 1992, s. 79; the application must be made within a year of the announcement of the result of the ballot: s. 79(3).

9   Ibid., ss. 80, 81, as amended by the Employment Relations Act 1999, Sch. 6. For the similar procedures in complaints over elections, see p. 611, above. There is an appeal on a point of law from the Certification Officer to the EAT: s.95.

10   Ibid., s. 82(1). The Certification Officer will supply a set of 'model rules' on request.

11   The suggested form of notice is contained in s 84.

12   *Birch v NUR* [1950] Ch 602, [1950] 2 All ER 253.

enquiries as he thinks fit, make an order for remedying the breach which has the status of an order of the county court[13].

Administration of the assets and liabilities of a political fund (when a political resolution is in force) is governed by the Trade Union and Labour Relations (Consolidation) Act 1992, section 83[14]. The only moneys that may be added to the fund are those from members' contributions, donations from other persons (but not from the union itself from its general funds) and anything accruing from the administration of the fund itself (e.g. interest on investments). All political expenditure must come out of the fund; the union may not 'top up' its political fund by transferring money from its general funds or by adding income which results from the investment of those funds, nor may it borrow money to finance its political activities or secure an overdraft on its political fund by charging the deficit to its general property[15]. If a union ceases to have a valid political resolution (e.g. if the necessary periodic reballoting shows a majority against the fund's continuation), the fund is frozen and the union must take the necessary steps to cease collecting the political contributions[16]. The choices then available to the union are to leave the fund frozen (in the hope that a subsequent ballot may approve a political resolution again and so revive the fund)[17], to spend it on non-political objects (which could be done simply by transferring it into the general funds), or, where the resolution has ceased because of an adverse re-balloting, to spend the money left in the fund (but without incurring an overdraft) on political objects within six months of the lapse of the ballot[18].

Whenever a political resolution is adopted (or renewed in a review ballot) the members must be informed of their right to contract out of paying the political levy; this they may do at any time (either on the standard form or in any other form to like effect), though if the notice of objection is given more than one month after the members were notified of their right to contract out it does not take effect until the first day of January following[19]. There is no statutory obligation to inform new members of their right to contract out, although the TUC's *Statement of Guidance* (issued in 1984 to stave off further legislation) requires TUC unions to provide new members with an information sheet explaining how to contract out. Where the political levy is collected separately there is little difficulty in

13 Ibid., s. 82(2); there is an appeal on a point of law to the EAT: s. 95. Confusingly, this form of complaint is in addition to the specific rights of action given by s. 72A (application of funds in breach of s. 71), s. 80 (failure to comply with ballot rules), s. 87 (failure to discontinue deductions of the political levy), and s. 90(4) (failure to discontinue collecting contributions after a resolution ceases to have effect). In 1998 the Certification Officer heard three complaints under s. 80 of the 1992 Act, and upheld one of them: *Annual Report of the Certification Officer*, 1998, p. 29.

14 Note that a political fund constitutes 'protected property' in that as long as it cannot be used to finance industrial action, it cannot be seized in order to satisfy a judgment against the union: Trade Union and Labour Relations (Consolidation) Act 1992, s. 23(2) (p. 699, below). This does not apply, however, to sequestration for failure to pay a fine imposed for contempt of court.

15 It may even be questioned whether a union may run an overdraft on its political fund *at all*, as technically an overdraft represents the addition of money to the fund which is neither a contribution nor income from investments: see Elias and Ewing, op. cit., p. 176.

16 Trade Union and Labour Relations (Consolidation) Act 1992, ss. 89–91. If contributions have been collected after the resolution has lapsed, a member may apply to have them refunded: s. 90(3). If the union does not discontinue collecting the contributions within a reasonable period, a member may complain to the High Court (but not, in this context, the Certification Officer) for a declaration and enforcement order: s. 90(4), (5).

17 The union may continue to administer a frozen fund: ibid., s. 91(1).

18 Ibid., s. 89(2).

19 Ibid., s. 84(4).

providing for the exemption of a contracted-out member. However, it may also be done by collecting one *combined* subscription and relieving the contracted-out members from that part of the subscription which is referable to the political levy[20]. The advantage for a union of the second method is that it may be operated through a 'check-off' system whereby the employer deducts the amount of the contribution from wages, on behalf of the union. One long-standing problem here is that an employer may be unwilling or unable to operate such a system on a differential basis for exempt members (i.e. Xp per week in the case of an ordinary member but X–Yp per week in the case of a contracted-out member). One widely-adopted solution to this problem was for the whole sum to be deducted from all, with the amount of the political levy subsequently refunded to contracted-out members. This was approved by the EAT under the 1913 Act[1], but the idea of refunding was unpopular with the previous Government and so the Trade Union Act 1984 made it unlawful for an employer to deduct the political levy where a contracted-out member has notified the employer in writing of his contracted-out status, in which case the employer must ensure that no amounts representing contributions to the political fund are deducted from his wages[2]; moreover, if the employer wishes to operate a check-off system he may not lawfully refuse to operate it in relation to contracted-out members while continuing to do so for other members[3], so that the employer must either be prepared to operate a differential system or no system at all. The practical significance of this particular conundrum has declined in recent years with the trend towards the collection of union subscriptions by direct debit rather than through the check-off[4].

7   UNION AMALGAMATIONS AND INTER-UNION DISPUTES

i)   Union amalgamations

It has in the past been a frequent criticism of trade unions in England and Wales that they have been too numerous. However, a rationalisation movement over several years has seen a marked decline in the number of unions[5], mainly as a result of union amalgamations, and in recent years the merger has come to be seen as an integral part of the modernisation process considered by many to be essential to the trade union movement, particularly in times of economic recession and falling membership[6]. At the end of 1997 there were 17 trade unions with over 100,000 members, accounting for nearly 82 per cent of the total union membership of 7.8 million, and over a half of all union members were

---

20   Ibid., s. 85(1).
1   *Reeves v TGWU* [1980] ICR 728, [1980] IRLR 307, EAT.
2   Trade Union and Labour Relations (Consolidation) Act 1992, s. 86. Complaint of a breach of s. 86 now lies to an employment tribunal which may make a declaration and, where appropriate, an order requiring the employer to pay any amount improperly deducted: ibid, s. 87, as substituted by the Employment Rights (Dispute Resolution) Act 1998, s. 15, Sch. 2.
3   Ibid., s. 86(3).
4   See p. 613.
5   The Certification Officer's figures show a total of 224 listed unions as at the end of 1998, with a further 23 unlisted unions submitting annual returns: *Annual Report of the Certification Officer*, 1998, Appendix 1; this is less than a fifth of the peak number of 1384 in 1920, and represents a fall of nearly 25 per cent since 1987. See Bland 'Trade union membership and recognition 1997-98' [1999] Labour Market Trends 343.
6   *ACAS Annual Report*, 1992, p. 19.

concentrated in the largest five unions[7]. At the other end of the scale, however, there were 164 unions (nearly two-thirds of the total number) with less than 2,500 members, accounting for less than 1 per cent of the total membership. At common law, there were difficulties in the way of mergers between unions, particularly the need to obtain the consent of every member of each of the merging organisations. For this reason, legislation was introduced at various times in the nineteenth century so as to mitigate the difficulties while still safeguarding to a reasonable extent the interests of individual members[8]. The current scheme was introduced by the Trade Union (Amalgamations, etc.) Act 1964, and is now contained in the Trade Union and Labour Relations (Consolidation) Act 1992, ss. 97–106[9].

Under the 1992 Act, two forms of merger are provided: amalgamation (where two or more unions merge to form a new union); and transfer of engagements (where one union transfers its members and property to another, losing its identity in the process). In either case, detailed statutory procedures must be followed[10]. First, the instrument of amalgamation or transfer must be approved by the Certification Officer. Secondly, the union must take all reasonable steps to secure that every voting paper supplied for voting in the ballot on the resolution is accompanied by a notice (approved by the Certification Officer), either setting out the instrument of amalgamation or transfer in full or giving a reasonably full explanation of it[11]. Thirdly, there must be a ballot of all the members[12] resulting in support for the proposed scheme[13]. Previous legislation had required special majorities or a minimum number of votes cast in order for a merger ballot to be effective, but now a simple majority suffices unless a union expressly adopts more restrictive rules. The requirements for a valid merger ballot were significantly amended by the Trade Union Reform and Employment Rights Act 1993[14] to bring them into line with the rules on union elections and political fund ballots, in particular by introducing compulsory postal ballots and a requirement of independent scrutiny. Finally, the instrument of amalgamation or transfer, once approved in the ballot, must be registered by the Certification Officer, who may not do so until six weeks have elapsed from the date of application for

---

7   *Annual Report of the Certification Officer*, 1998, Appendix 4. During 1993 the three largest public sector unions, NALGO, COHSE and NUPE, amalgamated to form UNISON: The Public Service Union, which with its 1.3m members is the largest UK trade union, with 17 per cent of total trade union membership.

8   Trade Union Act Amendment Act 1876, s. 12; Trade Union (Amalgamation) Act 1917; Societies (Miscellaneous Provisions) Act 1940, which introduced the idea of a transfer of engagements.

9   The statutory provisions are supported by the Trade Unions and Employers' Associations (Amalgamations, etc.) Regulations 1975, S.I. 1975 No. 536, as amended; *Harvey* R [28]. The required procedure is set out in the *Certification Officer's Guide to Transfers of Engagements and Amalgamations*.

10   Trade Union and Labour Relations (Consolidation) Act 1992, ss. 98–101.

11   Ibid., s. 99; the notice must not contain any statement making a recommendation or expressing an opinion about the proposed merger: s. 99(3A).

12   'Limited members' (e.g. former workers who have taken voluntary redundancy) are not necessarily 'members' for these purposes: *NUM (Yorkshire Area) v Millward* [1995] ICR 482, [1995] IRLR 411, EAT (overruling the Certification Officer on this point).

13   In the case of amalgamation this means a ballot of both unions; in the case of transfer, only a ballot of the transferor union is necessary.

14   Trade Union Reform and Employment Rights Act 1993, substituting Trade Union and Labour Relations (Consolidation) Act 1992, ss. 100–100E.

registration[15]. During that period, any member of the union may make a complaint of irregularities in the ballot to the Certification Officer, who will make such enquiries as he thinks fit[16]. If the Certification Officer finds the complaint justified he is required to make a declaration to that effect, and may also make an order specifying the steps which the union must take in order to rectify the irregularities in the ballot before registration is allowed[17]. Such complaints may only be brought before the Certification Officer, not before the courts, although there is an appeal on a point of law from his decision to the EAT[18].

Once the instrument is registered, the property of the original unions or the transferor union is automatically transferred 'without any conveyance, assignment or assignation' to the amalgamated union or transferee union, as the case may be (except for any property expressly excluded by the instrument, and any Government stocks and securities)[19]. The question of the political fund should be dealt with in the instrument of amalgamation or transfer; in an amalgamation of two unions each of which has valid political fund rules, the newly amalgamated union will be deemed to have passed a valid political resolution[20], subject to the ordinary periodic reballoting rules (see head 6 above); if, however, there is an amalgamation in which one of the original unions did not have a political fund, then the new union will have to hold a ballot of its new membership in order to instigate a new political fund.

Finally, it should be noticed that the 1992 Act does not cover the question of de-amalgamation. This will only arise occasionally but when it does it must be resolved under the relevant union rules, without recourse to statute; this may pose real difficulties if the unions on their amalgamation did not in fact provide for possible divorce in their rules, particularly as it has been held that the court's power to intervene does not extend to inventing a missing de-amalgamation rule[1].

ii)   Inter-union disputes

Inter-union disputes over membership could potentially be very damaging to the trade union movement, leading to poaching of members, fragmentation of bargaining units and floating memberships. To counter the undesirable effects of disputes over membership issues, the TUC drew up a set of principles in 1939 governing relations between affiliated unions, which have become known as the Bridlington Principles[2], after the 1939 Annual Congress at which they were adopted. The preface to the principles states that they are not intended to be a legally binding contract, but that they are 'accepted by all affiliated organisations

---

15   Trade Union and Labour Relations (Consolidation) Act 1992, s. 101. The Certification Officer is required to ensure that the rules of the transferee organisation are not inconsistent with the instrument of transfer: *R v Certification Officer, ex p AUEW (Engineering Section)* [1983] ICR 125, [1983] IRLR 113, CA.
16   Ibid, s.103, as amended by the Employment Relations Act 1999, Sch. 6.
17   Ibid., s. 103(3).
18   Ibid., s. 104.
19   Ibid., s. 105.
20   Ibid., s. 93(1).
1   *Burnley, Nelson, Rossendale and District Textile Workers' Union v Amalgamated Textile Workers' Union* [1987] ICR 69, [1986] IRLR 298; compare the approach taken to the implication of union rules following a merger in *McVitae v UNISON* [1996] IRLR 33; see p. 594, above.
2   The Principles have been supplemented and amended several times since 1939, most recently in 1993, and are contained in their present form in the TUC document, *TUC Disputes Principles and Procedures* (1993).

as a binding commitment for their continued affiliation to the TUC.' Each principle is supplemented by more detailed explanatory notes, which have equal status and validity with the main text of the Principles. The Principles are enforced by the TUC's Disputes Committee[3], which is empowered under TUC Rules to adjudicate on complaints of a breach of the Principles.

Until 1993, the Principles provided[4], inter alia, that no affiliated union should accept into membership a present or former member of another affiliated union without enquiring of that union whether the applicant has tendered his resignation, whether he is clear on the books, whether he is 'under discipline or penalty' and whether there are any other reasons why he should not be accepted. If the present or former union objected to the transfer, or if the enquiries revealed that the applicant was under discipline, engaged in a trade dispute or in arrears with contributions, the enquiring union was not to admit the applicant into membership, but if it considered the other union's objection to be unreasonable it could refer the matter to the TUC for adjudication by the Disputes Committee. The Principles also sought to regulate disputes over recognition, by providing that no union should commence organising activities at any establishment or undertaking in respect of any grade of workers in which another union has the majority of workers employed and negotiates wages and conditions, unless by arrangement with that union.

If the Disputes Committee decided that there had been a breach of the Principles it could order a union not to admit a person into membership, or to expel a member improperly recruited from another affiliated union. Affiliated unions were recommended to adopt a model rule which permitted the union's executive to expel members in order to comply with a ruling of the Disputes Committee, after the court in *Spring v NASDS*[5] refused to imply a power to expel in order to comply with such a ruling. Moreover, in *Cheall v APEX*[6], the House of Lords upheld the validity of the model rule, and rejected the argument that the Bridlington principles were contrary to public policy because they restricted the right of an individual to join and remain a member of a trade union of his or her choice. In that case the plaintiff, a dissatisfied member of the TGWU, resigned his membership and joined APEX, who knew of his previous membership of the TGWU. His membership of APEX was challenged by the TGWU under the Bridlington Principles, and the Disputes Committee upheld the challenge, ordering APEX to terminate his membership. This they did under their appropriate rule (based on the TUC's model rule) which allowed expulsion on six weeks' notice in order to comply with a ruling of the Disputes Committee. The plaintiff brought legal proceedings claiming that his expulsion was invalid. The House of Lords, reversing the decision of the Court of Appeal, upheld the validity of the model rule, and also held for good measure that the fact that the plaintiff had not been heard at the Disputes Committee hearing did not involve a denial of natural justice. Lord Diplock, in a strong affirmation of union autonomy over membership at common law, stated[7]:

3   On the working of the Disputes Committee, see Elgar and Simpson 'A Final Appraisal of "Bridlington"? An Evaluation of TUC Disputes Committee Decisions 1974–1991' (1994) BJIR 32.
4   For an analysis of the pre-1993 provisions, see Simpson 'Individualism versus Collectivism: an Evaluation of Section 14 of the Trade Union Reform and Employment Rights Act 1993' (1993) 22 ILJ 181.
5   [1956] 2 All ER 221, [1956] 1 WLR 585. See also *Rothwell v APEX* [1976] ICR 211, [1975] IRLR 375.
6   [1983] ICR 398, [1983] IRLR 215, HL, noted Simpson (1983) 46 MLR 635.
7   Ibid., at p. 218.

'My Lords, freedom of association can only be mutual; there can be no right of an individual to associate with other individuals who are not willing to associate with him ... I know of no existing rule of public policy that would prevent trade unions from entering into arrangements with one another which they consider to be in the interests of their members in promoting order in industrial relations and enhancing their members' bargaining power with their employers; nor do I think it a permissible exercise of your Lordships' judicial power to create a new rule of public policy to that effect. If this is to be done at all it must be done by Parliament.'

While the decision in *Cheall v APEX* endorsed the legitimacy of the Bridlington Principles at common law, in retrospect it was perhaps only a matter of time before the Conservative Government turned its attention to inter-union disputes in general and the Bridlington rules in particular, not least because of the potential impact of a decision of the Disputes Committee on the rights of individual union members. The Trade Union Reform and Employment Rights Act 1993 enacted a new right not to be excluded or expelled from a trade union[8], the practical effect of which was to make it impossible for a union lawfully to exclude or expel a member in order to comply with a ruling of the Disputes Committee[9]. Those measures were foreshadowed in the Green Paper, *Industrial Relations in the 1990s*[10], which was critical of the impact of the Bridlington Principles in restricting competition between trade unions and denying individuals the right to join the union of their choice. The TUC was therefore forced to revise the Principles in 1993 to take account of the new restrictions[11]. Under the modified provisions, TUC-affiliated unions are required to make a binding commitment, as a condition of their continued affiliation to the TUC, 'that they will not knowingly and actively seek to take into membership the present or recent members of another union by making recruitment approaches, either directly or indirectly, without the agreement of that organisation'[12], and must continue to include questions about past or present membership of other unions in their membership application forms. Where a dispute over membership arises, the unions concerned must attempt to resolve it by agreement, and the revised Principles require any such effort to include 'a moral obligation on the part of the respondent union to offer compensation to the complainant union for any loss of income that it has suffered' as a result of any knowing and active recruitment of its members. If the attempt to reach a negotiated settlement fails, the matter may be referred by the TUC to the Disputes Committee, which may order the respondent union to pay financial compensation to the complainant union, subject to a maximum of two years' loss of contributions, and may also censure the respondent union[13]. The Disputes Committee is however no longer empowered to order a union to expel a member admitted in breach of the Principles[14]. It is

---

8   See p. 601, above.
9   It is specifically provided that being or ceasing to be a member of another trade union is not a sufficient ground for the expulsion or exclusion of an individual: see p. 603, above.
10   Cm. 1602, 1991.
11   On the revised Principles, see Simpson, 'Bridlington 2' (1994) 23 ILJ 170.
12   *TUC Disputes, Principles and Procedures*, 1993, Principle 2.
13   The Disputes Committee may require the respondent union to publish the censure prominently in its journal.
14   This means that the model rule which was upheld in *Cheall v APEX* (see n. 6, above) is in effect now a dead letter.

questionable whether this financial disincentive is sufficient to dissuade unions from commencing recruitment campaigns targeted at the members of other unions[15].

15 Significantly, the DTI/PSI/ACAS survey in 1990 reported widespread potential for inter-union competition, but noted that actual competition was restrained by the Bridlington Principles: Millward, Stephens, Smart and Hawes *Workplace Industrial Relations in Transition* (1992) p. 84.

Chapter 11

Industrial action

1 INTRODUCTION[1]

Until the last quarter of the nineteenth century, important aspects of trade union aims and methods were in danger of being construed as criminal, either under certain statutes which outlawed certain forms of combination[2], or under the general law relating to conspiracy which was capable of rendering an agreement criminal even if the object of the agreement was in fact lawful. The Trade Union Act 1871 provided that the purposes of a union should not be deemed unlawful merely because they were in restraint of trade so as to render members liable to criminal prosecution for conspiracy or otherwise[3]. This, however, only covered one possible head of illegality, and the Criminal Law Amendment Act which was passed in the same year to liberalise the law relating to the use of non-violent means in a dispute was soon found to be ineffective. Thus, as late as 1872, servants of a gas company who had come out on strike as a protest against the dismissal of a fellow employee and who, in striking, had broken their contracts, could still be held guilty of criminal conspiracy[4]. The agitation which followed this decision led to the appointment of a Royal Commission, which in turn led to the passing of the Conspiracy and Protection of Property Act 1875, which repealed the Master and Servant legislation, codified the law relating to the use of intimidation and violence during industrial action and, most importantly in the present context, removed the possibility of a lawful combination of workmen constituting a criminal conspiracy by providing, in section 3, that an agreement or combination by two or more persons to do or procure to be done any act in contemplation or furtherance

---

1 See generally, Ewing *The Right to Strike* (1991); Auerbach *Legislating for Conflict* (1992); Millward, Bryson and Forth *All Change at Work? British Employee Relations 1980-1998* (2000).
2 Combination Act 1800; Molestation of Workmen Act 1825. For the history of the intervention of criminal law, see Wedderburn *The Worker and the Law* (3rd edn, 1986) pp. 513–521. On the history of trade union law generally, see Orth *Combination and Conspiracy: A Legal History of Trade Unionism 1721–1906* (1991).
3 See now the Trade Union and Labour Relations (Consolidation) Act 1992, s. 11.
4 *R v Bunn* (1872) 12 Cox CC 316. See generally Wallington, 'Criminal conspiracy and industrial conflict' (1975) 4 ILJ 69.

of a trade dispute was not to be indictable as a conspiracy if such an act when committed by one person alone would not be punishable as a crime[5]. Thus, the mere fact of combination or agreement is not criminal[6].

While the Conspiracy and Protection of Property Act 1875 had removed persons engaged in a trade dispute from the fear of prosecution for criminal conspiracy, it had no application to civil actions and so did not protect unions or their members from the payment of damages in a civil suit, and so, not unnaturally, it was to the civil remedy that aggrieved persons now turned. In *Allen v Flood*[7], the House of Lords prevented the evolution of one general tort of intentionally causing harm to a person without justification, by holding that an act lawful in itself is not converted by a malicious or bad motive into an unlawful act leading to civil liability. However, in this same period the courts did create or approve the specific torts of conspiracy[8] and inducement of breach of contract[9], so that if there was an element of combination (the 'magic of plurality') or contractual breach (both of which were missing in *Allen v Flood*), there could indeed be civil liability.

Moreover, in the famous *Taff Vale* case[10] the House of Lords held that a trade union could be sued in tort (in spite of not being a body corporate) and its assets could be taken in satisfaction of judgment. On one view this may have been no more than a refusal to put trade unions into a preferential position, but it created a genuine dilemma since all the funds of the union became attachable, including those to which members had subscribed for the receipt of benefits. A Royal Commission was set up under the chairmanship of Lord Dunedin which, in its report published in 1906, did not go as far as to recommend the reversal of the *Taff Vale* case, but instead made the more modest proposal that separate benefit funds should be established which would be protected from seizure. However, the Government went further and passed the Trade Disputes Act 1906 which (a) gave complete immunity to unions in respect of actions in tort, (b) gave immunity from liability for conspiracy and inducement of breach of contract to officers and members of unions provided they acted in 'contemplation or furtherance of a trade dispute' (the 'golden formula') and (c) gave statutory backing to *Allen v Flood* by declaring, for the avoidance of doubt, that an act done in contemplation or furtherance of a trade dispute is not actionable in tort simply because it interferes with the legitimate interests of another person. This statutory protection was extended in the Trade Disputes Act 1965 to give immunity (within the golden formula) from liability for the tort of intimidation which was exhumed and applied by the House of Lords in *Rookes v Barnard*[11].

The whole scheme was then altered by the Industrial Relations Act 1971 which removed the union's complete immunity and introduced certain 'unfair industrial practices' based on the old heads of civil liability[12]. In 1974, however,

5   This is still the criminal law position, though s. 3 was repealed by the Criminal Law Act 1977 as being no longer necessary, for s. 3 of that Act extends the principle to all conspiracies by restricting criminal conspiracies to agreements to commit crimes (with two exceptions, neither of which is relevant in industrial cases).

6   Agreements to commit acts which are themselves criminal are not protected, although summary offences may be disregarded in certain circumstances. See p. 683.

7   [1898] AC 1, HL.

8   *Mogul Steamship Co v McGregor, Gow & Co* [1892] AC 25, HL; *Quinn v Leathem* [1901] AC 495, HL.

9   *South Wales Miners' Federation v Glamorgan Coal Co* [1905] AC 239, HL.

10   *Taff Vale Rly Co v ASRS* [1901] AC 426, HL.

11   [1964] AC 1129, [1964] 1 All ER 367, HL.

12   For a discussion of the law under the 1971 Act, see Cooper's *Outlines of Industrial Law* (6th edn, 1972) ch. XI.

the pre-Industrial Relations Act law was reinstated by the Trade Union and Labour Relations Act 1974 and the immunities were further extended by the Trade Union and Labour Relations (Amendment) Act 1976, which widened the immunity from the tort of inducement of breach of contract to cover commercial contracts as well as contracts of employment (thereby removing possible liability for secondary boycotts and 'blackings'), and extended the immunity to cover the development of a new head of tortious liability, that of interference with contract (i.e. short of an actual breach). By 1976, therefore, the immunities appeared almost watertight. For a time in the late 1970s it seemed that the Court of Appeal had succeeded in restricting the scope of the immunities, not by finding loopholes in the individual immunities themselves, but instead by taking a more stringent approach to what fell within the golden formula, upon which the immunities depend; however, his approach was subsequently disapproved by the House of Lords in three landmark cases[13].

The incoming Conservative Government, elected in 1979 in the wake of the notorious 'winter of discontent', embarked on a relentless 'step-by-step' reform of the law on industrial action which lasted for 14 years and produced a remarkable transformation of industrial relations law. During that period there were no fewer than six Acts of Parliament affecting the law on industrial action, beginning with the Employment Act 1980, which contained complex provisions removing the immunities from most forms of secondary industrial action (i.e. action against employers not directly concerned in the dispute)[14]. This was accomplished by the notorious section 17 of the Employment Act 1980, which in effect reinstated much the same position as that reached by the Court of Appeal in the late 1970s. The Employment Act 1982 constituted a further stage in this process, with the narrowing of the definition of 'trade dispute' and the withdrawal of the immunities from union pressure to have union labour only and union recognition requirements inserted into commercial contracts and tenders. However, the most far-reaching reforms in that Act related to the position of a union itself. As stated above, the Trade Disputes Act 1906 made a union itself immune from an action in tort; any possible action by an employer lay against union officers and members (who themselves have specific immunities). However, the 1982 Act abolished that total immunity[15], so that a union now only has the same immunity as its individual officers and members, and introduced special rules as to when a union can be liable for the acts of its officials and committees, how much for, and from what funds.

This process was taken a stage further by the Trade Union Act 1984, but unlike section 17 of the 1980 Act, which limited the scope of lawful industrial action, the 1984 Act concentrated on the machinery for calling the strike or other industrial action. It did this by making a strike ballot mandatory in the case of official action; industrial action without such a ballot was thus made litigable at the suit of any employer (or, semble, any person) adversely affected, by a simple device of withdrawing the statutory immunities altogether. This step, no less radical for its being so simple, has had a considerable effect, and in the years since the introduction of the 1984 Act a significant proportion of actions brought

---

13   *NWL Ltd v Nelson* [1979] ICR 867, [1979] IRLR 478, HL; *Express Newspapers Ltd v McShane* [1980] 1 All ER 65, [1980] IRLR 35, HL; *Duport Steels Ltd v Sirs* [1980] 1 All ER 529, [1980] IRLR 116, HL.

14   Crucially, the 1980 Act did permit secondary action in certain specified circumstances: see below.

15   Employment Act 1982, s. 15. The immunity was previously contained in the Trade Union and Labour Relations Act 1974, s. 14.

or threatened by employers against unions in relation to industrial action (actual or impending) have been under the strike ballot provisions rather than under the provisions of the earlier Acts[16].

The next stage in this seemingly inexorable process was the Employment Act 1988 which, in addition to imposing extensive controls on internal union affairs (discussed in the previous chapter), removed the statutory immunities from industrial action taken to support or enforce union membership, thereby restricting a union's ability to defend a closed shop by means of industrial pressure. That Act also introduced a further refinement to the strike ballot provisions by requiring separate ballots to be held at each workplace unless certain stringent conditions were satisfied. Hard on the heels of the 1988 Act, the Employment Act 1990 contained a formidable series of measures designed to discourage secondary industrial action and unofficial industrial action. It removed the statutory immunities from virtually all forms of secondary action (repealing section 17 of the 1980 Act), significantly extended the range of circumstances where a union could be held responsible (and therefore potentially liable in tort) for the acts of its officials, committees and members, and completely removed the right to complain of unfair dismissal from those dismissed while taking part in unofficial industrial action.

To describe the state of the law on industrial action following the 1990 Act as confusing would be a considerable understatement. To gain a complete picture it was necessary to consult no fewer than nine statutes, stretching back as far as 1875, five of which had been enacted since 1980, all overlaid on a common law (i.e. the industrial torts) which was itself of great complexity. The decision to consolidate the whole of trade union law into one massive statute, the Trade Union and Labour Relations (Consolidation) Act 1992, was therefore greeted with relief by those toiling in the field, but in such a volatile area it was too much to hope that the consolidation would survive for long without further amendment. In fact, the Trade Union Reform and Employment Rights Act 1993 was introduced into the House of Commons within weeks of the 1992 Act coming into force; one can only wonder at the logic of proceeding with a major consolidation while further significant changes to the substantive law were in the pipeline. The 1993 Act contained several very significant and (needless to say) highly controversial reforms of the law on industrial action, some of which had been considered during the passage of earlier legislation and rejected as either unworkable or undesirable. Thus, there were major changes to the law on industrial action ballots, including compulsory postal ballots, independent scrutiny of the ballot process, and a requirement to give notice of a ballot, and of any subsequent industrial action, to the employers of those involved; furthermore, in a move influenced by the 'Citizen's Charter', the 1993 Act gave individuals a right (the Citizen's Right) to seek an injunction restraining unlawful industrial action where that action affects the supply of goods or services to that person. The potential impact of this development cannot be overestimated, for its effect is to extend the range of potential plaintiffs to embrace anyone adversely affected by unlawful industrial action, even those with no direct cause of action in tort (e.g. because the unlawful act was not directed at them). Having said that, to date very little use has been made of the Citizen's Right in practice, and it therefore remains something of an unexplored (unexploded?) weapon.

16　It has been argued that the frequent use of the strike ballot provisions by employers may initially have been at least partly due to the perceived effectiveness of legal sanctions during the miners' strike (albeit at the suit of working miners rather than employers): Benedictus (1985) 14 ILJ 176.

After 18 years of Conservative rule, any lingering hopes that a change of government might herald a return to the collective laissez-faire of the 1970s were dashed by the 1997 Labour general election manifesto, which made it clear that a new Labour Government would not repeal the key elements of the Conservative trade union laws[17]. In his Foreword to the 1998 White Paper, *Fairness at Work*, the Prime Minister stated: 'There will be no going back. The days of strikes without ballots, mass picketing, closed shops and secondary action are over'[18]. However, in that document the Government also signalled its intention to simplify the law on industrial action ballots and to extend unfair dismissal protection to those dismissed for taking part in lawfully organised official industrial action, and the Employment Relations Act 1999 duly enacted measures implementing those proposals. Taken together, the eleven changes made to the law on strike ballots represent a significant simplification, while leaving the main substance of the requirements largely intact; of far greater significance is the introduction of measures protecting workers from dismissal for taking part in lawful, official industrial action. These cannot be said to guarantee a 'right to strike' as such (on account of the qualified nature of the protection against dismissal, and the absence of any protection against victimisation short of dismissal), but they are undoubtedly the closest that UK law has ever come to such a right. It remains to be seen whether the new measures are sufficient to meet the International Labour Organisation's criticisms of our law in this area.

There is one further dimension to this issue, and that is the impact of the Human Rights Act 1998 on the law on industrial action. As seen in the previous chapter, Article 11 of the European Convention on Human Rights confers a right to freedom of association with others, including the right to form and join trade unions. Unlike the European Social Charter, Article 11 does not in terms confer a right to strike. In *Schmidt v Sweden*[19] the European Court of Human Rights described such a right as 'without any doubt one of the most important ... means' by which a state could seek to secure the protection of the Article 11 rights, but crucially the Court did not consider the right to strike to be 'indispensable' in order to guarantee 'the effective enjoyment of trade union freedom'. It is therefore unclear to what extent, if any, Article 11 could be used to challenge the qualified nature of the protection given to those taking industrial action by the 1999 Act. The right to freedom of peaceful assembly (also protected under Article 11) is however a different matter, and could conceivably be used to challenge some of the existing legal restrictions on picketing (e.g. the common law of trespass, and the recommendation in the Code of Practice on Picketing that pickets be limited to six at each entrance).

The complexity of the law on industrial action has in the past attracted adverse judicial comment on the basis that this is an area where it is particularly important that the players (the union leaders and managers) should know what the rules are and what is 'offside'[20]. The 1992 Consolidation Act helped to tidy up the structure of the legislation, but the law itself is still extremely difficult and complex. The approach adopted in this chapter is to look first at the effect of

17 *New Labour: Because Britain Deserves Better* (1997), p. 17.
18 Cm 3968, 1998.
19 (1976) 1 EHRR 632, ECtHR.
20 *Merkur Island Shipping Corpn v Laughton* [1983] ICR 178, [1983] IRLR 26, CA, per Sir John Donaldson MR, echoed by Lord Diplock in the House of Lords, n. 1, below.

industrial action on the individual participants, and then to consider the position of the organisers of the industrial action, including the industrial torts that may be committed during a trade dispute, the statutory immunities which apply where those torts are committed within the 'golden formula', and (most importantly in practice) the restrictions on those immunities enacted by successive Conservative governments during the 1980s and early 1990s. We then turn to the potential criminal liability for industrial action, and the law on picketing, including the specific statutory immunity for 'peaceful picketing'; we assess the extent to which a union is vicariously liable for the acts of its officials and committees; and finally, we examine the use of injunctions in industrial disputes, including the controversial 'Citizen's Right' introduced in 1993.

While it is necessary for the sake of exposition to split the subject up in this way, it must be remembered that any particular case may depend on the effect and interaction of several of these factors. Indeed, the recent reforms introduced by the Employment Relations Act 1999 have added to the complex interplay of issues by linking the protection against unfair dismissal to the legality of the industrial action. On the latter issue, it may help, when looking at the detail, to remember the three basic stages in an action in tort adopted by the House of Lords in *Merkur Island Shipping Corpn v Laughton*[1] : (i) does the industrial action in question give the plaintiff a cause of action in tort; (ii) if so, is that cause of action covered by the immunities in sections 219 or 220 of the Trade Union and Labour Relations (Consolidation) Act 1992; (iii) is the cause of action restored by anything in sections 222–234A of the Trade Union and Labour Relations (Consolidation) Act 1992?

2 THE EFFECT OF INDUSTRIAL ACTION ON THE INDIVIDUAL

As was seen in the introduction to this chapter, the approach traditionally taken in the law on industrial action has been to preserve the freedom to strike by providing immunities at the collective level (albeit within increasingly narrow boundaries) rather than by conferring any positive right to strike on the individual participants. At the collective level, the effect of industrial action on individual contracts of employment is primarily of importance in rendering the action 'unlawful' in the sense required by certain forms of the industrial torts, so opening the way to a successful civil action to stop the strike in any case where it can be argued that the statutory immunities do not apply[2]. Before turning to the collective dimension, however, it is necessary to examine more closely the effect of industrial action on the individual participants.

---

1   [1983] ICR 490, [1983] IRLR 218, HL.
2   Immunities are necessary because the very fact that a strike involves a breach of contract means that prima facie those organising it will be guilty of inducing a breach of contract, which may be tortious in itself and/or may provide the 'unlawful means' necessary for certain other torts (particularly indirect inducement of breach of commercial contracts or interference with the plaintiff's business); if the immunities are withheld (e.g. where there is no strike ballot), tortious liability will, in most cases, be easy to establish. One open question is whether the strikers' own breaches of contract can be 'unlawful means' in themselves, for the purposes of the economic torts; this is considered at p. 656, below.

i)   The effect of industrial action on individual contracts of employment

As the most fundamental contractual obligation of an employee is to be ready and willing to serve the employer, the action of going on strike[3] is likely to be regarded as constituting a breach of contract, giving the employer the right to dismiss summarily. In theory it may also entitle the employer to sue the employee for damages[4], although in practice the employer's common law power to withhold wages in respect of non-performance (or indeed partial performance) of contractual obligations is likely to be of far greater significance[5]. The orthodox view is that industrial action will be unlawful (as a breach of contract) however it is organised, and even if strike notice is given it will be construed merely as notice of an impending breach[6]. However, this orthodox view was challenged by Lord Denning MR in *Morgan v Fry*[7] where he suggested that where strike notice of adequate length (i.e. at least equal to the length required to terminate the contracts of employment) was given, the strike was not unlawful, since the notice had the effect of suspending the contracts, not breaking them:

> 'The truth is that neither employer nor workmen wish to take the drastic action of termination [of the contracts of employment] if it can be avoided. The men do not wish to leave their work for ever. The employers do not wish to scatter their labour force to the four winds. Each side is, therefore, content to accept a "strike notice" of proper length as lawful. It is an implication read into the modern law as to trade disputes. If a strike takes place, the contract of employment is not terminated. It is suspended during the strike and revives again when the strike is over[8].'

The Donovan Commission considered the possibility of introducing the concept of suspension through strike notice, but thought it surrounded by problems[9]; in spite of this, it was introduced by the Industrial Relations Act 1971, s. 147, but disappeared with the repeal of that Act in 1974. The whole question arose (obliquely) for consideration by the EAT in *Simmons v Hoover Ltd*[10] where, in reaffirming that an employer has a right to dismiss a striking employee (who is thereby disentitled to a redundancy payment), Phillips J held that there is no common law doctrine of suspension by strike notice, and refused to apply Lord Denning's views in *Morgan v Fry*. He considered that those views were out of line with the modern statutory provisions relating to strikes (in contexts such as unfair

---

3   Or taking industrial action short of a strike but still inconsistent with contractual obligations: see *British Telecommunications plc v Ticehurst* [1992] ICR 383, [1992] IRLR 219, CA, discussed in ch. 3, above.
4   *National Coal Board v Galley* [1958] 1 All ER 91, [1958] 1 WLR 16, CA; *Neil v Strathclyde Regional Council* [1984] IRLR 14 (not an industrial dispute case).
5   See p. 174, above.
6   See principally *Rookes v Barnard* [1964] AC 1129, [1964] 1 All ER 367, HL, at 1204 and 396 respectively, per Lord Devlin; *Stratford & Son Ltd v Lindley* [1965] AC 269, [1964] 2 All ER 209, CA, at 285 and 217 respectively, per Lord Denning MR.
7   [1968] 2 QB 710, [1968] 3 All ER 452, CA; Davies LJ supported Lord Denning's view, but Russell LJ did not and decided the case on other grounds. The case itself concerned an allegation of intimidation, though as the facts arose before the passage of the Trade Disputes Act 1965 the new immunity was not available.
8   Ibid., at 728 and 458, respectively.
9   (1968) Cmnd. 623, para. 943.
10   [1977] ICR 61, [1976] IRLR 266, EAT; applied in *Wilkins v Cantrell and Cochrane (GB) Ltd* [1978] IRLR 483, EAT and *Haddow v ILEA* [1979] ICR 202, EAT.

dismissal, redundancy claims and continuity of employment), which operate on the assumption that participation in a strike is repudiatory conduct entitling the employer to dismiss, and then graft on special rules (depending on the context). *Simmons v Hoover Ltd* shows a clear move back to the original view of strikes as breaches of contract[11], and any mitigation of the potential harshness of this must be found in the legislation.

ii) The effect of industrial action on statutory employment rights

Participation in a strike or other industrial action is likely to have a highly detrimental impact on an employee's statutory employment rights. The most serious consequence is likely to be the potential loss of the right to bring proceedings for unfair dismissal, discussed below; but other statutory rights of a striking employee will also be affected, in particular:

(a) the restrictions on deductions from pay do not apply to deductions in respect of a strike or other industrial action in which the employee took part[12];

(b) a striking employee's rights to a redundancy payment may be jeopardised[13];

(c) a week during which an employee takes part in a strike will not count for the purposes of calculating that employee's continuity of employment[14];

(d) an employee is not entitled to a statutory guarantee payment where the failure to provide work is in consequence of a strike, lock-out or other industrial action involving his employer or an associated employer[15];

(e) an employee may be disqualified from receiving statutory sick pay where there is a stoppage of work due to a trade dispute at his place of work[16];

(f) rights to state benefits (e.g. Jobseeker's Allowance) will be materially affected[17].

iii) Industrial action and unfair dismissal[18]

When employees strike, their employer has the contractual right to dismiss them[19], even if that right is infrequently exercised. However, while a dismissal in such circumstances is probably lawful at common law, it may still be unfair; indeed following the reforms introduced by the Employment Relations Act 1999, a dismissal may now be *automatically* unfair where the employee is dismissed for taking 'protected industrial action'. This new protection is however contingent

11 This view could be said to be implicit in the Trade Union and Labour Relations (Consolidation) Act 1992, s. 229(4), which requires a ballot paper to point out that a person who takes part in a strike or other industrial action may be in breach of his contract of employment. Note, however, the judgment of Saville J in *Boxfoldia Ltd v NGA (1982)* [1988] ICR 752, [1988] IRLR 383 to the effect that the question of whether a purported strike notice avoids a breach of contract is a matter of interpretation of the notice (which, in order to be effective, would have to be an unambiguous notice of termination of contracts by the strikers).

12 Employment Rights Act 1996, s. 14(5); see p. 216, above. For the common law power to withhold wages in such circumstances, see p. 174, above.

13 Ibid., s. 140; see p. 539, above.

14 Ibid., s. 216.

15 Ibid., s. 29(3). See p. 185, above.

16 Social Security Contributions and Benefits Act 1992, Sch. 11, paras. 2(g) and 7.

17 Jobseekers Act 1995, s. 14. See p. 546, above.

18 See *Harvey* D 14; Ewing, op cit., ch. 4.

19 *Simmons v Hoover Ltd* [1977] ICR 61, [1976] IRLR 266, EAT; *Wilkins v Cantrell and Cochrane (GB) Ltd* [1978] IRLR 483, EAT; *Haddow v ILEA* [1979] ICR 202, EAT.

on the industrial action in question being official (i.e. authorised or endorsed by the union), lawful (i.e. covered by the statutory immunities), and normally lasting for no longer than eight weeks[20]. Where these requirements are not satisfied, the pre-1999 law still applies, which means that in some circumstances an employment tribunal will have no jurisdiction to hear an unfair dismissal complaint, while in others the tribunal will only be able to consider the complaint on its merits if the employer has discriminated between the participants by selectively dismissing or re-engaging them. To gain a clear picture of the current position, it is necessary to explore how this highly intricate state of affairs has come about.

The approach of those responsible for drafting the original unfair dismissal legislation was to seek to protect the neutrality of the industrial tribunals by relieving them of the necessity of investigating the rights and wrongs of an industrial dispute, while at the same time preserving the employer's ultimate freedom to dismiss the participants. This was achieved by providing that where, at the date of dismissal, the employee was taking part in a strike or other industrial action, or the employer was conducting or instituting a lock-out, the tribunal would have no jurisdiction to hear an unfair dismissal complaint by that employee unless the employer had discriminated between the participants, either by selectively dismissing only some of them, or by selectively offering re-engagement[1]. In *Heath v J F Longman (Meat Salesmen) Ltd*[2], Sir Hugh Griffiths expressed the policy behind this as follows:

'... the manifest overall purpose of [the section] is to give a measure of protection to an employer if his business is faced with ruin by a strike. It enables him in those circumstances, if he cannot carry on business without a labour force, to dismiss the labour force on strike; to take on another labour force without the stigma of its being an unfair dismissal.'

The Thatcher government considered the principle of non-selectivity to be too restrictive on employers faced with industrial action, and so the relevant provisions were modified to allow some selectivity in dismissals. Thus, the Employment Act 1982[3] confined the non-selectivity principle to those still taking part in the industrial action at the date of the complainant's dismissal (thereby allowing an employer faced with a strike to wait to see who in fact returns to work before dismissing all those still holding out), and introduced a time limit on the re-engagement of dismissed strikers (in effect permitting selective re-engagement after a three-month period); and the Employment Act 1990 took matters much further, by completely removing the right to complain of unfair dismissal from those dismissed while taking part in unofficial industrial action[4]. Taken together, these reforms significantly weakened the protection which the non-selectivity principle had given to those taking part in industrial action. In its 1998 White

---

20   Action lasting for longer than eight weeks may still be protected in certain circumstances: see below. The new measures came into force on 24 April 2000.

1   See *Gallagher v Wragg* [1977] ICR 174, EAT, per Phillips J; the neutrality explanation is arguably undermined by the fact that, where a dismissal or re-engagement is selective, the tribunal will have to decide whether the dismissal was fair or unfair.

2   [1973] ICR 407, [1973] IRLR 214, at 410 and 215 respectively.

3   See Wallington 'The Employment Act 1982, s. 9 – a recipe for victimisation?' (1983) 46 MLR 310; Ewing 'Industrial action: another step in the "right" direction' (1982) 11 ILJ 209; Townshend-Smith 'Taking part in a strike or other industrial action' [1984] NLJ 194, 240.

4   See now the Trade Union and Labour Relations (Consolidation) Act 1992, s. 237

Paper, *Fairness at Work*, the incoming Labour Government signalled a major policy shift in this area by proposing to give employees dismissed for taking part in lawfully organised official industrial action the right to complain of unfair dismissal to a tribunal[5]. As seen above, the Employment Relations Act 1999 subsequently enacted measures designed to protect workers from being dismissed for taking part in lawful, official industrial action, by introducing the concept of protected industrial action (discussed below). The new provisions differ in several respects from the proposals contained in *Fairness at Work*; for example, the White Paper had not indicated any intention to restrict the protection temporally, whereas under the new provisions the protection normally only lasts for eight weeks. However, this limit on the protection is offset by the fact that under the new provisions, a dismissal during the protected period will be *automatically* unfair; in contrast, under the White Paper proposals, it would have been for a tribunal to decide whether the employer had acted fairly and reasonably in all the circumstances. On balance, the protection of an automatically unfair dismissal, albeit for a limited period, is likely in practice to be more advantageous to workers taking part in industrial action than protection for an unlimited period which is dependent on a tribunal finding on the facts that the dismissal was unfair. There are however some significant gaps in the new protection. As previously mentioned, it is contingent on the industrial action in question being both official and, more controversially, lawful, which may make reliance on the protection something of a gamble, as an individual union member has no way of knowing whether the union has in fact complied with the Byzantine laws governing industrial action[6]; moreover, the protection does not extend to detriment *short* of dismissal, so that an employee who is victimised by his employer (e.g. by being denied promotion) for taking part in lawfully organised official industrial action remains unprotected under English law.

a) Unofficial action

An employee has no right to bring an unfair dismissal complaint where at the time of the dismissal the employee was taking part in an unofficial strike or other unofficial industrial action[7]. The only exception is where it is shown that the dismissal was for family reasons, or because the employee has taken certain specified action in relation to health and safety, has acted as an employee representative, or has made a protected disclosure under the 'whistleblowing' provisions[8]. In such cases, the dismissal will be automatically unfair; in all other cases, the reason for the dismissal is wholly irrelevant. As seen above, the removal

---

5   Cm. 3968, 1998, paras. 4.21-4.23. The White Paper confirmed that the Government had no intention of changing the position in relation to those dismissed for taking unofficial action.

6   A satisfactory report on the ballot by the independent scrutineer (see p. 677 below) may provide some reassurance that the union has safely navigated the legal minefield, but it will probably come too late to be of any help, and in any event it does not guarantee that the industrial action is lawful.

7   Ibid., s. 237. In determining whether action is 'unofficial', the statutory test of vicarious liability in s. 20 of the 1992 Act applies (see p. 696, below), save that action will not be regarded as unofficial if none of those taking part are members of a trade union: s. 237(2). The meaning of 'taking part', 'strike' and 'industrial action' are considered below in respect of s. 238.

8   Ibid., s. 237(1A). The health and safety exception was introduced to alleviate fears that employees dismissed for refusing to work in circumstances of danger might be held to be taking part in industrial action, and therefore excluded from the protection against unfair dismissal.

of unfair dismissal protection from unofficial strikers was introduced in 1990 as part of a series of measures designed to discourage unofficial industrial action[9]. The effect of the provisions is that an employer may selectively dismiss the ringleaders of unofficial action without fear of having to defend an unfair dismissal complaint[10].

b)   Official action

Where the industrial action is official, the present position is that the dismissal will be automatically unfair[11] if the reason (or, if more than one, the principal reason) for the dismissal is that the employee took 'protected industrial action'[12], and one of the following three conditions is satisfied: (i) the dismissal took place within eight weeks[13] of the day on which the employee started to take protected industrial action[14]; (ii) the dismissal took place after the end of that eight week period, but the employee had stopped taking protected industrial action before the end of that period (thus protecting the participants against victimisation by the employer after they have returned to work); or (iii) the dismissal took place after the end of the eight week period and the employee had not stopped taking part in the industrial action before the end of that period, but the employer had failed to take reasonable procedural steps to resolve the dispute. Industrial action is 'protected' for those purposes if the employee is induced to take part in the industrial action 'by an act which by virtue of section 219 is not actionable in tort'[15]; in other words, the protection for the individual participants is contingent upon the union having complied with the complex legal requirements governing the organisation of industrial action, including the balloting requirements and the restrictions on certain forms of industrial action. As seen above, the unfair dismissal protection normally lasts for only eight weeks. However, a dismissal for taking protected industrial action will still be unfair where the industrial action has lasted for more than eight weeks, if the employer has failed to take 'such procedural steps as would have been reasonable for the purposes of resolving the dispute to which the protected industrial action relates'[16]. In deciding

---

9   The measures were canvassed in the Green Paper, *Unofficial Action and the Law* (Cm. 821, 1989), in which it was argued that the restrictions on selective dismissal impeded the employer's ability to take effective action against unofficial strikers (para. 3.3). For the other restrictions on unofficial action, see p. 670.

10   Green Paper, para. 3.7. Where industrial action is repudiated by the union under s. 21 of the 1992 Act, it does not become unofficial for present purposes before the end of the next working day after the day on which the repudiation takes place, in effect giving those involved a day's grace to decide whether to continue with the action.

11   The usual qualifying period and age restriction for unfair dismissal claims do not apply in complaints under s. 238A: s. 239(1). No reinstatement or re-engagement order may be made until after the end of the industrial action: s. 239(4).

12   Trade Union and Labour Relations (Consolidation) Act 1992, s. 238A, as inserted by the Employment Relations Act 1999, s. 16, with effect from 24 April 2000.

13   Eight weeks was considered by the government to be 'a period that allows reasonable time for parties to resolve their dispute and so avoid dismissals' (Minister of State, Standing Committee E, 9 March 1999, col. 289).

14   Note that the eight-week period runs from the day on which the dismissed employee started to take industrial action, not the day when the industrial action began; this has important implications where employees join in the action after it has already begun.

15   Trade Union and Labour Relations (Consolidation) Act 1992, s. 238A(1). On a strict interpretation, this could be taken to mean that if the industrial action is not tortious, or it involves the commission of a tort which is not covered by the s. 219 immunities, the unfair dismissal protection does not apply! See Ewing (1999) 28 ILJ 283, at p. 292.

16   Ibid., s. 238A(5).

whether the employer has taken reasonable procedural steps, the tribunal must have regard to whether the employer or the union had complied with the procedures laid down in any applicable collective agreement, and whether, after the start of the protected industrial action, either party had offered or agreed to commence or resume negotiations, had unreasonably refused to a request that conciliation services be used, or had unreasonably refused a request to use mediation services in relation to the procedures to be used to resolve the dispute[17].

Where the industrial action is official but is *not* 'protected' within the meaning of the new provisions, a tribunal will not have jurisdiction to consider an unfair dismissal complaint[18] where, at the date of dismissal[19], the employer was conducting or instituting a lock-out or the complainant was taking part in a strike or other industrial action, unless the employee shows that either:

(a) one or more relevant employees have not been dismissed; or

(b) a relevant employee has, before the expiry of the period of three months beginning with that employee's date of dismissal, been offered re-engagement and the complainant has not been offered re-engagement[20].

If the dismissals are selective, or only some of the relevant employees are selected for re-engagement, the tribunal will then have jurisdiction to consider the case in the ordinary way, which means that they must consider the reason for the dismissal[1], and, if it is a prima facie fair one, the reasonableness of the decision to sack or not to re-engage that particular employee in those circumstances (unless the reason for selection concerned union membership or activities, in which case the dismissal may be automatically unfair[2]); a selective dismissal is therefore not automatically unfair as such (unlike a dismissal for taking protected industrial action), and the employer may be able to show that it was reasonable in all the circumstances to dismiss or not to re-engage some of the strikers. If the dismissal is held to be unfair the tribunal is not entitled to take into account the mere act of participating in industrial action in deciding whether to reduce the award of compensation on the grounds of contributory fault, but the award may be reduced where there is individual blameworthy conduct by the applicant, additional to or separate from the mere act of participation in the industrial action, which contributed to the dismissal and which was sufficiently blameworthy to make it just and equitable for the tribunal to reduce the compensation (for example, if

17   Ibid., s. 238A(6). In determining whether the employer has taken reasonable procedural steps, the tribunal must disregard the merits of the dispute: s. 238A(7).

18   The reason for the dismissal in such a situation is usually irrelevant, although again there is an exception where the dismissal was for family reasons, or because the employee has taken certain specified action in relation to health and safety, or has acted as an employee representative: s. 238(2A).

19   This is defined in s. 238(5). See *Heath v J F Longman (Meat Salesmen) Ltd* [1973] ICR 407, [1973] IRLR 214, where it was taken to mean that the employee must be taking part in industrial action at the time of dismissal, and not merely on the same date. A dismissal before the industrial action has started (*Midland Plastics v Till* [1983] ICR 118, [1983] IRLR 9, EAT) or after it has ended (*Seed v Crowther (Dyers)* [1973] IRLR 199) will not fall within the section.

20   Re-engagement means taking the employee back into the same job or in a different job which would be reasonably suitable in his case: s. 238(4); the definition of 'job' (Employment Rights Act 1996, s. 235(1)) allows the employer a certain leeway on the precise terms on which he takes the employee back: see *Williams v National Theatre Board Ltd* [1982] ICR 715, [1982] IRLR 377, CA. An advertising campaign offering job vacancies is unlikely to be interpreted as an offer of re-engagement to a particular employee within the meaning of the section: *Crosville (Wales) Ltd v Tracey* [1993] IRLR 60, EAT.

1   See *Baxter v Limb Group of Companies* [1994] IRLR 572, CA.

2   Note however that the dismissal of a person while taking part in industrial action is unlikely to be automatically unfair under s.152 of the 1992 Act: see p. 578, above.

the applicant is a strike leader who has contributed to his own dismissal by his over-zealous or inflammatory actions)[3].

The interpretation of the above provisions has proved to be especially problematic, not least because a number of key phrases are not defined. There is no definition of 'lock-out' or 'other industrial action', and until 1992 there was no definition of 'strike' either. However, as part of the consolidation process, the definition of 'strike' from the strike ballot provisions was extended to the whole of the law on industrial action, so that now 'strike' is defined in this context as 'any concerted stoppage of work[4].' There are definitions of 'strike' and 'lock-out' in section 235 of the Employment Rights Act 1996, but it has previously been held that those definitions are only for the purposes of continuity of employment and so are not to be applied under section 238[5], although they may provide some guidance to the tribunal in interpreting the section. However, at the end of the day the words should be given their ordinary and natural meaning, and their interpretation remains strictly a question of fact for the tribunal. This is entirely in line with the modern anti-legalism approach and, as stated above[6], the unpredictability and inconsistency that it can produce was commented on adversely by Browne-Wilkinson P in *Naylor v Orton and Smith Ltd*[7]; however, that approach was reaffirmed by the Court of Appeal in *Express and Star Ltd v Bunday*[8] where May LJ said:

'What are the necessary elements of a lock-out, or for that matter of a bicycle or an elephant, is not in my opinion a question of law. Nor I think is it necessarily a question of law whether a court or tribunal was correct in thinking that the presence of a particular element or ingredient in a given state of affairs is necessary before that can be, for instance, a "lock-out". This may be a mixed question of law and fact. Alternatively it may be solely a question of fact, which it is for the expert tribunal to determine[9].'

The dangers inherent in this strongly fact-based approach are graphically illustrated by *Lewis and Britton v E Mason & Sons*[10], where the EAT upheld the finding of the industrial tribunal that one person acting alone was taking part in industrial action. In that case, the employee was dismissed after refusing to drive a heavy goods vehicle with no overnight heater from South Wales to Scotland in mid-December unless he was given an extra £5 for overnight bed and breakfast accommodation. The EAT held that whether the employee was taking part in industrial action was a question of fact for the tribunal alone, and that the tribunal's finding on that point was not perverse, as it was open to the tribunal to find that

---

3   *Tracey v Crosville Wales Ltd* [1997] ICR 862, [1997] IRLR 691, HL, overruling *TNT Express (UK) Ltd v Downes* [1994] ICR 1, [1993] IRLR 432, EAT. Contributory fault in unfair dismissal complaints is considered at p. 514, above.

4   Trade Union and Labour Relations (Consolidation) Act 1992, s. 246.

5   *McCormick v Horsepower Ltd* [1980] ICR 278, [1980] IRLR 182, EAT (upheld on other grounds on appeal) [1981] ICR 535, [1981] IRLR 217, CA and *Rasool v Hepworth Pipe Co Ltd* [1980] ICR 494, [1980] IRLR 88, EAT in relation to 'strike'; *Express and Star Ltd v Bunday* [1988] ICR 379, [1987] IRLR 422, CA in relation to 'lock-out'.

6   At p. 410.

7   [1983] ICR 665, [1983] IRLR 233, EAT.

8   N. 5, above.

9   At 388 and 425 respectively; this view can perhaps best be summed up by saying that the law needs a definitive interpretation of 'lock-out' like an elephant needs a bicycle. Glidewell LJ thought that 'the proper construction of a word or words in a statute is a matter of *law*' (at 390 and 427), but was in a minority on this point.

10 [1994] IRLR 4, EAT. See Dolding (1994) 23 ILJ 243.

one person acting alone was taking part in industrial action where that person's conduct was designed to coerce the employer to improve the terms and conditions of employment in some way. Taken to its logical conclusion, this line of reasoning would appear to mean that any employee who refused to carry out a lawful instruction of his employer in order to gain an improvement in his terms and conditions of employment could be held to be taking part in industrial action, thus enabling his employer to dismiss him without fear of having to defend an unfair dismissal complaint. The EAT's ruling sits uneasily with earlier dicta to the effect that industrial action is a collective act which involves the concerted action of more than one person[11], and it is difficult to reconcile with the wording of the section, which requires a person to be *taking part* in industrial action (implying the involvement of others), rather than merely *taking* industrial action. It is to be hoped that the adoption in 1992 of the definition of 'strike' as a 'concerted stoppage of work' makes it unlikely that the decision in *Lewis and Britton* will be followed in the future[12].

In some cases, the dominant consideration for the tribunals in determining whether the circumstances amount to a strike or other industrial action within the meaning of the Act has been the purpose for which the action in question was taken, and in particular whether it involved the application of pressure on the employer[13]. So for example, in *Rasool v Hepworth Pipe Co (No 2)*[14], the EAT held that attendance at an unauthorised union meeting during working hours did not amount to industrial action because the purpose was to discuss wages and not to apply pressure on the employer, even though the meeting did in fact result in some disruption of production. However, while it is undoubtedly true that industrial action will usually be taken for the purpose of putting pressure on the employer, there may be circumstances where action is taken for a social or political rather than an industrial motive (e.g. in protest at Government policy), and it is highly likely that such action would in practice be held to be industrial action. Greater emphasis is therefore likely to be placed on the nature and effect of the action, rather than on the reasons for it[15].

11   See *Tramp Shipping Corpn v Greenwich Marine Inc* [1975] ICR 261 at 266, CA, per Lord Denning: '... a strike is a concerted stoppage of work by men (sic) done with a view to improving their wages or conditions, or giving vent to a grievance or making a protest about something or other, or supporting or sympathising with other workmen in such endeavour'; see also *Coates v Modern Methods and Materials Ltd* [1982] ICR 763, [1982] IRLR 318, CA, per Eveleigh LJ: '... for a person to take part in a strike he must be acting jointly or in concert with others who withdraw their labour'; cf. *London Underground Ltd v RMT* [1995] IRLR 636, CA, per Millet LJ (on the strike ballot provisions): 'Industrial action is collective action. An individual does not take collective action; he takes part in it.'

12   *Lewis and Britton* was heard by the tribunal before the enactment of the 1992 Consolidation Act.

13   Cf. Stephenson LJ in *Power Packing Casemakers Ltd v Faust* [1983] ICR 292, [1983] IRLR 117, CA: 'the continued application of pressure is industrial action in the commonsense of the words.' See also *Fire Brigades Union v Knowles* [1996] IRLR 337, EAT (under s. 65(2)(a); see p. 605).

14   [1980] IRLR 137, EAT. The case is a good illustration of the potentially fine dividing line between union activity and industrial action: see p. 577. The EAT has held that the two situations are mutually exclusive: *Drew v St Edmundsbury Borough Council* [1980] ICR 513, [1980] IRLR 459.

15   Cf *Rasool v Hepworth Pipe Co (No 2)*, supra, where the EAT acknowledged that it was 'probably incorrect to attempt to interpret [industrial action] narrowly in terms of specific intention and that the nature and effect of the concerted action are probably of greater importance.'

It is clear that the technical question of whether the action is in breach of contract is not conclusive, although once again it may be taken into account as a factor. Usually a strike will involve a breach of contract, but the lack of a need to show such a breach could be important in the case of a lock-out or, more especially, in cases of 'other industrial action' – a wide phrase which has been held to cover not just actions arguably in breach (such as a go-slow, partial refusal of work or a work-to-rule), but also actions clearly *not* in themselves in breach, such as a refusal to work voluntary overtime which, if done collectively and with a coercive purpose, may constitute industrial action even though individually each employee was perfectly entitled to refuse it[16].

The right to complain of unfair dismissal is only removed from employees who were 'taking part' in a strike or other industrial action at the date of the dismissal. Here again the Court of Appeal has emphasised that the question of whether or not an individual is 'taking part' is ultimately a question of fact for the tribunal[17], but the cases nevertheless provide some guidance as to the correct approach. In *Coates v Modern Methods and Materials Ltd*[18], the employee had stayed away from work during the strike because she was frightened of crossing a picket line. The majority of the Court of Appeal held that the test to be applied is an objective one, focusing on what the employee in fact did, and not on her motivation; as Stephenson LJ put it: '... participation in a strike must be judged by what the employee does and not by what he thinks or why he does it[19].'

It follows that employees who are absent from work due to sickness or on holiday leave during the industrial action may still be held to be taking part in it, particularly if they associate themselves with the strike (e.g. by attending at the picket line)[20]. However, it seems that clear evidence of participation will be required before an employee who is off sick when the action begins will be found to be participating in it[1]. Just as the employee's subjective motivation is irrelevant, so also is subjective knowledge on the part of the employer, so that an employer's reasonable but mistaken belief that the employee is taking part in the industrial action will not be sufficient if the employee's actions and omissions do not justify the conclusion that he was in fact taking part in that action[2]. A threat to take industrial action does not of itself amount to taking part in industrial action within the meaning of the Act[3], but where an employee has stated his intention of joining in existing industrial action, he may be held to be taking part in that

16   *Power Packing Casemakers Ltd v Faust* [1983] ICR 292, [1983] IRLR 117, CA. The decision has been heavily criticised.

17   *Coates v Modern Methods and Materials Ltd* [1982] ICR 763, [1982] IRLR 318, CA; *Naylor v Orton and Smith Ltd* [1983] ICR 665, [1983] IRLR 233, EAT.

18   Ibid. See also *Bolton Roadways Ltd v Edwards* [1987] IRLR 392, EAT; *Manifold Industries Ltd v Sims* [1991] ICR 504, [1991] IRLR 242, EAT.

19   Kerr LJ expressed a similar view.

20   *Bolton Roadways Ltd v Edwards* [1987] IRLR 392, EAT, per Scott J. In *Hindle Gears Ltd v McGinty* [1985] ICR 111, [1984] IRLR 477, the EAT overturned as perverse the tribunal's decision that a sick employee who spent time talking to pickets while handing in his medical certificate was participating in the industrial action.

1   *Rogers v Chloride Systems Ltd* [1992] ICR 198, EAT.

2   *Bolton Roadways Ltd v Edwards*, supra; In *McKenzie v Crosville Motor Services Ltd* [1990] ICR 172, [1989] IRLR 516, the EAT held that the reasonable belief of the employer that the employee was participating would be sufficient, but this was rejected in favour of the approach in *Bolton* by the EAT in *Manifold Industries Ltd v Sims*, supra (followed in *Jenkins v P&O European Ferries (Dover) Ltd* [1991] ICR 652).

3   *Midland Plastics v Till* [1983] ICR 118, [1983] IRLR 9, EAT.

action before the time when he is contractually due to work in fact arrives[4]. In *Lewis and Britton v E Mason & Sons*[5], an employee was dismissed for refusing to drive a heavy goods vehicle which did not have an overnight heater unless he was given an allowance to cover the cost of overnight accommodation. On learning of the dismissal, one of his colleagues threatened the employer that there would be a strike the following day unless the dismissed employee was reinstated. The EAT controversially held that it was open to the tribunal to find that by making a definite threat not to come to work the following day, at a time when further negotiation could not have been expected to take place and where the work for the following day had been allocated by the employer, the employees were taking part in industrial action[6].

As seen above, where the industrial action is official but not 'protected' under the new provisions, the tribunal will have jurisdiction to determine the fairness of a dismissal where the employer has discriminated between 'relevant employees' by selectively dismissing[7] or selectively re-engaging them. As defined in section 238(3), 'relevant employees' means:
(a) in relation to a lock-out, employees who were directly interested in the dispute in contemplation or furtherance of which the lock-out occurred; and
(b) in relation to a strike or other industrial action, those employees at the establishment of the employer at or from which the complainant works who at the date of his dismissal were taking part in the action.

In the case of strikes and other industrial action, the definition of 'relevant employees' is restricted to those taking part in the action at the date of the complainant's dismissal. Before 1982, the definition of relevant employees included all those who had taken part *at any stage* in the industrial action, so that an employee who had been on strike but had returned to work before the dismissal occurred was still a relevant employee. Accordingly, in *Stock v Frank Jones (Tipton) Ltd*[8], the House of Lords held that there had been selectivity where the employer had not sacked two employees who had returned to work before the date of the dismissals, so that the applicant could bring her case. The Employment Act 1982 reversed the decision in that case, thus enabling an employer to issue an ultimatum to those taking industrial action to return to work or face dismissal and then to dismiss all those who fail to comply, while still retaining the protection

---

4 See *Winnett v Seamarks Bros Ltd* [1978] ICR 1240, [1978] IRLR 387, EAT, where an employee who had made clear his intention to join a strike when his next shift began was held to be taking part in industrial action from the time when he made that intention clear.

5 [1994] IRLR 4, EAT. See Dolding (1994) 23 ILJ 243.

6 The decision goes considerably further than *Winnett v Seamarks Bros Ltd*, above, because that case involved a threat to join an existing strike, rather than a threat to commence strike action. Cf Browne-Wilkinson J in *Midland Plastics v Till* (above, n. 3): 'The actual taking of industrial action is ... quite distinct from the stage at which the threat of it is being used as a negotiating weapon.'

7 The question of whether the dismissals are selective will be determined at the conclusion of the proceedings in which the tribunal determines whether or not it has jurisdiction: *P&O European Ferries (Dover) Ltd v Byrne* [1989] ICR 779, [1989] IRLR 254, CA; in that case the complainant was ordered to disclose the identity of an alleged relevant employee who had not been dismissed, thus enabling the employer to dismiss that employee before the conclusion of the hearing and so prevent the tribunal from acquiring jurisdiction to hear the complainant's case.

8 [1978] ICR 347, [1978] IRLR 87, HL.

of the section against unfair dismissal proceedings brought by the dismissed employees[9].

A second significant amendment made by the 1982 Act was to introduce a time limit on the re-engagement of relevant employees, so that the anti-discrimination provisions only apply where a relevant employee is offered re-engagement within three months of his dismissal; thereafter the employer is free to re-engage strikers selectively without conferring jurisdiction on the tribunal[10]. Before 1982, any such re-engagement would lay the employer open to an unfair dismissal complaint, even if the taking on was at some time in the future[11]. The time limit also enables the employer to make an initial limited offer of re-engagement – in effect sanctioning a 'cooling-off' period and a phased return to work – provided that all those dismissed have been offered re-engagement within three months of their dismissal[12]. The third amendment introduced by the 1982 Act dealt with the situation where there is industrial action at some or all of the plants of a multi-plant employer. Up to that time, if the industrial action all formed part of one dispute, the non-selectivity rule had to apply to all plants, so that an employer could not adopt a different response to the industrial action in different plants, e.g. by dismissing the workforce at one plant but not another. However, the 1982 Act restricted the definition of 'relevant employees' to those employed 'at the establishment of the employer at or from which the complainant works'[13], so that any application of the selectivity principle has to be done on an establishment-by-establishment basis. One further potential difficulty for a large employer operating from several sites is that an employee dismissed for taking part in industrial action might be mistakenly re-engaged at another site within the three-month period, so opening up the employer to unfair dismissal complaints by those not re-engaged. However, the EAT has held that for there to be an effective offer of re-engagement, the employer must have actual or constructive knowledge (in the sense that he has the means of finding out) of the job from which the employee was dismissed and the reason why he was dismissed[14].

The principle of non-selectivity was clearly weakened by the Employment Acts of 1982 and 1990, and has been further marginalised by the Employment Relations Act 1999, but where it still applies the basic concept remains that the employer

9   The restrictions in the 1982 Act only applied to strikes etc., not to lock-outs, so that in the case of the latter the definition of relevant employees remains considerably wider, and an employee who was locked-out but has returned to work by the time of the dismissal will still be a relevant employee: *Fisher v York Trailer Co Ltd* [1979] ICR 834, [1979] IRLR 385, EAT; *H Campey & Sons Ltd v Bellwood* [1987] ICR 311, EAT.

10   This could cause limitation problems where the complainant and the relevant employee's dismissals took place at the same time, for the normal limitation period for the claimant to bring his action is also three months. Because of this, the limitation period is extended to six months in a case where the complainant is relying on the re-engagement of a relevant employee as a ground for arguing that the s. 238 exclusion should not apply: Trade Union and Labour Relations (Consolidation) Act 1992, s. 239(2). The six-month limit also applies to complaints under s. 238A (protected industrial action).

11   See, e.g., *Sealey v Avon Aluminium Co Ltd* [1978] IRLR 285, IT, where the taking back of a dismissed striker five months later was held to remove the exclusion.

12   *Highland Fabricators Ltd v McLaughlin* [1985] ICR 183, [1984] IRLR 482, EAT.

13   There is no definition here of 'establishment'; it is used elsewhere (again without definition) in the context of redundancy consultation; for the case law there, which could by analogy apply here, see p. 67, above; see also the Equal Pay Act 1970, s. 1(6), and the Sex Discrimination Act 1975, s. 6.

14   *Bigham and Keogh v GKN Kwikform* [1992] ICR 113, [1992] IRLR 4, EAT; the EAT also confirmed that a re-engagement resulting from fraud on the part of the employee will not deprive the employer of the protection of the section.

must dismiss all or none if he is to rely on the exclusion. In most cases this narrows the scope of the exclusion in the employee's favour, but it has been argued that the whole concept of the exclusion is potentially too wide in a case where the employer is in fact willing to dispense with one whole group of employees, who may be deprived of their unfair dismissal rights in two ways – first, by the employer instituting a lock-out affecting them all, which is now treated in the same way as a strike[15]; and secondly, because the employer might try to goad the employees in question into taking industrial action and then dismiss them all. In *Thompson v Eaton Ltd*[16], Phillips J suggested that this second possibility might be countered by the concept of an 'engineered' strike (i.e. one produced by 'gross provocation' by the employer) which would not fall within the exclusion. However, in *Marsden v Fairey Stainless Ltd*[17], the EAT disapproved of the idea of an engineered strike, pointing out that the wording of the section simply requires the employee to have been dismissed *while* on strike[18], so that the exclusion will apply even if the industrial action was provoked by the employer[19]. In future, an employer tempted to indulge in such opportunistic behaviour is likely to be discouraged by the new protection for lawful, official industrial action introduced by the Employment Relations Act 1999.

3 LIABILITY IN TORT AND THE STATUTORY IMMUNITIES[20]

i) Conspiracy

a) The cause of action

That conspiracy is a head of civil, as well as criminal, liability was clearly established by the House of Lords at the turn of the century in the famous 'trilogy' of conspiracy cases[1]. The tort of conspiracy may take either of two forms. The first, 'conspiracy by lawful means'[2], is committed where two or more persons combine together with intent to injure the plaintiff by the employment of means which are *lawful* in

---

15 Compare the original drafting in the Trade Union and Labour Relations Act 1974, Sch. 1, para. 7.
16 [1976] ICR 336, [1976] IRLR 308, at 342 and 311, EAT respectively.
17 [1979] IRLR 103, EAT. See also *Wilkins v Cantrell and Cochrane (GB) Ltd* [1978] IRLR 483, EAT.
18 Phillips J had been able to argue for the concept of an engineered strike because, as originally drafted, the section provided that the real reason for dismissal must be that the employee was on strike; however, the requirement of such a causal link was removed by the Employment Protection Act 1975, Sch. 16, Part III, para. 13.
19 A particularly controversial application of the exclusion was in the dispute between the printing unions and News International; see Ewing and Napier 'The Wapping dispute and labour law' (1986) 45 CLJ 285, at p. 291. For an ingenious attempt to devise an argument avoiding this unfortunate state of affairs, see Elias 'The Strike and Breach of Contract: A Reassessment' in Ewing, Gearty and Hepple (eds.) *Human Rights and Labour Law: Essays for Paul O'Higgins* (1994).
20 See generally *Harvey*, N, para 2101 et seq; *Winfield and Jolowicz on Tort* (15th edn, 1998); *Clerk and Lindsell on Torts* (17th edn. 1995) ch. 15; Elias and Ewing 'Economic torts and labour law: old principles and new liabilities' (1982) 41 CLJ 321; Carty 'Intentional Violation of Economic Interests: The Limits of Common Law Liability' (1988) 104 LQR 250.
1 *Mogul Steamship Co v McGregor, Gow & Co* [1892] AC 25, HL; *Allen v Flood* [1898] AC 1, HL: *Quinn v Leathem* [1901] AC 495, HL.
2 This version of the tort, sometimes referred to as 'conspiracy to injure' or 'simple' conspiracy or 'conspiracy to effect an unlawful purpose', was described as an 'anomalous tort' in *Lonrho Ltd v Shell Petroleum Co Ltd (No 2)* [1982] AC 173, [1981] 2 All ER 456, HL.

themselves, but with a predominant purpose to harm the plaintiff rather than to advance the legitimate interests of the combiners. The second, 'conspiracy to use unlawful means', is committed where two or more persons combine together with intent to injure the plaintiff by the employment of means which are *unlawful* in themselves. In the case of the latter, its scope is as wide as the scope of unlawful means, and so a conspiracy to injure by means that are criminal[3] or tortious[4] is actionable. Thus, the respondents in *Rookes v Barnard*[5] were liable on the basis of a conspiracy to intimidate, since intimidation was not at the time covered by a statutory immunity. Until recently it was thought[6] that for both forms of the tort it was necessary to show that the predominant purpose of the combiners must be to injure the plaintiff. However, the House of Lords in *Lonrho plc v Fayed*[7] has made it clear that under the second form there is no such requirement, and that it is sufficient to show that the defendants acted with intent to injure the plaintiff.

The emergence of the first form, that of conspiracy by lawful means, could have constituted a serious impediment to the lawfulness of industrial action, particularly after *Quinn v Leathem*, for almost any strike will require concerted action and will lead to loss to the employer. This consideration led to the immunity which was first granted in the Trade Disputes Act 1906 (see below), but in fact, as the tort was developed in subsequent cases (in particular by the House of Lords in *Sorrell v Smith*[8] and *Crofter Hand Woven Harris Tweed Co Ltd v Veitch*[9]), it is arguable that the immunity is in fact unnecessary, for the courts have taken a liberal approach to what constitutes the legitimate interests of organised labour. If the union can show a genuine trade union reason for the industrial action[10], then the conspiracy will not be actionable, in spite of the loss caused to the employer, because the employer will be unable to show that the union's predominant purpose was to harm him[11]; it is this element of the tort of conspiracy by lawful means which has become dominant, whether it be called lack of an improper purpose or, more commonly, a defence of 'justification'. In the light of this, this particular head of liability has played little part in the modern cases.

---

3   It has however been held in another context that a crime which is not also an actionable wrong at the suit of the plaintiff does not constitute unlawful means for the purposes of the tort of conspiracy: see *Crédit Lyonnais Bank Nederland NV (formerly known as Generale Bank Nederland NV) v Export Credits Guarantee Department* [1998] 1 Lloyds Rep 19, CA (affd on other grounds, [1999] 1 All ER 929, HL); *Yukong Lines Ltd of Korea v Rendsburg Investments Corpn of Liberia (No 2)* [1998] 4 All ER 82.

4   In *Rookes v Barnard*, Lord Devlin said that although a breach of contract was unlawful means for the purposes of intimidation, this did not necessarily mean that it was so for the purposes of conspiracy: [1964] AC at 1210, [1964] 1 All ER at 400. In *Barretts & Baird (Wholesale) Ltd v IPCS* [1987] IRLR 3, Henry J thought there was an arguable case that breach of contract was unlawful means for the purposes of conspiracy.

5   [1964] AC 1129, [1964] 1 All ER 367, HL.

6   Based on a dictum of Lord Diplock in *Lonrho Ltd v Shell Petroleum Co Ltd (No 2)* [1982] AC 173, [1981] 2 All ER 456, HL.

7   [1992] 1 AC 448, [1991] 3 All ER 303, HL., overruling *Metall und Rohstoff AG v Donaldson Lufkin & Jenrette Inc* [1990] 1 QB 391, [1989] 3 All ER 14, CA. Cf. also *Lonrho plc v Fayed (No. 5)* [1994] 1 All ER 188, CA (the plaintiff must prove actual pecuniary or financial loss for both forms of the tort, as opposed e.g. to loss of reputation).

8   [1925] AC 700, HL.

9   [1942] AC 435, [1942] 1 All ER 142, HL.

10   See e.g. *Reynolds v Shipping Federation* [1924] 1 Ch 28 (action to enforce a closed shop); the *Crofters'* case, n. 9, above (action to force up wages); *Scala Ballroom (Wolverhampton) Ltd v Ratcliffe* [1958] 3 All ER 220, [1958] 1 WLR 1057, CA (action to stamp out a colour bar operated by the employer).

11   *Quinn v Leathem*, n. 1, above, is perhaps best explained as a rare case where the jury decided that the defendants' predominant purpose was vindictive; see also *Huntley v Thornton* [1957] 1 All ER 234, [1957] 1 WLR 321.

b)   The immunity

Section 219(2) of the Trade Union and Labour Relations (Consolidation) Act 1992 provides that an agreement or combination to do any act in contemplation or furtherance of a trade dispute is not actionable in tort if the act is one which, if done by one person alone, would not be actionable. This therefore gives protection from liability for conspiracy by lawful means (i.e. means which would not be actionable if done by only one person), but does *not* give immunity from suit for conspiracy by unlawful means (i.e. means which *would* be actionable if done by only one person), although in the latter case there may be an indirect immunity if the means are covered by one of the other immunities and are not therefore 'unlawful'. Thus, in most cases conspiracy will be a dead letter, but on the other hand it is not abolished, only held in abeyance while within the golden formula; if the act complained of is outside that formula, e.g. a personal vendetta or clear misuse of union power for improper purpose, conspiracy could still be used as a cause of action[12].

ii)   Inducement of breach of contract

a)   The cause of action

In the light of the relatively innocuous nature of conspiracy, reliance in modern industrial tort cases has been placed principally upon inducement of breach of contract, a cause of action established in *Lumley v Gye*[13] where a theatre owner induced an opera singer to break her existing contract so that she could sing for him instead. There are two forms of inducement – direct and indirect. Direct inducement is where the defendant induces X, a third party, to break an existing contract which X has with the plaintiff, who thereby suffers loss. The necessary elements are that (i) the conduct must be intentional (ii) there must be clear evidence of actual inducement, in the sense of 'pressure, persuasion or procuration' directed at one of the parties to the contract[14], and (iii) there must be actual knowledge on the part of the defendant of the contract which would be broken[15] or, according to later cases[16], the means of having that knowledge (e.g. through the possibility of discovery at an interlocutory stage). This form of inducement may arise where a defendant union leader calls upon union members

12   As in *Huntley v Thornton*, n. 11, above.
13   (1853) 2 E & B 216.
14   Lack of such evidence led to failure of the actions in *D C Thomson & Co Ltd v Deakin* [1952] Ch 646, [1952] 2 All ER 361, CA and *Camellia Tanker Ltd v ITWF* [1976] ICR 274, [1976] IRLR 190, CA. Pressure directed at *customers* of one of the parties will not suffice, although it may be actionable as an *indirect* inducement if unlawful means are used: *Middlebrook Mushrooms Ltd v TGWU* [1993] ICR 612, [1993] IRLR 232, CA (where the action failed as no unlawful means had been used).
15   *D C Thomson & Co Ltd v Deakin* n. 14, above. See also *TimePlan Education Group Ltd v National Union of Teachers* [1997] IRLR 457, CA (union could not be held to have intended to interfere with a contract of which it was unaware). There is no need for knowledge that the conduct induced will in fact lead to a breach of contract; thus the tort is committed even where the defendant believes that there will be no breach: *Solihull Metropolitan Borough v NUT* [1985] IRLR 211 (teachers' union withdrawing functions such as lunchtime supervision which they considered voluntary).
16   *J T Stratford & Son Ltd v Lindley* [1965] AC 269, [1964] 3 All ER 102, HL, at 332 and 112 respectively, per Lord Pearce; *Emerald Construction Co v Lowthian* [1966] 1 All ER 1013, [1966] 1 WLR 691, CA. Where action is threatened against the plaintiff, his solicitors could ensure the necessary knowledge by formally serving notice of the relevant contracts on the defendants.

to strike in breach of their contracts of employment, or directly puts pressure on one of the employer's suppliers to cease deliveries of vital supplies in breach of their commercial supply contract with the plaintiff. However, in the latter scenario (an example of 'secondary action' or 'blacking'), the tort more likely to be committed is *indirect* inducement. This arises where the defendant induces X (typically a union member) to do an unlawful act to Y (typically X's employer), thereby making Y break a commercial supply contract with the plaintiff who thereby suffers loss. The requirements of intention, inducement and knowledge are the same as for direct inducement, but the crucial difference between the two forms of the tort is that while direct inducement is wrongful in itself, indirect inducement must be by unlawful means (in order to keep it within any reasonable bounds) if it is to be actionable[17]. In diagrammatic form, this action could arise in an industrial dispute as follows:

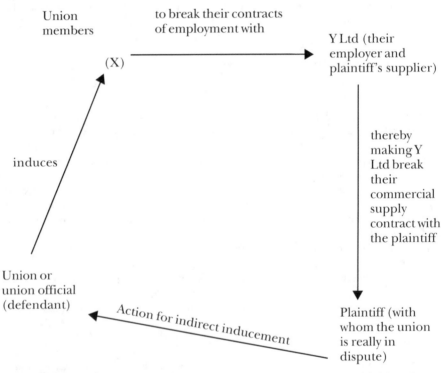

Questions of immunity aside, the tort of indirect inducement could arise where the union officials induce Y Ltd's employees to strike, or refuse to make deliveries to the plaintiff's factory, in breach of their contracts of employment, the inducement of the breach of those employment contracts prima facie being the unlawful means. In *J T Stratford & Son Ltd v Lindley*[18] the defendant union officials

17   *D C Thomson & Co Ltd v Deakin*, n. 14, above; *Torquay Hotel Co Ltd v Cousins* [1969] 2 Ch 106, [1969] 1 All ER 522, CA, per Lord Denning MR at 138 and 530 respectively, retracting his statement in *Daily Mirror Newspapers Ltd v Gardner* [1968] 2 QB 762, [1968] 2 All ER 163, CA that there was no difference between direct and indirect inducement.

18   [1965] AC 269, [1964] 3 All ER 102, HL. For other examples of indirect inducement, see the facts of *Associated Newspapers Group Ltd v Wade* [1979] ICR 664, [1979] IRLR 201, CA, or *Merkur Island Shipping Corpn v Laughton* [1983] ICR 490, [1983] IRLR 218, HL. *Dimbleby & Sons Ltd v NUJ* [1984] ICR 386, [1984] IRLR 161, HL is unusual in that the plaintiff was in fact in the position of Y Ltd in the above diagram, not in the usual position of the plaintiff as the one at the end of the line with whom the union is really in dispute.

induced some of their members to break their contracts of employment, thus causing their employers (Y) to break their commercial hiring contracts with the plaintiff company (which was associated with another company that was the real target of the defendants' actions). The House of Lords held that the plaintiff was entitled to an injunction to restrain this indirect inducement of breach of the commercial contracts, the essential unlawful means being found in the direct inducement of breaches of the employment contracts. The facts (but not the decision) were similar in *Thomson & Co Ltd v Deakin*[19] where the defendant union officials were in dispute with the plaintiff company over union recognition. The plaintiff company, printers, were supplied with paper by Bowaters Ltd (Y) and the defendants sought help with unions who dealt with that firm. When Bowaters discovered that some of their employees objected to loading and delivering supplies to the plaintiff company, they decided not to ask their employees to effect such loading and delivering, and ceased to supply, thus being in breach of their commercial contract. The plaintiff company sought an injunction against the defendants, restraining them from procuring breaches of contract between the plaintiff and Bowaters. The union officials replied (a) that in approaching other unions they had only asked for help and (b) that Bowaters' employees had not been instructed by them not to load or deliver paper. The Court of Appeal found for the defendant union officials for, although it was clear that an action would have lain had the defendants, with the relevant knowledge of the commercial contract, contrived by wrongful acts a situation in which it was impossible for Bowaters to perform the contract, on the actual facts of the case the plaintiff had failed to show either sufficient 'inducement' or that the defendants had caused Bowaters' employees actually to break their contracts (the necessary element of unlawful means therefore being missing).

Two further points should be noted in relation to inducement. The first is that there is still uncertainty as to the 'intention to injure' requirement. The orthodox view[20] is that such a requirement is an essential ingredient of the tort. However, in *Falconer v ASLEF and NUR*[1] inducement was found where the unions had taken action against British Rail in the course of an industrial dispute, thereby injuring the plaintiff who was unable to travel by train on the ticket that he had already bought; the union's argument that their intent was to harm British Rail, not the plaintiff, was rejected as 'naïve and divorced from reality'. This case therefore suggests that 'intent' is shown where the plaintiff (either individually or, as in this case, as one of a definable class) will foreseeably be injured even though the action is not actually aimed at him. This may be in line with concepts of intention elsewhere in the law[2], but it is inconsistent with other authority and

19 [1952] Ch 646, [1952] 2 All ER 361, CA.
20 As expressed by Jenkins LJ in *Thomson & Co Ltd v Deakin*, ibid.
1 [1986] IRLR 331, Co Ct; the case was not appealed by the union, in spite of (or because of?) the widespread publicity that it attracted. The question of intent to injure was vital because there had been no strike ballot, and as the immunities are withdrawn in toto in such a situation the union can only escape liability if it can show that no tort was committed in the first place.
2 Particularly in criminal law, where either 'wilful blindness' or the realisation that the consequence in question is almost certain to result from your action (*R v Hancock* [1986] AC 455, [1986] 1 All ER 641, CA) may justify an inference that you intended that consequence.

is capable of extending liability very widely[3]. At the other extreme, Henry J in *Barretts & Baird (Wholesale) Ltd v IPCS*[4] stated that, to establish the tort of interference with business (below), it must be shown that intent to injure the plaintiff was the 'predominant purpose' of the action. This vital point awaits authoritative determination. The second point is that there is a defence of justification available, but its scope is uncertain, and it is not as wide as that for conspiracy by lawful means. Thus, in *South Wales Miners' Federation v Glamorgan Coal Co Ltd*[5] it was held that there was no defence of justification available on the facts, in spite of the fact that the workers involved were merely acting in genuine furtherance of their own interests and bore no ill will towards the employers. It appears that exercise of a 'duty' may amount to justification, but mere self-interest cannot[6]; in *Brimelow v Casson*[7] the justification defence succeeded in highly unusual circumstances, the defence in that case being that the union had a duty, as a representative association, to secure the payment of reasonable wages by a theatrical manager in order that chorus girls in his employ could live without having to resort to immoral earnings. The idea of a 'duty' to act as providing justification for the tort of inducement is a nebulous one; it is theoretically capable of being extended to cover many union activities on the basis that a union officer may have certain legal and moral 'duties' towards the membership, but in practice the defence rarely succeeds[8].

b)   The immunity

Section 219(1)(a) of the Trade Union and Labour Relations (Consolidation) Act 1992 provides that an act done in contemplation or furtherance of a trade dispute is not actionable in tort on the ground only that it induces another person to break a contract. The immunity covers both direct and indirect inducement, and was significantly widened by the Trade Union and Labour Relations (Amendment) Act 1976, which extended the immunity to breach of *any* contract, not just a contract of employment, as had previously been the case; the effect of this was to extend the immunity to cover secondary boycotts and blackings aimed at breaking vital commercial contracts of the employer with whom the union is in dispute. Following this change in 1976 (and the inclusion

---

3   In some respects the argument in *Falconer* has been overtaken by events, in that the plaintiff in that case would now be able to apply for an injunction to restrain the unlawful industrial action under s. 235A of the Trade Union and Labour Relations (Consolidation) Act 1992 (the 'Citizen's Right'), whether or not he could himself sue in tort; see p. 703, below.

4   [1987] IRLR 3; note, however, that in *Lonrho plc v Fayed* [1990] 2 QB 479, [1989] 2 All ER 65, the Court of Appeal doubted whether for the tort of interference with business it is necessary to show that injury to the plaintiff was the predominant purpose; one explanation might simply be that the intent requirements for the two torts are different.

5   [1905] AC 239, HL; and see *British Motor Trade Association v Salvadori* [1949] Ch 556, [1949] 1 All ER 208.

6   See the *South Wales Miners'* case, in the Court of Appeal [1903] 2 KB 545, at 573 per Romer LJ and in the House of Lords [1905] AC 239 at 249 per Lord James; *Greig v Insole* [1978] 3 All ER 449, [1978] 1 WLR 302 at 491 and 340, respectively, per Slade J. See also *TimePlan Education Group Ltd v National Union of Teachers* [1997] IRLR 457, CA, per Peter Gibson LJ.

7   [1924] 1 Ch 302; *Camden Nominees Ltd v Forcey* [1940] Ch 352, [1940] 2 All ER 1. The suggestion in *British Industrial Plastics Ltd v Fergusson* [1938] 4 All ER 504, CA at 510 per Slesser LJ that a desire not to break the law might amount to justification must be doubtful.

8   *Posluns v Toronto Stock Exchange* (1964) 46 DLR (2d) 210 at 270, per Gale J. Cf. *Pete's Towing Services Ltd v NIUW* [1970] NZLR 32 at 51 per Speight J.

within the immunity of the tort of interference, discussed below), it appeared that the immunity itself was almost watertight, *provided* that the acts in question remained within the golden formula. It should be stressed that in spite of the legislative changes since 1980, the actual immunity in section 219(1) has remained unchanged. The rules on secondary action, strike ballots, etc., operate not by altering the basic immunity, but instead by suspending its operation in certain defined circumstances.

iii) Intimidation

a) The cause of action

The tort of intimidation is committed when the plaintiff suffers damage as a result of an unlawful threat made by the defendant with the intention of causing harm to the plaintiff. Typically, intimidation arises where the plaintiff is harmed by action taken by a third party, X, in response to an unlawful[9] threat by the defendant which is directed at X[10], but which is in reality intended to harm the plaintiff[11]. The case of *Rookes v Barnard*[12] resurrected this old action and established that it embraced not only threats of criminal or tortious conduct, but also threats to break contracts. The appellant was lawfully[13] dismissed by his employer as a result of an ultimatum from the respondent union officers threatening industrial action which would have involved breaches of their employment contracts by the participants (primarily because those contracts contained a 'no-strike' clause). It was held by the House of Lords that the respondents had committed the tort of intimidation in that the appellant had suffered damage (loss of employment) as a result of action taken by his employer (lawful dismissal) in response to an unlawful threat (threat to break their employment contracts) directed against the employer by the respondents. This decision opened up a potentially large area of liability in respect of industrial action which was not covered by the statutory immunities then contained in the Trade Disputes Act 1906; this was hardly surprising, since the tort had seen no development since 1793, when it appeared to be confined to threats of physical violence[14].

b) The immunity

In response to the threat posed by *Rookes v Barnard*, the Trade Disputes Act 1965 was passed creating a new immunity covering intimidation. This is now contained in section 219(1)(b) of the Trade Union and Labour Relations (Consolidation) Act 1992, which provides that an act done in contemplation or furtherance of a

9   Threats to take lawful action are not tortious: *Allen v Flood* [1898] AC 1, HL; *Hardie and Lane Ltd v Chilton* [1928] 2 KB 306, CA; *Thorne v Motor Trade Association* [1937] AC 797, HL.

10 I.e. indirect intimidation. There may also be liability for direct (or 'two-party') intimidation, i.e. where D makes an unlawful threat to P in order to make him act to his own detriment; in most instances, however, intimidation is unnecessary here as P could sue upon the threatened unlawful act itself.

11 To succeed, the plaintiff must show that the threats, although directed at the third party, were in fact intended to harm him: *News Group Newspapers Ltd v SOGAT '82 (No 2)* [1987] ICR 181, [1986] IRLR 337.

12 [1964] AC 1129, [1964] 1 All ER 367, HL.

13 Hence no action on the facts for for inducing breach of contract.

14 *Tarleton v M'Gawley* (1793) Peake 270.

trade dispute is not actionable in tort on the ground only that it consists in his threatening that a contract (whether one to which he is a party or not) will be broken or its performance interfered with, or that he will induce another person to break a contract or to interfere with its performance. As with section 219(1)(a), this provision was widened in 1976 to cover *any* contract, not just a contract of employment. On the particular facts of *Rookes v Barnard*, further protection would today be given by section 180, for this provides that no-strike clauses in collective bargains are not to be incorporated into individual contracts of employment unless the collective bargain (which must be readily accessible to the individual worker and must have been negotiated by an independent trade union) expressly states that the clause shall or may be incorporated, and the individual contract does incorporate it expressly or impliedly[15]. Once again, however, the whole scheme of the immunities is dependent upon the act in question being within the golden formula.

iv) Interference with contract, or with trade or business generally

a) The cause of action

The tort of inducing a breach of contract has long been established, but more recent authority has held that there is a further head of liability, namely *interfering* with the performance of a contract (short of causing an actual breach). This was put forward in *Torquay Hotel Co Ltd v Cousins*[16] where a problem arose because the oil supply contract which was the target of the union's activities in fact contained a *force majeure* clause excepting liability for labour disputes, thus giving rise to the argument that by stopping supplies the union had not actually caused a breach of the contract. Whereas Russell and Winn LJJ held that there was still a breach in spite of the clause and so the defendants could be liable for ordinary inducement, Lord Denning MR stated that there could be liability even if there was no breach – 'interference' (in the sense of conduct which prevents or hinders one party from performing his contract) is enough, even though it does not actually procure a breach, provided that it is deliberate and done with knowledge of the contract (or, at any rate, turning a blind eye to it). His Lordship then went on to divide interference into direct and indirect interference (by analogy with inducement), saying that direct interference is unlawful in itself, but indirect interference requires unlawful means. This, however, was doubtful, for any liability for simple interference which could be committed by lawful means (even if direct) would arguably have outflanked the central principle established in *Allen v Flood*[17] that the intentional infliction of harm without justification is not in itself tortious. However, in the subsequent case of *Acrow (Automatic) Ltd v Rex Chainbelt Inc*[18], Lord Denning restated the law in a different way, which requires both direct and indirect interference to be by unlawful means:

15   On no-strike clauses generally, see Lewis 'Strike-free deals and pendulum arbitration' (1990) 28 BJIR 32.
16   [1969] 2 Ch 106, [1969] 1 All ER 522, CA.
17   [1898] AC 1, HL.
18   [1971] 3 All ER 1175, [1971] 1 WLR 1676, CA; *Esso Petroleum Ltd v Kingswood Motors (Addlestone) Ltd* [1974] QB 142, [1973] 3 All ER 1057; cf. *Brekkes Ltd v Cattel* [1972] Ch 105, [1971] 1 All ER 1031.

'... if one person, without just cause or excuse, deliberately interferes with the trade or business of another, and does so by unlawful means, that is, by an act which he is not at liberty to commit, then he is acting unlawfully. He is liable in damages and, in a proper case, an injunction can be granted against him[19].'

This extension of the tort to interference with contract was finally sanctioned by the House of Lords in *Merkur Island Shipping Corpn v Laughton*[20], where Lord Diplock drew a clear parallel with inducement of *breach* of contract and stated that when Jenkins LJ referred to breach of contract in his authoritative judgment in *D C Thomson & Co Ltd v Deakin*[1] that was only because the facts of the case disclosed a clear breach; according to Lord Diplock, the judgment in its true intent applies to any *interference* with contract (of which actual breach is but one form), and this is then made certain by his Lordship's approval of Lord Denning's judgment in *Torquay Hotel Co Ltd v Cousins*[2] and by his reference to Parliament's extension in 1976 of the relevant immunity to cover interference as well as breach.

However, the law has moved on yet further in this volatile area, for it now appears (as envisaged in the above dictum by Lord Denning) that there has evolved (almost *sub silentio*) a wider, more generalised, head of civil liability in the form of a tort of interference with the plaintiff's *trade or business*[3], the theory being that inducement of breach of contract, interference with contract and indeed intimidation are themselves, in turn, simply manifestations of this 'supertort'. So far, it has not been a necessary part of the ratio of any of the cases to pronounce on the existence and extent of such a tort[4], but in *Merkur Island Shipping Corpn v Laughton* Lord Diplock argued (from effect to cause) that its existence could be divined from the existence in the Trade Union and Labour Relations Act 1974 s. 13(2), (3) of immunities apparently covering it[5]:

'... [T]he evidence also establishes a *prima facie* case of the common law tort, referred to in s. 13(2) and (3) of the 1974 Act, of interfering with the trade or business of another person by doing unlawful acts. To fall within the genus of torts the unlawful act need not involve procuring another person to break a subsisting contract or to interfere with the performance of a subsisting contract. The immunity granted by s. 13(2) and (3) I will call the "genus immunity". Where, however the procuring of another person to

---

19   Ibid., at 1181 and 1682, respectively; the reference to 'unlawful means' meaning simply 'an act which he is not at liberty to commit' is probably too wide; the better view is that the unlawful means must themselves constitute an actionable wrong against the third party in question: *Lonrho Ltd v Shell Petroleum Co Ltd (No 2)* [1982] AC 173, [1981] 2 All ER 456, HL (a conspiracy case); see *Harvey* N 14 H (2).

20   [1983] ICR 490, [1983] IRLR 218, HL. The decision in the case is strongly criticised by Wedderburn (1983) 46 MLR 632.

1   [1952] Ch 646, [1952] 2 All ER 361, CA.

2   See n. 16, above.

3   See, especially, Carty, 'Unlawful interference with trade' (1983) 3 LS 193.

4   It was pleaded as one of several causes of action in *Hadmor Productions Ltd v Hamilton* [1982] ICR 114, [1982] IRLR 102, HL, and likewise in *Shipping Co Uniform Inc v ITWF* [1985] ICR 245, [1985] IRLR 71, but in each case the eventual decision was largely on other grounds.

5   S. 13(2) stated 'For the avoidance of doubt it is hereby declared that an act done by a person in contemplation or furtherance of a trade dispute is not actionable in tort on the ground only that it is an interference with the trade, business or employment of another person ...'.

break a subsisting contract is the unlawful act involved, as it is in s. 13(1),
this is but one species of the wider genus of tort[6].'

The problems here are (a) that it is arguable that when Parliament originally
enacted what became the section 13(2) immunity (in the Trade Disputes Act
1906) it only did so ex abundante cautela *in case* such a tort was ever propounded[7],
and (b) that in any event section 13(2) and (3) were repealed by the Employment
Acts 1980 and 1982. Given, however, that the wider 'genus' tort does exist the
most important points to notice about it are (i) that there is the essential element
that the interference with trade or business must be by 'unlawful means' (were it
otherwise, it would clearly be inconsistent with the fundamental rule in *Allen v
Flood*[8]), and (ii) there appears to be a requirement of intent to injure the particular
plaintiff in question[9].

b)   The immunity

Prior to 1976, the development of a possible tort of interference with contract
was seen as a potential outflanking of the immunity then contained in section
13(1)(a) which only referred to *breach* of contract. However, the Trade Union and
Labour Relations (Amendment) Act 1976 removed this possibility (in cases within
the golden formula) by adding that an act is not to be actionable in tort on the
ground only that it interferes or induces another person to interfere with the
performance of a contract[10]. This covers both direct and indirect interference,
and once again is dependent upon the acts in question falling within the golden
formula and not falling within any of the circumstances in which the immunities
are suspended by sections 222–234A of the Trade Union and Labour Relations
(Consolidation) Act 1992. The wider 'genus' tort of interference with trade or
business is not specifically covered by an immunity, either generally[11] or by virtue
of the extension in 1976 (which only relates to interference with contract).
However, as seen above, the essence of this new tort is the use of unlawful means;
the result of this is that there may be *indirect* immunity if the means themselves

---

6   [1983] ICR at 507, [1983] IRLR at 222. Lord Diplock considered that the tort of
    interference with contract is a different tort from interference with business, rather than
    just an example of it; sed quaere?
7   *Rookes v Barnard* [1964] AC 1129, [1964] 1 All ER 367, HL, at 1177 and 379, respectively,
    per Lord Reid.
8   [1898] AC 1, HL; see p. 629, above. In *Barretts & Baird (Wholesale) Ltd v IPCS* [1987] IRLR
    3, Henry J thought it was arguable that the employees' own breaches of contract could
    constitute the requisite unlawful means in this context, but this is respectfully doubted;
    see Simpson (1987) 50 MLR 506. The plaintiffs in *Barretts* also argued that inducing
    breach of statutory duty (for which there is no immunity) constituted unlawful means, but
    failed on the facts; see below.
9   In *Barretts and Baird (Wholesale) Ltd v IPCS*, supra, Henry J imposed an 'intent' requirement
    as high as that in conspiracy, namely that the intent to injure the plaintiff must be the
    predominant purpose of the defendants' actions; however, in *Lonrho plc v Fayed* [1990] 2
    QB 479, [1989] 2 All ER 65, the Court of Appeal held that it was not necessary to show
    that the defendant's predominant purpose was to injure the plaintiff rather than to
    pursue his own self-interest (or in the case of a trade union, its members' interests). See
    also *Associated British Ports v TGWU* [1989] 3 All ER 796, [1989] IRLR 305, CA (reversed on
    other grounds, [1989] 3 All ER 822, [1989] IRLR 399, HL).
10 See now the Trade Union and Labour Relations (Consolidation) Act 1992, s. 219(1)(a).
11 The Trade Union and Labour Relations Act 1974, s. 13(2), n. 5, above, looked as though
    it provided an immunity, but the better view is that it was there in case an even more
    sweeping tort of interference by *lawful* means (but without justification) was developed.
    In any event, s. 13(2) was repealed by the Employment Act 1982.

are immune and therefore not 'unlawful'. This could arise where the means adopted consist of inducing the employees of someone in a business relationship (actual or potential) with the plaintiff to break their contracts of employment (e.g. by imposing a blacking); if that action itself is in contemplation or furtherance of a trade dispute and is immune, that means that any ensuing interference will be by lawful, not unlawful means[12]. As before, of course, any such (indirect) immunity is liable to be then removed if the action falls foul of sections 222–234A.

v) Outflanking the immunities – three further possibilities

It is clear from the above that much of the stimulus for the development of the industrial torts in the twentieth century has come from attempts to outflank the statutory immunities. The most significant development has undoubtedly been the evolution of the 'genus' tort of interference with trade or business, discussed above, but there are three further possibilities, considered here in ascending order of importance. The first concerns the importation into industrial disputes of the recently-developed contractual doctrine of 'economic duress', i.e. that if a party to a contract is obliged to enter into it, or to agree to certain terms, because of illegitimate coercion by the other party, he may claim that the contract is voidable for duress and so claim repayment of anything paid under it[13]. In *Universe Tankships Inc of Monrovia v International Transport Workers' Federation*[14] the ITWF, as part of its campaign against ships under flags of convenience, caused the blacking of the plaintiffs' ship until certain demands were met, including the payment of $6,480 to a seamen's welfare fund. Once the ship was released, the plaintiffs sought the return of this amount on the basis that it had been paid under duress. The House of Lords allowed recovery by a majority of three to two. The first point to note about this application of the doctrine of duress is that it does *not* constitute a new head of tort; rather, it gives rise to an action for restitution of moneys paid over, and given that such arrangements between unions and employers are not common, it is likely that in practice the occasions when such a claim will be brought will be few[15]. However, if a claim is brought, it raises an exceptionally difficult point – when does pressure by a union on an employer overstep the line between hard bargaining on the one hand and illegitimate coercion (giving rise to economic duress) on the other? The answer given by the House of Lords has at least the attribute of neatness – although the doctrine of duress does not give rise to an action in tort, so that the immunities in the Trade Union and Labour

---

12 This is because if the inducement is within s. 219(1) it is declared to be 'not actionable' and that means not actionable *by anyone*, i.e. lawful: *Hadmor Productions Ltd v Hamilton* [1982] ICR 114, [1982] IRLR 102, HL. Thus it cannot supply the unlawful means in an action by someone else; this used to be stated expressly by s. 13(3)(a) of the Trade Union and Labour Relations Act 1974, but that was repealed by the Employment Act 1980, s. 17(8).

13 Originally duress in contract law only covered threats of violence, but was widened to economic duress; see *North Ocean Shipping Co Ltd v Hyundai Construction Co Ltd* [1979] QB 705, [1978] 3 All ER 1170; *Pao On v Lau Yiu Long* [1980] AC 614, [1979] 3 All ER 65, PC; *Syros Shipping Co SA v Elaghill Trading Co* [1981] 3 All ER 189; *B & S Contracts and Design Ltd v Victor Green Publications Ltd* [1984] ICR 419, CA; *CTN Cash and Carry Ltd v Gallagher Ltd* [1994] 4 All ER 714, CA.

14 [1982] 2 All ER 67, [1982] ICR 262, HL, noted (1982) 45 MLR 556; see Sterling 'Actions for duress, seafarers and industrial disputes' (1982) 11 ILJ 156.

15 Although cf. *Dimskal Shipping Co SA v International Transport Workers' Federation, The Evia Luck (No 2)* [1992] ICR 37, [1992] IRLR 78, HL.

Relations (Consolidation) Act 1992, section 219 are not directly applicable, those immunities can be used *indirectly* to draw the line, the reasoning being that it would be contrary to Parliament's intention to hold voidable for duress actions which, had a suit been pleaded in tort, would have been covered by the statutory immunities. Thus, if an action would have been immune from a suit in tort, it will probably not be held to amount to economic duress. The majority went on to hold that the actions of the ITWF in fact would not have come within the statutory immunity, and so the plaintiffs could recover the money paid over by them. One possible problem with this approach (which certainly seems logical, given that economic duress has to be applied to industrial relations at all) is that the scope of the immunities may itself be subject to change by legislation and case law, and when this happens it will presumably also lead to a redrawing of the line on economic duress, a doctrine whose full effect in this context remains to be worked out.

The second possible development is the extension of the tort of inducement of breach of contract to other situations which involve the violation of legal rights, and in particular to inducement of breach of statutory duty[16]. The basis for the new tort was laid by the Court of Appeal in *Meade v London Borough of Haringey*[17] a case concerning the legality (under the Education Act 1944) of a decision by a local authority to close its schools because of strike action by caretakers and ancillary staff. In the course of their judgments, both Lord Denning MR and Eveleigh LJ stated obiter that it was tortious for the union to induce the local authority to be in breach of its statutory duty, and moreover that such tortious action would not be covered by the statutory immunities. The existence of the tort was subsequently confirmed by the Court of Appeal in *Associated British Ports v TGWU*[18], but with the important caveat that the statutory duty in question must be independently actionable[19]. The tort of inducement of breach of statutory duty could be of particular significance in the public sector, where employers are more likely to be under a statutory duty to provide and maintain goods or services, not least because there is no statutory immunity covering it.

The third possible development is of more general application, and concerns the central question of what amounts to unlawful means for present purposes. As seen above, while there is no specific immunity for the tort of interference with trade or business, in practice there may be an *indirect* immunity if the means adopted (e.g. inducing a breach of contract) are covered by an immunity and are therefore not unlawful[20]. An obvious way of outflanking this indirect immunity is by the development of types of unlawful means which are *not* themselves covered by an immunity. One such development was canvassed by Henry J in *Barretts &*

---

16 See also *Prudential Assurance Co Ltd v Lorenz* (1971) 11 KIR 78 (inducement of breach of equitable obligation).

17 [1979] 2 All ER 1016, [1979] ICR 494, CA. See also *Associated Newspapers Group Ltd v Wade* [1979] ICR 664, [1979] IRLR 201, CA and *Barretts & Baird (Wholesale) Ltd v IPCS* [1987] IRLR 3.

18 *Associated British Ports v TGWU* [1989] 3 All ER 796, [1989] IRLR 305, CA (reversed on other grounds, [1989] 3 All ER 822, [1989] IRLR 399, HL).

19 This is a matter of construction of the statute; to be independently actionable the plaintiff will usually need to show that the statute was passed for the benefit of a class which includes him, or that he has suffered some special damage: see *Cutler v Wandsworth Stadium Ltd* [1949] AC 398, HL; *Lonrho Ltd v Shell Petroleum Co Ltd (No 2)* [1982] AC 173, [1981] 2 All ER 465, HL. For an example of such an action being specifically written into a statute, see the Telecommunications Act 1984, s. 18(6)(b), noted Carty (1984) 13 ILJ 165.

20 See n. 12, above.

Baird (Wholesale) Ltd v IPCS[1] , where fatstock officers staffing private abattoirs took industrial action in a dispute with their employers, the Meat and Livestock Commission. The abattoir owners brought proceedings for injunctions against the union and against an individual fatstock officer; as against the former, the case relied on inducement to breach of statutory duty (above), but against the latter the argument was that the officers had interfered with the plaintiff's business, the unlawful means being quite simply their own breaches of employment contracts with their employer. If such an action were accepted it would have the astonishing result that the union officials organising a strike would be immune[2] , but the individual employees could be sued by anyone affected by their action. The problem here is that it has never been authoritatively decided whether or not simple breach of contract could be unlawful means for the torts of inducement and interference[3] . Henry J was therefore driven to conclude that it was arguable that simple breach could constitute unlawful means[4] . In the event he avoided finding the fatstock officers individually liable, on the basis, first, that they lacked the necessary intention to injure the plaintiff[5] , and secondly, that the remedy sought could not be granted against the individual employee defendant because of the statutory restrictions on the enforcement of contracts of employment against employees[6] . The result of the case therefore did not cause too much consternation, but the possibility of such an argument succeeding in the future cannot be discounted[7] . Another form of unlawful means which is of potentially great practical significance is the tort of inducement of breach of statutory duty. As seen above, this tort may provide a cause of action in its own right, but there its impact is restricted by the requirement that the breach of statutory duty be independently actionable at the suit of the plaintiff. However, in *Associated British Ports v TGWU*[8] , a majority of the Court of Appeal considered that it was 'strongly arguable' that for the purposes of the tort of interference with business, a breach of statutory duty could be relied upon as unlawful means even if not actionable at the suit of the plaintiff.

1   [1987] IRLR 3, noted Simpson (1987) 50 MLR 506, Napier (1987) 46 CLJ 222, Benedictus (1987) 16 ILJ 191.
2   Assuming there had been a ballot and that it remained primary action, the officials would have the protection of what is now s. 219(1) covering their inducement of the breaches of contract by the employees; that inducement would therefore not be actionable per se, nor would it constitute unlawful means, e.g. for the tort of interference on their part.
3   Breach of contract had been held to be unlawful means for the purposes of the tort of intimidation in *Rookes v Barnard* [1964] AC 1129, [1964] 1 All ER 367, HL, but it was not decided there that the same applied to the other economic torts, where the effect could be more drastic; s. 13(3)(b) of the Trade Union and Labour Relations Act 1974 used to state 'for the avoidance of doubt' that such a breach in contemplation or furtherance of a trade dispute was not to be treated as unlawful means, but that subsection was repealed by the Employment Act 1980.
4   In so deciding (at p. 9) the judge cites Wedderburn *The Worker and the Law* (3rd edn, 1986) at p. 637 where the author pointed out this danger of the repeal of s. 13(3)(b).
5   Henry J's view that the defendant's 'predominant purpose' must be to injure the plaintiff was however doubted by the Court of Appeal in *Lonrho plc v Fayed* [1990] 2 QB 479, [1989] 2 All ER 65. See above, p. 650.
6   Now contained in the Trade Union and Labour Relations (Consolidation) Act 1992, s. 236.
7   It has been referred to as 'a time-bomb in our labour law': Davies and Freedland *Labour Law Texts and Materials* (2nd edn, 1984) p. 755. The restriction on the enforcement of contracts of employment would not, of course, apply to an action for damages (actual or threatened) against employees taking industrial action.
8   [1989] 3 All ER 796, [1989] IRLR 305, CA (reversed on other grounds, [1989] 3 All ER 822, [1989] IRLR 399, HL).

The fact that these major areas of uncertainty exist (along with the other unresolved questions relating to the nature and extent of the established economic torts, referred to earlier), and are at least capable of development, shows how deeply unsatisfactory and unpredictable our current law on industrial action is.

vi)   The golden formula

It will be obvious from the discussion so far that the golden formula is crucial in any industrial tort case for, while the wording of the immunities has been fairly watertight (particularly since 1976), they can only be relied upon when the action in question takes place 'in contemplation or furtherance of a trade dispute'; if it falls outside that, the immunities fall and, in most cases, it will be easy for the plaintiff employer to show the elements of one or more of the above torts (particularly since the disapproval of the 'strike notice' theory in *Simmons v Hoover Ltd*[9]) and on that basis claim an interlocutory injunction to stop the industrial action. Thus, a crucial first stage in an employer's action for an injunction is to consider whether the golden formula applies – if it does not, the employer will probably be successful; if it does, the immunities apply, unless they are disapplied (to use the extremely inelegant word commonly adopted in this context) by anything in sections 222–234A of the Trade Union and Labour Relations (Consolidation) Act 1992. Moreover, as will be seen later, the exemption from liability given to pickets by section 220 is also reliant upon the formula.

To be within the protection of the golden formula, two matters must be shown – there must be a 'trade dispute', and the acts in question must be 'in contemplation or furtherance' of it.

a)   Is there a trade dispute?

The statutory definition of a trade dispute is contained in section 244 of the Trade Union and Labour Relations (Consolidation) Act 1992[10]. It is defined as a dispute between 'workers[11] and their employer' which relates 'wholly or mainly to' one or more of the following[12]:

---

9   [1977] ICR 61, [1976] IRLR 266, EAT.

10   For the history of the definition, and a clear and detailed investigation of its pre-1982 form, see Simpson, ' "Trade dispute" and "industrial dispute" in British labour law' (1977) 40 MLR 16; the latter term was the one adopted in the Industrial Relations Act 1971, s. 167, which also gave a more detailed definition. On the alterations in the Employment Act 1982, see Simpson, 'A not so golden formula' (1983) 46 MLR 463 and Ewing 'Another step in the "right" direction' (1982) 11 ILJ 209. The wider pre-1982 definition is retained by s. 218 for the purposes of Part IV of the 1992 Act, in particular for defining the powers of ACAS and Courts of Inquiry (see pp. 38 and 43, above). Given that the trade dispute disqualification for the jobseeker's allowance uses yet another definition (taken from the Trade Disputes Act 1906; see p. 546, above), we are now graced (or cursed?) with three definitions of trade dispute in industrial law.

11   'Worker' is defined in s. 296 and includes an independent contractor, provided he undertakes to perform work or services personally (other than in a professional capacity); *Broadbent v Crisp* [1974] ICR 248; cf. *Writers' Guild of Great Britain v BBC* [1974] ICR 234.

12   A dispute which relates to matters occurring outside the UK qualifies as a trade dispute only if those taking action within the UK are likely to be affected by the outcome of the dispute in relation to one or more of the matters specified in section 244(1)(a)–(g): s. 244(3).

(a) terms and conditions of employment[13], or the physical conditions in which any workers are required to work;
(b) engagement or non-engagement, or termination or suspension of employment, or the duties of employment[14], of one or more workers;
(c) allocation of work or the duties of employment between workers or groups of workers[15];
(d) matters of discipline;
(e) the membership or non-membership of a trade union on the part of a worker[16];
(f) facilities for officials of trade unions; and
(g) machinery for negotiation or consultation, and other procedures, relating to any of the above matters, including recognition of a union by an employer or employer's association[17].

It is further provided in section 244(4) that there can still be a 'dispute' even if the employer in fact submits to the union's demands, so that the initial making of the demands can still be considered as within the golden formula[18].

'Trade dispute' is thus given a wide definition, capable of covering many matters such as recognition and demarcation as well as more straightforward disputes over terms and conditions of employment, and therefore the actual definition will not normally be a significant legal restriction on a union's activities, provided it acts generally within an industrial relations context. If, however, it goes outside that and engages in what, for want of a better word, might be called 'political' action, then arguably it might be outside a trade dispute. Thus, industrial action taken *purely* as a protest against Government action might be of dubious legality[19]. However, the mere fact that there is a 'political' aspect will not

13 Although 'terms and conditions of employment' is a wide phrase, there must be some limitation of it to terms which regulate the relationship between employer and employee, excluding any matters extraneous to that relationship: *Universe Tankships Inc of Monrovia v International Transport Workers' Federation* [1982] 2 All ER 67, [1982] ICR 262, HL (note that Lord Scarman and Lord Brandon, dissenting, would have given the phrase a wider connotation).

14 A trade dispute arising out of fears for jobs in a period of high unemployment (involving, for example, a demand that what work there is should be done by existing employees, not by outside contractors) was said by Lord Diplock in *Hadmor Productions Ltd v Hamilton* [1982] 1 All ER 1042, [1982] ICR 114, HL to be a classic instance of a dispute covered by head (b); the Court of Appeal had held that there was no trade dispute in such a case.

15 This covers demarcation disputes, but note that the employer must be a party to such a dispute for it to qualify under head (c) because of the general requirement that the dispute be between 'workers and their employer'; moreover that requirement means that head (c) only applies to the allocation of work between the employer's own workers – it does not apply to a dispute over reallocation of work from the employer's own workers to an outside company: *Dimbleby & Sons Ltd v NUJ* [1984] ICR 386, [1984] IRLR 161, HL.

16 While the definition of trade dispute still includes disputes over non-membership, s. 222 provides that the immunities will be withdrawn where industrial action is taken to enforce union membership; see p. 669, below.

17 Recognition disputes also came within the original definition in the 1906 Act: *Beetham v Trinidad Cement Ltd* [1960] AC 132, [1960] 1 All ER 274, PC. However, the action must clearly be connected with the recognition issue, not just an aftermath: *J T Stratford & Son Ltd v Lindley* [1965] AC 269, [1964] 3 All ER 102, HL.

18 Nullifying statements to the contrary in *Cory Lighterage Ltd v TGWU* [1973] ICR 339, [1973] IRLR 152, CA.

19 *Associated Newspapers Group Ltd v Flynn* (1970) 10 KIR 17; in *National Sailors' and Firemen's Union v Reed* [1926] Ch 536, Astbury J held that the 1926 General Strike was illegal, sed quaere (see Goodhart, (1927) 36 Yale LJ 464). In *Sherard v AUEW* [1973] ICR 421, [1973] IRLR 188, CA, at 433 and 189 respectively, Lord Denning MR stated as his opinion that a dispute between the TUC and the Government (simpliciter) would not be trade dispute. See also *Express Newspapers v Keys* [1980] IRLR 247.

remove a dispute from the statutory definition, so that anti-Government action might still be included if there is a genuine trade aspect as, for example, where the Government is a significant employer of the union's members[20], or where those members may be directly affected by Government policies in question (e.g. on questions of nationalisation or privatisation of the industry concerned[1]). Until 1982 it was possible for industrial action to qualify as a trade dispute even if the action was taken for predominantly political or more widely social reasons, as long as there was some genuine connection with terms and conditions of employment or any of the other matters in (a) to (g). This was because the wording of the trade dispute definition at that time merely required that the dispute be 'connected with' one of the listed matters, and it seemed that the connection might be relatively slight. Only if the industrial action was wholly unconnected with any of the matters would it fall outside the statutory definition. So, for example, in *BBC v Hearn*[2] a threat to disrupt the broadcasting of the Cup Final to South Africa because of the union's anti-racialist policy was restrained by the Court of Appeal since it did not constitute a trade dispute; the union's argument that there should be read into the contracts of employment a term that employees would not be required to do anything to which they had a conscientious objection (thereby making it a trade dispute over terms and conditions) was not accepted. In contrast, Lord Diplock in *NWL Ltd v Nelson*[3] showed greater willingness to allow as a trade dispute a matter of basically a political nature, provided that it has some connection with terms and conditions of employment, and can be framed in such a way.

However, the Employment Act 1982 narrowed the trade dispute definition considerably by requiring that the dispute relate 'wholly or mainly to' one or more of the listed matters, rather than simply be 'connected with' them; this has made it far more difficult to alter the legal nature of a dispute by the way a demand is phrased, and its overall effect has been to throw the industrial/political distinction into much higher relief (rather than leaving it largely fudged, as was the case under the previous wording). The importance of this can clearly be seen in *Mercury Communications Ltd v Scott-Garner*[4]. The case concerned action taken by the union representing British Telecom workers to try to prevent the successful licensing of a private company by BT ('liberalisation'). The company brought proceedings for an injunction to restrain this action. The union pleaded

20   *Sherard v AUEW* [1973] ICR 421, [1973] IRLR 188, CA.
1   *General Aviation Services (UK) Ltd v TGWU* [1974] ICR 35, [1973] IRLR 355. Section 244(2) provides that a dispute between workers and a Government Minister who is not their employer will be treated as a trade dispute with their employer where the dispute cannot be settled without the Minister's involvement or approval: see e.g. *Wandsworth London Borough Council v NASUWT* [1993] IRLR 344, CA.
2   [1977] ICR 685, [1977] IRLR 273, CA, approved by Lord Scarman in *Express Newspapers Ltd v McShane* [1980] 1 All ER 65, [1980] ICR 42, HL.
3   [1979] ICR 867, [1979] IRLR 478, HL, at 878 and 483, respectively. In *Universe Tankships Inc of Monrovia v International Transport Workers' Federation* [1982] ICR 262, [1982] IRLR 200, HL, his Lordship stressed that there must still be some connection with one of the enumerated matters, even if it was not the predominant purpose of the defendant; Lord Cross was clearly against the idea of being able to frame a dispute in such a way as to transform it into a trade dispute.
4   [1984] ICR 74, [1983] IRLR 494, CA; the judge at first instance had failed to appreciate the significance of the altered wording and had refused to grant the injunction. The decision of the Court of Appeal to grant it was seen as a significant factor in the moves towards privatisation, which could have been at risk if the union had lawfully managed to frustrate the process of liberalisation (which was, incidentally, a technical term for franchising, not a politically loaded one).

the immunity, on the basis that this was a trade dispute concerning possible job losses. However, the Court of Appeal granted the injunction on the basis that the facts did not show that fear of job losses was the major factor behind the action (particularly as there was in existence a job security agreement with BT), and that on the facts the dispute related wholly or mainly to the union's political objection to liberalisation, which was seen as a precursor to the entire privatisation of BT (that in the event followed). The case is a good illustration of the difficulties faced by the courts in attempting to determine what a particular dispute is *mainly* about, in circumstances where there are a range of factors and issues involved which are inextricably linked. In practice much is likely to turn upon the way in which the union presents the dispute to its members and to the public at large. In *Wandsworth London Borough Council v NASUWT*[5], the Court of Appeal had to decide whether industrial action by teachers which included a boycott of testing under the national curriculum was a 'trade dispute' and therefore covered by the statutory immunities. The local authority argued that the main impetus for the dispute was the objection of the union and its members to the principle of testing, so that it was not wholly or mainly related to terms and conditions, etc., but on the facts the Court of Appeal accepted the union's argument that the dispute related mainly to the increased workload on teachers in conducting the tests (a point stressed by union leaders at every turn and also emphasised in the wording of the strike ballot), and held that there was in fact a trade dispute. The Court attached 'considerable importance' to the fact that the wording of the question posed in the ballot paper referred to 'protest against the excessive workload and unreasonable imposition made upon teachers' as a result of the new national curriculum assessment and testing requirements.

The second major change to the trade dispute definition by the Employment Act 1982 was to require that the dispute be between 'workers and their employer'. Previously it was possible to have a trade dispute between workers and employers (whether or not their own employer), or workers and workers[6], and there was deemed to be a dispute involving workers if a union was a party to the dispute, even if the actual workers were not[7]. The definition was thus extremely wide on the question of parties. Since 1982, however, the wording of the definition has required the existence of a dispute 'between workers and their employer', i.e. a dispute between the employer and workers currently employed by him[8]. The aim of these changes was to reinforce the need for there to be, somewhere along

---

5   [1994] ICR 81, [1993] IRLR 344, CA.
6   Thus a demarcation dispute between two unions which did not involve the employer directly could be a trade dispute. Presumably such a dispute could still comply if one or both of the unions were to make demands on the employer relating to the performance of the work in question.
7   This was particularly important in a case where it was the union itself which had a grievance against the employer even if it did not have the backing (or, indeed, the membership) of his employees (as in the case of the ITWF in its campaign against shipowners who use flags of convenience; see *Star Sea Transport Corpn of Monrovia v Slater* [1978] IRLR 507, CA and *NWL Ltd v Nelson* [1979] ICR 867, [1979] IRLR 478, HL). The changes in the 1982 Act were particularly significant in that sort of case.
8   Trade Union and Labour Relations (Consolidation) Act 1992, s. 244(5). A dispute concerning the terms and conditions to be enjoyed by *future* workers falls outside the definition: *University College London Hospitals NHS Trust v UNISON* [1999] IRLR 31, CA; a dispute between workers and their *former* employer will however qualify as a trade dispute where their employment was terminated in connection with the dispute or the termination of employment was one of the factors which gave rise to the dispute: s. 244(5).

the line, a genuine dispute between an employer and his employees[9]. At first sight, the tightening up of the trade dispute definition to disputes between an employer and his employees might seem to outlaw all secondary action, by rendering any action other than that taken against the employer in dispute outside the definition of a trade dispute. However, this is not the case, for section 244 only defines when a trade dispute is in existence; the legality of any action away from the centre of that dispute will depend upon whether it is 'in contemplation or furtherance' of that initial dispute, and whether it is lawful under other statutory provisions, particularly the restrictions on secondary action in section 224. So, for example, if employees of employer A take action purely in support of employees of employer B who are in dispute with their own employer, the only trade dispute is that with B, but the actions of A's employees may well be in contemplation or furtherance of that dispute (see below), and therefore within the golden formula; however, their action is now likely to fall foul of the restrictions on secondary action in section 224, and will therefore be unprotected[10]. The significance of the restricted trade dispute definition is that section 224 cannot be side-stepped by arguing that a fresh trade dispute has been created whenever and wherever industrial action is taken in support of the original dispute[11].

b)   Is the action 'in contemplation or furtherance'? Swings and roundabouts

It is not enough for there to be a trade dispute; to be within the golden formula, the action actually taken must be 'in contemplation or furtherance' of it. This phrase is a term of art, well known in industrial law, but at one crucially important time in the development of our modern law it was the subject of a major division of opinion between the Court of Appeal and the House of Lords as to its proper construction. Two preliminary points should be noted. First, it does *not* just mean 'connected with'; it has a more limited meaning than that. Second, it incorporates a time element, so that the trade dispute must either be about to or likely to happen ('contemplation'), or it must already be in existence ('furtherance'); thus, action could be too far in advance of any possible dispute to be in contemplation of it[12], and action taken after the conclusion of the dispute (for example to 'punish' certain participants in it or to regain prestige for the union) might be too late to be considered in furtherance of it[13]. In *Conway v Wade*[14], Lord Shaw said:

> '... the contemplation of such a dispute must be the contemplation of something impending or likely to occur and ... [it does] not cover the case of coercive interference in which the intervener may have in his own mind

9   The effect of the limitation to a dispute between workers and their own employer can be seen from *Dimbleby & Sons Ltd v NUJ*, n. 15, above.
10   Until 1990, secondary action enjoyed the protection of the immunities if it was aimed at the first customers or first suppliers of the employer in dispute: Employment Act 1980, s. 17. The restrictions on secondary action in s. 224, introduced in 1990, remove the immunities in virtually all cases of secondary action. See p. 665, below.
11   This is confirmed by s. 224(4), which provides that an employer shall not be treated as party to a dispute between another employer and workers of that employer, and where more than one employer is in dispute with his workers, the dispute between each employer and his workers shall be treated as a separate dispute.
12   *Bents Brewery Co Ltd v Hogan* [1945] 2 All ER 570.
13   *J T Stratford & Son Ltd v Lindley* [1965] AC 269, [1964] 3 All ER 102, HL; *Stewart v AUEW* [1973] ICR 128, [1973] IRLR 57, NIRC.
14   [1909] AC 506, HL at 522. The case remains good law on this point.

that if he does not get his own way he will thereupon take ways and means to bring a trade dispute into existence ... With regard to the term "furtherance" of a trade dispute, I think that must apply to a trade dispute in existence and that the act done must be in the course of it and for the purpose of promoting the interests of either party or both parties to it.'

Given that the timing was right and there was arguably a dispute in existence about industrial matters, it was thought at one time that the immunities were so widely drafted (especially after 1976) and the golden formula so widely construed that it was almost impossible for an employer to bring legal proceedings to stop industrial action. However, in a series of cases in the late 1970s (and particularly through the 'winter of discontent' preceding the 1979 election)[15] the Court of Appeal sought to alter that (and, in so doing, alter the bounds of permissible union activity) by looking anew at the phrase 'in contemplation or furtherance of a trade dispute' and establishing three requirements for that phrase to apply to industrial action. These were that: (a) the action must be taken for the 'proper motive' of pursuing a legitimate trade object, not for some extraneous motive (such as, for example, a campaign against flags of convenience by a seamen's union; (b) the action must not be too 'remote' from the centre of the dispute; (c) the action must be capable of furthering the trade objectives of one party to the dispute (the 'objective test').

Had they been accepted by the House of Lords, these three requirements, taken together, would have substantially narrowed the meaning of the phrase 'in contemplation or furtherance of a trade dispute', and enabled the judges to take a more active role in deciding what was and what was not within the golden formula. However, the Court of Appeal's innovations were very quickly set at nought when appeals were taken to the House of Lords, and all three requirements were disapproved[16], the House of Lords confirming in no uncertain terms that the question whether a person acts in contemplation or furtherance of a trade dispute is a subjective one which must be decided in the light of the intentions and beliefs of the actors; if a person has a genuine and honest belief that his actions will further the interests of one party to the dispute, the fact that those actions, considered objectively, are not reasonably capable of furthering the dispute will be relevant only in so far as it casts doubt on the genuineness of that person's subjective belief. In the words of Lord Scarman in *Express Newspapers Ltd v McShane*:

'It follows therefore that, once it is shown that a trade dispute exists, the person who acts, but not the court, is the judge of whether his acts will further the dispute. If he is acting honestly, Parliament leaves to him the choice of what to do. I confess that I am relieved to find that this is the law. It would be a strange and embarrassing task for a judge to be called upon to review the tactics of a party to a trade dispute and to determine whether in the view of the court the tactic employed was likely to further or advance

15 *Beaverbrook Newspapers Ltd v Keys* [1978] ICR 582, [1978] IRLR 34, CA; *Star Sea Transport Corpn of Monrovia v Slater, The Camilla M* [1978] IRLR 507, CA; *Associated Newspapers Group Ltd v Wade* [1979] ICR 664, [1979] IRLR 201, CA; *Express Newspapers Ltd v McShane* [1979] ICR 210, [1979] IRLR 79, CA.

16 *NWL Ltd v Nelson* [1979] ICR 867, [1979] IRLR 478, HL (disapproving the 'proper motive' requirement); *Express Newspapers Ltd v McShane* [1980] ICR 42, [1980] IRLR 35, HL (disapproving the objective test); *Duport Steels Ltd v Sirs* [1980] ICR 161, [1980] IRLR 116, HL (disapproving the 'remoteness' test).

that party's side of the dispute … It would need very clear statutory language to persuade me that Parliament intended to allow the courts to act as some sort of backseat driver in trade disputes[17].'

The result of these three House of Lords decisions was thus to negative completely the developments brought about by the activism of the Court of Appeal, and to establish clearly a subjective and pro-union interpretation of the phrase 'in contemplation or furtherance' of a trade dispute. That interpretation is still valid, and consequently this phrase is no longer a major limitation on the immunities; theoretically, it remains a stage in an action where it has to be established whether the immunities apply, but it is not normally an important hurdle for the defendant union or union official, except possibly in a rare case where the acts complained of bore no genuine relationship to a dispute whatsoever[18] or where there was no relationship in time between the acts and an existing dispute[19].

The developments in the Court of Appeal had, however, been very much in line with the political approach to industrial disputes of the incoming Conservative Government in 1979[20], and not surprisingly the re-establishment and strengthening of the previous law by the House of Lords was not to the Government's liking. The Government's response was to introduce into the 1980 Employment Bill a complicated provision (the notorious section 17, discussed below), which sought to reinstate much the same position as had been reached by the Court of Appeal, using much the same devices – in effect a statutory 'remoteness' test. However, crucially that section operated by imposing *additional* requirements, not by amending the phrase 'in contemplation or furtherance', which remains as the House of Lords left it. Ironically, section 17 was itself repealed by the Employment Act 1990 and replaced with an even narrower provision[1] which takes the restrictions on secondary industrial action considerably further than the Court of Appeal had proposed in those controversial cases a decade earlier.

4   RESTRICTIONS ON THE STATUTORY IMMUNITIES[2]

Even if industrial action passes the tests considered so far and thereby qualifies for protection under one of the statutory immunities, the final stage[3] in this involved progression is that it may still be rendered illegal and restrainable if it falls within one of the categories of industrial action from which the immunities

---

17   Ibid., at 64 and 78, respectively.

18   For example, where a defendant acted purely maliciously; *Express Newspapers Ltd v McShane* did retain a residual requirement that a defendant's purpose (whatever it might be in connection with the dispute) must be genuine and honest; if no reasonable person would have thought the acts in question capable of furthering the dispute, that may as a matter of evidence only call into question the defendant's bona fides.

19   See the dictum from *Conway v Wade* (see n. 14, above) which appears to be still good law.

20   Indeed, in the light of them, the Employment Bill of 1980 (as originally published) did not propose to alter the law on the immunities as the Court of Appeal appeared to have achieved the Government's objectives by its re-interpretation of the golden formula.

1   Now contained in s. 224 of the Trade Union and Labour Relations (Consolidation) Act 1992.

2   See Auerbach *Legislating for Conflict* (Oxford, 1992).

3   This means the final stage in theory: in practice it may be obvious in a particular case that (a) the action is prima facie tortious and that (b) the statutory immunities are applicable, in which case arguments may be almost entirely upon this 'final' point.

have been removed by the legislation introduced since 1980. The picture is a particularly complicated one, as there are now no fewer than seven separate circumstances where the immunities will be withdrawn; in some cases this will be on the grounds of the *scope* of the industrial action, as in the case of unlawful secondary action (s. 224) and (in part at least) unlawful picketing (s. 220(3)); in others it will be because the industrial action is taken for what is declared to be an impermissible *reason*, e.g. action to enforce union membership (s. 222), action taken because of the dismissal of unofficial strikers (s. 223), and pressure to impose union recognition requirements (s. 225); and, finally the immunities will be removed where the union has failed to comply with the mandatory *procedures* for official industrial action, e.g. where official action is taken without the support of a ballot (s. 226), or the union fails to give the requisite strike notice to employers (s. 234A). These are now considered.

i) Secondary action

Since 1980, the statutory immunities have been severely curtailed in the case of 'secondary action', i.e. action which is taken against an employer other than the employer in dispute (sometimes referred to as 'sympathy' or 'solidarity' action), reflecting the previous Conservative Government's belief that if trade unions must take industrial action at all, that action should be restricted to the employer in dispute, and not extended to other employers at one stage removed from the employer in dispute. The original restrictions on secondary action were contained in the notorious (and now repealed) section 17 of the Employment Act 1980[4], which attempted to strike a balance between, on the one hand, the interests of employers not party to the dispute to be protected from industrial action which does not directly concern them and, on the other, the desire of those taking industrial action to increase the pressure on the employer in dispute by widening their action to take in employers with a close relationship with that employer. Section 17 sought to achieve this by withdrawing the immunities in all cases of 'secondary action' as defined (see below), but then providing for three situations (the so-called 'gateways to freedom') in which secondary action was lawful, so that the immunities continued to apply. These were, first, where the purpose of the secondary action was to prevent or disrupt the supply of goods or services between the employer in dispute and his immediate customers or suppliers (the 'first customer/first supplier' exception); secondly, where the purpose of the secondary action was to prevent or disrupt the supply of goods or services during the dispute between an associated employer[5] of the employer in dispute and that associated employer's immediate customers or suppliers, where those goods or services were in substitution for those which would otherwise have been supplied to or by the employer in dispute (the 'associated employer' exception); and thirdly, where the secondary action was done in the course of peaceful picketing by a worker employed by the employer in dispute picketing his own place of work, or by a trade union official lawfully attending a picket line (the picketing exception).

The first of these, the 'first customer/first supplier' exception, can perhaps best be understood as an attempt to reintroduce in legislative form the remoteness test previously evolved by the Court of Appeal, and subsequently disapproved by

---

4   On s. 17 generally, see Bercusson (1980) 9 ILJ 215 and Wedderburn (1981) ILJ 113.
5   See p. 22, above.

the House of Lords. Its effect was to allow secondary action to be taken against a direct customer or supplier of the employer in dispute, but crucially, only where the supply of goods or services was *in pursuance of a contract between them subsisting at the time of the secondary action*. Thus it was the contractual link between the employer in dispute and the employer against whom the secondary action was taken that determined whether the action was protected by section 17. Action taken by a union against a supplier of a supplier, or a customer of a customer of the employer in dispute[6], or against a person or firm with no direct connection with the employer in dispute (as in the case of purely 'sympathy' action) was outside the protection of the section. The importance of the contractual link can be seen clearly from *Merkur Island Shipping Corpn v Laughton*[7] where a ship owned by A and sub-chartered to B was blacked while in port by the ITWF because of complaints of underpayment of the crew. The blacking was achieved by persuading tugmen to refuse to let the ship out, thereby breaking their contracts of employment with their employers, the tug company. The owners sought an injunction to restrain the blacking, which was granted, and upheld by the House of Lords. The point of the case was that the employer in dispute (the owner, A) and the employer subject to the secondary action (the tug company) were not in a direct contractual relationship, since when a chartered ship docks, the contract for the use of a facility such as tugs is between the tug company and the charterer (B); thus, the requirement of a subsisting contractual relationship between the employer in dispute and the employer subject to the secondary action was not satisfied, and the protection of section 17 was not available to the union officials.

The second exception, the 'associated employer' exception, was a narrow one, only covering the type of case where, because of a dispute, production is switched by the employer in dispute (employer A) to another employer within the same group (employer B); supplies relating to that switched production to or from employer B remained a valid target, even though the dispute was actually with employer A. However, for this exception to apply there was a clear requirement that the production must have been switched; it did not apply simply because the two employers were associated. This was illustrated by *Dimbleby & Sons Ltd v NUJ*[8] where the union was in (long-standing) dispute with T. Bailey Foreman Ltd and objected to the plaintiffs (local newspaper publishers) contracting to have their printing done by that company; they therefore took industrial action against the plaintiffs to prevent copy from being sent for printing. However, the problem then arose that in fact the printing contract was not with T. Bailey Foreman Ltd, but rather with TBF (Printers) Ltd, an associated company. As, however, there had been no switching of production, the associated employer exception did not apply and so, as the employer in dispute (T. Bailey Foreman Ltd) and the employer subject to the secondary action (the plaintiffs) were not in direct contractual relations, the action was unlawful secondary action and so illegal[9].

---

6   As, for example, on the facts of *Associated Newspapers Group Ltd v Wade* [1979] ICR 664, [1979] IRLR 201, CA and *Express Newspapers Ltd v McShane* [1980] 1 All ER 65, [1980] ICR 42, HL, itself.

7   [1983] ICR 490, [1983] IRLR 218, HL, approving the decision of the Court of Appeal in a case on almost identical facts: *Marina Shipping Ltd v Laughton, The Antama* [1982] ICR 215, [1982] IRLR 20, CA.

8   [1984] ICR 386, [1984] IRLR 161, HL.

9   The union also argued that the court should lift the veil of incorporation unilaterally and declare the two companies to be in effect one and the same, but the House of Lords refused to do so.

The third exception, the 'picketing' exception, was necessary in order to prevent the immunity for peaceful picketing[10] being rendered worthless as a result of the secondary 'ripple' effect which picketing activity is likely to have on commercial contracts. So, for example, where pickets lawfully attending outside their place of work in pursuance of a dispute with their employer, employer A, turn away lorries carrying supplies from B (thereby inducing B's driver to break his contract of employment and interfering with B's commercial supply contracts), there would be an immunity under the *first* exception if there was an existing supply contract for those goods between A and B; but if there was no such contract, or if the lorry in fact belonged to C, a haulage contractor, so that the pickets could be said to have interfered with the haulage contract between B and C (to which A is *not* a party), that action would not be protected under the first exception. Provided the pickets were employed by the employer in dispute and remained within the scope of the immunity for peaceful picketing, the third exception prevented such action from being illegal.

The provisions in section 17 proved to be exceptionally difficult and controversial in practice[11]. As the *Merkur Island Shipping Corpn* case (above) showed, a union had to be careful about the exact contractual relations involved if it were to avoid liability under section 17; and the *Dimbleby* case showed that it had to be equally careful about the exact corporate organisation of the employers concerned. Indeed, it proved all too easy for an employer to render union action unlawful under section 17 by the device of creating a 'buffer' organisation (such as an associated employer) between itself and its customers or suppliers, thereby breaking the contractual nexus which was necessary for the first exception to operate[12]. On the other hand, there were those who argued that secondary action should never be protected, and that 'there is no good reason why employers who are not party to a dispute should be at risk of having industrial action organised against them'[13]. In the event the Conservative Government were persuaded by the latter view; the Employment Act 1990 repealed section 17 and replaced it with a far more restrictive provision (now contained in section 224 of the Trade Union and Labour Relations (Consolidation) Act 1992), which removes the statutory immunities in all cases of secondary action[14] other than that occurring in the course of 'lawful picketing'[15] (i.e. within what was formerly the third exception).

10 Now contained in the Trade Union and Labour Relations (Consolidation) Act 1992, s. 220. The immunity for picketing is discussed at p. 691, below.
11 The section was described by Lord Denning in the Court of Appeal in *Hadmor Productions Ltd v Hamilton* [1981] ICR 690, [1981] IRLR 210, as 'the most tortuous section I have ever come across'; the discussion of s. 17 in the Court of Appeal (whose decision was reversed by the House of Lords, [1982] ICR 114, [1982] IRLR 102, HL), is best tactfully forgotten as being, at best, completely wrong and, at worst, incomprehensible.
12 This happened in the dispute between News International and the print unions: Ewing and Napier 'The Wapping dispute and labour law' (1986) 45 CLJ 285.
13 See the Green Paper *Removing Barriers to Employment* (Cm. 655, 1989), para. 3.10; ironically, the complexity of s. 17 was one of the justifications advanced in the Green Paper for its repeal (para. 3.10).
14 Under s. 17, the immunities were only removed where a person had induced a breach of or interfered with the performance of a *commercial* contract (or threatened to do so) by the use of secondary action; under the post-1990 provisions, the immunities are removed from the secondary action *itself*, whether or not that action results in breach or interference with commercial contracts.
15 Defined in s. 224(3) as peaceful picketing within the meaning of s. 220 by a worker employed (or last employed) by the employer in dispute or by a trade union official lawfully attending the picket line.

Section 224(2) provides that there is 'secondary action' in relation to a trade dispute when a person:

(a) induces another to break a contract of employment[16] or interferes or induces another to interfere with its performance; or

(b) threatens that a contract of employment under which he or another is employed will be broken or its performance interfered with, or that he will induce another to break a contract of employment or to interfere with its performance,

and the employer under the contract of employment is not the employer party to the dispute.

The gist of the definition is that to be secondary action the action must be directed against an employer *who is not a party to the trade dispute* and, moreover, must involve *interference with the contracts of employment* of that employer. Action which is in fact aimed at the employer in dispute, but which causes loss to that employer's customers or suppliers (i.e. 'primary action'[17] which has what might be termed secondary *effects*) is not 'secondary action' within the meaning of the section, and the legality of such action will be decided on ordinary principles[18]. One way of evading the restrictions on secondary action might have been for a union which was in dispute with employer A, but which wished to increase the pressure on employer A by taking action against employer B, to create a *fresh* trade dispute with B, and so avoid the potential application of the restrictions on secondary action. However, as seen above, the redrafting of the definition of 'trade dispute' by the Employment Act 1982 made this much more difficult, as the dispute with B would have to 'relate wholly or mainly' to the terms and conditions, etc., of the employees of B; simply acting in sympathy with, or promoting the cause of, A's employees would not be enough to generate a new trade dispute with B, so that the only dispute would be between the union and employer A, and any action against employer B would have to be judged according to section 224[19].

The result of the tightening of the restrictions on secondary action in 1990 is that, even more than before, the scope of lawful industrial action will be determined by the corporate structure of the employer in dispute[20]; and the refusal of the courts to lift the corporate veil means that action taken against another employer, even one in the same group as (or otherwise closely related to) the employer in dispute will not be covered by the statutory immunities, unless it is possible to identify a separate trade dispute with that employer.

ii)   Unlawful picketing

The second removal of the immunities occurs under section 219(3) of the Trade Union and Labour Relations (Consolidation) Act 1992, which removes all the

16   S. 224(6) adopts a wide definition of 'contract of employment' which includes self-employed and freelance workers, and others who personally do work or perform services for another.

17   As defined in s. 224(5).

18   See, for example, *Hadmor Productions Ltd v Hamilton* [1982] ICR 114, [1982] IRLR 102, HL.

19   Note also s. 224(4), which provides that for the purposes of the section an employer shall not be treated as party to a dispute between another employer and workers of that employer.

20   Cf. the obvious implications here of the break-up of the public utilities and the creation of NHS trusts.

section 219 immunities from acts done in the course of picketing falling outside the scope of the picketing immunity conferred by section 220[1]. Those whose attendance is not lawful within section 220 enjoy no immunity whatsoever for acts done in the course of picketing. As will be seen, many of the potential liabilities of pickets attract no immunity anyway (e.g. liability for trespass or nuisance), but picketing activity is also very likely to involve the commission of torts such as inducement of breach of contract and interference with trade or business. Normally such liability would be covered by the immunities in section 219; however, one of the aims of the Employment Act 1980 was to curb secondary picketing and to allow employers affected by it to bring actions to stop it. Accordingly, section 219(3) limits the immunities (in relation to the tortious effects of the picketing) to attendance rendered lawful by the 'narrow but real' immunity in section 220, and section 220(1) confines that picketing immunity to attendance *at or near a picket's own place of work*. The combined effect is that any picketing activity other than at the picket's own place of work which has tortious effects is deprived of the immunities and may be restrained by injunction.

iii) Action to enforce union membership

In an attempt to ensure that the stringent rules on the closed shop were not outflanked by practical measures designed to produce *de facto* requirements of union membership (in particular the use of 'contract compliance' by Labour-controlled local authorities to pressurise contractors into employing only union labour), the Conservative Government introduced in the Employment Act 1982 a series of restrictions on union membership requirements in commercial contracts. Thus, any term or condition of a contract for the supply of goods or services which requires that some or all of the work to be done under that contract should be done only by members of a trade union (or of a particular trade union) is rendered void[2], and it is unlawful to refuse to deal with a supplier of goods or services (for example, by the termination of a contract or the refusal to accept tenders or to enter a contract in the first place), on the grounds that the work under the contract would be done by non-union members[3]. Similar restrictions apply to contract terms requiring recognition of a trade union, and to a refusal to deal with a supplier of goods or services on the grounds of non-recognition of trade union[4]. The aim of these measures was to outlaw discrimination against employers employing non-union labour[5]. However, there remained the possibility that unions might seek to put industrial pressure on unsympathetic employers to attain these goals by taking or threatening to take industrial action,

1 See p. 691, below.
2 Trade Union and Labour Relations (Consolidation) Act 1992, s. 144. The restriction also applies to a requirement that the work be done by *non*-members of a trade union or of a particular trade union.
3 Ibid., s. 145. Failure to comply will be a breach of statutory duty, actionable at the suit of an aggrieved person.
4 Ibid., ss. 186 and 187; see p. 671, below.
5 Lewis and Simpson 'Disorganising industrial relations' (1982) 11 ILJ 227; Evans and Lewis 'Labour clauses: from voluntarism to regulation' (1988) 17 ILJ 209. The Conservative Government's opposition to the use of 'contract compliance' is also reflected in the Local Government Act 1988, s. 17, which bans the use of contract compliance by local authorities for the advancement of 'non-commercial' purposes, although s. 18 allows a certain measure of contract compliance by authorities seeking to discharge their duties under the Race Relations Act 1976, s. 71, to counteract racial discrimination.

and so the 1982 Act[6] withdrew the statutory immunities from action aimed at inducing an employer to act in contravention of the above restrictions; thus, for example, not only could an excluded tenderer sue the employer for failure to permit him to tender because of his employment of non-union labour, but he could also sue a union that had induced the employer to exclude him[7].

However, the relevant provisions then go considerably further, beyond issues of contract compliance, because section 222(1) of the Trade Union and Labour Relations (Consolidation) Act 1992 withdraws the immunities where the reason for the industrial action is the fact or belief that a particular employer (a) 'is employing, has employed or might employ a person' who is not a member of a trade union[8], or (b) 'is failing, has failed or might fail to discriminate against such a person'. This sweeping provision was introduced by the Employment Act 1988 as part of the attack on the closed shop[9], but while the main target of the 1988 Act was to outlaw industrial action taken in defence of a closed shop, in fact it went a great deal further by removing the immunities from *all* industrial action taken for reasons of non-union membership, irrespective of whether there is a closed shop in operation. By so doing it could be said to have fundamentally altered the boundaries of a lawful trade dispute, by outlawing industrial action on a matter which had previously been regarded as a legitimate basis for a dispute[10].

iv) Action taken because of the dismissal of unofficial strikers

As one of a series of measures designed to discourage unofficial industrial action, the Employment Act 1990 removed the right of those taking part in such action to complain of unfair dismissal[11]. In a related move, section 223 of the Trade Union and Labour Relations (Consolidation) Act 1992 aims to discourage a collective response to such dismissals by removing the statutory immunities where the reason (or *one* of the reasons) for the industrial action is the fact or belief that an employer has dismissed an employee taking part in unofficial industrial action. This will be the case even where the action in question has the support of a ballot. The result is that any industrial action taken by a union in support of members dismissed for taking part in unofficial action will be unprotected by the statutory immunities.

---

6   See now the Trade Union and Labour Relations (Consolidation) Act 1992, s. 222(3).
7   The torts of interference with contract or interference with trade or business might be particularly significant here.
8   Whether the person in question is not a member of any trade union or of a particular trade union or of one of a number of particular trade unions: s. 222(5).
9   There used to be a similar provision in s. 14 of the 1982 Act, but it only applied to action against employer A taken in order to impose a union-labour-only requirement on a *third party*, employer B (by disrupting commercial supplies between A and B). It did not apply to action in support of union membership taken *directly* against B. The provision introduced by the 1988 Act is stronger, in that it outlaws *all* industrial action aimed at establishing or preserving a closed shop, whether taken against A or B.
10   Cf. the trade dispute definition in s. 244, which still includes in subs. (1)(e) a dispute relating to 'a worker's membership *or non-membership* of a trade union'. See p. 658, above.
11   See p. 637, above, and the Green Paper, *Unofficial Action and the Law*, Cm. 821, 1989.

v) Pressure to impose union recognition requirements

In parallel with the restrictions on union *membership* requirements discussed above, the Employment Act 1982 introduced a similar set of restrictions on union *recognition* requirements in contracts for the supply of goods or services, and made it unlawful to refuse to deal with a supplier of goods or services on the grounds that the supplier does not or is not likely to recognise, negotiate or consult with a trade union[12]. Section 225 of the Trade Union and Labour Relations (Consolidation) Act 1992[13] removes the statutory immunities from industrial action taken to impose a union recognition requirement, so that action aimed at inducing an employer to breach any of the above restrictions (for example, by inserting a term requiring union recognition in a commercial contract) will be unprotected. That section also withdraws the immunities from industrial action taken against employer A which interferes with the supply of goods or services between that employer and the supplier, employer B (or can reasonably be expected to do so), where the reason or one of the reasons for the action is the fact or belief that the employer B does not or might not recognise, negotiate with or consult with one or more trade unions. This is similar to the restriction in section 222 on industrial action to enforce union membership, but with the important difference that in that context the immunities are withdrawn from *all* action to enforce union membership, whereas here only action aimed at securing recognition, etc., by a *third party* employer is affected.

vi) Action without the support of a ballot

Unquestionably the most impenetrable part of the labyrinth of legal requirements facing a union organising industrial action is the need to hold a secret ballot before taking official industrial action. Section 226 of the Trade Union and Labour Relations (Consolidation) Act 1992 provides[14] that the immunities in section 219 do not apply where an act is 'done by a trade union'[15] to induce a person to take part (or continue to take part) in industrial action[16], unless the industrial action has the support of a ballot. Thus, the action could in all other respects be perfectly lawful (i.e. within the immunities and lawful under heads i) to v) above), but be rendered immediately unlawful if there is no ballot, or there is a ballot but it does not meet the detailed statutory requirements[17]. Where

12   See now the Trade Union and Labour Relations (Consolidation) Act 1992, ss. 186 and 187.

13   Similar restrictions on the use of industrial pressure to enforce union membership are contained in s. 222. See p. 669, above.

14   Section 62 of the 1992 Act gives a trade union member the right to insist on a secret ballot before his union induces him to take official industrial action; the same ballot is capable of satisfying both sets of requirements: see p. 611, above.

15   I.e. the immunities are removed only from *official* industrial action; see p. 696, below. One very important consequence of the extension of the statutory vicarious liability test in 1990 to cover all officials and committees is that *most* industrial action will now be prima facie 'official', and will therefore need the support of a valid ballot if the immunities are to apply.

16   This is not defined for present purposes. For its interpretation in the context of dismissal of those taking part in industrial action, see p. 640, above.

17   The mandatory nature of the balloting requirements means that they still apply even if the union physically cannot comply with them; this may be the case with a purely federal union which has no individual members to ballot – according to *Shipping Co Uniform Inc v ITWF* [1985] ICR 245, [1985] IRLR 71 that is irrelevant and the immunities are still removed for failure to ballot.

the immunities are removed the full weight of the common law liabilities will be restored, and so anyone suffering loss or damage through a tort committed by the union could sue, even ordinary customers or suppliers of the employer in dispute[18]; until recently, the range of potential plaintiffs was restricted by the (probable) requirement that the defendant must have intended to injure the plaintiff, but under the 'Citizen's Right' introduced by the Trade Union Reform and Employment Rights Act 1993, a person has the right to seek an injunction restraining unlawful official industrial action where that action affects, or is likely to affect, the supply of goods or services to that person, irrespective of whether that person could bring an action in tort in his or her own right[19].

The balloting provisions were originally introduced in the Trade Union Act 1984, and were heavily amended by the Employment Acts 1988 and 1990 and the Trade Union Reform and Employment Rights Act 1993. In the White Paper, *Fairness at Work*, the new Labour Government signalled its intention to simplify the law on industrial action ballots, which it described as 'unnecessarily complex and rigid'[20], and invited suggestions on how this should be done. The Employment Relations Act 1999 subsequently enacted a series of changes to the balloting provisions, relaxing the requirements in several important respects[1]. These changes are considered below, but one of them is worth highlighting here, for it could have an impact on the way in which the law is used in industrial disputes. As will be seen below, the primary objective of a plaintiff in an industrial dispute case is usually to secure an injunction to stop the industrial action, and the complexity of the balloting requirements can provide ample scope for the employer's counsel to argue that there has been some technical infringement which justifies the granting of an injunction[2]. It is therefore important that the 1999 Act makes express provision for certain small[3] accidental failures in the conduct of the ballot to be disregarded[4]. The statutory dispensation is however restricted to certain types of failure (e.g. in relation to entitlement to vote and the supply of ballot papers); and given that under the old law a court might on occasion be persuaded to exercise its discretion against granting an injunction where the infringement was very minor or technical[5], it is unclear whether this change will have a significant impact on the practice of the courts in this area.

The Code of Practice on Industrial Action Ballots and Notice to Employers[6] gives guidance as to 'desirable practices' in relation to industrial action ballots.

---

18   See for example *Falconer v ASLEF and NUR* [1986] IRLR 331 (p. 649, above). Since the withdrawal of immunity is so immediate and so total, the only defence a union will have might be that no tort was committed in the first place; the existence of the strike-ballot laws may therefore have the effect of reawakening interest in the exact (?) definitions of the various, protean, economic torts.

19   Trade Union and Labour Relations (Consolidation) Act 1992, s. 235A; see p. 703, below.

20   Cm. 3968 (1998), para. 4.26.

1   Employment Relations Act 1999, Sch. 3, in force from 18 September 2000.

2   The use of injunctions in industrial cases is considered below at p. 699.

3   I.e. on a scale which is unlikely to affect the result of the ballot.

4   Trade Union and Labour Relations (Consolidation) Act 1992, s. 232B.

5   See e.g. *RJB Mining (UK) Ltd v National Union of Mineworkers)* [1997] IRLR 621; *British Railways Board v National Union of Railwaymen* [1989] ICR 678, [1989] IRLR 349, CA.

6   Revised in 1995 to take account of the new legislation in 1992 and 1993. See Simpson (1995) 24 ILJ 337. At the time of writing, the Government had issued a consultation document on a draft revised Code, designed to reflect the changes made by the 1999 Act and to make the Code 'easier to understand and more concise'. The discussion in the text refers to the 1995 Code.

As with previous Government-produced codes, it is a curious (and possibly objectionable) combination of a) useful advice as to the application of the statutory rules on balloting, on such matters as defining the constituency, the content of voting papers, unlawful interference and accurate counting, and b) an attempt at back-door legislation, adding requirements and practices which are not to be found in the statute. It is this second function that is open to criticism. Several recommendations of earlier versions of the Code have now found their way into law (for example, those relating to postal balloting and independent scrutiny), but there are still a number of areas in which the Code goes considerably further than the actual statutory requirements. So for example, the Code states that an industrial action ballot should not take place until any agreed procedures which might lead to the resolution of the dispute without the need for industrial action have been completed, or, where no such procedures are available or they have been exhausted, consideration has been given to resolving the dispute by other means, including seeking assistance from ACAS[7]; a union should only hold an industrial action ballot if it is contemplating authorising or endorsing industrial action (i.e. a ballot should not be used for purely tactical purposes), and only if the ballot (if properly conducted) would be capable of protecting the union against legal proceedings for organising the industrial action[8]; even after a vote in favour of industrial action, the union 'should consider all options other than authorising or endorsing industrial action as a means of resolving the dispute or potential dispute which led to the ballot being held'[9]; and a union should consider delaying any call for industrial action following a ballot until it has obtained the scrutineer's report on the ballot[10]. The legal difficulty is to see how, if at all, these purported extensions to the balloting rules in the Code could have any legal effect, since (although the Code is of course admissible in legal proceedings) the relevant statutory provisions do not require ballots to be 'in accordance with good industrial relations practice', nor do they use phrases such as 'fairness' or 'equity or the substantial merits of the case' which could be used as a legislative peg upon which to hang the Code's suggestions. Instead, they simply lay down detailed requirements for a valid ballot. The result is that either the union satisfies the Acts' requirements or it does not; failure to comply with one of the Code's extensions (as opposed to its advice as to the interpretation of one of the Act's substantive provisions, e.g. on defining the constituency) seems to be neither here nor there. To take one example, there appears to be no way that a failure to exhaust agreed procedures (strongly suggested by the Code, but not required by the Acts) could possibly render the ballot legally ineffective if it was otherwise properly conducted under the precise requirements of the statutory provisions. Furthermore, the exhortation not to use a ballot for tactical purposes flies in the face of industrial relations experience, which is that a positive ballot result has increasingly come to be seen by unions as an effective way of

---

7   Para. 8.
8   Para. 9. The implication is that a ballot should not be used to determine the level of support among members for industrial action falling outside the statutory immunities (e.g. secondary action, or action to support an employee dismissed while taking part in industrial action). Sed quaere?
9   Para. 58.
10   Para. 62. This would be particularly onerous in view of the strictly limited life-span of ballots, and the need to give the employer seven days' notice of the commencement of industrial action.

demonstrating collective strength, thereby improving a union's negotiating position[11].

a)   Entitlement to vote

The union must extend the entitlement to vote equally to 'all the members ... who it is reasonable at the time of the ballot for the union to believe will be induced to take part or ... to continue to take part in the industrial action in question, and to no others'[12]. The union must therefore be sure to define the balloting constituency carefully, for if a member is called out on strike who was denied entitlement to vote in the ballot, then the whole ballot may be invalidated and the immunity lost (subject to the new dispensation permitting small accidental failures to be disregarded)[13]. Even before the relaxation of the requirements in 1999, it had been recognised that it would be unrealistic to expect a union to achieve total compliance, and in one of the earliest cases on the strike ballot provisions the Court of Appeal held that an *inadvertent* failure to give someone the opportunity of voting (e.g. where some members are not supplied with voting papers) does not necessarily constitute a 'denial' of that person's entitlement to vote[14]. In such a case the correct approach is to ask whether the union has 'so far as is reasonably practicable' given every person who is entitled to vote a reasonable opportunity to do so[15]. Greater difficulty has arisen over the position of new members who did not join the union until after the ballot, and new employees who did not begin to work for the employer until after the ballot. In *Post Office v Union of Communication Workers*[16], Lord Donaldson suggested obiter that, de minimis apart, any call for industrial action should be limited to those who were employed by the employer and given an opportunity of voting at the time of the ballot. This was subsequently distinguished in *London Underground v RMT*[17], where the issue was whether the statutory immunities were lost because some 692 members who had joined the union since the date of the ballot were called upon to take part in the industrial action. The Court of Appeal held that the industrial action still had the support of a ballot within the meaning of section 226, because the union had balloted all those members who it was reasonable at the time of the ballot for the union to believe would be called upon to take part in the industrial action: 'The union is required to ballot those, *and only those, of its members* who *at the time of the ballot* it is reasonable to believe will be called upon to take part in the industrial action. It cannot identify future members, but even if it could it must not ballot them, since the ballot is confined to persons

---

11   In 1997, ACAS became aware of 1716 industrial action ballots, of which 1336 or nearly 78 per cent resulted in a majority vote in favour of industrial action: ACAS *Annual Report*, 1997.

12   Trade Union and Labour Relations (Consolidation) Act 1992, s. 227(1). A failure to comply will not be condoned simply because a union's complex structure makes full compliance difficult: *RJB Mining (UK) Ltd v National Union of Mineworkers* [1997] IRLR 621, QBD.

13   Ibid., s.232B; see p. 672.

14   *British Railways Board v National Union of Railwaymen* [1989] ICR 678, [1989] IRLR 349, CA.

15   This is the test in s. 230.

16   [1990] IRLR 143, CA.

17   [1995] IRLR 636, CA. Millett LJ also stated, obiter, that nothing in the statutory balloting provisions curtails a union's right to induce *non-members* to support industrial action called by the union, as those provisions are concerned exclusively with the relationship between the union and its members, and are intended for the protection of members, not the protection of the employer or the public.

who were members at the time of the ballot'[18]. This left unresolved the question of whether existing union members whose employment did not begin until after the ballot could be called upon to take part in the action. On one analysis, the balloting requirements should be held to be satisfied in such a case, since section 227(1) of the 1992 Act only requires the union to ballot those of its members who it is reasonable *at the time of the ballot* for the union to believe would be called upon to take part in the action, and in most circumstances that reasonable belief is unlikely to embrace members who were not employed by the employer in dispute at the time of the ballot. Against that, however, section 227(2) stated that the requirement in section 227(1) was not satisfied 'if any person who was a member of the trade union at the time when the ballot was held was denied entitlement to vote in the ballot'. Happily, the position was clarified by the Employment Relations Act 1999, which repealed section 227(2) and inserted a new provision in the 1992 Act which makes it clear that a union may call upon a person who was a member of the union at the time of the ballot to take part in the industrial action, unless it was reasonable at that time for the union to believe that he would be induced to take part in the industrial action[19].

The Employment Act 1988 added a further refinement to the rules on the balloting constituency by introducing a requirement of separate workplace ballots[20] where a union wishes to organise industrial action at more than one place of work, the aim apparently being to prevent a union from manipulating the outcome of a ballot by creating 'artificial' balloting constituencies, combining different (and perhaps unrelated) groups of workers together so as to ensure an overall vote in favour of industrial action. As an insistence on separate workplace ballots in every case would have been a recipe for industrial relations chaos, the 1988 Act permitted a union to hold one aggregated ballot across several workplaces where those to be balloted had some particular factor in common. The separate workplace ballot provisions, heavily criticised at the outset for their complexity, were revised in 1999 in the interests of greater clarity and simplicity (although it must be said that at first sight the redrafted provisions do not appear to have achieved either objective). It is now provided that a union may hold an aggregated ballot across more than one workplace[1] if one of the following is satisfied: (a) where each workplace concerned is the workplace of at least one member of the union who is 'affected by the dispute'[2]; (b) where the union reasonably believes that it is balloting all its members of a particular occupational description (or descriptions) who are employed by an employer (or employers) with whom the union is in dispute; or (c) where the union reasonably believes that it is balloting all its members who are employed by an employer (or employers) with whom the union is in dispute.

18 At p. 639. Millett LJ's emphasis.
19 Trade Union and Labour Relations (Consolidation) Act 1992, s. 232A.
20 See now the Trade Union and Labour Relations (Consolidation) Act 1992, ss. 228 and 228A, as substituted by the Employment Relations Act 1999, Sch. 3.
1   For these purposes, 'workplace' means, if the person works at or from a single set of premises, those premises, and in any other case, the premises with which the person's employment has the closest connection: s. 228(4). On the original (narrower) definition, which defined the place of work in terms of the premises 'occupied' by the employer, see *InterCity West Coast Ltd v RMT* [1996] IRLR 583. Under the pre-1999 provisions, it was held that the freedom to hold an aggregate ballot was not confined to situations where the different workplaces all belonged to the same employer (see *University of Central England v NALGO* [1993] IRLR 81), and this is believed still to be the case.
2   A member will be 'affected by a dispute' if, e.g., the dispute relates wholly or partly to a decision of the employer over a trade dispute matter, and the member is directly affected by that decision: s. 228A(5).

b)   The voting paper

The content of the voting paper is specified in great detail. There are four requirements: first, the voting paper must contain at least one of the two 'statutory questions', asking the voter to say, by answering 'yes' or 'no', whether he is prepared to take part in a 'strike', or in 'industrial action short of a strike'[3]. If the union contemplates taking both types of action these two questions must be put separately, and separate approval must be obtained for each type of action[4]. In *West Midlands Travel Ltd v TGWU*[5], the employers argued that where separate questions are put, the union must obtain a majority approval of all those who had participated in the voting process, including those who had abstained, and not just a simple majority in respect of each individual question on the ballot paper[6]; however, the Court of Appeal sensibly held that where separate questions are posed, one relating to strike action and the other to industrial action short of a strike, each question must be regarded as a separate matter to be voted on individually, and the result of the ballot in respect of each question must be considered separately. Secondly, the voting paper must contain a statement (a type of Government health warning?) informing members that industrial action may be unlawful. The statement was amended in 1999 to include information about the new protection against unfair dismissal during the protected period; it now reads as follows: 'If you take part in a strike or other industrial action, you may be in breach of your contract of employment. However, if you are dismissed for taking part in strike or other industrial action which is called officially and is otherwise lawful, the dismissal will be unfair if it takes place fewer than eight weeks after you started taking part in the action, and depending on the circumstances may be unfair if it takes place later.' This statement may not be qualified or commented on by anything else on the ballot paper[7], even if it is clear that the action in question does not involve a breach of contract (as, for example, in the case of withdrawal from voluntary overtime[8]). Thirdly, the voting paper must identify the person or persons authorised by the union to call upon members to take part in industrial action in the event of a vote in favour (a requirement introduced by the Employment Act 1990 to prevent union officials from jumping the gun unauthorisedly by calling on members to take industrial action before the leadership has give the go-ahead to do so – see below). Finally, the voting paper must give the name of the independent scrutineer[9]. If any of these requirements is omitted the industrial action will not be regarded as having

---

3   Overtime bans and call-out bans are to be treated as industrial action short of a strike for these purposes: Trade Union and Labour Relations (Consolidation) Act 1992, s. 229(2A), inserted by the Employment Relations Act 1999, Sch. 3 (reversing the effect of *Connex South Eastern Ltd v RMT* [1999] IRLR 249, CA).

4   *Post Office v Union of Communication Workers* [1990] ICR 258, [1990] IRLR 143, CA. Cf. *London Underground v National Union of Railwaymen* [1989] IRLR 341, noted by Simpson (1989) 18 ILJ 234, where it was held that several issues may not be rolled up in one single question where there are doubts over whether some of those issues are in fact the subject of a trade dispute; sed quaere?

5   [1994] ICR 978, [1994] IRLR 578, CA.

6   The wording of the statute is certainly ambiguous, in that s. 226(2) provides that 'the majority voting in [the] ballot' must have answered the relevant question affirmatively.

7   There does not appear to be anything to prevent a union from commenting on the statement in material enclosed with the voting paper, provided nothing appears on the voting paper itself.

8   *Power Packing Casemakers Ltd v Faust* [1983] ICR 292, [1983] IRLR 117, CA; see p. 642, above.

9   A requirement added by the Trade Union Reform and Employment Rights Act 1993, s. 20(2).

the support of a ballot, and the statutory immunities will be withdrawn. To facilitate a challenge on the ground of a defective ballot, a union is required to provide the employers of those entitled to vote in the ballot with a sample voting paper at least three days before the start of the ballot[10].

c) Conduct of the ballot

Until 1993 the requirements of a valid industrial action ballot differed significantly from those which applied to union elections and political fund ballots[11], for while ballots for either of those purposes have, since the Employment Act 1988, been required to be fully postal (i.e. ballot papers delivered and returned by post) and subject to independent scrutiny, a strike ballot could be held at the workplace[12] and was not subject to independent scrutiny. However, the requirements of postal balloting and independent scrutiny[13] were finally extended to industrial action ballots in 1993[14]. In retrospect it was perhaps surprising that workplace strike ballots survived for as long as they did, given the previous Government's well-known antipathy towards that practice. One of the reasons for their retention was the recognition that postal ballots take time to organise, and so might be inappropriate in an industrial action ballot where speed of response is often of the essence. There is also evidence to suggest that workplace balloting achieves a higher rate of participation than postal balloting[15]. However by 1993 the Government had been persuaded that fully postal voting was less susceptible to malpractice than other forms of balloting and provided the best security against interference and intimidation, and the extension of postal balloting to industrial action ballots became inevitable. There was pressure for an exception to be made in the case of ballots involving relatively few employees (the Green Paper which proposed the extension of postal balloting would not have required a postal ballot where no more than 50 members were involved[16]), but the 1993 Act made no such exception[17].

Members must be allowed to vote without interference from the union (although interference from other quarters will not invalidate the ballot), and, so far as reasonably practicable, the voting must be secret and at no direct cost to

---

10 Trade Union and Labour Relations (Consolidation) Act 1992, s. 226A(1). As a result of the 1999 Act, a union is now only required to send a sample of those voting papers which are to be sent to employees employed by that employer, not those which are to be sent only to the employees of other employers.

11 See pp. 607 and 617 respectively.

12 Although until its revision in 1995, the Code of Practice on Trade Union Ballots on Industrial Action recommended that fully postal balloting 'should be the preferred choice' (para. 20).

13 Independent scrutiny is not required in the case of a ballot involving no more than 50 members: s. 226(c). On independent scrutiny generally, see p. 610, above.

14 Trade Union Reform and Employment Rights Act 1993, ss. 17 and 20 amending the Trade Union and Labour Relations (Consolidation) Act 1992, s. 230 (postal ballots) and inserting new ss. 226B and 231B (independent scrutiny). Significantly, the 1993 Act repealed the provisions whereby unions could claim government funding for postal ballots (see p. 601).

15 See generally Undy and Martin *Ballots and Trade Union Democracy* (1984), and Leopold (1986) Ind Rels J 287.

16 *Industrial Relations in the 1990s* (Cm. 1602, 1991). See n. 13, above.

17 The only exception is for merchant seamen at sea or at a foreign port for some or all of the balloting period, who are allowed to vote on board ship or at the place where the ship is, where it is convenient for them to vote in this way: s. 230(2A), as amended by the Employment Relations Act 1999, Sch. 3.

those voting[18]. Votes must be fairly and accurately counted (although accidental errors may be disregarded if incapable of affecting the result), and the detailed results must be made known both to those voting and to their employers as soon as reasonably practicable after the holding of the ballot[19]. One particularly controversial requirement, introduced in 1993, is the need for a union to give the employers of those entitled to vote in the ballot at least seven days' notice in writing of the date of the ballot[20], the apparent aim being to enable employers to put the case against industrial action to their employees in advance of the ballot. As originally drafted, the ballot notice had to describe the employees to be balloted so that the employer 'can readily ascertain them'. During the passage of the 1993 Act, the minister sought to allay concerns that a union might be required to give the employer the names of those to be balloted (thereby increasing the risk of interference with the ballot and possible intimidation of those involved by an unscrupulous employer), declaring that he could 'envisage no circumstances' in which it would be necessary to do so[1]. However, in the first case on the notice provisions to come before the courts, *Blackpool and Fylde College v NATFHE*[2], the Court of Appeal controversially held that the union had to supply the employer with the names of those to be balloted in order to satisfy its statutory duty. In that case, the union had notified the college of its intention to 'hold a ballot of all our members in your institution'; the Court of Appeal accepted the employers' argument that this was not sufficiently precise to enable them readily to ascertain the employees involved, because they did not know which employees were in fact members of the union[3]. The incoming Labour Government gave notice of its intention to change the law to reverse the effect of this decision[4], and the law as amended in 1999 now requires the ballot notice to contain 'such information in the union's possession as would help the employer to make plans[5] and bring information to the attention of those of his employees who it is reasonable for the union to believe...will be entitled to vote in the ballot'[6]; in particular, where the union has 'information as to the number, category or work-place of the employees concerned, a notice must contain that information (at least)', but the redrafted provisions expressly state that the fact that the notice does not contain the names of any of the employees to be balloted is not a ground for holding that the notice requirements have not been met[7].

---

18   Trade Union and Labour Relations (Consolidation) Act 1992, s. 230. This means that the union must pay the postage (e.g. by providing pre-paid envelopes).
19   Ibid., ss 231 and 231A. As a result of the 1999 Act, the failure to inform some employers of the result of the ballot will no longer invalidate the whole ballot, but will merely result in the removal of the statutory immunities in relation to those employers: s. 226(3A), as amended by the Employment Relations Act 1999, Sch. 3.
20   Ibid., s. 226A, as amended by the Employment Relations Act 1999, Sch. 3. Unions must also give notice to employers before taking industrial action: see p. 680.
1   *Hansard*, House of Commons, Standing Committee F, 15 December 1992, col. 247.
2   [1994] ICR 648, [1994] IRLR 227, CA.
3   The trend away from the check-off of union subscriptions from pay has increased employer uncertainty over the level of union membership: see p. 613, above.
4   Cm. 3968 (1998), para. 4.27.
5   E.g. 'to help the employer to minimise the adverse effects of possible industrial action on his organisation, on his customers and on the general public' (Minister of State, *Hansard*, House of Lords, 16 June 1999, col. 299).
6   Trade Union and Labour Relations (Consolidation) Act 1992, s. 226A(2)(c), as amended by the Employment Relations Act 1999, Sch. 3.
7   Ibid., s. 226(3A).

d) The calling of industrial action

Where there has been a vote in favour of industrial action, that action must commence before the ballot ceases to be effective (i.e. before it reaches its statutory 'sell-by' date), otherwise the union will have to go through the whole process again[8]. An industrial action ballot normally ceases to be effective at the end of four weeks from the date of the ballot[9], but sensibly the Employment Relations Act 1999 amended the law to enable the employer and the union to agree an extension of up to four more weeks, thereby reducing pressure on a union to commence industrial action simply to prevent the ballot from becoming ineffective in circumstances where further negotiations might enable the parties to reach an agreement[10]. In *Monsanto plc v TGWU*[11], the Court of Appeal held that, provided the industrial action commences within the statutory time-limit, it may continue beyond that point, even if the union lifts the action during negotiations but then reimposes it if the negotiations prove unsuccessful, provided the dispute continues to be the same dispute as that in respect of which the original ballot was held.

Any strike call by the union in advance of the ballot will normally be fatal[12]; however, in determining whether there has been a 'call' by the union, the statutory test of vicarious liability applies[13]. This means that an unauthorised and unballoted call by, for example, a shop steward, will now be regarded as a call *by the union*, and the resulting action will consequently be denied the protection of the statutory immunities. The only way in which the union might avoid liability in such a case would be to repudiate the unauthorised call[14], but by doing so it exposes those who continue to take part in the action to the risk of selective dismissal[15]. To add to the complication, the Employment Act 1990 introduced the requirement that industrial action be called by a 'specified person'[16] (i.e. a person specified by the union on the voting paper), to prevent local officials unauthorisedly 'jumping the gun' by calling on members to take industrial action without waiting for the union leadership to decide whether or not to implement the ballot decision. If action is called by someone *other* than a specified person, that action will not be regarded as having the support of a ballot, even where there is a clear vote in favour of the action and all the other statutory requirements are satisfied. There

8   Ibid., s. 233(3)(b); 234(1).
9   See *RJB Mining (UK) Ltd v National Union of Mineworkers* [1995] IRLR 556, CA.
10   Ibid., s. 234(1), as amended by the Employment Relations Act 1999, Sch. 3; there is also a discretion in the court to extend the time-limit up to a maximum of 12 weeks from the date of the ballot where the union has been prohibited from calling or organising industrial action by a court order or an undertaking given to the court, and that order or undertaking has subsequently lapsed: ibid., s. 234(2).
11   [1987] ICR 269, [1986] IRLR 406, CA. But cf. *Post Office v Union of Communication Workers* [1990] ICR 258, [1990] IRLR 143, CA, where it was stated, obiter, that the action must continue without substantial interruption, so that a gap of nine months was considered too long; see also *Secretary of State for Scotland v Scottish Prison Officers' Association* [1991] IRLR 371 Ct of Sess.
12   Trade Union and Labour Relations (Consolidation) Act 1992, s. 233(3)(a). The prohibition on calling for industrial action before the date of the ballot is not infringed by a union recommendation to its members to vote in favour of industrial action: *Newham London Borough Council v NALGO* [1993] ICR 189, [1993] IRLR 83, CA.
13   Ibid., s. 20. See p. 696, below.
14   Ibid., s. 21. See p. 698, below.
15   Ibid., s. 237. See p. 637, above.
16   Ibid., s 233(1). The union can decide whom to specify, but the person (or description of persons) specified must come within the list of those for whom the union is deemed responsible under s. 20 (see p. 696, below).

are, however, signs that this requirement will be interpreted flexibly, and that some limited degree of delegation may be acceptable; in *Tanks and Drums Ltd v TGWU*[17], the Court of Appeal held that the section was satisfied where the specified person, the union's general secretary, authorised a district official to implement the industrial action if further negotiations with the employer the following day were not successful. Neill LJ stated that:

> 'in the field of industrial relations it would be impracticable to leave matters in such a way that there was no possibility for the exercise of judgment on the ground. Some matters must be left for the judgment of those on the ground who have to decide how and when as a matter of common sense the call for action is to be put into operation.'

However, Neill LJ also considered that a blanket delegation of authority to a local official would not be acceptable, and stressed the need for 'a close link in time between the call for the strike and the event, for example, an unsuccessful meeting which precipitates the final action'.

vii)   Notice of industrial action for employers

One of the most controversial of the reforms introduced by the Trade Union Reform and Employment Rights Act 1993 was the requirement for unions to give employers at least seven days' notice of official industrial action[18]. Apparently prompted by the disruption caused by random strikes in the public services (in particular a series of one-day strikes on the London Underground in 1989), the notice requirements apply to all types of industrial action, and across all sectors of employment. The notice must be in writing, must contain 'such information[19] in the union's possession as would help the employer to make plans and bring information to the attention of ...' the 'affected employees'[20], and must state whether industrial action is intended to be continuous or discontinuous. If the action is to be continuous, the notice must state when it is to start; if intended to be discontinuous (i.e. if the union does not intend to take action on all the days on which it could do so), the notice must specify the particular *dates* on which it is to take place. The result is that unions are no longer able to use the threat of random, discontinuous action to bring pressure to bear on employers, although there is still some potential for disruption in that, having given notice of the dates on which it intends the discontinuous action to take place, the union does not then have to call for that action to take place on all (or indeed any) of those dates. One potentially unfortunate consequence of the notice requirements in their original form was that where continuous industrial action was suspended, e.g. to allow further negotiations to take place, the union was required to give a further seven days' notice before resuming the action, which could act as a disincentive to attempts at negotiation during the action. The provisions were

---

17   [1992] ICR 1, [1991] IRLR 372, CA.
18   Trade Union and Labour Relations (Consolidation) Act 1992, s. 234A, as amended by the Employment Relations Act 1999, Sch. 3.
19   The information requirements in relation to notice of industrial action were amended by the Employment Relations Act 1999 in line with the amendments to the provisions requiring employers to be given notice of the ballot: see p. 678, above.
20   I.e. the employees of the employer whom the union intends to induce or has induced to take part, or continue to take part, in the industrial action: s. 234A(3).

therefore amended in 1999 so that where the industrial action has been suspended by joint agreement between the employer and the union, the action can be resumed after an agreed date ('the resumption date') without the need for the union to issue a fresh notice[1].

The earliest date that notice may be given is the day on which the employer is informed of the result of the ballot[2]. Given that a strike ballot normally only remains valid for four weeks *from the date of the ballot* (i.e. from the last day of voting), a further delay of seven days after disclosure of the results means that the 'window of opportunity' within which the ballot may be implemented is considerably shortened[3]. If the union fails to give the required notice the statutory immunities are withdrawn, but only as respects the employer of a person who is induced to take part in the action[4].

5 POTENTIAL CRIMINAL LIABILITY

As seen in the introduction to this chapter, criminal law does not play any significant role in the regulation of industrial action, outside the specialised law relating to picketing, and the application of the ordinary laws relating to violence and public order if a dispute gives rise to violence and disruption. Those matters are considered in the next section. Before turning to that, however, there are two contexts in which, in exceptional cases, there might be criminal liability. The first arises where employees occupy their employer's premises, for example by way of a sit-in or work-in. In civil law they become trespassers when they refuse to leave, and the employer may take civil action to regain possession of his factory[5]. However, English law has always been wary of imposing criminal sanctions for trespass, a position strengthened by the Criminal Law Act 1977, which provided that it could not be a criminal conspiracy for people to agree to commit an act which was merely tortious, such as trespass[6]. At the same time, Part II of that Act created several new trespass offences which could conceivably be committed by workers engaged in occupying the employer's premises, and in respect of which the police have powers of arrest and entry on to the property in question. Thus, it is an offence to use violence to secure entry when there is someone already on the premises[7], or to enter as a trespasser with a 'weapon of offence'[8]. In most sit-ins or work-ins, the former will not arise, as possession of the premises is usually

---

1   Ibid., s. 234A(7B), as inserted by the Employment Relations Act 1999, Sch. 3. The period of suspension may be extended by joint agreement.
2   Ibid., s. 234A(4).
3   Indeed, the Code of Practice (at para. 62) suggests that a call for industrial action following a ballot should be delayed until the union has received the scrutineer's report on the ballot, which would narrow the window of opportunity even further.
4   Ibid., s. 234A(1). Note however that in such a case the industrial action will still be regarded as an unlawful act for the purposes of the 'Citizen's Right', discussed at p. 703, below.
5   Under an expedited procedure: see RSC Ord. 113.
6   Criminal Law Act 1977, s. 1(1), overruling the decision of the House of Lords in *Kamara v DPP* [1974] AC 104, [1973] 2 All ER 1242, HL.
7   Criminal Law Act 1977, s. 6, as amended by the Criminal Justice and Public Order Act 1994, s. 72.
8   Criminal Law Act 1977, s. 8.

gained by failing to leave (or, at least, by entry by stealth)[9]; the occupiers may, however, be at risk under the latter, for many articles (even working tools) can constitute 'weapons of offence' if the person carrying them has the intention of using them to inflict injury on others. It is also an offence to resist bailiffs who are seeking to regain possession of the premises under a court order[10]. The other main trespass offence created by the 1977 Act, that of remaining in adverse possession after being requested to leave, is aimed essentially at squatting in residential property, and is therefore unlikely to be of any significance in an industrial context as it only applies where the person making the request is a 'displaced residential occupier' (or a 'protected intending occupier', as defined), which does not include a factory owner[11].

The second area of possible criminal liability is under certain remaining (and in some cases anomalous) statutory provisions creating offences which limit the freedom to take industrial action. Thus, industrial action by postal workers is of dubious legality because they may commit the offence of wilfully detaining or delaying any postal packet under the Post Office Act 1953[12], and it is possible that telecommunications workers may commit an offence if they intentionally intercept a communication in the course of its transmission[13]; likewise, there are punitive provisions in the merchant shipping legislation which may affect the legality of a strike by merchant seamen[14], and there are statutory restrictions on union membership[15] and the organisation of strike action in the police force[16], and on inducing prison officers to withhold their services or to commit breaches of discipline[17]. One further provision, dating from the Conspiracy and Protection of Property Act 1875[18] and now contained in the Trade Union and Labour Relations (Consolidation) Act 1992, section 240, makes it an offence for a person:

'... wilfully and maliciously [to break] a contract of service or hiring, knowing or having reasonable cause to believe that the probable consequences of his so doing, either alone or in combination with others, will be to endanger human life or cause serious bodily injury, or to expose valuable property, whether real or personal, to destruction or serious injury ...'

9   Indeed, once inside the occupiers could themselves be protected by s. 6, which will render criminal any attempt by the factory owner to use violence to enter to evict them! Note, however, the decision of the Scottish High Court of Justiciary that a work-in can constitute 'watching or besetting' (under the Trade Union and Labour Relations (Consolidation) Act 1992, s. 241, below) even though the people concerned are inside the premises: *Galt (Procurator Fiscal) v Philp* [1984] IRLR 156; this decision is potentially more damaging to occupations than the Criminal Law Act 1977.
10   Criminal Law Act 1977, s. 10.
11   Ibid., s. 7, as substituted by the Criminal Justice and Public Order Act 1994, s. 73.
12   Post Office Act 1953, ss. 58, 68; see *Gouriet v Union of Post Office Workers* [1978] AC 435; [1977] 3 All ER 70, HL.
13   Interception of Communications Act 1985, s. 1; see also the Telegraph Act 1863, s. 45 and the Telecommunications Act 1984, ss. 44, 45.
14   Merchant Shipping Act 1995, s. 58 (endangering a ship, life or limb) and s. 59 (disobedience at sea).
15   Police Act 1996, s. 64. A person who belonged to a union before becoming a member of a police force may continue to be a union member: ibid., s. 64(2).
16   Ibid., s. 91.
17   Criminal Justice and Public Order Act 1994, s. 127; the section operates by imposing a statutory duty owed to the Home Secretary, not by imposing criminal liability.
18   The 1875 Act also created certain offences pertinent to picketing; see p. 686, below.

This provision is potentially of great significance in industrial disputes, particularly in the context of industrial action by workers in the essential services such as nurses, doctors, firemen and ambulancemen. The penalty is small, and there appears to be no record of any prosecution under it, but it is conceivable that the main significance of such a provision could lie in its use as the basis of an application for an injunction to restrain a threatened breach of it, rather than in the possibility of prosecution directly under it. In *Gouriet v UPOW*[19] the plaintiff sought an injunction to prevent a threatened boycott of mail to South Africa, on the basis that the action would contravene the Post Office Act 1953. This was ultimately refused by the House of Lords, which reaffirmed the traditional limitation on this use of a civil law remedy to prevent anticipated breaches of criminal law – i.e. that an action may only be brought by the Attorney-General or by an individual whose private rights were about to be infringed or who would suffer 'special damage'. As the plaintiff in *Gouriet* had failed to persuade the Attorney-General to bring the action, and had brought it himself merely qua member of the general public, he did not have the necessary locus standi. An action for an injunction to restrain a threatened breach of the criminal law would, however, be open to someone who did have the necessary legal interest, and this could conceivably arise in the circumstances envisaged by section 240, e.g. where someone stands to risk personal injury or property damage as a result of a strike.

Finally, while the possibility of a lawful combination of workers constituting a criminal conspiracy has long since been removed[20], this protection does not extend to agreements to commit acts which are themselves criminal, and so if persons involved in industrial action agree among themselves to commit offences, e.g. to assault or intimidate people or destroy property, they may be prosecuted for those offences and also for criminal conspiracy[1], as in *R v Jones*[2] (the 'Shrewsbury pickets' case). However, there is an exception to this where the offence in question is a summary offence not punishable by imprisonment, as section 242 of the Trade Union and Labour Relations (Consolidation) Act 1992 provides[3] that any such offence which is committed in contemplation or furtherance of a trade dispute shall be disregarded for the purposes of the law of criminal conspiracy. Moreover, the Criminal Law Act 1977 places two significant limitations on the use of criminal conspiracy – first, it ties the penalty for conspiracy to the maximum for the crime conspired at, thus removing the criticism that conspiracy could be used (or misused) to put the penalty at large[4]; second, it requires the consent of the Director of Public Prosecutions before the prosecution may indict someone for conspiracy to commit an act which in itself is only a summary offence (e.g. intimidation)[5]. As a result of these limitations, criminal conspiracy is rarely of any relevance to industrial action in the present day.

---

19 See n. 12, above; see Feldman (1979) 42 MLR 369.
20 Originally by the Conspiracy and Protection of Property Act 1875, s. 3; see p. 628, above.
1   And perhaps, on the facts, other 'group offences' under the Public Order Act 1986, see below.
2   [1974] ICR 310, 59 Cr App Rep 120, CA.
3   Re-enacting Criminal Law Act 1977, s. 1(3).
4   Criminal Law Act 1977, s. 3. In *R v Jones*, n. 2, above, the three defendants found guilty of conspiracy to intimidate received sentences of nine months', two years' and three years' imprisonment, even though intimidation itself (a summary offence under s. 7 of the 1875 Act) then only carried three months.
5   Ibid., s. 4(1). Note, however, the Prosecution of Offences Act 1985, s. 1(6) which allows an ordinary Crown Prosecutor to exercise the DPP's functions in this respect.

6 PICKETING[6]

The act of picketing the premises of another person may not be unlawful in itself[7], but in reality it can very easily become so, either as a tort, such as public or private nuisance or trespass to the highway, or under one of several specific or general criminal offences. This is recognised in the statutory immunity for peaceful picketing during a trade dispute, now contained in the Trade Union and Labour Relations (Consolidation) Act 1992, section 220. It is necessary, therefore, to consider first the ways in which a picket may prima facie fall foul of the law and then the extent to which he is protected.

Picketing is a form of public demonstration carried on in an industrial context, and the imposition of restrictions on picketing has important civil liberties implications, particularly for freedom of assembly and freedom of speech. As was seen in the introduction to this chapter, the incorporation of the European Convention on Human Rights into English law by the Human Rights Act 1998 may well have important implications for the law affecting picketing, as the right to freedom of expression in Article 10 and the right to freedom of peaceful assembly in Article 11 could conceivably be used to challenge some of the existing legal restrictions on picketing. Indeed, even before the coming into force of the Human Rights Act, there is evidence that the courts are increasingly aware of the need to preserve these fundamental freedoms. So, for example, in *Middlebrook Mushrooms Ltd v TGWU*[8], where the plaintiffs, a firm of mushroom growers, sought an injunction restraining the union from distributing leaflets outside supermarkets supplied by the plaintiffs asking customers not to buy their mushrooms, in support of members dismissed by the plaintiffs for taking industrial action, the Court of Appeal emphasised the importance of keeping the civil law constraints on picketing within proper limits, Neill LJ stating that Article 10 should be taken into consideration 'in all cases which involve a proposed restriction on the right of free speech'[9]; similarly, in *DPP v Jones*[10], Lord Irvine LC expressed the view, obiter, that if English law did not give a right of peaceful assembly on the highway, Article 11 of the European Convention might in future require the common law to develop such a right.

---

6 See Wallington 'Policing the miners' strike' (1985) 14 ILJ 145; Auerbach 'Legal restraint of picketing: new trends; new tensions' (1987) 16 ILJ 227; Auerbach 'Injunctions against picketing' (1989) 18 ILJ 166.
7 *Hubbard v Pitt* [1975] 3 All ER 1, [1975] ICR 308, CA, per Lord Denning MR (dissenting); the majority decided the case on procedural points relating to interlocutory injunctions, not primarily upon the substantive law on picketing. See Wallington 'Injunctions and the right to demonstrate' (1976) 35 CLJ 86.
8 [1993] ICR 612, CA.
9 Ibid., at p. 620. The Court of Appeal discharged the injunction granted by the judge at first instance on the grounds that as the leaflets were directed at *customers* of the supermarkets and not at the supermarkets themselves, any interference with business was *indirect* rather than direct, and therefore required the use of unlawful means (not established on the facts) in order to be actionable.
10 [1999] 2 All ER 257, HL; see n.12, below. The case demonstrates the difficulties in store for the courts in interpreting Article 11, for Lord Slynn and Lord Hope saw no necessary conflict between the common law and the Convention on this point.

i) Potential civil liability

Picketing is not tortious per se, but in common with other forms of industrial action it is likely to involve the commission of one or more of the industrial torts discussed above, and may therefore be restrainable at the suit of the employer or some other person involved. For example, a picket who persuades a delivery driver to turn around and not to cross a picket line probably induces that driver to break his contract of employment, and may also indirectly induce a breach of (or at least interfere with) the commercial supply contracts of the driver's employer[11]. The presence of pickets may also give rise to the tort of trespass to the highway[12] or nuisance[13], and in *Thomas v NUM (South Wales Area)*[14], Scott J granted an injunction against mass picketing on the grounds of a new tort of 'harassment' (a variant of private nuisance) at the suit of working miners who were being prevented from going to work, even though they were not the owners of the land being picketed. The case also illustrates that an action can lie at the suit of people other than the employer in dispute. An injunction to prevent the unlawful picketing may have the effect of stopping the picketing altogether, or may instead impose conditions on picketing activity (e.g. on the numbers of pickets and their location; see below).

ii) Potential criminal liability

If picketing is violent, there will of course be criminal liability for e.g. assault, criminal damage and public order offences (see below), in the ordinary way, as seen most dramatically in the miners' strike of 1984/5[15]. Even if it is peaceful, however, picketing may constitute an obstruction of the highway[16], and any refusal to obey lawful police orders may constitute the offence of wilfully obstructing a police officer in the execution of his duty, contrary to the Police Act 1996, section 89. Picketing may also constitute the crime of harassment under the Protection

---

11 In *Union Traffic Ltd v TGWU* [1989] ICR 98, [1989] IRLR 127, the Court of Appeal held that the mere presence of pickets may constitute the tort of inducing breach of contract if it is clear that the presence of the pickets is intended to induce a breach of contract and it achieves its objective.

12 See *DPP v Jones* [1999] 2 All ER 457, a landmark case on the law on trespassory assemblies (p. 691, below) arising from a protest at Stonehenge, where the House of Lords held that there is a public right of peaceful assembly on the highway for any reasonable purpose, provided the activity does not obstruct the highway by unreasonably impeding the rights of others to pass and repass, and does not amount to a public or private nuisance.

13 *Hubbard v Pitt* [1975] 3 All ER 1, [1975] ICR 308, CA.

14 [1985] 2 All ER 1, [1985] IRLR 136. See Benedictus 'The use of the law of tort in the miners' dispute' (1985) 14 ILJ 176. In *News Group Newspapers Ltd v SOGAT '82 (No 2)* [1987] ICR 181, [1986] IRLR 337 Stuart-Smith J expressed obiter reservations about the invention of a tort of 'harassment' in *Thomas*, but in *Khorasandjian v Bush* [1993] QB 727, [1993] 3 All ER 669 (a non-industrial case involving the harassment of a woman by a former male friend), the Court of Appeal held that the tort does in fact exist.

15 During the course of the strike, 10,372 criminal charges were brought, including 468 for assaults of sorts, 360 for assaulting a police officer, 137 for riot, 509 for unlawful assembly, 21 for affray, 4,107 for conduct conducive to breach of the peace (Public Order Act 1936, s. 5), 1,019 for criminal damage, 352 for theft, 1,682 for obstructing a police officer, 640 for obstruction of the highway and 275 for intimidation. Subsequently, however, many of the major charges (especially those including riot) were not proceeded with.

16 Highways Act 1980, s. 137; see e.g. *Broome v DPP* [1974] 1 All ER 314, [1974] ICR 84, HL. It seems that picketing will only be an offence under the Highways Act where it involves an unreasonable use of the highway: see *Hubbard v Pitt* (n. 13, above).

from Harassment Act 1997[17], which makes it an offence for a person to pursue a 'course of conduct'[18] which amounts to harassment of another and which he knows or ought to know amounts to harassment of another[19]. Although primarily aimed at 'stalkers', the crime of harassment is clearly wide enough to apply to pickets; its significance in practice is likely to turn on the extent to which pickets are able to rely on the statutory defence 'that in the particular circumstances the pursuit of the course of conduct was reasonable.[20] '

In addition to the above, section 241 of the Trade Union and Labour Relations (Consolidation) Act 1992[1] makes it an offence for a person 'with a view to compelling[2] another person to abstain from doing or to do any act which that person has a legal right to do or abstain from doing, wrongfully and without legal authority' to:

(a) use violence to or intimidate[3] that person or his wife or children, or injure his property;

(b) persistently follow that person about from place to place[4];

(c) hide any tools, clothes or other property owned or used by that person, or deprive him of or hinder him in the use thereof[5];

(d) watch or beset[6] the house or other place where that person resides, works, carries on business or happens to be, or the approach to such house or place;

---

17 See Mullender (1998) 61 MLR 236. Section 3 of the Act provides a civil remedy for a person who is harassed or threatened with harassment. Section 4 creates a more serious offence of putting people in fear of violence, which applies where a person's course of conduct causes another to fear, on at least two occasions, that violence will be used against him; there is a defence, inter alia, where the accused can show that the pursuit of his course of conduct was reasonable for the protection of himself or another or for the protection of his or another's property: ibid., s. 4(3)(c).

18 This must involve conduct on at least two occasions: Protection from Harassment Act 1997, s. 7(3); 'conduct' in this context includes speech: ibid., s. 7(4).

19 Ibid., ss. 1(1), 2(1). 'Harassment' is not defined, save that references to harassing a person include alarming the person or causing the person distress: ibid., s. 7(2). A person convicted of an offence under these provisions may be subjected to a restraining order for the purpose of protecting the victim (or any other person named in the order) from further harassment: ibid., s. 5.

20 Ibid., s. 1(3)(c).

1   Re-enacting the Conspiracy and Protection of Property Act 1875, s. 7. The offence is not necessarily restricted to industrial cases: see e.g. *DPP v Todd* [1996] Crim LR 344 (anti-road protesters)

2   The defendant must have acted with a view to *compelling* someone to do something he had a right not to do, or vice versa; an intention to persuade is not enough: *DPP v Fidler* [1992] 1 WLR 91 (another non-industrial case involving a picket outside an abortion clinic).

3   Actual violence or threats of immediate personal injury are not necessary, but there must be some definite element of causing someone to feel afraid: *Judge v Bennett* (1887) 36 WR 103; *Gibson v Lawson* [1891] 2 QB 545; *Curran v Treleaven* [1891] 2 QB 545; *R v Jones* [1974] ICR 310, 59 Cr App Rep 120, CA.

4   *Smith v Thomasson* (1891) 16 Cox CC 740; *R v Wall* (1907) 21 Cox CC 401. For a rare example of a prosecution under this limb in Scotland, see *Elsey v Smith (Procurator Fiscal)* [1983] IRLR 292.

5   *Fowler v Kibble* [1922] 1 Ch 487, CA.

6   This limb is particularly relevant to picketing (see *R v Bonsall* [1985] Crim LR 150), and it is significant that the statutory immunity now contained in s. 220 of the 1992 Act was originally a proviso to s. 7 of the 1875 Act which deemed attendance for the purpose of obtaining or communicating information not to be watching or besetting. According to the Scottish High Court of Justiciary in *Galt (Procurator Fiscal) v Philp* [1984] IRLR 156 a person can be guilty of watching and besetting from inside the property, i.e. by occupying it, but this has been doubted.

(e) follow that person with two or more other persons in a disorderly manner in or through any street or road.

The inclusion of the words 'wrongful and without legal authority' means that the acts complained of under 1–5 above must already be unlawful (i.e. either tortious[7] or criminal) – the aim of the section is to make them amenable to summary trial in addition to any other unlawfulness:

> '[Section 242] legalises nothing, and it renders nothing wrongful that was not so before. Its object is solely to visit certain selected classes of acts which were previously wrongful, i.e. were at least civil torts, with penal consequences capable of being summarily inflicted[8].'

The offence under section 241 was rarely used until revived during the 1984/85 miners' strike; subsequently, it was upgraded somewhat by the Public Order Act 1986, which made it an arrestable offence and increased the maximum penalty to six months' imprisonment or a level 5 fine, or both[9].

iii) The importance of an anticipated breach of the peace

The discussion so far has centred on substantive offences which might be committed by pickets. However, one concept which, in practice, has tended to be dominant in the physical control of picketing by the police is that of breach of the peace[10] (either actual or reasonably apprehended), for it is a police officer's duty to prevent such a breach, if necessary by positive action to limit the numbers and placings of pickets. If a picket disregards an instruction from a police officer, and that officer can show grounds for reasonably anticipating[11] a breach of the peace at the time (e.g. through the imminent arrival of a lorry going into the picketed factory), then that picket is guilty of wilfully obstructing the police officer in the execution of his duty, contrary to section 89 of the Police Act 1996. Thus, breach of the peace acts as an umbrella head of liability which may justify

---

7   The converse of this is that the fact that the conduct in question constitutes an offence under this section does not automatically mean that it is an actionable tort: *Thomas v NUM (South Wales Area)* [1985] 2 All ER 1, [1985] IRLR 136. Cf. *Galt (Procurator Fiscal) v Philp*, n. 6, above, where it was held that tortious acts protected by the statutory immunities remain 'wrongful' for the purposes of these provisions. If correct, the decision could have profound implications for the legality of picketing.

8   *Ward Lock & Co Ltd v Operative Printers' Assistants' Society* (1906) 22 TLR 327, CA, at 329 per Fletcher Moulton LJ; *Fowler v Kibble* [1922] 1 Ch 487, CA; cf. *J Lyons & Sons v Wilkins* [1899] 1 Ch 255, where the Court of Appeal had previously held that the section created new offences complete in themselves. The approach in *Ward Lock* was preferred by Scott J in *Thomas v NUM (South Wales Area)*, n. 7, above.

9   The fact that the s. 241 offence is punishable with imprisonment means that it is capable of founding a charge of criminal conspiracy under the Criminal Law Act 1977, s. 1(1): Trade Union and Labour Relations (Consolidation) Act 1992, s. 242.

10 See *R v Howell (Errol)* [1982] QB 416, [1981] 3 All ER 383, CA, per Watkins LJ: 'There is a breach of the peace whenever harm is actually done or is likely to be done to a person or in his presence to his property or a person is in fear of being so harmed through an assault, an affray, a riot, an unlawful assembly or other disturbance.' The common law offence of breach of the peace was specifically retained by the Public Order Act 1986, s. 40(4).

11 See *Foulkes v Chief Constable of the Merseyside Police* [1998] 3 All ER 705, CA, per Beldam LJ: 'There must ... be a sufficiently real and present threat to the peace to justify the extreme step of depriving of his liberty a citizen who is not at the time acting unlawfully.'

the police in limiting numbers, as in *Piddington v Bates*[12], or holding back from the factory gates some, or even all, of the pickets[13] even if that means that there is little practical likelihood of the pickets (or their leaders) being able to converse with the lorry driver at all, provided that the drastic nature of any police action is justified by the magnitude of the risk of a breach of the peace. In the past, these powers have been used to control the activities of pickets at the premises being picketed. However, the miners' strike of 1984/5 saw a significant development when the police, faced with major disorders outside pits (particularly working pits in Nottinghamshire) began to close off areas altogether to would-be pickets, preventing them from reaching the premises in question at all, if necessary by the use of road blocks. Any pickets proceeding past such a barrier risked being arrested for obstruction of the police. The legality of such drastic measures was questioned in *Moss v McLachlan*[14] in the case of four such would-be pickets charged with obstruction for trying to pass a police cordon. They were convicted by magistrates and their appeal was dismissed by the Divisional Court which held that, on the facts, the police had reasonably anticipated a breach of the peace and so their preventive action was justified. One important holding was that in forming their reasonable anticipation the police were entitled to take into account their common knowledge of the course of the dispute and the likelihood of further major violence. The problem with the case as a precedent is that in fact the police cordon was only between one-and-a-half and four miles from four working pits within one area served by that particular road. Thus, the physical nexus between the cordon and the premises was relatively close. It is perhaps unfortunate that the legality of certain more controversial actions taken by the police (such as the stopping of Kent miners on their way to the northern coalfields at the Dartford tunnel) was not properly tested in the courts.

The large scale of the violence seen from an early stage of the miners' strike had the important legal effect of making further breaches of the peace easily foreseeable. Not only did this provide the basis for some otherwise extraordinary preventive tactics by the police, but it also (a) made the task of obtaining injunctions against mass picketing more easy; and (b) legitimised the imposition of stringent bail conditions on those arrested on violent picket lines, aimed at preventing them from returning; in *R v Mansfield Justices, ex p Sharkey*[15] the Divisional Court upheld the validity of what was then a common bail condition 'not to visit any premises or place for the purpose of picketing or demonstrating in connection with the current trade dispute between the NUM and the NCB other than peacefully to picket or demonstrate at his usual place of employment.'

12 [1960] 3 All ER 660, [1961] 1 WLR 162.
13 *Kavanagh v Hiscock* [1974] 2 All ER 177, [1974] ICR 282.
14 [1985] IRLR 76. Police powers to use roadblocks are now codified: Police and Criminal Evidence Act 1984, s. 4.
15 [1985] 1 All ER 193, [1984] IRLR 496. In the course of the strike, 32 charges were brought for breach of bail conditions and it was certainly possible for the defendant to receive a stiffer sentence for breach of bail than for the public order offence for which he was originally arrested. The effect of this particular condition has been likened to 'an injunction by another name', the difference being that it only applied to the individuals on bail.

iv) Public order offences[16]

As we have already seen, picketing which is not 'peaceful' may bring liability not only under specific criminal offences applying to industrial disputes, but also under the general laws relating to public order, which were subject to major amendment by the Public Order Act 1986. That Act had its origins in a review set up in 1979 to consider problems of public order generally, leading to a White Paper in 1985[17]; although the remit was wide, it was given added impetus by certain newsworthy industrial disputes, particularly the events of the 1984/85 miners' strike, and so several of the provisions in the Act were intended to affect picketing. The law on public order was further amended by the Criminal Justice and Public Order Act 1994 and the Crime and Disorder Act 1998, as successive governments of (supposedly) different political persuasions have resorted to increasingly draconian measures in an attempt to assuage public concern over a perceived deterioration in law and order. The measures relevant to picketing lie principally in the following areas – (i) offences against public order, (ii) controls over public processions and assemblies.`

Considering first the applicable offences, the Public Order Act abolished the common law offences of riot, rout, unlawful assembly and affray, and repealed the well-known statutory offence of 'threatening behaviour', replacing them with five graduated offences, all carrying powers of arrest; a further offence, that of causing intentional harassment, alarm or distress, was added by the Criminal Justice and Public Order Act 1994, and the Crime and Disorder Act 1998 imposed more severe penalties for certain of the offences where racially aggravated. The offences are as follows:[18]

a) *Riot*   Twelve or more persons present together using or threatening unlawful violence for a common purpose, their conduct being such as would cause a person of reasonable firmness present at the scene to fear for his personal safety[19]. Anyone using unlawful violence for the common purpose is liable on indictment to a maximum of ten years' imprisonment, a fine or both.

b) *Violent disorder*   Three or more persons present together using or threatening unlawful violence, their conduct being such as would cause a person of reasonable firmness present at the scene to fear for his personal safety[20]. Anyone using or threatening unlawful violence is liable on indictment to five years' imprisonment and/or a fine, or on summary conviction to six months' imprisonment and/or the maximum scale fine. This offence replaced the old common law offence of unlawful assembly, and is envisaged as being the major offence in practice in the case of serious disorder.

c) *Affray*   Using or threatening unlawful violence towards another, such as would cause a person of reasonable firmness present at the scene to fear for his personal

---

16   See Smith *Offences against Public Order* (1987); Wallington [1987] Crim LR 180; Carty 'The Public Order Act 1986: police powers and the picket line' (1987) 16 ILJ 146.
17   *Review of Public Order Law* (Cmnd 9510, 1985); also influential was the Law Commission's Report 'Offences relating to public order' (Law Com No. 123, 1983).
18   The following are condensed versions of the offences; for the full wording, see the text of the Act.
19   Public Order Act 1986, s. 1.
20   Ibid., s. 2.

safety[1]. The maximum penalty here is three years' imprisonment and/or a fine on indictment, or six months' imprisonment and/or the maximum scale fine on summary conviction.

d) *Violent behaviour* Using threatening, abusive, or insulting words or behaviour (or distributing or displaying anything to like effect) to another person with intent to cause that person to fear immediate unlawful violence (to himself or another) or to provoke that person or another to use immediate unlawful violence[2]. This offence is triable summarily only and carries a maximum penalty of six months' imprisonment and/or a level 5 fine[3].

e) *Intentional harassment* This offence, which was added by the Criminal Justice and Public Order Act 1994, is based on the existing offence of disorderly behaviour (see below), but with the additional requirements that the person must intend to cause, and the victim must actually be caused, harassment, alarm or distress[4]. It carries a much stiffer penalty than the non-intentional version (reflecting the intentional element), being punishable on summary conviction by up to six months' imprisonment and/or a level 5 fine[5]. Although apparently aimed at serious, persistent racial harassment, it is clearly of great potential significance to picketing.

f) *Disorderly behaviour* Using threatening, abusive or insulting words or behaviour, or disorderly behaviour (or displaying anything to like effect) within the hearing or sight of a person likely to be caused harassment, alarm or distress thereby, with the intention or the awareness that the words or behaviour may be threatening, abusive, insulting or disorderly[6]. This offence (perhaps best summed up colloquially as 'generally loutish behaviour') was particularly strongly criticised upon its introduction; it covers a multitude of sins, but is not of great importance in picketing cases since any such behaviour in that context is likely to lead to a breach of the peace (actual or reasonably apprehended), to which the present section probably adds little[7]. The offence is triable summarily only, with a maximum penalty of a level 3 fine[8].

Turning to the imposition of controls on public processions and assemblies, sections 11–13 of the Public Order Act 1986 allow the police to be given advance notice of public processions, and to impose conditions on them or to prohibit them altogether in order to prevent disorderly or intimidatory conduct. These powers are considered in full elsewhere[9] and are not of immediate application to picketing (except in the case of, for example, marches in support of pickets). Of more obvious relevance to picketing is the power to regulate public assemblies

1   Ibid., s. 3.
2   Ibid., s. 4. Violence includes violence to property; ibid., s. 8.
3   The penalties are more severe in the case of a racially aggravated offence: Crime and Disorder Act 1998. s. 31.
4   Public Order Act 1986, s. 4A. Compare the offence of harassment under the Protection from Harassment Act 1997, where it is enough to show that the accused ought to have known that his course of conduct amounted to harassment: see p. 686, above.
5   Again, the penalties are more severe in the case of a racially aggravated offence: see n. 3.
6   Public Order Act 1986, s. 5. The test of intention or awareness here is subjective: see *DPP v Clarke* (1991) 94 Cr App Rep 359.
7   Section 5 is principally aimed at conduct which is a social nuisance but which falls short of an actual breach of the peace because there is no actual or threatened harm to a person or his property; in that light, note the inclusion of mere 'disorderly behaviour'.
8   See n. 3.
9   See n. 16, above.

in section 14^{10}. This permits a senior police officer to impose conditions on a 'public assembly'[11], either in advance or at the scene, where the officer reasonably believes that:

> '(a) [the assembly] may result in serious public disorder, serious damage to property or serious disruption to the life of the community, or
> (b) the purpose of the persons organising it is the intimidation of others with a view to compelling them not to do an act they have a right to do, or to do an act they have a right not to do ...'

The potential application of this provision to picketing is obvious. If the police officer has such a reasonable belief, he may:

> 'give directions imposing on the persons organising or taking part in the assembly such conditions as to the place at which the assembly may be (or continue to be) held, its maximum duration, or the maximum number of persons who may constitute it, as appear to him necessary to avoid disorder, damage, disruption or intimidation.'

As we have seen above, the concept of breach of the peace (which remains unaffected by the 1986 Act) already gives a police officer on the spot some of these directional powers, but section 14 puts them into a wider, clearer and more comprehensive statutory form[12] (backed by criminal sanctions on those organising or taking part in an assembly in breach of conditions), and of course allows conditions to be attached in advance. Particularly significant are possible conditions as to place, time (not at times of shift changes for working employees?) and, of course as to numbers, where a provision in the Code of Practice on Picketing suggesting a limit of six pickets per entrance (considered below) assumes great significance.

v) The immunity

In view of the many and varied ways in which picketing can potentially fall foul of the law, the scope of the statutory immunity for picketing becomes of crucial significance, as it in effect defines the extent of the right to picket. Section 220 of the Trade Union and Labour Relations (Consolidation) Act 1992 provides that:

---

10   There is also a power to ban trespassory assemblies, introduced by the 1994 Act, which could conceivably be used where picketing (e.g. persistent mass picketing) results in 'serious disruption to the life of the community': Public Order Act 1986, s. 14A; see *DPP v Jones* [1999] 2 All ER 257, HL.

11   This is defined as 'an assembly of 20 or more persons in a public place which is wholly or partly open to the air' (s. 16), which clearly covers a picket line with that number of people (except in the unlikely event of it being entirely on private property). The requirement of advance notice and the power to ban (which apply to processions) do not apply to assemblies, although note the power to ban *trespassory* assemblies: see n. 10 above.

12   'The crucial difference is that reasons other than the need to preserve the peace may be relied upon, in particular the reasonable belief of the senior officer present that the picket organisers' purpose is to intimidate others' (Wallington, op. cit., n. 16; at p. 190).

'It is lawful for a person in contemplation or furtherance of a trade dispute to attend –

(a) at or near his own place of work, or

(b) if he is an official of a trade union, at or near the place of work of a member of the union whom he is accompanying and whom he represents[13],

for the purpose only of peacefully obtaining or communicating information, or peacefully persuading any person to work or abstain from working[14].'

It is important to appreciate that section 220 does not confer a 'right' to picket as such; it gives a limited right to *attend* for the stated purposes of peacefully obtaining or communicating information or peacefully persuading a person to work or abstain from working (i.e. 'peaceful picketing'), but it does not legitimise the *activities* of pickets. The section 220 immunity has therefore been described as 'narrow but real'[15] in that by protecting attendance for the purposes of peaceful picketing, it ensures that pickets will not incur either tortious liability (e.g. for nuisance) or criminal liability[16] (e.g. for obstruction of the highway or watching and besetting) from the mere fact of their attendance. Any liability which arises from the activities of pickets is protected, if at all, under the general trade dispute immunities contained in section 219 of the 1992 Act; the two provisions are however inextricably linked, as picketing which falls outside the section 220 immunity loses any protection which it might otherwise have enjoyed under section 219, while picketing which is within section 220 retains the section 219 immunities, even if it constitutes secondary action which would normally not be immune. The interrelationship of the immunities is discussed further below.

As seen above, the section 220 immunity applies to attendance for the purposes of peaceful picketing. It follows that if some other purpose can be inferred from the actions of the pickets (e.g. intimidation of those seeking to enter the workplace, or blockading the entrance), the immunity does not apply. Thus, in *Tynan v Balmer*[17] where pickets walked in a circle around the factory gates in such a way as to seal off the entrance from traffic, the court was able to infer a purpose other than one of those in the section. Similarly, in *Broome v DPP*[18] the House of Lords held that the defendant's purpose in standing in front of a lorry to prevent its passage (having failed to persuade the driver not to enter the picketed premises) was to obstruct rather than to persuade or communicate; the justices had acquitted the defendant on a charge of obstruction because they thought that he had only spent a reasonable time in trying to exercise his 'statutory right' of peaceful persuasion, a right which they considered would be meaningless if

---

13 An official who is elected or appointed to represent some members of the union is to be regarded as representing only those members: s. 220(4). This is to prevent the drafting in of large numbers of union officials, shop stewards, etc., from different parts of the country to do the picketing. A national officer, however, will be regarded as representing all members.

14 The 'persuasion' limb was introduced by the Trade Disputes Act 1906, s. 2; it had not been included in the immunity given by the Conspiracy and Protection of Property Act 1875: *J Lyons & Sons v Wilkins* [1899] 1 Ch 255, CA.

15 *Broome v DPP* [1974] 1 All ER 314, [1974] ICR 84, HL at 325 and 96 respectively, per Lord Salmon.

16 The Code of Practice of Picketing, para. 41, states that there is no immunity from the criminal law, but there are dicta in *Broome v DPP* to the contrary.

17 [1967] 1 QB 91, [1966] 2 All ER 133. The case is a good example of a trespass committed by an unreasonable user of the highway: see p. 685, above.

18 N. 15, above.

he was not allowed actually to stop the vehicle. The House of Lords held that this was entirely misconceived – the section gives no 'right' to picket, and certainly does not allow a picket to compel someone to stop and listen if that person does not wish to do so (a point reaffirmed shortly afterwards by the Divisional Court in *Kavanagh v Hiscock*[19]). Lord Salmon put it thus,

> '[The] words make it plain that it is nothing but the attendance of the pickets at the places specified which is protected; and then only if their attendance is for one of the specified purposes. The section gives no protection in relation to anything the pickets may say or do whilst they are attending if what they say or do is itself unlawful. But for the section, the mere attendance of pickets might constitute an offence under [section 241(1)(b) and (d) of the 1992 Act or under the Highways Act 1980] or constitute a tort, for example, nuisance. The section, therefore, gives a narrow but nevertheless real immunity to pickets. It clearly does no more.'

Before 1980, the statutory immunity for picketing applied so long as the attendance was for one of the stated purposes (i.e. peacefully obtaining or communicating information or peacefully persuading any person to work or abstain from working), and was within the golden formula. There were no restrictions on who could picket, or where, except that picketing a person's home was outside the immunity. This meant that those who engaged in so-called 'secondary picketing' enjoyed the full protection of the immunity. The phrase 'secondary picketing' is used to connote one of two things, either the attendance on picket lines of people who are not employed by the employer in dispute (sometimes referred to as sympathy picketing), or the placing of picket lines elsewhere than at the premises of the employer in dispute (particularly the use of so-called 'flying pickets'). The incoming Conservative Government in 1979 were determined to tackle secondary picketing, which was perceived as a major problem. The approach taken in the Employment Act 1980 was to restrict the scope of the immunity for peaceful picketing to a person picketing at or near[20] his *own* place of work[1] (and to a union representative accompanying such a person), so that the immunity no longer applies to secondary pickets engaged in sympathy picketing, or persons picketing a place other than their own place of work. As was mentioned above, crucially the 1980 Act also linked the immunity for *attendance* under section 220 with the immunities for the *activities* of pickets under section 219, by expressly removing the section 219 immunities from acts done in the course of picketing which falls outside the scope of section 220[2]

---

19 [1974] 2 All ER 177, [1974] ICR 282.
20 A realistic approach must be taken to the meaning of 'at or near': *Rayware Ltd v TGWU* [1989] ICR 457, [1989] IRLR 134, CA (pickets at the entrance to a private industrial estate which contained the employer's factory were held to be attending 'at or near' their place of work, even though 1,200 yards from their employer's premises).
1   Those with no fixed place of work, or whose workplace makes picketing impracticable (e.g. the proverbial lighthouse keeper), may picket 'any premises' from which they work or from which their work is administered: ibid., s. 220(2); see *Union Traffic Ltd v Transport and General Workers' Union* [1989] IRLR 127, CA. Workers who have been dismissed because of the dispute (and so who technically have no place of work) may picket their former place of work: ibid., s. 220(3), although note that if the employer moves production to a new plant, the dismissed workers may not lawfully picket that plant because it was never their place of work: *News Group Newspapers Ltd v SOGAT 1982 (No 2)* [1987] ICR 181, [1986] IRLR 337.
2   Trade Union and Labour Relations (Consolidation) Act 1992, s. 219(3); see p. 668, above.

(e.g. because it is not at that person's place of work, or is not peaceful). The effect of this is to allow an employer not a party to a dispute to obtain an injunction to stop employees of some other employer in dispute picketing his premises in the course of their dispute[3]. However, in one important respect the immunity for picketing is wider than the immunity for other forms of industrial action, because in certain circumstances pickets enjoy immunity for *secondary* action occurring during picketing[4]; indeed, following the tightening up of the law on secondary action by the Employment Act 1990, this is now the only form of secondary action which enjoys any statutory protection. This exception exists for the simple reason that without it the immunity for attendance conferred by section 220 would in practice be worthless. Workers peacefully picketing at their own place of work can very easily become involved in secondary action – for example, the actions of a picket who persuades a delivery driver not to cross a picket line (thereby probably inducing that driver to break his contract of employment and also indirectly interfering with the commercial supply contracts of the driver's employer) are likely to constitute secondary action if the driver is not employed by the employer in dispute. If there were no immunity for secondary action occurring during picketing, it would be virtually impossible for any lawful picketing to take place. Secondary action committed during peaceful picketing is therefore protected, but *only* as regards those employed (or last employed) by the employer in dispute, and union officials lawfully accompanying them. Those not employed by the employer in dispute (e.g. sympathy pickets who picket their own place of work in support of other workers) enjoy no protection against secondary action which occurs during picketing.

One other issue which in the past has been the cause of much controversy is mass picketing. Mass picketing such as that which occurred during the miners' strike in 1984/5 is not in itself unlawful, and section 220 places no limits on the numbers of pickets who may lawfully attend. However, the section does require that the picketing be 'peaceful', i.e. for the stated purposes of obtaining or communicating information or peacefully persuading any person to work or abstain from working. Thus, while mass picketing is not unlawful in itself, it is in the nature of things easier to infer a purpose other than that of peaceful communication or persuasion as the numbers grow larger. In *Broome v DPP*[5] Lord Salmon said that each case would depend on its facts, with the number of pickets being just one of the factors in deciding whether the attendance was for statutory purposes, but Lord Reid said, perhaps more realistically, that in a case of mass picketing 'it would not be difficult to infer as a matter of fact that pickets who assemble in unreasonably large numbers do have the purpose of preventing free passage', i.e. a purpose outside those permitted in section 220, an approach echoed in the judgment of Scott J in *Thomas v NUM (South Wales Area)*[6]. When the 1980 Employment Bill was going through Parliament, there was some pressure to supplement this general position with a statutory provision limiting numbers of pickets. This was not done in the Act, but in fact such a result was achieved

---

3   As in *Mersey Docks and Harbour Co v Verrinder* [1982] IRLR 152. One problem for an employer may be to identify the pickets in order to bring civil proceedings against them; it is no part of the police function to do so (see the Code of Practice on Picketing, para. 27).

4   Trade Union and Labour Relations (Consolidation) Act 1992, s. 244(3). The protection is, of course, subject to the other restrictions on the statutory immunities, such as the need to hold a valid ballot.

5   [1974] 1 All ER 314, [1974] ICR 84, HL.

6   [1985] 2 All ER 1, [1985] IRLR 136.

indirectly in the Code of Practice on Picketing, issued later in the year and revised in 1992[7]. Paragraph 47 states that 'the law does not impose a specific limit on the number of people who may picket at any one place; nor does this Code affect in any way the discretion of the police to limit the number of people on a particular picket line'. However, paragraph 51, after discussing the problems caused by large numbers, goes on to state that 'pickets and their organisers should ensure that in general the number of pickets does not exceed six at any entrance to, or exit from, a workplace; frequently a smaller number will be appropriate'. Although the Code itself is not legally binding it is expressly made admissible in tribunal or court proceedings[8], and this suggested maximum of six pickets per entrance has been seized upon by the courts as a guide 'to a sensible number for a picket line in order that the weight of numbers should not intimidate those who wish to go to work'[9]. It therefore seems likely that where the question arises whether picketing is 'peaceful', the presence of pickets in numbers greater than six may be taken to indicate a purpose outside those permitted by the section.

vi) The Code of Practice on Picketing

The Code was published in 1980 by the Secretary of State for Employment[10], and revised in 1992. The Code is not legally binding, and much of it is concerned with explaining the new law. However, as seen above, one aspect of the Code, the suggested maximum number of six pickets per entrance[11], is potentially of indirect legal effect as it may be taken into account by the courts when deciding whether the picketing was 'peaceful' and so within the immunity. Other than that, the Code's general exhortations as to prior consultations with the police and proper organisation of picketing by officials[12] are of little legal significance. The revised Code includes the following new recommendations: (1) where an entrance or exit is used jointly by the workers of more than one employer, pickets should not interfere with those workers or call upon them to join in the dispute; (2) picketing should be confined to a location or locations as near as practicable to the place of work; (3) a picket should not be designated as official unless it is actually organised by a trade union and the union is prepared to accept responsibility for it. Finally, one part of the Code is open to serious objection as a misuse of the idea of codes of practice. This is Section G (Essential Supplies and Services) which states that pickets should ensure that such supplies and services

---

7   The Code of Practice is discussed below.
8   Trade Union and Labour Relations (Consolidation) Act 1992, s. 207.
9   *Thomas v NUM (South Wales Area)*, n. 6, above, per Scott J; see also *News Group Newspapers Ltd v SOGAT 1982 (No 2)*, n. 1, above, per Stuart-Smith J. In *Thomas v NUM*, the terms of the injunction were clearly drafted with the Code of Practice in mind, for they restrained the organising of picketing at the colliery in question in numbers greater than six for any purpose other than peaceful persuasion or communication.
10   Under powers now contained in the Trade Union and Labour Relations (Consolidation) Act 1992, s. 203, which allows him to promulgate codes of practice (with Parliamentary approval) after consultation with ACAS. The Code of Practice is set out in *Harvey* S [602].
11   Para. 51.
12   One irony here is that, while the Code stresses the importance of good organisation and marshalling by officials, the law has never accepted that 'official pickets' should have any rights (other than the right of attendance) over and above ordinary pickets, e.g. a right to go through police cordons to talk to lorry drivers (see *Kavanagh v Hiscock*, n. 19, above).

are not impeded or prevented[13]. The problem is that it is difficult to see what legal effect this could have – it would be stretching several points to argue that picketing which did interfere with such services or supplies was thereby not 'peaceful', and it is the peaceful or other nature of it which is normally in issue in deciding whether or not the section 220 immunity can be relied upon. If it is correct that Section G has no legal effect, its inclusion can be seen either as merely pious hope or, more objectionably, an attempt to legislate by code of practice. If there are to be measures on something as important as the protection of essential supplies and services, it is surely not expecting too much that they should be properly enacted in a statute[14].

7 THE LIABILITY OF A UNION IN TORT

So far in this chapter we have been concerned with the legal gymnastics concerning the existence of a cause of action; the simplified position now is that industrial action by a union which has effects on commercial contracts or dealings is likely to be tortious, most of those torts are covered by immunities, but under the present legislation there are several major inroads into those immunities. However, the next major question concerns enforcement, which (criminal law aside) operates entirely in the civil law domain. This means that while the Government may legislate to create or permit causes of action, it is up to individuals to bring proceedings. Historically employers have been loath to do so. Perhaps one reason for this has been the nature of the defendant – given the blanket immunity afforded to unions in the Trade Disputes Act 1906, actions had to be brought, if at all, against named persons (usually union officers) and one problem has been that, although in the past injunctions have usually been obeyed by unions, if that was not the case the only remedy lay against the individual union official (on the complaint of the employer plaintiff) and could lead ultimately to imprisonment, which in turn could lead to the possibility of a serious clash between courts and unions which an employer would not wish to precipitate. In the light of this, it was of extreme importance that the previous Conservative Government not only restored major causes of action at the suit of the employer, but also abolished the blanket immunity of a trade union from liability in tort[15], leaving unions only with the same immunities (now contained in the Trade Union and Labour Relations (Consolidation) Act 1992, ss. 219 and 220), as were hitherto enjoyed by individual union officers and members. If those immunities do not apply, the union itself may now be the defendant in an action brought by an employer[16]. This means that there is less chance of the spectre arising of

13 Para. 62. Para. 63 lists such supplies and services as including pharmaceutical and medical products; hospitals; fuel for institutions; supplies needed in a crisis for public health and safety; goods and services necessary to the maintenance of plant and machinery; livestock; food and animal feeding stuffs; the operation of essential public services and mortuaries, burial and cremation services.

14 On industrial action in the essential services generally, see Morris *Strikes in Essential Services* (1986), and 'Industrial Action in Essential Services: The New Law' (1991) 29 ILJ 89.

15 Employment Act 1982, s. 15. See Ewing 'Industrial action: another step in the "right" direction' (1982) 11 ILJ 209.

16 In a further twist, the Trade Union and Labour Relations (Consolidation) Act 1992, ss. 235A–C (as inserted by the Trade Union Reform and Employment Rights Act 1993, s. 22) gives an individual the right to apply for an injunction restraining unlawful industrial action where an effect (or a likely effect) of that action will be to (i) prevent or delay the supply of goods or services to that individual, or (ii) reduce the quality of goods or services supplied to him; see p. 703, below.

imprisoned union leaders and that, in addition to the usual remedy of an injunction, the remedy of damages is now more than a mere technical possibility (being an action against the union funds, rather than against an individual). This raises three questions as to the legal effects: when is a union to be liable in tort for the acts of its officers and members; what remedies can be sought against it; and out of which union funds can an award of damages be satisfied?

Turning to the first of these points, before 1982 this problem had hardly ever arisen, for in the past a union itself could not be sued. However, the immunity had been temporarily removed by the Industrial Relations Act 1971, and the difficulties that could be caused became apparent, particularly in the case of *Heatons Transport Ltd v TGWU*[17], where the House of Lords had to decide upon the scope of the implied authority of a shop steward where the union rules were unclear on the point. In an attempt to avoid the problem of applying ordinary common law rules of vicarious liability, the Employment Act 1982 enacted a statutory test of vicarious liability governing when a union is to be liable for one of the economic torts[18]. That test deemed a union to be responsible for acts which had been 'authorised or endorsed by a responsible person', viz.: (a) the union's principal executive committee, (b) any other person empowered by the union rules to authorise or endorse such acts, (c) the president or general secretary, (d) any other employed official, or (e) any committee of the union to whom an employed official reports. In the case of the last two categories the union was not to be held responsible where the official or committee in question was prevented under the rules from authorising or endorsing industrial action, or where the action had been repudiated by the principal executive committee, the president or the general secretary. However, in an attempt to force trade unions to carry more responsibility for unofficial industrial action, the Employment Act 1990[19] extended the statutory test so as to make a trade union liable for the actions of *all* its committees and officials, including lay officials such as shop stewards, irrespective of anything to the contrary in the rules of the union. The 1990 Act even went so far as to make a union responsible for the actions of a 'group of persons', or any individual member of such a group, where an official of the union was a member of the group at the material time and the purposes of the group included organising or co-ordinating industrial action (e.g. an ad hoc strike committee)[20].

---

17 [1972] 3 All ER 101, [1972] ICR 308, HL; see Hepple, 'Union responsibility for shop stewards' (1972) 1 ILJ 197. One problem is that, in ordinary tort cases, one tends to think of vicarious liability operating from the top downwards, whereas within a union power tends to move upwards from the shop floor, particularly via the shop steward whose constitutional position may not be fully set out in the union's rules.

18 As originally enacted the statutory test applied to the economic torts but did not apply to contempt proceedings arising out of breach of an injunction granted on the basis of one of the economic torts: *Express and Star Ltd v NGA (1982)* [1986] ICR 589, [1986] IRLR 222, CA; however, the Employment Act 1990 applied the test to subsequent contempt proceedings. It still does not apply to any other form of liability, tortious or otherwise: *Thomas v NUM (South Wales Area)* [1985] ICR 886, [1985] IRLR 136 (nuisance). In such cases, the common law rules (as in *Heatons Transport*, n. 17, above) continue to apply.

19 Employment Act 1990, s. 6. See now the Trade Union and Labour Relations (Consolidation) Act 1992, s. 20. The proposals were advanced in the Green Paper, *Unofficial Action and the Law* (Cm. 821, 1989).

20 Trade Union and Labour Relations (Consolidation) Act 1992, s. 20(3)(b). As the section does not specify that the members of the group have to be members of the union, presumably this could render a union liable for the actions of a non-member in circumstances where the official who happens to belong to that group neither knows nor approves of that person's actions!

In view of this immense extension of responsibility, the ability of a union to repudiate unauthorised actions by its officials and committees becomes of crucial importance. The requirements for a valid repudiation are of truly Byzantine complexity[1]: (i) the repudiation must take place as soon as reasonably practicable after the relevant act has come to the knowledge of the repudiator; (ii) written notice of the repudiation must be given to the committee or official in question without delay; (iii) the union must 'do its best'[2] to give individual written notice of the fact and date of the repudiation, without delay, to every member of the union who the union has reason to believe is taking part (or might otherwise take part) in industrial action as a result of the act which is being repudiated, and to the employer of every such member; (iv) the notice to union members must contain the following statement: 'Your union has repudiated the call (or calls) for industrial action to which this notice relates and will give no support to unofficial industrial action taken in response to it (or them). If you are dismissed while taking unofficial industrial action, you will have no right to complain of unfair dismissal'[3]; (v) the repudiation will be deemed to be ineffective if the executive, president or general secretary subsequently behave in a manner which is inconsistent with the purported repudiation[4], or fail to confirm forthwith and in writing on request by a party to a commercial contract whose performance has been interfered with as a result of the act in question that it has been repudiated.

Given that a union may be liable under the above rules, what may it be liable for? Before the 1982 Act allowed an action in tort to be brought directly against a union, the aim of an action by an employer affected by industrial action was generally to obtain an injunction against named union leaders restraining them from organising the industrial action. To obtain such relief a full action for damages had in theory to be available, but in practice the prospect of an employer pursuing union leaders for damages was very remote. After the 1982 Act, an action in tort can now be brought against the union itself, which means that an action for damages (or, perhaps more to the point, the threat of an action for damages) is now a definite possibility, as the union is likely to have assets which could satisfy a judgment for damages. While the primary aim in most cases will still be an injunction, the possibility of unions having to pay damages raises one of the principal objections to laying unions open to actions in tort (ever since the *Taff Vale* decision[5] and the Trade Disputes Act 1906), namely that a strike or other industrial action could well cause vast losses by impeding production, losses which, if fully reflected in damages, could bankrupt the union. Section 22 of the Trade Union and Labour Relations (Consolidation) Act 1992 attempts to meet that argument by laying down maximum amounts of damages to be awarded against unions in tort actions (other than actions for personal injury or arising out of the ownership, occupation, possession, control or use of property, or product liability, where the statutory maxima do not apply). The limits are (a) £10,000 if the union has less than 5,000 members; (b) £50,000 if over 5,000 but

1   Ibid., s. 21. The actions of the principal executive committee, president or general secretary may not be repudiated, nor may those of a person acting under the authority of the rules.
2   The 'boy scout' test?
3   The draftsman somehow managed to resist the temptation to include the words 'you have been warned' in large capitals at the end.
4   For a case where a purported repudiation was held on the facts to have been a sham, see *Express and Star Ltd v NGA (1982)* [1985] IRLR 455 ('nods, winks, turning of blind eyes and similar clandestine methods of approval', per Skinner J).
5   See p. 629, above.

less than 25,000 members; (c) £125,000 if over 25,000 but less than 100,000 members; (d) £250,000 if over 100,000 members[6]. These amounts may be varied by the Secretary of State by statutory instrument.

Given that an award of damages is made against the union, how is it to be satisfied? It may be remembered[7] that the Royal Commission set up after the *Taff Vale* case did not recommend the total immunity for a union that was later enacted by the Trade Disputes Act 1906, but rather recommended that certain types of union funds should not be liable to seizure to satisfy awards of damages. Section 23 of the Trade Union and Labour Relations (Consolidation) Act 1992 effects a similar compromise, in that it creates a class of 'protected property' which may not be taken to satisfy any award of damages, costs or expenses. This covers any property (a) belonging to trustees of the union in any other capacity (including personally); (b) belonging to any union member (otherwise than jointly or in common with the other members); (c) belonging to any union official who is neither a member nor a trustee; (d) comprised in a political fund[8]; or (e) comprised in a provident benefits fund[9].

8 THE USE OF INJUNCTIONS IN INDUSTRIAL CASES

Although the establishment of a viable cause of action in an industrial dispute case could, in theory, lead to an award of damages against the defendant union or its leaders or members[10], the practical importance of such an action has always been that it permits the plaintiff to seek an injunction to *stop* the action. Moreover, as industrial disputes and stoppages may arise very quickly, the pattern has been for the plaintiff to apply for an interlocutory injunction as quickly as possible. Such an injunction may stop the industrial action; in theory, it only does so pending trial of the substantive action, but in practice the plaintiff has achieved his aim and so the vast majority of these cases never proceed to trial[11]. These cases are largely therefore dealt with at an interlocutory stage only. This raises two problems for a potential defendant. An interlocutory injunction may be sought and granted at great speed, and indeed can be sought *ex parte* even before the issue of a writ or

---

6   These are presumably the maximum amounts at the suit of one particular plaintiff, so that if there are several plaintiffs, damages up to the maximum can be awarded in the case of each successful plaintiff, even if the actions arise from the same event. The section is not specific on this point, merely referring to 'any proceedings in tort'. It is unclear whether, if two or more actions are consolidated, or one plaintiff brings separate actions for damages based on separate events during the dispute, those are separate proceedings. Note that the restrictions on amount in s. 22 only apply to damages; they do not apply to any interest awarded on damages (*Boxfoldia Ltd v National Graphical Association (1982)* [1988] IRLR 383) or to fines for contempt of court, and neither this section nor s. 23 on protected property prevents the sequestration of the whole of a union's property if a fine is not paid.

7   See p. 629, above.

8   The political fund must be subject to rules of the union which prevent its contents from being used for financing strikes or other industrial action: s. 23(2)(d). See p. 621.

9   'Provident benefits' are defined in s. 23(3) as including payments expressly authorised by the union rules, in respect of sickness, injury or unemployment; superannuation; accidents; loss of tools through fire or theft; funeral expenses; provision for the children of deceased members.

10 In *Huntley v Thornton* [1957] 1 All ER 234, [1957] 1 WLR 321 the plaintiff was awarded £500 damages for conspiracy.

11 See Anderman and Davies 'Injunction procedure in labour disputes' (1973) 2 ILJ 213 and (1974) 3 ILJ 30; Evans (1987) 25 BJIR 419.

originating summons in cases of 'urgency'[12]. The normal practice is for the plaintiff to show good reason why the court should proceed *ex parte*, i.e. in the absence of the defendant, and this is reinforced in industrial cases by the Trade Union and Labour Relations (Consolidation) Act 1992, section 221(1) which provides that a court shall not grant the injunction (in a case where the defendant is likely to claim that he acted in contemplation or furtherance of a trade dispute) unless it is 'satisfied that all steps which in the circumstances were reasonable have been taken with a view to securing that notice of the application and an opportunity of being heard with respect to the application have been given to [the defendant]'. It is probable that this provision does little other than repeat the normal procedure, for the avoidance of doubt.

The second problem is of more substance. In theory, an interlocutory application is not a trial of the issue, merely a decision whether to give certain temporary relief pending the action; if, however, the matter never goes any further (as in most industrial injunction cases) the interlocutory stage is the only one at which the defendant can put forward his case. It used to be thought that, to be granted an interlocutory injunction, the plaintiff had to show a 'prima facie' or 'strong prima facie' case that he would succeed at trial[13]; while this fell short of proof of his case on a balance of probabilities, it still meant that there was some examination of the substantive merits of the case. However, in *American Cyanamid Co v Ethicon Ltd*[14] the House of Lords held that this was incorrect – all that has to be shown by the plaintiff is an arguable case fit to go on trial; once that has been shown, the question whether to grant the injunction will be decided on the 'balance of convenience', i.e. whether the plaintiff will suffer more damage in the mean time if it is not granted than the defendant will suffer if it is. In ordinary cases, particularly of a commercial nature, this may make perfect sense and may be backed up by other devices such as an undertaking in damages by the successful plaintiff. In industrial cases, however, it means that there need be little investigation of the substantive merits of the case[15], and the dominant feature is the balance of convenience which is usually decided in the plaintiff employer's favour, for he can usually point to definite pecuniary loss if the strike is allowed to continue, whereas the defendant union can only point to the intangible 'damage' of loss of a tactical advantage in the dispute if the strike is stopped. In an attempt to meet the potential problem, the Employment Protection Act 1975 added a new requirement, now contained in section 221(2) of the Trade Union and Labour Relations (Consolidation) Act 1992, which provides that where an application is made to a court for an interlocutory injunction pending the trial of an action, and the party against whom the injunction is sought claims that he acted in contemplation or furtherance of a trade dispute:

12 RSC Ord. 29, r. 1.
13 *J T Stratford & Son Ltd v Lindley* [1965] AC 269, [1964] 3 All ER 102, HL.
14 [1975] AC 396, [1975] 1 All ER 504, HL. See *Hubbard v Pitt* [1975] 3 All ER 1, [1975] ICR 308, CA, the judgment of Henry J in *Barretts & Baird (Wholesale) Ltd v IPCS* [1987] IRLR 3 and Gray 'Interlocutory injunctions since *Cyanamid*' (1981) 40 CLJ 307.
15 It should however be acknowledged that in practice the courts do usually give some (albeit often hurried) consideration to the points of law involved, particularly on the applicability or otherwise of the immunities. *Barretts & Baird* (n. 14, above) is a good example of this, although for criticism of the uncertainty in this area, see the note on that case by Simpson (1987) 50 MLR 506, where it is pointed out, inter alia, that the injunction that Henry J discharged had been granted by another judge by telephone on a Sunday afternoon.

'the court shall, in exercising its discretion whether or not to grant the injunction, have regard to the likelihood of that party's succeeding at the trial of the action in establishing any matter which would afford a defence to the action.'

It is difficult to see what effect this subsection in fact has, for it only exhorts the court to 'have regard to the likelihood' of an immunity defence, which in practice it will almost certainly do anyway. In *Star Sea Transport Corpn of Monrovia v Slater*[16] Lord Denning MR said that the effect of section 221(2) was to remove industrial dispute cases from the ambit of the *American Cyanamid* case, and reapply to them the previous law whereby the court should look at the respective strengths of the plaintiff's and the defendant's cases when deciding whether to grant an interlocutory injunction. However, in practice section 221(2) has placed little restraint upon the granting of interlocutory injunctions: if there is little chance of the plaintiff succeeding in surmounting the immunities an injunction will not be given, but otherwise there is no bar to it, either (a) where the defendant will probably be unsuccessful in raising an immunity defence[17] or (b) where the question of liability is in the balance. Indeed, in *Slater's* case, where the success of an immunity defence was said to be a very open question, Brandon LJ said,

'[Section 221(2)] must be acted upon; but if in any particular case the merits of the defence are wide open, then it is obvious that even when one has applied that subsection it is not going to make any appreciable difference to the result[18].'

In either of these cases, the question then falls to be decided primarily on the balance of convenience, usually to the plaintiff's advantage in industrial dispute cases[19], particularly as it appears that the 'public interest' may in appropriate cases (e.g. of national strikes) be taken into account at this stage[20]. The House of Lords first considered section 221(2) in *NWL Ltd v Nelson*[1], where Lord Diplock acknowledged the likelihood that the application of the ordinary principles on interlocutory injunctions would heavily favour the employer in industrial dispute cases. In the light of that (and the fact that most such cases never in fact come to trial), he said that the section was enacted to enable judges to take into account the practical reality of industrial disputes when applying the 'balance of convenience' principle in the *American Cyanamid* case:

---

16 [1978] IRLR 507, CA; see also the judgment of Stephenson LJ. The decision in this case was overruled by the House of Lords in *NWL Ltd v Nelson* [1979] ICR 867, [1979] IRLR 478.

17 This is now much more likely, as a result of the narrowing of the immunities since 1980; see head 4, above. The development of torts *not* covered by an immunity (e.g. inducing breach of statutory duty) is also highly significant here, and it will usually not be difficult for the employer's counsel to put together an arguable case. See, for example, *Associated British Ports v TGWU* [1989] 3 All ER 796, [1989] IRLR 305, CA (reversed on other grounds, [1989] 3 All ER 822, [1989] IRLR 399, HL).

18 [1978] IRLR 507, at 513, CA. See also the discussion of the meaning of 'likelihood' by Lord Fraser in *NWL Ltd v Nelson* [1979] ICR 867, [1979] IRLR 478, HL.

19 See, e.g., *Beaverbrook Newspapers Ltd v Keys* [1978] ICR 582, [1978] IRLR 34, CA.

20 *Beaverbrook Newspapers Ltd v Keys* [1978] ICR 582, [1978] IRLR 34, CA; *United Biscuits (UK) Ltd v Fall* [1979] IRLR 110; *Express Newspapers Ltd v McShane* [1980] 1 All ER 65, [1980] IRLR 35, HL; *Associated British Ports v TGWU*, n. 17, above.

1 [1979] ICR 867, [1979] IRLR 478, HL.

'Subsection (2) [of section 221] ... appears to me to be intended as a reminder addressed to English judges that where industrial action is threatened that is prima facie tortious because it induces a breach of contract they should in exercising their discretion whether or not to grant an interlocutory injunction, put into the balance of convenience in favour of the defendant those countervailing practical realities and, in particular, that the grant of an injunction is tantamount to giving final judgment against the defendant ... My Lords, when properly understood, there is in my view nothing in the decision of this House in *American Cyanamid Co v Ethicon Ltd* to suggest that in considering whether or not to grant an interlocutory injunction the judge ought not to give full weight to all the practical realities of the situation to which the injunction will apply ... Cases of this kind are exceptional, but when they do occur they bring into the balance of convenience an important additional element ... it was clearly prudent of the draftsman of the section to state expressly that in considering whether or not to grant an interlocutory injunction the court should have regard to the likelihood of the defendant's succeeding in establishing that what he did or threatened was done and threatened in contemplation or furtherance of a trade dispute[2].'

However, this approach looked at what might be termed the 'practical realities' at that particular point in time; the problem is that such realities are subject to change, as indeed happened in 1982 with the removal of the union's immunity and the laying open of union funds (other than those specifically protected) to the possibility of an action for damages. Thus, it may no longer be a warranted assumption that the action against the union will proceed no further than an interlocutory injunction, and so there may now be no basis on which to argue that trade dispute cases should be viewed as an exception to the normal rules in *American Cyanamid*. In *Dimbleby & Sons Ltd v NUJ*[3] Lord Diplock stated that an action for damages is now a distinct possibility and resiled somewhat from his earlier statement on the grounds that, while section 221(2) still requires a court to 'have regard to the likelihood' of the defendant being able to rely on the immunities in the Trade Union and Labour Relations (Consolidation) Act 1992, sections 219 or 220,

'As respects all other issues raised by way of defence to the action the criterion to be applied in order to make recourse to the balance of convenience necessary is the ordinary criterion laid down in *American Cyanamid v Ethicon Ltd*: is there a serious question to be tried?[4]'

Finally, four points should be noticed; the first is that the position of an appellate court on an appeal from the granting or refusal of an interlocutory injunction was considered in *Hadmor Productions Ltd v Hamilton*[5] where Lord Diplock emphasised that the appellate court's function is one of review only; an interlocutory injunction is a discretionary remedy, lying essentially within the discretion of the trial judge, so that the appellate court should not on appeal treat the matter de novo and substitute its own view on the facts. The trial judge's

---

2   Ibid., at 879 and 484.
3   [1984] ICR 386, [1984] IRLR 161, HL.
4   At 406 and 164, respectively.
5   [1982] 1 All ER 1042, [1982] ICR 114, HL, applied in *Dimbleby & Sons Ltd v NUJ*, n. 3 above.

decision should only be reversed if there is a mistake of law, a misunderstanding of the facts adduced or if there has been a change of circumstances since the order was made; there may sometimes be cases where the judge's decision can be attacked as being 'aberrant' in that no reasonable judge could have reached the decision in question, but that will be rare. Thus, not only is the initial practical emphasis upon the application for an interlocutory injunction, but also the trial judge's decision may be difficult to challenge on appeal.

The second point is that events during the miners' strike of 1984/5 showed how potent a weapon an injunction[6] can be when it is granted against a union itself, not a named individual, for breach of or failure to comply with its contempt of court[7] for which the union may be fined (the fine not being subject to the statutory maxima on damages); if the fine is not paid, the plaintiff may apply for sequestration of the union's assets, and the fact of sequestration could give rise to a claim by disaffected union members for the union to be placed in receivership. Indeed, it has been argued that sequestration and, to a lesser extent, receivership are coming to be viewed as remedies in their own right (especially as sequestration is not merely an administrative means of gathering the fine, since even after the fine is recovered by the sequestrators the sequestration continues until the union purges its contempt).

The third point is that it must be remembered that an industrial dispute is an industrial relations problem, and at some stage the two sides will have to try to resume normal relations; this is unlikely to be helped by the service of writs, and a delicate balance may have to be preserved between the enforcement of legal rights in the short term, and the resolution of issues in the industrial relations context in the long term. ACAS have certainly found their collective conciliation efforts materially complicated in cases where there is the threat or actuality of legal proceedings, and at one point suggested that there should be some procedure whereby legal proceedings in industrial dispute cases could be temporarily stayed by the courts to allow at least an attempt at conciliation before final steps are taken[8], but the idea has not been taken up.

Finally, many employers faced with industrial action which is unlawful, and therefore potentially restrainable, choose not to pursue legal remedies for fear of inflaming an already difficult situation and reducing the chances of an early negotiated settlement. However, such a strategy on the part of an employer could in practice be frustrated by the Trade Union and Labour Relations (Consolidation) Act 1992, section 235A[9], which gives an individual who is deprived of goods or services[10] as a result of unlawful industrial action a right

---

6   The principal injunctions during the strike were in fact granted to working miners, not employers, but the principles are the same. See Ewing (1985) 14 ILJ at 170; Lightman (1987) 40 CLP 25.

7   On contempt of court and its remedies, see *Harvey* N 19G and Kidner 'Sanctions for contempt by a trade union' (1986) 6 LS 18. Exactly which funds are subject to sequestration may have to be worked out with care in the case of a union with a diverse or decentralised constitution: *News Group Newspapers Ltd v SOGAT 82* [1986] ICR 716, [1986] IRLR 227, CA. For an example of a contempt fine for half-hearted and delayed compliance with a court order, see *Kent Free Press v NGA* [1987] IRLR 267.

8   *ACAS Annual Report 1983*, paras. 1.16–1.18.

9   Introduced by the Trade Union Reform and Employment Rights Act 1993, s. 22.

10   The original proposals in the Green Paper, *Industrial Relations in the 1990s* (Cm. 1602, 1991), would have confined the right to customers of the public services within the scope of the Citizen's Charter, but as enacted the right goes considerably further.

(dubbed the 'Citizen's Right') to apply for an injunction restraining that action[11]. The right arises where 'an effect, or a likely effect, of the unlawful industrial action is or will be to (i) prevent or delay the supply of goods or services, or (ii) reduce the quality of goods or services supplied, to the individual making the claim'[12]. While the industrial action must be unlawful[13], it does not have to be actionable in tort on the part of the applicant, and it seems that he need not have suffered any quantifiable financial loss or damage as a result of it; moreover, it is immaterial whether or not the applicant is *entitled* to be supplied with the goods or services in question (this apparently designed to ensure that frustrated commuters stranded on station platforms are not denied the protection of the section by technical arguments over whether they have a contractual entitlement to travel on any particular train). The Citizen's Right is significant on two levels: first, it represents a breathtaking extension of liability, and could be said to render much of the earlier discussion on the scope of the economic torts irrelevant, for as long as the industrial action is in theory actionable by at least one person, anyone else adversely affected by that action may seek an injunction to restrain it; secondly, it could have a damaging effect on attempts to reach negotiated settlements to industrial disputes. In explaining the rationale of the Citizen's Right, the then minister of state posed the question, 'Why should citizens be inconvenienced because a gutless and spineless employer fails to see a remedy for unlawful action which results in loss?'[14], a view which arguably fails to recognise the industrial relations realities of the situation.

11   The section does not give a right to damages. Until recently such a plaintiff could seek financial assistance from the Commissioner for Protection Against Unlawful Industrial Action, but the Commissioner was abolished by the Employment Relations Act 1999 (see p. 46). The White Paper *Fairness at Work* (Cm. 3968), recorded that the Commissioner assisted only one applicant under these provisions, which did not lead to a court case (para. 4.31).
12   Trade Union and Labour Relations (Consolidation) Act 1992, s. 235A(1)(b).
13   Ibid., s. 235A(2), which provides that an act of inducement is unlawful if it is actionable in tort by any one or more persons (e.g. by the employer in dispute), or it could form the basis of an application by a member under s. 62 of the 1992 Act (which gives union members a right to be balloted before industrial action). The effect of this is that any non-excusable failure to comply with the detailed statutory requirements (e.g. on balloting) will render the industrial action restrainable by anyone adversely affected by it.
14   Minister of State, Mr Michael Forsyth, *Hansard*, H.C. (Standing Committee F),

Chapter 12

Industrial safety (1): compensation for industrial injury

I INTRODUCTION – FORMS OF COMPENSATION

Compensation for injuries suffered at work has long been an important area of substantive law, which contains at its heart the potentially difficult problem of the relationship between private compensation through the law of tort and the role of the state in providing compensation through the social security system. The importance of the civil action for industrial injuries can be seen in the legal significance of the industrial safety legislation which on its face usually only imposes criminal liabilities on those in breach of a relevant provision, but which has been primarily of significance to the lawyer as a highly practicable head of civil liability upon the employer through the development by the courts of the independent tort of breach of statutory duty to such an extent that it is now of greater practical importance than the common law action for negligence. Indeed, this has given rise to the criticism of the present system (certainly prior to the reforms in the Health and Safety at Work etc. Act 1974 and the 'Six Pack' of EC-based Regulations in the early 1990s) that the lawyers' approach has been to regard the industrial safety legislation primarily in the negative sense as a way of compensating an employee once he is injured, rather than as a positive means of preventing accidents in the first place. The law on civil liability for industrial injuries has seen much development (particularly since freed from the harsher effects of three common law defences – common employment, contributory negligence and volenti non fit injuria[1]) and in the light of the large amount of statute and case law it is easy for the lawyer to overlook the fact that it is only one of *two* aspects, for in quantitative terms the state compensation scheme (primarily the provision of incapacity and disablement benefits) is the senior partner, particularly for all but the most serious of work injuries. It is therefore important for the industrial lawyer to have a knowledge of the state scheme as well as a knowledge of the more traditional law on industrial tort claims.

---

1   The doctrine of common employment was abolished in 1948, and contributory negligence ceased to be a complete defence in 1949; the modern approach to contributory negligence and volenti is discussed under head 3, below.

The present system of compensation is thus a mixed one of state insurance (financed by compulsory national insurance contributions) and liability in tort (backed by widespread private insurance which, in the context of the liability of an employer to an injured employee, has been compulsory since 1969[2]); further, it is truly 'mixed' in that the injured employee does not have to elect to proceed under one scheme or the other – he may claim under both, though if eventually successful in the tort action, he can now be required to pay back the social security benefits he received in the meantime, out of the damages[3].

In the short term the practical remedy for the injured employee is to claim statutory sick pay while incapacitated from work; the state may also give compensation in the long term, through disablement benefit, but if his injuries are major or lasting, the employee may also wish to bring a civil action against his employer for damages[4]; in the case of the state scheme the question of fault is irrelevant but in the case of a civil action the plaintiff employee will normally have to prove fault of sorts. Over the years, the concept of fault liability has come under increasing criticism[5], and the principal arguments are well known – the fault-based tort action is slow, cumbersome and uncertain; it only compensates a small proportion of those in fact injured each year, and its method of compensating those few has always been in the past to give damages as a lump sum[6], often taking little or no account of future inflation; the risk of bringing an action is great, even with the substitution of no-win-no-fee arrangements to replace legal aid; proof of fault depends on the availability of evidence, and lack of such evidence may be fatal to the plaintiff's case, however badly injured he is; the system is extremely costly to run, certainly when compared to the low running costs of the state-run social security system. Such criticisms have been given impetus by the enactment of no-fault liability systems in other jurisdictions (either partial, for example in relation to motor accidents, or total); the obvious source for comparison has always been the New Zealand Accidents Compensation Scheme which provides comprehensive state insurance for all injuries (not just industrial ones) and bars any tort action for personal injuries caused by an accident[7]. With this background, the whole question of civil liability in this country

---

2   Employers' Liability (Compulsory Insurance) Act 1969. The area of motor vehicle accidents is also subject to compulsory insurance, which therefore covers the large majority of all tort actions, since 47 per cent of all tort claims concern work accidents and 41 per cent concern motor vehicles accidents: Report of the Royal Commission on Civil Liability Cmnd. 7054 (1978), para. 79.

3   Social Security (Recovery of Benefits) Act 1997.

4   In doing so, he may well receive assistance from his union if he is a member. For the union's liability in costs if the claim fails, see *Bourne v Colodense Ltd* [1985] ICR 291, [1985] IRLR 339, CA, noted Kidner (1985) 14 ILJ 124.

5   The literature is extensive. See Ison *The Forensic Lottery* (1967); Atiyah *Accidents, Compensation and the Law* (3rd edn, 1993); Jolowicz 'Liability for accidents' [1968] CLJ 50; Stoljar 'Accidents, costs and responsibility' (1973) 36 MLR 233; O'Connell, 'No-fault insurance for Great Britain' (1973) 2 ILJ 187; Parsons 'A no-fault system?: not proven' (1974) 3 ILJ 129; the Industrial Law Society 'Compensation for industrial injury' (1975) 4 ILJ 195; Sugarman, 'Personal injury law reform: a proposed first step' (1987) 16 ILJ 30.

6   There have, however, been some moves towards structured settlements, to meet the long-standing criticisms of lump sum damages.

7   Accident Compensation Act 1972, which came into force in 1974; it was based on the Report of the Royal Commission on Compensation for Personal Injury in New Zealand (1967), chaired by Woodhouse J, who also produced a similar report for the Australian Government in 1974. On the content and operation of the original New Zealand scheme, see Harris 'Accident Compensation in New Zealand: a comprehensive insurance system' (1974) 37 MLR 361; Palmer 'Accident Compensation in New Zealand; the first two years' (1977) 25 Am J Comp L 1; Szakats 'The re-emergence of common law principles in the

(including industrial injury) was reviewed by the Royal Commission on Civil Liability, under the chairmanship of Lord Pearson[8], which did not recommend abolition of the action in tort for personal injuries, but instead recognised and emphasised the inter-relationship of state insurance and the law of tort, envisaging that, although not abolished, the latter would increasingly become the 'junior partner'[9].

A detailed consideration of the Pearson Report is outside the scope of this book, but four particular suggested reforms should be mentioned and kept in mind when reading the rest of the chapter. The Report recommended, first, that the value of social security benefits should be deducted *in full* from subsequent tort damages, making it clear that the two systems are fully complementary[10]; second, that damages for non-pecuniary loss should not be recoverable for the first three months of injury[11] (emphasising the importance of the tort action in *serious* cases); third, that earnings related benefits under the industrial injuries scheme should be improved[12]; and fourth, that damages for future pecuniary loss should be through periodic payments (inflation-proofed, and subject to periodic review by the courts in the light of any changes in the plaintiff's medical condition) instead of the present lump sum, such a payment system to be obligatory in the case of death or lasting injury and discretionary in other cases[13]. However, the Report did not suggest alteration of the present basis of civil liability for industrial injuries and in particular did not recommend the imposition of strict liability as it did in the case of product liability and exceptionally hazardous operations[14]. Some cautious reforms were made in the Administration of Justice Act 1982, particularly in relation to the reassessment of damages at the suit of the plaintiff where an injury has worsened, but most of the other reforms were of a minor nature to deal with particular defects in the existing law (see head 3, below). Thus, the Report in fact produced little change in this area, which has remained curiously stable for many years (as to liability – procedure has been changed markedly by the Woolf reforms and the replacement of legal aid), as opposed to the frantic pace of change affecting most other areas of industrial law.

Bearing in mind the vital inter-relationship of state insurance and tort liability we must now look at the law relating to state benefits for those injured at work and the actions that may be maintained in tort by the injured employee, with the caveat in the case of the latter that, as the subject of industrial law has now become so specialised and substantial in its own right, that part of the chapter has been

---

New Zealand Accident Compensation scheme' (1978) 7 ILJ 216. In recent years, however, the New Zealand scheme has run into financial difficulties and has had to be pruned since 1992 (especially in relation to medical injuries where an element of fault has been reintroduced) and so is no longer a 'pure' alternative: Miller 'An analysis and critique of the 1992 changes to New Zealand and New Zealand's Accident Compensation Scheme' (1992) 5 Canta LR 1.

8   *Report of the Royal Commission on Civil Liability* (1978) Cmnd. 7054. See Corfield, Harris and Ogus, 'Pearson: principled reform or political compromise?' (1978) 7 ILJ 143; Fleming 'The Pearson Report: its "strategy" ' (1979) 42 MLR 249.

9   Report, para. 1732.

10 Ibid., paras. 467–483. This has now come about (see p. 721, below), but for very different reasons, i.e., simply to recoup the money.

11 Ibid., paras. 382–389.

12 Ibid., paras. 800–813. In fact, the earnings related supplement was abolished by the previous government (Social Security (No 2) Act 1980, s. 4), as was the short term industrial injury benefit (Social Security and Housing Benefits Act 1982, s. 39).

13 Ibid., paras. 550–614.

14 One of the major recommendations was that motor accidents should be covered by a no-fault state insurance scheme, closely modelled on that for industrial injuries.

confined to giving only an *outline* of an industrial tort action, and to pointing out what may be seen as the more specialised industrial aspects or applications of ordinary tort principles, with which it is assumed that the reader is already familiar.

2   STATE BENEFITS FOR THOSE INJURED AT WORK[15]

The present system of industrial injuries benefit grew out of the concept of workmen's compensation which, when first enacted in 1897, introduced the entirely new principle that in respect of certain employees and in relation to the risk of industrial injury, the employer became in effect the insurer of the employee's safety. The legislation provided for certain fixed benefits to be paid by the employer to an injured employee, either by periodic payments or a lump sum, whether or not the accident was the result of the employer's negligence. It thus provided the principal legal remedy for an injured employee, and the employer would cover his statutory liability by privately arranged insurance. While obviously much more available than redress through an ordinary tort action, the system was heavily criticised, primarily because of the huge amount of litigation that it caused, since the real parties to most claims were insurance companies and trade unions. The system of compensation was radically altered by the National Insurance (Industrial Injuries) Act 1946, which came into force in 1948 and changed the basis to one of state-run insurance, financed by compulsory contributions and administered by the relevant Government department and not through the courts. The scheme as it existed prior to 1983 was that where an employed earner suffered personal injury caused by an accident arising out of and in the course of employment, he or she was eligible for weekly payments of industrial injury benefit for a maximum of six months, and for disablement benefit if there was some long term loss of faculty.

The scheme thus drew two distinctions – between short term and longer term needs, and between those injured at work and those injured elsewhere or merely sick (who had to claim sickness benefit or, in the case of a lasting inability to work, invalidity benefit). The significance of the latter distinction was that, as a matter of policy, those injured at work were treated more generously than others. Thus, in 1948 injury benefit was 73 per cent higher than sickness benefit. However, by 1981 that preference had steadily declined to only 12 per cent, though the system still retained the complete separation of the two forms of benefit. Partly for that reason, and partly due to the then newly-introduced administrative provisions requiring the employer to pay (initially for eight weeks per year, but now for a maximum of 28 weeks per year) 'statutory sick pay'[16], the previous government decided upon what they saw as a rationalisation of the system. Thus, by virtue of the Social Security and Housing Benefits Act 1982, industrial injury benefit was abolished as from April 1983 and those injured at work are now subject to the same regime as those injured elsewhere or merely ill in relation to short-term income maintenance, namely statutory sick pay for the first 28 weeks if in employment and covered by that scheme, or the new incapacity benefit if not.

In the light of these changes it might have been thought that at last it would no longer be necessary to draw the often difficult distinction between an industrial

---

15   See Ogus Barendt & Wikeley *The Law of Social Security* (4th edn, 1995) ch. 7 for the basic structure and background; see also Lewis *Compensation for Industrial Injury* (1987).

16   See p. 179, above. This administrative scheme applies to employees who would previously have claimed injury benefit, as well as to those claiming sickness benefit.

injury and some other misfortune. Given that potential difficulty (and the enormous amount of case and statute law which has built up on it over the years), this would have been the greatest advantage of the supposed rationalisation and would have materially simplified this area of law. Unfortunately, however, that has not happened. The distinction has to continue because industrial disablement benefit has *not* been abolished – it was subject to major reforms in the Social Security Act 1986 which are considered below, but it remains payable to those who have suffered longer term loss of faculty as a result of an *industrial* injury. Moreover, initial suggestions by the present government that the industrial disablement scheme should be in effect privatised met with very strong opposition, and at the time of writing have not been proceeded with. It is therefore still necessary to define industrial accidents and industrial diseases, and it is to these that we now turn.

i) Industrial accidents

'Industrial accident' is a vital term which has produced a great volume of litigation, both under the old workmen's compensation legislation and the modern social security legislation, for both applied the same test, namely whether there was 'personal injury caused by an accident arising out of and in the course of employment'.

a) Personal injury

This will normally be self-evident and has been construed widely, excluding only damage to an artificial aid such as false teeth or an artificial leg[17]. It can include mental or nervous shock[18]. A disease could well constitute personal injury, but the danger then is that its contraction might not be viewed as an accident; to counter this, certain more common diseases are covered separately, and this is considered below.

b) Accident

There is no statutory definition of accident, even though as a concept it is essential in order to ensure that benefits are only payable in cases which are intended to be covered, not just in any case where there is some form of deterioration in health. The locus classicus has usually been said to be the dictum of Lord Macnaghten that an accident is 'an unlooked-for mishap or an untoward event which is not expected or designed'[19]. This must be applied from the viewpoint of the victim, so that even if injury is caused by an act, possibly criminal, which is entirely deliberate on the part of the perpetrator, that may still be an accident to the victim, as in *Trim Joint District School Board v Kelly*[20] where a master at an industrial school was killed by the deliberate acts of certain boys whom he had threatened to punish. This may also apply to acts of negligence by a third party or the victim:

17 R(I) 7/56. However, damage to an artificial hip joint was held to be personal injury in R(I) 8/81 on the basis that it constituted an integral part of the body.
18 *Yates v South Kirby Collieries Ltd* [1910] 2 KB 538, CA; *Re Drake* [1945] 1 All ER 576.
19 *Fenton v J Thorley & Co Ltd* [1903] AC 443, at 448, HL.
20 [1914] AC 667, HL; see CI 63/49; R(I) 30/58.

'Speaking generally ... an accident means any unintended and unexpected occurrence which produces hurt or loss. But it is often used to denote any unintended or unexpected loss or hurt apart from its cause; and if the cause is not known the loss or hurt itself would certainly be called an accident ... The great majority of what are called accidents are occasioned by carelessness; but for legal purposes it is often unimportant to distinguish carelessness from other unintended and unexpected events[1].'

It could indeed go as far as to cover suicide by the employee if there was a strong enough causal link between that and a work-related factor, for example producing depression or insanity leading to the death.

The personal injury must be caused by the accident in question. Questions of causation can cause much litigation, and principles well known to the law of tort (e.g. 'breaking the chain of causation') may be applicable here in more difficult cases, for example where the original accident put the claimant in a position where he was subjected to a further, non-industrial happening. However, for most purposes a fairly relaxed approach to causation has been taken in this context, and it is sufficient if the accident in question was more than a background factor and was at least a contributory cause, even if not the sole one. The practical importance of this is that the claimant may still succeed even if the reason for his disability was that the accident aggravated a pre-existing condition, or only produced the injury in question because of such a condition[2].

The major problem with the term 'accident' is to distinguish it from what is called a 'process', i.e. some process of bodily or mental degeneration which is not ascribable to any particular event. While an accident may remain genuinely such, even though its result is a disease of sorts[3], it may be that in such a case there is more likelihood of a finding that there was no discernible accident and that the case merely concerns the sort of ordinary illness that this scheme is not designed to cover. Perhaps the classic kind of accident is where one definite event, external to the claimant, clearly causes physical injury:

'It must be something external which has some physiological or psychological effect on that part of the sufferer's anatomy which sustains the actual trauma, or some bodily activity of the sufferer which would be perceptible to an observer ...[4]'

However, many cases are not as clear as that (e.g. where the claimant begins to feel internal pains after a period of time performing some particular operation at work), and in order that the concept of 'process' should not be applied too freely to disqualify too many people, the construction of accident has been broadened in two particular ways. The first is that, consistently with what was said above on causation, there can still be an accident where the event relied upon was merely the last in a chain of events or deteriorations, the proverbial last straw[5]. The second is that there may be no need to isolate one particular event, for a series of events may be sufficient to constitute an accident if they can

1   *Fenton v J Thorley & Co Ltd* [1903] AC 443, at 453, HL, per Lord Lindley. See *Harris v Associated Portland Cement Manufacturers Ltd* [1939] AC 71, HL.
2   R(I) 12/52; R(I) 19/63; cf. R(I) 6/82.
3   *Brintons Ltd v Turvey* [1905] AC 230, at 233, HL per Lord Halsbury LC.
4   *Jones v Secretary of State for Social Services* [1972] AC 944 at 1009, [1972] 1 All ER 145 at 184, HL, per Lord Diplock.
5   R(I) 54/53.

reasonably be viewed together, as with constant minor burns or repeated loud noises suffered while at work[6]; obviously the nature of the 'series' will be important, but so also might the time over which it occurred, so that if a particular condition arose over a short period, it might be more readily construed overall as an 'accident'[7].

However, this may be an area where the borderline between accident and process is at its thinnest, for a series of factors taking place over anything other than a relatively short period may soon look like the sort of ordinary health hazard which, however unfortunate, is not meant to be covered by the scheme[8]. Thus, a trainee nurse at a day nursery who developed infantile paralysis after contact with a child suffering from it was held to have suffered an industrial accident, but a doctor who contracted TB as a result of a series of penetrations of the lung by bacilli at various times was held not entitled to benefit[9]. More topically, it has been accepted that lung injury, allegedly from inhaling a fellow employee's tobacco smoke ('passive smoking'), could be an accident where it happened on six specific, documented occasions, though the Commissioner pointed out that *simple* passive smoking over a period of time would remain a process[10]. Similarly, post traumatic stress disorder suffered immediately after an abusive and aggressive incident with fellow workers who were on strike was held to be an 'accident'[11]. These are obviously wide questions of fact, and it must be stressed that, in this context and throughout the whole area of injury benefit, each case must depend heavily upon its facts and so, while there are many decided cases, they do not constitute a consistent body of case law to which detailed reference must be made on every occasion; it is certainly easy to point to certain decisions which, when put side by side, seem distinctly odd.

c) Arising out of and in the course of employment

This requirement has proved the most troublesome of all, and produced a disproportionate amount of litigation, both under the present state scheme and under the former workmen's compensation scheme. The usual approach has been that the phrase in fact contains two limbs; the requirement that the accident must arise 'in the course of employment' is a matter of the factual scope of the employment in question, while the requirement that it must arise 'out of' the employment is primarily a matter of causation. Thus, for example, in *Chief Adjudication Officer v Rhodes*[12] where a Benefits Agency officer was assaulted in her home by a neighbour whom she had reported for suspected benefit fraud, it was held that this 'accident' had arisen 'out of' her employment but *not* 'in the course of' it, and so her claim for benefit failed. Whether an accident is in the course of employment is a question of time, place and job content, and the Court of Appeal reaffirmed in *Nancollas v Insurance Officer*[13] that that question is largely

---

6   R(I) 24/54; R(I) 43/55.
7   R(I) 4/62; R(I) 31/52.
8   There may of course be tortious liability, even if no injury benefit, if the 'process' was caused by the employer's neglect.
9   CI 159/50 and CI 83/50 respectively.
10 R(I) 6/91.
11 CI2414/98.
12 [1999] IRLR 103, CA; the difficulty of drawing these distinctions is shown by the fact that the Court of Appeal split 2–1.
13 [1985] 1 All ER 833, CA; see e.g. R(I) 1/93. Note, however, that in *Smith v Stages* [1989] AC 928, [1989] 1 All ER 833, HL Lord Lowry said that this does not mean a total lack of principles or, at the least, applicable guidelines.

one of fact for the adjudicating authorities. Sir John Donaldson MR stressed that there is no single test to be applied (particularly not a test of the contractual obligations of the employee simpliciter), and that the previous case law can only provide general guidance as to factors that may be thought important in a particular case.

Bearing this clear warning in mind, some of that guidance may now be considered, and the starting point is that the question may more easily be answered in the case of a person with definite hours and a set place of work. Outside that (as in the case of *Nancollas* itself) the problems that have arisen are legion. Thus, when a home help, employed by a local council to make certain defined calls at certain defined times, was injured on her way to her first call of the day, it was held that this did not arise in the course of her employment, for her journey was merely preparatory to her first place of work[14]. On the other hand when a civil servant, employed to work partly in his office and partly by visiting homes as the need arose, was injured in a street accident within his defined area when about to make his first visit of the day, it was held that that was in the course of his employment, for it was during his normal hours and in the proper exercise of his discretion in performing his functions[15]. On the question of the time of the accident, a claimant need not be injured in actual working time to be successful, for normal break times may count, and he may be allowed a reasonable period before and after actually working before he ceases to be in the course of employment, as where a successful claimant arrived, as she usually did, half an hour early in order to change into her working clothes and have a meal in the canteen, where she was injured[16]. In that case, Lord Widgery CJ approved this extract from one of the old works on workmen's compensation:

> 'The course of employment may be taken to have commenced although the hour for actual work has not struck, if the workman's arrival on the premises is either not unreasonably early, or is necessitated by the circumstances of the employment, or if, at the time of the accident, he is doing something on the employer's premises which is necessary to be done to equip himself for his work.'

The question of the place of employment has caused much litigation, particularly where the claimant was not tied to any particular machine, room, etc. Normally the claimant may be successful if injured where he usually works in practice, or while using reasonable access to such a place; he may however fail if he was injured in a 'public zone', i.e. in a place to which in practice the public have general access (regardless of their strict legal rights)[17], on the basis that benefits are not payable for injuries which might have been suffered in the ordinary course of events by members of the public. Perhaps the most difficult aspect of the course of employment is the actual job content of the claimant, for it is clear that benefits are only payable for injuries sustained actually in the course of the claimant's work – it is not enough to show merely that at the material time he was legally engaged under a contract of employment. Thus if he was engaged in something outside the scope of his normal duties when injured, he may not be able to claim benefit. Even where a realistic view was taken of a claimant's duties,

14   R(I) 2/67; see also R(I) 12/75, R(I) 14/81 and R(I) 1/83.
15   R(I) 4/70.
16   *R v National Insurance Comr, ex p East* [1976] ICR 206; for the use of time after a shift, e.g. for bathing, see CI 22/49 and R(I) 22/51.
17   R(I) 1/68; cf. R(I) 3/72.

however, this test could work harshly, and one way to avoid that possibility was to look at the course of employment *and things reasonably incidental to it*[18]. Thus an employee may be doing something for his own purposes, such as having a break, taking a meal in the canteen or talking with other employees, but as long as it is something which he is not contractually disbarred from doing and may reasonably be said to be incidental to his actual work, he may still be in the course of his employment. This aspect was stressed by the Court of Appeal in *R v Industrial Injuries Comr, ex p AEU (No 2)*[19], but was subject to some restriction by that Court in the later case of *R v National Insurance Comr, ex p Michael*[20], where a policeman who was injured while representing his force in a football match was refused benefit, in spite of considerable support and encouragement being given to such sporting activities by the employing police authority. The Court of Appeal held that, while sports could in some cases be in the course of employment[1], that was not the case here, for it was not part of his ordinary work, nor was it 'reasonably incidental', for that was not part of the statutory test and, as a judicial gloss, should be restricted to cases where the injury occurred during some kind of interruption of the work which he was employed to do; it should not be used widely, to cover activities well outside the normal scope of the claimant's duties:

> 'This test of "reasonably incidental" is to be gathered from the speeches of Lord Sumner, Lord Parmoor and Lord Wrenbury in *Armstrong, Whitworth & Co Ltd v Redford* … It was followed by this court in *R v Industrial Injuries Comr, ex p AEU* … But in all these cases the workman was at the premises where he or she worked and was injured while on a visit to the canteen or other place, for a break. The words "reasonably incidental" should be read in that context, and limited to cases of that kind. They are not part of the statute and should not be extended to other cases without careful consideration[2].'

This is particularly relevant on the question of breaks in the employment; normal coffee and tea breaks will probably remain within the course of employment, as will meal breaks taken in the works canteen, though not breaks taken elsewhere purely at the choice of the employee. The rule here is in theory beneficial to the employee, for it was said in *R v Industrial Injuries Comr, ex p AEU (No 2)* that the employee would only be taken out of the course of his employment if he was engaged in some *material* interruption of his work[3]. However, the actual result of that case showed a rather stringent application of this, for the employee who had

18   *Charles R Davidson & Co v M'Robb* [1918] AC 304, HL; *Armstrong, Whitworth & Co Ltd v Redford* [1920] AC 757, HL.
19   [1966] 2 QB 31, [1966] 1 All ER 97, CA.
20   [1977] 2 All ER 420, [1977] ICR 121, CA; R(I) 2/80; cf. R(I) 3/81.
1   See ibid., at 135 and 431 respectively, per Lawton LJ; see also R(I) 13/66 where a fireman injured playing volleyball during a recreation period of a duty watch, which was encouraged as a way of keeping fit, was able to claim benefit. Cf. R(I) 3/81.
2   Ibid., at 423 and 126 respectively, per Lord Denning MR. In R(I) 10/80 a shop steward who was injured while attending a union course in pursuance of statutory time off work (see p. 581, above) was held not eligible as the connection with her work was not sufficient. On the other hand, in R(I) 1/93 an employee injured while attending a meeting at work to consider her RSI claim against the employer succeeded.
3   [1966] 2 QB 31, [1966] 1 All ER 97, CA, at 51 and 106, respectively, per Salmon LJ. In *R v National Insurance Comr, ex p Reed* (reported in the appendix to R(I) 7/80) a policeman injured whilst returning to the station from lunch at home was held eligible to claim by the Divisional Court, but the crucial factor was that while at home he was still on duty; this factor was missing in R(I) 5/81 in the case of a fireman killed whilst driving home who was merely on general call at any time in case of emergency.

been injured while still smoking in a corridor five minutes after the end of a ten minute tea break was held to have put himself outside the course of his employment and was not eligible for benefit.

Given that a particular injury happened in the course of employment, there is then the further requirement that it must have arisen out of that employment, for not every accident occurring during working time is actually referable to that work; it is a question of causation:

'Was it part of the injured man's employment to hazard, to suffer or to do that which caused his injury? ... To ask if the cause of the accident was within the sphere of the employment, or was one of the ordinary risks of the employment, or reasonably incidental to the employment ... are all different ways of asking whether it was a part of his employment that he should have acted as he was acting, or should have been in the position in which he was, whereby in the course of that employment he sustained injury[4].'

Thus, if an employee while at work takes medicine which has an adverse effect, that will not be an industrial accident, for it was not an employment risk[5], but where an employee was injured by an explosion when he attempted to light a cigarette close to a gas leak in the factory where he worked, it was held that he was eligible for benefit:

'... there were two causes of this accident: the act of the claimant in operating his lighter and the presence of an explosive mixture of gas and air. The latter was dangerous, and the danger was clearly a risk of the claimant's employment. Prima facie therefore the accident arose out of the employment. The remaining question is whether the claimant's act, which was done for his own personal purposes, added a *different* risk which was the real cause of the accident. In our judgment, his act did not do so ... The claimant's act ... converted the danger of an explosion into an actual explosion. It did not make it a different danger or create a fresh one. In our judgment there was here an amply sufficient causal connection between the employment and its risks on the one hand and the accident on the other[6].'

Apart from the ordinary problems of causation, two particular points have arisen in this context. The first is that the injury concerned may in fact have befallen anyone in the position of the claimant, whether or not employed to do his kind of work, as where a lorry driver is struck by a flying piece of grit, which could easily have hit a private motorist instead. In theory, an employee injured by a common hazard such as this should not be eligible for benefit[7], but it appears that more lenient decisions have been reached in some cases, by holding that the employment was the reason for the employee being in the particular circumstances in which that risk operated upon him, though the distinction is hardly a satisfactory one[8]. The second point is that the claimant's own conduct may have caused or contributed to his injuries, but here a relatively indulgent approach has been taken, for the claim will only fail on this ground if the claimant

4   *Lancashire and Yorkshire Rly Co v Highley* [1917] AC 352, at 372, HL per Lord Sumner.
5   R(I) 43/57.
6   R(I) 2/63, para. 29.
7   R(I) 62/53; R(I) 7/60; R(I) 6/82.
8   See Ogus Barendt, and Wikeley *The Law of Social Security* (4th edn, 1995) pp. 319–320.

created by his conduct a risk different from that inherent in his employment, and it was that different risk which in fact caused the accident (see the passage cited above from R(I) 2/63); if the claimant's contribution was less dramatic than that, his claim may still succeed, and there are no provisions for reduction of benefit on analogy with contributory negligence in the law of tort or contributory fault in unfair dismissal.

Some of the practical importance of having the two requirements of 'out of' and 'in the course of' employment has been to some extent lessened by a statutory provision[9] that an accident arising in the course of employment is presumed to have arisen out of that employment, in the absence of evidence to the contrary. Given a broad interpretation, this presumption could place the burden of proof on the 'out of employment' limb on the Agency officer in most cases, and thus diminish the claimant's difficulties, but a narrow view has been taken by the Divisional Court, so that if *any* evidence points to a contrary conclusion the presumption is inoperative:

> 'The words of the sub-section are not "in the absence of proof to the contrary" or "unless the contrary is proved"; the words of the sub-section are "in the absence of evidence to the contrary". That has been held by commissioners quite rightly ... to mean no more than that, if there is evidence before the commissioner that the accident does not arise out of or in the course of employment, then there is no presumption at all and it is left to the parties to prove the case in the ordinary way[10].'

If this is correct, the presumption will be of little effect, restricted in practice to those cases where no one knows how the accident happened, only that it arose in the course of employment. It would therefore be rash to state that the 'out of employment' limb is of waning importance, even though often criticised, and it certainly remains in principle as a device to ensure that only genuinely employment-linked accidents are covered by the industrial injuries scheme.

d) Special statutory provisions

The general principles discussed above have been supplemented by four special statutory provisions, covering four potential problems:
1) Where a claimant is injured whilst doing something in contravention of a relevant regulation or of any orders of the employer, that accident is still treated as arising out of and in the course of employment if (a) it would have been deemed so to have arisen if the claimant had not been in contravention, and (b) the 'illegal' act was done by the claimant for the purposes of and in connection with the employer's trade or business[11]. Thus, provided there remains a connection between the wrongful act and that which the claimant was employed to do, he may still succeed. In *Noble v Southern Rly Co*[12], Lord Maugham said that the approach should be to ask the following questions:

9   Social Security Contributions and Benefits Act 1992, s. 94(3).
10   *R v National Insurance Comr, ex p Richardson* [1958] 2 All ER 689 at 690, [1958] 1 WLR 851 at 855 per Lord Goddard CJ. See, e.g., the inapplicability of the presumption in R(I) 11/80.
11   Social Security Contributions and Benefits Act 1992, s. 98.
12   [1940] AC 583, at 591, HL; adopted in CI 210/50.

'First, looking at the facts proved as a whole, including any regulations or orders affecting the workman, was the accident one which arose out of and in the course of employment? Secondly, if the first question is answered in the negative, is the negative answer due to the fact that when the accident happened the workman was acting in contravention of some regulation or order? Thirdly, if the second question is answered in the affirmative, was the act which the workman was engaged in performing done by the workman for the purposes of and in connection with his employer's trade or business?'

The scope of this provision and the problems which arise can be seen by contrasting two cases. In R(I) 1/70 a dock labourer, employed in the loading of a ship, met with an accident while driving an electric truck to fetch two slings necessary for the loading. He was not authorised or permitted to drive the truck, which was owned by the port authorities and not by his employers. The Commissioner held that, by reason of the predecessor to section 98, the claimant could recover since in fetching the slings he was acting in the course of his employment, notwithstanding that he went about it in a prohibited manner. However, in an earlier case[13] a more restrictive view was taken. A dock labourer who, without authority or permission, decided to drive an unattended fork lift truck to remove an obstruction, and was injured whilst doing so, was held by the Commissioner to have taken himself outside the course of his employment, and beyond the scope of what is now section 98; this decision was affirmed by the Divisional Court. While it is true that section 98 will not avail someone who is injured while doing something which was clearly not his job, the distinction between these two cases is a thin one, and it could be argued that the more liberal approach in the later case is more in line with the policy behind the section.

2) An employee who is injured while travelling to work on transport operated by or for the employer (not being ordinary public transport) is eligible for benefit, even though he may have been under no obligation to use that particular transport[14]. This statutory provision covers the particular case of travelling on employer-provided transport; outside that provision, a case must be decided on general grounds. The question that arises here is the same as in the area of vicarious liability in tort (when is a travelling accident 'in the course of employment', so that the employer is liable?); in that context, valuable guidance has been given by Lord Lowry in *Smith v Stages*[15], which is set out at p. 732, below in that context, and to which reference may also be made for statutory purposes.

The social security case law amply demonstrates the problems here, for one starts from the general premise that an employee will not be eligible if injured on a journey to or from work which is merely for the purpose of going to his work or back from it, using a route also used by the general public. If he is injured whilst using a private access to his place of work, or whilst crossing land owned by the employer, he may be eligible[16] but once on the public

---

13   *R v D'Albuquerque, ex p Bresnahan* [1966] 1 Lloyd's Rep 69.
14   Social Security Contributions and Benefits Act 1992, s. 99. See Lewis 'Accidents on the way to work' [1981] NLJ 1218. The authority of the employer for the mode of transport is essential: R(I) 5/80.
15   [1989] AC 928, [1989] 1 All ER 833, HL, applied in R(I) 1/91.
16   *Weaver v Tredegar Iron and Coal Co Ltd* [1940] AC 955, at 983, HL per Lord Romer; R(I) 5/67.

highway, or in an area open to the public, his chances of claiming benefit are slim, *unless* he can show that his journey was in the performance of a duty to his employer, not merely preparatory to the performance of a duty[17]. Thus if the employee was ordered to make a particular journey or the journey was part of, or incidental to, the content of his job (wholly or in part), the employee may be covered by the scheme, even if the accident happens while he is travelling from home to his first appointment[18]. However, this will be more easily established in the case of a person without fixed hours or place of work, or with a discretion in the exercise of his function; where a person has a fixed work pattern at places other than the employer's premises (e.g. a home help), he or she may still be treated as an ordinary employee who is not eligible for benefit if injured when travelling to the first call[19].

3) An accident befalling an employee on the employer's premises while he is trying to rescue or protect people or avert serious damage to property in an actual or supposed emergency at the premises is deemed to arise out of and in the course of employment[20].

4) An accident arising in the course of employment which is caused by another person's 'misconduct, skylarking or negligence' or by steps taken in consequence of such matters is deemed to arise out of employment, and so give rise to a claim for benefit, provided the claimant did not 'directly or indirectly induce or contribute to' the accident by his own conduct[1]. This provision is designed to include the case where, although the claimant suffered from the actions of another while doing his job, there might be doubt as to whether the injury arose 'out of' his employment, as in *R v National Insurance Comr, ex p Richardson*[2] where a bus conductor who was assaulted on his bus was denied benefit on the basis that the attack was made on him simply as a person who happened to be there, not *qua* conductor, and so the injury did not arise 'out of' the employment. The present provision was first introduced in 1961 and covers acts consequent upon misconduct, etc., as well as direct results of it. Thus, in R(I) 3/67 the claimant was hit by a snowball thrown by a fellow employee during a smoke break; when he went after the perpetrator with intent to remonstrate, his hand was injured by a slammed door and the Commissioner held that he was eligible for benefit under the predecessor of section 101. The section also covers injury in the course of employment caused by the behaviour or presence of an animal or by being struck by any object or by lightning.

ii) Industrial diseases

While it is obvious that certain occupations may carry a risk of contracting certain diseases, these would in the main fall outside the basic industrial injury scheme which is reliant upon the physical injury in question being caused by an 'accident'; the gradual contraction of an industrial disease is prima facie a 'process' and so not covered. The answer to this has been to provide separate coverage for certain

17 *R v National Industrial Injury Benefit Tribunal, ex p Fieldhouse* (1974) 17 KIR 63; R(I) 12/75; R(I) 5/77.
18 R(I) 18/55; *Nancollas v Insurance Officer* [1985] 1 All ER 833, CA.
19 Contrast R(I) 4/70 and R(I) 3/72 with R(I) 2/67 and R(I) 12/75.
20 Social Security Contributions and Benefits Act 1992, s. 100.
1 Ibid., s. 101.
2 [1958] 2 All ER 689, [1958] 1 WLR 851.

specified diseases which experience has shown to be often caused by certain employments. The machinery provided by the legislation is that the Secretary of State may by regulation prescribe a particular disease if he is satisfied that it ought to be treated as a risk of the occupation in question, not just as a risk common to all persons, and that it is such that there will be reasonable certainty in any given case that contraction of the disease can fairly be ascribed to the employment[3]. Regulations have been made under this power which specify approximately 60 diseases[4], and once a disease is specified in relation to an employment, the remedies of a person contracting it lie under these particular provisions, not under the general 'personal injury by accident' provisions. Schedule 1 to the regulations contains a table of diseases and the occupations for which they are prescribed; a disease may be prescribed for one particular occupation, or for a general description of work, which may form part of a number of occupations. Thus, for example, ankylostomiasis is prescribed for 'work in or about a mine', whereas subcutaneous cellulitis of the hand is prescribed for any occupation involving 'manual labour causing severe or prolonged friction or pressure on the hand'. There are particularly detailed provisions applying to pneumoconiosis, byssinosis, diffuse mesothelioma and occupational deafness[5].

To claim benefit, a person suffering from an industrial disease must show three things. The first is that he is in fact suffering from the disease; this is a medical question, with a general right of appeal to a Medical Board and then an Appeal Tribunal. The second is that the disease is prescribed for his particular occupation; where the schedule prescribes it for a general activity, e.g. certain forms of manual labour, or contact with certain substances, he must show that his occupation included that activity to more than a purely minimal extent. The third is that contraction of the disease was caused by engaging in his particular occupation. Here the claimant is aided by a presumption that if the disease is prescribed for that occupation, it will be presumed to have been caused by it, unless the adjudication officer can prove the contrary, on a balance of probabilities[6]. This presumption will generally arise if the employee was in the relevant occupation on the date of development of the disease (as defined) or within one month previously.

iii)   Benefits

The state injuries scheme attempts to serve two different purposes in relation to injured employees – the provision of financial support while the employee is unable to work because of the injury or disease, and the provision of some form of compensation for a person who is left with a lasting disability after the accident, either total or partial. The short-term 'statutory sick pay' or 'incapacity benefit' covers the former, and the long-term 'disablement benefit' covers the latter.

---

3   Social Security Contributions and Benefits Act 1992, s. 108(2). For the difficulties inherent in industrial disease cases, see Wikeley 'Social security adjudication and occupational lung diseases' (1988) 17 ILJ 92.

4   Social Security (Industrial Injuries) (Prescribed Diseases) Regulations 1985, S.I. 1985 No. 967. See Wikeley 'Tinkering with tinpot legislation: reforms of the schedule of prescribed diseases' (1997) 26 ILJ 283.

5   See R(I) 7/76, RI 2/85 and R(I) 8/85 on occupational deafness; see also the Pneumoconiosis etc. (Workers' Compensation) Act 1979 and the Pneumoconiosis (Workers' Compensation) (Payment of Claims) Regulations 1985, S.I. 1985 No. 2035.

6   S.I. 1985 No. 967 (above), reg. 4(1); longer time periods are prescribed for certain diseases (such as deafness and pneumoconiosis) before the presumption can apply.

a) Income replacement benefits

Since the abolition of the special injury benefit for those suffering an accident or prescribed disease at work, the relevant claim became one for statutory sick pay for those still in work and short-term sickness benefit for those not. After 28 weeks of either, if still incapable of work, the person could claim invalidity benefit, which was the principal benefit for the long-term sick. To claim such benefit, the claimant had to show that he was in fact incapable, by reason of some specific disease or bodily or mental impairment, of work which he could reasonably be expected to do. Once it became clear that he could no longer hope to resume his normal work (e.g. because of heart or back problems), the question became whether there was other, usually lighter, work that he could be expected to do. Many of the appeals to appeal tribunals concerned exactly that point, i.e. in the jargon, whether the person was 'fit within limits' (a question akin to that of reasonable mitigation of damage in wrongful dismissal or personal injury cases).

Due to the previous government's concern over the increase in claims for invalidity benefit (from $^1/_2$ million in 1976 to one and a half million in 1992)[7], this whole system was subject to radical reform in 1995, with the abolition of sickness benefit and invalidity benefit and their replacement by the new incapacity benefit[8]. SSP is not affected, and so for the first 28 weeks the employee still in work will claim that. If not so entitled, the person can claim lower-rate, short-term incapacity benefit for that period, provided incapable of his own, normal work. The major change comes if still sick after 28 weeks. The person may then claim higher-rate, short-term incapacity benefit for the rest of the first year, and then long-term incapacity benefit for the future. However, after that initial 28 weeks, the claimant becomes subject to the new 'All work' test for incapability. This deliberately abandons any link with *actual* inability to work, and instead concentrates on supposedly objective medical effects of the condition in question, with points attached to each. There are 89 physical 'descriptors' under 14 headings (from walking through to episodes of lost consciousness) and 25 mental descriptors under 4 headings (completion of tasks, daily living, coping with pressure and interaction with others)[9]. If the claimant (after a prescribed medical procedure involving self-assessment, his own GP and a Benefit Agency medical officer) scores 15 points on the physical or 10 on the mental descriptors, they get the benefit, in principle irrespective of whether they are actually capable of work. Clearly this is meant to be a tougher test, in order to stop the increased expenditure on what was invalidity benefit. Early experience in the appeal tribunals suggested that it may not in fact have this effect, especially once the

---

7   The reasons for this increase are complex, and certainly wider than the general fear of fraud and malingering that seems to have been behind the general political impetus for change. High unemployment probably had a background effect, even though it should not have done (the benefit being payable for inability to perform work, not inability to get a job), and the Government's 'Care in the Community' policy has turned many from inmates into claimants. See generally Berthoud 'The medical assessment of incapacity' (1995) 2 JSSL 61.

8   Social Security (Incapacity for Work) Act 1994; Incapacity for Work (General) Regulations 1995, S.I. 1995 No. 311. See Wikeley, 'The Social Security (Incapacity for Work) Act 1994' (1995) 58 MLR 523; Bonner 'Incapacity for work: a new benefit and new tests' (1995) 2 JSSL 86.

9   Some descriptions qualify a person by themselves, e.g. inability to walk or not being able to stand unaided, each of which carries 15 points. Otherwise, the various lesser scores across several inabilities are aggregated.

factor of pain and variability ('good days and bad') is fully taken into account[10]. The present government have stated their desire to amend the system yet again, with a view to putting more emphasis on what a claimant can do, not what they cannot do, and so we are likely to see further change here.

b)   Disablement benefit

This is payable for loss of physical or mental faculty resulting from the accident or disease in question[11]. Causal connection between the loss of faculty and the accident or disease must be shown and this will be primarily a matter for the statutory authorities (adjudication officer, SSAT or Commissioner). However, assessment of the disability is the province of a medical board or appeal tribunal who may, if necessary, reopen the question of the causal connection[12]. Disablement benefit may not be paid until a minimum of 90 days (disregarding Sundays) after the accident[13]. Where it is payable, it is calculated by reference to a tariff set out in regulations[14], which lays down percentages for individual injuries (e.g. 7 per cent for loss of a little finger, 50 per cent for amputation of a leg below the knee, 100 per cent for loss of both legs); the relevant percentage for the claimant is established essentially by medical experts, and may be permanent or subject to a time limit if the disability is thought likely to end in that time; it is subject to review either upwards or downwards. Prior to 1986, the system for payment was that if the percentage of disability was less than 20 per cent, the benefit was payable as a lump sum gratuity of an amount fixed by regulations for that percentage; if 20 per cent or over, the benefit was payable as a weekly pension, the amount again fixed by regulations. However, by virtue of the amendments made by the Social Security Act 1986[15], benefit is only payable if the percentage disability is 20 per cent or over (though a percentage of 14 per cent to 19 per cent is now rounded up to 20 per cent)[16]. The effect is that injury of less than 14 per cent is now not compensated, and the lump sum gratuity disappears, being replaced by weekly pension payments in all new cases[17]. The rationale behind

---

10   The Act and Regulations are silent on pain and variability; in practice, such questions arise in the majority of the appeals now coming to social security appeal tribunals, especially in relation to back and neck injuries. BA doctors are told informally that they must be taken into account, and it has become common for tribunals to take them into account to a greater extent, in what has become a crucial gloss on the wording of the legislation, finally upheld by a Tribunal of Commissioners in CIB/14534/1996.

11   Social Security Contributions and Benefits Act 1992, s. 103.

12   Social Security Administration Act 1992, ss. 44, 45 and 60, reversing the decisions of the House of Lords in *Minister of Social Security v AEU* [1967] 1 AC 725, [1967] 1 All ER 210, HL and *Jones v Secretary of State for Social Services* [1972] AC 944, [1972] 1 All ER 145, HL.

13   Social Security Contributions and Benefits Act 1992, s. 103(6).

14   Social Security (General Benefit) Regulations 1982, S.I. 1982 No. 1408, Sch. 2.

15   See Lewis 'The government's philosophy towards reform of social security: the case of industrial injuries benefit' (1986) 15 ILJ 256 for details of the amendments and likely impact in practice.

16   Social Security Contributions and Benefits Act 1992, s. 103(3). The other principal changes were the abolition of (i) unemployability supplement (which had become superfluous in the light of other, earlier, changes), (ii) hospital treatment allowance, and (iii) industrial death benefit (industrial widows now being treated in the same way as those widowed by other causes).

17   Lewis (n. 15, above) points out that one of the gravest effects of the minimum percentage of 14 per cent may be in the area of certain industrial diseases where the link between the industrial process and the disease has been established (and incorporated into regulations) but the actual level of disability in many cases may be relatively small. Note, however, that certain chest diseases (pneumoconiosis, byssinosis and diffuse mesothelioma) are treated

the change was one that was claimed to be behind several of the major social security changes in the 1986 Act, namely better targeting of benefit on those in greatest need; however, it was highly criticised (particularly by the TUC), not just as a cost-cutting exercise but also as the removal of hard-won statutory rights for those involved in industrial accidents. Similar sentiments were again heard when the present government floated ideas of further changes to the benefit, in particular by making some version of it primarily the responsibility of the employer.

The amount of disablement benefit is thus linked to (a) the degree of disability and (b) a maximum fixed sum or sums; it is therefore not linked to any loss of income (so that, for example, it is unaffected by receipt of earnings or jobseeker's allowance). This could cause hardship where the accident has had an effect on the claimant's earning capabilities or ability to cope with life; the answer to this has been to provide certain further benefits. The old 'reduced earnings allowance' has been phased out (with no new claims permitted after 1990), but it remains the case that if a claimant suffers 100 per cent disability and is in need of constant attendance, he is eligible for a further flat rate benefit on that basis[18], and in cases of permanent grave disability for a flat rate 'exceptionally severe disablement allowance'[19].

iv) The overlap with damages

Receipt of state benefits for an industrial injury does not prejudice the claimant's rights to sue his employer for damages in the courts if he has a relevant cause of action. However, if he is successful in such an action the question arises whether the sums which he has already received in benefits should be taken into account in assessing his damages. Against deductions of state benefits, it could be argued that they were received under essentially an insurance scheme (albeit compulsory and state-run) which exists independently of the common law tort system, and so they should be treated as ordinary insurance moneys, which are not deducted[20]. On the other hand, a rule against deduction could be seen as sanctioning double compensation, and the insurance argument is heavily qualified by the fact that part of the contribution to the scheme comes from the employer (who then also has to pay the damages, through his premia to his insurer), so that it is not simply a question of the prudent employee benefiting from insurance moneys provided by his own premia, as is the case with private insurance. When the National Insurance system came into force in 1948 a compromise solution was enacted[1] whereby a court in assessing damages had to take into account one-half of the benefits received; this had the practical effect that the state paid the benefits, and the plaintiff and defendant shared the advantage, half each. The Royal Commission on Civil Liability, headed by Lord Pearson, recommended that benefits received should be deducted in full, as a matter of principle[2]. Total

separately, and still attract compensation if the level of disability is 1 per cent or more: Social Security (Industrial Injuries) (Prescribed Diseases) Regulations 1985, S.I. 1985 No. 967, reg. 20.

18   Ibid., s. 104.
19   Ibid., s. 105.
20   *Bradburn v Great Western Rly Co* (1874) LR 10 Exch 1; *Parry v Cleaver* [1970] AC 1, [1969] 1 All ER 555, HL; *Smoker v London Fire and Civil Defence Authority* [1991] 2 AC 502, [1991] 2 All ER 449, HL.
1   Law Reform (Personal Injuries) Act 1948, s. 2.
2   Report, 1978, Cmnd. 7054–1, vol. 1, paras. 277–280 and 467–483. The aim, as seen above, was to down-grade the tort action by making it less 'profitable', especially in smaller claims.

deductibility has now come about, by virtue of the Social Security Act 1989 (now the Social Security (Recovery of Benefits) Act 1997), however not as a matter of principle, but rather as a financial measure to allow the government to recoup the amounts paid out[3]. The basis of the scheme[4] is that a final settlement or award of a personal injury action is not to be made until the defendant (in practice, the insurer) has obtained from the DSS Compensation Recovery Unit a certificate of total benefits paid to the plaintiff; the defendant must then deduct that amount from the damages and account for it to that DSS department. The scheme has been subject to criticism; the power of recoupment is very broad[5], and the amount to be recouped may now be a significant factor in deciding on a settlement, especially where a considerable time has elapsed since the accident (i.e. where the amount of benefit received is substantial)[6]. One potentially unfair and highly criticised aspect of the original 1989 scheme was that benefit paid could be recouped for *any* damages awarded, if necessary biting into general damages for pain and suffering, etc. This was radically altered in the 1997 Act which splits damages into four – general damages, special damages for loss of earnings, compensation of cost of care and compensation for loss of mobility; the first head is *not* now subject to recoupment, and in relation to the other three it is provided that only benefits states to be relevant to them can be recouped from them (so that, for example, income support can only be recouped from damages for lost earnings and the care component of disability living allowance can only be recouped from compensation for care costs). This was an important reform, but there remains one other trap (not addressed by the 1997 Act), namely that if damages are reduced for contributory negligence, that fact does *not* affect the amount of benefit to be recouped, so that the recoupment requirement could weigh particularly heavily in such a case.

3   OUTLINE OF AN ACTION FOR DAMAGES

If an employee receives injuries from an industrial accident which are sufficiently serious and/or lasting, he may wish to consider bringing a civil action against his employer, in addition to receiving the essentially shorter-term remedy of incapacity benefit or disablement benefit. Such proceedings are brought in the normal way for an action in tort, for there is no special procedure and in most ways the form and substance of the action are governed by the ordinary rules of the law of tort[7].

3   The Government projection in 1989 was that it would apply to 120,000 compensation payments each year, recovering £55 million p.a.
4   For the details of the scheme, see DSS Booklet Z1 'Deduction from Compensation'.
5   One possible way to avoid recoupment is to argue that the benefit was not in fact paid because of the accident, but this will be difficult to prove; see, e.g. the appropriately named case of *Hassall v Secretary of State for Social Security* [1995] 3 All ER 909, [1995] 1 WLR 812, CA, applied in *Neal v Bingle* [1998] 2 All ER 58, CA.
6   One significant difference between this scheme and the long-established scheme for recouping benefit from unfair dismissal compensation (p. 513, above), on which it was partly based, is that this scheme applies to *settlements* as well as awards, and so cannot be avoided by settling; this caught the parties out in *Rees v West Glamorgan County Council* [1994] PIQR P37, CA. The existence of the scheme may place emphasis on earlier settlement (to keep the amount of benefit down), which could put pressure on the plaintiff to settle for less earlier. For the overall effects of the scheme, see Milton 'Recoupment planning' [1995] NLJ 784.
7   The standard work on industrial injuries cases is Munkman *Employer's Liability* (12th edn, 1995). More detailed coverage of the legislation can be found in Redgrave, Fife & Machin *Health and Safety* (2nd edn, 1993).

Thus, questions of proof of fault, causation, remoteness, the quantum of damages[8] and the special rules applying in case of a fatality are dealt with in basically the same way as in any other tort action. In spite of that, there is a tendency to think of industrial injury cases as sui generis and there is some justification for this since they comprise such a high proportion of all tort actions brought in any particular year (as with motor accident cases) and, while the legal principles may be the same as elsewhere, they have evolved in certain particular ways which can make this type of action distinctive. The aim of this head of this chapter, therefore, is to set out the *form* of the typical action (and, where appropriate, to point out certain rules which either are rules of general application which have particular significance in this type of action, or have evolved as separate rules in the industrial context), while assuming a working knowledge on the part of the reader of the basics of the law of tort.

Perhaps the two most distinctive features of an industrial injury case are the distillation of the general common law duty of care into certain well-defined duties upon the employer (in contract as well as tort) and the importance in practice of the action for breach of statutory duty. These are considered below. First, the four principal heads of liability upon an employer will be outlined, then the possible defences which he may be able to raise, and finally the question of insurance.

i) Liabilities upon the employer

a) The common law liability as 'master'

It has long been established that an employer has a duty of reasonable care towards his employee while the latter is in the course of his employment. This duty can in theory be viewed as contractual as well as tortious, for it is one of the implied terms which will be read into a contract of employment[9]; normally, however, there will be no advantage in pleading the case in contract, and so the action will be brought as an ordinary tort action. Its principal significance is that it is 'personal' to both employer and employee. This means that the duty upon the employer is non-delegable, so that the employer will remain liable for injury caused by breach of the duty even if he purported to leave the matter in question to others (e.g. to competent contractors); this was of great importance in the days when the employee's remedies were narrower than they are today (in particular, before the abolition of the doctrine of common employment in 1948), and remains of importance since it prevents the employer from claiming that he exercised due care simply by choosing competent people to whom to delegate his functions[10]. The personal nature of the duty further means that it is owed to each employee individually, not to the workforce as a whole, and so in applying the ordinary rules of tortious liability (e.g. the rules relating to the practicability of any precautions which could or should have been provided by the employer) the

---

8   A detailed discussion of the law on damages is outside the scope of this book. For authoritative treatment, see *McGregor on Damages* and *Kemp and Kemp on the Quantum of Damages* with its up-dating supplements and the regular 'Damages' heading in *Current Law*.

9   *Matthews v Kuwait Bechtel Corpn* [1959] 2 QB 57, [1959] 2 All ER 345, CA.

10   This also applies in a 'borrowed servant' case; if the employee is sent by his employer to work for Co X and is injured, his employer remains potentially liable, though able to seek a contribution or full indemnity from Co X: *Morris v Breaveglen Ltd* [1993] ICR 766, [1993] IRLR 350, CA; *Nelhams v Sandells Maintenance Ltd* (1995) Times, 15 June, CA.

court is entitled to look at the individual circumstances of the injured employee, and what it was reasonable to expect of the employer in *his* case (which may differ from the *average* or *usual* case)[11]. Naturally, there is a large body of case law on the employer's common law liability[12] and, although it is clear that there is in theory only one general duty of reasonable care, the tendency has been to treat that duty in practice as imposing upon the employer the obligation to use reasonable care to provide:

a)   safe and adequate plant and equipment[13];
b)   safe premises and/or place of work[14];
c)   competent and safe fellow employees[15]; and
d)   a safe system of work, in all the circumstances.

The last heading is a wide, residual one which shows how extensive the common law duty upon the employer may be, for it can cover the overall aspects of the organisation and supervision of the work (possibly including precautions to protect the employee partly from his own actions)[16], and clearly demonstrates the continuing nature of the obligation. Its application will vary greatly with the type of work in question, and factors such as the physical lay-out of the job, the sequence in which work is to be carried out and the provision of warnings, notices and special instructions may all be relevant; it can be equally applicable to the long-term lay-out of the job and to a procedure adopted in the short term for one particular job. Moreover, it is arguable that this heading may now take on renewed vitality in the light of the Management of Health and Safety at Work Regulations 1999 (see p. 762, below). These lay down important new legal duties on all employers, for example to undertake risk assessments. At a late stage a provision was inserted that these regulations do not support civil liability; this means that, for example, a failure to undertake a risk assessment (leading to injury) could not be used in a breach of statutory duty action *but* there appears to be no reason

11   *Paris v Stepney Borough Council* [1951] AC 367, [1951] 1 All ER 42, HL. If the plaintiff is to rely on any particular peculiarity or susceptibility, the employer must have known of it, or have had reasonable cause to know of it: *James v Hepworth and Grandage Ltd* [1968] 1 QB 94, [1967] 2 All ER 829, CA.

12   The leading authority is the decision of the House of Lords in *Wilsons and Clyde Coal Co Ltd v English* [1938] AC 57, [1937] 3 All ER 628 HL. It was reaffirmed in *McDermid v Nash Dredging and Reclamation Co Ltd* [1987] ICR 917, [1987] IRLR 334, HL. The duties can even apply where the employee was working abroad, but any question of *breach* must then be decided realistically: *Cook v Square D Ltd* [1992] ICR 262, [1992] IRLR 34, CA.

13   See Munkman, ch. 4. In this area it is particularly important to note that the obligation upon the employer will usually be to provide *and maintain* the equipment. Much of the common law on this heading is now superseded by the Employer's Liability (Defective Equipment) Act 1969, considered below.

14   This duty applies to the employee's place of work when it is outside the employer's premises (e.g. in another factory, a customer's home or, in the case of a window cleaner, on a windowsill); *General Cleaning Contractors v Christmas* [1953] AC 180, [1952] 2 All ER 1110, HL; *Wilson v Tyneside Window Cleaning Co Ltd* [1958] 2 QB 110, [1958] 2 All ER 265, CA; *Smith v Austin Lifts Ltd* [1959] 1 All ER 81, [1959] 1 WLR 100, HL. However, the duty remains one of reasonable care (only), so the fact that the accident happened outside the employer's premises may be a relevant factor.

15   This will cover the competence of supervisors and persons in charge of safety precautions. It also covers fellow employees, so that reasonable care should be taken to protect the employee in question from incompetents, homicidal maniacs and practical jokers: *Hudson v Ridge Manufacturing Co Ltd* [1957] 2 QB 348, [1957] 2 All ER 229. This common law duty may be important in an unfair dismissal action if the employer decides that the only way to protect the other employees is to dismiss the practical joker.

16   It may cover a duty to *warn* employees of work dangers where the employer is in a better position to appreciate them: *Pape v Cumbria County Council* [1992] 3 All ER 211, [1992] ICR 132.

why it could not be used in a *negligence* action, as failure to provide a safe system of work, using the obligations laid down in the regulations as *evidence* of that failure[17].

In the light of these well developed heads of liability, it is easy to imagine that compensation is fairly automatic once there is an industrial accident. However, that would be an over-simple view, for the above heads (wide as they are) only govern the sort of accident which *may* be the subject of compensation. Whether a particular accident *will* lead to a successful claim for damages depends on whether, on the facts of the case, the injured employee can clear the normal hurdles which must be cleared by the plaintiff in any tort action; the specialised *heads* of liability do not help him here. It must be remembered, therefore, that the burden of proof remains upon the employee, and that he must be able to prove fault.

The employee may discharge the burden of proof in the ordinary way by adducing the necessary evidence or, in a case where the precise details are unclear, by seeking to rely on the maxim res ipsa loquitur[18]. In an industrial accident case the plaintiff may in addition be able to rely on three special factors. The first is that if the employer can be shown to have acted contrary to the normal practice of the trade in question, that may raise an inference of negligence; this is not invariably so, for widespread adoption of a bad practice does not convert it into a good practice[19], but in the nature of things trade usages are likely to be of considerable evidential value, particularly in a trade or industry which is safety-conscious. Where the harm suffered is an industrial disease, rather than an accident, a difficulty may arise here in deciding from what date (the 'date of knowledge') it was reasonable for an employer to have realised the danger posed by the process or substance in question, especially where medical opinion on the matter gradually changed over a period of time[20]. The second is that the employee may be able to show that the employer has not complied with the recommendations of a relevant Code of Practice issued under the Health and Safety at Work etc. Act 1974. Section 17 of the Act expressly makes Codes of Practice admissible in criminal proceedings against the employer, but there is no reason why they should not be equally admissible in civil proceedings where relevant, though without the statutory presumption against the employer which applies in criminal proceedings by virtue of section 17(2). The third factor is that if the accident in question has been investigated by a health and safety inspector, information gathered by him may be released to a potential plaintiff for the purpose of bringing a civil action[1].

In these ways, the injured employee might be better placed than some other claimants on questions of proof, but he remains in the same position as any other claimant in a negligence action in that he must be able to prove *fault*. This means not only showing that there was a duty upon the employer (which in the light of the extensive case law may be easy), but also that the employer was in breach of

---

17   Smith, Goddard and Randall *Health and Safety – the New Legal Framework* (1993), ch. 4.
18   The actual effect of the maxim upon the trial of the issue is still a matter for legal dispute – see *Winfield and Jolowicz on Tort* (15th edn, 1998), p. 191.
19   This is equally important when applied in reverse, i.e. where the employer claims to have *complied* with standard practice and thereby to have discharged his duty of care.
20   One of the early cases was *Thompson v Smith Shiprepairers (North Shields) Ltd* [1984] QB 405 fixing the date of knowledge at 1963 (when Government recommendations were first published) for occupational deafness. In *Barclays Bank plc v Fairclough Building Ltd (No 2)* [1995] IRLR 605, CA the date for asbestos-related processes was fixed at 1988, and in a first instance decision reported in *The Times* on 16 January 1996 a claim by miners for vibration white finger was allowed back to 1975.
1   Health and Safety at Work etc. Act 1974, s 28(9).

that duty by not doing more to safeguard the employee, and that that breach of duty caused the injury which he suffered. In some cases this may raise difficult questions of the practicability of further safety precautions[2], and what knowledge the employer had or ought to have had of any defect which caused the injury. It is trite law to say that the duty upon the employer is only to take such care as is reasonable in the circumstances, not to *guarantee* the safety of the employee, but this can be a very real consideration in a common law action (explaining the preferability in many cases of the action for breach of statutory duty). This can be seen particularly from the cases on latent defects in tools and machinery used by the employee. As a 'latent defect' is one which could not be discovered by reasonable inspection, the employer is not in breach of his duty by not discovering it and, moreover, provided the employer used reasonable care in selecting the tool or machine (e.g. by buying a well known make from a reputable supplier) he will have discharged his duty and, if the tool later breaks or explodes causing injury to the employee, the employer will not be liable at common law[3]. It is true that the employee may have an action against the negligent manufacturer under the ordinary principles in *Donoghue v Stevenson*[4], but that is a less direct action which may raise practical problems of bringing the action and of proof (e.g. if the manufacturer is a foreign company). This particular problem in the common law led to the passage of the Employer's Liability (Defective Equipment) Act 1969 which provides that the employer is liable where the employee sustains personal injury in the course of his employment 'in consequence of a defect in equipment[5] provided by his employer for the purposes of the employer's business'. However, the liability is not strict, since the employee must be able to prove that 'the defect is attributable wholly or partly to the fault of a third party (whether identified or not)'; this will usually mean showing negligence on the part of the manufacturer, and if this can be shown the injured employee may proceed directly against his employer, leaving the employer to bring any further proceedings against the 'third party' for an indemnity for the damages which he has had to pay to the employee. This statute may provide valuable assistance to a plaintiff, particularly in a latent defect case, but it only applies to defective equipment and even then, as already stated, the plaintiff must be able to prove fault on the part of a third party, which may be particularly difficult where the nature of the 'defect' is not

2   This point may be of particular significance in an industrial accident case for, although the safety of the employee is a vital factor, the law cannot expect total safety if the price would be a decrease or cessation of industrial output out of proportion to the potential danger. The classic example here is *Latimer v AEC Ltd* [1953] AC 643, [1953] 2 All ER 449, HL. The concept of causation may also occasionally pose problems; see, e.g., *White v Holbrook Precision Castings Ltd* [1985] IRLR 215, CA where the plaintiff failed because the court took the view on the facts that even if the employer had given him a reasonable warning of the possible injurious effects of the work, the plaintiff would still have taken the job.
3   *Davie v New Merton Board Mills Ltd* [1959] AC 604, [1959] 1 All ER 346, HL. This does not jeopardise the principle that the duty upon the employer is non-delegable (*Wilsons and Clyde Coal Co Ltd v English* [1938] AC 57), for the manufacturer is not viewed as someone to whom the employer has delegated his functions; the obligation is still upon the employer to exercise care in selecting the equipment. The problem arises because no amount of reasonable care would have discovered the defect.
4   [1932] AC 562, HL. See, for example, *Hill v James Crowe (Cases) Ltd* [1978] 1 All ER 812, [1978] ICR 298. *Castree v E R Squibb & Sons Ltd* [1980] 2 All ER 589, [1980] 1 WLR 1248, CA, shows an application of the jurisdictional rules favourable to the claimant employee (or to a defendant employer wishing to issue third party proceedings against the manufacturers of defective equipment) where the equipment was manufactured abroad.
5   Defined as including 'any plant and machinery, vehicle, aircraft and clothing'. It includes a ship (*Coltman v Bibby Tankers Ltd* [1988] AC 276, [1988] ICR 67, HL) and also may include material being worked on, as well as the equipment being used (*Knowles v Liverpool County Council* [1993] 4 All ER 321, [1993] IRLR 588, HL).

obvious[6]; outside the Act's ambit the ordinary common law rule continues to apply, requiring the employee to show negligence on the part of the employer.

The above discussion has tended to concentrate on the traditional form of damage in employers' liability cases, physical injury from a definable accident. However, as in health and safety law generally, increased emphasis in recent years has been on extending these principles to diseases or other medical conditions caused by work, or to psychiatric injuries; by their very nature these areas are more difficult to deal with, being more difficult to define and potentially raising questions of causation[7]. Asbestos and its related problems of mesothelioma have become a serious concern of probable long-term effect, and the difficulties here can be seen from the example of repetitive strain injury (RSI) where there is even controversy over whether it exists, before getting to the question whether an employer can be liable in damages for it[8]. Nervous shock or post traumatic stress disorder caused by events at work are likely to cause increasing litigation[9]. However, perhaps the most important development has been in the area of mental stress from work causing psychiatric injury. In *Walker v Northumberland County Council*[10] a social worker succeeded at first instance in a claim for damages for common law negligence against his employers, based on the second, debilitating nervous breakdown that he suffered, due to the ever-increasing workload placed on him and the failure of the employer to provide help which had been promised after the first breakdown. This widely reported decision (unfortunately not appealed) caused considerable consternation in personnel circles (especially with the ruling that the employer could not raise a defence that the increased workload was caused by externally-imposed financial cutbacks), and raises the interesting prospect of the old common law rules on duties of care at work taking on a new role as possibly the only effective counterweight to what has seemed in recent years an irresistible movement in so many kinds of employment to demand more and more work of fewer and fewer employees and call it economic efficiency[11].

6   See Lang, 'The Employer's Liability (Defective Equipment) Act – lion or mouse?' (1984) 47 MLR 48 for a review of the practical difficulties of the Act and a suggestion that a statutory reversal of the burden of proof is essential if it is to work in the way originally intended.

7   Barrett 'Work-induced stress' (1995) 24 ILJ 343.

8   *Mughal v Reuters Ltd* [1993] IRLR 571 was widely reported due to remarks by the judge doubting the existence of RSI as such, and dismissing the plaintiff's claim, but there have also been (unreported) decisions where claims have succeeded: see Barrett (n. 7, above) at p. 345.

9   Employees have succeeded in actions against third parties who have put them in danger during their work, but the position against the employer is more uncertain. Ordinary nervous shock law, itself in a state of flux since the Hillsborough disaster litigation, makes a claim difficult where the employee was not himself in direct danger, even if he witnesses a horrifying work accident to others: *McFarlane v EE Caledonia Ltd* [1994] 2 All ER 1, CA; *Robertson v Forth Road Bridge Joint Board* [1995] IRLR 251, Ct of Sess. In a claim for nervous shock by police affected by the Hillsborough disaster, the House of Lords eventually held that there is *no* special duty owed to employees in this context, who therefore remain subject to the normal (restrictive) rules: *White v Chief Constable of South Yorkshire Police* [1999] 2 AC 455, [1999] 1 All ER 1, HL.

10 [1995] 1 All ER 737, [1995] IRLR 35.

11 This could be particularly so because of the large amounts of damages possible – a broken leg from an accident heals; a nervous breakdown may make the sufferer incapable of ever working again. An interesting parallel is with *Johnstone v Bloomsbury Health Authority* [1991] ICR 269, [1991] IRLR 118, CA (p. 99, above) where again there was a common law challenge (this time under the contract of employment and its implied obligations) to intolerable work requirements. These cases show the continuing vitality of the common law in areas not (yet) covered by protective legislation.

b)   Liability for breach of statutory duty

The action for breach of statutory duty may often be used to compensate for the defects and lack of certainty in the common law action against the employer. It is a device evolved by the courts to allow a claimant to sue for damages when the conduct of the defendant which caused the injury was in defiance of a duty cast upon him by statute, even though the statute itself will probably not even mention the question of civil liability, normally being concerned only to punish the transgression with criminal penalties (often in former times a fine of minute proportion). As the duty contained in the statute may be (a) stricter and (b) far more precise than the common law duty of reasonable care in all the circumstances, this action will tend in practice to be the primary one when pleading the injured employee's case, with the common law action in the past often little more than an afterthought or 'longstop' (a set of priorities which is not always reflected in tort texts). Although the result of this action may be more satisfactory for the claimant, its application is not automatic and so its constituent elements must be proved. To this extent, it can be a relatively technical action, and these elements must now be briefly summarised.

The first and most basic element is that the statutory provision upon which the plaintiff wishes to rely must be one which in law supports civil liability. This is not invariably so, and when a court has to consider the potential civil aspect of a section for the first time difficult questions may arise as to the presumed intention of Parliament, whether the statute was designed to give direct protection to people such as the plaintiff, what type of harm the statute was meant to prevent, and whether any criminal penalties which are provided are meant to give adequate protection on their own[12]. In most cases this exercise will now be unnecessary because of existing case law, and in industrial cases it has been well established (particularly after the decision of the Court of Appeal in *Groves v Lord Wimborne*[13]) that *safety* provisions in industrial legislation will usually support civil liability, though even this has exceptions, and moreover in the case of *health* or *welfare* provisions the position has been less certain. In the light of this uncertainty, the obvious point has been made that it would be preferable for the statutes in question to state whether they are intended to support civil liability[14]. In the past this has not usually been done[15], but this is in the process of changing. The Health and Safety at Work etc. Act 1974, section 47(2) states that regulations made under the Act are to be construed as giving rise to civil liability unless the regulation in question expressly provides otherwise. This is of particular importance now, with the coming into force on 1 January 1993 of the six new sets of EC-inspired regulations which largely replace the old factories legislation[16]. The 'head' regulations, the Management of Health and Safety at Work Regulations 1992 (reissued in 1999), do exclude civil liability, but there is no such exclusion in the other five, more specific, sets (applying to the workplace, work equipment, personal protective equipment, manual handling and VDUs), and so breaches of these *will* give rise to an action for breach of statutory duty.

---

12   For two examples of this problem (in non-industrial cases) see *McCall v Abelesz* [1976] QB 585, [1976] 1 All ER 727, CA; *Ex p Island Records Ltd* [1978] Ch 122, [1978] 3 All ER 824, CA.
13   [1898] 2 QB 402; *Butler v Fife Coal Co Ltd* [1912] AC 149, HL.
14   See, e.g., *Cutler v Wandsworth Stadium Ltd* [1949] AC 398, HL at 411 per Lord Du Parcq.
15   For rare examples, see the Resale Prices Act 1964, s. 4(2) and the Mineral Workings (Offshore Installations) Act 1971, s. 11.
16   See p. 762, below.

The second element is that the statutory duty in question must be owed to the claimant; this will depend upon the detailed wording of the section or regulation under which he wishes to sue. In the past, it was common to frame provisions as protecting 'persons employed' which clearly excludes independent contractors[17]. One of the main reasons for this was that many of the important detailed provisions were contained in regulations rather than in the principal statutes, and under the Factories Act 1961, section 76 regulations could only be made for the protection of 'persons employed' and so any regulation purporting to cover a wider class would have been ultra vires and void. Now, however, the power to make regulations is contained in the Health and Safety at Work etc. Act 1974, section 15 which is not so restricted, being a power to make regulations for any of the general purposes of the first Part of the Act[18]. The modern regulations under the Act (particularly the six that came into force on 1 January 1993) reflect this modern approach in full, not only applying to all employees across the board (subject to minor, specified exceptions), but also covering temporary workers[19] and placing duties on the self-employed to look after their own welfare. There should therefore be few problems in showing that a particular injured employee was within the scope of the new regulatory protection.

The third element is that the statutory duty must be imposed upon the defendant in the case. Under the old factory legislation, duties were normally cast on 'the occupier', which caused relatively few problems. Under the new regulations there should be even fewer, since (a) duties are generally placed, without more ado, on 'the employer', and (b) key concepts such as 'workplace', 'work equipment', 'personal protective equipment' and (VDU) 'workstation' are given broad, general definitions.

The fourth element is that the defendant must be in breach of duty. If there is one central principle in the law relating to breach of statutory duty it is that each case will depend ultimately on the detailed wording of the statutory provision in question. Thus, it is that wording which will determine the *level* of the duty, which will have the major effect on whether the defendant has breached it. If the duty is strict (e.g. that something 'shall be provided'), any failure to comply will constitute a breach and it will be no defence to say that the defendant acted reasonably, or could not have done otherwise, or even that the machine in question would be totally unusable if the statute were strictly applied[20]. A strict duty is thus clearly in the plaintiff's favour. However, a statutory duty may be cast in less mandatory terms, either by specifically providing the employer with a defence, or by specifying an alternative way to comply, or by imposing a lesser duty. In the last case, in the past the most common form of duty has been one to do or provide something as far as is 'practicable' or 'reasonably practicable', the former being

---

17 Hence the importance of the distinction between employment and self-employment in a case such as *Ferguson v John Dawson & Partners (Contractors) Ltd* [1976] 3 All ER 817, [1976] IRLR 346, CA (see p. 13, above). Such a restriction excludes not only independent contractors but also other non-employees lawfully on the premises, e.g. the fireman fighting a fire in *Hartley v Mayoh & Co* [1954] 1 QB 383, [1954] 1 All ER 375, CA. For an example in the context of the mines and quarries legislation, see *Thompson v National Coal Board* [1982] ICR 15, CA.

18 Sch. 3 sets out certain particular purposes for which health and safety regulations may be made, without prejudice to the generality of the regulation-making power.

19 In order to comply with the Temporary Workers Directive (91/383/EEC) in relation to health and safety.

20 *John Summers & Sons Ltd v Frost* [1955] AC 740, [1955] 1 All ER 870, HL; the extreme effect of this case had to be lessened by the Abrasive Wheel Regulations 1970, SI 1970 No. 535.

essentially a matter of technical feasibility and the latter being a wider concept, introducing more factors (including the cost of provision of a safeguard, in relation to the magnitude of the risk). Although the latter (in particular) may impose a standard of duty prima facie akin to the ordinary duty of care in common law negligence, there may still be one advantage for the employee in relying on such a statutory provision, since it has been held that if a dispute arises as to whether something was or was not practicable or reasonably practicable within the statute, the burden of proof in a civil action lies upon the employer to prove that it was not[1]. Moreover, recent case law has tended to view references to 'reasonable practicability' as being in the nature only of a defence to otherwise absolute obligations on employers, and to construe those references more narrowly than in the past[2]. Under the new regime of health and safety regulations, questions will arise as to the appropriate level of duty. This is because the drafting is a mixture of the older phrasing of practicability or reasonable practicability and new Euro-speak taken from the directives on which the regulations are based; the latter form of drafting tends to use phrases such as 'suitable and sufficient', 'suitable means' and 'adequate measures' which have not so far figured largely in domestic law and will need interpretation by the courts[3]. Clearly, the accompanying codes of practice and guidance notes will play a major role here, and in this context it is worth mentioning just how remarkably detailed the guidance contained therein is (including diagrams, flow charts, specific examples and cross-references to acceptable EC *product* standards, in relation particularly to work equipment and protective equipment).

The fifth element is that the damage done to the plaintiff must be the type of damage which the statute or regulation was designed to prevent[4]. Normally in an industrial accident case this will be perfectly obvious, but the rule produced one particular anomaly under the old factory legislation, for it was held that the fencing requirements for dangerous machines were, to put it at its simplest, meant to keep the employee out of the machine, not to keep the machine and the material in, so that if part of the machine or material flew out of the machine and injured the employee, the fencing provisions would not provide him with a cause of action (if the fencing was defective), since the harm suffered was not the type of harm which those particular provisions were designed to prevent[5]. It is to be

1   *Nimmo v Alexander Cowan & Sons Ltd* [1968] AC 107, [1967] 3 All ER 187, HL; *Larner v British Steel plc* [1993] ICR 551, [1993] IRLR 278, CA; in criminal proceedings under the Health and Safety at Work etc. Act 1974 there is an express, statutory reversal of the burden of proof on practicability or reasonable practicability: ibid, s. 40.
2   *Larner v British Steel plc*, n. 1, above; *R v British Steel plc* [1995] ICR 586 [1995] IRLR 311, CA; *Mains v Uniroyal Englebert Tyres Ltd* [1995] IRLR 544, Ct of Sess.
3   These phrases are often attached to obligations which are prima facie strict ('the employer *shall* provide *suitable and sufficient* means …'); the precise level of such a duty will doubtless give rise to litigation eventually. It may well be higher than reasonable practicability, since the *obligation* to provide is strict and the only argument is about what is suitable and sufficient, whereas under an old 'reasonably practicable' duty it could have been argued that it was not reasonably practicable to provide it *at all*. One obvious problem in the opposite direction is whether reg. 11 of the Provision and Use of Work Equipment Regulations 1992 (which replaces the famous s. 14 of the Factories Act 1961 which imposed a strict duty to fence dangerous parts of machinery) in fact *lowers* the level of the duty because of the Euro-speak involved; see Smith, Goddard and Randall *Health and Safety – the New Legal Framework* (1993), ch. 7.
4   *Gorris v Scott* (1874) LR 9 Exch 125.
5   *Nicholls v Austin (Leyton) Ltd* [1946] AC 493, [1946] 2 All ER 92, HL; *Close v Steel Co of Wales Ltd* [1962] AC 367, [1961] 2 All ER 953, HL; *Wearing v Pirelli Ltd* [1977] 1 All ER 339, [1977] 1 WLR 48, HL. For judicial criticism of this narrow approach, see *F E Callow (Engineers) Ltd v Johnson* [1971] AC 335, [1970] 3 All ER 639, HL.

hoped that there will be considerably less scope under the present regime of health and safety regulations for such fine distinctions, due to their wider approach and more general coverage, though it will still be important to sue under the right regulation (or combination of regulations).

The final element is that the injury must be caused by the defendant's breach. Causation is always important in the law of tort and it has been reaffirmed by the House of Lords that the action for breach of statutory duty is no exception. The claimant must therefore be able to show the causal link between his injury and the defendant's breach; there is no presumption of causation once the breach is shown[6]. The application of ideas of causation can lead to the employer being relieved of liability, in spite of a clear breach of statute, in two cases. The first is where the employer has failed to provide a safety precaution but it can be shown on a balance of probabilities that the employee would probably not have used it even if it had been available[7]. The second is where the defendant can show that he did everything in his power to comply with the statutory requirement (e.g. by providing all the necessary equipment, instructing the employee in its use and ordering him to use it) and the only reason why he was placed in breach was the act or omission of the claimant himself (e.g. in neglecting to use the equipment provided, in defiance of orders)[8]. In *Ross v Associated Portland Cement Manufacturers Ltd*[9] this was explained in terms of causation, whereas in the later case of *Boyle v Kodak Ltd*[10] the approach was to treat it as a specific defence to an action for breach of statutory duty:

'The plaintiff establishes a prima facie cause of action against his employer by proving the fact of non-compliance with a requirement of the regulation and that he suffered injury as a result. He need prove no more. No burden lies upon him to prove what steps should have been taken. But if the employer can prove that the only act or default of anyone which caused or contributed to the non-compliance was the act or default of the plaintiff himself, he establishes a good defence[11].'

It must be emphasised, however, that the key word is 'only', for the effect of the defence upon the plaintiff's claim is total and it should not be found in any but the clearest cases; if there is *any* fault on the part of the employer (e.g. failure to give proper orders, instruction or supervision) the defence will not be applicable and the case will be decided by the more sophisticated means of apportioning loss between the plaintiff and the defendant through the device of contributory negligence. It is interesting to note that the defence failed in both the *Ross* and the *Boyle* cases, and so the court went on to apportion the loss (the defendant employer bearing two-thirds and one-half of the loss respectively).

---

6   *Bonnington Castings Ltd v Wardlaw* [1956] AC 613, [1956] 1 All ER 615, HL; *Qualcast (Wolverhampton) Ltd v Haynes* [1959] AC 743, [1959] 2 All ER 38, HL. Human intervention between the breach by the defendant and the injury to the plaintiff could break the chain of causation: *McGovern v British Steel Corpn* [1986] ICR 608, [1986] IRLR 411, CA.

7   *Cummings v Sir William Arrol & Co Ltd* [1962] 1 All ER 623, [1962] 1 WLR 295, HL; *Wigley v British Vinegars Ltd* [1964] AC 307, [1962] 3 All ER 161, HL.

8   *Ginty v Belmont Building Supplies Ltd* [1959] 1 All ER 414.

9   [1964] 2 All ER 452, [1964] 1 WLR 768, HL.

10   [1969] 2 All ER 439, [1969] 1 WLR 661, HL.

11   At 446 and 672 respectively, per Lord Diplock. *Lineker v Raleigh Industries Ltd* [1980] ICR 83, CA.

c) Vicarious liability

The concept of vicarious liability means that if an employee injures someone in the course of his employment, that injured person may sue the employer for damages, a most useful action given the relative financial (and insurance) positions of the employee and employer. This action is normally thought of as giving redress to third parties (e.g. passers-by or customers), but it can also apply where the injured person is a fellow employee. This was not always so, for under the doctrine of common employment[12] the courts held that an employee could not sue his employer when injured by a fellow employee, for he was deemed to have consented to the risk of such injury. This harsh doctrine excluded what could have been a wide head of liability (since (a) most employers are corporate and therefore have to do things through their employees, and (b) vicarious liability can apply widely to cover acts of the employee which at first sight may appear to be outside what he is really employed to do, including for example fraud by the employee and acts done in defiance of the employer's orders[13]). This led to pressure to find alternative causes of action for the injured employee, and in particular explains the significance of the personal, non-delegable common law liabilities upon the employer (discussed above)[14]. The doctrine of common employment was finally abolished in 1948[15], and so now the employee who is injured by the negligence of a fellow employee has this additional cause of action against his employer.

The law on vicarious liability contains some well known difficulties, primarily on the question of what is in the course of employment; these are adequately covered in the tort texts[16]. Two specific points require mention here. The first is that one of the most difficult problems arises in relation to travelling time – is the employee in the course of his employment during it[17]? This matter arose in *Smith v Stages*[18] where a peripatetic worker travelling back from a particular job was held to be in the course of his employment (so that the employer was liable for the death of a fellow employee in a car accident caused by that worker's

---

12 *Priestley v Fowler* (1837) 3 M & W 1; *Hutchinson v York, Newcastle and Berwick Rly Co* (1850) 5 Exch 343.
13 See *Rose v Plenty* [1976] 1 All ER 97, [1976] 1 WLR 141, CA.
14 The duty to provide competent and safe fellow employees may still be particularly important, for if the fellow employee causes injury by a practical joke or an assault, that may take him outside the course of his employment, so that the employer will not be vicariously liable. If, however, the employer knew or ought to have known of the fellow employee's propensity for joking or violence, he may be liable for breach of his common law duty of care.
15 Law Reform (Personal Injuries) Act 1948, s. 1.
16 In addition to the standard textbooks, see McKendrick 'Vicarious liability and independent contractors – a re-examination' (1990) 53 MLR 770; Collins 'Independent contractors and the challenge of vertical disintegration to employment protection laws' (1990) 10 OJLS 353; Kidner, 'Vicarious liability: for whom should the employer be liable' (1995) 15 LS 47. For reaffirmation of the traditional test that the employer will be liable if the employee's act was either authorised by the employer or an unauthorised means of doing what he was authorised to do (but not if it fell outside what he was authorised to do), see *Heasmans v Clarity Cleaning Co Ltd* [1987] ICR 949, [1987] IRLR 286, CA; *Aldred v Nacanco* [1987] IRLR 292, CA (disapproving a wider reformulation suggested by Comyn J in *Harrison v Michelin Tyre Co Ltd* [1985] 1 All ER 918, [1985] ICR 696). Discrimination law, as a matter of legislative policy, operates on a wider basis than common law vicarious liability: *Jones v Tower Boot Co Ltd* [1997] ICR 254, [1997] IRLR 168, CA; *ST v North Yorkshire County Council* [1999] IRLR 98, CA.
17 A similar problem arises under the social security rules relating to industrial accidents, see p. 716, above.
18 [1989] AC 928, [1989] 1 All ER 833; the guidance from Lord Lowry is at 851, 956.

negligence). Although decisions in such cases are largely questions of fact, Lord Lowry gave the following guidance (which shows an interesting emphasis not only on job content but also on the payment system):

1) an employee travelling from his ordinary residence to his ordinary place of work is not in the course of his employment (unless obliged to use the employer's transport);

2) travelling in the employer's time between workplaces, or in the course of a peripatetic occupation, will be in the course of employment;

3) receipt of wages (though *not* simply of a travelling allowance) will indicate that the employee is travelling in the employer's time and for his benefit;

4) an employee travelling *in the employer's time* from his ordinary residence to a workplace *other* than his normal workplace, or on peripatetic work or to the scene of an emergency will be in the course of employment;

5) a deviation from or interruption of a journey in the course of employment (other than a merely incidental one) will take the employee out of the course of his employment;

6) return journeys are to be treated on the same footing as outward journeys.

The second point, as has already been made on p. 16, above, is that the test for the existence of vicarious liability in tort is not necessarily identical to that for the existence of a longer-term employment relationship (e.g. for the purpose of establishing a claim for unfair dismissal or some other employment protection right), even though ostensibly they are the same – is there a contract of employment? That the existence of an employment relationship and the incidence of vicarious liability may diverge is shown by the 'borrowed servant' cases[19], and the argument is advanced in chapter 1 that short-term factors such as control and supervision may be more important in the tort context, whereas longer-term factors may be more appropriate in the employment law context.

d) Liability as occupier

The employer, where he is the 'occupier' of industrial premises, owes the common duty of care to all visitors lawfully on those premises, under the Occupier's Liability Act 1957[20]. In the ordinary case of the employee working on the employer's premises, this will add little to the existing common law duties, but it may be important (a) for an independent contractor working on those premises (to whom the employer does not owe those general duties) and (b) for an employee working on someone else's premises (for in a case of injury he may be able to sue that other 'occupier' as well as his employer). If a person is present on premises 'in the exercise of his calling', the occupier may expect that he will 'appreciate and guard against any special risks ordinarily incident to it', but this

---

19   See *Mersey Docks and Harbour Board v Coggins and Griffiths Ltd* [1947] AC 1, [1946] 2 All ER 345, HL; *Donovan v Laing, Wharton and Down Construction Syndicate* [1893] 1 QB 629; *Denham v Midland Employers' Mutual Assurance* [1955] 2 QB 437, [1955] 2 All ER 561, CA; *Cross v Redpath Dorman Long (Contracting) Ltd* [1978] ICR 730. For the possible application of the Unfair Contract Terms Act 1977 to a clause apportioning liability as between the two employers, see Morris (1987) 16 ILJ 264.

20   A person not lawfully on the land, i.e. a trespasser, used to be owed the lesser 'duty of common humanity' (*British Railways Board v Herrington* [1972] AC 877, [1972] 1 All ER 749, HL); but this was altered to a duty of reasonable care in *all* the circumstances (including the trespassory status) by the Occupiers' Liability Act 1984. For the circumstances in which such a duty is imposed by the statute, see s. 1(3).

should only apply to such specialised risks and not to any overall conditions of the premises which may pose risks generally[1].

One aspect of occupiers' liability which has caused some difficulty in the past is the exclusion of liability for personal injury (by contractual term or by notice); this appeared to be effective when done properly[2] and, although factually unlikely to be applied to the occupier's own employees (who could still sue under the common law duties anyway), it was of significance to independent contractors coming on to the occupier's land. Now, however, such exclusion of liability for death or personal injury resulting from negligence (which includes the common duty of care under the 1957 Act) is ineffective, under the Unfair Contract Terms Act 1977, section 2 (whether by contract term or notice), provided the exclusion arises in a business context, which will of course be so where it relates to the occupier's business premises.

ii) Defences for the employer

The most obvious 'defence' for the defendant employer is that one of the essential elements of the plaintiff's cause of action is missing; thus, for example, we have seen that causation must be proved and if for any reason it cannot be (e.g. if, in a breach of statutory duty action, the employer successfully argues that the only act causing the employer to be in breach was that of the plaintiff himself), then the plaintiff's claim will fail. There are, however, three substantive defences which deserve mention (volenti, contributory negligence and limitation), though once again it is assumed that the reader is familiar with the basic law relating to each.

a) Volenti non fit injuria

Whatever may be the position in other branches of the law of tort, volenti will rarely ever succeed at common law in an industrial injury case, even though it is theoretically available[3]. Two particular rules relating to volenti are chiefly responsible for this, for they take on particular significance when applied to the employment context. The first is the rule that sciens is not volens, so that it will not be enough for the employer simply to point to continuance at work by the employee with knowledge of the risk as establishing consent on his part[4]. The second is the rule that consent must be freely given; this will rarely be the case where the plaintiff is an employee, either because he will have been acting under orders, or because he was not in a position (economically or otherwise) to refuse to do the act in question, or because the act in question was one which in practice he had to do in order to discharge his work duties[5].

1 Occupiers' Liability Act 1957, s. 2(3)(b); *Woollins v British Celanese Ltd* (1966) 1 KIR 438, CA. See also s. 2(4)(b) which may exonerate an employer who has had work, maintenance, etc., done by a reputable independent contractor: *Ferguson v Welsh* [1987] 3 All ER 777, [1988] IRLR 112, HL.
2 *Ashdown v Samuel Williams & Sons Ltd* [1957] 1 QB 409, [1957] 1 All ER 35, CA; *White v Blackmore* [1972] 2 QB 651, [1972] 3 All ER 158, CA; Occupiers' Liability Act 1957, s. 2(1).
3 It is expressly retained in occupiers' liability actions (Occupiers' Liability Act 1957, s. 2(5)). It is not to be used to circumvent the ban on clauses or notices excluding liability for death or personal injury: Unfair Contract Terms Act 1977, s. 2(3).
4 *Smith v Baker & Sons* [1891] AC 325, HL.
5 *Bowater v Rowley Regis Corpn* [1944] KB 476, [1944] 1 All ER 465, CA; *Burnett v British Waterways Board* [1973] 2 All ER 631, [1973] 1 WLR 700, CA.

Turning from common law actions to that for breach of statutory duty the position is even clearer, for it has been held that volenti does not apply *at all* to an action for breach of a statutory duty laid upon the employer by the relevant legislation[6], the principal reason being that it would be contrary to public policy to allow an employee by agreement or consent to 'contract out' of his statutory protection (particularly as some of the legislation is designed to protect him from his own defaults as well as those of his employer). However, the House of Lords in *ICI Ltd v Shatwell*[7] held that this does not apply where the employer is not in breach of a statutory duty on himself[8], but is only liable vicariously for breach by another person. In that case, two shotfirers were injured when they agreed to test equipment in a manner that was contrary to statutory regulations which applied to *them* (as well as contrary to the employer's express instructions). One of them sued the employer for damages (accepting 50 per cent contributory negligence) on the basis that the employer was vicariously liable for the breach of statutory duty by the other shotfirer. The House of Lords held that in these circumstances, as there was no direct breach of statutory duty by the employer, the defence of volenti was available and indeed decided the case against the plaintiff.

Thus, volenti is of restricted application in employment cases; where, however, the plaintiff does run risks with full knowledge, that may still constitute contributory negligence (leading to a decrease in his damages against the employer), but that may be considered a more satisfactory approach to the problem for it is based upon the more modern approach of apportionment of blame and does not rule the plaintiff out altogether, unlike the more blunt instrument of volenti.

b) Contributory negligence

Before the Law Reform (Contributory Negligence) Act 1945, contributory negligence by the plaintiff used to be a complete defence. Now it leads to a reduction of damages to 'such extent as the court thinks just and equitable having regard to the [plaintiff's] share in the responsibility for the damage'. This shows the modern approach to multiple causation of trying to reach an equitable apportionment instead of seeking to lay the blame wholly on one party or the other, and as such it is analogous to the modern rules on apportionment between joint tortfeasors, which proceed on similar principles[9].

In the industrial injury context, four particular points about the application of contributory negligence should be noticed. The first is that, unlike volenti, it applies to all cases of breach of statutory duty[10], as well as to common law actions.

---

6   *Baddeley v Earl of Granville* (1887) 19 QBD 423; *Wheeler v New Merton Board Mills* [1933] 2 KB 669, CA.

7   [1965] AC 656, [1964] 2 All ER 999, HL; in this case the House approved the general principle laid down in *Baddeley* and *Wheeler*. For a rare example of the application of volenti to an industrial injury on this basis, see *McMullen v National Coal Board* [1982] ICR 148; cf. *Storey v National Coal Board* [1983] 1 All ER 375, [1983] ICR 156; see Holgate (1983) 12 ILJ 185.

8   And, semble, provided he is not vicariously liable for a breach by someone placed upon the plaintiff (e.g. a foreman or manager), since in such a case the employee may not have been free to consent to the breach (per Lord Pearce).

9   Civil Liability (Contribution) Act 1978, ss. 1(1) and 2(1).

10   *Caswell v Powell Duffryn Associated Collieries Ltd* [1940] AC 152, [1939] 3 All ER 722, HL. There is no rule that once a breach of statutory duty is shown there cannot be 100 per cent contributory negligence in an appropriate case where the accident was entirely the employee's fault: *Jayes v IMI (Kynoch) Ltd* [1985] ICR 155, CA.

The second is that breach of a statutory duty by the *employee* (e.g. failure to use a safety device, contrary to a duty to do so laid upon him by regulation) can constitute contributory negligence on his part if it contributes to the accident[11]. Under the modern law of health and safety, the following statutory obligations are placed on employees:

1) to take reasonable care for the health and safety of himself and others, and to co-operate with his employers so far as is necessary to enable the employers to comply with their statutory duties[12];

2) not, intentionally or recklessly, to interfere with or misuse anything provided in the interests of health, safety or welfare[13];

3) to use anything provided by his employers (under their statutory duties) in accordance with training and instructions and to inform the employers of any work situation representing a serious and imminent danger to health and safety, and of any shortcomings in the employer's protection arrangements[14];

4) to use personal protective equipment provided, in accordance with training and instructions, to take all reasonable steps to return it, and to report forthwith any loss of or obvious defect in it[15];

5) to make full and proper use of any system for manual handling provided by the employers[16].

Breach of these obligations, as well as potentially incurring criminal liability on the employee, could well give rise to a defence of contributory negligence (in spite of the fact that 1 to 3 come from statutory provisions which themselves do not support civil liability).

The third point is that, on general principles, to be held to have been contributorily negligent the plaintiff must have shown definite lack of care for his own safety. One ramification of this in the employment context is that disobedience of orders (e.g. going into part of the premises declared by the employer to be out of bounds) will not necessarily constitute contributory negligence, unless the employee should have foreseen that the act of disobedience in question would place him in danger[17].

The fourth point is that the courts may be prepared to expect a lower standard of care by the plaintiff for his own safety in industrial accident cases, and so either find contributory negligence less easily or make a smaller deduction from damages. This is certainly so as regards breach of statutory duty. In *Caswell v Powell Duffryn Associated Collieries Ltd*[18] (the case which established that contributory negligence applies to breach of statutory duty actions), Lord Atkin said:

11   *Norris v Syndic Manufacturing Co* [1952] 2 QB 135, [1952] 1 All ER 935, CA.
12   Health and Safety at Work etc. Act 1974, s. 7.
13   Ibid., s. 8.
14   Management of Health and Safety at Work Regulations 1999, reg. 14; see generally ch. 13, below. Note that an employee making such complaints is now protected from dismissal by the Employment Rights Act 1996, s. 100 and from action short of dismissal by s. 44, both originally enacted by the Trade Union Reform and Employment Rights Act 1993; see p. 494, above.
15   Personal Protective Equipment at Work Regulations 1992, regs. 10 and 11.
16   Manual Handling Operations Regulations 1992, reg. 5.
17   *Westwood v Post Office* [1974] AC 1, [1973] 3 All ER 184, HL.
18   N. 10, above; the following dicta are at pp. 214 and 178. See Fagelson 'The last bastion of fault? Contributory negligence in actions for employers' liability' (1979) 42 MLR 646. For a rare example of a finding of 100 per cent contributory negligence in an industrial injury case, see *Jayes v IMI (Kynoch) Ltd* n. 10, above.

'I am of the opinion that the care to be expected of the plaintiff in the circumstances will vary with the circumstances; and that a different degree of care may well be expected from a workman in a factory or a mine from that which might be taken by an ordinary man not exposed continually to the noise, strain and manifold risks of factory or mine.'

Lord Wright said:

'What is all important is to adapt the standard of what is negligence to the facts, and to give due regard to the actual conditions under which men work in a factory or mine, to the long hours and the fatigue, to the slackening of attention which naturally comes from constant repetition of the same operation, to the noise and confusion in which the man works, to his preoccupation in what he is actually doing at the cost perhaps of some inattention to his own safety.'

However, doubt has been expressed whether this more lenient standard is to apply to the common law negligence action, particularly in *Staveley Iron and Chemical Co Ltd v Jones*[19] where Lord Reid declined to decide whether it applied outside actions for breach of statutory duty, and Lord Tucker said[20]:

'... while accepting without question this and other dicta to similar effect [i.e. in favour of the more lenient standard] which have been used in this House in relation to cases under the Factories Acts and other statutes imposing absolute obligations on employers or occupiers of premises, I doubt very much whether they were ever intended or could properly be applied to a simple case of common law negligence such as the present where there was no evidence of work-people performing repetitive work under strain or for long hours at dangerous machines'.

On its face, this is capable of two interpretations – that the lenient standard is never applicable to contributory negligence as a defence to a common law action, or that it is applicable *if* there is positive evidence of factors such as strain, long hours, noise, etc., which are capable of justifying it. It is submitted that the latter view is preferable, particularly as it would give greater uniformity between the common law and statutory actions which may, of course, be tried together.

c) Limitation

The normal rule in actions for personal injury or death is that the action must be commenced within three years of the date of the accident. While a time limit is obviously necessary, a rigid one was seen to work injustice in certain cases where the damage did not manifest itself until a considerable time after it had been sustained; certain industrial diseases were prime examples of this. The Limitation Act 1963 attempted to alleviate this, allowing the limitation rule to be ignored in certain circumstances. The position was further improved by the Limitation Act 1975 which introduced new provisions which, with the consolidation of the limitation statutes in 1980, are now contained in the Limitation Act 1980, sections 11, 14 and 33. These new sections give to a claimant more scope to avoid the

19 [1956] AC 627, [1956] 1 All ER 403, HL.
20 At 647 and 413 respectively.

standard three-year period, in two ways. First, sections 11 and 14 provide that the three year period runs from either the date on which the cause of action accrued *or* the date (if later) of 'the plaintiff's knowledge'; this is defined as the date on which he first had knowledge of the following facts: (a) that the injury in question was significant; (b) that it was attributable in whole or in part to the act or omission relied upon; (c) the identity of the defendant and (d) the identity of any relevant third party (and the facts supporting the action against him). This includes not just facts within his actual knowledge, but also any facts which could have been ascertained by him with the help of expert advice (where it was reasonable for him to seek it). Second, section 33 gives the court a residual discretion, independently of sections 11 and 14, to allow an action to go ahead out of time where it is equitable to do so, having regard to factors such as the reasons for the delay, the effect it may have had on the cogency of the evidence, any dilatory conduct by the defendant, any period of disability suffered by the plaintiff after the accident, whether the plaintiff acted promptly once he realised he might have a cause of action against the defendant and whether the plaintiff took steps to obtain expert advice (and, if so, the nature of the advice which he received)[1].

iii) Insurance

It has always been the practice of the prudent employer to cover his 'employer's liability' with insurance under a policy covering at the least his potential liability to his own employees. However, not all employers were prudent and the result of a failure to insure might prejudice the ability of an injured employee to recover from a bankrupt employer.

Statutory provision has been made to oblige an employer to insure against his liability for personal injury to his employees, in the Employer's Liability (Compulsory Insurance) Act 1969; the Act covers all employers except local authorities, statutory corporations, nationalised industries and certain others exempted by regulations[2]. The duty is to maintain an approved policy with authorised insurers covering bodily injury or disease of an employee arising out of and in the course of employment[3] in Great Britain. The details defining such concepts as 'approved policy' and 'authorised insurers' are provided by regulations made under the Act[4] (for example, they prohibit certain conditions of exemption of the insurers from liability).

Those to be covered by such insurance are defined by the Act as individuals working under a contract of service or apprenticeship 'whether by way of manual labour, clerical work or otherwise, whether such contract is expressed or implied,

---

1   This discretion under s. 33 was construed widely by the Court of Appeal in *Firman v Ellis* [1978] QB 886, [1978] 2 All ER 851, CA, but doubt was cast on that construction by the decision of the House of Lords in *Walkley v Precision Forgings Ltd* [1979] 2 All ER 548, [1979] 1 WLR 606, HL which overruled the decision in *Firman v Ellis*. However, both of those cases were on a slightly different point and when the matter came directly before the House of Lords in *Thompson v Brown Construction (Ebbw Vale) Ltd* [1981] 2 All ER 296, [1981] 1 WLR 744, HL, they made it clear that the discretion is unfettered.
2   Employers' Liability (Compulsory Insurance) Act 1969, s. 3
3   This is the same phrase as that used in the industrial injuries scheme – see head 2, above.
4   Employers' Liability (Compulsory Insurance) Regulations 1998, S.I. 1998 No. 2573. The amount for which the employer must be insured is £5 million in respect of claims relating to one or more employees arising out of any one occurrence: reg. 3.

oral or in writing'[5]. Close relatives are excluded, as are those not ordinarily resident in Great Britain although regulations make exceptions to the latter category[6]. The Act provides that certificates of insurance must be issued; the regulations govern the form of the certificate and require that it shall be displayed at the employer's place of business[7]. Also, such certificates have to be produced to an inspector or to the Health and Safety Executive upon request, and failure to do so is a summary offence. Failure to insure is itself of course also backed by the criminal sanction of a summary offence of strict liability;[8] where the employer is a corporation, any officer who consented to, connived at, or facilitated by his negligence the failure to insure is also liable to be prosecuted.

Insurance against liability towards injured employees is thus made compulsory, and wider 'public liability' insurance (primarily covering vicarious liability towards third parties as a result of an employee's negligence) is also common, though not compulsory[9]. This means that when an action is brought by an injured person against the employer, it will in fact be an insurance company which will have control over negotiations for a settlement of the claim, and over any ensuing litigation, even though such litigation will be defended in the name of the employer[10]. In the light of this modern emphasis on insurance[11] and its practical importance in the smooth running of our present system of recovery of damages for individual fault, it is perhaps permissible to wonder whether the insurance point in *Lister v Romford Ice and Cold Storage Co Ltd*[12] would have been decided the same way if the case had arisen today, or whether the courts would have held that there was indeed an implied term that the employer would 'look after the whole matter of insurance', and not just restrict himself to that which was legally obligatory, particularly in the light of the broader approach taken to possible obligations on an employer to inform and advise an employee (of matters not fully in the latter's knowledge) in *Scally v Southern Health and Social Services Board*[13].

5   S. 2(1).
6   S. 2(2); see also the Offshore Installations and Pipeline Works (Management and Administration) Regulations 1995, S.I. 1995 No. 738, reg. 21.
7   Reg. 5.
8   Section 5. An attempt to interpret the Act as supporting civil liability as well (so that a claimant injured by the employer but prejudiced by the latter's failure to insure could sue for that breach of the Act) failed in *Richardson v Pitt-Stanley* [1995] QB 123, [1995] 1 All ER 460, CA.
9   If different policies with different insurance companies cover these matters, the exact legal status of the person injured can become a vital point in deciding which company is to indemnify the employer: *Denham v Midland Employers' Mutual Assurance Ltd* [1955] 2 QB 437, [1955] 2 All ER 561, CA.
10   This is because of the doctrine of subrogation, on which see *Morris v Ford Motor Co Ltd* [1973] QB 792, [1973] 2 All ER 1084, CA. It will also normally be for the insurer to operate the civil recoupment system, p. 722, above.
11   This is now to be seen in both of the major types of tort actions – those for industrial injuries and those for motor accidents.
12   [1957] AC 555, [1957] 1 All ER 125, HL; see p. 109, above.
13   [1991] ICR 771, [1991] IRLR 52, HL; see p. 127 above.

Chapter 13

Industrial safety (2): health and safety at work

I INTRODUCTION

There is no aspect of industrial law more important than those rules, which are largely statutory, that attempt to ensure the health and safety of workers at their place of work[1]. Such legislation has a long history[2]; the first Factory Act, a substantial measure, was passed in 1802. Since that date the law to protect health and safety at work saw a steady flow of statute law. Later, particularly in the second half of the 20th century concepts in the common law, especially the development of the torts of negligence and breach of statutory duty, have done much to help to protect the worker from injury. The possibility that the employer, or most usually his insurer, might have to pay large damages undoubtedly was a powerful pressure towards a safe working environment, but a pressure that was not as effective against the marginal employer as it might have been.

It has to be said, however, that despite this long history, there have been over the years relatively long periods with only slow development. There has been a strong tendency for legislation to lag behind developments in work practices, and the introduction and increasing use of increasingly dangerous processes and substances. So, while the old-fashioned factory was reasonably well covered by protective legislation, modern safeguards were slow to appear and statutes have tended to remain on the statute book while becoming increasingly outdated and ineffective.

The kernel of the law before the 1970s was a handful of major pieces of legislation. The first Factories Act of 1802 has already been mentioned. The last Act was the Factories Act 1961; a glance at its format shows clearly that it has as its backbone the nineteenth-century factory with boiler house, prime mover, transmission machinery and individual machines. This is long after the typical place of work was filled with newer dangers – dangers such as electricity, the

---

1   Recent figures show 1.6 m accidents at work each year; 2.2 m people suffer ill health caused or worsened by work; in total, 33 m working days are lost each year. Moreover, 80,000 people retire each year on grounds of ill-health.
2   For an excellent exposition of the history, see Cornish and Clark *Law and Society in England 1750–1950* (1989), pp. 301–308 and 483–541.

fumes from a host of newly introduced chemicals and mobile handling of materials with tractors and fork-lift trucks. Many of these dangers were at times covered, in part at least, by statutory regulations but the law was fragmented and particular, lacking both general principles and catch-all duties of care.

Other similar major statutes must be noted. Perhaps the most comprehensive, and certainly the best respected and most carefully followed, was the Mines and Quarries Act 1954, itself the result of a long line of previous statutes stretching back into the nineteenth century. A relative latecomer was the equally comprehensive Offices, Shops and Railway Premises Act 1963. Indeed, those three statutes formed a formidable, if somewhat rigid code protecting safety and they were backed by a considerable weight of subsidiary legislation in the form of regulations, made under the statutes.

The law was comprehensively reviewed by the Robens Committee on Safety and Health at Work[3] which recognised the importance of the existing law but was equally aware of the basic defects. The report itself led to the passing of the reforming Health and Safety at Work etc. Act 1974, a major piece of modern legislation which is dealt with in the next section.

As far as the Committee was concerned it foresaw three levels of control – legislation, regulations and statutory or approved codes of practice, supplemented by voluntary codes and rules within individual establishments. As far as the crucial legislation was concerned it indicated the need to deal with the issues in a general way, laying down basic principles of wide application. That was indeed the purpose of the Health and Safety at Work etc. Act 1974 which followed. It supplemented and, in effect, overarched the major pieces of employment-type statutes mentioned in the preceding paragraph. Development was envisaged as both top down – Parliament insisting on basic standards; and bottom up – growing from individual experience leading employers and workers, through their trade unions, to develop from good practice voluntary codes which might themselves, as indication of good practice, give the impetus for new legally binding regulations or approved codes of practice. This involved a shift of emphasis, which was not at the time universally popular, from particular types of places of work – mine, office or factory, to the idea of 'a workplace' for most of the general protections.

Important steps of reform almost always require appropriate administrative changes and new attitudes to the enforcement of law. The inspectorates under the major pieces of legislation had an excellent record and provided an ideal base for improvements. To ensure this, the Committee's Report led to the speedy establishment of the Health and Safety Commission and its Executive which have ensured that there has been a focal point for the development of the law, particularly codes of practice, and especially of good health and safety monitoring. It is in the area of legislation itself, however, as has been already indicated, where progress has until recently been disappointingly slow. The Health and Safety at Work etc. Act 1974 was speedily put into place; an essential first step. Its expression of duties in general terms was unfamiliar and not particularly to the liking of many lawyers, but it was an important general basis for the law giving a clear indication that detailed control had to be matched by an overall duty to look generally at health and safety, and ensure that possible dangers were guarded against.

The following years did not continue the initial impetus in the form of legislation. Not only was there little attempt to revise the existing statute law, admittedly a long and difficult exercise, even though the existing legislation was

3   Report of the Committee 1970–1972, Cmnd. 5034.

rapidly becoming both outdated and, more seriously, completely deficient in its control of the newer dangers that were arising. Such changes as there were came through the steady stream of statutory regulations and codes of practice. But progress was very slow.

Health and safety was, not unnaturally, a subject that became of central concern to the European Community. A social topic of importance to both employers and workers, it was an obvious area for major initiatives from the Community. It believes, with justification, that it 'is now recognised as the main force in the development of new safety and health legislation[4].' Directives on individual dangers have indeed had an influence on national legislation after a start which has to be described as somewhat slow[5]. In the last decade and a half, however, as a result of the Single European Act of 1987, which, in Article 118a, aimed at encouraging improvements, especially in the work environment, as regards the health and safety of workers, progress has accelerated. Following the 1987 Act a programme concerning safety, hygiene and health at work was instituted, and a group of directives was transmitted to the Council.

Those directives were adopted by the Community and at the beginning of 1993 became incorporated into English law by means of regulations and codes of practice[6]. There seems every likelihood that this most important development represents the way forward for future reform and it is likely to lead to a comprehensive spring cleaning of the English law in this area that is long overdue. To take just one example, this is clear from the section in one of the regulations – Provision and Use of Work Equipment Regulations 1992[7] ('PUWER') – dealing with its relationship with the existing health and safety legislation[8]. It is worth quoting paras. 10–12 because the principles expressed apply to all the 1993 Regulations, discussed below in section 3:

'PUWER amplifies and makes more explicit the general duties on employers, the self-employed and persons in control to provide safe plant and equipment. Virtually all the requirements already exist somewhere in the law, or constitute good practice. PUWER brings together these requirements and applies them across all industrial, commercial and service sectors.

This means that employers with well chosen and well maintained equipment should need to do little more than before. Some older equipment may need to be up-graded to meet the requirements, and there is until 1 January 1997 to do the necessary work[9]. Much old legislation – 17 codes of regulations, seven sections of the Factories Act 1961, one section of the Offices, Shops and Railway Premises Act 1963 and two sections of the Mines and Quarries Act 1954 – is being replaced, in full or in part, by PUWER although most will continue to apply to existing equipment until 1 January 1997 when the transitional period ends.

PUWER will overlap many existing requirements but where this occurs compliance with the existing requirement should normally be sufficient to

4   Social Europe – Health and Safety at work in the European Community, 2/90.
5   The years 1974–1985 saw two Commission Action Programmes and a number of directives and draft directives.
6   See section 3 below.
7   S.I. 1992 No. 2932, derived from the European instrument 89/655/EEC; reissued in 1998 – S.I. 109 No. 2306.
8   At p. 2.
9   It is impossible to say such legislation is draconian.

comply with PUWER. For example, the requirement concerning isolation from sources of energy (regulation 19) is, so far as electricity is concerned, dealt with by the Electricity at Work Regulations 1989. Another example is that scaffolds which have been properly maintained under the Construction (Working Places) Regulations 1966 will also meet the requirements for maintenance under PUWER.'

The next section of this chapter deals in some detail with the Health and Safety at Work etc. Act 1974 itself. The basic statutes mentioned above – the Mines and Quarries Act 1954, the Factories Act 1961 and the Offices, Shops and Railway Premises Act 1963 – have now finally disappeared (after a transitional period), and so the third section of the chapter will concentrate on the new regulations[10].

2   THE HEALTH AND SAFETY AT WORK ETC. ACT 1974

i)   The Robens Committee

The regulation of hours of work, health, safety and welfare in factories and workshops was one of the earliest statutory interventions for the regulation of industry[11]. The first statute was as early as 1802 and the process continued throughout the nineteenth century. The earliest regulations applied to textile mills but the scope of the later provisions applied to a widening range of employment. The legislation was firmly based on types of work and upon premises. Parallel legislation on mines and quarries started in 1842. Other major areas followed: railways (1900), shop employees (1886). Agriculture lagged behind but it became similarly covered in 1956.

A great deal of the legislation sprang from the efforts of dedicated reformers. Some were the result of accidents which attracted publicity and wide concern. For example the regulation of fire precautions in factories only reached an acceptable level in the Factories Act 1959 which followed a tragic mill fire at Keighley. This important subject had never been looked at in a wide-ranging way until the Labour Government, as almost one of its last acts in 1970, set up a Committee, chaired by Lord Robens, to review the whole field. Its report was published two years later and has formed the basis of renewed interest and activity in this important area.

It is important to summarise the principal findings of the Robens Committee before turning to the subsequent legislation. The initial criticism was of the existing state of the law. In paragraphs 24–26 the Committee identified 11 major statutes[12] and pointed out that there were nearly 500 supplementary statutory instruments. This body of law was continually increasing and in the view of the

10   For discussion of the old factory legislation, see the fourth edition of this book, ch. 11.
11   There is a useful summary of the history in Appendix 5 of the *Report of the Committee on Safety and Health at Work* (the Robens Committee) (1972) Cmnd. 5034. On the report generally, see Howells 'The Robens Report' (1972) 1 ILJ 185; Woolf 'The Robens Report – the wrong approach?' (1973) 2 ILJ 88.
12   Factories Act 1961, Offices, Shops and Railway Premises Act 1963, Mines and Quarries Act 1954, Agriculture (Poisonous Substances) Act 1952 and Agriculture (Safety, Health and Welfare Provisions) Act 1956 – all supported by extensive statutory regulations; Explosives Acts 1875 and 1923, Petroleum (Consolidation) Act 1928, Nuclear Installations Act 1965 and 1969 – those dealing with dangerous substances; and the Radioactive Substances Act 1960 and the Alkali, etc., Works Regulation Act 1906 – dealing with dangerous emissions.

Committee it could be said that there was too much law[13]. Not only that, the law itself was found to be badly structured, largely because it had been assembled piecemeal with little regard to principle. Indeed the leading statute, the Factories Act 1961, reflected closely the needs of the typical nineteenth century textile mill and bore little close relevance to, say, a modern chemical plant.

The responsibility for this legislation was split between a number of separate government departments with little or no co-ordination. Employment, Environment, Agriculture, Trade and Industry and the Home Office, all had a major responsibility. There were seven inspectorates – factories, mines and quarries, agriculture, explosives, radioactivity, chemical and alkali[14].

It was inevitable that the Committee would propose rationalisation of both the law and its administration. Before making its proposals the Committee looked at several general issues. The one which raised most controversy concerned the main line of approach to be adopted. Some felt that the best results could be achieved by more protective law and stricter enforcement. Although the Robens Committee accepted that there must be a legal code, properly enforced, it sought improvement by means of self-regulation[15]. In line with that approach, and also with the modern way of looking at industrial matters, the Committee felt that the basic relationship upon which to build the new safety and health code was that of employment. The previous bases, premises and substances for example, would remain as part of the code but the basic concept should be that of the employer's duty to his employee and the concomitant duty of the employee to look after himself[16].

The Committee made fairly specific proposals for a new statutory framework. The law was to be brought together into four broad categories. These differed largely in scope and stretched between the broad, wide-ranging provisions such as the Factories Act 1961 to statutes of much narrower scope dealing with special dangers, e.g. Boiler Explosions Acts 1882 and 1890 and the Mines and Quarries (Tips) Act 1969[17]. Unified law was to be accompanied by a unified administration headed by a national body with overall responsibility[18].

The Committee commented upon the form and content of the new legislation. The major proposal was the enactment of a major statute setting out general principles. The Committee clearly had in mind the common law duties, developed in the law of negligence and outside the code of statutory regulation and enforcement[19]. It is this proposal that provided the principal provisions in the subsequent Health and Safety at Work etc. Act 1974. The Committee had interesting views upon subordinate legislation. It felt that over the whole field there was an important place for statutory regulation. The hope was expressed that this would provide a flexible and responsive method of dealing with individual and detailed dangers[20]. Finally encouragement was given to the development of non-statutory codes of practice. This process was said to be central to the proposals, as it built on the concept of self regulation[1].

13　Para. 28.
14　See paras. 32 and 33.
15　This approach underlies chs. 2 and 3. It is an approach that met with criticism after the publication of the report.
16　Chapter 4.
17　Paras. 100–109. The last mentioned statute resulted from the tragic Aberfan disaster and illustrated the reactive nature of much of the legislation.
18　Paras. 110–124.
19　See ch. 12, head 3, above.
20　Paras. 134–140.
1　Paras. 148–154.

The Committee, in looking at the law, saw the possibility of countervailing pressures. The importance of satisfactory compensation is obvious but there was said to be evidence that this tended to lessen the attention paid to prevention. Indeed the Committee, in Appendix 7, went further and suggested that the pressure in the field of compensation to narrow the application of the law was in contradiction of the clear need, in the interests of prevention, to adopt, wherever the matter is doubtful, the wider interpretation. The Committee did not feel able to do more than indicate its concern and suggest further consideration. In due course the matter was taken up by the Pearson Committee[2]. Its report shows again the problem of reconciling the two facets of prevention and compensation and does not greatly assist those seeking greater concern for prevention.

The Robens Committee dealt with a wide range of additional matters. It proposed two relatively new methods of enforcement – improvement notices[3] and prohibition notices[4]. It looked at public safety[5], special topics such as fire and toxic substances[6], occupational medicine[7], training[8] and research[9].

The other major change recommended by the Committee, not surprisingly in view of the criticisms of the situation it found, was concerned with the administrative structure to supervise the whole fabric of health and safety legislation and its application[10]. Its approach has been followed in subsequent legislation and a discussion of the changes is best left until the new law is considered.

The Report ended, and this is very much the product of the Chairman's personality, with a Programme of Action[11]. This was not wishful thinking, for by 1973 the Conservative Government had proposed and introduced a bill. That bill was lost as a result of the 1974 general election leading to a change of government early in 1974. However an almost identical bill was immediately re-introduced and became the Health and Safety at Work etc. Act 1974[12], which must now be considered.

ii)   The Health and Safety at Work etc. Act

a)   General

The Act, at the outset in section 2(1), lays down the basic general duty placed upon employers, and does so with simple clarity. 'It shall be the duty of every employer to ensure, so far as is reasonably practicable, the health, safety and welfare of all his employees.' This provision has a positive aspect which is

---

2   *Report of the Royal Commission on Civil Liability* (1978) Cmnd. 7054; see ch. 12, head 1, above.
3   Para. 269.
4   Para. 276.
5   Chapter 10.
6   Chapter 11.
7   Chapter 12 – a rather superficial treatment of an area of growing concern.
8   Chapter 13.
9   Chapter 14.
10 Chapters 4 and 7.
11 Chapter 19.
12 The odd, but not unprecedented 'etc.' is present because the Act in Part III covers 'Building Regulations and Amendments of Building (Scotland) Act 1959.' This was merely because the bill provided a suitable vehicle for these extraneous, but important and necessary matters. The oddities of Parliament's concept of a businesslike approach are not infrequent.

comprehensive and wide to an extent that has given rise to criticism and fear. In its negative aspect, as far as is reasonably practicable, it has been criticised as imprecise and flawed. Both aspects need to be considered in turn.

The section continues, without detracting from the general duty of section 2(1) to particularise the duties, covered again in terms laying down areas of responsibility. These are the provision and maintenance of plant and systems of work so that they are safe and without risk to health[13]; the handling, storage and transport of articles and substances[14]; the provision of information, instructions, training and supervision[15]; the maintenance of places of work under the employer's control in a safe condition with safe and risk-free means of access and egress[16]; the provision and maintenance of a safe, risk-free working environment with adequate welfare facilities and arrangements[17]. Each of these provisions is qualified by the familiar phrase 'as far as is reasonably practicable'.

A detailed discussion of these responsibilities placed upon the employer would require a full discussion of the previous law on common law negligence and breach of statutory duty[18]. Only the most salient points can be considered here. The basis of the general duties is the relationship of employer and employee. Employee is defined as an individual who works under a contract of employment[19]. The legal rules as to scope and extent of employment will obviously be of importance. The restriction of the duty to the bounds of reasonable practicability raises again a concept well known in the law of tort and breach of statutory duty. The prime effect is to ensure that the duties are not absolute, as so many have historically been under the various statutory codes such as the Factories Act 1961 or the Mines and Quarries Act 1954.

It must be emphasised that these duties fulfil two functions but not the third. Above all they ensure that employers have to think about their responsibilities in a wide range of areas, many of which e.g. training, would be relatively new to many. This is in line with the Robens philosophy. Secondly the duties are enforceable by the inspectorate. The way this is done will be considered below but the ultimate sanction is criminal prosecution. That gives the duties a backing which ensures they receive close consideration. Finally these statutory duties are *not* the basis for civil actions by those injured as a result of breach. Alternative grounds for action might be available, but the Health and Safety at Work Act duties are not such. This is specifically stated in section 47 of the Act which not only states that sections 2–8 do not confer rights of action but also makes the important provision that neither must those rights be construed as affecting other existing statutory provisions[20]. The other duties set out in section 2 concern matters involving participation between employers and trade unions and employees.

The structure of all the duties under the Act is complex and wide-ranging. For example the employer himself has an additional duty outside the field of

13 S. 2(2)(a).
14 S. 2(2)(b).
15 S. 2(2)(c).
16 S. 2(2)(d).
17 S. 2(2)(e).
18 For much of this see ch. 12, head 3, above.
19 For a full discussion of the status of employment see p. 9, above. The status of trainees under Government work experience schemes has been clarified by regulation – see S.I. 1988 No. 1222.
20 S. 47(1)(a), (b). Regulations made under the Act are similarly dealt with – they are to support civil liability unless they specifically provide otherwise: s. 47(2).

employment. This is to conduct his undertaking so as to ensure as far as is reasonably practicable that persons, other than his employees, who might be affected are not exposed to risks to health and safety[1]. A precisely similar duty is placed upon self-employed persons[2]. A self-employed person is defined as anyone who works for gain or reward otherwise than under a contract of employment and whether or not he himself employs others[3]. Power is given to make regulations under the Act requiring both employers and the self-employed to provide information to others on the way the undertaking is conducted where their health and safety may be affected[4].

The previous statutory codes had often been based on premises. This approach was continued by provision of a general duty applying to those in control of premises to any extent. This duty covers non-employees and those who make use of non-domestic premises as a place of work or for using things available there[5]. One of the problems aimed at was premises such as launderettes where quite dangerous machines and processes (those involving dry cleaning fluids which produce noxious fumes for example) were left untended for unsupervised use by the general public. The duty laid down is to ensure as far as is reasonably practicable the safety of the premises and machines and processes and the absence of risks to health[6]. Control is widely drawn to cover those who, under a tenancy or by contract, have responsibility for the maintenance of the premises or access and egress to them, or for the safety and absence of risk concerning the plant or substances used on premises[7]. The section applies to those carrying on a business, whether for profit or not[8].

The theme of protection of those other than employees by those in control of premises, is continued in section 5 which lays down general duties in respect of emissions into the atmosphere. The duty is to use the best practical means for preventing emissions of noxious or offensive substances and to render harmless and inoffensive any such substances as are emitted[9]. It is specifically provided that the means to be adopted include the method of use of plant and supervision of emissions[10]. Provision is made for the designation of noxious or offensive substances by regulation[11].

An even wider and more basic set of duties is laid down to cover the designer, manufacturer, importer or supplier of articles for use at work[12]. This section attempts to tackle safety at the earliest stage. It lays down, in the now familiar pattern of terminology, the duty to ensure that design and construction are safe and without risks to health. Information has also to be made available to indicate adequately the uses for which the article has been made and tested and setting out conditions necessary for safe and risk-free use. The designer and

1   S. 3(1). See *R v Swan Hunter Shipbuilders Ltd* [1982] 1 All ER 264, [1981] ICR 831. He may be responsible for defective equipment, left by a contractor, but available for use by his employees: *R v Mara* [1987] ICR 165, [1987] IRLR 154, CA.
2   S. 3(2).
3   S. 53.
4   S. 3(3).
5   S. 4(1)(a), (b). *Westminster City Council v Select Management Ltd* [1985] 1 All ER 897, [1985] 1 WLR 576, CA.
6   S. 4(2); *Austin Rover Group Ltd v HM Inspector of Factories* [1990] ICR 133, [1989] IRLR 404, HL, noted (1990) 19 ILJ 43.
7   S. 4(3).
8   S. 4(4).
9   S. 5(1).
10   S. 5(2).
11   S. 5(3).
12   S. 6(1), strengthened by the Consumer Protection Act 1987.

manufacturer are under a duty to undertake or arrange for necessary research aimed at discovering and eliminating or minimising dangers and risks[13]. The erector or installer is placed under a similar duty in relation to the way he carries out his task[14].

A similar pattern of duties is placed on the manufacturer, importer or supplier of substances used at work[15]. A substance for use at work is defined as any substance intended to be used by persons at work, which again is a definition noticeable for its breadth rather than its precision[16]. The duties laid down include testing, supplying adequate information upon use and conditions to be observed in use[17], and research to discover and eliminate or minimise danger and risk[18]. As far as research is concerned it is permissible to rely upon the work of others where such an approach is reasonable[19] and reliance may be placed upon the written undertaking that the recipient will himself take care of the various steps to be taken to fulfil these duties[20].

It will be observed that these duties comprise an overlapping structure. A solvent for use in a dry-cleaning machine, imported by a wholesaler and supplied to a laundry which also uses it in a launderette open to the public, will involve duties on very many people. The overlapping, although it might be said to complicate the question of liability in the common law sense, which of course has been stressed, is not affected by the Act. From the angle of safety the more people involved in a duty to avoid danger or risk, the less chance of an accident. In one particular case[1] it was held that a shipbuilder had a duty to inform workers of a sub-contractor of the dangers of the build up of oxygen. The argument that since the sub-contractor had a duty the shipbuilder need not act was firmly rejected.

This interlocking matrix is made even more secure by the provisions of section 7 which clearly place similar general duties upon the employee. Again the language is wide and important. It can usefully be quoted. The duty on every employee while at work is:

'a) to take reasonable care for the health and safety of himself and of other persons who may be affected by his acts and omissions at work; and

b) as regards any duty or requirement imposed on his employer or any other person by or under any of the relevant statutory provisions, to co-operate with him so far as is necessary to enable that duty or requirement to be performed or complied with.'

This section brings the employee's duty firmly within the group of duties enforceable by the inspectorate. That provision is of far less practical significance than the clear statement of the duty itself. It is within the context of works rules and disciplinary procedures that the real impact will lie. There is finally a duty on the employee not to interfere with or misuse anything provided in the interests of health, safety or welfare, under any of the relevant statutory provisions[2].

13 S. 6(2).
14 S. 6(3).
15 S. 6(4).
16 S. 53(1).
17 S. 6(4).
18 S. 6(5).
19 S. 6(6).
20 S. 6(8).
1   *R v Swan Hunter Shipbuilders Ltd* [1982] 1 All ER 264, [1981] ICR 831, CA.
2   S. 8. The employer must not charge for such items: s. 9.

b)   Interpretation of the Act

After a relative dearth of case law on the interpretation of the 1974 Act, we have now seen some very important decisions of the higher courts, showing a willingness to interpret it on its own terms, and in order to achieve its overall protective aim. Two particular themes can be discerned, both important from the point of view of legal involvement in actually trying to avoid accidents.

The first is the emphasis on *risk* of harm, not just on proved damage or injury. Although many of the legislative provisions start from the common law duties (and in practice many prosecutions will arise from actual accidents), the Act is *not* concerned with compensation for injury. It goes much wider than that, which can be seen particularly in the wide duties to the public in section 3. In *R v Board of Trustees of the Science Museum*[3] an inspection showed that legionella bacteria in the cooling system could be a danger to the public outside the building, due to faulty maintenance and monitoring. The museum, convicted on indictment under section 3 of failing to secure, as far as reasonably practicable, that persons not in their employment were not exposed to risks to their health and safety, appealed; they argued that the prosecution had failed to prove that any members of the public had *actually* been put at risk. Such an argument has strong common law foundations (where is the proved damage, caused by the defendant's default?), but was strongly disapproved by the Court of Appeal who held that the key to section 3 lies in the creation of a risk of *possible* harm; citing the Robens Report and the wide administrative powers granted to inspectors by the Act, they held that to restrict the section to cases of actual danger or injury would result in a substantial emasculation of a central part of the Act. It is argued that this purposive approach is particularly appropriate in the light of the new statutory duties in the Six Pack (see p. 762), especially the requirements of risk assessments in the Management Regulations, the Personal Protective Equipment Regulations, the Manual Handling Regulations and the Display Screen Regulations. This emphasis on forward looking, pro-active measures against possible future risks is likely to be a feature of health and safety law, and failure to adopt such measures may well become central in civil claims too, with the Six Pack establishing the obligations on which the action for breach of statutory duty will be based. It also fits in with the reviewed emphasis (above) placed on the common law obligation to provide a safe *system* of work.

The second theme is the willingness of the courts to break free of interpretations of the Act based on the old common law concepts in this area. The old view that the Act merely adopted those civil law ideas and duties, and criminalised them (for the purposes of administrative enforcement) was a pervasive one for a long time[4]. The restrictive effects of this view could be seen as late as in the case of *RMC Roadstone Products Ltd v Jester*[5]. Independent subcontractors working on the defendants' premises suggested a method of work that in the event killed one of them; it had been assented to by one of the defendants' managers. The defendants were convicted under section 3 but their appeal was allowed by the Divisional Court, on the basis that the section only applied to 'conducting his undertaking' and that, on a traditional view, the

---

3   [1993] ICR 876, [1993] IRLR 853, CA. A similar approach can be seen, under s. 2, in *Bolton Metropolitan Borough Council v Malrod Insulations Ltd* [1993] ICR 358, [1993] IRLR 274, Div Ct.

4   It could be seen, e.g., in old editions of Munkman's *Employer's Liability*, and in dicta in *R v Swan Hunter Shipbuilders Ltd* [1982] 1 All ER 264, [1981] ICR 831, CA.

5   [1994] ICR 456, [1994] IRLR 330, DC.

'employer' was not liable for or to independent contractors, and so the only undertaking in question here was that of the subcontractors, who had been reasonably chosen by the defendants and were not subject to any exceptional powers of control[6]. However within six months there arose the seminal case of *R v Associated Octel Ltd*[7] which shows a very different approach indeed and overrules *Jester*. In this case, the defendants ran a chemical plant and each year hired a particular contractor to do repair work during the annual shut down. One of the contractor's employees was sent into a chemical tank to clean it; the lamp he took was not a safety lamp, there was no containment of the acetone cleaner being used and no forced ventilation provided. When the bulb broke the result was a flash fire in which the employee was badly injured. The defendants were convicted under section 3 and heavily fined. They appealed, relying on *Jester* (i.e. that liability under section 3 was conterminous with common law liability, and that they were not liable for the acts of their contractors) but this time the appeal was dismissed. The Court of Appeal[8] stated that section 3 and its crucial phrasing of 'conducting his undertaking' is to be construed as it stands, and is wider than the old common law duties, being concerned with the creation of risks. The legislative intent is deliberately protective, and here the cleaning and repairing of the plant *was* part of the conducting of the undertaking, whether done by the defendant's own employees or a contractor. Thus, if a risk was created (and, a fortiori, if an accident actually happened) there was prima facie liability on the defendant, subject to the *defence* of reasonable practicability[9]. It is that defence, they said, that provides the counterweight to ensure that a defendant employer is not subject to unfair liability, especially where contractors are involved. On further appeal, the House of Lords strongly adopted the same approach to the meaning of conducting an undertaking. Emphasising the direct nature of the duty on an employer under the statute, and contrasting that with common law rules on vicarious liability, Lord Hoffman said:

> '... section 3 is not concerned with vicarious liability. It imposes a duty on the employer himself. That duty is defined by reference to a certain kind of activity, namely the conduct by the employer of his undertaking. It is indifferent to the nature of the contractual relationships by which the employer chooses to conduct it'.

---

6   The defendants' argument was accepted that this was a penal statute and there were no reasons of policy why the duties imposed should extend beyond the existing common law duties.

7   [1996] ICR 972, [1997] IRLR 123, HL.

8   [1995] ICR 281, [1994] IRLR 540, CA.

9   The wide approach to 'undertaking' can also be seen in the earlier case of *R v Mara* [1987] 1 All ER 478, [1987] ICR 165, CA. The idea of the strict duty, subject to a reasonable practicability defence (itself to be construed relatively narrowly) can also be seen in the contemporaneous decisions (on both the Act and civil liability) in the *Science Museum* case (n. 3 above), *R v British Steel plc* [1995] ICR 586, [1995] IRLR 310, CA, *Larner v British Steel plc* [1993] 4 All ER 102, [1993] IRLR 278, CA and *Mains v Uniroyal Engelbert Tyres Ltd* [1995] IRLR 544, Ct of Sess. The one exceptional case here so far has been s. 4 (making non-domestic premises available as a place of work) which was held in *Austin-Rover Group plc v HM Inspector of Factories* [1990] 1 AC 619, [1989] 2 All ER 1087, HL not to impose strict liability. This can be distinguished on the basis that that section is drafted very differently (with two references to reasonable practicability); on the other hand, it is interesting to notice that the dissenting speech of Lord Goff is much more in line with the recent approach to ss. 2 and 3.

Given their decision, the House of Lords did not have to consider in detail the defence of reasonable practicability, and so it is still primarily the decision of the Court of Appeal that governs that point. Obviously, there will be cases where the contracted-out work is so specialised that it is not reasonably practicable for the employer to supervise it, and so the defence will be available[10]. However, that will be a question of fact in each case, and what is fundamental is that the employer is no longer simply *exonerated* by the involvement of contractors. This decision, and the emphasis it clearly shows on the protective intent of the legislation (which is not to be compromised by reliance on old common law doctrines), could be of great importance for the future and, again, it is very much in line with the modern approach in the Six Pack.

c) The Health and Safety Commission and Executive

The Act set up a Health and Safety Commission and an Executive. The Commission is appointed by the Secretary of State for Employment and consists of a Chairman and between six and nine members[11]. Before making the appointments various interest groups must be consulted – as to three, employers' organisations: as to three others, organisations representing employees and as to the rest a series of bodies such as local authorities and professional associations[12]. The Commission has been in existence since 1975 and its policies and actions can be followed in detail through the annual reports[13]. The Executive comprises three persons, one appointed as Director[14].

The functions of the Commission and the Executive are set out in section 11 and have been added to by accepted practices. The Commission is under a duty to assist and encourage all the purposes of the general provisions of the Act: to encourage research and its publication and safety training, to ensure wide dissemination of advice and information particularly to those practically concerned in this field and to prepare and propose regulations[15]. The Commission has said that its basic strategy was based on three themes – the promotion of positive attitudes to health and safety at work, better information on the analysis of the cause and scale of hazards and the development of a better database and the review of the legislation[16].

The Commission is independent, though it receives its finances from government. The Secretary of State is given supervisory control and may give the Commission directions as to the discharge of its statutory functions[17]. The Commission itself is given the necessary wide legal powers for it to function efficiently. It may delegate its functions to government departments or in turn undertake work for them[18]. It may set up committees of advice and indeed its

---

10   There is an interesting analogy with the Occupiers Liability Act 1957, s. 2(4)(b) (liability for repairs, etc., carried out by an independent contractor) and the case of *Heseldine v Daw & Son Ltd* [1941] 2 KB 343, [1941] 3 All ER 156, CA where it was reasonable to delegate entirely the maintenance of a lift.

11   These are statutory requirements of Sch. 2, para. 15 of the Act. Sch. 2 sets out the details regulating both the Commission and the Executive. The Annual Reports appear with a considerable and unfortunate delay.

12   S. 10(2).

13   S. 10(3).

14   S. 10(5).

15   S. 11(2).

16   Set out in the first Report.

17   S. 12.

18   S. 13(1)(b).

Reports show a considerable number[19]. It may order investigations or inquiries, one of the major ways in which understanding of problems is advanced[20]. The Act lays down outline powers and provides for regulations to provide and govern the powers of those conducting an enquiry or investigation[1].

One of the important functions of the Secretary of State[2] in this field is the making of regulations. The general statutory control of this power is set out in section 50 which also includes a duty upon the Commission, before submitting a proposed regulation, to consult government departments or other appropriate bodies[3]. The purposes for which regulations can be made are set out in some detail in section 15. Overall, the power lies within the purposes of Part I of the Act which are set out in section 1. This is a general statement in straightforward language covering securing health, safety and welfare; protection against danger and risks to health at work: controlling explosives and highly flammable or dangerous substances and controlling emissions into the atmosphere of noxious or offensive substances[4]. Regulations are intended as a continuing and important method of providing detailed legal regulation where it is felt that this is required. It means, in effect, continuation of previous practice.

A novel approach is set out in section 16 by means of the concept of approved codes of practice. The Robens Committee, within its philosophy of self regulation, encouraged the idea of voluntary codes of practice. This provision enables these codes, where appropriate, to be integrated into the fabric of legal control. To supplement the provisions of duties laid down in sections 2–7 the Commission is empowered to approve and issue suitable codes of practice[5]. Consent of the Secretary of State is required as is the process of consultation with government departments or other appropriate bodies[6]. Such codes have to be formally dated and published but provision is made for their revision or withdrawal[7].

Of great interest are the provisions as to the use of those codes[8]. It is specifically stated that failure to observe the code will not make a person liable to either civil or criminal proceedings. This is to say the code itself cannot form the basis of legal action. However, where criminal proceedings for the enforcement of a duty are being taken reference may be made to any relevant provision in a code of practice. Proof of failure to meet the requirements of the code will be enough to establish a contravention unless the accused can show to the satisfaction of the court that the requirement was complied with in another way[9].

Enforcement is the responsibility of the Executive which has the duty to make adequate arrangements[10]. The Annual Reports of the Commission include a report from the Executive from which the re-structuring of the inspectorates and

19   E.g. on Major Hazards, on Arbitrations and a Medical Advisory Committee.
20   S. 14.
1   S. 14(2).
2   When the Department of Employment was abolished in 1995 the health and safety functions were transferred to the Secretary of State for the Environment.
3   S. 50(3).
4   S. 1(1)(a)–(d).
5   S. 16(1).
6   S. 16(3).
7   S. 16(4), (5).
8   There are, of course, important precedents e.g. the Highway Code in road traffic law and the Industrial Relations Codes. The use of codes in health and safety law is taken to new lengths in the six new sets of EC-inspired provisions which came into force on 1 January 1993 (head 3, below), in which the regulations are short, but filled out extensively with practical advice in the codes or guidance notes to each.
9   S. 17(1), (2).
10   S. 18(1).

the principles upon which they work can be seen. The Act empowers the Secretary of State to transfer the duty of enforcement to local authorities[11]. The appointment of inspectors is the duty of the enforcing authority[12].

The inspector has to be appointed in writing, setting out those of the statutory powers he is entitled to exercise[13]. The powers are detailed in section 20(2) of the Act and are aimed at ensuring that he can legally overcome obstruction to his lawful work. He is given, for example, power of entry at any reasonable time or at any time where there is danger. He may make examinations and investigations and may direct that matters be left undisturbed as long as is necessary for him to complete them. He can measure, take photographs, samples and so on. He has the power to ask for relevant information and to require the production of books and documents, both those required to be kept by statute and any other[14]. He has a duty to consult appropriate persons to ensure that nothing he proposes to do is, unknown to him, dangerous[15].

d)   Administrative and criminal enforcement

One of the fundamental dilemmas in the pursuit of health and safety is the balance achieved by the enforcement agencies between consultancy and advisory roles and use of enforcement powers. These powers fall into three categories. The improvement notice is established by section 21. An inspector who believes that one of the statutory provisions is being contravened and that this is likely to be continued or repeated can serve a notice on the person he regards as responsible. This improvement notice must specify the provisions in question and give reasons why the inspector thinks there is a breach. The notice requires the person upon whom it is served to remedy the contravention within a stated period[16]. Where an inspector is of the opinion that activities are being carried on, or are about to be, which are covered by statutory provision and which involve a risk of serious personal injury then he may issue a prohibition notice under section 22. The notice must specify the matters giving rise to the risk and set out the provisions which the inspector believes are being contravened. The notice directs that the activities specified should not be carried on until the matters specified have been remedied. Such a notice may be of immediate effect or take effect after a period set out. The Act indicates ways in which these two sorts of notice – improvement and prohibition – may be framed[17]. For example the inspector may refer to any approved code of practice. He may offer the person upon whom the notice is served alternative ways of dealing with the danger in question. Provision is made for an appeal where the person on whom the notice of either sort is served wishes to challenge it[18]. An appeal has the effect of suspending the operation of an improvement notice until the issue is determined.

11   S. 18(2).
12   S. 19(1).
13   S. 19(2).
14   S. 20(2). Safeguards upon disclosure of information so obtained are set out in s. 28. The Commission and Executive are given powers of access to information: s. 27.
15   S. 20(5).
16   S. 22(4).
17   S. 23. Obviously the choice will depend upon the nature and imminence of the danger. As a matter of policy, an inspector cannot be sued in negligence for exercising these notice-issuing powers, even if an appeal is successful: *Harris v Evans* [1998] 3 All ER 522, [1998] 1 WLR 1285, CA.
18   S. 24. There are very few such appeals. Non-compliance is a strict offence: *Deary (HMI) v Mansion Hide Upholstery Ltd* [1983] ICR 610, [1983] IRLR 195.

A prohibition notice remains effective unless the tribunal accepts an application that it should be suspended[19]. These issues are dealt with by the industrial tribunals whose sole function is to determine the technical validity of the notice. In addition an inspector is given executive powers to deal with articles or substances in premises which he believes threaten imminent danger of serious personal injury[20].

It will be obvious that the use of notices is aimed at direct enforcement by the elimination of danger to health and safety. Considerable use is made of both types of action – in 1997/98 there were approximately 4,500 of each issued. They are plainly proving to be a useful bridge between exhortation and advice and actual prosecution. So far very few cases have occurred of challenge before the industrial tribunals and especially of successful challenge.

The provisions for prosecution are based on the terms of section 33 which lay down a long list of offences under the Act. It should be remembered that the specific legislation also provides for large numbers of similar offences. In short it is only necessary to say that section 33 makes breach of the various duties laid down in sections 2–9 and of regulations an offence. It protects the other methods of enforcement by making breach of the prohibition and improvement notices also an offence. There is a further series of offences aimed at protecting an inspector and ensuring that he is not obstructed or deceived. The usual pattern of procedure is provided for. An offence may be tried, depending upon its gravity, either summarily only or either summarily or on indictment.

This possibility of trial by judge and jury, with the attendant publicity and stigma if convicted, was very much in line with the Robens twin-track approach to criminal prosecution, namely that the aim is to use it only in serious cases (often where other means have failed) *but* to ensure that it is seen to be a serious matter if it has to be resorted to[1]. At the time of writing, the government are proposing a general increase in penalties by (a) making the majority of offences in section 33 triable either way and (b) where that is the case, increasing the maximum fine on summary conviction to £20,000. Most offences also carry six months' imprisonment on summary conviction. On conviction on indictment, the penalties are imprisonment for a term not exceeding two years, an unlimited fine, or both. Where a criminal prosecution is being brought, it is specifically provided that the onus of proof in relation to what was or was not reasonably practicable is reversed on to the defendant[2].

The penalties available are thus considerable (especially when defence costs are added), but a particularly live issue in recent years has been how these powers should be exercised, because prosecution *policy* plays a major role here. We have already seen that there will often be an emphasis on *not* prosecuting except as a last resort. Once a decision to prosecute is taken[3], however, three further questions of some sensitivity and topicality arise:

19 S. 24(3) (a) and (b).
20 S. 25. He must if possible give a sample to a responsible person on the premises and he has to prepare a written report on his action.
1 This can cause problems when prosecuting a small firm, which could be severely affected by a large fine. In *R v Howe & Son (Engineers) Ltd* [1999] IRLR 434 the Court of Appeal laid down sentencing guidelines, saying that in the case of a small firm there has to be a balance between imposing a fine high enough to affect the owners/shareholders, but not so high as to risk bankrupting the firm and losing jobs.
2 Health and Safety at Work Act 1974, s. 40.
3 Factors taken into account will include the gravity of the offence, the general record and approach of the offender, public effect (including deterrence) and realistic prospect of conviction (adopting the CPS approach).

i) Who should be prosecuted? The very existence of the punishment of imprisonment shows that the prosecution of individuals is envisaged, and in the early years of the 1974 Act it produced a considerable *in terrorem* effect among managers. However, such prosecutions in practice have proved to be relatively rare. The HSE have tended to take the view that, although an individual may be prosecuted if the facts are strong enough, that could be counter-productive because in many cases a health and safety breach will be the result of the negligence of a whole chain of people, rather than one named director, manager or employee. Indeed, simply to go for the individual in a case of managerial failure may be unfair[4]. Thus, the emphasis is on prosecuting the firm or organisation (where, for example, the stigma effect may be greatest), and this leads to the second question.

ii) For what is the company or organisation liable? Vicarious liability is well developed in the law of tort, but has always raised real problems in criminal law. How do you establish corporate liability? Traditionally, this has been done by the 'identification doctrine', i.e. that the company acts through its 'guiding brains' only, usually meaning at board level. Thus, in the leading case of *Tesco Supermarkets Ltd v Nattrass*[5] a supermarket chain was not liable for breaches of the Trade Descriptions Act by the manager of one of its stores. Clearly, to apply that doctrine to health and safety cases could be disastrous because many dangerous practices evolve at shop floor level, so that at board level the company would often be able to deny knowledge and hence liability. In two important cases, the Court of Appeal have held that *Tesco Supermarkets* is *not* to apply under the Health and Safety at Work Act. In *R v British Steel plc*[6] they stressed this as a matter of protective policy, based themselves on the *strict* liability (subject only to the defence of reasonable practicability) imposed by the Act, and said that to apply the identification doctrine would 'drive a juggernaut' through the Act.

Likewise, in *R v Gateway Foodmarkets Ltd*[7] (a case of a fatality through a dangerous practice growing up in a particular supermarket, of which the board had no knowledge) a similar result was achieved, stating that the policy in the recent case law on sections 2 and 3 was to impose liability on 'the employer', that there was no need to show that the company itself was to blame (hence the inapplicability of the identification doctrine) and that (although there might be further problems as to the eventual *depth* of a company's responsibility within its organisation) it was certainly the case that safety lapses at local managerial level *were* to be attributed to the company as employer. In both cases the company was convicted and its appeal rejected[8]. One glitch in this analysis occurred in *R v Nelson Group Services (Maintenance) Ltd*[9], an important test case for the HSE concerning the liability of post-

---

4   For example, the only successful prosecution following the Zeebrugge ferry disaster was of the individual bosun who had left the bow doors open on that occasion; the organisation which had allowed that to happen was not convicted.

5   [1972] AC 153, [1971] 2 All ER 127, HL.

6   [1995] IRLR 310, CA.

7   [1997] IRLR 189, CA.

8   Note that the 1974 Act s. 37 adopts a very standard legislative provision that where a body corporate commits an offence with the consent or connivance of, as attributable to the neglect of, 'any director, manager, secretary or other similar officer', that individual may also be prosecuted. However, that only applies to senior, decision-making management: *R. v Boal* [1992] QB 591, [1992] 3 All ER 177, CA.

9   [1999] IRLR 646, CA.

privatisation gas maintenance organisations under both the Act and the relevant gas regulations. One of the defendant company's fitters had failed to connect a domestic appliance properly, leaving a dangerous situation. The fitter had clearly not done everything reasonably practicable to ensure safety, but the company argued that at *its* level it had indeed done that which was reasonably practicable by training and instructing the fitter well – they were therefore not to be made liable by an individual failing by a fitter. The Court of Appeal agreed (drawing support from the fact that under the gas regulations the fitter himself could also be liable). In a sense, this case only explored further the loose end in *Gateway Foodmarkets* (which was relied on) as to depth of responsibility, but in as much as it established that the reasonable practicability defence has to be operated at a relatively high level in the company (albeit not actually at board level, given that the court did not apply *Tesco Supermarkets*), it could be seen as contrary to the strict/protective intent of the Act. In the light of this, the case was effectively reversed when the Management of Health and Safety at Work Regulations were reissued in 1999, the new reg. 21 providing:

> 'Nothing in the relevant statutory provisions[10] shall operate so as to afford an employer a defence in any criminal proceedings for a contravention of those proceedings by reason of any act or default of ... an employee of his ... .'

iii) Where does liability lie in a fatal accident case? It is, however, when we turn to liability in industrial death cases that the most controversial problems have arisen. Clearly, there can be a prosecution under the Act in the normal way, but the controversy has been whether the law should go further and hold the company liable for manslaughter, on ordinary principles. The HSE have no power to prosecute for this common law crime, and so have to liaise with the CPS; to that end, they entered into a protocol with them in April 1998 as to such liaison, modes of investigation and how prosecutions are to be co-ordinated (including the involvement of the police)[11]. In the past, however, a manslaughter charge has been rare, and the usual result of a death has been a health and safety offence conviction with (even on indictment) the perception that the company has evaded the full rigour of the law[12]. There are, on the other hand, two good reasons for this. The first is that, from the HSE's point of view, the mischief to be aimed at is the health and safety breach itself, not the fact that it has caused death. Without being heartless, the difference between a death and a near miss can be one of

---

10 'Relevant statutory provisions' means (a) the provisions of Part I (i.e. the general health and safety provisions) of the 1974 Act and any health and safety regulations and (b) the existing statutory provisions: s. 53. In this context, it is the 'reasonable practicability' defences throughout the provisions that are particularly relevant.

11 [1998] NLJ 910, 1007.

12 An analogy may be drawn here with road traffic death cases; technically, in many of them there could be a manslaughter charge but in practice the likelihood is of the charge 'only' being the statutory offence of causing death by dangerous driving, with the public perception of light sentencing, a point often commented on in the media by relatives of the deceased.

fortune and inches[13]. The principal health and safety aim is to ensure that the lapse itself does not recur; here, once again, health and safety law and the common law (wanting punishment and perceived retribution) part company. The second reason is that the common law of manslaughter has been notoriously difficult to apply to a corporate defendant; when tried, it has usually failed. Thus, a health and safety charge as an alternative has always had the practical advantage that it may well actually *succeed*, and that in the longer term that will be the stronger deterrent to neglect by companies (which, after all, is the policy aim of the HSE). This second point has now been dramatically reaffirmed in *A-G's Reference (No 2 of 1999)*[14] which arose from the acquittal of a train operating company on multiple manslaughter charges after the Southall rail disaster in 1997. The company had pleaded guilty to health and safety offences, and had been fined £1.5m. However, on the manslaughter point the Court of Appeal held that 'a non-human defendant cannot be convicted of manslaughter by gross negligence in the absence of evidence establishing the guilt of an identified human being for the same crime'[15]. That was because at common law the identification doctrine (*Tesco Supermarkets*) applies in a manslaughter case; the relaxation of this rule under the 1974 Act in *British Steel* and *Gateway Foodmarkets* was only possible as a matter of statutory interpretation, and could not be translated into the common law. At the end of his judgment, Rose LJ pointed to what the court saw as the real way forward, namely (overdue) Parliamentary action on the Law Commission Report No. 237 (1996) which suggests, as part of the overall reform of the law of manslaughter, a new statutory offence of corporate killing based on 'management failure', *not* involving the doctrine of identification. At the time of writing, the present government have shown interest in this proposal, which could form the basis of a major change in this area during the currency of this edition, especially in the light of public concern over the two recent rail disasters.

e)   Joint regulation

It cannot be said that the Act, despite the major impact it has had, introduced many new ways of regulating health and safety by law. So far all that has been discussed has been basically a restructuring and development of the established approach. In one respect, however, there was a major shift in emphasis. This lay in the statutory provision for integration of the workforce in the machinery aimed at securing health and safety. This was sought to be done principally through the creation of statutory safety representatives and safety committees. Neither concept

---

13   A good example of this is the regulatory scheme on compulsory reporting to the HSE, which covers accidents, illnesses *or dangerous occurrences*, the point being that the latter are considered potentially just as serious, with a need to rectify the factors causing the danger. It all goes back to the emphasis (seen above) in modern health and safety law on *risk*, not actual harm. For an example of this, see Ecclestone (Solicitor to the HSE) 'Work related deaths' [1998] NLJ 910, and for a criticism based on traditional common law grounds, see the letter in reply by Professor Celia Wells: [1998] NLJ 1007.

14   [2000] IRLR 417, CA. The decision coincided with the publication of the report into the rail disaster in question, and was immediately said to mean that no manslaughter charges would be brought in relation to the Paddington rail disaster in 1999.

15   Again, the point is that many major accidents will be the result of a complex chain of events/neglects, not attributable to a particular individual, especially not one at 'guiding brain' level. A further result would be that convictions would only be likely against very small companies, run by one or two people, leaving large concerns immune.

was new – the safety representative was familiar in mining and safety committees were a fairly common voluntary device, widely spread especially in manufacturing industry. The Act put these methods of ensuring practical concern with routine health and safety into a prominent place in the reformed structure. For reasons which will be explained, the significance of joint regulation seemed to be on the wane in recent years, but events and EC law have had the effect of reviving interest in it. It is necessary first, however, to set out the scheme as originally set up in the Act.

The first provision in this respect, set out in section 2(3), is for the preparation by an employer of a notice. This has to cover two points. It must set out the employer's general policy on health and safety. It must also describe the organisation and arrangements set up by the employer in order to carry out his policy. The notice and any revisions of it must be made known to all the employees. In this way the Act seeks to ensure that the employer gives thought to his responsibilities and that the workforce is made aware of what is being done[16].

The detailed rules on safety representatives and safety committees have been laid down in regulations. The Act in section 2 merely sets out the framework. This provides for the appointment by recognised trade unions[17] of safety representatives from amongst the employees concerned. These representatives have the right to represent the employees in consultation with the employer and the powers are set out by regulation. There is a corresponding duty on the employer to consult the representatives so appointed[18]. The purpose of such consultation is said to be co-operation in promoting and developing ways of ensuring health and safety and checking their effectiveness.

Safety Committees have to be formed by an employer when he is asked to do so by the safety representatives. The function of the Committee, set out in the Act, is said to be the monitoring of the measures taken to ensure health and safety. Other functions may be prescribed by regulations and it is to these regulations that attention must be turned.

Safety Representative and Safety Committees Regulations were promulgulated in 1976 and were accompanied by a Code of Practice[19]. These deal first with the appointment of safety representatives. Recognised trade unions are given the right to appoint safety representatives. The obvious basis for appointments is the bargaining unit but an indication is given that trade unions might jointly appoint a representative. The process is tied into the existing industrial relations structure[20]. Guidance notes on this area set out useful criteria, rather than lay

16 S. 2(3) provides for exceptions to this duty to be prescribed by regulation. Employers with less than five employees are excepted by the Employers' Health and Safety Policy Statements (Exception) Regulations 1975, S.I. 1975 No. 1584; see *Osborne v Bill Taylor of Huyton Ltd* [1982] ICR 168, [1982] IRLR 17. This requirement of writing is taken further in some of the Six Pack regulations, with their emphasis on risk assessment and information (see head 3).

17 See ch. 2, head 3. The right of employees to *elect* such representatives, as well as the power of appointment by a recognised trade union, was provided for in s. 2(5). This provision was repealed by s. 125, of the Employment Protection Act 1975 – a rather sad example of the (then) aim of trade union growth taking precedence over another working aim. It is in this context that we are to see changes (below).

18 S. 2(6).

19 The Health and Safety Commission publishes a useful booklet with both the regulations and the code conveniently set out in parallel. The regulations and code came into force in 1978 and were slightly amended by the Management of Health and Safety at Work Regulations 1992 in order to comply with the 'Framework Directive' (89/391/EEC), see head 3, below.

20 Code, para. 3.

down rules to be followed. Disputes are to be settled under the industrial relations machinery[1]. The emphasis is upon flexibility so that adequate arrangements are made. This is particularly so in respect of numbers. Nowhere is specific guidance given. The regulations do lay down one important qualification. A safety representative must, as far as reasonably practicable, have two years experience either with the employer or in similar employment[2].

The functions of the safety representatives are set out in some detail[3]. Generally there is the task of consulting with the employer on health and safety matters. To perform this detailed functions are set out[4]. These are to investigate potential hazards and the causes of accidents; to investigate employee complaints; to raise matters on health, safety and welfare with the employer; to carry out inspections; to consult with the various inspectors and enforcement authorities; to receive information and to attend meetings of safety committees. Provision is made that the representative should be given time off with pay to perform these functions[5] with the protection of recourse to an industrial tribunal[6]. The Code emphasises the positive use of these functions and the need for the development of expertise[7].

Special powers are given to safety representatives in respect of inspections of the workplace, and conditions are set out[8]. Written notice must be given to the employer of the intention to inspect. Inspections at less than three-month intervals can only be made by agreement with the employer or where there has been a substantial change in conditions of work or where new information has been published by the Commission or Executive as to hazards. Inspections may be carried out in addition where there has been a notifiable accident or disease and inspection is safe and the represented employees' interests are involved[9]. The employer has to provide facilities and assistance where there is such an inspection. The guidance notes indicate some of the principal aims of inspections e.g. general tours, sampling of dangerous processes, monitoring of dangerous activities. Similar powers are laid down in respect of inspection of documents and the right to information[10].

Safety Committees have only brief mention in the Regulations. The employer must, if asked, establish such a committee in consultation with the safety representatives making the request, within three months, and he must post a notice drawing attention to the committee and the area of the workplace it covers[11]. The guidance notes take the matter little further, but express the view that a committee should evolve from the particular needs.

The original aim was to link these structures firmly into the existing industrial relations machinery. However, once that machinery itself came under attack in the 80s and 90s, and union membership and recognition declined substantially that original model in fact became a source of weakness. Of course it has always

---

1   E.g. reference to conciliation.
2   Reg. 2(4). For special employment see reg. 8.
3   Regs. 4(1) and 4A.
4   Reg. 4(1)(a) to (h).
5   Reg. 4(2). The calculation of pay is laid down in the Schedule.
6   Reg. 11.
7   Code, para. 5. A great deal of effort has been made to train representatives – much under the auspices of the TUC.
8   Reg. 5.
9   Reg. 6.
10   Reg. 7.
11   Reg. 9.

been open to an employing concern to have a safety representative or committee system even where there was no recognised union, but the evidence showed another important move away from joint regulation – not only was there the decline in formal union recognition, but there was also a move in any event to view health and safety matters as an element of the increasingly dominant 'human resource management' philosophy, i.e. to reclaim it as an area of managerial prerogative[12]. This has however changed due to EC law. There was no challenge directly in this area, but the problem was the indirect effect of the decision in *EC Commission v United Kingdom*[13] by the ECJ that, in the areas of collective redundancies and transfers of undertakings the restriction of consultation rights to cases where there are recognised trade unions does not meet the requirements of the backing directives in those areas to consult with 'workers or their representatives'. The point was that similar requirements exist in the Framework Directive[14] which lies behind the Management of Health and Safety at Work Regulations 1992 (considered below). As a result, the previous government felt obliged to introduce the Health and Safety (Consultation with Employees) Regulations 1996[15] which broadens the obligation on an employer to consult on health and safety matters. Where there is a recognised trade union, the original 1977 Regulations continue to apply *but* where that is not the case the 1996 Regulations require consultation with elected 'representatives of employee safety'[16], and to give them such information as is 'necessary to enable them to participate fully and effectively in the consultation'[17]. The employer must provide reasonable training and facilities and an elected representative is allowed paid time off work to perform the functions; employment protection (against detriment or dismissal) is extended to representatives. While these provisions are not as extensive as those applying to safety representatives under the 1977 Regulations (for example, not giving positive powers of inspection or the right to require a safety committee), they have revitalised the question of *joint* regulation of health and safety in the workplace but, as with collective redundancies and transfers of undertakings, it is interesting to see that the proposed model for this is not the old one of trade unions as the sole conduit[18].

3 EUROPEAN INSPIRED REGULATIONS AND CODES

Statutory regulations have long been an essential method of supplementing statutes that seek to protect health and safety at work. They enable detailed legislative rules to be prepared under the aegis of the basic statute, from time to time, as needs determine. By their nature such regulations have tended to be precise and detailed, dealing with specific difficulties and dangers. They attract

12 Millward et al. *Workplace Industrial Relations in Transition* (1992), pp. 159–164. It remained the case that accident rates were higher in companies that did not have jointly appointed representatives or committees.
13 Cases C-382/92, 383/92 [1994] ICR 664, [1994] IRLR 392, ECJ. This led to the Collective Redundancies and Transfers of Undertakings (Protection of Employment) (Amendment) Regulations 1995, S.I. 1995 No. 2587, which require consultation with recognised trade unions *or* directly elected employee representatives, see pp. 64 and 71, above.
14 Council Directive 89/391/EEC.
15 S.I. 1996 No. 1513.
16 Reg. 4; the alternative is to consult the employees directly.
17 Reg. 5.
18 James & Walters 'Non-union involvement: the case of health and safety at work' (1997) 26 ILJ 35.

little legal controversy as their requirements have generally been clearly drafted and disputes have normally concerned their application, rather than their meaning. Of recent years as the work environment has become more diverse and complicated, with many new dangers, the flow of regulations has increased. The aim of the European Community to establish common factors throughout the member states has, over the last decade, increased that flow. Health and safety is an obvious and important concern for the Community, and it is an area in which the setting of common standards, covering essential questions of health and safety, based on technical considerations and proved practice, was relative easy and fitted well into the overall aim of basing competition upon uniform conditions (the economic 'level playing field' argument).

After a relatively slow trickle of regulations, the process has more recently changed into top gear. At the beginning of 1993 six major regulations and their accompanying codes of practice came into effect[19]. The Health and Safety Executive has issued six booklets (the 'Six Pack') setting out provisions of the regulations and approved codes of practice, along with a considerable amount of detailed guidance. Two of the sets of regulations have since been reissued in slightly extended form.

These fall into two categories – three are very general and apply to most, if not all, places of work and cover very large numbers of employed persons. They are: Management of Health and Safety at Work Regulations, 1999[20]; Workplace (Health, Safety and Welfare) Regulations 1992[1]; and the Provision and Use of Work Equipment Regulations 1998[2]. The titles indicate the width of these regulations. The other three deal with slightly more specific issues. They are: Personal Protective Equipment (EC Directive) Regulations 1992[3]; Manual Handling Operations Regulations 1992[4]; and the Health and Safety (Display Screen Equipment) Regulations 1992[5].

The Management of Health and Safety at Work Regulations 1999 are backed by an Approved Code of Practice and guidance filling in details and giving helpful examples of what should be done. Since there are regulations governing 'workplaces' these regulations are important in their coverage of temporary and mobile sites. It is the pattern of the regulations, rather than their detail, which is of crucial importance. Regulation 3, for example, makes it clear that these regulations are the responsibility of the employer, in respect of his own employees and also of those not employed by him but involved arising out of the conduct of the undertaking. They also are the responsibility of a person who is self-employed in respect of his own position and that of those employed by him. It provides that the basic task is risk assessment, which must be repeated whenever there is reason to believe that the original is no longer valid, or where there have been significant changes. Moreover, these general duties were expanded in the 1999 reissuing of the Regulations to include the 'principles of prevention', taken from the Framework Directive. The steps to be taken to ensure the protection of health and safety are expressed in very general terms in regulation 5 as such

---

19   Smith, Goddard and Randall *Health and Safety – the New Legal Framework* (1993); Eberlie 'The new health and safety legislation of the European Community' (1990) 19 ILJ 81.
20   S.I. 1999 No 3242 derived from the European instruments 89/391/EEC 'The Framework Directive' and 91/383/EEC.
1   S.I. 1992/3004 – derived from the European instrument 89/654/EEC.
2   S.I. 1998/2306 – derived from the European instrument 89/655/EEC.
3   S.I. 1992/2966 – derived from the European instrument 89/656/EEC.
4   S.I. 1992/2793 – derived from the European instrument 90/269/EEC.
5   S.I. 1992/2792 – derived from the European instrument 90/270/EEC.

arrangements 'as are appropriate with particular reference to the size'. Where five or more are employed on site the arrangements have to be recorded. In the same way 'as is appropriate' there has to be health surveillance and the protection of health is further described in regulation 6 which provides for one or more competent person to be made responsible, with co-operation secured where there is more than one and with adequate time allowed for the duties to be discharged[6]. Those have to be provided with the necessary knowledge of the dangers and with proper training. Serious and imminent dangers, or areas of danger, are specially dealt with in a similar way with the additional duty to restrict access, and to deal with anyone who is exposed to danger who has to be told and allowed to stop work and go to a place of safety[7]. By the new regulation 9, necessary contact must be maintained with external agencies, particularly as regards first aid, emergency medical care and rescue work. Particular attention is given to ensuring that employees know of the risks, of the relevant preventive and protective measures and the procedures to be adopted. The same applies to outside employees or to the self-employed[8]. Where workplaces are shared, there has to be co-operation. There is an overall duty, in entrusting tasks to workers, to ensure that their capabilities, as regards matters of health and safety, are taken into account. Training has to be given on recruitment and repeated periodically. It has to be reinforced where there are new factors or increased risks[9]. Regulation 14 stresses that the employee has to use the workplace in accordance with the instructions and training, and to make known serious or immediate dangers[10]. Finally, regulation 22 makes the important point that breach of the regulations does not, of itself, give rise to a civil action.

The Workplace (Health, Safety and Welfare) Regulations 1992 and the accompanying Approved Code of Practice has a similar framework. Its scope is huge, applying as it does to every workplace with few exceptions[11]. Regulation 4 puts the duty to ensure compliance with these regulations upon the employer. The basic duty, again in general terms, is to maintain the place of work, equipment, devices and systems. They have to be cleaned as appropriate, and maintained in an efficient state, working order and good repair[12]. The regulations go on to cover matters such as ventilation, temperature in indoor workplaces – which must be reasonable and not involve the discharge of fumes that are injurious or offensive, lighting, cleanliness, working space, workstations, floor and traffic routes[13]. Regulation 13 deals with the prevention of falls and falling objects, and dangers likely to cause scalds, burns, and from substances that may scald, burn, or are poisonous or corrosive. The level of detail is best illustrated from the notes of guidance which cover well-known hazards such as ladders, roofwork, stacking, and the loading and unloading of vehicles. Attention is paid to windows, doors and skylights. Cleaning itself has to be done in a safe manner[14]. Regulation 17 deals with the organisation of traffic routes, so as to enable pedestrians and vehicles to circulate safely. The Approved Code of Practice and guidance notes

6   Reg. 7.
7   Reg. 8.
8   Regs. 9 and 11.
9   Reg. 13.
10   Reg. 14(2); reg. 15 covers temporary workers.
11   Reg. 3. It does not apply to a ship, building operations or any construction within s. 176 of the Factories Act 1961. The regulations discussed in the previous paragraph will, of course, have to be taken into account.
12   Reg. 5.
13   Regs. 6 to 12, respectively.
14   Regs. 14–16. Doors and gates are reg. 18.

go into greater detail on special dangers, for example drawings illustrating a safe loading bay are provided[15]. The remaining regulations[16] deal with a variety of aspects – escalators, moving walkways, sanitary conveniences, drinking water, facilities for clothing and for eating meals. The fully comprehensive nature of these regulations clearly indicates their importance and the width of protection they seek to ensure.

The same can be said of the Provision and Use of Work Equipment Regulations 1998. Their primary objective is to ensure, as their title indicates, the provision of safe work equipment and its safe usage. By now the structure will be obvious from the discussion in previous paragraphs of the other regulations. Duties are placed both on the employer and employees, and apply also to the self-employed[17]. These duties form two groups: one covers selection of suitable equipment, its maintenance, information as to its use and appropriate training[18]; the other deals with equipment to deal with special dangers such as contact with dangerous parts, fires, explosions, contact with hot and cold surfaces, and instability of materials[19]. The purpose of these regulations is to amplify the regulation and to make general duties more explicit. It is explained that most of the old law is being replaced. Despite many repeals there is likely to remain some overlap, but it will be obvious that since the aim of the regulations is protection that is not a matter of real concern. There is even an element of vagueness in that the guidance to the regulations include a list of some 38 articles, ranging from dumper trucks to hammers and meat cleavers, but expressly stated not to be an exhaustive list[20]. The duties cover suitability of equipment, its maintenance, specific risks, and the need to give information of risks and to train those likely to use the equipment[1]. Regulation 10 makes the important point that these general regulations are said to be read as in conformity with other detailed Community directives, principally on product standards. Schedule 1 lists some of these covering 20 years' legislative work[2].

The Personal Protective Equipment (EC Directive) Regulations 1992 covers its topic in a similar way, showing the basic intent very clearly and dealing with a most comprehensive range of matters. An interesting underlying general principle concerning the provision of protective equipment is made clear – that such provision is to be regarded as the 'last resort' to be used only where there is no practical way of obviating the danger itself[3]. That said, the now familiar approach is used to cover capability, assessment, maintenance and provision for storage. Information, instruction and training are equally provided for[4]. The employer has a duty to see that the equipment is properly used and the employee has a duty to report any defect in, or loss of, the equipment.

A rather different approach is adopted in the Manual Handling Operation Regulations 1992. These regulations make it clear that they are put forward

---

15 Reg. 17.
16 Regs. 19–21.
17 Reg. 4.
18 Regs. 5–10. Significantly, in the first case in the Court of Appeal on the Work Equipment Regulations, the maintenance requirement in reg 6 was held to impose strict liability: *Stark v Post Office* (2000) 144 Sol Jo LB 150, CA.
19 Regs. 11–24.
20 Reg. 2.
1   Regs. 5–9.
2   E.g. electric equipment: 72/23/EEC, and electromagnets: 92/31/EEC.
3   Reg. 4.
4   Reg. 4.

largely as guidance, since they, of necessity, cover an infinitely wide range of actions that a worker might be called upon to take in the course of his work. For this reason the regulations take the form of a flow chart of questions that have to be asked and considered – does the work involve manual handling? Is there a risk of injury? Is it practicable to avoid the handling? Can the process be automated or mechanised? If these questions still leave manual handling then the obvious safety safeguards have to be put in place. In other words each task must be assessed and a way devised to perform it in a way that reduces the risk to a minimum. Measures to introduce this must then be considered to see if the risk that remains is acceptable. Once a system is devised, again one of the classic dangers has to be guarded against – any change in conditions must be the trigger for a review.

The Health and Safety (Display Screen Equipment) Regulations 1992 cover a modern development that is becoming an increasing feature of work, as this edition of the textbook could well illustrate. Their application basically is made to depend upon the intensity of use and the regulations give careful guidance as to this, rather than a definitive definition. Some work is said to be clearly within scope – that involving word processing, or as a secretary, journalist or librarian, the categories mentioned as examples likely to have regular screen work. Another list indicates categories of work where the use may well cause the individual user to be covered by the regulations if the time spent so dictates – client manager, scientist, building society manager, receptionist, airways clerk. Finally others, such as a senior manager, may have access to a screen but will, because of infrequency of use, be basically a non-user. Again it is stressed that the possibility of a reduction of the risks has to be assessed. Daily exposure has to be monitored, care given to the health of eyes and eyesight, and training given and information that may be helpful given.

As indicated at the start of this chapter these regulations show clearly both a pattern of regulation and above all an attitude as to what is expected. It will be difficult to resist breaches of regulations if there has not been a considerable amount of forethought, careful consideration of risks and how to protect against them. There must be repeated inspection, information and training Two final, general comments may be made. The first is that responsibilities here overlap so that both the employer and the employee may have a concurrent responsibility. If that gives a headache to the civil lawyers looking at compensation aspects, so be it; the regulations are concerned at prevention which must be accorded undoubted priority. It is a very healthy development in the law. The second comment is that the previous government made some political capital out of taking to themselves in the Deregulation and Contracting Out Act 1994 a power to repeal (by an expedited procedure) health and safety legislation which, they said, was a burden on business. If anyone actually believed that large parts of the above, recent legislation would be swept aside in a blaze of deregulatory zeal, they will have been sadly disappointed because one of the novel aspects of these regulations is that they are of course entrenched by EC Directives. Thus, when in 1995 we finally had a repealing order it swept aside a grand total of 12 pieces of legislation including (crucially) the Home Work (Lampshades) Order 1929 and the Horizontal Milling Machines (Amendment) Regulations 1934. Given that this whole subject of industrial law is an area in which substantial gaps between political invective and employment reality are not exactly unknown, that is perhaps not a bad note on which to conclude.

Index